Hippocre...
Practical ...

Portuguese-English
English-Portuguese

D1010250

Hippocrene Practical Dictionaries

Portuguese-English
English-Portuguese

Revised with Glossary
of Menu Terms

HIPPOCRENE BOOKS, New York

Revised Hippocrene edition, 1991, 1993, 1994, 1996.

First Hippocrene edition, 1987

Copyright © by Antonio Houaiss and Ismael
Cardim

For information, address:
HIPPOCRENE BOOKS, INC.
171 Madison Avenue
New York, NY 10016

ISBN 0-87052-980-3 (revised paperback)
ISBN 0-87052-440-2 (hardback edition)

Printed in the United States of America.

PREFACE

This book is designed as a small and practical bilingual dictionary of both English and Portuguese languages.

As almost all bilingual dictionaries, it does not give definitions, but does give "synonims" from one to the other language concerned, that is, the word or words or phrases used as corresponding sense equivalent in *Portuguese*-English and *English*-Portuguese alphabetical order.

This dictionary is based on the larger size and number of entries dictionaries of Record publishers — the *Webster's Dicionário Inglês-Português,* by Antônio Houaiss, Ismael Cardim and *alii* (928 pages) and the *Webster's Portuguese-English Dictionary,* by James L. Taylor (revised edition, 657 pages). So, this dictionary represents a new and original selection of entries which we hope will respond to the spirit of modern usages in English and Portuguese.

The phonetic symbols aim to give main phonological traces of each word in the simplest way, but a previous careful acquaintance of these symbols is strongly recommended to consultants.

We deeply hope this dictionary will be of good usage among its readers and consultants from whom we shall receive suggestions of corrections and improvements with great recognition.

PHONEMIC TRANSCRIPTION

All the entries of this dictionary are followed by their phonemic transcription between vertical parallels. The signals of this system of transcription with their phonemic values are the following:

Vowels

| a | Eng. c*a*rpet
| e | Eng. rail | reil |
| ɛ | Eng. s*e*t
| i | Eng. s*ee*
| ɪ | Eng. *it* (variable sound from | e | to | i |)
| o | Eng. go | goʋ |
| ω | Eng. j*a*w, f*ou*r, d*oo*r
| u | Eng. t*oo*th, d*o*
| ʋ | Eng. f*u*ll (variable sound from | o | to | u |)
| ã | F. ˙ch*an*t, ch*am*p, v*an*ter
| ẽ | F. v*in*, f*in*, s*ym*phonie
| ĩ | nasal *i*
| ῖ | variable sound from | ẽ | to | ĩ |
| õ | F. m*on*de, prof*on*d, c*om*parer
| ũ | nasal *u*
| ῦ | variable sound from | õ | to | ũ |

Diphtongs and triphtongs

| ay | Eng. fl*y*, *i*ce, n*i*ght
| ey | Eng. *a*pe, ra*i*l, s*a*y
| ɛy | diphtong of the *e* of s*e*t and the *y* of pr*e*y
| oy | Eng. b*o*y with the *o* of s*ou*l
| ωy | Eng. b*o*y, t*o*y
| uy | stressed Eng. *u(oo)* with the *y* of d*a*y
| aw | Eng. h*ow*, *ou*t
| ew | stressed Eng. *e* of *e*nd with the end of Eng. v*ow*
| ɛw | stressed Eng. *e* in r*e*d with the end of Eng. v*ow*

Phonemic transcription

| ow |	Eng. g*o*, sh*ow*
| iw |	as in v*iew* with stress in the *i*
| āy |	as *ay* above, but nasal as if *ā*ȳ
| ēy |	as *ey* above, but nasal as if *ē*ȳ
| õy |	as *oy* above, but nasal as if *õ*ȳ
| ūy |	as *uy* above, but nasal as if *ū*ȳ
| āw |	as *aw* above, but nasal as if *ā*w̃
| wi |	Eng. w*i*th, w*i*ll
| way |	Eng. *why*
| wey |	Eng. *way*, *wai*t, *wai*ter
| wow |	Amer. Eng. *vow*
| wãw |	as *ãw* above precided with *w*
| wõy |	as *õy* above precided with *w*

Consonants

| b |	Eng. *b*ad
| d |	Eng. *d*add*y*
| f |	Eng. *f*ear
| g |	Eng. *g*ood
| k |	Eng. *c*attle
| l |	Eng. *l*ive
| m |	Eng. *m*other
| n |	Eng. *n*ight
| p |	Eng. *p*eace
| r |	Eng. c*r*uel
| R |	F. cha*r*, *r*ue
| s |	Eng. *s*aint
| t |	Eng. *t*able
| v |	Eng. *v*ouch
| z |	Eng. *z*ero
| w |	Eng. *w*agon, *w*ord
| y |	Eng. *y*outh
| N |	F. vi*gn*e, It. biso*gn*o, Sp. espa*ñ*ol
| L |	It. pa*gl*ia, Cast. *ll*ave
| x |	Eng. *sh*ame
| j |	Eng. mea*s*ure, vi*s*ion

Phonemic transcription

| ζ | it is a signal corresponding to I s I, I z I, I x I and I j I according to a variable: rule explained in the note (*) below.

Stress

Tonic or stressed syllable is marked by a reversed comma or apostrophe before the syllable; v.g.: corpo I 'koʀpʊ I (body); alfaiate I alfay'atı I (taylor); animal I ani'mal I (animal); não I 'nãw I (no, not); sílaba I 'silaba I (syllable); modelo I mo'del I (model); cadeira I ka'deyra I (chair).

Note

(*) I ζ I is a transcription for written *s*, *z* or *x* ending syllables, e.g. a*s*, e*s*ta*s*, po*s*tura, atri*z*, atro*z*, e*x*portar, e*x*pansão. The pronunciation of I ζ I has two patterns: 1) as I s I or I x I in a*s* fada*s*, e*s*pera; 2) as I z I or I j I in meu*s* dado*s*.

ABREVIATIONS USED IN THIS DICTIONARY

a.	adjective
abbrev.	abbreviation; abbreviated
adv.	adverb
(aeron.)	aeronautics
(Afr.)	African
(agric.)	agriculture
(Amer.)	American
(anat.)	anatomy
(anthropol.)	anthropology
(arch.)	architecture
(archaeol., archeol)	archaeology
(arith.)	arithmetic
art.	article
(astrol.)	astrology
(astron.)	astronomy
(atom. ener.)	atomic energy
aug.	augmentative
aux.	auxiliary
(bact., bacteriol.)	bacteriology
(Bib.)	Bible; Biblical
(biochem.)	biochemistry
(biol.)	biology
(bot.)	botanic
(Braz.)	Brazilian
(Brit.)	British
cap.	capital; capitalized
(carp.)	carpentry
(Cath.)	Catholic
(chem.)	chemistry
(cine.)	cinema; cinematic
(colloq.)	colloquial
(com.)	commerce; commercial
compar.	comparative
conj.	conjunction

imp.	impersonal
(Ind.)	Indian
indef.	indefinite
inf.	infinitive
interj.	interjection
(internat. law)	international law
(irreg.)	irregular; irregularly
(It.)	Italian
(journal.)	journalism
(L., Lat.)	Latin
(ling.)	linguistics
(lit.)	literature; literal
m.	masculine
(mach.)	machinery
(manuf.)	manufacturing
(mason.)	masonry
(math.)	mathematics
(med.)	medicine
(metal.)	metallurgy
(meteor.)	meteorology
(mil.)	military
(min.)	mining
(mineral.)	mineralogy
mpl.	masculine plural
(mus.)	music
(myth.)	mythology
(naut.)	nautical
(neol.)	neologism
(nuclear phys.)	nuclear physics
num.	numeral
(numis.)	numismatics
(obs.)	obsolete
(opt.)	optics
(ornith.)	ornithology
(pej.)	pejorative
(phar., pharm.)	pharmacy; pharmacology
(philol.)	philology
(philos.)	philosophy

Abreviations used in this dictionary

(constr.)	construction
contr.	contraction
def.	definite
demonst.	demonstrative
(dent.)	dentistry
dim.	diminutive
(diplom.)	diplomacy
(eccles.)	ecclesiastical
(econ.)	economy
(e.g.)	for example
(elect.)	electricity
(electron.)	electronics
(Eng.)	English
(eng., engin.)	engineering
(entom.)	entomology
(Esp.)	Spanish
(esp.)	especially
(etc.)	et cetera
f.	feminine
(F.)	French
(fig.)	figurative; figuratively
(fin.)	finance
(fort.)	fortification
fpl.	feminine plural
(G.)	German
(gen.)	generally
(geneal.)	genealogy
(genet.)	genetics
(geog.)	geography
(geol.)	geology
(geom.)	geometry
(Gr.)	Greek
(Gr. Brit.)	Great Britain
(gram.)	grammar
(her., herald.)	heraldry
(hist.)	history
(hort.)	horticulture
(ichth.)	ichthyology

(phon., phonet.)	phonetics
(photog.)	photography
(phys.)	physics
(physiol.)	physiology
pl.	plural
(poet.)	poetic
(polit.)	politics
(Port.)	Portuguese
poss.	possessive
p.p.	past participle
pref.	prefix
prep.	preposition
pron.	pronoun
(psychiat.)	psychiatry
(psychol.)	psychology
(rad.)	radio
rel.	relative
(rel., relig.)	religion
(rhet.)	rhetoric
(Rom.)	Roman
(R.R.)	railroad
s.	substantive
(sculp.)	sculpture
sing.	singular
(sociol.)	sociology
(specif.)	specifically
(stat.)	statistics
suf.	suffix
superl.	superlative
(surg.)	surgery
(surv.)	surveying
(tech.)	technical
(teleg.)	telegraphy
(teleph.)	telephony
(tex.)	textiles
(theat.)	theatre
(theol.)	theology
(topog.)	topography

Abreviations used in this dictionary

(trigon.)	trigonometry
(TV)	television
(typog.)	typography
(unc.)	uncommon
(US)	United States
v	verb
V.	vide
(var,)	variant
v. aux.	auxiliary verb
(vet., veter.)	veterinary science
vi.	intransitive verb
v. imp.	inpersonal verb
vr.	reflexive verb
vt.	transitive verb
(vulg.)	vulgarism
(zool.)	zoology

Portuguese-English

A

a | a | *f. def. art.* the / *pron.* her; the one that; the one who / *prep.* in; to; at; by; for; on

à | a sometimes 'a | (*pl.* às) *contr.* of the *prep.* a and the *f. def. art.* a at the, to the, for the etc.

aba | 'aba | *sf.* brim (of a hat); edge, rim; flap (of a coat); flange, ledge

abacate | aba'katı | *sm.* (bot.) avocado, alligator pear

abacaxi | abaka'xi | *sm.* (bot.) pineapple

abade | a'badı | *sm.* abbot

abadessa | aba'desa | *sf.* abbess

abadia | aba'dia | *sf.* abbey

abafado -da | aba'fadʋ | *a.* airless, stuffy; muggy; hollow (sound)

abafar | aba'faʀ | *vt.* to smother (fire); to muffle (sound); to hush up; to cover

abaixar | abay'xaʀ | *vt.* to lower

abaixo | a'bayxʋ | *adv.* below; down; under

abaixo-assinado | a'bayxʋasi'nadʋ | *sm.* petition signed by several persons; the undersigned

abajur | aba'juʀ | *sm.* lampshade

abalado -da | aba'ladʋ | *a.* loose, unsteady; (fig.) moved

abalar | aba'laʀ | *vt.* to shake (loose); to stir; to upset

abalizado -da | abali'zadʋ | *a.* competent, distinguished

abalo | a'balʋ | *sm.* shock; concussion, commotion

abanar | aba'naʀ | *vt.* to fan

abandonar | abãdo'naʀ | *vt.* to abandon

abandono | abã'donʋ | *sm.* abandonment (also law), desertion

abano | a'banʋ | *sm.* fire-fan

abarcar | abaʀ'kaʀ | *vt.* to embrace; to enclose

abarrotar | abaʀo'taʀ | *vt.* to crowd, to cram, to stuff

abastado -da | abaʃ'tadʋ | *a.* well-to-do

abastança | abaʃ'tãsa | *sf.* abundance, wealth

abastecer | abaʃte'seʀ | *vt.* to supply; to fuel. -a. de to provide with

abastecimento | abaʃtesi'mẽtʋ | *sm.* provisioning, supplying; refuelling

abater | aba'teʀ | *vt.* to lower; to weaken; to knock down; to slaughter (cattle)

abatido -da | aba'tidʋ | *a.* depressed; slaughtered (cattle)

abatimento | abati'mẽtʋ | *sm.* depression; decrease; (com.) reduction, discount

abdicação | abdika'sãw | *sf.* abdication

abdicar | abdi'kaʀ | *vt. vi.* to abdicate; to give up

abdome, abdômen | ab'dome ab'domẽy | *sm.* abdomen

a-bê-cê | abe'se | *sm.* ABC; alphabet card, primer

abecedário | abese'darıʋ | *sm.* the alphabet

abelha | a'beLa | sf. bee

abençoar | abēsv'aR | vt. to bless

aberração | abeRa'sãw | sf. aberration

aberto -ta | a'beRtv | a. open

abertura | abeR'tura | sf. opening; aperture

abeto | a'betv | sm. fir

abismado -da | abiʒ'madv | a. astonished; greatly surprised

abismar | abiʒ'maR | vt. to amaze, to astound

abismo | a'biʒmv | sm. abysm, precipice

abjeto -ta | ab'ʒetv | a. abject

abjuração | abjura'sãw | sf. abjuration, repudiation

abjurar | abju'raR | vt. to abjure, to repudiate

ablação | abla'sãw | sf. ablation

abnegação | abnega'sãw | sf. abnegation, self-denial

abnegado -da | abne'gadv | sm. unselfish person / a. altruistic

abóbada | a'bʊbada | sf. vault

abóbora | a'bʊbʊra | sf. pumpkin

abolição | abʊli'sãw | sf. abolition; extinction

abolir | abv'liR | vt. to abolish; to suppress

abominar | abomi'naR | vt. to abominate, to execrate

abonar | abo'naR | vt. to warrant, to guarantee

abono | a'bonv | sm. guarantee; bonus

abordar | aboR'daR | vt. (naut.) to board; to accost

aborrecer | abvRe'seR | vt. to bore

aborrecido -da | abvRɪ'sidv | a. bored; annoyed; tiresome

aborrecimento | abvRɪsi'mētv | sm. annoyance; worry, trouble; bóredom

aborto | a'boRtv | sm. abortion; miscarriage

abotoadura | abvtva'dura | sf. cuff-link

abotoar | abvtv'aR | vt. to button (up) / vi. to button; (bot.) to bud

abraçar | abra'saR | vt. to hug, to embrace; to encircle; to adopt (principles, ideas)

abraço | a'brasv | sm. hug, embrace

abrandar | abrã'daR | vt. to soften; to mitigate / vi. to become calm; to soften

abranger | abrã'jeR | vt. to encircle; to include

abrasador -dora | abraza'doR | a. blazing, burning

abrasileirar | abraziley'raR | vt. to Brazilianize

abreviação | abrɪvi'sãw | sf. abbreviation

abreviar | abrɪvi'aR | vt. to abbreviate; to shorten

abreviatura | abrɪvia'tura | sf. abbreviation

abridor | abri'doR | sm. opener

abrigar | abri'gaR | vt. to shelter; to protect

abrigo | a'brigv | sm. shelter, cover

abril | a'bril | sm. April

abrir | a'briR | vt. to open; to cut or tear open / vi. to open; to be opened

abscesso | ab'sɛsv | sm. abscess

absoluto -ta | abso'lutv | a. absolute

absolver | absol'veR | vt. to absolve, to acquit

absorção | absoR'sãw | sf. absorption

absorto -ta | ab'soRtv | a. absorbed, deep (in thought)

absorver | absoR'veR | vt. (also a.-se) to absorb; to imbibe

abstêmio -mia | abʒ'temiv | smf. teetotaler, abstainer / a. abstemious

abster-se | abʒ'teRsɪ | vr. to abstain, to refrain from

abstinência | abʒti'nẽsia | sf. abstinence

abstração | abʒtra'sãw | sf. abstraction; abscence of mind

abstrair | abʒtra'iR | vt. to abstract. -a.-se to concentrate

absurdo -da | ab'suRdʊ | *sm.* absurdity, nonsense / *a.* absurd

abundância | abū'dãsia | *sf.* abundance, plenty

abundante | abū'dãtɩ | *a.* abundant, plentiful

abundar | abū'daR | *vi.* to abound in

abusar | abu'zaR | *vi.* to abuse; to mistreat; to violate

abuso | a'buzʊ | *sm.* abuse, misuse

abutre | a'butrɩ | *sm.* vulture

acabado -da | aka'badʊ | *a.* finished, complete; (fig.) worn out

acabamento | akaba'mētʊ | *sm.* finish, finishing, final touch

acabar | aka'baR | *vt.* to finish, to conclude

acabrunhado -da | akabru'Nadʊ | *a.* down-hearted

acabrunhar | akabru'NaR | *vt.* to afflict; to distress

academia | akade'mia | *sf.* academy

acadêmico -ca | aka'demikʊ | *sm.* academician; university student / *a.* academic

acalmar | akal'maR | *vt.* to calm; to soothe

acamado -da | aka'madʊ | *a.* sick abed; (geol.) stratified

açambarcar | asãbaR'kaR | *vt.* to monopolize

acampamento | akãpa'mētʊ | *sm.* camp, encampment, bivouac

acampar | akã'paR | *vt.* (also a.-se) *vi.* to camp

acanhado -da | aka'Nadʊ | *a.* shy, timid; tight

acanhamento | akaNa'mētʊ | *a.* shyness, timidity

ação | a'sãw | *sf.* action, deed; (com.) share of stock; legal action

acarajé | akara'jɛ | *sm.* (Braz.) a fried cake of cooked beans and palm oil

acariciar | akarisi'aR | *vt.* to caress, to fondle

acarretar | akaRe'taR | *vt.* to carry; to give rise to

acaso | a'kazʊ | *sm.* hazard, fate. **-ao a.** at random / *adv.* perhaps, possibly

acatamento | akata'mētʊ | *sm.* deference, respect

acatar | aka'taR | *vt.* to respect

acautelar | akawte'laR | *vt.* to caution / *vi.* to be cautious

aceder | ase'deR | *vi.* to accede, to acquiesce

aceitação | aseyta'sãw | *sf.* acceptance, approbation

aceitar | asey'taR | *vt.* to accept; to admit

aceitável | asey'tavɩl | *a.* acceptable

aceleração | aselera'sãw | *sf.* acceleration

acelerar | asele'raR | *vt.* to accelerate; to speed up / *vi.* to increase in speed

acenar | ase'naR | *vi.* to beckon

acender | asẽ'deR | *vt.* to light; to switch on (light etc.); (fig.) to provoke, to enchant

acento | a'sẽtʊ | *sm.* accent (also gram., mus.)

acentuação | asẽtua'sãw | *sf.* accentuation

acentuar | asẽtu'aR | *vt.* to accentuate; (fig.) to emphasize

acepção | asep'sãw | *sf.* meaning, sense

acerca de | a'seRka dɩ | *prep.* about, concerning

acercar | aseR'kaR | *vt.* (also a.-se) to approach, to draw near (to)

acertado -da | aseR'tadʊ | *a.* correct, exact

acertar | aseR'taR | *vt.* to hit (mark, target etc.); to hit upon (the right answer, the right way; to fit, to adjust / *vi.* to hit the mark or target; to think or act wisely

aceso -sa | a'sezʊ | *a.* lighted, lit; excited, inflamed

acessível | ase'sivɩl | *a.* accessible

acesso | a'sɛsʊ | *sm.* access; attack; outburst

acessório -ria | ase'sɔriʊ | *sm.* accessory, attachment / *a.* accessory, supplementary

acetona | ase'tona | *sf.* acetone

achacar | axa'kaʀ | *vt.* to extort, to steal by threatening

achado-da | a'xadʊ | *sm.* find, discovery / *a.* found, discovered

achaque | a'xakı | *sm.* chronic ailment

achar | a'xaʀ | *vt.* to find; to consider. **-a.-se** to be

achatar | axa'taʀ | *vt.* to flatten

achegar | axe'gaʀ | *vt.* to draw or bring near

acidentado -da | asidẽ'tadʊ | *smf.* victim of an accident / *a.* rugged, rough

acidental | asidẽ'tal | *a.* accidental

acidente | asi'dẽtı | *sm.* accident

acidez | asi'deʒ | *sf.* acidity, sourness

ácido -da | 'asidʊ | *smf.* acid / *a.* acid, sour

acima | a'sima | *adv.* above / *prep.* (with **de**) above, on top of, beyond

acinte | a'sĩtı | *sm.* spite, grudge

acionar | asio'naʀ | *vt.* to operate, to set in motion; (law) to sue

acionista | asio'niʃta | *smf.* stockholder, shareholder

aclamação | aklama'sãw | *sf.* acclamation, applause

aclamar | akla'maʀ | *vt. vi.* to acclaim, to applaud

aclarar | akla'raʀ | *vt.* to elucidate; to illuminate / *vi.* to clear up

aclimação | aklima'sãw | *sf.* acclimation, acclimatization

aclimar | akli'maʀ | *vt.* to acclimatize

aclimatar | aklima'taʀ | *vt.* = *aclimar*

aço | 'asʊ | *sm.* steel

acocorar-se | akoko'raʀsı | *vr.* to crouch, to squat

açoitar | asoy'taʀ | *vt.* to whip, to lash

acolá | akʊ'la | *adv.* there, over there

acolhedor -dora | akoʟe'doʀ | *smf.* welcomer / *a.* welcoming

acolher | ako'ʟeʀ | *vt.* to welcome; to harbo(u)r

acometer | akome'teʀ | *vt.* to assault, to charge

acomodação | akomoda'sãw | *sf.* accomodation; lodging

acomodar | akomo'daʀ | *vt.* to accomodate; to lodge. **-a.-se** to lodge; to adjust oneself

acompanhamento | akõpaNa'mẽtʊ | *sm.* accompaniment (also mus.); side-dish

acompanhar | akõpa'naʀ | *vt.* to accompany (also mus.); to attend, to escort; to keep up with

aconchegar | akõxe'gaʀ | *vt.* (also **a.-se**) to cuddle, to nestle; to draw or pull up (as covers, against the cold)

acondicionar | akõdisio'naʀ | *vt.* to condition; to wrap up, to pack

aconselhar | akõse'ʟaʀ | *vt.* to advise. **-a.-se** to seek or take counsel

acontecer | akõte'seʀ | *vi.* to happen, to occur, to take place

acontecimento | akõtesi'mẽtʊ | *sm.* happening, occurrence; remarkable occasion

acordar | akoʀ'daʀ | *vt.* to wake, to awake, to awaken; to agree with / *vi.* to wake, to awaken

acorde | a'kɔʀdı | *sm.* chord

acordeão | akoʀdı'ãw | *sm.* accordion

acordo | a'kɔʀdʊ | *sm.* agreement

acorrentar | akoʀẽ'taʀ | *vt.* to chain, to enchain

acostumado -da | akʊʃtu'madʊ | *a.* accustomed, used to

acostumar | akʊʃtu'maʀ | *vt.* to accustom, to habituate. **-a.-se a** to get used to

acotovelar | akʊtʊve'laʀ | *vt.* to elbow; to nudge; to poke

açougue | a'sowgı | *sm.* butcher's shop

açougueiro | asow'geyrʊ | *sm.* butcher

acre | 'akrı | *sm.* acre / *a.* acrid, bitter

acreditar | akredi'taʀ | *vt. vi.* to believe; to have faith or confidence in

acrescentar | akresen'taʀ | *vt.* to augment, to add

acréscimo | a'krɛsimʊ | *sm.* increase; addition

acrimônia | akri'monia | *sf.* acrimony

acrobata | akro'bata | *smf.* acrobat

açu | a'su | *a.* (Tupi) large, big

acuar | aku'aʀ | *vt.* to corner, to drive into a corner / *vi.* to draw back

açúcar | a'sukaʀ | *sm.* sugar

açucareiro -ra | asuka'reyrʊ | *sm.* sugar bowl / *a.* of or pertaining to sugar

açude | a'sudı | *sm.* dam

acudir | aku'diʀ | *vt. vi.* to help, to succor

açular | asu'laʀ | *vt.* to instigate; to set on (a dog)

acumulação | akumula'sãw | *sf.* accumulation

acumular | akumu'laʀ | *vt.* to accumulate, to amass / *vi.* to increase, to grow

acusação | akuza'sãw | *sf.* accusation, charge

acusar | aku'zaʀ | *vt.* to accuse; to blame; to indicate. **-a. o recebimento de** to acknowledge the receipt of

acústica | a'kuʃtika | *sf.* acoustics

adaga | a'daga | *sf.* dagger

adaptação | adapta'sãw | *sf.* adaptation, adjustment

adaptar | adap'taʀ | *vt.* to adapt. **-a.-se** to accustom oneself to

adega | a'dɛga | *sf.* wine-cellar

adejar | ade'jaʀ | *vi.* to flutter; to flap (wings)

adelgaçar | adelga'saʀ | *vt.* to thin; to make sparse / *vi.* (also **a.-se**) to become thin

adentro | a'dẽtrʊ | *adv.* indoors.

-pela porta a. in through the doors

adepto | a'dɛptʊ | *sm.* follower

adequado -da | ade'kwadʊ | *a.* adequate, proper

adereço | ade'resʊ | *sm.* adornment, jewelled ornament

aderir | ade'riʀ | *vt.* to join; to attach / *vi.* to adhere

adesão | ade'zãw | *sf.* adhesion

adesivo -va | ade'zivʊ | *sm. a.* adhesive

adestrar | adeʃ'traʀ | *vt.* to train, to instruct

adeus | a'dewʃ | *sm.* goodbye, farewell, bye-bye

adiamento | adia'mẽtʊ | *sm.* postponement, adjournment

adiantado -da | adiã'tadʊ | *a.* advanced; fast (clock) / *adv.* ahead, in advance

adiantamento | adiãta'mẽtʊ | *sm.* advancement, anticipation; progress

adiantar | adiã'taʀ | *vt.* to advance; to anticipate. **-a.-se** to get or go ahead; to run fast (clock)

adiante | adi'ãtı | *adv.* ahead; forward; farther on. **-levar a.** to carry on

adiar | adi'aʀ | *vt.* to postpone, to adjourn

adição | adi'sãw | *sf.* addition; sum

adicionar | adisio'naʀ | *vt.* to add

adido | a'didʊ | *sm.* attaché

aditamento | adita'mẽtʊ | *sm.* addition, addendum

adivinhação | adiviɴa'sãw | *sf.* soothsaying; puzzle; guessing

adivinhar | adivi'ɴaʀ | *vt.* to guess; to divine

adivinho | adi'viɴʊ | *sm.* fortune-teller, soothsayer

adjacente | adja'sẽtı | *a.* adjacent

adjetivo -va | adje'tivʊ | *sm.* (gram.) adjective / *a.* (gram., law) adjective, additional

adjunto -ta | ad'jũtʊ | *sm.* adjunct; assistant / *a.* adjunct, adjoined

administração | adminiʒtra'sãw *sf.* administration, management, executive department

administrador -dora | adminiʒtra'doʀ | *smf.* administrator, manager / *a.* administrative

administrar | adminiʒ'traʀ | *vt.* to administer, to manage; to apply, to give (medicine etc.)

admiração | admira'sãw | *sf.* admiration, wonder

admirado | admi'radʋ | *a.* astonished, surprised

admirador -dora | admira'doʀ | *smf.* admirer

admirar | admi'raʀ | *vt.* to admire; to be astonished at / *vi.* to be awed

admirável | admi'ravɩl | *a.* admirable

admissão | admi'sãw | *sf.* admission, entrance; secondary school examination

admitir | admi'tiʀ | *vt.* to admit; to allow; to tolerate

admoestação | admʋeʒta'sãw | *sf.* admonition

admoestar | admʋeʒ'taʀ | *vt.* to admonish

adoçar | ado'saʀ | *vt.* to sweeten

adocicar | adosi'kaʀ | *vt.* to make sweetish

adoecer | adʋe'seʀ | *vi.* to become sick

adoentado -da | adʋē'tadʋ | *a.* indisposed, sickish

adolescente | adole'sētɩ | *smf.a.* adolescent

adoração | adora'sãw | *sf.* adoration, worship

adorar | ado'raʀ | *vt.* to adore, to worship

adormecer | adoʀme'seʀ | *vt.* to lull, to put to sleep / *vi.* to fall asleep

adornar | adoʀ'naʀ | *vt.* to adorn, to ornament

adorno | a'doʀnʋ | *sm.* adornment, ornament

adotar | ado'taʀ | *vt.* to adopt

adquirir | adki'riʀ | *vt.* to acquire; to obtain; to get

adro | 'adrʋ | *sm.* church square; churchyard

aduana | adu'ana | *sf.* customs, custom-house

aduaneiro -ra | adua'neyrʋ | *smf.* custom-house employee / *a.* of or pertaining to customs

adubar | adu'baʀ | *vt.* to fertilize, to manure

adubo | a'dubʋ | *sm.* fertilizer, manure

adular | adu'laʀ | *vt.* to flatter

adulterar | adulte'raʀ | *vt.* to adulterate; to counterfeit

adultério | adul'tɛriʋ | *sm.* adultery

adúltero -ra | a'dulterʋ | *sm.* adulterer; *sf.* adulteress / *a.* adulterous, adulterate

adulto -ta | a'dultʋ | *sm.* adult / *a.* adult, mature

aduzir | adu'ziʀ | *vt.* to adduce, to bring forward

advento | ad'vētʋ | *sm.* advent, coming, arrival

advérbio | ad'vɛrbiʋ | *sm.* adverb

adversário -ria | adveʀ'sariʋ | *smf.* adversary, opponent

adversidade | adveʀsi'dadɩ | *sf.* adversity, hardship

adverso -sa | ad'vɛʀsʋ | *a.* adverse, contrary

advertência | adveʀ'tēsia | *sf.* advertence; warning; observation

advertir | adveʀ'tiʀ | *vt.* to admonish; to give heed to / *vi.* to advert; to take notice

advogado -da | advo'gadʋ | *smf.* lawyer, barrister, attorney

advogar | advo'gaʀ | *vt.* to advocate; (law) to plead / *vi.* to practice law

aéreo -rea | a'ɛriʋ | *a.* air, aerial. **-via aérea** by air mail

aerodinâmico -ca | aerodi'namikʋ | *a.* aerodynamic

aeromoço -ça | aero'mosʋ | *sm.* air steward; *sf.* air stewardess

aeronáutico -ca | aero'nawtikʊ | a. aeronautic

aeronave | aero'navɪ | sf. aircraft

aeroporto | aero'pɔRtʊ | sm. airport

afã | a'fã | sm. diligence

afabilidade | afabili'dadɪ | sf. affability, friendliness

afagar | afa'gaR | vt. to caress; to pet

afago | a'fagʊ | sm. caress

afamado -da | afa'madʊ | a. famous, celebrated

afastado -da | afaʒ'tadʊ | a. remote, distant; apart; away from

afastar | afaʒ'taR | vt. to remove; to separate; to chase away. **-a.-se** to go away

afável | a'favɪl | a. affable, amiable

afazeres | afa'zerɪʒ | smpl. tasks, duties

afeição | afey'sãw | sf. affection, fondness, liking

afeiçoar | afeysʊ'aR | vt. to shape, to form. **-a.-se** to take a liking to

afeito -ta | a'feytʊ | a. accustomed (to), used (to)

aferir | afɪ'riR | vt. to gauge; to check; to estimate

aferrado -da | afe'Radʊ | a. persistent, obstinate

aferrar | afe'RaR | vt. to grapple, to grasp. **-a.-se** to grab, to cling to

aferrolhar | afeRo'LaR | vt. to lock, to bolt

afetado -da | afe'tadʊ | a. affected, artificial; afflicted

afetar | afe'taR | vt. to affect, to feign

afeto -ta | a'fɛtʊ | sm. affection / a. affectionate

afetuoso -sa | afetu'ozʊ -'ωza | a. affectionate, warm-hearted

afiançar | afiã'saR | vt. to guarantee; to affirm; to go bail for

afiar | afi'aR | vt. to sharpen

afilhado -da | afi'Ladʊ | smf. godchild; sm. godson; protegé; sf. goddaughter; protegée

afiliar | afili'aR | vt. to affiliate

afim | a'fĩ | a. akin / sm. relative (by marriage etc.)

afinado -da | afi'nadʊ | a. (mus.) in tune, tuned up

afinal | afi'nal | adv. at last, after all. **-a. de contas** after all

afinar | afi'naR | vt. (mus.) to tune up; to taper; (fig.) to harmonize / vi. to become thin

afinco | a'fĩkʊ | sm. persistence, tenacity

afinidade | afini'dadɪ | sf. affinity, rapport

afirmação | afiRma'sãw | sf. affirmation; statement

afirmar | afiR'maR | vt. to affirm, to declare, to assert

afirmativo -va | afiRma'tivʊ | a. affirmative

afivelar | afive'laR | vt. to buckle

afixar | afi'ksaR | vt. to post (bills, notices etc.)

aflição | afli'sãw | sf. affliction, distress; anguish

afligir | afli'jiR | vt. to afflict, to grieve. **-a.-se** to worry

aflorar | aflo'raR | vi. to appear on the surface, to emerge

afluência | aflu'ẽsia | sf. affluence; abundance; crowd

afluente | aflu'ẽtɪ | sm. affluent, tributary / a. affluent

afluir | aflu'iR | vi. to flock together; to flow to, to flow in

afobar | afo'baR | vt. to hasten; to confuse. **-a.-se** to be in a hurry, to be confused

afogar | afo'gaR | vt. to drown; to asphyxiate. **-a.-se** to drown

afoito -ta | a'foytʊ | a. bold

afora | a'fωra | adv. outside, out into. **-rua a.** out into the street / prep. except, save

afortunado -da | afʊRtu'nadʊ | a. fortunate, lucky

afresco | a'freʒkʊ | sm. (fine arts) fresco

africano -na | afri'kanʊ | smf. a. African

afronta | a'frõta | *sf.* affront, outrage

afrontar | afrõ'taR | *vt.* to affront, to insult; to face, to defy

afrouxar | afrow'xaR | *vt.* to loosen; to slacken / *vi.* to slack up; to slow down

afugentar | afujẽ'taR | *vt.* tò drive away, to chase

afundar | afũ'daR | *vt.* to sink; to deepen

agachar-se | aga'xaRsɩ | *vr.* to crouch, to squat

agarrar | aga'RaR | *vt.* to seize, to grab; to catch; to hold on or to

agasalho | aga'zaLʋ | *sm.* warm clothing; hospitality

agência | a'jẽsia | *sf.* agency, office

agenciar | ajẽsi'aR | *vt.* to seek to obtain; to be an agent for

agenda | a'jẽda | *sf.* agenda; engagement book

agente | a'jẽtɩ | *sm.* agent

ágil | 'ajil | *a.* agile, nimble, limber

agilidade | ajili'dadɩ | *sf.* agility

agiota | aji'ωta | *smf.* usurer, money-lender

agir | a'jiR | *vi.* to act; to do

agitação | ajita'sãw | *sf.* agitation; excitement

agitar | aji'taR | *vt.* to agitate; to trouble

aglomerar | aglʋme'RaR | *vt.* to agglomerate

agonia | agʋ'nia | *sf.* agony, anguish

agonizante | agʋni'zãtɩ | *smf.* dying person

agonizar | agʋni'zaR | *vi.* to agonize, to be at the point of death

agora | a'gωra | *sm.* now, the present time / *adv.* now. **-a. mesmo** right now. **-até á.** up to now. **-de a. em diante** from now on / *conj.* now; however

agosto | a'goʃtʋ | *sm.* August

agouro | a'gowrʋ | *sm.* omen

agraciar | agrasi'aR | *vt.* to decorate with (medal etc.)

agradar | agra'daR | *vt.* to please; to flatter. **-a.-se de** to be pleased with / *vi.* to be pleasing

agradável | agra'davɩl | *a.* agreeable, delightful, pleasant

agradecer | agrade'seR | *vt.* to thank for / *vi.* to give thanks

agradecimento | agradɩsi'mẽtʋ | *sm.* gratitude

agrado | a'gradʋ | *sm.* pleasure, liking

agravar | agra'vaR | *vt.* to aggravate / *vi.* (law) to make an appeal

agravo | a'gravʋ | *sm.* grievance, offense; (law) appeal

agredir | agrɩ'diR | *vt.* to attack, to assault; to provoke

agregado | agre'gadʋ | *sm.* aggregate; tenant farmer / *a.* aggregate

agregar | agre'gaR | *vt.* (also **a.-se**) to aggregate; to add; to associate

agremiação | agremia'sãw | *sf.* association

agressão | agre'sãw | *sf.* aggression, offense

agreste | a'grɛʃtɩ | *sm.* arid zone in northeastern Brazil / *a.* rustic, rural

agrião | agri'ãw | *sm.* watercress

agrícola | a'grikʋla | *a.* agricultural

agricultor -tora | agrikul'toR | *smf.* farmer; farm-hand

agricultura | agrikul'tura | *sf.* agriculture, farming

agrilhoar | agrilʋ'aR | *vt.* to shackle, to fetter

agropecuária | agrʋpeku'aria | *sf.* farming and cattle raising

agrupar | agru'paR | *vt.* to group. **-a.-se** to form a group

água | 'agwa | *sf.* water. **-á. doce** fresh water. **-á. potável** drinking water. **-à flor d'á.** on the surface

aguaceiro | agwa'seyrʋ | *sm.* downpour, shower

água-de-colônia | 'agwa dɩ ko'lonia | *sf.* cologne

aguado -da | a'gwadʋ | *a.* watery, watered

aguar | a'gwaʀ | *vt.* t̓o water / *vi.* (colloq.) to water (said of the mouth)

aguardar | agwaʀ'daʀ | *vt.* to wait for; to expect / *vi.* to wait for

aguardente | agwaʀ'dẽtι | *sf.* sugar cane alcoholic liquor; any alcoholic liquor

açuçar | agu'saʀ | *vt.* to sharpen

agudez, agudeza | agu'deʒ agu'deza | *sf.* sharpness

agudo -da | a'gudʋ | *sm.* (mus.) a sharp / *a.* acute (also geom., med., gram.); sharp (also mus., fig.)

agüentar | agwẽ'taʀ | *vt.* to endure, to tolerate; to resist / *vi.* to hold out

águia | 'agia | *sf.* eagle

aguilhão | agi'Lãw | *sm.* goad (also fig.)

aguilhoada | agiLo'ada | *sf.* prick, poke (with a goad)

agulha | a'guLa | *sf.* needle

ai | 'ay | *sm.* oh!, moan; sigh / *interj.* oh!, ah!, alas!, ouch! -**a. de mim!** alas!, woe is me!

aí | a'i | *adv.* there; (Braz.) at that moment. -**a. está** there you are. -**a. mesmo** right there. -**por a.** over there / *interj.* stop!, good!

ainda | a'ĩda | *adv.* still; some day. -**a. agora** just now. -**a. assim** nevertheless. -**a. há pouco** just a little while ago. -**a. não** not yet

aipim | ay'pĩ | *sm.* sweet cassava

aipo | 'aypʋ | *sm.* celery

ajantarado | ajãta'radʋ | *sm.* single (heavy) Sunday meal

ajeitar | ajey'taʀ | *vt.* to arrange, to fix up; to adapt. -**a.-se** to arrange with or for

ajoelhar | ajʋe'Laʀ | *vi.* (also **a.-se**) to kneel

ajuda | a'juda | *sf.* aid, assistance. -**dar uma a.** to give a hand

ajudante | aju'dãtι | *smf.* assistant; aide (also mil.)

ajudar | aju'daʀ | *vt.* to help, to aid, to assist

ajuizado -da | ajui'zadʋ | *a.* judicious; reasonable

ajuntamento | ajũta'mẽtʋ | *sm.* reunion, congregation; gathering

ajuntar | ajũ'taʀ | *vt.* to gather, to collect; to bring together; to accumulate

ajustar | aju'taʀ | *vt.* to adjust, to adapt; to fit; to settle (accounts)

ajuste | a'juʃtι | *sm.* adjustment; agreement, pact

ala | 'ala | *sf.* ale, row, rank; (mil.) flank; (mil., arch., sports) wing

alagar | ala'gaʀ | *vt.* to flood, to inundate

alambique | alã'bikι | *sm.* still, retort, alembic

alameda | ala'meda | *sf.* tree-lined street; arrow of trees

álamo | 'alamʋ | *sm.* poplar, aspen, alamo

alaranjado -da | alarã'jadʋ | *sm.* orange (colour) / *a.* orange (colour)

alarde | a'laʀdι | *sm.* ostentation, parade, boasting

alargar | alar'gaʀ | *vt.* to enlarge, to widen, to broaden; to extend. -**a.-se** to widen, to broaden

alarido | ala'ridʋ | *sm.* clamour, tumult

alarma | a'laʀma | *sm.* alarm, alert

alastrar | alaʃ'tʀaʀ | *vt.* to spread, to diffuse. -**a.-se** to spread

alavanca | ala'vãka | *sf.* lever; crowbar

albergue | al'bɛʀgι | *sm.* inn, hostelry

álbum | 'albũ | *sm.* album

alça | 'alsa | *sf.* loop, ring, shoulder strap. -**a. de mira** backsight (of a gun)

alcachofra | alka'xofra | *sf.* artichoke

alçada | al'sada | *sf.* jurisdiction, judicial competence; authority

alcançar | alkã'saʀ | *vt.* to reach; to

arrive at; to get, to obtain / *vi.* to reach, to obtain

alcance | al'kãsɪ | *sm.* reach, range; (fig.) understanding, importance. **-de longo a.** far--reaching

alçapão | alsa'pãw | *sm.* trapdoor; (Braz.) bird trap

alcaparra | alka'paʀa | *sf.* caper

alçar | al'saʀ | *vt.* to lift, to raise. **-a.-se** to raise; to become haughty. **-a. vôo** (aeron.) to take off; to fly (birds)

alcatrão | alka'trãw | *sm.* tar; pitch

alce | 'alsɪ | *sm.* (zool.) elk, moose

álcool | 'alkool | *sm.* alcohol

alcoólatra | alko'ωlatra | *smf.* alcoholic

alcoólico -ca | alko'ωlikʋ | *smf. a.* alcoholic

alcoviteiro -ra | alkovi'teyrʋ | *sm.* procurer, pimp; *sf.* procuress

alcunha | al'kuna | *sf.* sobriquet, nickname

aldeão -deã | aldɪ'ãw | *smf.* peasant / *a.* rustic, rural

aldeia | al'deya | *sf.* village

aldraba | al'draba | *sf.* knocker; latch (of the door)

alecrim | alɪ'krĩ | *sm.* (bot.) rosemary

alegação | alega'sãw | *sf.* allegation, claim

alegar | ale'gaʀ | *vt.* to allege, to assert, to affirm; to offer in excuse

alegoria | alego'ria | *sf.* allegory

alegrar | ale'graʀ | *vt.* to gladden, to cheer. **-a.-se** to rejoice

alegre | a'lɛgrɪ | *a.* glad, happy; slightly intoxicated

alegria | alɪ'gria | *sf.* cheerfulness, gladness, joy

aleijado -da | aley'jadʋ | *smf.* cripple / *a.* crippled, lame

aleijar | aley'jaʀ | *vt.* to cripple; to disable; to mutilate

aleitar | aley'taʀ | *vt.* to nurse

além | a'lẽy | *sm.* distant place; the hereafter / *adv.* beyond. **-a. de** farther; besides. **-muito a.** far beyond

alemão -mã | ale'mãw | *sm.* (ling.) German; *smf. a.* German

além-mar | alẽy'maʀ | *sm. adv.* overseas

alento | a'lẽtʋ | *sm.* breath, breathing; courage, spirit

alergia | aleʀ'jia | *sf.* allergy

alerta | a'lɛʀta | *sm.* alert / *a.* alert, alive / *adv.* alertly, watchfully / *interj.* attention!

alfabeto | alfa'bɛtʋ | *sm.* alphabet, ABC's

alface | al'fasɪ | *sf.* lettuce

alfaiataria | alfayata'ria | *sf.* tailoring shop

alfaiate | alfay'atɪ | *sm.* tailor

alfândega | al'fãdɪga | *sf.* customs; custom-house

alfange | al'fãjɪ | *sm.* scimitar

alfarrábio | alfa'ʀabiʋ | *sm.* old second-hand book

alfazema | alfa'zema | *sf.* lavender

alferes | al'fɛrɪʃ | *sm.* (mil.) (former) army rank corresponding to second lieutenant

alfinete | alfi'netɪ | *sm.* pin

alforje | al'fʋʀjɪ | *sm.* saddle-bag

alforria | alfʋ'ʀia | *sf.* emancipation (esp. of slaves)

alga | 'alga | *sf.* seaweed

algarismo | alga'riʃmʋ | *sm.* figure, number, digit

algazarra | alga'zaʀa | *sf.* clamo(u)r, tumult, outcry

algema | al'jema | *sf.* (usu. *pl.*) handcuffs, shackles

algemar | alje'maʀ | *vt.* to handcuff; (fig.) to dominate, to oppress

algo | 'algʋ | *adv.* something, somewhat

algodão | algʋ'dãw | *sm.* cotton

algoz | al'goʒ | *sm.* executioner; torturer

alguém | al'gẽy | *indef. pron.* someone, somebody

alguidar | algi'daʀ | *sm.* a shallow earthen bowl

algum -ma | al'gũ -'guma | *indef. a.* a, an. any, one; (*pl.*) some, several, a few. **-alguma coisa**

something. **-de modo a.** not at all

alheio -lheia | a'Leyʋ a'Leya | *a.* someone else's; alien, foreign; absorbed; enraptured / *sm.* what belongs to someone else

alho | 'aLʋ | *sm.* garlic

alho-poró | 'aLʋpo'ɾω | *sm.* (Braz.) leek

ali | a'li | *adv.* there

aliado -da | ali'adʋ | *smf.* ally / *a.* allied

aliança | ali'ãsa | *sf.* alliance; wedding ring

aliar | ali'aR | *vt.* (also **a.-se**) to ally; to unite, to join

aliás | ali'aʒ | *adv.* otherwise; besides; as a matter of fact

álibi | 'alibi | *sm.* alibi

alicate | ali'katɩ | *sm.* pliers

alicerce | ali'sɛRsɩ | *sm.* (gen. *pl.*) foundation, base

aliciar | alisi'aR | *vt.* to entice, to attract

alienação | aliena'sãw | *sf.* alienation; transfer of title; madness, lunacy

alienado -da | alie'nadʋ | *smf.* insane person / *a.* abstracted; enraptured; lunatic, mad

alienar | alie'naR | *vt.* to alienate; to transfer title; to remove, to withdraw; to deviate; to hallucinate, to madden. **-a.-se** to become insane; to divert oneself from reality

alijar | ali'jaR | *vt.* to discard, to throw off

alimentação | alimẽta'sãw | *sf.* nourishment, nutrition

alimentar | alimẽ'taR | *a.* alimentary, nutritive / *vt.* to feed, to nourish

alimentício -cia | alimẽ'tisiʋ | *a.* nourishing

alimento | ali'mẽtʋ | *sm.* food, nourishment; (*pl.*) alimony

alinhado -da | ali'Nadʋ | *a.* aligned, lined up; (Braz.) spruce; correct

alinhamento | aliNa'mẽtʋ | *sm.* alignment

alinhar | ali'NaR | *vt.* to align, to line up, to range

alinhavar | aliNa'vaR | *vt.* to baste; to do hastily and carelessly

alisar | ali'zaR | *vt.* to smooth; to unwrinkle; (colloq.) to caress, to pet

alistamento | aliʒta'mẽtʋ | *sm.* recruiting, enlistment; roll, list

alistar | aliʒ'taR | *vt.* to enlist, to enroll; to draft, to recruit. **-a.-se** to enlist, to join

aliviar | alivi'aR | *vt.* to alleviate, to relieve / *vi.* to deliver oneself of; to lessen

alívio | a'liviʋ | *sm.* relief, appeasement

alma | 'alma | *sf.* soul, spirit; core; bore (of a gun). **-criar a. nova** to regain one's spirit

almanaque | alma'nakɩ | *sm.* almanac

almejar | alme'jaR | *vt.* to yearn, to crave

almirante | almi'rãtɩ | *sm.* admiral

almoçar | almʋ'saR | *vi.* to have lunch

almoço | al'mosʋ | *sm.* lunch, luncheon

almofada | almʋ'fada | *sf.* cushion; pillow; (typog.) ink roll or pad

almofariz | almofa'riʒ | *sm.* mortar

almôndega | al'mõdɩga | *sf.* meat ball

almoxarifado | almʋxari'fadʋ | *sm.* stock-room

alô | a'lo | *interj.* hello!

alocução | aloku'sãw | *sf.* allocution, brief address

alojamento | aloja'mẽtʋ | *sm.* lodging; (mil.) quarters, barracks

alojar | alo'jaR | *vt. vi.* to quarter, to billet; to shelter. **-a.-se** to lodge

alongar | alõ'gaR | *vt.* to elongate, to extend; to prolong. **-a.-se** to talk or write at long length

alourar | alow'raʀ | *vt.* to bleach, to make or become blond; to brown (meat)

alpercata | alpeʀ'kata | *sf.* espadrille, footwear of canvas upper and hemp sole

alpiste | al'piʃtɩ | *sm.* birdseed

alquebrar | alke'braʀ | *vt. vi.* to bend, to break (as with age or weakness)

alqueire | al'keyrɩ | *sm.* surface measure (with local variations)

alta | 'alta | *sf.* rise, increase; discharge (from a hospital)

alta-fidelidade | 'alta fideli'dadɩ | *sf.* high-fidelity, hi-fi

altaneiro -ra | alta'neyrʊ | *a.* towering; proud

altar | al'taʀ | *sm.* altar

alta-roda | alta'ʀʊda | *sf.* high society

altear | altɩ'aʀ | *vt.* to heighten; to elevate

alteração | altera'sãw | *sf.* alteration, modification; disturbance, unrest

alterar | alte'raʀ | *vt.* to alter, to modify; to falsify, to adulterate. **-a. -se** to change; (colloq.) to become upset

altercação | alteʀka'sãw | *sf.* altercation, dispute

alternar | alteʀ'naʀ | *vt. vi.* to alternate

alternativa | alteʀna'tiva | *sf.* alternative, option

alteza | al'teza | *sf.* (*cap.*) Highness

altitude | alti'tudɩ | *sf.* altitude, height

altivez | alti'veʒ | *sf.* pride, haughtiness

alto -ta | 'altʊ | *sm.* height, altitude; top, summit. **-de a. a baixo** from top to bottom / *a.* high, tall; loud; superior / *adv.* loud, loudly / *interj.* halt!

alto-falante | 'altʊfa'lãtɩ | *sm.* loud-speaker

alto-forno | 'altʊ'foʀnʊ | *sm.* blast furnace

altruísmo | altru'iʃmʊ | *sm.* altruism

altura | al'tura | *sf.* height, altitude; occasion, moment; (mus.) pitch. **-à a. de** at the height of; (fig.) up to; worthy of. **-a certa a.** at a certain point

alucinação | alusina'sãw | *sf.* hallucination

alugar | alu'gaʀ | *vt.* to rent, to lease, to hire, to charter, to let

aluguel | alu'gɛl | *sm.* rent; leasing, chartering. **-de a.** for rent, for (on) hire

aluir | alu'iʀ | *vi.* to collapse, to fall

alumiar | alumi'aʀ | *vt.* to illuminate, to light / *vi.* to light, to give light

alumínio | alu'miniʊ | *sm.* aluminium, aluminum

aluno -na | a'lunʊ | *smf.* pupil, student

alusão | alu'zãw | *sf.* allusion, reference

alvará | alva'ra | *sm.* license, permit

alvejar | alve'jaʀ | *vt.* to whiten, to blanch; to take aim; to shoot at

alvenaria | alvena'ria | *sf.* masonry, stonework

alvéolo | al'vɛʊlʊ | *sm.* (anat., zool.) alveolus; honey-comb cell

alvissareiro -ra | alvisa'reyrʊ | *a.* favorable, propicious

alvitre | al'vitrɩ | *sm.* proposition, suggestion

alvo -va | 'alvʊ | *sm.* target; goal / *a.* white

alvorada | alvo'rada | *sf.* dawn, daybreak; (mil.) reveille

alvoroçar | alvoro'saʀ | *vt.* to excite, to arouse, to agitate. **-a. -se** to be excited

alvoroço | alvo'rosʊ | *sm.* excitement; commotion

alvura | al'vura | *sf.* whiteness; purity

ama | 'ama | *sf.* nurse

amabilidade | amabili'dadɩ | *sf.* amiability, politeness

amaciar | amasi'aʀ | *vt.* to soften, to smooth

ama-de-leite | 'amadɪ'leytɪ | *sf.* wet-nurse

amado -da | a'madʊ | *smf. a.* beloved, darling

amador -dora | ama'doʀ | *smf.* amateur; lover

amadurecer | amadure'seʀ | *vt. vi.* to ripen; to season, to age

amadurecimento | amaduresi'mẽtʊ | *sm.* ripening, maturing, aging

âmago | 'amagʊ | *sm.* kernel, core, heart

amainar | amay'naʀ | *vi.* to decrease, to diminish (wind, storm, rain, anger etc.) / *vt.* to furl (sails)

amaldiçoar | amaldisʊ'aʀ | *vt.* to curse

amálgama | a'malgama | *smf.* amalgam

amalgamar | amalga'maʀ | *vt.* to amalgamate. -a.-se to join, to associate with

amamentar | amamẽ'taʀ | *vt.* to nurse, to brest-feed

amaneirado | amaney'radʊ | *a.* affected; finical

amanhã | ama'nã | *sm. adv.* tomorrow. -depois de a. the day after tomorrow

amanhar | ama'naʀ | *vt.* to till, to cultivate

amanhecer | amane'seʀ | *sm.* dawn, daybreak. -ao a. at dawn / *vi.* to dawn; to wake up

amansar | amã'saʀ | *vt.* to tame, to domesticate / *vi.* (also a.-se) to calm down

amante | a'mãtɪ | *smf.* lover; *sf.* mistress / *a.* fond of; loving, admiring

amar | a'maʀ | *vt.* to love / *vi.* to be in love

amarelo -la | ama'rɛlʊ | *sm. a.* yellow (colour, dye, person)

amargar | amaʀ'gaʀ | *vt.* to make bitter (also fig.). -a.-se to be or to become embittered / *vi.* to be bitter or disagreeable, to taste bitter. -de a. (colloq.) terrible

amargo -ga | a'maʀgʊ | *sm. a.* bitter; (fig.) bitter, harsh

amargura | amaʀ'gura | *sf.* sorrow, grief; bitterness

amargurar | amaʀgu'raʀ | *vt.* to embitter, to grieve, to afflict. -a.-se to suffer anguish

amarrar | ama'ʀaʀ | *vt.* to tie (up), to fasten / *vi.* (naut.) to moor

amarrotar | amaʀo'taʀ | *vt.* to wrinkle, to crease, to crush

ama-seca | ama'seka | *sf.* dry-nurse

amassar | ama'saʀ | *vt.* to knead (dough, clay etc.); to crease, to wrinkle

amável | a'mavɪl | *a.* kind, pleasant; amiable, lovable

amazona | ama'zona | *sf.* Amazon; horsewoman; riding-habit

âmbar | 'ãbaʀ | *sm.* amber

ambição | ãbi'sãw | *sf.* ambition; aspiration

ambicionar | ãbisio'naʀ | *vt.* to crave, to desire, to long for

ambicioso -sa | ãbisi'ozʊ -'ɔza | *smf.* ambitious / *a.* ambitious, greedy

ambiente | ãbi'ẽtɪ | *sm.* environment, atmosphere / *a.* ambient, surrounding

ambíguo -gua | ã'bigwʊ | *a.* ambiguous, equivocal

âmbito | 'ãbitʊ | *sm.* ambit, field

ambos | 'ãbʊʃ | *a.* both / *pron.* both, both of them

ambulância | ãbu'lãsia | *sf.* ambulance

ambulante | ãbu'lãtɪ | *a.* roving, wandering. -vendedor a. street paddler

ameaça | amɪ'asa | *sf.* threat, menace

ameaçar | amɪa'saʀ | *vt.* to threaten, to menace / *vi.* to threaten; to impend

ameaço | amɪˈasʊ | *sm.* (fig.) symptom

amedrontar | amedrõˈtaʀ | *vt.* to frighten, to scare. **-a.-se** to become afraid

ameixa | aˈmeyxa | *sf.* plum

amêndoa | aˈmẽdʊa | *sf.* almond; kernel

amendoim | amẽdʊˈĩ | *sm.* peanut

amenidade | ameniˈdadɪ | *sf.* amenity, mildness

amenizar | ameniˈzaʀ | *vt.* to assuage, to soothe; to gentle

ameno -na | aˈmenʊ | *a.* pleasant, agreeable

americano -na | ameriˈkanʊ | *smf. a.* American

amerissar | ameriˈsaʀ | *vi.* (aeron.) to alight on water

amesquinhar | amɪʃkiˈnaʀ | *vt.* to belittle; to discredit. **-a.-se** to demean oneself

amestrar | ameʃˈtraʀ | *vt.* to train (animals)

ametista | ameˈtiʃta | *sf.* amethyst

amianto | amiˈãtʊ | *sm.* amianthus

amido | aˈmidʊ | *sm.* starch

amiga | aˈmiga | *sf.* female friend; (vulg.) mistress

amigado -da | amiˈgadʊ | *a.* (vulg.) in a state of illicit cohabitation

amigável | amiˈgavɪl | *a.* friendly, repeated

amígdala | aˈmigdala | *sf.* tonsil

amigo -ga | aˈmigʊ | *sm.* male friend; *sf.* V. *amiga / a.* fond of; friend

amistoso -sa | amiʃˈtozʊ-ˈtɔza | *a.* friendly, amicable, cordial

amiudado -da | amiuˈdadʊ | *a.* frequent, repeated

amiúde | amiˈudɪ | *adv.* frequently, often

amizade | amiˈzadɪ | *sf.* friendship, friendliness, amity; regard

amo | ˈamʊ | *sm.* master

amoedar | amʊeˈdaʀ | *vt.* to coin, to mint

amofinar | amʊfiˈnaʀ | *vt.* to afflict, to trouble, to bother. **-a.-se** to become upset

amolação | amolaˈsãw | *sf.* (Braz.) bother, nuisance; sharpening, whetting

amolar | amoˈlaʀ | *vt.* to hone, to sharpen; (colloq.) to bother

amoldar | amolˈdaʀ | *vt.* to adjust, to adapt. **-a. -se** to accommodate, to conform

amolecer | amoleˈseʀ | *vt.* to soften; to weaken

amontoar | amõtʊˈaʀ | *vt.* to pile, to heap up. **-a.-se** to pile up / *vi.* to pile, to heap

amor | aˈmoʀ | *sm.* love; beloved, darling; (*pl.*) affairs, love affairs

amora | aˈmɔra | *sf.* mulberry; blackberry

amordaçar | amoʀdaˈsaʀ | *vt.* to muzzle; to gag, to silence

amornar | amoʀˈnaʀ | *vt.* to make lukewarm

amoroso -sa | amoˈrozʊ-ˈrɔza | *a.* amorous, loving

amor-perfeito | aˈmoʀpeʀˈfeytʊ | *sm.* pansy

amortalhar | amoʀtaˈʟaʀ | *vt.* to shroud

amortecer | amoʀteˈseʀ | *vt.* to deaden; to muffle; to cushion, to absorb; to dim, to decrease; to numb / *vi.* to die away; to weaken

amortização | amoʀtizaˈsãw | *sf.* amortization

amostra | aˈmoʃtra | *sf.* sample, pattern; specimen

amotinar | amʊtiˈnaʀ | *vt.* to mutiny, to revolt

amparar | ãpaˈraʀ | *vt.* to support, to sustain; to help, to assist. **-a.-se** to lean on

amparo | ãˈparʊ | *sm.* support, protection

ampliação | ãpliaˈsãw | *sf.* enlargement (also photog.); amplification

ampliar | ãpliˈaʀ | *vt.* to amplify, to enlarge; to extend; (photog.) to blow up

amplidão | ăpli'dãw | sf. amplitude

amplificação | ăplifika'sãw | sf. amplification

amplitude | ăpli'tudɩ | sf. amplitude, spaciousness

amplo -pla | 'ăplʋ | a. ample; liberal, copious; extensive

ampola | ă'pola | sf. ampoule; blister

ampulheta | ăpu'Leta | sf. sand-glass

amputar | ăpu'taR | vt. to amputate

amuar | amu'aR | vi. to sulk. -a.-se to become sullen

amuleto | amu'letʋ | sm. amulet, talisman

amuo | a'muʋ | sm. ill-humo(u)r, sullenness

amurada | amu'rada | sf. (naut.) gunwale, gunnel

anágua | a'nagwa | sf. petticoat, underskirt

anais | a'nayʒ | smpl. annals

analfabetismo | analfabe'tiʒmʋ | sm. illiteracy

analfabeto -ta | analfa'bɛtʋ | smf. a. illiterate

analisar | anali'zaR | vt. to analyse; to examine, to study accurately

análise | a'nalizɩ | sf. analysis

analista | ana'liʃta | smf. analyst

analítico -ca | ana'litikʋ | a. analytical

analogia | analo'jia | sf. analogy

ananás | ana'naʒ | sf. pineapple

anão -nã | a'nãw -'nã | smf. a. dwarf

anarquia | anaR'kia | sf. anarchy

anarquismo | anaR'kiʒmʋ | sm. anarchism

anátema | a'natema | sm. anathema; condemnation

anatomia | anato'mia | sf. anatomy

anca | 'ãka | sf. rump; croup

ancestral | ăseʒ'tral | smf. ancestor / a. ancestral

anchova | ă'xova | sf. anchovy

ancião -ciã | ăsi'ãw -'ã | sm. venerable old man / a. ancient, old

ancinho | ă'siN ʋ | sm. rake

âncora | 'ăkora | sf. anchor

ancoradouro | ăkora'dowrʋ | sm. anchorage

ancorar | ăko'raR | vt. vi. to anchor

andaime | ă'daymɩ | sm. scaffolding

andamento | ăda'mẽtʋ | sm. progress, course; (mus.) tempo

andar | ă'daR | sm. walk, gait, pace; storey, floor. -a. térreo ground floor / vi. to walk, to go on foot; to act, to behave. -a. alegre (triste etc.) to be happy (worried etc.). -a. de automóvel (trem, ônibus etc.) to ride a car (train, bus etc.) / vt. to travel all over / interj. -anda! move!

andarilho | ăda'riL ʋ | sm. walker, hiker; vagabond, vagrant

andor | ă'doR | sm. litter for bearing religious images

andorinha | ădʋ'riNa | sf. swallow

andrajo | ă'drajʋ | sm. (gen. pl.) rags, tatters

anedota | ane'dʊta | sf. joke; anecdote

anel | a'nɛl | sm. ring; link, loop

anelar | ane'laR | a. annular / vt. to desire, to crave; to long for; to curl / vi. to pant, to gasp

anelo | a'nɛlʋ | sm. longing, craving, yearning

anexação | aneksa'sãw | sf. annexation

anexar | ane'ksaR | vt. to annex; to attach. -a.-se to incorporate

anexo -xa | a'nɛksʋ | sm. annex; appendage / a. annexed, added

anfíbio -bia | ă'fibiʋ | smf. amphibian / a. amphibious

anfiteatro | ăfitɩ'atrʋ | sm. amphitheatre, amphitheater

anfitrião -oa | ăfitri'ãw | smf. host, hostess

angariar | ăgari'aR | vt. to collect, to solicit

angina | ã'jina | *sf.* quinsy, pharyngitis. **-a. do peito** angina pectoris

angolano -na, angolense | ãgo'lanʋ, ãgo'lẽsι | *smf. a.* native of or pertaining to Angola

angra | 'ãgra | *sf.* inlet, bay

angu | ã'gu | *sm.* (Braz.) cornflour mush

angular | ãgu'laʀ | *a.* angular. **-pedra a.** corner-stone

ângulo | 'ãgulʋ | *sm.* angle; corner

angústia | ã'guʃtia | *sf.* anguish

anil | a'nil | *sm.* indigo

animação | anima'sãw | *sf.* animation, liveliness

animal | ani'mal | *sm. a.* animal

animar | ani'maʀ | *vt.* to animate; to stimulate; to awake. **-a. -se** to be encouraged. **-a. -se** a to dare, to venture

ânimo | 'animʋ | *sm.* disposition; courage; resolution / *interj.* courage!

animosidade | animozi'dadι | *sf.* animosity

animoso -sa | ani'mozʋ -'mɔza | *a.* spirited, courageous

aninhar | ani'naʀ | *vt. vi.* (also **a. -se**) to nest, to nestle; to lodge

aniquilar | aniki'laʀ | *vt.* to annihilate, to destroy

anis | a'niʃ | *sm.* anise; anisette

anistia | aniʃ'tia | *sf.* amnesty

aniversário | aniveʀ'sariʋ | *sm.* birthday, anniversary

anjo | 'ãjʋ | *sm.* angel

ano | 'anʋ | *sm.* year. **-a.bissexto** leap-year. **-a.letivo** academic year. **-fazer anos** to have or celebrate a birthday

anoitecer | anoyte'seʀ | *sm.* nightfall / *vt.* to darken / *vi.* to become dark, to fall (night)

anomalia | anoma'lia | *sf.* anomaly

anônimo -ma | a'nonimʋ | *smf.* anonym / *a.* anonymous

anormal | anoʀ'mal | *smf.* abnormal / *a.* abnormal, irregular

anotação | anota'sãw | *sf.* annotation, note

anotar | ano'taʀ | *vt.* to annotate, to make notes on; to write down

ânsia | 'ãsia | *sf.* anxiety

ansiar | ãsi'aʀ | *vi.* to long for, to desire

ansiedade | ãsie'dadι | *sf.* anxiety, apprehension

ansioso -sa | ãsi'ozʋ -'ɔza | *a.* anxious, apprehensive

anta | 'ãta | *sf.* (zool.) tapir

antagonismo | ãtagʋ'niʒmʋ | *sm.* antagonism, hostility

ante | 'ãtι | *prep.* before

antebraço | ãtι'brasʋ | *sm.* forearm

antecâmara | ãtι'kamara | *sf.* antechamber

antecedência | ãtese'dẽsia | *sf.* antecedence. **-com a.** in advance

antecedente | ãtese'dẽtι | *sm.* antecedent; (*pl.*) antecedents / *a.* antecedent, preceding

antecessor -sora | ãtese'soʀ | *smf.* antecessor; (*pl.*) ancestors

antecipação | ãtιsipa'sãw | *sf.* anticipation

antecipar | ãtιsi'paʀ | *vt.* to anticipate, to foresee; to be or to do in advance

antemão | ãtι'mãw | *adv.* used in the expression **de a.** beforehand, previously

antena | ã'tena | *sf.* antenna; (*pl.*, zool.) antennae

anteontem | ãtι'õtẽy | *adv.* the day before yesterday

anteparo | ãtι'parʋ | *sm.* bulwark, shield, screen; protection

antepassado | ãtιpa'sadʋ | *sm.* ancestor, forefather

anterior | ãteri'oʀ | *a.* preceding; earlier, former; front part

antes | 'ãtιʃ | *adv.* before; rather, preferably. **-a. de tudo** above all

ante-sala | ãtι'sala | *sf.* vestibule; antechamber

antiaéreo -rea | ãtia'ɛrιʋ | *a.* anti-aircraft

anticoncepcional | ãtikõsepsio'nal | *sm. a.* contraceptive

antídoto | ã'tidʋtʋ |*sm.* antidote, counterpoison

antigo -ga | ã'tigʋ | *a.* ancient, antique, old; former

antílope | ã'tilopι | *sm.* antelope

antipatia |ãtipa'tia|*sf.* antipathy, aversion; dislike

antipático -ca | ãti'patikʋ | *a.* displeasing, unpleasant

antiquado-da |ãti'kwadʋ|*a.* antiquated, old-fashioned

antiquário | ãti'kwariʋ | *sm.* antiquary

antítese | ã'titezι | *sf.* antithesis

antolhos | ã'tʊʟʊʒ | *smpl.* blinkers

antologia | ãtolo'jia | *sf.* anthology

antro | 'ãtrʋ | *sm.* cave, cavern

antropologia | ãtropolo'jia | *sf.* anthropology

antropólogo -ga | ãtro'pʊlogʋ | *smf.* anthropologist

anual | anu'al | *a.* annual, yearly

anuário | anu'ariʋ |*sm.* year-book

anuidade | anui'dadι | *sf.* annuity

anuir | anu'ir | *vi.* to assent to

anulação | anula'sãw | *sf.* invalidation, cancellation

anular |anu'lar |*sm.* ring finger / *a.* annular / *vt.* to annul, to cancel

anunciação | anũsia'sãw | *sf.* announcement

anunciar | anũsi'ar | *vt.* to announce; to advertise

anúncio | a'nũsiʋ | *sm.* advertisement; announcement

anuviar |anuvi'ar|*vt.* to cloud, to darken

anzol | ã'zʊl | *sm.* fish-hook, hook. **-cair no a.** to be tricked

ao | 'aw |*contr.* of the *prep.* **a** *and* the *m. def. art.* **o** at; in the; on, upon

aonde |a'õdι |*adv.* whereto; (colloq.) where, whence

apagado-da |apa'gadʋ |*a.* extinguished; erased; dull

apagar|apa'gar|*vt.* (also **a.-se**) to extinguish; to turn off; to erase

apaixonado-da |apayxo'nadʋ|*a.* passionate

apaixonar |apayxo'nar |*vt.* to inflame, to fill with enthusiasm. **-a.-se por** to fall madly in love with

apalpar |apal'par| *vt.* to palpate, to feel, to touch

apanhar |apa'nar| *vt.* to catch; to pick; to lift, to seize / *vi.* to be beaten up

apara | a'para | *sf.* fragment; (*pl.*) shavings

aparador |apara'dor|*sm.* buffet, sideboard

aparafusar | aparafu'zar | *vt.* to screw

aparar | apa'rar | *vt.* to catch (something thrown or fallen); to trim

aparato | apa'ratʋ | *sm.* pomp, ostentation

aparecer |apare'ser | *vi.* to appear; to show up

aparecimento | aparesi'mẽtʋ |*sm.* appearance

aparelhagem | apare'ʟajẽy | *sf.* equipment; gear

aparelhar | apare'ʟar | *vt.* to equip, to outfit; to prepare; (naut.) to rig

aparelho | apa'reʟʋ | *sm.* equipment, apparatus; machine; (*pl.*) set (dishes etc.); (anat.) system (e.g. *aparelho digestivo* digestive system); (Braz.) telephone

aparência | apa'rẽsia | *sf.* appearance, air, aspect

aparentado -da | aparẽ'tadʋ | *a.* related

aparentar | aparẽ'tar | *vt.* to appear, to seem; to affect / *vi.* to pretend to be

aparente | apa'rẽtι | *a.* apparent; supposed; evident

aparição | apari'sãw | *sf.* apparition, vision

apartado-da |apar'tadʋ|*a.* separate; secluded

apartamento | aparta'mẽtʋ | *sm.* flat, apartment; separation

apartar | apaʀ'taʀ | vt. to separate; to set aside; to part (combatants)

aparte | a'paʀtɩ | sm. aside; side remark

apartear | apaʀtɩ'aʀ | vt. to interrupt (a speaker)

apascentar | apasẽ'taʀ | vt. to pasture, to lead to pasture

apatia | apa'tia | sf. apathy

apático -ca | a'patikʋ | a. apathetic; sluggish

apavorar | apavo'raʀ | vt. to terrify

apaziguamento | apazigwa'mẽtʋ | sm. pacification, conciliation

apaziguar | apazi'gwaʀ | vt. to pacify; to reconcile

apear | apɩ'aʀ | vi. to dismount; to disembark

apedrejar | apedre'jaʀ | vt. to stone, to lapidate

apegar | ape'gaʀ | vt. to attach to. **-a.-se** to attach oneself to

apego | a'pegʋ | sm. attachment, affection

apelação | apela'sãw | sf. (law) appeal

apelar | ape'laʀ | vi. to appeal (also law)

apelidar | apɩli'daʀ | vt. (also **a.-se**) to nickname

apelido | apɩ'lidʋ | sm. nickname

apelo | a'pelʋ | sm. appeal

apenas | a'penaʃ | adv. only, scarcely / conj. as soon as

apêndice | a'pẽdisɩ | sm. appendix (also anat.); supplement

aperceber-se | apeʀse'beʀsɩ | vr. to take into account

aperfeiçoamento | apeʀfeysʋa'mẽtʋ | sm. improving, perfecting

aperfeiçoar | apeʀfeysʋ'aʀ | vt. to improve, to perfect

aperitivo-va | apɩri'tivʋ | sm. aperitif / a. aperitive

apertado -da | apeʀ'tadʋ | a. tight, close; rigorous

apertão | apeʀ'tãw | sm. tight squeeze

apertar | apeʀ'taʀ | vt. to tighten; to squeeze. **-a. a mão** to shake hands / vi. to become tight; to become more intense

aperto | a'peʀtʋ | sm. tightening; squeezing; affliction

apesar de | ape'zaʀ dɩ | loc. in spite of

apetecer | apete'seʀ | vt. to long for, to desire / vi. to appeal to; to like, to please

apetite | apɩ'titɩ | sm. appetite; desire

apetitoso -sa | apɩti'tozʋ -'tɔza | a. appetizing; tempting

apetrecho | ape'trexʋ | sm. equipment, gear

apiário | api'ariʋ | sm. apiary

ápice | 'apisɩ | sm. apex, summit

apiedar-se | apie'daʀsɩ | vr. to pity, to have compassion for

apimentar | apimẽ'taʀ | vt. to pepper

apinhar | api'ɴaʀ | vt. (also **a.-se**) to crowd, to cram; to pile up

apitar | api'taʀ | vt. to blow a whistle / vi. to whistle

apito | a'pitʋ | sm. whistle (instrument, sound)

aplacar | apla'kaʀ | vt. to placate, to appease / vi. to become calm

aplainar | aplay'ɴaʀ | vt. to plane, to level

aplanar | apla'ɴaʀ | vt. to level, to flatten

aplaudir | aplaw'diʀ | vt. to applaud; to praise

aplauso | a'plawzʋ | sm. applause

aplicação | aplika'sãw | sf. application; use; assiduity

aplicar | apli'kaʀ | vt. to apply; to use. **-a.-se** to be diligent

apoderar-se | apode'raʀsɩ | vr. to take possession, to seize control of

apodrecer | apodre'seʀ | vi. to rot, to decompose

apodrecimento | apodresi'mẽtʋ | sm. rotteness, putrefaction

apogeu | apo'jew | sm. (astron., geom.) apogee; acme; prime

apoiar | apoy'aR | *vt.* to support; to lean, to rest. **-a.-se** to depend, to lean; to base

apoio | a'poyʊ | *sm.* support

apólice | a'pʊlisɩ | *sf.* (fin.) policy, bond, share

apologia | apolo'jia | *sf.* apology, defense; panegyric

apólogo | a'pʊloɡʊ | *sm.* apologue, fable

apontador | apõta'doR | *sm.* pointer; sharpener; foreman

apontamento | apõta'mẽtʊ | *sm.* note, memorandum; annotation

apontar | apõ'taR | *vt.* to sharpen; to point out; to aim (gun etc.) / *vi.* to emerge

apoquentar | apokẽ'taR | *vt.* to badger, to annoy

após | a'pʊʃ | *adv.* after, since /*prep.* after; behind; since

aposentado -da | apozẽ'tadʊ | *a.* retired

aposentar | apozẽ'taR | *vt.* to pension off. **-a.-se** to retire

aposento | apo'zẽtʊ | *sm.* room, alcove

apossar-se | apo'saRsɩ | *vr.* to take possession (of)

aposta | a'pʊʃta | *sf.* bet

apostar | apoʃ'taR | *vt.* to bet

apostila | apʊʃ'tila | *sf.* class notes

apóstolo | a'pʊʃtʊlʊ | *sm.* apostle

apoucar | apow'kaR | *vt.* to lessen; (fig.) to belittle

aprazar | apra'zar | *vt.* to summon; to set (a specific date or time)

apreçar | apre'saR | *vt.* to price

apreciação | apresia'sãw | *sf.* appreciation, estimation

apreciar | aprɩsi'aR | *vt.* to value; to enjoy

apreço | a'presʊ | *sm.* appreciation, esteem, consideration

apreender | aprɩẽ'deR | *vt.* to apprehend, to seize

apreensão | aprɩẽ'sãw | *sf.* apprehension; anxiety

apreensivo -va | aprɩẽ'sivʊ | *a.* apprehensive; anxious

apregoar | apreɡʊ'aR | *vt.* to proclaim

aprender | aprẽ'deR | *vt.* to learn

aprendiz -diza | aprẽ'diʒ -'diza | *smf.* apprentice, novice

aprendizagem | aprẽdi'zajẽy | *sf.* apprenticeship

apresentação | aprezẽta'sãw | *sf.* presentation, introduction; show, showing

apresentar | aprezẽ'taR | *vt.* to present; to introduce; to exhibit; to show

apressado -da | apre'sadʊ | *a.* hurried; hasty

apressar | apre'saR | *vt.* to hurry, to hasten

aprestar | apreʒ'taR | *vt.* to equip. **-a.-se** to get ready

aprestos | a'prɛʃtʊʃ | *smpl.* (unc. *sing.*) equipment; preparation

aprisionar | aprizio'naR | *vt.* to imprison; to capture

aprofundar | aprʊfũ'daR | *vt.* to deepen

aprontar | aprõ'taR | *vt.* to prepare, to get ready

apropriar | apropri'aR | *vt.* to appropriate. **-a.-se** to appropriate, to take as one's own

aprovação | aprova'sãw | *sf.* approval, approbation

aprovar | apro'vaR | *vt.* to approve; to pass (a student, in an exam)

aproveitamento | aprʊveyta'mẽtʊ | *sm.* utilization; making good use of

aproveitar | aprʊvey'taR | *vt.* to benefit by; to take advantage of; to seize (opportunity); to use. **-a.-se de** to take advantage of

aproveitável | aprʊvey'tavɩl | *a.* utilizable; serviceable

aproximação | aprosima'sãw | *sf.* approximation; close estimate

aproximado -da | aprosi'madʊ | *a.* approximate

aproximar | aprosi'maR | *vt.* to approach, to bring near. **-a.-se** to approach; to draw near; to come up to

aprumar | apru'maʀ | *vt.* to erect, to place upright

aptidão | apti'dãw | *sf.* aptitude, aptness

apto -ta | 'aptʋ | *a.* apt, able, fit

apunhalar | apuɴa'laʀ | *vt.* to stab

apupar | apu'paʀ | *vt.* to hiss, to jeer, to boo

apuração | apura'sãw | *sf.* verification; counting (votes)

apurado -da | apu'radʋ | *a.* refined; counted

apurar | apu'raʀ | *vt.* to perfect; to verify; to count (votes); to make (money); to thicken (as soup etc.)

apuro | a'purʋ | *sm.* refinement, elegance; (usually *pl.*) **-estar em apuros** to be in trouble

aquário | a'kwariʋ | *sm.* aquarium

aquartelar | akwaʀte'laʀ | *vt.* to billet, to quarter

aquecer | ake'seʀ | *vt.* to warm. **-a.-se** to warm up, to warm oneself

aquecimento | akɪsi'mẽtʋ | *sm.* heating

aquele -la | a'kelɪ -'kɛla | *a.* (*m.f.*) that; (*pl.*) those

àquele-la | a'kelɪ-'kɛla | *contr.* of the *prep.* **a** with the *pron.* **aquele-la** (*m.f.*) to that (one); (*pl.*) to those

aqui | a'ki | *adv.* here. **-eis a.** here it is

aquietar | akie'taʀ | *vt.* to quiet; to appease / *vi.* to be still

aquilo | a'kilʋ | *neuter demonst. pron.* that (near person or object spoken of)

àquilo | a'kilʋ | *contr.* of the *prep.* **a** with the *pron.* **aquilo** (*neuter*) to that (one)

aquinhoar | akiɴʋ'aʀ | *vt.* to apportion, to allot

aquisição | akizi'sãw | acquisition

ar | 'ar | *sm.* air; appearance; resemblance

árabe | 'arabɪ | *sm.* (ling.) Arabic; *smf.* Arab / *a.* Arabian

arado -da | a'radʋ | *sm.* plow / *a.* plowed

aragem | a'rajẽy | *sf.* breeze

arame | a'ramɪ | *sm.* wire. **-a. farpado** barbed wire

aranha | a'raɴa | *sf.* spider

arapuca | ara'puka | *sf.* (Braz.) bird trap; (fig.) shady deal

arar | a'raʀ | *vt.* to plow

arara | a'rara | *sf.* macaw

araucária | araw'karia | *sf.* Brazilian pine, Paraná pine

arauto | a'rawtʋ | *sm.* herald

arbitragem | aʀbi'trajẽy | *sf.* arbitration; (sports) refereeing

arbitrar | aʀbi'traʀ | *vt.* to arbitrate, to judge, to settle; (sports) to referee

arbitrariedade | aʀbitrarie'dadɪ | *sf.* arbitrariness; iniquity

arbitrário -ria | aʀbi'trariʋ | *a.* arbitrary

arbítrio | aʀ'bitriʋ | *sm.* arbitrary resolution. **-livre a.** free will

árbitro | 'aʀbitrʋ | *sm.* arbitrator; mediator; (sports) referee

arbusto | aʀ'buʃtʋ | *sm.* shrub

arca | 'aʀka | *sf.* chest, ark

arcada | aʀ'kada | *sf.* arcade; (mus.) bowing

arcaico -ca | aʀ'kaykʋ | *a.* archaic

arcar | aʀ'kaʀ | *vt.* to arch, to bend / *vi.* to grapple, to struggle. **-a. com a responsabilidade** to shoulder the responsibility

arcebispo | aʀsɪ'biʃpʋ | *sm.* archbishop

arco | 'aʀkʋ | *sm.* arc; arch; bow

ardente | aʀ'dẽtɪ | *a.* ardent; burning

arder | aʀ'deʀ | *vi.* to burn, to blaze

ardil | aʀ'dil | *sm.* trick, ruse

ardor | aʀ'doʀ | *sm.* ardour, zeal, vivacity

árduo -dua | 'aʀduʋ | *a.* arduous, difficult

área | 'arɪa | *sf.* area; (Braz.) yard, court

areal | arɪ'al | *sm.* stretch of sand

areia | a'reya | *sf.* sand. **-a. movediça** quicksand

arejar | are'jaʀ | *vt.* to air, to ventilate / *vi.* to get fresh air

arenga | a'ʀẽga | *sf.* harangue

arenoso -sa | are'nozʊ -'nωza | *a.* sandy

arenque | a'ʀẽkɪ | *sm.* herring

aresta | a'ʀɛʃta | *sf.* edge, corner, angle (also geom.)

arfar | aʀ'faʀ | *vi.* to pant, to gasp; to palpitate

argamassa | aʀga'masa | *sf.* mortar, cement

argentino -na | aʀjẽ'tinʊ | *smf.* Argentine, Argentinean / *a.* Argentine; argentine (of silver)

argila | aʀ'jila | *sf.* clay

argola | aʀ'gωla | *sf.* ring, metal ring

argúcia | aʀ'gusia | *sf.* astuteness

argueiro | aʀ'geyrʊ | *sm.* speck of dust

argüição | aʀgwi'sãw | *sf.* questioning; inquisition; arguing

argüir | aʀ'gwiʀ | *vt.* to examine (orally); to impugne, to argue; to censure

argumentação | aʀgumẽta'sãw | *sf.* argumentation, reasoning

argumentar | aʀgumẽ'taʀ | *vi.* to argue; to hold or carry on an argument

argumento | aʀgu'mẽtʊ | *sm.* argument; film or story plot

arguto -ta | aʀ'gutʊ | *a.* ingenious, subtle

ária | 'aria | *sf.* (mus.) aria; *sm.a.* Aryan, Arian

aridez | ari'deʒ | *sf.* aridity

árido -da | 'aridʊ | *a.* arid

arisco -ca | a'riʃkʊ | *a.* coltish, wild; unsociable

aritmética | arit'mɛtika | *sf.* arithmetic

arlequim | aʀlɪ'kĩ | *sm.* harlequin

arma | 'aʀma | *sf.* weapon, arm (also fig.)

armação | aʀma'sãw | *sf.* frame, framework; structure; rigging (of a ship)

armada | aʀ'mada | *sf.* fleet, navy

armadilha | aʀma'diLa | *sf.* trap, snare

armador | aʀma'doʀ | *sm.* shipowner; one who arms; framer

armadura | aʀma'dura | *sf.* armour; frame

armamento | aʀma'mẽtʊ | *sm.* armament

armar | aʀ'maʀ | *vt.* to arm (also fig.); to supply with weapons; to cock a gun; to assemble

armarinho | aʀma'riNʊ | *sm.* haberdashery, notions store; small cabinet

armário | aʀ'mariʊ | *sm.* closet; cabinet; cupboard; locker

armazém | aʀma'zẽy | *sm.* warehouse; grocery store

armazenar | aʀmaze'naʀ | *vt.* to store, to put away; to stock

armeiro | aʀ'meyrʊ | *sm.* gunsmith

armistício | aʀmiʃ'tisiʊ | *sm.* armistice

aro | 'arʊ | *sm.* hoop, ring; rim of a wheel

aroma | a'roma | *sm.* aroma, perfume

aromático -ca | aro'matikʊ | *a.* aromatic

arpão | aʀ'pãw | *sm.* harpoon

arpoar | aʀpʊ'aʀ | *vt.* to harpoon

arquear | aʀkɪ'aʀ | *vt.* to arch, to bend, to bow

arquejar | aʀke'jaʀ | *vi.* to pant, to gasp

arqueologia | aʀkɪolo'jia | *sf.* archaeology

arquibancada | aʀkibã'kada | *sf.* bleachers, grandstand

arquiteto | aʀki'tɛtʊ | *sm.* architect

arquitetura | aʀkite'tura | *sf.* architecture

arquivar | aʀki'vaʀ | *vt.* to file; to record; to shelve

arquivo | aʀ'kivʊ | *sm.* file; archives; file cabinet

arrabalde | aʀa'baldɪ | *sm.* suburbs, outskirts

arraia | a'ʀaya | *sf.* ray, skate; paper kite

arraial | aRay'al | *sm.* hamlet, small village

arraigado -da | aRay'gadʊ | *a.* deep-rooted; ingrained

arrancada | aRã'kada | *sf.* jerk, sudden pull; acceleration

arrancar | aRã'kaR | *vt.* to pull (up, out, away, off), to pluck; to tear up or away / *vi.* to depart in haste; to start (motor)

arranco | a'Rãkʊ | *sm.* pull, jerk; sudden start

arranha-céu | aRaNa'sɛw | *sm.* skyscraper

arranhadura | aRaNa'dura | *sf.* = *arranhão*

arranhão | aRa'Nãw | *sm.* scratch

arranhar | aRa'NaR | *vt.* to scratch

arranjar | aRã'jaR | *vt.* to arrange (also mus.); to put in order; to obtain. **-a.-se** to take care of oneself

arranjo | a'Rãjʊ | *sm.* arrangement (also mus.); good order; adjustment; solution

arrasar | aRa'zaR | *vt.* to raze, to demolish

arrastão | aRaʒ'tãw | *sm.* drag-net, trawl

arrastar | aRaʒ'taR | *vt.* to drag; to haul. **-a.a asa** (colloq.) to court / *vi.* to crawl, to creep

arrazoado -da | aRazʊ'adʊ | *sm.* defense, plea / *a.* reasoned, justified

arrear | aRɪ'aR | *vt.* to harness, to saddle

arrebatamento | aRebata'mẽtʊ | *sm.* rapture, transport; furor, rage

arrebatar | aReba'taR | *vt.* to carry away; to snatch; to enrapture

arrebentar | aRebẽ'taR | *vt.* *vi.* to burst, to blast; to blow up

arrecadação | aRekada'sãw | *sf.* exaction; collection

arrecadar | aReka'daR | *vt.* to collect, to gather; to exact

arredar | aRe'daR | *vt.* to move away or back

arredio -dia | aRɪ'diʊ | *a.* apart, aloof

arredondar | aRedõ'daR | *vt.* to round off, to round out

arredor | aRe'dʊR | *sm.* (esp. *pl.*) surroundings, vicinity / *adv.* around, about

arrefecer | aRefe'seR | *vt.* *vi.* to cool off, to round out

arregaçar | aRega'saR | *vt.* to roll up, to tuck up, to turn up

arreganhar | aRega'NaR | *vt.* to grin, to bare one's teeth

arreio | a'Reyʊ | *sm.* (esp. *pl.*) harness

arrematar | aRema'taR | *vt.* to finish up, to give the last touch to; to buy at an auction / *vi.* to finish, to end

arremedar | aReme'daR | *vt.* to ape, to mock, to mimic

arremedo | aRe'medʊ | *sm.* imitation, mockery; appearance

arremessar | aReme'saR | *vt.* to throw, to cast, to hurl

arremesso | aRe'mesʊ | *sm.* throwing, casting

arremeter | aReme'teR | *vt.* to charge, to assail, to attack. **-a. contra** to dash against

arremetida | aReme'tida | *sf.* attack, assault

arrendar | aRẽ'daR | *vt.* to lease, to rent, to hire

arrendatário -ria | aRẽda'tariʊ | *smf.* tenant, lessee

arrepender-se | aRepẽ'deRsɪ | *vr.* to regret, to repent (of); to change one's mind

arrependimento | aRepẽdi'mẽtʊ | *sm.* regret, repentance

arrepiar | aRɪpi'aR | *vt.* to ruffle, to muss (hair, feathers, fur); to cause goose-flesh

arrepio | aRɪ'piʊ | *sm.* chiver, chill; goose-flesh

arrevesado -da | aReve'zadʊ | *a.* obscure; cross-grained

arrevesar | aReve'zaR | *vt.* to reverse, to make intricate

arriar | aRi'aR | *vt.* to lower; (naut.) to haul in, to furl / *vi.* to weaken; to become discouraged; to yield

arribar | aʀiˈbaʀ | *vi.* to touch land; (naut.) to put in or into port; (fig.) to recover

arrimo | aˈʀimʊ | *sm.* support. **-a. de família** the support of a family

arriscar | aʀiʃˈkaʀ | *vt.* to risk, to hazard; to endanger. **-a.-se** to venture, to take a chance

arrochar | aʀoˈxaʀ | *vt.* to tighten

arrogância | aʀoˈɡãsia | *sf.* arrogance

arrogante | aʀoˈɡãtɩ | *a.* arrogant, insolent

arrogar | aʀoˈɡaʀ | *vt.* to arrogate, to claim. **-a.-se o direito de to arrogate to oneself the right to

arroio | aˈʀoyʊ | *sm.* brook, streamlet

arrojado-da | aʀoˈjadʊ | *a.* daring, brave

arrojar | aʀoˈjaʀ | *vt.* to throw, to fling. **-a.-se** to dash against; to dare, to venture

arrojo | aˈʀojʊ | *sm.* boldness, intrepidity

arrolhar | aʀoˈLaʀ | *vt.* to cork

arromba | aˈʀõba | *sf.* used in the expression **de a.** terrific, excellent

arrombar | aʀõˈbaʀ | *vt.* to break in or down; to crack open

arrostar | aʀoʃˈtaʀ | *vt.* to face, to front, to brave. **-a. com** to cope with

arrotar | aʀoˈtaʀ | *vt. vi.* to belch; (fig.) to brag

arroubo | aˈʀowbʊ | *sm.* rapture, transport

arroz | aˈʀoʃ | *sm.* rice

arroz-doce | aˈʀoʃˈdosɩ | *sm.* rice pudding

arruaça | aʀuˈasa | *sf.* street fight, street brawl

arruaceiro -ra | aʀuaˈseyrʊ | *smf.* street fighter, hooligan

arruela | aʀuˈɛla | *sf.* (mech.) washer

arrufar | aʀuˈfaʀ | *vt.* to annoy.

-a.-se to be annoyed

arruinar | aʀuiˈnaʀ | *vt.* to ruin, to destroy. **-a.-se** to ruin oneself / *vi.* to fall into ruin; to decay

arrulhar | aʀuˈLaʀ | *vi.* to coo

arrulho | aˈʀuLʊ | *sm.* coo, cooing

arrumação | aʀumaˈsãw | *sf.* arrangement, disposition, tidying up

arrumar | aʀuˈmaʀ | *vt.* to arrange, to dispose; to clean; (colloq.) to get, to obtain

arte | ˈaʀtɩ | *sf.* art; craft; cunning; (colloq.) mischief

artefato, artefacto | aʀteˈfa(k)tʊ | *sm.* artifact; (*pl.*) manufactured goods

arteiro -ra | aʀˈteyrʊ | *a.* (colloq.) mischievous, naughty

artelho | aʀˈtɛLʊ | *sm.* ankle

artéria | aʀˈtɛria | *sf.* (anat.) artery (also fig.)

artesanato | aʀtezaˈnatʊ | *sm.* craftsmanship

articulação | aʀtikulaˈsãw | *sf.* articulation; pronunciation

articular | aʀtikuˈlaʀ | *vt.* to articulate; to enunciate, to pronounce

artífice | aʀˈtifisɩ | *sm.* artisan, craftsman

artifício | aʀtiˈfisiʊ | *sm.* artifice; contrivance; trick. **-fogos de a.** fireworks

artigo | aʀˈtigʊ | *sm.* article (also gram.); clause, item; (*pl.*) goods

artilharia | aʀtiLaˈria | *sf.* artillery

artimanha | aʀtiˈmaNa | *sf.* trick, artifice, ruse

artista | aʀˈtiʃta | *smf.* artist; actor, actress; performer

arvorar | aʀvoˈʀaʀ | *vt.* to hoist. **-a.-se** to claim to be, to set oneself up as

árvore | ˈaʀvʊrɩ | *sf.* tree; (mech.) axle, shaft

arvoredo | aʀvoˈredʊ | *sm.* grove of trees

ás | ˈaʃ | *sm.* ace

asa | ˈaza | *sf.* wing; handle

ascendência | asẽ'dẽsia | *sf.* ancestry; ascendency

ascendente | asẽ'dẽtɩ | *smf.* ancestor / *a.* rising, upward

ascensão | asẽ'sãw | *sf.* ascension, ascent; promotion, elevation

ascensor | asẽ'soʀ | *sm.* lift, elevator

ascensorista | asẽso'riʃta | *smf.* lift operator

asco | 'aʃkʊ | *sm.* repugnance; disgust, nausea

asfalto | aʃ'faltʊ | *sm.* asphalt

asfixiar | aʃfiksi'aʀ | *vt. vi.* (also **a.-se**) to choke, to suffocate

asiático -ca | azi'atikʊ | *smf.a.* Asian, Asiatic

asilar | azi'laʀ | *vt.* to give asylum to, to protect. **-a.-se** to take refuge

asilo | a'zilʊ | *sm.* asylum; shelter, refuge; home, institution (for orphans etc.)

asneira | aʃ'neyra | *sf.* nonsense, stupidity; folly

asno | 'aʃnʊ | *sm.* ass; donkey

aspa | 'aʃpa | *sf.* horn, antler; St. Andrew's cross; (*pl.*, *gram.*) quotation marks

aspargo | aʃ'paʀgʊ | *sm.* = *espargo*

aspecto, aspeto | aʃ'pɛ(k)tʊ | *sm.* aspect, air

aspereza | aʃpe'reza | *sf.* roughness, asperity; harshness, severity

áspero -ra | 'aʃperʊ | *a.* rough, coarse; harsh; severe

aspiração | aʃpira'sãw | *sf.* aspiration; ambition; breathing; inhaling

aspirador -dora | aʃpira'doʀ | *sm.* aspirator. **-a. de pó** vacuum cleaner / *a.* aspirating

aspirante | aʃpi'rãtɩ | *sm.* cadet / *a.* aspirant

aspirar | aʃpi'raʀ | *vt.* to inhale, to breathe in, to aspirate / *vi.* to aspire; to breathe

aspirina | aʃpi'rina | *sf.* aspirin

asqueroso -sa | aʃke'rozʊ -'rʊza |

a. disgusting, repulsive

assado -da | a'sadʊ | *sm.* roast / *a.* roast, roasted, baked

assadura | asa'dura | *sf.* chafe, chafing

assaltante | asal'tãtɩ | *smf.* brigand; assailant / *a.* assaulting, attacking, assailing

assaltar | asal'taʀ | *vt.* to assault, to attack

assalto | a'saltʊ | *sm.* assault, attack, aggression, holdup

assanhado -da | asa'Nadʊ | *sm.* fresh, bold; *sf.* provocative / *a.* ardent, impetuous; excited

assanhar | asa'Naʀ | *vt.* to enrage, to infuriate; to provoke, to excite

assar | a'saʀ | *vt.* to roast; to bake; to irritate (skin) / *vi.* to roast

assassinar | asasi'naʀ | *vt.* to assassinate, to murder

assassinato, assassínio | asasi'natʊ, asa'siniʊ | *sm.* assassination, killing

assassino -na | asa'sinʊ | *sm.* assassin, killer, murderer / *a.* murderous

assaz | a'saʃ | *adv.* enough, rather, sufficiently

assear | asɩ'aʀ | *vt.* to clean, to tidy up

assediar | asedi'aʀ | *vt.* to besiege; to annoy; to molest (with questions)

assegurar | asɩgu'raʀ | *vt.* to assure, to guarantee; to affirm

asseio | a'seyʊ | *sm.* cleanliness; neatness

assembléia | asẽ'blɛya | *sf.* assembly; congress, legislative body

assemelhar | aseme'laʀ | *vt.* to make similar; to liken, to compare. **-a.-se** to resemble, to be like

assentada | asẽ'tada | *sf.* (law) session. **-de uma a.** in one sitting; in a row

assentado -da | asẽ'tadʊ | *a.* seated; set, firm; settled

assentar | asẽ'taʀ | *vt.* to seat; to lay, to place; to set down; to register; to stipulate. **-a.-se** to sit down. **-a. praça** (mil.) to enlist / *vi.* to settle; to go well with

assentimento | asẽti'mẽtʊ | *sm.* assent, acquiescence

assento | a'sẽtʊ | *sm.* seat, base; bottom

asserção | aseʀ'sãw | *sf.* assertion, claim

assessor -sora | ase'soʀ | *smf.* adviser, attendant

assessorar | aseso'raʀ | *vt.* to advise, to attend, to assist

assiduidade | asidui'dadɪ | *sf.* assiduity

assíduo -dua | a'sidʊʊ | *a.* assiduous; diligent

assim | a'sĩ | *adv.* so, like this, thus. **-ainda a.** even so. **-a. que** as soon as

assimilação | asimila'sãw | *sf.* assimilation

assimilar | asimi'laʀ | *vt.* to assimilate

assinalar | asina'laʀ | *vt.* to mark; to point out. **-a.-se** to distinguish oneself

assinante | asi'nãtɪ | *smf.* subscriber

assinar | asi'naʀ | *vt.* to sign; to subscribe; to determine. **-a.-se** to sign oneself

assinatura | asina'tura | *sf.* signature; subscription

assistência | asiʃ'tẽsia | *sf.* attendance; assembly, audience; aid; (colloq.) ambulance

assistente | asiʃ'tẽtɪ | *smf.* assistant, adjutant / *a.* assistant, assisting; auxiliary

assistir | asiʃ'tir | *vt.* to assist; to help / *vi.* to attend, to be present at; to assist, to help

assoalho | asʊ'aʌʊ | *sm.* floor, flooring

assoar | asʊ'aʀ | *vt.* (also **a.-se**) to blow (one's nose)

associação | asosia'sãw | *sf.* association; society

associado -da | asosi'adʊ | *smf.* associate; member / *a.* associated; connected

associar | asosi'aʀ | *vt.* to associate / *vi.* to mingle, to mix

assolar | aso'laʀ | *vt.* to devastate, to destroy

assomar | aso'maʀ | *vi.* to appear; to emerge. **-a. a** to appear at (a window etc.)

assombração | asõbra'sãw | *sf.* apparition, ghost

assombrar | asõ'braʀ | *vt.* (also **a.-se**) to astonish; to frighten, to terrify

assombro | a'sõbrʊ | *sm.* wonder, marvel

assombroso -sa | asõ'brozʊ -'brɔza | *a.* astonishing, amazing

assomo | a'somʊ | *sm.* fit of anger, exasperation

assoviar | asʊvi'aʀ | *vt. vi.* to whistle; to hiss

assovio | asʊ'viʊ | *sm.* whistle (sound, act or instrument)

assumir | asu'mir | *vt.* to assume, to undertake; to adopt

assunção | asũ'sãw | *sf.* assumption

assunto | a'sũtʊ | *sm.* subject matter

assustar | asuʃ'taʀ | *vt.* (also **a.-se**) to startle, to frighten, to scare

astro | 'aʃtrʊ | *sm.* star, planet; famous person (esp. movie actor)

astronauta | aʃtro'nawta | *sm.* astronaut

astronáutica | aʃtro'nawtika | *sf* astronautics

astronáutico -ca | aʃtro'nawtikʊ | *a.* astronautical

astronomia | aʃtrono'mia | *sf.* astronomy

astrônomo | aʃ'tronomʊ | *sm.* astronomer

astúcia | aʃ'tusia | *sf.* cunning, shrewdness

astucioso -sa | aʃtusi'ozʊ -'ɔza | *a.* shrewd, cunning, astute

ata | 'ata | *sf.* record, minute; (bot.) sweetsop

atacadista | ataka'diʒta | *smf.* wholesaler / *a.* wholesale

atacado -da | ata'kadʋ | *a.* attacked, assaulted. **-por a.** wholesale

atacante | ata'kãtɩ | *smf.* (sports) offensive player / *a.* attacking, aggressive

atacar | ata'kaʀ | *vt.* to attack, to assault; to charge; to corrode

atadura | ata'dura | *sf.* bandage

atalaia | ata'laya | *smf.* sentinel, watch; *sf.* watch-tower

atalhar | ata'ʟaʀ | *vt.* to stop, to check; to cut down; to intercept / *vi.* to take a short cut; to interrupt

atalho | a'taʟʋ | *sm.* short cut

ataque | a'takɩ | *sm.* attack (also med.). **-a. aéreo** air raid

atar | a'taʀ | *vt.* to tie (up), to fasten

atarefado -da | atare'fadʋ | *a.* busy

atarraxar | ataʀa'xaʀ | *vt.* to screw

ataúde | ata'udɩ | *sm.* coffin

ataviar | atavi'aʀ | *vt.* to ornament, to adorn. **-a.-se** to attire

atávico -ca | a'tavikʋ | *a.* atavistic

até | a'tɛ | *adv.* although, even. **-a. aqui, tudo bem** so far, so good/ *prep.* until, to, up to the time. **-a. agora** as yet, up to the day. **-a. que ponto?** how far? **-a. logo** good-bye

atear | atɩ'aʀ | *vt.* to kindle, to light. **-a. fogo a** to set fire to

ateísmo | atɛ'iʒmʋ | *sm.* atheism

atemorizar | atemori'zaʀ | *vt.* to frighten; to intimidate. **-a.-se** to be frightened

atenção | atẽ'sãw | *sf.* attention; civility, courtesy / *interj.* attention!, look out!

atencioso -sa | atẽsi'ozʋ -'ωza | *a.* attentive; thoughtful; courteous

atender | atẽ'deʀ | *vt.* to listen (to); to answer (telephone, door etc.); to serve. **-a. pelo nome de** to answer to the name of

atentado | atẽ'tadʋ | *sm.* criminal attack

atentar | atẽ'taʀ | *vt.* to pay attention to, to observe / *vi.* to observe attentively; to ponder

atento -ta | a'tẽtʋ | *a.* attentive, alert; courteous

atenuação | atenua'sãw | *sf.* attenuation

atenuante | atenu'ãtɩ | *sf.* (law) attenuating circumstance / *a.* attenuating

atenuar | atenu'aʀ | *vt.* to attenuate, to diminish

aterrado -da | ate'ʀadʋ | *sm.* filled-in land / *a.* filled, leveled (land); (aeron.) landed; terrified, frightened

aterrar | ate'ʀaʀ | *vt.* to cover, to fill (with earth); to frighten / *vi.* (aeron.) to land

aterrissagem | ateʀi'sajẽy | *sf.* (aeron.) landing

aterrissar | ateʀi'saʀ | *vi.* (aeron.) to land

aterro | a'teʀʋ | *sm.* earth embankment

atestado -da | ateʒ'tadʋ | *sm.* certificate / *a.* full, brimful

atestar | ateʒ'taʀ | *vt.* to attest, to certify; to fill (up), to fill to the brim

ateu -éia | a'tew -'tɛya | *smf.* atheist / *a.* atheistic

atiçar | ati'saʀ | *vt.* to poke (a fire); to incite, to provoke

atilado -da | ati'ladʋ | *a.* keen, sharp

atinado -da | ati'nadʋ | *a.* intelligent, astute

atinar | ati'naʀ | *vt.* to guess (com, at), to find (out) / *vi.* to discover (by conjecture)

atingir | atĩ'jiʀ | *vt.* to hit; to touch (on, upon); to reach; to understand

atiradeira | atira'deyra | *sf.* sling-shot, boy's catapult

atirar | ati'raʀ | *vt.* to throw, to cast / *vi.* to shoot, to fire

atitude | ati'tudɩ | *sf.* attitude

ativo -va | a'tivʋ | *sm.* (com.) assets / *a.* active

atlas | 'atlaʒ | *sm.* atlas (also anat.); (*cap.*) Atlas

atleta | a'tlɛta | *smf.* athlete

atmosfera | atmoʒ'fɛra | *sf.* atmosphere

ato | 'atʊ | *sm.* act

à-toa | a'toa | *a.* worthless; easy; vile. **-coisa à.** (colloq.) a trifling problem. **-mulher à.** (colloq.) prostitute

atolar | ato'laʀ | *vt.* to stick down in mud. **-a.-se** to stick in mud, to bog down

atoleiro | ato'leyrʊ | *sm.* bog, marsh, swamp

atômico-ca | a'tomikʊ | *a.* atomic, atomical

átomo | 'atomʊ | *sm.* atom

atônito -ta | a'tonitʊ | *a.* amazed, astonished

ator | a'toʀ | *sm.* actor

atordoado -da | atʊʀdʊ'adʊ | *a.* stunned; astonished

atordoamento | atʊʀdʊa'mētʊ | *sm.* numbness, dizziness

atormentar | atoʀmē'taʀ | *vt.* to torment; to tease, to badger

atração | atra'sãw | *sf.* attraction, affinity; magnetism

atracar | atra'kaʀ | *vt.* (naut.) to moor, to dock; to come alongside

atraente | atra'ētɪ | *a.* attractive, charming

atraiçoar | atraysʊ'aʀ | *vt.* to betray

atrair | atra'iʀ | *vt.* to attract; to allure, to entice

atrapalhar | atrapa'laʀ | *vt.* to confuse, to disturb. **-a.-se** to become confused, to get mixed up / *vi.* to cause confusion; to be upsetting

atrás | a'traʒ | *adv.* back; before, prior to; behind; ago. **-a de** after; behind

atrasado-da | atra'zadʊ | *a.* under-developed; delayed; late or overdue (in payment of bills); obsolete; slow (watch)

atrasar | atra'zaʀ | *vt.* to hold back; to delay; to postpone; to set an earlier hour. **-a.-se** to remain behind; to neglect payment on time

atraso | a'trazʊ | *sm.* backwardness; delay; late or overdue payments (of bills)

através | atra'vɛʒ | *adv.* used in the expression **a. de** through, across

atravessar | atrave'saʀ | *vt.* to traverse, to cross over or through; to place across / *vi.* to move across

atrelar | atre'laʀ | *vt.* to leash; to harness; to yoke

atrever-se | atre'veʀsɪ | *vr.* to dare, to venture

atrevido -da | atrɪ'vidʊ | *a.* bold, intrepid; impudent; brash

atrevimento | atrɪvi'mētʊ | *sm.* boldness, daring; impudence

atribuição | atribui'sãw | *sf.* attribution, assignment; (*pl.*) powers, rights

atribuir | atribu'iʀ | *vt.* to attribute, to ascribe

atributo | atri'butʊ | *sm.* attribute

átrio | 'atriʊ | *sm.* courtyard; vestibule

atrito | a'tritʊ | *sm.* friction, clash of temperament or opinion

atriz | a'triʒ | *sf.* actress

atroar | atrʊ'aʀ | *vt.* to resound, to thunder, to roar

atrocidade | atrosi'dadɪ | *sf.* atrocity, cruelty

atrofiar-se | atrofi'aʀsɪ | *vr.* to become atrophied

atropelamento | atropela'mētʊ | *sm.* trampling, running over

atropelar | atrʊpe'laʀ | *vt.* to run down or over; to trample, to knock down

atropelo | atrʊ'pelʊ | *sm.* trampling, overturning; hustle

atroz | a'trɔʒ | *a.* atrocious; excruciating

atuação | atua'sãw | *sf.* performance, acting

atual | atu'al | *a.* present, current

atualidade | atuali'dadɩ | *sf.* the present, nowadays; (*pl.*) news, news-reel

atuar | atu'aʀ | *vt.* to actuate, to influence / *vi.* to act

atulhar | atu'ʟaʀ | *vt.* to cram, to pack (in), to stuff full

atum | a'tũ | *sm.* tunny, tuna

aturar | atu'ʀaʀ | *vt.* to bear, to tolerate / *vi.* to remain, to last

aturdido -da | atuʀ'didʊ | *a.* perplexed, bewildered

aturdir | atuʀ'diʀ | *vt.* to bewilder, to perplex

audácia | aw'dasia | *sf.* boldness, daring; effrontery

audacioso -sa | awdasi'ozʊ-'ɔza | *a.* bold, daring; impudent

audição | awdi'sãw | *sf.* hearing, audition

audiência | awdi'ẽsia | *sf.* hearing (also law); audition; formal interview; court session

auditório | awdi'tɔriʊ | *sm.* audience, auditorium

audível | aw'divɩl | *a.* audible

auferir | awfɩ'ʀiʀ | *vt.* to benefit; to receive (benefits)

auge | 'awjɩ | *sm.* height, peak

augurar | awgu'ʀaʀ | *vt.* to augur, to predict

aula | 'awla | *sf.* class. **-dar a.** to teach, to have a class

aumentar | awmẽ'taʀ | *vt.* to increase; to raise, to intensify / *vi.* to increase, to augment, to grow

aumento | aw'mẽtʊ | *sm.* rise, increase; expansion, growth. **-a. de salário** salary increase

aura | 'awra | *sf.* aura (also med.); breeze; renown, fame

áureo -rea | 'awrɩʊ | *a.* golden

auréola | aw'rɛʊla | *sf.* halo

aurora | aw'rɔra | *sf.* dawn

ausência | aw'zẽsia | *sf.* absence; want

ausentar-se | awzẽ'taʀsɩ | *vr.* to be absent; to absent oneself

ausente | aw'zẽtɩ | *smf.* absentee / *a.* absent, away; missing

austeridade | awʃteri'dadɩ | *sf.* austerity

austero -ra | awʃ'tɛrʊ | *a.* austere, severe

austral | awʃ'tral | *a.* southern

australiano -na | awʃtrali'anʊ | *smf. a.* Australian

austríaco -ca | awʃ'triakʊ | *smf. a.* Austrian

autenticar | awtẽti'kaʀ | *vt.* to authenticate; to countersign. **-a. em cartório** to notarize

autêntico -ca | aw'tẽtikʊ | *a.* authentic, genuine

auto | 'awtʊ | *sm.* (short for) automobile; kind of play or drama; solemnity; (*pl.*, law) records, papers of legal proceedings

auto-estrada | 'awtʊɩʃ'trada | *sf.* highway

autógrafo -fa | aw'tɔgrafʊ | *sm.* autograph / *a.* autographic

automática | awto'matika | *sf.* semi-automatic pistol

automático -ca | awto'matikʊ | *a.* automatic

automatização | awtomatiza'sãw | *sf.* automatization; automation

automóvel | awto'mɔvɩl | *sm.* car, automobile / *a.* automotive

autonomia | awtono'mia | *sf.* autonomy, self-government; independency

autônomo -ma | aw'tonomʊ | *a.* autonomous; free

autópsia | aw'tɔpsia | *sf.* autopsy, post-mortem

autor -tora | aw'toʀ | *smf.* author

auto-retrato | 'awtʊʀe'tratʊ | *sm.* self-portrait

autoria | awtʊ'ria | *sf.* authorship

autoridade | awtori'dadɩ | *sf.* authority; (*pl.*) authorities, officials

autoritário -ria | awtori'tariʊ | *a.* authoritarian

autorização | awtoriza'sãw | *sf.* authorization

autorizado -da | awtori'zadʊ | *a.* authorized; authoritative; respected

autorizar | awtori'zaʀ | *vt.* to authorize, to permit; to grant

auxiliar | awsili'aR | *smf.* auxiliary, assistant / *a.* auxiliary, adjunct / *vt.* to aid; to help out

auxílio | aw'siliv | *sm.* aid, help, assistance

avacalhação | avakaLa'sãw | *sf.* (vulg.) demoralization

aval | a'val | *sm.* (law) co-signer's agreement; moral support

avaliação | avalia'sãw | *sf.* evaluation, appraisal

avaliar | avali'aR | *vt.* to evaluate, to estimate; to price, to value; to calculate

avalista | ava'liʃta | *smf.* co-signer

avalizar | avali'zaR | *vt.* to co-sign, to guarantee

avançar | avã'saR | *vt.* to advance, to move forward. **-a. o sinal** to go against the red light / *vi.* to advance, to progress, to lay hands on, to steal

avarento -ta | ava'rẽtv | *smf.* miser, niggard / *a.* avaricious, tight-fisted

avareza | ava'reza | *sf.* avarice, greed

avaria | ava'ria | *sf.* damage (also maritime law)

ave | 'avι | *sf.* bird, fowl. **-a. de rapina** bird of prey

aveia | a'veya | *sf.* oat(s); oatmeal

avelã | ave'lã | *sf.* hazel-nut

avenca | a'vẽka | *sf.* (bot.) Venus's hair

avença | a'vẽsa | *sf.* agreement

avenida | avι'nida | *sf.* avenue

avental | avẽ'tal | *sm.* apron

aventura | avẽ'tura | *sf.* adventure. **-a. amorosa** love affair

aventurar | avẽtu'raR | *vt.* to venture, to risk

aventureiro -ra | avẽtu'reyrv | *sm.* adventurer; *sf.* adventuress / *a.* adventurous

averiguação | averigwa'sãw | *sf.* investigation, verification

averiguar | averi'gwaR | *vt.* to investigate, to verify

aversão | aveR'sãw | *sf.* aversion, repugnance

avessas | a'vesaʃ | *sfpl.* used in the expression **às a.** inside out, backwards, the other way round

avesso -sa | a'vesv | *sm.* reverse, wrong side / *a.* contrary, opposite

avestruz | avιʃ'truʃ | *smf.* ostrich

aviação | avia'sãw | *sf.* aviation

aviador -dora | avia'doR | *smf.* flyer, pilot

aviamento | avia'mẽtv | *sm.* filling (prescription); dispatching, shipping; (*pl.*) notions (in dress-making)

avião | avi'ãw | *sm.* aircraft, airplane

aviar | avi'aR | *vt.* to dispatch, to send off, to ship; to execute, to carry out; to fill (prescription)

avidez | avi'deʃ | *sf.* avidity; greediness

ávido -da | 'avidv | *a.* avid; greedy; voracious

aviltar | avil'taR | *vt.* to debase, to degrade. **-a.-se** to demean oneself

avinagrado -da | avina'gradv | *a.* sourish, vinegar-like

avisado -da | avi'zadv | *a.* notified, warned; prudent, judicious

avisar | avi'zaR | *vt.* to notify, to give notice of; to caution

aviso | a'vizv | *sm.* notice, warning, signal

avistar | aviʃ'taR | *vt.* to see, to catch sight of. **-a.-se** to have an interview with

avivar | avi'vaR | *vt.* to enliven; to renew, to refresh; to quicken

avizinhar | avizi'ɴaR | *vt.* to approximate, to place close to. **-a.-se** to approach

avo | 'avv | *sm.* (arith.) an "eenth", a fraction

avô -vó | a'vo -'vɔ | *sm.* grandfather; *sf.* grandmother; (*pl.*) | a'vɔʃ | grandparents, forefathers

avolumar | avvlu'maR | *vt.* to augment (volume). **-a.-se** to bulk, to increase in volume / *vi.* to be voluminous

avulso -sa | a'vulsv | *a.* extracted; detached, loose

avultado -da | avul'tadʋ | *a.* bulky, voluminous

avultar | avul'taʀ | *vt.* to augment, to increase; to show in relief / *vi.* to stand out

axila | a'ksila | *sf.* armpit; axilla

azáfama | a'zafama | *sf.* bustle, ado, fuss

azálea, azaléia | a'zalɪa aza'lɛya | *sf.* (bot.) azalea

azar | a'zaʀ | *sm.* bad luck. -**jogo de a.** game of chance

azarado -da | aza'radʋ | *a.* unlucky, unfortuned, jinxed

azedar | aze'daʀ | *vi.* (also **a.-se**) to sour; to become irritated

azedo -da | a'zedʋ | *sm.* sourness / *a.* sour, acid; acrimonious

azedume | aze'dumɪ | *sm.* sourness; acrimony, irritation

azeite | a'zeytɪ | *sm.* olive oil

azeitona | azey'tona | *sf.* olive

azeviche | azɪ'vixɪ | *sm.* jet, pitch coal

azia | a'zia | *sf.* heartburn

aziago -ga | azi'agʋ | *a.* unlucky, ill-fated

ázimo -ma | 'azimʋ | *a.* unleaved

azinhavre | azi'Navrɪ | *sm.* verdigris

azoto | a'zotʋ | *sm.* (chem.) = *nitrogênio*

azougue | a'zowgɪ | *sm.* quicksilver, mercury; (colloq.) dynamic person

azucrinar | azukri'naʀ | *vt.* (colloq.) to annoy, to pester

azul | a'zul | *sm.* the colour blue / *a.* blue

azulejo | azu'lejʋ | *sm.* glazed tile

B

baba | 'baba | *sf.* slobber, dribbling saliva

babá | ba'ba | *sf.* nanny, nursemaid

babaçu | baba'su | *sm.* (bot.) babassu palm

bacalhau | baka'Law | *sm.* cod, codfish, dried codfish

bacana | ba'kana | *a.* (slang) smart, tops, terrific

bacharel -rela | baxa'rɛl -'rɛla | *smf.* bachelor or graduate at the university level; law school graduate

bacia | ba'sia | *sf.* basin (also geog., geol.); (anat.) pelvic cavity

bacilo | ba'silʋ | *sm.* bacillus

baço -ça | 'basʋ | *sm.* (anat.) spleen / *a.* tarnished, dull

báculo | 'bakulʋ | *sm.* crosier

badalada | bada'lada | *sf.* stroke (of a bell), clang

badalar | bada'laʀ | *vi.* to ring, to peal; (colloq.) to gossip; to knock about

badalo | ba'dalʋ | *sm.* bell clapper

bafejar | bafe'jaʀ | *vt.* to warm with the breath; to whiff; to favour / *vi.* to exhale

bafio | ba'fiʋ | *sm.* mustiness, fustiness

bafo | 'bafʋ | *sm.* breath, whiff, exhalation

baforada | bafo'rada | *sf.* puff, whiff (of tobacco smoke)

baga | 'baga | *sf.* (bot.) berry; bead, drop (perspiration)

bagaceira | baga'seyra | *sf.* bagasse dump; marc brandy; waste, junk

bagaço | ba'gasʋ | *sm.* bagasse; crushed skins, pips etc. (of fruit)

bagageiro -ra | baga'jeyrʋ | *sm.* baggage car / *a.* baggage carrying

bagagem | ba'gajẽy | *sm.* baggage, luggage

bagatela | baga'tɛla | *sf.* trifle, bagatelle

bago | 'bagυ | *sm.* grain; grape; small lead pellet (shot); (slang) testicle

bagre | 'bagrι | *sm.* catfish

bagunça | ba'gūsa | *sf.* mess, disorder

baia | 'baya | *sf.* stall (in a stable)

baía | ba'ia | *sf.* bay; harbour

bailado | bay'ladυ | *sm.* ballet, dance

bailarino -na | bayla'rinυ | *smf.* ballet dancer; *sf.* ballerina

baile | 'baylι | *sm.* ball, dance

bainha | ba'iNa | *sf.* scabbard; sheath (also bot., anat.); hem

baioneta | bayo'neta | *sf.* bayonet. **-b. calada** fixed bayonet

bairro | 'bayRυ | *sm.* quarter (of a town), city district

baixa | 'bayxa | *sf.* decrease, reduction; drop (in price); stock market dip; (mil.) discharge; (*pl.*) casualties

baixada | bay'xada | *sf.* lowland, bottomland

baixar | bay'xaR | *vt.* to lower / *vi.* to go down, to come down; to decrease; to fall, to drop

baixeza | bay'xeza | *sf.* lowness, vileness, baseness

baixio | bay'xiυ | *sm.* sandbar, shoal

baixo -xa | 'bayxυ | *sm.* shoal; (mus.) bass, basso / *a.* low; short; shallow; vile, base; (mus.) low-pitched

baixo-relevo | 'bayxυRe'levυ | *sm.* low relief

bala | 'bala | *sf.* bullet; hard candy, caramel

balada | ba'lada | *sf.* ballad

balaio | ba'layυ | *sm.* kind of basket made of split bamboo

balança | ba'lãsa | *sf.* scale, balance

balançar | balã'saR | *vt.* to swing, to oscillate, to rock back and

forth; to balance / *vi.* to oscillate, to swing

balanço | ba'lãsυ | *sm.* oscillation, swinging; rolling (of a ship); swing; (com.) balance sheet

balão | ba'lãw | *sm.* baloon; (chem.) flask

balaustrada | balauʒ'trada | *sf.* balustrade, banisters

balbuciar | balbusi'aR | *vt. vi.* to babble, to prattle; to stammer

balbúrdia | bal'buRdia | *sf.* hubbub; tumult; confusion

balcão | bal'kãw | *sm.* counter; balcony (also theat.)

balcão-nobre | bal'kãw'nωbrι | *sm.* (theat.) dress circle, mezzanine

baldar | bal'daR | *vt.* to frustrate, to defeat, to thwart

balde | 'baldι | *sm.* bucket, pail

baldeação | baldιa'sãw | *sf.* trans-shipment

baldear | baldι'aR | *vt.* to bail (water); to transfer (passengers or baggage), to trans-ship

baldio -dia | bal'diυ | *a.* uncultivated, unused. **-terreno b.** vacant lot, waste land

balear | balι'aR | *vt.* to wound with a bullet

baleeiro -ra | balι'eyrυ | *sm.* whaler; whaling ship; *sf.* sportive row-boat

baleia | ba'leya | *sf.* whale

balido | ba'lidυ | *sm.* bleat, baa

baliza | ba'liza | *sf.* landmark; buoy; seamark; delimitation; drum major or majorette

balneário-ria | balnι'ariυ | *sm.* balneary, bath; bathing beach; watering place / *a.* balneary

balofo -fa | ba'lofυ | *a.* puffy; adipose; bloated

balouço | ba'lowsυ | *sm.* swinging; rolling, pitching (of a ship)

balsa | 'balsa | *sf.* raft; ferryboat; balsa (also bot.)

bálsamo | 'balsamυ | *sm.* balm, balsam (also fig.); aroma

baluarte | balu'aRtι | *sm.* bulwark,

bastion

balzaquiana | balzaki'ana | *sf.* (colloq.) a woman in her thirties

balzaquiano -na | balzaki'anʊ | *a.* related to Balzac or to his style

bamba | 'bãba | *sm.* (colloq.) expert, shark, tough guy

bambo -ba | 'bãbʊ | *a.* slack, loose

bambolear | bãbʊlɪ'aʀ | *vt.* (also **b.-se**) *vi.* to wiggle (one's hips); to swagger

bamboleio | bãbo'leyʊ | *sm.* wiggling (of the hips); shimmy (of the front wheels)

bambu | bã'bu | *sm.* bamboo

banal | ba'nal | *a.* banal, trivial, commonplace

banana | ba'nana | *sf.* banana; obscene gesture of contempt; stick of dynamite; *sm.* weakling

bananada | bana'nada | *sf.* confection made of bananas and sugar

bananeira | bana'neyra | *sf.* banana plant

banca | 'bãka | *sf.* examining board; craftsman bench; market stall; lawyer's office; the bank (at gambling); news-stand

bancada | bã'kada | *sf.* craftsman bench; a congressional bloc

bancar | bã'kaʀ | *vt.* (colloq.) to pretend to be, to act / *vi.* to bank (gambling)

bancário -ria | bã'karɪʊ | *smf.* bank clerk / *a.* of or pertaining to banks

bancarrota | bãka'ʀota | *sf.* bankruptcy

banco | 'bãkʊ | *sm.* bench, stool; bank (fin., geol.); reef, shoal

banda | 'bãda | *sf.* band (also mus., rad.); side, flank; ribbon, sash. **-pôr de b.** to discard, to cast aside

bandeira | bã'deyra | *sf.* flag, banner; colonial exploratory expedition in Brazil

bandeirante | bãdey'rãtɪ | *sm.* member of a colonial expedi-

tion in Brazil; *sf.* girl scout / *a.* pertaining to the State of São Paulo

bandeja | bã'deja | *sf.* tray

bandido | bã'didʊ | *sm.* outlaw, robber, brigand

bando | 'bãdʊ | *sm.* band; gang; flock; cloud

bandoleiro -ra | bãdo'leyrʊ | *smf.* outlaw bandoleer

bandolim | bãdʊ'lĩ | *sm.* mandolin

banha | 'baNa | *sf.* lard, animal fat

banhado -da | ba'Nadʊ | *sm.* swamp, marsh / *a.* bathed; wet

banhar | ba'Naʀ | *vt.* to bathe

banheira | ba'Neyra | *sf.* bath-tub

banheiro | ba'Neyrʊ | *sm.* bathroom

banhista | ba'Niʃta | *smf.* bather; *sm.* life-guard

banho | 'baNʊ | *sm.* bath, bathing; (usu. *pl.*) banns (of marriage)

banho-maria | 'baNʊma'ria | *sf.* double boiler

banqueiro | bã'keyrʊ | *sm.* (fin., games) banker; (games) dealer, croupier

banquete | bã'ketɪ | *sm.* banquet

banzé | bã'zɛ | *sm.* (colloq.) disorder, disturbance

baque | 'bakɪ | *sm.* thud, thump; (fig.) disaster

baquear | bakɪ'aʀ | *vi.* to tumble, to fall heavily

barafunda | bara'fũda | *sf.* mess, confusion

baralhar | bara'laʀ | *vt.* to shuffle (cards); to disorder, to jumble

baralho | ba'ralʊ | *sm.* deck (of cards)

barão | ba'rãw | *sm.* baron

barata | ba'rata | *sf.* cockroach

barato -ta | ba'ratʊ | *sm.* housetake (gambling house) / *a.* cheap, inexpensive

barba | 'baRba | *sf.* beard (also *pl.*). **-fazer a b.** to shave

barbante | baR'bãtɪ | *sm.* string, twine

barbaridade | baRbari'dadɪ | *sf.* barbarity; cruelty; (fig.)

absurdity

bárbaro -ra |'baʀbaʀʋ| *smf*. Barbarian / *a*. barbarous, savage

barbatana|baʀba'tana|*sf*. fin (of a fish)

barbear|baʀbɪ'aʀ|*vt*. (also **b.-se**) to shave

barbearia|baʀbɪa'ria|*sf*. barber-shop

barbeiragem | baʀbey'rajěy | *sf*. (colloq.) bad driving

barbeiro | baʀ'beyrʋ |*sm*. barber; (entom.) the barber bug; (colloq.) bad driver

barca | 'baʀka | *sf*. ferryboat; barge

barcaça | baʀ'kasa | *sf*. a large barge

barco | 'baʀkʋ |*sm*. boat, ship

bardo | 'baʀdʋ |*sm*. bard, poet

barômetro | ba'rometrʋ | *sm*. barometer

barqueiro | baʀ'keyrʋ |*sm*. boatman, bargeman

barra|'baʀa|*sf*. bar; hem of a garment; bar of a harbour

barraca|ba'ʀaka|*sf*. tent; stall (in market); beach umbrella

barracão|baʀa'kãw|*sm*. shanty, roughly-built dwelling

barragem | ba'ʀajěy | *sf*. barrage (also mil.); dam

barranco | ba'ʀãkʋ |*sm*. ravine, steep bank

barreira | ba'ʀeyra | *sf*. barrier, barricade; obstacle

barrica|ba'ʀika|*sf*. cask

barricada | baʀi'kada | *sf*. barricade

barriga | ba'ʀiga | *sf*. belly; (fig.) bulge. **-b. da perna** calf of the leg

barril | ba'ʀil |*sm*. barrel

barro | 'baʀʋ |*sm*. clay; mud

barulhento -ta |baru'Lětʋ | *a*. noisy

barulho | ba'ruLʋ |*sm*. noise; brawl, tumult

base |'bazɪ | *sf*. base (also mil., chem., geom., math.); foundation; basis

basear|bazɪ'aʀ|*vt*. (also **b.-se**) to base

basta |'baʃta |*sm*. only in expressions such as **dar o b.** (colloq.) to put a stop to / *interj*. enough!

bastante | baʃ'tãtɪ | *a*. enough, sufficient / *adv*. sufficiently, quite

bastão | baʃ'tãw | *sm*. staff; walking stick

bastar | baʃ'taʀ | *vi*. to suffice, to be enough

bastardo -da | baʃ'taʀdʋ | *smf*. bastard / *a*. bastard, illegitimate

bastidor | baʃti'doʀ |*sm*. embroidery frame; (*pl*., theat.) wings

basto -ta | 'baʃtʋ |*a*. dense, thick, bushy

batalha|ba'taLa|*sf*. battle, combat; (mil.) action

batalhão | bata'Lãw | *sm*. (mil.) batallion

batata|ba'tata|*sf*. potato. **-na b.** (colloq.) certainly

batedeira | bate'deyra | *sf*. mixer; churn

batedor|bate'doʀ|*sm*. beater (also in hunt); mixer; (mil.) scout; forerunner. **-b. de carteiras** pickpocket

bate-estacas | 'batɪʃ'takaʃ | *sm*. (*sing*. and *pl*.) pile-driver

batelada|bate'lada|*sf*. boatload

bate-papo |'batɪ'papʋ|*sm*. chat

bater | ba'teʀ | *vt*. to beat; to knock; to strike (also hours, coins); to hit. **-b.-se** to fight. **-b. palmas** to applaud. **-b. papo** (colloq.) to chat / *vi*. to beat; to slam; to bump; to pulsate

bateria | bate'ria | *sf*. (elect., mil.) battery; (mus.) percussion instruments. **-b. de cozinha** set of kitchen-ware

batida | ba'tida | *sf*. collision; knock; striking (clocks); police raid; a kind of rum sour

batido | ba'tidʋ | *a*. beaten; commonplace

batina | ba'tina | *sf*. cassock

batizado | bati'zadʋ | *sm.* baptism, christening

batizar | bati'zaʀ | *vt.* to baptize, to christen

batom | ba'tõ | *sm.* lipstick

batoque | ba'tʊkɩ | *sm.* bung, stopper, plug

batuque | ba'tukɩ | *sm.* generic designation of Afro-Brazilian dances

batuta | ba'tuta | *sf.* (mus.) baton; *smf.* (colloq.) expert

baú | ba'u | *sm.* trunk, chest

baunilha | baw'niLa | *sf.* vanilla

bazófia | ba'zʋfia | *sf.* boast, brag

bê-a-bá | bea'ba | *sm.* spelling exercise

beatice | bea'tisɩ | *sf.* bigotry

beato -ta | be'atʋ | *smf.* (theol.) beatified person / *a.* beatified

bêbado -da | 'bebadʋ | *smf. a.* = **bêbedo**

bebê | be'be | *sm.* baby

bebedeira | bebe'deyra | *sf.* drunkenness, drinking bout

bêbedo -da | 'bebedʋ | *smf.* drunkard, drunk / *a.* drunk

bebedouro | bebe'dowrʋ | *sm.* drinking fountain; watering through

beber | be'beʀ | *vt.* to drink; to absorb (also fig.); to imbibe

bebida | bɩ'bida | *sf.* drink, beverage

beca | 'bɛka | *sf.* judge's robe, academic gown

beça | 'bɛsa | *sf.* used only in the expression à b. (colloq.) a lot, a great deal

beco | 'bekʋ | *sm.* alley; court. **-b. sem saída** blind alley

bedelho | be'deLʋ | *sm.* door bolt, latch. **-meter o b.** (colloq.) to interfere

beiço | 'beysʋ | *sm.* lip. **-dar o b.** (colloq.) to leave without paying

beija-flor | 'beyja'floʀ | *sm.* humming-bird

beijar | bey'jaʀ | *vt.* to kiss

beijo | 'beyjʋ | *sm.* kiss

beira | 'beyra | *sf.* edge, rim; vicinity. **-à b. de** at the edge of

beira-mar | 'beyra'maʀ | *sf.* sea-shore, seaside

beirar | bey'raʀ | *vt.* to follow the edge of; to approach

beleza | be'leza | *sf.* beauty

belga | 'bɛlga | *smf. a.* Belgian

beliche | be'lixɩ | *sm.* berth, bunk

bélico -ca | 'bɛlikʋ | *a.* warlike, military

beligerante | belije'rãtɩ | *smf. a.* belligerent

beliscar | bɩlɩʃ'kaʀ | *vt.* to pinch; to nibble at (food)

belo -la | 'bɛlʋ | *sm.* beauty; anything beautiful / *a.* beautiful; lovely; fine

beltrano | bel'tranʋ | *sm.* So-and-so, John Doe

bem | 'bẽy | *sm.* a good, that which is good; benefit; a beloved person; (*pl.*) belongings / *adv.* well, rightly; much, very, quite. **-ainda b. que** fortunately. **-estar b.** to feel well

bem-disposto -ta | bẽydiʃ'poʃtʋ -'pʊʃta | *a.* with good appearance, in good health

bem-estar | bẽyɩʃ'taʀ | *sm.* well-being; comfort

bem-humorado -da | bẽyumo'radʋ | *a.* good-humoured, cheerful

bem-passado -da | bẽypa'sadʋ | *a.* (cookery) well-done

bem-vindo -da | bẽy'vĩdʋ | *a.* welcome

bem-visto -ta | bẽy'viʃtʋ | *a.* well-liked; respected

bênção | 'bẽsãw | *sf.* blessing

bendito -ta | bẽ'ditʋ | *a.* blessed

beneficência | benefi'sẽsia | *sf.* beneficence, charity

beneficiamento | benefisia'mẽtʋ | *sm.* processing (agricultural products)

beneficiar | benɩfisi'aʀ | *vt.* to benefit; to better; to process (agricultural products etc.)

benefício | benɩ'fisiʋ | *sm.* benefaction, charity; (eccles.) benefice

benéfico -ca | be'nɛfikʊ | *a.* beneficial; advantageous; healthy

benemérito -ta | bene'mɛritʊ | *smf.* benefactor / *a.* well-deserving

beneplácito | bene'plasitʊ | *sm.* approval, sanction

benevolência | benevo'lẽsia | *sf.* benevolence

benfeitor -tora | bẽfey'toR | *sm.* benefactor; *sf.* benefactress

benfeitoria | bẽfeytʊ'ria | *sf.* improvement (of property)

bengala | bẽ'gala | *sf.* cane, walking-stick; (tex.) bengaline

benigno -na | be'nignʊ | *a.* benign; indulgent; mild

benquisto -ta | bẽ'kiʃtʊ | *a.* well-liked, esteemed

bens | 'bẽyʃ | *smpl.* property. **-b. de raiz** real estate

benzer | bẽ'zeR | *vt.* to bless. **-b. -se** to cross oneself

berçário | beR'sariʊ | *sm.* nursery (in hospital)

berço | 'beRsʊ | *sm.* cradle; source

berinjela | bɪrĩ'jɛla | *sf.* (bot.) egg-plant

berro | 'bɛRʊ | *sm.* shout, scream, yell

besouro | bɪ'zowrʊ | *sm.* beetle

besta | 'bɛʃta | *sf.* work animal; ass, imbecile. **-fazer-se de b.** (colloq.) to be pretentious or arrogant

besteira | beʃ'teyra | *sf.* (colloq.) stupidity

bestial | beʃti'al | *a.* beastly, brutal

besuntar | bɪzũ'taR | *vt.* (colloq.) to grease, to smear

beterraba | bete'Raba | *sf.* beet

bétula | 'bɛtula | *sf.* white, gray or poplar birch

betume | bɪ'tumɪ | *sm.* bitumen, asphalt

bexiga | bɪ'xiga | *sf.* bladder; (*pl.*) pock-marks

bezerro -ra | bɪ'zeRʊ | *smf.* calf; *sm.* calfskin

bíblia | 'biblia | *sf.* Bible

bibliografia | bibliogra'fia | *sf.* bibliography

biblioteca | biblio'tɛka | *sf.* library

bibliotecário -ria | bibliote'kariʊ | *smf.* librarian

biboca | bi'bʊka | *sf.* shanty, straw hut

bica | 'bika | *sf.* tap, faucet

bicar | bi'kaR | *vt.* to peck

bicha | 'bixa | *sf.* intestinal worm; leach; (slang) fag

bicheiro | bi'xeyrʊ | *sm.* bookmaker in illegal lottery

bicho | 'bixʊ | *sm.* animal (also fig.); insect, bug. **-jogo do b.** illegal lottery

bicho-do-pé | 'bixʊdʊ'pɛ | *sm.* chigoe, jigger

bicicleta | bisi'klɛta | *sf.* bicycle

bico | 'bikʊ | *sm.* beak, bill; nipple; (colloq.) sideline

bidê | bi'de | *sm.* bidet

bife | 'bifɪ | *sm.* steak, beefsteak

bifurcação | bifuRka'sãw | *sf.* bifurcation, branch

bigode | bi'gʊdɪ | *sm.* moustache, mustache

bigorna | bi'gʊRna | *sf.* anvil

bijuteria | bijute'ria | *sf.* costume jewelry; jewelry store

bilha | 'biʎa | *sf.* jug, pitcher; (mech.) a ball-bearing

bilhar | bi'ʎaR | *sm.* billiards; billiard table; billiard room

bilhete | bi'ʎetɪ | *sm.* note; ticket. **-b. de loteria** lottery ticket

bilheteria | biʎete'ria | *sf.* ticket window, box-office

bilião, bilhão | bili'ãw bi'ʎãw | *sm.* milliard; billion

bílis | 'biliʃ | *sf.* bile

binóculo | bi'nʊkulʊ | *sm.* binoculars; field glasses

biografia | biogra'fia | *sf.* biography

biólogo -ga | bi'ʊlogʊ· | *smf.* biologist

biombo | bi'õbʊ | *sm.* screen

biopse, biópsia | bi'ωpsι bi'ωpsia | sf. biopsy

bioquímica | bio'kimika | sf. biochemistry

bioquímico -ca | bio'kimikυ | smf. biochemist / a. biochemical

biqueira | bi'keyra | sf. tip, cap, ferrule; cleat (on toes of shoes)

birra | 'bira | sf. aversion, dislike; stubbornness. **-deb.** out of spite

bis | 'biζ | sm. encore; (mus.) repeat / adv. bis, twice / interj. encore!, again!

bisavô -vó | biza'vo-'vω | sm. great grandfather; sf. great grandmother

bisbilhoteiro -ra | biζbiLo'teyrυ | smf. meddler, tattler

biscate | biζ'katι | sm. odd job; minor task

biscoito | biζ'koytυ | sm. cookie, biscuit

bisnaga | biζ'naga | sf. tube (of paint, tooth paste etc.); (colloq.) French bread

bisneto -ta | biζ'netυ | sm. great grandson; sf. great granddaughter

bisonho -nha | bi'zoNυ | smf. beginner, greenhorn / a. inexperienced; timid, shy

bispo | 'biζpυ | sm. bishop

bisturi | biζtu'ri | sm. scalpel

bitola | bi'tωla | sf. gauge (also R.R.); standard measure; norm

bizarria | biza'Ria | sf. gallantry

blasfemar | blaζfe'maR | vt. vi. to blaspheme

blasfêmia | blaζ'femia | sf. blasphemy

blindagem | blĩ'dajěy | sf. armour-plating

bloco | 'blωkυ | sm. block; writing pad; (dent.) inlay. **-em b.** in quantity; in a group; en bloc

bloquear | blokι'aR | vt. to blockade

bloqueio | blo'keyυ | sm. blockade

blusa | 'bluza | sf. blouse

boa | 'boa | sf. (zool.) boa / a. (f. of bom) good; (slang) sexy

boa-noite | boa'noytι | interj. good evening!, good night!

boa-pinta | boa'pĩta | smf. a. good-looking

Boas-festas | boaζ'fεζtaζ | interj. Season's greetings!, Merry Christmas!

boas-vindas | boaζ'vĩdaζ | sfpl. welcome / interj. welcome!

boa-tarde | boa'taRdι | interj. good afternoon!

boato | bυ'atυ | sm. rumo(u)r, gossip

bobagem | bo'bajěy | sf. nonsense, foolishness. **-que b.!** what nonsense!

bobina | bυ'bina | sf. bobbin; reel; spool; (elect.) coil

bobo -ba | 'bobυ | smf. fool, idiot; sm. buffoon / a. foolish

boca | 'boka | sf. mouth; entrance; hole

bocado | bυ'kadυ | sm. mouthful; bit; little while

bocal | bυ'kal | sm. mouth (of a jar, pitcher etc.); (mus.) mouthpiece

boçal | bo'sal | smf. stupid, ignorant / a. stupid, ignorant; coarse

bocejar | bυse'jaR | vi. to yawn, to gape

bochecha | bυ'xexa | sf. cheek

bochechar | bυxe'xaR | vt. to rinse the mouth

boda | 'boda | sf. wedding, marriage; (pl.) wedding anniversary

bode | 'bωdι | sm. billy-goat. **-b.** expiatório scapegoat

bodega | bυ'dεga | sf. tavern; (slang) junk, trash

bofe | 'bωfι | sm. (colloq.) lung; (colloq.) ugly person; (pl.) lights and other viscera (of animals)

bofetada | bυfe'tada | sf. slap in the face; insult

boi | 'boy | sm. ox

bóia | 'bωya | sf. buoy, marker; float

boiada | boy'ada | *sf.* herd of cattle

boiadeiro | boya'deyrʋ | *sm.* cowhand; cattle herder

boião | boy'ãw | *sm.* a large-mouthed jar

boiar | boy'aʀ | *vi.* to float; (colloq.) to have no idea

boina | 'boyna | *sf.* beret

bojo | 'bojʋ | *sm.* bulge; bilge (also naut.); protuberance

bojudo -da | bʋ'judʋ | *a.* bulging, bulgy

bola | 'bɔla | *sf.* ball, sphere, globe; bolus or poisoned dog food. **-levar b.** (slang) to be bribed. **-dar b.** (slang) to lead on, to flirt; to bribe someone

bola-ao-cesto | 'bʋlaw'seʃtʋ | *sm.* basketball

bolacha | bʋ'laxa | *sf.* cracker; (colloq.) a slap in the face

bolada | bo'lada | *sf.* hit with a ball; (colloq.) a pile (of money)

bolar | bo'laʀ | *vt. vi.* (colloq.) to plan, to scheme; to invent

boletim | bʋlɪ'tĩ | *sf.* bulletin; periodic publication; school report card

bolha | 'bɔla | *sf.* bubble; blister

boliviano -na | bʋlivi'anʋ | *smf. a.* Bolivian; *sm.* boliviano (monetary unit)

bolo | 'bolʋ | *sm.* cake. **-dar o b. em alguém** (colloq.) to fail to show up

bolor | bo'loʀ | *sm.* mo(u)ld, mildew

bolorento -ta | bolo'rẽtʋ | *a.* mo(u)ldy, mildewed

bolsa | 'bolsa | *sf.* purse, bag, handbag; scholarship, fellowship; stock market, stock exchange

bolsista | bol'siʃta | *smf.* scholarship holder

bolso | 'bolsʋ | *sm.* pocket

bom | 'bõ | *a.* (*f.* **boa**, *compar.* and *superl.* **melhor**, also *superl.* **ótimo, boníssimo**) good; kind / *sm.* good person / *interj.* good! **-b. humor** good humo(u)r,

good mood. **-b. partido** good catch (in marriage)

bomba | 'bõba | *sf.* bomb; pump; cream puff; (fig.) great surprise. **-levar b.** (colloq.) to fail in an examination. **-b. de gasolina** petrol pump, fuel pump, filling station

bombardear | bõbaʀdɪ'aʀ | *vt.* to bomb, to shell

bombardeio | bõbaʀ'deyʋ | *sm.* bombing, shelling

bombástico -ca | bõ'baʃtikʋ | *a.* bombastic, pompous; booming

bombeiro | bõ'beyrʋ | *sm.* fireman; plumber

bombom | bõ'bõ | *sm.* chocolate sweetmeat

bombordo | bõ'bʋrdʋ | *sm.* (naut.) larboard (left side of a ship)

bom-dia | bõ'dia | *interj.* good morning!, good day!

bom-gosto | bõ'goʃtʋ | *sm.* good taste

bom-senso | bõ'sẽsʋ | *sm.* common sense, discernment

bonança | bo'nãsa | *sf.* calm (after a storm)

bondade | bõ'dadɪ | *sf.* kindness, goodness

bonde | 'bõdɪ | *sm.* streetcar

bondoso -sa | bõ'dozʋ -'dʋza | *a.* kind, good, benevolent

boné | bo'nɛ | *sm.* cap

boneco -ca | bʋ'nɛkʋ | *smf.* doll, puppet

bonito -ta | bʋ'nitʋ | *sm.* (ichth). bonito / *a.* pretty, good-looking

bonus | 'bonuʒ | *sm.* (*sing.* and *pl.*) bonus; (fin.) bond, debenture; allowance, reduction

boquiaberto -ta | bokia'bɛʀtʋ | *a.* open-mouthed, astonished

boquinha | bo'kiɴa | *sf.* small mouth. **-fazer uma b.** to have a snack

borboleta bʋrbo'leta | *sf.* butterfly; turnstile; bow-tie; wing nut

borbulhar | bʊʀbu'laʀ | *vt.* to bubble; to gush / *vi.* to bubble up; to gush out

borco | 'boʀkʊ | *sm.* used in the expression **de b.** face down, wrong side up

borda | 'bʊʀda | *sf.* edge; rim, fringe; bank (of a stream)

bordado -da | boʀ'dadʊ | *sm.* embroidery / *a.* embroidered

bordão | boʀ'dãw | *sm.* staff

bordar | boʀ'daʀ | *vt.* to embroider

bordejar | boʀde'jaʀ | *vt.* (naut.) to tack / *vi.* (naut.) to tack; to pursue a zigzag course

bordel | boʀ'dɛl | *sm.* brothel

bordo | 'bʊʀdʊ | *sm.* board; side. **-a b.** on board

bordo | 'boʀdʊ | *sm.* silver maple

bordoada | bʊʀdʊ'ada | *sf.* blow with a staff

boreal | bore'al | *a.* boreal, northern

bornal | boʀ'nal | *sm.* haversack

borra | 'boʀa | *sf.* sediment; lees, dregs

borracha | bʊ'ʀaxa | *sf.* rubber; eraser

borracheira | bʊʀa'xeyra | *sf.* drunkenness

borrachudo -da | bʊʀa'xudʊ | *sm.* buffalo gnat, turkey gnat / *a.* rubbery

borralho | bʊ'ʀalʊ | *sm.* embers, ash fire; (fig.) hearth, home

borrão | bo'ʀãw | *sm.* blot, blotch

borrar | bo'ʀaʀ | *vt.* to blot, to blotch; to dirty, to smear

borrasca | bo'ʀaʃka | *sf.* storm, hurricane

borrifar | bʊʀi'faʀ | *vt.* to sprinkle, to spray

borrifo | bʊ'ʀifʊ | *sm.* sprinkling; sprinkle, spray

bosque | 'bʊʃkɪ | *sm.* thicket, grove

bossa | 'bʊsa | *sf.* bump; protuberance; (slang) knack, talent. **-b. nova** new style of popular Brazilian music

bosta | 'bʊʃta | *sf.* dung, animal excrement

bota | 'bʊta | *sf.* boot

bota-fora | 'bʊta'foʀa | *sm.* (*sing.* and *pl.*) going-away party; (colloq.) send-off

botânica | bo'tanika | *sf.* botany

botânico -ca | bo'tanikʊ | *smf.* botanist / *a.* botanical

botão | bʊ'tãw | *sm.* button; knob; bud

botar | bo'taʀ | *vt.* to put; to place; to lay; to set

bote | 'bʊtɪ | *sm.* row-boat; spring, leap (of attacking animal)

botequim | bʊtɪ'kĩ | *sm.* cheap bar, joint

boticão | bʊti'kãw | *sm.* dentist's forceps

botija | bʊ'tija | *sf.* jug

botina | bʊ'tina | *sf.* high shoes

boto | 'bʊtʊ | *sm.* (zool.) porpoise

boxe | 'bʊksɪ | *sm.* boxing

boxeador | boksɪa'doʀ | *sm.* boxer, pugilist

brabo -ba | 'brabʊ | *a.* fierce; wild, savage; furious

braça | 'brasa | *sf.* (naut.) fathom

braçada | bra'sada | *sf.* stroke (in swimming)

bracelete | brase'letɪ | *sm.* bracelet

braço | 'brasʊ | *sm.* arm; hand worker; branch (also of a river). **-de b. dado** arm in arm. **-ficar de braços cruzados** to be idle

bradar | bra'daʀ | *vt. vi.* to shout, to bawl, to yell

brado | 'bradʊ | *sm.* shout

braguilha | bra'giLa | *sf.* fly (of pants)

bramido | bra'midʊ | *sm.* bellow, roar

bramir | bra'miʀ | *vi.* to roar, to bellow (as a wild beast); to howl

branco -ca | 'brãkʊ | *sm.* white (colo[u]r); white man; *sf.* white woman / *a.* white; pale

brancura | brã'kura | *sf.* whiteness

brandir | brã'diʀ | *vt.* to brandish

brando -da | 'bradʊ | *a.* soft; mild; gentle; tender; (cookery) low

(flame, heat)

brandura | brã'dura | *sf.* softness; mildness; gentleness

branquear | brãkı'aʀ | *vt.* to whiter / *vi.* to turn white

branquidão | brãki'dãw | *sf.* = *brancura*

brasa | 'braza | *sf.* live coal, ember; (*pl.*) charcoal. **-em b.** glowing, red hot. **-puxar a b. para a sua sardinha** to feather one's nest. **-estar sobre brasas** or **pisar em brasas** to be on pins and needles

brasão | bra'zãw | *sm.* coat of arms, heraldic shield

braseiro | bra'zeyrʋ | *sm.* a heap of live coals; brazier

brasileiro -ra | brazi'leyrʋ | *smf. a.* Brazilian

bravata | bra'vata | *sf.* bravado, boast, boasting

bravio -via | bra'viʋ | *a.* ferocious, fierce; wild, savage

bravo -va | 'bravʋ | *a.* courageous; wild; furious / *interj.* bravo!

bravura | bra'vura | *sf.* courage, bravery; wildness

breca | 'brɛka | *sf.* used in the expression **com a b!** damn it!

brecha | 'brɛxa | *sf.* breach, opening; gap

brejeiro -ra | bre'jeyrʋ | *a.* coquettish, provocative

brejo | 'brɛjʋ | *sm.* swamp, marsh, bog

breu | 'brew | *sm.* tar, pitch

breve | 'brɛvı | *a.* brief; short (also phon.); concise / *adv.* soon, shortly. **-até b.** see you soon. **-(dentro) em b.** soon, shortly

brevê | bre've | *sm.* pilot's license

brevidade | brevi'dadı | *sf.* brevity, briefness

briga | 'briga | *sf.* fight; quarrel. **-puxar b.** to pick a fight

brigada | bri'gada | *sf.* brigade

brigadeiro | briga'deyrʋ | *sf.* a general in the air force

brigar | bri'gaʀ | *vi.* to fight, to come to blows; to quarrel; to sever relations

brilhante | bri'ʟãtı | *sm.* diamond / *a.* bright; brilliant

brilhar | bri'ʟaʀ | *vi.* to shine

brilho | 'briʟʋ | *sm.* brightness, brilliance; splendour

brincadeira | brĩka'deyra | *sf.* game; joke, jest; amusement **-fora de b.** seriously

brincar | brĩ'kaʀ | *vi.* to play; to joke, to jest

brinco | 'brĩkʋ | *sm.* ear-ring

brindar | brĩ'daʀ | *vt.* to drink to; to give a gift to

brinde | 'brĩdı | *sm.* toast; gift; offering

brinquedo | brĩ'kedʋ | *sm.* toy, plaything; children's play, game; play, fun

brio | 'briʋ | *sm.* dignity; pride; self-respect

brioso -sa | bri'ozʋ -'ɔza | *a.* full of self-respect; dignified, proud

brisa | 'briza | *sf.* breeze

britânico -ca | bri'tanikʋ | *smf. a.* British

broa | 'broa | *sf.* corn cake or muffin

broca | 'brɔka | *sf.* drill; bit; (entom.) borer

brocar | bro'kaʀ | *vt.* to drill; to become spoiled (by plant or tree borers)

broche | 'brɔxı | *sm.* brooch, pin

brochura | brʋ'xura | *sf.* brochure, pamphlet; paperback

brócolos, brócolis | 'brɔkʋluʒ 'brɔkʋliʒ | *smpl.* (bot.) broccoli

bronca | 'brõka | *sf.* (slang) scolding, dressing down

bronco -ca | 'brõkʋ | *a.* coarse; rustic

bronquite | brõ'kitı | *sf.* bronchitis

brotar | bro'taʀ | *vt. vi.* to bud, to sprout; to gush out

broto | 'brotʋ | *sm.* bud, sprout; (colloq.) teenager

brotoeja | brʋtʋ'eja | *sf.* prickly heat

broxa | 'brɔxa | *sf.* a large brush for white-washing; *sm. a.* (vulg.) an impotent man

bruços | 'brusʊʒ | *smpl.* used in the expression **de b.** lying prone

bruma | 'bruma | *sf.* fog, mist (esp. at sea)

brumoso -sa | bru'mozʊ -'mɔza | *a.* foggy, misty, hazy

brunir | bru'niʀ | *vt.* to burnish, to polish

brusco -ca | 'bruʃkʊ | *a.* rough, harsh; sudden

brutal | bru'tal | *a.* brutal, violent

brutalidade | brutali'dadɩ | *sf.* brutality, violence

bruto -ta | 'brutʊ | *smf.* brute, beast / *a.* brute, brutal; ill--mannered; inorganic; huge; rough. **-em b.** raw (materials); unfinished

bruxaria | bruxa'ria | *sf.* witchcraft

bruxo -xa | 'bruxʊ | *sm.* sorcerer, wizard; *sf.* witch, sorcerer

bruxulear | bruxulɩ'aʀ | *vi.* to flicker

bucha | 'buxa | *sf.* wad; plug

bucho | 'buxʊ | *sm.* animal's stomach

buço | 'busʊ | *sm.* down, fuzz (on upper lip)

bueiro | bu'eyrʊ | *sm.* culvert; air duct; drain hole

bufar | bu'faʀ | *vt. vi.* to puff; to breathe hard; to get mad

bugiganga | buji'gãga | *sf.* trinket, bauble; odds and ends

bugio | bu'jiʊ | *sm.* howling monkey

bujão | bu'jãw | *sm.* threaded cap or stopper

bula | 'bula | *sf.* directions (on a bottle of medicine); papal bull; bulla seal

bule | 'bulɩ | *sm.* teapot, coffee--pot

bulha | 'buʟa | *sf.* noise; riot, brawl

bulício | bu'lisiʊ | *sm.* stir, tumult; agitation

bulir | bu'liʀ | *vt. vi.* to stir, to move; to touch. **-b. com** to tease. **-b. em** to touch

bunda | 'bũda | *sf.* (vulg.) buttocks

buraco | bu'rakʊ | *sm.* hole

burguês -guesa | buʀ'geʃ -'geza | *smf.* bourgeois

burguesia | buʀgɩ'zia | *sf.* bourgeoisie

burilar | buri'laʀ | *vt.* to engrave (with a burin); to perfect

burla | 'buʀla | *sf.* hoax; fraud, swindle

burlar | buʀ'laʀ | *vt.* to trick, to hoax; to mock

burlesco -ca | buʀ'leʃkʊ | *a.* burlesque; ludicrous; mocking

burocracia | burokra'sia | *sf.* bureaucracy

burocrata | buro'krata | *smf.* bureaucrat

burra | 'buʀa | *sf.* female donkey; money chest

burrice | bu'ʀisɩ | *sf.* stupidity

burro -ra | 'buʀʊ | *smf.* ass, donkey; nitwit / *a.* stupid, idiotic. **-pra b.** (colloq.) lots, tons, extremely

busca | 'buʃka | *sf.* search

buscar | buʃ'kaʀ | *vt.* to seek, to search, to look for; to bring, to get, to fetch

bússola | 'busʊla | *sf.* compass

busto | 'buʃtʊ | *sm.* bust; torso; a woman's breasts

buzina | bu'zina | *sf.* horn; automobile horn

buzinar | buzi'naʀ | *vi.* to blow a horn; to honk (automobile horn)

C

cá | 'ka | *adv*. here

caatinga | kaa'tĩga | *sf*. region of spare vegetation typical of northeastern Brazil

cabaça | ka'basa | *sf*. gourd, calabash

cabana | ka'bana | *sf*. hut, cabin

cabeça | ka'besa | *sf*. head; top; common sense; *sm*. head, chief (of a revolution etc.)

cabeçada | kabe'sada | *sf*. blow with the head; blunder. **-dar uma c.** to blunder

cabeçalho | kabe'saʌʋ | *sm*. masthead of a newspaper; letterhead

cabecear | kabesɪ'aʀ | *vi*. to nod (in drowsiness)

cabeceira | kabe'seyra | *sf*. head, top (of bed, table etc.). **-à c. de** at the bedside of

cabeçudo -da | kabe'sudʋ | *a*. big-headed; stubborn

cabedal | kabe'dal | *sm*. fund, capital; experience; (*pl*.) resources

cabeleira | kabe'leyra | *sf*. head of hair; wig

cabeleireiro | kabeley'reyrʋ | *sm*. hairdresser

cabelo | ka'belʋ | *sm*. hair

caber | ka'beʀ | *vi*. to go in or into; to befit, to suit; to fall to. **-não c. em si de alegria** to be beside oneself with joy

cabide | ka'bidɪ | *sm*. hanger, coat-hanger, peg

cabimento | kabi'mẽtʋ | *sm*. fitness, suitableness. **-não ter c.** to be outrageous

cabina, cabine | ka'bina ka'binɪ | *sf*. cabin

cabineiro | kabi'neyrʋ | *sm*. lift operator

cabisbaixo -xa | kabiʒ'bayxʋ | *a*. crestfallen, downcast

cabo | 'kabʋ | *sm*. cape; handle; cable; cordage; corporal. **-aoc. de** at the end of. **-levar a c.** to complete, to conclude

caboclo -cla | ka'boklʋ | *smf*. acculturated Brazilian Indian; Brazilian half-breed of white and Indian / *a*. copper coloured; of or pertaining to the acculturated Brazilian Indian

cabotagem | kabo'tajẽy | *sf*. coastwise navigation

cabra | 'kabra | *sf*. she-goat; *sm*. half-breed; a fellow

cabra-cega | 'kabra'sega | *sf*. (games) blindman's buff

cabrito | ka'britʋ | *sm*. kid

cabrocha | ka'brʋxa | *sf*. mulatto girl

caça | 'kasa | *sf*. hunt chase; shooting; game; *sm*. (aeron.) chaser. **-c. grossa (miúda)** big (small) game

caçador -dora | kasa'doʀ | *sm*. hunter; *sf*. huntress

cação | ka'sãw | *sm*. shark

caçar | ka'saʀ | *vt*. to hunt, to chase, to pursue; to shoot game

cacarejar | kakare'jaʀ | *vt*. *vi*. to cackle

caçarola | kasa'rɔla | *sf*. casserole, saucepan

cacau | ka'kaw | *sm*. cocoa bean; fruit of the cacao-tree

cacetada | kase'tada | *sf*. a blow with a cudgel; (colloq.) nuisance, annoyance

cacete | ka'setɪ | *sm*. club, cudgel; bore / *a*. boring

cachaça | ka'xasa | *sf*. kind of Brazilian white rum

cachimbo | ka'xĩbʋ | *sm*. pipe

cacho | 'kaxʋ | *sm*. bunch (of bananas etc.); curl (of hair)

cachoeira | kaxʊ'eyra | *sf.* waterfall. falls

cachorro | ka'xoRʊ | *sm.* dog

cachorro-quente | ka'xoRʊ'kẽtɪ | *sm.* hot dog

cacimba | ka'sĩba | *sf.* water-hole

cacique | ka'sikɪ | *sm.* Indian chief

caco | 'kakʊ | *sm.* splinter, shiver (of glass)

caçoada | kasʊ'ada | *sf.* banter, jest

caçoar | kasʊ'aR | *vt.* to tease, to make fun of

cacoete | kakʊ'etɪ | *sm.* nervous tic

cacto | 'kaktʊ | *sm.* cactus

caçula | ka'sula | *smf.* youngest child

cada | 'kada | *a.* each, every

cadafalso | kada'falsʊ | *sm.* gallows, scaffold

cadáver | ka'davɪR | *sm.* corpse

cadê | ka'de | *interrog.* (colloq.) where is?, what has happened to?

cadeado | kadɪ'adʊ | *sm.* padlock

cadeia | ka'deya | *sf.* chain; (fig.) jail

cadeira | ka'deyra | *sf.* chair; subject (academic); (*pl.*) hips

cadela | ka'dɛla | *sf.* bitch

cadência | ka'dẽsia | *sf.* cadence (also mus.), rhythm

caderneta | kadɛR'neta | *sf.* notebook; school register. -c. de poupança bank-book; savings account

caderno | ka'dɛRnʊ | *sm.* notebook

cadete | ka'detɪ | *sm.* cadet

cadinho | ka'diNʊ | *sm.* crucible, melting pot

caduco -ca | ka'dukʊ | *a.* senile; (law) lapsed, null and void

cafajeste | kafa'jɛʃtɪ | *smf.* vulgar person

café | ka'fɛ | *sm.* coffee; café. -c. da manhã breakfast

cafeteira | kafe'teyra | *sf.* coffee--pot

cafezinho | kafɛ'ziNʊ | *sm.* demi-

tasse (coffee)

cágado | 'kagadʊ | *sm.* a kind of fresh-water turtle

caiar | kay'aR | *vt.* to whitewash

cãibra | 'kãybra | *sf.* cramp

caído -da | ka'idʊ | *a.* fallen, dropped; prostrate; hanging

caipira | kai'pira | *smf.* a man or a woman of the backwoods / *a.* rustic, rough

cair | ka'iR | *vi.* to fall; to drop; to decay; to fall on (said of a holiday etc.). -c. fora (slang) to scram. -c. nas graças de to come into favour with

cais | 'kayʃ | *sm.* pier, quay

caixa | 'kayxa | *sf.* box, case, chest; cashier's booth. -c. do correio mailbox. -c. econômica savings bank. -c. postal post office box; *smf.* teller

caixão | kay'xãw | *sm.* box, chest, case; coffin

caixeiro-viajante | kay'xeyrʊ via'jãtɪ | *sm.* travel(l)ing salesman

caixilho | kay'xiLʊ | *sm.* frame (of a window)

caixote | kay'xʊtɪ | *sm.* case, packing case

cajado | ka'jadʊ | *sm.* shepherd's staff or crook

caju | ka'ju | *sm.* cashew

cal | 'kal | *sf.* whitewash, lime. -c. viva quick lime. -c. extinta slaked lime

calabouço | kala'bowsʊ | *sm.* dungeon

calado -da | ka'ladʊ | *sm.* draft (of a vessel) / *a.* quiet, silent

calafetar | kalafe'taR | *vt.* to ca(u)lk

calamidade | kalami'dadɪ | *sf.* calamity, disaster

calão | ka'lãw | *sm.* jargon, slang. -baixo c. vulgar language

calar | ka'laR | *vt.* to silence, to hush / *vi.* to be silent

calçada | kal'sada | *sf.* sidewalk

calçadeira | kalsa'deyra | *sf.* shoehorn

calçado -da | kal'sadυ | sm. foot-wear / a. paved

calcanhar | kalka'naʀ | sm. heel

calção | kal'sãw | sm. shorts, trunks. **-c. de banho** bathing trunks

calcar | kal'kaʀ | vt. to press down, to compress; to tread, to step

calçar | kal'saʀ | vt. to put on (shoes, socks etc.); to pave; to skid (a wheel)

calças | 'kalsaʃ | sfpl. trousers, pants

calcinhas | kal'siɲaʃ | sfpl. pant-ies, underpants

cálcio | 'kalsiυ | sm. calcium

calço | 'kalsυ | sm. block, wedge

calculador | kalkula'doʀ | sm. cal-culator (also fig.); computer, calculating machine

calcular | kalku'laʀ | vt. vi. to cal-culate, to figure; to estimate

cálculo | 'kalkulυ | sm. (med.) stone; calculation, estimate, computation

calda | 'kalda | sf. syrup; (pl.) hot springs

caldeira | kal'deyra | sf. boiler

caldeirão | kaldey'rãw | sm. large kettle

caldo | 'kaldυ | sm. broth, soup; juice

calefrio, calafrio | kale'friυ ka-la'friυ | sm. chill, shiver

calejar | kale'jaʀ | vt. vi. (also **c.-se**) to develop calluses

calendário | kalẽ'dariυ | sm. calendar

calha | 'kaʟa | sf. roof gutter

calhar | ka'ʟaʀ | vi. to coincide; to fit together; to suit. **-vir a c.** to come in handy

calhau | ka'ʟaw | sm. pebble; stone

calibre | ka'librɪ | sm. calibre, cali-ber; bore; caliper

cálice | 'kalisɪ | sm. liquor glass; small wine glass; chalice

caligrafia | kaligra'fia | sf. calli-graphy; handwriting

calma | 'kalma | sf. self-posses-sion; serenity, tranquility

calmante | kal'mãtɪ | sm. sedative / a. calming

calmaria | kalma'ria | sf. calm (al-so naut.)

calmo -ma | 'kalmυ | a. calm, quiet

calo | 'kalυ | sm. corn; callus

calor | ka'loʀ | sm. heat; warmth; vivacity

caloria | kalo'ria | sf. calorie

caloroso -sa | kalo'rozυ -'rωza | a. warm; ardent

calote | ka'lωtɪ | sm. a bad debt. **-passar um c. em** to cheat, to evade payment

caloteiro -ra | kalo'teyrυ | smf. swindler, welsher

calouro | ka'lowrυ | sm. freshman, beginning student

calúnia | ka'lunia | sf. calumny, slander

calva | 'kalva | sf. bald spot

calvário | kal'variυ | sm. calvary; suffering

calvície | kal'visiɪ | sf. baldness

calvo -va | 'kalvυ | smf. bald-headed person / a. bald; bare

cama | 'kama | sf. bed. **-estar de c.** to be bedridden

camada | ka'mada | sf. coat (of paint etc.); layer; (geol.) stratum

camaleão | kamalɪ'ãw | sm. chamaleon

câmara | 'kamara | sf. chamber (also of firearms), room, stateroom; camera. **-c. ardente** funeral chamber

camarada | kama'rada | smf. com-rade; companion, friend / a. friendly

camaradagem | kamara'dajẽy | sf. comradeship

camarão | kama'rãw | sm. shrimp, prawn

camareiro -ra | kama'reyrυ | smf. steward; chamber-maid

camarim | kama'rĩ | sm. (theat.) dressing-room

camarote | kama'rωtɪ | sm. cabin; (theat.) box

cambada | kã'bada | sf. bundle;

gang, mob

cambalear | kãbalι'aʀ | *vi.* to totter; to wobble, to stagger

cambalhota | kãba'ʟωta | *sf.* somersault

cambial | kãbi'al | *sf.* (com.) bank acceptance; (com.) bill of exchange

câmbio | 'kãbiυ | *sm.* exchange, change, conversion (of currency); (fin.) rate of exchange

câmbio-negro | 'kãbiυ'negrυ | *sm.* black market

cambista | kã'biʒta | *smf.* money--changer; (colloq.) ticket scalper

camelo | ka'melυ | *sm.* camel

camelô | kame'lo | *sm.* street vendor of gadgets

caminhada | kami'Nada | *sf.* walking, stroll

caminhão | kami'Nãw | *sm.* truck, lorry, van

caminhar | kami'NaʀR | *vi.* to walk; to proceed

caminho | ka'miNυ | *sm.* way, road, path; course

caminhonete | kamiNo'nɛtι | *sf.* station-wagon, small van

camisa | ka'miza | *sf.* shirt; (mech.) case

camiseta | kami'zeta | *sf.* undershirt, T-shirt

camisola | kami'zωla | *sf.* night-gown, night-dress

campa | 'kãpa | *sf.* gravestone, tombstone

campainha | kãpa'iNa | *sf.* bell, buzzer

campanha | kã'paNa | *sf.* campaign

campeão -peã | kãpι'ãw | *smf.* champion

campeonato | kãpιo'natυ | *sm.* championship

campestre | kã'pɛʃtrι | *a.* country, rural

campina | kã'pina | *sf.* field, meadow; plain, prairie

campo | 'kãpυ | *sm.* field, open country, meadow. **-c. de ação**

field of activity; range

camponês-nesa | kãpo'neʒ -'neza | *smf.* peasant; *sm.* country man; *sf.* country woman / *a.* rural

camuflagem | kamu'flajẽy | *sf.* camouflage

camundongo | kamũ'dõgυ | *sm.* mouse

camurça | ka'muʀsa | *sf.* chamois

cana | 'kana | *sf.* cane, sugar-cane. **-ir em c.** (slang) to go to jail

cana-de-açúcar | 'kanadιa'sukaʀ | *sf.* sugar-cane

canadense | kana'dẽsι | *smf. a.* Canadian

canal | ka'nal | *sm.* canal (also anat.); channel (also rad., TV)

canalha | ka'naʟa | *smf.* scoundrel; *sf.* canaille, rabble / *a.* base, vile

canalização | kanaliza'sãw | *sf.* piping

canalizar | kanali'zaʀ | *vt.* to canalize, to channel; to pipe; to pipeline

canário | ka'narιυ | *sm.* canary

canavial | kanavi'al | *sm.* sugar--cane plantation

canção | kã'sãw | *sf.* song

cancela | kã'sɛla | *sf.* wooden gate; barrier at a railroad crossing

cancelamento | kãsela'mẽtυ | *sm.* cancellation

cancelar | kãse'laʀ | *vt.* to cancel, to call off

candeeiro | kãdι'eyrυ | *sm.* oil--lamp

candente | kã'dẽtι | *a.* red-hot; fiery (said of words etc.)

candidatar-se | kãdida'taʀsι | *vr.* to present oneself as a candidate

candidato -ta | kãdi'datυ | *smf.* candidate; applicant

candidatura | kãdida'tura | *sf.* candidacy, candidature

cândido -da | 'kãdidυ | *a.* candid, sincere, naïve

candomblé | kãdõ'blɛ | *sm.* Brazilian voodoo

candura | kã'dura | *sf.* candor; purity, innocence

caneca | ka'nɛka | *sf.* mug, tankard

canela | ka'nɛla | *sf.* cinnamon; shin, shin-bone

canelada | kane'lada | *sf.* kick on the shin

canelado -da | kane'ladʋ | *a.* grooved

caneta | ka'neta | *sf.* fountain--pen; penholder. **-c. esferográfica** ball-pen

cânfora | 'kãfora | *sf.* camphor

canga | 'kãga | *sf.* yoke

cangaceiro | kãga'seyrʋ | *sm.* bandit, outlaw, highwayman

cangote | kã'gʋtɪ | *sm.* nape, back of the neck

cânhamo | 'kaNamʋ | *sm.* hemp

canhão | ka'Nãw | *sm.* cannon; (geog.) canyon

canhoto -ta | ka'Nɔtʋ -'Nɔta | *smf.* left-handed person; *sm.* the stub left in a cheque-book; *sf.* the left hand

caniço | ka'nisʋ | *sm.* cane, reed; fishing-rod

canícula | ka'nikula | *sf.* dog days

canil | ka'nil | *sm.* kennel

canivete | kani'vetɪ | *sm.* penknife

canja | 'kãja | *sf.* chicken soup; (colloq.) cinch

cano | 'kanʋ | *sm.* pipe, tube; gun barrel; leg of boot

canoa | ka'noa | *sf.* dug-out, canoe

cansaço | kã'sasʋ | *sm.* fatigue, tiredness

cansado -da | kã'sadʋ | *a.* tired

cansar | kã'saR | *vt.* to tire, to weary; to harass / *vi.* (also c.-se) to become tired

cansativo-va | kãsa'tivʋ | *a.* tiring; tedious

canseira | kã'seyra | *sf.* toil, hard work

cantada | kã'tada | *sf.* (slang) sweet talk

cantar | kã'taR | *sm.* singing / *vt. vi.* to sing

cântaro | 'kãtarʋ | *sm.* water jug. **-chover a cântaros** to rain

buckets

cantarolar | kãtaro'laR | *vt. vi.* to hum

canteiro | kã'teyrʋ | *sm.* bed (of flowers)

cântico | 'kãtikʋ | *sm.* hymn, chant

cantiga | kã'tiga | *sf.* song, air

cantil | kã'til | *sm.* canteen, flask

cantina | kã'tina | *sf.* canteen

canto | 'kãtʋ | *sm.* song, chant; corner

cantor -tora | kã'toR | *smf.* singer

canudo | ka'nudʋ | *sm.* slender tube; drinking straw

cão | 'kãw | *sm.* dog; hammer (of a gun)

caótico -ca | ka'ɔtikʋ | *a.* chaotic

capa | 'kapa | *sf.* raincoat; cape, cloak; cover (of a book)

capacete | kapa'setɪ | *sm.* helmet

capacho | ka'paxʋ | *sm.* doormat

capacidade | kapasi'dadɪ | *sf.* capacity; competence, talent

capanga | ka'pãga | *sm.* bodyguard; *sf.* knapsack

capataz | kapa'taʒ | *sm.* foreman, gang boss

capaz | ka'paʒ | *a.* capable, able; capacious

capela | ka'pɛla | *sf.* chapel; shrine

capelão | kape'lãw | *sm.* chaplain

capenga | ka'pẽga | *smf.* lame, cripple

capeta | ka'peta | *sm.* the devil; mischievous child

capim | ka'pĩ | *sm.* grass

capinar | kapi'naR | *vt.* to weed, to hoe

capital | kapi'tal | *sm.* capital; *sf.* capital (city) / *a.* capital, fundamental

capitalista | kapita'liʒta | *smf. a.* capitalist

capitanear | kapitanɪ'aR | *vt.* to captain, to command

capitão | kapi'tãw | *sm.* captain, skipper

capitulação | kapitula'sãw | *sf.* capitulation, surrender

capitular | kapitu'laR | *sf.* display type face / *vi.* to capitulate, to surrender

capítulo | ka'pitulʊ | *sm.* chapter

capoeira | kapʊ'eyra | *sm.* an adept of a certain method of bodily assault; *sf.* hen-coop; brush, second growth; Afro-Brazilian method of bodily assault

capota | ka'pɔta | *sf.* top, roof (of a car or carriage)

capotar | kapo'taR | *vi.* to capsize, to overturn

capote | ka'pɔtɪ | *sm.* overcoat; cloak

capricho | ka'prixʊ | *sm.* caprice, whim. **-a c.** carefully

caprichoso-sa | kapri'xozʊ-'xʊza | *a.* capricious, fanciful; meticulous

cápsula | 'kapsula | *sf.* capsule; cartridge shell

captar | kap'taR | *vt.* to captivate; to impound (water); (rad., TV) to receive

capturar | kaptu'raR | *vt.* to capture, to catch

capuz | ka'puʒ | *sm.* hood

caqui | ka'ki | *sm.* persimmon

cara | 'kara | *sf.* face; aspect, appearance; *sm.* (slang) fellow, guy

carabina | kara'bina | *sf.* rifle; carbine

caracol | kara'kʊl | *sm.* snail; ringlet (of hair)

característica | karakte'riʃtika | *sf.* characteristic, feature, attribute

característico -ca | karakte'riʃtikʊ | *a.* characteristic, distinctive

caracterização | karakteriza'sãw | *sf.* characterization; (theat.) make-up

caracterizar | karakteri'zaR | *vt.* to characterize, to distinguish

caramanchão | karamã'xãw | *sm.* bower, pergola

caramelo | kara'mɛlʊ | *sm.* toffee, caramel candy

caramujo | kara'mujʊ | *sm.* periwinkle

caranguejo | karã'gejʊ | *sm.* crab

carapinha | kara'piNa | *sf.* kinky hair

carapuça | kara'pusa | *sf.* cap, hood. **-enfiar a c.** (fig.) to make the cap fit

caráter | ka'rateR | *sm.* (*pl.* **caracteres** | karak'terɪʒ |) character

caravela | kara'vɛla | *sm.* caravel; Portuguese man-of-war

carbono | kaR'bonʊ | *sm.* carbon; carbon paper

carburador | kaRbura'doR | *sm.* carburettor

carcaça | kaR'kasa | *sf.* carcass; skeleton

cárcere | 'kaRsɪrɪ | *sm.* prison

carcereiro -ra | kaRse'reyrʊ | *smf.* warder, jailer

carcomido -da | kaRkʊ'midʊ | *a.* worm-eaten, rotten

cardápio | kaR'dapiʊ | *sm.* menu, bill of fare

cardeal | kaRdɪ'al | *sm.* (eccles.) cardinal (also ornith.) / *a.* cardinal, principal

cardíaco | kaR'diakʊ | *smf.* person with heart disease / *a.* cardiac

cardinal | kaRdi'nal | *a.* cardinal, principal

cardume | kaR'dumɪ | *sm.* shoal (of fish)

careca | ka'rɛka | *smf.* (colloq.) bald person; *sf.* bald spot

carecer | kare'seR | *vi.* (used with the *prep.* **de**) to want, to be short of

carência | ka'rẽsia | *sf.* need, lack, want

carestia | karɪʒ'tia | *sf.* expensiveness, high prices

careta | ka'reta | *sf.* grimace; (slang) conventional person or thing

carga | 'kaRga | *sf.* load, cargo, freight; burden; charge

cargo | 'kaRgʊ | *sm.* charge, duty, office; responsibility. **-a c. de** in charge of. **-ter a c.** to be in charge of

cargueiro | kaR'geyrʊ | *sm.* cargo ship or train

caricatura | karika'tura | *sf*. caricature; cartoon

caricia | ka'risia | *sf*. caress

caridade | kari'dadɪ | *sf*. charity; pity

cárie | 'kariɪ | *sf*. (dent.) cavity

carimbar | karĩ'baR | *vt*. to rubber-stamp; to seal

carimbo | ka'rĩbʊ | *sm*. stamp, rubber stamp

carinho | ka'riNʊ | *sm*. tenderness, affection; caress

carinhoso -sa | kari'Nozʊ -'Nwza | *a*. loving, affectionate, tender

carioca | kari'ɔka | *smf*. native of the city of Rio de Janeiro / *a*. of or pertaining to the city of Rio de Janeiro

carnal | kaR'nal | *a*. carnal; full (brother etc.)

carnaúba | karna'uba | *sf*. carnauba (tree); carnauba wax

carnaval | karna'val | *sm*. carnival

carne | 'kaRnɪ | *sf*. flesh; meat

carneiro | kaR'neyrʊ | *sm*. sheep; burial niche. **-carne de c.** mutton

carniça | kaR'nisa | *sf*. carrion

carniceiro -ra | kaRni'seyrʊ | *sm*. butcher / *a*. carnivorous; sanguinary

carnificina | kaRnifi'sina | *sf*. massacre, carnage

carnívoro -ra | kaR'nivʊrʊ | *sm*. carnivore / *a*. carnivorous

carnudo -da | kaR'nudʊ | *a*. fleshy, meaty

caro -ra | 'karʊ | *a*. expensive; dear, beloved / *adv*. dearly

carochinha | karɔ' xina | *sf*. used in the expressions **conto** or **história da c.** fairy-tale

caroço | ka'rosʊ | *sm*. stone (of fruit); lump

carona | ka'rona | *smf*. (colloq.) hitch-hiker, gate-crasher; *sf*. (colloq.) ride, lift

carpintaria | kaRpĩta'ria | *sf*. carpentry; carpenter's shop

carpinteiro | kaRpĩ'teyrʊ | *sm*. carpenter

carranca | ka'Rãka | *sf*. a stern, forbidding look; figure-head

carrancudo -da | kaRã'kudʊ | *a*. frowning, scowling

carrapato | kaRa'patʊ | *sm*. tick, jigger

carrapicho | kaRa'pixʊ | *sm*. bur, burr, beggar's-lice

carrasco | ka'Raʃkʊ | *sm*. executioner, hangman

carregado | kaRe'gadʊ | *a*. loaded; sombre; dark (colour)

carregador | kaRega'doR | *sm*. porter, bearer

carregamento | kaRega'mẽtʊ | *sm*. loading, load; cargo

carregar | kaRe'gaR | *vt*. to load; to carry; to charge. **-c.-se** to become dark or overcast (sky) / *vi*. to intensify; to press on

carreira | ka'Reyra | *sf*. career; running; race; row. **-às carreiras** in a hurry

carreta | ka'Reta | *sf*. cart, wagon

carretel | kaRe'tɛl | *sm*. spool, bobbin

carretilha | karɪ'tiLa | *sf*. spool, bobbin; reel

carreto | ka'Retʊ | *sm*. cartage, portage

carrinho | ka'RiNʊ | *sm*. small cart, small automobile. **-c. de mão** wheelbarrow

carro | 'kaRʊ | *sm*. car, automobile. **-c. de boi** oxcart. **-c. fúnebre** hearse

carruagem | kaRu'aȷ̃ey | *sf*. carriage, coach

carta | 'kaRta | *sf*. letter; map, chart; card (also games); constitution; menu; (*pl*.) mail

cartão | kaR'tãw | *sm*. cardboard; card; visiting-card. **-c. postal** postcard

cartaz | kaR'taʃ | *sm*. poster; (theat.) playbill

carteira | kaR'teyra | *sf*. wallet, pocket-book; desk. **-c. de identidade** identification papers

carteiro | kaR'teyrʊ | *sm*. postman

cartilha | kaR'tiLa | *sf*. first reader,

primer
cartolina | kaʀtʊ'lina | *sm.* light cardboard
cartório | kaʀ'tɔriʊ | *sm.* notary's office; registry
cartucho | kaʀ'tuxʊ | *sm.* shot-gun shell; cartridge; paper cone
caruncho | ka'rũxʊ | *sm.* dry rot
carvalho | kaʀ'vaLʊ | *sm.* oak-tree
carvão | kaʀ'vãw | *sm.* charcoal; coal
casa | 'kaza | *sf.* house; home; buttonhole; square (on a chess-board); commercial establishment. **-c. e comida** board and lodging. **-c. de saúde** private hospital
casaca | ka'zaka | *sf.* dress coat, tailcoat, tails. **-virar a c.** to change sides
casaco | ka'zakʊ | *sm.* coat, jacket
casal | ka'zal | *sm.* married couple; any couple
casamento | kaza'mẽtʊ | *sm.* marriage; wedding
casar | ka'zaʀ | *vt. vi.* to marry, to wed; to mate, to pair. **-c.-se com** to get married
casarão | kaza'rãw | *sm.* mansion, a big house
casca | 'kaʃka | *sf.* rind, peel; crust; bark; shell (of egg, nut etc.)
cascalho | kaʃ'kaLʊ | *sm.* crushed rock, gravel
cascata | kaʃ'kata | *sf.* cascade, waterfall; (slang) bullshit
cascavel | kaʃka'vɛl | *sf.* rattlesnake
casco | 'kaʃkʊ | *sm.* hoof; (naut.) hull; empty bottle (beer etc.)
casebre | ka'zɛbrɪ | *sm.* shanty, shack, hut
caseiro -ra | ka'zeyrʊ | *smf.* overseer (of an estate) / *a.* domestic, home-loving
caserna | ka'zɛʀna | *sf.* barracks
casimira | kazi'mira | *sf.* light-weight woolen cloth

casmurro -ra | kaʃ'muʀʊ | *a.* gloomy, taciturn
caso | 'kazʊ | *sm.* case; instance, event; story, tale; (colloq.) love affair. **-vir ao c.** to come to the point
caspa | 'kaʃpa | *sf.* dandruff
cassar | ka'saʀ | *vt.* (law) to annul, to cancel; (law) to discharge
cassino | ka'sinʊ | *sm.* casino, gambling house
casta | 'kaʃta | *sf.* caste; lineage, breed
castanha | kaʃ'taNa | *sf.* chestnut
castanha-de-caju | kaʃ'taNadɪ-ka'ju | *sf.* cashew nut
castanha-do-pará | kaʃ'taNadʊ-pa'ra | *sf.* Brazil nut
castanho -nha | kaʃ'taNʊ | *sm. a.* chestnut-brown, chestnut (colour)
castanholas | kaʃta'Nɔlaʃ | *sfpl.* castanets
castelhano -na | kaʃte'Lanʊ | *sm.* (ling.) Castilian, Spanish; *smf. a.* Castilian
castelo | kaʃ'tɛlʊ | *sm.* castle
castiçal | kaʃti'sal | *sm.* candlestick
castiço -ça | kaʃ'tisʊ | *a.* pure; correct; of good origin or lineage
castidade | kaʃti'dadɪ | *sf.* chastity
castigar | kaʃti'gaʀ | *vt.* to punish; to discipline
castigo | kaʃ'tigʊ | *sm.* punishment
casto -ta | 'kaʃtʊ | *a.* chaste
castor | kaʃ'toʀ | *sm.* beaver
castrado -da | kaʃ'tradʊ | *a.* castrated
castrar | kaʃ'traʀ | *vt.* to castrate, to geld
casual | kazu'al | *a.* accidental, fortuitous
casualidade | kazuali'dadɪ | *sf.* chance, hazard, accident. **-por c.** by chance
casulo | ka'zulʊ | *sm.* cocoon; seed capsule
cata | 'kata | *sf.* search; mine; grading of coffee beans. **-à c.**

de ın search of

catadura | kata'dura | *sf.* mien; aspect. **-de má c.** of evil aspect

catálogo | ka'talʊgʊ | *sm.* catalogue, catalog. **-c. telefônico** telephone book

cataplasma | kata'plaʒma | *sf.* poultice

catar | ka'taʀ | *vt.* to search; to pick (out). **-c. arroz (café etc.)** to cull rice (coffee etc.) by hand

catarata | kata'rata | *sf.* waterfall; cataract (also med.)

catarro | ka'taʀʊ | *sm.* catarrh

catástrofe | ka'taʒtrʊfɪ | *sf.* catastrophe, calamity

cata-vento | kata'vẽtʊ | *sm.* weather-vane, weathercock

catecismo | katɪ'siʒmʊ | *sm.* catechism

catedral | kate'dral | *sf.* cathedral

catedrático | kate'dratikʊ | *sm.* full professor

categoria | katego'ria | *sf.* category, class. **-de alta c.** first-rate

catinga | ka'tĩga | *sf.* (vulg.) offensive body odo(u)r; stench

cativar | kati'vaʀ | *vt.* to captivate, to fascinate

cativeiro | kati'veyrʊ | *sm.* captivity, bondage; slavery

catolicismo | katoli'siʒmʊ | *sm.* Catholicism

católico -ca | ka'tʊlikʊ | *smf. a.* Roman Catholic

catorze | ka'tɔʀzɪ | *sm. num.* fourteen

catre | 'katrɪ | *sm.* cot; folding bed

caturra | ka'tuʀa | *smf.* person who clings to out-moded ideas

caução | kaw'sãw | *sf.* surety bond. **-sob c.** on bail

cauda | 'kawda | *sf.* tail; tail end

caudaloso -sa | kawda'lozʊ -'lɔwza | *a.* high, swollen (of a river); abundant

caule | 'kawlɪ | *sm.* stalk, stem

causa | 'kawza | *sf.* cause (also law); motive; factor, account; sake. **-por c. de** because of

causar | kaw'zaʀ | *vt.* to cause; to originate; to give rise to

cautela | kaw'tɛla | *sf.* caution, care. **-c. de penhor** pawn ticket

cauteloso -sa | kawte'lozʊ -'lɔwza | *a.* cautious, prudent

cavala | ka'vala | *sf.* a mackerel

cavalaria | kavala'ria | *sf.* cavalry; herd of horses

cavalariça | kavala'risa | *sf.* stable

cavaleiro -ra | kava'leyrʊ | *sm.* rider, horseman; knight; *sf.* horsewoman

cavalete | kava'letɪ | *sm.* easel

cavalgar | kaval'gaʀ | *vt.* to mount (a horse) / *vi.* to ride horseback

cavalheiro | kava'ʟeyrʊ | *sm.* gentleman / *a.* gentlemanly

cavalo | ka'valʊ | *sm.* horse; horsepower; knight (chess). **-a c.** on horseback

cavalo-vapor | ka'valʊva'poʀ | *sm.* horsepower

cavanhaque | kava'Nakɪ | *sm.* goatee

cavaquinho | kava'kiNʊ | *sm.* small guitar

caveira | ka'veyra | *sf.* skull

caverna | ka'vɛʀna | *sf.* cavern (also med.), cave

cavidade | kavi'dadɪ | *sf.* cavity

cavilha | ka'viʟa | *sf.* peg, dowell

cavo -va | 'kavʊ | *a.* hollow, cavernous, deep (also voice)

caxumba | ka'xûba | *sf.* mumps, parotitis

cear | sɪ'aʀ | *vt. vi.* to have supper

cearense | sɪa'rẽsɪ | *smf.* native of Ceará / *a.* of or pertaining to the State of Ceará

cebola | se'bola | *sf.* onion

ceder | se'deʀ | *vt.* to yield, to give up; to succumb / *vi.* to cave in; to give way

cedilha | sɪ'diʟa | *sf.* cedilla

cedo | 'sedʊ | *adv.* early; soon. **-o mais c. possível** as soon as possible

cedro | 'sɛdrʊ | *sm.* cedar

cédula | 'sedula | *sf.* note, banknote, bill; ballot

cegar | se'gaʀ | *vt.* to blind; to dull (a blade etc.) / *vi.* to become blind

cego -ga | 'sɛgʊ | *smf.* blind man, blind woman / *a.* blind; dull, edgeless (of blades). **-às cegas** blindly

cegonha | se'goɴa | *sf.* storck

cegueira | se'geyra | *sf.* blindness

ceia | 'seya | *sf.* supper

ceifar | sey'faʀ | *vt.* to harvest, to mow

cela | 'sɛla | *sf.* cell; cubicle

celebração | selebra'sãw | *sf.* celebration

celebrar | sele'braʀ | *vt.* to celebrate, to commemorate / *vi.* to celebrate (mass)

célebre | 'sɛlɪbrɪ | *a.* celebrated, renowned

celebridade | selebri'dadɪ | *sf.* celebrity, fame

celeiro | se'leyrʊ | *sm.* barn, granary

celerado -da | sele'radʊ | *smf.* criminal / *a.* criminal, perverse

célere | 'sɛlɪrɪ | *a.* swift, fleet, rapid

celestial | sele'ʒti'al | *a.* celestial, heavenly, divine

celibato | sɪli'batʊ | *sm.* celibacy

célula | 'sɛlula | *sf.* cell; cellule

cem | 'sẽy | *sm. num.* hundred

cemitério | sɪmi'tɛriʊ | *sm.* graveyard, cemetery

cena | 'sena | *sf.* scene; sight; stage

cenário | se'nariʊ | *sm.* (theat.) scenery

cenoura | sɪ'nowra | *sf.* carrot

censo | 'sẽsʊ | *sm.* census

censor | sẽ'soʀ | *sm.* censor

censura | sẽ'sura | *sf.* censorship; censure, reprimand

centavo | sẽ'tavʊ | *sm.* centavo (hundredth part of one cruzeiro); cent

centeio | sẽ'teyʊ | *sm.* rye

centelha | sẽ'teLa | *sf.* spark

centena | sẽ'tena | *sf.* hundred; hundredth

centenário -ria | sẽte'nariʊ | *smf.* centenarian; *sm.* centennial,

century / *a.* centennial

centésimo -ma | sẽ'tezimʊ |*sm.a.*. centesimal, hundredth

centígrado -da | sẽ'tigradʊ | *a.* centigrade

cento | 'sẽtʊ | *sm.* hundred. **-por c.** (%) percent

centopeia, centopéia | sẽto'peya sẽto'peya | *sf.* centipede

central | sẽ'tral | *sf.* central office (telephone, police etc.) / *a.* central

centralizar | sẽtrali'zaʀ | *vt.* to centralize

centro | 'sẽtrʊ | *sm.* centre, center. **-c. da cidade** downtown

cepa | 'sepa | *sf.* grape-vine, vine-stock

cepo|'sepʊ|*sm.* stump; block, log

cepticismo, ceticismo | septi'siʒmʊ seti'siʒmʊ | *sm.* scepticism, skepticism

cera | 'sera | *sf.* wax

cerâmica|se'ramika|*sf.* ceramics

cerca | 'seʀka | *sf.* fence, fencing / *adv.* about, nearly. **-c. de** about, approximately

cercado -da|seʀ'kadʊ|*sm.* enclosure / *a.* fenced, enclosed. **-c. de** amidst

cercania | seʀka'nia | *sf.* (gen. *pl.*) vicinity, outskirts, surroundings

cercar | seʀ'kaʀ | *vt.* to fence; to enclose, to encircle; to besiege

cercear|seʀsɪ'aʀ|*vt.* to restrict, to cut

cerco | 'seʀkʊ | *sm.* encirclement; siege

cerda | 'seʀda | *sf.* bristle

cereal | sɪrɪ'al | *sm.* cereal

cérebro | 'sɛrebrʊ | *sm.* brain

cereja | se'reja | *sf.* cherry

cerimônia | sɪri'monia | *sf.* ceremony; solemnity. **-fazer c.** to stand on ceremony. **-sem c.** informal

cerimonial | sɪrimoni'al |*sm.* cerimonial; etiquette; official department in charge of ceremonies

cerimonioso -sa | sɪrimoni'ozʊ -'ωza | *a.* ceremonious, formal

cerração | seʀa'sãw | *sf.* fog, mist

cerrado -da | se'ʀadʊ | *sm.* waste land with stunted twisted trees / *a.* closed, locked; overcast, cloudy; dense, thick; hard to understand (pronunciation etc.)

cerrar | se'ʀaʀ | *vt.* to close, to shut; to clench; to grit (one's teeth); to terminate / *vr.* to close in (referring to the weather)

cerro | 'seʀʊ | *sm.* small, craggy hill

certa | 'sɛʀta | *sf.* a certainty. **-na c.** certainly, surely

certame, certâmen | seʀ'tamɪ seʀ'tamẽ(y) | *sm.* contest, competition

certeiro -ra | seʀ'teyrʊ | *a.* well--aimed, exact

certeza | seʀ'teza | *sf.* certitude; assurance, conviction. **-com c.** certainly; (colloq.) probably

certidão | seʀti'dãw | *sf.* certificate. **-c. de nascimento** birth certificate

certificado | seʀtifi'kadʊ | *sm.* attestation, certificate. **-c. de reservista** (mil.) discharge papers

certificar | seʀtifi'kaʀ | *vt.* to certify. **-c.-se** to be (make) sure

certo-ta | 'sɛʀtʊ | *sm.* certainty. **-ao c.** for certain, for sure. **-de c.** certainly / *a.* certain; correct; just; exact. **-está c.** all right, sure / *adv.* certainly, surely

cerveja | seʀ'veja | *sf.* beer. **-fábrica de c.** brewery

cervejaria | seʀveja'ria | *sf.* beer hall; pub; brewery

cervo | 'sɛʀvʊ | *sm.* stag, hart

cerzideira | sɪʀzi'deyra | *sf.* darner, mender

cessação | sesa'sãw | *sf.* cessation, discontinuance, extinction

cessão | se'sãw | *sf.* cession; (law) assignment

cessar | se'saʀ | *vi.* to cease; to discontinue

cesta | 'seʃta | *sf.* basket. **-c. de**

papéis waste-paper basket

cesto | 'seʃtʊ | *sm.* basket, hamper

cetim | sɪ'tĩ | *sm.* satin

cetro | 'setrʊ | *sm.* scepter

céu | 'sɛw | *sm.* sky, heaven. **-c. da boca** palate, roof of the mouth

cevada | se'vada | *sf.* barley, barleycorn

cevado -da | se'vadʊ | *sm.* hog fattened for slaughter / *a.* fattened

cevar | se'vaʀ | *vt.* to fatten; to chum (fish). **-c.-se** to satisfy one's desire

chá | 'xa | *sm.* tea (also beverage, party); any similar infusion

chacal | xa'kal | *sm.* jackal

chácara | 'xakara | *sf.* country place

chacina | xa'sina | *sf.* slaughtering

chacota | xa'kωta | *sf.* jeer, mock

chafariz | xafa'riʒ | *sm.* public fountain

chaga | 'xaga | *sf.* wound; ulcer

chaleira | xa'leyra | *sf.* kettle

chama | 'xama | *sf.* flame

chamada | xa'mada | *sf.* call, calling; roll call; (typog.) catch line. **-c. telefônica** telephone call

chamar | xa'maʀ | *vt.* to call; to summon; to convoke. **-c.-se** to be called, to be named / *vi.* to call, to beckon

chamariz | xama'riʒ | *sm.* decoy; attraction

chamejar | xame'jaʀ | *vt.·vi.* to blaze; to glow, to gleam

chaminé | xami'nɛ | *sm.* chimney; stove pipe

chamuscar | xamuʒ'kaʀ | *vt.* to singe

chancela | xã'sɛla | *sf.* seal; official seal; rubber stamp

chantagem | xã'tajẽy | *sf.* backmail

chão, chã | 'xãw 'xã | *sm.* ground, soil; floor. **-de pé no c.** (colloq.) barefoot / *a.* plain, down to earth

chapa | 'xapa | *sf.* plate (photog., typog., dent.); metal plate; li-

cense plate. **-c. eleitoral** slate,
ticket. **-bater uma c.** to take a
photograph. **-de c.** in full, flatly

chapada | xa'pada | *sf.* plateau,
plain

chapelaria | xapela'ria | *sf.* hatter's shop, hattery

chapeleiro -ra | xape'leyrʋ | *smf.*
hatter; *sf.* hat box

chapéu | xa'pɛw | *sm.* hat. **-tirar o
c. a** (colloq.) to praise

chapéu-de-chuva | xa'pɛwdɩ'xuva | *sm.* umbrella

chapinhar | xapi'ɴaʀ | *vt.* to splash
water; to slosh water

charanga | xa'rãga | *sf.* brass band

charco | 'xaʀkʋ | *sm.* stagnant
pool, mud puddle

charlatão -tona | xaʀla'tãw -'tona |
smf. charlatan, faker

charneca | xaʀ'nɛka | *sf.* moor,
heath; tract of waste land

charque | 'xaʀkɩ | *sm.* jerked beef

charuto | xa'rutʋ | *sm.* cigar

chata | 'xata | *sf.* barge

chatear | xatɩ'aʀ | *vt.* (colloq.) to
bore; to pester, to bother

chato -ta | 'xatʋ | *sm.* (vulg.) crab-louse; (colloq.) annoying
person / *a.* flat; (fig.) dull;
(colloq.) annoying

chave | 'xavɩ | *sf.* key; wrench;
(fig.) solution. **-c. de parafuso**
screwdriver. **-c. inglesa**
monkey-wrench

chaveiro | xa'veyrʋ | *sm.* key-ring;
key maker; keeper of the keys

chefe | 'xɛfɩ | *sm.* chief; head,
leader

chegada | xe'gada | *sf.* arrival

chegar | xe'gaʀ | *vt.* to bring near.
-c.-se to come near / *vi.* to arrive; to come; to reach; to be
enough. **-c. a ser** to become, to
get to be

cheia | 'xeya | *sf.* flood

cheio, cheia | 'xeyʋ | *a.* full; filled;
crowded. **-acertar em c.** to hit
the bull's-eye

cheirar | xey'raʀ | *vt. vi.* to smell;
to scent. **-c. a** to smell of

cheiro | 'xeyrʋ | *sm.* smell; perfume, fragrance

cheiroso -sa | xey'rozʋ -'ɾwza | *a.*
scented, fragrant

cheiro-verde | 'xeyrʋ'veʀdɩ | *sm.*
(cookery) parsley and shallot

cheque | 'xɛkɩ | *sm.* cheque, check.
-c. ao portador bearer cheque.
-c. visado certified cheque

chiar | xi'aʀ | *vi.* to squeak; to
chirp; to sizzle

chibata | xi'bata | *sf.* switch, whip

chicana | xi'kana | *sf.* chicane,
chicanery

chiclete | xi'klɛtɩ | *sm.* chewing-gum

chicote | xi'kʋtɩ | *sm.* whip

chifre | 'xifrɩ | *sm.* horn

chileno -na | xi'lenʋ | *smf. a.*
Chilean

chilreio | xil'ʀeyʋ | *sm.* peep,
chirp; trill

chinelo -la | xi'nɛlʋ | *smf.* house
slipper

chinês -nesa | xi'neʃ -'neza | *smf.
a.* Chinese

chinó | xi'nɔ | *sm.* wig

chique | 'xikɩ | *a.* chic, smart,
elegant

chiqueiro | xi'keyrʋ | *sm.* pigsty

chispa | 'xiʃpa | *sf.* flash, spark

chispar | xiʃ'paʀ | *vi.* to sparkle;
(colloq.) do dash, to run

chita | 'xita | *sf.* calico

choça | 'xwsa | *sf.* hut, shack

chocalhar | xʋka'laʀ | *vt.* to rattle,
to jingle

chocalho | xʋ'kalʋ | *sm.* rattle

chocante | xo'kãtɩ | *a.* shocking

chocar | xo'kaʀ | *vt.* to hatch, to incubate, to brood; to shock.
-c.-se to collide; to be shocked

chocho -cha | 'xoxʋ | *a.* empty;
dull, insipid

choco -ca | 'xokʋ 'xwka | *sm.* incubation period / *a.* brooding;
spoiled (egg)

chocolate | xoko'latɩ | *sm.* cocoa;
chocolate

chofer | xo'fɛʀ | *sm.* driver

chofre | 'xofrɩ | *sm.* sudden strike.

-de c. suddenly

chope | 'xopɪ | sm. draught beer, draft beer

choque | 'xωkɪ | sm. shock; crash; battle

choramingar | xòramĩ'gaR | vt. vi. to whimper, to cry; to complain

chorão-rona | xo'rãw-'rona | smf. weeper, whiner; sm. weeping willow / a. crying, whining

chorar | xo'raR | vt. to cry for; to mourn for; to deplore / vi. to cry

choro | 'xorʊ | sm. crying; a kind of popular Brazilian tune

choupana | xow'pana | sf. hut, shanty, cot

choupo | 'xowpʊ | sm. poplar

chouriço | xow'risʊ | sm. smoked sausage

chover | xʊ'veR | vi. to rain. -c. a cântaros to rain buckets

chuchu | xu'xu | sm. (bot.) chayote

chulice | xu'lisɪ | sf. crude expression

chumaço | xu'masʊ | sm. padding, stuffing

chumbo | 'xũbʊ | sm. lead

chupar | xu'paR | vt. to suck

chupeta | xu'peta | sf. dummy, rubber nipple

churrasco | xu'Raʃkʊ | sm. barbecued beef; barbecue

chutar | xu'taR | vt. vi. to kick

chute | 'xutɪ | sm. kick

chuva | 'xuva | sf. rain

chuveiro | xu'veyrʊ | sm. shower, shower-bath

chuviscar | xuviʃ'kaR | vi. to drizzle

chuvoso -sa | xu'vozʊ -'vωza | a. rainy

cicatriz | sika'triʃ | sf. scar

ciciar | sisi'aR | vt. vi. to murmur, to whisper; to rustle

ciclista | si'kliʃta | smf. bicycle rider, cyclist

ciclo | 'siklʊ | sm. cycle

ciclone | si'klonɪ | sm. cyclone; hurricane

cidadão -dã | sida'dãw -'dã | smf. citizen

cidade | si'dadɪ | sf. city, town

cidadela | sida'dela | sf. citadel

ciência | si'êsia | sf. science; knowledge

ciente | si'êtɪ | sm. endorsement, initials / a. notified, aware

científico -ca | siê'tifikʊ | a. scientific

cientista | siê'tiʃta | smf. scientist

cifra | 'sifra | sf. cipher; total; code

cifrão | si'frãw | sm. monetary symbol ($)

cifrar | si'fraR | vt. to cipher, to code

cigano -na | si'ganʊ | smf. a. gypsy

cigarra | si'gaRa | sf. cicada; (elect.) buzzer

cigarreira | sɪga'Reyra | sf. cigarette case

cigarro | si'gaRʊ | sm. cigarette

cilada | si'lada | sf. ambush

cilindro | si'lĩdrʊ | sm. cylinder; roller

cílio | 'siliʊ | sm. eyelash

cima | 'sima | sf. top, summit (gen. used in adv. loc.). -ainda por c. in addition. -lá em c. upstairs. -para c. up, upward. -para c. de more than, over, in excess of

cimentar | simê'taR | vt. to cement; to consolidate

cimento | si'mêtʊ | sm. cement; concrete; uniting element. -c. armado armoured concrete

cimo | 'simʊ | sm. top, summit

cinco | 'sĩkʊ | sm. num. five

cinema | si'nema | sm. cinema, motion picture theatre; movies

cinematografar | sinematogra'faR | vt. to film

cingir | sĩ'jiR | vt. to gird (on); to encircle; to restrict. -c.-se a to hold (restrict) oneself to

cínico -ca | 'sinikʊ | smf. cynic / a. cynical; impudent

cinismo | si'niʃmʊ | sm. cynicism

cinqüenta | sĩ'kwêta | sm. num. fifty

cinta | 'sĩta | sf. girdle; mailing wrapper (for newspapers etc.).

-à c. fastened to the belt

cintilar | sĩti‘laʀ | *vt. vi.* to scintillate; to twinkle; to glitter

cinto | ‘sĩtʊ | *sm.* belt. -c. de segurança safety belt, seat-belt

cintura | sĩ‘tura | *sf.* waist

cinza | ‘sĩza | *sf.* ash; (*pl.*) ashes, mortal remains / *a.* grey (colour)

cinzeiro | sĩ‘zeyrʊ | *sm̥.* ashtray; ash-bin, ashpan

cinzel | sĩ‘zɛl | *sm.* chisel

cinzelar | sĩze‘laʀ | *vt.* to chisel; to engrave

cinzento -ta | sĩ‘zẽtʊ | *a.* grey, ashen (colo[u]r)

cio | ‘siʊ | *sm.* heat, rut

cioso -sa | si‘ozʊ -‘ωza | *a.* zealous, solicitous

cipó | si‘pω | *sm.* liana, vine

cipreste | si‘prɛʂtↄ | *sm.* cypress

ciranda | si‘rãda | *sf.* children's game (similar to ring-around-the-rosy); folk-dance and music

circo | ‘siʀkʊ | *sm.* circus

circuito | siʀ‘kuytʊ | *sm.* circuit (also elect.)

circulação | siʀkula‘sãw | *sf.* circulation; distribution

circular | siʀku‘laʀ | *sf.* circular letter / *a.* circular / *vt.* to encircle / *vi.* to circulate; to walk around

círculo | ‘siʀkulʊ | *sm.* circle; club

circuncisão | siʀkũsi‘zãw | *sf.* circumcision

circundar | siʀkũ‘daʀ | *vt.* to surround, to encircle

circunferência | siʀkũfe‘rẽsia | *sf.* circumference

circunflexo | siʀkũ‘flɛksʊ | *sm. a.* circumflex

circunscrever | siʀkũʂkre‘veʀ | *vt.* to circumscribe; to limit

circunspecção, circunspeção | siʀkũʂpek‘sãw siʀkũʂpe‘sãw | *sf.* circumspection

circunspecto, circunspeto -ta | siʀkũʂ‘pɛktʊ siʀkũʂ‘pɛtʊ | *a.* circumspect, cautious

circunstância | siʀkũʂ‘tãsia | *sf.* circumstance, situation

circunstante | siʀkũʂ‘tãtↄ | *smf.* bystander; *smpl.* audience

circunvizinho -nha | siʀkũviˈziɴʊ | *a.* neighbo(u)ring; surrounding; adjacent

círio | ‘siriʊ | *sm.* large candle

cirurgia | siruʀ‘jia | *sf.* surgery

cirurgião -giã | siruʀji‘ãw | *smf.* surgeon

cisão | si‘zãw | *sf.* dissension

cisco | ‘siʂkʊ | *sm.* speck of dust

cisma | ‘siʂma | *sf.* musing, day-dream; obsession, fixation; schism

cismar | siʂ‘maʀ | *vt.* to brood over; to ponder; (colloq.) to imagine / *vi.* to brood

cisne | ‘siʂnↄ | *sm.* swan

cisterna | siʂ‘tɛrna | *sf.* cistern, water tank

cisto | ‘siʂtʊ | *sm.* cyst

citação | sita‘sãw | *sf.* quotation; (law) summons

citar | si‘taʀ | *vt.* to quote; to summon; to mention

ciúme | si‘umↄ | *sm.* jealousy

ciumento -ta | siu‘mẽtↄ | *a.* jealous

civil | si‘vil | *smf.* civilian / *a.* civil (also law); civilian

civilidade | sivili‘dadↄ | *sf.* civility, courtesy

civilização | siyiliza‘sãw | *sf.* civilization

civilizado -da | sivili‘zadʊ | *a.* civilized

civilizar | sivili‘zaʀ | *vt.* to civilize

civismo | si‘viʂmʊ | *sm.* public spirit; civic pride

clamar | kla‘maʀ | *vt..* to clamo(u)r; to cry out for / *vi.* to clamo(u)r, to cry out

clamor | kla‘moʀ | *sm.* outcry

clamoroso -sa | klamo‘rozʊ -‘rωza | *a.* clamorous

clandestino -na | klãdeʂ‘tinʊ | *smf.* stowaway / *a.* clandestine, concealed

clara | ‘klara | *sf.* egg-white

clarabóia | klara‘bωya | *sf.*

skylight

clarão | kla'rãw | *sm.* flash of light, dazzling light

clarear | kları'aR | *vt.* to clear (up); to light (up) / *vi.* to grow light

clareira | kla'reyra | *sf.* clearing, opening, glade

clareza | kla'reza | *sf.* clearness, clarity

claridade | klari'dadı | *sf.* clarity; clearness

clarificar | klarifi'kaR | *vt.* to clarify, to purify

clarim | kla'rĩ | *sm.* clarion; bugle; bugler

claro -ra | 'klarʊ | *sm.* space, gap; opening / *a.* clear; light; light--coloured. **-c. que não** of course not. **-c. que sim** of course, certainly / *adv.* clearly, certainly, surely

classe | 'klası | *sf.* class; group

clássico -ca 'klasikʊ | *sm.* classic author; (*pl.*) the classics / *a.* classic

classificação | klasifika'sãw | *sf.* classification

classificar | klasifi'kaR | *vt.* to classify, to arrange

claudicar | klawdi'kaR | *vi.* to limp, to hobble; (fig.) to blunder

claustro | 'klawʃtrʊ | *sm.* cloister

cláusula | 'klawzula | *sf.* clause (also gram.), article, condition

clausura | klaw'zura | *sf.* seclusion; monastic life

clave | 'klavı | *sf.* (mus.) key, clef

clavícula | kla'vikula | *sf.* clavicle, collar-bone

clemência | kle'mẽsia | *sf.* clemency, mercy

clemente | kle'mẽtı | *a.* clement, merciful

clérigo | 'klɛrigʊ | *sm.* clergyman, cleric, priest

clero | 'klerʊ | *sm.* clergy

clichê | kli'xe | *sm.* printing plate, cliché (also fig.)

cliente | kli'ẽtı | *sm.* client; customer, patron

clientela | klĩ'tɛla | *sf.* clientele; customers

clima | 'klima | *sm.* climate

clínica | 'klinika | *sf.* the practice of medicine; clinic

clínico -ca | 'klinikʊ | *smf.* physician, doctor / *a.* clinical

clube | 'klubı | *sm.* club

coabitar | cʊabi'taR | *vi.* to cohabit, to live together

coação | kʊa'sãw | *sf.* coaction, force

coador | kʊa'doR | *sm.* strainer

coagir | kʊa'jiR | *vt.* to coerce, to compel

coagular | kʊagu'laR | *vt. vi.* (also c.-se) to coagulate, to curdle, to clot

coágulo | kʊ'agulʊ | *sm.* clot

coalhada 'kʊa'Ladaı | *sf.* curd, curdled milk

coalhado -da | kʊa'Ladʊ | *a.* curdled, clotted

coar | kʊ'aR | *vt.* to strain; to filter / *vi.* to filter

coaxar | kʊa'xaR | *vi.* to croak (as a frog)

cobaia | ko'baya | *sf.* guinea-pig

coberto -ta | kʊ'bɛrtʊ | *sm.* covered area; *sf.* bedspread; (naut.) deck / *a.* covered; overcast (sky)

cobertor | kʊbeR'toR | *sm.* blanket

cobertura | kʊbeR'tura | *sf.* cover, covering; penthouse

cobiça | kʊ'bisa | *sf.* greed, covetousness

cobiçar | kʊbi'saR | *vt.* to covet; to desire ardently

cobiçoso -sa | kʊbi'sozʊ -'sʊza | *a.* greedy, covetous

cobra | 'kʊbra | *sf.* snake

cobrador -dora | kobra'doR | *smf.* collector (of debts etc.); ticket--collector

cobrança | ko'brãsa | *sf.* collection (of bills)

cobrar | ko'braR | *vt.* to collect; to regain (courage)

cobre | 'kʊbrı | *sm.* copper

cobrir | kʊ'briR | *vt.* to cover; to

protect; to roof (house). **-c.-se** to cover oneself; to put on a hat; to become overcast (sky)

coça | ˈkʊsa | *sf.* (colloq.) beating, thrashing

cocada | koˈkada | *sf.* coconut candy or dessert

coçado -da | koˈsadʊ | *a.* threadbare, worn thin

cocaína | kokaˈina | *sf.* cocaine

coçar | koˈsaʀ | *vt.* to scratch. **-c.-se** to scratch oneself / *vi.* to itch

cócegas | ˈkʊsɪgaʒ | *sfpl.* tickles; (fig.) impatience. **-fazer c.** to tickle

coche | ˈkoxɪ | *sm.* carriage, coach

cocheira | koˈxeyra | *sf.* stable

cocheiro | koˈxeyrʊ | *sm.* coachman

cochichar | kʊxiˈxaʀ | *vt. vi.* to whisper

cochilar | kʊxiˈlaʀ | *vi.* to doze, to nap

côco | ˈkokʊ | *sm.* coconut

cócoras | ˈkʊkʊraʒ | *sfpl.* used only in the expression **de c.** squatting

código | ˈkʊdigʊ | *sm.* code

codorna | koˈdʊʀna | *sf.* quail

coelho | kʊˈeʟʊ | *sm.* rabbit

coerência | koeˈrẽsia | *sf.* coherence

coesão | koeˈzãw | *sf.* cohesion

cofre | ˈkʊfrɪ | *sm.* safe, chest

cogitar | kojiˈtaʀ | *vt. vi.* to cogitate, to meditate

cogumelo | kʊguˈmɛlʊ | *sm.* mushroom

coibir | koiˈbiʀ | *vt.* to restrain

coice | ˈkoysɪ | *sm.* a backward kick; recoil (of gun)

coincidência | koĩsiˈdẽsia | *sf.* coincidence

coincidir | koĩsiˈdiʀ | *vt.* to coincide

coisa | ˈkoyza | *sf.* thing

coitado -da | koyˈtadʊ | *smf.* unfortunate person / *a.* poor, unfortunate / *interj.* poor fellow!, poor thing!

cola | ˈkʊla | *sf.* glue, adhesive

colaboração | kolaboraˈsãw | *sf.* collaboration

colaborar | kolaboˈraʀ | *vi.* to collaborate

colar | koˈlaʀ | *sm.* necklace; neckchain / *vt.* to stick, to glue

colarinho | kʊlaˈrinʊ | *sm.* shirt collar

colcha | ˈkolxa | *sf.* bedspread

colchete | kolˈxetɪ | *sm.* hook and eye fastener; (typog.) bracket

colchoaria | kolxʊaˈria | *sf.* mattress factory or store

coleção | koleˈsãw | *sf.* collection

colecionador -dora | kolesionaˈdoʀ | *smf.* collector

colecionar | kolesioˈnaʀ | *vt.* to collect

colega | koˈlɛga | *smf.* colleague

colégio | kʊˈlɛjiʊ | *sm.* grammar school; secondary school, high school

coleira | koˈleyra | *sf.* collar (for dogs etc.)

cólera | ˈkʊlera | *sf.* wrath, ire; (med.) cholera

colete | kʊˈletɪ | *sm.* waistcoat, vest

colheita | koˈʟeyta | *sf.* harvest, crop

colher | kʊˈʟɛʀ | *sf.* spoon

colher | koˈʟɛʀ | *vt.* to gather; to pick; to catch

colherada | kʊʟeˈrada | *sf.* spoonful

colibri | koliˈbri | *sm.* humming-bird

cólica | ˈkʊlika | *sf.* colic

colidir | koliˈdiʀ | *vi.* to collide, to clash

coligação | koligaˈsãw | *sf.* alliance, coalition

coligir | koliˈjiʀ | *vt.* to collect, to gather

colina | kʊˈlina | *sf.* hill

colisão | koliˈzãw | *sf.* collision, crash

colméia, colmeia | kolˈmeya kolˈmeya | *sf.* beehive

colo | ˈkʊlʊ | *sm.* gorge; neck; lap. **-ao c.** in someone's lap

colocação | koloka'sãw | *sf.* situation; position, job; placing

colocar | kolo'kaR | *vt.* to place, to put, to set; to employ / *vr.* to get a job

colônia | ko'lonia | *sf.* colony (also biol.), settlement; eau-de--Cologne

colonização | koloniza'sãw | *sf.* colonization

colonizar | koloni'zaR | *vt.* to colonize

colono -na | ko'lonʋ | *smf.* settler; *sm.* farm-hand

coloquialismo | kolokia'liʒmʋ | *sm.* colloquialism

colorir | kolo'riR | *vt.* to colo(u)r; to brighten

colossal | kolo'sal | *a.* colossal

coluna | kʋ'luna | *sf.* column, pillar. **-c. vertebral** spinal column

colunista | kʋlu'niʒta | *smf.* (journal.) columnist

com | 'kũ | *prep.* with

comadre | kʋ'madrɪ | *sf.* godmother; (colloq.) midwife

comandante | komã'dãtɪ | *sm.* commander; captain (of a ship or aircraft)

comandar | komã'daR | *vt.* to command

comando | ko'mãdʋ | *sm.* command; control; (mil.) commando

comarca | ko'maRka | *sf.* district, county

combalir | kõba'liR | *vt.* to weaken, to debilitate, to enfeeble

combate | kõ'batɪ | *sm.* combat, battle

combater | kõba'teR | *vt. vi.* to combat, to battle; to fight

combinação | kõbina'sãw | *sf.* combination; agreement; underskirt

combinar | kõbi'naR | *vt.* to combine; to unite; to agree / *vi.* to be in agreement, to harmonize. **-c. com** to match

comboiar | kõboy'aR | *vt.* to convoy

comboio, combóio | kõ'boyʋ kõ'bwyʋ | *sm.* convoy

combustão | kõbuʃ'tãw | *sf.* combustion, ignition

combustível | kõbuʃ'tivɪl | *sm.* fuel / *a.* combustible

começar | kome'saR | *vt. vi.* to begin; to commence

começo | kʋ'mesʋ | *sm.* beginning, start

comédia | ko'mɛdia | *sf.* comedy

comediante | komedi'ãtɪ | *smf.* comedian

comedido -da | kome'didʋ | *a.* moderate, temperate

comedir | komɪ'diR | *vt.* to moderate, to temper

comemoração | komemora'sãw | *sf.* commemoration, celebration

comemorar | komemo'raR | *vt.* to commemorate, to celebrate

comensal | komẽ'sal | *smf.* table guest

comentar | komẽ'taR | *vt.* to comment; to interpret

comentário | komẽ'tariv | *sm.* commentary; comment

comentarista | komẽta'riʒta | *smf.* commentator; columnist

comer | kʋ'meR | *vt.* to eat; to consume

comercial | kʋmeRsi'al | *a.* commercial

comerciante | kʋmeRsi'ãtɪ | *smf.* trader, merchant, dealer

comerciário -ria | kʋmeRsi'arivʋ | *smf.* commercial employee

comércio | kʋ'meRsivʋ | *sm.* commerce, trade

comestível | kʋmeʒ'tivɪl | *a.* edible / *sm.* (usu. *pl.*) food, food products

cometa | ko'meta | *sm.* comet

cometer | kome'teR | *vt.* to commit, to perpetrate

comichão | kʋmi'xãw | *sf.* itch

comício | ko'misivʋ | *sm.* political meeting

cômico -ca | 'komikʋ | *smf.* comedian / *a.* comic

comida | kʊ'mida | *sf.* food; meals. **-casa e** c. room and board

comido -da | kʊ'midʊ | *a.* eaten

comigo | kʊ'migʊ | *pron.* with me

comilão -lona | kʊmi'lãw -'lona | *smf.* glutton / *a.* gluttonous

comissão | kʊmi'sãw | *sf.* commission; committee; (com.) percentage

comissário -ria | kʊmi'sariʊ | *smf.* commissioner; commissary; steward, air hostess

comitê | komi'te | *sm.* committee

comitiva | komi'tiva | *sf.* escort, entourage, retinue

como | 'komʊ | *adv.* how, how much. **-c. vai?** how are you? / *conj.* as; like; since. **-c. assim?** how come? **-c. não** certainly, of course. **-c.?** I beg your pardon?

comoção | komo'sãw | *sf.* commotion; turmoil, tumult

cômoda | 'komoda | *sf.* chest of drawers

comodidade | komodi'dadɪ | *sf.* comfort; convenience

comodista | komo'diʒta | *smf.* self-indulgent person

cômodo -da | 'komʊdʊ | *sm.* accomodation; room / *a.* comfortable

comovente | komo'vẽtɪ | *a.* moving, touching

comover | komo'veʀ | *vt.* to move, to affect

compacto -ta | kõ'paktʊ | *a.* compact; massive

compadecer | kõpade'seʀ | *vt.* to pity. **-c.-se de** to take pity on

compadre | kʊ'padrɪ | *sm.* godfather; (colloq.) intimate friend

compaixão | kõpay'xãw | *sf.* compassion, pity

companheiro -ra | kʊpa'ɴeyrʊ | *smf.* companion, mate

companhia | kõpa'ɴia | *sf.* company; firm

comparação | kõpara'sãw | *sf.* comparison

comparar | kõpa'ʀaʀ | *vt.* to compare

comparecer | kõpare'seʀ | *vi.* to appear

comparecimento | kõpaʀesi'mẽtʊ | *sm.* attendance

compartilhar | kõpaʀti'LaʀR | *vt.* to partake

compartimento | kõpaʀti'mẽtʊ | *sm.* compartment, room

compasso | kõ'pasʊ | *sm.* drawing compass; (mus.) beat, time, measure

compatibilidade | kõpatibili'dadɪ | *sf.* compatibility

compatível | kõpa'tivɪl | *a.* compatible

compatriota | kõpatri'ɷta | *smf.* fellow-citizen, compatriot

compelir | kõpɪ'liʀ | *vt.* to compel, to coerce

compenetração | kõpenetra'sãw | *sf.* deep conviction; gravity

compenetrar | kõpene'traʀ | *vt.* to convince. **-c.-se** to be conscious of (one's duties etc.)

compensação | kõpẽsa'sãw | *sf.* compensation; balance. **-em c.** on the other hand

compensar | kõpẽ'saʀ | *vt.* to compensate; to counterbalance

competência | kõpe'tẽsia | *sf.* competence; capacity

competente | kõpe'tẽtɪ | *a.* competent, capable; suitable

competição | kõpɪti'sãw | *sf.* competition, contest

competir | kõpɪ'tiʀ | *vi.* to compete. **-c. com** to compete with

compilar | kõpi'laʀ | *vt.* to compile

complacência | kõpla'sẽsia | *sf.* indulgence

compleição | kõpley'sãw | *sf.* constitution, physical make-up (of a person)

complemento | kõple'mẽtʊ | *sm.* complement

completar | kõple'taʀ | *vt.* to complete, to finish

completo -ta | kõ'plɛtʊ | *a.* complete; whole

complexidade | kõpleksi'dadɪ |*sf.* complexity

complexo -xa | kõ'plɛksʊ | *sm.* complex / *a.* complex, intricate

complicação | kõplika'sãw | *sf.* complication

complicar | kõpli'kar | *vt.* to complicate

componente | kõpo'nētɪ | *sm. a.* component

compor | kõ'poʀ |*vt.* to compose; to constitute; to calm / *vr.* to be composed of; to compose oneself

comporta | kõ'pʊʀta | *sf.* sluice--gate, floodgate

comportamento | kõpoʀta'mẽtʊ | *sm.* behaviour, conduct

comportar | kõpoʀ'taʀ | *vt.* to hold, to contain. **-c.-se** to behave

composição | kõpozi'sãw | *sf.* composition

compositor -tora| kõpozi'toʀ |*smf.* composer; (typog.) type-setter

composto -ta | kõ'poʃtʊ-'pɔʃta | *sm.* compound / *a.* composed; compound

compostura | kõpʊʒ'tura | *sf.* composure; composition

compota | kõ'pʊta | *sf.* compote, preserved fruit

compra | 'kõpra | *sf.* purchase. **-fazer compras** to go shopping

comprador -dora | kõpra'doʀ | *smf.* buyer, purchaser

comprar | kõ'praʀ | *vt.* to buy, to purchase

compreender |kõprɪ̃e'deʀ |*vt.* to understand; to include; to comprise

compreensão| kõprɪ̃e'sãw |*sf.* understanding, comprehension

compreensivo-va | kõprɪ̃e'sivʊ | *a.* understanding, comprehensive

compressa | kõ'prɛsa | *sf.* compress

comprido-da | kʊ̃'pridʊ |*a.* long; lengthy. **-ao c.** lengthwise

comprimento | kũpri'mẽtʊ | *sm.* length

comprimido -da | kõpri'midʊ | *sm.* tablet, medicine tablet / *a.* compressed

comprimir | kõpri'miʀ | *vt.* to compress; to press

comprometer | kõprome'teʀ | *vt.* to compromise, to jeopardize; to implicate. **-c.-se** to pledge one's words

compromisso | kõpro'misʊ | *sm.* appointment; pledge; compromise

comprovar | kõpro'vaʀ | vt. to confirm; to corroborate

compulsão | kõpul'sãw | *sf.* compelling; compulsion

compulsória | kõpul'sɔria | *sf.* compulsory retirement

compulsório -ria| kõpul'sɔriʊ |*a.* compulsory

computação | kõputa'sãw | *sf.* computation, calculation; estimate

computador -dora| kõputa'doʀ | *sm.* computer / *a.* computing

computar | kõpu'taʀ | *vt.* to compute, to calculate

comum | ko'mũ | *a.* common, public; usual; coarse; trivial; ordinary. **-em c.** together

comungar | kʊmũ'gaʀ | *vi.* to partake of the Holy Communion; to share (beliefs, opinions etc.)

comunhão | komu'nãw | *sf.* communion; Holy Communion. **-c. de bens** common property (in marriage)

comunicação|kʊmunika'sãw|*sf.* communication; message; connecting passage

comunicado-da | kʊmuni'kadʊ | *sm.* official communiqué / *a.* communicated

comunicar| kʊmuni'kaʀ | *vt. vi.* to communicate; to transmit

comunicativo-va |kʊmunika'tivʊ| *a.* communicative, expansive

comunidade | kʊmuni'dadɪ | *sf.* community

comunismo | kʊmu'niʒmʊ | *sm.* communism

comunista | kʊmu'niʒta | smf. a. communist

comutador | kʊmuta'doʀ | sm. (elect.) switch

comutar | kʊmu'taʀ | vt. to commute; (law) to reduce (a sentence)

côncavo-va | 'kõkavʊ | a. concave, hollow

conceber | kõse'beʀ | vt. to conceive, to imagine; to become pregnant

conceder | kõse'deʀ | vt. to concede, to grant

conceito | kõ'seytʊ | sm. notion, concept; reputation

conceituado -da | kõseytu'adʊ | a. respected, ⋅idered, deemed

concelho | kõ'seʟʊ | sm. council

concentração | kõsẽtra'sãw | sf. concentration; centralization

concentrar | kõsẽ'traʀ | vt. to concentrate; to centralize

concepção | kõsep'sãw | sf. conception; idea, imagination

concertar | kõseʀ'taʀ | vt. to concert; to plan; to settle / vi. to agree; to harmonize

concerto | kõ'seʀtʊ | sm. concert; consonance, harmony

concessão | kõse'sãw | sf. concession; permission, grant

concha | 'kõxa | sf. shell; conch; ladle

concidadão -dã | kõsida'dãw-'dã | smf. fellow-citizen

conciliação | kõsilia'sãw | sf. conciliation; reconciliation

conciliar | kõsili'aʀ | vt. to conciliate; to reconcile

concílio | kõ'siliʊ | sm. (eccles.) council

concisão | kõsi'zãw | sf. conciseness, brevity

conciso-sa | kõ'sizʊ | a. concise, brief

concludente | kõklu'dẽtɩ | a. conclusive

concluir | kõklu'iʀ | vt. to conclude, to finish; to deduce

conclusão | kõklu'zãw | sf. conclusion, end; deduction

conclusivo-va | kõklu'zivʊ | a. conclusive, decisive, final

concomitante | kõkomi'tãtɩ | a. concomitant, concurrent

concordância | kõkoʀ'dãsia | sf. concordance, harmony

concordar | kõkoʀ'daʀ | vi. to agree

concordata | kõkoʀ'data | sf. (law, com.) composition (of creditors)

concórdia | kõ'kωʀdia | sf. concord; harmony

concorrência | kõkʊ'ʀẽsia | sf. competition, rivalry; concourse

concorrente | kõkʊ'ʀẽtɩ | smf. competitor

concorrer | kõkʊ'ʀeʀ | vi. to concur; to contribute; to compete; to run for

concretizar | kõkreti'zaʀ | vt. to render concrete

concreto -ta | kõ'krɛtʊ | sm. concrete / a. concrete, real, solid

concurso | kõ'kuʀsʊ | sm. contest, competition; concourse; civil service exam

condão | kõ'dãw | sm. magic power. -varinha de c. magic wand

conde | 'kõdɩ | sm. earl, count

condecoração | kõdekora'sãw | sf. decoration, medal

condecorar | kõdeko'raʀ | vt. to decorate, to award a decoration to

condenação | kõdena'sãw | sf. condemnation, conviction; censure

condenar | kõde'naʀ | vt. to condemn, to sentence; to censure

condensar | kõdẽ'saʀ | vt. to condense; to compress; to abridge

condescendência | kõdesẽ'dẽsia | sf. indulgence, tolerance

condescender | kõdesẽ'deʀ | vi. to comply, to acquiesce

condessa | kõ'desa | sf. countess

condição | kŏdiˈsãw | *sf.* condition circumstances; social rank, class; stipulation. -em condições able

condicional | kŏdisioˈnal | *smf.* condition; *sm.* conditional mood / *a.* conditional

condimentar | kŏdimẽˈtaR | *vt.* to season, to spice, to flavo(u)r

condizer | kŏdiˈzeR | *vi.* to match, to correspond

condoer-se | kŏdvˈeRsɩ | *vr.* to pity, to commiserate

condolências | kŏdoˈlẽsiaʃ | *sfpl.* condolences, expressions of sympathy

condomínio | kŏdoˈminiv | *sm.* joint ownership

condômino | kŏˈdominv | *sm.* joint owner

condução | kŏduˈsãw | *sf.* conduction, transmission; transportation

conduta | kŏˈduta | *sf.* behaviour, conduct, manners

conduto | kŏˈdutv | *sm.* duct, conduit

condutor -tora | kŏduˈtoR | *sm.* conductor; guide driver

conduzir | kŏduˈziR | *vt.* to conduct; to guide; to transport. -c.-se to behave

cone | ˈkonɩ | *sm.* cone

cônego | ˈkonegv | *sm.* canon

conexão | koneˈksãw | *sf.* connection, connexion; relationship

confecção | kŏfekˈsãw | *sf.* preparing, making; ready-made article of clothing

confeccionar | kŏfeksioˈnaR | *vt.* to make, to prepare

confederação | kŏfederaˈsãw | *sf.* confederation

confeitaria | kŏfeytaˈria | *sf.* candy-store, pastry shop

conferência | kŏfeˈrẽsia | *sf.* conference; lecture; verification

conferenciar | kŏferẽsiˈaR | *vi.* to confer, to hold a conference; to give a public lecture

conferencista | kŏferẽˈsiʧta | *smf.* lecturer

conferir | kŏfɩˈriR | *vt.* to confer; to grant; to compare; to verify

confessar | kŏfeˈsaR | *vt.* to confess; to admit

confessor -sora | kŏfeˈsoR | *smf.* confessor; *sm.* father confessor

confiado-da | kŏfiˈadv | *a.* trusting; (colloq.) pushy

confiança | kŏfiˈãsa | *sf.* trust, confidence; assurance; (colloq.) familiarity.-tomar c. to get disrespectful

confiar | kŏfiˈaR | *vt.* to confide to trust / *vi.* to trust; to believe

confidência | kŏfiˈdẽsia | *sf.* confidence, trust; secret. -em c. secretly

confidencial | kŏfidẽsiˈal | *a.* confidential

confidente | kŏfiˈdẽtɩ | *smf.* confidant, confident

confinar | kŏfiˈnaR | *vt.* to confine; to imprison. -c. com to have a common boundary with

confins | kŏˈfĩʃ | *smpl.* boundaries

confirmação | kŏfiRmaˈsãw | *sf.* confirmation

confirmar | kŏfiRˈmaR | *vt.* to confirm; to ratify

confiscar | kŏfiʃˈkaR | *vt.* to confiscate

confisco | kŏˈfiʃkv | *vt.* confiscation

confissão | kŏfiˈsãw | *sf.* confession; avowal

conflagração | kŏflagraˈsãw | *sf.* conflagration

conflito | kŏˈflitv | *sm.* conflict, struggle

confluência | kŏfluˈẽsia | *sf.* confluence

conformação | kŏfoRmaˈsãw | *sf.* conformation, configuration; resignation

conformar | kŏfoRˈmaR | *vt.* to conform, to fit. -c.-se to conform; to resign oneself

conforme | kŏˈfɔRmɩ | *a.* conformable; acquiescent; analogous / *adv.* conformably, accordingly / *conj.* as, according to; it depends

conformidade | kõfoRmi'dadι | *sf.* conformity; conformability (also geol.). **-de c. com** in accordance with

confortar | kõfoR'taR | *vt.* to comfort, to console

confortável | kõfoR'tavιl | *a.* comfortable

conforto | kõ'foRtυ | *sm.* comfort

confrontação | kõfrõta'sãw | *sf.* confrontation; comparison

confrontar | kõfrõ'taR | *vt.* to confront; to compare. **-c. se com** to face

confronto | kõ'frõtυ | *sm.* confrontation

confundir | kõfũ'diR | *vt.* to confuse; to mistake; to embarrass. **-c. -se** to become confused or embarrassed

confusão | kõfu'zãw | *sf.* confusion; embarrassment

confuso -sa | kõ'fuzυ | *a.* confused; entangled; embarrassed; obscure

congelar | kõje'laR | *vt.* to freeze

congênito -ta | kõ'jenitυ | *a.* congenital

congestão | kõjeʒ'tãw | *sf.* congestion; abnormal accumulation (traffic, population etc.)

congestionamento | kõjeʒtiona'mētυ | *sm.* congestion. **-c. de trânsito** traffic jam

congratulações | kõgratula'sõyʒ | *sfpl.* congratulations

congratular | kõgratu'laR | *vt.* to congratulate. **-c.-se com** to rejoice with

congregação | kõgrega'sãw | *sf.* congregation (also eccles.), assembly

congressista | kõgre'siʒta | *smf.* member of the Congress

congresso | kõ'grεsυ | *sm.* congress, assembly

conhaque | ko'Nakι | *sm.* cognac, brandy

conhecedor -dora | koNese'doR |

sm. connoisseur, expert / *a.* experienced

conhecer | kυNe'seR | *vt.* to know; to meet; to be familiar with

conhecido -da | koNe'sidυ | *smf.* acquaintance / *a.* known

conhecimento | koNesi'mētυ | *sm.* knowledge; acquaintanceship; (*pl.*) learning, knowledge. **-tomar c. de** to take cognizance of

conivência | koni'vēsia | *sf.* connivance

conjetura | kõje'tura | *sf.* conjecture; surmise

conjugação | kõjuga'sãw | *sf.* conjugation

conjugar | kõju'gaR | *vt.* to conjugate

cônjuge | 'kõjujι | *smf.* consort, spouse

conjunção | kõjũ'sãw | *sf.* conjunction

conjunto -ta | kõ'jũtυ | *sm.* whole; assemblage, collection, body. **-em c. as a whole. -no c. in all** / *a.* conjoined

conjuntura | kõjũ'tura | *sf.* circumstances; situation

conjuração | kõjura'sãw | *sf.* conspiracy

conluio | kõ'luyυ | *sm.* collusion, conspiracy, plot

conosco | ko'noʃkυ kõ'noʃkυ | *pron.* with us

conquanto | kõ'kwãtυ | *conj.* although, though

conquista | kõ'kiʒta | *sf.* conquest

conquistar | kõkiʒ'taR | *vt.* to conquer; to captivate

consagração | kõsagra'sãw | *sf.* consecration

consagrar | kõsa'graR | *vt.* to consecrate, to dedicate / *vr.* to devote oneself; to be sanctioned (by usage etc.)

consangüíneo -nea | kõsã'gwinιυ | *a.* related by blood

consciência | kõsi'ēsia | *sf.* conscience; consciousness, awareness. **-em sã c. in all conscience**

consciencioso -sa | kõsiẽsi'ozυ -'ωza | *a.* conscientious

consciente | kõsi'ẽtι | *a.* conscious; aware

conscrição | kõʒkri'sãw | *sf.* conscription

consecução | kõseku'sãw | *sf.* attainment; consecution

consecutivo -va | kõseku'tivυ | *a.* consecutive, successive

conseguinte | kõsι'gĩtι | *a.* consecutive; consequent. **-por c.** consequently

conseguir | kõsι'giR | *vt.* to obtain, to get; to achieve; to succeed in

conselheiro -ra | kõse'Leyrυ | *smf.* adviser, counselor

conselho | kõ'seLυ | *sm.* advice, exhortation; council, board, assembly. **-c. de guerra** court-martial

consentimento | kõsẽti'mẽtυ | *sm.* consent

conseqüência | kõse'kwẽsia | *sf.* consequence. **-arcar com as conseqüências** to take the consequences

consertar | kõseR'taR | *vt.* to repair, to mend

conserto | kõ'seRtυ | *sm.* repair, mend

conserva | kõ'seRva | *sf.* conserve; canned food

conservação | kõseRva'sãw | *sf.* conservation; maintenance

conservador -dora | kõseRva'doR | *smf.* curator, keeper; (polit.) conservative / *a.* conservative

conservar | kõseR'vaR | *vt.* to conserve, to preserve, to keep up, to maintain. **-c.-se** to remain

consideração | kõsidera'sãw | *sf.* consideration, concern; (*pl.*) reasons

considerado -da | kõside'radυ | *a.* considered; considerate; respected

considerar | kõside'raR | *vt.* to consider. **-c.-se** to regard oneself as / *vi.* to consider, to reflect

considerável | kõside'ravιl | *a.* considerable

consignar | kõsig'naR | *vt.* to consign; to register

consigo | kũ'sigυ | *pron.* with (to) himself (herself, itself, themselves)

consistência | kõsiʒ'tẽsia | *sf.* consistency; stability

consistente | kõsiʒ'tẽtι | *a.* consisting (of); dense, firm

consoante | kõsυ'ãtι | *sf.a.* consonant / *prep.* according to

consolação | kõsola'sãw | *sf.* consolation

consolar | kõso'laR | *vt.* to console, to comfort

consolidação | kõsolida'sãw | *sf.* consolidation

consolidar | kõsoli'daR | *vt.* to consolidate; to codify (laws) / *vi.* to consolidate

consolo | kõ'solυ | *sm.* consolation, solace

consonância | kõso'nãsia | *sf.* consonance; harmony

consórcio | kõ'sωRsiυ | *sm.* partnership; marriage; (com.) association of buyers

consorte | kõ'sωRtι | *smf.* consort, partner; spouse

conspícuo -cua | kõʒ'pikwυ | *a.* conspicuous; illustrious

conspiração | kõʒpira'sãw | *sm.* conspiracy, plot

conspirador- dora | kõʒpira'doR | *smf.* conspirator, plotter / *a.* conspiring

conspirar | kõʒpi'raR | *vt.* to plot / *vi.* to conspire, to act in collusion

constância | kõʒ'tãsia | *sf.* constancy; persistence, perseverance

constante | kõʒ'tãtι | *a.* constant, unchangeable. **-c. de** consisting of

constar | kõʒ'taR | *vi.* to be recorded, to appear in a record

constatar | kõʒta'taR | *vt.* to verify

constelação | kõʒtela'sãw | *sf.* constellation

consternação | kõˈʒteʀnaˈsãw | sf. consternation

constipação | kõˈʒtipaˈsãw | sf. constipation; (colloq.) common cold

constitucional | kõˈʒtitusioˈnal | a. constitutional

constituição | kõˈʒtituiˈsãw | sf. constitution

constituir | kõˈʒtituˈiʀ | vt. to constitute; to elect to office

constranger | kõˈʒtrãˈjeʀ | vt. to compel; to make (someone) ill at ease

constrangimento | kõˈʒtrãjiˈmẽtʋ | sm. constraint, restraint

construção | kõˈʒtruˈsãw | sf. construction

construir | kõˈʒtruˈiʀ | vt. to construct, to build; to construe

construtor -tora | kõˈʒtruˈtoʀ | smf. constructor / a. constructing, constructive

cônsul | ˈkõsul | sm. consul

consulado | kõsuˈladʋ | sm. consulate

consulta | kõˈsulta | sf. consultation. -obra de c. reference book

consultar | kõsulˈtaʀ | vt. to consult. -c.-se com to consult, to take advice

consultor -tora | kõsulˈtoʀ | smf. consultant, adviser

consultório | kõsulˈtɔriʋ | sm. doctor's office, consultation room

consumação | kõsumaˈsãw | sf. consummation; food and drinks consumed in a restaurant

consumado -da | ˈkõsuˈmadʋ | a. consummate, perfect

consumar | kõsuˈmaʀ | vt. to consummate

consumidor -dora | kõsumiˈdoʀ | smf. consumer

consumir | kõsuˈmiʀ | vt. to consume; to waste to use up / vr. to chafe; to languish

consumo | kõˈsumʋ | sm. consumption, use. -artigos de c.

consumer goods

conta | ˈkõta | sf. calculation; account; bill, check. -fazer de c. que to pretend that. -tomar c. de to take charge of. -não é da sua c. it is none of your business. -afinal de contas after all. -no fim das contas in the long run

contabilidade | kõtabiliˈdadɪ | sf. accounting, bookkeeping

contador -dora | kõtaˈdoʀ | smf. accountant; sm. instrument for measuring

contagem | kõˈtajẽy | sf. count; score

contagiar | kõtajiˈaʀ | vt. to infect, to contaminate

contágio | kõˈtajiʋ | sm. contagion, infection

contagioso -sa | kõtajiˈozʋ -ˈɔza | a. contagious

conta-gotas | ˈkõtaˈgotaʒ | sm. medicine dropper

contaminar | kõtamiˈnaʀ | vt. to contaminate, to infect

contanto que | kõˈtãtʋˈkɪ | conj. provided that

contar | kõˈtaʀ | vt. to count; to tell, to narrate; to number / vi. to count (calculate); to intend. -c. com to count on

contato, contacto | kõˈtatʋ kõˈtaktʋ | sm. contact. -em c. com in touch with

contemplação | kõtẽplaˈsãw | sf. contemplation

contemplar | kõtẽˈplaʀ | vt. to contemplate; to gaze upon

contemporâneo -nea | kõtẽpoˈranɪʋ | smf.a. contemporary

contemporizar | kõtẽporiˈzaʀ | vi. to temporize

contenção | kõtẽˈsãw | sf. contention; restraint

contenda | kõˈtẽda | sf. dispute

contentar | kõtẽˈtaʀ | vt. to content. -c.-se to be contented

contente | kõˈtẽtɪ | a. pleased, satisfied; contented

contento | kõ'tẽtʊ | *sm.* used in the expression **a c.** satisfactorily

conter | kõ'teʀ | *vt.* to contain, to hold; to restrain, to hold back. **-c.-se** to restrain oneself

conterrâneo -nea | kõte'ʀanɪʊ | *smf.* fellow-countryman

contestar | kõteʒ'taʀ | *vt.* to contest; to contradict

conteúdo | kõte'udʊ | *sm.* content(s)

contexto | kõ'teʒtʊ | *sm.* context

contido -da | kõ'tidʊ | *a.* contained; restrained

contigo | kʊ'tigʊ | *pron.* with you

contíguo -gua | kõ'tigwʊ | *a.* contiguous, adjacent

continência | kõti'nẽsia | *sf.* continence; (mil.) salute

continente | kõti'nẽtɪ | *sm.* continent

contingência | kõtĩ'jẽsia | *sf.* contingency; circumstance

contingente | kõtĩ'jẽtɪ | *sm. a.* contingent

continuação | kõtinua'sãw | *sf.* continuation

continuar | kõtinu'aʀ | *vt. vi.* to continue, to persist, to go on / *vi.* to continue, to endure, to last

continuidade | kõtinui'dadɪ | *sf.* continuity

contínuo -nua | kõ'tinuʊ | *sm.* office-boy / *a.* continuous, continual

contista | kõ'tiʒta | *smf.* short story writer

conto | 'kõtʊ | *sm.* short story, tale. **-c. da carochinha** fairy-tale

conto-do-vigário | kõtʊdʊvi'garɪʊ | *sm.* (colloq.) swindle

contorção | kõtoʀ'sãw | *sf.* contortion

contornar | kõtoʀ'naʀ | *vt.* to contour; to by-pass

contorno | kõ'toʀnʊ | *sm.* contour; circuit

contra | 'kõtra | *sm.* rebuke / *adv.* contrary / *prep.* against; facing; versus

contra-almirante | kõtr(a)almi'ʀatɪ | *sm.* rear-admiral

contrabalançar | kõtrabalã'saʀ | *vt.* to counterbalance

contrabando | kõtra'bãdʊ | *sm.* smuggling, contraband

contração | kõtra'sãw | *sm.* contraction

contradição | kõtradi'sãw | *sf.* contradiction

contraditório-ria | kõtradi'tɔrɪʊ | *a.* contradictory

contradizer | kõtradi'zeʀ | *vt.* to contradict; to refute

contrafação | kõtrafa'sãw | *sf.* counterfeiting; forgery

contrafazer | kõtrafa'zeʀ | *vt.* to counterfeit; to forge

contrafeito -ta | kõtra'feytʊ | *a.* constrained; uneasy; annoyed

contrair | kõtra'iʀ | *vt.* to contract; to acquire (habit); to incur (debt). **-c.-se** to shrink

contramestre | kõtra'mɛʒtrɪ | *sm.* (naut.) quartermaster; foreman

contrapeso | kõtra'pezʊ | *sm.* counterweight

contrapor | kõtra'poʀ | *vt.* to contrapose, to set over against

contraproducente | kõtraprodu'sẽtɪ | *a.* producing the opposite result

contrariar | kõtrari'aʀ | *vt.* to oppose, to contradict; to refute; to annoy

contrariedade | kõtrarie'dadɪ | *sf.* setback, disappointment

contrário -ria | kõ'trariʊ | *smf.* opponent, adversary; *sm.* contrary / *a.* contrary; unfavourable. **-ao c.** or **pelo c.** on the contrary. **-do c.** otherwise, if not

contraste | kõ'traʒtɪ | *sm.* contrast

contratante | kõtra'tãtɪ | *smf.* contractant / *a.* contracting

contratar | kõtra'taʀ | *vt.* to contract / *vi.* to contract, to make a contract

contrato | kõ'tratʊ | *sm.* contract,

pact, agreement

contravenção | kõtravē'sãw | *sf.* contravention, infraction

contribuição | kõtribui'sãw | *sf.* contribution; tax

contribuinte | kõtribu'ĩtι | *smf.* contributor; taxpayer

contribuir | kõtribu'iʀ | *vt. vi.* to contribute

contrição | kõtri'sãw | *sf.* contrition, repentance

contristar | kõtriʒ'taʀ | *vt.* to grieve, to sadden

contrito -ta | kõ'tritυ | *a.* contrite

controlar | kõtro'laʀ | *vt.* to control. -c.-se to control oneself

controle | kõ'trolι | *sm.* control; domination

controvérsia | kõtro'vɛʀsia | *sf.* controversy, dispute

contudo | kõ'tudυ | *conj.* nevertheless, however

contumaz | kõtu'maʒ | *a.* contumacious, insubordinate

contundir | kõtũ'diʀ | *vt.* to bruise, to batter

contusão | kõtu'zãw | *sf.* contusion, bruise

convalescença | kõvale'sẽsa | *sf.* convalescence

convalescer | kõvale'seʀ | *vi.* to convalesce

convenção | kõvẽ'sãw | *sf.* convention; pact, agreement

convencer | kõvẽ'seʀ | *vt* to convince / *vr.* to be convinced

convencido -da | kõvĩ'sidυ | *a.* convinced; (colloq.) conceited

convencional | kõvẽsio'nal | *smf.* delegate to a political convention / *a.* conventional

conveniência | kõveni'ẽsia | *sf.* convenience; (*pl.*) social conventions

conveniente | kõveni'ẽtι | *a.* convenient; advisable; appropriate

convênio | kõ'veniυ | *sm.* convention; agreement

convento | kõ'vẽtυ | *sm.* convent, monastery

convergir | kõveʀ'jiʀ | *vi.* to

converge

conversa | kũ'vɛʀsa | *sf.* conversation; chat; cock-and-bull story

conversação | kũveʀsa'sãw | *sf.* conversation

conversão | kõveʀ'sãw | *sf.* conversion (all senses)

conversar | kõveʀ'saʀ | *vi.* to converse, to chatter

conversível | kõveʀ'sivιl | *sm.* convertible (car) / *a.* convertible

converter | kõveʀ'teʀ | *vt.* to convert / *vr.* to be converted

convertido -da | kõveʀ'tidυ | *smf.* convert

convés | kõ'vɛʒ | *sm.* deck

convicção | kõvik'sãw | *sf.* conviction, certainty

convidado -da | kũvi'dadυ | *smf.* invited guest, guest / *a.* invited

convidar | kũvi'daʀ | *vt.* to invite

convidativo -va | kũvida'tivυ | *a.* inviting

convincente | kõvĩ'sẽtι | *a.* convincing

convir | kõ'viʀ | *vi.* to suit (be suitable, be proper); to agree (on)

convite | kõ'vitι | *sm.* invitation

convivência | kõvi'vẽsia | *sf.* living together; familiarity; close association

conviver | kõvi'veʀ | *vi.* to live together; to have a daily relationship with

convocação | kõvoka'sãw | *sf.* convocation; military conscription

convocar | kõvo'kaʀ | *vt.* to convoke, to call

convosco | kõ'voʒkυ | *pron.* with you

convulsão | kõvul'sãw | *sf.* convulsion; tumult, commotion

convulsionar | kõvulsio'naʀ | *vt.* to convulse

cooperação | koopera'sãw | *sf.* co--operation

cooperar | koope'raʀ | *vi.* to co--operate

cooperativa | koopera'tiva | *sf.* co-

-operative (society, association etc.)

cooperativo -va | koopera'tivʋ | a. co-operative

coordenação | koorⅾena'sãw | sf. co-ordination

coordenadas | koorⅾe'nadaʒ | sfpl. co-ordinates

coordenar | koorⅾe'naʀ | vt. to co-ordinate

copa |'kʋpa| sf. pantry; crown (of hat or tree); (pl., card suit) hearts

copeiro -ra | ko'peyrʋ | sm. pantryman, waiter; sf. serving maid

cópia |'kʋpia| sf. copy; reproduction; imitation; abundance

copiar | kopi'aʀ | vt. to copy; to imitate

copioso -sa | kopi'ozʋ -'ʋza | a. copious, abundant

copo |'kʋpʋ| sm. glass

coque |'kʋkι| sm. coke; a rap on the head

coqueiro | ko'keyrʋ | sm. coconut palm-tree

coqueluche | kokι'luxι | sf. whooping cough

coquetel | kokι'tɛl | sm. cocktail

cor |'kʋʀ | sm. used in the expression **de c.** by heart

cor | 'kor |sf. colo(u)r; complexion. **-de c.** colo(u)red, non--white (person)

coração | kora'sãw | sm. heart

coragem | ko'rajẽy | sf. courage

corajoso -sa |kora'jozʋ-'jʋza |a. courageous, brave

corar | ko'raʀ | vt. to colo(u)r; to bleach (washed clothes) by sunning / vi. to blush

corça |'kʋʀsa|sf. doe, female roe--deer

corcova | koʀ'kʋva | sf. hump; buck (of a horse)

corcovado -da | koʀko'vadʋ | a. hunchbacked

corcunda | kʋʀ'kũda | smf. hunchback; sf. hump (deformity) / a. hunchbacked

corda | 'kʋʀⅾa | sf. rope; string (also mus.); chord; cord. **-dar c. (a um relógio)** to wind (watch)

cordão | koʀ'dãw |sm. cord, twine. **-c. de sapato** shoe-lace

cordeiro | koʀ'deyrʋ | sm. lamb

cor-de-rosa | koʀⅾe'ʀʋza koʀ-dι'ʀʋza | a. (sing. and pl.) pink (colo[u]r)

cordial | koʀdi'al | sm. cordial (drink) / a. cordial, warm

cordialidade | koʀdiali'dadι | sf. cordiality

cordilheira | koʀdi'ᴌeyra | sf. mountain ridge, cordillera

coreto | ko'retʋ | sm. bandstand

corisco | kʋ'riʒkʋ | sm. flash (as of lightning)

corista | ko'riʒta | sf. showgirl

corja | 'kʋʀja | sf. rabble, mob

corneta | koʀ'neta | sf. bugle, trumpet, horn

coro | 'korʋ |sm. chorus; choir

coroa | ko'roa | sf. crown (also dent., numis.)

coroação | koroa'sãw | sf. coronation

coroar | korʋ'aʀ | vt. to crown; (fig.) to acclaim

coronel | koro'nɛl |sm. colonel

coronha | ko'roɴa | sf. gun-stock, butt (of shot-gun, rifle etc.)

corpo |'koʀpʋ|sm. body; corpse; consistency; corps. **-c. a c.** arm to arm (fighting)

corporação | koʀpora'sãw | sf. corporation; fraternity

corpulento -ta | koʀpu'lẽtʋ | a. stout, corpulent

correção | koʀe'sãw | sf. correction, rectification

corredor -dora | koʀe'doʀ | smf. runner, racer; sm. corridor / a. running

córrego | 'kʋʀιgʋ | sm. streamlet, brook

correia | ko'ʀeya | sf. belt; leather strap; leash

correio | ko'ʀeyʋ | sm. courier; post office; mail. **-c. aéreo** air mail. **-caixa de c.** mailbox

corrente | ko'Rɛtɪ | *sf.* chain; current (water, air, electricity etc.); flow / *a.* current; fluent; usual

correnteza | koRẽ'teza | *sf.* current, flow (of water)

correr | ko'RER | *vt.* to run; to be exposed to risk; to run (the hand, the eyes) over; to chase away; to draw (the curtain) / *vi.* to run (also fig.); to go; to flow

correspondência | koRɛʃpõ'dẽsia | *sf.* correspondence; mail; letters

correspondente | koRɛʃpõ'dẽtɪ | *smf.* correspondent / *a.* corresponding

corresponder | koRɛʃpõ'deR | *vi.* to correspond; to retribute, to reciprocate. **-c.-se com** to correspond with

correto -ta | ko'Rɛtʊ | *a.* correct, exact, right, proper

corretor -tora | koRe'toR | *smf.* broker; commission agent. **-c. de imóveis** real estate broker

corrida | ku'Rida | *sf.* race. **-de c.** race (horse, car etc.); in a hurry

corrigir | kuRi'jiR | *vt.* to correct; to reform; to discipline

corrimão | kuRi'mãw | *sm.* banister, handrail

corriqueiro-ra | kuRi'keyrʊ | *a.* common, trivial

corroborar | koRobo'raR | *vt.* to corroborate, to confirm

corroer | koRo'eR | *vt.* to corrode; to eat away

corromper | koRõ'peR | *vt.* to corrupt; to deprave, to pervert

corrupção | koRup'sãw | *sf.* corruption

corrupto -ta | ko'Ruptʊ | *a.* corrupt; depraved

corsário | koR'sariʊ | *sm.* pirate

cortante | koR'tãtɪ | *a.* cutting; sharp (also sound); piercing (wind)

cortar | koR'taR | *vt.* to cut (up, off, out, open etc.); to shutt off (electricity, water etc.)

corte | 'kɔRtɪ | *sm.* cut (also tailoring); incision; sharpness (of a blade)

corte | 'koRtɪ | *sf.* court; (*pl.*) houses of parliament

cortejar | koRte'jaR | *vt.* to court; to flatter

cortês | koR'teʃ | *a.* courteous

cortesia | koRtɪ'zia | *sf.* courtesy, civility

cortiça | kuR'tisa | *sf.* cork

cortiço | kuR'tisʊ | *sm.* beehive; doss-house

cortina | kuR'tina | *sf.* curtain; screen

coruja | ku'ruja | *sf.* owl

corvo | 'koRvʊ | *sm.* crow; raven

cós | 'kɔʃ | *sm.* waistband

coser | ku'zeR | *vt.* to sew, to stitch

cosmético -ca | koʃ'mɛtikʊ | *sm. a.* cosmetic

cosmopolita | koʃmopo'lita | *smf. a.* cosmopolitan

costa | 'koʃta | *sf.* coast, shore; (*pl.*) back

costear | koʃtɪ'aR | *vt.* to follow the coast / *vi.* to sail close to the coast

costela | kuʃ'tela | *sf.* rib

costeleta | kuʃte'leta | *sf.* cutlet, chop (pork, lamb etc.); (*pl.*) sideburns

costume | kuʃ'tumɪ | *sm.* habit, custom, practice; (*pl.*) social customs and habits, behavio(u)r. **-como de c.** as usual

costura | kuʃ'tura | *sf.* sewing; stitching; seam; dressmaking; (med.) suture

costurar | kuʃtu'raR | *vt.* to sew; to suture

costureiro -ra | kuʃtu'reyrʊ | *smf.* dressmaker

cota | 'kɔta | *sf.* share, quota, allotment; coat of mail

cotação | kota'sãw | *sf.* quotation; assessment; valuation; (colloq.) prestige

cotão | ko'tãw | *sm.* fuzz, down, fluff

cotar | ko'taR | *vt.* to quote (prices), to fix the price at

cotejar | kote'jaʀ | *vt.* to compare, to collate

cotidiano -na | kotidi'anʊ | *sm.* quotidian; daily newspaper / *a.* daily

coto |'kotʊ| *sm.* stump

cotó | ko'tʷo | *smf.* bobtail / *a.* bobtailed

cotovelo | kʊtʊ'velʊ | *sm.* elbow; bend of a road or river

cotovia | koto'via | *sf.* lark, sky--lark

couraça | kow'rasa | *sf.* cuirass; armo(u)r

couraçado -da | kowra'sadʊ | *sm.* battleship / *a.* armo(u)red, cuirassed

couro | 'kowrʊ | *sm.* leather, hide. **-c. cabeludo** scalp

couve |'kowvɪ | *sf.* kale, cole

couve-flor | 'kowvɪ'floʀ | *sf.* cauliflower

cova |'kɔva | *sf.* hole; grave; dimple; cave

covarde | ko'vaʀdɪ | *smf.* coward, poltroon / *a.* coward; vile

covardia | kovaʀ'dia | *sf.* cowardice; treacherousness

covil | ko'vil | *sm.* den, lair

covinha | kʊ'viɴa | *sf.* dimple

coxa |'koxa |*sf.* thigh

coxo-xa |'koxʊ | *smf.* cripple, lame person

cozer | kʊ'zeʀ | *vt.* = cozinhar

cozido -da | kʊ'zidʊ | *sm.* a dish of boiled vegetables, beef etc. / *a.* cooked, boiled

cozinha | kʊ'ziɴa | *sf.* kitchen; cookery; cuisine

cozinhar | kʊzi'ɴaʀ |*vt.* to cook, to boil

cozinheiro -ra | kʊzi'ɴeyrʊ | *smf.* cook, chef

crânio | 'kranɪʊ | *sm.* skull

crápula | 'krapula | *sm.* scoundrel

craque |'krakɪ | *sm.* person of great ability (esp. in sports); a crack racing horse; financial crash

crase |'krazɪ | *sf.* (gram.) crasis

crasso -sa |'krasʊ | *a.* crass, coarse; dense. **-erro c.** a blunder

cratera | kra'tɛra | *sf.* crater

cravar | kra'vaʀ | *vt.* to thrust in (nail, dagger, stake etc.); to set gems; to fix

cravo |'kravʊ |*sm.* horseshoe nail; (bot.) carnation; (bot.) clove; blackhead; harpsichord

creche | 'krɛxɪ | *sf.* day nursery, crèche

credenciais | kredẽsi'ayʃ | *sfpl.* credentials

crediário | kredi'arɪʊ | *sm.* installment plan

crédito | 'krɛditʊ | *sm.* credit (also fin.); faith, trust. **-dar c.** to believe

credor -dora | kre'doʀ | *smf.* creditor

crédulo -la |'krɛdulʊ |*smf.* dupe / *a.* credulous, gullible

cremalheira | krema'ʎeyra | *sf.* cog rail; cog-wheel

cremar | kre'maʀ | *vt.* to cremate

creme |'krɛmɪ | *sm.* cream; custard / *a.* cream-colo(u)red

crença |'krẽsa | *sf.* belief

crendice | krẽ'disɪ | *sf.* foolish belief, superstition

crente | 'krẽtɪ | *smf.* believer; (col-loq.) dupe / *a.* believing

crepúsculo | kre'puʃkulʊ | *sm.* twilight, dusk

crer | 'kreʀ | *vt.* to believe; to suppose / *vi.* to have faith

crescente | kre'sẽtɪ | *sm.* crescent / *a.* increasing, growing. **-quarto c.** quarter moon

crescer | kre'seʀ | *vi.* to grow (up), to increase; to progress

crescido -da | krɪ'sidʊ | *a.* grown up

crescimento | krɪsi'mẽtʊ | *sm.* growth, growing, increase

crespo -pa | 'kreʃpʊ | *a.* wavy, curly; rough (sea)

crestar | kreʃ'taʀ | *vt.* to singe; to parch

cretino -na | kre'tinʊ |*smf.* cretin; stupid person

cretone | kre'tonɪ | *sm.* cretonne

cria |'kria |*sf.* young (of animals);

(colloq.) foster child

criação | kria'sãw | *sf.* creation; invention; bringing-up; breeding

criado -da | kri'adʊ | *sm.* servant; *sf.* servant girl, maid / *a.* created, born, produced

criador -dora | kria'doʀ | *smf.* breeder (of cattle); *sm.* The Creator / *a.* creative

criança | kri'ãsa | *sf.* child, baby

criar | kri'aʀ | *vt.* to create; to rear, to raise, to bring up; to breed (cattle)

criatura | kria'tura | *sf.* creature, being, person

crime | 'krimɛ | *sm.* crime

criminoso -sa | krimi'nozʊ '-nɯza | *smf. a.* criminal

crina | 'krina | *sf.* horse's mane; horsehair (mane, tail)

crioulo -la | kri'owlʊ | *smf.* any Negro; creole / *a.* creole; said of animals without race

crise | 'krizɛ | *sf.* crisis

crisma | 'kriʃma | *sf.* (eccles.) confirmation

crista | 'kriʃta | *sf.* cock's comb; crest, ridge

cristal | kriʃ'tal | *sm.* crystal; (*pl.*) crystalware

cristalino -na | kriʃta'linʊ | *sm.* (anat.) crystalline lens / *a.* crystalline

cristandade | kriʃtã'dadɛ | *sf.* Christendom; Christianity

cristão -tã | kriʃ'tãw-'tã | *smf. a.* Christian

cristianismo | kriʃtia'niʒmʊ | *sm.* Christianism

Cristo | 'kriʃtʊ | *sm.* Christ

critério | kri'tɛriʊ | *sm.* criterion; common sense

crítica | 'kritika | *sf.* criticism; critical article; review

criticar | kriti'kaʀ | *vt.* to criticize; to review (book, play etc.); to judge

crítico -ca | 'kritikʊ | *smf.* critic / *a.* critical, judicious; precarious

crivar | kri'vaʀ | *vt.* to sift; to riddle (as with shot)

crocodilo | kroko'dilʊ | *sm.* crocodile

crônica | 'kronika | *sf.* chronicle; annals; (journal.) literary column

crônico -ca | 'kronikʊ | *a.* (med.) chronic; inveterate

cronista | kro'niʃta | *smf.* chronicler; newspaper columnist

cronológico -ca | krono'lɯjikʊ | *a.* chronological

croqui | kro'ki | *sm.* outline, sketch

crosta | 'krɔʃta | *sf.* crust

cru, crua | 'kru 'krua | *a.* raw; crude

crucificação | krusifika'sãw | *sf.* crucifixion

crucificar | krusifi'kaʀ | *vt.* to crucify

crucifixo -xa | krusi'fiksʊ | *sm. a.* crucifix

cruel | kru'ɛl | *a.* cruel

crueldade | kruel'dadɛ | *sf.* cruelty

cruento -ta | kru'ẽtʊ | *a.* bloody (battle etc.); cruel

cruz | 'kruʃ | *sf.* cross; (fig.) trial / *interj.* Good Heavens!

cruzada | kru'zada | *sf.* crusade

cruzado -da | kru'zadʊ | *sm.* crusader / *a.* crossed, crisscross

cruzamento | kruza'mẽtʊ | *sm.* crossing; crossroads; cross-breeding

cruzar | kru'zaʀ | *vt.* to cross; to lay or to place across; to cruise; to cross-breed

cruzeiro | kru'zeyrʊ | *sm.* large cross; cruise; cruiser; cruzeiro (monetary unit of Brazil)

cubano -na | ku'banʊ | *smf. a.* Cuban

cubículo | ku'bikulʊ | *sm.* cubicle, cell

cubo | 'kubʊ | *sm.* cube

cuco | 'kukʊ | *sm.* cuckoo

cuecas | ku'ɛkaʃ | *sfpl.* shorts (men's underwear)

cueiro | ku'eyrʊ | *sm.* swaddling band; diaper

cuia | 'kuya | *sf.* vessel made from a

gourd; vessel (of any material) resembling a gourd

cuíca | ku'ika | *sf.* Afro-Brazilian percussion instrument

cuidado -da | kuy'dadʋ | *sm.* care; diligence; concern / *a.* thought out / *interj.* look out!

cuidar | kuy'daʀ | *vt.* to care (**de, for**), to take care (**de, of**); to attend (**de, to**)

cujo -ja | 'kujʋ | *rel. poss. pron.* whose, of whom, of which / *poss. a.* which, this, that

culatra | ku'latra | *sf.* gun breech

culote | ku'lɷtɪ | *sm.* riding breeches

culpa | 'kulpa | *sf.* guilt, blame; fault

culpabilidade | kulpabili'dadɪ | *sf.* culpability, guilt

culpado -da | kul'padʋ | *a.* guilty

culpar | kul'paʀ | *vt.* to blame, to incriminate

cultivar | kulti'vaʀ | *vt.* to cultivate; to farm, to grow

culto -ta | 'kultʋ | *sm.* cult, worship / *a.* cultured, refined, cultivated

cultura | kul'tura | *sf.* culture (also biol.), cultivation (also agric.); civilization

cultural | kultu'ral | *a.* cultural

cumbuca | kũ'buka | *sf.* gourd bottle

cume | 'kumɪ | *sm.* peak, top, summit

cumeeira | kumɪ'eyra | *sf.* ridge, roof-tree

cúmplice | 'kũplisɪ | *sm.* accomplice, co-operator in a criminal action

cumprimentar | kũprimẽ'taʀ | *vt.* to greet, to salute; to congratulate

cumprimento | kũpri'mẽtʋ | *sm.* greeting; compliment; congratulation; accomplishment

cumprir | kũ'priʀ | *vt.* to accomplish, to fulfill; to execute. **-c.-se** to happen. **-c. com a palavra** to keep one's word. **-c. pena**

to serve a sentence

cúmulo | 'kumulʋ | *sm.* culmination, height. **-é o c!** that's the limit!

cunha | 'kuna | *sf.* wedge

cunhado -da | ku'nadʋ | *sm.* brother-in-law; *sf.* sister-in-law

cunhar | ku'naʀ | *vt.* to coin, to mint

cupim | ku'pĩ | *sm.* termite, white ant

cupom | ku'põ | *sm.* coupon

cura | 'kura | *sf.* cure, healing; recovery; *sm.* vicar

curador -dora | kura'doʀ | *smf.* guardian, trustee; (law)curator

curandeiro -ra | kurã'deyrʋ | *sm.* medicine-man, charlatan; healer

curar | ku'raʀ | *vt.* to heal, to cure; to preserve (cheese etc.). **-c.-se** to cure oneself / *vi.* to heal

curativo -va | kura'tivʋ | *sm.* dressing; curative / *a.* curative

curinga | ku'rĩga | *sm.* joker (cards)

curiosidade | kuriozi'dadɪ | *sf.* curiosity; curio, oddity, rarity

curioso -sa | kuri'ozʋ'-ωza | *smf.* curious, inquisitive individual; bystander; practician / *a.* curious, inquisitive; strange, odd

curral | ku'ral | *sm.* corral

currículo | ku'Rikulʋ | *sm.* curriculum

cursar | kuʀ'saʀ | *vt.* to attend, to study at (a university etc.); to travel (over)

curso | 'kuʀsʋ | *sm.* course; direction; course of studies; current. **-dar c. a** to give (something) free rein. **-em c.** current, in circulation

curtir | kuʀ'tiʀ | *vt.* to tan; to harden; to suffer, to endure; (slang) to take pleasure in doing something

curto -ta | 'kuʀtʋ | *a.* short, brief / *sm.* = *curto-circuito*

curto-circuito | 'kuʀtʋsiʀ'kuytʋ |

sm. (elect.) short circuit

curtume | kuʀ'tumι | sm. tannery; tanning

curva | 'kuʀva | sf. curve (also math.), bend, turn

curvar | kuʀ'vaʀ | vt. to curve, to bend. **-c.-se** to curve, to bend, to bow

curvatura | kuʀva'tura | sf. curvature, bend

cuspir | kuʃ'piʀ | vt. to spit; to eject / vi. to spit

cuspo, cuspe | 'kuʃpυ 'kuʃpι | sm. spittle, saliva, spit

custa | 'kuʃta | sf. cost, expense; (pl., law) costs. **-à c. de** at the expense of

custar | kuʃ'taʀ | vt. to cost, to be priced at / vi. to cost; to be difficult or painful

custear | kuʃtι'aʀ | vt. to pay, to finance

custo | 'kuʃtυ | sm. price, cost; trouble, pain. **-a muito c.** with great difficulty

custódia | kuʃ'tωdia | sf. custody; protection; (law) detention; (eccles.) monstrance

cutelaria | kutela'ria | sf. cutlery

cutia | ku'tia | sf. (zool.) agouti

cutícula | ku'tikula | sf. cuticle

cutilada | kuti'lada | sf. slash, stroke with a sabre etc.

cútis | 'kutiʃ | sf. cutis; skin (esp. of the face); complexion

cutucar | kutu'kaʀ | vt. to poke, to nudge

D

da | da | contr. de + a of the, from the

dactilografar, datilografar | da(k)-tilogra'faʀ | vt. to type

dactilógrafo -fa, datilógrafo -fa | da(k)ti'lωgrafυ | smf. typist

dádiva | 'dadiva | sf. gift

dadivoso -sa | dadi'vozυ -'vωza | a. generous, open-handed

dado | 'dadυ | sm. datum, basic fact; (pl.) data; (games) die; (pl., games) dice. **-os dados estão lançados** the die is cast

daí | da'i | contr. de + aí from there; from that; for that reason. **-d. em** or **por diante** from then on; thereafter, ever since. **-e d.?** (colloq.) so what?

dama | 'dama | sf. lady; (games) the queen (at cards or chess); female partner (at a ball); (pl., games) checkers. **-d. de companhia** lady-in-waiting

damasco | da'maʃkυ | sm. apricot; (tex.) damask

danação | dana'sãw | sf. damnation; fury, rage

danado -da | da'nadυ | smf. damned; (colloq.) keen, clever / a. damned; rabid, hydrophobic; furious

dança | 'dãsa | sf. dance

dançar | dã'saʀ | vt. vi. to dance / vi. (slang) to get the sack

dançarino -na | dãsa'rinυ | smf. professional dancer

daninho -nha | da'niɴυ | a. damaging, harmful

dano | 'danυ | sm. damage, injury; loss

danoso -sa | da'nozυ -'nωza | a. damaging; detrimental

dantes | 'dãtιʃ | contr. de + antes formerly

daqui | da'ki | contr. de + aqui from here, from now. **-d. em diante** from now on, henceforth

dar | 'daʀ | vt. to give, to bestow, to present; to strike (someone, the hour etc.). **-d. a entender** to let (something) be understood. **-d. certo** to come out well. **-d. corda** to wind (clock, toy etc.). **-d. margem a** to make way for, to allow. **-d. à luz** to give birth. **-d. -se conta de** to realize, to become aware of. **-d. um jeito** to find a way; to fix something up; (colloq.) to strain (a muscle). **-d. um nó** to make a knot. **-d. um passeio** to take a walk; to go for a ride. **-d. um pulo** (colloq.) to drop in

dardejar | daʀdeˈjaʀ | *vt.* to dart (intense glances) at; to shoot out (rays of heat or light)

dardo | ˈdaʀdʊ | *sm.* dart, javelin

data | ˈdata | *sf.* date. **-até esta d.** down to date. **-com d. de** under date of

de | ˈdɪ | *prep.* of, from, by, in, at; on, about, as, with, for

deão | dɪˈãw | *sm.* dean

debaixo | dɪˈbayxʊ | *adv.* under, underneath, below, beneath

debalde | dɪˈbaldɪ | *adv.* in vain

debandar | debãˈdaʀ | *vi.* to disband, to disperse

debate | deˈbatɪ | *sm.* debate, discussion

debater | debaˈteʀ | *vt.* to debate, to discuss. **-d. -se** to struggle, to trash about

debelar | debeˈlaʀ | *vt.* to put down, to overcome

débil | ˈdɛbil | *a.* weak, feeble. **-d. mental** feeble-minded person

debilidade | debiliˈdadɪ | *sf.* weakness, debility

debitar | debiˈtaʀ | *vt.* to debit

débito | ˈdɛbitʊ | *sm.* debit

debochar | deboˈxaʀ | *vt.* (colloq.) to mock

debruçar | debruˈsaʀ | *vt.* (also **d. -se**) to lean out

debrum | dɪˈbrũ | *sm.* hem, edging

debulhar | debuˈlaʀ | *vt.* to thresh (grain); to shell (corn). **-d. -se em lágrimas** to dissolve into tears

década | ˈdɛkada | *sf.* decade

decadência | dekaˈdẽsia | *sf.* decadence, decadency, decay

decadente | dekaˈdẽtɪ | *smf.* decadent, decaying

decair | dekaˈiʀ | *vt.* to decay, to decline; to droop

decano -na | deˈkanʊ | *smf.* elder, senior (of a corporation); dean

decantar | dekãˈtaʀ | *vt.* to decant (liquids); to sing the praises of

decapitar | dekapiˈtaʀ | *vt.* to decapitate, to behead

decência | deˈsẽsia | *sf.* decency, decorum; cleanliness

decente | deˈsẽtɪ | *a.* decent, decorous, proper

decepar | deseˈpaʀ | *vt.* to sever; to amputate; to chop off

decepção | desepˈsãw | *sf.* disappointment, disenchantment; deception

decerto | dɪˈseʀtʊ | *adv.* certainly

decidido -da | dɪsiˈdidʊ | *a.* resolute, determined; decided

decidir | dɪsiˈdiʀ | *vt.* to decide; to settle, to conclude. **-d. -se** to make up one's mind / *vi.* to decide, to reach a decision

decifrar | dɪsiˈfraʀ | *vt.* to decipher

décimo -ma | ˈdesimʊ | *sm. a.* tenth

decisão | dɪsiˈzãw | *sf.* decision

decisivo -va | dɪsiˈzivʊ | *a.* decisive, conclusive

declamar | deklaˈmaʀ | *vt. vi.* to declaim

declaração | deklaraˈsãw | *sf.* declaration; statement

declarar | deklaˈraʀ | *vt.* to declare, to state; to proclaim

declinação | deklinaˈsãw | *sf.* declination; inclination

declinar | dekliˈnaʀ | *vt.* to decline; to refuse / *vi.* to decline, to ebb

declínio | deˈkliniʊ | *sm.* decline, decadence, decay

declive | deˈklivɪ | *sm.* declivity, downward slope

decolagem | dekoˈlajẽy | *sf.* (aeron.) take off

decolar | deko'laʀ | *vi.* (aeron.) to take off

decomposição | dekõpozi'sãw | *sf.* decomposition, rotteness

decoração | dekora'sãw | *sf.* decoration, ornamentation

decorar | deko'raʀ | *vt.* to decorate; to memorize

decorativo -va | dekora'tivʊ | *a.* decorative

decoro | de'korʊ | *sm.* decorum, decency

decoroso -sa | deko'rozʊ-'rwza | *a.* proper, decorous

decorrer | deko'ʀeʀ | *vi.* to pass, to elapse (said of time); to arise, to originate

decote | de'kwtɪ | *sm.* neckline, low neckline

decrépito -ta | de'krɛpitʊ | *a.* decrepit, feeble

decrescente | dekre'sẽtɪ | *a.* diminishing, decreasing

decrescer | dekre'seʀ | *vi.* to decrease, to abate, to diminish

decrescimento, decréscimo | dekresi'mẽtʊ de'krɛsimʊ | *sm.* decrease, lessening

decretar | dekre'taʀ | *vt. vi.* to decree

decreto | de'krɛtʊ | *sm.* decree, edict, mandate

decurso -sa | de'kuʀsʊ | *sm.* course, lapse of time / *a.* past, elapsed

dedal | dɪ'dal | *sm.* thimble; bit, small quantity

dédalo | 'dɛdalʊ | *sm.* labyrinth, maze

dedicação | dɪdika'sãw | *sf.* dedication, devotion

dedicar | dedi'kaʀ | *vt.* to dedicate, to devote; to inscribe (a book). **-d. -se a** to devote oneself to

dedicatória | dɪdika'twria | *sf.* dedication, inscription

dedo | 'dedʊ | *sm.* finger; toe; bit, small portion. **-d. anular** ring finger. **-d. indicador** forefinger. **-d. médio** middle finger. **-d. mínimo** little finger. **-d.**

polegar thumb. **-nós dos dedos** knuckles

dedução | dedu'sãw | *sf.* deduction; abatement, discount

deduzir | dedu'ziʀ | *vt.* to deduce; to subtract / *vi.* to deduce, to infer

defeito | de'feytʊ | *sm.* defect, imperfection, flaw

defeituoso -sa | defeytu'ozʊ -'wza | *a.* defective; faulty

defender | defẽ'deʀ | *vt.* to defend, to protect; to maintain

defensiva | defẽ'siva | *sf.* defensive

defensor -sora | defẽ'soʀ -'sora | *smf.* defender; (law) defensor / *a.* defensive

deferência | defe'rẽsia | *sf.* deference, regard

deferimento | deferi'mẽtʊ | *sm.* approval, grant

deferir | defɪ'riʀ | *vt.* to concede, to grant (a request)

defesa | de'feza | *sf.* defence, defense (also law); protection; apology

deficiência | defisi'ẽsia | *sf.* deficiency; lack; imperfection

deficiente | defisi'ẽtɪ | *a.* deficient, insufficient

definhar | dɪfi'naʀ | *vi.* to emaciate, to waste away; to droop

definição | dɪfini'sãw | *sf.* definition

definir | dɪfi'niʀ | *vt.* to define, to describe precisely

definitivo -va | dɪfini'tivʊ | *a.* definitive, conclusive

deformação | defoʀma'sãw | *sf.* deformation, distortion

deformar | defoʀ'maʀ | *vt.* to deform, to distort

deformidade | defoʀmi'dadɪ | *sf.* deformity, distortion

defraudar | defraw'daʀ | *vt.* to defraud, to swindle

defrontar-se | defrõ'taʀsɪ | *vr.* to face

defronte | dɪ'frõtɪ | *adv.* facing. **-d. de** in front of

defumar | defu'maʀ | *vt.* to smoke

(fish, meat etc.), to smoke-cure

defunto-ta | dɪ'fũtʊ | *sm.* dead person / *a.* deceased, dead, the late

degelar | deje'laʀ | *vt.* to defrost / *vi.* to thaw

degelo | de'jelʊ | *sm.* thawing, thaw

degenerar | dejene'raʀ | *vi.* to degenerate

deglutir | dɪglu'tiʀ | *vt.* to swallow

degolar | dego'laʀ | *vt.* to cut the throat of; to decapitate

degradação | degrada'sãw | *sf.* degradation

degradar | degra'daʀ | *vt.* to degrade, to debase

degrau | de'graw | *sm.* stair.step; rung of a ladder

degredar | degre'daʀ | *vt.* to exile, to banish

degredo | de'gredʊ | *sm.* exile, banishment

degustar | deguʒ'taʀ | *vt.* to taste, to savo(u)r

deitada | dey'tada | *sf.* (colloq.) a lying down

deitado -da | dey'tadʊ | *a.* in bed; lying down

deitar | dey'taʀ | *vt.* to lay, to lay down; to put; to put to bed; to tilt. **-d. -se** to lie down, to go to bed. **-d. sangue** to bleed. **-d. a perder** to cause the ruin of

deixa | 'deyxa | *sf.* actor's cue, hint

deixar | dey'xaʀ | *vt.* to leave; to abandon; to let, to allow; to lay aside; to bequeath. **-d. em paz** to let alone, to let in peace. **-d. escapar** to let slip. **-d. estar** to wait and see / *vi.* to stop, to cease. **-d. de** to abstain from

delator -tora | dela'toʀ | *smf.* informer, denouncer

delegação | delega'sãw | *sf.* delegation

delegacia | delega'sia | *sf.* police headquarters

delegado | dele'gadʊ | *sm.* delegate; deputy, commissioner. **-d. de polícia** district chief of police

delegar | dele'gaʀ | *vt.* to delegate, to commission

deleitar | deley'taʀ | *vt.* to delight. **-d. -se** to delight oneself

deleite | de'leytɪ | *sm.* delight, pleasure

delgado -da | del'gadʊ | *a.* slim, slender, lean

deliberação | delibera'sãw | *sf.* deliberation; decision

deliberar | delibe'raʀ | *vt.* to deliberate; to decide / *vi.* to deliberate, to consider

delicadeza | delika'deza | *sf.* politeness, courtesy; fragility

delicado -da | deli'kadʊ | *a.* courteous, urbane; delicate, fragile; critical, dangerous

delícia | dɪ'lisia | *sf.* delight

delicioso -sa | dɪlisi'ozʊ -'ɔza | *a.* delicious, delightful

delimitação | dɪlimita'sãw | *sf.* delimitation, demarcation

delinear | dɪlinɪ'aʀ | *vt.* to delineate, to outline

delinqüência | dɪlĩ'kwẽsia | *sf.* delinquency

delinqüente | dɪlĩ'kwẽtɪ | *smf.* delinquent; criminal

delirante | dɪli'rãtɪ | *a.* delirious

delirar | dɪli'raʀ | *vi.* to be delirious

delírio | dɪ'lirɪʊ | *sm.* delirium; frenzy; (psychiat.) delusion

delito | de'litʊ | *sm.* delict, crime

delonga | de'lõga | *sf.* delay. **-sem mais delongas** without further delay

demagogo -ga | dema'gogʊ | *smf.* demagogue, demagog; agitator

demais | dɪ'mayʒ | *adv.* too much; excessively; moreover, besides; furthermore. **-assim é d.!** that's the limit!

demanda | de'mãda | *sf.* lawsuit (civil), plea; demand, claim (also law). **-em d. de** in search of

demandar | demã'daʀ | *vt.* to demand; to ask for; to go in search for; to sue at law

demão | dɪ'mãw | *sf.* coat (of paint etc.)

demasia | dema'zia | *a.* surplus, excess

demasiado -da | dɩmazi'advɩ | *a.* too much, too many; excessive / *adv.* too much, too many

demência | de'mẽsia | *sf.* madness, insanity

demente | de'mẽtɩ | *smf.* insane person / *a.* demented, insane, mad

demissão | dɩmi'sãw | *sf.* dismissal, discharge. **-pedir d.** to resign

demitir | dɩmi'tiR | *vt.* to dismiss, to discharge. **-d. -se** to resign

democracia | demokra'sia | *sf.* democracy

democrata | demo'krata | *smf.* democrat

democrático -ca | demo'kratikɩ | *a.* democratic

demolição | demoli'sãw | *sf.* demolition

demolir | demo'liR | *vt.* to demolish

demônio | de'moniɩ | *sm.* demon, devil. **-como o d.** very much

demonstração | demõʃtra'sãw | *sf.* demonstration; manifestation

demonstrar | demõʃ'traR | *vt.* to demonstrate, to prove; to manifest

demonstrativo -va | demõʃtra'tivɩ | *a.* demonstrative

demora | dɩ'mɔra | *sf.* delay; postponement; deferment; detention

demorar | dɩmo'raR | *vt.* to delay, to slow down; to defer. **-d. -se** to linger, to delay

demover | demo'veR | *vt.* to dissuade

dendê | dẽ'de | *sm.* Afro-Brazilian oil-palm (tree, fruit and oil)

dengoso -sa | dẽ'gozɩ -'gɔza | *a.* coy and coquettish; affected

dengue | 'dẽgɩ | *sm.* affectation, daintiness

denominação | denomina'sãw | *sf.* denomination, designation

denotar | deno'taR | *vt.* to denote, to express

densidade | dẽsi'dadɩ | *sf.* density; heaviness

denso -sa | 'dẽsɩ | *a.* dense; thick; heavy

dentada | dẽ'tada | *sf.* bite; bite (wound)

dentado -da | dẽ'tadɩ | *a.* toothed; dentate, cogged

dentadura | dẽta'dura | *sf.* denture, set of teeth. **-d. postiça** false teeth

dente | 'dẽtɩ | *sm.* tooth; tusk, fang; gear tooth; indentation; clove (of garlic)

dentista | dẽ'tiʃta | *smf.* dentist

dentro | 'dẽtrɩ | *adv.* in, inside; indoors. **-d. de** or **-d. em** within; inside of. **-d. em breve** soon

denúncia | de'nũsia | *sf.* denunciation (also law), accusation; (law) indictment

denunciar | denũsi'aR | *vt.* to denounce, to denunciate (also law); to disclose

deparar | depa'raR | *vt.* to meet, to come upon. **-d. -se com** to fall across

departamento | depaRta'mẽtɩ | *sm.* department

depenar | depe'naR | *vt.* to pluck (feathers)

dependência | depẽ'dẽsia | *sf.* dependence; subordination; dependency

depender | depẽ'deR | *vi.* (used with *prep.* **de**) to depend on

deplorar | deplo'raR | *vt.* to deplore, to lament

deplorável | deplo'ravɩl | *a.* deplorable, lamentable

depoimento | depoi'mẽtɩ | *sm.* deposition (also law), testimony; statement

depois | dɩ'poyʃ | *adv.* after, afterwards; later, later on; besides, moreover. **-d. de** after that, following

depor | de'poR | *vt.* to depose, to dethrone; to set aside; to depose, to testify under oath; to lay down (arms)

deportar | depoR'taʀ | *vt.* to banish, to exile

deposição | depozi'sãw | *sf.* deposition, overthrow; statement

depositar | depozi'taʀ | *vt.* to deposit. **-d. -se** to precipitate

depósito | de'pɔzitʊ | *sm.* deposit (also geol., chem.); depository; depot, warehouse; tank, bin

depravação | deprava'sãw | *sf.* depravity, corruption

depravado -da | depra'vadʊ | *a.* depraved, corrupt

depreciar | depresi'aʀ | *vt.* to depreciate; to devaluate

depredação | depreda'sãw | *sf.* depredation

depressa | dɪ'prɛsa | *adv.* fast, quickly / *interj.* hurry up!

depressão | depre'sãw | *sf.* depression

deprimente | depri'mẽtɪ | *a.* depressing, depressive

deprimir | depri'miʀ | *vt.* to depress; to dispirit

depuração | depura'sãw | *sf.* purification

deputado -da | depu'tadʊ | *sm.* congressman; *sf.* congresswoman; *smf.* deputy, representative

derivar | deri'vaʀ | *vt.* to derive; to deflect; (naut.) to drift

derradeiro -ra | deʀa'deyrʊ | *a.* last

derramamento | deʀama'mẽtʊ | *sm.* pouring; spilling; shedding (of blood)

derramar | deʀa'maʀ | *vt.* to spill; to shed (water, tears, blood); to pour out

derrame | de'ʀamɪ | *sm.* spreading; hemorrhage. **-d. cerebral** brain hemorrhage

derrapagem | deʀa'pajẽy | *sf.* skidding, skid

derrapar | deʀa'paʀ | *vi.* to skid

derredor | dɪʀe'dɔʀ | *adv.* around, about

derreter | deʀe'teʀ | *vt.* to melt; to liquefy; to soften

derrocar | deʀo'kaʀ | *vt.* to demolish, to destroy, to raze

derrota | de'ʀɔta | *sf.* defeat, beating

derrubada | deʀu'bada | *sf.* downfall; clearing (of land)

derrubar | deʀu'baʀ | *vt.* to throw or to knock down; to overthrow

desabafar | dɪzaba'faʀ | *vt.* to free (from obstructions); to get something off one's chest

desabar | dɪza'baʀ | *vi.* to collapse, to crumble

desabitado -da | dɪzabi'tadʊ | *a.* uninhabited

desabotoar | dɪzabʊtʊ'aʀ | *vt.* to unbutton

desabrido -da | dɪza'bridʊ | *a.* rude, rough; insolent

desabrochar | dɪzabro'xaʀ | *vi.* to bloom, to blossom

desacato | dɪza'katʊ | *sm.* disrespect, disregard, contempt

desacerto | dɪza'seʀtʊ | *sm.* mistake, blunder

desacordo | dɪza'koʀdʊ | *sm.* disagreement

desacostumado -da | dɪzakʊʒtu'madʊ | *a.* unaccustomed

desacreditado -da | dɪzakredi'tadʊ | *a.* discredited; disreputable

desafeto | dɪza'fɛtʊ | *sm.* foe, enemy

desafiar | dɪzafi'aʀ | *vt.* to defy, to challenge / *vi.* to become blunt

desafinado -da | dɪzafi'nadʊ | *a.* out of tune, off-key

desafinar | dɪzafi'naʀ | *vi.* to get out of tune, to play out of tune

desafio | dɪza'fiʊ | *sm.* challenge, defiance

desafogar | dɪzafo'gaʀ | *vt.* to relieve, to ease

desafogo | dɪza'fogʊ | *sm.* ease, relief; comfort, abundance

desaforado -da | dɪzafo'radʊ | *a.* impudent, insolent

desaforo | dɪza'forʊ | *sm.* impudence, insolence

desagradar | dɪzagra'daʀ | *vt.* to

displease. **-d. -se** to be displeased

desagradável | dɪzagra'davɪl | a. disagreeable, unpleasant

desagrado | dɪza'gradʊ | sm. displeasure

desagravo | dɪza'gravʊ | sm. redress, satisfaction, reparation

desaguar | dɪza'gwaʀ | vi. to empty, to flow into

desairoso -sa | dɪzay'rozʊ -'rʊza | a. inelegant; indecorous; discreditable

desajeitado -da | dɪzajey'tadʊ | a. clumsy, awkward

desajustado -da | dɪzajuʃ'tadʊ | smf. a. misfit, maladjusted

desajuste | dɪza'juʃtɪ | sm. maladjustment; desagreement

desalentado -da | dɪzalē'tadʊ | a. disheartened

desalento | dɪza'lētʊ | sm. discouragement, despondency

desalinho | dɪza'liNʊ | sm. disorder, untidiness

desalmado -da | dɪzal'madʊ | smf. cruel, inhuman person / a. merciless, ruthless

desalojar | dɪzalo'jaʀ | vt. to dislodge; to displace; to force out

desalugado -da | dɪzalu'gadʊ | a. vacant, unrented

desamarrar | dɪzama'ʀaʀ | vt. to untie, to unfasten

desamparado -da | dɪzãpa'radʊ | a. abandoned, unprotected

desamparar | dɪzãpa'raʀ | vt. to abandon, to leave defenseless

desandar | dɪzã'daʀ | vi. to degenerate; to separate (said of beaten egg-whites etc.); (colloq.) to go bad

desanimar | dɪzani'maʀ | vt. to dispirit, to dishearten / vi. to be or to become disheartened

desânimo | dɪ'zanimʊ | sm. despondency; discouragement, depression

desanuviar | dɪzanuvi'aʀ | vt. to make clear. **-d. -se** to clear up

desaparecer | dɪzapare'seʀ | vt. to

disappear, to vanish; to fade away

desaparecimento | dɪzaparɪsi'mētʊ | sm. disappearance

desapego | dɪza'pegʊ | sm. detachment, unconcern

desapertar | dɪzapeʀ'taʀ | vt. to unfasten, to untie; to alleviate. **-d.-se** to come loose; (slang) to come out of a tight spot

desapontamento | dɪzapõta'mētʊ | sm. disappointment

desapontado -da | dɪzapõ'tadʊ | a. disappointed

desapontar | dɪzapõ'taʀ | vt. to deceive; to disappoint; to disenchant

desapropriar | dɪzapropri'aʀ | vt. to dispossess, to expropriate

desaprovar | dɪzapro'vaʀ | vt. tó disapprove; to reprove

desarmamento | dɪzaʀma'mētʊ | sm. disarmament

desarmar | dɪzaʀ'maʀ | vt. to disarm; to disassemble, to dismantle

desarmonia | dɪzaʀmʊ'nia | sf. disharmony; discordance

desarraigar | dɪzaʀay'gaʀ | vt. to uproot, to eradicate

desarranjar | dɪzaʀã'jaʀ | vt. to disarrange, to disturb; to upset

desarranjo | dɪza'ʀãjʊ | sm. disarrangement, disorder; disturbance; (colloq.) diarrhea

desarrumação | dɪzaʀuma'sãw | sf. disorder; untidiness

desarrumado -da | dɪzaʀu'madʊ | a. untidy, messy; deranged

desarrumar | dɪzaʀu'maʀ | vt. to disarrange; to mess; to unpack (baggage)

desarticular | dɪzaʀtiku'laʀ | vt. to disarticulate, to disjoint; to disconnect

desassossego | dɪzasʊ'segʊ | sm. disquiet, uneasiness

desastrado -da | dɪzaʃ'tradʊ | a. awkward, clumsy

desastre | dɪ'zaʃtrɪ | sm. disaster; accident

desastroso -sa | dɪzaʒ'trozʋ
-'trʋza | a. disastrous

desatar | dɪza'taR | vt. to untie, to
undo (a knot). **-d. a rir** to break
out laughing

desatarraxar | dɪzataRa'xaR | vt. to
unscrew

desatencioso -sa | dɪzatēsi'ozʋ
-'ωza | a. inattentive, inconsiderate; uncivil

desatento -ta | dɪza'tētʋ | a.
absent-minded, distracted;
negligent

desatinado -da | dɪzati'nadʋ | smf.
a. wild, mad

desatino | dɪza'tinʋ | sm. folly,
madness

desavença | dɪza'vēsa | sf. disagreement, misunderstanding

desbancar | dɪʒbã'kaR | vt. to surpass, to outclass, to supplant

desbaratar | dɪʒbara'taR | vt. to
squander, to waste; to destroy

desbastar | dɪʒbaʒ'taR | vt. to
trim; to shape; to thin

desbocado -da | dɪʒbo'kadʋ | a.
foul-mouthed, unrestrained

desbotar | dɪʒbo'taR | vi. to fade,
to become colo(u)rless

desbragamento | dɪʒbraga'mētʋ |
a. excess, immoderation

desbravar | dɪʒbra'vaR | vt. to
open up (the wilderness)

descabelado -da | dɪʒkabe'ladʋ |
a. dishevel(l)ed

descabido -da | dɪʒka'bidʋ | a. unsuitable, inappropriate

descalabro | dɪʒka'labrʋ | sm. calamity, disaster; breakdown,
ruin; damage

descalçar | dɪʒkal'saR | vt. to take
off, to remove (shoes, gloves
etc.)

descalço -ça | dɪʒ'kalsʋ | a. barefoot, shoeless

descambar | dɪʒkã'baR | vi. to top-
.ple, to fall; to slide

descampado -da | dɪʒkã'padʋ |
sm. barren plain, open desolate
land

descansado -da | dɪʒkã'sadʋ | a.

relaxed, at ease or leisure; calm

descansar | dɪʒkã'saR | vt. to give
rest to / vi. to rest. **-d.!** (mil.) at
easy!

descanso | dɪʒ'kãsʋ | sm. rest, repose; ease, leisure

descarado -da | dɪʒka'radʋ | a.
shameless, impudent

descarga | dɪʒ'kaRga | sf. discharge; (mil.) firing; (mech.)
exhaust; unloading (of cargo)

descargo | dɪʒ'kaRgʋ | sm. ease,
relief; acquittal

descarregar | dɪʒkaRe'gaR | vt. to
unload; to discharge; to unburden; to fire a gun; to relieve (of
cares); to give vent (to anger)

descarrilar | dɪʒkaRi'laR | vt. to derail / vi. to jump the track

descascar | dɪʒka'kaR | vt. to
peel; to bark (trees); to shell
(nuts) / vi. to peel (said of the
skin)

descendência | desē'dēsia | sf. descent, extraction; offspring

descendente | desē'dētɪ | smf. descendant / a. descending

descender | desē'deR | vi. to descend from

descer | de'seR | vi. to descend, to
go down, to be lowered; to
disembark

descerrar | dese'RaR | vt. to open;
to reveal

descida | dɪ'sida | sf. descent; fall,
drop

desclassificar | dɪʒklasifi'kaR | vt.
to disqualify; to declassify; to
discredit

descoberta | dɪʒkʋ'beRta | sf.
discovery

descoberto -ta | dɪʒkʋ'beRtʋ | a.
uncovered, exposed, open; discovered. **-a d.** openly; (com.)
overdrawn

descobridor -dora | dɪʒkʋbri'doR |
smf. discoverer

descobrimento | dɪʒkʋbri'mētʋ |
sm. discovery, finding

descobrir | dɪʒkʋ'briR | vt. to discover; to reveal, to disclose; to find out

descolar | dɪʃko'laʀ | vt. vi. to unglue

descolorar | dɪʃkolo'ʀaʀ | vt. to discolo(u)r / vi. to fade

descomedido -da | dɪʃkome'didʊ | a. immoderate, intemperate

descompor | dɪʃkõ'poʀ | vt. to discompose, to disarrange; (fig.) to insult, to dress down

descompostura | dɪʃkõpʊʃ'tura | sf. discomposure; dressing down

descomunal | dɪʃkomu'nal | a. colossal, enormous, monstrous

desconcertante | dɪʃkõseʀ'tãtɪ | a. disconcerting; confusing

desconcertar | dɪʃkõseʀ'taʀ | vt. to disconcert; to perplex, to confuse

desconexo -xa | dɪʃko'nɛksʊ | a. disconnected; disjointed, incoherent

desconfiado -da | dɪʃkõfi'adʊ | a. suspicious, distrustful

desconfiança | dɪʃkõfi'ãsa | sf. suspicion, distrust

desconfiar | dɪʃkõfi'aʀ | vi. to be distrustful. **-d.** de to distrust

desconforto | dɪʃkõ'foʀtʊ | sm. discomfort, uneasiness of body or mind

desconhecer | dɪʃkone'seʀ | vt. not to know; not to recognize; to ignore

desconhecido -da | dɪʃkone-'sidʊ | smf. stranger / a. unknown

desconjuntado -da | dɪʃkõjũ'tadʊ | a. disjointed; ramshackle

desconjuntar | dɪʃkõjũ'taʀ | vt. to disjoint, to disarticulate; to unhinge. **-d. -se** to come apart

desconsolado -da | dɪʃkõso'ladʊ | a. disconsolate, desolate

descontar | dɪʃkõ'taʀ | vt. to discount, to deduct. **-d. um cheque** to cash a cheque

descontentamento | dɪʃkõtẽta-'mẽtʊ | sm. discontent; dissatisfaction

descontente | dɪʃkõ'tẽtɪ | a. discontented, unsatisfied

desconto | dɪʃ'kõtʊ | sm. discount, reduction

descontrole | dɪʃkõ'trolɪ | sm. lack of control

descorado -da | dɪʃko'radʊ | a. discolo(u)red; pale; faded

descortês | dɪʃkoʀ'teʃ | a. discourteous, impolite

descortinar | dɪʃkoʀti'naʀ | vt. to reveal, to disclose to view; to catch sight of

descoser | dɪʃkʊ'zeʀ | vt. to unsew, to unstitch / vi. to come apart at the seams

descrédito | dɪʃ'kredɪtʊ | sm. discredit, disrepute

descrença | dɪʃ'krẽsa | sf. disbelief; incredulity

descrever | dɪʃkre'veʀ | vt. to describe

descrição | dɪʃkri'sãw | sf. description, representation, portrayal

descuidado -da | dɪʃkuy'dadʊ | a. careless, negligent, heedless; lazy

descuidar | dɪʃkuy'daʀ | vt. to neglect, to disregard / vi. to be careless

descuido | dɪʃ'kuydʊ | sm. carelessness, negligence; oversight

desculpa | dɪʃ'kulpa | sf. excuse, apology, pretext. **-pedir d.** to apologize

desculpar | dɪʃkul'paʀ | vt. to excuse, to pardon, to forgive. **-d. -se** to apologize; to excuse oneself

desculpe | dɪʃ'kulpɪ | interj. excuse me!, pardon me!

desde | 'deʒdɪ | prep. since, from. **-d. agora** from now on. **-d. então** (ever) since, since then

desdém | deʒ'dẽ | sm. disdain

desdenhar | dɪʒde'naʀ | vt. to disdain, to scorn

desdenhoso -sa | deʒde'nozʊ -'nɔza | a. disdainful, scornful

desdita | dɪʃ'dita | sf. misfortune; unhappiness

desdobrar | dɪʒdo'braʀ | *vt.* to unfold; to extend; to divide into parts

desejar | deze'jaʀ | *vt. vi.* to desire, to wish

desejo | de'zejʊ | *sm.* desire; wish; longing

desejoso -sa | deze'jozʊ -'jʊza | *a.* desirous

desembainhar | dɪzĩbai'naʀ | *vt.* to unsheathe

desembaraçado -da | dɪzĩbara-'sadʊ | *a.* clear, unencumbered, unobstructed; alert, active

desembaraçar | dɪzĩ bara'saʀ | *vt.* to free, to clear, to disentangle

desembaraço | dɪzĩ ba'rasʊ | *sm.* dexterity, ease; quickness

desembarcar | dɪzĩbaʀ'kaʀ | *vt.* to disembark; to unload / *vi.* to disembark, to go ashore

desembarque | dɪzĩ 'baʀkɪ | *sm.* disembarkation, landing

desembocadura | dɪzĩ boka'dura | *sf.* mouth (of a river)

desembocar | dɪzĩ bo'kaʀ | *vi.* to empty; to run into (street)

desembolsar | dɪzĩ bol'saʀ | *vt.* to disburse

desembrulhar | dɪzĩ bru'LaʀR | *vt.* to unwrap; to unfold; to uncover

desempatar | dɪzĩ pa'taʀ | *vt.* to cast the deciding vote; (sports) to play or to shoot off a tie; to decide

desempenhar | dɪzĩ pe'naʀ | *vt.* to redeem (something pawned); to execute (a duty). **-d. um papel** to play a part

desempenho | dɪzĩ 'penʊ | *sm.* execution (of a duty); performance; redemption (of something pawned)

desempregado -da | dɪzĩpre'gadʊ | *smf.* unemployed person / *a.* unemployed

desemprego | dɪzĩ 'pregʊ | *sm.* unemployment

desencadear | dɪzĩ kadɪ'aʀ | *vt.* to unchain; to disconnect; (fig.) to arouse. **-d. -se** to break out (storm)

desencaixotar | dɪzĩ kayxo'taʀ | *vt.* to unbox, to unpack

desencaminhar | dɪzĩ kami'naʀ | *vt.* to misguide, to mislead. **-d. -se** to go astray

desencantar | dɪzĩ kã'taʀ | *vt.* to disenchant, to disillusion

desencontro | dɪzĩ'kõtrʊ | *sm.* failure to meet; discordance, disagreement

desenfreado -da | dɪzĩfre'adʊ | *a.* unbraidled, uncontrolled

desenganar | dɪzĩ ga'naʀ | *vt.* to disillusion; to give up (someone) as incurable. **-d. -se** to realize the truth (of something)

desengano | dɪzĩ 'ganʊ | *sm.* disillusionment

desengonçado -da | dɪzĩ gõ'sadʊ | *a.* clumsy, awkward

desenhar | deze'naʀ | *vt.* to design, to draw; to show (in outline)

desenhista | deze'nɪʃta | *smf.* designer; draftsman

desenho | de'zenʊ | *sm.* design, sketch, drawing

desenlace | dɪzĩ 'lasɪ | *sm.* epilogue, outcome; upshot, end

desenrolar | dɪzĩ ʀo'laʀ | *vt.* to unroll; to unwind; to develop (story, plot) / *vi.* to unfold; to come to pass (events). **-d. -se** to uncoil (as a snake)

desentendido -da | dɪzĩ tẽ'didʊ | *a.* misunderstood. **-fazer-se de d.** to do as if one did not understand

desentendimento | dɪzĩ tẽdi'mẽtʊ | *sm.* misunderstanding

desenterrar | dɪzĩ te'ʀaʀ | *vt.* to unearth, to dig up; to disinter

desentranhar | dɪzĩ tra'naʀ | *vt.* to remove from the innermost part; to disembowel

desentupir | dɪzĩ tu'piʀ | *vt.* to unstop (as a pipe), to unclog, to clear open (a passage)

desenvolto -ta | dɪzĩ 'voltʊ | *a.* unrestrained, uninhibited; agile

desenvoltura | dιzĩvol'tura | *sm.* nimbleness, vivacity; ease

desenvolver | dιzĩ vol'veʀ | *vt.* to develop

desenvolvimento | dιzĩ volvi'mẽtυ | *sm.* development; growth; expansion

desequilibrado -da | dιzιkili'bradυ | *a.* unbalanced

desequilibrar | dιzιkili'braʀ | *vt.* to unbalance, to put out of balance

deserção | dιzeʀ'sãw | *sf.* desertion

deserdar | dιzeʀ'daʀ | *vt.* to disinherit

desertar | dιzeʀ'taʀ | *vt.* to desert, to abandon / *vi.* (mil.) to desert

deserto -ta | dι'zeʀtυ | *sm.* desert, wasteland / *a.* deserted, abandoned

desesperado -da | dιzιʃpe'radυ | *smf.* desperate person / *a.* desperate

desesperança | dιzιʃpe'rãsa | *sf.* despair

desesperar | dιzιʃpe'raʀ | *vt.* to cause to despair / *vi.* to despair; to grow desperate

desespero | dιzιʃ'perυ | *sm.* despair

desfaçatez | dιʃfasa'teʃ | *sf.* insolence, impudence

desfalcar | dιʃfal'kaʀ | *vt.* to embezzle; to break a set, to leave a gap in

desfalecer | dιʃfale'seʀ | *vi.* to faint; to weaken

desfalque | dιʃ'falkι | *sm.* embezzlement

desfavorável | dιʃfavo'ravιl | *a.* unfavo(u)rable, adverse

desfazer | dιʃfa'zeʀ | *vt.* to undo, to unmake; to break, to dissolve. **-d. -se** to become undone, to fall apart. **-d. -se de** to get rid of

desfechar | dιʃfe'xaʀ | *vt.* to fire (a gun); to let fly (blow, arrow); to hurl (an insult) / *vi.* to break

(storm, tragedy)

desfecho | dιʃ'fexυ | *sm.* conclusion, epilogue, end

desfeita | dιʃ'feyta | *sf.* insult, offense, affront

desfeito -ta | dιʃ'feytυ | *a.* undone; annuled; fragmented

desfiar | dιʃfi'aʀ | *vt.* to fray; to unthread; to relate in detail. **-d. -se** to become frayed

desfigurar | dιʃfigu'raʀ | *vt.* to disfigure; to distort

desfilar | dιʃfi'laʀ | *vi.* to parade; to file by, to defile

desfile | dιʃ'filι | *sm.* parade; pageant, procession

desfolhar | dιʃfo'Laʀ | *vt.* to strip (of leaves or petals)

desforra | dιʃ'fωra | *sf.* revenge, retaliation

desfraldar | dιʃfral'daʀ | *vt.* to unfurl (flag, sails)

desfrutar | dιʃfru'taʀ | *vt.* to enjoy, to relish

desgarrar | dιʃga'ʀaʀ | *vi.* (naut.) to go off course; to go astray

desgastar | dιʃgaʃ'taʀ | *vt.* to wear out; to erode. **-d. -se** to become worn out

desgaste | dιʃ'gaʃtι | *sm.* wear, wear and tear

desgostar | dιʃgoʃ'taʀ | *vt.* to displease; to upset. **-d. -se** to be or to become displeased. **-d. de** to dislike

desgosto | dιʃ'goʃtυ | *sm.* displeasure; grief, sorrow

desgraça | dιʃ'grasa | *sf.* misfortune; disaster, calamity

desgraçado -da | dιʃgra'sadυ | *smf.* wretch / *a.* unfortunate, wretched; (colloq.) clever, shrewd

desgrenhado -da | dιʃgre'Nadυ | *a.* tousled (hair)

desidratar | dιzidra'taʀ | *vt.* to dehydrate

designar | dιzig'naʀ | *vt.* to designate; to appoint; to denote

desigual | dιzi'gwal | *a.* unequal; uneven (ground)

desilusão | dₑzilu'zãw | *sf.* desillusionment, disenchantment

desimpedir | dₑzĩpₑ'diʀ | *vt.* to disencumber, to unclog

desinchar | dₑzĩ'xaʀ | *vt.* to reduce (a swelling) / *vi.* to become unswollen

desinfetante | dₑzĩfe'tãtₑ | *sm. a.* disinfectant, antiseptic

desinfetar | dₑzĩfe'taʀ | *vt.* to disinfect

desintegrar | dₑzĩte'graʀ | *vt.* to disintegrate. **-d. -se** to disintegrate, to fall apart

desinteligência | dₑzĩteli'jẽsia| *sf.* disagreement, misunderstanding

desinteressante | dₑzĩtere'sãtₑ | *a.* uninteresting, dull, flat

desinteresse | dₑzĩte'resₑ | *sm.* disinterest, unconcern, apathy

desistência | dₑziʃ'tẽsia | *sf.* abandonment (also law); cancellation

desistir | dₑziʃ'tiʀ | *vi.* (used with *prep.* **de**) to desist, to give up, to abandon

desleal | dₑʃli'al | *a.* disloyal; treacherous

desleixo | dₑʃ'leyxʊ | *sm.* negligence, carelessness; untidiness

desligar | dₑʃli'gaʀ | *vt.* to disconnect; to sever; to hang up (telephone); to turn off (electricity etc.); to release from

deslindar | dₑʃlĩ'daʀ | *vt.* to disentangle, to unravel; to clear up (a mistery, a plot)

deslizar | dₑʃli'zaʀ | *vi.* to glide, to slip, to slide

deslize | dₑʃ'lizₑ | *sm.* lapse, fault, error

deslocar | dₑʃlo'kaʀ | *vt.* to displace; to dislocate (arm, leg etc.). **-d. -se** to become dislocated; to move

deslumbrante | dₑʃlũ'brãtₑ | *a.* dazzling; fascinating

deslumbrar | dₑʃlũ'braʀ | *vt.* to dazzle (by excess of light); to fascinate. **-d. -se** to be dazzled

desmaiar| dₑʃmay'aʀ| *vi.* to faint;

to discolo(u)r

desmaio | dₑʃ'mayʊ | *sm.* faint, fainting spell

desmamar| dₑʃma'maʀ | *vt. vi.* to wean

desmanchar | dₑʃmã'xaʀ | *vt.* to undo; to rip up (as a garment); to take to pieces; to break up (as a marriage engagement); to dissolve. **-d. -se** to come undone; to fall apart

desmantelar|dₑʃmãte'laʀ|*vt.* to dismantle. **-d. -se** to fall apart

desmascarar | dₑʃmaʃka'raʀ | *vt.* to unmask

desmazelo|dₑʃma'zelʊ|*sm.* sloppiness, negligence

desmedido -da | dₑʃme'didʊ | *a.* immense; excessive

desmemoriado -da | dₑʃmemori'adʊ | *a.* forgetful; amnesic

desmentir | dₑʃmĩ'tiʀ | *vt.* to give the lie to; to deny the truth of

desmerecer | dₑʃmere'seʀ | *vi.* to lose merit; to fade (cloth)

desmesurado -da | dₑʃmezu'radʊ | *a.* immense, enormous

desmiolado -da | dₑʃmio'ladʊ | *smf.* scatterbrain / *a.* brainless, scatterbrained

desmobilização | dₑʃmobiliza'sãw | *sf.* demobilization

desmontar|dₑʃmõ'taʀ|*vt.* to dismount; to dismantle, to disassemble / *vi.* to dismount

desmoralizar|dₑʃmorali'zaʀ|*vt.* to demoralize

desmoronar|dₑʃmoro'naʀ|*vt.* to demolish. **-d. -se** to tumble down, to collapse

desnecessário -ria|dₑʃnese'sariʊ| *a.* unnecessary

desnível | dₑʃ'nivₑl | *sm.* unevenness, drop, fall

desnortear | dₑʃnoʀte'aʀ | *vt.* to disorient, to confuse. **-d.-se** to become confused; to get lost

desnudar | dₑʃnu'daʀ | *vt.* to denude, to undress; to bare

desobedecer | dₑzobₑde'seʀ | *vi.* to disobey

desobediência | dɪzobɪdi'ẽsia | *sf.* disobedience

desocupado -da | dɪzoku'padʊ | *a.* unoccupied; idle

desocupar | dɪzoku'paʀ | *vt.* to disoccupy; to vacate (a house)

desodorizante | dɪzodori'zãtɪ | *sm.* deodorant / *a.* deodorizing

desolação | dɪzola'sãw | *sf.* desolation, ruin; grief; bereavement

desolar | dɪzo'laʀ | *vt.* to desolate; to afflict, to distress; to bereave

desonesto -ta | dɪzo'nɛʧʊ | *a.* dishonest; immoral; obscene, indecent

desonra | dɪ'zõʀa | *sf.* dishono(u)r, disgrace; shame

desonrar | dɪzõ'ʀaʀ | *vt.* to disgrace, to dishono(u)r

desoras | de'zɔraʒ | *sfpl.* used in the expression **a d.** in the wee hours, late at night

desordem | dɪ'zɔʀdẽy | *sf.* disorder, disorganization; confusion; tumult

desorganizar | dɪzoʀgani'zaʀ | *vt.* to disorganize

desorientar | dɪzoriẽ'taʀ | *vt.* to disorientate, to disorient; to throw off course. **-d. -se** to become confused

desova | dɪ'zɔva | *sf.* spawning

despachante | dɪʃpa'xãtɪ | *smf.* forwarding clerk, shipping clerk

despachar | dɪʃpa'xaʀ | *vt.* to dispatch, to send off; to render decisions on (official business); to fill (a prescription); (colloq.) to dismiss

despacho | dɪʃ'paxʊ | *sm.* dispatch; message; clearance (at customs etc.); decision (in official documents)

despedaçar | dɪʃpeda'saʀ | *vt.* to shatter, to smash, to tear into pieces

despedida | dɪʃpɪ'dida | *sf.* farewell, parting; dismissal, firing

despedir | dɪʃpɪ'diʀ | *vt.* to dismiss, to fire; to send away; to send off. **-d. -se de** to bid farewell to

despeito | dɪʃ'peytʊ | *sm.* resentment, spite. **-a d. de** in spite of

despejar | dɪʃpe'jaʀ | *vt.* to pour out; to clear (of rubble); (law) to evict, to dispossess

despejo | dɪʃ'pejʊ | *sm.* clearing, evacuation; pouring out, emptying; litter, garbage

despencar | dɪʃpẽ'kaʀ | *vt.* to pick apart (as a bunch of bananas) / *vi.* to break off and fall; (colloq.) to fall (from a great height)

despenhadeiro | dɪʃpeɲa'deyrʊ | *sm.* precipice, cliff

despensa | dɪʃ'pẽsa | *sf.* pantry, larder

despenteado -da | dɪʃpẽtɪ'adʊ | *a.* uncombed

desperdiçar | dɪʃpeʀdi'saʀ | *vt.* to waste, to dissipate

desperdício | dɪʃpeʀ'disɪʊ | *sm.* waste, dissipation

despertador | dɪʃpeʀta'doʀ | *sm.* alarm clock

despertar | dɪʃpeʀ'taʀ | *vt.* to awake, to wake, to arouse / *vi.* to awaken, to wake up

despesa | dɪʃ'peza | *sf.* expense, cost, charge

despir | dɪʃ'piʀ | *vt.* to undress, to unclothe; to denude

despistar | dɪʃpiʒ'taʀ | *vt.* to mislead; to throw off the track

despojar | dɪʃpo'jaʀ | *vt.* to despoil, to strip (of possessions); to deprive. **-d.-se de** to dispose of one's belongings

despojo | dɪʃ'pojʊ | *sm.* spoil, booty (usu. *pl.*). **-despojos mortais** mortal remains

despontar | dɪʃpõ'taʀ | *sm.* dawn, emergence / *vi.* to appear, to emerge

desporto | dɪʃ'poʀtʊ | *sm.* = *esporte*

desposar | dɪʃpo'zaʀ | *vt.* to marry. **-d. -se** to get married

déspota | 'dɛʃpota | *smf.* despot,

tyrant

despovoado -da | dɪʃpovʊ'adʊ | *a.*
uninhabited, deserted

desprazer | dɪʃpra'zeR | *sm.*
displeasure

despregar | dɪʃpre'gaR | *vt.* to un-
fix, to remove (something
which has been nailed or fastened on). **-d. -se** to become
loose or separated

desprendido -da | dɪʃprẽ'didʊ |
a. generous, unselfish; unfas-
tened, loose

despreocupado -da | dɪʃprɪo-
kʊ'padʊ | *a.* unconcerned,
carefree

despretensioso -sa | dɪʃpretẽ-
si'ozʊ -'ωza | *a.* modest;
unpretentious

desprevenido -da | dɪʃprɪvɪ'nidʊ |
a. unprepared, off-guard; (colloq.) out of money

desprezar | dɪʃpre'zaR | *vt.* to de-
spise; to disregard; to disdain

desprezível | dɪʃpre'zivɪl | *a.* con-
temptible; vile, base; negligible

desprezo | dɪʃ'prezʊ | *sm.* con-
tempt, disdain

despropósito | dɪʃpro'pωzitʊ |
sm. unreasonableness, absurdity; excess

desprovido -da | dɪʃpro'vidʊ | *a.*
lacking, wanting. **-d. de** desti-
tute of, devoid of

desquitar-se | dɪʃki'taRsɪ | *vr.* to
separate legally (man and wife)

desquite | dɪʃ'kitɪ | *sm.* legal sepa-
ration which does not dissolve
the marriage

desregrado -da | dɪʃRe'gradʊ | *a.*
intemperate; unruly; disorder-
ly

desrespeitar | dɪʃRe'pey'taR | *vt.*
to disrespect, to affront; to
disregard

desse -sa | 'desɪ 'dɛsa | *contr.* **de** +
esse -sa of that, from that; (*pl.*)
of those, from those

destacado | dɪʃta'kadʊ | *a.*
outstanding

destacamento | dɪʃtaka'mẽtʊ |
sm. detachment (also mil.)

destacar | dɪʃta'kaR | *vt.* to de-
tach, to unfasten and remove
(from); to singularize. **-d. -se** to
become detached; to stand out

destampar | dɪʃtã'paR | *vt.* to take
off the lid of, to uncap

destaque | dɪʃ'takɪ | *sm.* distinc-
tion, eminence, notability,
note

deste -ta | 'deʃtɪ 'dɛʃta | *contr.* **de**
+ **este -ta** of this, from this;
(*pl.*) of these, from these

destemido -da | dɪʃtɪ'midʊ | *a.*
fearless; daring, bold

destempero | dɪʃtẽ'perʊ | *sm.* dis-
order, disarrangement; (col-
loq.) diarrh(o)ea

desterrar | dɪʃte'RaR | *vt.* to exile,
to expatriate, to banish

desterro | dɪʃ'teRʊ | *sm.* exile,
banishment

destilar | dɪʃti'laR | *vt.* to distil;
(fig.) to dribble, to trickle

destilaria | dɪʃtila'ria | *sf.*
distillery

destinar | dɪʃti'naR | *vt.* to destine,
to predetermine; to reserve for.
-d. -se to devote oneself to. **-d.
-se a** to be bound for

destinatário -ria | dɪʃtina'tariʊ |
smf. addressee

destino | dɪʃ'tinʊ | *sm.* destiny,
fate, fortune; destination;
use, application. **-com d: a**
bound for

destituição | dɪʃtitui'sãw | *sf.* dis-
missal from office

destituir | dɪʃtitu'iR | *vt.* to deprive
(of position or dignity), to
dismiss

destoar | dɪʃtʊ'aR | *vi.* to discord,
to be out of tune; to disagree

destorcer | dɪʃtoR'seR | *vt.* to un-
twist, to untwine

destrancar | dɪʃtrã'kaR | *vt.* to un-
lock, to unbolt

destratar | dɪʃtra'taR | *vt.* to mis-
treat, to abuse, to insult

destravar | dɪʃtra'vaR | *vt.* to re-
lease the brake; to release the

safety-catch (of a gun)

destreinado -da | dɪʒ'trey'nadʋ | *a.* untrained; out of practice, out of shape

destreza | deʒ'treza | *sf.* dexterity, skill

destroçar | dɪʒtro'saʀ | *vt.* to smash, to ruin; to defeat; to wreck

destroço | dɪʒ'trosʋ | *sm.* destruction, havoc; (*pl.*) rubble, ruins

destronar | dɪʒtro'naʀ | *vt.* to dethrone

destroncar | dɪʒtrõ'kaʀ | *vt.* to sprain (ankle etc.); to dismember; to disarticulate

destruição | dɪʒtrui'sãw | *sf.* destruction, demolition

destruir | dɪʒtru'iʀ | *vt.* to destroy

desumano -na | dɪzu'manʋ | *a.* inhuman, brutal, cruel

desunião | dɪzuni'ãw | *sf.* disunion, disunity

desunir | dɪzu'niʀ | *vt.* to disunite, to dissociate; to disconnect

desusado -da | dɪzu'zadʋ | *a.* disused, obsolete; unusual

desuso | dɪ'zuzʋ | *sm.* disuse

desvairado -da | dɪʒvay'radʋ | *a.* wild, frantic, mad

desvalorização | dɪʒvaloriza'sãw | *sf.* devaluation, depreciation

desvalorizar | dɪʒvalori'zaʀ | *vt.* to devaluate. **-d. -se** to devaluate; to lose one's worth or value

desvanecer | dɪʒvane'seʀ | *vt.* to disperse, to dissipate; to fill with pride or vanity. **-d. -se** to vanish

desvantagem | dɪʒvã'tajẽy | *sf.* disadvantage, drawback

desvario | dɪʒva'riʋ | *sm.* folly, hallucination, delirium

desvelar | dɪʒve'laʀ | *vt.* to unveil. **-d. -se** to be full of zeal or solicitude

desvelo | dɪʒ'velʋ | *sm.* devotion; care; zeal

desvendar | dɪʒvẽ'daʀ | *vt.* to reveal, to disclose

desventura | dɪʒvẽ'tura | *sf.* misfortune, misadventure; unhappiness

desviar | dɪʒvi'aʀ | *vt.* to deviate, to turn aside; to turn, to change the position of; to separate; to avert, to evade; to embezzle (money). **-d. -se** to avoid, to flee from

desvio | dɪʒ'viʋ | *sm.* deviation, deflection, detour; embezzlement

desvirtuar | dɪʒvɪʀtu'aʀ | *vt.* to disparage; to misrepresent; to pervert

detalhar | deta'LaʀF | *vt.* to detail, to particularize

detalhe | de'taLɪ | *sm.* detail, particularity

detenção | detẽ'sãw | *sf.* detention, imprisonment

deter | de'teʀ | *vt.* to detain, to hold back; to hold or keep in custody. **-d. -se** to linger; to stop

detergente | deteʀ'jẽtɪ | *sm. a.* detergent

deterioração | deteriora'sãw | *sf.* deterioration

deteriorar | deterio'raʀ | *vi.* to deteriorate, to spoil. **-d. -se** to deteriorate

determinação | deteʀmina'sãw | *sf.* determination, resolution; instruction, order

determinar | deteʀmi'naʀ | *vt.* to determine, to decide; to cause

detestar | deteʒ'taʀ | *vt.* to detest, to abhor

detestável | deteʒ'tavɪl | *a.* horrible, abominable

detetive, detective | dete(k)'tivɪ | *smf.* detective; police inspector

detidamente | dɪtida'mẽtɪ | *adv.* minutely, carefully

detonar | deto'naʀ | *vi.* to detonate

detrás | dɪ'traʒ | *adv.* behind. **-d. de** behind, in back of

detrito | de'tritʋ | *sm.* (gen. *pl.*) remains, debris

deturpar | detuʀ'paʀ | *vt.* to distort; to defile; to adulterate; to pervert

Deus | 'dewʒ | *sm.* God (also *l.c.*). -D. (me, nos etc.) livre! God forbid! -graças a D.! thanks be to God!

deusa | 'dewza | *sf.* goddess

deus-dará | dewʒda'ra | *sm.* used in the expression **ao d.** haphazardly

devagar | dɪva'gaʀ | *adv.* slowly

devanear | devanɪ'aʀ | *vi.* to day--dream, to muse

devaneio | deva'neyʋ | *sm.* day--dream, dream, reverie

devassa | de'vasa | *sf.* inquiry, judicial investigation

devassado -da | deva'sadʋ | *a.* exposed, open to public view

devassidão | devasi'dãw | *sf.* licentiousness; debauchery

devasso -sa | de'vasʋ | *smf.* libertine, debauchee / *a.* depraved, debauched

devastar | deva ʒ'taʀ | *vt.* to devastate

devedor -dora | deve'doʀ | *smf.* debtor / *a.* owing, in debt

dever | de'veʀ | *sm.* duty, obligation

deveras | dɪ'veraʒ | *adv.* truly, indeed, really

devido -da | dɪ'vidʋ | *sm.* due, debt; right / *a.* owing, due. -d. a due to

devoção | devo'sãw | *sf.* devotion

devolução | devolu'sãw | *sf.* devolution, restitution

devolver | devol'veʀ | *vt.* to return, to refund, to give back

devorar | devo'raʀ | *vt.* to devour

devotamento | devota'mẽtʋ | *sm.* devotion, dedication

devoto -ta | de'vʋtʋ | *smf.* devotee; church-goer / *a.* devout, religious

dez | 'dɛʒ | *sm. num.* ten

dezembro | de'zẽbrʋ | *sm.* December

dezena | de'zena | *sf.* ten, group of ten

dezenove | dɪze'nʋvɪ | *sm. num.*

nineteen

dezesseis | dɪze'seyʒ | *sm. num.* sixteen

dezessete | dɪze'setɪ | *sm. num.* seventeen

dezoito | dɪ'zoytʋ | *sm. num.* eighteen

dia | 'dia | *sm.* day; daytime, daylight. -andar em d. to be up to date. -até o d. de hoje to this day. -d. sim, d. não every other day. -hoje em d. today; nowadays, in our days

diabo | di'abʋ | *sm.* devil. -como o d. like the devil. -pintar o d. to raise the devil. -pobre d. poor devil

diabrura | dia'brura | *sf.* mischief of a child, deviltry

diagnóstico | diag'nʋʒtikʋ | *sm.* diagnosis

dialeto | dia'lɛtʋ | *sm.* dialect

diálogo | di'alʋgʋ | *sm.* dialogue, dialog

diamante | dia'mãtɪ | *sm.* diamond. -d. bruto rough diamond

diâmetro | di'ametrʋ | *sm.* diameter

diante | di'ãtɪ | *adv. prep.* before; in front. -daqui em d. from here on, from now on. -d. de before, in front of

dianteira | diã'teyra | *sf.* foreside, front; vanguard. -estar na d. to be ahead

diária | di'aria | *sf.* daily wages; daily expenses or rate (hotel etc.)

diário -ria | di'ariʋ | *sm.* diary; daily, journal. -d. de bordo logbook / *a.* daily

diarréia | dia'ʀeya | *sf.* diarrh(o)ea

dicção | dik'sãw | *sf.* diction

dicionário | disio'nariʋ | *sm.* dictionary

dieta | di'ɛta | *sf.* diet

difamação | difama'sãw | *sf.* libel, difamation

difamar | difa'maʀ | *vt.* to defame; (colloq.) to slander, to calumniate

diferença | dife'rēsa | *sf.* difference

diferençar | diferē'saʀ | *vt.* to differentiate, to distinguish

diferente | dife'rētι | *a.* different

diferir | difι'riʀ | *vt.* to defer, to delay / *vi.* to differ, to disagree

difícil | di'fisil | *a.* difficult

dificuldade | difikul'dadι | *sf.* difficulty; obstacle; (*pl.*) trouble

dificultar | difikul'taʀ | *vt.* to make difficult

difteria | difte'ria | *sf.* diphteria

difundir | difũ'diʀ | *vt.* to diffuse, to spread

difusão | difu'zāw | *sf.* diffusion

digerir | dijι'riʀ | *vt.* to digest

digestão | dijeζ'tāw | *sf.* digestion

dignar-se | dig'naʀsι | *vr.* to deign, to condescend

dignidade | digni'dadι | *sf.* dignity, self-respect; high office

dignitário -ria | digni'tariv | *smf.* dignitary

digno -na | 'dignv | *a.* deserving, worthy

digressão | digre'sāw | *sf.* digression

dilacerar | dilase'raʀ | *vt.* to lacerate

dilatação | dilata'sāw | *sf.* dilatation

dilatar | dila'taʀ | *vt.* to dilate, to expand; to delay. **-d. -se** to dilate

diligência | dili'jēsia | *sf.* diligence, assiduity; judicial proceeding; stage-coach

diligente | dili'jētι | *a.* diligent, active, sedulous

diluir | dilu'iʀ | *vt. vi.* to dilute / *vr.* to dissolve

dilúvio | di'luviv | *sm.* deluge, flood

dimensão | dimē'sāw | *sf.* dimension

diminuição | diminui'sāw | *sf.* diminution, decrease

diminuir | diminu'iʀ | *vt.* to diminish, to make smaller; to de-

duct, to subtract / *vi.* (also **d.-se**) to diminish, to decrease

diminutivo -va | diminu'tivv | *sm. a.* diminutive (also gram.)

dinamarquês -quesa | dinamaʀ'keζ -'keza | *smf.* Dane; *sm.* (ling.) Danish; Great Dane (dog) / *a.* Danish

dinâmica | di'namika | *sf.* dynamics

dinâmico -ca | di'namikv | *a.* dynamic, dynamical

dinamite | dina'mitι | *sf.* dynamite

dínamo | 'dinamv | *sm.* dynamo, generator

dinastia | dinaζ'tia | *sf.* dynasty

dinheiro | di'Neyrv | *sm.* money, cash, currency

diploma | di'ploma | *sm.* diploma, certificate

diplomacia | diploma'sia | *sf.* diplomacy

diplomata | diplo'mata | *smf.* diplomat

diplomático -ca | diplo'matikv | *a.* diplomatic, diplomatical

dique | 'dikι | *sm.* dike. **-d. seco** dry dock

direção | dire'sāw | *sf.* direction, way; management; course; guidance; steering wheel

direita | di'reyta | *sf.* right side, right hand; (polit.) right wing

direito -ta | di'reytv | *sm.* law; right; fairness, justice; (*pl.*) tax, duty / *a.* right

direto -ta | di'rɛtv | *a.* direct, straight; express, nonstop

diretor-tora | dire'toʀ | *smf.* director / *a.* directing

dirigente | diri'jētι | *smf.* director / *a.* directing

dirigir | diri'jiʀ | *vt.* to direct, to conduct; to drive; to address. **-d. -se** to direct oneself. **-d. -se a** to address. **-d. -se para** to go to

dirimir | diri'miʀ | *vt.* to put on an end to, to settle (questions)

discernimento | diseʀni'mētv | *sm.* discernment; discretion

disciplina | disi'plina | *sf.* discipline; course of study

disciplinar | disipli'naʀ | a. disciplinary / vt. to discipline

discipulo-la | di'sipulu |smf. disciple; follower

disco | 'diʃkʊ | sm. disc, disk; phonograph, record. **-d. voador** flying saucer

discordância | diʃkoʀ'dãsia | sf. disagreement; discordance

discordar | diʃkoʀ'daʀ | vi. to disagree, to dissent

discórdia | diʃ'kʊʀdia | sf. discord, disagreement

discorrer | diʃko'ʀeʀ | vi. to reason. **-d. sobre** or **acerca de** to discourse on or about

discoteca | diʃko'teka | sf. phonograph record collection; discothèque (dancing club)

discrepância | diʃkre'pãsia | sf. discrepancy, incongruity

discreto-ta |diʃ'kretʊ |a. discreet, judicious; tactful

discrição | diʃkri'sãw | sf. discretion, tact

discriminar |diʃkrimi'naʀ | vt. vi. to discriminate

discursar | diʃkuʀ'saʀ | vt. vi. to discourse

discurso | diʃ'kuʀsʊ | sm. speech, discourse, address

discussão | diʃku'sãw | sf. discussion; debate, dispute

discutir | diʃku'tiʀ | vt. vi. to discuss; to argue

disenteria | dizĩ te'ria | sf. dysentery

disfarçar | diʃfaʀ'saʀ | vt. to disguise, to conceal

disfarce | diʃ'faʀsɪ | sm. disguise, pretense

disforme | diʃ'fʊʀmɪ | a. deformed, distorted

disparar | diʃpa'ʀaʀ | vt. to discharge, to fire (a gun); to cast, to let fly / vi. to dash, to dart

disparatado -da | diʃpara'tadʊ |a. nonsensical, absurd

disparate | diʃpa'ʀatɪ | sm. nonsense, absurdity

disparo |diʃ'paʀʊ |sm. discharge, shot; blast-off (of a rocket)

dispêndio | diʃ'pẽdiʊ | sm. expenditure

dispendioso -sa | diʃpẽdi'ozʊ -'ɔza | a. expensive, costly

dispensa | diʃ'pẽsa | sf. exemption, dispense, dispensation

dispensar | diʃpẽ'saʀ | vt. to dispense; to exempt; to distribute; to dismiss

dispensário | diʃpẽ'sariʊ | sm. dispensary

dispersar | diʃpeʀ'saʀ | vt. vi. to disperse, to scatter

displicência | diʃpli'sẽsia | sf. negligence, carelessness

disponível |diʃpo'nivɪl | a. available, ready

dispor |diʃ'pʊʀ | vt. to dispose, to arrange, to place in order / vi. (allways followed by the *prep.* **de**) to dispose (of) / sm. only in the expression **ao seu d.** at your disposal

disposição | diʃpozi'sãw | sf. disposition (also law), arrangement; ordering, disposal; inclination

disposto -ta | diʃ'pʊʃtʊ -'pɔʃta | a. disposed, inclined

disputa | diʃ'puta | sf. dispute, quarrel; argument

disputar | diʃpu'taʀ | vt. to dispute, to contend; to struggle (compete) for

dissabor | disa'bʊʀ | sm. displeasure; vexation

dissecar | dise'kaʀ | vt. to dissect

disseminar |disemi'naʀ |vt. to disseminate, to spread

dissertação | diseʀta'sãw | sf. dissertation, essay, thesis

dissertar | diseʀ'taʀ | vi. to discourse, to give a dissertation

dissidente | disi'dẽtɪ | smf. a. dissident

dissimulação | disimula'sãw | sf. dissimulation

dissimular | disimu'laʀ | vt. vi. to dissimulate, to feign

dissipação | disipa'sãw |*sf.* dissipation; waste; dissoluteness

dissipar | disi'paʀ |*vt.* to dissipate; to waste, to squander. -d. -se to vanish

disso | 'disυ | *contr.* de + isso of that, of it. -além d. besides. -apesar d. even so

dissolução | disolu'sãw |*sf.* dissolution; dismissal (of an assembly)

dissoluto -ta | disυ'lutυ | *a.* dissolute

dissolver | disol'veʀ |*vt. vi.* (also d. -se) to dissolve

dissuadir | disua'diʀ | *vt.* to dissuade, to discourage

distância | diʒ'tãsia |*sf.* distance

distante | diʒ'tãtι | *a.* distant, far; reserved, cool

distinção | diʒtĩ'sãw | *sf.* distinction; difference; award

distinguir | diʒtĩ'giʀ | *vt.* to distinguish, to differentiate; to hono(u)r. -d. -se to distinguish oneself

distintivo -va | diʒtĩ'tivυ | *sm.* badge, emblem / *a.* distinctive, characteristic

distinto -ta | diʒ'tĩtυ | *a.* distinct; distinguished, illustrious, eminent

disto | 'diʒtυ | *contr.* de + isto of this, of it

distração | diʒtra'sãw |*sf.* distraction, abstractedness; amusement, recreation

distraído -da | diʒtra'idυ | *a.* inattentive, absent-minded

distrair | diʒtra'iʀ | *vt.* to distract, to divert; to entertain, to amuse

distribuição | diʒtribui'sãw | *sf.* distribution; arrangement

distribuir | diʒtribu'iʀ | *vt.* to distribute, to apportion, to allot

distrito | diʒ'tritυ | *sm.* district; region, section; police precinct

distúrbio | diʒ'tuʀbiυ | *sm.* disturbance; disorder

ditado | di'tadυ | *sm.* dictation; saying, proverb

ditador -dora | dita'doʀ | *smf.* dictator

ditadura | dita'dura | *sf.* dictatorship

ditar | di'taʀ |*vt. vi.* to dictate

dito | 'ditυ | *sm.* saying, sentence; witticism

ditongo | di'tõgυ | *sm.* diphthong

divã | di'vã | *sm.* couch

divagar | diva'gaʀ | *vi.* to ramble, to wander; to digress

divergência | diveʀ'jẽsia | *sf.* divergence, divergency; disagreement

divergir | diveʀ'jiʀ | *vi.* to diverge; do differ, to disagree

diversão | diveʀ'sãw | *sf.* diversion, amusement, recreation

diversidade | diveʀsi'dadι | *sf.* diversity, difference

diverso -sa | di'veʀsυ | *a.* diverse, varied; (*pl.*) various, several

divertido -da | divιʀ'tidυ | *a.* amusing, funny

divertimento | diveʀti'mẽtυ | *sm.* amusement, entertainment

divertir | diveʀ'tiʀ | *vt.* to amuse, to entertain. -d. -se to amuse oneself, to have a good time

dívida | 'divida | *sf.* debt, obligation, debit

dividendo | divi'dẽdυ |ɪ|*sm* dividend (also math., com.), bonus

dividir | divi'diʀ | *vt.* to divide, to split

divino -na | di'vinυ | *a.* divine, heavenly

divisa | di'viza |*sf.* motto, legend, slogan; boundary; (*pl.*) foreign exchange credits; (mil.) stripes

divisão | divi'zãw |*sf.* division (also arith., mil.), separation; section

divisar | divi'zaʀ |*vt.* to discern; to catch a glimpse of

divorciar | divoʀsi'aʀ |*vt.* to divorce; to separate. -d. -se to divorce, to get divorced

divórcio | di'voʀsiυ |*sm.* divorce

divulgar | divul'gaʀ |*vt.* to divulge, to disclose; to propagate, to publicize

dizer | di'zeʀ | *sm.* a saying; manner of speech; (*pl.*) inscription / *vt.* to say, to speak; to tell; to signify. **-d. -se** to call oneself. **-digamos** let's say, shall we say. **-quer d.** that is to say / *vi.* to say, to speak. **-por assim d.** so to speak. **-como disse?** I beg your pardon?

do | 'dʊ | *contr.* **de** + **o** of the, from the; of what

dó | 'dɔ | *sm.* (mus.) C, do; pity, mercy; compassion

doação | dʊa'sãw | *sf.* donation, gift, benefaction

doar | dʊ'aʀ | *vt. vi.* to donate, to bestow

dobra | 'dɔbra | *sf.* fold; corrugation; act of folding

dobradiça | dobra'disa | *sf.* hinge, joint

dobrar | do'braʀ | *vt.* to double; to fold; to flex; to round (corner, cape) / *vi.* to double, to duplicate; to toll

dobro | 'dobrʊ | *sm.* double

doca | 'dɔka | *sf.* dock

doce | 'dɔsɪ | *sm.* candy, confection / *a.* sweet; mild; pleasant; fresh (said of water); melodious

docente | do'sẽtɪ | *smf.* professor / *a.* teaching. **-corpo d.** teaching staff

dócil | 'dɔsil | *a.* docile

documentação | dʊkumẽta'sãw | *sf.* documentation; document

documento | dʊku'mẽtʊ | *sm.* document, paper

doçura | dʊ'sura | *sf.* sweetness; gentleness

doença | dʊ'ẽsa | *sf.* illness, sickness, ailment; disease

doente | dʊ'ẽtɪ | *smf.* sick person, patient / *a.* ill, sick

doentio -tia | dʊẽ'tiʊ | *a.* sickly, morbid, unhealthy

doer | dʊ'eʀ | *vi.* to hurt, to ache. **-d. -se** to feel sorry; to feel offended

dogmático -ca | dog'matikʊ | *a.* dogmatic

doidice | doy'disɪ | *sf.* madness, foolishness, folly

doido -da | 'doydʊ | *smf.* (colloq.) a demented person / *a.* mad, insane, crazy

dois | 'doyʃ | *sm. num.* two

dólar | 'dɔlaʀ | *sm.* dollar

doloroso -sa | dolo'rozʊ -'rɔza | *a.* painful, aching; grievous, afflicting, sorrowful

doloso -sa | do'lozʊ -'lɔza | *a.* (law) deliberated misfeading

dom | 'dõ | *sm.* gift, endowment; Dom (honorific title)

domar | do'maʀ | *vt.* to tame, to subdue

domesticar | domeʃti'kaʀ | *vt.* to domesticate

doméstico -ca | do'mɛʃtikʊ | *smf.* servant / *a.* domestic

domicílio | dʊmi'siliʊ | *sm.* domicile, residence

dominação | domina'sãw | *sf.* domination

dominante | domi'nãtɪ | *a.* dominant, predominant; prevailing

dominar | domi'naʀ | *vt.* to dominate, to control; to overcome; to overlook (as from a superior position). **-d. -se** to control oneself

domingo | dʊ'mĩgʊ | *sm.* Sunday

domínio | do'miniʊ | *sm.* dominion, domain, domination; control

dona | 'dona | *sf.* owner; lady (also *cap.*); title before Christian name of a woman

dona-de-casa | donadɪ'kaza | *sf.* housewife

donativo | dona'tivʊ | *sm.* donation, gift

donde | 'dõdɪ | *adv.* from where, whence

dono -na | 'donʊ | *smf.* owner, proprietor; V. *dona*

dor | 'doʀ | *sf.* pain, ache; grief, sorrow

doravante | dora'vãtɪ | *adv.* henceforth, from now on

dormir | dʊʀ'miʀ | *vi.* to sleep. **-d. a sono solto** to sleep very soundly

dormitar | dʊʀmi'taʀ | *vi.* to doze

dormitório | dʊʀmi'tʊʀiʋ | *sm.* dormitory

dosar | do'zaʀ | *vt.* to dose

dose | 'dɔzι | *sf.* dose

dossel | do'sεl | *sm.* canopy

dotar | do'taʀ | *vt.* to endow; to give as a dowry

dote | 'dɔtι | *sm.* dowry; *(pl.)* natural gifty

dourar | dow'ʀaʀ | *vt.* to gild; (cookery) to brown

douto -ta | 'dowtʋ | *a.* learned, erudite

doutor-tora | dow'toʀ | *smf.* doctor (title given to any person holding a university degree)

doutorado | dowto'ʀadʋ | *sm.* doctorate

doutrina | dow'trina | *sf.* doctrine

doutrinar | dowtri'naʀ | *vt.* to indoctrinate

doze | 'dozι | *sm. num.* twelve

draga | 'dʀaga | *sf.* dredge

dragão | dʀa'gãw | *sm.* dragon; (mil.) dragoon

drama | 'dʀama | *sm.* drama

dramaturgo -ga | dʀama'tuʀgʋ | *smf.* dramatist, playwright

drenar | dʀe'naʀ | *vt.* to drain

droga | 'dʀɔga | *sf.* drug; (colloq.) any worthless thing, trash, junk. **-dar em d.** (colloq.) to come to naught

drogaria | dʀoga'ʀia | *sf.* pharmacy (selling medicines but no compound drugs)

duas | 'duaʃ | *sf. a.* two

dúbio -bia | 'dubiʋ | *a.* dubious, ambiguous

dublagem | du'blajẽy | *sf.* (cine., TV) dub, dubbing

ducha | 'duxa | *sf.* shower bath

duelo | du'εlʋ | *sm.* duel

dueto | du'etʋ | *sm.* (mus.) duet

duna | 'duna | *sf.* dune, sand dune

dupla | 'dupla | *sf.* couple

duplicar | dupli'kaʀ | *vt. vi.* to duplicate

duplicata | dupli'kata | *sf.* a duplicate copy; a certified and negotiable copy of an invoice

duplicidade | duplisi'dadι | *sf.* duplicity

duplo -pla | 'duplʋ | *sm.* double, duplication / *a.* double

duque -sa | 'dukι -'keza | *sm.* duke ; *sf.* duchess

duração | dura'sãw | *sf.* duration

durante | du'ʀãtι | *prep.* during

durar | du'ʀaʀ | *vi.* to last, to be durable; to continue

durável | du'ʀavιl | *a.* durable, lasting

dureza | du'ʀeza | *sf.* hardness; rigo(u)r, severity

duro -ra | 'durʋ | *a.* hard; severe

dúvida | 'duvida | *sf.* doubt, uncertainty; disbelief; hesitation

duvidar | duvi'daʀ | *vt. vi.* to doubt

duvidoso -sa | duvi'dozʋ -'dɔza | *a.* doubtful; questionable; suspicious

duzentos -tas | du'zẽtʋʃ | *smf. num.* two hundred

dúzia, 'duzia , *sf.* dozen. **-às dúzias** by dozens. **-d. de frade** baker's dozen. **-meia d.** half dozen, small quantity

E

e | ι | *conj.* and

ébano | 'εbanʋ | *sm.* ebony

ébrio -bria | 'εbriʋ | *a.* drunk, intoxicated

ebulição | ιbuli'sãw | *sf.* ebullience; boiling

eclipse | e'klipsι | *sm.* eclipse

eclosão | eklo'zãw | *sf.* emergence;

hatching

eco | 'ɛkʊ | *sm.* echo

economia | ekono'mia | *sf.* economy; thrift; (*pl.*) savings. **-fazer economias** to save

econômico -ca | eko'nomikʊ | *a.* economic; economical; inexpensive

economista | ekono'miʃta | *smf.* economist

ecumênico -ca | ɪku'menikʊ | *a.* ecumenical, universal

edição | ɪdi'sãw | *sf.* publication (of a book etc.); edition, issue

edificação | ɪdifika'sãw | *sf.* building, construction; edification (moral)

edificar | ɪdifi'kaʀ | *vt.* to construct, to build; to edify

edifício | ɪdi'fisiʊ | *sm.* building, edifice; apartment house

edital | ɪdi'tal | *sm.* (law) official notice

editar | ɪdi'taʀ | *vt.* to publish, to print (books etc.)

édito | 'ɛditʊ | *sm.* public (published) legal notice, proclamation or court order

edito | e'ditʊ | *sm.* edict, decree

editor -tora | ɪdi'toʀ | *smf.* publisher; editor; *sf.* publishing house / *a.* publishing

educação | ɪduka'sãw | *sf.* education, instruction; upbringing; good manners

educar | ɪdu'kaʀ | *vt.* to educate; to bring up

efeito | e'feytʊ | *sm.* effect; result, purpose. **-com e.** in fact, as a matter of fact

efervescente | efeʀve'sẽtɪ | *a.* effervescent

efetuar | efetu'aʀ | *vt.* to accomplish, to achieve, to bring about. **-e.-se** to take place

eficácia | efi'kasia | *sf.* efficacy, effectiveness

eficaz | efi'kaʃ | *a.* effective; powerful

eficiência | efisi'ẽsia | *sf.* efficiency

eficiente | efisi'ẽtɪ | *a.* efficient

efusivo -va | efu'zivʊ | *a.* effusive, expansive

égide | 'ɛʒidɪ | *sf.* sponsorship, patronage

egípcio -cia | ɪ'jipsiʊ | *smf. a.* Egyptian

egoísmo | ego'iʒmʊ | *sm.* egoism, selfishness

egoísta | ego'iʃta | *smf.* egoist / *a.* egoistic, selfish

égua | 'ɛgwa | *sf.* mare

eis | 'eyʃ | *adv.* here is, here are; behold

eixo | 'eyxʊ | *sm.* axle, shaft; axis

ela | 'ɛla | *pron. f.* she, it; (*pl.*) they

elaboração | elabora'sãw | *sf.* elaboration, development

elaborar | elabo'raʀ | *vt.* to elaborate, to organize, to develop

elasticidade | elaʃtisi'dadɪ | *sf.* elasticity

elástico -ca | e'laʃtikʊ | *sm.* rubber band / *a.* elastic

ele | 'elɪ | *pron. m.* he, it; (*pl.*) they

electri-, electro- V. formas em **eletri-, eletro-**

elefante -ta | ele'fãtɪ | *smf.* elephant

elegância | ele'gãsia | *sf.* elegance

elegante | ele'gãtɪ | *a.* elegant, graceful; smart; refined

eleger | ele'jeʀ | *vt.* to elect (by vote); to choose

eleição | eley'sãw | *sf.* election; choice

eleito -ta | e'leytʊ | *smf.* elected, chosen person / *a.* elected, chosen

eleitor -tora | eley'toʀ | *smf.* elector, voter

eleitorado | eleyto'radʊ | *sm.* electorate

elementar | elemẽ'taʀ | *a.* elementary

elemento | ele'mẽtʊ | *sm.* element; constituent, ingredient, component (part)

elenco | e'lẽkʊ | *sm.* (theat.) cast; list, index

eletricidade | eletrisi'dadɪ | *sf.* electricity

eletricista | eletri'siʒta | smf. electrician / a. electrical

elétrico -ca | e'lɛtrikʊ | a. electric

eletrificar | elɪtrifi'kaʀ | vt. to electrify

eletrizar | elɪtri'zaʀ | vt. to electrify, to thrill. **-e.-se** to be electrified

eletrônica | ele'tronika | sf. electronics

eletrônico -ca | ele'tronikʊ | a. electronic

elevação | eleva'sãw | sf. elevation; height; altitude

elevador | eleva'doʀ | sm. lift, elevator

elevar | ele'vaʀ | vt. to raise; to erect; to augment, to increase (prices etc.). **-e.-se** to rise; to exalt oneself

eliminação | ɪlimina'sãw | sf. elimination

eliminar | ɪlimi'naʀ | vt. to eliminate

elo | 'ɛlʊ | sm. link

elogiar | elʊji'aʀ | vt. to praise; to extol

elogio | elʊ'jiʊ | sm. praise; eulogy

eloqüência | elo'kwẽsia | sf. eloquence

eloqüente | elo'kwẽtɪ | a. eloquent

elucidação | ɪlusida'sãw | sf. elucidation, explanation

elucidar | ɪlusi'daʀ | vt. to elucidate, to clarify

em | ẽỹĩ | prep. in, into, on, by, at

emagrecer | ɪmagre'seʀ | vt. to make thin / vi. to reduce, to lose weight

emanar | ema'naʀ | vi. to emanate

emancipar | ɪmãsi'paʀ | vt. to emancipate

emaranhar | emara'naʀ | vt. to entangle; to complicate. **-e.-se** to become entangled

embaçar | ĩ ba'saʀ | vt. to blur, to dim. **-e.-se** to become dimmed

embainhar | ĩ bai'naʀ | vt. to sheathe (a sword); to hem (a garment or piece of cloth)

embaixada | ĩbay'xada | sf. embassy; ambassadorship

embaixador -dora | ĩ bayxa'doʀ | sm. ambassador; sf. ambassadress

embaixatriz | ĩbayxa'triʒ | sf. wife of the ambassador; ambassadress

embaixo | ĩ'bayxʊ | adv. under, underneath, down, below. **-lá e.** down below, downstairs

embalagem | ĩba'lajẽy | sf. packaging

embalar | ĩba'laʀ | vt. to lull to sleep; to pack (goods); to accelerate (vehicle); (mil.) to load (rifle or hand-gun)

embalsamar | ĩbalsa'maʀ | vt. to embalm

embaraçar | ĩbara'saʀ | vt. to embarrass; to obstruct; to entangle

embaraço | ĩba'rasʊ | sm. embarrassment; entanglement; obstacle

embarcação | ĩbaʀka'sãw | sf. boat

embarcadiço | ĩbaʀka'disʊ | sm. seafarer, seafaring (man)

embarcar | ĩbaʀ'kaʀ | vt. to put on board, to load / vi. to embark

embargo | ĩ'baʀgʊ | sm. embargo, hindrance; (law) attachment

embarque | ĩ'baʀkɪ | sm. embarkation; shipment (of goods)

embasbacar | ĩbaʒba'kaʀ | vt. to stupefy. **-e.-se** to be stupefied / vi. to be stupefied, to be flabbergasted

embate | ĩ'batɪ | sm. impact; collision

embebedar | ĩbebe'daʀ | vt. to make drunk. **-e.-se** to get drunk

embeber | ĩbe'beʀ | vt. to soak; to plunge (a dagger etc.) in. **-e.-se** to become absorbed of

embelezar | ĩbele'zaʀ | vt. to embellish, to beautify. **-e.-se** to adorn oneself

embevecer | ĩbeve'seʀ | vt. to enrapture; to ravish. **-e.-se** to be enraptured

embirrar | ĩbi'RaR | vi. (used with prep. **com**) to dislike, to show aversion (for)

emblema | ĩ'blema | sm. emblem, badge

embocadura | ĩboka'dura | sf. (mus.) mouthpiece; bit (of a bridle); mouth (of a river)

êmbolo | 'ẽbulu | sm. piston

embolsar | ĩbol'saR | vt. to pocket

embora | ĩ'bwra | adv. even so / conj. though, although. -ir(-se) e. to go away

emboscada | ĩboʃ'kada | sf. ambush

embotar | ĩbo'taR | vt. to blunt, to dull

embranquecer | ĩbrãke'seR | vt. to whiten, to make white / vi. (also e.-se) to grow white

embreagem | ĩbre'ajẽy | sf. (mech.) clutch

embrenhar-se | ĩbre'naRsι | vr. to penetrate deep into the woods

embriagar | ĩbria'gaR | vt. to make drunk. -e.-se to become drunk

embriaguez | ĩbria'geʒ | sf. drunkeness

embrião | ĩbri'ãw | sm. embryo

embromar | ĩbro'maR | vt. (colloq.) to cheat, to swindle

embrulhar | ĩbru'LaR | vt. to wrap up, to pack up; to complicate; to upset (the stomach); (colloq.) to cheat

embrulho | ĩ'bruLu | sm. package, parcel; (colloq.) confusion; (colloq.) swindle

embrutecer | ĩbrute'seR | vt. to stupidify. -e.-se to become brutish, to grow stupid

emburrar | ĩbu'RaR | vi. (colloq.) to sulk

embuste | ĩ'buʃtι •| sm. hoax, fraud

embusteiro -ra | ĩbuʒ'teyru | smf. deceiver, swindler, impostor

embutido-da | ĩbu'tidu | sm. inlay work, mosaic / a. built in

emenda | ι'mẽda | sf. correction; splice; amendment (also law)

emendar | ιmẽ'daR | vt. to amend, to correct; to splice. -e.-se to repent, to mend one's ways

emergência | emeR'jẽsia | sf. emergency; emergence

emergir | emeR'jiR | vi. to emerge, to arise; to rise out of

emigração | emigra'sãw | sf. emigration; (zool.) migration

emigrante | emi'grãtι | smf. a. emigrant

emigrar | emi'graR | vi. to emigrate; (zool.) to migrate

eminência | emi'nẽsia | sf. eminence, height; (cap.) Eminence (a cardinal's title)

eminente | emi'nẽtι | a. eminent; outstanding

emissão | emi'sãw | sf. emission; (rad.) broadcast; issue of paper currency

emissora | emi'sora | sf. radio station, broadcasting station

emitir | emi'tiR | vt. to emit; to issue (bank notes etc.)

emoção | emo'sãw | sf. emotion

emocionante | emosio'nãtι | a. moving; exciting

emocionar | emosio'naR | vt. to move; to thrill. -e.-se to be moved

emoldurar | emoldu'raR | vt. to frame

empacotar | ĩpako'taR | vt. to pack up, to wrap up; to package; to bale, to put into a bundle; to incase, to box

empada | ĩ'pada | sf. patty; pastry filled with meat or shrimp or fish or the like; (colloq.) meddlesome person

empáfia | ĩ'pafya | sf. haughtiness; pride, arrogance, self-esteem, conceit; presumption; conceited person

empalar | ĩpa'laR | vt. to impale; (fig.) to torture

empalhador -dora | ĩpaLa'doR | sm. person who covers or packs or stuffs with straw; cane-worker / a. lazy, idle, truant

empalhar | ĩpa'LaR | *vt.* to pack with straw (fruits etc.); to stuff with straw (animals); to cover with straw (bottles, glasses); to put straw seats in chairs; (fig.) to delay, to defer, to procrastinate

empalidecer | ĩpalide'seR | *vi.* to become pale; to blanch; (fig.) to fade

empalmador -dora | ĩpalma'doR | *sm.* palmer, prestidigitator; pilferer, thief, swindler

empalmar | ĩpal'maR | *vt.* to palm, to snatch, to hide in the hand

empanar | ĩpa'naR | *vt.* to dull, to tarnish

empanturrar | ĩpãtu'RaR | *vt.* to stuff, to gorge (with food). -e.-se to gorge, to glut

empanzinar | ĩpãzi'naR | *vt.* to surfeit, to stuff, to glut, to gorge. -e.-se to fill one's bell, to eat one's fill

empapar | ĩpa'paR | *vt.* to soak, to drench

empapelar | ĩpape'laR | *vt.* to wrap in paper, to pack up in parcels; to paper (wall)

empapuçado -da | ĩpapu'sadʋ | *a.* pounchy, puffed up, swollen

emparedar | ĩpare'daR | *vt.* to wall in, to cloister, to shut up between walls

emparelhar | ĩpare'LaR | *vt.vi.* to pair, to couple, to yoke, to make equal or alike; to match, to mate; to fit, to suit, to make suitable; to resemble, to be like, to be similar; to stand on a par

empatar | ĩpa'taR | *vt.* to stalemate; to tie (a score etc.); to tie up (money) in an investment; to snell (on a fish-hook)

empate | ĩ'patɩ | *sm.* tie, stalemate; parity (of votes); snell

(on a fish-hook). -e. de capital money tied-up in investment

empedernido -da | ĩpedeR'nidʋ | *a.* hardened; heartless

empedrar | ĩpe'draR | *vt.* to pave; to cover with stones

empenar | ĩpe'naR | *vi.* to become covered with feathers; to warp, to take a set

empenhar | ĩpe'NaR | *vt.* to pawn. -e.-se to run into debt; (fig.) to strive, to make every effort. -e. a palavra to pledge one's word

empenho | ĩ'peNʋ | *sm.* pawn; pledge, promise; perseverance; zeal

emperrar | ĩpe'RaR | *vi.* to stick, to jam

empertigar-se | ĩpeRti'gaRsɩ | *vr.* to stand up straight; to become haughty

empilhar | ĩpi'LaR | *vt.* to pile, to heap up; to amass

emplacar | ĩpla'kaR | *vt.* to register (a vehicle)

emplastro | ĩ'plaʃtrʋ | *sm.* (phar.) plaster

empobrecer | ĩpobre'seR | *vt.* to impoverish / *vi.* to become poor

empobrecimento | ĩpobrɩsi'mẽtʋ | *sm.* impoverishment

empoeirar-se | ĩpʋey'raRsɩ | *vr.* to become dust-covered

empola | ĩ'pola | *sf.* blister

empolgante | ĩpol'gãtɩ | *a.* breath-taking, exciting

empolgar | ĩpol'gaR | *vt.* to grasp; to absorb, to enrapture

empossar | ĩpo'saR | *vt.* to install in office. -e.-se to assume office

empreendimento | ĩprɩẽdi'mẽtʋ | *sm.* undertaking, enterprise

empregado -da | ĩpre'gadʋ | *smf.* employee; servant; *sf.* housemaid / *a.* used, employed

empregar | ĩpre'gaR | *vt.* to employ; to invest, to spend (time, money etc.). -e.-se to get a job

emprego | ĩ'pregʋ | *sm.* job, occupation; use, usage

empreitada | ĩprey'tada | *sf.* contract work

empreiteiro | ĩprey'teyrυ | *sm.* contractor

empresa | ĩ 'preza | *sf.* enterprise; firm, company

empresário -ria | ĩpre'zariυ | *smf.* (theat.) impresario; owner of a business enterprise

emprestar | ĩpreʒ'taʀ | *vt.* to lend, to loan; to impart

empréstimo | ĩ'preʒtimυ | *sm.* loan; lending; borrowing

empunhar | ĩpu'ɴaʀ | *vt.* to grasp, to hold by the handle

empurrão | ĩpu'ʀãw | *sm.* push, shove. **-aos empurrões** violently, forcibly

empurrar | ĩpu'ʀaʀ | *vt.* to push, to shove

emudecer | ɪmude'seʀ | *vt.* to silence / *ví.* to grow mute; to be silent

enaltecer | ɪnalte'seʀ | *vt.* to exalt

enamorado -da | ɪnamo'radυ | *a.* in love

encadeamento | ĩkadɪa'mẽtυ | *sm.* connection, concatenation

encadear | ĩkadɪ'aʀ | *vt.* to enchain; to subjugate; to link. **-e.-se** to form a chain, to form a series

encadernação | ĩkadeʀna'sãw | *sf.* bookbinding

encaixar | ĩkay'xaʀ | *vt.* to fit or to set one part into another; to mortise / *vi.* to fit perfectly

encaixe | ĩ'kayxɪ | *sm.* mortise, socket

encaixotar | ĩkayxo'taʀ | *vt.* to box, to pack in boxes

encalço | ĩ'kalsυ | *sm.* pursuit. **-ir ao e. de** to be on the heels or track (of)

encalhar | ĩka'LaʀR | *vt.* (naut.) to run ashore / *vi.* to beach, to run ashore; to get stuck (said of unsold merchandise)

encaminhar | ĩkami'ɴaʀ | *vt.* to guide; to orientate. **-e.-se** to make one's way (to)

encanamento | ĩkana'mẽtυ | *sm.* plumbing, piping

encanecer | ĩkane'seʀ | *vi.* to grow grey (with age)

encantamento | ĩkãta'mẽtυ | *sm.* charm; incantation, magic

encantar | ĩkã'taʀ | *vt.* to enchant; to delight; to charm, to fascinate

encanto | ĩ'kãtυ | *sm.* grace, loveliness; appeal, allurement

encapelar | ĩkape'laʀ | *vi.* to become rough (the sea). **-e.-se** to rise (the sea)

encarar | ĩka'raʀ | *vt.* to face; to look straight at

encarcerar | ĩkaʀse'raʀ | *vt.* to incarcerate, to imprison

encarecer | ĩkare'seʀ | *vt.* to raise the price of; to stress / *vi.* to increase in price

encargo | ĩ'kaʀgυ | *sm.* responsibility, burden; mission

encarnação | ĩkaʀna'sãw | *sf.* incarnation

encarnado -da | ĩkaʀ'nadυ | *a.* incarnate; red. scarlet

encarniçado -da | ĩkaʀni'sadυ | *a.* bloodthirsty, sanguinary; cruel

encarregado -da | ĩkaʀe'gadυ | *smf.* person in charge, foreman / *a.* in charge (of), intrusted (with)

encarregar | ĩkaʀe'gaʀ | *vt.* to put in charge of; to entrust with. **-e.-se** to take upon oneself

encenação | ĩsena'sãw | *sf.* (theat., TV) staging; acting up

encenar | ĩse'naʀ | *vt.* to stage (a play)

enceradeira | ĩsera'deyra | *sf.* floor polisher or waxer (machine)

encerar | ĩse'raʀ | *vt.* to wax

encerramento | ĩseʀa'mẽtυ | *sm.* closing, conclusion; confinement

encerrar | ĩse'ʀaʀ | *vt.* to contain, to encompass; to confine; to terminate. **-e.-se** to terminate; to shut oneself up

encetar | ĩse'taʀ | *vt.* to begin, to start

encharcar | ĩxaR'kaR| *vt.* to drench, to soak. **-e.-se** to become drenched

enchente | ĩ'xẽtι | *sf.* flood; a full house

encher | ĩ'xeR | *vt.* to fill, to fill up / *vi.* to fill up; to overflow; (slang) to bore someone

enchimento | ĩxi'mẽtυ | *sm.* filling, filler, stuffing

enchova | ĩ'xova | *sf.* (ichth.) bluefish

enciclopédia | ĩsiklo'pεdia | *sf.* encyclopaedia

encoberto -ta | ĩkυ'bεRtυ | *a.* concealed; dull, overcast (sky)

encobrir | ĩkυ'briR | *vt.* to hide, to conceal / *vr.* to cloud, to darken (sky)

encolerizar | ĩkoleri'zaR | *vt.* to anger, to make angry. **-e.-se** to become angry

encolher | ĩko'LeR | *vi.* to shrink, to contract, to diminish

encomenda | ĩko'mẽda | *sf.* order (for goods); object ordered. **-feito de e.** made to order

encomendar | ĩkomẽ'daR | *vt.* to order (something) to be made or sent

encontrar | ĩkõ'traR | *vt.* to meet, to encounter; to find

encontro | ĩ'kõtrυ | *sm.* encounter, meeting; date; engagement

encorajar | ĩkora'jaR | *vt.* to encourage

encosta | ĩ'kωζta | *sf.* slope, hillside

encostar | ĩkoζ'taR | *vt.* to lean on; to place against; to touch; to pull up (a vehicle). **-e.-se** to lean on

encosto | ĩ'koζtυ | *sm.* support; back of a chair

encrenca | ĩ'krẽka | *sf.* snag, difficulty; confusion

encrespar | ĩkreζ'paR | *vt.* to curl; to ripple (the sea). **-e.-se** to become curly; to become rough (the sea); (fig.) to become irritated

encruzilhada | ĩkruzi'Lada | *sf.* crossroads

encurralar | ĩkυra'laR | *vt.* to fence in, to drive into a corner

encurtar | ĩkυR'taR | *vt.* to shorten, to curtail

endereçar | ĩdere'saR | *vt.* to address (a letter etc.); to direct

endereço | ĩde'resυ | *sm.* address

endiabrado | ĩdia'bradυ | *a.* devilish; mischievous

endireitar | ĩdirey'taR | *vt.* to straighten (out); to rectify, to correct; to repair. **-e.-se** to straighten oneself up

endividar | ĩdivi'daR | *vt.* to make one run into debt. **-e.-se** to run into debt

endoidecer | ĩdoyde'seR | *vt.* to madden / *vi.* to go mad

endossar | ĩdo'saR | *vt.* to endorse

endosso | ĩ'dosυ | *sm.* endorsement

endurecer | ĩdure'seR | *vt. vi.* to harden

energia | eneR'jia | *sf.* energy, strength; drive

enérgico -ca | e'nεRjikυ | *a.* energetic, vigorous, active

enervante | eneR'vãtι | *a.* enervating, nerve-racking

enevoar | enevυ'aR | *vt.* to mist; to darken; to dim, to blur

enfadar | ĩfa'daR | *vt.* to bore; to annoy. **-e.-se** (with *prep.* com or de) to be bored (with)

enfado | ĩ'fadυ | *sm.* boredom, weariness, tediousness

enfadonho -nha | ĩfa'doNυ | *a.* boring, tiresome, tedious

enfaixar | ĩfay'xaR | *vt.* to bandage; to band, to belt

enfaro | ĩ'farυ | *sm.* disgust, aversion (to food), repugnance

enfarte | ĩ'faRtι | *sm.* (med.) infarct

ênfase | 'ẽfazι | *sm.* emphasis

enfastiar | ĩfaζti'aR | *vt.* to weary, to bore; to annoy. **-e.-se** to be bored (with)

enfático -ca | ĩ'fatikυ | *a.* emphatic

enfeitar | ĩ fey'taR | *vt.* to adorn, to

embellish. **-e.-se** to adorn oneself

enfeite | ĩ'feytɩ | *sm.* ornament, trimming

enfeitiçar | ĩfeyti'saʀ | *vt.* to bewitch

enfeixar | ĩfey'xaʀ | *vt.* to bundle; to bunch, to clump (together)

enfermaria | ĩfeʀma'ria | *sf.* infirmary; hospital ward

enfermeiro -ra | ĩfeʀ'meyrʋ | *smf.* nurse

enfermidade | ĩfeʀmi'dadɩ | *sf.* illness, disease, sickness

enfermo -ma | ĩ'feʀmʋ | *smf.* sick person, patient / *a.* sick, ill

enferrujar | ĩfeʀu'jaʀ | *vi.* to rust

enfezar | ĩfe'zaʀ | *vt.* to dwarf; to peeve. **-e.-se** to decay; to become peeved

enfiada | ĩfi'ada | *sf.* string, row; series (of things, happenings etc.). **-de e.** in a row

enfiar | ĩfi'aʀ | *vt.* to thread, to string; to slip on; to pierce (as with a sword). **-e. em** to insert in

enfileirar | ĩfiley'raʀ | *vt.* to line up

enfim | ĩ'fĩ | *adv.* at last, finally; in short; after all. **-até que e.** at last

enforcar | ĩfoʀ'kaʀ | *vt.* to hang

enfraquecer | ĩfrake'seʀ | *vt.* to weaken / *vi.* to weaken, to go feeble

enfrentar | ĩfrẽ'taʀ | *vt.* to face; to brave, to defy

enfurecer | ĩfure'seʀ | *vt.* to infuriate, to enrage. **-e.-se** to become furious

enganar | ĩga'naʀ | *vt.* to deceive, to fool; to seduce. **-e.-se** to fool oneself; to make a mistake

engano | ĩ'ganʋ | *sm.* error, mistake, oversight; delusion, fraud

engarrafamento | ĩgarafa'mẽtʋ | *sm.* process of bottling. **-e. de trânsito** traffic jam

engarrafar | ĩgara'faʀ | *vt.* to bottle (up) / *vi.* to jam (traffic)

engasgar | ĩgaʒ'gaʀ | *vi.* to swallow the wrong way; to choke

engastar | ĩgaʒ'taʀ | *vt.* to set (precious stone)

engaste | ĩ'gaʒtɩ | *sm.* setting, mounting (of gems)

engatar | ĩga'taʀ | *vt.* to couple together (as railway cars); to fasten together (with a clamp)

engatilhar | ĩgati'laʀ | *vt.* to cock (a gun)

engatinhar | ĩgati'naʀ | *vi.* to crawl (on hands and knees)

engelhar | ĩje'laʀ | *vt. vi.* to wrinkle

engendrar | ĩjẽ'draʀ | *vt.* to engender, to beget; to hatch (a plot)

engenharia | ĩjena'ria | *sf.* engineering

engenheiro -ra | ĩje'neyrʋ | *smf.* engineer

engenho | ĩ'jenʋ | *sm.* ingenuity, inventiveness; machine; sugar-mill

engenhoca | ĩje'nɔka | *sf.* gadget, any simple mechanical apparatus

engenhoso -sa | ĩje'nozʋ -'nɔza | *a.* ingenious, inventive; resourceful; clever

engessar | ĩje'saʀ | *vt.* to plaster; to put in a plaster cast

englobar | ĩglo'baʀ | *vt.* to gather in a whole; to embody

engodo | ĩ'godʋ | *sm.* ground-bait; allurement

engolir | ĩgʋ'liʀ | *vt.* to swallow

engomar | ĩgo'maʀ | *vt.* to starch and iron clothes

engordar | ĩgoʀ'daʀ | *vt.* to fatten / *vi.* to gain weight, to become fat

engraçado -da | ĩgra'sadʋ | *a.* funny, comical; spirited, witted

engrandecer | ĩgrãde'seʀ | *vt.* to aggrandize; to enlarge; to hono(u)r, to exalt / *vi.* to become powerful or rich or famous

engravidar | ĩgravi'daʀ | *vt.* to make pregnant / *vi.* to be or to become pregnant

engraxar | ĩgra'xaR | *vt.* to grease; to shine (shoes)

engraxate | ĩgra'xatɩ | *sm.* shoe-black, bootblack

engrenagem |ĩgre'nájēy |*sf.* gear, gearings

engrenar |ĩgre'naR |*vt.* to gear, to mesh, to throw in gear

engrossar | ĩgro'saR | *vt.* to thicken / *vi.* to thicken; to grow stronger; (slang) to become rude

enguia |ĩ'gia |*sf.* eel

enguiçar | ĩgi'saR | *vi.* to break down, to be out of order (car, machine etc.)

enguiço | ĩ'gisʊ |*sm.* breakdown (of a motor); impediment, snag

enjaular |ĩjaw'laR |*vt..*to cage

enjeitado -da | ĩjey'tadʊ | *smf.* foundling / *a.* rejected

enjeitar |ĩjey'taR | *vt.* to reject, to repudiate; to abandon (a child)

enjoar |ĩjʊ'aR | *vt.* to nauseate, to sicken / *vi.* to be seasick

enjôo |ĩ'jоʊ |*sm.* nausea, seasickness; boredom

enlaçar |ĩla'saR |*vt.* to entwine, to enlace; to bind, to tie

enlace | ĩ'lasɩ | *sm.* enlacement, concatenation; marriage

enlatar |ĩla'taR | *vt.* to can (foods etc.)

enlear |ĩlɩ'aR | *vt.* to confuse, to perplex; to bind

enleio |ĩ'leyʊ |*sm.* entanglement; embarrassment

enlevo | ĩ'levʊ | *sm.* rapture, enchantment

enlouquecer | ĩlowke'seR | *vt.* to madden, to drive insane / *vi.* to go mad

enobrecer | ɩnobre'seR | *vt.* to ennoble

enojar |ɩno'jaR | *vt.* to disgust, to nauseate

enorme |ɩ'nʊRmɩ | *a.* enormous

enormidade | ɩnɔRmi'dadɩ | *sf.* enormity

enovelar | ɩnove'laR | *vt.* to wind (thread) in a ball

enquadrar | ĩkwa'draR | *vt.* to frame

enquanto | ĩ'kwãtʊ | *conj.* while; as long as. **-por e.** for the time being

enraivecido -da | ĩRayvɩ'sidʊ | *a.* infuriated, furious

enraizado -da | ĩRai'zadʊ | *a.* rooted; inveterate, deep--rooted

enredar |ĩRe'daR |*vt.* to net; to entangle; to embroil (in plot)

enredo | ĩ'Redʊ | *sm.* (theat., lit.) plot; intrigue

enrijar |ĩRi'jaR | *vt. vi.* to harden

enriquecer | ĩRike'seR | *vt.* to enrich / *vi.* to become rich

enrolar | ĩRo'laR | *vt.* to wind, to roll up; to twist; (colloq.) to confuse

enroscar |ĩRoʃ'kaR| *vt.* to twist; to screw (a nut); to wind around

enrugar | ĩRu'gaR | *vt.* to wrinkle, to crease

ensaboar | ĩsabʊ'aR | *vt.* to soap, to lather

ensaiar | ĩsay'aR | *vt.* to rehearse; to experiment, to test

ensaio | ĩ'sayʊ | *sm.* test, trial; attempt; (theat.) rehearsal; (lit.) essay

ensaísta |ĩsa'iʃta | *smf.* essayist

ensangüentar | ĩsãgwẽ'taR | *vt.* to stain with blood

enseada | ĩsɩ'ada | *sf.* small bay, inlet

ensejo | ĩ'sejʊ | *sm.* opportunity, occasion

ensinar | ĩsi'naR | *vt.* to teach, to instruct; to show (where etc.)

ensino | ĩ'sinʊ | *sm.* teaching, instruction, education

ensolarado -da | ĩsola'radʊ | *a.* sunny

ensopar | ĩso'paR | *vt.* to drench, to soak; to stew (meat, fish etc.)

ensurdecer | ĩsuRde'seR | *vt.* to deafen / *vi.* to grow deaf

entabular |ĩtabu'laR | *vt.* to initiate, to begin. **-e. negociações** to engage in negotiations

entalar | ĩta'laʀ | *vt.* to put between splints; to push, to stick; to put in a tight spot

entalhar | ĩta'laʀ | *vt.* to carve (wood); to engrave, to incise

entalhe | ĩ'talɪ | *sm.* groove; notch, carving

entanto | ĩ'tãtʊ | *adv.* meanwhile. **-no e.** nevertheless, yet

então | ĩ'tãw | *adv.* then, at that time; in that case. **-desde e.** ever since. **-pois e.** in that case / *interj.* well?, how about it?

ente | 'ẽtɪ | *sm.* being, creature

enteado-da | ẽtɪ'adʊ | *sm.* stepson; *sf.* stepdaughter

entender | ĩtẽ'deʀ | *vt.* to understand, to comprehend, to perceive / *vi.* to know, to have an understanding (of). **-dar a e.** to insinuate

entendido -da | ĩtẽ'didʊ | *smf.* expert / *a.* understood; expert, skilled

entendimento | ĩtẽdi'mẽtʊ | *sm.* understanding, perception; agreement

enternecer | ĩteʀne'seʀ | *vt.* to move, to touch. **-e.-se** to be moved

enterrar | ĩte'ʀaʀ | *vt.* to bury

enterro | ĩ'teʀʊ | *sm.* burial; funeral

entesar | ĩte'zaʀ | *vt.* to tighten, to make taut; to stiffen / *vi.* to stiffen

entidade | ẽti'dadɪ | *sf.* entity, being; collective group, body

entoar | ĩtʊ'aʀ | *vt.* to intone; to tune (voice etc.): to sing in tune

entontecer | ĩtõte'seʀ | *vt.* to dazzle, to stun, to dizzy / *vi.* to be dizzy

entornar | ĩtoʀ'naʀ | *vt.* to spill, to pour out

entorpecente | ĩtoʀpe'sẽtɪ | *sm. a.* narcotic

entorpecer | ĩtoʀpe'seʀ | *vt.* to make torpid, to be numb

entorpecimento | ĩtoʀpesi'mẽtʊ |

sm. numbness, torpor

entortar | ĩtoʀ'taʀ | *vt.* to crook, to twist, to bend

entrada | ĩ'trada | *sf.* entrance (also theat.); admission; doorway; (com.) down payment; ticket. **-dar e.** to file an application etc.

entranha | ĩ'traɲa | *sf.* any of the viscera; (*pl.*) entrails

entranhar | ĩtra'ɲaʀ | *vt.* to make penetrate / *vi.* to penetrate (as a perfume). **-e.-se em** to go deep into

entrar | ĩ'traʀ | *vi.* to enter, to go in, to come in. **-e. em vigor** to go into effect

entravar | ĩtra'vaʀ | *vt.* to block, to impede

entre | 'ẽtrɪ | *prep.* between; among, amongst. **-por e.** through

entreabrir | ẽtrɪa'briʀ | *vt.* to open slightly (eyes, door etc.); to set ajar (door)

entreato | ẽtrɪ'atʊ | *sm.* (theat.) intermission

entrecho | ĩ'trexʊ | *sm.* (theat., lit.) plot

entrecortar | ẽtrɪkoʀ'taʀ | *vt.* to interrupt (from time to time). **-e.-se** to intersect

entrecosto | ẽtre'koʃtʊ | *sm.* ribs of beef

entrega | ĩ'trɛga | *sf.* delivery, handing over. **-pagamento contra e.** cash on delivery, C.O.D.

entregar | ĩtre'gaʀ | *vt.* to deliver, to hand over; to give back. **-e.-se** to surrender

entrelaçar | ĩtrela'saʀ | *vt.* to interlace, to interweave

entreluzir | ĩtrelu'ziʀ | *vi.* to glimmer; to shine through

entremear | ĩtremi'aʀ | *vt.* to intermingle, to mix; to alternate

entrementes | ĩtre'mẽtɪʃ | *adv.* meanwhile

entreolhar-se | ẽtrɪo'laʀsɪ | *vr.* to eye one another; to exchange glances

entretanto | ĩtre'tãtʊ | *adv.* meanwhile, in the meantime / *conj.* however, nevertheless

entreter | ĩtre'teʀ | *vt.* to amuse, to entertain; to keep up; to harbour (hopes etc.)

entrevar | ĩtre'vaʀ | *vt. vi.* to paralyze, to cripple

entrever | ĩtre'veʀ | *vt.* to glimpse, to catch sight of

entrevista | ĩtre'viʃta | *sf.* interview; meeting; appointment

entrevistar | ĩtreviʃ'taʀ | *vt.* to interview / *vi.* to have an interview with

entrincheirar | ĩtrixey'raʀ | *vt.* to entrench / *vr.* to entrench oneself

entristecer | ĩtriʃte'seʀ | *vt.* to sadden / *vi.* to become sad

entroncamento | ĩtrõka'mẽtʊ | *sm.* junction (of railways etc.); articulation

entroncar | ĩtrõ'kaʀ | *vt.* to join, to connect / *vi.* to branch out; to become corpulent

entronizar | ĩtroni'zaʀ | *vt.* to enthrone

entrosar | ĩtro'zaʀ | *vt.* to branch together; to fit (one part into another). **-e.-se** to be adapted to

entrudo | ĩ'trudʊ | *sm.* carnival merry-making; revelry

entulho | ĩ'tuLʊ | *sm.* debris, rubble

entupir | ĩtu'piʀ | *vt.* to clog, to stop up, to obstruct / *vi.* to choke

entusiasmar | ĩtuziaʃ'maʀ | *vt.* to fill with enthusiasm; to thrill. **-e.-se** to fill enthusiastic

entusiasmo | ĩtuzi'aʃmʊ | *sm.* enthusiasm, excitement, fervo(u)r

entusiasta | ĩtuzi'aʃta | *smf.* enthusiast / *a.* enthusiastic

enumerar | enume'raʀ | *vt.* to enumerate (one by one)

enunciar | enũsi'aʀ | *vt.* to enun-

ciate; to proclaim, to declare

envaidecer | ĩvayde'seʀ | *vt.* to make vain. **-e.-se** to grow vain; to become proud

envelhecer | ĩveLe'seʀ | *vt.* to age, to make old / *vi.* to become old

envenenar | ĩvene'naʀ | *vt.* to poison

enveredar | ĩvere'daʀ | *vi.* to make one's way toward

envergadura | ĩveʀga'dura | *sf.* spread (of a sail, of a bird's wings, of an aircraft); scope, extent

envergar | ĩveʀ'gaʀ | *vt.* to bend, to curve; to put on (jacket, dress etc.) / *vi.* to bend, to curve

envergonhar | ĩveʀgo'ɲaʀ | *vt.* to shame. **-e.se** to be ashamed

envernizar | ĩveʀni'zaʀ | *vt.* to varnish

enviado -da | ĩvi'adʊ | *smf.* envoy, representative

enviar | ĩvi'aʀ | *vt.* to send; to dispatch

envidar | ĩvi'daʀ | *vt.* to endeavour, to strive. **-e. esforços** to put forth one's best

envidraçar | ĩvidra'saʀ | *vt.* to fit with glass (as a window)

enviesado -da | ĩvie'zadʊ | *a.* oblique, diagonal

envio | ĩ'viʊ | *sm.* sending, dispatch; remittance

enviuvar | ĩviu'vaʀ | *vi.* to become a widow or widower

envolto -ta | ĩ'voltʊ | *a.* wrapped

envoltório | ĩvol'tɔriʊ | *sm.* wrapper, cover

envolver | ĩvol'veʀ | *vt.* to wrap, to cover; to surround; to encompass, to involve; to implicate

enxada | ĩ'xada | *sf.* hoe

enxaguar | ĩxa'gwaʀ | *vt.* to rinse (clothes etc.)

enxame | ĩ'xamɪ | *sm.* swarm of bees

enxaqueca | ĩxa'keka | *sf.* migraine

enxergão | ĩxeʀ'gãw | *sm.* wire mattress

enxergar | ĩ xeʀˈgaʀ | *vt.* to discern, to perceive, to see

enxertar | ĩ xeʀˈtaʀ | *vt.* to graft (also surg.)

enxerto | ĩ ˈxeʀtʊ | *sm.* (bot., surg.) graft

enxó | ĩ ˈxω | *sm.* adze

enxofre | ĩ ˈxofrɩ | *sm.* sulphur

enxotar | ĩ xoˈtaʀ | *vt.* to expel, to oust

enxoval | ĩ xoˈval | *sm.* trousseau (of bride); layette (of infant)

enxovalhar | ĩ xovaˈLaʀ | *vt.* to wrinkle; to soil; to affront, to insult. **-e.-se** to wrinkle one's clothes; to degrade oneself

enxugar | ĩ xuˈgaʀ | *vt.* to dry; to wipe dry / *vi.* to become dry

enxurrada | ĩ xuˈʀada | *sf.* spate, torrent of rain water

enxuto -ta | ĩ ˈxutʊ | *a.* dry; dried

épico -ca | ˈεpikʊ | *a.* epic, epical / *sm.* an epic poet

epidemia | ɩpidɩˈmia | *sf.* epidemic

epilepsia | ɩpilepˈsia | *sf.* epilepsy

epílogo | eˈpilogʊ | *sm.* epilogue

episódio | ɩpiˈzωdiʊ | *sm.* episode

epístola | eˈpiʃtola | *sf.* epistle, letter

epitáfio | ɩpiˈtafiʊ | *sm.* epitaph

época | ˈεpʊka | *sf.* epoch, period, time

equador | ekwaˈdoʀ | *sm.* equator

eqüidade | ekwiˈdadɩ | *sf.* equity, impartiality

equilibrar | ɩkiliˈbraʀ | *vt.* to balance

equilíbrio | ɩkiˈlibriʊ | *sm.* balance. **-perder o e.** to lose one's balance

equipagem | ɩkiˈpajēy | *sf.* ship's crew; equipment

equipamento | ɩkipaˈmẽtʊ | *sm.* equipment; gear, tackle

equipar | ɩkiˈpaʀ | *vt.* to equip, to outfit

equiparar | ɩkipaˈraʀ | *vt.* to put on a level with

equipe | eˈkipɩ | *sf.* team, staff. **-trabalho de e.** team-work

equitação | ɩkitaˈsãw | *sf.* riding, horsemanship

equitativo -va | ɩkitaˈtivʊ | *a.* equitable, fair

equivalente | ɩkivaˈlẽtɩ | *sm. a.* equivalent

equivaler, eqüivaler | ɩkivaˈleʀ ɩkwivaˈleʀ | *vi.* to be equivalent, to correspond

equivocado -da | ɩkivoˈkadʊ | *a.* mistaken

equivocar-se | ɩkivoˈkaʀsɩ | *vr.* to make a mistake

equívoco -ca | ɩˈkivokʊ | *sm.* misunderstanding, mistake / *a.* equivocal, ambiguous

era | ˈεra | *sf.* era, age

eremita | ereˈmita | *sm.* hermit

ereto -ta | eˈrεtʊ | *a.* erect

erguer | eʀˈgeʀ | *vt.* to raise, to erect, to build; to lift. **-e.-se** to rise

eriçado -da | ɩriˈsadʊ | *a.* bristled; ruffled

erigir | ɩriˈjiʀ | *vt.* to erect; to build

ermo -ma | ˈεʀmʊ | *sm.* desert, wilderness / *a.* desert; abandoned

erosão | eroˈzãw | *sf.* erosion, corrosion

erótico -ca | eˈrωtikʊ | *a.* erotic

erradicar | eʀadiˈkaʀ | *vt.* to eradicate, to uproot

errado -da | eˈʀadʊ | *a.* wrong; mistaken; erroneous

errante | eˈʀãtɩ | *a.* vagrant, nomadic, erring

errar | eˈʀaʀ | *vt.* to miss; to make a mistake. **-e. o alvo** to miss the target. **-e. o caminho** to lose one's way / *vi.* to wander; to roam; to err

erro | eˈʀʊ | *sm.* mistake, error. **-e. crasso** a blunder

errôneo -nea | eˈʀonɩʊ | *a.* erroneous, mistaken

erudição | erudiˈsãw | *sf.* erudition, knowledge, learning

erudito -ta | eruˈditʊ | *smf.* scholar / *a.* erudite, learned, scholar

erupção | erupˈsãw | *sf.* eruption; skin eruption, rash

erva | 'ɛRvɐ | *sf.* herb, grass; (slang) dough, money

erva-doce | 'ɛRvɐ'dosɪ | *sf.* anise

erva-mate | 'ɛRvɐ'matɪ | *sf.* maté, Paraguay tea

ervilha | eR'viLɐ | *sf.* (bot.) pea

esbaforido -da | ɪʒbɐfu'ridʊ | *a.* breathless, panting

esbanjar | ɪʒbã'jaR | *vt.* to waste, to dissipate, to squander

esbarrão | ɪʒba'Rãw | *sm.* bump, collision

esbarrar | ɪʒba'RaR | *vi.* (with *prep.* em) to bump into, to run into

esbeltez, esbelteza | ɪʒbel'teʒɪʒbel- 'teza | *sf.* slenderness, slimness

esbelto -ta | ɪʒ'bɛltʊ | *a.* slender, gracile, svelte

esboçar | ɪʒbo'saR | *vt.* to sketch, to outline

esboço | ɪʒ'bosʊ | *sm.* sketch (also lit.); first draft, outline

esbofetear | ɪʒbʊfetɪ'aR | *vt.* to slap (esp. in the face)

esbranquiçado-da | ɪʒbrãki'sadʊ | *a.* whitish; discolo(u)red

esbravejar | ɪʒbrave'jaR | *vi.* to rage, to shout, to rave

esbugalhar | ɪʒbuga'LaR | *vt.* to goggle, to open wide (the eyes)

esburacar | ɪʒbura'kaR | *vt.* to pierce with holes

escabeche | ɪʒka'bɛxɪ | *sm.* a kind of marinade

escabroso -sa | ɪʒka'brozʊ -'brɔza | *a.* indecorous, improper; rough, harsh

escada | ɪʒ'kada | *sf.* staircase, stairs, flight of steps; ladder. **-e. rolante** escalator

escadaria | ɪʒkada'ria | *sf.* a flight of stairs; a wide stair

escafandrista | ɪʒkafã'driʒtɐ | *sm.* diver (wearing a diving-suit)

escafandro | ɪʒka'fãdrʊ | *sm.* diving-suit; diver (wearing a diving-suit)

escala | ɪʒ'kala | *sf.* scale (also mus., tech., phys.); rank; (naut., aeron.) place of call

escalada | ɪʒka'lada | *sf.* climb; (mil.) escalade

escaldar | ɪʒkal'daR | *vt.* to scald, to burn

escaler | ɪʒka'lɛR | *sm.* (naut.) lifeboat

escalfar | ɪʒkal'faR | *vt.* to poach (eggs)

escalonamento | ɪʒkalona'mẽtʊ | *sm.* staggering

escalope | ɪʒka'lɔpɪ | *sm.* (cookery) a thin slice of meat (gen. veal)

escalpelo | ɪʒkal'pelʊ | *sm.* scalpel

escama | ɪʒ'kama | *sf.* scale (of fish, reptiles etc.)

escamotear | ɪʒkamʊtɪ'aR | *vt.* to snatch, to swipe, to palm

escancarar | ɪʒkãka'raR | *vt.* to open wide

escândalo | ɪʒ'kãdalʊ | *sm.* scandal

escandaloso -sa | ɪʒkãda'lozʊ -'lɔza | *a.* scandalous

escandinavo -va | ɪʒkãdi'navʊ | *smf. a.* Scandinavian

escangalhar | ɪʒkãga'LaR | *vt.* to ruin, to wreck, to break

escanhoar | ɪʒkaNʊ'aR | *vt.* to shave against the grain

escaninho | ɪʒka'niNʊ | *sm.* small partition within a drawer or chest; pigeon-hole

escapar | ɪʒka'paR | *vi.* to escape

escapatória | ɪʒkapa'tɔrɪa | *sf.* (colloq.) way out; excuse

escapulir | ɪʒkapu'liR | *vi.* to slip away; to escape

escaramuça | ɪʒkara'musa | *sf.* skirmish

escarcéu | ɪʒkaR'sɛw | *sm.* clamo(u)r; uproar, tumult

escarlate | ɪʒkaR'latɪ | *sm.* scarlet (also the colo(u)r)

escarlatina | ɪʒkaRla'tina | *sf.* scarlet fever

escarnecer | ɪʒkaRne'seR | *vi.* to mock, to jeer, to scorn

escarpa | ɪʒ'kaRpa | *sf.* steep slope

escarranchar | ɪʒkarã'xaR | *vt. vr.* to straddle; to spread out (the legs)

escarrar | ιʃka'ʀaʀ | *vi.* to expectorate

escarro | ιʃ'kaʀʊ | *sm.* phlegm, mucus

escassear | ιʃkasι'aʀ | *vt.* to grow scarce, to diminish

escassez | ιʃka'seʃ | *sf.* scarcity, shortage, lack

escasso -sa | ιʃ'kasʊ | *a.* scarce, scant, meager

escavação | ιʃkava'sãw | *sf.* excavation

escavar | ιʃka'vaʀ | *vt.* to excavate, to dig

esclarecer | ιʃklaɾι'seʀ | *vt.* to clarify, to explain

esclarecimento | ιʃklaɾιsi'mẽtʊ | *sm.* elucidation; information; explanation

esclerose | ιʃkle'ɾɔzι | *sf.* sclerosis

escoadouro | ιʃkʊa'dowɾʊ | *sm.* drain; trench, ditch

escoar | ιʃkʊ'aʀ | *vt.* to drain (off) / *vi.* to flow off or away; to ooze

escocês -sa | ιʃko'seʃ -'seza | *sm.* Scots (dialect); Scotsman; *smf.* Scot / *a.* Scottish

escoicear | ιʃkoysι'aʀ | *vt. vi.* to kick (as a horse)

escola | ιʃ'kɔla | *sf.* school; college

escolado -da | ιʃko'ladʊ | *a.* (colloq.) wise, shrewd

escolar | ιʃko'laʀ | *smf.* student, pupil / *a.* school

escolha | ιʃ'koLa | *sf.* choice

escolher | ιʃko'LeʀR | *vt.* to choose, to select

escolho | ιʃ'koLʊ | *sm.* reef, shoal; obstacle

escolta | ιʃ'kɔlta | *sf.* escort, convoy, guard

escoltar | ιʃkol'taʀ | *vt.* to escort, to convoy, to guard

escombro | ιʃ'kõbɾʊ | *sm.* (gen. *pl.*) ruins, debris

esconder | ιʃkõ'deʀ | *vt.* to hide, to conceal

esconderijo | ιʃkõde'ɾijʊ | *sm.* hiding place, cover

escondidas | ιʃkõ'didaʃ | *sfpl.*

used in the expression **às e.** furtively

esconjurar | ιʃkõju'ʀaʀ | *vt.* to conjure; to exorcise

escopo | ιʃ'kopʊ | *sm.* aim, purpose

escopro | ιʃ'kopɾʊ | *sm.* chisel

escora | ιʃ'kɔɾa | *sf.* brace, support

escorchar | ιʃkoʀ'xaʀ | *vt.* to strip, to peel; to gouge (on prices)

escória | ιʃ'kɔɾia | *sf.* slag; dross, refuse

escorpião | ιʃkoʀpi'ãw | *sm.* scorpion

escorregadela | ιʃkʊʀega'dɛla | *sf.* false step; slip; mistake

escorregadio -dia | ιʃkʊʀega'diʊ | *a.* slippery

escorregar | ιʃkʊʀe'gaʀ | *vi.* to slip, to slide

escorrer | ιʃko'ʀeʀ | *vt. vi.* to drain; to trickle, to drip

escoteiro -ra | ιʃko'teyɾʊ | *sm.* Boy Scout / *a.* travel(l)ing without baggage; going alone

escova | ιʃ'kova | *sf.* brush. **-e. de dentes** tooth-brush

escovar | ιʃko'vaʀ | *vt.* to brush

escravatura | ιʃkrava'tura | *sf.* slavery; enslavement

escravidão | ιʃkravi'dãw | *sf.* slavery; servitude

escravizar | ιʃkravi'zaʀ | *vt.* to enslave

escravo -va | ιʃ'kravʊ | *smf. a.* slave

escrever | ιʃkre'veʀ | *vt. vi.* to write. **-e. à máquina** to typewrite

escrevinhar | ιʃkɾιvi'ɴaʀ | *vt.* to scribble

escrita | ιʃ'krita | *sf.* writing, handwriting; bookkeeping

escrito -ta | ιʃ'kritʊ | *sm.* writing; (*pl.*) writings. **-por e.** in writing/ *a.* written

escritor-tora | ιʃkri'toʀ | *smf.* writer, author

escritório | ιʃkri'tʊɾiʊ | *sm.* office; bureau

escritura | ιʃkri'tura | *sf.* deed, legal document. **-e. de uma casa** conveyance of a house. **-Sagradas Escrituras** the Holy Writ

escrituração | ιʃkritura'sãw | *sf.* bookkeeping

escriturar | ιʃkritu'raʀ | *vt.* to keep books

escriturário -ria | ιʃkritu'rariυ | *smf.* clerk

escrivaninha | ιʃkriva'niɴa | *sf.* desk, writing table

escrivão -vã | ιʃkri'vãw | *smf.* notary; clerk (in a court of justice)

escroque | ιʃ'kʀɔkι | *smf.* crook, swindler

escrúpulo | ιʃ'krupulυ | *sm.* scruple, hesitation, qualm

escrupuloso -sa | ιʃkrupu'lozυ -'lωza | *a.* scrupulous

escrutínio | ιʃkru'tiniυ | *sm.* balloting; ballot counting

escudar | ιʃku'daʀ | *vt.* to shield, to protect

escudo | ιʃ'kudυ | *sm.* shield; Portuguese monetary unit

esculhambação | ιʃkuʟãba'sãw | *sf.* (vulg.) dressing-down; (vulg.) disorder, mess

esculpir | ιʃkul'piʀ | *vt.* to sculpture; to carve

escultor -tora | ιʃkul'toʀ | *smf.* sculptor

escultura | ιʃkul'tura | *sf.* sculpture

escuna | ιʃ'kuna | *sf.* schooner

escuras | ιʃ'kuraʃ | *sfpl.* used in the expression **às e.** in the dark

escurecer | ιʃkure'seʀ | *vt.* to darken, to make dark / *vi.* to cloud, to overcast (weather); to get dark

escuridão | ιʃkurí'dãw | *sf.* darkness

escuro -ra | ιʃ'kurυ | *sm.* dark / *a.* dark, obscure; dim

escusa | ιʃ'kuza | *sf.* excuse; apology

escuso -sa | ιʃ'kuzυ | *a.* shady, questionable

escutar | ιʃku'taʀ | *vt. vi.* to listen, to listen to; to hear

esfacelar | ιʃfase'laʀ | *vt.* to smash; to ruin, to destroy

esfalfar | ιʃfal'faʀ | *vt.* to exhaust, to fatigue

esfaquear | ιʃfakι'aʀ | *vt.* to knife, to stab

esfarrapado -da | ιʃfaʀa'padυ | *a.* tattered, ragged

esfera | ιʃ'fɛra | *sf.* sphere; field, range

esférico -ca | ιʃ'fɛrikυ | *a.* spherical, globular

esfinge | ιʃ'fĩjι | *sf.* sphinx

esfolar | ιʃfo'laʀ | *vt.* to flay, to skin (also slang); to scratch (the skin)

esforçar-se | ιʃfoʀ'saʀsι | *vr.* to make an effort; to exert oneself

esforço | ιʃ'foʀsυ | *sm.* effort; straining

esfregão | ιʃfre'gãw | *sm.* mop, dish rag

esfregar | ιʃfre'gaʀ | *vt.* to scrub; to rub

esfriar | ιʃfri'aʀ | *vt.* to cool, to chill / *vi. vr.* to grow cold; to lose enthusiasm

esganar | ιʃga'naʀ | *vt.* to strangle, to suffocate

esgar | ιʃ'gaʀ | *sm.* grimace

esgarçar | ιʃgaʀ'saʀ | *vi.* to become frayed with use (cloth)

esgotamento | ιʃgota'mẽtυ | *sm.* exhaustion, draining; breakdown. **-e. nervoso** nervous breakdown

esgotar | ιʃgo'taʀ | *vt.* to drain; to exhaust; to wear out. **-e.-se** to be exhausted, to be worn out; to be out of print; to be sold out

esgoto | ιʃ'gotυ | *sm.* sewer. **-rede de e.** sewerage system

esgrima | ιʃ'grima | *sf.* (sports) fencing

esgrimir | ιʃgri'miʀ | *vt.* to brandish (sword, sabre etc.) / *vi.* to fence

esgueirar-se | ιʃgey'raʀsι | *vr.* to sneak out, to sneak off

esguelha | ιʃ'geʟa | *sf.* slant. **-de e.**

obliquely, aslant

esguichar | ιʒgiˈxaʀ | *vt. vi.* to spurt; to gush

esguicho | ιʒˈgixʊ | *sm.* squirt; waterspout; hose

esguio -a | ιʒˈgiʊ | *a.* slim, tall and slender

eslavo -va | ιʒˈlavʊ | *sm.* (ling.) Slavic; *smf. a.* Slav

esmagar | ιʒmaˈgaʀ | *vt.* to crush, to squash; to overwhelm; to oppress

esmalte | ιʒˈmaltι | *sm.* enamel. **-e. de unhas** nail varnish

esmerado -da | ιʒ meˈradʊ | *a.* accomplished, painstaking

esmeralda | ιʒmeˈralda | *sf.* emerald

esmerar | ιʒmeˈʀaʀ | *vt.* to perfect, to finish. **-e.-se** to do one's best

esmeril | ιʒmeˈril | *sm.* emery

esmero | ιʒˈmerʊ | *sm.* refinement, perfection; accuracy, neatness

esmigalhar | ιʒmigaˈLaʀ | *vt.* to crumble, to crush

esmiuçar | ιʒmiuˈsaʀ | *vt.* to mince; to investigate in great detail; to recount in detail

esmo | ˈeʒmʊ | *sm.* estimate, rough guess. **-a e.** at random

esmola | ιʒˈmɔla | *sf.* alms

esmolambado -da | ιʒmʊlãˈbadʊ | *a.* ragged, tattered

esmorecer | ιʒmoreˈseʀ | *vt.* to discourage / *vi.* to lose heart; to grow weak

esmurrar | ιʒmuˈʀaʀ | *vt.* to punch, to strike (with closed fist)

esnobe | ιʒˈnɔbι | *smf.* snob / *a.* snobbish

espaçar | ιʒpaˈsaʀ | *vt.* to space; to slow down

espacial | ιʒpasiˈal | *a.* spatial

espaço | ιʒˈpasʊ | *sm.* space (also mus., typog.). **-a espaços** from time to time

espaçoso -sa | ιʒpaˈsozʊ -ˈsɔwza | *a.* spacious, roomy

espada | ιʒˈpada | *sf.* sword; (*pl.*, card suit) spades

espadaúdo -da | ιʒpadaˈudʊ | *a.* broad-shouldered

espadim | ιʒpaˈdĩ | *sm.* rapier

espádua | ιʒˈpadua | *sf.* shoulder--blade

espaguete | ιʒpaˈgetι | *sm.* spaghetti

espairecer | ιʒpayreˈseʀ | *vi.* to divert, to relax

espalhafato | ιʒpaLaˈfatʊ | *sm.* fuss, noise, commotion

espalhar | ιʒpaˈLaʀ | *vt.* to scatter; to spread out; to spill; to distribute

espanador | ιʒpanaˈdoʀ | *sm.* feather duster

espanar | ιʒpaˈnaʀ | *vt.* to dust; to brush away the dust

espancar | ιʒpãˈkaʀ | *vt.* to thrash, to beat, to spank

espanhol -la | ιʒpãˈNɔl | *sm.* (ling.) Spanish; *smf.* Spaniard / *a.* Spanish

espantalho | ιʒpãˈtaLʊ | *sm.* scarecrow

espantar | ιʒpãˈtaʀ | *vt.* to frighten, to scare; to astonish / *vi.* to be astonishing

espanto | ιʒˈpãtʊ | *sm.* amazement, astonishment; fright, scare

espantoso -sa | ιʒpãˈtozʊ -ˈtɔwza | *a.* frightful, fearful; terrible; extraordinary

esparadrapo | ιʒparaˈdrapʊ | *sm.* (med.) adhesive tape

espargir | ιʒpaʀˈjiʀ | *vt.* to spill; to sprinkle, to spray

espargo | ιʒˈpaʀgʊ | *sm.* asparagus

esparramar | ιʒpaʀaˈmaʀ | *vt.* to spread out, to scatter

esparrela | ιʒpaˈʀɛla | *sf.* snare, trap

espasmo | ιʒˈpaʒmʊ | *sm.* (med.) spasm

espatifar | ιʒpatiˈfaʀ | *vt.* to shatter, to smash to bits

especial | ιʒpesiˈal | *a.* special

especialidade | ιʒpesialiˈdadι | *sf.* speciality; particularity; special branch

especialista | ιʃpesia'liʃta | *smf. a.* specialist

especializar | ιʃpesiali'zaʀ | *vt.* to specialize

especiaria | ιʃpesia'ria | *sf.* spices

espécie | ιʃ'pesιε | *sf.* kind, sort, class, genre. **-causar e.** to be strange or peculiar. **-em e.** in specie, in kind (also law)

especificar | ιʃpesifi'kaʀ | *vt.* to specify

espécime | ιʃ'pεsimι | *sm.* specimen, example

espectador -dora | ιspekta'doʀ | *smf.* spectator

espectro | ιʃ'pεktrʊ | *sm.* specter, ghost; (phys.) spectrum

especulação | ιʃpekula'sãw | *sf.* speculation; exploration

especular | ιʃpeku'laʀ | *vi.* to speculate (also in business)

espelho | ιʃ'peLʊ | *sm.* mirror, looking-glass

espelunca | ιʃpe'lũka | *sf.* den, joint; gambling hell

espera | ιʃ'pεra | *sf.* wait, delay; expectation; ambush. **-sala de e.** waiting-room

esperança | ιʃpe'rãsa | *sf.* hope

esperar | ιʃpe'raʀ | *vt.* to expect, to await, to wait for; to hope for

espertalhão -lhona | ιʃpeʀta'lãw -'Lona | *smf.* crook, scoundrel

esperteza | ιʃpeʀ'teza | *sf.* shrewdness, cleverness; cunning

esperto -ta | ιʃ'pεʀtʊ | *a.* shrewd, smart, clever

espesso -sa | ιʃ'pesʊ | *a.* dense, thick

espessura | ιʃpe'sura | *sf.* thickness, denseness

espetacular | ιʃpetaku'laʀ | *a.* spectacular

espetáculo | ιʃpe'takulʊ | *sm.* spectacle; sight; show, performance

espetar | ιʃpe'taʀ | *vt.* to prick; to poke; to impale (as on a spit); (slang) to put on credit

espeto | ιʃ'petʊ | *sm.* spit, broach; pointed stick

espiada | ιʃpi'ada | *sf.* peep, glance

espião -ã | ιʃpi'ãw -'ã | *smf.* spy

espiar | ιʃpi'aʀ | *vt.* to spy on, to watch carefully; to observe

espichar | ιʃpi'xaʀ | *vt.* to stretch out; to stick out (as the neck) / *vi.* (slang) to die

espiga | ιʃ'piga | *sf.* spike, ear (of corn, wheat etc.). **-e. de milho** corn-cob

espinafre | ιʃpi'nafrι | *sm.* spinach

espingarda | ιʃpĩ'gaʀda | *sf.* shot-gun

espinha | ιʃ'piNa | *sf.* spine, spinal column; fish bone; pimple

espinho | ιʃ'piNʊ | *sm.* thorn, prickle

espinhoso -sa | ιʃpi'Nozʊ -'Nωza | *a.* thorny, prickly, spiny; arduous, difficult

espionagem | ιʃpio'najẽy | *sf.* espionage, spying

espionar | ιʃpio'naʀ | *vt.* to spy

espiritismo | ιʃpiri'tiʃmʊ | *sm.* spiritism

espirito | ιʃ'piritʊ | *sm.* spirit, soul, mind; wit; vigo(u)r, enthusiasm. **-E. Santo** Holy Ghost

espiritual | ιʃpiritu'al | *a.* spiritual

espirituoso-sa | ιʃpiritu'ozʊ -'ωza | *a.* witty, clever; spirituous

espirrar | ιʃpi'ʀaʀ | *vi.* to sneeze; to gush (water, blood etc.)

espirro | ιʃ'piʀʊ | *sm.* sneeze

esplêndido -da | ιʃ'plẽdidʊ | *a.* splendid; excellent; magnificent

espojar-se | ιʃpo'jaʀsι | *vr.* to wallow, to roll in the ground

espoleta | ιʃpo'leta | *sf.* fuse, detonator; primer; percussion cap

espoliar | ιʃpoli'aʀ | *vt.* to plunder, to despoil, to rob

espólio | ιʃ'pωliʊ | *sm.* estate, assets, property of a deceased person; booty

esponja | ιʃ'põja | *sf.* sponge

esponjoso -sa | ιʃpõ'jozʊ -'jωza | *a.* spongy

espontaneidade | ιʃpõtaney'dadι | *sf.* spontaneity

espontâneo -nea | ιʃpõ'tanιυ | *a.* spontaneous

espora | ιʃ'pʊɾa | *sf.* spur

esporádico -ca | ιʃpo'ɾadikυ | *a.* sporadic

esporte | ιʃ'pʊʀtι | *sm.* sport

esportivo -va | ιʃpoʀ'tivυ | *a.* sporting

esposa | ιʃ'poza | *sf.* wife

esposar | ιʃpo'zaʀ | *vt.* to marry, to wed; to support, to adopt (a cause etc.)

esposo | ιʃ'pozυ | *sm.* husband; (*pl.*) man and wife

espraiar | ιʃpray'aʀ | *vi. vr.* to stretch out, to spread out (as a river)

espreguiçadeira | ιʃpɾιgisa'deyɾa | *sf.* deck-chair, lounge chair

espreguiçar | ιʃpɾιgi'saʀ | *vi. vr.* to stretch one's limbs

espreitar | ιʃpɾey'taʀ | *vt.* to spy (out); to pry into; to observe (in secret), to peep

espremer | ιʃpɾe'meʀ | *vt.* to squeeze

espuma | ιʃ'puma | *sf.* foam

espumante | ιʃpu'mãtι | *sm.* sparkling wine / *a.* foamy, foaming

esquadra | ιʃ'kwadɾa | *sf.* fleet

esquadria | ιʃkwa'dɾia | *sf.* door and window frames; a right angle

esquadrilha | ιʃkwa'dɾiʟa | *sf.* (naut.) flotilla; (aeron.) air squadron

esquadrinhar | ιʃkwadɾi'naʀ | *vt.* to search accurately; to scrutinize

esquadro | ιʃ'kwadɾυ | *sm.* square (instrument for drawing right angles)

esquecer | ιʃke'seʀ | *vt. vr.* to forget

esquecimento | ιʃkιsi'mẽtυ | *sm.* forgetfulness; omission

esqueleto | ιʃke'letυ | *sm.* skeleton; framework

esquema | ιʃ'kema | *sm.* diagram, design; scheme

esquentar | ιʃkẽ'taʀ | *vt.* to heat (up); to warm (up)

esquerda | ιʃ'keʀda | *sf.* the left (side, hand); (polit.) left wing

esquerdo -da | ιʃ'keʀdυ | *sm.* left foot / *a.* left

esqui | ιʃ'ki | *sm.* ski

esquilo | ιʃ'kilυ | *sm.* squirrel

esquimó | ιʃki'mɔ | *smf.* *'a.* Eskimo

esquina | ιʃ'kina | *sf.* corner. **-dobrar a e.** to turn the corner

esquisito -ta | ιʃki'zitυ | *a.* odd, queer; (colloq.) singular, quaint; slightly deteriorated (meat, fish)

esquivar-se | ιʃki'vaʀsι | *vr.* to dodge, to sidestep; to shun

esquivo -va | ιʃ'kivυ | *a.* elusive, evasive; timid

essa | 'ɛsa | *a.* (*f.*) that (near the person spoken to); *pron. f.* that one; (*pl.*) those. V. **esta**

esse | 'esι | *a.* (*m.*) that (near the person spoken to); *pron. m.* that one; (*pl.*) those. V. **este**

essência | e'sẽsia | *sf.* essence, perfume

essencial | esẽsi'al | *a.* essential

esta | 'ɛʃta | *a.* (*f.*) this (near the speaker); *pron. f.* this one; (*pl.*) these. V. **essa**

estabelecer | ιʃtabele'seʀ | *vt.* to establish, to found; to set up

estabelecimento | ιʃtabιlιsi'mẽtυ | *sm.* establishment; institution, settlement. **-e. de ensino** a school. **-e. comercial** a shop

estabilidade | ιʃtabili'dadι | *sf.* stability; (law) tenure (in a job)

estábulo | ιʃ'tabulυ | *sm.* stable, barn

estaca | ιʃ'taka | *sf.* stake, post

estacada | ιʃta'kada | *sf.* palisade, picket fence

estação | ιʃta'sãw | *sf.* season, period; station (train, bus etc.)

estacar | ιʃta'kaʀ | *vt.* to stop, to halt; to stake, to support with stakes / *vi.* to stop suddenly

estacionamento | ιʃtasiona'mẽtʋ | *sm.* parking

estacionar | ιʃtasio'naʀ | *vt.* to park (automobiles) / *vi.* to stop in a place, to come to a standstill

estada | ιʃ'tada | *sf.* stay, sojourn

estádio | ιʃ'tadιʋ | *sm.* stadium

estado | ιʃ'tadʋ | *sm.* state (also polit.), condition; status, position, situation. **-e. civil** marital status

estadual | ιʃtadu'al | *a.* of or pertaining to a state

estafa | ιʃ'tafa | *sf.* fatigue, exhaustion

estafante | ιʃta'fãtι | *a.* fatiguing, tiring, wearying

estafermo | ιʃta'feʀmʋ | *sm.* simpleton

estafeta | ιʃta'feta | *sm.* messenger, courier; messenger boy

estagiário -ria | ιʃtaji'arιʋ | *smf.* probationer, trainee

estágio | ιʃ'tajιʋ | *sm.* probation, a period of professional training

estagnação | ιʃtagna'sãw | *sf.* stagnation

estalagem | ιʃta'lajẽy | *sf.* inn, hostelry

estalar | ιʃta'laʀ | *vt.* to crack, to snap / *vi.* to crack, to snap; to break, to split; to break out suddenly (as handclapping or revolution)

estaleiro | ιʃta'leyrʋ | *sm.* shipyard

estalido | ιʃta'lidʋ | *sm.* snap, crack, click

estalo | ιʃ'talʋ | *sm.* snap, crack, pop; small firework that cracks by impact

estampa | ιʃ'tãpa | *sf.* printed picture, print

estampar | ιʃtã'paʀ | *vt.* to print, to imprint; to cold stamp (metal)

estampido | ιʃtã'pidʋ | *sm.* explosion, detonation, loud report

estampilha | ιʃtã'piʟa | *sf.* revenue stamp

estancar | ιʃtã'kaʀ | *vt.* to stanch (esp. blood); to check, to stop; to bring to a halt / *vi.* to stop running

estância | ιʃ'tãsia | *sf.* cattle ranch (esp. in S. Brazil); sojourn, rest; stanza, strophe. **-e. balneária** seaside resort. **-e. hidromineral** watering-place

estandarte | ιʃtã'daʀtι | *sm.* banner, flag, standard

estanho | ιʃ'taɴʋ | *sm.* tin

estanque | ιʃ'tãkι | *a.* watertight; tight, impervious

estante | ιʃ'tãtι | *sf.* bookcase; book-rest; music stand

estapafúrdio -dia | ιʃtapa'fuʀdιʋ | *a.* extravagant; odd, queer

estar | ιʃ'taʀ | *vi.* to be. V. *ser*

estatística | ιʃta'tiʃtika | *sf.* statistics

estatístico -ca | ιʃta'tiʃtikʋ | *smf.* statistician / *a.* statistical

estátua | ιʃ'tatua | *sf.* statue

estatura | ιʃta'tura | *sf.* stature, height

estatuto | ιʃta'tutʋ | *sm.* statute; act, law; (fig.) code

estável | ιʃ'tavιl | *a.* stable, firm, steady

este | 'eʃtι | *sm.* east

este | 'eʃtι | *a.* (m.) this (near the speaker); *pron. m.* this one; (*pl.*) these. V. *esse*

esteio | ιʃ'teyʋ | *sm.* stay, prop, support

esteira | ιʃ'teyra | *sf.* mat, matting; (naut.) wake, backwash

estender | ιʃtẽ'deʀ | *vt.* to extend, to stretch out; to prolong; to spread

estenoda(c)tilógrafo -fa | ιʃtenʋda(k)ti'lɔgrafʋ | *smf.* shorthand-typist

estenografia | ιʃtenogra'fia | *sf.* stenography, shorthand

esterco | ιʃ'teʀkʋ | *sm.* manure, dung, fertilizer

estéril | ιʃ'terιl | *a.* sterile, barren; fruitless

estética | ιʃ'tεtika | *sf.* aesthetics

estiar | ιʃti'aʀ | *vi.* to stop raining

estibordo | ιʃti'bωʀdυ | *sm.* starboard

esticar | ιʃti'kaʀ | *vt.* to stretch (out); (slang) to die

estilhaço | ιʃti'Lasυ | *sm.* splinter, fragment

estilo | ιʃ'tilυ | *sm.* style; manner; fashion

estima | ιʃ'tima | *sf.* esteem, appreciation, regard

estimativa | ιʃtima'tiva | *sf.* estimate, evaluation, appraisal, judgement

estimulante | ιʃtimu'lãtι | *sm.* stimulant / *a.* stimulating

estimular | ιʃtimu'laʀ | *vt.* to stimulate, to incite, to stir up

estímulo | ιʃ'timulυ | *sm.* stimulus; incentive

estio | ιʃ'tiυ | *sm.* summer

estipular | ιʃtipu'laʀ | *vt.* to stipulate

estirar | ιʃti'raʀ | *vt.* to stretch (out)

estirpe | ιʃ'tiʀpι | *sf.* stock, lineage, ancestry

estivador | ιʃtiva'doʀ | *sm.* stevedore, longshoreman

estocada | ιʃto'kada | *sf.* stab, thrust

estofador -dora | ιʃtofa'doʀ | *smf.* upholsterer

estofar | ιʃto'faʀ | *vt.* to upholster; to pad

estóico -ca | ιʃ'tωykυ | *sm.* stoic / *a.* stoic, stoical

estojo | ιʃ'tojυ | *sm.* case, kit, set

estômago | ιʃ'tomagυ | *sm.* stomach

estontear | ιʃtõtι'aʀ | *vt.* to stun, to dazzle

estopa | ιʃ'topa | *sf.* tow, oakum

estopim | ιʃto'pĩ | *sm.* fuse, blasting fuse

estoque | ιʃ'tωkι | *sm.* stock, supply; rapier

estore | ιʃ'tωrι | *sm.* window shade, blind

estorvar | ιʃtoʀ'vaʀ | *vt.* to hinder, to impede, to hamper

estorvo | ιʃ'toʀvυ | *sm.* hindrance, impediment, encumbrance

estourar | ιʃtow'raʀ | *vt.* to burst, to blast, to explode / *vi.* to burst; to explode; to stampede (said of cattle)

estouro | ιʃ'towrυ | *sm.* burst, explosion; outbreak; stampede

estouvado -da | ιʃtow'vadυ | *a.* scatter-brained, clumsy, awkward

estrábico -ca | ιʃ'trabikυ | *smf. a.* cross-eyed

estrabismo | ιʃtra'biʃmυ | *sm.* squint, cross-eyed

estraçalhar | ιʃtrasa'laʀ | *vt.* to shatter, to tear to pieces

estrada | ιʃ'trada | *sf.* road, highway. **-e. de ferro** railroad, railway. **-e. de rodagem** highway

estrado | ιʃ'tradυ | *sm.* raised platform, dais; mattress frame

estragar | ιʃtra'gaʀ | *vt.* to spoil, to ruin, to damage; to corrupt. **-e.-se** to deteriorate

estrago | ιʃ'tragυ | *sm.* damage; spoilage, havoc; devastation

estrangeiro -ra | ιʃtrã'jeyrυ | *sm.* foreign countries (collectively); *smf.* foreign, stranger, alien / *a.* foreign

estrangular | ιʃtrãgu'laʀ | *vt.* to strangle, to choke

estranhar | ιʃtra'ɴaʀ | *vt.* to find strange or peculiar

estranho -nha | ιʃ'traɴυ | *smf.* stranger, outsider / *a.* strange, odd, queer

estratagema | ιʃtrata'jema | *sm.* stratagem, trick

estrategia, estratégia | ιʃtrate'jia ιʃtra'tεjia | *sf.* strategy; strategics

estrear | ιʃtrι'aʀ | *vt.* to use or to wear for the first time; to open (a film, play etc.). **-e.-se** to make one's debut

estrebaria | ιʃtreba'ria | *sf.* stable

estrebuchar | ιʃtrιbu'xaʀ | *vi.* to struggle, to toss (about)

estréia | ɩʃ'tɾɛya | sf. opening, debut; the first use of anything. -noite de e. opening night

estreitar | ɩʃtɾey'taʀ | vt. to narrow; to tighten; to clasp, to embrace

estreiteza | ɩʃtɾey'teza | sf. narrowness

estreito -ta | ɩʃ'tɾeytʋ | sm. (geog.) strait / a. narrow, tight; narrow-minded

estrela | ɩʃ'tɾela | sf. star; destiny; fate; (cine., theat., TV) leading lady

estrelado -da | ɩʃtɾe'ladʋ | a. starry, starred. -ovosestrelados fried eggs

estremecer | ɩʃtɾeme'seʀ | vi. to tremble, to quake; to vibrate

estrépito | ɩʃ'tɾɛpitʋ | sm. loud noise; rattle

estriado -da | ɩʃtɾi'adʋ | a. grooved, rifled

estribilho | ɩʃtɾi'biLʋ | sm. refrain

estribo | ɩʃ'tɾibʋ | sm. stirrup; boarding step (of a train)

estridente | ɩʃtɾi'dɛtɩ | a. strident, shrill

estrofe | ɩʃ'tɾɔfɩ | sf. strophe, stanza

estróina, estroina | ɩʃ'tɾɔyna ɩʃ'tɾoyna | smf. spendthrift, wastrel / a. dissipated, wanton

estrondo | ɩʃ'tɾõdʋ | sm. roar, blast, rumble

estrondoso -sa | ɩʃtɾõ'dozʋ -'dɔza | a. roaring, thundering; boisterous, blatant

estropiado -da | ɩʃtɾopi'adʋ | a. crippled, mutilated

estrume | ɩʃ'tɾumɩ | sm. manure

estrutura | ɩʃtɾu'tura | sf. structure

estudante | ɩʃtu'dãtɩ | smf. student, pupil

estudar | ɩʃtu'daʀ | vt. to study

estúdio | ɩʃ'tudiʋ | sm. studio; working room (as of a painter, photographer etc.)

estudioso -sa | ɩʃtudi'ozʋ -'ɔza | smf. scholar / a. studious

estudo | ɩʃ'tudʋ | sm. study; (mus.) étude; (pl.) course of studies

estufa | ɩʃ'tufa | sf. stove, heater; hot house; sterilizer

estugar | ɩʃtu'gaʀ | vt. used in the expression e. o passo to quicken one's step

estupefato-ta | ɩʃtupe'fatʋ | a. stupefied; amazed

estupendo -da | ɩʃtu'pẽdʋ | a. stupendous; extraordinary

estupidez | ɩʃtupi'deʃ | sf. stupidity; (colloq.) coarseness, rudeness

estúpido-da | ɩʃ'tupidʋ | a. stupid; (colloq.) rude, coarse

estupor | ɩʃtu'poʀ | sm. stupor, lethargy; (colloq.) ugly and stupid person

estupro | ɩʃ'tuprʋ | sm. rape

estuque | ɩʃ'tukɩ | sm. plaster, stucco

esvaecimento | ɩʃvaesi'mẽtʋ | sm. evanescence, vanishing; weakening, enfeeblement

esvair-se | ɩʃva'iʀsɩ | vr. to vanish; to faint. -e. em sangue to bleed to death

esvaziar | ɩʃvazi'aʀ | vt. to empty

esverdeado -da | ɩʃveʀdɩ'adʋ | a. greenish

esvoaçar | ɩʃvʋa'saʀ | vi. to fly about

etapa | e'tapa | sf. stopping place; stage, phase

eternidade | eteʀni'dadɩ | sf. eternity

eterno-na | e'tɛʀnʋ | a. eternal

ética | 'ɛtika | sf. ethics (also philos.)

ético -ca | 'ɛtikʋ | a. ethic, ethical

etimologia | etimolo'jia | sf. etymology

etiqueta | eti'keta | sf. etiquette; label

eu | 'ew | pron. I. -como e. like me; as I. -e. mesmo I myself

eucarístico -ca | ewka'riʃtikʋ | a. Eucharistic, Eucharistical

europeu -péia | ewro'pew -'pɛya |

smf. a. European

evacuar | evaku'aʀ | *vt. vi.* to evacuate

evadir | eva'diʀ | *vt.* to evade, to avoid. **-e.-se** to escape

evangelho | evã'jɛLu | *sm.* Gospel

evangelista | evãje'liʃta | *smf.* evangelist (also *čap.*)

evaporação | evapora'sãw | *sf.* evaporation

evaporar | evapo'raʀ | *vt.* to evaporate. **-e.-se** to evaporate; to vanish

evasão | eva'zãw | *sf.* escape; evasion, subterfuge

evasiva | eva'ziva | *sf.* evasion, subterfuge

evasivo -va | eva'zivu | *a.* evasive

eventual | evẽtu'al | *a.* fortuitous

evidência | evi'dẽsia | *sf.* evidence

evidenciar | evidẽsi'aʀ | *vt.* to make evident, to make clear

evidente | evi'dẽtɩ | *a.* evident, clear, obvious

evitar | ɩvi'taʀ | *vt.* to avoid, to evade, to elude

evocar | evo'kaʀ | *vt.* to evoke, to call forth

evolução | evʋlu'sãw | *sf.* evolution; maneuver

evoluir | evʋlu'iʀ | *vi.* to evolve, to develop; to maneuver

exacerbar | ɩzaseʀ'baʀ | *vt.* to irritate, to exacerbate

exagerar | ɩzaje'raʀ | *vt. vi.* to exaggerate; to overstate

exagero | ɩza'jerʋ | *sm.* exaggeration

exalação | ɩzala'sãw | *sf.* exhalation

exalar | ɩza'laʀ | *vt.* to exhale, to give off (smell); to breathe out

exaltar | ɩzal'taʀ | *vt.* to exalt, to elevate; to praise, to glorify. **-e.-se** to get excited, angry or irritated

exame | ɩ'zamɩ | *sm.* examination; test. **-e. vestibular** university entrance examination

examinar | ɩzami'naʀ | *vt.* to examine; to inspect

exarar | eza'raʀ | *vt.* to write down (esp. on official papers). **-e. um despacho** to render decisions on (official papers)

exasperar | ɩzaʃpe'raʀ | *vt.* to exasperate

exatidão | ɩzati'dãw | *sf.* exactitude, accuracy; punctuality

exato -ta | ɩ'zatu | *a.* exact, accurate; punctual

exaurir | ɩzaw'riʀ | *vt.* to exhaust. **-e.se** to become exhausted

exausto -ta | e'zawʃtʋ | *a.* exhausted, worn-out

exceção | ese'sãw | *sf.* exception. **-com (a) e. de** except for, excluding

excedente | ese'dẽtɩ | *smf. a.* excess, surplus

exceder | ese'deʀ | *vt. vi.* to exceed, to surpass. **-e.-se** to overdo; to behave improperly

excelência | ese'lẽsia | *sf.* excellence, superiority. **-Vossa E.** Your Excellency

excelente | ese'lẽtɩ | *a.* excellent

excentricidade | esẽtrisi'dadɩ | *sf.* eccentricity

excêntrico -ca | e'sẽtrikʋ | *a.* eccentric

excepcional | esepsio'nal | *a.* exceptional; odd, unusual / *smf. a.* mentally or sensorially deficient person

excessivo -va | ese'sivʋ | *a.* excessive, extravagant, immoderate

excesso | e'sɛsʋ | *sm.* excess, surplus; extravagance, immoderation

exceto | e'sɛtʋ | *prep.* except, save

excitação | esita'sãw | *sf.* excitation, excitement

excitado -da | esi'tadʋ | *a.* excited; irritated

excitante | esi'tãtɩ | *sm.* excitant, stimulant / *a.* exciting, stimulating

excitar | esi'taʀ | *vt.* to excite, to stimulate

exclamação | ɩʃklama'sãw | *sf.* exclamation

exclamar | ιʒkla'maʀ | *vt. vi.* to exclaim; to shout

excluir | ιʒklu'iʀ | *vt.* to exclude; to expel

exclusive | ιʒklu'zivι | *adv.* exclusive of, not including

exclusivo -va | ιʒklu'zivυ | *a.* exclusive, private

excomungar | ιʒkυmū'gaʀ | *vt.* to excommunicate

excursão | ιʒkuʀ'sãw | *sf.* excursion, trip, tour

execrar | eze'kraʀ | *vt.* to execrate, to detest

execução | ezeku'sãw | *sm.* execution (also law); performance

executar | ezeku'taʀ | *vt.* to execute (also law); to accomplish; to perform

executivo -va | ezeku'tivυ | *sm.* executive branch of government; *smf. a.* executive

exemplar | ezē'plaʀ | *sm.* specimen, model, copy / *a.* exemplary

exemplificar | ezēplifi'kaʀ | *vt.* to exemplify

exemplo | e'zēplυ | *sm.* example; instance. **-dar o e.** to set a good example. **-por e.** for instance, for example

exéquias | e'zεkiaʒ | *sfpl.* funeral rites, obsequies

exercer | ezeʀ'seʀ | *vt.* to exercise (as influence on); to practise; to exert

exercício | ezeʀ'sisiυ | *sm.* exercise; practice; fiscal year. **-em e.** acting (in office)

exercitar | ezeʀsi'taʀ | *vt.* to exercise, to practice

exército | e'zεʀsitυ | *sm.* army

exibição | ιzibi'sãw | *sf.* exhibition; exposition

exibir | ιzi'biʀ | *vt.* to exhibit, to display

exigente | ιzi'jētι | *a.* exacting; demanding

exigir | ιzi'jiʀ | *vt.* to demand, to claim, to require

exíguo -gua | ι'zigwυ | *a.* scanty, small, exiguous

exilado -da | ιzi'ladυ | *smf.* exile / *a.* exiled

exilar | ιzi'laʀ | *vt.* to exile, to banish

exílio | ι'ziliυ | *sm.* exile, banishment

exímio -mia | ι'zimiυ | *a.* expert, skilled

eximir | ιzi'miʀ | *vt.* to exempt. **-e.-se** to shun

existência | ιziʒ'tēsia | *sf.* existence

existir | ιziʒ'tiʀ | *vi.* to exist, to be

êxito | 'ezitυ | *sm.* success

exoneração | ezonera'sãw | *sf.* exoneration; dismissal, discharge

exonerar | ezone'raʀ | *vt.* to exonerate, to release; to discharge (from office). **-e.-se** to resign (from office)

exorbitante | ezoʀbi'tãtι | *a.* exorbitant, extravagant

exortação | ezoʀta'sãw | *sf.* exhortation

exortar | ezoʀ'taʀ | *vt.* to exhort; to warn, to admonish

exótico -ca | e'zωtikυ | *a.* exotic; foreign

expansão | ιʒpã'sãw | *sf.* expansion; expansiveness; increase

expectativa | ιʒpekta'tiva | *sf.* expectation, hopes

expedição | ιʒpedi'sãw | *sf.* expedition (also mil.); shipment; delivery department

expedicionário -ria | ιʒpedisio'nariυ | *smf.* member of an expedition

expediente | ιʒpedi'ētι | *sm.* business hours, office hours; expedient, resource

expedir | ιʒpι'diʀ | *vt.* to ship (goods); to send out (letters etc.); to dispatch

expelir | ιʒpι'liʀ | *vt.* to expel, to eject

experiência | ιʒperi'ēsia | *sf.* experience; experiment; practice

experiente | ιʒperi'ētι | *a.* experienced, skillful

experimentado -da | ιʃpιrimẽ'tadʋ | *a.* experienced

experimentar | ιʃpιrimẽ'taR | *vt.* to experiment, to try, to test; to taste; to try on (as shoes)

expiar | ιʃpi'aR | *vt.* to expiate

expirar | ιʃpi'raR | *vi.* to expire, to exhale, to breathe / *vi.* to expire, to die

explanar | ιʃpla'naR | *vt.* to explain, to elucidate

explicação | ιʃplika'sãw | *sf.* explanation; justification; apology

explicar | ιʃpli'kaR | *vt.* to explain; to justify; to teach. **-e.-se** to make one's meaning clear

explícito -ta | ιʃ'plisitʋ | *a.* explicit

explodir | ιʃplʋ'diR | *vt. vi.* to explode

exploração | ιʃplora'sãw | *sf.* exploration; exploitation

explorar | ιʃplo'raR | *vt.* to explore; to exploit

explosão | ιʃplʋ'zãw | *sf.* explosion, blast; outburst

explosivo -va | ιʃplʋ'zivʋ | *sm. a.* explosive

expor | ιʃ'poR | *vt.* to expose, to exhibit; to risk; to explain; to reveal. **-e.-se** to expose oneself (to risks)

exportação | ιʃpoRta'sãw | *sf.* exportation, export

exportar | ιʃpoR'taR | *vt.* to export

exposição | ιʃpozi'sãw | *sf.* exposition, exhibition; explanation; exposure

exposto -ta | ιʃ'poʃtʋ -'pωʃta | *smf.* foundling / *a.* exposed; open to, bare, unprotected

expressão | ιʃpre'sãw | *sf.* expression

expressar | ιʃpre'saR | *vt.* = *exprimir*

expresso -sa | ιʃ'presʋ | *sm.* express (train, bus etc.) / *a.* expressed, express; clear, explicit

exprimir | ιʃpri'miR | *vt.* to express

expulsão | ιʃpul'sãw | *sf.* expulsion, expelling; ejection

expulsar | ιʃpul'saR | *vt.* to expel; to excrete

expurgar | ιʃpuR'gaR | *vt.* to expurgate, to purge; to cleanse

êxtase | 'eʃtazι | *sm.* ecstasy, rapture

extensão | ιʃtẽ'sãw | *sf.* extension; expansion; range, extent

extenso -sa | ιʃ'tẽsʋ | *a.* extensive, extended; vast. **-por e.** written out in full

extenuar | ιʃtenu'aR | *vt.* to exhaust, to debilitate

exterior | ιʃteri'oR | *sm.* exterior, foreign lands collectively; outside; appearance / *a.* exterior, external

exteriorizar | ιʃteriori'zaR | *vt.* to express

exterminar | ιʃteRmi'naR | *vt.* to exterminate

extermínio | ιʃteR'miniʋ | *sm.* extermination

externato | ιʃteR'natʋ | *sm.* day school

externo -na | ιʃ'teRnʋ | *sm.* external, exterior. **-aluno e.** day student

extinção | ιʃtĩ'sãw | *sf.* extinction; destruction

extinguir | ιʃtĩ'giR | *vt.* to extinguish; to suppress; to abolish

extinto -ta | ιʃ'tĩtʋ | *smf.* deceased / *a.* extinct, extinguished; dead

extirpar | ιʃtiR'paR | *vt.* to extirpate, to root out

extorquir | ιʃtoR'kiR | *vt.* to extort

extorsão | ιʃtoR'sãw | *sf.* extortion

extração | ιʃtra'sãw | *sf.* extraction; drawing (lottery); lineage

extradição | ιʃtradi'sãw | *sf.* extradition

extrair | ιʃtra'iR | *vt.* to extract, to remove; to pull out; to distill

extraordinário -ria | ιʃtraoRdi'nariʋ | *a.* extraordinary; outstanding; special

extrato | ιʃ'tratʋ | *sm.* extract; excerpt; (colloq.) perfume

extravagância | ιʃtrava'gãsia | *sf.* extravagance; eccentricity, oddity; dissipation

extravagante | ιʃtrava'gătι | *a*. extravagant; eccentric, odd

extraviar | ιʃtravi'aʀ | *vt*. to lead or send astray. **-e.-se** to go astray

extravio | ιʃtra'viʊ | *sm*. loss; going astray

extremidade | ιʃtremi'dadι | *sf*. extremity, tip, end

extremo -ma | ιʃ'tremʊ | *sm*. extreme; extremity, end / *a*. extreme, most remote; final, last; remotest. **-ao e.** extremely

extremoso -sa | ιʃtre'mozʊ -'mωza | *a*. extremely loving, devoted

extroversão | ιʃtroveʀ'sãw | *sf*. extroversion

exuberante | ιzube'rătι | *a*. exuberant; copious; lush; effusive, full of life

exultante | ιzul'tătι | *a*. exultant, jubilant, elated

exultar | ιzul'taʀ | *vi*. to exult, to rejoice

exumar | ιzu'maʀ | *vt*. to exhume

F

fá | 'fa | *sm*. (mus.) fa (in England, U.S. and Germany, the fourth tone in the scale of C)

fã | 'fã | *smf*. fan (esp. of a movie star)

fábrica | 'fabrika | *sf*. factory, plant, works

fabricação | fabrika'sãw | *sf*.-fabrication, manufacture

fabricante | fabri'kătι | *smf*. manufacturer, maker

fabricar | fabri'kaʀ | *vt*. to manufacture, to make, to fabricate

fábula | 'fabula | *sf*. fable, tale; legend

faca | 'faka | *sf*. knife

facada | fa'kada | *sf*. knifing, stab; (slang) touch (for money)

façanha | fa'saɴa | *sf*. prowess, feat, exploit

facão | fa'kãw | *sm*. machete, large and heavy knife

facção | fak'sãw | *sf*. faction

face | 'fasι | *sf*. face; cheek; surface. **-em f. de** by (in) virtue of. **-fazer f. a** to make a stand against

faceiro -ra | fa'seyrʊ | *a*. coquettish, foppish

fachada | fa'xada | *sf*. façade, face of a building

facho | 'faxʊ | *sm*. torch

fácil | 'fasil | *a*. easy, simple, effortless

facilidade | fasili'dadι | *sf*. ease, easiness, facility; (*pl*.) means, facilities

facilitar | fasili'taʀ | *vt*. to facilitate, to make easy / *vi*. to expose oneself to danger

facínora | fa'sinora | *sm*. criminal, gangster

faculdade | fakul'dadι | *sf*. faculty, capacity; a university school. **-f. de Direito** law school. **-faculdades mentais** lights, wits

facultativo -va | fakulta'tivʊ | *sm*. physician / *a*. facultative, optional

fada | 'fada | *sf*. fairy. **-conto de fadas** fairy tale

fadado -da | fa'dadʊ | *a*. bound, doomed

fadiga | fa'diga | *sf*. fatigue, exhaustion; (*pl*.) hardships, drudgery

fagueiro -ra | fa'geyrʊ | *a*. agreeable; pleased, glad

fagulha | fa'guʟa | *sf*. spark, flash, flashing

faia | 'faya | *sf*. beech

faina | 'fayna | sf. toil, task

faisão -soa | fay'zãw -'zoa | smf. pheasant

faísca | fa'iʃka | sf. spark, flash

faiscar | faiʃ'kaʀ | vt. to prospect for gold or diamonds / vi. to glitter, to sparkle, to flash

faixa | 'fayxa | sf. stripe, streak; waistband; zone, area

fala | 'fala | sf. speech; talk; voice; (theat.) line

faladeira | fala'deyra | sf. tattler (woman), gossip, chatterbox / a. talkative

falador -dora | fala'doʀ | smf. gabbler / a. very talkative

falar | fa'laʀ | vt. vi. to speak, to talk. -f. claro to be frank. -f. pelos cotovelos (colloq.) to talk one's head off. -por f. nisso by the way. -falou! (slang) O.K.!, all right!

falcão -coa | fal'kãw -'koa | smf. hawk, falcon

falcatrua | falka'trua | sf. swindle, fraud

falecer | fale'seʀ | vi. to die, to pass away

falecimento | falɪsi'mẽtʊ | sm. death, decease

falência | fa'lẽsia | sf. bankruptcy, insolvency

falha | 'faʟa | sf. flaw, imperfection

falhar | fa'ʟaʀ | vi. to fail; to miss; to misfire

falho -lha | 'faʟʊ | a. faulty, defective

falir | fa'liʀ | vi. to go bankrupt, to fail (in business)

falível | fa'livɪl | a. fallible

falsário -ria | fal'sariʊ | smf. forger, counterfeiter

falsidade | falsi'dadɪ | sf. falseness; hypocrisy, duplicity

falsificar | falsifi'kaʀ | vt. to falsify; to forge

falso -sa | 'falsʊ | a. false; disloyal; counterfeit, fraudulent. -f. testemunho calumny, slanderous report

falta | 'falta | sf. need, lack; fault, failure; absence; mistake; (sports) foul. -sem f. without fail. -sentir f. de to miss (person or thing). -estar em f. to be in default

faltar | fal'taʀ | vi. to be lacking, to be wanting; to miss; to fail. -f. a to be absent from. -f. à palavra to go back on one's word. -faltam cinco para as cinco it's five minutes to five

fama | 'fama | sf. fame, reputation, renown

famélico -ca | fa'mɛlikʊ | a. starving

família | fa'milia | sf. family

familiar | famili'aʀ | smf. a relative / a. familiar, domestic; common; well-known

familiarizar | familiari'zaʀ | vt. to familiarize; to accustom. -f.-se com to familiarize oneself with, to become acquainted with

faminto -ta | fa'mĩtʊ | a. hungry, starving

famoso -sa | fa'mozʊ -'mwza | a. famous; renowned, celebrated

fanático -ca | fa'natikʊ | smf. fanatic / a. fanatical

fanatismo | fana'tiʃmʊ | sm. fanaticism

fanfarrão -rona | fãfa'ʀãw -'ʀona | sm. boaster, bragger / a. boastering, bragging

fanhoso -sa | fa'nozʊ -'nwza | a. nasal, twangy

fantasia | fãta'zia | sf. fantasy, imagination; caprice; costume for Carnival

fantasma | fã'taʃma | sm. ghost, spectre, phantom

fantástico -ca | fã'taʃtikʊ | a. fantastic; fanciful, imaginary

fantoche | fã'twxɪ | sm. puppet

faqueiro | fa'keyrʊ | sm. cutlery case

farda | 'faʀda | sf. uniform (esp. military)

fardo | 'faʀdʊ | sm. bale, bundle; load, burden

farejar | fare'jaʀ | vt. to scent, to

sniff, to smell

farfalhar | faʀfa'laʀ | vi. to rustle

farinha | fa'riɲa | sf. flour; meal; manioc flour

farmacêutico -ca | faʀma'sewtiku | smf. pharmacist, druggist / a. pharmaceutical, pharmaceutical

farmácia | faʀ'masia | sf. pharmacy; chemist's shop

farnel | faʀ'nɛl | sm. provisions for a journey

faro | 'faʀʋ | sm. sense of smell (of animals)

farofa | fa'rɔfa | sf. manioc flour browned in butter or oil

farol | fa'rɔl | sm. lighthouse; beacon; headlight (of a car, train etc.)

farpa | 'faʀpa | sf. splinter (of wood); barb (of an arrow, fish-hook, harpoon)

farra | 'faʀa | sf. frolic, drinking-bout; orgy

farrapo | fa'ʀapʋ | sm. rag; tatter

farsa | 'faʀsa | sf. farce; imposture

farsante | faʀ'sãtɪ | smf. impostor, fake

fartar | faʀ'taʀ | vt. to satiate. -f.-se to gorge oneself; to become tired

farto -ta | 'faʀtʋ | a. satiated; abundant; tired, weary, sick (of)

fartura | faʀ'tura | sf. abundance, plenty

fascinação | fasina'sãw | sf. fascination, charm

fascinar | fasi'naʀ | vt. to fascinate; to charm

fase | 'fazɪ | sf. phase; grade, stage

fastidioso -sa | faʃtidi'ozʋ -'ɔza | a. tedious, tiresome, boring

fastio | faʃ'tiʋ | sm. lack of appetite; boredom, tedium

fatal | fa'tal | a. fatal, deadly; ruinous

fatalidade | fatali'dadɪ | sf. fatality; disaster

fatia | fa'tia | sf. slice; piece

fatigante | fati'gãtɪ | a. tiresome, fatiguing; wearysome

fatigar | fati'gaʀ | vt. to tire, to fatigue, to exhaust; to annoy

fato | 'fatʋ | sm. fact, event, occurrence. -de f. in fact, as a matter of fact. -ir às vias de f. to come to grips

fatura | fa'tura | sf. invoice, bill

faturar | fatu'raʀ | vt. to invoice, to bill; (slang) to bag, to secure

fausto -ta | 'fawʃtʋ | sm. pageantry, pomp / a. fortunate; happy

fava | 'fava | sf. broad bean; bean pod

favela | fa'vɛla | sf. slum (usually on a hill), shanty town

favo | 'favʋ | sm. honeycomb

favor | fa'voʀ | sm. favo(u)r; kindness, benefit. -a f. de or em f. de to the advantage of; on behalf of. -faça o f. de be so kind as to. -por f. please

favorável | favo'ravɪl | a. favo(u)rable; auspicious

favorecer | favore'seʀ | vt. to favo(u)r; to benefit, to aid

favorito -ta | favo'ritʋ | smf. favo(u)rite / a. favo(u)rite, darling

faxina | fa'xina | sf. a cleanup

faxineiro -ra | faxi'neyrʋ | smf. cleaner (person who cleans rooms, houses etc.)

fazenda | fa'zẽda | sf. farm, plantation, ranch; public treasure; cloth, fabric. -Ministério da F. Treasury Department

fazendeiro -ra | fazẽ'deyrʋ | smf. farmer, planter; owner of a large estate

fazer | fa'zeʀ | vt. to make; to do. -f. a barba to shave. -f. as pazes to make up, to be reconciled. -f. cerimônia to stand on ceremony. -f. de conta que to pretend that

fé | 'fɛ | sf. faith, belief. -dar f. to certify

febre | 'fɛbrɪ | sf. fever

febril | fe'bril | a. feverish, febrile

fechadura | fexa'dura | sf. lock (of door, drawer etc.)

fechar | fe'xaʀ | *vt.* to close, to shut (up, down); to settle (a business deal); to cut off (a car). -f. à chave to lock

fecho | 'fexʋ | *sm.* lock, latch; clip; closure; close (of a letter). -f. ecler zipper

fedelho -lha | fe'deʟʋ | *smf.* brat

feder | fe'deʀ | *vi.* (vulg.) to stink

federação | federa'sãw | *sf.* federation

fedor | fe'doʀ | *sm.* (vulg.) stink, stench

feição | fey'sãw | *sf.* aspect; form, shape; (*pl.*) facial features

feijão | fey'jãw | *sm.* bean

feijoada | feyjʋ'ada | *sf.* dish of black beans stewed with pork, dried meat, sausages etc.

feio, feia | 'feyʋ | *smf.* ugly person / *a.* ugly

feira | 'feyra | *sf.* fair; open-air market

feita | 'feyta | *sf.* deed, act; time. -de uma f. once

feitiçaria | feytisa'ria | *sf.* witchcraft, sorcery

feiticeiro -ra | feyti'seyrʋ | *sm.* sorcerer, warlock; medicine man; *sf.* witch / *a.* charming

feitiço | fey'tisʋ | *sm.* magic spell; enchantment

feitio | fey'tiʋ | *sm.* shape; fashion; temperament; labo(u)r (of a tailor, dressmaker etc.)

feito -ta | 'feytʋ | *sm.* feat / *conj.* (colloq.) like. -f. louco like mad / *a.* done, made; settled. -bem f.! it serves you (him, her, them) right!

feitor | fey'toʀ | *sm.* foreman (esp. of slaves in a plantation)

feixe | 'feyxɩ | *sm.* bunch, bundle (also bot., anat.); faggot; (rad.) beam (also of light)

fel | 'fɛl | *sm.* bile, gall; gall bladder (of animals); bitterness

felicidade | fɩlisi'dadɩ | *sf.* happiness, joy, contentment

felicitação | felisita'sãw | *sf.* congratulation. -felicitações! congratulations!

feliz | fɩ'liʒ | *a.* happy; lucky; fortunate

felpudo -da | fel'pudʋ | *a.* fluffy, downy; fuzzy

feltro | 'feltrʋ | *sm.* felt

fêmea | 'femɩa | *sf.* female

feminino -na | fɩmi'ninʋ | *a.* feminine; female

fenda | 'fẽda | *sf.* crack, flaw; fissure

fender | fẽ'deʀ | *vt.* to crack, to split, to cleave

feno | 'fenʋ | *sm.* hay

fenômeno | fe'nomenʋ | *sm.* phenomenon

fera | 'fɛra | *sf.* beast of prey

féretro | 'fɛretrʋ | *sm.* bier, coffin

féria | 'fɛria | *sf.* daily or weekly wage; income of a business establishment; (*pl.*) holidays, vacation

feriado | feri'adʋ | *sm. a.* holiday

ferida | fɩ'rida | *sf.* sore, wound

ferido -da | fɩ'ridʋ | *smf.* wounded person / *a.* wounded

ferimento | fɩri'mẽtʋ | *sm.* wound, injury

ferir | fɩ'riʀ | *vt.* to wound, to hurt (also fig.). -f.-se to wound oneself; to become offended

fermentação | feʀmẽta'sãw | *sf.* fermentation

fermentar | feʀmẽ'taʀ | *vt. vi.* to ferment

fermento | feʀ'mẽtʋ | *sm.* ferment, leaven, yeast

ferocidade | ferosi'dadɩ | *sf.* ferocity

feroz | fe'rwʒ | *a.* ferocious, fierce; savage

ferradura | feʀa'dura | *sf.* horseshoe

ferragem | fe'ʀajẽy | *sf.* hardware; iron fittings. -loja de ferragens hardware store

ferramenta | feʀa'mẽta | *sf.* tool, instrument, implement

ferrão | fe'ʀãw | *sm.* spike; sting (of an insect)

ferrar | fe'ʀaʀ | *vt.* to shoe horses;

to mark with a branding iron; to set the hook

ferreiro | fe'Reyrʋ | *sm.* blacksmith, smith

ferrenho -nha | fe'Renʋ | *a.* stubborn, inflexible

ferro | 'feRʋ | *sm.* iron; surgery or dentistry instrument; electric iron; anchor (also *pl.*). -**lançar ferros** to drop anchor. -**f. fundido** cast iron. -**f. batido** wrought iron

ferroada | feRʋ'ada | *sf.* sting, prick

ferrolho | fe'Rolʋ | *sm.* bolt (also of rifles)

ferro-velho | 'feRʋ'velʋ | *sm.* junk, scrap

ferroviário -ria | feRovi'ariʋ | *smf.* railwayman, railway employee / *a.* of or pertaining to railways

ferrugem | fe'Rujẽy | *sf.* rust

fértil | 'fertil | *a.* fertile, fecund, productive

fertilidade | fertili'dadɩ | *sf.* fertility, productivity

fertilizar | fertili'zaR | *vt.* to fertilize

ferver | feR'veR | *vt. vi.* to boil; to bubble

fervilhar | fɩRvi'LaR | *vi.* to swarm; to pullulate, to teem

fervor | feR'voR | *sm.* fervo(u)r; zeal; eagerness

fervoroso -sa | feRvo'rozʋ -'rωza | *a.* fervent; zealous

fervura | feR'vura | *sf.* boiling

festa | 'fєʃta | *sf.* party; celebration; festival; (*pl.*) caresses; Christmas presents. -**Boas Festas!** Season's Greetings! -**fazer festas a** to caress; to welcome warmly

festejar | feʃte'jaR | *vt.* to feast, to give a party for; to celebrate, to commemorate

festejo | feʃ'tejʋ | *sm.* festivity, celebration; warm welcome, caress

festim | feʃ'tĩ | *sm.* banquet. -**tiro de f.** blank cartridge shot

festival | feʃti'val | *sm.* festival

festividade | feʃtivi'dadɩ | *sf.* festivity

fetiche | fe'tixɩ | *sm.* fetish

fétido -da | 'fєtidʋ | *sm.* stench / *a.* fetid

feto | 'fєtʋ | *sm.* foetus; embryo

feudal | few'dal | *a.* feudal

fevereiro | feve'reyrʋ | *sm.* February

fezes | 'fєzɩʃ | *sfpl.* excrement; dregs

fiação | fia'sãw | *sf.* spinning; spinning mill

fiado -da | fi'adʋ | *a.* spun; trustful; bought or sold on credit

fiador -dora | fia'doR | *smf.* warrantor, surety; *sm.* bondsman

fiança | fi'ãsa | *sf.* bail, bond; security, warranty

fiapo | fi'apʋ | *sm.* small piece of thin thread

fiar | fi'aR | *vt.* to spin (thread); to sell on credit. -**f.-se** to trust / *vi.* to sell on credit

fiasco | fi'aʃkʋ | *sm.* fiasco, failure

fibra | 'fibra | *sf.* fibre; filament, thread

ficar | fi'kaR | *vi.* to stay; to remain; to be located; to be left. -**f. com** to keep; to get (ill, jealous etc.). -**f. de** to be supposed or expected to. -**f. bem** to fit; to look well

ficção | fik'sãw | *sf.* fiction, imagination

ficha | 'fixa | *sf.* chip, counter (gambling); index card, file card

fichado -da | fi'xadʋ | *a.* on file; having a police record

fichar | fi'xaR | *vt.* to record (on file cards); to enter in a file

fichário | fi'xariʋ | *sm.* file cabinet

fictício -cia | fik'tisiʋ | *a.* fictitious, imaginary; false

fidalgo -ga | fi'dalgʋ | *smf.* aristocrat / *a.* noble, magnanimous

fidedigno -na | fide'dignʋ | *a.* trustworthy, dependable, reliable

fidelidade | fideli'dadι | *sf.* fidelity, faithfulness, loyalty

fieira | fi'eyra | *sf.* string; string (of things tied together)

fiel | fi'ɛl | *smf.* believer; *sm.* pointer (of a scale) / *a.* faithful; accurate

figa | 'figa | *sf.* an amulet (a tight--fisted hand with the thumb between the index and the middle finger)

fígado | 'figadʊ | *sm.* liver

figo | 'figʊ | *sm.* fig

figura | fi'gura | *sf.* figure (all senses); image; appearance

figurar | figu'raʀ | *vt.* to figure, to represent / *vi.* to figure, to appear; to have a part or a role in

figurino | figu'rinʊ | *sm.* fashion magazine; pattern, model

fila | 'fila | *sf.* queue, line. **-fazer f.** to queue up. **-cão de f.** mastiff. **-f. brasileiro** Brazilian mastiff

filantropia | filãtro'pia | *sf.* philanthropy, humanity

filar | fi'laʀ | *vt.* (colloq.) to cadge, to mooch, to bum

filatelia | filate'lia | *sf.* philately, stamp collecting

filé | fi'lɛ | *sm.* fil(l)et (of meat or fish)

fileira | fi'leyra | *sf.* line, row, rank, file; (gen. *pl.*) military service

filete | fi'letι | *sm.* thin thread

filha | 'fiʎa | *sf.* daughter

filharada | fiʎa'rada | *sf.* large family, many children

filho | 'fiʎʊ | *sm.* son. **-f. natural** illegitimate child

filhote | fi'ʎɔtι | *sm.* young animal

filiação | filia'sãw | *sf.* filiation; affiliation; subordination

filial | fili'al | *sf.* branch store or office / *a.* filial

filmar | fil'maʀ | *vt.* to film

filme | 'filmι | *sm.* film, motion picture

filosofia | filozo'fia | *sf.* philosophy

filósofo -fa | fi'lɔzʊfʊ | *smf.* philosopher

filtrar | fil'traʀ | *vt.* to filter

filtro | 'filtrʊ | *sm.* filter

fim | 'fĩ | *sm.* end; aim, purpose. **-a f. de que** in order that, so that. **-ao** or **no f. de contas** after all

finado -da | fi'nadʊ | *smf. a.* deceased, dead. **-dia de finados** All Soul's Day

final | fi'nal | *sm.* end, finish, close; last

finalizar | finali'zaʀ | *vt. vi.* to end, to conclude, to finish

finanças | fi'nãsaʃ | *sfpl.* finances; public funds

financeiro -ra | finã'seyrʊ | *a.* financial

finaciador -dora | finãsia'doʀ | *smf.* financial backer

financiamento | finãsia'mẽtʊ | *sm.* financing

financiar | finãsi'aʀ | *vt.* to finance, to back

fincar | fĩ'kaʀ | *vt.* to drive (as a stake in the ground); to thrust in

fineza | fi'neza | *sf.* fineness; finesse; courtesy

fingimento | fĩji'mẽtʊ | *sm.* pretense; hypocrisy; affectation

fingir | fĩ'jiʀ | *vt.* to pretend to, to simulate; to affect. **-f.-se** to pretend to be

finlandês -desa | fĩlã'deʃ | *sm.* (ling.) Finnish; *smf.* Finn / *a.* Finnish

fino -na | 'finʊ | *a.* fine; slender; shrewd; choice

fio | 'fiʊ | *sm.* thread, string; wire; edge (of a blade); a fine thread of any liquid

firma | 'fiʀma | *sf.* firm, business; signature

firmar | fiʀ'maʀ | *vt.* to make firm; to sign (a contract etc.)

firme | 'fiʀmι | *a.* firm, stable; fast (said of colo[u]rs)

firmeza | fiʀ'meza | *sf.* firmness; determination; stability

fiscal | fiʃ'kal | *smf.* inspector; controller / *a.* fiscal

fiscalizar | fiʃkali'zaʀ | *vt.* to supervise, to control, to inspect

fisco | 'fiʃkʋ | *sm.* treasury, exchequer

fisga | 'fiʃga | *sf.* harpoon, fishing spear

física | 'fizika | *sf.* physics

físico -ca | 'fizikʋ | *sm.* physique, build; *smf.* physicist / *a.* physical; material

fisionomia | fizionoʻmia | *sf.* face, countenance, appearance

fissura | fiʻsura | *sf.* fissure, crevice

fita | 'fita | *sf.* ribbon; tape; motion picture film. **-fazer f.** to act, to pretend

fitar | fiʻtaR | *vt.* to stare at

fito | 'fitʋ | *sm.* aim; purpose

fivela | fiʻvɛla | *sf.* buckle

fixar | fiʻksaR | *vt.* to fix; to fix (one's attention, eyes etc.); to determine, to set (a date etc.); to remember, to retain

fixo -xa | 'fiksʋ | *a.* fixed, steady; fast (colo[u]r)

flácido -da | 'flasidʋ | *a.* flaccid, flabby, drooping, lax

flagelar | flajeʻlaR | *vt.* to scourge

flagrante | flaʻgrãtɩ | *sm.* instant, moment, the very act; (photog.) snapshot. **-em f.** in the act

flamejar | flameʻjaR | *vi.* to flame, to glow

flâmula | 'flamula | *sf.* pennant, streamer, banneret

flanco | 'flãkʋ | *sm.* flank

flanela | flaʻnela | *sf.* flannel

flauta | 'flawta | *sf.* flute

flecha | 'flexa | *sf.* arrow

flerte | 'flɛRtɩ | *sm.* flirtation

flexibilidade | fleksibiliʻdadɩ | *sf.* flexibility

flexível | fleʻksivɩl | *a.* flexible

floco | 'flɔkʋ | *sm.* snowflake; flake, flock, tuft (of wool)

flor | 'flɔR | *sf.* flower. **-a fina f.** the cream (of anything). **-em f.** flowering, blooming

florescer | floreʻseR | *vi.* to flower, to blossom; to prosper

floresta | floʻrɛʃta | *sf.* forest, woods

florista | floʻriʃta | *smf.* florist

fluência | fluʻẽsia | *sf.* fluency

fluente | fluʻẽtɩ | *a.* fluent

fluido -da | 'fluydʋ | *sm. a.* fluid, liquid

fluir | fluʻiR | *vi.* to flow

fluminense | flumiʻnẽsɩ | *smf.* native of the State of Rio de Janeiro / *a.* of or pertaining to the State of Rio de Janeiro

flutuante | flutuʻãtɩ | *a.* floating, buoyant

flutuar | flutuʻaR | *vi.* to float

fluvial | fluviʻal | *a.* fluvial

fluxo | 'fluksʋ | *sm.* flux, flow

foca | 'fɔka | *sf.* (zool.) seal

focalizar | fokaliʻzaR | *vt.* to focalize, to focus

focinho | fʋʻsiNʋ | *sm.* snout, muzzle

foco | 'fɔkʋ | *sm.* focus; focal point, center

fofo -fa | 'fofʋ | *a.* fluffy; soft; smooth

fogão | fʋʻgãw | *sm.* stove

fogo | 'fogʋ | *sm.* fire. **-abrir f.** to open fire. **-fogos de artifício** fireworks

fogoso -sa | foʻgozʋ -ʻgwza | *a.* spirited (said of a horse); ardent, fiery

fogueira | fʋʻgeyra | *sf.* bonfire, campfire

foguete | fʋʻgetɩ | *sm.* rocket; (mil.) missile

foguista | foʻgiʃta | *sm.* fireman, stoker

foice | 'foysɩ | *sf.* scythe. **-a talho de f.** just right

folclore | folkʻlɔrɩ | *sm.* folklore

fole | 'fɔlɩ | *sm.* bellows

fôlego | 'folɩgʋ | *sm.* breath, respiration. **-obra de f.** extensive work (esp. literary)

folga | 'fɔlga | *sf.* rest, work pause; (mech.) slack; (mech.) clearance. **-estar de f.** to be off duty. **-dia de f.** free day

folgado -da | folʻgadʋ | *a.* loose, baggy; loose-fitting; rested; easygoing; (slang) unpleasantly familiar

folgar | fol'gaʀ | *vt.* to rest, to be off duty; to loosen, to slacken / *vi.* to rejoice; to rest; to amuse oneself

folha | 'foLa | *sf.* leaf; blade; sheet (as of paper). **-f. de pagamento** pay-roll. **-f. de serviço** service record

folhagem | fo'Lajẽy | *sf.* foliage

folhear | foLí'aʀ | *vt.* to leaf through (the pages of a book); to veneer; to plate

folhetim | foLe'tĩ | *sm.* daily chapter of a newspaper serial

folheto | foLe'tʊ | *sm.* leaflet; pamphlet

folhinha | fʊ'Lina | *sf.* leaflet; tear--off calendar

folia | fʊ'lia | *sf.* frolic; Carnival merrymaking

folião -ona | fʊli'ãw -'ona | *smf.* Carnival dancer; reveler, carouser

fome | 'fomí | *sf.* hunger; famine; avidity. **-estar com f.** or **ter f.** to be hungry

fomentar | fomẽ'taʀ | *vt.* to foment, to promete, to stimulate

fomento | fo'mẽtʊ | *sm.* stimulation, encouragement; development

fone | 'foní | *sm.* telephone receiver; earphone

fonética | fo'nɛtika | *sf.* phonetics

fonético -ca | fo'nɛtikʊ | *a.* phonetic

fonte | 'fõtí | *sf.* fountain; spring, source; temple (side of forehead). **-f. de renda** source of revenue

fora | 'fɔra | *adv.* out, outside; abroad. **-botar f.** to throw away. **-lá f.** out there / *prep.* except. **-f. de si** beside oneself / *interj.* out!, get out!

foragido -da | fora'jidʊ | *smf.* fugitive; outlaw

forasteiro -ra | foraʃ'teyrʊ | *smf.* foreigner, stranger

forca | 'foʀka | *sf.* gallows

força | 'foʀsa | *sf.* strength, power, force (also mil.). **-à f.** forcibly, by force. **-à f. de** by dint of

forçar | foʀ'saʀ | *vt.* to force, to compel; to obtain by force; to strain (eyes, voice etc.)

forçoso -sa | foʀ'sozʊ -'sɔza | *a.* necessary; inevitable

forja | 'foʀja | *sf.* foundry, furnace; ironworks

forjar | foʀ'jaʀ | *vt.* to forge (metal); to falsify

forma | 'foʀma | *sf.* form, shape; manner. **-da mesma f.** in the same manner. **-de f. que** so that

fôrma | 'foʀma | *sf.* mould; foundry mould; shoe-last; cake or pudding mould

formação | foʀma'sãw | *sf.* formation; education

formado -da | foʀ'madʊ | *a.* formed; graduated (from college)

formal | foʀ'mal | *a.* formal, explicit; conventional

formalidade | foʀmali'dadí | *sf.* formality, ceremony

formão | foʀ'mãw | *sm.* chisel

formar | foʀ'maʀ | *vt.* to form, to shape; to constitute. **-f.-se** to develop; to graduate (from college)

formatura | foʀma'tura | *sf.* graduation

formidável | foʀmi'davíl | *a.* formidable; amazing; excellent

formiga | fʊʀ'miga | *sf.* ant

formigar | fʊʀmi'gaʀ | *vi.* to itch; to swarm

formigueiro | fʊʀmi'geyrʊ | *sm.* antheap, anthill

formoso -sa | foʀ'mozʊ -'mɔza | *a.* lovely, beautiful

formosura | foʀmʊ'zura | *sf.* loveliness, beauty

fórmula | 'foʀmula | *sf.* formula

formular | foʀmu'laʀ | *vt.* to formulate; to prescribe (a recipe)

fornalha | foʀ'naLa | *sf.* furnace

fornecer | foʀne'seʀ | *vt.* to supply, to provide

forno | 'foRnʋ | *sm.* oven; kiln

foro | 'fɔrʋ | *sm.* forum, law court; jurisdiction; (*pl.*) rights, privileges

foro | 'forʋ | *sm.* (law) ground-rent; right, privilege

forquilha | foR'kiʟa | *sf.* forked stick; crotch

forragem | fo'Rajẽy | *sf.* forage, fodder

forrar | fo'RaR | *vt.* to line (the inside of); to overlay; to cover (as a floor with carpets)

forro -ra | 'foRʋ | *sm.* lining; covering; sheathing; ceiling / *a.* freed (said of a slave, esp. a Negro)

fortalecer | foRtale'seR | *vt.* to fortify, to strengthen; to encourage

fortaleza | foRta'leza | *a.* force, vigo(u)r; fortitude; fortress

forte | 'fɔRtɪ | *sm.* fort, fortress / *a.* strong; courageous; healthy; sturdy

fortificar | foRtifi'kaR | *vt.* to fortify

fortuito -ta | foR'tuytʋ | *a.* fortuitous, accidental

fortuna | fʋR'tuna | *sf.* fortune; chance, luck; fate; riches

fosco -ca | 'foʒkʋ | *a.* dull, dim; mat

fosforescente | foʒfore'sẽtɪ | *a.* phosphorescent

fósforo | 'foʒfʋrʋ | *sm.* (chem.) phosphorus; match. **-riscar um f.** to strike a match

fossa | 'fɔsa | *sf.* pit; cesspool; (anat.) cavity; (slang) depression. **-fossas nasais** nostrils

fóssil | 'fɔsil | *sm. a.* fossil

foto | 'fɔtʋ | *sf.* (colloq.) photo, snapshot

fotocópia | foto'kɔpia | *sf.* photocopy, photostat

fotografar | fotogra'faR | *vt.* to photograph

fotografia | fotogra'fia | *sf.* photography; photograph

fotógrafo | fo'tɔgrafʋ | *smf.* photographer

foz | 'fɔʒ | *sf.* mouth of a river

fração | fra'sãw | *sf.* fraction

fracassar | fraka'saR | *vi.* to fail, to miscarry

fracasso | fra'kasʋ | *sm.* failure, fiasco

fraco -ca | 'frakʋ | *a.* weak; thin, watery; of poor quality

frade | 'fradɪ | *sm.* friar

fragata | fra'gata | *sf.* (naut.) frigate

frágil | 'frajil | *a.* fragile, breakable; frail, delicate

fragmento | frag'mẽtʋ | *sm.* fragment; bit; splinter

fragor | fra'goR | *sm.* crack, crash, din

fragoroso -sa | frago'rozʋ -'rɔza | *a.* cracking; loud, noisy; overwhelming

fragrância | fra'grãsia | *sf.* fragrance; perfume, aroma

framboesa | frãbʋ'eza | *sf.* raspberry

francês -cesa | frã'seʒ -'seza | *sm.* (ling.) French; Frenchman; *sf.* Frenchwoman / *a.* French

franco -ca | 'frãkʋ | *sm.* franc (monetary unit); (hist.) Frank / *a.* frank, sincere, outspoken. **-f. de porte** postpaid. **-entrada franca** free admission. **-seja f.!** be honest!

frangalho | frã'gaʟʋ | *sm.* rag, tatter

frango | 'frãgʋ | *sm.* chicken

franja | 'frãja | *sf.* fringe; bangs (hair)

franquear | frãkɪ'aR | *vt.* to frank, to exempt from duties; to facilitate the passage of; to grant, to concede

franqueza | frã'keza | *sf.* frankness, sincerity

franquia | frã'kia | *sf.* franchise; exemption; immunity

franzino -na | frã'zinʋ | *a.* thin, slender; feeble, frail

franzir | frã'ziR | *vt.* to ruffle, to gather; to wrinkle. **-f. a testa** or **as sobrancelhas** to frown

fraque | 'frakı | *sm.* man's morning coat and striped trousers, morning dress

fraqueza | fra'keza | *sf.* weakness, frailty, feebleness

frasco | 'fraʃkʊ | *sm.* flask

frase | 'frazı | *sf.* phrase, sentence, expression. -**f. feita** stock phrase

fraternidade | frateRni'dadı | *sf.* fraternity, brotherhood

fraterno -na | fra'teRnʊ | *a.* fraternal, brotherly

fratura | fra'tura | *sf.* fracture, break

fraturar | fratu'raR | *vt.* to fracture

fraude | 'frawdı | *sf.* fraud

fraudulento -ta | frawdu'lẽtʊ | *a.* fraudulent

freada | frı'ada | *sf.* sudden braking (of a car)

frear | frı'aR | *vt.* to brake; to slow down; to restrain

freguês -guesa | fre'geʃ | *smf.* customer, client

freguesia | frıgı'zia | *sf.* customers (collectively); (eccles.) parish

frei | 'frey | *sm.* (*cap.*) Friar

freio | 'freyʊ | *sm.* brake; bit (of a bridle); check, control, restraint

freira | 'freyra | *sf.* nun

freixo | 'freyxʊ | *sm.* (bot.) ash

fremir | fre'miR | *vi.* to flutter, to rustle; to tremble, to quiver

frêmito | 'fremitʊ | *sm.* roar, rustle; shudder, quiver

frenesi | frene'zi | *sm.* frenzy

frenético -ca | fre'nɛtikʊ | *a.* frantic, delirious, excited

frente | 'frẽtı | *sf.* front; façade. -**à f. ahead**, in front, before. -**à f. de** in front of

freqüência | fre'kwẽsia | *sf.* attendance; frequency; periodicity. -**com f. often**

freqüentar | frekwẽ'taR | *vt.* to frequent, to attend regularly

freqüente | fre'kwẽtı | *a.* frequent

fresco -ca | 'freʃkʊ | *sm.* fresh air; (fine arts) fresco; (vulg.) homosexual / *a.* fresh, cool; not stale; wet (paint). -**de f. freshly**

frescura | freʃ'kura | *sf.* freshness; coolness; (vulg.) effeminate behavio(u)r; (vulg.) finicalness

fresta | 'freʃta | *sf.* crack, slit; gap, aperture

fretar | fre'taR | *vt.* to charter

frete | 'frɛtı | *sm.* **freight**, freightage

frevo | 'frevʊ | *sm.* Carnival dance and music (typical of the State of Pernambuco)

friagem | fri'ajẽy | *sf.* cold weather or wind

fricção | frik'sãw | *sf.* friction, rubbing; massaging

frieira | fri'eyra | *sf.* athlete's foot; eczema between the toes

frieza | fri'eza | *sf.* coolness, coldness, indifference

frigideira | friji'deyra | *sf.* frying-pan

frigorífico -ca | frigo'rifikʊ | *sm.* cold storage plant / *a.* refrigerative; frigorific

frincha | 'frĩxa | *sf.* crack, narrow gap

frio -a | 'friʊ | *sm.* cold; (*pl.*) cold cuts / *a.* cool, cold; indifferent

friorento -ta | frio'rẽtʊ | *a.* sensitive to cold

frisa | 'friza | *sf.* theatre box (on the main floor)

frisar | fri'zaR | *vt.* to curl, to frizzle; to stress, to emphasize

friso | 'frizʊ | *sm.* (arch.) frieze; (arch.) fillet (also typog.)

fritada | fri'tada | *sf.* kind of omelette with shrimp or chopped meat etc.

fritar | fri'taR | *vt.* to fry

frito -ta | 'fritʊ | *a.* fried

frívolo -la | 'frivʊlʊ | *a.* frivolous

frondoso -sa | frõ'dozʊ -'dwza | *a.* leafy

fronha | 'froNa | *sf.* pillowcase

fronte | 'frõtı | *sf.* forehead

fronteira | frõ'teyra | *sf.* frontier, border

frota | 'frwta | *sf.* fleet

frouxo -xa | 'frowxʊ | *a.* loose,

slack; weak, feeble; coward, irresolute

frugalidade | frugali'dadɪ | *sf.* frugality

fruir | fru'iʀ | *vi.* to enjoy, to have fruition of

frustração | fruʃtra'sãw | *sf.* frustration; disappointment

frustrar | fruʃ'tʀaʀ | *vt.* to frustrate; to disappoint

fruta | 'fruta | *sf.* fruit

fruta-de-conde | 'frutadɪ'kõdɪ | *sf.* sweet-sop

fruteiro-ra | fru'teyrʊ | *smf.* dealer in fruit; *sf.* fruit tree, fruit bowl

frutífero -ra | fru'tiferʊ | *a.* fruit-bearing

fruto | 'frutʊ | *sm.* fruit; result, product; profit. **-dar f.** to fructify

fubá | fu'ba | *sm.* ground maize

fuçar | fu'saʀ | *vt.* to root (as a pig)

fuga | 'fuga | *sf.* escape

fugaz | fu'gaʃ | *a.* passing, transitory

fugir | fu'jiʀ | *vi.* to flee, to escape; to avoid, to shun

fugitivo -va | fuji'tivʊ | *smf.* fugitive / *a.* fugitive, fleeting

fulano-na | fu'lanʊ | *smf.* fellow, guy, girl, gal; So-and-So

fulgor | ful'goʀ | *sm.* brilliance, gleam

fuligem | fu'lijẽy | *sf.* soot

fulminar | fulmi'naʀ | *vt.* to fulminate, to kill instantaneously

fumaça | fu'masa | *sf.* smoke

fumacento -ta | fuma'sẽtʊ | *a.* smoky

fumada | fu'mada | *sf.* smoking; a puff (on a cigarrette, pipe etc.)

fumar | fu'maʀ | *vt.* to smoke (tobacco). **-proibido f.** no smoking

fumegar | fume'gaʀ | *vi.* to emit smoke; to steam

fumigar | fumi'gaʀ | *vt.* to fumigate

fumo | 'fumʊ | *sm.* tobacco, tobacco plant; smoke

função | fũ'sãw | *sf.* function; of-

fice, duty; show (in a circus, theatre etc.)

funcionalismo | fũsiona'liʃmʊ | *sm.* civil service, civil servants

funcionar | fũsio'naʀ | *vi.* to function; to work, to operate

funcionário -ria | fũsio'narɪʊ | *smf.* civil servant; (colloq.) employee, clerk. **-f. público** civil servant

funda | 'fũda | *sf.* sling (for hurling stones); truss (for hernias)

fundação | fũda'sãw | *sf.* foundation; base; an endowed institution

fundamentado -da | fũdamẽ'tadʊ | *a.* well-grounded, well-founded

fundamental | fũdamẽ'tal | *a.* fundamental

fundamento | fũda'mẽtʊ | *sm.* foundation; basis; reason

fundar | fũ'daʀ | *vt.* to found, to establish

fundição | fũdi'sãw | *sf.* foundry; smelter; fusion

fundir | fũ'diʀ | *vt.* to cast (metal); to fuse, to melt; to merge. **-f.-se** to fuse, to melt

fundo -da | 'fũdʊ | *sm.* bottom; depth; end; back, background; base, foundation; (*pl.*) capital, funds. **-a f.** deeply. **-f. de agulha** eye of a needle. **-ir ao f.** to sink. **-artigo de f.** principal editorial in a newspaper / *a.* deep

fúnebre | 'funɪbrɪ | *a.* funereal, mortuary

funesto -ta | fu'nɛʃtʊ | *a.* fatal; doleful

fungar | fũ'gaʀ | *vi.* to sniff

funil | fu'nil | *sm.* funnel

funileiro | funi'leyrʊ | *sm.* tinker

furacão | fura'kãw | *sm.* hurricane

furão -rona | fu'rãw -'rona | *sm.* ferret / *a.* hard-working, laborious

furar | fu'raʀ | *vt.* to pierce; to drill; to puncture

fúria | 'furia | *sf.* fury; rage; fierceness

furibundo -da | furi‘būdʋ | *a.* furious, raging

furioso -sa | furi‘ozʋ -‘ωza | *a.* furious, infuriated

furna | ‘fuRna | *sf.* cave, cove, den

furo | ‘furʋ | *sm.* hole; orifice; (colloq.) journalistic hit, news scoop

furor | fu‘ror | *sm.* fury, frenzy. **-fazer f.** (colloq.) to make a great success

furtar | fuR‘taR | *vt.* to steal. **-f.-se** to avoid, to shun

furtivo -va | fuR‘tivʋ | *a.* furtive, clandestine

furto | ‘fuRtʋ | *sm.* theft, stealing; stolen goods

furúnculo | fu‘rūkulʋ | *sm.* furuncle, boil

fusão | fu‘zãw | *sf.* fusion; melting; consolidation

fusco -ca | ‘fuʃkʋ | *a.* dusky, dark

fuselagem | fuze‘lajěy | *sf.* (aeron.) fuselage, body

fusível | fu‘zivʋl | *sm.* (elect.) fuse, safety fuse

fuso | ‘fuzʋ | *sm.* spindle

fustão | fuʃ‘tãw | *sm.* (tex.) piqué

fustigar | fuʃti‘gaR | *vt.* to flog, to whip

futebol | futɪ‘bωl | *sm.* (sports) soccer, association football. **-f. americano** football, rugby football

fútil | ‘futil | *a.* futile

futilidade | futili‘dadɪ | *sf.* futility; frivolity

futuro -ra | fu‘turʋ | *sm.* future; future tense / *a.* future, forthcoming

fuzil | fu‘zil | *sm.* military rifle

fuzilar | fuzi‘laR | *vt.* to execute by shooting / *vi.* to flash (as lightning); (fig.) to get furious

fuzilaria | fuzila‘ria | *sf.* fusillade, steady fire

fuzileiro | fuzi‘leyrʋ | *sm.* fusilier, fusileer. **-f. naval** marine

G

gabar | ga‘baR | *vt.* to praise. **-g.-se** to boast, to brag

gabinete | gabi‘netɪ | *sm.* cabinet, private office; ministry, body of ministers

gado | ‘gadʋ | *sm.* cattle, livestock. **-g. leiteiro** dairy cattle. **-g. vacum** beef cattle

gafanhoto | gafa‘Notʋ | *sm.* locust, grasshopper

gafe | ‘gafɪ | *sf.* blunder, gaffe

gafieira | gafi‘eyra | *sf.* (colloq.) popular dancing club

gaforinha | gafʋ‘riNa | *sf.* (colloq.) Negro's bushy head of hair

gagá | ga‘ga | *a.* (colloq.) decrepit, senile

gago -ga | ‘gagʋ | *smf.* stammerer / *a.* stammering

gaguejar | gage‘jaR | *vt. vi.* to stammer, to stutter

gaiola | gay‘ωla | *sf.* birdcage; Amazon River steamboat

gaita | ‘gayta | *sf.* bamboo or tin fife; harmonica; (slang) money

gaita-de-foles | ‘gaytadɪ‘fωlɪʃ | *sf.* bagpipe

gaivota | gay‘vωta | *sf.* gull, seagull

gala | ‘gala | *sf.* gala dress; pomp, ostentation. **-uniforme de g.** full-dress uniform

galã | ga‘lã | *sm.* (cine.,theat., TV) leading man; gallant, lover

galante | ga‘lãtɪ | *a.* elegant, graceful; gallant, chivalrous

galantear | galãtɪ‘aR | *vt.* to court / *vi.* to play the gallant; to pay compliments

galanteio | galã'teyʋ | *sm.* courtliness (to ladies); flattery, adulation

galão | ga'lãw | *sm.* galloon, trimming; (mil.) stripe; gallon (liquid measure)

galardão | galaR'dãw | *sm.* prize, reward

galego -ga | ga'legʋ | *sm.* (ling.) Galician (of Spain); *smf.* Galician (of Spain); (pej.) Portuguése (person) / *a.* Galician of Spanish Galicia)

galera | ga'lɛra | *sf.* (naut.) galley; (slang, soccer) group of rooters or cheerers

galeria | gale'ria | *sf.* gallery; gangway (in mining)

galês -sa | ga'leʃ | *sm.* (ling.) Welsh; Welshman; *smf.* Welsh / *a.* Welsh

galgar | gal'gaR | *vt.* to climb, to reach the top of; to gain rapidly (high office etc.)

galgo | 'galgʋ | *sm.* greyhound

galhardia | galaR'dia | *sf.* gallantry; grace

galheteiro | gaLe'teyrʋ | *sm.* cruet stand

galho | 'gaLʋ | *sm.* branch (of tree). -quebrar um g. (colloq.) to solve a problem

galhofa | ga'Lʋfa | *sf.* mockery, derision

galinha | ga'liNa | *sf.* hen

galinha-d'angola | ga'liNadã'gʋla | *sf.* guinea-fowl, guinea-hen

galinheiro | gali'Neyrʋ | *sm.* poultry-yard

galo | 'galʋ | *sm.* rooster, cock; (colloq.) bump (on the head)

galocha | ga'lʋxa | *sf.* galosh, rubber overshoe

galopar | galo'paR | *vi.* to gallop

galope | ga'lʋpɪ | *sm.* gallop. -a g. at a gallop, at full speed

galpão | gal'pãw | *sm.* storage shed

galvanizar | galvani'zaR | *vt.* to galvanize

gama | 'gama | *sf.* gamut; range (of sizes etc.)

gamão | ga'mãw | *sm.* gammon, backgammon

gambá | gã'ba | *smf.* opossum

gamela | ga'mɛla | *sf.* large wooden vessel

gamo | 'gamʋ | *sm.* fallow deer

gana | 'gana | *sf.* craving desire; hate

ganância | ga'nãsia | *sf.* greediness

ganancioso -sa | ganãsi'ozʋ -'ʋza | *a.* greedy

gancho | 'gãxʋ | *sm.* hook; gaff

gandaia | gã'daya | *sf.* idleness, dissōlute life

gangorra | gã'goRa | *sf.* seesaw

gangrena | gã'grena | *sf.* gangrene

ganha-pão | gaNa'pãw | *sm.* means of livelihood

ganhar | ga'NaR | *vt.* to win; to earn, to gain; to receive; to attain

ganho -nha | 'gaNʋ | *sm.* gain, profit, earnings / *a.* gáined, profited, earned

ganir | ga'niR | *vi.* to yelp

ganso | 'gãsʋ | *sm.* goose, gander

garagem | ga'rajẽy | *sf.* garage

garantia | garã'tia | *sf.* guarantee; guaranty

garantir | garã'tiR | *vt.* to guarantee, to assure, to vouch for

garatujar | garatu'jaR | *vt. vi.* to scribble, to scrawl

garbo | 'gaRbʋ | *sm.* elegance; gallantry; distinction

garboso -sa | gaR'bozʋ -'bʋza | *a.* elegant; gallant; distinguished

garça | 'gaRsa | *sf.* heron

garçom | gaR'sõ | *sm.* waiter

garçonete | gaRso'nɛtɪ | *sf.* waitress

garfada | gaR'fada | *sf.* forkful

garfo | 'gaRfʋ | *sm.* fork

gargalhada | gaRga'Lada | *sf.* burst of laughter, guffaw

gargalo | gaR'galʋ | *sm.* bottle-neck

garganta | gaR'gãta | *sf.* throat; ravine, gorge

gargarejo | gaRga'rejʋ | *sm.* gargle, gargling

gari | ga'ri | *sm.* street cleaner

garimpeiro | garĩ'peyrʋ | *sm.* prospector (for gold, precious stones etc.)

garoa | ga'roa | *sf.* drizzle

garota | ga'rota | *sf.* young girl; (colloq.) girl-friend, sweetheart

garoto | ga'rotʋ | *sm.* boy, kid; urchin

garra | 'gaRa | *sf.* claw, talon

garrafa | ga'Rafa | *sf.* bottle

garrafão | gaRa'fãw | *sm.* large bottle

garrancho | ga'Rãxʋ | *sm.* scribble, scrawl; gnarled or twisted shrub

garupa | ga'rupa | *sf.* hindquarters, crupper (of a horse). **-ir na g.** to ride pillion (horse, motor cycle etc.)

gás | 'gaʃ | *sm.* gas. **-g.** lacrimogêneo tear-gas

gasolina | gazʋ'lina | *sf.* petrol, gasoline, gas. **-bomba de g.** petrol-pump, gasoline pump, filling station

gasômetro | ga'zometrʋ | *sm.* gasometer

gasoso -sa | ga'zozʋ -'zwza | *a.* gaseous

gastar | gaʃ'taR | *vt.* to spend; to wear out; to squander

gasto -ta | 'gaʃtʋ | *sm.* expenditure; waste; (*pl.*) expenses / *a.* worn-out

gastrônomo -ma | gaʃ'tronʋmʋ | *smf.* gastronome

gata | 'gata | *sf.* she-cat

gatilho | ga'tiLʋ | *sm.* trigger

gato | 'gatʋ | *sm.* cat

gatuno -na | ga'tunʋ | *smf.* thief

gaúcho -cha | ga'uxʋ | *smf.* native of the State of Rio Grande do Sul / *a.* of or pertaining to the State of Rio Grande do Sul

gaveta | ga'veta | *sf.* drawer

gavião | gavi'ãw | *sm.* hawk

gaze | 'gazɪ | *sf.* (tex.) gauze.

-atadura de g. bandage

gazela | ga'zɛla | *sf.* gazelle

gazeta | ga'zeta | *sf.* gazette, periodical, newspaper. **-fazer g.** to play truant

gazua | ga'zua | *sf.* picklock's toll; false key

geada | jɪ'ada | *sf.* frost

geladeira | jela'deyra | *sf.* refrigerator, icebox

gelado -da | je'ladʋ | *a.* iced, frozen

gelar | je'laR | *vt. vi.* to cool; to freeze. **-g. -se** to become frozen

geléia | je'lɛya | *sf.* jelly; jam. **-g. de laranja** marmalade, orange marmalade

geleira | je'leyra | *sf.* glacier

gelo | 'jelʋ | *sm.* ice

gema | 'jema | *sf.* yolk (of an egg)

gêmeo -mea | 'jemɪʋ | *smf. a.* twin

gemer | je'meR | *vi.* to moan, to groan

gemido | jɪ'midʋ | *sm.* moan, groan

general | jene'ral | *sm.* (mil.) general

generalidade | jenerali'dadɪ | *sf.* generality

generalizar | jenerali'zaR | *vt.* to generalize / *vr.* to spread, to become general

gênero | 'jenerʋ | *sm.* kind, sort; (gram.) gender; genre (also lit. and fine arts); (*pl.*) produce. **-gêneros alimentícios** foodstuff

generosidade | jenerozi'dadɪ | *sf.* generosity

generoso -sa | jene'rozʋ -'rwza | *a.* generous

gengibre | jẽ'jibrɪ | *sm.* ginger

gengiva | jẽ'jiva | *sf.* gum (of the mouth)

genial | jeni'al | *a.* of or pertaining to genius. **-g.!** (slang) splendid!, marvellous!

gênio | 'jenɪʋ | *sm.* genius, great talent; temperament; (myth.) genie. **-de mau g.** ill-natured. **-de bom g.** good-natured

genro | 'jẽʀʊ | *sm.* son-in-law

gente | 'jẽtɪ | *sf.* people; mankind; family. **-g. grande** grown-up. **-a g. we**

gentil | jẽ'til | *a.* polite, courteous; gentle, kind

gentileza | jẽti'leza | *sf.* politeness, courtesy; kindness

gentio | jẽ'tiʊ | *sm.* heathen, pagan

genuíno-na | jenu'inʊ | *a.* genuine, authentic

geografia | jeogra'fia | *sf.* geography

geógrafo -fa | je'ωgrafʊ | *smf.* geographer

geologia | jeolo'jia | *sf.* geology

geólogo -ga | je'ωlʊgʊ | *smf.* geologist

geometria | jeome'tria | *sf.* geometry

geração | jera'sãw | *sf.* generation

gerador -dora | jera'doʀ | *sm.* (elect.) generator / *a.* generative

geral | je'ral | *sm.* generality; superior (of a religious order); *sfpl.* bleacher seats. **-em g.** in general / *a.* general, universal

gerar | je'ʀaʀ | *vt.* to generate; to procreate; to engender; to create; to originate

gerência | je'rẽsia | *sf.* management

gerente | je'rẽtɪ | *smf.* manager

geringonça | jɪrĩ'gõsa | *sf.* contraption, rattletrap; jargon, slang

gerir | je'ʀiʀ | *vt.* to manage

germe | 'jɛʀmɪ | *sm.* germ

germinar | jeʀmi'naʀ | *vi.* to germinate, to sprout

gesso | 'jesʊ | *sm.* plaster of Paris

gestação | jeʃta'sãw | *sf.* gestation, pregnancy

gestante | jeʃ'tãtɪ | *sf.* pregnant woman / *a.* pregnant

gestão | jeʃ'tãw | *sf.* administration

gesticular | jeʃtiku'laʀ | *vi.* to gesticulate

gesto | 'jɛʃtʊ | *sm.* gesture; deed (conspicuous act)

giba | 'jiba | *sf.* hump

gibão | ji'bãw | *sm.* (zool.) gibbon. **-g. de couro** kind of leather jacket worn by the cowboys in the northeastern Brazil

gigante -ta | ji'gãtɪ | *smf. a.* giant

gigantesco -ca | jigã'teʃkʊ | *a.* gigantic

gilete | ji'lɛtɪ | *sf.* safety razor blade

gim | 'jĩ | *sm.* gin

ginásio | ji'naziʊ | *sm.* secondary school, high school; gymnasium

gingar | jĩ'gaʀ | *vi.* to swing, to sway from side to side while walking; to move the hips

girafa | ji'rafa | *sf.* giraffe

girar | ji'raʀ | *vi.* to turn (around), to revolve; to spin / *vt. vi.* to rotate

girassol | jira'sωl | *sm.* sunflower

gíria | 'jiria | *sf.* slang, jargon

giro | 'jirʊ | *sm,* circuit, turn; gyre, whirl. **-dar um g.** to go for a stroll

giz | 'jiʃ | *sm.* chalk

glacial | glasi'al | *a.* glacial, freezing

glândula | 'glãdula | *sf.* gland

glicerina | glise'rina | *sf.* glycerine

globo | 'globʊ | *sm.* globe. **-g. ocular** eyeball. **-g. terrestre** terrestrial globe

glória | 'glωria | *sf.* glory (cap. also eccles.)

glorificar | glorifi'kaʀ | *vt.* to glorify, to exalt; to extol

glorioso -sa | glori'ozʊ -'ωza | *a.* glorious

glossário | glo'sariʊ | *sm.* glossary

gluglu | glu'glu | *sm.* gurgle

glutão -tona | glu'tãw -'tona | *sm.* glutton (also zool.) / *a.* gluttonous, voracious

goela | gʊ'ɛla | *sf.* gullet, gorge

goiaba | goy'aba | *sf.* guava

goiabada | goya'bada | *sf.* guava paste (confection)

gol | 'gol | *sm.* (soccer, sports) goal

gola | 'gɔla | *sf.* collar; neckband (of shirt)

gole | 'gɔlɪ | *sm.* mouthful, gulp. **-de um só g.** at one gulp

goleiro | go'leyrʊ | *sm.* goalkeeper

golfada | gol'fada | *sf.* gushing, spewing

golfe | 'golfɪ | *sm.* golf

golfinho | gol'fiɲʊ | *sm.* (zool.) dolphin; miniature golf

golfo | 'golfʊ | *sm.* gulf

golpe | 'gɔlpɪ | *sm.* blow, hit, stroke. **-de um g.** at one dash. **-com um só g.** with a single blow. **-g. de Estado** *coup d'état*

golpear | golpɪ'aR | *vt.* to strike, to hit

golpista | gol'piʃta | *smf.* swindler, crook; (polit., pej.) one who advocates a coup

goma | 'goma | *sf.* gum; starch (for linen). **-g. de mascar** chewing-gum

gomo | 'gomʊ | *sm.* segment (of citrus fruit); (sewing) gore

gorar | go'raR | *vi.* to fail to hatch (egg); to miscarry (plans)

gordo -da | 'goRdʊ | *a.* fat; plump; greasy

gordura | guR'dura | *sf.* fat, fatness; lard; grease

gorduroso -sa | guRdu'rozʊ -'rɔza | *a.* greasy, oily, oleaginous

gorila | gu'rila | *sm.* gorilla

gorjear | goRjɪ'aR | *vi.* to warble

gorjeta | guR'jeta | *sf.* tip (gratuity). **-dar g.** to tip

gorro | 'goRʊ | *sm.* cap, beret

gostar | goʃ'taR | *vi.* (with **de**) to like, to enjoy, to be fond of. **-não g. de** to dislike

gosto | 'goʃtʊ | *sm.* taste, flavo(u)r; pleasure; inclination

gostoso -sa | goʃ'tozʊ -'tɔza | *a.* tasteful, delicious

gostosura | goʃtu'zura | *sf.* (colloq.) delight, joy

gota | 'gota | *sf.* drop; (med.) gout

goteira | go'teyra | *sf.* leak (in the roof), roof gutter

gotejar | gote'jaR | *vt. vi.* to drop, to drip, to dribble

gótico -ca | 'gɔtikʊ | *a.* Gothic

governador -dora | guveRna'doR | *smf.* governor

governar | guveR'naR | *vt.* to govern, to rule; to guide, to steer

governo | gu'veRnʊ | *sm.* government; administration; control; steering

gozar | go'zaR | *vt.* to enjoy; (colloq.) to make fun of / *vi.* to enjoy (life etc.); to experience pleasure (esp. sexual)

gozo | 'gozʊ | *sm.* joy, delight; possession

graça | 'grasa | *sf.* grace (also eccles.), favo(u)r; clemency; wit; joke, pleasantry; (*pl.*) thanks. **-dar graças a Deus** to be thankful to God. **-ter g.** to be funny, witty. **-de g.** free, gratis. **-qual a sua g.?** what is your name, please?

gracejar | grase'jaR | *vi.* to joke, to jest

gracejo | gra'sejʊ | *sm.* jest, joke

grade | 'gradɪ | *sf.* grating, bars; (*pl.*, colloq.) jail

grade -da | 'gradʊ | *sm.* only used in the expressions **de bom g.** willingly, with good grace; **de mau g.** unwillingly, with bad grace / *a.* important, well received. **-pessoa grada** *persona grata*

graduação | gradua'sãw | *sf.* gradation; grade; graduation

graduar | gradu'aR | *vt.* to graduate; to grade, to classify. **-g.-se** to graduate (at college), to take a degree

gráfica | 'grafika | *sf.* print-shop

gráfico -ca | 'grafikʊ | *sm.* graph, chart; printer, typographer / *a.* graphic. **-artes gráficas** graphic arts

grã-fino -na | grã'finʊ | *smf.* socialite; snob / *a.* fashionable; snobbish

grafologia | grafolo'jia | *sf.* graphology

gralha | 'graLa | *sf.* (ornith.) magpie;

(ornith.) any of various jays;
(typog.) misprint

grama | 'grama | *sf.* grass; *sm.*
gram

gramado | gra'madυ | *sm.* lawn,
green; (colloq.) soccer field

gramática | gra'matika | *sf.* grammar; grammar book

gramático -ca | gra'matikυ | *smf.*
grammarian

grampeador | grãpιa'doR | *sm.*
stapler, stapling machine

grampo | 'grãpυ | *sm.* clamp; staple. -g. de cabelo hairpin. -g. de
papel paper-clip

granada | gra'nada | *sf.* grenade,
bomb. -g. de mão hand grenade

grande | 'grãdι | *a.* large, big, tall;
huge; great. -à g. a lot; on a
grand scale

grandeza | grã'deza | *sf.* greatness;
largeness; splendo(u)r

grandioso -sa | grãdi'ozυ -'ωza | *a.*
grandiose, imposing, magnificent

granel | gra'nεl | used in the expression a g. in bulk; loose; in great
quantity

granito | gra'nitυ | *sm.* granite

granizo | gra'nizυ | *sm.* hail

granja | 'grãja | *sf.* small farm;
grange

granjear | grãjι'aR | *vt.* to obtain, to attract, to win
(sympathy etc.)

grão | 'grãw | *sm.* grain; grit; corn

grão-de-bico | grãwdι'bikυ | *sm.*
chick-pea

grasnar | graʒ'naR | *vi.* to caw (as a
crow); to quack (as a duck)

gratidão | grati'dãw | *sf.* gratitude

gratificação | gratifika'sãw | *sf.*
tip; bonus

gratificar | gratifi'kaR | *vt.*
to tip; to reward

gratis | 'gratiʒ | *adv.* free, gratis

grato -ta | 'gratυ | *a.* grateful,
thankful; pleasant

gratuito -ta | gra'tuytυ | *a.* free,
gratis; groundless, baseless

grau | 'graw | *sm.* degree; extent;

grade. -colar g. to take a degree

graúdo -da | gra'udυ | *a.* (colloq.)
large, big

gravação | grava'sãw | *sf.* engraving; recording; record

gravador -dora | grava'doR | *smf.*
engraver; *sm.* tape-recorder

gravar | gra'vaR | *vt.* to engrave; to record; to imprint, to
stamp; to fix (in the memory);
(law) to burden

gravata | gra'vata | *sf.* necktie, tie.
-g. borboleta bow tie

grave | 'gravι | *a.* grave, serious;
deep, bass (voice). -acento g.
grave accent

graveto | gra'vetυ | *sm.* twig

gravidade | gravi'dadι | *sf.* gravity
(also phys.), seriousness

gravidez | gravi'deʒ | *sf.*
pregnancy

grávida | 'gravida | *a.* pregnant

gravitação | gravita'sãw | *sf.*
gravitation

gravura | gra'vura | *sf.* engraving;
print; picture

graxa | 'graxa | *sf.* grease; shoe
polish

grego -ga | 'gregυ | *smf. a.* Greek;
sm. Greek (language)

grelha | 'grελa | *sf.* grill

grelhar | gre'LaR | *vt.* to grill, to
broil

grelo | 'grelυ | *sm.* sprout

grêmio | 'gremiυ | *sm.* guild, fraternity, society

grenha | 'grεna | *sf.* mop (of hair)

greta | 'greta | *sf.* fissure, crack

greve | 'grεvι | *sf.* strike. -entrarem
g. to go on strike

grevista | gre'viʒta | *smf.* striker

grifado -da | gri'fadυ | *a.* italicized

grifar | gri'faR | *vt.* to italicize; to
underline

grilhão | gri'Lãw | *sm.* chain; (*pl.*)
fetters

grilo | 'grilυ | *sm.* cricket; (slang)
problem

grinalda | gri'nalda | *sf.* garland

gringo -ga | 'grĩgυ | *smf.* (colloq.,
pej.) any foreigner

gripe | 'gripɪ | *sf*. grippe, influenza, flu

grisalho -lha | gri'zaʟʊ | *a*. grey-headed, grey-bearded

gritar | gri'taʀ | *vt*. *vi*. to shout, to yell, to scream. **-g. com alguém** to shout at someone

gritaria | grita'ria | *sf*. shouting, screaming

grito | 'gritʊ | *sm*. shout, scream, yell, cry

grosa | 'grɔza | *sf*. gross; (carp.) rasp

groselha | gro'zɛʟa | *sf*. gooseberry; currant; gooseberry syrup

grosseiro -ra | gro'seyrʊ | *a*. rough, crude; coarse, vulgar

grosseria | grose'ria | *sf*. incivility, rudeness, coarseness

grosso -sa | 'grosʊ 'grɔsa | *a*. thick; rough; deep (voice); (slang) impolite. **-fazer vista grossa** to pretend not to see / *sm*. the main part

grossura | gro'sura | *sf*. thickness; (slang) rudeness

grotesco -ca | gro'te ʃkʊ | *a*. grotesque; farcical

grua | 'grua | *sf*. crane, derrick

grudar | gru'daʀ | *vt*. to glue; to stick together / *vi*. *vr*. to cling, to stick

grude | 'grudɪ | *sm*. glue, paste; (slang) chow, food

grumete | gru'metɪ | *sm*. apprentice seaman

grunhido | gru'ɴidʊ | *sm*. grumble, grunt

grunhir | gru'ɴiʀ | *vi*. to grunt (as a pig); to grumble

grupo | 'grupʊ | *sm*. group, order; bunch (of people)

gruta | 'gruta | *sf*. cave; grotto

guaraná | gwara'na | *sm*. (bot.) guarana (also soft drink)

guarda | 'gwaʀda | *sm*. constable, guardian, warden; *sf*. guard, watch; custody

guarda-chuva | 'gwaʀda'xuva | *sm*. umbrella

guarda-civil | 'gwaʀdasi'vil | *sm*. constable, policeman

guarda-costas | 'gwaʀda'kɔ ʃtaʃ | *sm*. bodyguard

guarda-freios | 'gwaʀda'freyʊʃ | *sm*. brakeman, railway brakeman

guarda-livros | 'gwaʀda'livrʊʃ | *smf*. bookkeeper

guardanapo | gwaʀda'napʊ | *sm*. napkin

guardar | gwaʀ'daʀ | *vt*. to keep, to retain; to guard, to protect; to watch

guarda-roupa | 'gwaʀda'rowpa | *sm*. clothes closet; wardrobe

guarda-sol | 'gwaʀda'sɔl | *sm*. parasol

guarida | gwa'rida | *sf*. den; place of refuge. **-dar g.** to give shelter

guarnecer | gwaʀne'seʀ | *vt*. to adorn; to furnish; to provide with troops

guarnição | gwaʀni'sãw | *sf*. (mil.) garrison; (naut.) crew; (sewing) trim; (cookery) side-dish

gude | 'gudɪ | *sm*. marbles (game) **-bola de g.** marble

guelra | 'gɛʟʀa | *sf*. fish gill

guerra | 'gɛʀa | *sf*. war, warfare. **-conselho de g.** court martial. **-estar em pé de g.** to be up in arms

guerrear | geʀɪ'aʀ | *vt*. to battle / *vi*. to wage war

guerreiro -ra | ge'ʀeyrʊ | *smf*. warrior / *a*. warlike

guia | 'gia | *smf*. guide, leader; *sm*. directory, manual; *sf*. guiding, guidance; delivery note; way-bill

guiar | gi'aʀ | *vt*. to guide, to lead; to drive (an automobile); to advise

guichê | gi'xe | *sm*. window (in a ticket office, bank etc.)

guidom | gi'dõ | *sm*. handlebar (of a bicycle)

guilhotina | giʟo'tina | *sf*. guillotine

guinada | gi'nada | *sf*. veer, lurch;

sudden change of position

guincho | 'gĩxʊ | *sm.* screech, shriek; small crane, winch

guindar | gĩ'daʀ | *vt.* to hoist; to lift

guindaste | gĩ'daʒtɩ | *sm.* crane, derrick, hoist

guisado -da | gi'zadʊ | *sm.* stew

guitarra | gi'taʀa | *sf.* guitar

guizo | 'gizʊ | *sm.* sleigh-bell

gula | 'gula | *sf.* gluttony

gulodice | gulʊ'disɩ | *sf.* gluttony; delicacy, morsel

guloso -sa | gu'lozʊ -'lʊza | *a.* gluttonous, glutton

gume | 'gumɩ | *sm.* edge, knife--edge

guri | gu'ri | *sm.* (colloq.) a boy, a kid

guria | gu'ria | *sf.* (colloq.) a girl, a young girl

gurizada | guri'zada | *sf.* (colloq.) bunch of kids

H

hábil | 'abil | *a.* handy, dexterous; capable; (law) legally qualified

habilidoso -sa | abili'dozʊ -'dʊza | *a.* skilled, dexterous; able; ingenious

habilitação | abilita'sãw | *sf.* qualification, competence; capability, aptitude

habilitar | abili'taʀ | *vt.* to enable, to capacitate; to prepare

habitação | abita'sãw | *sf.* dwelling, place of residence

habitante | abi'tãtɩ | *smf.* inhabitant

habitar | abi'taʀ | *vt.* to inhabit, to live in

hábito | 'abitʊ | *sm.* custom, habit; dress (of monastic orders), habit

habitual | abitu'al | *a.* usual, customary; ordinary

habituar | abitu'aʀ | *vt.* to habituate, to accustom

hálito | 'alitʊ | *sm.* breath; exhalation

harmonia | aʀmʊ'nia | *sf.* harmony (also mus.)

harmônico -ca | aʀ'monikʊ | *a.* harmonic, harmonious

harmonioso -sa | aʀmoni'ozʊ 'ʊza | *a.* harmonious

harpa | 'aʀpa | *sf.* harp

haste | 'aʒtɩ | *sf.* rod, shaft; stem

hastear | aʒtɩ'aʀ | *vt.* to hoist, to raise to the top (as a flag)

havaiano -na | avay'anʊ | *smf. a.* Hawaiian

haver | a'veʀ | *v.imp.* to exist, there to be. **-há um ano** a year ago. **-não há de quê** (colloq.) not at all, you're welcome. **-que há de novo?** what's new? / *vi.* = *ter* / *v. aux.* to have to. **-deve h.** there ought to be, there should be

haveres | a'verɩʃ | *smpl.* possessions, assets, personal effects

hediondo -da | edi'õdʊ | *a.* hideous; horrid, horrible

hélice | 'ɛlisɩ | *sf.* propeller

helicóptero | eli'kʊpterʊ | *sm.* helicopter

hemisfério | emiʒ'fɛriʊ | *sm.* hemisphere

hemorragia | emoʀa'jia | *sf.* hemorrhage

hera | 'ɛra | *sf.* ivy

herança | e'rãsa | *sf.* inheritance, heritage

herdar | eʀ'daʀ | *vt.* to inherit

herdeiro -ra | eʀ'deyrʊ | *sm.* heir; *sf.* heiress

hereditário -ria | eredi'tariʊ | *a.*

hereditary

herege | e'rɛjι |*smf.* heretic

heresia | ere'zia | *sf.* heresy

herético -ca | e'rɛtikʊ |*smf.* heretic / *a.* heretical

herói | e'rɔwy |*sm.* hero

heróico -ca | e'rɔwykʊ | *a.* heroic, valiant

heroína | erʊ'ina | *sf.* heroine; (phar.) heroin

heroísmo|erʊ'iʃmʊ |*sm.* heroism

hesitação | ezita'sãw | *sf.* hesitation

hesitar | ezi'taʀ | *vi.* to hesitate

heterogêneo -nea | etero'jenιʊ | *a.* heterogeneous

híbrido -da | 'ibridʊ | *smf. a.* hybrid

hidráulica | i'drawlika | *sf.* hydraulics

hidráulico -ca | i'drawlikʊ | *a.* hydraulic

hidrelétrico -ca | idre'lɛtrikʊ | *a.* hydroelectric

hidroavião | idrʊavi'ãw | *sm.* (aeron.) hydroplane

hidrogênio | idro'jeniʊ | *sm.* hydrogen

hiena | i'ena |*sf.* hyena

hierarquia | ieraʀ'kia | *sf.* hierarchy

hífen | 'ifen 'ifẽy |*sm.* hyphen

higiene | iji'enι |*sf.* hygiene; sanitation

higiênico -ca|iji'enikʊ|*a.* hygienic, sanitary

hindu | ĩ'du | *smf. a.* Hindu, Indian

hino |'inʊ|*sm.* hymn. -**h. nacional** national anthem

hípico -ca | 'ipikʊ | *a.* of or pertaining to horses

hipnotismo | ipno'tiʃmʊ | *sm.* hypnotism

hipocrisia | ipokri'zia | *sf.* hypocrisy

hipócrita | i'pʊkrita |*smf.* hypocrite / *a.* hypocritical

hipódromo | i'pʊdrʊmʊ |*sm.* race track, hippodrome

hipopótamo | ipo'pʊtamʊ | *sm.* hippopotamus

hipoteca | ipo'tɛka | *sf.* mortgage

hipotecar | ipote'kaʀ | *vt.* to mortgage

hipótese| i'pʊtιzι |*sf.* hypothesis, theory, assumption

histeria | iʃte'ria | *sf.* hysteria, hysterics

história | iʃ'tʊria | *sf.* history; story, tale. -**h. em quadrinhos** comic strip

historiador -dora | iʃtoria'doʀ | *smf.* historian

histórico -ca | iʃ'tʊrikʊ | *sm.* account, report / *a.* historic, historical

historieta | iʃtori'eta | *sf.* anecdote, tale

hoje | 'ojι |*adv.* today. -**h. em dia** nowadays. -**de h. em diante** from now on. -**de h. para amanhã** overnight, from one day to the next

holandês -desa | olã'deʃ | *sm.* (ling.) Dutch; Dutchman; *smf.* Hollander / *a.* Dutch

holofote | olo'fʊtι | *sm.* searchlight, floodlight

homem | 'omẽy |*sm.* man; mankind. -**h. de bem** honest man. -**h. feito** grown man. -**o h.** (slang) the boss

homenagem | ome'najẽy | *sf.* homage. -**prestar h.** to render homage (to)

homicídio |omi'sidiʊ |*sm.* homicide, assassination, murder

homogêneo -nea | omo'jenιʊ | *à.* homogeneous

homossexual |omoseksu'al |*smf. a.* homosexual

homossexualismo | omoseksua'liʃmʊ |*sm.* homosexuality

honestidade | oneʃti'dadι | *sf.* honesty, integrity

honesto -ta | o'nɛʃtʊ | *a.* honest, hono(u)rable

honorário -ria | ono'rariʊ | *sm.* (usu. *pl.*) fees, honorarium / *a.* honorary

honra | 'õRa | *sf.* hono(u)r; (*pl.*) hono(u)rs

honradez | õRa'deʒ | *sf.* honesty, integrity

honrado -da | õ'Radʊ | *a.* hono(u)rable, honest

honrar | õ'RaR | *vt.* to hono(u)r; to venerate; to do credit to

honroso -sa | õ'Rozʊ -'Rwza | *a.* hono(u)rable; creditable

hora | 'ωra | *sf.* hour; time. **-a altas horas** in the wee hours. **-em cima da h.** at the exact moment. **-que horas são?** what time is it? **-horas a fio** hours on end

horário | o'rariʊ | *sm.* timetable, schedule / *a.* hourly

horda | 'ωRda | *sf.* horde, mob, gang

horizonte | ori'zõtɩ | *sm.* horizon

horrendo -da | o'Rẽdʊ | *a.* horrible, dreadful

horripilante | oRipi'lãtɩ | *a.* horrifying; blood-curdling

horripilar | oRipi'laR | *vt.* to horrify

horrível | o'Rivɩl | *a.* horrible, awful, hideous

horror | o'RoR | *sm.* horror. **-ter h. a** to hate (someone or something)

horrorizar | oRori'zaR | *vt.* to horrify, to terrify; to shock

horroroso -sa | oRo'Rozʊ -'Rwza | *a.* horrible, dreadful, frightful

horta | 'ωRta | *sf.* vegetable garden

hortaliça | oRta'lisa | *sf.* vegetable, vegetables

hortelã | oRte'lã | *sf.* (bot.) mint

hortelã-pimenta | oRte'lãpi'mẽta | *sf.* peppermint

hospedagem | oʃpe'dajẽy | *sf.* lodging, accommodation

hospedar | oʃpe'daR | *vt.* to lodge, to house

hospedaria | oʃpeda'ria | *sf.* boarding-house; inn

hóspede | 'ωʃpɩdɩ | *smf.* guest; lodger

hospício | oʃ'pisiʊ | *sm.* mental hospital

hospital | oʃpi'tal | *sm.* hospital

hospitaleiro -ra | oʃpita'leyrʊ | *a.* hospitable

hospitalidade | oʃpitali'dadɩ | *sf.* hospitality

hospitalizar | oʃpitali'zaR | *vt.* to hospitalize

hóstia | 'ωʃtia | *sf.* (eccles.) Host

hostil | oʃ'til | *a.* hostile, inimical

hostilidade | oʃtili'dadɩ | *sf.* hostility, enmity

hotel | o'tɛl | *sm.* hotel

hoteleiro -ra | ote'leyrʊ | *smf.* hotel-keeper; hotel-owner

hulha | 'uLa | *sf.* coal

humanidade | umani'dadɩ | *sf.* humanity, mankind; (fig.) kindness; (*pl.*) the humanities

humanitário -ria | umani'tariʊ | *sm.* humanitarian, philanthropist / *a.* humanitarian, philanthropic

humanizar | umani'zaR | *vt.* to humanize; to civilize

humano -na | u'manʊ | *sm.* human, human being / *a.* human; humane

humildade | umil'dadɩ | *sf.* humility, humbleness

humilde | u'mildɩ | *a.* humble, meek; modest, plain

humilhação | umiLa'sãw | *sf.* humiliation

humilhante | umi'Lãtɩ | *a.* humiliating

humilhar | umi'LaR | *vt.* to humiliate, to humble. **-h.-se** to demean oneself, to stoop

humor | u'moR | *sm.* disposition, mood; wit; humo(u)r. **-de bom h.** in high spirits. **-de mau h.** in bad temper

humorístico -ca | umo'riʃtikʊ | *a.* humoristic, witty

húngaro -ra | 'ũgarʊ | *smf. a.* Hungarian

I

ianque | iˈãkɪ | *smf. a.* Yankee, American

iate | iˈatɪ | *sm.* yacht

ida | ˈida | *sf.* departure, going, leaving. **-i. e volta** round trip. **-idas e vindas** comings and goings

idade | iˈdadɪ | *sf.* age; epoch, era, period. **-ser maior de i.** to be of age. **-ser menor de i.** to be under age. **-qual a sua i.?** how old are you?

ideal | idɪˈal | *sm. a.* ideal

idealismo | idɪaˈliʒmʊ | *sm.* idealism

idealista | idɪaˈlista | *smf.* idealist / *a.* idealistic

idealizar | idɪaliˈzaR | *vt.* to idealize

idear | idɪˈaR | *vt.* to imagine; to plan, to contrive

idéia | iˈdɛya | *sf.* idea; thought; opinion; belief; notion. **-fazer i.** to imagine. **-mudar de i.** to change one's mind. **-ter i.** to remember

idêntico -ca | iˈdẽtikʊ | *a.* identical

identidade | idẽtiˈdadɪ | *sf.* identity

identificação | idẽtifikaˈsãw | *sf.* identification

ideologia | idɪoloˈjia | *sf.* ideology

idílio | iˈdiliʊ | *sm.* idyll

idioma | idiˈoma | *sf.* language. **-i. estrangeiro** foreign language

idiota | idiˈɔta | *smf.* idiot, fool / *a.* idiotic

idiotice | idioˈtisɪ | *sf.* silliness, foolish act

idiotismo | idioˈtiʒmʊ | *sm.* idiotism; idiomatic expression

idolatrar | idolaˈtraR | *vt.* to idolize; (*fig.*) to love excessively

idolatria | idolaˈtria | *sf.* idolatry

ídolo | ˈidʊlʊ | *sm.* idol

idoneidade | idoneyˈdadɪ | *sf.* aptness; suitableness; competence

idôneo -nea | iˈdonɪʊ | *a.* competent, fit; capable; apt

idoso -sa | iˈdozʊ -ˈdɔza | *a.* aged, elderly, old

Iemanjá | iemãˈja | *sf.* Afro-Brazilian goddess of the sea

ignição | igniˈsãw | *sf.* ignition

ignomínia | ignoˈminia | *sf.* ignominy, dishono(u)r

ignorado -da | ignoˈradʊ | *a.* unknown; obscure

ignorância | ignoˈrãsia | *sf.* ignorance

ignorante | ignoˈrãtɪ | *smf.* ignoramus, ignorant person / *a.* ignorant

ignorar | ignoˈraR | *vt.* to ignore; to be ignorant (unaware) of

ignoto -ta | igˈnotʊ -ˈnɔta | *a.* unknown; obscure

igreja | iˈgreja | *sf.* church; (*cap.*) the Roman Catholic Church

igual | iˈgwal | *smf.* equal / *a.* equal, same, identical; even, level. **-sem i.** matchless

igualar | igwaˈlaR | *vt. vi.* to equal, to equalize; to match; to level, to make even

igualdade | igwalˈdadɪ | *sf.* equality; uniformity

iguaria | igwaˈria | *sf.* table delicacy

ilegal | ileˈgal | *a.* illegal

ilegítimo -ma | ileˈjitimʊ | *a.* illegitimate

ilegível | ileˈjivɪl | *a.* illegible

ileso -sa | iˈlɛzʊ | *a.* safe, unharmed

iletrado -da | ileˈtradʊ | *smf. a.* illiterate

ilha | ˈiLa | *sf.* island; isle

ilharga | iˈLaRga | *sf.* flank

ilhéu -lhoa | iˈLɛw iˈLoa | *smf.*

islander (esp. an Azorian)

ilhota | i'Lɔta | *sf*. islet

ilícito -ta | i'lisitʋ | *a*. illicit, unlawful

ilimitado -da | ilimi'tadʋ | *a*. unlimited

ilógico -ca | i'lɔjikʋ | *a*. illogical

iludir | ilu'diR | *vt*. to deceive, to delude; to dupe. **-i.-se** to deceive oneself

iluminação | ilumina'sãw | *sf*. illumination

iluminar | ilumi'naR | *vt*. to illuminate, to light up; to enlighter. (the understanding)

iluminura | ilumi'nura | *sf*. illumination (of manuscripts)

ilusão | ilu'zãw | *sf*. illusion, delusion

ilustração | iluʃtra'sãw | *sf*. illustration; knowledge, learning

ilustrado -da | iluʃ'tradʋ | *a*. illustrated (with designs, pictures etc.); cultured, educated

ilustrador -dora | iluʃtra'doR | *smf*. illustrator

ilustrar | iluʃ'traR | *vt*. to illustrate with pictures; to render illustrious. **-i.-se** to become illustrious; to instruct oneself

ilustre | i'luʃtrɩ | *a*. illustrious, distinguished

imã | 'imã | *sm*. magnet

imaculado -da | imaku'ladʋ | *a*. immaculate

imagem | i'majēy | *sf*. image, likeness, figure; idea

imaginação | imajina'sãw | *sf*. imagination

imaginar | imaji'naR | *vt*. to imagine, to devise; to conceive, to picture; to suppose. **-i.-se** to picture oneself as

imaginário -ria | imaji'narɩʋ | *a*. imaginary

imaginativo -va | imajina'tivʋ | *a*. imaginative

imaturo -ra | ima'turʋ | *a*. immature; premature

imbecil | ĩbe'sil | *smf. a*. imbecile

imberbe | ĩ'bɛRbɩ | *a*. beardless;

youthful

imbuir | ĩbu'iR | *vt*. to imbue, to inspire (with ideas, feelings etc.). **-i.-se de** to become imbued with (sentiments, ideas etc.)

imediações | imedia'sõys | *sfpl*. neighbo(u)rhood

imediato -ta | imedi'atʋ | *sm*. (naut.) first mate, the second in command; the next in line / *a*. immediate; near, close

imensidade | imẽsi'dadɩ | *sf*. immensity; (fig.) a great quantity

imenso -sa | i'mẽsʋ | *a*. immense; huge, enormous

imerecido -da | imerɩ'sidʋ | *a*. undeserved

imersão | imeR'sãw | *sf*. immersion

imerso -sa | i'mɛRsʋ | *a*. immersed; (fig.) absorbed

imigração | imigra'sãw | *sf*. immigration

imigrante | imi'grãtɩ | *smf. a*. immigrant

imigrar | imi'graR | *vi*. to immigrate

iminente | imi'nẽtɩ | *a*. imminent, impending

imiscuir-se | imiʃku'iRsɩ | *vr*. to mix in with; to interfere (meddle) with

imitação | imita'sãw | *sf*. imitation; copy

imitar | imi'taR | *vt*. to imitate; to copy; to counterfeit; to mimic

imobiliária | imobili'aria | *sf*. real state agency

imobiliário -ria | imobili'arɩʋ | *a*. (law) pertaining to real property

imobilidade | imobili'dadɩ | *sf*. immobility

imobilizar | imobili'zaR | *vt*. to immobilize. **-i.-se** to become immobile

imoderado -da | imode'radʋ | *a*. immoderate, unrestrained

imodesto -ta | imo'dɛʃtʋ | *a*. immodest

imolar | imo'laʀ | vt. to immolate, to sacrifice

imoral | imo'ral | a. immoral

imoralidade | imorali'dadι | sf. immorality

imorredouro -ra | imoʀe'dowrυ | a. immortal, imperishable, undying

imóvel | i'mɔvυl | sm. real property (houses etc.) / a. immobile, immovable, motionless

impaciência | ĩpasi'ẽsia | sf. impatience, impetuosity; irritability

impaciente | ĩpasi'ẽtι | a. impatient; impetuous; restless

impacto | ĩ'paktυ | sm. impact; shock; a hit by a bomb or bullet

impagável | ĩpa'gavιl | a. priceless; unpayable; very funny

impalpável | ĩpal'pavιl | a. impalpable; intangible

impaludismo | ĩpalu'diʒmυ | sm. malaria

ímpar | 'ĩpaʀ | a. odd, uneven (number); matchless

imparcial | ĩpaʀsi'al | a. impartial, fair, unbiased

impassível | ĩpa'sivιl | a. impassible; insensitive; unruffled; expressionless

impávido -da | ĩ'pavidυ | a. intrepid, fearless

impecável | ĩpe'kavιl | a. impeccable, faultless

impedido -da | ĩpι'didυ | a. interrupted, obstructed; (sports, soccer) offside

impedimento | ĩpιdi'mẽtυ | sm. obstruction, obstacle; (sports, soccer) offside

impedir | ĩpι'diʀ | vt. to obstruct, to hinder, to impede

impelir | ĩpι'liʀ | vt. to impel, to push; to incite

impenetrável | ĩpene'travιl | a. impenetrable; impervious

impensado -da | ĩpẽ'sadυ | a. unpremeditated, inconsiderate, thoughtless

imperador | ĩpera'doʀ | sm. emperor

imperar | ĩpe'raʀ | vi. to reign, to rule; to predominate

imperativo -va | ĩpera'tivυ | sm. imperative (also gram.) / a. imperative; commanding, authoritative

imperatriz | ĩpera'triʃ | sf. empress

imperceptível | ĩpeʀsep'tivιl | a. imperceptible; minute, very small

imperdoável | ĩpeʀdυ'avιl | a. unforgivable; inexcusable

imperfeição | ĩpeʀfey'sãw | sf. imperfection, defect, flaw

imperfeito -ta | ĩpeʀ'feytυ | sm. imperfect verb tense / a. imperfect, defective

imperial | ĩperi'al | a. imperial

imperialismo | ĩperia'liʒmυ | sm. imperialism

impericia | ĩpι'risia | sf. lack of skill, awkwardness

império | ĩ'pεriυ | sm. empire; domination

imperioso -sa | ĩperi'ozυ -'ωza | a. imperious

impermeabilização | ĩpeʀmιabiliza'sãw | sf. impermeabilization; waterproofing

impermeabilizar | ĩpeʀmιabili'zaʀ | vt. to waterproof

impermeável | ĩpeʀmι'avιl | sm. raincoat / a. impermeable; waterproof

impertinência | ĩpeʀti'nẽsia | sf. impertinence

impertinente | ĩpeʀti'nẽtι | a. impertinent, uncivil, petulant; irrelevant, not pertinent

imperturbável | ĩpeʀtuʀ'bavιl | a. imperturbable, cool, calm

impessoal | ĩpesυ'al | a. impersonal (also gram.)

impetrar | ĩpe'traʀ | vt. to entreat, to enter a plea (in court)

impetuoso -sa | ĩpetu'ozυ -'ωza | a. impetuous

impiedoso -sa | ĩpie'dozυ -'dωza | a. pitiless, merciless

impingem | ĩ'pĩʒẽy | sf. the common name for almost any skin blemish; tetter

impingir | ĩpĩ'jiR | *vt.* to impose fraudulently (thing or idea etc. on person), to inflict (something unpleasant) upon, to foist

ímpio -pia | 'ĩpiʋ | *a.* impious, ungodly, blasphemous

implacável | ĩpla'kavɪl | *a.* implacable, relentless, inexorable

implantar | ĩplã'taR | *vt.* to implant; to insert, to introduce

implemento | ĩple'mẽtʋ | *sm.* implement; (*pl.*) material, accessories, tackle, tools

implicação | ĩplika'sãw | *sf.* implication; connotation

implicância | ĩpli'kãsia | *sf.* ill will, ill nature, grudge. **-estar de i. com** (colloq.) to pick on

implicar | ĩpli'kaR | *vt.* to implicate, to involve; to connote, to presuppose / *vi.* to tease, to annoy. **-i. com alguém** to pick on someone

implícito -ta | ĩ'plisitʋ | *a.* implicit

implorar | ĩplo'raR | *vt.* to implore, to supplicate, to beg

impolidez | ĩpoli'deʒ | *sf.* impoliteness, rudeness, incivility

imponderado -da | ĩpõde'radʋ | *a.* thoughtless, ill-considered

imponência | ĩpo'nẽsia | *sf.* magnificence, grandeur

imponente | ĩpo'nẽtɪ | *a.* imposing, impressive, majestic

impontual | ĩpõtu'al | *a.* unpunctual

impopular | ĩpopu'laR | *a.* unpopular

impor | ĩ'poR | *vt.* to impose; to lay on (hands); to enforce; to oblige to accept. **-i.-se** to impose oneself, to impose one's authority

importação | ĩpoRta'sãw | *sf.* import, importation

importador -dora | ĩpoRta'doR | *smf.* importer; *sf.* (colloq.) shop of imported goods / *a.* importing

importância | ĩpoR'tãsia | *sf.* importance, significance; sum, amount. **-dar** or **ligar i. a** to attach importance to. **-não tem i.** it doesn't matter

importante | ĩpoR'tãtɪ | *a.* important

importar | ĩpoR'taR | *vt.* to import / *vi.* to matter, to be of importance. **-i.-se** to take notice of, to take into consideration; to care about

importunar | ĩpʋRtu'naR | *vt.* to importune, to annoy, to pester

importuno -na | ĩpʋR'tunʋ | *smf.* an annoying person / *a.* importunate, annoying

imposição | ĩpʋzi'sãw | *sf.* imposition

impossibilidade | ĩposibili'dadɪ | *sf.* impossibility

impossibilitar | ĩposibili'taR | *vt.* to render impossible; to preclude; to incapacitate, to disable

impossível | ĩpʋ'sivɪl | *a.* impossible; (colloq.) insufferable

imposto | ĩ'poʃtʋ | *sm.* tax; duty. **-i. de consumo** sales tax. **-i. de renda** income tax

impostor -tora | ĩpoʒ'toR | *smf.* impostor

impostura | ĩpʋʒ'tura | *sf.* imposture, fraud, humbug

impotência | ĩpo'tẽsia | *sf.* impotence

impotente | ĩpo'tẽtɪ | *smf.* impotent person / *a.* impotent, powerless

imprecação | ĩpreka'sãw | *sf.* curse, imprecation

imprecisão | ĩprɪsi'zãw | *sf.* inaccuracy, inexactness; vagueness

impregnar | ĩpreg'naR | *vt.* to impregnate, to saturate, to soak

imprensa | ĩ'prẽsa | *sf.* printing-press; press, journalism

imprescindível | ĩpresĩ'divɪl | *a.* indispensable, essential

impressão | ĩpre'sãw | *sf.* impression, effect; imprint; edition. **-i. digital**

fingerprint

impressionante | īpresio'nātɩ | *a.* impressive; stirring; thrilling

impressionar | īpresio'naʀ | *vt.* to impress; (photog.) to expose; to create an impression upon. **-i.-se com** to be impressed by; to be affected by / *vi.* (photog.) to expose. **-i.-se** to be affected by light (film or paper)

impresso -sa | ī'prɛsʋ | *sm.* pamphlet, circular; (*pl.*) printed matter in general / *a.* printed

impressor -sora | īpre'soʀ | *sm.* printer; *sf.* printing-press

imprestável | īpreʒ'tavɩl | *smf.* (colloq.) egoistic person, useless person / *a.* useless

impreterível | īprete'rivɩl | *a.* that cannot be postponed, imperative

imprevisão | īprevi'zãw | *sf.* lack of foresight; negligence, carelessness

imprevisível | īprevi'zivɩl | *a.* unpredictable

imprevisto -ta | īpre'viʃtʋ | *sm.* something unexpected or unforeseen / *a.* unforeseen, sudden

imprimir | īpri'miʀ | *vt.* to impress; to stamp; to print; to transmit, to communicate

improcedente | īprose'dētɩ | *a.* baseless, groundless (also law)

improdutivo -va | īprodu'tivʋ | *a.* unproductive

impropério | īpro'pɛriʋ | *sm.* coarse or insulting word

impróprio -pria | ī'prɔpriʋ | *a.* unsuitable, unfit; improper, indecorous

improvável | īpro'vavɩl | *a.* improbable

improvisação | īproviza'sãw | *sf.* improvisation

improvisado -da | īprovi'zadʋ | *a.* improvised, makeshift, offhand

improvisar | īprovi'zaʀ | *vt.* to improvise

improviso -sa | īpro'vizʋ | *sm.* impromptu, improvisation / *a.* sudden. **-de i.** unexpectedly

imprudência | īpru'dẽsia | *sf.* imprudence, carelessness

imprudente | īpru'dētɩ | *smf.* imprudent person / *a.* imprudent, careless; indiscreet

impudência | īpu'dẽsia | *sf.* impudence, insolence, effrontery

impudente | īpu'dētɩ | *a.* impudent; shameless

impudico -ca | īpu'dikʋ | *a.* lewd; wantom

impugnar | īpug'naʀ | *vt.* to impugn; to refute; to contest, to contradict

impulsionar | īpulsio'naʀ | *vt.* to impel, to propel; to animate, to stimulate

impulsivo -va | īpul'sivʋ | *a.* impulsive; impetuous

impulso | ī'pulsʋ | *sm.* impulse, impetus, push. **-tomar i.** to gather way

impune | ī'punɩ | *a.* unpunished

impunidade | īpuni'dadɩ | *a.* impunity

impureza | īpu'reza | *sf.* impurity; sediment; unchasteness

impuro -ra | ī'purʋ | *a.* impure; unchaste

imputar | īpu'taʀ | *vt.* to impute, to ascribe (to), to attribute (to)

imundície | imũ'disiɩ | *sf.* filthiness, dirtiness

imundo -da | i'mũdʋ | *a.* filthy, dirty

imune | i'munɩ | *a.* immune

imunidade | imuni'dadɩ | *sf.* immunity; prerogative, privilege

imutável | imu'tavɩl | *a.* unchangeable; immutable

inabalável | inaba'lavɩl | *a.* steadfast, immovable; (fig.) inflexible, adamant

inábil | i'nabil | *a.* inapt, inexpert; clumsy

inabilidade | inabili'dadɩ | *sf.* inability; clumsiness

inabilitar | inabili'taʀ | vt. to disqualify; to incapacitate
inabitado -da | inabi'tadʊ | a.
uninhabited
inacabado-da | inaka'badʊ | a. unfinished, incomplete
inaceitável | inasey'tavɪl | a. unacceptable; inadmissible
inacessível | inase'sivɪl | a. inaccessible, unapproachable
inacreditável | inakredi'tavɪl | a.
unbelievable, incredible
inadequado -da | inade'kwadʊ |
a inadequate, inappropriate, ill
-suited
inadiável | inadi'avɪl | a. non
-postponable; urging, pressing
inadvertido -da | inadveʀ'tidʊ | a.
inadvertent
inalar | ina'laʀ | vt. to inhale
inalcançável | inalkã'savɪl | a.
unattainable, unreachable
inalterável | inalte'ravɪl | a. unalterable, immutable, unchangeable; (fig.) undisturbed, serene
inanimado -da | inani'madʊ | a.
inanimate, inert, lifeless
inaptidão | inapti'dãw | sf. incapacity, lack of aptitude
inapto -ta | i'naptʊ | a. unqualified, incapable
inapreciável | inapresi'avɪl | a.
inestimable, invaluable
inaproveitável | inaprʊvey'tavɪl |
a. unusable
inatingível | inatĩ'jivɪl | a. inaccessible; unattainable
inativo -va | ina'tivʊ | a. inactive,
idle
inato-ta | i'natʊ | a. innate, inbred,
inherent
inaudito -ta | inaw'ditʊ | a.
unheard-of, unprecedented
inauguração | inawgura'sãw | sf.
inauguration, opening
inaugurar | inawgu'raʀ | vt. to
inaugurate; to initiate
incalculável | ĩkalku'lavɪl | a. incalculable, unnumbered
incandescente | ĩkãde'sẽtɪ | a.

incandescent
incansável | ĩkã'savɪl | a. tireless,
indefatigable
incapaz | ĩka'paʒ | a. incapable;
incompetent; unable
incauto -ta | ĩ'kawtʊ | a. careless,
heedless
incendiar | ĩsẽdi'aʀ | vt. vi. to set
fire to; to burn (up, down).
-i.-se to catch fire
incêndio | ĩ'sẽdiʊ | sm. fire.
-extintor de i. fire extinguisher
incenso | ĩ'sẽsʊ | sm. incense
incentivo | ĩsẽ'tivʊ | sm. incentive,
stimulus
incerteza | ĩseʀ'teza | sf. incertitude, uncertainty, doubt
incerto -ta | ĩ'sɛʀtʊ | a. doubtful,
dubious, uncertain
incessante | ĩse'sãtɪ | a. unceasing,
incessant
incesto | ĩ'sɛʃtʊ | sm.incest
inchação | ĩxa'sãw | sf. swelling
inchado -da | ĩ'xadʊ | a. swollen
inchar | ĩ'xaʀ | vt. vi. to swell, to inflate. -i.-se to swell up
incidente | ĩsi'dẽtɪ | sm. a. incident
incinerar | ĩsine'raʀ | vt. to incinerate, to cremate
incisão | ĩsi'zãw | sf. incision (also
surg.)
incisivo -va | ĩsi'zivʊ | sm. (dent.)
incisor, foretooth / a. incisive,
keen
incitar | ĩsi'taʀ | vt. to incite, to
excite, to arouse, to instigate
incivil | ĩsi'vil | a. uncivil, rude,
discourteous
inclemência | ĩkle'mẽsia | sf. severity, harshness, inclemency
inclemente | ĩkle'mẽtɪ | a. severe,
harsh, inclement
inclinação | ĩklina'sãw | sf. inclination, tilt; propensity,
disposition
inclinar | ĩkli'naʀ | vt. to incline; to
bow, to tilt. -i.-se to incline, to
slope; to bow; to stoop; to show
a tendency
ínclito -ta | 'ĩklitʊ | a. famous,
illustrious

incluir | ĩklu'iʀ | *vt.* to include, to embody; to cover; to enclose

inclusão | ĩklu'zãw | *sf.* inclusion

inclusive | ĩklu'zivɪ | *adv.* inclusively

incluso -sa | ĩ'kluzʊ | *a.* included, enclosed; herewith (in letter)

incoerente | ĩkoe'ɾẽtɪ | *a.* incoherent

incógnita | ĩ'kʊgnita | *sf.* (math.) unknown quantity

incógnito -ta | ĩ'kʊgnitʊ | *a.* unknown; incognito

incolor | ĩko'loʀ | *a.* colo(u)rless

incólume | ĩ'kʊlumɪ | *a.* safe and sound, unharmed

incomensurável | ĩkomẽsu'ɾavɪl | *a.* immeasurable, immense

incomível | ĩkʊ'mivɪl | *a.* uneatable

incomodar | ĩkomo'daʀ | *vt.* to bother, to molest; to annoy, to disturb. **-i.-se** to trouble, to bother (oneself); to become annoyed or disturbed

incômodo -da | ĩ'komʊdʊ | *sm.* inconvenience, nuisance, disturbance; indisposition / *a.* inconvenient, uncomfortable; annoying, disturbing

incomparável | ĩkõpa'ɾavɪl | *a.* incomparable, matchless

incompatibilidade | ĩkõpatibili'dadɪ | *sf.* incompatibility

incompatível | ĩkõpa'tivɪl | *a.* incompatible

incompetência | ĩkõpe'tẽsia | *sf.* incompetence

incompetente | ĩkõpe'tẽtɪ | *a.* incompetent

incompleto -ta | ĩkõ'plɛtʊ | *a.* incomplete, unfinished; defective

incompreensível | ĩkõprɪẽ'sivɪl | *a.* incomprehensible

incomum | ĩko'mũ | *a.* uncommon, unusual

incomunicável | ĩkʊmuni'kavɪl | *a.* incommunicable; incommunicado (said of prisoner)

inconcebível | ĩkõsɪ'bivɪl | *a.* inconceivable

inconciliável | ĩkõsili'avɪl | *a.* irreconcilable

incondicional | ĩkõdisio'nal | *a.* unconditional

inconfidência | ĩkõfi'dẽsia | *sf.* unfaithfulness, disloyalty. **-I. Mineira** patriotic movement against the Portuguese domination in Brazil (1789)

inconfidente | ĩkõfi'dẽtɪ | *sm.* a. partisan of the *Inconfidência Mineira* / *a.* unfaithful, disloyal

inconformado -da | ĩkõfoʀ'madʊ | *a.* malcontent, discontented

inconfundível | ĩkõfũ'divɪl | *a.* unmistakable

inconquistável | ĩkõkiʃ'tavɪl | *a.* unconquerable

inconsciência | ĩkõsi'ẽsia | *sf.* unconsciousness

inconsciente | ĩkõsi'ẽtɪ | *sm.* the unconscious / *a.* unconscious

inconseqüente | ĩkõse'kwẽtɪ | *a.* inconsequent

inconsistente | ĩkõsiʃ'tẽtɪ | *a.* inconsistent

inconsolável | ĩkõso'lavɪl | *a.* inconsolable

inconstante | ĩkõʃ'tãtɪ | *a.* inconstant, changeable

incontestável | ĩkõteʃ'tavɪl | *a.* incontestable, unquestionable

incontido -da | ĩkõ'tidʊ | *a.* unrestrained

incontinente | ĩkõti'nẽtɪ | *smf.* a. incontinent; unrestrained; licentious

incontrolável | ĩkõtro'lavɪl | *a.* uncontrollable, ungovernable

inconveniência | ĩkõvɪni'ẽsia | *sf.* inconvenience, annoyance; impropriety

inconveniente | ĩkõvɪni'ẽtɪ | *sm.* drawback, disadvantage; difficulty / *a.* inconvenient, inopportune; unbecoming

incorporar | ĩkoʀpo'ʀaʀ | *vt.* to incorporate; to embody; to form into a corporation. **-i.-se** to become part of; to join

incorrer | ĩko'ReR | *vi.* to incur; to run into; to become liable to

incorreto -ta | ĩko'Rɛtʊ | *a.* incorrect, wrong; inaccurate; improper

incorrigível | ĩkoRi'jivɪl | *a.* incorrigible

incorruptível | ĩkʊRup'tivɪl | *a.* incorruptible

incorrupto -ta | ĩkʊ'Ruptʊ | *a.* incorrupt

incrédulo -la | ĩ'krɛdulʊ | *smf.* unbeliever / *a.* incredulous

incrementar | ĩkremẽ'taR | *vt.* to further, to develop; to increase, to augment

incremento | ĩkre'mẽtʊ | *sm.* increase; growth, development

incriminar | ĩkrimi'naR | *vt.* to incriminate, to inculpate

incrível | ĩ'krivɪl | *a.* unbelievable, incredible

inculpar | ĩkul'paR | *vt.* to accuse; to blame

inculto -ta | ĩ'kultʊ | *a.* uncultivated, uncultured; ignorant

incumbir | ĩkũ'biR | *vt.* to commit, to assign, to entrust / *vi.* to be the duty of, to be entrusted with. **-i.-se de** to take upon oneself

incurável | ĩku'ravɪl | *a.* incurable

incúria | ĩ'kuria | *sf.* carelessness, negligence

incursão | ĩkuR'sãw | *sf.* incursion, attack, raid

incutir | ĩku'tiR | *vt.* to instill, to impress (on, upon)

indagação | ĩdaga'sãw | *sf.* investigation, search; speculation; interrogation

indagar | ĩda'gaR | *vt.* to ask; to search, to inquire into, to investigate

indecência | ĩde'sẽsia | *sf.* indecency

indecente | ĩde'sẽtɪ | *a.* indecent

indecisão | ĩdɪsi'zãw | *sf.* indecision, vacillation, irresolution

indeciso -sa | ĩdɪ'sizʊ | *a.* irresolute, indecisive, hesitant

indeferido -da | ĩdɪfɪ'ridʊ | *a.* denied, not granted (said of a petition or request)

indefeso -sa | ĩde'fezʊ | *a.* helpless, defenceless

indefinido -da | ĩdɪfi'nidʊ | *a.* indefinite; undefined

indelével | ĩde'lɛvɪl | *a.* indelible

indelicado -da | ĩdɪli'kadʊ | *a.* discourteous, impolite; tactless; coarse

indenização | ĩdeniza'sãw | *sf.* reimbursement, indemnity; reparation

indenizar | ĩdeni'zaR | *vt.* to indemnify, to compensate, to reimburse

independência | ĩdepẽ'dẽsia | *sf.* independence; self-sufficiency

independente | ĩdepẽ'dẽtɪ | *a.* independent, self-sufficient

indescritível | ĩdɪʃkri'tivɪl | *a.* indescribable, extraordinary

indesculpável | ĩdɪʃkul'pavɪl | *a.* inexcusable

indesejável | ĩdeze'javɪl | *smf. a.* undesirable

indestrutível | ĩdɪʃtru'tivɪl | *a.* indestructible

indevido -da | ĩdɪ'vidʊ | *a.* undue, improper, unsuitable

indiano -na | ĩdi'anʊ | *smf. a.* Indian, Hindu

indicação | ĩdika'sãw | *sf.* indication; evidence; designation, appointment

indicador -dora | ĩdika'doR | *sm.* indicator; any gauge or dial for measuring or testing; the index finger / *a.* indicating

indicar | ĩdi'kaR | *vt.* to indicate, to denote, to point out; to appoint, to designate; to suggest

índice | 'ĩdisɪ | *sm.* table of contents; index. **-i. remissivo** cross index

indício | ĩ'disiʊ | *sm.* sign, indication, vestige, trace

indiferença | ĩdife'rẽsa | *sf.* indifference; unconcern; apathy

indiferente | ĩdife'rẽtɪ | *a.* indifferent; nonchalant, unconcerned

indígena | ĭ'dijɩna | *smf.* native, aborigine / *a.* indigenous, native, aboriginal

indigestão | ĭdijeʒ'tãw | *sf.* indigestion

indignação | ĭdigna'sãw | *sf.* indignation

indignado -da | ĭdig'nadʋ | *a.* indignant

indignar | ĭdig'naR | *vt.* to cause indignation; to anger; to revolt, to incite. **-i.-se** to become indignant

indignidade | ĭdigni'dadɩ | *sf.* indignity, affront, outrage

indigno -na | ĭ'dignʋ | *a.* undeserving, unworthy, base, low

índio -dia | 'ĭdiʋ | *smf. a.* Indian

indireta | ĭdi'rɛta | *sf.* cutting remark, veiled and malevolent allusion

indireto -ta | ĭdi'rɛtʋ | *a.* indirect; equivocal, roundabout

indisciplina | ĭdisi'plina | *sf.* insubordination, indiscipline

indiscreto -ta | ĭdiʃ'krɛtʋ | *a.* indiscreet; tactless

indiscrição | ĭdiʃkri'sãw | *sf.* indiscretion, blunder

indiscutível | ĭdiʃku'tivɩl | *a.* incontrovertible, certain

indispensável | ĭdiʃpẽ'savɩl | *a.* indispensable, essential

indisponível | ĭdiʃpo'nivɩl | *a.* unavailable, not disposable

indispor | ĭdiʃ'poR | *vt.* to indispose, to disarrange; to upset; to turn one against (someone else). **-i.-se** to become ruffled, to turn against

indisposição | ĭdiʃpozi'sãw | *sf.* indisposition; slight ailment

indisposto -ta | ĭdiʃ'poʃtʋ -'poʃta | *a.* indisposed; out of sorts; averse

indistinto -ta | ĭdiʃ'tĭtʋ | *a.* indistinct, vague, hazy

individual | ĭdividu'al | *a.* individual

indivíduo | ĭdi'viduʋ | *sm.* individual, person; (colloq.) fellow, guy

indivisível | ĭdivi'zivɩl | *a.* indivisible

indizível | ĭdi'zivɩl | *a.* unspeakable, indescribable

indócil | ĭ'dɯsil | *a.* indocile, unmanageable; excited

índole | 'ĭdʋlɩ | *sf.* temperament, disposition; character

indolência | ĭdo'lẽsia | *sf.* indolence

indolente | ĭdo'lẽtɩ | *a.* indolent

indolor | ĭdo'loR | *a.* painless

indomável | ĭdo'mavɩl | *a.* untameable, indomitable

indômito -ta | ĭ'domitʋ | *a.* unconquered, unbowed

indubitável | ĭdubi'tavɩl | *a.* indubitable, doubtless

indulgência | ĭdul'jẽsià | *sf.* indulgence, leniency

indultar | ĭdul'taR | *vt.* (law) to reduce or to extinguish a sentence

indulto | ĭ'dultʋ | *sm.* (law) pardon, amnesty

indumentária | ĭdumẽ'taria | *sf.* dress, cloth, clothing

indústria | ĭ'duʃtria | *sf.* industry

industrial | ĭduʃtri'al | *smf.* industrialist / *a.* industrial

industrialização | ĭduʃtrializa'sãw | *sf.* industrialization

industrializar | ĭduʃtriali'zaR | *vt.* to industrialize

industrioso -sa | ĭduʃtri'ozʋ -'ɯza | *smf.* industrious, operose

induzir | ĭdu'ziR | *vt.* to induce; to cause, to occasion; to constrain. **-i.em erro** to lead into error

inebriante | inebri'ãtɩ | *a.* intoxicating, inebriating

inédito -ta | i'nɛditʋ | *sm.* unpublished work / *a.* unpublished; unprecedented, unheard-of

inefável | ine'favɩl | *a.* ineffable, indescribable

ineficaz | inefi'kaʒ | *a.* inefficacious, ineffectual

ineficiente | inefisi'ẽtɩ | *a.* inefficient

inegável | ine'gav↓l | *a.* undeniable, irrefutable

inelutável | inelu'tav↓l | *a.* ineluctable, inevitable

inépcia | i'nɛpsia | *sf.* ineptitude

inepto -ta | i'nɛpt↓ | *a.* inept, clumsy

inequívoco -ca | ine'kivʊkʊ | *a.* clear, unmistakable

inércia | i'nɛRsia | *sf.* inertia (also phys.); sluggishness

inerente | ine'Rẽt↓ | *a.* inherent

inerme | i'nɛRm↓ | *a.* **defenceless,** unarmed

inerte | i'nɛRt↓ | *a.* inert, inactive, sluggish

inesgotável | ine꜀go'tav↓l | *a.* inexhaustible

inesperado -da | ine꜀pe'radʊ | *a.* unexpected, sudden

inesquecível | ine꜀ke'siv↓l | *a.* unforgettable

inestimável | ine꜀ti'mav↓l | *a.* inestimable, priceless

inevitável | inevi'tav↓l | *a.* inevitable, unavoidable

inexatidão | inezati'dãw | *sf.* inaccuracy, error

inexato -ta | ine'zatʊ | *a.* inexact, inaccurate

inexcedível | inese'div↓l | *a.* unsurpassable

inexistente | inezi꜀'tẽt↓ | *a.* inexistent, nonexistent

inexperiência | ine꜀peri'ẽsia | *sf.* inexperience

inexperiente | ine꜀peri'ẽt↓ | *a.* inexperienced; ingenuous, naïve

inexplicável | ine꜀pli'kav↓l | *a.* inexplicable

inexplorado -da | ine꜀plo'radʊ | *a.* unexplored

inexpressivo -va | ine꜀pre'sivʊ | *a.* inexpressive, meaningless

infalível | ĩfa'liv↓l | *a.* infallible; unerring; sure-fire

infame | ĩ'fam↓ | *smf.* infamous person / *a.* infamous, vile

infâmia | ĩ'famia | *sf.* infamy

infância | ĩ'fãsia | *sf.* childhood, infancy

infantaria | ĩfãta'ria | *sf.* infantry

infante | ĩ'fãt↓ | *sm.* baby, infant; infantry soldier

infantil | ĩfã'til | *a.* childish, infantile

infantilidade | ĩfãtili'dad↓ | *sf.* childishness

infatigável | ĩfati'gav↓l | *a.* indefatigable

infecção | ĩfek'sãw | *sf.* infection

infeccionar | ĩfeksio'naR | *vt.* to infect, to contaminate. **-i.-se** to become infected

infeccioso -sa | ĩfeksi'ozʊ-'ɔza | *a.* (med.) infectious

infelicidade | ĩf↓lisi'dad↓ | *sf.* unhappiness, misfortune

infeliz | ĩf↓'li꜀ | *a.* unhappy, unfortunate

inferior | ĩferi'oR | *a.* inferior, lower, nether, under; cheap

inferioridade | ĩferiori'dad↓ | *sf.* inferiority

inferir | ĩf↓'RiR | *vt.* to infer, to conclude, to deduce

infernizar | ĩfeRni'zaR | *vt.* to afflict, to torment

inferno | ĩ'feRnʊ | *sm.* hell

infestar | ĩfe꜀'taR | *vt.* to infest; to swarm over; to plague

infidelidade | ĩfideli'dad↓ | *sf.* infidelity

infiel | ĩfi'ɛl | *a.* unfaithful; (relig.) infidel; inexact, untrue

infiltrar | ĩfil'traR | *vt.* to infiltrate. **-i.-se** to infiltrate, to enter gradually and imperceptibly

ínfimo -ma | 'ĩfimʊ | *a.* undermost, lowermost; negligible; vilest

infinidade | ĩfini'dad↓ | *sf.* infinity; endless number

infinito -ta | ĩfi'nitʊ | *sm.* infinite; (gram.) infinitive / *a.* infinite, boundless; innumerable

inflação | ĩfla'sãw | *sf.* inflation

inflacionar | ĩflasio'naR | *vt.* (econ.) to inflate, to bring about inflation of

inflamação | ĩflama'sãw | *sf.* inflammation

inflamar | ĩfla'maR | *vt.* to inflame, to excite; to set afire / vi. to become swelled and infected

inflamável | ĩfla'mavɩl | a. inflammable

inflar | ĩ'flaʀ | vt. to inflate; to puff up

inflexível | ĩfle'ksivɩl | a. inflexible, unbending; inexorable

infligir | ĩfli'jiʀ | vt. to inflict, to impose (punishment)

influência | ĩflu'ẽsia | sf. influence, importance, ascendance

influenciar | ĩfluẽsi'aʀ | vt. to influence

influenciável | ĩfluẽsi'avɩl | a. capable of being influenced

influente | ĩflu'ẽtɩ | a. influential

influir | ĩflu'iʀ | vt. to induce, to inspire. -i.em (para, sobre) to influence, to have influence on

influxo | ĩ'fluksv | sm. influx, inflow; influence

informação | ĩfoʀma'sãw | sf. information

informante | ĩfoʀ'mãtɩ | smf. informer, informant

informar | ĩfoʀ'maʀ | vt. to inform, to notify; to report, to communicate. -i.-se to inform (oneself) about

informe | ĩ'fɷʀmɩ | sm. report; information / a. shapeless, amorphous

infortúnio | ĩfoʀ'tuniv | sm. misfortune, adversity

infração | ĩfra'sãw | sf. infraction, infringement, breach; (sports) foul

infringir | ĩfrĩ'jiʀ | vt. to infringe, to break, to transgress. -i.a lei to break the law

infrutífero -ra | ĩfru'tifɩrv | a. fruitless; useless

infundado -da | ĩfũ'dadv | a. unfounded, baseless, groundless

infundir | ĩfũ'diʀ | vt. to infuse, to instil, to inculcate

infusão | ĩfu'zãw | sf. infusion; brewage, brew

ingenuidade | ĩjenui'dadɩ | sf. ingenuousness, simplicity, art-

lessness, naïvety

ingênuo -nua | ĩ'jenuʋ | .a. ingenuous, artless, naïve

inglês -glesa | ĩ'gleʓ | sm. (ling.) English; Englishman; sf. Englishwoman / a. English. -i.mal falado broken English. -povo i. the British

ingratidão | ĩgrati'dãw | sf. ingratitude

ingrato -ta | ĩ'gratv | a. ungrateful; unpleasant, to no advantage; sterile, barren (soil)

ingrediente | ĩgrɩdi'ẽtɩ | sm. ingredient

íngreme | 'ĩgrɩmɩ | a. steep; arduous

ingressar | ĩgre'saʀ | vt. to enter, to go into; to join, to become a member of

ingresso | ĩ'gresv | sm. entry, entrance; admission ticket

inhame | i'ɴamɩ | sm. yam

inibição | inibi'sãw | sf. inhibition

inibir | ini'biʀ | vt. to inhibit, to hinder. -i.-se to become inhibited

iniciação | inisia'sãw | sf. initiation; novitiate

inicial | inisi'al | sf. initial, first letter of a word; (law) initial petition; (pl.) first letters of person's names / a. initial

iniciar | inisi'aʀ | vt. to initiate; to begin, to start, to commence

iniciativa | inisia'tiva | sf. initiative. -i. privada free enterprise

início | i'nisiʋ | sm. beginning, start

inimigo -ga | ini'migʋ | smf. enemy / a. inimical, hostile

inimitável | inimi'tavɩl | a. inimitable

inimizade | inimi'zadɩ | sf. enmity, disaffection; hostility

ininteligível | inĩteli'jivɩl | a. unintelligible, incomprehensible

ininterrupto -ta | inĩte'ʀuptv | a. uninterrupted, continuous, incessant

iníquo -qua | i'nikwv | a. iniquitous; inequitable, unjust

injeção | ĩje'sãv | *sf.* injection

injetado-da | ĩje'tadv | *a.* injected; bloodshot ([esp. *pl.*] said of eyes)

injúria | ĩ'juria | *sf.* injury, insult, defamation, slander

injuriar | ĩjuri'aR | *vt.* to defame, to slander, to insult

injurioso -sa | ĩjuri'ozv -'ωza | *a.* offensive, insulting

injustiça | ĩjuʒ'tisa | *sf.* injustice

injustificável | ĩjuʒtifi'kavɩl | *a.* unjustifiable

injusto -ta | ĩ'juʒtv | *a.* unjust, unfair

inocência | ino'sẽsia | *sf.* innocence; guiltlessness; chastity

inocentar | inosẽ'taR | *vt.* to acquit, to declare innocent

inocente | ino'sẽtɩ | *smf.* innocent; (law) not guilty / *a.* innocent

inocular | inoku'laR | *vt.* to inoculate

inofensivo -va | inofẽ'sivv | *a.* inoffensive, harmless

inolvidável | inolvi'davɩl | *a.* unforgettable

inoportuno -na | inopoR'tunv | *a.* inopportune, inconvenient

inóspito -ta | i'nωʃpitv | *a.* inhospitable (place)

inovação | inova'sãw | *sf.* innovation

inoxidável | inoksi'davɩl | *a.* stainless. **-aço i.** stainless steel

inqualificável | ĩkwalifi'kavɩl | *a.* unqualifiable; unspeakably bad

inquebrantável | ĩkebrã'tavɩl | *a.* adamant; unfailing; unflagging

inquebrável | ĩke'bravɩl | *a.* unbreakable

inquérito | ĩ'kɛritv | *sm.* inquiry, enquiry, examination

inquietação | ĩkieta'sãw | *sf.* uneasiness, anxiety; unrest

inquietar | ĩkie'taR | *vt.* to upset, to trouble, to disturb. **-i.-se** to worry

inquieto -ta | ĩki'ɛtv | *a.* unquiet, restless, uneasy, agitated

inquilino -na | ĩki'linv | *smf.* tenant, lodger

inquirição | ĩkiri'sãw | *sf.* inquiry, investigation, interrogation

inquirir | ĩki'riR | *vt.* to inquire, to question, to interrogate

inquisitivo -va | ĩkizi'tivv | *a.* inquisitive, curious

insaciável | ĩsasi'avɩl | *a.* insatiable, insatiate

insalubre | ĩsa'lubrɩ | *a.* unhealthy, insalubrious

insanável | ĩsa'navɩl | *a.* irremediable, irreparable

insanidade | ĩsani'dadɩ | *sf.* insanity

insano -na | ĩ'sanv | *a.* insane, demented, mad

insatisfação | ĩsatiʒfa'sãw | *sf.* dissatisfaction; inquietude, anxiety

insatisfeito -ta | ĩsatiʒ'feytv | *a.* insatisfied, dissatisfied

inscrever | ĩʃkre'veR | *vt.* to inscribe (also geom.). **-i.-se** to register, to matriculate oneself

inscrição | ĩʃkri'sãw | *sf.* inscription; registration

insegurança | ĩsɩgu'rãsa | *sf.* insecurity, incertitude

insensatez | ĩsẽsa'teʃ | *sf.* foolishness; folly

insensato -ta | ĩsẽ'satv | *a.* foolish, senseless, unreasonable

insensibilidade | ĩsẽsibili'dadɩ | *sf.* insensibility; insensitiveness

insensível | ĩsẽ'sivɩl | *a.* insensible; insensitive

inseparável | ĩsepa'ravɩl | *a.* inseparable

inserir | ĩsɩ'riR | *vt.* to insert, to introduce

inseticida | ĩseti'sida | *sm. a.* insecticide

inseto | ĩ'setv | *sm.* insect

insigne | ĩ'signɩ | *a.* illustrious, celebrated, noted, famous

insígnia | ĩ'signia | *sf.* badge, emblem; (*pl.*) insignia

insignificante |ĩsignifi'kãtι| *a.* insignificant, negligible

insincero -ra |ĩsĩ'sɛrυ| *a.* insincere

insinuação | ĩsinua'sãw | *sf.* insinuation

insinuante | ĩsinu'ãtι | *a.* insinuative, ingratiating

insinuar | ĩsinu'ar | *vt.* to insinuate; to hint, to suggest. **-i.-se** to insinuate oneself; to work oneself into

insípido -da | ĩ'sipidυ | *a.* insipid, tasteless

insistir | ĩsiʃ'tir | *vi.* to insist; to persist; to importune

insolação | ĩsola'sãw | *sf.* sunstroke; insolation

insolente | ĩso'lẽtι | *a.* insolent

insólito -ta | ĩ'sωlitυ | *a.* unusual, uncommon

insolúvel | ĩso'luvιl | *a.* insoluble; inextricable

insolvência | ĩsol'vẽsia | *sf.* insolvency

insondável |ĩsõ'davιl| *a.* fathomless; unfathomable

insônia | ĩ'sonia | *sf.* insomnia

insosso -sa | ĩ'sosυ | *a.* unsalted, saltless; tasteless, insipid

inspeção | ĩʃpe'sãw | *sf.* inspection, examination

inspecionar | ĩʃpesio'nar | *vt.* to inspect, to examine

inspetor -tora |ĩʃpe'tor| *smf.* inspector; supervisor

inspiração | ĩʃpira'sãw | *sf.* inspiration; inhalation

inspirar | ĩʃpi'rar | *vt.* to inspire; to inhale

instabilidade | ĩʃtabili'dadι | *sf.* instability; inconstancy

instalação | ĩʃtala'sãw | *sf.* installation; settlement; (*pl.*) equipment, fittings

instalar |ĩʃta'lar| *vt.* to install, to establish; to locate. **-i.-se** to lodge oneself

instância |ĩʃ'tãsia | *sf.* urging, insisting request, entreaty; (law) instance, court. **-em última i.** in last resort

instantâneo -nea | ĩʃtã'tanιυ | *sm.* (photog.) snapshot / *a.* instantaneous, immediate

instante |ĩʃ'tãtι | *sm.* instant, moment / *a.* urgent, pressing

instar |ĩʃ'tar | *vt. vi.* to insist (**com** with; **em** upon); to request insistently; to entreat

instaurar | ĩʃtaw'rar | *vt.* to institute, to establish

instável | ĩʃ'tavιl | *a.* unstable, unsteady

instigar | ĩʃti'gar | *vt.* to instigate, to incite; to provoke

instilar | ĩʃti'lar | *vt.* to instil (l) (also fig.)

instintivo -va | ĩʃtĩ'tivυ | *a.* instinctive; spontaneous

instinto | ĩʃ'tĩtυ | *sm.* instinct

instituição | ĩʃtitui'sãw | *sf.* institution; institute

instituir |ĩʃtitu'ir | *vt.* to institute, to establish

instituto | ĩʃti'tutυ | *sm.* institute

instrução | ĩʃtru'sãw | *sf.* instruction, education, schooling; (*pl.*) briefing (also mil.), directions

instruído -da | ĩʃtru'idυ | *a.* learned; instructed

instruir | ĩʃtru'ir | *vt.* to instruct, to teach; to give instructions. **-i.-se** to acquire learning or information

instrumento | ĩʃtru'mẽtυ | *sm.* instrument; tool, utensil. **-i. de cordas** string instrument. **-i. de sopro** wind instrument

instrutor -tora | ĩʃtru'tor | *smf.* instructor, coach, trainer

insubmisso -sa | ĩsub'misυ | *sm.* draft dodger; (mil.) deserter / *a.* unsubmissive

insubordinação | ĩsubordina'sãw | *sf.* insubordination; mutiny, revolt

insucesso | ĩsu'sɛsυ | *sm.* failure

insuficiência | ĩsufisi'ẽsia | *sf.* insufficiency

insuficiente |ĩsufisi'ẽtι| *a.* insufficient; unsatisfactory; deficient

insuflar | īsu'flaʀ | *vt.* to insufflate; to incite, to instigate

insular | īsu'laʀ | *smf.* islander / *a.* insular

insultar | īsul'taʀ | *vt.* to insult, to affront; to outrage

insulto | ĩ'sultυ | *sm.* insult, outrage, affront; (med.) attack

insuperável | īsupe'ravιl | *a.* insuperable

insuportável | īsupoʀ'tavιl | *a.* intolerable, unbearable

insurgente | īsuʀ'jētι | *smf. a.* insurgent

insurgir-se | īsuʀ'jiʀsι | *vr.* to revolt, to rebel

insurreição | īsuʀey'sãw | *sf.* insurrection, rebellion, revolt

insustentável | īsuʃtē'tavιl | *a.* unsustainable, untenable

intangível | ītã'jivιl | *a.* intangible

intato -ta | ĩ'tatυ | *a.* intact, untouched

íntegra | 'ītegra | *sf.* integral text. **-na í.** in full, verbatim

integração | ītegra'sãw | *sf.* integration

integral | ĩte'gral | *a.* integral, complete, whole

integridade | ītegri'dadι | *sf.* integrity; entirety; moral uprightness

íntegro -gra | 'ītegrυ | *a.* upright, righteous; whole, complete

inteirar | ītey'raʀ | *vt.* to complete; to inform completely. **-i.-se** to inform oneself completely about

inteiriço -ça | ītey'risυ | *a.* of one piece, solid

inteiro -ra | ĩ'teyrυ | *a.* entire, whole, complete; not gelded, uncastrate

intelecto | īte'lektυ | *sm.* intellect

intelectual | ītelektu'al | *smf. a.* intellectual

inteligência | ītιli'jēsia | *sf.* intelligence; intellect, mind

inteligente | ītιli'jētι | *a.* intelligent, bright, clever

inteligível | ītιli'jivιl | *a.* intelligible

intemperança | ītēpe'rãsa | *sf.* intemperance

intempérie | ĩtē'periι | *sf.* inclemency (of weather)

intempestivo -va | ĩtēpeʃ'tivυ | *a.* untimely, ill-timed

intenção | ĩtē'sãw | *sf.* intention; purpose, design, object

intencional | ītēsio'nal | *a.* intentional, intended, deliberate

intendência | ĩtē'dēsia | *sf.* intendancy; an administrative department of headquarters (in the army, navy and air force)

intendente | ĩtē'dētι | *sm.* (mil.) an officer attached to the administrative department of headquarters

intensidade | ītēsi'dadι | *sf.* intensity

intensificar | ītēsifi'kaʀ | *vt.* to intensify, to increase

intenso -sa | ĩ'tēsυ | *a.* intense, vivid

intentar | ĩtē'taʀ | *vt.* to intend, to aim at; to attempt, to undertake

intento | ĩ'tētυ | *sm.* intent, intention, design, purpose

intercalar | īteʀka'laʀ | *vt.* to intercalate, to insert between

intercâmbio | īteʀ'kãbiυ | *sm.* interchange; commerce

interceder | īteʀse'deʀ | *vi.* to intercede, to plead (in behalf of another)

intercepção | īteʀsep'sãw | *sf.* interception

interceptar | īteʀsep'taʀ | *vt.* to intercept; to interrupt

intercessão | īteʀse'sãw | *sf.* intercession

interessado -da | ītere'sadυ | *smf.* an interested or concerned person; (com.) profit-sharer / *a.* interested, concerning

interessante | ītere'sãtι | *a.* interesting; significant; attractive. **-em estado i.** pregnant

interessar | ītere'saʀ | *vt.* to interest (em in). **-i.-se** to take an interest; to concern oneself / *vi.* to be of interest. **-a quem possa i.** to whom it may concern

interesse | ĩteʹrɛsɪ | *sm.* interest (also com.), benefit; concern, regard

interesseiro -ra | ĩtereʹseyrʊ | *a.* self-seeking

interestadual | ĩterɪʒtaduʹal | *a.* interstate

interferência | ĩteRfeʹrẽsia | *sf.* interference

interferir | ĩteRfɪʹrir | *vi.* to interfere, to intervene

ínterim | ʹĩterĩ | *sm.* interim, meantime. **-nesse í.** meanwhile

interino -na | ĩteʹrinʊ | *a.* provisional, temporary

interior | ĩteriʹoR | *sm.* interior, inside; inner nature; inland / *a.* interior; internal; inland

interjeição | ĩteRjeyʹsãw | *sf.* interjection, exclamation

intermediário -ria | ĩteRmediʹariʊ | *smf.* intermediary; *sm.* (com.) middleman / *a.* intermediate

intermédio | ĩteRʹmɛdiʊ | *sm.* intermediation, intervention. **-por i. de** by means of, through

interminável | ĩteRmiʹnavɪl | *a.* interminable, endless

intermitente | ĩteRmiʹtẽtɪ | *a.* intermittent

internacional | ĩteRnasioʹnal | *a.* international

internar | ĩteRʹnaR | *vt.* to intern; to place in a boarding-school; to place in a hospital. **-i.-se** to penetrate, to enter (deeply) into; to go to a hospital

internato | ĩteRʹnatʊ | *sm.* boarding-school

interno -na | ĩʹteRnʊ | *smf.* intern; boarder (student) / *a.* internal; inner, inside; boarding (student)

interpelar | ĩteRpeʹlaR | *vt.* to interpellate (also law); to summon, to cite; to challenge

interpor | ĩteRʹpoR | *vt.* to interpose, to place between. **-i.-se** to place oneself between. **-i. um recurso** (law) to lodge an appeal

interpretação | ĩteRpretaʹsãw | *sf.* interpretation

interpretar | ĩteRpreʹtaR | *vt.* to interpret; to render; to explain

intérprete | ĩʹtɛRprɪtɪ | *smf.* interpreter

interrogação | ĩteRogaʹsãw | *sf.* interrogation; interrogation mark or point

interrogar | ĩteRoʹgaR | *vt.* to interrogate, to question

interrogatório | ĩteRogaʹtɔriʊ | *sm.* interrogatory

interromper | ĩteRõʹpeR | *vt.* to interrupt, to stop, to cut off; to obstruct

interrupção | ĩteRupʹsãw | *sf.* interruption, discontinuity

interruptor | ĩteRupʹtoR | *sm.* interrupter; electric switch

interseção | ĩteRseʹsãw | *sf.* intersection

interurbano | ĩteruRʹbanʊ | *sm.* long-distance telephone call / *a.* interurban

intervalo | ĩteRʹvalʊ | *sm.* interval, intermission

intervenção | ĩteRvẽʹsãw | *sf.* intervention, interference

intervir | ĩteRʹviR | *vi.* to intervene; to intermeddle; to mediate

intestino -na | ĩtɪʒʹtinʊ | *sm.* intestine, bowels / *a.* intestine, internal

intimação | ĩtimaʹsãw | *sf.* citation, notification

intimar | ĩtiʹmaR | *vt.* to notify; to summon, to cite

intimidade | ĩtimiʹdadɪ | *sf.* intimacy, familiarity; privacy

intimidar | ĩtimiʹdaR | *vt.* to intimidate, to frighten, to bully

íntimo -ma | ʹĩtimʊ | *sm.* core, innermost part; *smf.* intimate, close friend / *a.* intimate, familiar, close

intitular | ĩtituʹlaR | *vt.* to entitle, to give a title to. **-i.-se** to entitle (call) oneself

intolerância | ĩtoleʹrãsia | *sf.* intolerance

intolerável | ĭtoleˈrav⟨l | *a*. intolerable, unbearable

intoxicação | ĭtoksikaˈsãw | *sf*. intoxication, poisoning

intoxicar | ĭtoksiˈkaʀ | *vt*. to intoxicate, to poison. **-i.-se** to poison oneself; to take stupefying drugs

intraduzível | ĭtraduˈzív⟨l | *a*. untranslatable; inexpressible

intragável | ĭtraˈgav⟨l | *a*. unpalatable (also fig.)

intranqüilo -la | ĭtrãˈkwil⟨ | *a*. restless

intransigente | ĭtrãziˈjɛt⟨ | *smf*. intransigent; intolerant

intransitável | ĭtrãziˈtav⟨l | *a*. impassable (road, street); (fig.) untractable

intransponível | ĭtrãʒpʋˈniv⟨l | *a*. unsurmountable

intratável | ĭtraˈtav⟨l | *a*. intractable, unmanageable, unsociable, unapproachable

intrépido -da | ĭˈtrɛpidʋ | *a*. intrepid, fearless, bold

intriga | ĭˈtriga | *sf*. intrigue; malicious gossip

intrigar | ĭtriˈgaʀ | *vt*. to intrigue; to perplex, to puzzle / *vi*. to scheme, to intrigue

intrincado -da | ĭtrĭˈkadʋ | *a*. intricate, complex, complicated

intrínseco -ca | ĭˈtrĭsɨkʋ | *a*. intrinsic, inherent, ingrained

introdução | ĭtrʋduˈsãw | *sf*. introduction

introduzir | ĭtrʋduˈziʀ | *vt*. to introduce; to insert; to bring in; to bring into use. **-i.-se** to penetrate

intrometer-se | ĭtromeˈteʀsɨ | *vr*. to meddle, to interfere in, to intrude

intrometido -da | ĭtrʋmɨˈtidʋ | *smf*. meddler, intruder / *a*. meddlesome, intrusive

intromissão | ĭtrʋmiˈsãw | *sf*. intrusion, meddling

intrujão -jona | ĭtruˈjãw -ˈjona | *smf*. swindler, impostor; (slang) fence, receiver of stolen goods

intrujar | ĭtruˈjaʀ | *vt*. to dupe; to inveigle / *vi*. to tell tall tales

intruso -sa | ĭˈtruzʋ | *smf*. intruder; gatecrasher / *a*. intrusive

intuição | ĭtuiˈsãw | *sf*. intuition

intuito | ĭˈtuytʋ | *sm*. aim, purpose, intention

inumano -na | inuˈmanʋ | *a*. inhuman(e)

inumerável | inumeˈrav⟨l | *a*. innumerable, countless

inundação | inũdaˈsãw | *sf*. flood, inundation

inundar | inũˈdaʀ | *vt*. to inundate, to flood

inútil | iˈnutil | *a*. useless

inutilidade | inutiliˈdad⟨ | *sf*. uselessness

inutilizar | inutiliˈzaʀ | *vt*. to render useless, to destroy; to incapacitate, to disable

invadir | ĭvaˈdiʀ | *vt*. to invade; to trespass

invalidar | ĭvaliˈdaʀ | *vt*. to invalidate, to nullify

invalidez | ĭvaliˈdeʒ | *sf*. invalidity; disability

inválido -da | ĭˈvalidʋ | *smf*. invalid / *a*. invalid, disabled

invariável | ĭvariˈav⟨l | *a*. invariable, unchanging

invasão | ĭvaˈzãw | *sf*. invasion

invasor -sora | ĭvaˈzoʀ | *smf*. *a*. invader

invectiva | ĭvekˈtiva | *sf*. invective

inveja | ĭˈveja | *sf*. envy

invejar | ĭveˈjaʀ | *vt*. to envy, to covet; to grudge

invejoso -sa | ĭveˈjozʋ -ˈjɔza | *smf*. envious person / *a*. envious, grudging

invenção | ĭvẽˈsãw | *sf*. invention, discovery

invencível | ĭvẽˈsiv⟨l | *a*. invincible, unconquerable

inventar | ĭvẽˈtaʀ | *vt*. to invent; to devise, to contrive; to fabricate

inventariante | ĭvẽtariˈãt⟨ | *smf*. (law) executor, one who makes an inventory / *a.* inventorying

inventariar | ĩvẽtari'aR | *vt.* to inventory

inventário | ĩvẽ'tariʋ | *smf.* inventory, detailed list of property (esp. of a deceased person)

invento | ĩ'vẽtʋ | *sm.* invention

inventor -tora | ĩvẽ'toR | *smf.* inventor; discoverer

inverno | ĩ'vɛRnʋ | *sm.* winter

inverossímil | ĩvero'simil | *a.* unlikely, improbable

inverso -sa | ĩ'vɛRsʋ | *smf. a.* inverse, reverse

inverter | ĩvɛR'teR | *vt.* to invert, to reserve; to invest (capital)

invés | ĩ'vɛʒ | *sm.* the opposite. **-ao i.** on the contrary. **-ao i. de** instead of, rather than

investida | ĩvɨʒ'tida | *sf.* charge, sally, attack

investigação | ĩvɨʒtiga'sãw | *sf.* investigation

investigar | ĩvɨʒti'gaR | *vt.* to investigate

investir | ĩvɨʒ'tiR | *vt.* to attack, to assail; to invest

inveterado -da | ĩvete'radʋ | *a.* inveterate, confirmed

invicto -ta | ĩ'viktʋ | *a.* undefeated, unbeaten

inviolado -da | ĩvio'ladʋ | *a.* inviolate, unbroken

inviolável | ĩvio'lavɨl | *a.* inviolable

invisível | ĩvi'zivɨl | *a.* invisible

invocar | ĩvo'kaR | *vt.* to invoke, to call upon

invólucro | ĩ'vʊlukrʋ | *sm.* covering, wrapper

involuntário -ria | ĩvolũ'tariʋ | *a.* involuntary; unintentional

invulgar | ĩvul'gaR | *a.* uncommon, unusual

invulnerável | ĩvulne'ravɨl | *a.* invulnerable

iodo | i'odʋ | *sm.* iodine

ir | 'iR | *vi.* to go; to proceed; to travel, to journey. **-i.a pé** to walk. **-i. a pique** to sink. **-i. às vias de fato** to come to blows. **-i. bem** to be doing well. **-i. de** to go

by (train, plane etc.). **-i. embora** to go away / *v. aux.* to be going (*vou escrever* I'm going to write). **-i. andando** or **indo** to be getting along (well)

ira | 'ira | *sf.* anger, rage, wrath

irascível | ira'sivɨl | *a.* irascible, irritable

íris | 'iriʒ | *smf.* (anat., bot.) iris

irmã | iR'mã | *sf.* sister

irmandade | iRmã'dadɨ | *sf.* brotherhood, fraternity

irmão | iR'mãw | *sm.* brother

ironia | iro'nia | *sf.* irony

irônico -ca | i'ronikʋ | *a.* ironic, ironical

irracional | iRasio'nal | *a.* irrational

irradiar | iRadi'aR | *vt.* to irradiate; to radiate; to broadcast

irreal | iRɨ'al | *a.* unreal, imaginary

irreconhecível | iRekoNe'sivɨl | *a.* unrecognizable

irrefletido -da | iRefle'tidʋ | *a.* inconsiderate, thoughtless

irreflexão | iRefle'ksãw | *sf.* thoughtlessness

irregular | iRegu'laR | *a.* irregular

irrelevante | iRele'vãtɨ | *a.* irrelevant, immaterial

irremediável | iRemɨdi'avɨl | *a.* irreparable; irremediable

irreparável | iRepa'ravɨl | *a.* irreparable

irrepreensível | iRʋprɨẽ'sivɨl | *a.* irreproachable, blameless

irreprimível | iRepri'mivɨl | *a.* irrepressible

irrequieto -ta | iRɨki'ɛtʋ | *a.* restless, unquiet

irresistível | iRɨzi'ʒtivɨl | *a.* irresistible

irresoluto -ta | iRezʋ'lutʋ | *a.* irresolute, hesitant, undecided

irresponsável | iReʒpõ'savɨl | *a.* irresponsible

irrestrito -ta | iReʒ'tritʋ | *a.* unrestricted, unlimited

irreverente | iReve'rẽtɨ | *a.* irreverent, disrespectful

irrevogável | iRevo'gavɨl | *a.*

irrevocable

irrigar | iʀi'gaʀ | *vt.* to irrigate

irrisório -ria | iʀi'zɔriʋ | *a.* scornful, derisive, ludicrous; petty

irritação | iʀita'sãw | *sf.* irritation, exasperation; itching, burning (of the skin)

irritadiço -ça | iʀita'disʋ | *a.* irritable, cranky, crabby; peevish

irritante | iʀi'tãtɪ | *a.* irritant, irritative, irritating

irritar | iʀi'taʀ | *vt.* to irritate, to annoy; to provoke. **-i.-se** to become angry

irromper | iʀõ'peʀ | *vi.* to burst forth; to irrupt; to break forth (as an epidemic, a fire etc.). **-i. em** to burst into

isca |'iʃka | *sf.* fishing bait; lure; tinder; (*pl.*) dish of strips of fried liver

isenção |izẽ'sãw | *sf.* exemption; immunity; freedom of character

isentar | izẽ'taʀ | *vt.* to exempt; to except; to acquit

isento -ta |i'zẽtʋ | *a.* exempt, free, not liable

isolamento |izola'mẽtʋ | *sm.* isolation, detachment; (elect.) insulation

isolar |izo'laʀ | *vt.* to isolate, to separate; (elect.) to insulate; (colloq.) to knock on wood. **-i.-se** to isolate oneself

isqueiro | iʃ'keyrʋ | *sm.* cigarette-lighter

isso |'isʋ | *neuter demonst. pron.* it, that (near person spoken to). **-é i.** that's it, that's right. **-i. mesmo** that's it, exactly

isto |'iʃtʋ | *neuter demonst. pron.* it, this (near person speaking). **-i. é** that is (to say). **-por i.** this is why. **-que é i.?** what's this?

italiano -na |itali'anʋ | *smf. a.* Italian

itálico -ca |i'talikʋ | *sm.* italic(s)

item |'itẽy | *sm.* item, article (of a written contract etc.)

itinerário -ria | itine'rariʋ | *sm. a.* itinerary

J

já | 'ja | *adv.* now, at once, immediately; already. **-j. em** as early as. **-j. j.** right now, immediately. **-j. não** no longer. **-j. vou!** coming!, I'm coming! **-j. que** since, seeing that

jabuti | jabu'ti | *sm.* kind of land turtle

jabuticaba |jabuti'kaba|*sf.* jaboticaba (sweet cherrylike fruit of the jaboticaba tree)

jaca | 'jaka | *sf.* jack (fruit of the jack tree)

jacá | ja'ka | *sm.* wicker hamper

jacarandá | jakarã'da | *sm.* rosewood. **-j. cabiúna** or **j. preto** Brazilian rosewood

jacaré | jaka 'rɛ | *sm.* alligator, cayman

jacente | ja'sẽtɪ | *sm.* bridge girder / *a.* recumbent, lying

jacinto | ja'sĩtʋ | *sm.* (bot.) hyacinth; (mineral.) jacinth, zircon

jactância | jak'tãsia |*sf.* boasting, conceit

jactar-se | jak'taʀsɪ |*vr.* to boast, to brag

jaez | ja'eʒ | *sm.* harness, bard; (fig.) sort, kind

jaguar | ja'gwaʀ | *sm.* jaguar

jaguatirica | jagwati'rika | *sf.* variety of American ocelot

jamais | ja'mayʒ | *adv.* never

janeiro | ja'neyru | sm. January
janela | ja'nɛla | sf. window; opening
jangada | jã'gada | sf. raft; seaworthy sailing raft used by fishermen of northwestern Brazil
janota | ja'nɔta | sm. dandy, fop, dude / a. foppish, dapper
jantar | jã'taR | sm. dinner. **-j. americano** buffet supper / vt. vi. to dine. **-hora de j.** dinner time
japonês -nesa | japo'neʃ | smf. a. Japanese
jaqueta | ja'keta | sf. short jacket
jaquetão | jake'tãw | sm. double--breasted jacket
jararaca | jara'raka | sf. pit viper; (colloq.) harridan
jarda | 'jaRda | sf. yard (36 inches)
jardim | jaR'dĩ | sm. garden. **-j. zoológico** zoo. **-j. de infância** kindergarten
jardineira | jaRdi'neyra | sf. woman gardener; flower-bed
jardineiro | jaRdi'neyru | sm. gardener
jarra | 'jaRa | sf. pitcher; vase (esp. for flowers)
jarro | 'jaRu | sm. pitcher, jug; vase (esp. for flowers)
jasmim | jaʒ'mĩ | sm. jasmine
jato | 'jatu | sm. jet, spurt, gush; jet plane. **-avião a j.** jet plane, jet
jaula | 'jawla | sf. cage (esp. for wild animals)
javali | java'li | sm. wild boar, boar
jazer | ja'zeR | vi. to lie (in the grave etc.)
jazida | ja'zida | sf. large deposit of ore, mine
jazigo | ja'zigu | sm. grave, tomb, sepulcher, burial monument
jeca | 'jɛka | smf. (pej.) back-woodsman; boor / a. rustic, boorish, of bad taste (esp. clothes)
jeito | 'jeytu | sm. manner, way; skill, dexterity; knack; appearance. **-com j.** adroitly; tact-

fully. **-dar um j.** to manage, to fix; to find a way
jeitoso -sa | jey'tozu -'tɔza | a. skillful; comely
jejuar | jeju'aR | vi. to fast
jejum | je'jũ | sm. fast, fasting
jibóia | ji'bɔya | sf. boa constrictor; python
jiló | ji'lɔ | sm. kind of smaller and bitter egg-plant
jipe | 'jipɪ | sm. jeep
joalheiro | jʋa'Leyru | sm. jewel(l)er
joalheria | jʋaLe'ria | sf. jewel(l)ry
joaninha | jʋa'niNa | sf. ladybird, ladybug
joão-de-barro | jʋ'ãwdɪ'baRu | sm. oven-bird
jocoso -sa | jo'kozu -'kɔza | a. facetious, droll, playful
joelho | jʋ'eLu | sm. knee. **-de joelhos** kneeling
jogada | jo'gada | sf. act or action in a game; play, move; throw; bet
jogador -dora | joga'doR | smf. player; gambler
jogar | jo'gaR | vt. to throw, to cast; to play (a game, a card); to gamble / vi. to roll, to pitch, to lurch (ship)
jogatina | joga'tina | sf. gambling, vice of gambling
jogo | 'jogu | sm. game, play; gambling; set (of dishes, tools etc.); tossing, pitching (of vessels); (mech.) looseness. **-j. de azar** game of chance. **-j. de palavras** pun, play of words. **-j. do bicho** illegal popular gambling related to the lottery
joguete | jo'getɪ | sm. toy, plaything; dupe
jóia | 'jɔya | sf. jewel, gem, entrance fee (for new club members). **-tudo j.** (slang) everything OK
joio | 'joyu | sm. darnel. **-separar o j. do trigo** to separate the wheat from the tares, to separate the good from the bad

jóquei | 'jʊkey | *sm.* jockey

jornada | joR'nada | *sf.* journey, trip; day's journey. **-j. de trabalho** a day's work

jornal | joR'nal | *sm.* newspaper; newsreel. **-banca de jornais** news-stand

jornaleiro | joRna'leyrʊ | *sm.* newspaper seller, news- -vendor; day-labo(u)rer

jornalismo | joRna'liʒmʊ | *sm.* journalism

jornalista | joRna'liʃta | *smf.* journalist

jorrar | jo'RaR | *vi.* to spurt, to spout, to gush

jorro | 'joRʊ | *sm.* gush, spout, jet

jovem | 'jʊvẽy | *smf.* youth; *sm.* young man; *sf.* young lady / *a.* young, youthful

jovial | jovi'al | *a.* merry, jolly, jovial

juba | 'juba | *sf.* lion's mane

jubilar | jubi'laR | *a.* pertaining to a jubilee / *vt.* to pension off, to grant retirement (to a teacher, professor etc.)

jubileu | jubi'lew | *sm.* jubilee

júbilo | 'jubilʊ | *sm.* joy, satisfaction, jubilation

judeu -dia | ju'dew -'dia | *sm.* Jew; *sf.* Jewess / *a.* Jewish

judiação | judia'sãw | *sf.* mistreatment, abuse, cruelty

judiar | judi'aR | *vi.* (with **de** or **com**) to mistreat, to ill-treat, to maltreat

judicial | judisi'al | *a.* judicial

judicioso -sa | judisi'ozʊ -'ɔza | *a.* judicious

jugo | 'jugʊ | *sm.* yoke

juiz -íza | ju'iʒ | *sm.* judge, magistrate; arbiter; *sf.* female judge; arbitress; *smf.* referee

juízo | ju'izʊ | *sm.* judg(e)ment; good sense; good behavio(u)r; law court. **-j. perfeito** sound mind. **-em j.** in a law court

julgamento | julga'mẽtʊ | *sm.* judg(e)ment, trial

julgar | jul'gaR | *vt.* to judge; to

sentence; to suppose; to consider

julho | 'julʊ | *sm.* July

jumento -ta | ju'mẽtʊ | *sm.* donkey, ass; *sf.* female donkey

junção | jũ'sãw | *sf.* junction; connection; juncture

junco | 'jũkʊ | *sm.* (bot.) rush; (naut.) junk

jungir | jũ'jiR | *vt.* to yoke; to unite

junho | 'juɲʊ | *sm.* June

júnior | 'junioR | *sm. a.* junior

junta | 'jũta | *sf.* joint, union; pair, couple; council, board; (anat.) articulation. **-j. de bois** yoke of oxen

juntar | jũ'taR | *vt.* to couple, to connect. **-j.-se** to unite with, to join

junto -ta | 'jũtʊ | *a.* joined; adjoining / *adv.* jointly. **-j. a** attached to; next to. **-j. de** next to

jurado -da | ju'radʊ | *smf.* (law) juror, member of a jury / *a.* sworn, declared under oath. **-inimigo j.** sworn enemy

juramento | jura'mẽtʊ | *sm.* oath

jurar | ju'raR | *vt.* to swear, to take an oath; to vow

júri | 'juri | *sm.* jury

jurídico -ca | ju'ridikʊ | *a.* legal, juridical, judicial

jurisconsulto | juriʃkõ'sultʊ | *sm.* jurist, legal counsellor

jurisdição | juriʒdi'sãw | *sf.* jurisdiction

jurisprudência | juriʃpru'dẽsia | *sf.* jurisprudence

jurista | ju'riʃta | *sm.* jurist

juro | 'jurʊ | *sm.* (com., fin.) interest

justeza | juʃ'teza | *sf.* exactness, correctness, precision

justiça | juʃ'tisa | *sf.* justice; lawyers or magistrates collectively; judicial power

justificação | juʃtifika'sãw | *sf.* justification

justificar | juʃtifi'kaR | *vt.* to justify. **-j. se** to justify oneself

justo -ta | 'juʒtʊ | *a.* just, fair, impartial; tight-fitting

juvenil | juve'nil | *a.* juvenile, young

juventude | juvẽ'tudɪ | *sf.* youth; young people

K

K, k | 'ka | *sm.* it is only used in names and words derived from foreign names (e.g. *kantiano, kafkiano* etc.)

L

lá | 'la | *sm.* (mus.) la (in England, U.S. and Germany, the sixth tone in the scale of C) / *adv.* there, over there; yonder

lã | 'lã | *sf.* wool; woolen cloth

labareda | laba'reda | *sf.* flame, blaze

lábia | 'labia | *sf.* smooth talk, well-oiled tongue

lábio | 'labiʊ | *sm.* lip

labirinto | labi'rĩtʊ | *sm.* labyrinth; maze

labor | la'boR | *sm.* toil, work, labo(u)r

laboratório | labora'tɔriʊ | *sm.* laboratory

laborioso -sa | labori'ozʊ -'ɔza | *a.* hard-working; laborious

labrego -ga | la'bregʊ | *smf.* (pej.) peasant / *a.* rustic, rough, crude

labuta | la'buta | *sf.* toil, hard work, drudgery

labutar | labu'taR | *vi.* to work hard; to work long hours, to toil

laca | 'laka | *sf.* lacquer

laçada | la'sada | *sf.* slip-knot; loop

lacaio | la'kayʊ | *sm.* lackey, footman

laçar | la'saR | *vt.* to lasso, to catch with lasso

laço | 'lasʊ | *sm.* slip-knot, bow; lasso; bond; snare, trap. **-armar um l.** to set a trap. **-laços de sangue** blood ties

lacônico -ca | la'konikʊ | *a.* laconic, brief, concise

lacraia | la'kraya | *sf.* centipede, earwig

lacrar | la'kraR | *vt.* to seal with sealing-wax

lacre | 'lakrɪ | *sm.* sealing-wax

lacrimejante | lakrime'jãtɪ | *a.* tearful, watery (eyes)

lacrimoso -sa | lakri'mozʊ -'mɔza | *a.* tearful

lacuna | la'kuna | *sf.* lacuna, gap; omission

ladainha | lada'iɴa | *sf.* litany; (fig.) rigmarole

ladear | ladɪ'aR | *vt.* to flank, to go alongside of; to accompany; to evade, to get around

ladeira | la'deyra | *sf.* slope; steep street

ladino -na | la'djɴʊ | *a.* astute, clever, cunning

lado | 'ladʊ | *sm.* side, flank; direction; faction, party. **-ao l. de** next to, at the side of. **-de um l. para o outro** (colloq.) to and fro. **-por outro l.** on the other hand

ladrão -dra | la'drãw 'ladra | *smf.* thief, robber

ladrar | la'draʀ | *vi.* = *latir*

ladrilho | la'driʟʋ | *sm.* tile

lagarta | la'gaʀta | *sf.* caterpillar. **-l. de trator** (mech.) caterpillar tread

lagartixa | lagaʀ'tixa | *sf.* small lizard (esp. the gecko)

lagarto | la'gaʀtʋ | *sm.* lizard; a cut of beef

lago | 'lagʋ | *sm.* lake

lagoa | la'goa | *sf.* lagoon, small lake

lagosta | la'goʃta | *sf.* lobster

lágrima | 'lagrima | *sf.* tear

laguna | la'guna | *sf.* lagoon

laia | 'laya | *sf.* (pej.) kind, sort. **-gente da mesma l.** birds of a feather

laivo | 'layvʋ | *sm.* stain, spot, blemish; (*pl.*) a smattering of something

laje | 'lajɪ | *sf.* flagstone; (constr.) cover slab (roof); any large flat rock

lajear | lajɪ'aʀ | *vt.* to pave with flagstones

lama | 'lama | *sf.* mud

lamaçal | lama'sal | *sm.* marsh, bog, mud hole

lamacento -ta | lama'sẽtʋ | *a.* muddy

lambada | lã'bada | *sf.* lashing, whipping

lamber | lã'beʀ | *vt.* to lick

lambuzar | lãbu'zaʀ | *vt.* to daub, to stain, to smear. **-l. -se** to soil one's *face*, hands or clothes with grease, food etc.

lamentável | lamẽ'tavɪl | *a.* lamentable, deplorable

lamento | la'mẽtʋ | *sm.* lament; moan; complaint

lâmina | 'lamina | *sf.* blade; thin plate or sheet. **-l. de barbear** razor-blade

lâmpada | 'lãpada | *sf.* lamp; light bulb

lamparina | lãpa'rina | *sf.* small

lamp; oil-lamp

lampejar | lãpe'jaʀ | *vi.* to flash

lampião | lãpi'ãw | *sm.* lantern, lamp; street lamp

lamúria | la'muria | *sf.* lamentation; wail; whining

lança | 'lãsa | *sf.* lance, spear

lançadeira | lãsa'deyra | *sf.* shuttle; (fig.) a restless person

lançamento | lãsa'mẽtʋ | *sm.* throw, cast; entry (in book-keeping); (naut.) launching; release

lançar | lã'saʀ | *vt.* to cast, to throw; to launch; to introduce; (com.) to enter; to publish

lance | 'lãsɪ | *sm.* throwing, casting; play (in a game); bidding (at an auction); incident, event

lancha | 'lãxa | *sf.* motor boat; launch

lanche | 'lãxɪ | *sm.* afternoon snack. **-fazer um l.** to have a snack

languescer | lãge'seʀ | *vi.* to languish

languidez | lãgi'deʒ | *sf.* languor

lânguido -da | 'lãgidʋ | *a.* languid

lanho | 'laɴʋ | *sm.* gash, slash, cut

lanterna | lã'teʀna | *sf.* lantern. **-l. elétrica** electric torch

lapa | 'lapa | *sf.* rock cave or den

lapela | la'pɛla | *sf.* lapel

lapidação | lapida'sãw | *sf.* cutting, polishing (of gems); lapidation, stoning

lapidar | lapi'daʀ | *a.* lapidary, suitable for inscriptions; concise, well-expressed (said of writing or speech) / *vt.* to lapidate, to stone; to cut and polish (gems)

lápis | 'lapiʃ | *sm.* (*sing.* and *pl.*) pencil

lapiseira | lapi'zeyra | *sf.* mechanical pencil

lapso | 'lapsʋ | *sm.* lapse of time; oversight

lar | 'laʀ | *sm.* home

laranja | la'rãja | *sf.* orange

laranjada | larã'jada | *sf.* orangeade

laranjal | larã'jal | *sm.* orange grove

laranjeira | larã'jeyra | *sf.* orange tree

larápio -pia | la'rapiʊ | *smf.* sneak thief

lareira | la'reyra | *sf.* fireplace, hearth

larga | 'laʀga | *sf.* loosing, releasing. **-à l.** generously. **-dar largas a** to give free rein to

largar | laʀ'gaʀ | *vt.* to let go, to release; to put down / *vi.* to set out to sea, to set sail

largo -ga | 'laʀgʊ | *sm.* small public square / *a.* wide; broad; loose, baggy (clothing); generous, liberal. **-largos anos** many years. **-passar de (ao) l.** to pass at a distance

largueza | laʀ'geza | *sf.* generosity, liberality

largura | laʀ'gura | *sf.* width, breadth

laringe | la'rĩjɪ | *smf.* larynx

lasca | 'laʃka | *sf.* chip, fragment; splinter

lascívia | laʃ'sivia | *sf.* lasciviousness

lascivo -va | la'sivʊ | *a.* lascivious, lewd

lassidão | lasi'dãw | *sf.* lassitude

lástima | 'laʃtima | *sf.* pity, compassion. **-que l.!** what a pity!

lastimar | laʃti'maʀ | *vt.* to deplore, to lament, to regret. **-l.-se** to complain

lastimável | laʃti'mavɪl | *a.* lamentable, deplorable

lastro | 'laʃtrʊ | *sm.* ballast; (fin.) gold reserve for currency

lata | 'lata | *sf.* can, tin can, tin plate. **-dar a l. em alguém** (colloq.) to can someone, to discard a lover

latada | la'tada | *sf.* trellis; trellised vine

latão | la'tãw | *sm.* brass; a large can

latejar | late'jaʀ | *vt.* to pulsate, to throb, to beat

latente | la'tẽtɪ | *a.* latent

laticínio | lati'siniʊ | *sm.* any food prepared from milk; (*pl.*) dairy products

latido | la'tidʊ | *sm.* bark, barking

latim | la'tĩ | *sm.* Latin

latino -na | la'tinʊ | *smf. a.* Latin

latir | la'tiʀ | *vi.* to bark

latitude | lati'tudɪ | *sf.* latitude

lato -ta | 'latʊ | *a.* ample, broad. **-em sentido l.** in a broad sense

latrocínio | latrʊ'siniʊ | *sm.* armed robbery, hold-up

lauda | 'lawda | *sf.* each side of a sheet of paper; page (of a book)

laudo | 'lawdʊ | *sm.* (law) report of an arbiter or board of inquiry, expert's report

láurea | 'lawrɪa | *sf.* laurel wreath; laurel; academic hono(u)r

lauto -ta | 'lawtʊ | *a.* opulent, magnificent, plentiful

lava | 'lava | *sf.* lava

lavadeira | lava'deyra | *sf.* laundress, washerwoman; dragon-fly

lavagem | la'vajẽy | *sf.* washing enema; hog-wash; (sports, colloq.) victory by a large score

lavanda | la'vãda | *sf.* (bot.) lavender; finger-bowl

lavanderia | lavãde'ria | *sf.* laundry

lavar | la'vaʀ | *vt.* to wash

lavatório | lava'tɔriʊ | *sm.* lavatory; wash-basin

lavável | la'vavɪl | *a.* washable

lavor | la'voʀ | *sm.* work; handiwork; fancy needlework; ornate carving

lavoura | la'vowra | *sf.* agriculture, farming

lavra | 'lavra | *sf.* work; farming; mining; mine (of gold or diamonds)

lavrador -dora | lavra'doʀ | *smf.* agricultural worker, peasant; farmer

lavrar | la'vraʀ | *vt.* to plow, to till,

to chisel, to carve (wood etc.); to engrave; to embroider; to draw up (a document) / *vi.* to spread (as fire)

laxante | la'xãtι | *sm. a.* laxative

lazer | la'zeʀ | *sm.* leisure. **-horas de l.** spare time

leal | lι'al | *a.* loyal, faithful

lealdade | lιal'dadι | *sf.* loyalty, fidelity, sincerity

leão | lι'ãw | *sm.* lion

lebre | 'lεbrι | *sf.* hare

lecionar | lesio'naʀ | *vt.* to teach

legação | lega'sãw | *sf.* legation

legado | le'gadυ | *sm.* legate; legacy; bequest; ambassador, envoy

legal | le'gal | *a.* legal, lawful; (slang) OK, perfect; fine

legalizar | legali'zaʀ | *vt.* to legalize, to give legal validity to

legar | le'gaʀ | *vt.* to bequeath

legatário -ria | lega'tariυ | *smf.* legatee

legenda | le'ʒēda | *sf.* inscription; caption; (cine.) subtitle

legião | lιʒi'ãw | *sf.* legion

legislação | lιʒiʒla'sãw | *sf.* legislation

legislador-dora | lιʒiʒla'doʀ | *smf.* legislator / *a.* legislative

legislar | lιʒiʒ'laʀ | *vt. vi.* to legislate

legislativo -va | lιgiʒla'tivυ | *sm.* the legislative power / *a.* legislative

legislatura | lιʒiʒla'tura | *sf.* legislature

legista | lι'ʒiʃta | *smf.* medical examiner, coroner

legitimar | lιʒiti'maʀ | *vt.* to legitimate

legítimo -ma | lι'ʒitimυ | *a.* legitimate, genuine, authentic. **legítima defesa** self-defence

legível | lι'ʒivιl | *a.* legible

légua | 'legwa | *sf.* league (unit of distance, approx. 4 miles in Brazil)

legume | lι'gumι | *sm.* vegetable

lei | 'ley *sf.* law; rule, statute. **-ma-**

deira de l. hardwood. **-projeto de l.** bill (in the legislature)

leigo -ga | 'leygυ | *smf.* layman; outsider / *a.* lay, secular; nonexpert

leilão | ley'lãw | *sm.* auction

leitão -toa | ley'tãw - 'toa | *smf.* suckling pig

leite | 'leytι | *sm.* milk

leiteiro -ra | ley'teyrυ | *sm.* milkman / *a.* milk yielding. **-gado l.** dairy cattle

leiteria | leyte'ria | *sf.* dairy, creamery

leito | 'leytυ | *sm.* bed; couch, berth; river bed

leitor-tora | ley'toʀ | *smf.* reader / *a.* reading

leitoso -sa | ley'tozυ -'tωza | *a.* milky; resembling milk

leitura | ley'tura | *sf.* reading

lema | 'lema | *sm.* motto

lembrança | lē'brãsa | *sf.* remembrance, souvenir; recollection; gift, token; (*pl.*) greetings

lembrar | lē'braʀ | *vt. vi.* to recall, to remember; to remind. **-l. -se de** to remember

leme | 'lemι | *sm.* rudder, helm

lenço | 'lēsυ | *sm.* handkerchief; scarf

lençol | lē'sωl | *sm.* sheet

lenda | 'lēda | *sf.* fable, legend

lendário -ria | lē'dariυ | *a.* legendary

lenha | 'leNa | *sf.* firewood

lenhador | leNa'doʀ | *sm.* lumberjack, lumberman

lenho | 'leNυ | *sm.* log, tree trunk

lenitivo -va | lιni'tivυ | *a.* soothing

lente | 'lētι | *sf.* lens; *sm.* (obs.) college professor

lentidão | lēti'dãw | *sf.* slowness; sluggishness

lentilha | lē'tiʌa | *sf.* lentil

lento -ta | 'lētυ | *a.* slow, sluggish

leoa | lι'oa | *sf.* lioness

leopardo | lιo'paʀdυ | *sm.* leopard

lépido -da | 'lεpidυ | *a.* agile, swift, nimble

lepra | 'lεpra | *sf.* leprosy

leproso -sa | leˈprozʊ -ˈprɔza | smf. leper

leque | ˈlɛkɩ | sm. fan

ler | ˈleʀ | vt. to read

lerdo -da | ˈlɛʀdʊ | a. slow, dull, stupid

lesão | leˈzãw | sf. lesion, hurt, injury; grievance

lesar | leˈzaʀ | vt. to hurt; to wrong; to cheat

lesma | ˈleʒma | sf. slug; (colloq.) sluggard

leste | ˈlɛʃtɩ | sm. east

lesto -ta | ˈlɛʃtʊ | a. agile, active, nimble

letárgico -ca | leˈtaʀjikʊ | a. lethargic

letivo -va | leˈtivʊ | a. of or pertaining to lessons. **-ano l.** school year

letra | ˈletra | sf. letter, character; (typog.) type; handwriting; (mus.) lyrics; (com.) note; (pl.) literature. **-ao pé da l.** literally. **-l. de câmbio** (com.) bill of exchange

letrado -da | leˈtradʊ | smf. man of letters, scholar / a. learned

letreiro | leˈtreyrʊ | sm. sign; lettering; inscription

léu | ˈlew | sm. idleness; chance. **-ao l.** at random, aimlessly

levadiço -ça | levaˈdisʊ | a. mobile, portable, easily lifted

levado -da | leˈvadʊ | a. mischievous, devilish (child)

levantamento | levãtaˈmẽtʊ | sm. lifting, raising; survey; revolt, insurrection

levantar | levãˈtaʀ | vt. to raise (up), to lift (up), to elevate; to erect; to excite, to stir up; to discontinue (a session etc.). **-l. -se** to stand up; to rebel. **-l. vôo** to take off / vi. to arise; to raise. **-l. o tempo** to clear (said of the weather)

levante | leˈvãtɩ | sm. mutiny, rebellion; (cap.) Levant, East, Orient

levar | leˈvaʀ | vt. to take (away); to transport; to conduct; to lead; to require, to need (time); to induce. **-l. adiante** to carry forward. **-l. à cena** to stage (a play). **-l. a mal** to take offence. **-l. a melhor** to gain the upper hand

leve | ˈlevɩ | a. light; simple; tenuous. **-de l.** lightly

levedura | leveˈdura | sf. yeast

leveza | leˈveza | sf. lightness, buoyancy

leviandade | leviãˈdadɩ | sf. frivolity; carelessness

leviano -na | leviˈanʊ | a. frivolous

lhe | ˈʎɩ | oblique pron. 3rd pers. sing. (indirect object) to him, to her, to it, to you; (pl.) to them, to you

libélula | liˈbɛlula | sf. dragon-fly

liberal | libeˈral | smf. liberal / a. liberal, generous

liberalidade | liberaliˈdadɩ | sf. liberality

liberar | libeˈraʀ | vt. to release; to deliver; to free (from obligation)

liberdade | liberˈdadɩ | sf. liberty, freedom

libertador -dora | libeʀtaˈdoʀ | smf. liberator / a. liberating

libertar | liberˈtaʀ | vt. to liberate, to set free

libertino -na | liberˈtinʊ | smf. a. libertine

libra | ˈlibra | sf. pound (money; weight). **-l. esterlina** pound sterling

liça | ˈlisa | sf. arena, lists

lição | liˈsãw | sf. lesson; school work; reproof, scolding

licença | liˈsẽsa | sf. licence, permit; approval; leave of absence; excessive liberty. **-com l.** excuse me, allow me; may I? **-l. médica** sick leave

licenciar | lisẽsiˈaʀ | vt. to licence, to register; to grant permission to; to grant leave of absence to

licencioso -sa | lisẽsiˈozʊ -ˈɔza | a. licentious

liceu | li'sew | sm. secondary school, high school

lícito -ta | 'lisitʊ | sm. that which is lawful or permitted / a. licit, permitted, lawful

licor | li'koR | sm. liqueur, cordial; liquor (any liquid)

lida | 'lida | sf. drudgery; chore

lidar | li'daR | vi. to struggle, to toil. -l. com to deal with

líder | 'lideR | smf. leader, chief, head

liderança | lide'rãsa | sf. leadership, command

liga | 'liga | sf. league; alloy; garter

ligação | liga'sãw | sf. union, connection, liaison

ligadura | liga'dura | sf. ligature; bandage

ligar | li'gaR | vt. to tie, to bind; to link, to connect. -l. a luz (o gás, a televisão etc.) to turn on the light (the gas, the television etc.) -l. para to telephone to. -não l. importância a to attach no importance to

ligeireza | lijey'reza | sf. lightness; agility; superficiality

ligeiro -ra | li'jeyrʊ | a. swift, speedy, light

lilás, lilá | li'laʃ li'la | sm. (bot.) lilac (also the colo[u]r) /a. lilac (colo[u]r)

lima | 'lima | sf. file (tool); variety of sweet lime

limão | li'mãw | sm. lemon, lime

limar | li'maR | vt. to file, to smooth

limiar | limi'aR | sm. threshold, doorstep; entrance, beginning

limitação | limita'sãw | sf. limitation, restriction

limitar | limi'taR | vt. to limit, to restrict

limite | li'mitɪ | sm. limit; boundary

limo | 'limʊ | sm. slime, sludge; mire

limoeiro | limʊ'eyrʊ | sm. lemon tree

limonada | limo'nada | sf.

lemonade

limpar | lĩ'paR | vt. to clean (up) /vi. to clear up

limpeza | lĩ'peza | sf. cleanliness; cleaning; neatness; purity

limpo -pa | 'lĩpʊ | a. clean; clear; neat, tidy. -passar a l. to make a clean copy of. -tirar a l. to get at the bottom of the matter

lince | 'lĩsɪ | sm. lynx

linchar | lĩ'xaR | vt. to lynch

lindeza | lĩ'deza | sf. beauty, prettiness

lindo -da | 'lĩdʊ | a. beautiful, lovely; graceful

lingote | lĩ'gʊtɪ | sm. ingot, bar iron, pig iron

língua | 'lĩgwa | sf. tongue; language, speech. -l. afiada sharp tongue. -l. suja foul-mouthed person. -l. geral a lingua franca based on Tupi

linguado | lĩ'gwadʊ | sm. flounder; sole

linguagem | lĩ'gwajẽy | sf. language, speech

linguajar | lĩgwa'jaR | sm. mode of speech; dialect

lingüeta | lĩ'gweta | sf. latch (of a door); bolt (of a lock); tongue (of a shoe)

lingüiça | lĩ'gwisa | sf. kind of sausage. -encher l. (colloq.) to use dilatory talking or writing

lingüística | lĩ'gwiʃtika | sf. linguistics

lingüístico -ca | lĩ'gwiʃtikʊ | a. linguistic

linha | 'liNa | sf. line; thread; row, rank; telephone or telegraph line; track, rail; (fig.) correct demeanor

linhaça | li'Nasa | sf. linseed

linhagem | li'Najẽy | sf. lineage, ancestry; pedigree

linho | 'liNʊ | sm. linen; flax

linóleo | li'nʊlɪʊ | sm. linoleum

liquidação, liqüidação | likida'sãw -kwi- | sf. liquidation; special sale of merchandise

liquidar, liqüidar | liki'daR -kwi- |

vt. to liquidate, to settle; to sell out; to finish off, to kill

liquidificador, liqüidificador | likidifika'doʀ -kwi- | *sm.* liquefier, blender

liquidificar, liqüidificar | likidifi'kaʀ -kwi- | *vt.* to liquefy

líquido -da, líqüido -da | 'likidʊ -kwi- | *sm.* liquid, fluid / *a.* liquid; net (prices, profits etc.)

lira | 'lira | *sf.* lyre; lira (monetary unit of Italy)

lírico -ca | 'likirʊ | *sm.* lyric poet / *a.* lyric; operatic

lírio | 'liriʊ | *sm.* lily

lirismo | li'riʒmʊ | *sm.* lyricism

liso -sa | 'lizʊ | *a.* smooth; even, flat; straight (hair); (slang) broke, pennyless

lisonja | li'zõja | *sf.* flattery, adulation

lisonjear | lizõjɪ'aʀ | *vt.* to flatter

lisonjeiro -ra | lizõ'jeyrʊ | *a.* flattering, complimentary

lista | 'liʃta | *sf.* list, enumeration, roll. **-l. telefônica** telephone book

listra | 'liʃtra | *sf.* stripe, streak

liteira | li'teyra | *sf.* litter (vehicle)

literário -ria | lite'rariʊ | *a.* literary

literato -ta | lite'ratʊ | *sm.* man of letters; *sf.* authoress

literatura | litera'tura | *sf.* literature

litigar | liti'gaʀ | *vt. vi.* to litigate, to contend

litígio | li'tijiʊ | *sm.* (law) litigation; dispute

litoral | lito'ral | *sm.* littoral, shore / *a.* coastal

litro | 'litrʊ | *sm.* litre; one-litre bottle

lívido -da | 'lividʊ | *a.* livid, pale

livramento | livra'mẽtʊ | *sm.* deliverance, liberation. **-l. condicional** (law) parole

livrar | li'vraʀ | *vt.* to free; to release, to deliver; to liberate. **-l. -se de** to get rid of; to escape from. **-Deus me livre!** (colloq.) Heaven forbid!

livraria | livra'ria | *sf.* bookshop

livre | 'livrɪ | *a.* free; exempt, clear; vacant; loose, licentious. **-ao ar l.** in the open air

livreiro -ra | li'vreyrʊ | *smf.* bookseller

livro | 'livrʊ | *sm.* book. **-l. brochado** paperback. **-l. de bordo** (naut.) log-book. **-l. de consulta** reference book. **-l. de endereços** directory

lixa | 'lixa | *sf.* sandpaper

lixo | 'lixʊ | *sm.* garbage, refuse, litter

lobinho | lo'biNʊ | *sm.* wolf-cub; Cub Scout

lobisomem | lobi'zomẽy | *sm.* werewolf

lobo -ba | 'lobʊ | *sm.* wolf; *sf.* she-wolf

lobo-do-mar | lobʊdʊ'maʀ | *sm.* old sea-dog; (zool.) seal

lobrigar | lʊbri'gaʀ | *vt.* to discern, to catch sight of (indistinctly), to see in the distance

lóbulo | 'lʊbulʊ | *sm.* lobe

locação | loka'sãw | *sf.* leasing

local | lo'kal | *sm.* place, premise, site; locality / *a.* local

localidade | lokali'dadɪ | *sf.* locality, place; district, small community

localizar | lokali'zaʀ | *vt.* to locate, to situate

loção | lo'sãw | *sf.* lotion; hair lotion

locatário -ria | loka'tariʊ | *smf.* tenant, lodger, lessee

locomotiva | lokomo'tiva | *sf.* engine, locomotive

locomover-se | lokomo'veʀsɪ | *vr.* to move about

locução | loku'sãw | *sf.* idiom, idiomatic expression

locutor -tora | loku'toʀ | *smf.* speaker, radio or television announcer

lodo | 'lodʊ | *sm.* slime, sludge, mud

lógico -ca | 'lʊjikʊ | *smf.* logician; *sf.* logic / *a.* logical

logo | 'lɔgʊ | *adv.* immediately, right away; soon. -até l. good by!, so long! -l. após thereupon. -tão l. as soon as / *conj.* therefore, consequently, then. -penso, l. existo I think, therefore I am

logradouro | logra'dowrʊ | *sm.* public park, square, street etc.

lograr | lo'graR | *vt.* to attain, to achieve; to succeed in; to deceive, to dupe. -l. (bom) êxito to meet with success

logro | 'logrʊ | *sm.* deceit, bluff, cheat

loja | 'lɔja | *sf.* shop, store; masonic lodge

lojista | lo'jiʃta | *smf.* shopkeeper

lomba | 'lõba | *sf.* ridge, slope, crest (of hill or mountain)

lombo | 'lõbʊ | *sm.* back (of an animal); loin

lona | 'lona | *sf.* canvas

londrino -na | lõ'drinʊ | *smf.* Londoner / *a.* of or pertaining to London

longe | 'lõjɪ | *a.* remote, distant, detached / *adv.* away, far, afar. -ao l. away, afar off. -de l. from far, by far. -de l. em l. at long intervals. -ir l. demais to go too far

longevidade | lõjɪvi'dadɪ | *sf.* longevity

longínquo -qua | lõ'jĩkwʊ | *a.* distant, remote, far-off

longitude | lõji'tudɪ | *sf.* longitude

longo -ga | 'lõgʊ | *a.* long, lengthy. -ao l. de by, along, all along

lontra | 'lõtra | *sf.* otter

loquaz | lo'kwaʃ | *a.* talkative, loquacious, verbose

lotação | lota'sãw | *sf.* capacity; number of employees allotted to an office. -l. esgotada all seats booked

lote | 'lɔtɪ | *sm.* lote, allotment, portion; building lot, parcel of land

loteamento | lotɪa'mẽtʊ | *sm.* parcels (of land)

loteria | lote'ria | *sf.* lottery

louça | 'lowsa | *sf.* china, china ware; earthenware; dishes collectively

louco -ca | 'lowkʊ | *sm.* madman; *sf.* madwoman. -l. varrido raving mad / *a.* mad, crazy

loucura | low'kura | *sf.* insanity, madness; folly

loureiro | low'reyrʊ | *sm.* laurel tree, bay tree

louro -ra | 'lowrʊ | *sm.* laurel, bay; *smf.* blond / *a.* fair, fair-haired, blond

lousa | 'lowza | *sf.* slate; gravestone

louvar | low'vaR | *vt.* to praise; to glorify

louvável | low'vavɪl | *a.* laudable, praiseworthy

louvor | low'voR | *sm.* praise

lua | 'lua | *sf.* moon. -l. de mel honeymoon

luar | lu'aR | *sm.* moonlight

lubricidade | lubrisi'dadɪ | *sf.* lasciviousness, lechery

lubrificante | lubrifi'kãtɪ | *sm.* lubricant / *a.* lubricating

lubrificar | lubrifi'kaR | *vt.* to lubricate

lúcido -da | 'lusidʊ | *a.* lucid; clear-headed, sane

lúcio | 'lusiʊ | *sm.* (ichth.) pike

lucrar | lu'kraR | *vt. vi.* to profit; to gain; to benefit

lucro | 'lukrʊ | *sm.* profit, gain

ludibriar | ludibri'aR | *vt.* to deceive, to dupe, to cheat

lufada | lu'fada | *sf.* gust of wind

lugar | lu'gaR | *sm.* place; site, spot; locality; job; seat (as in a theatre). -dar l. a to give occasion to. -em l. de in place of; for

lugarejo | luga'rejʊ | *sm.* small village, hamlet

lúgubre | 'lugubrɪ | *a.* lugubrious, gloomy, dismal

lula | 'lula | *sf.* cuttlefish, squid

lume | 'lumɪ | *sm.* fire, flame; light. -dar a l. to publish

luminar | lumi'naR | *smf.* luminary, illustrious person / *a.* illuminant

luminoso -sa | lumiˈnozʊ -ˈnʊza | *a.* luminous; clear, acute

luneta | luˈneta | *sf.* monocular telescope; (obs.) eyeglass

lupa | ˈlupa | *sf.* magnifying glass

lupanar | lupaˈnaʀ | *sm.* brothel

lúpulo | ˈlupulʊ | *sm.* (bot.) hop

lusco-fusco | luʃkʊˈfuʃkʊ | *sm.* dusk; twilight

luso-sa | ˈluzʊ | *smf. a.* Lusitanian, Portuguese

luso-brasileiro | ˈluzʊbraziˈleyrʊ | *smf. a.* Portuguese-Brazilian

lustrar | luʃˈtraʀ | *vt.* to polish

lustre | ˈluʃtrɪ | *sm.* chandelier; gloss; varnish

lustro | ˈluʃtrʊ | *sm.* luster, brightness, glossiness; lustrum, quinquennium

luta | ˈluta | *sf.* fight, struggle; wrestling; toil, effort

lutar | luˈtaʀ | *vi.* to fight, to struggle; to wrestle

luto | ˈlutʊ | *sm.* mourning. **-de l.** in mourning

luva | ˈluva | *sf.* glove; (mech.) sleeve; (*pl.*) extra payment

luxo | ˈluxʊ | *sm.* luxury. **-de l.** de luxe

luxuoso -sa | luxuˈozʊ -ˈʊza | *a.* luxurious, de luxe, sumptuous

luxúria | luˈxuria | *sf.* lecherousness, lechery; lust

luxuriante | luxuriˈãtɪ | *a.* luxuriant, exuberant

luz | ˈluʃ | *sf.* light; (*pl.*) knowledge, education. **-à l. de** in the light of. **-dar à l.** to give birth to; to bring forth; to publish

luzidio -dia | luziˈdiʊ | *a.* shiny, glossy, sleek

luzir | luˈziʀ | *vi.* to shine, to sparkle, to glitter / *vt.* to parade, to display ostentatiously

M

maca | ˈmaka | *sf.* stretcher; sailor's hammock

maça | ˈmasa | *sf.* mace; club

maçã | maˈsã | *sf.* apple. **-m. do rosto** cheek-bone

macacão | makaˈkãw | *sm.* overalls

macaco-ca | maˈkakʊ | *smf.* monkey, ape; *sm.* (mech.) jack

maçada | maˈsada | *sf.* nuisance, bore

macambúzio -zia | makãˈbuziʊ | *a.* sad, depressed; sullen, morose

maçaneta | masaˈneta | *sf.* knob, doorknob

maçante | maˈsãtɪ | *a.* annoying, bothering, boring

macaquear | makakɪˈaʀ | *vt.* to ape, to mimic

maçar | maˈsaʀ | *vt.* to pester, to bother, to annoy

maçarico | masaˈrikʊ | *sm.* blowtorch, blowpipe; (ornith.) ruddy turnstone

macarrão | makaˈʀãw | *sm.* macaroni

macete | maˈsetɪ | *sm.* small mallet; (slang) key, trick

machadinha | maxaˈdina | *sf.* hatchet

machado | maˈxadʊ | *sm.* axe

machão | maˈxãw | *sm.* (slang) he--man

macho | ˈmaxʊ | *sm.* male (also mech.) / *a.* male, masculine, virile

machucado -da | maxuˈkadʊ | *sm.* bruise, contusion / *a.* bruised

machucar | maxuˈkaʀ | *vt.* to hurt; to mash, to pound; to wound

maciço-ça | ma'sisυ | *sm.* (geol.) massif / *a.* massive (also geol.), solid, compact

macieira | masi'eyra | *sf.* apple tree

maciez, macieza | masi'eʒ masi'eza | *sf.* softness, smoothness

macilento-ta | masi'lẽtυ | *a.* emaciated, gaunt; haggard

macio -cia | ma'siυ | *a.* soft, smooth (to the touch)

maço | 'masυ | *sm.* bundle; package (cigarettes etc.); wooden mallet; mace

maçonaria | masona'ria | *sf.* Freemasonry

maconha | ma'koNa | *sf.* marijuana

má-criação | makria'sãw | *sf.* rudeness, impoliteness

mácula | 'makula | *sf.* blotch, stain; infamy, dishonour

macumba | ma'kũba | *sf.* kind of voodooism

madeira | ma'deyra | *sf.* wood, timber, lumber; (*cap.*) Madeira wine. **-m. de lei** hardwood

madeixa | ma'deyxa | *sf.* lock of hair, curl, ringlet; small skein

madrasta | ma'draʃta | *sf.* stepmother (also fig.) / *a.* unkind, cruel. **-sorte m.** bad fate

madre | 'madrι | *sf.* nun, sister, mother superior

madrepérola | madrι'pεrυla | *sf.* mother-of-pearl

madrinha | ma'driNa | *sf.* godmother; patroness; lead mare, lead cow

madrugada | madru'gada | *sf.* dawn, daybreak; early morning

madrugar | madru'gaR | *vi.* to rise very early

madureza | madu'reza | *sf.* ripeness; maturity

maduro-ra | ma'durυ | *a.* ripe; mature

mãe | 'mãy | *sf.* mother

mãe-benta | mãy'bẽta | *sf.* cup-cake made of rice flour, coco-nut milk and eggs

má-fé | ma'fε | *sf.* bad faith

magia | ma'jia | *sf.* magic; sorcery; enchantment

mágico -ca | 'majikυ | *smf.* magician; wizard; *sf.* magic / *a.* magic, magical; enchanting

magistério | majiʃ'teriυ | *sm.* teaching; teachers collectively; professorate; professorship

magistrado -da | majiʃ'tradυ | *smf.* magistrate

magistral | majiʃ'tral | *a.* masterly; perfect, exemplary

magistratura | magiʃtra'tura | *sf.* magistracy

magnânimo-ma | mag'nanimυ | *a.* magnanimous

magnata | mag'nata | *sm.* magnate

magnético -ca | mag'nεtikυ | *a.* magnetic

magnífico -ca | mag'nifikυ | *a.* magnificent, splendid

mago | 'magυ | *sm.* magician, sorcerer. **-reis magos** the Magi, the Three Wise Men from the East

mágoa | 'magwa | *sf.* grief, woe, heartache

magoar | magυ'aR | *vt.* to hurt, to afflict, to offend

magreza | ma'greza | *sf.* thinness, leanness

magro -gra | 'magrυ | *a.* thin, lean; meagre, poor, scanty

maio | 'mayυ | *sm.* May

maiô | may'o | *sm.* woman's bathing-suit

maior | may'ωR | *smf.* adult; the greatest / *a.* bigger, greater, larger; adult. **-de m. idade** of age

maioral | mayo'ral | *sm.* chief, leader; topman

maioria | mayυ'ria | *sf.* majority

maioridade | mayori'dadι | *sf.* majority, full age. **-atingir a m.** to come of age

mais | 'mayʒ | *sm.* rest, remainder / *a.* more/ *adv.* more; any more, furthermore; also, besides. **-a m.** in excess, to much;

superfluous. **-as m. das vezes** more often than not. **-de m. a m.** besides, anyhow. **- logo m.** later on. **- m. adiante** further on. **- m. cedo ou m. tarde** sooner or later. **- m. ou menos** more or less

maiúscula | may'uʒkula | *sf. a.* capital (letter)

majestade | majeʒ'tadɪ | *sf.* majesty

majestoso -sa | majeʒ'tozʊ-'tɔwza | *a.* majestic

major | ma'jʊR | *sm.* major (military rank or officer)

mal | 'mal | *sm.* bad, evil, wrong; harm, damage; disease / *adv.* scarcely, hardly; no sooner had; badly, poorly. **-de m. a pior** from bad to worse. **- não faz m.** never mind; no matter. **-sentir-se m.** to feel bad. **- levar a m.** to take offence, to take umbrage

mala | 'mala | *sf.* suitcase; trunk; (*pl.*) luggage. **- fazer as malas** to pack

malabarista | malaba'riʒta | *smf.* juggler, trickster

mal-agradecido -da | malagradɪ'sidʊ | *smf.* ingrate / *a.* ungrateful

malagueta | mala'geta | *sf.* bush red pepper

malandragem | malã'drajẽy | *sf.* idleness; roguery; trickery

malandro -dra | ma'lãdrʊ | *smf.* rogue, rascal; idler, trickster

malária | ma'laria | *sf.* malaria

mal-assombrado -da | malasõ'bradʊ | *a.* haunted

mal-comportado -da | malkõpoR'tadʊ | *a.* naughty

malcriação | malkria'sãw | *sf.* = *má-criação*

malcriado -da | malkri'adʊ | *a.* rude, impolite; ill-bred

maldade | mal'dadɪ | *sf.* wickedness; cruelty; mischievousness, naughtiness; evil

maldição | maldi'sãw | *sf.* curse

maldito -ta | mal'ditʊ | *a.* cursed, accursed, damned

maldizer | maldi'zeR | *vt. vi.* to curse; to slander, to defame

maldoso -sa | mal'dozʊ-'dɔwza | *a.* malicious, malevolent; evil-minded

maléavel | malɪ'avɪl | *a.* malleable, ductile, flexible

maledicência | malɪdi'sẽsia | *sf.* slander, defamation, evil talk

mal-educado-da | malɪdu'kadʊ | *a.* ill-mannered, ill-bred, uncivil, impolite

maléfico -ca | ma'lɛfikʊ | *a.* malignant, malevolent; harmful

maleita | ma'leyta | *sf.* malaria

mal-empregado -da | malĩ pre'gadʊ | *a.* wasted, misapplied

mal-encarado -da | malĩ ka'radʊ | *a.* cross-looking, sullen looking

mal-entendido -da | malĩ tẽ'didʊ | *sm.* misunderstanding / *a.* misunderstood

mal-estar | malɪʒ'taR | *sm.* indisposition, ailment; uneasiness, discomfort

maleta | ma'leta | *sf.* handbag, small suitcase

malfadado -da | malfa'dadʊ | *a.* unlucky, ill-fated

malfeitor-tora | malfey'toR | *smf.* criminal; evil doer

malgrado | mal'gradʊ | *prep.* notwithstanding, in spite of

malha | 'maLa | *sf.* mesh; stitch; mail (of armo[u]r); spot, dapple; patch (in colo[u]ring of animals). **- artigos de m.** knitted articles. **- jogo de m.** kind of game of quoits

malhado -da | ma'Ladʊ | *a.* specked, spotted, mottled, dapple. **- cavalo m.** dappled horse

malhar | ma'LaR | *vt. vi.* to hammer, to maul; to criticize harshly

malho | 'maLʊ | *sm.* mallet; sledge hammer. **- meter o m.** to criticize harshly

mal-humorado -da | malumo'radσ | *a.* ill-humoured; irritable; sullen

malícia | ma'lisia | *sf.* malice; slyness

malicioso -sa | malisi'ozσ-'ωza | *smf.* full of malice (person); malicious gossiper / *a.* malicious; artful

maligno -na | ma'lignσ | *a.* malignant

malmequer | malmι'kεR | *sm.* marigold

malogrado -da | malo'gradσ | *a.* unsuccessful; frustrate

malograr | malo'graR | *vt.* (also **m.-se**) to fail, to miscarry; to be in vain, to come to naught

malogro | ma'logrσ | *sm.* failure, frustration

malparado -da | malpa'radσ | *a.* hazardous, perilous, risky

malquisto- ta | mal'kiξtσ | *a.* disliked; ill-famed

malsoante | malsσ'ātι | *a.* harsh, dissonant

malta | 'malta | *sf.* gang, mob. **-andar à m.** to loaf

malte | 'maltι | *sm.* malt

maltrapilho -lha | maltra'piLσ | *smf.* ragamuffin / *a.* ragged, tattered

maltratar | maltra'taR | *vt.* to maltreat; to mishandle, to misuse; to insult, to outrage

maluco -ca | ma'lukσ | *smf.* mad person; (slang) a nut / *a.* crazy, mad, insane

maluquice | malu'kisι | *sf.* madness, crazyness; nonsense, something foolish

malvado -da | mal'vadσ | *smf.* wicked person / *a.* mean, bad; malicious, malevolent

malvisto-ta | mal'viξtσ | *a.* looked--upon with dislike or suspicion; ill-regarded

mamadeira | mama'deyra | *sf.* nursing bottle, baby's milk bottle

mamãe | ma'mãy | *sf.* (colloq.) mammy, mamma

mamão | ma'mãw | *sm.* papaya

mamar | ma'maR | *vt.* to suckle, to take the breast; to suck (as on a cigar)

mamífero -ra | ma'miferσ | *sm.* (zool.) mammal, mammalian / *a.* mammiferous, mammalian

mamona | ma'mona | *sf.* castor bean. **-óleo de m.** castor oil

manada | ma'nada | *sf.* herd, flock

manancial | manãsi'al | *sf.* fountain, spring; source

manar | ma'naR | *vt.* to pour out, to shed / *vi.* to flow out, to ooze

mancada | mã'kada | *sf.* (colloq.) error, blunder, gaffe

mancar | mã'kaR | *vi.* to limp, to hobble; to fail to keep a promise, to break one's word

mancebo | mã'sebσ | *sm.* (obs.) lad, youth

mancha | 'mãxa | *sf.* spot, stain

manchar | mã'xaR | *vt.* to spot, to stain; to tarnish (reputation)

manchete | mã'xεtι | *sf.* (journal.) headline

manco -ca | 'mãkσ | *a.* crippled, lame; hobbling, halting

mancomunar-se | mãkσmu'naRsι | *vr.* to practice collusion

mandachuva | mãda'xuva | *sm.* (colloq.) big shot; political boss

mandado-da | mã'dadσ | *sm.* warrant, edict, sending; order. **- m. de busca** search warrant. **- m. de despejo** eviction notice. **- m. de prisão** warrant of arrest / *a.* sent, ordered, commanded

mandamento | mãda'mẽtσ | *sm.* commandment, precept of the church; command, order. **-os dez mandamentos** the Ten Commandments

mandar | mã'daR | *vt.* to send; to command, to order. **-m. embora** to send away, to throw out. **-m. fazer** to have (something) made to order / *vi.* to command, to govern; to be the boss

mandato | mã'datσ | *sm.* mandate;

order

mandíbula | mã'dibula | *sf.* lower jawbone

mandinga | mã'dĩga | *sf.* witchcraft, sorcery

mandioca | mãdi'ɷka | *sf.* (bot.) cassava, manioc

mando | 'mãdʋ | *sm.* power, authority; command. **- a m. de** by order of

mandriar | mãdri'aʀ | *vi.* to idle, to loaf

maneira | ma'neyra | *sf.* manner, way, method; mode, form, style; (*pl.*) manners. **- de m. que** so as to, in order to. **- de qualquer m.** anyway, one way or another

manejar | mane'jaʀ | *vt.* to handle, to manage

manejo | ma'nejʋ | *sm.* handling, control, manipulation; (*pl.*) tricks, machinations

manequim | manɩ'kĩ | *sm.* mannequin, model; dummy; size (of woman's garment)

maneta | ma'neta | *smf.* one--handed person / *a.* one--handed

manga | 'mãga | *sf.* sleeve (also mech.); glass chimney (for a lamp); (bot.) mango. **- em mangas de camisa** in shirt--sleeves

manganês | mãga'neʃ | *sm.* manganese (metal or ore)

mangar | mã'gaʀ | *vt. vi.* (colloq.) to mock, to jeer

mangue | 'mãgɩ | *sm.* mangrove; mangrove swamp; red-light district in Rio (in former times)

mangueira | mã'geyra | *sf.* rubber hose; mango-tree

manha | 'maɴa | *sf.* slyness, shrewdness; bad habit, vice; whining of children

manhã | ma'ɴã | *sf.* morning

manhoso -sa | ma'ɴozʋ -'ɴɷza | *a.* cunning, foxy; vicious (said of a horse); whimsical

mania | ma'nia | *sf.* mania; obses-

sion; excentricity; passion, craze

maníaco-ca | ma'niakʋ | *smf.* maniac / *a.* maniac, maniacal; insane; obsessed

manicômio | mani'komiʋ | *sm.* insane asylum

manicuro -ra | mani'kurʋ | *smf.* manicure

manifestação | manifeʃta'sãw | *sf.* manifestation; public demonstration

manifestar | manifeʃ'taʀ | *vt.* to manifest, to declare, to display. **- m.-se** to manifest itself

manifesto -ta | mani'fɛʃtʋ | *sm.* manifest; manifesto, open letter / *a.* manifest, evident

manipulação | manipula'sãw | *sf.* manipulation, handling

manivela | mani'vɛla | *sf.* crank, handle

manjar | mã'jaʀ | *sm.* tidbit, delicacy / *vt.* (slang) to get it, to perceive, to be in the know

manjericão | mãjɩri'kãw | *sm.* (bot.) basil

mano -na | 'manʋ | *sm.* (colloq.) brother; *sf.* (colloq.) sister

manobra | ma'nɷbra | *sf.* maneuver (also mil., naut.); manipulation; skillful move; machination

manobrar | mano'braʀ | *vt.* to manoeuvre, to maneuver; to manipulate / *vi.* to manoeuvre, to maneuver; to function; to handle

mansão | mã'sãw | *sf.* mansion, manor-house

mansidão | mãsi'dãw | *sf.* tameness, docility; meekness, gentleness

manso -sa | 'mãsʋ | *a.* tame, docile, gentle

manta | 'mãta | *sf.* blanket; saddle blanket; wrap, shawl

manteiga | mã'teyga | *sf.* butter

manteigueira | mãtey'geyra | *sf.* butter dish

manter | mã'teʀ | *vt.* to maintain,

to support

mantimento | mãti'mẽtʋ | *sm.* maintenance, support; (*pl.*) provisions

manto | 'mãtʋ | *sm.* cape, cloak

manual | manu'al | *sm.* handbook, guide / *a.* manual

manufatura | manufa'tura | *sf.* manufacture; factory

manuscrito-ta | manuʃ'kritʋ | *sm.* manuscript / *a.* handwritten

manusear | manuzι'aʀ | *vt.* to handle; to leaf through (a book)

manutenção | manutẽ'sãw | *sf.* maintenance

mão | 'mãw | *sf.* hand; paw; coat of paint. - **abrir m. de** to give up. - **dar m. forte a** to give total support to. - **não ter mãos a medir** to do one's utmost. - **de mãos abanando** empty-handed. - **mãos à obra!** let's get to work!

mão-de-obra | mãwdι'ωbra· | *sf.* hand labo(u)r; labo(u)r cost; workmanship

maometano-na | maʋme'tanʋ | *smf. a.* Mohammedan, Muhammadan, Mahometan

mapa | 'mapa | *sm.* map, chart

maquilagem | maki'lajẽy | *sf.* make-up, cosmetics

máquina | 'makina | *sf.* machine; engine. - **m. fotográfica** camera. - **m. de costura** sewing machine. -**m. de escrever** typewriter

maquinação | makina'sãw | *sf.* machination, plot

maquinal | maki'nal | *a.* mechanical, automatic

maquinaria | makina'ria | *sf.* machinery

maquinismo | maki'niʃmʋ | *sm.* mechanism, machinery

maquinista | maki'niʃta | *sm.* machinist; locomotive engineer

mar | 'maʀ | *sm.* sea. - **alto m.** high sea. - **m. encapelado** rough sea. -**fazer-se ao m.** to put out to sea

maracujá | maraku'ja | *sm.*

passion-fruit

maravilha | mara'vιla | *sf.* marvel, wonder. - **às mil maravilhas** marvelously, wonderfully

maravilhar | maravi'laʀ | *vt.* to amaze, to astonish. - **m. -se** to marvel, to wonder at

maravilhoso-sa | maravi'lozʋ -'lωza | *a.* marvelous, wonderful; amazing, extraordinary

marca | 'maʀka | *sf.* mark, marking, sign; brand, make. - **m. registrada** trademark

marcar | maʀ'kaʀ | *vt.* to mark, to label; to stamp, to brand. -**m. hora** to make an appointment. -**m. lugar** to book (a seat etc.); to make a reservation

marceneiro | maʀsι'neyrʋ | *sm.* cabinet-maker

marcha | 'maʀxa | *sf.* march; pace, step; course; military march. - **m. à ré** reverse gear. - **pôr-se em m.** to set out, to start

marchar | maʀ'xaʀ | *vi.* to march

marchetar | maʀxe'taʀ | *vt.* to inlay, to do marquetry work on

marcial | maʀsi'al | *a.* martial, military. - **lei m.** martial law

marco | 'maʀkʋ | *sm.* landmark; boundary, limit; milestone; (numis.) German mark. - **m. miliar** or **miliário** milestone

março | 'maʀsʋ | *sm.* March

maré | ma'rε | *sf.* tide. - **m. alta** or **m. cheia** high tide. - **m. baixa** or **m. vazante** low tide

marear | marι'aʀ | *vt.* to sail, to steer; to make seasick / *vi.* to become seasick; to sail; to navigate

marechal | mare'xal | *sm.* marshal

marfim | maʀ'fĩ | *sm.* ivory

margarida | maʀga'rida | *sf.* daisy

margarina | maʀga'rina | *sf.* margarine

margem | 'maʀjẽy | *sf.* margin; edge; shore, river bank; brink. -**dar m. a** to give occasion to

marido | ma'ridʋ | *sm.* husband

marimbondo | marĩ'bõdʋ | *sm.*

wasp, hornet

marinha | ma'riɴa | *sf.* navy; (fine arts) seascape

marinheiro | mari'ɴeyrʊ | *sm.* sailor, seaman

marinho -nha | ma'riɴʊ | *a.* marine, sea

mariposa | mari'poza | *sf.* moth; butterfly

marisco | ma'riʒkʊ | *sm.* mussel; any edible shellfish

marítimo -ma | ma'ritimʊ | *sm.* sailor, seaman / *a.* maritime, marine

marmelada | maʀme'lada | *sf.* quince marmalade; (colloq.) fixed game, crooked deal

marmelo | maʀ'mɛlʊ | *sm.* quince

marmita | maʀ'mita | *sf.* deep metal pot with lid; lunch pail

mármore | 'maʀmʊrɪ | *sm.* marble

maroto-ta | ma'rotʊ | *smf.* rogue, scoundrel / *a.* roguish; malicious

marquês -quesa | maʀ'keʒ-'keza | *sm.* marquis, marquess; *sf.* marchioness; kind of sofa

marreco -ca | ma'ʀɛkʊ | *smf.* general name of several wild ducks

marreta | ma'ʀeta | *sf.* mallet, maul, small sledge hammer

marrom | ma'ʀõ | *sm. a.* brown (colo[u]r)

martelada | maʀte'lada | *sf.* hammer-blow

martelar | maʀte'laʀ | *vt.* to hammer

martelo | maʀ'tɛlʊ | *sm.* hammer

mártir | 'maʀtiʀ | *smf.* martyr

martírio | maʀ'tiriʊ | *sm.* martyrdom; torment, affliction

martirizar | maʀtiri'zaʀ | *vt.* to martyrize (also fig.)

marujo | ma'ruʒʊ | *sm.* sailor

marulho | ma'rulʊ | *sm.* roaring of the sea, dashing of the waves

mas | 'maʒ | *conj.* but

mascar | maʒ'kaʀ | *vt. vi.* to chew without swallowing (as gum, tobacco etc.)

máscara | 'maʃkara | *sf.* mask

mascate | maʒ'katɪ | *sm.* peddler (of small wares)

mascote | maʒ'kɔtɪ | *sf.* mascot

masculino -na | maʒku'linʊ | *a.* masculine

másculo -la | 'maʃkulʊ | *a.* masculine, male, manly

masmorra | maʒ'mɔʀa | *sf.* dungeon

massa | 'masa | *sf.* mass (also phys.); dough; paste (also cookery); (slang) money, dough

massacrar | masa'kraʀ | *vt.* to massacre

massagem | ma'sajẽy | *sf.* massage

massudo -da | ma'sudʊ | *a.* bulky, massive; heavy, tedious (said of speech etc.)

mastigar | maʃti'gaʀ | *vt.* to chew, to masticate

mastim | maʒ'tĩ | *sm.* mastiff

mastro | 'maʃtrʊ | *sm.* (naut.) mast. **- m. de bandeira** flag-pole

mata | 'mata | *sf.* woods, forest

mata-borrão | matabo'ʀãw | *sm.* blotting-paper

matadouro | mata'dowrʊ | *sm.* slaughterhouse

matagal | mata'gal | *sm.* thicket, dense wood

matança | ma'tãsa | *sf.* massacre, slaughtering

matar | ma'taʀ | *vt.* to kill; to appease (hunger etc.); to quench (thirst)

mate | 'matɪ | *sm.* (bot.) maté; checkmate (in chess) / *a.* mat, dull

matemática | mate'matika | *sf.* mathematics

matemático -ca | mate'matikʊ | *smf.* mathematician / *a.* mathematical

matéria | ma'teria | *sf.* matter, substance; topic, subject; course of study

material | materi'al | *sm.* material; material goods; apparatus, equipment. **- m. bélico** arms and equipment used in war.

- m. de escritório stationery

matéria-prima | ma'tɛria'prima | sf. raw material

maternal | mateʀ'nal | a. maternal, motherly

maternidade | mateʀni'dadɪ | sf. maternity, motherhood, maternity hospital

matilha | ma'tiʟa | sf. pack of hounds

matinal | mati'nal | a. morning, early

matiz | ma'tiʒ | sm. hue, tint, shade; nuance; blend of colo(u)rs

mato | 'matʋ | sm. thicket, brush; undergrowth

matraca | ma'traka | sf. wooden rattle

matreiro -ra | ma'treyrʋ | a. foxy, shrewd

matrícula | ma'trikula | sf. matriculation; enrollment, admission; registration or tuition fee

matrimônio | matri'moniʋ | sm. matrimony, marriage

matriz | ma'triʒ | sf. origin, source; cast, mold; head office; matrix, womb

maturidade | maturi'dadɪ | sf. maturity

matutino -na | matu'tinʋ | sm. morning paper / a. morning; early-rising

matuto -ta | ma'tutʋ | smf. boor, rustic person / a. backwoods, backcountry; timid, shy

mau má | 'maw 'ma | a. bad, evil, ill; harmful; poor, inferior; cruel, mean. - m. humor ill humour, bad mood. -de má vontade unwillingly. -má sorte bad luck

mavioso -sa | mavi'ozʋ -'ɔza | a. smeet-sounding, mellow

maxilar | maksi'laʀ | sm. jaw-bone / a. maxillary

máxima | 'masima 'maksima | sf. maxim, aphorism

máximo-ma | 'masimʋ 'maksimʋ | smf. maximum / a. maxi-

mum, greatest

maxixe | ma'xixɪ | sm. (bot.) variety of gherkin; popular dance (of former times)

mazela | ma'zɛla | sf. (colloq.) ailment (esp. pl.)

me | mɪ | oblique pron. 1st pers. sing. (direct object) me; (indirect object) to me, to myself; reflexive pron. 1st pers. sing. myself

meada | mɪ'ada | sf. skein (of yarn, thread etc.)

meado | mɪ'adʋ | sm. middle, mid. - em meados de in the middle of (month, year, century)

mecânica | me'kanika | sf. mechanics

mecânico -ca | me'kanikʋ | sm. mechanic / a. mechanical

mecanismo | meka'niʒmʋ | sm. mechanism, machine

mecha | 'mɛxa | sf. wick (of a lamp); fuse; lock of hair

medalha | me'daʟa | sf. medal; religious medal (image of a saint etc.)

média | 'mɛdia | sf. average, mean; (colloq.) large cup of hot milk and coffee. -em m. on the average

mediano -na | mɪdi'anʋ | a. median, medial, medium

mediante | mɪdi'ãtɪ | prep. for, by, by means of

mediar | medi'aʀ | vi. to be in the middle, to lie between; to mediate, to be a mediator

medicação | medika'sãw | sf. medication

medicamento | medika'mẽtʋ | sm. medicine, remedy

medicina | mɪdi'sina | sf. medicine, medical science

médico -ca | 'mɛdikʋ | smf. physician / a. medical

medida | mɪ'dida | sf. measure, measurement; size; degree, extent; (pl.) steps, means to an end. - à m. que as, while. - feito sob m. made to order, custom made

médio -dia | 'mɛdiʊ | *a.* medium, middle; intermediate

mediocridade | mɪdiokri'dadɪ | *sf.* mediocrity

medir | mɪ'diR | *vt.* to measure; to appraise

meditar | mɪdi'taR | *vt. vi.* to meditate; to muse, to ponder. **-m. em** or **sobre** to think about

medo | 'medʊ | *sm.* fear, fright, dread. **-com m. de** afraid of; for fear that. **- meter m.** to frighten

medonho -nha | me'doNʊ | *a.* frightful, awful, dreadful

medrar | me'draR | *vi.* to thrive, to flourish; (slang) to show fear

medroso -sa | me'drozʊ-'drɷza | *a.* fearful; timorous

medula | me'dula | *sf.* marrow; core, heart. **- m. espinhal** spinal cord

meia | 'meya | *sf.* stocking, sock

meia-noite | meya'noytɪ | *sf.* midnight

meigo -ga | 'meygʊ | *a.* loving, tender, gentle

meiguice | mey'gisɪ | *sf.* affection, gentleness, sweetness

meio, meia | 'meyʊ | *sm.* middle; center; means, resources; milieu, environment; (*pl.*) riches; (*pl.*) ways and means. **- ao m.** in half, in the middle, in two. **- m. de vida** livelihood. **- por m. de** by, through / *a.* half; middle; semi, demi / *adv.* half, halfway; somewhat, rather, not completely

meio-dia | meyʊ'dia | *sm.* noon, midday

meio-fio | meyʊ'fiʊ | *sm.* curb line of a sidewalk

mel | 'mɛl | *sm.* honey

melaço | me'lasʊ | *sm.* molasses

melado -da | me'ladʊ | *sm.* molasses / *a.* sticky, gummy

melancia | melã'sia | *sf.* watermelon

melancólico -ca | melã'kɷlikʊ | *a.* melancholy, sad, despondent

melão | me'lãw | *sm.* melon

melar | me'laR | *vi.* to become sticky or gummy

melhor | mɪ'LɷR | *a. adv.* better, best. **- ainda m.** even better. **- bem m.** much better

melhora | mɪ'Lɷra | *sf.* improvement, betterment

melhoramento | mɪLora'mẽtʊ | *sm.* improvement

melhorar | mɪLo'raR | *vt.* to make better, to ameliorate / *vt. vi.* to improve / *vi.* to get better

melindrar | mɪli'draR | *vt.* to offend, to hurt (pride, feelings). **-m. -se** to take offence

melindre | mɪ'lĩdrɪ | *sm.* affectation; susceptibility, touchiness (esp. *pl.*)

melodia | melo'dia | *sf.* melody

meloso -sa | me'lozʊ-'lɷza | *a.* sticky; honeylike; (colloq.) excessively sentimental

melro | 'mɛlrʊ | *sm.* blackbird; any of a number of orioles

membro | 'mẽbrʊ | *sm.* member; limb (of the body); (*pl.*) arms and legs

memória | me'mɷria | *sf.* memory; remembrance, recollection; fame; report; (*pl.*) memoirs. **-de m.** by heart

memorizar | memori'zaR | *vt.* to memorize

menção | mẽ'sãw | *sf.* mention, reference; gesture, sign

mencionar | mẽsio'naR | *vt.* to mention

mendigar | mĩdi'gaR | *vt.* to beg (alms) / *vi.* to ask humbly

mendigo -ga | mĩ'digʊ | *smf.* beggar

menear | menɪ'aR | *vt.* to shake, to wag (as the head, tail etc.); to flourish (as a sword)

meneio | me'neyʊ | *sm.* shaking, wagging; swaying (of the body or a part of it)

meninice | mɪni'nisɪ | *sf.* childhood, infancy; boyhood, girlhood

menino -na | mɪ'ninʊ | *sm.* boy; young man, lad; *sf.* girl; young girl, maiden

menor | me'nɔR | *smf.* minor / *a.* minor; smaller, smallest; lesser, least

menoridade | menori'dadɪ | *sf.* minority

menos | 'menʊʃ | *a.* less, not so many, not so much / *adv.* less; not so much. **- ao (pelo) m.** at least / *sm.* the least / *prep.* but, except, save

menosprezar | menʊʃpre'zaR | *vt.* to underrate; to belittle; to disdain

mensageiro -ra | mẽsa'jeyrʊ | *smf.* messenger

mensagem | mẽ'sajẽy | *sf.* message

mensal | mẽ'sal | *a.* monthly

mensalidade | mẽsali'dadɪ | *sf.* monthly payment

menta | 'mẽta | *sf.* (bot.) mint

mente | 'mẽtɪ | *sf.* mind; understanding. **- ter em m.** to have or to bear in mind

mentecapto -ta | mẽte'kaptʊ | *smf. a.* demented, idiot, crackbrained

mentir | mĩ'tiR | *vi.* to lie

mentira | mĩ'tira | *sf.* lie, falsehood

mentiroso -sa | mĩti'rozʊ-'rɔza | *smf.* liar / *a.* lying, false

mercado | meR'kadʊ | *sm.* market; market place; commerce. **- m. negro** black market

mercador | meRka'doR | *sm.* merchant, trader

mercadoria | meRkadʊ'ria | *sf.* merchandise; goods

mercante | meR'kãtɪ | *a.* merchant, commercial

mercê | meR'se | *sf.* favo(u)r; mercy; grant, benefice. **- à m. de** at the mercy of

mercearia | meRsɪa'ria | *sf.* grocery store

mercenário -ria | meRse'narɪʊ | *smf. a.* mercenary

mercúrio | meR'kurɪʊ | *sm.* mercury

merecer | mere'seR | *vt.* to deserve, to merit

merecimento | mɪrɪsi'mẽtʊ | *sm.* merit, worth; capability, competence

merenda | me'rẽda | *sf.* school lunch; afternoon snack

meretriz | mere'triʃ | *sf.* prostitute, harlot

mergulhar | meRgu'LaR | *vt.* to plunge / *vi.* to dive

mergulho | meR'guLʊ | *sm.* dive, plunge; (hort.) layer

meridiano -na | mɪridi'anʊ | *sm. a.* meridian

meridional | mɪridio'nal | *a.* southern

mérito | 'mɛritʊ | *sm.* merit; moral or intellectual worth

mero -ra | 'mɛrʊ | *sm.* jewfish / *a.* mere, simple

mês | 'meʃ | *sm.* month

mesa | 'meza | *sf.* table. **- cama e m.** room and board. **- m. telefônica** switchboard

mesada | me'zada | *sf.* monthly allowance

mesa-de-cabeceira | 'mezadɪkabɪ'seyra | *sf.* night table

mesmo-ma | 'meʃmʊ | *smf.* same. **- dar no m.** or **na mesma** to end the same way / *a.* same, identical. **-ele m.** hễ himself. **-é m.?** is it true? / *adv.* exactly, precisely; even; really. **- agora m.** right now, immediately. **-aqui m.** right here

mesquinharia | mɪʃkiNa'ria | *sf.* miserliness, niggardliness, pettiness

mesquinho -nha | mɪʃ'kiNʊ | *a.* miserly, niggardly; petty

mesquita | mɪʃ'kita | *sf.* mosque

messias | mɪ'siaʃ | *sm.* messiah (also *cap.*)

mestiço -ça | mɪʃ'tisʊ | *smf.* mestizo, half-breed; mongrel / *a.* half-breed, of mixed blood

mestre -tra | 'mɛʃtrɪ | *smf.* teacher, instructor; *sm.* schoolmaster;

foreman; (naut.) boat-swain / *a.* master, main

mestre-de-obras | 'mɛstrɪdɪ'ωbraʒ | *sm.* construction foreman

mestria | meʒ'tria | *sf.* mastery, great skill

mesura | mɪ'zura | *sf.* bow, curtsy, curtsey

meta | 'mɛta | *sf.* aim, goal; finishing line, end post

metade | me'tadɪ | *sf.* half; middle. **- pela m.** half full; in the middle

metal | me'tal | *sm.* metal. **- m. sonante** hard cash, coins. **- m. amarelo** brass

meteoro | mete'ωrυ | *sm.* meteor

meter | me'teR | *vt.* to introduce, to insert; to thrust; to place between. **- m.-se** to put oneself in; to get in. **- m.-se a** to set oneself up as

metódico -ca | me'tωdikυ | *a.* methodical, systematic

método | 'mɛtυdυ | *sm.* method, manner

metodologia | metodolo'jia | *sf.* methodology

metragem | me'trajẽy | *sf.* length in meters. **- filme de curta m.** short film. **- filme de longa m.** feature film

metralhadora | metraʟa'dora | *sf.* machine-gun

métrica | 'mɛtrika | *sf.* metrics

métrico -ca | 'mɛtrikυ | *a.* metric, metrical

metro | 'mɛtrυ | *sm.* metre, meter; verse metre. **- m. de carpinteiro** folding ruler

metrô | me'tro | *sm.* underground railway, subway

metrópole | me'trωpυlɪ | *sf.* metropolis

metropolitano -na | metropoli'tanυ | *sm.* metropolitan bishop; underground railway / *a.* metropolitan

meu | 'mew | *poss. a.* my. **-a m. ver** in my opinion / *poss. pron.* mine

mexer | me'xeR | *vt.* to move, to stir; to mix by stirring; to touch, to disturb. **-m.-se** to budge, to stir; to get a move on. **-m. em** to disturb, to disarrange. **-m. com** to tease

mexerica | mɪxɪ'rika | *sf.* tangerine

mexericar | mɪxɪri'kaR | *vi.* to gossip

mexerico | mɪxɪ'rikυ | *sm.* gossip, tattle

mexeriqueiro -ra | mɪxɪri'keyrυ | *smf.* gossip, tattler

mexicano -na | mexi'kanυ | *smf. a.* Mexican

mexido-da | mɪ'xidυ | *a.* mixed, stirred. **- ovos mexidos** scrambled eggs

mexilhão -lhona | mɪxi'ʟãw-'ʟona | *sm.* mussel; *smf.* meddler, busybody

miado | mi'adυ | *sm.* meow, miaow, mew

miar | mi'aR | *vi.* to mew (as a cat)

mico | 'mikυ | *sm.* any capuchin monkey

micróbio | mi'krωbiυ | *sm.* microbe

microfone | mikro'fonɪ | *sm.* microphone

microscópico -ca | mikroʒ'kωpikυ | *a.* microscopic, microscopical

microscópio | mikroʒ'kωpiυ | *sm.* microscope

mictório | mik'tωriυ | *sm.* public urinal, lavatory

micuim | miku'ĩ | *sm.* small tick

migalha | mi'gaʟa | *sf.* crumb; (*pl.*) small bits, table scraps

migração | migra'sãw | *sf.* migration

migrar | mi'graR | *vi.* to migrate

mijar | mi'jaR | *vi.* (vulg.) to piss

mil | 'mil | *sm. num.* thousand

milagre | mi'lagrɪ | *sm.* miracle

milagroso -sa | mila'grozυ-'grωza | *a.* miraculous

milênio | mi'leniυ | *sm.* millennium

milha | 'miʟa | *sf.* mile

milhagem | mɪˈLajèy | *sf.* mileage

milhão | miˈLãw | *sm.* million

milhar | miˈLaʀ | *sm.* thousand.
- **aos milhares** by the thousands

milharal | miLaˈral | *sm.* cornfield, maize field

milheiro | miˈLeyrʊ | *sm.* one thousand

milho | ˈmiLʊ | *sm.* corn, maize

miligrama | miliˈgrama | *sm.* milligram, milligramme

milímetro | miˈlimetrʊ | *sm.* millimetre, millimeter

milionário -ria | milioˈnariʊ | *smf. a.* millionaire

militante | miliˈtãtɪ | *a.* militant

militar | miliˈtaʀ | *smf.* a military person / *a.* military / *vi.* to serve as a soldier; to fight; to be engaged in a political party

mim | ˈmĩ | *oblique pron. 1st pers. sing.* (object of a *prep.*) me, myself

mimar | miˈmaʀ | *vt.* to caress, to fondle; to pamper, to spoil; to mimic

mimo | ˈmimʊ | *sm.* caress, fondling; keepsake

mimosa | miˈmɔza | *sf.* any plant of the genus *Mimosa*

mimoso -sa | miˈmɔzʊ-ˈmɔza | *a.* dainty, delicate; soft, tender

mina | ˈmina | *sf.* mine (also mil.); (fig.) bonanza. - **m. de ouro** gold mine (also fig.)

minar | miˈnaʀ | *vt.* to mine (also mil.); to sap, to undermine

mineiro -ra | miˈneyrʊ | *sm.* miner; *smf.* a native of the State of Minas Gerais / *a.* mining; of or pertaining to the State of Minas Gerais

minerador | mineraˈdoʀ | *sm.* miner

mineral | mineˈral | *sm. a.* mineral

minério | miˈnériʊ | *sm.* ore

mingau | mĩˈgaw | *sm.* pap, porridge, gruel

míngua | ˈmĩgwa | *sf.* want, lack, scarcity. - **à m. de** for want or lack of

minguar | mĩˈgwaʀ | *vi.* to decrease, to dwindle, to wane

minha | ˈmiNa | *poss. a.* my / *poss. pron.* mine

minhoca | miˈNʊka | *sf.* earthworm

miniatura | miniaˈtura | *sf.* miniature

mínima | ˈminima | *sf.* minim, half-note

mínimo -ma | ˈminimʊ | *sm.* minimum; (eccles.) minim. - **nom.** at least. - **dedo m.** little finger

ministério | miniˈʃteriʊ | *sm.* ministry; cabinet; (U.S.) department

ministro | miˈniʃtrʊ | *smf.* minister; magistrate; (cap. U.S.) Secretary; *sm.* pastor, clergyman

minoria | minʊˈria | *sf.* minority

minúcia | miˈnusia | *sf.* minute detail, minuteness, trifle; (pl.) minutiae, trivia

minucioso -sa | minusiˈozʊ-ˈɔza | *a.* detailed, meticulous

minúscula | miˈnuʃkula | *sf.* minuscule, lower case or small letter

minúsculo-la | miˈnuʃkulʊ | *a.* minuscule

minuta | miˈnuta | *sf.* minute, draft of a document; dish cooked to order (in restaurants)

minuto | miˈnutʊ | *sm.* minute

miolo | miˈolʊ | *sm.* core, kernel, pith; soft part of bread; (pl.) brains (esp. as food)

míope | ˈmiwpɪ | *a.* myopic, nearsighted, shortsighted

miopia | miʊˈpia | *sf.* myopia, nearsightedness, shortsightedness

mira | ˈmira | *sf.* sight; gunsight; aim, object

miraculoso -sa | mirakuˈlozʊ -ˈlɔza | *a.* miraculous

mirada | miˈrada | *sf.* look, glance

miragem | miˈrajèy | *sf.* mirage

mirante | miˈrãtɪ | *sm.* belvedere; high point providing a fine prospect

mirar | mi'raʀ | vt. to snare at, to gaze at; to observe. **- m.-se** to look at oneself in the mirror / vi. to aim, to take aim; to gaze

mirim | mi'rĩ | a. small, tiny (Tupian word used alone or as suffix)

mirrado -da | mi'ʀadʋ | a. thin, skinny, underdeveloped; shrunken

miscelânea | mise'lanɪa | sf. miscellany

miserável | mize'ravɪl | smf. miserable being, unfortunate person, wretch / a. miserable, wretched; miserly

miséria | mi'zɛria | sf. misery, wretchedness; privation, extreme poverty

misericórdia | mizɪri'kɔʀdia | sf. mercy, clemency; compassion

misericordioso -sa | mizɪrikoʀdi'ozʋ -'oza | a. merciful, clement

missa | 'misa | sf. (eccles., mus.) Mass, mass. **- dizer m.** to celebrate mass. **- ouvir m.** to attend mass

missão | mi'sãw | sf. mission

missionário -ria | misio'nariʋ | smf. missionary

mister | miʃ'teʀ | sm. occupation, trade; duty; necessity, need. **- ser m.** to be imperative that

mistério | miʃ'tɛriʋ | sm. mystery

misterioso -sa | miʃteri'ozʋ-'oza | a. mysterious

mística | 'miʃtika | sf. mysticism

místico -ca | 'miʃtikʋ | smf. a. mystic

misto-ta | 'miʃtʋ | sm. mixture, compound; ham and cheese sandwich / a. mixed, blended; carrying passengers and freight

mistura | miʃ'tura | sf. mixture, blend

misturar | miʃtu'raʀ | vt. to mix, to blend

mitigar | miti'gaʀ | vt. to mitigate, to alleviate

mito | 'mitʋ | sm. myth

mitologia | mitolo'jia | sf. mythology

miudeza | miu'deza | sf. littleness, smallness; (pl.) odds and ends

miúdo -da | mi'udʋ | sm. small change; (pl.) giblets, viscera / a. little, small

mixórdia | mi'xoʀdia | sf. mess, mix-up, hodgepodge

mó | 'mɔ | sf. millstone, grandstone

mobilhar, mobiliar | mobi'Laʀ mobili'aʀ | vt. to furnish

mobília | mʋ'bilia | sf. furniture

mobilizar | mobili'zaʀ | vt. to mobilize (also mil.)

moça | 'mosa | sf. girl. young woman; (colloq.) maiden

moção | mo'sãw | sf. motion; proposal

mochila | mʋ'xila | sf. knapsack, haversack, rucksack

mocho -cha | 'moxʋ | sm. owl / a. hornless; hammerless (firearms)

mocidade | mosi'dadɪ | sf. youth; young people

moço -ça | 'mosʋ | sm. young man; sf. young woman / a. young, youthful

moda | 'mɔda | sf. fashion; mode; rage, fad. **- em m.** fashionable, in style

modelar | mode'laʀ | a. model, ideal / vt. to model; to form, to shape

modelo | mo'delʋ | sm. model; pattern; sf. mannequin

moderado -da | mode'radʋ | a. moderate; self-restrained

moderar | mode'raʀ | vt. to moderate; to restrain; to reduce. **-m. -se** to be moderate or temperate

modernizar | modeʀni'zaʀ | vt. vi. to modernize

moderno -na | mo'dɛʀnʋ | a. modern

modéstia | mo'dɛ tia | sf.

modesty

modesto -ta | moˈdɛʃtʊ | *a.* modest, simple, unpretending

módico -ca | ˈmɔdikʊ | *a.* low--priced, moderate

modificar | modifiˈkaʀ | *vt.* to modify, to alter

modinha | mʊˈdiNa | *sf.* tune, popular song

modista | moˈdiʃta | *sf.* dressmaker

modo | ˈmʊdʊ | *sm.* manner, mode, way, style; (gram.) mood, mode; (*pl.*) manners. **-de m. que** so that, in order to. **-de m. algum** not at all, in no way

modorra | moˈdoʀa | *sf.* sleepiness, drowsiness

moeda | mʊˈɛda | *sf.* coin; currency, money. **-m. corrente** currency. **-casa da m.** the Mint

moela | mʊˈɛla | *sf.* gizzard

moer | mʊˈɛʀ | *vi.* to grind, to pound; to batter, to bruise

mofar | moˈfaʀ | *vi.* to mo(u)ld, to mildew. **-m. de** to mock at, to sneer at

mofo | ˈmofʊ | *sm.* mo(u)ld, mildew

moído -da | mʊˈidʊ | *a.* ground, milled; tired-out, exhausted

moinho | mʊˈiNʊ | *sm.* mill; grinder

moita | ˈmoyta | *sf.* bush, thicket. **-estar** or **ficar na m.** (slang) to queep quiet

mola | ˈmɔla | *sf.* spring

molambo | mʊˈlãbʊ | *sm.* rag, tatter

molar | moˈlaʀ | *sm.* molar tooth

moldar | molˈdaʀ | *vt.* to mo(u)ld

molde | ˈmɔldɪ | *sm.* mo(u)ld, cast

moldura | mʊlˈdura | *sf.* frame, picture frame

mole | ˈmɔlɪ | *sf.* large mass / *a.* soft, yielding; (colloq.) lazy; (slang) easy

molecagem | mʊleˈkajẽy | *sf.* roguery, roguishness

moleque -ca | mʊˈlɛkɪ -ˈlɛka |

sm. (obs.) Negro boy; rogue; scoundrel; street urchin; *sf.* (obs.) Negro girl / *a.* joking, roguish

molestar | moleʃˈtaʀ | *vt.* to molest; to annoy

moléstia | mʊˈlɛʃtia | *sf.* illness, disease

moleza | moˈleza | *sf.* softness (also fig.); weakness; lazyness; (slang) easiness

molhar | moˈʎaʀ | *vt.* to wet, to soak; to moisten

molheira | moˈʎeyra | *sf.* sauce--boat

molho | ˈmoʎʊ | *sm.* bundle, bunch. **-m. de chaves** bunch of keys

molho | ˈmɔʎʊ | *sm.* sauce, gravy

momentâneo -nea | momẽˈtanʊ | *a.* momentary, transitory

momento | moˈmẽtʊ | *sm.* moment, instant; (mech.) momentum

monarca | moˈnaʀka | *sm.* monarch, sovereign

monarquia | monaʀˈkia | *sf.* monarchy

monetário -ria | moneˈtarɪʊ | *a.* monetary

monge -ja | ˈmõjɪ | *sm.* monk; *sf.* nun

monopólio | monoˈpɔliʊ | *sm.* monopoly

monossílabo -ba | monoˈsilabʊ | *sm.* monosyllable / *a.* monosyllabic

monótono -na | moˈnʊtʊnʊ | *a.* monotonous, monotone

monstro | ˈmõʃtrʊ | *sm.* monster

montagem | mõˈtajẽy | *sf.* mounting (also theat., typog.); (mech.) assembly; (cine., photog.) montage, stage setting. **-linha de m.** assembly line

montanha | mõˈtaNa | *sf.* mountain

montanhoso -sa | mõtaˈNozʊ--ˈNɔza | *a.* montainous

montante | mõˈtãtɪ | *sm.* amount, sum; high tide; (obs.) broadsword. **-a** m. upstream / a. mounting, rising. **-maré** m. rising tide

montão | mõ'tãw | sm. pile, heap

montar | mõ'taʀ | vt. to mount (a horse); to assemble, to set up; to install / vi. to ride horseback; to amount or to come to, to reach

montaria | mõta'ria | sf. saddle horse; big game hunting; dug-out canoe in the Amazon

monte | 'mõtɪ | sm. hill; mountain; heap, pile, large quantity

montepio | mõtɪ'piʋ | sm. mutual insurance, pension society

monturo | mõ'tuʀʋ | sm. garbage heap; dunghill; pile of repulsive things

monumento | monu'mẽtʋ | sm. monument

moqueca | mʋ'kɛka | sf. dish of fish (or shellfish) with palm-oil and hot peppers

morada | mo'rada | sf. residence, home, dwelling-place

morador -dora | mora'doʀ | smf. resident, dweller / a. residing, dwelling

moral | mo'ral | sm. morality; morale; sf. morals, ethics; the morals of a story / a. moral, ethical

morango | mʋ'rãgʋ | sm. strawberry

morar | mo'raʀ | vi. to reside, to live; (slang) to understand, to get the point

mórbido -da | 'mɔʀbidʋ | a. morbid

morcego | mʋʀ'segʋ | sm. bat

mordaça | moʀ'dasa | sf. gag, muzzle

mordaz | moʀ'daʒ | a. biting, caustic, sarcastic

morder | moʀ'deʀ | vt. to bite; (colloq.) to borrow money from

mordomo | moʀ'domʋ | sm. butler; house steward

morena | mo'rena | sf. brunette; (geol.) esker, eskar

moreno -na | mo'renʋ | a. dark-complexioned, brown

morfina | mʋʀ'fina | sf. morphine

moribundo -da | mʋri'bũdʋ | smf. dying person / a. moribund

moringa | mʋ'rĩga | sf. water jug made of porous clay

mormaço | moʀ'masʋ | sm. hazy sun, sultry weather, muggy weather

mormente | moʀ'mẽtɪ mʋʀ'mẽtɪ | adv. chiefly, mostly

morno -na | 'moʀnʋ 'mʋʀna | a. lukewarm, tepid

moroso -sa | mo'rozʋ-'rʋza | a. slow, sluggish

morrer | mo'ʀeʀ | vi. to die; to perish; to die out (said of sound)

morro | 'moʀʋ | sm. hill, hillock

mortal | moʀ'tal | sm. mortal, human being; (pl.) mankind / a. deadly, lethal

mortalha | moʀ'taʟa | sf. shroud

mortalidade | moʀtali'dadɪ | sf. mortality; death rate

mortandade | moʀtã'dadɪ | sf. slaughter

morte | 'mʋʀtɪ | sf. death

mortiço -ça | moʀ'tisʋ | a. dimming, going out; spiritless

mortífero -ra | moʀ'tiferʋ | a. deadly, mortal

mortificar | moʀtifi'kaʀ | vt. to mortify; to humiliate. **-m.-se** to mortify oneself

morto -ta | 'moʀtʋ 'mʋʀta | smf. dead person / a. dead; forgotten. **-m. de cansaço** tired to death

mosaico -ca | mo'zaykʋ | sm. mosaic / a. Mosaic, related to Moses

mosca | 'moʃka | sf. fly; bull's-eye (of a target). **-às moscas** empty, with few customers

mosquiteiro | mʋʃki'teyrʋ | sm. mosquito-net (esp. over a bed)

mosquito | mʋʃ'kitʋ | sm. mosquito, gnat

mostarda | mʋʃ'taʀda | sf. mustard

mosteiro | moʒ'teyrʋ | *sm.* monastery

mostra | 'mɔʒtra | *sf.* exhibition, display. **-à m.** on view. **-dar mostras de** to give signs of

mostrador | moʒtra'doR | *sm.* dial (of a timepiece, radio etc.); display window

mostrar | moʒ'traR | *vt.* to show, to display; to manifest

motejar | mote'jaR | *vi.* to jest, to joke, to mock

motejo | mo'tejʋ | *sm.* mockery, derision

motim | mʋ'tĩ | *sm.* mutiny

motivar | moti'vaR | *vt.* to motivate, to cause

motivo | mʋ'tivʋ | *sm.* motive, cause, reason; (mus.) motif. **-dar m. a** to give rise to

motocicleta | motʋsi'kleta | *sf.* motor cycle

motor | mo'toR | *sm.* motor, engine. **-m. de popa** outboard motor

motorista | moto'riʒta | *smf.* motorist, driver

motriz | mo'triʒ | *a.* motive. **-força m.** motive power

mourão | mow'rãw | *sm.* post, stake. **-m. de cerca** fence post

movediço -ça | mʋvɪ'disʋ | *a.* moving; shifting. **-areia movediça** quicksand

móvel | 'mɔvɪl | *sm.* piece of furniture; prime motive; (*pl.*) furniture / *a.* movable

mover | mo'veR | *vt.* to move, to set in motion; to propel. **-m. uma ação contra** to start a lawsuit

movimentado-da | mʋvimẽ'tadʋ | *a.* lively, active, busy

movimento | mʋvi'mẽtʋ | *sm.* movement, motion; activity (esp. on a street)

muamba | mu'ãba | *sf.* kind of magic spell related to voodoo; (colloq.) contraband

muar | mu'aR | *smf. a.* mule

muco | 'mukʋ | *sm.* mucus

muçulmano -na | musul'manʋ | *smf. a.* Moslem, Muslim

muda | 'muda | *sf.* molt (of birds); (hort.) cutting scion; change of clothes

mudança | mu'dãsa | *sf.* removal; transference; change; alteration; (mech.) gearbox

mudar | mu'daR | *vt.* to move, to displace; to alter. **-m.-se** to move elsewhere / *vi.* to move away, to change. **-m. de idéia** to change one's mind

mudo -da | 'mudʋ | *smf.* mute person / *a.* dumb, mute; silent

mugido | mu'jidʋ | *sm.* mooing, moo

mugir | mu'jiR | *vi.* to moo

muito -ta | 'mũytʋ | *a.* much, a great deal of; (*pl.* **many**). **-muitas vezes** often / *adv.* very; much; a lot; greatly; too much. **-m. bem!** very good! **-quando m.** at most

mula | 'mula | *sf.* she-mule

mulato -ta | mu'latʋ | *smf.* mulatto person / *a.* mulatto

muleta | mu'leta | *sf.* crutch

mulher | mu'LɛR | *sf.* woman; wife. **-m. da vida** prostitute

multa | 'multa | *sf.* fine

multicor | multi'koR | *a.* multicolo(u)red

multidão | multi'dãw | *sf.* crowd, multitude

multiplicar | multipli'kaR | *vt. vi.* to multiply

mundano -na | mũ'danʋ | *a.* worldly / *sf.* a woman of easy virtue

mundial | mũdi'al | *a.* world-wide, global

mundo | 'mũdʋ | *sm.* world. **-todo o m.** everybody

mungir | mũ'jiR | *vt.* to milk

munição | muni'sãw | *sf.* ammunition

municipal | munisi'pal | *a.* municipal / *sm.* (cap. colloq.) municipal theatre

municipalidade | munisipali'dadɪ |

sf. municipality; city council

município | muni'sipiʋ | *sm.* municipal district (corresponding roughly to a county)

munir | mu'niʀ | *vt.* to provide, to supply

muralha | mu'raʟa | *sf.* bulward, rampart

murchar | muʀ'xaʀ | *vi.* to wither, to shrivel, to wilt

murmurar | muʀmu'raʀ | *vt. vi.* to murmur, to mutter, to mumble

murmúrio | muʀ'muriʋ | *sm.* murmur; sound of many quiet voices; whisper

muro | 'murʋ | *sm.* outside wall, garden wall

murro | 'muʀʋ | *sm.* blow with the fist, punch

músculo | 'muʃkulʋ | *sm.* muscle

museu | mu'zew | *sm.* museum

musgo | 'muʃgʋ | *sm.* moss

música | 'muzika | *sf.* music

musicista | muzi'siʃta | *smf.* musician

músico -ca | 'muzikʋ | *sm.* musician / *a.* musical

mutação | muta'sãw | *sf.* mutation; alteration

mutilado -da | muti'ladʋ | *a.* mutilated; disabled

mutilar | muti'laʀ | *vt.* to mutilate; to mutilate in order to misrepresent; to distort

mútuo -tua | 'mutuʋ | *a.* mutual, reciprocal

muxoxo | mu'xoxʋ | *sm.* noise made with the tongue to indicate annoyance, doubt, disgust etc.

N

nabo | 'nabʋ | *sm.* turnip

nação | na'sãw | *sf.* nation

nacional | nasio'naʟ | *a.* national. **-artigo n.** domestic merchandise. **-hino n.** national anthem

nacionalidade | nasionali'dadɪ | *sf.* nationality

nacionalizar | nasionali'zaʀ | *vt.* to nationalize; to naturalize

naco | 'nakʋ | *sm.* chunk

nada | 'nada | *sm.* nothing; nothingness; trifle; naught. **-n. feito** (colloq.) no deal. **-antes de mais n.** first of all. **-de n.** not at all, you're welcome

nadadeira | nada'deyra | *sf.* (ichth.) fin; flipper

nadador -dora | nada'doʀ | *smf.* swimmer

nadar | na'daʀ | *vi.* to swim

nádega | 'nadɪga | *sf.* buttock

nadinha | na'diɴa | *sm.* bit, trifle. **-um n.** a wee bit, a drop

nado | 'nadʋ | *sm.* swim, swimming. **-a n.** (by) swimming

naipe | 'naypɪ | *sm.* suit (of cards)

namorado -da | namo'radʋ | *sm.* sweetheart, boy-friend; an edible percoid marine fish; *sf.* sweetheart, girl-friend

namorar | namo'raʀ | *vt.* to court, to flirt; to look at longingly

namoro | na'morʋ | *sm.* courting, love affair

não | 'nãw | *sm.* no, denial / *adv.* no, not, in no manner. **-com o n.** of course, certainly. **-pois n.!** certainly!, of course!

narciso | naʀ'sizʋ | *sm.* daffodil

narcótico -ca | naʀ'kɔtikʋ | *sm. a.* narcotic

narigudo -da | nari'gudʋ | *a.* big-nosed

narina | na'rina | *sf.* nostril

nariz | na'riʃ | *sm.* nose. **-torcer o n.** to turn up one's nose (at). **-assoar o n.** to blow one's nose

narração | naʀa'sãw | *sf.* narration, narrative

narrador -dora | naRa'doR | *smf.* narrator

narrar | na'RaR | *vt.* to narrate, to relate, to tell

narrativa | naRa'tiva | *sf.* narrative, narration

nasal | na'zal | *sf. a.* nasal

nascença | na'sẽsa | *sf.* birth; origin, beginning. **-de n.** by birth

nascente | na'sẽti | *sm.* east (point of sunrise); *sf.* source; spring / *a.* beginning; nascent

nascer | na'seR | *vi.* to be born; to begin, to originate; to rise (sun, moon)

nascido -da | na'sidv | *a.* born

nascimento | nasi'mẽtv | *sm.* birth; beginning. **-de n.** by birth

nata | 'nata | *sf.* cream (also fig.)

natação | nata'sãw | *sf.* swimming

natal | na'tal | *sm.* (cap.) Christmas / *a.* native. **-país n.** native land. **-terra n.** birthplace

natalício -cia | nata'lisiv | *sm.* birthday / *a.* of or referring to the birthday

natalidade | natali'dadɪ | *sf.* birth rate

nativo -va | na'tivv | *smf.* native / *a.* native, natural

nato -ta | 'natv | *a.* born; innate

natural | natu'ral | *sm.* native; disposition, temperament / *a.* natural; spontaneous; unaffected. **-de tamanho n.** life size. **-filho n.** illegitimate child

naturalidade | naturali'dadɪ | *sf.* simplicity, unaffectedness; nativeness

naturalização | naturaliza'sãw | *sf.* naturalization

naturalizar | naturali'zaR | *vt.* to naturalize. **-n. -se** to become a citizen of

natureza | natu'reza | *sf.* nature (also fig.). **-n. morta** (fine arts) still life

nau | 'naw | *sf.* (obs.) ship, vessel

naufragar | nawfra'gaR | *vi.* to be shipwrecked; to suffer failure

naufrágio | naw'frajiv | *sm.* shipwreck

náufrago -ga | 'nawfragv | *smf.* shipwrecked person

náusea | 'nawzɪa | *sf.* nausea; seasickness

nauseabundo -da | nawzɪa'būdv | *a.* nauseating, sickening; disgusting

náutica | 'nawtika | *sf.* art of navigation

náutico -ca | 'nawtikv | *a.* nautical

naval | na'val | *a.* naval, nautical

navalha | na'vaLa | *sf.* razor

nave | 'navɪ | *sf.* nave (in church); (obs.) ship, vessel

navegação | navega'sãw | *sf.* navigation; maritime commerce. **-n. costeira** coasting cabotage

navegar | nave'gaR | *vi.* to navigate

navegável | nave'gavɪl | *a.* navigable

navio | na'viv | *sm.* ship, liner, boat. **-n. cargueiro** freighter. **-n. de guerra** warship

neblina | ne'blina | *sf.* fog, mist

nebulosa | nebu'lɔza | *sf.* nebula

nebuloso -sa | nebu'lɔzv -'lɔza | *a.* cloudy, misty, hazy; vague; obscure

necessário -ria | nese'sariv | *sm. a.* necessary, essential

necessidade | nɪsɪsi'dadɪ | *sf.* necessity, need; poverty. **-fazer suas necessidades** to relieve nature

necessitar | nesesi'taR | *vt.* to need, to want

necrológio | nekro'lɔjiv | *sm.* obituary; obituary notice

necrotério | nekro'tɛriv | *sm.* morgue

nefando -da | ne'fãdv | *a.* nefarious

nefasto -ta | ne'faʃtv | *a.* ominous, inauspicious; tragic

negação | nega'sãw | *sf.* negation; denial. **-ser uma n.** (colloq.) to be inept

negar | ne'gaR | *vt.* to deny; to refuse. **-n. -se a** to refuse to

negativa | nega'tiva | *sf.* negative; denial; refusal

negativo -va |nega'tivʋ | *a.* negative

negligência | nɪgli'jẽsia | *sf.* negligence, carelessness

negligente | nɪgli'jẽtɪ | *a.* negligent, careless

nego -ga |'negʋ | *contr.* of **negro** (colloq.) expression of endearment signifying my darling, my dear friend etc.

negociação | negosia'sãw | *sf.* negociation

negociante|negosi'ãtɪ|*smf.* business man or woman; trader

negociar | negosi'aR |*vt. vi.* to negotiate; to deal; to trade

negociata | negosi'ata | *sf.* shady business; swindle

negociável | negosi'avɪl | *a.* negotiable

negócio | ne'gʋsiʋ | *sm.* trade, commerce; transaction; deal, agreement; business; (colloq.) thing; any subject. **-a negócios** on business. **-n. à vista** cash business

negreiro | ne'greyrʋ | *sm.* slave- -trader

negro -gra|'negrʋ|*sm.* black (colour); *smf.* Negro / *a.* black

negrura | ne'grura | *sf.* black, blackness

nem | 'nẽy | *adv.* not, not even / *conj.* nor; neither ... nor. **-que n.** (colloq.) just like

nenê|ne'ne|*sm.* baby

nenem|ne'nẽy|*sm.* = *nenê*

nenhum -ma | ne'nũ -'numa | *a.* not one, not any, no, none / *pron.* no one, nobody, none

neófito | ne'ωfitʋ | *sm.* beginner, novice

nervo | 'neRvʋ | *sm.* nerve; strength

nervosismo | neRvo'ziʒmʋ | *sm.* nervousness, nervous irritability

nervoso -sa | neR'vozʋ -'vωza | *a.* nervous; sinewy; (colloq.) ex-

citable, irritable

nesga | 'neʒga | *sf.* small piece; small space. **-n. de terra** strip of land

nêspera | 'neʒpera | *sf.* medlar; loquat

nesse -sa|'nesɪ'nesa|*contr.* of **em** + **esse -sa** in that, on that; (*pl.*) in those, on those

neste -ta | 'neʃtɪ'nesta | *contr.* of **em** + **este -ta** in this, on this; (*pl.*) in these, on these

neto -ta | 'netʋ | *sm.* grandson, grandchild; *sf.* granddaughter, grandchild

neurose | new'rωzɪ | *sf.* neurosis

neurótico -ca|new'rωtikʋ|*smf. a.* neurotic

neutralidade | newtrali'dadɪ | *sf.* neutrality

neutro -tra | 'newtrʋ | *sm.* (gram.) neuter / *a.* neutral, neuter

nevar|ne'vaR|*vi.* to snow

neve | 'nevɪ | *sf.* snow

névoa | 'nevva | *sf.* fog; mist

nevoeiro | nevʋ'eyrʋ | *sm.* dense fog, heavy mist

nevralgia | nevral'jia | *sf.* neuralgia

nexo | 'neksʋ | *sm.* nexus, coherency

nicho | 'nixʋ |*sm.* niche

ninar | ni'naR | *vt.* to lull to sleep. **-cantiga de n.** lullaby

ninfa | 'nĩfa | *sf.* nymph

ninguém | nĩ'gẽy | *indef. pron.* nobody, no one

ninhada | ni'Nada | *sf.* brood, litter, nestful

ninharia | ni'Naria | *sf.* trifle

ninho | 'niNʋ | *sm.* nest

níquel | 'nikɪl | *sm.* nickel; (colloq.)coin. **-não valer um n.** to be worthless

niquelar | nike'laR | *vt.* to nickel- -plate

nisso| 'nisʋ |*contr.* of **em** + **isso** in that, on that, in it, on it

nisto | 'niʃtʋ |*contr.* of **em** + **isto** in this, on this, in it, on it

nitidez | niti'deʒ | *sf.* clearness;

(opt.) definition, sharpness

nítido -da | ˈnitidʋ | *a.* bright, sharp, clear

nível | ˈnivɪl | *sm.* level (also mech., carp.); standard, degree. **-ao n.** on a par. **-n. de vida** standard of living

nivelar | niveˈlaʀ | *vt.* to level

no, na | ˈnʋ ˈna | *contr.* of **em + o, a** in the, on the, at the, into the

nó | ˈnɔ | *sm.* knot; tie; knot, nautical mile. **-n. corrediço** slip knot. **-ter um n. na garganta** to have a lump in the throat. **-nós dos dedos** knuckles

nobilitar | nobiliˈtaʀ | *vt.* to ennoble

nobre | ˈnɔbrɪ | *smf. a.* noble

nobreza | noˈbreza | *sf.* nobility

noção | noˈsãw | *sf.* notion, idea; succint information

nocaute | noˈkawtɪ | *sm.* (boxing) knock-out, K.O.

nocivo -va | noˈsivʋ | *a.* harmful, pernicious, noxious

nódoa | ˈnɔdʋa | *sf.* stain, blot, blotch

nodoso -sa | noˈdozʋ -ˈdʋza | *a.* nodose, knotty

nogueira | noˈgeyra | *sf.* walnut (tree and wood)

noitada | noyˈtada | *sf.* all-night party; a whole night

noite | ˈnoytɪ | *sf.* night. **-à (de) n.** at night, by night

noivado | noyˈvadʋ | *sm.* engagement period; wedding feast

noivo -va | ˈnoyvʋ | *sm.* bridegroom, fiancé; *sf.* bride, fiancée; (*pl.*) engaged couple, bride and groom

nojento -ta | noˈjẽtʋ | *a.* disgusting, repulsive

nojo | ˈnojʋ | *sm.* repugnance; disgust, loathing

nome | ˈnomɪ | *sm.* name, family name; fame, renown; (gram.) noun. **-de n.** by name. **-n. de batismo** Christian name. **-n. de família** family or last name

nomeação | nomɪaˈsãw | *sf.* nomination, appointment

nomear | nomɪˈaʀ | *vt.* to nominate; to appoint; to name

nono -na | ˈnonʋ | *smf. a.* ninth

nora | ˈnɔra | *sf.* daughter-in-law

nordeste | noʀˈdɛʃtɪ | *sm. a.* northeast

nordestino -na | noʀdeʃˈtinʋ | *smf.* northeastern / *a.* northeastern; of or pertaining to northeastern Brazil

norma | ˈnɔʀma | *sf.* norm, rule, precept

normal | noʀˈmal | *a.* normal. **-escola n.** normal school

normalidade | noʀmaliˈdadɪ | *sf.* normality

normalizar | noʀmaliˈzaʀ | *vt.* to normalize. **-n. -se** to return to normal

noroeste | norʋˈɛʃtɪ | *sm. a.* northwest

norte | ˈnɔʀtɪ | *sm.* north; guide, direction / *a.* north

norte-americano -na | noʀtɪameriˈkanʋ | *smf. a.* North--American, American

nortista | noʀˈtiʃta | *smf.* northerner / *a.* northern; of or pertaining to northern Brazil

norueguês -guesa | nʋrueˈgeʃ | *smf. a.* Norwegian

nos | nʋʃ | *oblique pron. 1st pers. pl.* (direct object) us; (indirect object) to us, to ourselves; *reflexive pron. 1st pers. pl.* ourselves

nós | ˈnɔʃ | *pron. 1st pers. pl.* we; (colloq.) us; (with any *prep.*) us

nosso -sa | ˈnʋsʋ | *poss. a.* our / *poss. pron.* ours. **-os nossos** our folks, our people, our team etc.

nota | ˈnɔta | *sf.* note (also mus.); grade, mark; banknote; restaurant chek

notar | noˈtaʀ | *vt.* to note, to observe; to notice. **-é de n.** it is worth noting

notário | noˈtarivʋ | *sm.* notary, notary public

notável | no'tavɪl | a. outstanding, remarkable

notícia | nʋ'tisia | sf. news, notice; announcement; (pl.) news

noticiário | nʋtisi'ariʋ | sm. news; (rad., TV) newscast

notificar | notifi'kaʀ | vt. to notify; to summon

notoriedade | notorie'dadɪ | sf. quality of being public, known to all; notoriety

notório -ria | no'tʊriʋ | a. publicly known, notorious. **-público en.** well-known

noturno -na | nʋ'tuʀnʋ | sm. (mus.) nocturne; (R. R.) night train / a. nocturnal, nightly

noutro-tra | 'nowtrʋ | contr. of em + outro -tra in the other (one); (pl.) in the other (or other ones), on the other (or other ones)

nova | 'nʋva | sf. news. **-boa(s) n.** (s) good news

novato -ta | no'vatʋ | smf. novice, beginner, greenhorn / a. inexperienced

nove | 'nʋvɪ | sm. num. nine

novecentos -tas | novɪ'sẽtʋʃ | smf. num. nine hundred

novela | no'vela | sf. (obs.) novelette, story of moderate length; (rad., TV) soap opera, sentimental serial

novelista | nove'liʃta | smf. (rad., TV) author of soap operas; (obs.) fictionist

novelo | no'velʋ | sm. ball of yarn, skein

novembro | no'vẽbrʋ | sm. November

noventa | no'vẽta | sm. num. ninety

noviciado | novisi'adʋ | sm. noviciate, apprenticeship

noviço -ça | no'visʋ | sm. novice; beginner, greenhorn / a. inexperienced

novidade | novi'dadɪ | sf. novelty; news; rarity, curiosity

novilho -lha | nʋ'viʎʋ | sm. calf, bullock; sf. heifer

novo -va | 'novʋ 'nʋva | a. new; young. **-de n.** again. **-n. em folha** brand new

noz | 'nʋʒ | sf. nut

noz-moscada | 'nʋʒmoʒ'kada| sf. nutmeg

nu, nua | 'nu 'nua | sm. nude / a. naked, nude; bare, barren. **-n. em pêlo** stark naked

nublar | nu'blar | vt. to cloud, to becloud. **-n. -se** to become cloudy

nuca | 'nuka | sf. nape of the neck

núcleo | 'nuklɪʋ | sm. nucleus (also chem., phys.); core, heart

nudez | nu'deʒ | sf. nudity, nakedness

nulidade | nuli'dadɪ | sf. nullity, invalidity; nonentity (person)

nulo -la | 'nulʋ | a. null, void

num, numa | nũ 'numa | contr. of em + um uma in a, on a, at a, into a

numeração | numera'sãw | sf. numbering; size (of garments etc.)

numerar | nume'raʀ | vt. to number

numerário | nume'rariʋ | sm. money, cash

numérico -ca | nu'mɛrikʋ | a. numerical

número | 'numɪrʋ | sm. number (also gram.), numeral; size (of garments etc.); quantity; copy, issue; number of a show

numeroso -sa | nume'rozʋ -'rwza | a. copious, abundant

nunca | 'nũka | adv. never. **-n. mais** never more, not ever

núpcias | 'nupsiaʃ | sfpl. wedding, marriage

nutrição | nutri'sãw | sf. nutrition

nutrido -da | nu'tridʋ | a. well-nourished; plump

nutrir | nu'triʀ | vt. to nourish, to feed; to cherish (hopes etc.)

nutritivo -va | nutri'tivʋ | a. nourishing, nutritious

nuvem | 'nuvẽy | sf. cloud. **-cair das nuvens** to be flabbergasted

O

oásis | ʋ'aziʃ | *sm.* oasis

obcecação | obseka'sãw | *sf.* obduracy; obfuscation; delusion

obedecer | obede'seʀ | *vi.* to obey, to comply with

obediência | obɪdi'ẽsia | *sf.* obedience, submission

obediente | obɪdi'ẽtɪ | *a.* obedient, submissive

obesidade | obezi'dadɪ | *sf.* obesity

óbito | 'ɷbitʋ | *sm.* death. **-atestado de ó.** death certificate

objeção | obje'sãw | *sf.* objection

objetivo-va | obje'tivʋ | *sm.* objective; (mil.) target; *sf.* (opt.) a system of lenses / *a.* objective

objeto | ob'jɛtʋ | *sm.* object, thing; purpose

oblíquo -qua | o'blikwʋ | *a.* oblique, aslant, askew

obra | 'ɷbra | *sf.* work, literary composition; a building under construction or repair; deed. **-o. de consulta** reference work. **-em obras** under repair

obra-prima | 'ɷbra'prima | *sf.* masterpiece

obrar | o'braʀ | *vi.* to work, to act

obreiro -ra | o'breyrʋ | *smf.* worker, labo(u)rer / *a.* working

obrigação | obriga'sãw | *sf.* duty, obligation; (fin.) bond

obrigado -da | obri'gadʋ | *a.* constrained; obliged, grateful / *interj.* thank you!, thanks!

obrigar | obri'gaʀ | *vt.* to oblige, to compel, to constrain. **-o.-se a** to assume an obligation

obrigatório -ria | obriga'tɷriʋ | *a.* compulsory, obligatory

obsceno-na | ob'senʋ | *a.* obscene, indecent

obscurecer | obʃkure'seʀ | *vt.* to obscure, to darken

obscuridade | obʃkuri'dadɪ | *sf.* obscurity

obscuro -ra | obʃ'kurʋ | *a.* obscure; humble

obsequiar | obzeki'aʀ | *vt.* to oblige, to favo(u)r. **-o. com** to present with

obséquio | ob'zɛkiʋ | *sm.* favo(u)r, kindness. **-por o.** please

obsequioso-sa | obzeki'ozʋ-'ɷza | *a.* obliging, polite

observação | obseʀva'sãw | *sf.* observation; remark, comment

observador -dora | obseʀva'doʀ | *smf.* observer / *a.* observing; attentive

observância | obseʀ'vãsia | *sf.* observance

observar | obseʀ'vaʀ | *vt.* to observe

observatório | obseʀva'tɷriʋ | *sm.* observatory

obsessão | obse'sãw | *sf.* obsession

obsoleto -ta | obso'letʋ obso'lɛtʋ | *a.* obsolete, outmoded

obstáculo | obʃ'takulʋ | *sm.* obstacle, obstruction, hindrance

obstante | obʃ'tãtɪ | *a.* hindering, obstructive. **-não o.** despite, notwithstanding

obstar | obʃ'taʀ | *vt.* to obstruct ,to impede, to oppose

obstinação | obʃtina'sãw | *sf.* obstinacy

obstinado -da | obʃti'nadʋ | *a.* obstinate; stubborn

obstinar-se | obʃti'naʀsɪ | *vr.* to be obstinate. **-o.-se em** to persist in

obstrução | obʃtru'sãw | *sf.* obstruction

obstruir | obʃtru'iʀ | *vt.* to obstruct, to block, to stop up

obtenção | obtẽ'sãw | *sf.* procurement; attainment

obter | ob'teʀ | *vt.* to obtain, to acquire

obturar | obtu'raʀ | *vt.* to obturate, to plug (an opening). **-o.**

um dente to fill a tooth

obtuso -sa | ob'tuzʋ | *a.* obtuse

obviar | obvi'aʀ | *vt.* to obviate, to prevent

óbvio -via | 'ωbviʋ | *a.* obvious

ocasião | okasi'ãw | *sf.* occasion; opportunity

ocasionar | okazio'naʀ | *vt.* to cause, to give rise to

ocaso | o'kazʋ | *sm.* sunset; decline, decadence

oceano | osɪ'anʋ | *sm.* ocean

ocidental | osidẽ'tal | *smf.* Occidental / *a.* occidental (also *cap.*); Western

ócio | 'ωsiʋ | *sm.* idleness; leisure, spare time

ocioso -sa | osi'ozʋ -'ωza | *a.* idle, inactive; superfluous

oco -ca | 'okʋ | *sm.* hollow, hole / *a.* hollow, empty

ocorrência | okʋ'ʀẽsia | *sf.* occurrence, event, happening

ocorrer | okʋ'ʀeʀ | *vi.* to occur, to befall, to happen

ocre | 'ωkrɪ | *sm.* ochre, ocher

ocular | oku'laʀ | *smf. a.* ocular. **-testemunha o.** eyewitness

oculista | oku'liʃta | *smf.* oculist, eye specialist

óculo | 'ωkulʋ | *sm.* telescope; (*pl.*) glasses, spectacles. **-óculos escuros** sun-glasses

ocultar | okul'taʀ | *vt.* to conceal, to hide

oculto -ta | o'kultʋ | *a.* occult; concealed, hidden, secret

ocupação | okupa'sãw | *sf.* occupancy (also law, mil.); occupation (also mil.), employment, business

ocupado -da | oku'padʋ | *a.* busy; occupied, taken

ocupar | ʋku'paʀ | *vt.* to occupy; to inhabit. **-o.-se** de to busy oneself with

odiar | odi'aʀ | *vt.* to hate

ódio | 'ωdiʋ | *sm.* hate, hatred

odioso -sa | odi'ozʋ -'ωza | *a.* odious, hateful, detestable

odor | o'doʀ | *sm.* odo(u)r, smell; fragrance

oeste | ʋ'εʃtɪ | *sm.* west

ofegante | ofe'gãtɪ | *a.* panting, out of breath

ofegar | ofe'gaʀ | *vi.* to pant, to gasp, to breathe hard

ofender | ofẽ'deʀ | *vt.* to offend, to insult; to injure, to hurt. **-o.-se** to take offence

ofensa | o'fẽsa | *sf.* offence, offense, abuse; affront. **-o. corporal** bodily injury

ofensiva | ofẽ'siva | *sf.* (mil.) attack

ofensivo -va | ofẽ'sivʋ | *a.* offensive, abusive; injurious

ofensor -sora | ofẽ'soʀ | *smf.* offender / *a.* offending

oferecer | ofere'seʀ | *vt.* to offer; to present. **-o.-se** to present itself or oneself; to occur, to happen. **-o.-se para** to volunteer

oferecimento | ofɪrɪsi'mẽtʋ | *sm.* offer, offering

oferta | o'fɛʀta | *sf.* offer, offering, gift; bid (also com., law). **-o. e procura** supply and demand

oficial | ofisi'al | *sm.* official; (mil.) officer; artisan / *a.* official

oficialidade | ofisiali'dadɪ | *sf.* body or staff of officers

oficializar | ofisiali'zaʀ | *vt.* to make official; to approve or to sanction officially

oficiar | ofisi'aʀ | *vi.* to officiate (at mass); to address an official letter to

oficina | ofi'sina | *sf.* workshop

ofício | o'fisiʋ | *sm.* craft, trade; occupation; (eccles.) office; official correspondence

oficioso -sa | ofisi'ozʋ -'ωza | *a.* unofficial; obliging

ofuscar | ofuʃ'kaʀ | *vt.* to dazzle, to daze; to outshine (others)

oitavo -va | oy'tavʋ | *sm.* eighth; *sf.* eighth; musical octave / *a.* eighth

oitenta | oy'tẽta | *sm. num.* eighthy

oito | 'oytʊ | *sm. num.* eight

oitocentos -tas | oytʊ'sẽtʊʃ | *smf. num.* eight hundred

olá | o'la | *interj.* hello!, hi!

olaria | ola'ria | *sf.* brick factory; pottery (workshop)

oleado -da | olɪ'adʊ | *sm.* oilcloth/ *a.* oiled

oleiro | o'leyrʊ | *sm.* potter, pottery worker

óleo | 'ᴐlɪʊ | *sm.* oil; oil painting

oleoso -sa | olɪ'ozʊ -'ᴐza | *a.* oily, greasy

olfato | ol'fatʊ | *sm.* sense of smell

olhada | o'ʟada | *sf.* glance. **-dê uma o.** have a glance

olhar | o'ʟaʀ | *sm.* look, aspect, mien / *vt.* to look at; to take care of; to examine / *vi.* to look, to try to see. **-o. por** to take care of

olheiras | o'ʟeyraʃ | *sfpl.* dark circles under the eyes

olho | 'oʟʊ *pl.* 'ᴐʟʊʃ | *sm.* eye. **-a o. nu** with the naked eye. **-não ver com bons olhos** to take a dim view of. **-num abrir e fechar de olhos** in a twinkling of an eye. **-bons olhos o vejam!** welcome!

oliveira | oli'veyra | *sf.* olive-tree

olmo | 'olmʊ | *sm.* elm

olor | o'loʀ | *sm.* perfume, scent, fragrance

olvidar | olvi'daʀ | *vt.* to forget

ombreira | õ'breyra | *sf.* shoulder (of a garment)

ombro | 'õbrʊ | *sm.* shoulder. **-o. a o.** side by side. **-dar de ombros** to shrug the shoulders

omelete | ome'letɪ | *sm.* omelette, omelet

ominoso -sa | omi'nozʊ -'nᴐza | *a.* ominous

omissão | omi'sãw | *sf.* omission, oversight; (law) non-feasance

omitir | omi'tiʀ | *vt.* to omit; to neglect, to leave out

omoplata | omo'plata | *sf.* shoulder-blade

onça | 'õsa | *sf.* any of various wild felines (esp. the jaguar and the puma); ounce (weight)

onda | 'õda | *sf.* wave

onde | 'õdɪ | *adv.* where. **-o. quer que** wherever

ondear | õdɪ'aʀ | *vt.* to wave / *vi.* to wave, to undulate

ondulação | õdula'sãw | *sf.* undulation; corrugation. **-o. permanente** permanent (hair) wave

ondulante | õdu'lãtɪ | *a.* waving, undulating

ondular | õdu'laʀ | *vt.* to wave (the hair)

onerar | one'raʀ | *vt.* to burden (esp. with taxes)

ônibus | 'onibʊʃ | *sm. (sing.* and *pl.)* omnibus, bus. **-ponto de ô.** bus-stop

ontem | 'õtẽy | *adv.* yesterday. **-o. à noite** last night

onze | 'õzɪ | *sm. num.* eleven

opaco -ca | o'pakʊ | *a.* opaque

opção | op'sãw | *sf.* option, choice

ópera | 'ᴐpera | *sf.* opera

operação | opera'sãw | *sf.* operation

operador -dora | opera'doʀ | *smf.* operator; surgeon

operar | ope'raʀ | *vt.* to operate (also surg.); to effect / *vi.* to function

operariado | operari'adʊ | *sm.* working classes

operário -ria | ope'rarɪʊ | *sm.* worker, workman; *sf.* woman factory worker

opinar | opi'naʀ | *vt. vi.* to hold or express an opinion

opinião | opini'ãw | *sf.* opinion; conviction, belief

ópio | 'ᴐpɪʊ | *sm.* opium

opíparo | o'piparʊ | *a.* sumptuous, splendid

oponente | opo'nẽtɪ | *smf.* opponent, adversary / *a.* opposing

opor | o'poʀ | *vt.* to oppose. **-o. a** to set against. **-o.-se a** to oppose; to resist

oportunidade | opoʀtuni'dadɪ | *sf.* opportunity

oportuno -na | opoʀ'tunʋ | *a.* opportune; favo(u)rable, convenient

oposição | opozi'sãw | *sf.* opposition (also polit.); antagonism

oposto -ta | o'poʃtʋ -'pwʒta | *smf.* opposite / *a.* opposed; opposite, facing; contrary

opressão | opre'sãw | *sf.* oppression, tyranny; suffocation

opressivo -va | opre'sivʋ | *a.* oppressive

opressor -sora | opre'soʀ | *smf.* oppressor / *a.* oppressive

oprimir | opri'mir | *vt.* to oppress / *vi.* to tyrannize over

opróbrio | o'pʀɔbriʋ | *sm.* opprobrium, ignominy, disgrace

optar | op'taʀ | *vt.* to opt, to choose

óptica | 'ɔptika | *sf.* optics

óptico -ca | 'ɔptikʋ | *smf.* optician / *a.* optic, optical

opulência | opu'lẽsia | *sf.* opulence, wealth; plentifulness

opúsculo | o'puʃkulʋ | *sm.* pamphlet, booklet

ora | 'ɔra | *adv.* now, presently. **-por o.** for the time being / *conj.* but, however / *interj.* well!, now then! **-o. essa!** well now!

oração | ora'sãw | *sf.* prayer; oration, speech; (gram.) simple sentence

oráculo | o'rakulʋ | *sm.* oracle

orador -dora | ora'doʀ | *smf.* orator, speaker

oral | o'ral | *a.* oral

orar | o'raʀ | *vi.* to pray

orbe | 'ɔrbɪ | *sm.* orb, sphere, globe

órbita | 'ɔrbita | *sf.* orbit; eye socket

orçamento | orsa'mẽtʋ | *sm.* budget; estimate

ordeiro -ra | oʀ'deyrʋ | *á.* orderly; peaceable

ordem | 'oʀdẽy | *sf.* order; disposition; command; (*pl.*) holy orders. **-às ordens de** at the disposal of. **-de primeira o.**

first-rate

ordenação | oʀdena'sãw | *sf.* ordination (also eccles.); arrangement, disposition

ordenado -da | oʀde'nadʋ | *sm.* salary / *a.* orderly, methodical

ordenança | oʀde'nãsa | *sm.* (mil.) orderly

ordenar | oʀde'naʀ | *vt.* to order, to arrange; to command; (relig.) to ordain. **-o.-se** to take holy orders

ordenhar | oʀde'naʀ | *vt.* to milk

ordinário -ria | oʀdi'nariʋ | *a.* ordinary, common; average; cheap; vulgar

orelha | o'reLa | *sf.* ear

orelhão | ore'Lãw | *sm.* (colloq.) public telephone (in the streets of Rio de Janeiro)

orfanato | oʀfa'natʋ | *sm.* orphanage

órfão -fã | 'oʀfãw 'oʀfã | *smf.* orphan

orfeão | oʀfɪ'ãw | *sm.* choral society

organismo | oʀga'niʒmʋ | *sm.* organism; organization

organização | oʀganiza'sãw | *sf.* organization

organizar | oʀgani'zaʀ | *vt.* to organize

órgão | 'oʀgãw | *sm.* organ

orgia | oʀ'jia | *sf.* orgy, bacchanal; (colloq.) Carnival merriment

orgulho | oʀ'gulʋ | *sm.* pride; haughtiness

orgulhoso -sa | oʀgu'lozʋ -'Lwza | *a.* proud; haughty

orientação | oriẽta'sãw | *sf.* orientation, direction; guidance

oriental | oriẽ'tal | *smf.* Oriental / *a.* oriental (also *cap.*), Eastern; Uruguayan

orientar | oriẽ'taʀ | *vt.* to orient, to guide, to direct. **-o.-se** to determine how one stands

oriente | ori'ẽtɪ | *sm.* orient, east; (*cap.*) the East. **-O. Médio** Middle East

orifício | ori'fisiʋ | *sm.* orifice,

aperture

origem | o'rijēy | *sf.* origin; source

original | oriji'nal | *sm.* manuscript, typescript / *a.* original; odd, curious

originar | oriji'naʀ | *vt.* to originate; to generate

originário -ria | oriji'narɪʋ | *a.* derived from; native of

oriundo -da | ori'ũdʋ | *a.* deriving from; resulting from

orla | 'ɔʀla | *sf.* edge, rim, fringe

ornamentar | oʀnamē'taʀ | *vt.* to ornament, to adorn

ornamento | oʀna'mētʋ | *sm.* ornament, decoration, garnish

ornar | oʀ'naʀ | *vt.* to adorn

orquestra | oʀ'kɛʃtra | *sf.* orchestra

ortodoxo -xa | oʀto'dɔksʋ | *a.* orthodox

ortografia | oʀtogra'fia | *sf.* spelling, orthography

orvalho | oʀ'vaʟʋ | *sm.* dew

oscilar | osi'laʀ | *vt. vi.* to sway, to oscillate; to hesitate

ósculo | 'oʃkulʋ | *sm.* (unc.) kiss

ossada | o'sada | *sf.* bones, skeleton

osso | 'osʋ *pl.* 'ɔsʋʃ | *sm.* bone

ossudo -da | o'sudʋ | *a.* bony, big-boned

ostensivo -va | oʃtē'sivʋ | *a.* ostensible, apparent

ostentação | oʃtēta'sãw | *sf.* ostentation, display, vanity

ostentar | oʃtē'taʀ | *vt.* to exhibit, to display, to parade

ostentoso -sa | oʃtē'tozʋ -'tʋza | *a.* ostentatious

ostra | 'oʃtra | *sf.* oyster

otário -ria | o'tarɪʋ | *smf.* (slang) dupe

ótico -ca | 'ɔtikʋ | *a.* otical (used frequently instead of **óptico**)

otimismo | oti'miʒmʋ | *sm.* optimism

otimista | oti'miʃta | *smf.* optimist / *a.* optimistic

ótimo -ma | 'ɔtimʋ | *sm.* optimum

/ *a.* excellent, splendid / *interj.* excellent!

ou | 'ow | *conj.* or, either

ouriço | ow'risʋ | *sm.* hedgehog; sea-urchin

ourives | ow'rivɪʃ | *smf.* goldsmith

ourivesaria | owriveza'ria | *sf.* goldsmithery; goldsmith's shop

ouro | 'owrʋ | *sm.* gold; (*pl.*, card suit) diamonds. **-o. de lei** 18-carat gold. **-o. maciço** solid gold

ouropel | owro'pɛl | *sm.* tinsel; pretence

ousadia | owza'dia | *sf.* daring, boldness; impudence

ousar | ow'zaʀ | *vt.* to dare

outeiro | ow'téyrʋ | *sm.* hillock, small hill

outono | ow'tonʋ | *sm.* autumn; (U.S.) fall

outorgar | owtoʀ'gaʀ | *vt.* to grant, to concede

outrem | 'owtrēy | *pron.* somebody else

outro -tra | 'owtrʋ | *indef. a.* and *pron.* the other (one), another; (*pl.*) the others. **-um ao o.** each other, one another. **-um ou o.** one or the other

outrora | ow'trʋra | *adv.* formerly; in olden times

outrossim | owtrʋ'sĩ | *adv.* also, besides

outubro | ow'tubrʋ | *sm.* October

ouvido | ow'vidʋ | *sm.* the (inner) ear; sense of hearing. **-de o.** by ear

ouvinte | ow'vĩtɪ | *smf.* listener

ouvir | ow'viʀ | *vt.* to hear, to listen (to). **-o. dizer** or **falar que** to hear it said that. **-o. falar de** to hear of (about) / *vi.* to hear, to obey

ovação | ova'sãw | *sf.* ovation, applause

ovelha | o'veʟa | *sf.* sheep, ewe

ovo | 'ovʋ *pl.* 'ɔvʋʃ | *sm.* egg. **-ovos estrelados** fried eggs.

-ovos mexidos scrambled eggs.

-ovos quentes soft-boiled eggs

oxalá | oxaˈla | *interj.* God willing!, let's hope so!

oxigenar | oksijeˈnaʀ | *vt.* to oxygenate. **-o. os cabelos** to bleach (hair) with peroxide

oxigênio | oksiˈjeniʋ | *sm.* oxygen

P

pá | ˈpa | *sf.* shovel, spade; blade (of an oar, fan, propeller etc.); shoulder (of an animal)

paca | ˈpaka | *sf.* paca

pacato -ta | paˈkatʋ | *a.* peaceful, quiet

pachorrento -ta | paxoˈʀẽtʋ | *a.* sluggish, slow, easy-going

paciência | pasiˈẽsia | *sf.* patience, resignation; solitaire (card game)

paciente | pasiˈẽtɪ | *smf. a.* patient

pacificação | pasifikaˈsãw | *sf.* pacification

pacificar | pasifiˈkaʀ | *vt.* to pacify. **p.-se** to become peaceful

pacífico -ca | paˈsifikʋ | *sm.* (cap.) Pacific (Ocean) / *a.* peaceful, calm

paçoca | paˈsʋka | *sf.* maniocmeal pounded with bits of meat; crushed peanuts mixed with sugar and manioc flour

pacote | paˈkʋtɪ | *sm.* package, parcel

pacto | ˈpaktʋ | *sm.* pact, agreement

pactuar | paktuˈaʀ | *vt. vi.* to make a pact with

padaria | padaˈria | *sf.* bakery

padecer | padeˈseʀ | *vt. vi.* to suffer

padecimento | padesiˈmẽtʋ | *sm.* suffering

padeiro | paˈdeyrʋ | *sm.* baker

padiola | padiˈʋla | *sf.* stretcher

padrão | paˈdrãw | *sm.* standard; pattern, model; example. **-p. de vida** standard of living

padrasto | paˈdraʃtʋ | *sm.* stepfather

padre | ˈpadrɪ | *sm.* priest

padre-nosso | padrɪˈnʋsʋ | *sm.* paternoster (Our Father)

padrinho | paˈdriɲʋ | *sm.* godfather; best man; second (in a duel); protector

padroeiro -ra | padrʋˈeyrʋ | *smf.* patron (also eccles.); patron saint

padronizar | padroniˈzaʀ | *vt.* to standardize

paga | ˈpaga | *sf.* pay, payment, wages

pagamento | pagaˈmẽtʋ | *sm.* payment

pagão -gã | paˈgãw | *smf. a.* pagan

pagar | paˈgaʀ | *vt.* to pay. **-p. à vista** to pay at sight. **-p. em prestações** to pay in instalments / *vi.* to pay; to suffer for another's misdoings. **-p. caro** to pay dear

página | ˈpajina | *sf.* page

pago -ga | ˈpagʋ | *a.* paid

pai | ˈpay | *sm.* father; (*pl.*) parents

paina | ˈpayna | *sf.* silk cotton (from the silk cotton tree); kapok

paineira | payˈneyra | *sf.* silk cotton tree

painel | payˈnel | *sm.* panel. **-p. de instrumentos** control panel

paio | ˈpayʋ | *sm.* thick smoked sausage

paiol | payˈʋl | *sm.* powder magazine; granary

pairar | payˈraʀ | *vi.* to hover; to flutter; to be impending

país | pa'iʃ | sm. country, nation

paisagem | pay'zajēy | sf. landscape, view

paisano -na | pay'zanʊ | smf. civilian; sf. civilian clothes. -à paisana in civilian clothes / a. civilian

paixão | pay'xãw | sf. passion

pajem | 'pajēy | sm. page (attendant)

pala | 'pala | sf. eye-shade; brim (of a hat); sm. poncho

palácio | pa'lasiʊ | sm. palace

paladar | pala'daR | sm. taste; palate

paladino | pala'dinʊ | sm. paladin, champion

palanque | pa'lãkɪ | sm. stand; raised platform

palavra | pa'lavra | sf. word; term; statement. -p. dada pledged word. -cumprir a p. to keep one's word. -dirigir a p. a to address another (person) / interj. I give you my word!

palavrão | pala'vrãw | sm. coarse word

palco | 'palkʊ | sm. stage

palerma | pa'lɛRma | smf. simpleton, fool / a. stupid, foolish

palestra | pa'lɛʃtra | sf. chat, conversation; lecture

palestrar | paleʃ'traR | vi. to chat

paleta | pa'leta | sf. palette

paletó | palɪ'tɔ | sm. man's coat, jacket

palha | 'paLa | sf. straw

palhaçada | paLa'sada | sf. clowning

palhaço -ça | pa'Lasʊ | smf. clown

palheiro | pa'Leyrʊ | sm. haystack

palhoça | pa'Lɔsa | sf. straw-thatched hut; shanty

paliativo -va | palia'tivʊ | sm. a. palliative

paliçada | pali'sada | sf. palisade, stockade

palidez | pali'deʃ | sf. paleness, pallor

pálido -da | 'palidʊ | a. pale, colo(u)rless

palito | pa'litʊ | sm. toothpick. -p. de fósforo match

palma | 'palma | sf. palm; palm leaf; (pl.) handclapping, applause. -bater palmas to clap, to applaud

palmada | pal'mada | sf. slap, smack

palmeira | pal'meyra | sf. palm tree

palmito | pal'mitʊ | sm. heart of palm, palmetto

palmo | 'palmʊ | sm. span (of the hand). -p. a p. inch by inch

palpável | pal'pavɪl | a. palpable, tangible

pálpebra | 'palpebra | sf. eyelid

palpitante | palpi'tãtɪ | a. palpitating; exciting, stirring

palpitar | palpi'taR | vt. to guess, to offer advice (often wrong) / vi. to palpitate, to pulsate

palpite | pal'pitɪ | sm. guess; hunch; suggestive remark

palustre | pa'luʃtrɪ | a. swampy, marshy. -febre p. malarial fever

pamonha | pa'moNa | sf. kind of pudding made of green corn paste and rolled in corn husks; smf. (colloq.) simpleton

panarício | pana'risiʊ | sm. (med.) felon

pança | 'pãsa | sf. belly, paunch

pancada | pã'kada | sf. blow, stroke; gust (of rain)

pândego -ga | 'pãdɪgʊ | smf. merrymaker, carouser; sf. revelry, carousal

pandeiro | pã'deyrʊ | sm. kind of tambourine

panela | pa'nɛla | sf. pot, casserole

panfleto | pã'fletʊ | sm. pamphlet

panificação | panifika'sãw | sf. bakery

pano | 'panʊ | sm. cloth, fabric; (naut.) sail; (theat.) stage curtain. -a todo o p. (colloq.) under full sail (also fig.)

panorama | pano'rama | sm. panorama; landscape, view

pântano | 'pãtanʊ | sm. swamp, marsh, bog

pantanoso -sa | pãta'nozʊ-'nɔwza |
a. swampy, marshy, boggy

pão | 'pãw | *sm.* bread; loaf of
bread. **-p. de forma** loaf of
bread. **-p. francês** French
bread, roll bread

pão-de-ló | pãwdɪ'lↄ | *sm.* sponge
cake

pão-duro | pãw'durʊ | *sm.* miser,
niggard, stingy person

pãozinho | pãw'ziNʊ | *sm.* roll,
bread roll

papa | 'papa | *sm.* the Pope; *sf.*
pap, gruel. **-não ter papas na
língua** to be outspoken

papado | pa'padʊ | *sm.* Papacy

papagaio | papa'gayʊ | *sm.* parrot;
paper kite

papai | pa'pay | *sm.* (colloq.) dad,
daddy, papa, pa. **-Papai Noel**
Santa Claus

papão | pa'pãw | *sm.* bogey,
bogeyman

papar | pa'paʀ | *vt.* (colloq.) to
gobble (food)

papel | pa'pɛl | *sm.* paper; role;
(*pl.*) documents. **-no p. de** in the
role of. **-p. higiênico** toilet-
-páper

papelada | pape'lada | *sf.* heap of
papers

papelão | pape'lãw | *sm.* card-
board, carton

papelaria | papela'ria | *sf.* statio-
nery shop

papo | 'papʊ | *sm.* crop (of birds);
goitre; (colloq.) paunch. **-bater
p.** (colloq.) to chat

papoula | pa'powla | *sf.* poppy

par | 'paʀ | *sm.* pair, couple; peer;
dancing partner. **-ao p.** (com.,
fin.) at par. **-estar a p.** to be in-
formed about. **-p. ou ímpar**
even or odd / *a.* equal; even
(said of numbers)

para | 'para | *prep.* for, to,
toward, in, into. **-estar p.** to be
about to. **-p. já** for now. **-p.
quê?** what for? / *conj.* in order
to. **-p. que** so that

parabéns | para'bẽyʒ | *smpl.*
congratulations

parábola | pa'rabʊla | *sf.* (geom.)
parabola; parable

pára-brisa | para'briza | *sf.*
windshield

pára-choque | para'xↄkɪ | *sm.*
bumper; buffer

parada | pa'rada | *sf.* stop; halt;
pause; (mil.) parade; (gam-
bling) stake. **-p. de ônibus** bus-
-stop

paradeiro | para'deyrʊ | *sm.*
whereabouts, stopping place

parado -da | pa'radʊ | *a.* still,
motionless

paradoxo | para'dↄksʊ | *sm.*
paradox

parafina | para'fina | *sf.* paraffin
wax

paráfrase | pa'rafrazɪ | *sf.* para-
phrase

parafuso | para'fuzʊ | *sm.* screw;
(aeron.) tail spin. **-p. de porca**
bolt

paragem | pa'rajẽy | *sf.* place, lo-
cation. **-nestas paragens**
hereabouts

parágrafo | pa'ragrafʊ | *sm.*
paragraph

paraguaio -ia | para'gwayʊ | *smf.
a.* Paraguayan

paraíso | para'izʊ | *sm.* paradise

pára-lama | para'lama | *sm.* mud-
guard (of an automobile etc.)

paralelo -la | para'lɛlʊ | *smf. a.*
parallel

paralisar | parali'zaʀ | *vt.* to
paralyse

paralisia | parali'zia | *sf.* paralysis

paramento | para'mẽtʊ | *sm.* (ec-
cles.) vestment

paraninfo -fa | para'nĩfʊ | *smf.* the
hono(u)red spokesman or
spokeswoman for a graduating
class; *sm.* best man

parapeito | para'peytʊ | *sm.* para-
pet, rampart; window sill

pára-quedas | para'kɛdaʒ | *sm.*
parachute

pára-quedista | parake'diʒta | *sm.*
parachutist

parar | pa'raʀ | vt. to stop; to discontinue; to intercept / vi. to stop; to halt, to pause; to cease

pára-raios | para'ʀayʋʒ | sm. lightning-conductor, lightning-rod

parasita | para'zita | smf. parasite

parati | para'ti | sm. = *cachaça*; (ichth.) a kind of mullet

parceiro -ra | paʀ'seyrʋ | smf. partner (in a game, in song-writing etc.)

parcela | paʀ'sɛla | sf. fragment, small part; (arith.) numbers of a sum

parceria | paʀse'ria | sf. partnership, association

parcial | paʀsi'al | a. partial; one-sided

parcialidade | paʀsiali'dadɩ | sf. parciality, favo(u)ritism

parcimônia | paʀsi'monia | sf. parsimony; moderation

parco -ca | 'paʀkʋ | a. meagre; frugal; sparing

pardal | paʀ'dal | sm. sparrow

pardieiro | paʀdi'eyrʋ | sm. decayed old house

pardo-da | 'paʀdʋ | smf. mulatto / a. brownish, dun-colo(u)red

parecer | pare'seʀ | sm. appearance; judg(e)ment, written opinion (esp. juridical) / vt. to resemble, to look like / vi. to seem, to appear

parecido -da | parɩ'sidʋ | a. resembling, similar

paredão | pare'dãw | sm. high and thick external wall

parede | pa'redɩ | sf. wall; strike, work stoppage

parelha | pa'rɛɫa | sf. team (of horses); pair, brace

parente | pa'rētɩ | smf. relative; (pl.) relatives, kinsfolk

parentela | parē'tɛla | sf. (pej.) one's relatives collectively

parentesco | parē'teʒkʋ | sm. kinship; relationship; connection

parêntese, parêntesis | parē'tɩzɩ pa'retɩziʒ | sm. parenthesis

páreo | 'parɩʋ | sm. horse-race; dispute, rivalry

pária | 'paria | sm. pariah, social outcast

paridade | pari'dadɩ | sf. parity, equality; (fin.) par

parir | pa'riʀ | vt. vi. to give birth to (esp. animals)

parisiense | parizi'ẽsɩ | smf. a. Parisian

parlamentar | paʀlamē'taʀ | smf. member of a parliament; parliamentarian / a. parliamentary / vi. to parley; to negotiate

parlamento | paʀla'mētʋ | sm. parliament

pároco | 'parʋkʋ | sm. parish priest

parmesão | paʀme'zãw | sm. Parmesan cheese

paródia | pa'rʋdia | sf. parody

paróquia | pa'rʋkia | sf. parish

paroquiano -na | paroki'anʋ | smf. parishioner

parque | 'paʀkɩ | sm. park

parreira | pa'ʀeyra | sf. vine, grape-vine, trellised vine

parte | 'paʀtɩ | sf. part (also theat., math.); share; report (oral or written); opponent in a lawsuit (esp. pl.). **-da p. de** from. **-de p. a p.** reciprocally. **-em toda p.** everywhere

parteiro -ra | paʀ'teyrʋ | smf. obstetrician; sf. midwife

participação | paʀtisipa'sãw | sf. participation; announcement; copartnership

participante | paʀtisi'pãtɩ | smf. participant, partaker / a. participating

participar | paʀtisi'paʀ | vt. to announce, to communicate / vi. to participate, to partake

particípio | paʀti'sipiʋ | sm. participle

particular | paʀtiku'laʀ | smf. private individual; (pl.) details. **-em p.** in private; particularly / a. particular; individual, private

partida | paʀ'tida | sf. departure;

game, match; start (motors); (com.) shipment. **-estar de p.** to be about to leave. **-p. de futebol** football match

partidário -ria | paʀti'dariʊ | *smf.* partisan, devotee, follower

partido-da | paʀ'tidʊ | *sm.* (polit.) party, faction; advantage. **-bom p.** good catch (for marriage). **-tirar p. de** to take advantage of / *a.* divided, broken

partilha | paʀ'tiLa | *sf.* partition (also law), division

partilhar | paʀti'LaʀR | *vt.* to share; to partake; (law) to partition

partir | paʀ'tiʀ | *vt.* to break, to divide / *vi.* to depart from, to leave, to go away. **-a p. de agora** from now on

partitura | paʀti'tura | *sf.* (mus.) score

parto | 'paʀtʊ | *sm.* childbirth, delivery

parvo-va | 'paʀvʊ | *smf.* fool, simpleton / *a.* stupid

Páscoa | 'paʃkʊa | *sf.* Easter

pasmado -da | paʃ'madʊ | *a.* astounded, amazed

pasmar | paʃ'maʀ | *vt.* to astonish, to astound / *vi.* to stand in awe of

pasmo | 'paʃmʊ | *sm.* astonishment, amazement / *a.* (colloq.) = *pasmado*

paspalhão -lhona | paʃpa'Lãw | *smf.* simpleton

pasquim | paʃ'kĩ | *sm.* cheap newspaper; lampoon

passa | 'pasa | *sf.* raisin

passada | pa'sada | *sf.* step, stride, pace

passadeira | pasa'deyra | *sf.* runner, carpet; ironer (person); ring, circular band of any material

passadiço | pasa'disʊ | *sm.* (naut.) bridge; passageway

passadio | pasa'diʊ | *sm.* daily food; diet

passado -da | pa'sadʊ | *sm.* past

(also gram.) / *a.* past; former; overdone; stale. **-bem p.** well--done (said of meat). **-mal p.** rare (said of meat)

passageiro -ra | pasa'jeyrʊ | *smf.* passenger, travel(l)er / *a.* passing, ephemeral

passagem | pa'sajẽy | *sf.* passage; alley, passageway; fare, ticket. **-de p.** in passing, passing through

passante | pa'sãtɪ | *smf.* passer, passer-by

passaporte | pasa'pɔʀtɪ | *sm.* passport

passar | pa'saʀ | *vt.* to pass, to go (beyond, across, through); to spend (time); to undergo; to send (telegram); to be approved (examination). **-p. -se** to pass, to happen. **-p. roupa** or **p. a ferro** to iron clothes / *vi.* to pass, to go by; to be over. **-como tem passado?** how have you been?

passarinho | pasa'riNʊ | *sm.* any small bird

pássaro | 'pasarʊ | *sm.* bird

passatempo | pasa'tẽpʊ | *sm.* passtime, recreation, hobby

passe | 'pasɪ | *sm.* pass, permit; passing of the hand (by a hypnotist etc.); (soccer, sports) passing the ball; (soccer) transference of a player

passear | pasɪ'aʀ | *vi.* to take a walk, to promenade

passeata | pasɪ'ata | *sf.* public demonstration

passeio | pa'seyʊ | *sm.* walk, stroll; drive; trip; sidewalk. **-dar um p.** to take a walk

passivo -va | pa'sivʊ | *sm.* (com.) liability / *a.* passive

passo | 'pasʊ | *sm.* step; pace; pass; action, measure. **-ao p. que** while. **-a p.** slowly. **-a um p. de** on the verge of

pasta | 'paʃta | *sf.* paste; briefcase, portfolio (also the office of a minister of state). **-p. de dentes** toothpaste

pastagem | paʒ'tajēy | *sf.* pasture; herbage, grass

pastar | paʒ'taʀ | *vt. vi.* to graze

pastel | paʒ'tɛl | *sm.* pie; kind of rissole; (fine arts) pastel

pastelão | paʃte'lãw | *sm.* large pie; (theat.) low comedy

pastilha | paʒ'tiʟa | *sf.* tablet, lozenge, pastille

pasto | 'paʃtʋ | *sm.* pasture, pasturage; food

pastor -tora | paʒ'toʀ | *sm.* shepherd (also relig.); parson; *sf.* shepherdess

pata | 'pata | *sf.* paw, foot; duck (female)

pataca | pa'taka | *sf.* old silver coin. **-de meia p.** (colloq.) of insignificant value

patada | pa'tada | *sf.* pawing (by an animal), kick

patamar | pata'maʀ | *sf.* landing (of a staircase)

patente | pa'tẽtɪ | *sf.* patent, privilege; military rank / *a.* patent, evident

patentear | patẽtɪ'aʀ | *vt.* to make patent; to manifest; to patent (an invention). **-p.-se** to become evident

paterno -na | pa'tɛʀnʋ | *a.* paternal, fatherly

pateta | pa'tɛta | *smf.* simpleton, nitwit

patético -ca | pa'tɛtikʋ | *a.* pathetic, affecting, moving

patíbulo | pa'tibulʋ | *sm.* scaffold, gallows

patife | pa'tifɪ | *sm.* scoundrel, rogue, rascal

patim | pa'tĩ | *sm.* skate. **-p. de rodas** roller-skate

pátio | 'patiʋ | *sm.* courtyard, inner court

pato | 'patʋ | *sm.* duck, drake. **-pagar o p.** to take the blame, to pay the piper

patrão -troa | pa'trãw-'troa | *smf.* boss, owner (of a business establishment etc.); *sm.* (naut.) skipper; (rowing) coxswain

pátria | 'patria | *sf.* native land, fatherland, motherland

patriarca | patri'aʀka | *sm.* patriarch

patrício -cia | pa'trisiʋ | *sm.* countryman; *sf.* countrywoman

patrimônio | patri'moniʋ | *sm.* patrimony; heritage, inheritance. **-p. nacional** state property

patriota | patri'ʋta | *smf.* patriot

patriótico -ca | patri'ʋtikʋ | *a.* patriotic

patriotismo | patrio'tiʒmʋ | *sm.* patriotism

patroa | pa'troa | *sf.* boss's wife; mistress (of a house, shop etc.); landlady; (colloq.) wife

patrocinar | patrosi'naʀ | *vt.* to patronize, to sponsor

patrocínio | patrʋ'siniʋ | *sm.* sponsorship, patronage; support. **sob o p. de** under the auspices of

patrulha | pa'truʟa | *sf.* patrol

pau | 'paw | *sm.* stick; cudgel; piece of wood; tree; (*pl.*, card suit) clubs. **-meter o p. em** to squander. **-levar p.** to fail (an exam) / *a.* (colloq.) boring, tedious

paulada | paw'lada | *sf.* blow with a club; cudgeling

paulatino -na | pawla'tinʋ | *a.* gradual, little by little

pausa | 'pawza | *sf.* pause, interval, rest

pauta | 'pawta | *sf.* schedule; guide-line; (mus.) staff

pavão | pa'vãw | *sm.* peacock

pavilhão | pavi'ʟãw | *sm.* pavilion; flag, banner; ward (of a hospital); exhibitor's building

pavimento | pavi'mẽtʋ | *sm.* paving; floor, story (of a building)

pavio | pa'viʋ | *sm.* wick. **-de fio a p.** from beginning to end

pavoa | pa'voa | *sf.* peahen

pavonear-se | pavonɪ'aʀsɪ | *vr.* to strut, to swagger

pavor | pa'voʀ | *sm.* fright, dread, horror

pavoroso -sa | pavo'rozʋ -'rʋza |

a. frightful, dreadful

paz | 'pa∫ | *sf.* peace; calm, quiet. **-deixe-me em p.!** leave me alone!

pé | 'pε | *sm.* foot; hind foot of a horse; bottom; tree; state of affairs; (colloq.) excuse (for doing something). **-andar a p.** to walk. **-ao p. da letra** literally. **-dar p.** to be shallow; (slang) to be possible

peão | pɩ'ãw | *sm.* horse tamer; (chess) pawn

peça | 'pεsa | *sf.* piece, part; room of a house; (theat.) play; (colloq.) practical joke. **-p. de vestuário** garment. **-pregar uma p.** to play a practical joke. **-peças sobressalentes** spare parts

pecado | pe'kadʋ | *sm.* sin

pecador -dora | peka'doR | *smf.* sinner

pecaminoso -sa | pekami'nozʋ -'nʷza | *a.* sinful

pecar | pe'kaR | *vi.* to sin

pechincha | pɩ'xĩxa | *sf.* (colloq.) bargain, buy

peçonha | pe'soɴa | *sf.* poison

peçonhento -ta | peso'ɴẽtʋ | *a.* poisonous, venomous

pecuária | peku'aria | *sf.* cattle raising

pecuário -ria | peku'ariʋ | *a.* of or pertaining to cattle

peculiar | pekuli'aR | *a.* particular, special, characteristic

pecúlio | pe'kuliʋ | *sm.* savings, money reserve

pedaço | pe'dasʋ | *sm.* piece, portion, fragment

pedágio | pe'dajiʋ | *sm.* toll (on road, bridge etc.)

pedal | pe'dal | *sm.* pedal

pedante | pe'dãtɩ | *smf.* pedant / *a.* pedantic; pretentious

pé-de-meia | 'pedɩ'meya | *sm.* nest egg, savings

pé-de-moleque | 'pedɩmʋ'lεkɩ | *sm.* kind of peanut brittle; pavement made of stones of ir-

regular form

pedestal | pede∫'tal | *sm.* pedestal, base

pedestre | pe'dε∫trɩ | *smf. a.* pedestrian

pedicuro | pedi'kurʋ | *sm.* chiropodist

pedido | pɩ'didʋ | *sm.* request; order (for goods); petition

pedinte | pɩ'dĩtɩ | *smf.* beggar, mendicant

pedir | pɩ'diR | *vt.* to solicit, to ask for; to request. **-p. desculpas** to apologize. **-p. emprestado** to borrow. **-p. a mão** to ask the hand of (in marriage)

pedra | 'pεdra | *sf.* stone. **-p. angular** cornerstone. **-p. de amolar** grindstone

pedra-pomes | pεdra'pomɩ∫ | *sf.* pumice, pumice-stone

pedra-sabão | pεdrasa'bãw | *sf.* soapstone

pedregoso -sa | pedre'gozʋ -'gʷza | *a.* rocky, stony

pedreira | pe'dreyra | *sf.* quarry, stone pit

pedreiro | pe'dreyrʋ | *sm.* mason, stoneworker

pega | 'pεga | *sf.* tweezer-like electrical connection; setting of concrete; (colloq.) riot (with police repression)

pega | 'pega | *sf.* magpie

pegada | pe'gada | *sf.* footprint; (soccer) catch made by a goalkeeper

pegado -da | pe'gadʋ | *a.* taken; near, close by, next door (house)

pegar | pe'gaR | *vt.* to catch; to stick; to grab, to seize; to contract (disease); (colloq.) to understand / *vi.* to stick, to adhere; to take root; to start (motor)

pego -ga | 'pεgʋ | *a.* (colloq.) = *pegado -da*

peitilho | pey'tiʟʋ | *sm.* shirt-front

peito | 'peytʋ | *sm.* chest; breast, bosom; (colloq.) courage. **-p.**

do pé instep. -tomar a p. to take to heart

peitoril | peytʋ'ril | sm. window-ledge; parapet

peixada | pey'xada | sf. fish stew

peixaria | peyxa'ria | sf. shop where fishes are sold

peixe | 'peyxɩ | sm. fish

peixeiro | pey'xeyrʋ | sm. fishmonger

pejo | 'pejʋ | sm. shyness; shame. -ter p. to be ashamed

pejorativo -va | pejora'tivʋ | a. pejorative

pelada | pe'lada | sf. (colloq.) informal soccer game; bald spot

pelado -da | pe'ladʋ | a. bald; bare; (colloq.) naked

pelanca | pe'lãka | sf. trimmings, inedible tag ends of meat; loose fold of skin

pelar | pe'laR | vt. to skin, to peel; to scald, to burn; to fleece

pele | 'pɛlɩ | sf. skin; hide; fur; rind, peel

peleja | pe'leja | sf. fight, struggle, battle

pelejar | pele'jaR | vi. to fight, to struggle; to toil

pelica | pɩ'lika | sf. kid leather

pelicano | pɩli'kanʋ | sm. pelican

película | pɩ'likula | sf. film; motion picture; pellicle

pelintra | pɩ'lĩtra | sm. dandy, fop / a. dandy, foppish

pelo -la | pelʋ | contr. of por + o, a for the; on the; at the; from the; of the; in the; through the. -p. amor de Deus for the love of God; (colloq.) for Christ's sake!

pêlo | 'pelʋ | sm. hair; fur. -em p. (colloq.) naked. -montar em p. to ride bareback

pelotão | pelo'tãw | sm. platoon, squad

pelourinho | pelow'riɴʋ | sm. pillory, stocks

pelúcia | pe'lusia | sf. plush

peludo -da | pɩ'ludʋ | a. hairy, furry; (colloq.) extremely lucky

pena | 'pena | sf. feather; writing pen; punishment; (law) sentence; compassion; grief, pain. -dar or fazer p. to arouse pity. -não valer a p. to not be worth bothering about. -p. d'água water gauge. -p. de morte death sentence. -que p.! what a pity!

penacho | pe'naxʋ | sm. crest; tuft of feathers

penal | pe'nal | a. penal

penalidade | penali'dadɩ | sf. penalty

penar | pe'naR | vi. to suffer

penca | 'pẽka | sf. bunch (of bananas, keys). -em p. (colloq.) galore

pendão | pẽ'dãw | sm. banner, flag

pendência | pẽ'dẽsia | sf. contention, quarrel, dispute

pendente | pẽ'dẽtɩ | sm. pendant / a. hanging, drooping; pending (action etc.)

pender | pẽ'deR | vi. to hang, to be suspended from; to incline; to tend to; to be pending

pendor | pẽ'doR | sm. inclination, propensity

pêndulo | 'pẽdulʋ | sm. pendulum

pendurar | pẽdu'raR | vt. to hang; (colloq.) to pawn

penedo | pe'nedʋ | sm. rock, cliff

peneira | pe'neyra | sf. sieve, sifter

peneirar | peney'raR | vt. to sift / vi. (colloq.) to drizzle

penetra | pe'nɛtra | smf. (colloq.) intruder, gatecrasher

penetração | penetra'sãw | sf. penetration; perspicacity

penetrar | pene'traR | vt. to penetrate; to pierce; (colloq.) to intrude

penha | 'peɴa | sf. rock, cliff

penhasco | pe'ɴaʃkʋ | sm. cliff, crag

penhor | pe'ɴoR | sm. pledge, pawn; deposit; bond. -casa de penhores pawnshop

penhorado -da | peɴo'radʋ | a. pledged; obliged, indebted

penhorar | peNO'raR | *vt.* to pledge; to distrain (goods); to put under obligation

península | pe'nĩsula | *sf.* peninsula

penitência | peni'tẽsia | *sf.* penitence, contrition

penitenciária | penitẽsi'aria | *sf.* penitentiary

penitenciário -ria | penitẽsi'ario | *a.* of or pertaining to a penitentiary

penitente | peni'tẽtɩ | *smf. a.* penitent

penoso -sa | pe'nozo -'nɔza | *a.* painful; distressing

pensado -da | pẽ'sado | *a.* deliberate

pensador -dora | pẽsa'doR | *smf.* thinker

pensamento | pẽsa'mẽto | *sm.* thought; thinking; opinion

pensão | pẽ'sãw | *sf.* pension, allowance; boarding-house, board. **-p. de alimentos** (law) alimony

pensar | pẽ'saR | *vt.* to think; to consider, to ponder / *vi.* to think; to meditate; to intend. **-só em p.** at the very thought

pensativo -va | pẽsa'tivo | *a.* pensive, thoughtful

pente | 'pẽtɩ | *sm.* comb

penteadeira | pẽtɩa'deyra | *sf.* dressing-table

penteado | pẽtɩ'ado | *sm.* way hair is dressed, hair-do

pentear | pẽtɩ'aR | *vt.* to comb

penugem | pe'nujẽy | *sf.* down, fuzz

penúltimo -ma | pe'nultimo | *a.* penultimate, next to the last

penumbra | pe'nũbra | *sf.* dusk, half-light, twilight

penúria | pe'nuria | *sf.* penury, poverty

pepino | pɩ'pino | *sm.* cucumber; gherkin

pepita | pɩ'pita | *sf.* gold nugget

pequenez | pɩkɩ'neʒ | *sf.* smallness

pequenino -na | pɩkɩ'nino | *smf.* little one / *a.* tiny

pequeno -na | pɩ'keno | *sm.* boy; boy-friend; *sf.* girl; girl--friend / *a.* small, little

pêra | 'pera | *sf.* pear; goatee

peralta | pe'ralta | *sm.* mischievous child; fop, dandy, idler / *a.* mischievous

perambular | perãbu'laR | *vi.* to stroll; to wander, to roam

perante | pe'rãtɩ | *prep.* before, in the presence of

percalço | peR'kalso | *sm.* drawback, disadvantage

perceber | peRse'beR | *vt.* to perceive; to notice; to receive, to draw (salary)

percentagem | peRsẽ'tajẽy | *sf.* percentage

percepção | peRsep'sãw | *sf.* perception; receiving (salary, fees etc.)

percevejo | peRse'vejo | *sm.* bedbug; thumbtack, drawing--pin

percorrer | peRko'ReR | *vt.* to travel all over; to go through; to examine; to glance over, to peruse

percurso | peR'kuRso | *sm.* course, route, way

percussão | peRku'sãw | *sf.* percussion. **-instrumento de p.** percussion instrument

perda | 'peRda | *sf.* loss; damage, waste

perdão | peR'dãw | *sm.* pardon, forgiveness / *interj.* sorry!

perder | peR'deR | *vt.* to lose; to ruin; to miss (train, chance etc.). **-p.-se** to go astray; to disgrace oneself. **-p. de vista** to lose sight of

perdição | peRdi'sãw | *sf.* perdition; wreck, ruin

perdigueiro -ra | peRdi'geyro | *smf.* retriever, bird dog (esp. the pointers)

perdiz | peR'diʒ | *sf.* partridge

perdoar | peRdo'aR | *vt.* to pardon, to forgive; to excuse

perdulário -ria | peʀdu'larıʋ | *smf.*
waster, squanderer / *a.* prod-
igal, wasteful

perdurar | peʀdu'raʀ | *vi.* to last
long, to abide

perecer | pere'seʀ | *vi.* to perish; to
die

peregrinação | pɩrɩgrina'sãw | *sf.*
pilgrimage

peregrino -na | pɩrɩ'grinʋ | *smf.*
pilgrim

pereira | pe'reyra | *sf.* pear-tree

peremptório -ria | perẽp'tɔrıʋ | *a.*
peremptory, decisive, final

perene | pe'renɩ | *a.* perennial,
lasting, enduring

perereca | pere'rɛka | *sf.* tree-frog,
tree-toad

perfazer | peʀfa'zeʀ | *vt.* to com-
plete; to make up (the required
number etc.)

perfeição | peʀfey'sãw | *sf.*
perfection

perfeito -ta | peʀ'feytʋ | *a.* perfect;
complete

perfídia | peʀ'fidia | *sf.* perfidy,
treachery

perfil | peʀ'fil | *sm.* profile; outline

perfilar | peʀfi'laʀ | *vt.* to draw the
profile of. **-p.-se** to stand up
straight

perfilhar | peʀfi'laʀ | *vt.* (law) to
legitimate (a child); to adopt
(principle etc.)

perfumar | peʀfu'maʀ | *vt.* to per-
fume, to scent

perfumaria | peʀfuma'ria | *sf.* per-
fume shop

perfume | peʀ'fumɩ | *sm.* per-
fume, fragrance

perfuração | peʀfura'sãw | *sf.* per-
foration, drilling

perfurar | peʀfu'raʀ | *vt.* to perfo-
rate, to drill; to puncture

pergaminho | peʀga'minʋ | *sm.*
parchment; (colloq.) university
diploma

pergunta | peʀ'gũta | *sf.* question.
-p. de algibeira tricky question

perguntar | peʀgũ'taʀ | *vt.* to ask,
to inquire; to question, to

interrogate

perícia | pɩ'risia | *sf.* skill; (law)
examination by experts

periferia | pɩrifɩ'ria | *sf.* periphery

perigar | pɩrɩ'gaʀ | *vi.* to be in
danger

perigo | pɩ'rigʋ | *sm.* danger; (*pl.*)
perils. **-pôr em p.** to endanger

perigoso -sa | pɩrɩ'gozʋ -'gʋza | *a.*
dangerous; risky, hazardous

periódico -ca | pɩrı'ɔdikʋ | *sm. a.*
periodical

período | pɩ'rıʋdʋ | *sm.* period;
era; (gram.) sentence

peripécia | pɩrı'pɛsia | *sf.* vicissi-
tude; adventure

periquito | pɩrı'kitʋ | *sm.* par(r)a-
keet; any small parrot

periscópio | pɩrıʃ'kʋpiʋ | *sm.*
periscope

perito -ta | pɩ'ritʋ | *smf.* expert / *a.*
expert; experienced

perito-contador | pɩ'ritʋkõta'doʀ |
sm. accountant

perjurar | peʀju'raʀ | *vi.* to com-
mit perjury

perjúrio | peʀ'juriʋ | *sm.* perjury

permanecer | peʀmane'seʀ | *vi.* to
remain, to stay; to last, to
continue

permanência | peʀma'nẽsia | *sf.*
permanence; stay, sojourn

permanente | peʀma'nẽtɩ | *sm.*
free pass or ticket; *sf.* perma-
nent wave (hair) / *a.* perma-
nent; lasting, enduring

permeio | peʀ'meyʋ | *adv.* midst.
-de p. between

permissão | peʀmi'sãw | *sf.* per-
mission; permit

permitir | peʀmi'tiʀ | *vt.* to permit,
to allow, to let

permuta | peʀ'muta | *sf.* ex-
change; barter; transfer

permutar | peʀmu'taʀ | *vt.* to per-
mute, to exchange

perna | 'pɛrna | *sf.* leg

perneta | peʀ'neta | *smf.* one-
-legged person

pernicioso -sa | peʀnisi'ozʋ -'ʋza |
a. pernicious, harmful

pernil | peʀˈnil | *sm.* hind leg (of pork, mutton or veal)

pernilongo -ga | pɪʀniˈlõgʊ | *sm.* any long-legged mosquito / *a.* long-legged

pernoitar | peʀnoyˈtaʀ | *vi.* to stay overnight

pérola | ˈpeʀʊla | *sf.* pearl / *a.* of the colo(u)r of a pearl

perpetuidade | peʀpetuiˈdadɪ | *sf.* perpetuity

perpétuo -tua | peʀˈpɛtuʊ | *a.* perpetual

perplexidade | peʀpleksiˈdadɪ | *sf.* perplexity, bewilderment

perplexo -xa | peʀˈplɛksʊ | *a.* perplexed, bewildered, puzzled

persa | ˈpɛʀsa | *smf. a.* Persian

perseguição | pɪʀsɪgiˈsãw | *sf.* pursuit; persecution

perseguidor -dora | pɪʀsɪgiˈdoʀ | *smf.* pursuer; persecutor / *a.* pursuing

perseguir | pɪʀsɪˈgiʀ | *vt.* to pursue; to persecute; to harass

perseverança | peʀseveˈrãsa | *sf.* perseverance, persistence

perseverar | peʀseveˈraʀ | *vi.* to persevere, to persist

persiana | peʀsiˈana | *sf.* Venetian blind

persignar-se | peʀsigˈnaʀsɪ | *vr.* to cross oneself

persistente | peʀsiʒˈtẽtɪ | *a.* persistent, persevering

persistir | peʀsiʒˈtiʀ | *vt.* to persist, to persevere

personagem | peʀsoˈnajẽy | *smf.* character (in a play etc.); personage

personalidade | peʀsonaliˈdadɪ | *sf.* personality

perspectiva | peʀʒpekˈtiva | *sf.* perspective; prospect. **-ter em p.** to expect

perspicaz | peʀʒpiˈkaʒ | *a.* perspicatious, keen, acute, shrewd

persuadir | peʀsuaˈdiʀ | *vt.* to persuade, to convince

persuasão | peʀsuaˈzãw | *sf.* persuasion

persuasivo -va | peʀsuaˈzivʊ | *a.* persuasive, convincing

pertencente | peʀtẽˈsẽtɪ | *a.* belonging; appertaining

pertencer | peʀtẽˈseʀ | *vi.* to belong; to concern

pertinácia | peʀtiˈnasia | *sf.* pertinacity; obstinacy

pertinaz | peʀtiˈnaʒ | *a.* pertinacious; obstinate

pertinente | peʀtiˈnẽtɪ | *a.* pertinent, relevant

perto | ˈpɛʀtʊ | *adv.* near, nearby, close. **-conhecer de p.** to be well--acquainted

perturbação | peʀtuʀbaˈsãw | *sf.* disturbance, agitation; ailment

perturbar | peʀtuʀˈbaʀ | *vt.* to disturb, to upset

peru | pɪˈru | *sm.* turkey

perua | pɪˈrua | *sf.* hen turkey

peruano -na | pɪruˈanʊ | *smf. a.* Peruvian

peruca | pɪˈruka | *sf.* peruke, wig

perversão | peʀveʀˈsãw | *sf.* perversion

perversidade | peʀveʀsiˈdadɪ | *sf.* perversity, wickedness

perverso -sa | peʀˈvɛʀsʊ | *smf.* wicked person / *a.* perverse, wicked

perverter | peʀveʀˈteʀ | *vt.* to pervert, to corrupt

pesadelo | pezaˈdelʊ | *sm.* nightmare

pesado -da | peˈzadʊ | *a.* heavy; indigestible; rich (food); vulgar; expensive

pêsames | ˈpezamɪʒ | *smpl.* condolences, sympathy

pesar | peˈzaʀ | *sm.* sorrow, grief, regret / *vt. vi.* to weigh. **-p. na balança** to have influence

pesaroso -sa | pezaˈrozʊ -ˈrʊza | *a.* sorry, regretful

pesca | ˈpɛʃka | *sf.* fishing; (sport) angling

pescada | peʃˈkada | *sf.* any of various weakfishes; hake

pescado | peʃˈkadʊ | *sm.* any fish (esp. for food)

pescador -dora | peʒka'doʀ | *sm.* fisherman; *sf.* fisherwoman; *smf.* (sport) angler / *a.* fishing

pescar | peʒ'kaʀ | *vt.* to fish

pescoço | peʃ'kosʊ | *sm.* neck

peso | 'pezʊ | *sm.* weight; burden; peso (monetary unit). **-p. líquido** net weight. **-p. bruto** gross weight

pesquisa | pɪʃ'kiza | *sf.* research

pêssego | 'pesɪgʊ | *sm.* peach

pessimista | pɪsi'miʃta | *smf.* pessimist / *a.* pessimistic

péssimo -ma | 'pɛsimʊ | *a.* very badly

pessoa | pe'soa | *sf.* person, individual. **-p. física** person having a civil status. **-p. jurídica** legal entity

pessoal | pesʊ'al | *sm.* personnel; (colloq.) people / *a.* personal

pestana | peʃ'tana | *sf.* eyelash. **-queimar as pestanas** to burn the midnight oil. **-tirar um a p.** to take a nap

pestanejar | peʃtane'jaʀ | *vi.* to blink

peste | 'pɛʃtɪ | *sf.* plague; nuisance, pest

peta | 'peta | *sf.* fib, lie

pétala | 'pɛtala | *sf.* petal

peteca | pe'tɛka | *sf.* sort of shuttlecock played with the palm of the hand

petição | pɪti'sãw | *sf.* petition; appeal

peticionar | petisio'naʀ | *vi.* to petition

petiscar | pɪtiʃ'kaʀ | *vt.* to nibble, to eat tidbits

petisco | pɪ'tiʃkʊ | *sm.* tidbit, morsel, dainty

petiz | pɪ'tiʃ | *sm.* child

petrechos | pe'trexʊʃ | *smpl.* equipment, outfit, gear

petrificar | petrifi'kaʀ | *vt.* to petrify

petroleiro | petro'leyrʊ | *sm.* oil tanker

petróleo | pe'trɔlɪʊ | *sm.* petroleum, oil

petulância | petu'lãsia | *sf.* insolence, flippancy, boldness

petulante | petu'lãtɪ | *a.* insolent, impertinent

pia | 'pia | *sf.* sink, wash basin. **-p. batismal** baptismal font

piada | pi'ada | *sf.* joke; gag

pianista | pia'niʃta | *smf.* pianist

piano | pi'anʊ | *sm.* piano. **-p. de cauda** grand piano

pião | pi'ãw | *sm.* top (toy)

piar | pi'aʀ | *vi.* to peep, to cheep

picada | pi'kada | *sf.* prick (of needle etc.); sting (of insect); (aeron.) nose dive; narrow pass cut through a forest. **-p. de cobra** snake bite

picadeiro | pika'deyrʊ | *sm.* circus ring; riding arena (as in a circus)

picadinho | pika'diɴʊ | *sm.* minced meat, hash

picado -da | pi'kadʊ | *a.* punctured; stung; chopped; pock-marked; choppy (sea)

picante | pi'kãtɪ | *a.* piquant, sharp; peppery; malicious, spicy

pica-pau | pika'paw | *sm.* woodpecker

picar | pi'kaʀ | *vt.* to sting, to bite; to prick; to puncture; to spur; to mince. **-p.-se** to prick oneself; to take offence / *vi.* to itch; to dive (an aircraft)

picaresco -ca | pika'reʃkʊ | *a.* picaresque; ludicrous

picareta | pika'reta | *sf.* pick; *smf.* (colloq.) swindler

piche | 'pixɪ | *sm.* pitch

pico | 'pikʊ | *sm.* peak, summit; sharp point. **-e p.** (colloq.) and a bit, about

picolé | piko'lɛ | *sm.* popsicle (ice cream on a stick)

piedade | pie'dadɪ | *sm.* piety; pity, compassion

piedoso -sa | pie'dozʊ -'dɔza | *a.* pious, devote; compassionate

piegas | pi'ɛgaʃ | *a.* namby-pamby, maudlin, silly

pieguice | pie'gisι | *sf.* namby-pamby, sentimentality

pifão | pi'fãw | *sm.* (colloq.) binge, drinking-bout

pifar | pi'faʀ | *vi.* (colloq.) to conk out, to fail to function

pigarrear | pigaʀι'aʀ | *vi.* to clear the throat

pigarro | pi'gaʀυ | *sm.* a clearing of the throat

pigmeu -méia | pig'mew -'mɛya | *smf. a.* pigmy

pijama | pi'jama | *sm.* pajamas

pilão | pi'lãw | *sm.* pestle; heavy wooden mortar (for pounding grain etc.)

pilar | pi'laʀ | *sm.* pillar / *vt.* to pestle, to pound

pileque | pi'lɛkι | *sm.* (colloq.) drinking-bout, binge

pilha | 'piLa | *sf.* pile, heap; (elect.) battery

pilhagem | pi'Lajẽy | *sf.* plunder, rapine

pilhar | pi'laʀ | *vt.* to plunder; (colloq.) to catch. **-p.-se** to find oneself (in a given condition)

pilhéria | pi'Lɛria | *sf.* joke, jest

pilotar | pilo'taʀ | *vt.* to pilot; to steer a vessel or an aircraft

pilotis | pilo'tiʃ | *smpl.* stilts (for a building)

piloto | pi'lotυ | *sm.* pilot

pílula | 'pilula | *sf.* pill / *interj.* (*pl.*, colloq.) shucks!

pimenta | pi'mẽta | *sf.* pepper

pimenta-do-reino | pi'mẽta-dυ'ʀeynυ | *sf.* black pepper

pimenta-malagueta | pi'mẽtamala'geta | *sf.* red pepper

pimentão | pimẽ'tãw | *sm.* pimiento, sweet pepper

pimpolho | pĩ'poLυ | *sm.* (colloq.) child, baby

pináculo | pi'nakulυ | *sm.* pinnacle, summit

pinça | 'pĩsa | *sf.* tweezers; pincers

píncaro | 'pĩkarυ | *sm.* pinnacle, summit, highest point

pincel | pĩ'sɛl | *sm.* paintbrush, brush. **-p. de barba** shaving-brush

pincelada | pĩse'lada | *sf.* brush stroke

pinga | 'pĩga | *sf.* (colloq.) = *cachaça*

pingar | pĩ'gaʀ | *vt.* to sprinkle / *vi.* to drip; to leak; to sprinkle (rain)

pingente | pĩ'jẽtι | *sm.* pendent, pendant (jewelry); (colloq.) hanger-on (on trains etc.)

pingo | 'pĩgυ | *sm.* drop

pingue-pongue | 'pĩgι'põgι | *sm.* ping-pong, table tennis

pingüim | pĩ'gwĩ | *sm.* penguin

pinha | 'piNa | *sf.* pine-cone; sweet-sop

pinheiro | pi'Neyrυ | *sm.* pine, pine tree

pinho | 'piNυ | *sm.* pine, pine timber, pine tree

pino | 'pinυ | *sm.* (mech.) peg, pin; the highest point. **-a p.** upright. **-com o sol a p.** at high noon

pinote | pi'nɔtι | *sm.* a horse's curvet; buck, leap

pinta | 'pĩta | *sf.* spot; mole; (colloq.) characteristic, expression of the face; (colloq.) fellow, guy

pintar | pĩ'taʀ | *vt.* to paint; to portray, to represent; to tint (hair). **-p.-se** to use make-up. **-p. o sete** to paint the town red / *vi.* (colloq.) to turn grey (hair); (slang) to give signals of; (slang) to show up

pinto | 'pĩtυ | *sm.* chick; (slang) easy thing

pintor -tora | pĩ'toʀ | *smf.* painter

pintura | pĩ'tura | *sf.* painting, picture in paint; make-up. **-p. a óleo** oil painting

pio -a | 'piυ | *sm.* chirp; call (of a bird); birdcall (also the device). **-não dar um p.** to not utter a sound / *a.* pious

piolho | pi'oLυ | *sm.* louse

pioneiro -ra | pio'neyrυ | *smf. a.* pioneer

pior | pi'ɔʀ | *a. adv.* worse, worst

piorar | pio'ʀaʀ | *vt. vi.* to worsen,

to make or to become worse

pipa | ˈpipa | *sf.* cask, barrel; paper kite

piparote | pipaˈrɔtɪ | *sm.* flick

pipi | piˈpi | *sm.* (baby talk and colloq.) urine; child's sex. **-fazer p.** to urinate

pipoca | piˈpɔka | *sf.* popcorn

pique | ˈpikɪ | *sm.* home base (in the game of tag); game of tag; a small puncture. **-a p.** upright. **-ir a p.** to sink. **-a p. de** about to

piquê | piˈke | *sm.* nose dive (of an aircraft)

piquenique | pikɪˈnikɪ | *sm.* picnic

pirâmide | piˈramidɪ | *sf.* pyramid

pirão | piˈrãw | *sm.* manioc mush; purée

pirata | piˈrata | *smf. a.* pirate

pirataria | pirataˈria | *sf.* piracy

pires | ˈpirɪʒ | *sm.* (*sing* and *pl.*) saucer

pirilampo | piriˈlãpʊ | *sm.* firefly

piroga | piˈrɔga | *sf.* piragua, dug-out canoe

pirotecnia | pirotekˈnia | *sf.* pyrotechnics

pirraça | piˈʀasa | *sf.* spite; obstinacy. **-fazer (algo) de p.** to do (something) out of spite

pirralho -lha | piˈʀaʎʊ | *smf.* child, brat

pirulito | piruˈlitʊ | *sm.* lollypop, lollipop

pisada | piˈzada | *sf.* footstep, footprint

pisado -da | piˈzadʊ | *a.* stepped on; bruised; crushed

pisar | piˈzaʀ | *vt.* to tread on; to crush; to bruise / *vi.* to step

piscar | piʃˈkaʀ | *vt. vi.* to wink, to blink; to twinkle

piscina | piˈsina | *sf.* swimming-pool

piso | ˈpizʊ | *sm.* ground floor, pavement

pista | ˈpiʃta | *sf.* track, trail; trace, clue; race track; landing strip

pistão | piʃˈtãw | *sm.* piston; (mus.) trumpet

pistola | piʃˈtɔla | *sf.* pistol

pistolão | piʃtoˈlãw | *sm.* (colloq.) strong recommendation; influent person that can get someone a job etc.

pistoleiro | piʃtoˈleyrʊ | *sm.* gunman, hired gun

pitada | piˈtada | *sf.* pinch (of snuff, salt etc.)

piteira | piˈteyra | *sf.* cigarette-holder, mouthpiece (of a pipe)

pitéu | piˈtɛw | *sm.* delicacy, tidbit

pito | ˈpitʊ | *sm.* (colloq.) tobacco pipe; (colloq.) scolding, rebuke. **-passar um p.** to scold

pitoresco -ca | pitoˈreʃkʊ | *a.* picturesque

pitu | piˈtu | *sm.* large freshwater prawn

pixaim | pixaˈĩ | *sm.* (colloq., pej.) kinky hair. / *a.* kinky

placa | ˈplaka | *sf.* plate (thin sheet of metal); plaque; insignia, badge; automobile licence plate

placar | plaˈkaʀ | *sm.* (sports) score; score-board

plácido -da | ˈplasidʊ | *a.* placid, calm

plagiar | plajiˈaʀ | *vt.* to plagiarize

plaina | ˈplayna | *sf.* plane, jack-plane

planador | planaˈdoʀ | *sm.* (aeron.) glider

planalto | plaˈnaltʊ | *sm.* plateau, tableland

planar | plaˈnaʀ | *vi.* to glide

planejamento | planejaˈmẽtʊ | *sm.* planning, projecting

planejar | planeˈjaʀ | *vt.* to plan

planeta | plaˈneta | *sm.* planet

plangente | plãˈjẽtɪ | *a.* plaintive, mournful

planície | plaˈnisiɪ | *sf.* plain; prairie

plano -na | ˈplanʊ | *sm.* plan, scheme, project / *a.* plane, level; even

planta | ˈplãta | *sf.* plant; plan, blueprint. **-p. do pé** sole of the foot

plantação | plãtaˈsãw | *sf.* plantation; planting

plantão | plã'tãw | *sm.* late shift at a hospital, night shift. **-de p.** on duty

plantar | plã'taʀ | *vt.* to plant; to cultivate; to set up; to establish

plantio | plã'tiʋ | *sm.* planting

plástica | 'plaʃtika | *sf.* plastic surgery; shape (of the body)

plástico -ca | 'plaʃtikʋ | *sm.* plastic / *a.* plastic, pliable

plataforma | plata'fɷʀma | *sf.* platform; political platform. **-p. continental** continental shelf

platéia | pla'tɛya | *sf.* main floor of a theatre; the audience on the main floor. **-cadeira de p.** orchestra seat

platina | pla'tina | *sf.* platinum

plausível | plaw'zivɪl | *a.* plausible, reasonable

plebe | 'plɛbɪ | *sf.* populace, the common herd, the masses

plebeu-béia | ple'bew-'beya | *smf. a.* plebeian

plebiscito | plɪbi'sitʋ | *sm.* plebiscite

pleitear | pleytɪ'aʀ | *vt.* to seek, to strive for; to plead; to litigate

pleito | 'pleytʋ | *sm.* (law) plea; lawsuit; contest

plenário -ria | ple'nariʋ | *sm.* plenary assembly or council / *a.* plenary, full. **-sessão plenária** plenary seating, plenary meeting

plenitude | pleni'tudɪ | *sf.* fullness, completeness

pleno -na | 'plenʋ | *a.* full, complete; high, broad. **-em p. mar** on the high seas. **-plenos poderes** full powers. **-sessão plena** plenary session

pluma | 'pluma | *sf.* feather, plume

plumagem | plu'majẽy | *sf.* plumage, feathers

plutocrata | pluto'krata | *smf.* plutocrat / *a.* plutocratic

pneu | 'pnew colloq. pɪ'new | *sm.* tire (short for pneumatic tire)

pneumática | pnew'matika | *sf.*

(phys.) pneumatics

pneumático -ca | pnew'matikʋ | *sm.* pneumatic tire / *a.* pneumatic

pó | 'pɷ | *sm.* powder; dust. **-fermento em p.** baking powder. **-tirar o p.** to dust

pobre | 'pɷbrɪ | *smf.* beggar / *a.* poor, needy; barren (soil). **-p. de espírito** simple-minded

pobreza | po'breza | *sf.* poverty, need, want, penury

poça | 'posa | *sf.* shallow pool, puddle (of water)

poção | pʋ'sãw | *sm.* potion; deep hole in a river

pocilga | pʋ'silga | *sf.* pigpen; dirty place

poço | 'posʋ *pl.* 'pɷsʋʒ | *sm.* well; pool (in a river); shaft, pit

podar | po'daʀ | *vt.* to prune, to clip

pó-de-arroz | 'pɷdɪa'ʀoʒ | *sm.* face powder

poder | po'deʀ | *sm.* power, capacity; authority; (*pl.*) procuration. **-em p. de** in the hands of / *vt.* (followed by an infinitive) to be able / *vi.* to have the power of or to. **-a mais não p.** to the utmost

poderio | pʋde'riʋ | *sm.* power, force

poderoso -sa | pode'rozʋ -'ɷza | *a.* powerful, mighty; vigorous

podre | 'podrɪ | *a.* rotten, putrid; corrupt. **-p. de rico** (colloq.) filthy rich

podridão | pʋdri'dãw | *sf.* rottenness, decay

poeira | pʋ'eyra | *sf.* dust

poeirento -ta | pʋey'rẽtʋ | *a.* dusty

poema | pʋ'ema | *sm.* poem

poente | pʋ'ẽtɪ | *sm.* sunset / *a.* setting (sun)

poesia | pʋɪ'zia | *sf.* poetry; short poem

poeta | pʋ'eta | *sm.* poet

poético -ca | pʋ'etikʋ | *a.* poétic, poetical

poetisa | pᴠe'tiza | *sf.* poetess

pois | 'poyʒ | *adv.* so, then, consequently. **-p. bem** very well. **-p. é** well, well then, that's right. **-p. sim** (ironically) oh sure! **-p. não** (colloq.) of course!, certainly! / *conj.* for, because; as, since, so that

polaco -ca | po'lakᴠ | *smf. a.* (pej.) Pole, Polish

polainas | po'laynaʒ | *sfpl.* spats

poldro -dra | 'poldrᴠ | *sm.* colt; *sf.* filly

polegada | pᴠle'gada | *sf.* inch

polegar | pᴠle'gaʀ | *sm.* thumb; big toe

poleiro | pᴠ'leyrᴠ | *sm.* perch; (colloq.) top gallery in a theatre

polêmica | po'lemika | *sf.* controversy, polemics

polêmico -ca | po'lemikᴠ | *a.* polemic, polemical

pólen | 'pᴐlěy | *sm.* pollen

polichinelo | pᴠlixi'nɛlᴠ | *sm.* punchinello, a Punch

polícia | pᴠ'lisia | *sf.* police, police force; *sm.* constable, policeman

policial | pᴠlisi'al | *sm.* constable, policeman; *sf.* police woman / *a.* police

polidez | pᴠli'deʒ | *sf.* courtesy, politeness, civility

polido -da | pᴠ'lidᴠ | *a.* polished; polite, courteous

poliglota | poli'glᴐta | *smf. a.* polyglot

polimento | pᴠli'mětᴠ | *sm.* polishing, polish, gloss

polir | pᴠ'liʀ | *vt.* to polish

política | pᴠ'litika | *sf.* politics; policy; sagacity

político -ca | pᴠ'litikᴠ | *smf.* politician / *a.* political

politiqueiro -ra | pᴠliti'keyrᴠ | *smf.* petty politician

pólo | 'pᴐlᴠ | *sm.* pole; (sports) polo. **-p. aquático** water polo

polonês -nesa | polo'neʒ -'neza | *sm.* (ling.) Polish; *smf. a.* Pole

polpa | 'polpa | *sf.* pulp, soft mass

polpudo -da | pᴠl'pudᴠ | *a.* pulpy; fleshy; abundant

poltrão -trona | pol'trãw -'trona | *sm.* coward, poltroon / *a.* cowardly, craven

poltrona | pol'trona | *sf.* easy chair; orchestra seat

poluição | pᴠlui'sãw | *sf.* pollution

poluir | pᴠlu'iʀ | *vt.* to pollute

polvilhar | polvi'laʀ | *vt.* to powder, to besprinkle

polvilho | pᴠl'viLᴠ | *sm.* fine tapioca powder

polvo | 'polvᴠ | *sm.* octopus

pólvora | 'pᴐlvᴠra | *sf.* gunpowder

pomada | pᴠ'mada | *sf.* balm, ointment

pomar | po'maʀ | *sm.* orchard

pombal | põ'bal | *sm.* dovecote

pombo -ba | 'põbᴠ | *smf.* pigeon, dove

pombo-correio | 'põbᴠko'ʀeyᴠ | *sm.* carrier pigeon, homing pigeon

pomo | 'pomᴠ | *sm.* pome, apple. **-p. da discórdia** bone of contention

pompa | 'põpa | *sf.* pomp, gala, pageantry

pomposo -sa | põ'pozᴠ -'pᴡza | *a.* pompous

ponderação | põdera'sãw | *sf.* careful consideration; deliberation

ponderado -da | põde'radᴠ | *a.* considerate, sober, judicious

ponderar | põde'raʀ | *vt. vi.* to ponder, to cogitate, to consider; to make a thoughtful statement

ponta | 'põta | *sf.* point; top, peak; end, extremity; butt (of a cigarette). **-estar de p. com alguém** (colloq.) to be at odds with someone. **-na ponta dos pés** on tiptoes. **-fazer uma p.** to play a minor role

pontão | põ'tãw | *sm.* floating bridge, pontoon

pontapé | põta'pɛ | *sm.* kick

pontaria | põta'ria | *sf.* aim. **-fazer**

p. to take aim

ponte | 'põtι | *sf.* bridge. **-p. aérea** (aeron.) air shuttle. **-p. levadiça** lift bridge. **-p. pênsil** suspension bridge

pontear | põtι'aʀ | *vt.* to dot; to stitch to finger (a stringed instrument)

ponteira | põ'teyra | *sf.* tip (as of a cane or umbrella)

ponteiro | põ'teyrʊ | *sm.* hand (of a watch, clock· etc.); point chisel

pontiagudo | põtia'gudʊ | *a.* pointed; peaked

pontificado | põtifi'kadʊ | *sm.* pontificate

pontífice | põ'tifisι | *sm.* pontiff. **-Sumo P.** the Pope

pontilhar | põti'LaR | *vt.* to dot

pontinha | põ'tiNa | *sf.* (colloq.) little bit. **-ser da p.** (colloq.) to be excellent

pontinho | põ'tiNʊ | *sm.* short stitch; speck; (*pl.*, typog.) dots, ellipsis

ponto | 'põtʊ | *sm.* point; dot; stitch; (gram.) full stop, period; spot, place; (theat.) prompter; (*pl.*) subject, matter; (sports) points, score. **-a p. de** on the verge of. **-a tal p. que** to the point of. **-p. de ônibus** bus-stop. **-p. de interrogação** question mark. **-p. e vírgula** semicolon

pontuação | põtua'sãw | *sf.* punctuation

pontual | põtu'al | *a.* punctual

pontualidade | põtuali'dadι | *sf.* punctuality

popa | 'popa | *sf.* stern. **-à p.** astern, aft. **-de vento em p.** (colloq.) flourishing

população | pʊpula'sãw | *sf.* population

popular | pʊpu'laR | *smf.* one of the people / *a.* popular, of the people; admired by the people; common, current

popularidade | pʊpulari'dadι | *sf.* popularity

populoso-sa | pʊpu'lozʊ-'lɔza | *a.* populous, thickly inhabited

pôquer | 'pokeR | *sm.* poker (game of cards)

por | pʊR pʊr | *prep.* by; for; through; per; around; in; to. **-p. assim dizer** so to speak. **-p. atacado** wholesale. **-p. enquanto** for the time being. **-p. extenso** in full, not abbreviated. **-p. volta de** around. **-p. mais que** no matter how. **-p. quê?** why?, for what reason?

pôr | 'poR | *vt.* to put, to place; to set, to lay. **-p. -se** to place oneself; to set (sun). **-p. -se a** to start, to begin. **-p. a mesa** to set the table. **-p. em dia** to bring up to date. **-p. a salvo** to place in safety. **-p. de parte** to set aside. **-p. na rua** to discharge, to fire (an employee) / *vi.* to lay (eggs)

porão | pʊ'rãw | *sm.* (naut.) hold; basement (of a house)

porca | 'pʊRka | *sf.* (zool.) sow; (mech.) nut

porção | pʊR'sãw | *sf.* portion; slice, serving; (colloq.) large quantity

porcaria | pʊRka'ria | *sf.* filth; mess, bungled job; rubbish

porcelana | pʊRse'lana | *sf.* porcelain, china

porcentagem | pʊRsẽ'tajẽy | *sf.* = *percentagem*

porco -ca | 'pʊRkʊ 'pʊRka | *sm.* pig, hog; *sf.* (zool.) sow; (mech.) nut (of a screw). **-carne de p.** pork / *a.* dirty, filthy

porco-do-mato | 'pʊRkʊdʊ'matʊ | *sm.* peccary

porco-espinho | 'pʊRkʊιʃ'piNʊ | *sm.* porcupine

pôr-do-sol | pʊRdʊ'sɔl | *sm.* sunset, sundown

porém | po'rẽy | *conj.* but, however, yet

porfia | pʊR'fia | *sf.* contention, dispute; pertinacity. **-à p.** in a spirit of rivalry

porfiar | pʊRfi'aR | *vi.* to contend,

to dispute; to persist

pormenor | puʀme'nʊʀ | sm. detail, particular

pormenorizar | poʀmenori'zaʀ | vt. to detail, to particularize

poro | 'pʊʀʊ | sm. pore

poroso -sa | po'rozʊ -'rʊza | a. porous

porquanto | pʊʀ'kwãtʊ | conj. as, since, inasmuch as

porque | pʊʀ'kɪ | conj. because, since, as

porquê | pʊʀ'ke | sm. cause, reason, motive. **-o p.** the reason why

porre | 'pɔʀɪ | sm. (colloq., vulg.) drinking spree. **-de p.** (colloq., vulg.) drunk

porrete | pʊ'ʀetɪ | sm. club, cudgel

porta | 'pɔʀta | sf. door; entrance; gateway. **-p. corrediça** sliding door. **-p. da rua** front door. **-por portas travessas** (colloq.) by devious means

porta-aviões | 'pɔʀt(a)avi'õyʒ | sm. aircraft carrier

porta-chaves | 'pɔʀta'xavɪʒ | sm. key-ring

portador -dora | poʀta'doʀ | smf. bearer; messenger

porta-jóias | 'pɔʀta'ʒʊyaʒ | sm. jewel case

portal | poʀ'tal | sm. doorway

porta-luvas | 'pɔʀta'luvaʒ | sm. glove compartment (in a car)

porta-malas | 'pɔʀta'malaʒ | sm. boot, baggage compartment (of a car)

porta-níqueis | 'pɔʀta'nikeyʒ | sm. coin purse

portanto | pʊʀ'tãtʊ | conj. therefore, and so

portão | poʀ'tãw | sm. large gate, gateway; front entrance

portar | poʀ'taʀ | vt. to carry. **-p.-se** to behave

porta-retratos | 'pɔʀtaʀe'tratʊʒ | sm. picture frame

portaria | poʀta'ria | sf. vestibule; reception desk; a government directive, edict or regulation

portátil | poʀ'tatil | a. portable

porta-voz | 'pɔʀta'vɔʒ | sm. megaphone; spokesman

porte | 'pɔʀtɪ | sm. transportation; freightage (fee); postage; deportment, demeanor. **-p. pago** post-paid. **-de grande p.** large; of large tonnage

porteira | poʀ'teyra | sf. gate (of a pasture, farm etc.)

porteiro -ra | poʀ'teyrʊ | smf. door-keeper, janitor, porter

portento | poʀ'tẽtʊ | sm. prodigy; person of uncommon learning or intelligence

portentoso -sa | poʀtẽ'tozʊ -'tʊza | a. marvellous, prodigious

pórtico | 'pɔʀtikʊ | sm. (arch.) portico, porch

portinhola | poʀti'ɴʊla | sf. small door (esp. of a carriage)

porto | 'pɔʀtʊ | sm. port, harbo(u)r; port wine; (cap.) Oporto. **-p. de escala** port of call

porto-franco | 'pɔʀtʊ'frãkʊ | sm. free port

porto-riquenho -nha | 'pɔʀtʊ-ʀi'keɴʊ | smf. a. Puerto Rican, Porto Rican

portuário -ria | poʀtu'ariʊ | smf. dock worker / a. port

português -guesa | pʊʀtu'geʒ -'geza | smf. a. Portuguese

porventura | pʊʀvẽ'tura | adv. perhaps; by any chance

porvir | pʊʀ'viʀ | sm. time to come, future

posar | po'zaʀ | vi. to pose, to sit as a model; to pose affectedly

pose | 'pɔzɪ | sf. pose, posture; act of posing as a model; (photog.) exposure. **-fazer p.** to behave affectedly

pós-escrito | pɔzɪʃ'kritʊ | sm. postscript, P.S.

pós-graduado -da | 'pɔʃgradu'a-dʊ | smf. a. postgraduate

posição | pʊzi'sãw | sf. position, place; posture; circumstances; social rank

positivo -va | puzi'tivʋ | *sm.* positive / *a.* positive; sure, clear, categorical

possante | po'sãtɩ | *a.* powerful, mighty

posse | 'pɔsɩ | *sf.* possession, ownership; (law) appropriation; investiture; (*pl.*) means, wealth. **-tomar p.** to take office

possessão | pose'sãw | *sf.* possession; dominion

possesso -sa | po'sɛsʋ | *a.* possessed, demoniac; mad, furious

possibilidade | posibili'dadɩ | *sf.* possibility

possibilitar | pʋsibili'taʀ | *vt.* to make possible, to facilitate

possível | pʋ'sivɩl | *a.* possible; feasible. **-fazer o p.** to do one's best, to do everything possible

possuidor -dora | pʋsui'doʀ | *smf.* possessor / *a.* possessing

possuir | pʋsu'iʀ | *vt.* to possess, to own; to have

posta | 'pɔsta | *sf.* slice of fish, meat etc. **-p. de peixe** fish stake

postal | poʃ'tal | *sm.* post card, postal card / *a.* postal

postar | poʃ'taʀ | *vt.* to post (a sentinel etc.); to mail. **-p.-se** to place oneself

posta-restante | 'pɔʃtaʀeʃ'tãtɩ | *sf.* general delivery (department in post office)

poste | 'pɔʃtɩ | *sm.* post, pole. **-p. de iluminação** lamppost

postergar | pʋʃteʀ'gaʀ | *vt.* to postpone; to disregard

posteridade | poʃteri'dadɩ | *sf.* posterity; offspring, progeny

posterior | poʃteri'oʀ | *sm.* (colloq.) buttocks / *a.* posterior; farther; hind

posteriormente | poʃterioʀ'mẽtɩ | *adv.* subsequently, afterwards

postiço -ça | pʋʃ'tisʋ | *a.* false; artificial

postigo | pʋʃ'tigʋ | *sm.* small opening in a door or window

posto, -ta | 'poʃtʋ 'pɔʃta | *sm.* po-

sition, place; (mil.) post; (mil.) rank. **-p. de bombeiros** fire-station. **-p. de salvamento** life-guard. **-p. de gasolina** service station / *a.* placed, put; set (said of the sun) / *conj.* although, since, even though. **-p. que** although, since, even though

póstumo -ma | 'pɔʃtumʋ | *a.* posthumous

postura | pʋʃ'tura | *sf.* posture, position; deportment; laying (eggs); municipal ordinance

potassa | po'tasa | *sf.* potash

potável | po'tavɩl | *a.* drinkable

pote | 'pɔtɩ | *sm.* pot, jug, jar

potência | po'tẽsia | *sf.* potency; might; a power (nation); virility

potencial | potẽsi'al | *sm. a.* potential

potente | po'tẽtɩ | *a.* potent; mighty; virile

potro | 'potrʋ | *sm.* colt

pouca-vergonha | powkaveʀ'goNa | *sf.* (colloq.) shameful behaviour

pouco -ca | 'powkʋ | *sm.* little; short time / *a.* little; (*pl.*) few. **-muito p.** very little or few. **-p. caso** disdain / *adv.* slightly, not much; in a small degree. **-daqui a p.** in a little while. **-fazer p. de** to disdain. **-há p.** recently. **-por p.** almost. **-p. a p.** little by little

poupança | pow'pãsa | *sf.* thrift; savings; parsimony. **-medidas de p.** economy measures

poupar | pow'paʀ | *vt.* to save, to economize / *vi.* to stint, to be sparing. **-p.-se** to spare oneself

pouquinho | pow'kiNʋ | *sm.* a wee bit

pousada | pow'zada | *sf.* lodge, inn

pousado -da | pow'zadʋ | *a.* perched, resting

pousar | pow'zaʀ | *vt.* to lay, to put, to set down / *vi.* to perch, to roost; to stay overnight; to settle; (aeron.) to land

pouso | 'powzʋ | *sm.* resting place;

(aeron.) landing

povinho | po'viNʊ | *sm.* rabble, mass

povo | 'povʊ *pl.* 'ρωνυζ | *sm.* people; population; public

povoação | pʊvʊa'sãw | *sf.* village, settlement; population; settling

povoado -da | pʊvʊ'adʊ | *sm.* village, settlement / *a.* populated

povoar | pʊvʊ'aR | *vt.* to people; to stock, to fill with (fish, game etc.)

pra | 'pra | *prep.* and *conj.* colloquial contraction of **para**

praça | 'prasa | *sf.* public square; (com.) market; (mil.) enlisted man. **-assentar** or **sentar p.** to enlist in the army. **-p. forte** fortress

prado | 'pradʊ | *sm.* meadow; field; race-track

praga | 'praga | *sf.* curse, plague; pest; vermin

pragmático -ca | prag'matikʊ | *a.* pragmatic

praguejar | prage'jaR | *vt. vi.* to curse

praia | 'praya | *sf.* beach, shore

prancha | 'prãxa | *sf.* plank; board; gangplank; surf-board

pranto | 'prãtʊ | *sf.* weeping, crying

prata | 'prata | *sf.* silver

prataria | prata'ria | *sf.* silverware

pratarraz | prata'Raζ | *sm.* dish heaped with food

prateado -da | pratɪ'adʊ | *a.* silvery

prateleira | pratɪ'leyra | *sf.* shelf

prática | 'pratika | *sf.* practice, use, usage; training; experience

praticante | prati'kãtɪ | *smf.* apprentice, trainee / *a.* practicing

praticar | prati'kaR | *vt.* to practice; to perform; to commit (a crime); to cut (as an opening in a wall) / *vi.* to act; to exercise (a profession); to train

praticável | prati'kavɪl | *a.* practi-cable, feasible; negotiable (that can be crossed etc.)

prático -ca | 'pratikʊ | *sm.* practician (without a diploma); harbo(u)r pilot / *a.* practical

prato | 'pratʊ | *sm.* dish; plate; course (of a meal); pan (of scales); (*pl.*, mus.) cymbals

praxe | 'praxɪ | *sf.* usage, custom, tradition

prazenteiro -ra | prazẽ'teyrʊ | *a.* jolly, jovial, merry

prazer | pra'zeR | *sm.* pleasure, enjoyment, delight. **-muito p.** how do you do? (greeting on being introduced)

prazo | 'prazʊ | *sm.* term, span; given period of time. **-a p.** in installments. **-vender a p. to sell** on time

preâmbulo | prɪ'ãbulʊ | *sm.* introduction, preface

pré-aviso | prea'vizʊ | *sm.* advance notice, prior notice; forewarning

prebenda | pre'bẽda | *sf.* (eccles.) prebend; (colloq.) bothersome obligation

precário -ria | pre'karɪʊ | *a.* precarious, uncertain; insecure

precaução | prekaw'sãw | *sf.* precaution

precaver | preka'veR | *vt.* to warn, to caution. **-p.-se** to be cautious

prece | 'prɛsɪ | *sf.* prayer

precedência | prese'dẽsia | *sf.* precedence, precedency

preceder | prese'deR | *vt.* to precede, to forerun

preceito | pre'seytʊ | *sm.* precept; rule, principle

preceptor -tora | presep'toR | *smf.* preceptor, tutor

preciosidade | prɪsiozi'dadɪ | *sf.* preciousness, preciosity

precioso -sa | prɪsi'ozʊ - 'ωza | *a.* precious, dear; pretentious, affected

precipício | prɪsi'pisiʊ | *sm.* precipice, abyss

precipitação | prɪsipita'sãw | *sf.*

precipitation

precipitar | prɪsipi'taʀ | *vt. vi.* to precipitate (also chem.); to throw headlong; to hasten. **-p.-se** to rush headlong; to hurl oneself upon

precisão | prɪsi'zãw | *sf.* precision, accuracy; (obs.) need, necessity

precisar | prɪsi'zaʀ | *vt.* to particularize, to specify; to need, to require / *vi.* to be in need

preciso -sa | prɪ'sizʊ | *a.* necessary; precise, accurate

preço | 'presʊ | *sm.* price, cost; value. **-a p. de custo** at cost. **-p. de ocasião** bargain price

precoce | pre'kɔsɪ | *a.* premature, early; precocious

preconceito | prekõ'seytʊ | *sm.* prejudice, bias

preconizar | prekoni'zaʀ | *vt.* to commend publicly, to extol

precursor -sora | prekuʀ'soʀ | *smf.* precursor, forerunner, predecessor

predatório -ria | preda'tɔriʊ | *a.* predatory, plundering

predecessor -sora | predese'soʀ | *smf.* predecessor

predestinado -da | prɪdɪʃti'nadʊ | *a.* predestinate, predestined

predial | predi'al | *a.* of or pertaining to buildings

predicado | prɪdi'kadʊ | *sm.* quality; attribute; (gram.) predicate

predição | prɪdi'sãw | *sf.* prediction, prophecy

predileção | prɪdile'sãw | *sf.* predilection, preference; fondness

predileto -ta | prɪdi'letʊ | *smf. a.* beloved, darling, favourite

prédio | 'predɪʊ | *sm.* building, construction, house

predispor | prediʃ'poʀ | *vt.* to predispose

predizer | predi'zeʀ | *vt.* to predict, to foretell

predominância | predomi'nãsia | *sf.* predominance

predominar | predomi'naʀ | *vi.* to predominate, to prevail

predomínio | predo'miniʊ | *sm.* predominance, supremacy

preencher | prɪĩ'xeʀ | *vt.* to fill in or up; to fulfil, to accomplish; to comply with

prefácio | pre'fasiʊ | *sm.* preface, prologue, introduction

prefeito | pre'feytʊ | *sm.* mayor

prefeitura | prefey'tura | *sf.* City Hall

preferência | prefe'rẽsia | *sf.* preference, choice; priority. **-de p.** preferably

preferir | prɪfɪ'riʀ | *vt.* to prefer

prega | 'prɛga | *sf.* fold, pleat

pregador -dora | prega'doʀ | *smf.* preacher. **-p. de roupa** clothespin

pregão | pre'gãw | *sm.* street vendor's cry; (oral) public proclamation; (pl.) bans of marriage

pregar | pre'gaʀ | *vt.* to nail; to fasten, to fix (as with nails); to deliver (a sermon); to preach (the gospel). **-p. mentiras** to tell lies. **-p. um botão** to sew on a button. **-p. um susto em alguém** to give someone a fright

prego | 'prɛgʊ | *sm.* nail; (slang) pawnshop; (slang) exhaustion. **-pôr no p.** (slang) to pawn. **-dar o p.** (slang) to poop out

pregoeiro | pregʊ'eyrʊ | *sm.* crier; auctioneer

preguiça | prɪ'gisa | *sf.* laziness, indolence; (zool.) sloth

preguiçoso -sa | prɪgi'sozʊ -'sɔza | *a.* lazy, indolent

preito | 'preytʊ | *sm.* homage, token of respect

prejudicar | prɪjudi'kaʀ | *vt.* to damage, to injure, to impair

prejuízo | prɪʒu'izʊ | *sm.* damage; harm, loss

prelado | pre'ladʊ | *sm.* prelate

preleção | prele'sãw | *sf.* lecture

preliminar | prɪlimi'naʀ | *smf. a.* preliminary

prelo | 'prelʊ | *sm.* printing-press. **-no p.** about to be published

prematuro -ra | prema'turʊ | *a.*

premature

premeditado -da | premedi'tadʋ | *a.* deliberate

premeditar | premedi'taʀ | *vt.* to premeditate

premente | pre'mẽtι | *a.* pressing, urgent

premer | pre'meʀ | *vt.* to press

premiar | premi'aʀ | *vt.* to award a prize; to reward

prêmio | 'premiʋ | *sm.* prize, award; (insurance) premium

premissa | pre'misa | *sf.* premiss

prenda | 'prẽda | *sf.* gift, present; talent, endowment. **-prendas domésticas** occupation of a housewife

prendado-da | prẽ'dadʋ | *a.* talented, gifted

prender | prẽ'deʀ | *vt.* to fasten, to attach; to arrest; to imprison; to delay; to captivate

prenhe | 'prɛɲι | *a.* pregnant; full, replete

prenome | pre'nomι | *sm.* first name, Christian name

prensa | 'prẽsa | *sf.* press; printing press

prensar | prẽ'saʀ | *vt.* to press, to compress

prenúncio | pre'nũsιʋ | *sm.* advance sign, sign (of a coming event)

preocupação | prιokupa'sãw | *sf.* concern, worry; preoccupation

preocupar | prιʋku'paʀ | *vt.* to preoccupy; to worry. **-não se preocupe** don't worry

preparação | prepara'sãw | *sf.* preparation

preparar | prepa'raʀ | *vt.* to prepare, to make ready

preparativos | prepara'tivʋʒ | *smpl.* preparations

preparatório -ria | prepara'tɔrιʋ | *sm. (pl.,* obs.) preparatory studies / *a.* preparatory, preparative

preparo | pre'parʋ | *sm.* preparation; (colloq.) education, learning

preponderância | prepõde'rãsia | *sf.* preponderance

preposição | prepʋzi'sãw | *sf.* preposition

prerrogativa | preʀoga'tiva | *sf.* prerogative, privilege

presa | 'preza | *sf.* prize (in war); canine tooth; tusk, fang; claw (of bird of prey)

prescindir | prιsĩ'diʀ | *vt.* (with *prep.* de) to do without, to dispense with

prescindível | prιsĩ'divιl | *a.* dispensable

prescrever | preʃkre'veʀ | *vt.* to prescribe / *vi.* (law) to become outlawed (by prescription)

prescrição | prιʃkri'sãw | *sf.* (law) prescription, order; precept

presença | pre'zẽsa | *sf.* presence; attendance; bearing. **-p. de espírito** presence of mind

presenciar | prezẽsi'aʀ | *vt.* to witness, to be present at (an occurrence)

presente | pre'zẽtι | *sm.* present, now; gift; present tense; (*pl.*) people who are present. **-fazer p. de** to give as a gift

presentemente | prezẽtι'mẽtι | *adv.* at present

presépio | pre'zɛpiʋ | *sm.* Nativity scene, crib

preservação | prezeʀva'sãw | *sf.* preservation

preservar | prezeʀ'vaʀ | *vt.* to preserve; to protect

presidência | prιzi'dẽsia | *sf.* presidency

presidente | prιzi'dẽtι | *sm.* president; chairman / *a.* presiding

presidiário -ria | prιzidi'arιʋ | *smf.* inmate of a penitentiary

presídio | prι'zidiʋ | *sm.* military prison; jail, prison

presidir | prιzi'diʀ | *vt.* to preside; to direct, to guide

presilha | prι'ziʟa | *sf.* loop, tab, tag (for fastening)

preso -sa | 'prezʋ | *smf.* prisoner; convict / *a.* imprisoned, arrested; seized, caught

pressa | 'prɛsa | *sf.* hurry, haste. **-à(s) pressa(s)** in a hurry. **-estar com p.** to be in a hurry

presságio | pre'sajiʋ | *sm.* omen, sign

pressão | pre'sãw | *sf.* pressure; oppression; (colloq.) snap fastener

pressentimento | presẽti'mẽtʋ | *sm.* presentiment, foreboding

pressentir | presĩ'tiʀ | *vt.* to have a presentiment, to perceive beforehand; to have a hunch

pressuroso -sa | presu'rozʋ -'rωza | *a.* eager, anxious; hasty

prestação | preʃta'sãw | *sf.* instalment, installment. **-à p.** in instalments. **-p. de contas** rendering of accounts. **-p. de serviços** service rendering

prestar | preʃ'taʀ | *vt.* to render, to give. **-p.-se** to lend oneself to. **-p. atenção** to pay attention. **-p. contas** to render accounts. **-p. juramento** to take an oath / *vi.* to be good for, to be suitable. **-não p.** to be no good

prestativo -va | preʃta'tivʋ | *a.* helpful, obliging

prestes | 'prɛʃtɪʃ | *a.* ready, willing / *adv.* about to, at the point of

presteza | preʃ'teza | *sf.* readiness, promptness

prestígio | prɪʃ'tijiʋ | *sm.* prestige, influence

préstimo | 'prɛʃtimʋ | *sm.* utility, usefulness. **-oferecer préstimos** to offer assistance

préstito | 'prɛʃtitʋ | *sm.* pageant; (*pl.*) pageant, spectacular procession during the Carnival merriments

presumir | prɪzu'miʀ | *vt.* to presume, to suppose / *vi.* to be conceited

presunção | prezũ'sãw | *sf.* presumption, supposition; arrogance, presumptuousness

presunçoso -sa | prezũ'sozʋ -'sωza | *a.* presumptuous, arrogant

presuntivo-va | prezũ'tivʋ | *a.* presumptive

presunto | prɪ'zũtʋ | *sm.* ham

pretendente | pretẽ'dẽtɪ | *smf.* pretendent; applicant; claimant

pretender | pretẽ'deʀ | *vt.* to pretend, to claim; to aspire to; to intend, to purpose

pretensão | pretẽ'sãw | *sf.* pretension, claim; ostentation, affectation

preterir | prete'riʀ | *vt.* to pretermit, to pass over (without mention)

pretérito -ta | pre'tɛritʋ | *sm.* preterit, past (definite) / *a.* bygone, former

pretexto | pre'teʃtʋ | *sm.* pretext, pretence; excuse

pretidão, pretura | preti'dãw pre'tura | *sf.* (colloq.) blackness; darkness

preto, preta | 'pretʋ | *sm.* black (colo[u]r); Negro / *a.* black; dark; Negro

pretoria | pretʋ'ria | *sf.* magistrate's court

prevalecer | prevale'seʀ | *vi.* to prevail. **-p.-se** de to take advantage of

prevaricar | prevari'kaʀ | *vi.* to deviate from rectitude

prevenção | prevẽ'sãw | *sf.* prevention; precaution; prejudice. **-estar com p. contra** to be prejudiced against

prevenido-da | prɪvɪ'nidʋ | *a.* forewarned, cautious

prevenir | prɪvɪ'niʀ | *vt.* to prevent; to warn, to caution. **-p.-se** to take precautions

prever | pre'veʀ | *vt.* to foresee, to anticipate

previdência | prɪvi'dẽsia | *sf.* prudence, precaution. **-p. social** social welfare

prévio -via | 'prɛviʋ | *a.* previous, prior. **-aviso p.** prior notice

previsão | previ'zãw | *sf.* prevision, foresight; forecast. **-p. do**

tempo weather forecast

previsto -ta | pre'viʃtʋ | *a.* foreseen

prezado -da | pre'zadʋ | *a.* dear; highly esteemed. **-P. Senhor** Dear Sir (in letters)

prezar | pre'zaʀ | *vt.* to esteem, to value, to hold deer. **-p.-se** to have self-respect

primar | pri'maʀ | *vi.* to be superior, to stand out. **-p. pelo saber** to excel in knowledge

primário -ria | pri'mariʋ | *a.* primary; primitive

primavera | prima'vera | *sf.* spring; (bot.) primrose

primazia | prima'zia | *sf.* primacy; supremacy; advantage

primeiro -ra | pri'meyrʋ | *smf.* the first one; *sf.* (mech.) low gear / *a.* first; foremost; fundamental, elementary. **-de primeira** first rate, top quality. **-p. plano** foreground

primitivo -va | primi'tivʋ | *smf. a.* primitive person; a primitive (artist) / *a.* primitive; primeval, aboriginal

primo -ma | 'primʋ | *smf.* cousin. **-p. em segundo grau** second cousin / *a.* prime, first. **-número p.** prime number

primogênito -ta | primo'jenitʋ | *smf. a.* first-born

primo-irmão -mã | prim(ʋ)ɪʀ'mãw | *smf.* first cousin

primor | pri'moʀ | *sm.* perfection, excellence, beauty

primordial | primoʀdi'al | *a.* primordial, primitive; primal, fundamental

primoroso -sa | primo'rozʋ -'rɔza | *a.* perfect, excellent

princesa | prĩ'seza | *sf.* princess

principado | prĩsi'padʋ | *sm.* principality

principal | prĩsi'pal | *smf.* principal (also com.) / *a.* principal, main, first

príncipe | 'prĩsipɩ | *sm.* prince

principiante | prĩsipi'ãtɩ | *smf.* beginner, novice

principiar | prĩsipi'aʀ | *vt. vi.* to begin, to start

princípio | prĩ'sipiʋ | *sm.* beginning, start; principle. **-a p.** at first. **-por p.** on principle

prioridade | priori'dadɩ | *sf.* priority; precedence

prisão | pri'zãw | *sf.* prison, jail; imprisonment; arrest; bondage. **-dar ordem de p.** to put someone under arrest. **-p. perpétua** life imprisonment. **-p. de ventre** constipation

prisioneiro -ra | prizio'neyrʋ | *smf.* prisoner

privação | priva'sãw | *sf.* privation, destitution, want; (*pl.*) hardships, privations

privada | pri'vada | *sf.* water--closet

privado -da | pri'vadʋ | *sm.* favourite, intimate friend / *a.* private, deprived

privar | pri'vaʀ | *vt.* to deprive of. **-p.-se de** to abstain from. **-p. com** to be on intimate terms with

privativo -va | priva'tivʋ | *a.* privative, exclusive

privilegiado -da | privileji'adʋ | *a.* privileged; exceptional

privilégio | privi'lɛjiʋ | *sm.* privilege

pró | 'prɔ | *sm.* pro, advantage. **-os prós e os contras** the pros and the cons / *adv.* pro; in favo(u)r of, for. **-nem p. nem contra** neither for nor against

proa | 'proa | *sf.* prow, bow; (colloq.) conceit. **-figura de p.** figurehead

probabilidade | probabili'dadɩ | *sf.* probability

problema | pro'blema | *sm.* problem

probo -ba | 'prɔbʋ | *a.* honest

procedência | prose'dẽsia | *sf.* origin, source. **-sem p.** without foundation (in fact)

proceder | prose'deʀ | *sm.* behavio(u)r / *vi.* to proceed, to arise from; to conduct oneself

procedimento | prosɪdi'mētʋ | *sm.* procedure; behavio(u)r, conduct

processar | prose'saR | *vt.* to process; to action at law; to sue

processo | pro'sɛsʋ | *sm.* process, procedure; (law) lawsuit

procissão | prʋsi'sãw | *sf.* procession (esp. a religious one)

proclamação | proklama'sãw | *sf.* proclamation, announcement

proclamar | prokla'maR | *vt.* to proclaim, to promulgate

procriar | prokri'aR | *vt.* to procreate, to breed

procura | prʋ'kura | *sf.* search, quest; demand, call (also econ.). **-à p. de** in search of

procuração | prʋkura'sãw | *sf.* power of attorney, proxy. **-por p.** by proxy

procurador -dora | prʋkura'doR | *smf.* proxy; attorney, solicitor

procurar | prʋku'raR | *vt.* to look for, to search, to seek; to strive for, to aim at; to call on

prodígio | pro'diʒiʋ | *sm.* prodigy

prodigioso -sa | prodiʒi'ozʋ -'ωza | *a.* prodigious, extraordinary, marvellous

pródigo -ga | 'prωdigʋ | *a.* prodigal, dissipated, wanton, extravagant

produção | prʋdu'sãw | *sf.* production; product, produce

produtivo -va | prʋdu'tivʋ | *a.* productive, fertile; active

produto | prʋ'dutʋ | *sm.* product; produce; offspring. **-p. derivado** by-product

produzir | prʋdu'ziR | *vt.* to produce

proeminência | proemi'nẽsia | *sf.* prominence; protuberance

proeminente | proemi'nẽtɪ | *a.* prominent; important

proeza | prʋ'eza | *sf.* prowess, feat, exploit

profanar | profa'naR | *vt.* to profane, to desecrate, to defile

profano -na | pro'fanʋ | *sm.* profane, laic or secular thing / *a.* profane, secular; irreverent; unholy; uninitiated

profecia | profɪ'sia | *sf.* prophecy

proferir | profɪ'riR | *vt.* to utter, to pronounce. **-p. sentença** to pronounce judg(e)ment. **-p. um discurso** to deliver a speech

professar | profe'saR | *vt.* to profess, to declare openly; to exercise a profession / *vi.* to profess, to take religious vows

professor -sora | profe'soR | *smf.* professor; teacher. **-p. catedrático** full professor

professorado | profeso'radʋ | *sm.* professorate; teaching staff; teachers collectively

profeta | pro'feta | *sm.* prophet

profetizar | profɪti'zaR | *vt. vi.* to prophesy, to foretell

proficiência | profisi'ẽsia | *sf.* proficiency, competence, skill

proficiente | profisi'ẽtɪ | *a.* proficient, competent, skilled

profissão | profi'sãw | *sf.* profession; occupation

profissional | profisio'nal | *smf. a.* professional

profundidade | prʋfũdi'dadɪ | *sf.* depth, deepness, profundity

profundo -da | prʋ'fũdʋ | *a.* deep, profound; penetrating

profuso -sa | prʋ'fuzʋ | *a.* profuse, abundant

progênie | pro'jeniɪ | *sf.* progeny; lineage

prognosticar | prognoʃti'kaR | *vt.* to prognosticate; to foresee, to presage / *vi.* (med.) to make a prognosis

prognóstico | prog'nωʃtikʋ | *sm.* prognostic, prognosis (also med.); forecast

programa | pro'grama | *sf.* programme, program

programar | progra'maR | *vt.* to programme, to program, to schedule

progredir | progrɪ'diR | *vi.* to progress, to advance

progresso | pro'grɛsʋ | *sm.* progress

proibição | proibi'sãw | *sf.* prohibition, forbidding, ban

proibir | prʋi'biʀ | *vt.* to forbid, to prohibit

projeção | proje'sãw | *sf.* projection

projetar | proje'taʀ | *vt.* to project; to throw; to plan

projetil, projétil | proje'til pro'jetil | *sm.* projectile, missile

projeto | pro'jɛtʋ | *sm.* project, plan, design. **-p. de lei** draft (legislative) bill

projetor | proje'toʀ | *sm.* projector, searchlight

prol | 'prɔl | *sm.* benefit. **-em p. de** in behalf of

prole | 'prɔlɨ | *sf.* issue, offspring

proletariado | proletari'adʋ | *sm.* proletariat

proletário -ria | prole'tarɪʋ | *smf. a.* proletarian

prolífico -ca | pro'lifikʋ | *a.* prolific; productive

prolixo -xa | pro'liksʋ | *a.* prolix, wordy, long-winded

prólogo | 'prɔlʋgʋ | *sm.* prologue

prolongamento | prolõga'mẽtʋ | *sm.* extension, prolongation

prolongar | prolõ'gaʀ | *vt.* to extend, to lengthen, to prolong

promessa | pro'mesa | *sf.* promise

prometer | prome'teʀ | *vt.* to promise

promiscuidade | promiʃkui'dadɨ | *sf.* promiscuity, promiscuousness

promissão | promi'sãw | *sf.* promise. **-Terra da P.** Promised Land

promissor -sora | promi'soʀ | *a.* promising

promissória | promi'sɔria | *sf.* promissory note

promissório -ria | promi'sɔriʋ | *a.* promissory

promoção | promo'sãw | *sf.* promotion. **-p. de vendas** sales promotion

promontório | promõ'tɔriʋ | *sm.* promontory, headland

promotor-tora | promo'toʀ | *smf.* promoter. **-p. público** (law) district attorney, public prosecutor / *a.* promoting, advancing

promover | promo'veʀ | *vt.* to promote; to foment, to foster

promulgar | promul'gaʀ | *vt.* to promulgate, to proclaim

pronome | pro'nomɨ | *sm.* pronoun

prontidão | prõti'dãw | *sf.* promptitude, readiness; (mil.) alert

pronto -ta | 'prõtʋ | *a.* prompt, ready; prepared; immediate / *adv.* promptly. **-de p.** immediately. / *interj.* ready!, here!

pronto-socorro | 'prõtʋso'koʀʋ | *sm.* first aid clinic

pronúncia | prʋ'nũsia | *sf.* pronunciation; accent; (law) indictment

pronunciamento | prʋnũsia'mẽtʋ | *sm.* pronouncement, manifesto, pronunciamento

pronunciar | prʋnũsi'aʀ | *vt.* to pronounce; (law) to indict. **-p.-se** to declare one's opinion. **-p. um discurso** to make a speech

propagação | propaga'sãw | *sf.* propagation; dissemination, diffusion

propaganda | propa'gãda | *sf.* propaganda; advertising. **-p. eleitoral** electioneering. **-fazer p.** to advertise

propagar | propa'gaʀ | *vt.* to propagate; to disseminate

propensão | propẽ'sãw | *sf.* propensity, inclination

propenso -sa | pro'pẽsʋ | *a.* prone, inclined, given

propício | pro'pisiʋ | *a.* propitious, favo(u)rable

propina | prʋ'pina | *sf.* tip, gratuity (esp. of drink money)

propor | pro'poʀ | *vt.* to propose, to suggest

proporção | propoʀ'sãw | *sf.*

proportion

proporcionado -da | propoRsio'nadʊ | *a.* proportioned; proportionate

proporcionar | propoRsio'naR | *vt.* to provide, to supply; to adjust

proposição | propozi'sãw | *sf.* proposition, proposal

propósito | pro'pɔzitʊ | *sm.* purpose, aim, intention. **-a p.** by the way. **-a p. de** in connection with. **-de p.** on purpose

proposta|pro'pɔʃta|*sf.* proposition, proposal, offer

propriamente | prɔpria'mētɪ | *adv.* properly; exactly. **-p. dito** strictly speaking

propriedade | proprie'dadɪ | *sf.* property; capability; ownership; estate; propriety; proper speech

proprietário -ria | proprie'tariʊ | *sm.* proprietor, owner; landlord; *sf.* proprietress; landlady

próprio -pria | 'prɔpriʊ | *sm.* individual characteristic, peculiar feature (of something or someone). **-p. de** pertaining to. **-p. para** fit for. **-a si p.** to oneself / *a.* private; peculiar; proper; precise

propulsão | propul'sãw | *sf.* propulsion

propulsor -sora|propul'soR|*sm.* propeller / *a.* propellent

prorrogação | proRoga'sãw | *sf.* prorogation; extension

prorrogar | proRo'gaR | *vt.* to prorrogue, to extend the time limit

prorromper | proRõ'peR | *vi.* to burst, to break out

prosa|'prɔza|*sf.* prose; chat / *a.* conceited

prosador -dora|proza'doR|*smf.* prose-writer

prosaico -ca | pro'zaykʊ | *a.* prosaic; pedestrian; matter-of-fact

proscrito -ta | proʃ'kritʊ | *smf.* exile; outlaw; outcast

prosear | prozi'aR | *vi.* to chat, to talk, to converse

prospecto, prospeto|proʃ'pɛktʊ pros'pɛtʊ | *sm.* prospectus, informative literature

prosperar | proʃpe'raR | *vi.* to prosper, to thrive

prosperidade|proʃpɪri'dadɪ|*sf.* prosperity, success

próspero -ra | 'prɔʃperʊ|*a.* prosperous; successful; **favo(u)rable**

prosseguimento | prʊsɪgi'mētʊ | *sm.* continuation

prosseguir | prosɪ'giR | *vi.* to proceed, to carry on

prostituir | prʊʃtitu'iR | *vt.* to prostitute

prostituta | prʊʃti'tuta | *sf.* prostitute

prostração | proʃtra'sãw | *sf.* prostration, depression; exhaustion

prostrar | proʃ'traR | *vt.* to prostrate. **-p.-se** to prostrate oneself

protagonista | protago'niʃta | *smf.* protagonist

proteção | prote'sãw | *sf.* protection, shelter; favo(u)r, patronage

proteger | prote'jeR | *vt.* to protect, to patronize; to shield, to shelter

protegido -da | prʊtɪ'jidʊ | *sm.* protegé; *sf.* protegée / *a.* protected

proteína|prote'ina|*sf.* protein

protelar | prote'laR | *vt.* to postpone; to delay

protestante | proteʃ'tãtɪ|*smf. a.* protestant

protestar|proteʃ'taR|*vt.* to protest (also com.) / *vi.* to protest, to object

protesto | pro'tɛʃtʊ | *sm.* protest (also com.); protestation; complaint; asseveration

protetor -tora | prote'toR | *smf.* protector, guardian / *a.* protective

protocolo | proto'kɔlʊ | *sm.* pro

tocol; register; etiquette

protótipo | pro'tωtipυ | *sm.* prototype

protuberância | prυtube'rãsia | *sf.* protuberance

prova | 'prωva | *sf.* proof; examination; experiment; (typog.) proof sheet; taste. **-a toda p.** uncontestable. **-à p. d'água** waterproof

provação | prova'sãw | *sf.* affliction, tribulation, suffering

provar | pro'vaʀ | *vt.* to prove; to test, to try; to try on (as a garment)

provável | pro'vavιl | *a.* provable; probable, likely

provedor -dora | prove'doʀ | *smf.* purveyor; provider

proveito | prυ'veytυ | *sm.* profit; advantage. **-em p. de** for the benefit of. **-bom p.!** enjoy your meal!

proveitoso -sa | prυvey'tozυ -'tωza | *a.* profitable; advantageous

proveniência | provιni'ẽsia | *a.* source, origin

proveniente | provιni'ẽtι | *a.* coming from, originating in

prover | pro'veʀ | *vt.* to provide; to supply

provérbio | pro'vεʀbiυ | proverb, saying

providência | provi'dẽsia | *sf.* Providence; foresight. **-tomar providências** to take the right steps

providenciar | providẽsi'aʀ | *vt.* to take steps or measures / *vi.* to make arrangements

provido -da | prυ'vidυ | *a.* well--supplied

província | pro'vĩsia | *sf.* province

provir | pro'viʀ | *vi.* to derive from, to result from

provisão | provi'zãw | *sf.* provision; supply; (*pl.*) provisions

provisório -ria | provi'zωriυ | *a.* provisional, temporary

provocação | provoka'sãw | *sf.* provocation

provocante | provo'kãtι | *a.* provoking, provocative

provocar | provo'kaʀ | *vt.* to provoke; to cause; to tempt

proximidade | prosimi'dadι | *sf.* proximity, nearness; (*pl.*) neighbo(u)rhood, surroundings

próximo -ma | 'prωsimυ | *sm.* fellow man / *a.* near, close; neighbo(u)ring; next, following. **-o mais p.** the hithermost. **-parente p.** close relation

prudência | pru'dẽsia | *sf.* prudence; discretion; caution

prudente | pru'dẽtι | *a.* prudent; careful

prumo | 'prumυ | *sm.* prummet, plumb. **-a p.** vertically

prurido | pru'ridυ | *sm.* itch, itching; burning desire

psicanálise | psika'nalizι | *sf.* psychoanalysis

psicologia | psikolo'jia | *sf.* psychology

psicológico -ca | psiko'lωjikυ | *a.* psychologic, psychological

psicólogo -ga | psi'kωlυgυ | *smf.* psychologist

psiquiatra | psiki'atra | *smf.* psychiatrist

psiquiatria | psikia'tria | *sf.* psychiatry

psiu | 'psiw | *interj.* pst!, hey!

pua | 'pua | *sf.* bit; auger; thorn. **-arco de p.** brace and bit

publicação | publika'sãw | *sf.* publication; edition, print, issue

publicar | publi'kaʀ | *vt.* to publish; to announce, to publicize

publicidade | publisi'dadι | *sf.* publicity; advertising

publicitário -ria | publisi'tariυ | *smf.* person who works in advertising

público -ca | 'publikυ | *sm. a.* public. **-serviço p.** civil service

púcaro | 'pukarυ | *sm.* earthen pot with a handle

pudera | pu'dεra | *interj.* no wonder!, of course!

pudim | pu'dĩ | *sm.* pudding

pudor | pu'doR | *sm.* pudency, modesty, shyness

pueril | pue'ril | *a.* childish, puerile

pugilismo | puji'liʒmʋ | *sm.* boxing

puido -da | pu'idʋ | *a.* threadbare, worn smooth

pujante | pu'jãtɩ | *a.* vigorous, strong; powerful

pular | pu'laR | *vt.* to jump, to leap over / *vi.* to jump, to leap

pulga | 'pulga | *sf.* flea

pulmão | pul'mãw | *sm.* lung

pulo | 'pulʋ | *sm.* jump, leap, bound. **-dar um p.** or **um pulinho em algum lugar** (colloq.) to drop by somewhere. **-de um p.** in a flash

pulsação | pulsa'sãw | *sf.* pulsation, beat, beating

pulsar | pul'saR | *vi.* to pulsate, to beat, to throb

pulseira | pul'seyra | *sf.* bracelet

pulso | 'pulsʋ | *sm.* wrist; (med.) pulse; strength, vigo(u)r. **-a p.** by force. **-obra de p.** work of great importance

pulverizar | pulveri'zaR | *vt.* to grind to powder, to pulverize; to spray

punção | pũ'sãw | *sm.* punch (tool); *sf.* (surg.) puncture

pundonor | pũdo'noR | *sm.* sense of hono(u)r; dignity

pungente | pũ'jẽtɩ | *a.* pungent; heartbreaking, afflictive

pungir | pũ'jiR | *vt.* to prick, to sting; to afflict, to distress

punhado | pu'ɴadʋ | *sm.* handful

punhal | pu'ɴal | *sm.* dagger

punhalada | puɴa'lada | *sf.* stab

punho | 'puɴʋ | *sm.* fist; wrist; handle; handcuff. **-de próprio p.** in one's own handwriting. **-em p.** in hand

punição | puni'sãw | *sf.* punishment; penalty

punir | pu'niR | *vt.* to punish

pupila | pu'pila | *sf.* (anat.) pupil

pupilo -la | pu'pilʋ | *smf.* ward, pupil; protegé

purê | pu're | *sm.* purée. **-p. de batatas** mashed potatoes

pureza | pu'reza | *sf.* purity; chastity

purgante | puR'gãtɩ | *sm. a.* purgative

purgatório | puRga'tɔriʋ | *sm.* purgatory

purificação | purifika'sãw | *sf.* purification, purifying

purificar | purifi'kaR | *vt.* to purify; to clean, to purge

purista | pu'riʃta | *smf.* purist

puro -ra | 'purʋ | *a.* pure; clean, immaculate; chaste; simple

puro-sangue | 'purʋ'sãgɩ | *smf. a.* thoroughbred

púrpura | 'puRpura | *sf.* purple

pus | 'puʃ | *sm.* pus, purulence

pusilânime | puzi'lanimɩ | *a.* faint-hearted, timid

puxa | 'puxa | *interj.* why!, upon my soul! **-p. vida!** by Jove!, holy mackerel!

puxador | puxa'doR | *sm.* knob, pull; drawer handle

puxão | pu'xãw | *sm.* pull; haul; tug

puxar | pu'xaR | *vt.* to pull, to draw; to haul. **-p. conversa** to strike up a conversation. **-p. saco** (vulg.) to be toady

Q

quadra | 'kwadra | *sf.* street block; quatrain; (sports) court; period, season

quadrado -da | kwa'dradʋ | *sm. a.*

square

quadriculado -da | kwadriku'la-dʊ | a. checkered. **-papel** q. graph paper

quadril | kwa'dril | sm. hip; haunch

quadrilha | kwa'driLa | sf. gang of robbers; square dance, quadrille (also mus.)

quadrimotor | kwadrimo'toR | sm. four-engined plane / a. four-engined

quadro | 'kwadrʊ | sm. picture, painting; blackboard; table, list, schedule; scene; (sports) team. **-q. de avisos** bulletin board.

quadro-negro | 'kwadrʊ'negrʊ | sm. blackboard

qual | 'kwal | rel. pron. who, whom, which, that; interrog. pron. what?, which? / conj. as / interj. nonsense! **-q. o quê!** not at all! **-tal e q.** just as. **-cada q.** each one

qualidade | kwali'dadɪ | sf. quality. **-na q. de** in the capacity of. **-de q.** of good quality

qualificação | kwalifika'sãw | sf. qualification

qualificar | kwalifi'kaR | vt. to qualify. **-q. de** to label, to call

qualquer | kwal'kɛR | a. pron. any, anyone, either. **-q. pessoa** anybody, anyone. **-q. coisa** anything. **-q. um** anyone. **-a q. hora** any time. **-de q. maneira** anyhow; anyway

quando | 'kwãdʊ | adv. conj. when. **-de vez em q.** once in a while. **-desde q.?** since when? **-q. muito** at the most, at best

quantia | kwã'tia | sf. amount, sum; quantity

quantidade | kwãti'dadɪ | sf. quantity. **-em q.** (colloq.) galore

quanto -ta | 'kwãtʊ | a. pron. all that, as much as; (pl.) as many as; interrog. a. how much? / adv. how, as. **-q. a** as for. **-q. a**

mim as far as I am concerned. **-q. antes** as soon as possible. **-q. mais** let alone, especially. **-tanto q.** as far as; as much as

quarenta | kwa'rẽta | sm. num. forty

quarentão -tona | kwarẽ'tãw -'tona | smf. a person in his forties

quarentena | kwarẽ'tena | sf. quarantine; a period of forty days

quaresma | kwa'rɛsma | sf. Lent

quarta | 'kwaRta | sf. = quarta-feira

quarta-feira | kwaRta'feyra | sf. Wednesday

quarteirão | kwaRtey'rãw | sm. city block

quartel | kwaR'tɛl | sm. quarter; barracks, quarters. **-luta sem q.** merciless combat

quartel-general | kwaR'tɛljene'ral | sm. general headquarters

quarteto | kwaR'tetʊ | sm. (mus.) quartet; (poetry) quatrain

quartilho | kwaR'tiLʊ | sm. pint

quarto -ta | 'kwaRtʊ | sm. quarter; room; quarter-hour; watch (turn of duty) / a. fourth

quase | 'kwazɪ | adv. almost. **-q. nunca** seldom

quatro | 'kwatrʊ | sm. num. four

quatrocentos -tas | kwatrʊ'sẽtʊʃ | smf. num. four hundred

que | 'kɪ | pron. who, whom, which, that / conj. that. **-q. pena!** what a pity! **-q. é q.** what's?, what are?

quê | 'ke | sm. something. **-não há de q.** not at all, don't mention it. **-um certo q.** a certain something / interrog. pron. (at the end of a sentence) **-para q.?** what for? **-por q.?** why?

quebra | 'kɛbra | sf. break, breakage; bankruptcy. **-de q.** (colloq.) in the bargain

quebra-cabeça | 'kɛbraka'besa | sm. puzzle, enigma; jigsaw puzzle

quebradiço -ça | kebra'disʊ | *a.* fragile, brittle

quebrado-da | ke'bradʊ | *sm.* fraction; (colloq.) a breaking; (*pl.*, colloq.) small change / *a.* broken

quebra-luz | kɛbra'luʒ | *sm.* lampshade

quebra-mar | kɛbra'maR | *sm.* jetty, breakwater

quebra-nozes | kɛbra'nɔzɪʒ | *sm.* nutcracker

quebranto | ke'brãtʊ | *sm.* weakness, exhaustion; magic spell inflicted by an "evil eye"

quebra-quebra | 'kɛbra'kɛbra | *sm.* street riot

quebrar | ke'braR | *vt.* to break; to interrupt; to make bankrupt; to weaken; to bend (street); to modify (water temperature). **-q. um galho** (slang) to get someone (something) out of trouble / *vi.* to break; to go bankrupt

queda | 'kɛda | *sf.* fall, drop; tendency, inclination. **-q. para** or **por** weakness for; aptitude for

queda-d'água | 'kɛda'dagwa | *sf.* waterfall

queijo | 'keyjʊ | *sm.* cheese

queijo-de-minas | 'keyjʊdɪ'minaʒ | *sm.* kind of white cheese

queijo-do-reino | 'keyjʊdʊ'Reynʊ | *sm.* Dutch-type cheese

queimadura | keyma'dura | *sf.* burn, burning

queimar | key'maR | *vt.* to burn; to scorch, to singe. **-q. as pestanas** (colloq.) to burn the midnight oil

queima-roupa | keyma'Rowpa | *sf.* used in the expression à q. point-blank

queixa | 'keyxa | *sf.* complaint (also law)

queixada | key'xada | *sf.* jaw-bone; white-lipped peccary

queixar-se | key'xaRsɪ | *vr.* to complain; to grumble

queixo | 'keyxʊ | *sm.* chin

queixoso -sa | key'xozʊ -'xɔza | *smf.* (law) complainant; plain-

tiff / *a.* complaining; lamenting

quem | 'kẽy | *rel. pron.* who, whom, anybody who. **-de q.** whose, of whom, from whom. **-q. dera!** I wish! **-q. quer que** whoever

quente | 'kẽtɪ | *a.* hot; warm; ardent

quer | 'kɛR | *conj.* either; whether; or **-q. chova, q. não chova** whether it rains or not. **-o que q.** whatever (may be). **-quem q. que** whoever

querela | ke'rɛla | *sf.* indictment; altercation; dispute

querer | ke'reR | *vt.* to want, to desire, to wish. **-q. bem a** to love. **-q. mal a** to hate. **-quer dizer** that is to say / *vi.* to want. **-por q.** on purpose. **-sem q.** accidentally

querido -da | kɪ'ridʊ | *a.* dear, beloved

querosene | kero'zenɪ | *sm.* kerosene

quesito | kɪ'zitʊ | *sm.* query, question

questão | keʒ'tãw | *sf.* question; subject; dispute; lawsuit; interrogation. **-fazer q. de** to insist on

questionar | keʒtio'naR | *vt.* to question; to object to / *vi.* to dispute, to wrangle; to bicker

questionário | keʒtio'narɪʊ | *sm.* questionnaire

quiabo | ki'abʊ | *sm.* (bot.) okra (pod or plant)

quiçá | ki'sa | *adv.* perhaps; who knows?

quieto -ta | ki'ɛtʊ | *a.* quiet, still; silent

quietude | kie'tudɪ | *sf.* quietness; tranquillity

quilate | ki'latɪ | *sm.* carat

quilha | 'kiLa | *sf.* keel

quilo | 'kilʊ | *sm.* kilo, kilogram

quilômetro | ki'lometrʊ | *sm.* kilometre, kilometer

quimera | ki'mɛra | *sf.* chimera; fancy, day-dream

química | 'kimika | *sf.* chemistry

químico -ca | ˈkimikʊ | *smf.* chemist / *a.* chemical

quina | ˈkina | *sf.* sharp edge (as of a table); corner (as of a wall); chinchona (bark)

quinau | kiˈnaw | *sm.* (colloq.) correction. **-dar q.** to supply the correct answer

quindim | kĩˈdĩ | *sm.* kind of coconut candy

quinhão | kiˈNãw | *sm.* share; portion

quinhentos -tas | kiˈNẽtʊʃ | *smf. num.* five hundred

quinina | kiˈnina | *sf.* quinine

quinquilharia | kĩkiLaˈria | *sf.* trinket, bauble

quinta | ˈkĩta | *sf.* country seat, grange, rural residence (esp. in Portugal); = *quinta-feira*

quinta-feira | ˈkĩtaˈfeyra | *sf.* Thursday

quinto -ta | ˈkĩtʊ | *sm. a.* fifth

quinze | ˈkĩzɪ | *sm. num.* fifteen

quinzena | kĩˈzena | *sf.* period of fifteen days; fortnight

qüiproquó | kwiprɔˈkwɔ | *sm.* misunderstanding

quiromante | kiroˈmãtɪ | *smf.* chiromancer, palmist

quisto | ˈkiʃtʊ | *sm.* cyst, wen

quitação | kitaˈsãw | *sf.* acquittal; receipt (for payment)

quitanda | kiˈtãda | *sf.* (colloq.) vegetable market, greengrocery

quitandeiro -ra | kitãˈdeyrʊ | *smf.* greengrocer

quitar | kiˈtaR | *vt.* to free (of an obligation); to quit, to release (from)

quite | ˈkitɪ | *a.* clear, free. **-estar q.** to be even with

quitute | kiˈtutɪ | *sm.* delicacy, tidbit

quota | ˈkwɔta | *sf.* quota, share, portion; instalment payment. V. *cota*

R

rã | ˈRã | *sf.* frog

rabada | Raˈbada | *sf.* oxtail (used as food); tail end of anything

rabanada | Rabaˈnada | *sf.* kind of French toast; a blow with the tail

rabanete | Rabaˈnetɪ | *sm.* radish

rabeca | Raˈbɛka | *sf.* (mus., obs.) fiddle

rabecão | Rabeˈkãw | *sm.* (mus., obs.) bass fiddle; (colloq.) van for conveying corpses to the morgue

rabicho | Raˈbixʊ | *sm.* pigtail (hair); crupper (of a harness); (colloq.) infatuation

rabicó | Rabiˈkɔ | *a.* (colloq.) bobtailed

rabino | Raˈbinʊ | *sm.* rabbi

rabiscar | RabiʃˈkaR | *vt. vi.* to scribble, to scrawl

rabo | ˈRabʊ | *sm.* tail; (vulg.) buttocks. **-r. do olho** corner of the eye

rabugento -ta | Rabuˈjẽtʊ | *a.* sour; crabby; peevish

rabugice | Rabuˈjisɪ | *sf.* peevishness, sullenness, sulkiness

rábula | ˈRabula | *smf.* pettifogger

raça | ˈRasa | *sf.* race, breed, strain. **-de r.** thoroughbred

ração | Raˈsãw | *sf.* ration

racha | ˈRaxa | *sf.* split, fissure; *sm.* (colloq.) informal soccer match

rachadura | Raxaˈdura | *sf.* fissure (also in the skin, bone etc.), split, crack

rachar | Ra'xaʀ | *vt.* to split; to crack; (colloq.) to share (expenses, profits etc.) / *vi.* to crack. **-calor de r.** very strong heat

raciocinar | Rasiosi'naʀ | *vi.* to reason

raciocínio | Rasio'siniʋ | *sm.* reasoning

racional | Rasio'nal | *a.* rational

racionamento | Rasiona'mẽtʋ | *sm.* rationing

racionar | Rasio'naʀ | *vt.* to ration

radiador | Radia'doʀ | *sm.* radiator

radiante | Radi'ãtɪ | *a.* radiant; joyous, gleeful

radicado -da | Radi'kadʋ | *a.* rooted; living in a country (definitively [said of a foreign citizen])

radical | Radi'kal | *sm.* root or stem of a word / *a.* radical; extreme

radicar | Radi'kaʀ | *vt.* to root / *vr.* to take root; to settle

rádio | 'Radiʋ | *sm.* radio; (chem.) radium; (anat.) radius; *sf.* broadcasting station

radioemissor -sora | Radiʋemi-'soʀ | *sm.* broadcaster; *sf.* broadcasting station

radiografia | Radiogra'fia | *sf.* radiography

radiograma | Radio'grama | *sm.* radiogram, radiotelegram

radiologia | Radiolo'jia | *sf.* radiology

radioso -sa | Radi'ozʋ -'ωza | *a.* radiant, bright

raia | 'Raya | *sf.* line, scratch; race course; (ichth.) skate, ray; (*pl.*) the limit of something (as folly, nonsense etc.). **-tocar as raias** to reach the limit

raiar | Ray'aʀ | *vt.* to stripe; to rifle (a gun barrel) / *vi.* to emit rays, to shine; to come into sight. **-ao r. do sol** at sunrise

rainha | Ra'iɲa | *sf.* queen

raio | 'Rayʋ | *sm.* ray; radius; lightning; spoke (of a wheel). **-como um r.** quickly. **-r. de ação** range of action / *interj.* (*pl.*) blast it!

raiva | 'Rayva | *sf.* anger, rage, fury; (med.) hydrophobia, rabies

raivoso -sa | Ray'vozʋ -'vωza | *a.* angry, rabid, furious; hydrophobic

raiz | Ra'iʃ | *sf.* root; origin, source. **-bens de r.** real estate. **-r. da serra** foot of a mountain

rajada | Ra'jada | *sf.* gust of wind. **-r. de metralhadora** a burst of machine-gun fire

rajado -da | Ra'jadʋ | *a.* striped, streaked

ralador | Rala'doʀ | *sm.* grater

ralar | Ra'laʀ | *vt.* to grate (cheese etc.); to scrape; to annoy

ralé | Ra'lɛ | *sf.* mob, rabble, the common herd

ralhar | Ra'Laʀ | *vi.* to scold, to reprimand, to admonish

ralo -la | 'Ralʋ | *sm.* grater; sprinkling nozzle; grating / *a.* sparse, thin; wattery (said of coffee, soup etc.)

rama | 'Rama | *sf.* foliage; branches. **-algodão em r.** raw cotton. **-pela r.** superficially

ramagem | Ra'majẽy | *sf.* branches, foliage; (*pl.*) leaf pattern (on clothing)

ramal | Ra'mal | *sm.* branch (of a railway etc.); telephone extension line

ramalhete | Rama'Letɪ | *sm.* bunch of flowers, bouquet

ramerrão | Rame'Rãw | *sm.* everyday routine, daily grind

ramificar-se | Ramifi'kaʀsɪ | *vr.* to branch out, to spread out

ramo | 'Ramʋ | *sm.* branch, ramification; limb, bough; bunch of flowers. **-r. de negócios** trade, line of business

rampa | 'Rãpa | *sf.* ramp, incline, slope

rancho | 'Rãxʋ | *sm.* shanty; organized group of Carnival merrymakers; food (for soldiers or sailors)

rancor | Rã'koʀ | *sm.* rancour,

spite, grudge, hate

rançoso -sa | Rã'sozʋ -'sωza | a. rancid

ranger | Rã'jeR | vi. to creak, to squeak. **-r. os dentes** to grind the teeth

rangido | Rã'jidʋ | sm. creak, squeak

ranhura | Ra'Nura | sf. groove, slot, slit

ranzinza | Rã'zĩza | a. grouchy, cranky

rapadura | Rapa'dura | sf. hard square of raw brown sugar

rapagão | Rapa'gãw | sm. strapping young man

rapapé | Rapa'pɛ | sm. servile bowing and scraping

rapar | Ra'paR | vt. to scrape, to rasp; to shave close

rapariga | Rapa'riga | sf. (obs.) girl, lass

rapaz | Ra'paʒ | sm. young man, lad. **-bom r.** nice fellow

rapaziada | Rapazi'ada | sf. the boys; group of youngsters; prank

rapé | Ra'pɛ | sm. snuff

rapidez | Rapi'deʒ | sf. speed, velocity; quickness; brevity

rápido -da | 'Rapidʋ | sm. swift current; express train / adv. rapidly, quick, quickly

rapina | Ra'pina | sf. rapine, ravening. **-ave de r.** bird of prey

raposo -sa | Ra'pozʋ | sm. male fox; sf. fox; fox skin; foxy person

raptar | Rap'taR | vt. to abduct, to kidnap

rapto | 'Raptʋ | sm. (colloq.) abduction, kidnapping; (fig.) rapture, ecstasy; (law) abduction of an honest woman with libidinous intentions

raquete | Ra'ketɪ | sf. (sports) racket, racquet

raquítico -ca | Ra'kitikʋ | a. (med.) rachitic, rickety; (colloq.) underdeveloped

raquitismo | Raki'tiʒmʋ | sm. ra-

chitis, rickets

rarear | Rarɪ'aR | vi. to be scarce, to be rare

raridade | Rari'dadɪ | sf. rarity

raro -ra | 'Rarʋ | a. rare; scarce; extraordinary

rasante | Ra'zãtɪ | sf. (aeron.) hedge-hop / a. sweeping, grazing

rascunhar | Raʃku'NaR | vt. to sketch, to outline, to draft

rascunho | Raʃ'kuNʋ | sm. rough draft; sketch, outline

rasgado -da | Raʒ'gadʋ | a. torn, ripped. **-cumprimentos rasgados** effusive greetings

rasgão | Raʒ'gãw | sm. tear, rip, slit

rasgar | Raʒ'gaR | vt. to tear, to rip; to open with a lancet

rasgo | 'Raʒgʋ | sm. tear, rip; (fig.) dash, spirit; (fig.) an impulsive deed

raso -sa | 'Razʋ | a. level, plain, flat; brimful; shallow. **-soldado r.** (mil.) private. **-campo r.** open country

raspa | 'Raʒpa | sf. shaving; rasp, scraper

raspadeira | Raʒpa'deyra | sf. scraper

raspão | Raʒ'pãw | sm. scratch, slight scrape or abrasion. **-atingir de r.** to sideswipe

raspar | Raʒ'paR | vt. to scrape; to grate; to erase, to rub out. **-r.-se** to shave oneself; (colloq.) to get away

rasteira | Raʒ'teyra | sf. a tripping up (of someone). **-dar** or **passar uma r. em** (colloq.) to trip someone; to fool

rasteiro -ra | Raʒ'teyrʋ | a. creeping, crawling; humble, low

rastejar | Raʒte'jaR | vt. to track / vi. to creep, to crawl; (fig.) to degrade oneself

rastilho | Raʒ'tiLʋ | sm. fuse; train (of gunpowder)

rasto | 'Raʒtʋ | sm. track, footprint, trace, mark. **-de rastos**

creeping, crawling

rastreamento | Raʃtrɪa'mētʊ | sm. act of following the trail or tracks of

rastrear | Raʃtrɪ'aR | vt. = rastejar (vt.); to follow the trail or tracks of

rastro | 'Raʃtrʊ | sm. = rasto

rasura | Ra'zura | sf. erasure; act of scraping or grating

ratazana | Rata'zana | sf. rat

ratear | Ratɪ'aR | vt. to apportion, to divide pro rate / vi. to miss (said of a motor)

rateio | Ra'teyʊ | sm. apportionment, proration

ratificar | Ratifi'kaR | vt. to ratify, to confirm

rato | 'Ratʊ | sm. rat

ratoeira | Ratʊ'eyra | sf. mousetrap, rattrap

razão | Ra'zãw | sf. reason, mind, sense; cause, motive; reasoning; rate; ratio. **-à r. de** at the rate of. **-dar r. a** to agree with

razoável | Razʊ'avɪl | a. reasonable; open-minded; fair

ré | 'Rɛ | sf. female defendant; (naut.) stern; sm. (mus.) D. **-à r.** astern. **-dar marcha à r.** to move backwards

reabastecer | Rɪabaʃte'seR | vt. to replenish, to restock

reabilitar | Rɪabili'taR | vt. to rehabilitate; to regenerate

reação | Rɪa'sãw | sf. reaction; response

reagir | Rɪa'jiR | vi. to react; to resist

reajustamento | Rɪajuʃta'mētʊ | sm. readjustment; (colloq.) adjustment of wages

reajustar | Rɪajuʃ'taR | vt. to readjust

real | Rɪ'al | sm. reality / a. real, actual; royal

realçar | Rɪal'saR | vt. to accentuate, to emphasize

realce | Rɪ'alsɪ | sm. enhancement; emphasis. **-dar r. a** to enhance; to emphasize

realejo | Rɪa'lejʊ | sm. barrel-organ, hurdy-gurdy

realeza | Rɪa'leza | sf. royalty

realidade | Rɪali'dadɪ | sf. reality. **-na (em) r.** really, actually

realista | Rɪa'liʃta | smf. a. realist; royalist

realização | Rɪaliza'sãw | sf. realization, achievement

realizar | Rɪali'zaR | vt. to realize (also fin.), to accomplish, to achieve, to perform. **-r. -se** to take place

realmente | Rɪal'mētɪ | adv. really, in fact, actually

reanimar | Rɪani'maR | vt. to reanimate, to revive. **-r. -se** to become reanimated; to cheer up

reapresentação | Rɪaprezēta'sãw | sf. new presentation; new introduction; (cine., theat., TV) rerun

reatar | Rɪa'taR | vt. to re-establish relations; to resume

reator | Rɪa'toR | sm. (nuclear phys., elect.) reactor

reavaliação | Rɪavalia'sãw | sf. reappraisal

reaver | Rɪa'veR | vt. to recover, to get back

rebaixamento | Rebayxa'mētʊ | sm. lowering; abasement; debasement; degradation

rebaixar | Rebay'xaR | vt. to lower; to debase, to discredit; to depreciate. **-r. -se** to debase oneself

rebanho | Re'baNʊ | sm. herd, flock

rebarba | Re'baRba | sf. barb; (mech.) burr, rough edge

rebarbativo -va | Rebarba'tivʊ | a. sullen, crabbed; disagreeable

rebater | Reba'teR | vt. to strike again; to parry (a blow); to refute; to kick back (a soccer ball)

rebelar | Rebe'laR | vt. to incite to rebellion. **-r. -se** to rebel, to revolt

rebelde | Re'bɛldɪ | smf. rebel, insurgent / a. rebellious, insurgent; (med.) refractory

rebeldia ˌRebel'dia ˌ *sf.* rebelliousness; opposition, resistance

rebelião ˌRɛbeli'ãw ˌ *sf.* rebellion; mutiny, insurrection

rebentação ˌRebẽta'sãw ˌ *sf.* line of breaking of waves

rebentar ˌRebẽ'taR ˌ *vt.* to break, to burst / *vi.* to burst; to explode

rebento ˌRe'bẽtʋ ˌ *sm.* shoot, bud; offspring

rebitar ˌRebi'taR ˌ *vt.* to rivet

rebite ˌRe'bitɩ ˌ *sm.* rivet

reboar ˌRebʋ'aR ˌ *vi.* to resound, to resonate

rebocador ˌReboka'doR ˌ *sm.* tugboat; plasterer

rebocar ˌRebo'kaR ˌ *vt.* to tow; to plaster

reboco ˌRe'bokʋ ˌ *sm.* plaster

rebolado ˌRebo'ladʋ ˌ *sm.* swinging of the hips. **-perder o r.** (slang) to be embarrassed

rebolar ˌRebo'laR ˌ *vt.* to swing the hips; to waddle; (slang) to have a hard time

rebolo ˌRe'bolʋ ˌ *sm.* grindstone

reboque ˌRe'bɔkɩ ˌ *sm.* trailer; tow. **-levar a r.** to take in tow

rebordo ˌRe'boRdʋ ˌ *sm.* turned edge; flange

rebuliço ˌRebu'lisʋ ˌ *sm.* stir; commotion, fuss

rebuscado-da ˌRebuʃ'kadʋ ˌ *a.* affected; far-fetched; finical

rebuscar ˌRebuʃ'kaR ˌ *vt.* to search thoughly; to adorn excessively

recado ˌRe'kadʋ ˌ *sm.* message; errand. **-deixar r.** to leave a message. **-dar conta do r.** (colloq.) to handle the matter

recaída ˌReka'ida ˌ *sf.* relapse

recalcitrante ˌRekalsi'trãtɩ ˌ *a.* recalcitrant

recambiar ˌRekãbi'aR ˌ *vt.* to send back; to return (something) to the sender

recanto ˌRe'kãtʋ ˌ *sm.* corner, nook; place of retirement

recapitular ˌRekapitu'laR ˌ *vt.* to recapitulate

recatado -da ˌReka'tadʋ ˌ *a.* shy; prudent, circumspect

recato ˌRe'katʋ ˌ *sm.* modesty, bashfulness; circumspection

recauchutar ˌRekawxu'taR ˌ *vt.* to recap (tires)

recear ˌResɩ'aR ˌ *vt. vi.* to fear, to be afraid

receber ˌRese'beR ˌ *vt.* to receive; to take; to accept / *vi.* to entertain, to receive guests

recebimento ˌResebi'mẽtʋ ˌ *sm.* receiving; acceptance; reception

receio ˌRe'seyʋ ˌ *sm.* uncertainty; fear. **-não tenha r.** have no fear

receita ˌRe'seyta ˌ *sf.* revenue, income, receipts; (phar.) prescription; recipe (for cooking). **-r. pública** budget

receitar ˌResey'taR ˌ *vt. vi.* (med.) to prescribe

recém-casado -da ˌRe'sẽyka'zadʋ ˌ *smf. a.* newly-wed

recém-chegado -da ˌRe'sẽyxe'gadʋ ˌ *smf.* newcomer / *a.* newly arrived

recém-nascido -da ˌRe'sẽyna'sidʋ ˌ *smf.* newborn child, baby

recenseamento ˌResẽsɩa'mẽtʋ ˌ *sm.* census

recente ˌRe'sẽtɩ ˌ *a.* recent, new, fresh

receoso -sa ˌResɩ'ozʋ -'ɔza ˌ *a.* afraid, apprehensive

recepção ˌResep'sãw ˌ *sf.* reception; party; reception room; receipt (of letter, goods etc.)

recepcionista ˌResepsio'niʃta ˌ *smf.* receptionist

receptar ˌResep'taR ˌ *vt.* to receive or to hide (stolen goods)

receptor ˌResep'toR ˌ *sm.* receiver (radio)

recesso ˌRe'sɛsʋ ˌ *sm.* recess, nook; secluded place; recess (of Parliament, courts etc.)

rechear ˌRexɩ'aR ˌ *vt.* to stuff (a turkey, a cake etc.)

recheio ˌRe'xeyʋ ˌ *sm.* stuffing;

filling

rechonchudo -da | Rexõ'xudʋ | *a.*
plump, chubby

recibo | Rɪ'sibʋ | *sm.* receipt

recife | Rɪ'sifɪ | *sm.* reef, shoal

recinto | Rɪ'sĩtʋ | *sm.* premises; en-
closure, enclosed place

recipiente | Rɪsipi'ẽtɪ | *sm.* recepta-
cle, container

reciprocar | Resipro'kaR | *vt. vi.* to
reciprocate

reciprocidade | Rɪsiprosi'dadɪ | *sf.*
reciprocity

recíproco -ca | Re'siprʋkʋ | *a.* re-
ciprocal; mutual

récita | 'Rɛsita | *sf.* (theat.) per-
formance; recital

recitação | Rɪsita'sãw | *sf.* recita-
tion, declamation

recital | Rɪsi'tal | *sm.* (mus.) recital

recitar | Resi'taR | *vt.* to recite, to
declaim

reclamação | Reklama'sãw | *sf.*
complaint; protest

reclamar | Rekla'maR | *vt.* to com-
plain of or about, to protest / *vi.*
to complain

reclame | Re'klamɪ | *sm.* (obs.)
advertising, publicity

reclinar | Rekli'naR | *vt.* to recline,
to lay back. **-r. -se** to recline, to
lay down

recluso -sa | Re'kluzʋ | *smf.* rec-
luse; prisoner in solitary con-
finement / *a.* secluded

recobrar | Reko'braR | *vt.* to re-
cover, to regain. **-r. -se** to get
well again

recolher | Reko'LeR | *vt.* to gath-
er, to collect; to lodge. **-r. -se** to
go to bed; to retire / *vi.* to go
home, to go to bed

recolhimento | RekoLi'mẽtʋ | *sm.*
retirement, withdrawal; seclu-
sion; meditation

recomendação | Rekomẽda'sãw |
sf. recommendation; (*pl.*) greet-
ings, regards

recomendar | Rekomẽ'daR | *vt.* to
recommend; to advise; to
commend. **-r. -se** to send one's

regards

recompensa | Rekõ'pẽsa | *sf.* re-
ward; recompense

recompensar | Rekõpẽ'saR | *vt.* to
recompense, to reward

reconciliar | Rekõsili'aR | *vt.* to
reconcile. **-r. -se** to become
reconciled

recôndito -ta | Re'kõditʋ | *a.*
recondite, secret, hidden

reconhecer | Rekoɲe'seR | *vt.* to
recognize; to acknowledge, to
admit; to show appreciation of;
to reconnoitre. **-r. uma firma** to
witness a signature

reconhecido -da | Rekoɲɪ'sidʋ | *a.*
grateful, thankful; recog-
nized; admitted

reconhecimento | Rekoɲɪsi'mẽtʋ |
sm. recognition; (mil.) reconnais-
sance; gratitude

reconquistar | Rekõkiʃ'taR | *vt.* to
regain, to recapture, to recover

reconsiderar | Rekõside'raR | *vt.* to
reconsider

reconstituir | Rekõʃtitu'iR | *vt.* to
reconstitute; to re-establish

reconstruir | Rekõʃtru'iR | *vt.* to
reconstruct, to rebuild

recordação | RekoRda'sãw | *sf.* re-
membrance, recollection; keep-
sake

recordar | RekoR'daR | *vt.* to re-
member, to recollect, to recall

recorde | Re'kɔRdɪ | *sm.* record
(esp. sports). **-bater** or. to break
the record

recorrer | Reko'ReR | *vt.* to re-
trace, to go back over. **-r. a** to
resort to, to have recourse to; to
make use of. **-r. de** (law) to
appeal from

recortar | RekoR'taR | *vt.* to clip, to
cut out; to silhouette; to renew
an old garment

recorte | Re'kɔRtɪ | *sm.* clip,
clipping; cut-out

recostar | Rekoʃ'taR | *vt.* to lay, to
lean. **-r. -se** to recline, to lay
down

recreação | Rekrɪa'sãw | *sf.* recreation

recrear | Rekrɩ'aR | *vt*. to amuse, to divert, to entertain

recreio | Re'kreyʋ | *sm*. recreation, diversion; playground. **-hora do r.** playtime. **-viagem de r.** pleasure trip

recriminação | Rɩkrimina'sãw | *sf*. recrimination

recruta | Re'kruta | *sm*. recruit, draftee

recrutar | Rekru'taR | *vt*. to recruit; (fig.) to enlist (new members)

recuado-da | Reku'adʋ | *a*. set back

recuar | Reku'aR | *vi*. to move back / *vi*. to recoil; to retreat; to back down or out

recuo | Re'kuʋ | *sm*. backward movement; recoil (esp. of a gun); (mil.) retreat

recuperar | Rekupe'raR | *vt*. to recuperate, to recover, to regain. **-r. -se** to recover

recurso | Re'kuRsʋ | *sm*. resource, resort; appeal (also law); (*pl*.) resources, means

recusa | Re'kuza | *sf*. refusal, denial

recusar | Reku'zaR | *vt*. to refuse, to reject, to deny

redação | Reda'sãw | *sf*. redaction; composition exercise; editorial staff or room

redargüir | RedaR'gwiR | *vt*. to retort, to reply

redator -tora | Reda'toR | *smf*. editor (esp. of a newspaper)

rede | 'Redɩ | *sf*. net; fish-net; hair net; mesh; network (of roads, canals etc.); hammock; trap

rédea | 'Redɩa | *sf*. reins. **-à r. larga** or **solta** headlong, (at) full tilt. **-dar rédeas** to give full reins

redemoinho | Redemʋ'iɴʋ | *sm*. whirl; whirlpool; whirlwind; swirl

redenção | Redẽ'sãw | *sf*. redemption

redentor -tora | Redẽ'toR | *smf*. redeemer; *sm*. (cap.) Redeemer, Jesus Christ / *a*. redeeming

redigir | Rɩdi'jiR | *vt*. to write, to compose, to redact

redobrar | Redo'braR | *vt*. to refold; to increase; to intensify; to peal over and over again (said of bells)

redoma | Re'doma | *sf*. bell-jar, bell-glass

redondeza | Redõ'deza | *sf*. roundness; (*pl*.) surroundings

redondo -da | Re'dõdʋ | *a*. round; (typog.) roman

redor | Re'dʋR | *sm*. used in the éxpression **ao** or **em r. (de)** round, around, about

redução | Redu'sãw | *sf*. reduction, decrease

reduto | Re'dutʋ | *sm*. redoubt, stronghold

reduzir | Rɩdu'ziR | *vt*. to reduce; to abridge; to submit

reembolsar | Reẽbol'saR | *vt*. to reimburse, to repay, to refund

reembolso | Reẽ'bolsʋ | *sm*. reimbursement, repayment

reentrância | Reẽ'trãsia | *sf*. hollow, recess

refazer | Refa'zeR | *vt*. to remake. **-r. -se** to recover

refeição | Refey'sãw | *sf*. meal

refeito -ta | Re'feytʋ | *a*. remade; repaired; recovered

refeitório | Refey'tʋriʋ | *sm*. refectory, dining hall

referência | Refe'rẽsia | *sf*. reference, mention, allusion; (*pl*.) information

referente | Refe'rẽtɩ | *a*. regarding, concerning

referido -da | Refɩ'ridʋ | *a*. said, above-mentioned

referir | Refɩ'riR | *vt*. to report, to relate; to connect (one thing with another). **-r. -se a** to mention

refinação | Refina'sãw | *sf*. refining; mill (esp. of sugar)

refinado -da | Refi'nadʋ | *a*. refined; downright, thorough. **-um patife r.** a downright scoundrel

refinamento | Refina'mētʊ | *sm.* refinement

refinar | Refi'naʀ | *vt.* to refine, to purify; to improve

refinaria | Refina'ria | *sf.* refinery. **-r. de petróleo** oil refinery

refletir | Reflɪ'tiʀ | *vt.* to reflect; to reveal; to reproduce / *vi.* to reflect, to meditate; to resound

refletor -tora | Refle'toʀ | *sm.* reflector; searchlight / *a.* reflecting

reflexão | Refle'ksãw | *sf.* reflection; meditation

reflexo -xa | Re'fleksʊ | *sm. a.* reflex

reflorestamento | Refloreʃ-ta'mētʊ | *sm.* reforestation, reforestment

reflorestar | Refloreʃ'taʀ | *vt.* to reforest

refogado -da | Refo'gadʊ | *sm.* onion and tomato gravy / *a.* sautéed in onion and tomato gravy

reforçado -da | Refoʀ'sadʊ | *a.* reinforced

reforçar | Refoʀ'saʀ | *vt.* to reinforce, to strengthen

reforço | Re'foʀsʊ | *sm.* reinforcement; (mil.) relief, replacement (esp. *pl.*)

reforma | Re'fɔʀma | *sf.* reform, reformation (also *cap.*); (mil.) retirement (of an officer)

reformador -dora | Refoʀma'doʀ | *smf.* reformer, reformist

reformar | Refoʀ'maʀ | *vt.* to reform; to rebuild; (mil.) to put on the retired list (an officer); (law) to reverse (a legal decision)

refrão | Re'frãw | *sm.* refrain, chorus; saying

refrear | Refrɪ'aʀ | *vt.* to restrain, to control

refrescante | Refreʃ'kãtɪ | *a.* refreshing

refrescar | Refreʃ'kaʀ | *vt.* to refresh, to cool; to revive (the memory) / *vi.* to grow cool

refresco | Re'freʃkʊ | *sm.* refresh-ment; soft drink, cool drink

refrigeração | Refrijera'sãw | *sf.* refrigeration; air-conditioning

refrigerador | Refrijera'doʀ | *sm.* refrigerator, icebox

refrigerante | Refrije'rãtɪ | *sm.* (colloq.) soft drink

refrigerar | Refrije'raʀ | *vt.* to refrigerate

refugiado -da | Refuji'adʊ | *smf.* refugee; expatriate

refugiar-se | Refuji'aʀsɪ | *vr.* to seek refuge, to take refuge; to expatriate oneself

refúgio | Re'fujiʊ | *sm.* refuge; shelter

refugo | Re'fugʊ | *sm.* reject, waste

refulgir | Rɪful'jiʀ | *vi.* to shine, to glitter

refutar | Refu'taʀ | *vt.* to refute, to contradict

regador | Rega'doʀ | *sm.* sprinkler, watering-can

regalar | Rega'laʀ | *vt.* to regale; to delight. **-r. -se** to regale oneself

regalia | Rega'lia | *sf.* privilege, prerogative

regalo | Re'galʊ | *sm.* regalement; pleasure, delight

regar | Re'gaʀ | *vt.* to water, to irrigate; to moisten; (cookery) to baste

regatear | Regatɪ'aʀ | *vt.* to bargain, to stint / *vi.* to dicker (over prices)

regato | Re'gatʊ | *sm.* stream, creek

regelar | Reje'laʀ | *vi.* (also **-r. -se**) to freeze

regeneração | Rejenera'sãw | *sf.* regeneration

regenerar | Rejene'raʀ | *vt.* to regenerate

regente | Re'jētɪ | *smf.* regent; (mus.) conductor / *a.* governing

reger | Re'jeʀ | *vt.* to rule, to govern; to conduct (an orchestra)

região | Reji'ãw | *sf.* region

regime | Rɪ'jimɪ | *sm.* regime, regimen (also med.); government (also gram.); diet

regimento | Rɪji'mẽtʋ | *sm.* (mil.) regiment; rule. **-r. interno** bylaws and statutes

régio -gia | 'Rɛjiʋ | *a.* regal, royal

registrar | Rɪgiʃ'traR | *vt.* to register (also mail), to record

registro | Rɪ'jiʃtrʋ | *sm.* registration (also of mail); registry; register; gauge (of gas, water etc.)

rego | 'Regʋ | *sm.* ditch, channel

regozijar-se | Regʋzi'jaRsɪ | *vr.* to rejoice

regozijo | Rɪgʋ'zijʋ | *sm.* rejoicing, delight, joy

regra | 'Rɛgra | *sf.* rule; precept; norm; (*pl.*) menstruation. **-em r.** generally, ordinarily. **-via der.** as a rule

regressar | Regre'saR | *vi.* to return

regresso | Re'grɛsʋ | *sm.* return. **-de r.** back (returned)

régua | 'Rɛgwa | *sf.* ruler. **-r. de cálculo** slide-rule. **-r. T** T-square

regulador-dora | Regula'doR | *sm.* (mech.) regulator / *a.* regulating

regulagem | Regu'lajẽy | *sf.* adjustment (of machines, motors etc.)

regulamentação | Regulamẽta'sãw | *sf.* regulation

regulamentar | Regulamẽ'taR | *a.* regulation / *vt.* to regulate

regulamento | Regula'mẽtʋ | *sm.* regulations, rules

regular | Regu'laR | *a.* regular, normal; average / *vt.* to regulate; to adjust; to control / *vi.* to run properly (as a watch). **-não r. bem** to be a little mad

regularidade | Regulari'dadɪ | *sf.* regularity

regularizar | Regulari'zaR | *vt.* to regularize, to regulate. **-r. -se** to become normal

rei | 'Rey | *sm.* king. **-reis magos** the Magi. **-dia de Reis** Epiphany

reimprimir | rũpri'miR | *vt.* to reprint

reinado | Rey'nadʋ | *sm.* reign; predominance, supremacy

reinar | Rey'naR | *vi.* to reign; to predominate; to spread, to rage

reino | 'Reynʋ | *sm.* kingdom; realm

reintegrar | Reĩte'graR | *vt.* to reinstate, to restore

reiterar | Reyte'raR | *vt.* to reiterate, to repeat

reitor -tora | Rey'toR | *sm.* rector (head of a university), headmaster; *sf.* headmistress

reivindicar | Reyvĩdi'kaR | *vt.* to claim, to demand (privileges, property etc.)

rejeitar | Rejey'taR | *vt.* to reject; to refuse

rejuvenescer | Rejuvene'seR | *vt. vi.* to rejuvenate

relação | Rela'sãw | *sf.* relation; ratio, proportion; list; (*pl.*) connections, acquaintances

relacionar | Relasio'naR | *vt.* to enumerate, to itemize; to relate, to associate

relâmpago | Re'lãpagʋ | *sm.* lightning, flash of lightning

relampejar | Relãpe'jaR | *vi.* to lighten, to flash like lightning

relance | Re'lãsɪ | *sm.* look, glance, glimpse. **-de r.** at a glance

relancear | Relãsɪ'aR | *vt.* to cast a quick glance

relapso -sa | Re'lapsʋ | *smf.* backslider; recidivist

relatar | Rela'taR | *vt.* to relate, to narrate; to give an account of

relativo -va | Rela'tivʋ | *a.* relative

relato | Re'latʋ | *sm.* account, report

relatório | Rela'tʋriʋ | *sm.* written report

relaxado -da | Rela'xadʋ | *smf.* careless person, slouch / *a.* relaxed; slovenly

relaxamento | Relaxa'mẽtʋ | *sm.* relaxation, easement; negligence; slovenliness

relaxar | Rela'xaR | *vt.* to loosen, to slacken; to moderate. **-r. -se** to become negligent and lazy

relegar | Rele'gaR | *vt.* to relegate, to consign to some inferior position

relembrar | Relẽ'braR | *vt.* to remind, to recollect

relento | Re'lẽtʋ | *sm.* dampness of the night. **-ao r.** outdoors

reles | 'Rɛlɩʃ | *a.* vulgar; disreputable

relevante | Rele'vãtɩ | *a.* relevant, pertinent; important, significant

relevar | Rele'vaR | *vt.* to forgive, to excuse; to put in relief / *vi.* to import, to matter

relevo | Re'levʋ | *sm.* relief; distinction, importance

religião | Rɩliji'ãw | *sf.* religion

religioso-sa | Rɩliji'ozʋ-'ʋza | *smf.* a member of a religious order / *a.* religious, devout

relinchar | Relĩ'xaR | *vi.* to neigh, to whinny

relíquia | Rɩ'likia | *sf.* relic; (*pl.*) remains

relógio | Re'lʋjiʋ | *sm.* clock, watch; meter (for gas, water etc.). **-r. de sol** sun dial

relojoaria | Relʋjʋa'ria | *sf.* watchmaking; watchmaking shop; shop where watches are sold

relojoeiro | Relʋjʋ'eyrʋ | *sm.* watchmaker

relutância | Relu'tãsia | *sf.* reluctance

reluzente | Relu'zẽtɩ | *a.* sparkling, glittering

reluzir | Relu'ziR | *vi.* to shine, to glitter, to gleam

relva | 'Rɛlva | *sf.* grass, lawn

remada | Re'mada | *sf.* stroke of an oar

remanso | Re'mãsʋ | *sf.* eddy, slack water

remar | Re'maR | *vt. vi.* to row

rematado | Rema'tadʋ | *a.* complete, perfect

remate | Re'matɩ | *sm.* finish, finishing touch

remediado-da | Remedi'adʋ | *a.* remedied; neither rich nor poor

remediar | Remedi'aR | *vt.* to remedy, to relieve

remédio | Re'mɛdiʋ | *sm.* medicine; remedy; help. **-que r.?** (colloq.) what can I do?

remela | Re'mela | *sf.* (vulg.) secretion from the eyes

remendar | Remẽ'daR | *vt.* to mend, to patch

remendo | Re'mẽdʋ | *sm.* patch

remessa | Re'mɛsa | *sf.* remittance; shipment

remetente | Reme'tẽtɩ | *sm.* sender; return address

remeter | Reme'teR | *vt.* to remit, to send; to dispatch, to despatch

reminiscência | Rɩmini'sẽsia | *sf.* reminiscence, remembrance

remissão | Rɩmi'sãw | *sf.* remission, absolution; cross reference

remo | 'remʋ | *sm.* oar; paddle

remoção | Remo'sãw | *sf.* removal

remoçar | Remo'saR | *vt. vi.* to rejuvenate

remodelar | Remode'laR | *vt.* to remodel; to reconstruct

remoer | Remo'eR | *vt.* to regrind; to ruminate; to brood over

remontar | Remõ'taR | *vt.* to remount; to ascend; to return (to the past). **-r.-se** to refer to times gone by

remorso | Re'mʋRsʋ | *sm.* remorse

remoto -ta | Re'mʋtʋ | *a.* remote, far, distant

remover | Remo'veR | *vt.* to remove

remuneração | Remunera'sãw | *sf.* remuneration, pay

remunerador -dora | Remunera'doR | *a.* remunerative

remunerar | Remune'raR | *vt.* to remunerate, to pay (salary etc.)

rena | 'Rena | *sf.* reindeer

renascença | Rena'sẽsa | *sf.* renaissance (also *cap.*)

renascer | Rena'seR | *vi.* to be born again; to revive

renascimento | Renasi'mẽtʋ | *sm.* (*cap.*) Renaissance; rebirth

renda | 'Rẽda | *sf.* income, revenue; rent; lace. **-r. bruta** gross income. **-r. líquida** net income

rendeiro -ra | Rẽ'deyrʋ | *smf.* tenant farmer; lacemaker

render | Rẽ'deR | *vt.* to produce (profits etc.); to subdue; to take the place of. **-r.-se** to surrender. **-r. graças a** to render thanks to / *vi.* to be productive; to pay; to last

rendição | Rẽdi'sãw | *sf.* surrender, capitulation

rendimento | Rẽdi'mẽtʋ | *sm.* profit, interest; income; output; efficiency (of motors etc.)

rendoso -sa | Rẽ'dozʋ -'dωza | *a.* profitable, productive

renegado -da | Rene'gadʋ | *smf.* renegade; turncoat

renegar | Rene'gaR | *vt.* to abjure; to deny, to renounce

renhido -da | Re'Nidʋ | *a.* hard-fought, bitterly contested; relentless

renitente | Reni'tẽtɩ | *a.* recalcitrant, stubborn

renome | Re'nomɩ | *sm.* renown, fame

renovação | Renova'sãw | *sf.* renovation, renewal

renovar | Reno'vaR | *vt.* to renew, to renovate

renque | 'Rẽkɩ | *sm.* row, file, rank

rente | 'Rẽtɩ | *adv.* close; even with. **-cortar r.** to cut close

renúncia | Re'nũsia | *sf.* renunciation; resignation; relinquishment

renunciar | Renũsi'aR | *vt.* to renounce; to resign

reorganizar | RɩoRgani'zaR | *vt.* to reorganize

reparação | Repara'sãw | *sf.* reparation; repair; amends, satisfaction

reparar | Repa'raR | *vt.* to repair; to make amends for / *vi.* to notice, to observe, to remark

reparo | Re'parʋ | *sm.* reparation, repairing; censure, objection

repartição | Reparti'sãw | *sf.* partition; distribution; civil service department or office

repartir | RepaR'tiR | *vt.* to divide; to share. **-r. o cabelo** to part the hair

repassar | Repa'saR | *vt.* to pass again; to read over again (a lesson etc.); to iron again (garments)

repatriar | Repatri'aR | *vt.* to repatriate

repelão | Repe'lãw | *sm.* rough pull

repelir | Repɩ'liR | *vt.* to repel, to rebuff, to reject

repente | Re'pẽtɩ | *sm.* impulsive act or utterance; suddenness; improvised verse. **-de r.** suddenly

repentino -na | Repẽ'tinʋ | *a.* sudden, unexpected

repercussão | RepeRku'sãw | *sf.* repercussion; (fig.) effect

repercutir | RepeRku'tiR | *vt.* to reflect; to reverberate; to re-echo / *vi.* to resound

repertório | RepeR'tωriʋ | *sm.* repertoire, repertory

repetição | Rɩpɩti'sãw | *sf.* repetition

repetir | Rɩpɩ'tiR | *vt.* to repeat

repicar | Rɩpi'kaR | *vt.* to mince, to chop again / *vi.* to ring, to peal (bells)

repimpado | Rɩpĩ'padʋ | *a.* lolling, stretched out (as in an easy chair)

repique | Rɩ'pikɩ | *sm.* pealing (of church bells)

repisar | Rɩpi'zaR | *vt.* to repeat, to reiterate; to insist on

repleto -ta | Re'pletʋ | *a.* replete, brimming; crowded

réplica | 'Rɛplika | *sf.* retort, reply; refutation; (fine arts) reproduction

replicar | Rɩpli'kaR | *vt. vi.* to reply, to retort

repolho | Re'poλʋ | *sm.* cabbage

repor | Re'poR | *vt.* to replace; to make restitution

reportagem | RepoR'tajẽy | *sf.* (journal.) reporting; reporters collectively

reportar-se | Repor'tarsı | *vr.* to refer to

reposição | Repozi'sãw | *sf.* replacement. **-peças de r.** spare parts

reposteiro | Repoʃ'teyrʋ | *sm.* hangings, *portière*, door curtain

repousante | Repow'zãtı | *a.* restful; soothing

repousar | Repow'zaR | *vi.* to repose, to rest

repouso | Re'powzʋ | *sm.* rest, repose

repreender | Reprıẽ'deR | *vt.* to reprehend, to admonish

repreensão | Reprıẽ'sãw | *sf.* reprehension, rebuke, scolding

represa | Re'preza | *sf.* dam; reservoir

represália | Repre'zalia | *sf.* reprisal, retaliation

representação | Reprezẽta'sãw | *sf.* representation; performance; allowance of money

representante | Reprezẽ'tãtı | *smf.* representative

representar | Reprezẽ'taR | *vt.* to represent

representativo -va | Reprezẽta'tivʋ | *a.* representative

repressão | Repre'sãw | *sf.* repression

reprimenda | Repri'mẽda | *sf.* reprimand, rebuke

reprimir | Rıpri'miR | *vt.* to repress; to restrain. **-r. -se** to hold oneself back

reprise | Re'prizı | *sf.* rerun (of a film, play etc.)

reprodução | Reprʋdu'sãw | *sf.* reproduction

reprodutor -tora | Reprʋdu'toR | *smf.* reproducer / *a.* reproducing

reproduzir | Reprʋdu'ziR | *vt.* to reproduce

reprovação | Reprova'sãw | *sf.* reproval, reproof; failure (in an examination)

reprovar | Repro'vaR | *vt.* to reprove; to reject; to disapprove of

réptil | 'Rɛptil *pl.* 'Rɛpteyʃ | *sm.* reptile

república | Re'publika | *sf.* republic

republicano -na | Republi'kanʋ | *smf. a.* republican

repudiar | Repudi'aR | *vt.* to repudiate, to reject; to disavow

repúdio | Re'pudiʋ | *sm.* repudiation; disavowal

repugnância | Repug'nãsia | *sf.* repugnance, disgust, aversion

repugnante | Repug'nãtı | *a.* repugnant, disgusting

repugnar | Repug'naR | *vt.* to cause repugnance to; to feel repugnance for / *vi.* to be repugnant

repulsa | Re'pulsa | *sf.* repulse; aversion, repugnance

repulsivo -va | Repul'sivʋ | *a.* repulsive, disgusting

reputação | Reputa'sãw | *sf.* reputation

reputar | Repu'taR | *vt.* to repute, to regard, to consider

repuxar | Repu'xaR | *vt.* to jerk or draw back; to draw tightly / *vi.* to gush, to spout

repuxo | Re'puxʋ | *sm.* jet of water (in an ornamental fountain); the act of drawing back

requebrado | Reke'bradʋ | *sm.* voluptuous movement of the hips

requebrar | Reke'braR | *vt. vi.* (also **r. -se**) to walk with a swaying motion; to wiggle one's hips

requeijão | Rekey'jãw | *sm.* cream cheese

requerente | Reke'rẽtı | *smf.* applicant, petitioner

requerer | Reke'reR | *vt.* to solicit, to petition for

requerimento | Rekeri'mẽtʋ | *sm.* petition, request

requintar | Rekĩ'taR | *vt.* to perfect, to refine to the highest degree

requinte | Rı'kĩtı | *sm.* refinement

requisição | Rɪkizi'sãw | *sf.* requisition

requisitar | Rɪkizi'taR | *vt.* to requisition; to demand

requisito | Rɪki'zitʋ | *sm.* requisite, requirement

rês | 'reʃ | *sf.* head of cattle (for slaughtering); (*pl.*) livestock

rescindir | Rɪsĩ'diR | *vt.* to rescind; to annul

rés-do-chão | 'Rɛʃdʋ'xãw | *sm.* ground floor

resenha | Re'zeNa | *sf.* report; summary

reserva | Re'zɛRva | *sf.* reserve; reservation; (mil.) retirement (of an officer); discretion; substitute

reservado -da | RezeR'vadʋ | *sm.* lavatory / *a.* reserved; confidential, secret

reservar | RezeR'vaR | *vt.* to reserve; to book; to save, to keep

reservatório | RezeRva'tɔriʋ | *sm.* reservoir; tank

resfolegar | Reʃfole'gaR | *vi.* to pant, to puff, to gasp for breath

resfriado -da | Rɪʃfri'adʋ | *sm.* common cold / *a.* having a cold; cooled

resfriar | Rɪʃfri'aR | *vt.* to cool. **-r. -se** to catch a cold

resgatar | Reʃga'taR | *vt.* to ransom, to redeem

resgate | Reʃ'gatɪ | *sm.* ransom; redemption

resguardar | ReʃgwaR'daR | *vt.* to safeguard; to shelter, to protect

resguardo | Reʃ'gwaRdʋ | *sm.* guard, defence; protection; secrecy

residência | Rɪzi'dẽsia | *sf.* residence

residente | Rɪzi'dẽtɪ | *smf. a.* resident

residir | Rɪzi'diR | *vi.* to reside, to live

resíduo | Rɪ'ziduʋ | *sm.* residue

resignação | Rɪzigna'sãw | *sf.* resignation

resignar | Rɪzig'naR | *vt.* to resign.

-r. -se to resign oneself

resina | Rɪ'zina | *sf.* resin

resistência | Rɪziʃ'tẽsia | *sf.* resistance

resistente | Rɪziʃ'tẽtɪ | *a.* resistant; tough, hardy, knockabout

resistir | Rɪziʃ'tiR | *vt.* to resist, to oppose, to withstand / *vi.* to endure, to last

resma | 'Reʃma | *sf.* ream (of paper)

resmungar | Rɪʃmũ'gaR | *vt. vi.* to grouch, to mumble

resolução | Rezʋlu'sãw | *sf.* resolution; solution; determination

resoluto -ta | Rɪzʋ'lutʋ | *a.* resolute, firm, determined

resolver | Rezol'veR | *vt.* to solve, to unravel; to determine. **-r. -se** to make up one's mind

respectivo -va | Reʃpek'tivʋ | *a.* respective

respeitar | Reʃpey'taR | *vt.* to respect, to hono(u)r; to spare

respeitável | Reʃpey'tavɪl | *a.* respectable; hono(u)rable; considerable

respeito | Reʃ'peytʋ | *sm.* respect, regard; aspect; (*pl.*) respects, greetings. **-a -r.** concerning about. **-com r. a** concerning

respeitoso -sa | Reʃpey'tozʋ -'twza | *a.* respectful

respingar | Rɪʃpĩ'gaR | *vi.* to sprinkle, to splash

respingo | Rɪʃ'pĩgʋ | *sm.* sprinkle

respiração | Rɪʃpira'sãw | *sf.* breathing, respiration

respirar | Rɪʃpi'raR | *vt. vi.* to breathe

resplandecente | Reʃplãde'sẽtɪ | *a.* resplendent, shining

resplandecer | Reʃplãde'seR | *vi.* to shine resplendently

resplendor | Reʃplẽ'doR | *sm.* splendo(u)r, refulgence; halo; glory

respondão -dona | Reʃpõ'dãw -'dona | *a.* insolent. saucy

responder | Reʃpõ'deR | *vt.* to answer / *vi.* to answer, to reply. **-r.**

por to answer for

responsabilidade | Reʃpõsabili'dadɩ | *sf.* responsibility

responsabilizar | Reʃpõsabili'zaR | *vt.* to entrust, to hold responsible for; to blame. **-r. -se por** to answer for

responsável | Reʃpõ'savɩl | *smf.* responsible person / *a.* responsible

resposta | Reʃ'pʊʃta | *sf.* answer; reply; refutation

resquício | Rɩʃ'kisiʊ | *sm.* grain, vestige, trace

ressabiado -da | Resabi'adʊ | *a.* distrustful, suspicious

ressaca | Re'saka | *sf.* rough condition of the sea; (colloq.) hangover

ressaltar | Resal'taR | *vt.* to throw into relief, to emphasize / *vi.* to stand out

ressalva | Re'salva | *sf.* exception; reservation; safety clause

ressarcir | Resar'siR | *vt.* to indemnify, to repair

ressecado -da | Rese'kadʊ | *a.* parched, dried up

ressentido -da | Resĩ'tidʊ | *a.* resentful

ressentimento | Resĩti'mẽtʊ | *sm.* resentment

ressentir | Resĩ'tiR | *vt.* to resent. **-r.-se** to be resentful

ressoar | Resʊ'aR | *vt. vi.* to resound, to echo

ressonância | Reso'nãsia | *sf.* resonance

ressonar | Reso'naR | *vi.* to snore; to breathe regularly during sleep

ressurgimento | Resurji'mẽtʊ | *sm.* resurgence, revival

ressurreição | Resurey'sãw | *sf.* resurrection

ressuscitar | Resusi'taR | *vt. vi.* to resuscitate; to revive

restabelecer | Reʃtabele'seR | *vt.* to re-establish, to restore. **-r.-se** to recover

restante | Reʃ'tãtɩ | *smf.* remainder, rest

restar | Reʃ'taR | *vi.* to remain, to be left over

restauração | Reʃtawra'sãw | *sf.* restoration

restaurante | Reʃtaw'rãtɩ | *sm.* restaurant

restaurar | Reʃtaw'raR | *vt.* to restore

réstia | 'Rɛʃtia | *sf.* string of onions or garlic; beam, ray of light

restinga | Rɩʃ'tĩga | *sf.* sand bank; salt marsh

restituição | Rɩʃtitui'sãw | *sf.* restitution

restituir | Rɩʃtitu'iR | *vt.* to return, to give back, to reimburse

resto | 'Rɛʃtʊ | *sm.* remainder, rest; (*pl.*) remains. **-de r.** besides, moreover

restrição | Rɩʃtri'sãw | *sf.* restriction, limitation

restringir | Rɩʃtrĩ'jiR | *vt.* to restrict, to limit

restrito -ta | Rɩʃ'tritʊ | *a.* restricted, limited

resultado -da | Rezul'tadʊ | *sm.* result

resultar | Rezul'taR | *vi.* to result, to arise, to follow

resumido -da | Rezu'midʊ | *a.* resumed, reduced, abridged

resumir | Rezu'miR | *vt.* to summarize, to condense; to abridge

resumo | Re'zumʊ | *sm.* summary. **-em r.** in brief

resvalar | Reʃva'laR | *vi.* to slip, to slide

resvés | Reʃ'vɛʃ | *adv.* close, even with; flush; exactly, justly; right at the bottom

reta | 'Rɛta | *sf.* straight line

retaguarda | Reta'gwarda | *sf.* rear, back part; (mil.) rear guard

retalhar | Reta'LaR | *vt.* to slasn, to cut (into pieces)

retalho | Re'taLʊ | *sm.* piece, remnant; a patch of cloth. **-ar.** at retail; by bits

retaliação | Retalia'sãw | *sf.* retaliation; tit for tat

retardar | Retar'dar | *vt.* to retard, to delay

retardatário -ria | Retarda'tariv | *smf.* late comer, straggler

retenção | Retẽ'sãw | *sf.* retention

reter | Re'ter | *vt.* to retain; to delay; to hold back

retesar | Rete'zar | *vt.* to tighten

retificar | Retifi'kar | *vt.* to rectify; to correct; (chem.) to purify (alcohol etc.)

retinir | Ríti'nir | *vi.* to tinkle, to jingle

retinto -ta | Rí'tĩtv | *a.* deep-dyed; very dark

retirada | Ríti'rada | *sf.* (mil.) retreat; withdrawal; retirement

retirado -da | Ríti'radv | *a.* secluded, retired

retirante | Ríti'rãtí | *a.* retiring, retreating / *smf.* migrant from the drought areas of northeastern Brazil

retirar | Ríti'rar | *vt.* to pull back, to take off; to retract (something said). **-r. -se** to withdraw, to retire

retiro | Rí'tirv | *sm.* seclusion; retreat

reto -ta | 'Retv | *sm.* (anat.) rectum /*a.* right, straight, upright

retocar | Reto'kar | *vt.* to retouch, to touch up

retomar | Reto'mar | *vt.* to retake; to resume

retoque | Re'tɔkí | *sm.* finishing touch, retouching

retorcer | Retor'ser | *vt.* to twist back; to interpret malevolently. **-r. -se** to contort oneself

retórica | Re'tɔrika | *sf.* rhetoric

retórico | Re'tɔrikv | *sm.* rhetorician

retornar | Retor'nar | *vt.* to give back, to return / *vi.* to return

retorno | Re'tornv | *sm.* return; restoration, recurrence

retorquir | Retor'kir | *vt. vi.* to retort, to reply

retraido -da | Retra'idv | *a.* retracted; bashful, reserved

retraimento | Retrai'mẽtv | *sm.* restraint, reserve; bashfulness; seclusion

retrair | Retra'ir | *vt.* to retract, to draw back / *vr.* to withdraw

retrasado -da | Retra'zadv | *a.* before last. **-o ano r.** the year before last

retratar | Retra'tar | *vt.* to portray; to photograph; to mirror, to reflect. **-r. -se** to confess one's error

retrato | Re'tratv | *sm.* portrait; likeness

retribuição | Rítribui'sãw | *sf.* recompense, reward

retribuir | Rítribu'ir | *vt.* to give in return, to reciprocate

retroceder | Retrose'der | *vi.* to retrocede, to retrograde

retrós | Re'trɔʃ | *sm.* fine sewing thread

retrucar | Rítru'kar | *vt.* to retort, to reply; to talk back

retumbante | Retũ'bãtí | *a.* resonant, rumbly. **-vitória r.** smashing victory

retumbar | Retũ'bar | *vi.* to resound, to rumble

réu | 'Rεw | *sm.* (law) defendant, accused

reumatismo | Rewma'tiʒmv | *sm.* rheumatism

reunião | Ríuni'ãw | *sf.* reunion; meeting; gathering

reunir | Ríu'nir | *vt.* to reunite; to gather; to bring together. **-r. -se** to meet together

revalidação | Rívalida'sãw | *sf.* restoration of validity

revalidar | Rívali'dar | *vt.* to revalidate, to reconfirm

revelação | Revela'sãw | *sf.* revelation; disclosal; (photog.) development

revelar | Reve'lar | *vt.* to reveal, to disclose; to develop (a photograph)

revelia | Rívε'lia | *sf.* default. **-à r. de** without the knowledge of. **-julgamento à r.** judgement by default

rever | Re'veR | *vt.* to see again; to check; to read proofs

reverência | Reve'rẽsia | *sf.* reverence; bow. **-fazer uma r.** to bow

reverenciar | Reverẽsi'aR | *vt.* to revere, to venerate

reverendo -da | Reve'rẽdʋ | *sm.* (*cap.*) Reverend Father / *a.* reverend

reverente | Reve'rẽtɩ | *a.* reverent, reverential

reversão | ReveR'sãw | *sf.* reversion; (law) devolution

reversível | ReveR'sivɩl | *a.* reversible

reverso -sa | Re'veRsʋ | *sm.* reverse, the other side

reverter | ReveR'teR | *vi.* to revert, to return

revés | Re've ʃ | *sm.* reverse, back; setback, misfortune. **-ao r.** inside out; on the contrary

revestido -da | Rɩviʃ'tidʋ | *a.* covered, coated

revestimento | Rɩvɩʃti'mẽtʋ | *sm.* covering, coating

revestir | Rɩviʃ'tiR | *vt.* to coat, to cover; to endow (with authority etc.)

revezar | Reve'zaR | *vt. vi.* to alternate, to rotate. **-r. -se** to take turns

revidar | Rɩvi'daR | *vt.* to strike back; to pay back (insults etc.)

revirar | Rɩvi'raR | *vt.* to turn over and over; to turn inside out; to roll (the eyes)

revisão | Rɩvi'zãw | *sf.* revision; proof-reading, proof-reading room

revisar | Rɩvi'zaR | *vt.* to revise; to proof-read

revisor -sora | Rɩvi'zoR | *smf.* proof-reader; reviewer, examiner

revista | Rɩ'viʃta | *sf.* magazine, journal; review (also mil.); (theat.) revue; ransacking

revistar | Rɩviʃ'taR | *vt.* to search, to ransack

revogar | Revo'gaR | *vt.* to revoke, to annul

revolta | Re'vʋlta | *sf.* revolt, rebellion

revoltar | Revol'taR | *vt.* to disgust; to stir up revolt; to make indignant. **-r. -se** to revolt, to rebel

revolto -ta | Re'voltʋ | *a.* agitated; stormy (sea); dishevelled (hair)

revolução | Revʋlu'sãw | *sf.* revolution; (mech.) gyration

revolucionar | Revʋlusio'naR | *vt.* to revolutionize

revolucionário -ria | Revʋlusio'narɩʋ | *smf. a.* revolutionary

revolver | Revol'veR | *vt.* to turn over; to stir; to whirl. **-r. -se** to roll / *vi.* to revolve

revólver | Re'vʋlveR | *sm.* revolver

reza | 'Reza | *sf.* prayer; magic formula to protect against diseases, the evil eye etc.

rezar | Re'zaR | *vt. vi.* to pray; to read (thus and so [said of a law, a notice etc.])

riacho | Ri'axʋ | *sm.* brook, creek

ribalta | Ri'balta | *sf.* footlights

ribanceira | Ribã'seyra | *sf.* steep slope, ravine

ribeirinho -nha | Ribey'riNʋ | *a.* riparian

ribombar | Ribõ'baR | *vi.* to thunder, to resound

ricaço -ça | Ri'kasʋ | *smf.* (pej.) rich person

riçar | Ri'saR | *vt.* to curl, to frizzle, to crimp (the hair)

ricino | 'Risinʋ | *sm.* castor oil plant or bean. **-óleo de r.** castor oil

rico -ca | 'Rikʋ | *a.* rich, wealthy; abundant; tasty

ridículo -la | Ri'dikulʋ | *sm.* ridicule, ridiculousness / *a.* ridiculous

rifa | 'Rifa | *sf.* raffle

rifão | Ri'fãw | *sm.* proverb

rigidez | Riji'deʃ | *sf.* rigidity, stiffness; severity

rígido -da | 'ʀiʒidu | *a.* rigid, stiff; severe

rigor | ʀi'goʀ | *sm.* rigo(u)r, severity. **-a r.** strictly; formally dressed. **-traje de r.** formal dress

rigoroso -sa | ʀigo'ʀozu -'ʀɔza | *a.* rigorous, strict, harsh, tough

rijo -ja | 'ʀiʒu | *a.* rigid, hard

rim | 'ʀĩ | *sm.* kidney

rima | 'ʀima | *sf.* rhyme

rimar | ʀi'maʀ | *vt. vi.* to rhyme

rinchar | ʀĩ'xaʀ | *vi.* = **relinchar**

rinoceronte | ʀinose'ʀõtɪ | *sm.* rhinoceros

rio | 'ʀiʊ | *sm.* river

ripa | 'ʀipa | *sf.* lath. **-meter a r.** (colloq.) to criticize harshly

riqueza | ʀi'keza | *sf.* wealth, riches; opulence

rir | 'ʀiʀ | *vi. vr.* to laugh. **-r. à socapa** to laugh in one's sleeve. **-fazer r.** to amuse

risada | ʀi'zada | *sf.* laughter

risca | 'ʀiʃka | *sf.* line; stripe. **-à r.** to the letter

riscar | ʀiʃ'kaʀ | *vt.* to cross (out), to delete; to make lines. **-r. um fósforo** to strike a match

risco | 'ʀiʃku | *sm.* risk, hazard; dash, mark

riso | 'ʀizu | *sm.* laughter

risonho -nha | ʀi'zoɲu | *a.* smiling, cheerful

ríspido -da | 'ʀiʃpidu | *a.* rude, harsh, dry

ritmo | 'ʀitmu | *sm.* rhythm

rito | 'ʀitu | *sm.* rite, ritual, ceremony

rival | ʀi'val | *smf. a.* rival. **-sem r.** peerless

rivalidade | ʀivali'dadɪ | *sf.* rivalry

rivalizar | ʀivali'zaʀ | *vt.* to rival. **-r. com** to vie with

rixa | 'ʀixa | *sf.* brawl, scuffle

robustecer | ʀubuʃte'seʀ | *vt.* to make robust, to strengthen

robusto -ta | ʀu'buʃtu | *a.* robust, vigorous

roca | 'ʀɔka | *sf.* distaff, spinning--wheel

roça | 'ʀɔsa | *sf.* cleared land (for planting); small planting; country (as opposed to "city")

roçar | ʀo'saʀ | *vt.* to grub land for planting; to touch lightly in passing

roceiro -ra | ʀo'seyru | *smf.* peasant / *a.* (pej.) of or pertaining to the backwoods

rocha | 'ʀɔxa | *sf.* rock, large boulder

rochedo | ʀo'xedu | *sm.* cliff, crag

roda | 'ʀɔda | *sf.* wheel; circle; social circle. **-à r. de** around, about. **-brincar de r.** to play ring-around-a-rosy

rodagem | ʀo'daʒẽy | *sf.* set of wheels; wheeling. **-estrada de r.** highway

roda-gigante | 'ʀɔdaʒi'gãtɪ | *sf.* Ferris wheel

rodapé | ʀoda'pɛ | *sm.* skirting--board

rodar | ʀo'daʀ | *vt.* to cause to turn. **-r. um filme** to make a motion picture / *vi.* to turn; to cruise (in a vehicle)

roda-viva | 'ʀɔda'viva | *sf.* flurry, bustle, ado

rodear | ʀodɪ'aʀ | *vt.* to surround, to encircle

rodeio | ʀo'deyu | *sm.* circumlocution, subterfuge; cattle roundup. **-falar sem rodeios** to come to the point

rodela | ʀo'dɛla | *sf.* small wheel; washer; round slice. **-r. de limão** slice of lemon

rodo | 'ʀodu | *sm.* wooden rake (without teeth); squeegee. **-a r. galore**

rodopiar | ʀodopi'aʀ | *vi.* to spin, to swirl, to twirl

rodovia | ʀodo'via | *sf.* highway

rodoviário -ria | ʀodovi'arɪu | *a.* highway

roedor -dora | ʀue'doʀ | *sm.* (zool.) rodent / *a.* gnawing

roer | ʀu'eʀ | *vt.* to gnaw, to corrode, to erode. **-r. a corda** (colloq.) to go back on one's word

rogar | Ro'gaʀ | *vt.* to beg, to pray for; to implore. **-r. pragas** to call down curses on. **-fazer-se r.** to play hard to get

rogo | 'Rogʋ | *sm.* supplication, entreaty

rojão | Ro'jãw | *sm.* sky-rocket. **-agüentar o r.** (colloq.) to have endurance

rol | 'Rɔl | *sm.* roll, list. **-r. de roupa** laundry list

rola | 'Rola | *sf.* turtle-dove

rolamento | Rola'mētʋ | *sm.* rolling; (mech.) ball-bearing

rolar | Ro'laʀ | *vt. vi.* to roll, to turn, to revolve

roldana | Rol'dana | *sf.* grooved pulley

roldão | Rol'dãw | *sm.* confusion. **-de r.** tumultuously carried along

rolha | 'Rola | *sf.* cork; stopper

roliço -ça | Rʋ'lisʋ | *a.* cylindrical; chubby, plump

rolo | 'Rolʋ | *sm.* roll, cylinder; roller; (slang) scuffle

romã | Ro'mã | *sf.* pomegranate

romance | Ro'mãsι | *sm.* novel; romantic love affair. **-r. policial** detective story

romancear | Romãsι'aʀ | *vt.* to write down in form of a novel; (fig.) to exaggerate

romancista | Romã'siʃta | *smf.* novelist

romântico -ca | Ro'mãtikʋ | *smf. a.* romantic

romantismo | Romã'tiʒmʋ | *sm.* romanticism

romaria | Roma'ria | *sf.* pilgrimage

romãzeira | Romã'zeyra | *sf.* pomegranate tree

rombo -ba | 'Rõbʋ | *sm.* large hole; / *a.* dull, blunt

romeiro -ra | Ro'meyrʋ | *smf.* pilgrim; *sf.* = *romãzeira*

romeno -na | Ro'menʋ | *sm.* (ling.) Romanian; *smf. a.* Romanian, Rumanian, Roumanian

rompante | Rõ'pãtι | *sm.* fit of temper

romper | Rõ'peʀ | *vt.* to rip, to tear; to break (open, through, down) / *vi.* to burst out; to erupt; to break off (relations) with

rompimento | Rõpi'mētʋ | *sm.* rupture, breaking

roncar | Rõ'kaʀ | *vi.* to snore; to grunt (as a pig)

ronco | 'Rõkʋ | *sm.* snore, snoring; grunt (of a pig); roar

ronda | 'Rõda | *sf.* patrol, watch; circuit, rounds

rondar | Rõ'daʀ | *vt.* to patrol; to lurk, to prowl about / *vi.* to veer around (said of the wind)

ronqueira | Rõ'keyra | *sf.* wheeze

ronronar | Rõro'naʀ | *vi.* to purr (like a cat)

rosa | 'Rωza | *sf.* rose; *sm.* rose (colo[u]r) / *a.* rose, rosy, rose-colo(u)red

rosado -da | Ro'zadʋ | *a.* rosy, pink

rosário | Ro'zariʋ | *sm.* rosary (prayer beads)

rosbife | Roʃ'bifι | *sm.* roast beef

rosca | 'Roʃka | *sf.* screw thread; twisted ring (as of bread or pastry)

roseira | Ro'zeyra | *sf.* rose-bush

róseo -sea | 'Rωzιʋ | *a.* rose, rosy, rose-colo(u)red

rosnar | Roʃ'naʀ | *vt. vi.* to snarl, to growl; to mutter

rosto | 'Roʃtʋ | *sm.* face. **-lançar em r.** to fling at (someone's) face

rota | 'Rωta | *sf.* route, course, direction

rotação | Rota'sãw | *sf.* rotation, revolution

roteiro | Ro'teyrʋ | *sm.* itinerary; schedule; guidebook; (cine.) script

rotina | Ro'tina | *sf.* routine; routine procedure

roto -ta | 'Rotʋ | *a.* torn, ragged; shabby

rótula | 'Rωtula | *sf.* kneecap; trellis, jalousie

rótulo | 'Rωtulʋ | *sm.* label

roubalheira | Rowba'Leyra | *sf.*

(colloq.) embezzlement (esp. of public funds)

roubar | ʀow'baʀ | *vt.* to rob, to plunder; to embezzle

roubo | 'ʀowbʋ | *sm.* robbery, burglary

rouco -ca | 'ʀowkʋ | *a.* hoarse, husky, raucous

roupa | 'ʀowpa | *sf.* clothes, clothing. **-r. branca** or **de baixo** underclothes. **-r. de banho** bathing-suit. **-r. de cama** bed clothes

roupão | ʀow'pãw | *sm.* bathrobe, dressing-gown

rouparia | ʀowpa'ria | *sf.* wardrobe (department of a hospital, boarding-school etc.)

rouquidão | ʀowki'dãw | *sf.* hoarseness

rouxinol | ʀowxi'nʋl | *sm.* nightingale

roxo -xa | 'ʀoxʋ | *sm. a.* purple, violet

rua | 'ʀua | *sf.* street / .*interj.* get out!

rubi | ʀu'bi | *sm.* ruby

rubor | ʀu'boʀ | *sm.* blush, glow, redness

ruborizar | ʀubori'zaʀ | *vt.* to make red. **-r. -se** to blush

rubrica | ʀu'brika | *sf.* abbreviated signature; autograph initials; rubric

rubricar | ʀubri'kaʀ | *vt.* to sign or to initial the pages of a document; to countersign

rubro -bra | 'ʀubrʋ | *a.* blood-red, crimson

ruço -ça | 'ʀusʋ | *sm.* dense fog / *a.* faded; faded gray; (colloq.) sandy-haired

rude | 'ʀudɪ | *a.* rude, rough; primitive

rudez, rudeza | ʀu'deʒ ʀu'deza | *sf.* rudeness, roughness

rudimentar | ʀudimẽ'taʀ | *a.*

rudimentary

rudimento | ʀudi'mẽtʋ | *sm.* (gen. *pl.*) rudiments

ruela | ʀu'ɛla | *sf.* little street, alley

rufar | ʀu'faʀ | *vt.* to ruffle, to beat (a drum)

rufião | ʀufi'ãw | *sm.* pimp

ruga | 'ʀuga | *sf.* wrinkle; crease (in clothes)

rugido | ʀu'ʒidʋ | *sm.* roar

rugir | ʀu'ʒiʀ | *vt. vi.* to roar, to bellow

ruído | ʀu'idʋ | *sm.* noise, sound, clatter

ruidoso -sa | ʀui'dozʋ -'dɔza | *a.* noisy, boisterous

ruim | ʀu'ĩ | *a.* bad, evil; wicked; spoiled

ruína | ʀu'ina | *sf.* ruin, destruction; (*pl.*) ruins, debris

ruindade | ʀuĩ'dadɪ | *sf.* wickedness; nastiness

ruir | ʀu'iʀ | *vi.* to crash, to fall, to tumble

ruivo -va | 'ʀuyvʋ | *smf.* redhead / *a.* red-haired

rumo | 'ʀumʋ | *sm.* (naut.) course, direction. **-sem r.** aimless. **-r. a** bound for

rumor | ʀu'moʀ | *sm.* noise, rustle; rumo(u)r

rumorejar | ʀumore'ʒaʀ | *vi.* to rustle (leaves); to murmur (brook)

ruptura | ʀup'tura | *sf.* rupture; break

rural | ʀu'ral | *a.* rural

rusga | 'ʀuʒga | *sf.* quarrel, squabble; disagreement

russo -sa | 'ʀusʋ | *sm.* (ling.) Russian / *smf. a.* Russian

rústico -ca | 'ʀuʒtikʋ | *a.* rustic; rough

rutilante | ʀuti'lãtɪ | *a.* glittering, gleaming

rutilar | ʀuti'laʀ | *vi.* to glitter, to gleam

S

sábado | 'sabadʊ | *sm.* Saturday

sabão | sa'bãw | *sm.* soap

sabatina | saba'tina | *sf.* weekly school examination

sabedor -dora | sabe'doʀ | *a.* aware; learned. -**s.** de cognizant of

sabedoria | sabɪdʊ'ria | *sf.* wisdom, knowledge

saber | sa'beʀ | *sm.* knowledge, learning / *vt.* to know; to know how to. -**s. ler** to know how to read. -**a s.** namely

sabiá | sabi'a | *sm.* any of several thrushes of the turdoid family

sabichão -chona | sabi'xãw -'xona | *smf.* (pej.) know-it-all, know-all

sabido -da | sa'bidʊ | *a.* (colloq.) shrewd, foxy

sábio -bia | 'sabiʊ | *smf.* savant, sage; scholar / *a.* wise, learned

sabonete | sabo'netɪ | *sm.* toilet soap

sabor | sa'boʀ | *sm.* flavo(u)r, taste. -**ao s. de** at the whim of

saborear | saborɪ'aʀ | *vt.* to savo(u)r, to relish

saboroso -sa | sabo'rozʊ -'rɔza | *a.* tasty, palatable; delicious

sabotagem | sabo'taʒẽy | *sf.* sabotage

sabotar | sabo'taʀ | *vt.* to sabotage

sabugo | sa'bugʊ | *sm.* tender flesh below nails; corn-cob

saca | 'saka | *sf.* sack, bag (esp. a large one)

sacar | sa'kaʀ | *vt.* to draw, to draw out, to take out

sacarina | saka'rina | *sf.* saccharin

saca-rolha | 'saka'ʀola | *sm.* corkscrew

sacerdócio | saseʀ'dɔsiʊ | *sm.* priesthood

sacerdote | saseʀ'dɔtɪ | *sm.* priest

saciar | sasi'aʀ | *vt.* to satiate, to satisfy

saco | 'sakʊ | *sm.* sack; bag. -**encher o s. (de alguém)** (vulg.) to exasperate (someone)

sacolejar | sakʊle'ʒaʀ | *vt. vi.* to shake (up and down)

sacramento | sakra'mẽtʊ | *sm.* sacrament

sacrificar | sakrifi'kaʀ | *vt.* to sacrifice

sacrifício | sakri'fisiʊ | *sm.* sacrifice

sacrilégio | sakri'lɛʒiʊ | *sm.* sacrilege

sacrílego -ga | sa'krilegʊ | *a.* sacrilegious

sacristão | sakriʃ'tãw | *sm.* sacristan; sexton

sacro -cra | 'sakrʊ | *a.* sacred, holy

sacudida, sacudidela | saku'dida sakudi'dɛla | *sf.* shake, jerk, jolt

sacudido -da | saku'didʊ | *a.* shaken, agitated; (colloq.) vigorous

sacudir | saku'diʀ | *vt.* to shake (up, off, out)

sadio -dia | sa'diʊ | *a.* healthy, sound, sane

safado -da | sa'fadʊ | *smf.* (colloq.) shameless person / *a.* (colloq.) impudent, shameless

safar | sa'faʀ | *vt.* to pull out, to set free. -**s. -se** to get away

safira | sa'fira | *sf.* sapphire

safra | 'safra | *sf.* harvest

sagacidade | sagasi'dadɪ | *sf.* sagacity

sagaz | sa'gaʃ | *a.* shrewd, sagacious

sagrado -da | sa'gradʊ | *a.* sacred, holy

saguão | sa'gwãw | *sm.* vestibule, entrance-hall

saia | 'saya | *sf*. skirt

saibro | 'saybrʊ | *sm*. mixture of clay and sand

saída | sa'ida | *sf*. departure; exıt; way out, escape; outlet; remark, sally

sair | sa'ıʀ | *vi*. to go out; to come out; to leave; to issue from; to be published; to turn out. **-s. a alguém** to take after someone. **-s. à luz** to appear, to be published. **-s.(-se) bem** to come off well. **-s.(-se) com a alguém** to come out with (an unexpected remark)

sal | 'sal | *sm*. salt. **-s. grosso** bay salt

sala | 'sala | *sf*. large room; hall

salada | sa'lada | *sf*. salad; (fig.) mess, confusion

salão | sa'lãw | *sm*. large hall; ballroom; large drawing-room; salon (art exhibit). **-s. de barbeiro** barber shop. **-s. de beleza** beauty parlo(u)r

salário | sa'larıʊ | *sm*. salary, wages, pay

saldar | sal'daʀ | *vt*. to settle, to adjust (accounts)

saldo | 'saldʊ | *sm*. (com.) balance, remainder; (*pl.*) bargain sale

saleiro | sa'leyrʊ | *sm*. salt-cellar

saleta | sa'leta | *sf*. small waiting-room; small parlo(u)r

salgadinhos | salga'diNʊʃ | *smpl*. hors-d'oeuvres or canapés

salgado -da | sal'gadʊ | *a*. salted, salty; (fig.) piquant

salgar | sal'gaʀ | *vt*. to salt

sal-gema | sal'jema | *sm*. rock-salt

salgueiro | sal'geyrʊ | *sm*. willow, weeping willow

saliência | sali'ẽsia | *sf*. salience, prominence; (fig., colloq.) impudence

salientar | saliẽ'taʀ | *vt*. to point out, to stress, to accentuate. **-s.-se** to distinguish oneself

saliente | sali'ẽtı | *a*. salient, prominent; (colloq.) saucy, impudent

salina | sa'lina | *sf*. saltworks

salino -na | sa'linʊ | *a*. saline, salty

salitre | sa'litrı | *sm*. saltpetre, saltpeter, nitrate

saliva | sa'liva | *sf*. saliva, spittle

salmão | sal'mãw | *sm*. salmon

salmo | 'salmʊ | *sm*. psalm

salmoura | sal'mowra | *sf*. brine

salobro -bra | sa'lobrʊ | *a*. brackish

salpicar | salpi'kaʀ | *vt*. to sprinkle, to spatter

salsa | 'salsa | *sf*. parsley

salsicha | sal'sixa | *sf*. sausage

saltado -da | sal'tadʊ | *a*. protruding, projecting. **-olhos saltados** goggle eyes

saltar | sal'taʀ | *vt*. to jump, to jump over; to skip. **-s. uma página** to skip a page / *vi*. to jump; to get down; to leap, to pop up. **-s. aos olhos** to strike the eye

salteado -da | saltı'adʊ | *a*. intermittent, skipped. **-saber de core** s. to know by heart

salteador -dora | saltıa'doʀ | *smf*. highwayman

saltimbanco | saltĩ'bãkʊ | *sm*. juggler, acrobat

saltitar | salti'taʀ | *vi*. to hop, to skip about

salto | 'saltʊ | *sm*. jump, leap, bound; drop (of a waterfall); heel (of a shoe). **-dar um s. em** (colloq.) to drop in on. **-s. mortal** somersault

salubre | sa'lubrı | *a*. healthy, salubrious

salutar | salu'taʀ | *a*. salutary

salva | 'salva | *sf*. gun salute, salvo; simultaneous discharge (of guns); salver. (bot.) sage. **-s. de palmas** round of applause

salvação | salva'sãw | *sf*. salvation; deliverance; saving, rescue

salvador -dora | salva'doʀ | *smf*. *a*. savio(u)r

salvados | sal'vadʊʃ | *smpl*. salvage, salvaged goods

salvaguarda | salva'gwaʀda | *sf.* safeguard, protection; safe conduct

salvamento | salva'mẽtʊ | *sm.* saving, rescue; deliverance

salvar | sal'vaʀ | *vt.* to save, to rescue; to salvage; to salu̯te with a salvo

salva-vidas | salva'vidaʃ | *sm.* (*sing.* and *pl.*) life-saver. **-bote s.** life raft

salve | 'salvɪ | *interj.* hail!

salvo -va | 'salvʊ | *a.* safe. **-a s.** out of harm's way. **-a s. de** safe from. **-são e s.** safe and sound / *prep.* save, except

salvo-conduto | 'salvʊkõ'dutʊ | *sm.* safe-conduct

samambaia | samã'baya | *sf.* any of various polypodies (brake, fern etc.)

samba | 'sãba | *sm.* samba, the typical Brazilian dance

sambar | sã'baʀ | *vi.* to dance the samba

sanar | sa'naʀ | *vt.* to remedy (a situation etc.)

sanatório | sana'tɔriʊ | *sm.* hospital (esp. for tuberculars)

sancionar | sãsio'naʀ | *vt.* to sanction, to approve

sandália | sã'dalia | *sf.* sandal

sanduíche | sãdu'ixɪ | *sm.* sandwich

saneamento | sanɪa'mẽtʊ | *sm.* sanitation

sanear | sanɪ'aʀ | *vt.* to sanitize, to make sanitary, to disinfect

sanfona | sã'fona | *sf.* kind of small accordion

sangrar | sã'graʀ | *vt.* to bleed, to open a vein; to let flow (water from a dam) / *vi.* to bleed

sangrento-ta | sã'grẽtʊ | *a.* bloody, bleeding; rare (as of meat)

sangria | sã'gria | *sf.* (med.) blood-letting; sangaree, *sangría* (beverage)

sangue | 'sãgɪ | *sm.* blood

sanguessuga | sãgɪ'suga | *sf.* leech

sangüinário -ria | sãgwi'nariʊ | *a.* cruel, bloodthirsty

sangüíneo -nea | sã'gwinɪʊ | *a.* blood-colo(u)red; ruddy (complexion); sanguine (temperament). **-vaso s.** blood vessel

sanha | 'saNa | *sf.* rage, fury

sanidade | sani'dadɪ | *sf.* health, sanitation, health conditions

sanitário -ria | sani'tariʊ | *a.* sanitary, hygienic. **-água sanitária** hypochlorine

santidade | sãti'dadɪ | *sf.* sanctity, saintliness. **-Sua S.** His Holiness (the Pope)

santificar | sãtifi'kaʀ | *vt.* to sanctify, to make holy

santo -ta | 'sãtʊ | *smf.* saint / *a.* saintly, sainted, holy. **-dia s.** holy day. **-todo s. dia** (colloq.) day after day

santuário | sãtu'ariʊ | *sm.* sanctuary, shrine

são | 'sãw | *sm.* (*abbr.* of **santo**) (*cap.*) Saint (*e.g.* **São Pedro** Saint Peter)

são, sã | 'sãw 'sã | *a.* healthy, sound, wholesome. **-s. e salvo** safe and sound

sapador | sapa'doʀ | *sm.* (mil.) sapper

sapataria | sapata'ria | *sf.* shoe store, shoe shop

sapatear | sapatɪ'aʀ | *vi.* to tap-dance; to stamp

sapateiro -ra | sapa'teyrʊ | *sm.* shoemaker, cobbler; *sf.* shoe closet

sapato | sa'patʊ | *sm.* shoe. **-sapatos de tênis** sneakers

sapé, sapê | sa'pɛ sa'pe | *sm.* sape grass (used for thatching)

sapo | 'sapʊ | *sm.* toad

sapoti | sapʊ'ti | *sm.* sapodilla fruit

saque | 'sakɪ | *sm.* sack, looting, rapine; bank draft; (sports, tennis) service

saquear | sakɪ'aʀ | *vt.* to sack, to plunder, to loot

saracotear | sarakʊtɪ'aʀ | *vi.* to swing the hips; to rambler, to saunter along

saracura | saraˈkura | *sf.* (ornith.) any of various wood rails

saraiva | saˈrayva | *sf.* (meteor.) hail

sarampo | saˈrãpʊ | *sm.* measles

sarapatel | sarapaˈtɛl | *sm.* a dish made of sheep's or pig's viscera and blood

sarapintar | sarapĩˈtaR | *vt.* to dot, to speckle, to mottle

sarar | saˈraR | *vt. vi.* to heal, to cure

sarará | saraˈra | *smf. a.* (colloq.) person of mixed negro blood having reddish kinky hair; albino (person)

sarau | saˈraw | *sm.* evening party, soirée. **-s. musical** evening concert

sarcasmo | saRˈkaʒmʊ | *sm.* sarcasm

sarda | ˈsaRda | *sf.* (ichth.) spanish mackerel; freckle

sardinha | saRˈdiNa | *sf.* sardine

sargento | saRˈjẽtʊ | *sm.* (mil.) sergeant; screw clamp

sarilho | saˈriLʊ | *sm.* windlass, winch; (colloq.) confusion, disorder

sarja | ˈsaRja | *sf.* (tex.) serge

sarjeta | saRˈjeta | *sf.* gutter

sarna | ˈsaRna | *sf.* scabies; mange

sarrafada | saraˈfada | *sf.* (colloq.) blow, kick

sarrafo | saˈRafʊ | *sm.* lath, slat. **-meter** or **baixar o s.** to criticize severely; (sports, esp. soccer) to play with violence

sarro | ˈsaRʊ | *sm.* tartar (deposit on the teeth and in wine casks); fur (on tongue); tar deposit in a pipe

satélite | saˈtɛlitɪ | *sm. a.* satellite

sátira | ˈsatira | *sf.* satire

satírico -ca | saˈtirikʊ | *a.* satiric, satirical

sátiro | ˈsatirʊ | *sm.* satyr

satisfação | satiʒfaˈsãw | *sf.* satisfaction

satisfazer | satiʒfaˈzeR | *vt.* to satisfy

saturar | satuˈraR | *vt.* to saturate, to soak

saudação | sawdaˈsãw | *sf.* salutation, salute; (*pl.*) greetings

saudade | sawˈdadɪ | *sf.* longing, yearning; homesickness. **-ter s. de** to miss, to long for; to be nostalgic for

saudar | sawˈdaR | *vt.* to greet; to welcome

saudável | sawˈdavɪl | *a.* healthy, wholesome, sound

saúde | saˈudɪ | *sf.* health / *interj.* health!, cheers!

saudoso -sa | sawˈdozʊ -ˈdɷza | *a.* longing; homesick, nostalgic; deeply missed

saúva | saˈuva | *sf.* any of a number of leaf-cutting ants

saveiro | saˈveyrʊ | *sm.* kind of fishing boat

se | ˈsɪ | *conj.* if, whether. **-como s.** as if. **-s. ao menos** if only, if just. **-s. bem que** although

se | ˈsɪ | *reflexive pron.* 3rd pers. sing. himself, herself, itself, oneself, yourself; (*pl.*) themselves, yourselves, each other, one another; (impersonal) one, they, you

sé | ˈsɛ | *sf.* cathedral; see. **-Santa S.** Holy See

seara | sɪˈara | *sf.* harvest; (fig.) field, area of study

sebe | ˈsɛbɪ | *sf.* hedge

sebento -ta | seˈbẽtʊ | *a.* dirty, greasy

sebo | ˈsebʊ | *sm.* tallow, fat (esp. of beef); (colloq.) second-hand bookstore

seca | ˈseka | *sf.* drought; long dry spell

secador | sekaˈdoR | *sm.* drier, dryer

seção, secção | seˈsãw sekˈsãw | *sf.* section

secar | seˈkaR | *vt.* to dry (up). **-s.-se** to become dry / *vi.* to dry (up, out)

seco -ca | ˈsekʊ | *sm.* (only *pl.*) dry foodstuffs / *a.* dry; arid, parched; lean, skinny

secreção | sekre'sãw | *sf.* secretion

secretaria | sekreta'ria | *sf.* secretariat; government department, ministry or bureau

secretário -ria | sekre'tariʋ | *smf.* secretary; *sf.* desk

secreto -ta | se'krɛtʋ | *a.* secret

secular | seku'laʀ | *a.* secular, lay, temporal; agelong

século | 'sɛkulʋ | *sm.* century

secundar | sekũ'daʀ | *vt.* to second; to back up; to repeat

secundário -ria | sekũ'dariʋ | *a.* secondary, subordinate

secura | se'kura | *sf.* dryness; (fig.) coldness

seda | 'seda | *sf.* silk

sedativo -va | seda'tivʋ | *sm. a.* sedative

sede | 'sɛdɪ | *sf.* seat, headquarters, home office; plantation house. **-s. de governo** seat of a government. **-s. de um clube** club-house

sede | 'sedɪ | *sf.* thirst; (fig.) strong desire. **-matar a s.** to quench one's thirst

sedentário -ria | sedẽ'tariʋ | *a.* sedentary

sedento -ta | se'dẽtʋ | *a.* thirsty

sedição | sɪdi'sãw | *sf.* sedition

sedicioso -sa | sɪdisi'ozʋ -'ωza | *a.* seditious

sedimento | sɪdi'mẽtʋ | *sm.* sediment

sedoso -sa | se'dozʋ -'dωza | *a.* silky

sedução | sedu'sãw | *sf.* seduction, attraction, allurement

sedutor -tora | sedu'toʀ | *sm.* seducer; *sf.* seductress / *a.* seductive, alluring, enticing

seduzir | sedu'ziʀ | *vt.* to seduce, to allure; (law) to deprive of virginity

sega | 'sɛga | *sf.* harvest

segadeira | sega'deyra | *sf.* scythe. **-s. mecânica** reaping machine

segar | se'gaʀ | *vt.* to harvest, to mow, to scythe

segmento | seg'mẽtʋ | *sm.* segment, part, section

segredar | segre'daʀ | *vt. vi.* to whisper

segredo | se'gredʋ | *sm.* secret; mystery; secret combination of a safe

segregação | segrega'sãw | *sf.* segregation

segregar | segre'gaʀ | *vt.* to segregate, to set apart; (physiol.) to secrete

seguida | sɪ'gida | *sf.* following. **-em s.** soon after, immediately after

seguido -da | sɪ'gidʋ | *a.* followed; continued; continuous; immediate. **-dias seguidos** day after day

seguimento | sɪgi'mẽtʋ | *sm.* following; sequence, continuation. **-dar s.** to continue

seguinte | sɪ'gĩtɪ | *a.* following, next

seguir | sɪ'giʀ | *vt.* to follow; to attend closely; to take as an example. **-s.-se** to follow (in order), to succeed; to result from / *vi.* to follow; to continue; to proceed; to carry on. **-fazer s.** to forward, to send on

segunda | sɪ'gũda | *sf.* = *segunda--feira*

segunda-feira | sɪ'gũda'feyra | *sf.* Monday

segundo -da | sɪ'gũdʋ | *sm.* second; moment; *smf.* second / *a.* second. **-de** or **em segunda mão** second--hand / *adv.* in second place / *prep.* according to

segurança | sɪgu'rãsa | *sf.* security, safety; assurance; bodyguards; *sm.* (colloq.) body guard. **-com s.** assuredly

segurar | sɪgu'raʀ | *vt.* to hold, to grasp, to seize; to insure

seguro -ra | sɪ'gurʋ | *sm.* insurance, assurance / *a.* secure, safe; certain, confident; fixed, stable. **-estar s.** to be sure

seio | 'seyʋ | *sm.* bosom; breast; depth, innermost recesses. **-no**

s. de in the midst of

seis | ˈseyʃ | *sm. num.* six

seiscentos -tas | seyˈsẽtuʃ | *smf. num.* six hundred

seita | ˈseyta | *sf.* sect; faction

seiva | ˈseyva | *sf.* sap; (fig.) blood, strength

seixo | ˈseyxu | *sm.* pebble

sela | ˈsɛla | *sf.* saddle

selar | seˈlaR | *vt.* to saddle; to seal; to stamp (for mailing)

seleção | seleˈsãw | *sf.* selection; choice

seleta | seˈlɛta | *sf.* (lit.) anthology

seleto -ta | seˈlɛtu | *a.* select, choice

selim | sɩˈlĩ | *sm.* bicycle seat

selo | ˈselu | *sm.* postage stamp; seal

selva | ˈsɛlva | *sf.* jungle, rain forest

selvagem | selˈvajẽy | *smf.* savage / *a.* savage, wild

sem | ˈsẽy | *prep.* without. **-s. conta** countless

semana | seˈmana | *sf.* week

semanal | semaˈnal | *a.* weekly

semblante | sẽˈblãtɩ | *sm.* face, countenance

semear | semɩˈaR | *vt.* to sow, to seed

semelhança | semeˈlãsa | *sf.* similarity, likeness, resemblance. **-à s. de** like, in the manner of

semelhante | semeˈlãtɩ | *smf.* fellow creature / *a.* similar, like, resembling; such

semelhar | semeˈlaR | *vt. vr.* to resemble, to look like

semente | seˈmẽtɩ | *sf.* seed

sementeira | semẽˈteyra | *sf.* seed-bed; seed field

semestre | seˈmɛʃtrɩ | *sm.* semester, half-year

seminário | semiˈnariu | *sm.* seminary

seminu -nua | semiˈnu | *a.* half-naked

sem-número | sẽyˈnumeru | *sm.* countless number

sem-par | sẽyˈpaR | *a.* peerless, unequaled

sempre | ˈsẽprɩ | *adv.* always, ever.

-como s. as ever. **-para s.** for ever. **-quase s.** ordinarily

sem-vergonha | sẽyveRˈgona | *smf.* shameless person / *a.* shameless, impudent

senado | seˈnadu | *sm.* senate

senador -dora | senaˈdoR | *sm.* senator, congressman; *sf.* congresswoman

senão | sɩˈnãw | *sm.* defect, flaw / *conj.* or else, otherwise; save, but, except

senda | ˈsẽda | *sf.* path, trail

senha | ˈseNa | *sf.* password; (mil.) parole; theatre ticket stub

senhor | sɩˈNoR | *sm.* mister, sir; gentleman; (*cap.*) God. **Senhor** (preceded by the article o) form of address translated by the pronoun you. **-Prezado S.** Dear Sir

senhora | sɩˈNora | *sf.* mistress; wife, lady of the house. **Senhora** (preceded by the article a) form of address translated by the pronoun you

senhorio -ria | sɩNuˈriu | *sm.* landlord; *sf.* landlady

senhorita | sɩNuˈrita | *sf.* miss

senil | seˈnil | *a.* senile

senilidade | seniliˈdadɩ | *sf.* senility

sensação | sẽsaˈsãw | *sf.* sensation, feeling

sensacional | sẽsasioˈnal | *a.* sensational

sensato -ta | sẽˈsatu | *a.* judicious, sensible, wise

sensibilidade | sẽsibiliˈdadɩ | *sf.* sensibility, sensitiveness, sensitivity

sensibilizar | sẽsibiliˈzaR | *vt.* to touch, to move; (chem., photog.) to sensitize

sensitiva | sẽsiˈtiva | *sf.* the sensitive plant

sensitivo -va | sẽsiˈtivu | *a.* sensitive

sensível | sẽˈsivɩl | *a.* sensitive; compassionate; sensible; noticeable; sore

senso | ˈsẽsu | *sm.* sense. **-s. comum**

common sense

sensual | sẽsu'al | *a.* sensual; sensuous

sentar | sẽ'taʀ | *vt.* to seat. **-s.-se** to sit down. **-s. praça** to enlist (as a soldier)

sentença | sẽ'tẽsa | *sf.* sentence, decision; maxim, axiom

sentenciar | sẽtẽsi'aʀ | *vt.* to sentence, to condemn

sentido -da | sĩ'tidʊ | *sm.* sense; meaning; feeling; direction, course. **-perder os sentidos** to faint / *a.* grieved; sorry; sad / *interj.* (mil.) attention!

sentimental | sẽtimẽ'tal | *smf.* sentimentalist / *a.* sentimental

sentimento | sẽti'mẽtʊ | *sm.* sentiment; feeling; tender feeling; (*pl.*) condolences. **-apresentar sentimentos a** to extend one's sympathy to

sentinela | sẽti'nɛla | *sf.* sentinel, sentry. **-de s.** on sentry duty

sentir | sĩ'tiʀ | *vt.* to feel, to perceive; to experience; to regret; to resent. **-s.-se** to feel, to experience. **-s. falta de alguém** to miss someone

senzala | sẽ'zala | *sf.* (hist.) slave quarters on a plantation

separação | separa'sãw | *sf.* separation

separado -da | sepa'radʊ | *a.* separated, detached. **-em s.** under separate cover

separar | sepa'raʀ | *vt.* to separate. **-s.-se de** to separate oneself from, to part with

separata | sepa'rata | *sf.* offprint, reprint (of articles)

sepulcro | se'pulkrʊ | *sm.* sepulcher, tomb

sepultar | sepul'taʀ | *vt.* to bury, to inter

sepultura | sepul'tura | *sf.* grave, tomb

seqüência | se'kwẽsia | *sf.* sequence, succession

sequer | sɩ'kɛʀ | *adv.* even, so much as. **-nem s.** not even

seqüestrar | sekwɛʃ'traʀ | *vt.* to sequester, to sequestrate; to abduct, to kidnap

seqüestro | se'kwɛʃtrʊ | *sm.* abduction, kidnapping; sequestration; confiscation

sequioso -sa | seki'ozʊ -'ɔza | *a.* avid, eager; thirsty

séquito, séqüito | 'sɛkitʊ 'sɛkwitʊ | *sm.* entourage, retinue

ser | 'seʀ | *sm.* a being / *vi.* to be. **-s. capaz de** to be able to. **-s. brasileiro, inglês** etc. to be Brazilian, English etc. **-s. contra** to be against. **-s. de** to belong to; to be from

serão | se'rãw | *sm.* night work; overtime work; evening party

sereia | se'reya | *sf.* mermaid, siren; siren of fire or police vehicles

serenar | sere'naʀ | *vi.* to calm, to placate / *vt.* to grow calm; to drizzle

serenata | sere'nata | *sf.* serenade

serenidade | sereni'dadɩ | *sf.* serenity, calmness

sereno -na | se'renʊ | *sm.* mist, dew / *a.* clear, unclouded (weather); serene, calm

seresta | se'rɛʃta | *sf.* serenade

seresteiro | sereʃ'teyrʊ | *sm.* serenader

seriado | seri'adʊ | *sm.* cinema film or TV program presented in series / *a.* seriate, arranged in a series

série | 'sɛriɩ | *sf.* series; succession; grade (in school etc.). **-produção em s.** mass production

seriedade | serie'dadɩ | *sf.* seriousness; graveness, austerity

seringa | sɩ'rĩga | *sf.* syringe; rubber latex (in the Amazon region)

seringal | sɩrĩ'gal | *sm.* rubber plantation

seringueira | sɩrĩ'geyra | *sf.* rubber tree

seringueiro | sɩrĩ'geyrʊ | *sm.* rubber-gatherer

sério -ria | 'sɛriv | *sm.* seriousness, graveness / *a.* serious, grave; solemn. **-a** s. seriously

sermão | seR'mãw | *sm.* sermon

serpente | seR'pɛ̃tɪ | *sf.* serpent, snake

serpentear | seRpẽtɪ'aR | *vi.* to crawl (as a snake); to meander

serpentina | seRpẽ'tina | *sf.* coil of a still; paper streamer (used at Carnival)

serra | 'sɛRa | *sf.* saw; sierra (also ichth.). **-subir a s.** (colloq.) to get very angry

serralheiro | seRa'Leyrv | *sm.* locksmith

serrano -na | se'Ranv | *a.* mountain, of or pertaining to the mountain

serrar | se'RaR | *vt.* to saw

serraria | seRa'ria | *sf.* sawmill

serrote | se'Rwtɪ | *sm.* handsaw

sertanejo -ja | seRta'nejv | *smf.* dweller of the back country / *a.* of or pertaining to the back country

sertão | seR'tãw | *sm.* back country, backwoods

servente | seR'vẽtɪ | *smf.* cleaner; unskilled assistant

serviçal | seRvi'sal | *smf.* servant / *a.* obliging; complying; servile

serviço | seR'visv | *sm.* service; set of dishes; cover charge; (colloq.) job. **-de s.** (mil.) on duty

servidão | sɪRvi'dãw | *sf.* servitude, bondage

servido -da | sɪR'vidv | *a.* served; used, worn

servil | seR'vil | *a.* base, servile

servir | sɪR'viR | *vt.* to serve; to attend. **-s.-se** to help oneself; to take advantage / *vi.* to serve; to be of use; to fit; to wait on

servo -va | 'seRvv | *smf.* serf

sesmaria | seʒma'ria | *sf.* land grant in colonial Brazil

sessão | se'sãw | *sm.* session (also cine.); meeting

sessenta | se'sẽta | *sm. num.* sixty

sesta | 'sɛʃta | *sf.* siesta, afternoon nap

seta | 'sɛta | *sf.* arrow

sete | 'sɛtɪ | *sm. num.* seven

setecentos -tas | sɛtɪ'sẽtuʃ | *smf. num.* seven hundred

setembro | se'tẽbrv | *sm.* September

setenta | se'tẽta | *sm. num.* seventy

setentrional | setẽtrio'nal | *a.* northern

sétimo -ma | 'sɛtimv | *smf. a.* seventh

seu | 'sew | *sm. poss. a.* his, her, its, your, yours; (*pl.*) their, your / *poss. pron.* his, hers, its, yours; (*pl.*) theirs, yours

severidade | severi'dadɪ | *sf.* severity, harshness

severo -ra | se'vɛrv | *a.* severe, harsh, austere

sexo | 'sɛksv | *sm.* sex. **-o belos.** the fair sex

sexta | 'seʃta | *sf.* = *sexta-feira*

sexta-feira | 'seʃta'feyra | *sf.* Fryday

sexto -ta | 'seʃtv | *smf. a.* sixth

sexual | seksu'al | *a.* sexual

sezão | se'zãw | *sf.* malaria, intermittent fever

si | 'si | *pron. 3rd pers. sing.* himself, herself, itself, oneself, yourself; (*pl.*) yourselves, themselves

si | 'si | *sm.* (mus.) B, si (in England, the U.S. and Germany the seventh tone in the scale of C)

sibilar | sibi'laR | *vi.* to hiss; to zip (a bullet)

sicrano -na | si'kranv | *smf.* Mr., Mrs. or Miss so-and-so. **-Fulano, Beltrano e S.** Tom, Dick and Harry

siderurgia | sideruR'jia | *sf.* metallurgy of iron and steel

sidra | 'sidra | *sf.* cider

sifão | si'fãw | *sm.* siphon

sigilo | si'jilv | *sm.* secret; secrecy

signatário -ria | signa'tariv | *smf.* signatory

significação | signifika'sãw | *sf.* significance, meaning, sense

significado | signifi'kadʊ | sm. meaning

significar | signifi'kaʀ | vt. to signify, to denote, to mean

significativo -va | signifika'tivʊ | a. significative

signo | 'signʊ | sm. sign (esp. astron.)

sílaba | 'silaba | sf. syllable

silenciar | silēsi'aʀ | vt. to silence / vi. to become or to remain silent

silêncio | si'lēsiʊ | sm. silence

silencioso -sa | silēsi'ozʊ -'ωza | a. silent, quiet

silhueta | siʟu'eta | sf. silhouette

silvestre | sil'vɛʒtrɪ | a. wild, uncultivated

silvícola | sil'vikʊla | smf. indian, aborigine

silvo | 'silvʊ | sm. whistle; hiss (esp. of snakes); a shrill sound

sim | 'sī | sm. yes. **-dar o s.** to say yes, to consent / adv. yes. **-claro que s.!** of course! **-poiss.!** that's what you think! (ironically); also, simply, all right

símbolo | 'sībʊlʊ | sm. symbol

simetria | sime'tria | sf. symmetry

similar | simi'laʀ | a. similar, alike

simpatia | sīpa'tia | sf. sympathy, liking, affinity; (colloq.) magic spell

simpático -ca | sī'patikʊ | a. likable, attractive, pleasing

simpatizar | sīpati'zaʀ | vt. to like, to get on with

simples | 'sīpliʒ | a. simple; unadorned, bare, austere

simplicidade | sīplisi'dadɪ | sf. simplicity; naturalness, artlessness; simple-mindedness

simplificar | sīplifi'kaʀ | vt. to simplify

simplório -ria | sī'plωriʊ | smf. a simpleton / a. simple, simple-minded

simulacro | simu'lakrʊ | sm. pretence, imitation

simular | simu'laʀ | vt. to simulate

simultâneo -nea | simul'tanɪʊ | a. simultaneous

sina | 'sina | sf. (colloq.) fate, fortune

sinagoga | sina'gωga | sf. synagogue

sinal | si'nal | sm. signal, sign; mark, indication; down payment; omen; mole, skin blemish; traffic light. **-fazer s.** to beckon. **-sinais particulares** scars, moles etc.

sinalização | sinaliza'sãw | sf. signalizing; traffic signals and signs

sinalizar | sinali'zaʀ | vt. vi. to signal

sinceridade | sīseri'dadɪ | sf. sincerity

sincero -ra | sī'sɛrʊ | a. sincere, honest, frank

síncope | 'sīkʊpɪ | sf. syncope. **-s. cardíaca** heart stroke

sincronizar | sīkroni'zaʀ | vt. to synchronize

sindicância | sīdi'kãsia | sf. investigation, inquiry, probe

sindicato | sīdi'katʊ | sm. trade union, labo(u)r union; syndicate

síndico -ca | 'sīdikʊ | smf. resident manager of a co-operative apartment building

sinecura | sine'kura | sf. sinecure

sineiro | si'neyrʊ | sm. bell-ringer; bell-founder

sineta | si'neta | sf. small bell

sinete | si'netɪ | sm. seal, signet

sinfonia | sīfo'nia | sf. symphony

singelez, singeleza | sīje'leʒ sīje-'leza | sf. simplicity; artlessness; naïvety

singelo -la | sī'jɛlʊ | a. single; simple, unadorned

singrar | sī'graʀ | vi. (unc.) to sail, to navigate

singular | sīgu'laʀ | sm. (gram.) singular / a. singular, individual; extraordinary, unique, peculiar

singularidade | sīgulari'dadɪ | sf. singularity; peculiarity

sinhá | si'Na | sf. (colloq.) Missis,

Missus (negro slave corruption of se**nhora**)

sinhô | si'NO | *sm.* Massa (negro slave corruption of **senhor**)

sinistro -tra | si'niʒtrʋ | *sm.* disaster; wreck / *a.* sinister

sino | 'sinʋ | *sm.* bell

sinônimo -ma | si'nonimʋ | *sm.* synonym / *a.* synonymous

sinopse | si'nɔpsι | *sf.* synopsis

sintaxe | sĩ'taksι | *sf.* syntax

sintese | 'sĩtezι | *sf.* synthesis

sintético -ca | sĩ'tεtikʋ | *a.* synthetic, synthetical

sintoma | sĩ'toma | *sm.* symptom

sintonizar | sĩtoni'zaR | *vt.* (rad.) to tune

sinuca | si'nuka | *sf.* snooker, pool. **-estar numa s.** (slang) to be on a tight spot

sinuoso -sa | sinu'ozʋ -'ωza | *a.* sinuous

siri | si'ri | *sm.* crab

sírio -ria | 'siriʋ | *smf. a.* Syrian

siso | 'sizʋ | *sm.* prudence, good sense, judgment; (colloq.) wisdom tooth

sistema | siʒ'tema | *sm.* system

sisudez | sizu'deʒ | *sf.* gravity, seriousness

sitiante | siti'ãtι | *smf.* besieger; owner of a small farm / *a.* besieging

sitiar | siti'aR | *vt.* to besiege

sítio | 'sitiʋ | *sm.* site, location; small farm; siege. **-estado de s.** state of siege

situação | situa'sãw | *sf.* situation; position

situar | situ'aR | *vt.* to situate, to locate

smoking | 'smokĩ(g) | *sm.* dinner--jacket, man's evening dress; tuxedo

só | 'sω | *a.* alone; single; solitary. **-por si s.** by himself; by or in itself; alone / *adv.* only

soalho | sʋ'aLʋ | *sm.* wooden floor

soar | sʋ'aR | *vi.* to sound. **-s. bem** to ring true; (fig.) to give a good impression

sob | sob(i) | *prep.* under, subject to. **-s. a capa de** under cover of. **-s. medida** made-to-order. **-s. pena de** on pain of

sobejo -ja | so'bejʋ | *a.* surplus; leftover. **-de s.** excessively / *sm.* (*pl.*) leftovers

soberania | sobera'nia | *sf.* sovereignty

soberano -na | sobe'ranʋ | *smf. a.* sovereign

soberba | so'beRba | *sf.* haughtiness, arrogance

soberbo -ba | so'beRbʋ | *a.* superb; haughty; sumptuous

sobra | 'sωbra | *sf.* excess, surplus; (*pl.*) leftovers. **-de s.** more than enough

sobrado -da | so'bradʋ | *sm.* (obs.) house of two or more stories / *a.* leftover

sobranceiro -ra | sobrã'seyrʋ | *a.* towering, overlooking; haughty, proud

sobrancelha | sobrã'seLa | *sf.* eyebrow. **-franzir as sobrancelhas** to frown

sobrar | so'braR | *vi.* to be more than enough; to be left over

sobre | 'sobrι | *prep.* over, above; on, upon; concerning

sobreaviso | sobrιa'vizʋ | *sm.* precaution. **-de s.** on the alert

sobrecarga | sobrι'kaRga | *sf.* overcharge

sobrecarregado -da | sobrιkaRe'gadʋ | *a.* overloaded

sobrecarregar | sobrιkaRe'gaR | *vt.* to overload

sobrecenho | sobrι'seNʋ | *sm.* scowl, frown

sobre-humano -na | sobrιu'manʋ | *a.* superhuman

sobreloja | sobrι'lωja | *sf.* mezzanine

sobremaneira | sobrιma'neyra | *adv.* exceedingly, excessively

sobremesa | sobrι'meza | *sf.* dessert

sobrenatural | sobrιnatu'ral | *a.* supernatural

sobrenome|sobrɪ'nomɪ|*sm.* surname, family name

sobrepor|sobrɪ'poR|*vt.* to superpose; to superimpose; to overlay. **-s.-se** a to overcome

sobrepujar | sobrɪpu'jaR | *vt.* to surpass; to overcome

sobrescrever | sobrɪʃkre'veR | *vt.* to superscribe; to address (mail)

sobrescritar|sobrɪʃkri'taR|*vt.* to address (mail)

sobrescrito -ta | sobrɪʃ'kritʊ | *sm.* envelope, wrapping (for mail)

sobressair|sobrɪsa'iR|*vi.* to stand out

sobressalente, sobresselente | sobrɪsa'lẽtɪ sobrɪse'lẽtɪ | *sm.* spare (part) / *a.* spare, extra

sobressaltar | sobrɪsal'taR | *vt.* to startle, to take unawares. **-s.-se** to be startled

sobressalto | sobrɪ'saltʊ | *sm.* surprise, start; freight

sobretaxa | sobrɪ'taxa | *sf.* additional charge

sobretudo | sobrɪ'tudʊ | *sm.* overcoat / *adv.* especially, above all

sobrevir | sobrɪ'viR | *vi.* to supervene; to follow; to befall, to happen

sobrevivente | sobrɪvi'vẽtɪ | *smf.* survivor / *a.* surviving

sobreviver | sobrɪvi'veR | *vi.* to survive

sobriedade | sobrie'dadɪ | *sf.* soberness, sobriety; temperance

sobrinho -nha | sʊ'briɴʊ | *sm.* nephew; *sf.* niece

sobrinho-neto, sobrinha-neta | sʊ'briɴʊ'netʊ | *sm.* grandnephew; *sf.* grandniece

sóbrio -bria | 'sɔbriʊ | *a.* frugal; moderate; sober; abstemious

sobrolho|soʼbroʟʊ|*sm.* eyebrow

socador|soka'doR|*sm.* pounder; tamper

socapa | so'kapa | *sf.* used in the expression **a.s.** furtively, on the sly

socar | so'kaR | *vt.* to hit (with the fist), to sock; to smash, to pound

socavão | soka'vãw | *sm.* cave; hideaway

sociabilidade | sosiabili'dadɪ | *sf.* sociability

social | sosi'al | *a.* social

socialismo | sosia'liʒmʊ | *sm.* socialism

socialização | sosializa'sãw | *sf.* socialization

socializar | sosiali'zaR | *vt* to socialize

sociável | sosi'avɪl | *a.* sociable

sociedade | sosie'dadɪ | *sf.* society; association; (com.) firm, partnership. **-s. anônima** (com.) corporation

sócio -cia | 'sɔsiʊ | *smf.* partner, associate; member. **-s. comanditário** silent partner

sociologia | sosiolo'jia | *sf.* sociology

soco|'sokʊ|*sm.* punch, blow with the fist

soco | 'sɔkʊ | *sm.* clog, wooden shoe

soçobrar | soso'braR | *vi.* to sink, to go under, to be shipwrecked

socorrer|soko'ReR|*vt.* to help; to rescue. **-s.-se de** to resort to

socorro | so'koRʊ | *sm.* help, aid; rescue. **-primeiros socorros** first aid

soda | 'sɔda | *sf.* soda; barilla; seltzer. **-s. limonada** lemon squash

soerguer | sʊeR'geR | *vt.* to raise or lift slightly

sofá | so'fa | *sf.* sofa, couch

sofisma | so'fiʒma | *sm.* sophism

sofrear | sofrɪ'aR | *vt.* to rein (in); to check, to restrain

sôfrego -ga | 'sofregʊ | *a.* avid, eager; impatient

sofreguidão | sofregi'dãw | *sf.* avidity, eagerness; impatience

sofrer | so'freR | *vt.* to suffer, to undergo. **-s. do coração** to have a heart condition / *vi.* to suffer, to endure

sofrimento | sʊfri'mẽtʊ | *sm.*

suffering; distress

sofrível | svˈfrivɪl | *a.* endurable, tolerable, fair

sogro -gra | ˈsogrʊ ˈsɔgra | *sm.* father-in-law; *sf.* mother-in-law

soja | ˈsɔja | *sf.* soya, soya bean. **-molho de s.** soy

sol | ˈsɔl | *sm.* sun; sunlight. **-fazer s.** to be sunny. **-nascer do s.** sunrise

sola | ˈsɔla | *sf.* shoe sole; sole of the foot

solapar | solaˈpaʀ | *vt.* to undermine

solar | soˈlaʀ | *sm.* manor-house / *a.* solar / *vt.* to sole (shoes) / *vi.* to play a solo; to fly solo

solavanco | svlaˈvãkʊ | *sm.* jolt, jerk, bump

solda | ˈsɔlda | *sf.* solder; weld

soldado -da | solˈdadʊ | *sm.* soldier / *a.* soldered

soldar | solˈdaʀ | *vt.* to solder; to weld / *vi.* (also **s.-se**) to weld, to unite

soldo | ˈsoldʊ | *sm.* soldier's pay. **-a s.** mercenarily

soleira | soˈleyra | *sf.* threshold; doorstep; (colloq.) scorching sun

solene | soˈlenɪ | *a.* solemn

solenidade | soleniˈdadɪ | *sf.* solemnity, ceremony

solenizar | soleniˈzaʀ | *vt.* to solemnize

soletrar | soleˈtraʀ | *vt.* to spell, to spell out (orally); to read slowly

solicitar | solisiˈtaʀ | *vt.* to solicit; to request; to petition, to apply for

solícito -ta | soˈlisitʊ | *a.* solicitous; concerned

solicitude | solisiˈtudɪ | *sf.* solicitude, concern

solidão | soliˈdãw | *sf.* solitude, loneliness; wilderness

solidariedade | solidarieˈdadɪ | *sf.* solidarity

solidário -ria | soliˈdarɪv | *a.* interdependent; mutual; understanding

solidez | soliˈdeʒ | *sf.* solidity; stability

sólido -da | ˈsɔlidʊ | *sm.* solid; (geom.) body / *a.* solid, firm; strong

solista | soˈliʃta | *smf.* soloist

solitário -ria | soliˈtarɪv | *sm.* solitaire (ring); hermit; *sf.* (colloq.) taenia; solitary (cell) / *a.* solitary; deserted

solo | ˈsɔlʊ | *sm.* ground; soil; (aeron., mus.) solo

soltar | solˈtaʀ | *vt.* to loosen, to unfasten; to let loose, to let go; to release; to let out (a cry etc.). **-s.-se** to get loose; to come undone

solteirão -rona | soltey'rãw -'rona | *sm.* (colloq.) a confirmed bachelor; *sf.* (colloq.) spinster, old maid

solteiro -ra | solˈteyrʊ | *sm.* bachelor, single man; *sf.* single woman

solto -ta | ˈsoltʊ | *a.* loose, free, released. **-às soltas** at large. **-dormir a sono s.** to sleep soundly

solução | svluˈsãw | *sf.* solution

soluçar | svluˈsaʀ | *vi.* to sob; to hiccup

solucionar | svlusioˈnaʀ | *vt.* to solve; to unravel

soluço | svˈlusʊ | *sm.* sob; hiccup

solúvel | svˈluvɪl | *a.* soluble

solvência | solˈvẽsia | *sf.* solvency

solver | solˈveʀ | *vt.* to solve; to dissolve; to settle (a debt)

som | ˈsõ | *sm.* sound. **-ao s. de** to the sound of

soma | ˈsoma | *sf.* sum, total, amount; addition

somar | soˈmaʀ | *vt.* to add, to sum up / *vi.* to ammount to

sombra | ˈsõbra | *sf.* shadow, shade; trace, tinge. **-nem por s.** not by the remotest chance

sombrear | sõbrɪˈaʀ | *vt.* to shade

sombrinha | sõˈbriɴa | *sf.* parasol

sombrio -bria | sõˈbriv | *a.* somber; shady; cloudy; dark, dull

somenos | so'menʋʒ | *a.* petty, worthless. **-questão de s.** unimportant matter

somente | sʋ'mẽtɪ so'mẽtɪ | *adv.* only, merely

sonâmbulo -la | so'nãbulʋ | *smf.* sleepwalker / *a.* sleepwalking

sonante | so'nãtɪ | *a.* sounding. **-moeda** s. hard cash

sonda | 'sõda | *sf.* sounding lead; (surg.) sound, probe; drilling rig (as for oil)

sondagem | sõ'dajẽy | *sf.* sounding; (surg., fig.) probe; drilling (as for oil)

sondar | sõ'daʀ | *vt.* to fathom; to probe; to sound out (surg., fig.); to drill (as for oil)

soneca | so'nɛka | *sf.* nap. **-tirar uma s.** to take a nap

sonegar | sone'gaʀ | *vt.* to evade (taxes etc.); to conceal, to withhold (as income etc.)

soneto | so'netʋ | *sm.* sonnet

sonhador -dora | soɲa'doʀ | *smf.* dreamer / *a.* dreaming

sonhar | so'ɲaʀ | *vi.* to dream

sonho | 'soɲʋ | *sm.* dream; kind of fried cake

sono | 'sonʋ | *sm.* sleep. **-a s. solto** fast asleep. **-estar com s.** to be sleepy

sonolência | sono'lẽsia | *sf.* sleepiness

sonolento -ta | sono'lẽtʋ | *a.* sleepy, drowsy, somnolent

sonoro -ra | so'nɔrʋ | *a.* sonorous, sounding, resonant

sonso -sa | 'sõsʋ | *a.* sly, artful

sopa | 'sopa | *sf.* soup. **-isto é s.** (colloq.) that's a cinch. **-dar s.** (slang) to make things easy

sopapo | sʋ'papʋ | *sm.* punch; cuff

sopé | sʋ'pɛ | *sm.* foot, base (of a mountain, hill etc.)

sopeira | so'peyra | *sf.* soup tureen

sopesar | sope'zaʀ | *vt.* to weigh or balance (in one's hand)

soprar | so'praʀ | *vt.* to blow; to prompt (a student) / *vi.* to blow

sopro | 'soprʋ | *sm.* blowing; gust,

puff. **-instrumento de s.** wind instrument

sórdido -da | 'sɔʀdidʋ | *a.* sordid, filthy

soro | 'sorʋ | *sm.* (med.) serum; whey (of milk)

sorrateiro -ra | soʀa'teyrʋ | *a.* sneaky, sly

sorridente | soʀi'dẽtɪ | *a.* smiling

sorrir | sʋ'ʀiʀ | *vi.* to smile

sorriso | so'ʀizʋ | *sm.* smile. **-s. amarelo** forced smile

sorte | 'sɔʀtɪ | *sf.* luck, fortune; fate; sort, kind. **-tirar a s. grande** to hit the jackpot. **-tirar às.** to draw lots. **-de s. que** so that

sortear | soʀtɪ'aʀ | *vt.* to draw lots; to raffle

sorteio | soʀ'teyʋ | *sm.* raffle or other drawing of lots

sortido -da | sʋʀ'tidʋ | *a.* assorted; stocked

sortilégio | soʀti'lɛjiʋ | *sm.* sorcery

sortimento | sʋʀti'mẽtʋ | *sm.* assortment

sorumbático -ca | sʋrũ'batikʋ | *a.* somber, gloomy

sorvedouro | soʀve'dowrʋ | *sm.* whirlpool (also fig.)

sorver | soʀ'veʀ | *vt.* to sip; to absorb

sorvete | soʀ'vetɪ | *sm.* ice cream; sherbet

sós | 'sɔʒ | *adv.* used in the expression **a s.** alone, all alone, all by themselves

sósia | 'sɔzia | *smf.* double (of person)

soslaio | soʒ'layʋ | *sm.* used in the expression **de s.** sideways, aslant

sossegado -da | sʋse'gadʋ | *a.* quiet, calm, peaceful

sossegar | sʋse'gaʀ | *vt.* to quiet, to tranquilize / *vi.* to calm down, to rest

sossego | sʋ'segʋ | *sm.* calm, quiet, quietude

sotaina | so'tayna | *sf.* cassock

sótão | 'sɔtãw | *sm.* attic, garret

sotaque | sʋ'takɪ | *sm.* accent,

brogue

soterrar | sʊteˈRaR | *vt.* to bury

sova | ˈsɔva | *sf.* (colloq.) beating, thrashing

sovaco | sʊˈvakʊ | *sm.* (vulg.) armpit

sovar | soˈvaR | *vt.* to beat, to spank; to knead

sovela | sʊˈvɛla | *sf.* shoemaker's awl

soviético -ca | soviˈɛtikʊ | *a.* soviet (also *cap.*)

sovina | sʊˈvina | *smf.* miser, niggard / *a.* miserly

sozinho -nha | soˈziNʊ soˈziNʊ | *a.* alone, all alone

sua | ˈsua | *poss. a.* his, her, its, your; (*pl.*) their, your / *poss. pron.* his, hers, its, yours; (*pl.*) theirs, yours

suar | suˈaR | *vi.* to sweat, to perspire

suave | suˈavι | *a.* soft, mild, gentle

suavidade | suaviˈdadι | *sf.* softness, mildness, gentleness

suavizar | suaviˈzaR | *vt.* to sweeten, to soften, to assuage

subalterno -na | subalˈtɛRnʊ | *smf.* subaltern / *a.* subaltern; subordinate

subdesenvolvido -da | subdιZιvolˈvidʊ | *a.* underdeveloped

subentender | subιˈtẽdeR | *vt.* to discern (something not clear); to perceive; to gather

subestimar | subιʒtiˈmaR | *vt.* to underestimate, to underrate

subida | suˈbida | *sf.* ascent, climb; rise

subir | suˈbiR | *vt.* to climb, to go up; to raise / *vi.* to mount, to ascend

súbito -ta | ˈsubitʊ | *a.* sudden, unexpected / *adv.* suddenly

subjugar | subjuˈgaR | *vt.* to subjugate, to subdue

sublevar | subleˈvaR | *vt.* to raise up; to stir up revolt. **-s.-se** to revolt

sublime | suˈblimι | *a.* sublime; magnificent

sublinhar | subliˈNaR | *vt.* to underline; to emphasize, to stress

sublocação | sublokaˈsãw | *sf.* sublease, subtenancy

sublocar | subloˈkaR | *vt.* to sublet, to sublease

submarino -na | submaˈrinʊ | *sm.* submarine / *a.* submarine, underwater

submergir | submeRˈjiR | *vt. vi.* (also **s.-se**) to submerge

submeter | submeˈteR | *vt.* to subdue. **-s. a** to submit (something to someone [for approval etc.]). **-s.se** to submit

submissão | submiˈsãw | *sf.* submission

submisso -sa | subˈmisʊ | *a.* submissive; obedient, acquiescent

subnutrição | subnutriˈsãw | *sf.* malnutrition

subordinar | suboRdiˈnaR | *vt.* to subordinate, to subject. **-s.-se** to submit

subornar | suboRˈnaR | *vt.* to bribe, to suborn

suborno | suˈboRnʊ | *sm.* bribe, bribery

sub-reptício -cia | subRepˈtisiʊ | *a.* surreptitious

subscrever | subʒkreˈveR | *vt.* to subscribe. **-s.-se** to sign one's name / *vi.* to approve

subscrição | subʒkriˈsãw | *sf.* subscription

subserviente | subseRviˈẽtι | *a.* servile

subsídio | subˈsidiʊ | *sm.* grant, subsidy

subsistência | subsιʒˈtẽsia | *sf.* subsistence; livelihood

substância | subʒˈtãsia | *sf.* substance

substantivo | subʒtãˈtivʊ | *sm.* substantive, noun

substituir | subʒtituˈiR | *vt.* to substitute, to replace

substituto -ta | subʒtiˈtutʊ | *smf. a.* substitute

subterfúgio | subteRˈfujiʊ | *sm.* subterfuge, evasion

subterrâneo -nea | subte'ʀanɩʋ | *sm.* subterranean cave or passage / *a.* subterranean, underground

subtração | subtra'saw | *sm.* subtraction, deduction

subtrair | subtra'iʀ | *vt.* to subtract, to deduct. **-s.-se** to avoid

subúrbio | su'buʀbiʋ | *sm.* suburb; (*pl.*) outskirts

subvencionar | subvẽsio'naʀ | *vt.* to subsidize, to grant a subvention to

subversão | subveʀ'saw | *sf.* subversion; overthrow, upset

subversivo -va | subveʀ'sivʋ | *smf. a.* subversive

subverter | subveʀ'teʀ | *vt.* to subvert, to overthrow

sucata | su'kata | *sf.* scrap iron

succção | suk'saw | *sf.* suction

sucedâneo -nea | suse'danɩʋ | *sm. a.* substitute

suceder | suse'deʀ | *vi.* to happen, to occur, to take place

sucessão | suse'saw | *sf.* succession; series, sequence

sucessivo -va | suse'sivʋ | *a.* successive

sucesso | su'sɛsʋ | *sm.* success

sucessor -sora | suse'soʀ | *smf.* successor, follower

súcia | 'sucia | *sf.* mob, gang, pack of rogues

sucinto -ta | su'sĩtʋ | *a.* succinct, concise

suco | 'sukʋ | *sm.* juice; sap

suculento -ta | suku'lẽtʋ | *a.* succulent, juicy

sucumbir | sukũ'biʀ | *vt.* to succumb; to give in; to die

sucuri | suku'ri | *sf.* South American anaconda, water boa

sucursal | sukuʀ'sal | *sf. a.* (com.) branch

sudeste, sueste | su'dɛʃtɩ su'ɛʃtɩ | *sm.* southeast, southeast wind

súdito -ta | 'suditʋ | *smf.* subject, vassal / *a.* subject (under the power or dominion of another)

sudoeste | sudʋ'ɛʃtɩ | *sm.* southwest; southwest wind

sueco -ca | su'ɛkʋ | *sm.* (ling.) Swedish; *smf.* Swede / *a.* Swedish

suficiência | sufisi'ẽsia | *sf.* sufficiency; ability, capacity

suficiente | sufisi'ẽtɩ | *a.* sufficient, enough, plenty

sufixo | su'fiksʋ | *sm.* suffix

sufocante | sufo'kãtɩ | *a.* suffocating

sufocar | sufo'kaʀ | *vt.* to strangle to death; (fig.) to repress / *vt. vi.* to suffocate, to stifle

sufrágio | su'frajiʋ | *sm.* suffrage, vote

sugar | su'gaʀ | *vt.* to suck

sugerir | suje'riʀ | *vt.* to suggest

sugestão | suʒeʃ'taw | *sf.* suggestion

suíças | su'isaʒ | *sfpl.* sideburns

suicida | sui'sida | *smf.* one who commits suicide / *a.* suicidal

suicidar-se | suisi'daʀsɩ | *vr.* to commit suicide

suicídio | sui'sidiʋ | *sm.* suicide

suíço -ça | su'isʋ | *smf. a.* Swiss

suíno -na | su'inʋ | *sm.* swine, pig

sujar | su'jaʀ | *vt.* to dirty, to soil, to stain

sujeição | sujey'saw | *sf.* subjection

sujeira | su'jeyra | *sf.* filth, dirt; (colloq.) dirty trick

sujeitar | sujey'taʀ | *vt.* to subject, to submit; to subdue. **-s.-se** a to submit

sujeito -ta | su'jeytʋ | *sm.* (gram.) subject; fellow, guy / *a.* subject, liable to. **-estar s. a** to be exposed to

sujo -ja | 'sujʋ | *a.* dirty, soiled

sul | 'sul | *sm.* south

sulcar | sul'kaʀ | *vt.* to plow, to make furrows in; to groove

sulco | 'sulkʋ | *sm.* furrow; groove

suma | 'suma | *sf.* summary. **-em s.** in short

sumário -ria | su'mariʋ | *sm. a.* summary

sumiço | su'misʋ | *sm.* (colloq.) disappearance

sumir | su'miʀ | *vi*. (also **s.-se**) tɔ disappear, to vanish; to sink; tɔ fade away

sumo -ma | 'sumʋ | *sm*. juice / *a*. highest, supreme. **-s. pontífice** the Pope

sunga | 'sũga | *sf*. swimming trunks; men's short underpants

suntuoso -sa | sũtu'ozʋ -'ωza | *a*. sumptuous; luxurious

suor | su'ωʀ | *sm*. sweat, perspiration

superabundância | superabũ'dãsia | *sf*. superabundance

superar | supe'ʀaʀ | *vt*. to surmount, to surpass; to overcome

superestimar | superɪʃti'maʀ | *vt*. to overestimate

superfície | supeʀ'fisiɪ | *sf*. surface

supérfluo -flua | su'pɛʀfluʋ | *a*. superfluous, excessive

superintendente | superĩte'dẽtɪ | *smf*. superintendent

superior -ora | superi'oʀ | *smf*. superior; head of a monastery / *a*. superior, upper; higher, better

superioridade | superiori'dadɪ | *sf*. superiority

superlotado -da | supeʀlo'tadʋ | *a*. overcrowded

supermercado | supeʀmeʀ'kadʋ | *sm*. supermarket

superprodução | supeʀprʋdu'sãw | *sf*. overproduction

supersônico -ca | supeʀ'sonikʋ | *a*. supersonic

superstição | supeʀʃti'sãw | *sf*. superstition

supervisão | supeʀvi'zãw | *sf*. supervision

supervisionar | supeʀvizio'naʀ | *vt*. to supervise

supetão | supe'tãw | *sm*. used in the expression **de s.** suddenly

suplantar | suplã'taʀ | *vt*. to surpass, to surmount

suplemento | suple'mẽtʋ | *sm*. supplement

suplente | su'plẽtɪ | *smf*. substitute

súplica | 'suplika | *sf*. supplica-

tion; petition, appeal

suplicar | supli'kaʀ | *vt. vi*. to supplicate, to beg, to entreat

suplício | su'plisiʋ | *sm*. torture; torment

supor | su'poʀ | *vt*. to suppose

suportar | supoʀ'taʀ | *vt*. to support; to sustain; to endure, to suffer; to tolerate

suporte | su'pωʀtɪ | *sm*. support; stay, brace; base, foundation

suposição | supʋzi'sãw | *sf*. supposition

supositório | supʋzi'tωriʋ | *sm*. suppository

suposto -ta | su'poʃtʋ -'pωʃta | *a*. supposed; conjectural, presumed

supremacia | suprema'sia | *sf*. supremacy

supremo -ma | su'premʋ | *a*. supreme -

supressão | supre'sãw | *sf*. suppression

suprimento | supri'mẽtʋ | *sm*. supply; subsidy; suppliment

suprimir | supri'miʀ | *vt*. to suppress, to withhold

suprir | su'priʀ | *vt*. to supply; to substitute; to fill (a need)

supurar | supu'raʀ | *vi*. to suppurate

surdez | suʀ'deʒ | *sf*. deafness

surdo -da | 'suʀdʋ | *smf*. deaf person; *sm*. bass drum / *a*. deaf; muffled, dull (said of sounds). **-s. como uma porta** stone deaf

surdo-mudo surda-muda | 'suʀdʋ'mudʋ | *smf. a*. deaf mute (person)

surgir | suʀ'jiʀ | *vi*. to arise, to emerge, to appear, to spring up

surpreendente | suʀprɪẽ'dẽtɪ | *a*. surprising, astonishing

surpreender | suʀprɪẽ'deʀ | *vt*. to surprise, to take unawares; to astonish

surpresa | suʀ'preza | *sf*. surprise; astonishment

surpreso -sa | suʀ'prezʋ | *a*. surprised; astonished

surra | 'suRa | *sf*. beating, spanking

surrar | su'RaR | *vt*. to beat, to spank; to wear out (garments)

surripiar | suRipi'aR | *vt*. to pilfer, to filch

surtir | suR'tiR | *vt*. to give rise to, to occasion. **-s. efeito** to produce the desired result

surto -ta | 'suRtʊ | *sm*. outbreak, eruption / . *a*. anchored, at anchor

sururu | suru'ru | *sm*. an edible mussel; (colloq.) brawl, riot

suscetível | suse'tivιl | *a*. susceptible, sensitive

suscitar | susi'taR | *vt*. to raise, to call forth; to suggest. **-s. dúvidas** to raise doubts

suspeita | suʃ'peyta | *sf*. suspicion, distrust

suspeitar | suʃpey'taR | *vt*. to suspect, to distrust

suspeito -ta | suʃ'peytʊ | *smf*. suspect / *a*. suspect; suspicious

suspender | suʃpẽ'deR | *vt*. to discontinue; to stop or to dismiss temporarily; to postpone; to hang

suspensão | suʃpẽ'sãw | *sf*. suspension; interruption; temporary dismissal

suspenso -sa | suʃ'pẽsʊ | *a*. suspended, hanging; temporarily dismissed

suspensórios | suʃpẽ'sʊriʃ | *smpl*. men's braces, suspenders

suspirar | suʃpi'raR | *vi*. to sigh. **-s. por** to sigh for; to long for

suspiro | suʃ'pirʊ | *sm*. sigh; baked meringue

sussurrar | susu'RaR | *vt*. *vi*. to whisper, to murmur; to rustle

sussurro | su'suRʊ | *sm*. whisper, murmur; rustle

sustar | suʃ'taR | *vt*. to halt, to stop

sustentar | suʃtẽ'taR | *vt*. to support; to sustain; to uphold. **-s.-se** to maintain oneself

sustento | suʃ'tẽtʊ | *sm*. maintenance; sustenance

suster | suʃ'teR | *vt*. (also **s.-se**) to support, to hold up; to restrain, to hold back

susto | 'suʃtʊ | *sm*. fright; scare

sutiã | suti'ã | *sm*. brassière; (colloq.) bra

sutil | su'til | *a*. subtle

sutileza | suti'leza | *sf*. subtleness

T

taba | 'taba | *sf*. Indian settlement

tabacaria | tabaka'ria | *sf*. tobacco shop

tabaco | ta'bakʊ | *sm*. tobacco

tabefe | ta'bɛfι | *sm*. slap, cuff

tabela | ta'bela | *sf*. list, schedule. **-t. de horário** timetable. **-por t.** (colloq.) indirectly

tabelião | tabιli'ãw | *sm*. notary public

taberna | ta'bɛRna | *sf*. tavern; cheap eating-place

tabique | ta'bikι | *sm*. wooden partition (of rooms)

tablado | ta'bladʊ | *sm*. raised plat-

form; dais; stage

tábua | 'tabwa | *sf*. board, plank; table, list

tabuada | tabu'ada | *sf*. multiplication table

tabuleiro | tabu'leyrʊ | *sm*. shallow baking tin; tray; board (for games). **-t. de xadrez** chess-board

tabuleta | tabu'leta | *sf*. signboard; name-plate

taça | 'tasa | *sf*. drinking cup with stem; trophy cup

tacada | ta'kada | *sf*. stroke with a club or cue. **-daruma boat.** (colloq.) to hit the jackpot

tacanho -nha | ta'kaɴʋ | *a.* narrow-minded; petty; miserly

tacão | ta'kãw | *sm.* shoe heel

tacha | 'taxa | *sf.* tack, small nail; boiler for sugar-cane juice

tachar | ta'xaʀ | *vt.* to stigmatize. **-t. de** to brand as

tacho | 'taxʋ | *sm.* large shallow pan

tácito -ta | 'tasitʋ | *a.* tacit

taciturno -na | tasi'tuʀɴʋ | *a.* taciturn; reserved

taco | 'takʋ | *sm.* golf club; billiard cue; parquet block; large bite

tagarela | taga'rela | *a.* talkative, chattering; gossiping

tagarelar | tagare'laʀ | *vi.* to chatter, to gabble; to gossip

tainha | ta'iɴa | *sf.* mullet

taipa | 'taypa | *sf.* lath-and-plaster wall. **-casa de t.** mud hut

tal | 'tal | *a.* such, like, similar. **-a t. ponto** to such an extent. **-que t.?** how about it? **-t. pai, t. filho** like father, like son. **-fulano de t.** John Doe. **-um t.** such a / *adv.* such, thus, so, as. **-t. como** just as. **-t. qual** exactly, precisely

tala | 'tala | *sf.* leather strap

talão | ta'lãw | *sm.* claim check, ticket. **-t. de bagagens** baggage check. **-t. de cheques** cheque--book

talco | 'talkʋ | *sm.* talc; talcum powder

talento | ta'lẽtʋ | *sm.* talent, gift

talha | 'taʟa | *sf.* large earthen jug; chisel(l)ing, carving

talhada | ta'ʟada | *sf.* slice

talhadeira | taʟa'deyra | *sf.* chisel

talhar | ta'ʟaʀ | *vt.* to cut, to slash, to slice; to carve / *vt. vi.* to sour, to curdle

talharim | taʟa'rĩ | *sm.* thin noodles

talhe | 'taʟɪ | *sm.* figure, form, shape

talher | ta'ʟɛʀ | *sm.* knife, fork and spoon; a table place for one person

talho | 'taʟʋ | *sm.* a cut or act of cutting; butcher shop; form, shape

talo | 'talʋ | *sm.* (bot.) stalk, stem

talvez | tal'veʒ | *adv.* perhaps, maybe

tamanco | ta'mãkʋ | *sm.* open--toed wooden clog

tamanduá | tamãdu'a | *sm.* South American ant-eater, tamanoir

tamanho -nha | ta'maɴʋ | *sm.* size / *a.* so big, so great, such big

tâmara | 'tamara | *sf.* (bot.) date

também | tã'bẽy | *adv.* also, too, as well

tambor | tã'boʀ | *sm.* drum; metal barrel; revolver magazine

tampa | 'tãpa | *sf.* lid, cover

tampar | tã'paʀ | *vt.* to cover with a lid; to cork, to plug

tampinha | tã'piɴa | *sf.* bottle cap; *smf.* (colloq.) dumpy person

tampouco | tã'powkʋ | *adv.* either, neither

tanga | 'tãga | *sf.* loincloth, G--string

tanger | tã'jeʀ | *vt.* to pluck (a harp); to strike (a gong); to drive (animals)

tangerina | tãjɪ'rina | *sf.* tangerine

tanque | 'tãkɪ | *sm.* reservoir; tank (also mil.); concrete wash tub

tanto | 'tãtʋ | *sm.* indeterminate amount. **-um t.** somewhat, a little bit. **-outro t.** as much again / *a.* so much; as much; so many / *adv.* to such a degree or extent; in such quantity; in such a way. **-não t. assim** not so much. **-t. melhor** so much the better. **-t. um como o outro** both of them

tão | 'tãw | *adv.* so; as. **-t. bom como** as good as

tão-só tão-somente | tãw'sɔ tãwsɔ'mẽtɪ | *adv.* only

tapa | 'tapa | *sf.* slap, blow with palm of hand

tapar | ta'paʀ | *vt.* to cover; to stop (up); to plug

tapear | tapɪ'aʀ | *vt.* (colloq.) to deceive, to cheat

tapeçaria | tapesaʻria | sf. tapestry

tapete | taʻpetɪ | sm. carpet

tapume | taʻpumɪ | sm. boarding; hedge

taquara | taʻkwara | sf. any bamboo (esp. of the smaller species)

taquigrafia | takigraʻfia | sf. stenography, shorthand

tarado-da |taʻradʊ|smf.(colloq.) degenerate person, sexual criminal

tardar | taʀʻdaʀ | vt. to delay / vi. to delay; to be late in coming. -o mais t. at the latest. -sem mais t. without further delay

tarde | ʻtardɪ | sf. afternoon. -boa t. good afternoon / adv. late

tardinha | taʀʻdiɴa | sf. (colloq.) late afternoon

tardio -dia | taʀʻdiʊ | a. late, untimely

tarefa | taʻrɛfa | sf. task; contract job

tarifa | taʻrifa |sf. tariff. -t. alfandegária custom-house tariff

tarimba | taʻrĩba | sf. soldier's wooden bunk; (fig.) practice

tarja | ʻtaʀja |sf. ornamental border (on something); black border on stationary

tarrafa |taʻʀafa |sf. casting net

tartaruga |tartaʻruga |sf. turtle

tasca | ʻtaʃka | sf. cheap tavern; (slang) bite (of something one is eating)

tatear | tatɪʻaʀ | vt. to feel, to probe / vi. to grope, to feel one's way

tática | ʻtatika |sf. tactics

tático -ca | ʻtatikʊ | a. tactic, tactical

tato | ʻtatʊ | sm. sense of touch; feeling; tact, diplomacy

tatu | taʻtu | sm. armadillo

tatuagem | tatuʻajẽy |sf. tattooing, tattoo mark

tatuí | tatuʻi | sm. sand bug

taxa | ʻtaxa |sf. tax, tribute; rate. -t. de câmbio exchange rate

taxar | taʻxaʀ | vt. to tax

táxi | ʻtaksɪ | sm. taxi, cab

te | ʻtɪ | oblique pron. 2nd pers. sing. (direct object) you, thee; (indirect object)to you, to thee, to yourself, to thyself; reflexive pron. 2nd pers. sing. yourself, thyself

tear | tɪʻaʀ | sm. loom

teatral | tɪaʻtral | a. theatrical

teatro | tɪʻatrʊ | sm. theatre, theater

tecelagem | teseʻlajẽy | sf. weaving; textile industry

tecer | teʻseʀ | vt. to weave

tecido -da | tɪʻsidʊ | sm. fabric, cloth; (med.) tissue / a. woven

tecla | ʻtɛkla | sf. key (of a piano, typewriter etc.)

teclado | teʻkladʊ | sm. keyboard

técnica | ʻtɛknika | sf. technique

técnico -ca | ʻtɛknikʊ |smf. technician / a. technical

teco-teco |tɛkʊʻtɛkʊ |sm.(colloq.) small single-motor airplane

tédio | ʻtɛdiʊ | sm. boredom; tediousness

tedioso -sa | tediʻozʊ -ʻoza | a. tedious

teia | ʻteya | sf. web; texture, network. -t. de aranha cobweb

teimar | teyʻmaʀ | vi. to be stubborn; to persist, to insist

teimoso -sa | teyʻmozʊ -ʻmoza | a. stubborn; obstinate

tela | ʻtela | sf. woven fabric; canvas (for painting or a finished painting); screen

telefonar | telefoʻnaʀ | vt. vi. to telephone

telefone |teleʻfonɪ| sm. telephone

telefonema | telefoʻnema | sm. telephone call

telefonista | telefoʻniʃta | smf. telephone operator, operator

telegrafar | telegraʻfaʀ | vt. vi. to telegraph, to wire, to cable

telegrama | teleʻgrama | sm. telegram, cable

teleguiado -da | telegiʻadʊ | sm. ballistic missile / a. remote control

telescópio | teleʃʻkʊpiʊ | sm.

telescope

televisão | televi'zãw | *sf.* television; (colloq.) TV

telha | 'teʌa | *sf.* tile

telhado | te'ʌadʋ | *sm.* roof

telheiro | te'ʌeyrʋ | *sm.* open tile--covered shed

tema | 'tema | *sm.* theme, subject; topic; (mus.) motif

temer | te'meʀ | *vt.* to fear; to be afraid of

temerário -ria | teme'rariʋ | *a.* bold, daring, risky

temeridade | temeri'dadı | *sf.* temerity, rashness

temível | te'mivıl | *a.* fearsome, fearful, frightful

temor | te'moʀ | *sm.* fear, dread

têmpera | 'tẽpera | *sf.* (metal.) temper; (fine arts) tempera; (fig.) mettle

temperado -da | tẽpe'radʋ | *a.* temperate; spiced, seasoned

temperamento | tẽpera'mẽtʋ | *sm.* temperament

temperança | tẽpe'rãsa | *sf.* temperance, moderation

temperar | tẽpe'raʀ | *vt.* to season, to flavo(u)r; to moderate; (metal.) to temper

temperatura | tẽpera'tura | *sf.* temperature

tempero | tẽ'perʋ | *sm.* seasoning; flavo(u)ring

tempestade | tẽpeʃ'tadı | *sf.* storm, tempest. **-t. em copo d'água** storm in a teacup

tempestuoso -sa | tẽpeʃtu'ozʋ -'ωza | *a.* stormy, tempestuous

templo | 'tẽplʋ | *sm.* temple; church

tempo | 'tẽpʋ | *sm.* time; period; opportunity; proper time; weather; (gram.) tense. **-a. t.** in time, on time. **-ao mesmo t.** at the same time. **-há quanto t.?** how long ago?

temporada | tẽpo'rada | *sf.* period of time; season

temporal | tẽpo'ral | *sm.* storm / *a.* temporal; temporary

temporário -ria | tẽpo'rariʋ | *a.* temporary

tenacidade | tenasi'dadı | *sf.* tenacity, persistence

tenaz | te'naʃ | *sf.* tongs (esp. of a blacksmith) / *a.* tenacious, stubborn, obstinate

tenção | tẽ'sãw | *sf.* intention, intent

tencionar | tẽsio'naʀ | *vt.* to intend, to plan

tenda | 'tẽda | *sf.* tent; (colloq.) small shop

tendão | tẽ'dãw | *sm.* tendon, sinew

tendência | tẽ'dẽsia | *sf.* tendency, inclination

tendencioso -sa | tẽdẽsi'ozʋ -'ωza | *a.* biassed, tendentious

tender | tẽ'deʀ | *vi.* to tend, to incline. **-t. para** to tend towards

tenebroso -sa | tene'brozʋ -'brωza | *a.* dark; gloomy; appalling

tenente | te'nẽtı | *sm.* lieutenant

tênia | 'tenia | *sf.* tapeworm

tênis | 'teniʃ | *sm.* tennis; tennis shoe

tenro -ra | 'tẽʀʋ | *a.* tender, soft; frail, delicate

tensão | tẽ'sãw | *sf.* tension. **-t. elétrica** voltage

tenso -sa | 'tẽsʋ | *a.* tense; taut

tentação | tẽta'sãw | *sf.* temptation

tentáculo | tẽ'takulʋ | *sm.* tentacle

tentador -dora | tẽta'doʀ | *smf.* tempter; *sf.* temptress / *a.* tempting

tentar | tẽ'taʀ | *vt.* to try, to attempt; to tempt, to lure

tentativa | tẽta'tiva | *sf.* attempt

tentear | tẽtı'aʀ | *vt.* to probe; to sound, to explore; to play (fish)

tento | 'tẽtʋ | *sm.* attention, heed; (soccer, sports) goal, score

tênue | 'tenuı | *a.* tenuous, slender; subtle

teologia | teolo'jia | *sf.* theology, divinity

teológico -ca | teo'lωjikʋ | *a.* theological

teor | te'oʀ | *sm.* tenor, meaning; content (esp. chemical). **-t. alcoólico** alcohol content. **-do seguinte t.** to the following effect

teoria | tɪo'ria | *sf.* theory

teórico -ca | tɪ'ɔriku | *a.* theoretical

tépido -da | 'tɛpidu | *a.* tepid, lukewarm

ter | 'teʀ | *vt.* to have; to possess; to beget (offspring). **-t. de** to have to. **-t. em vista** to have in mind. **-que é que você tem?** what's wrong? **-que tem isso?** what does that matter? **-tenha paciência!** come now! **-não tem de quê** not at all, you're welcome

terça | 'teʀsa | *sf.* = *terça-feira*

terça-feira | 'teʀsa'feyra | *sf.* Tuesday

terceiro -ra | teʀ'seyru | *a.* third

terço | 'teʀsu | *sm.* a third; chaplet (third of a rosary)

terçol | teʀ'sɔl | *sm.* (med.) sty, stye

terminar | teʀmi'naʀ | *vt.* to finish, to conclude / *vi.* to cease, to end

término | 'teʀminu | *sm.* end; close, finish

termo, termos | 'teʀmu 'teʀmuʃ | *smf.* thermos bottle

termo | 'teʀmu | *sm.* term; limit; period of time; end, finish; word, vocable. **-meio t.** moderately. **-pôr t. a** to put a stop to

termômetro | teʀ'mometru | *sm.* thermometer

terno -na | 'teʀnu | *sm.* man's suit; three of anything forming a group / *a.* tender, loving

ternura | teʀ'nura | *sf.* tenderness, affection; gentleness

terra | 'teʀa | *sf.* land, soil; earth, world; country, nation. **-ir à t.** to go ashore

terra-a-terra | 'teʀa(a)'teʀa | *a.* commonplace, trivial

terraço | te'ʀasu | *sm.* terrace

terreiro | te'ʀeyru | *sm.* open terrace (for drying coffee beans etc.); place where voodoo rites are practiced

terremoto | teʀe'mɔtu | *sm.* earthquake

terreno -na | te'ʀenu | *sm.* ground; tract of land / *a.* terrestrial; mundane

térreo -rea | 'teʀɪu | *a.* ground. **-andar t.** ground floor. **-casa térrea** one-story house

terrestre | te'ʀɛʃtrɪ | *a.* terrestrial; earthy

terrina | te'ʀina | *sf.* tureen

território | teʀi'tɔriu | *sm.* territory

terrível | te'ʀivɪl | *a.* terrible

terror | te'ʀoʀ | *sm.* terror; terrorism

tese | 'tɛzɪ | *sf.* thesis

teso -sa | 'tɛzu | *a.* taut, stiff, rigid; (slang) broke

tesoura | tɪ'zowra | *sf.* scissors; shears

tesourar | tɪzow'ʀaʀ | *vt.* to scissor; to shear; (colloq.) to backbite

tesouraria | tɪzowra'ria | *sf.* treasury

tesoureiro -ra | tɪzow'reyru | *smf* treasurer

tesouro | tɪ'zowru | *sm.* treasure; treasury. **-t. público** treasury, exchequer

testa | 'tɛʃta | *sf.* forehead, brow. **-à t. de** at the head of

testa-de-ferro | 'tɛʃtadɪ'feʀu | *sm.* figurehead, strawman

testamento | teʃta'mẽtu | *sm.* testament, will

testar | teʃ'taʀ | *vt.* to bequeath; to test, to experiment / *vi.* to make one's will

teste | 'tɛʃtɪ | *sm.* test; trial, experiment

testemunha | teʃtɪ'muɴa | *sf.* witness. **-t. ocular** eye witness

testemunhar | teʃtɪmu'naʀ | *vt.* to testify, to bear witness to / *vi.* to witness

testemunho | teʃtɪ'muɴu | *sm.* testimony, deposition

teta | ʹteta | *sf.* udder; teat, nipple

teto | ʹtɛtʋ | *sm.* ceiling; roof

tétrico -ca | ʹtɛtrikʋ | *a.* lugubrious; horrible, gruesome

teu | ʹtew | *poss. a.* your (familiar), thy, thyne. **-o** *t.*, **os teus** yours

têxtil | ʹteʃtil | *a.* textile

texto | ʹteʃtʋ | *sm.* text

textura | teʃʹtura | *sf.* texture

tez | ʹteʃ | *sf.* complexion; skin. **-t. clara** fair complexion

ti | ʹti | *oblique pron. 2nd pers. sing.* (object of a *prep.*) you, yourself, thee

tico-tico | tikʋʹtikʋ | *sm.* kind of crown sparrow. **-serra t.** jig saw

tifo | ʹtifʋ | *sm.* typhus

tigela | tiʹjela | *sf.* bowl

tigre | ʹtigrɛ | *sm.* tiger

tijolo | tiʹjolʋ | *sm.* brick

til | ʹtil | *sm.* tilde, the sign( )

tilintar | tiliʹtaʀ | *vt. vi.* to tinkle, to jingle, to ring

timão | tiʹmãw | *sm.* helm, tiller

timbrado -da | tiʹbradʋ | *a.* crested (said of stationary). **-papel** t. letterhead

timbre | ʹtĩbrɛ | *sm.* crest (on a coat of arms); letterhead; (mus.) tone

time | ʹtimɛ | *sm.* team

timidez | timiʹdeʃ | *sf.* timidity

tímido -da | ʹtimidʋ | *a.* timid; coy; shy

timoneiro | timoʹneyrʋ | *sm.* helmsman, coxswain, cox

tina | ʹtina | *sf.* tub

tinhorão | tiɲoʹrãw | *sm.* (bot.) common caladium

tingir | tĩʹjiʀ | *vt.* to dye, to colo(u)r, to stain

tinir | tiʹniʀ | *vi.* to tinkle, to jingle

tino | ʹtinʋ | *sm.* judg(e)ment, discernment, sense

tinta | ʹtĩta | *sf.* ink; paint; dye, tint. **-t. a óleo** oil-colo(u)r

tinteiro | tĩʹteyrʋ | *sm.* ink-well

tinto -ta | ʹtĩtʋ | *a.* dyed, stained; red (said of wine, grapes etc.)

tintura | tĩʹtura | *sf.* dye; tincture

(also phar.); (fig.) smattering

tinturaria | tĩturaʹria | *sf.* the cleaner's; dry cleaner

tio, tia | ʹtiʋ | *sm.* uncle; *sf.* aunt

tio-avô, tia-avó | tiʋaʹvo tia(a)ʹv⊍ | *sm.* granduncle; *sf.* grandaunt

típico -ca | ʹtipikʋ | *a.* typical

tipo | ʹtipʋ | *sm.* type, model; printing type; (colloq.) fellow, guy

tipografia | tipograʹfia | *sf.* printing; printing-works

tipógrafo -fa | tiʹpʊgrafʋ | *smf.* typographer, printer

tipóia | tiʹpʊya | *sf.* arm sling

tique | ʹtikɛ | *sm.* (med.) tic. **-t. nervoso** nervous tic

tira | ʹtira | *sf.* strip (of paper, cloth etc.); band; (slang) detective

tiracolo | tiraʹkʊlʋ | *sm.* used in the expression **a t.** worn over the shoulder and across the chest

tirada | tiʹrada | *sf.* long stretch (of time, road etc.); tirade

tiragem | tiʹrajẽy | *sf.* circulation; number printed (of newspaper, books etc.), printing; draft of a chimney

tirania | tiraʹnia | *sf.* tiranny, despotism

tirano -na | tiʹranʋ | *sm.* tyrant / *a.* tyrannic

tirante | tiʹrãtɛ | *sm.* strap or trace (of a harness); (constr.) binding beam, brace / *a.* drawing, pulling / *prep.* except. **-t. a** like, resembling

tirar | tiʹraʀ | *vt.* to take, to remove; to pull (cart); to extract; to win (lottery); to issue. **-t. a mesa** to clear the table. **-t. férias** to take vacations

tiritar | tiriʹtaʀ | *vi.* to shiver, to shake (with cold)

tiro | ʹtirʋ | *sm.* shot; act of shooting; discharge of a gun. **-t. ao alvo** target practice. **-cavalo de t.** draft horse

tirocínio | tiroʹsinʋ | *sm.* practice in a profession; experience; apprenticeship

tiroteio | tiro'teyʋ | sm. gun fight; firing, gunfire

tísico -ca | 'tizikʋ | smf. a. consumptive

títere | 'titɩrɩ | sm. puppet; marionette

titio -a | ti'tiʋ | sm. (colloq.) uncle; sf. (colloq.) auntie, aunty

titubear | titubɩ'aʀ | vi. to stagger, to totter; to hesitate; to stammer

titular | titu'laʀ | smf. titled person / a. titular, nominal / vt. to entitle

título | 'titulʋ | sm. title; title of rank; bond, stock or similar certificate. **-a t. de experiência** by way of trial

toa | 'toa | sf. (naut.) tow; (naut.) towline. **-à t.** aimlessly

toada | tʋ'ada | sf. tune, air

toalete | tʋa'letɩ | sm. dressing-room, lavatory / sf. toilet, style of dress

toalha | tʋ'aLa | sf. towel. **-t. de mesa** table-cloth

toca | 'tωka | sf. burrow, den, hole

toca-discos | 'tωka'diʃkʋʃ | sm. record-player

tocaia | to'kaya | sf. ambush; hunter's blind

tocante | to'kãtɩ | a. touching, moving. **-no t. a** as for, as regarding

tocar | to'kaʀ | vt. to touch; to play; to ring (bell); to drive (cattle). **-t. para** (colloq.) to give (someone) a ring, to telephone. **-t. a** to be someone's turn. **-t. em** to call at (port)

tocha | 'tωxa | sf. torch

toco | 'tokʋ | sm. stump (of tree etc.)

todavia | toda'via | conj. however, nevertheless, yet

todo, toda | 'todʋ | smf. whole; (pl.) everybody; all. **-ao t.** in the whole. **-no t.** in all, on the whole. **-o t.** the whole / a. all, whole; any; any one. **-em t. caso** in any case. **-t. espécie de** all

kinds of. **-t. (o) mundo** everyone, every one, everybody

todo-poderoso | 'todʋpode'rozʋ | a. almighty / sm. (cap.) the Almighty (God)

toldo | 'toldʋ | sm. awning; sun blind (of a shop); canopy

tolerância | tole'rãsia | sf. tolerance; toleration, indulgence. **-casa de t.** brothel

tolerante | tole'rãtɩ | a. tolerant

tolerar | tole'raʀ | vt. to tolerate, to allow; to bear with

tolher | to'LeR | vt. to hinder, to impede; to restrain

tolice | tʋ'lisɩ | sf. foolishness; nonsense / interj. nonsense!

tolo -la | 'tolʋ | smf. fool / a. foolish, silly, senseless

tom | 'tõ | sm. tone; shade, hue; (mus.) key

tomada | to'mada | sf. taking, capture: (elect.) socket

tomar | to'maʀ | vt. to take; to seize; to capture; to drink; to deprive of. **-t. conta de** to take charge of; to take care of. **-t. conta** (colloq.) to dominate. **-t. emprestado** to borrow (something). **-t. por testemunha** to call as witness. **-t. posse** to be seated (inaugurated) in office

tomara | to'mara | interj. (colloq.) I hope so!

tomate | tʋ'matɩ | sm. tomato

tombar | tó'baʀ | vt. to cause to fall; to record, to register (esp. in official collection of registers) / vi. to fall

tombo | 'tõbʋ | sm. fall, tumble; archives, records

tomo | 'tomʋ | sm. tome, volume

tona | 'tona | sf. surface. **-à t.** on the surface

tonel | to'nɛl | sm. large cask, vat

tonelada | tone'lada | sf. ton

tônico -ca | 'tonikʋ | sm. tonic / a. tonic (also gram., mus.)

tontas | 'tõtaʃ | sfpl. used in the expression **às t.** thoughtlessly, heedlessly

tontear | tõtι'aʀ | *vt.* to make dizzy
/ *vi.* to feel dizzy

tonteira | tõ'teyra | *sf.* dizziness

tonto -ta | 'tõtυ | *a.* dizzy

topada | to'pada | *sf.* trip, stumble

topar | to'paʀ | *vt.* to run across, to
fall upon; (colloq.) to accept
(an invitation, a challenge etc.).
-topo! (colloq.) it's a deal!

topázio | to'paziυ | *sm.* topaz

tope | 'tωpι | *sm.* top, summit

topete | tυ'petι | *sm.* forelock, tuft
of hair; (colloq.) impudence

tópico -ca | 'tωpikυ | *sm.* topic / *a.*
topical

topo | 'topυ | *sm.* top, summit,
peak

toque | 'tωkι | *sm.* touch, contact;
bugle call; dash (of something);
test, assay. **-a t. de caixa** in a
great hurry

tora | 'tωra | *sf.* log, trunk of a tree;
large slice

torcedor -dora | toʀse'doʀ | *smf.*
rooter (esp. of a soccer team)

torcedura | toʀsι'dura | *sf.* twist;
sprain (of wrist etc.)

torcer | toʀ'seʀ | *vt.* to twist; to dis-
tort (the meaning). **-t. -se** to
writhe (as in pain); to squirm.
-t. o pé to sprain one's foot. **-t. o
nariz a** to turn up one's nose;
to frown / *vi.* to cheer, to root

torcicolo | toʀsi'kωlυ | *sm.* crick,
wry neck

torcida | tυʀ'sida | *sf.* wick;
(sports) act of rooting; group of
rooters

torcido -da | tυʀ'sidυ | *a.* twisted

tordo | 'toʀdυ | *sm.* thrush

tormenta | toʀ'mẽta | *sf.* storm,
tempest

tormento | toʀ'mẽtυ | *sm.* torture,
torment: anguish

tornar | toʀ'naʀ | *vt.* to render, to
make; to convert. **-t. -se** to become / *vi.* to return; to answer

tornear | toʀnι'aʀ | *vt.* to turn (on a
lathe); to shape neatly; (fig.) to
perfect

torneio | toʀ'neyυ | *sm.*

tournament

torneira | toʀ'neyra | *sf.* faucet,
tap

torneiro | toʀ'neyrυ | *sm.* lathe
worker, turner

torniquete | toʀni'ketι | *sm.*
(med.) tourniquet; turnstile

torno | 'toʀnυ | *sm.* (mech.) lathe;
(mech.) vice, vise. **-em t.**
around, about

tornozelo | tυʀnυ'zelυ | *sm.* ankle

toró | to'rω | *sm.* (colloq.)
downpour

torpe | 'toʀpι | *a.* base, mean, sor-
did, vile

torquês | toʀ'keʒ | *sf.* tongs,
pincers

torrada | to'ʀada | *sf.* toast

torradeira | toʀa'deyra | *sf.* toaster

torrado -da | to'ʀadυ | *a.* toasted;
scorched

torrão | to'ʀãw | *sm.* clod; hard
lump of soil. **-t. natal** native
land

torrar | to'ʀaʀ | *vt.* to toast, to
roast (coffee); (colloq.) to sell
out

torre | 'toʀι | *sf.* tower; belfry; tur-
ret; rook (in chess)

torrente | to'ʀẽtι | *sf.* torrent

torresmo | to'ʀeʒmυ | *sm.* crack-
ling (crisp, browned pork fat)

tórrido -da | 'tωʀidυ | *a.* torrid

torta | 'tωʀta | *sf.* pie

torto -ta | 'toʀtυ 'tωʀta | *a.* bent;
crooked. **-a t. e a direito** (colloq.) indiscriminately, left and
right

tortuoso -sa | toʀtu'ozυ -'ωza |
a. winding; tortuous

tortura | tυʀ'tura | *sf.* torture;
torment

torturar | tυʀtu'raʀ | *vt.* to tor-
ture, to torment

torvelinho | tυʀvι'liɲυ | *sm.* swirl,
whirl; whirlpool

tosar | to'zaʀ | *vt.* to shear, to clip,
to crop

tosco -ca | 'toʃkυ | *a.* crude,
coarse; rough

tosquiar | toʃki'aʀ | *vt.* to fleece,

to shear; (fig.) to criticize severely (a book etc.)

tosse | 'tɔsɪ | sf. cough

tossir | tʊ'siʀ | vi. to cough

tostão | tʊʃ'tãw | sm. former Brazilian small coin. **-sem t.** penniless

tostar | toʃ'taʀ | vt. to toast, to brown. **-t. -se** (fig.) to tan

total | to'tal | sm. total, whole, all / a. total, complete

totalitário -ria | totali'tariʊ | a. totalitarian

touca | 'towka | sf. bonnet; small brimless cap; nun's coif. **-t. de banho** bathing cap

toucador | towka'doʀ | sm. dressing-table; dressing-room **-artigos de t.** cosmetic preparations

toucinho, toicinho | tow'siɴʊ toy'siɴʊ | sm. pork fat. **-t. defumado** smoked bacon

toupeira | tow'peyra | sf. ground mole

tourada | tow'rada | sf. bullfight

toureiro | tow'reyrʊ | sm. bullfighter

touro | 'towrʊ | sm. bull

tóxico -ca | 'tɔksikʊ | sm. toxin; poison / a. toxic

toxicômano -na | toksi'komanʊ | smf. drug addict

trabalhador -dora | trabaLa'doʀ | smf. worker, labo(u)rer / a. hard-working

trabalhar | traba'LaʀR | vt. to shape; to perfect / vi. to work, to toil; to function (as a motor etc.)

trabalho | tra'baLʊ | sm. work; job, occupation; work product. **-trabalhos forçados** hard labo(u)r

trabalhoso -sa | traba'Lozʊ -'Lɔza | a. hard, difficult, laborious

traça | 'trasa | sf. moth, clothes moth

traçado -da | tra'sadʊ | sm. tracing; drawing; plan / a. traced, drafted; planned

tração | tra'sãw | sf. traction, pull

traçar | tra'saʀ | vt. to sketch, to draft, to delineate. **-t. planos** to make plans

traço | 'trasʊ | sm. trace, line; stroke (of a pen, pencil etc.); trait, feature; (pl.) trace, vestige. **-t. de união** hyphen

tradição | tradi'sãw | sf. tradition

tradução | tradu'sãw | sf. translation

tradutor -tora | tradu'toʀ | smf. translator

traduzir | tradu'ziʀ | vt. to translate. **-t. -se** to become manifest

trafegar | trafe'gaʀ | vi. to pass or go through, to come and go (esp. on a vehicle)

tráfego | 'trafɪgʊ | sm. traffic; trade; transport, transit

traficar | trafi'kaʀ | vt. to traffic, to trade (esp. fraudulently)

tráfico | 'trafikʊ | sm. traffic, trade (esp. of an illicit nature)

tragar | tra'gaʀ | vt. to devour, to swallow; to inhale (tobacco smoke)

tragédia | tra'jedia | sf. tragedy

trágico -ca | 'trajikʊ | sm. tragedian; sf. tragedienne / a. tragic

trago | 'tragʊ | sm. gulp, swallow. **-de um t.** at one gulp. **-tomar um t.** to have a drink

traição | trai'sãw | sf. treason, treachery, betrayal. **-à t.** treacherously

traiçoeiro -ra | traysʊ'eyrʊ | a. treacherous

traidor -dora | trai'doʀ | smf. traitor / a. treacherous

trair | tra'iʀ | vt. to betray

traje, trajo | 'trajɪ 'trajʊ | sm. dress, clothing, garb, attire. **-t. de rigor** formal evening attire. **-trajes menores** underclothes

trajeto | tra'jɛtʊ | sm. course, route, way

tralha | 'traLa | sf. (colloq.) trash, junk; cumbersome equipment

trama | 'trama | sf. woof, weft; weave, web; plot

tramar | tra'maʀ | *vt.* to plot, to conspire

trambolhão | trãbʊ'lãw | *sm.* (colloq.) tumble, heavy fall

trambolho | trã'bolʊ | *sm.* (colloq.) hindrance

tramela | tra'mɛla | *sf.* wooden door latch

trâmite | 'tramitɪ | *sm.* (esp. *pl.*) proper procedures. **-trâmites legais** legal procedures

tramóia | tra'mɔya | *sf.* (colloq.) swindle

trampolim | trãpʊ'lĩ | *sm.* spring board

tranca | 'trãka | *sf.* bar, crossbar (on a door)

trança | 'trãsa | *sf.* braid, braid of hair; (colloq.) intrigue

trancar | trã'kaʀ | *vt.* to lock up, to shut up. **-t.-se** to shut oneself up

trançar | trã'saʀ | *vt.* to braid, to plait

tranco | 'trãkʊ | *sm.* jolt, jounce; jump (of a horse); push

tranqüilidade | trãkwili'dadɪ | *sf.* tranqui(l)lity, quietness

tranqüilizante | trãkwili'zãtɪ | *sm.* (med.) tranqui(l)lizer / *a.* tranqui(l)lizing

tranqüilizar | trãkwili'zaʀ | *vt.* to tranqui(l)lize. **-t.-se** to calm down

tranqüilo -la | trã'kwilʊ | *a.* tranquil; reassured; calm

transa | 'trãza | *sf.* (slang) business; shady business; relationship; sexual intercourse

transação | trãza'sãw | *sf.* transaction; business deal

transar | trã'zaʀ | *vt.* (slang) to do (something); to face (something); to deal with (something); to have sexual intercourse with

transatlântico -ca | trãza'tlãtikʊ | *sm.* ocean liner / *a.* transatlantic

transbordar | trãzboʀ'daʀ | *vi.* to overflow, to overrun

transcender | trãsẽ'deʀ | *vt.* to transcend; to surpass

transcorrer | trãʃko'ʀeʀ | *vi.* to elapse

transcrever | trãʃkre'veʀ | *vt.* to transcribe, to copy

transcurso | trãʃ'kuʀsʊ | *sm.* passage (of time, of a given date)

transe | 'trãzɪ | *sm.* trance; ordeal, anguish. **-a todo t.** at all costs

transeunte | trãzɪ'ũtɪ | *smf.* passer, passer-by

transferir | trãʃfɪ'riʀ | *vt.* to transfer

transfigurar | trãʃfigu'raʀ | *vt.* to transfigure, to transform

transformação | trãʃfoʀma'sãw | *sf.* transformation

transformar | trãʃfoʀ'maʀ | *vt.* to transform, to convert

transfusão | trãʃfu'zãw | *sf.* transfusion

transgredir | trãʃgrɪ'diʀ | *vt.* to transgress, to trespass

transgressão | trãʃgre'sãw | *sf.* transgression, trespass

transgressor -sora | trãʃgre'soʀ | *smf.* transgressor, trespasser

transição | trãzi'sãw | *sf.* transition

transigência | trãzi'jẽsia | *sf.* tolerance; compliance

transigir | trãzi'jiʀ | *vi.* to compromise, to come to terms

transitar | trãzi'taʀ | *vi.* to transit; to pass over, through or across; to journey

trânsito | 'trãzitʊ | *sm.* transit. **-guarda de t.** traffic policeman. **-sinal de t.** traffic sign. **-t. impedido** no thoroughfare. **-passageiro em t.** transit passenger

transitório -ria | trãzi'tɔriʊ | *a.* transitory

transmissão | trãʒmi'sãw | *sf.* transmission

transmitir | trãʒmi'tiʀ | *vt.* to transmit, to convey; (rad., TV) to broadcast

transparente | trãʃpa'rɛtɪ | *a.* transparent

transpirar | trãʃpi'raʀ | *vi.* to perspire; to transpire; (fig.) to leak out (news)

transplante | trãʒ'plãtι | sm. transplant, transplantation (also surg.)

transpor | trãʒ'poR | vt. to traverse; to cross over; to transpose

transportar | trãʒpoR'taR | vt. to transport; to carry, to convey; to entrance, to enrapture. **-t. -se** to be transported (also fig.)

transporte | trãʒ'pωRtι | sm. transport, transportation

transtornar | trãʒtoR'naR | vt. to upset, to disturb; to derange

transtorno | trãʒ'toRnυ | sm. disturbance, upset, inconvenience

transversal | trãʒveR'sal | a. transverse, cross

transviar | trãʒvi'aR | vt. to lead astray. **-t. -se** to go astray

trapaça | tra'pasa | sf. swindle, fraud

trapacear | trapasι'aR | vt. vi. to cheat, to swindle

trapaceiro -ra | trapa'seyrυ | smf. swindler

trapalhada | trapa'Lada | sf. (colloq.) mess, imbroglio

trapalhão -lhona | trapa'Lãw -'Lona | smf. blunderer; swindler

trapiche | tra'pixι | sm. pier warehouse; pier

trapo | 'trapυ | sm. rag

traquejo | tra'kejυ | sm. experience, skill

traquinas | tra'kinaʒ | smf. a naughty child / a. mischievous (said of children)

trás | 'traʒ | adv. and prep. behind, after; back. **-para t.** backward(s). **-por t. de** behind

traseiro -ra | tra'zeyrυ | sm. the behind; sf. rear, hind part / a. back, rear, hind

trasladar | traʒla'daR | vt. to transfer; to postpone; to transcribe

traslado | traʒ'ladυ | sm. copy;

transcript

traspassar | traʒpa'saR | vt. to pass over or through, to transfix; to transfer or sublet (property)

traspasse | traʒ'pasι | sm. passing over, transfer, transferring

traste | 'traʒtι | sm. (unc.) household furniture or utensils; (fig.) old household article; (colloq.) worthless person

tratado | tra'tadυ | sm. treaty; pact; treatise

tratamento | trata'mẽtυ | sm. treatment; attendance; mode of address

tratante | tra'tãtι | smf. swindler; sm. knave, rogue

tratar | tra'taR | vt. to treat; to arrange for; to care for (medically). **-de que se trata?** what is it about? **-trata-se de** it is a question of/ vi. to treat, to discourse on. **-t. com** to deal with. **-t. alguém de** to address as

tratável | tra'tavιl | a. treatable; affable; docile

trato | 'tratυ | sm. deal; usage, handling; caring for; manner of dealing (with other persons); manners. **-pessoa de t.** a well-bred person. **-maus tratos** maltreatment

trator | tra'toR | sm. tractor. **-t. de esteira** caterpillar tractor

trava | 'trava | sf. fetterlock; brake; lock for a wheel; safety (as in a firearm)

travar | tra'vaR | vt. to brake; to clog, to block. **-t. batalha** to join battle. **-t. conversa** to engage in conversation (with)

trave | 'travι | sf. wooden beam, crossbar

través | tra'veʒ | sm. bias, slant. **-de t.** aslant; crosswise

travessa | tra'vesa | sf. platter, serving dish; cross street; barrette, comb

travessão | trave'sãw | sm. dash; (typog., mus.) bar

travesseiro | travι'seyrυ | sm.

pillow

travessia | travɩ'sia | *sf.* crossing; voyage

travesso -sa | tra'vesʋ | *a.* naughty, mischievous

travessura | travɩ'sura | *sf.* naughtiness, mischievousness

travo | 'travʋ | *sm.* tartness, sourness (also fig.)

trazer | tra'zeʀ | *vt.* to bring; to get; to bring about; to wear. **-t. à baila** to bring (a matter) up for discussion. **-t. de presente** to bring (something) as a gift

trecho | 'trexʋ | *sm.* space, distance; passage (musical or literary)

trégua | 'trɛgwa | *sf.* truce; respite

treinador-dora | treyna'doʀ | *smf.* trainer (also sports), coach

treinar | trey'naʀ | *vt. vi.* to train, to practice, to exercise

treino | 'treynʋ | *sm.* (sports) training

trejeito | tre'jeytʋ | *sm.* twitch, quirk; grimace

trela | 'trɛla | *sf.* dog leash. **-dar t. a** (colloq.) to encourage familiarity

trem | 'trẽy | *sm.* train. **-t. de cozinha** kitchen utensils. **-t. de aterrissagem** landing gear

trema | 'trema | *sm.* (gram.) dieresis

tremelicar | trɩmɩli'kaʀ | *vi.* to shiver; to quake

tremendo -da | tre'mẽdʋ | *a.* tremendous; frightful; formidable

tremer | tre'meʀ | *vi.* to tremble, to shudder, to quiver

tremor | tre'moʀ | *sm.* tremor, shaking. **-t. de terra** earthquake

trempe | 'trẽpɩ | *sf.* trivet

tremular | tremu'laʀ | *vi.* to flutter (as a flag); to glimmer (as stars); to vibrate

trêmulo -la | 'tremulʋ | *a.* tremulous

trena | 'trena | *sf.* tape-measure

trenó | tre'nɔ | *sm.* sled, sleigh

trepadeira | trepa'deyra | *sf.* climbing plant

trepador -deira | trepa'doʀ | *sm.* climbing bird / *a.* climbing, creeping

trepar | tre'paʀ | *vt. vi.* to climb; (vulg.) to have sexual intercourse

trepidação | trepida'sãw | *sf.* trepidation

trepidar | trepi'daʀ | *vi.* to vibrate, to tremble

três | 'treʃ | *sm. num.* three

tresloucado -da | treʃlow'kadʋ | *smf.* mad person / *a.* mad, crazed

trevas | 'trɛvaʃ | *sfpl.* darkness (also fig.)

trevo | 'trevʋ | *sm.* clover

treze | 'trezɩ | *sm. num.* thirteen

trezentos -tas | tre'zẽtʋʃ | *smf. num.* three hundred

triângulo | tri'ãgulʋ | *sm.* triangle

tribo | 'tribʋ | *sf.* tribe

tribulação | tribula'sãw | *sf.* tribulation, misfortune

tribuna | tri'buna | *sf.* tribune

tribunal | tribu'nal | *sm.* tribunal, court

tributação | tributa'sãw | *sf.* taxation

tributar | tribu'taʀ | *vt.* to tax; to pay tribute to

tributário -ria | tribu'tariʋ | *sm. a.* tributary, confluent

tributo | tri'butʋ | *sm.* tribute, tax

trigésimo -ma | tri'jɛzimʋ | *sm. a.* thirtieth

trigo | 'trigʋ | *sm.* wheat

trilar | tri'laʀ | *vi.* to trill, to warble

trilha | 'triʟa | *sf.* trail, track. **-t. sonora** sound track

trilhar | tri'ʟaʀ | *vt.* to tread, to follow (a path); to travel on foot

trilho | 'triʟʋ | *sm.* rail, steel rail; track, trail

trimestre | tri'mɛʃtrɩ | *sm.* trimester, quarter year

trinar | tri'naʀ | *vi.* to trill, to warble, to chirp

trinca | 'trĩka | *sf.* set of three (of

anything)

trincar | trī'kaʀ | *vt.* to bite, to munch. **-t. -se** to crack (porcelain)

trinchar | trī'xaʀ | *vt.* to carve, to cut up (meat, fowl etc.)

trincheira | trī'xeyra | *sf.* trench

trinco | 'trīkʋ | *sm.* catch, latch

trindade | trī'dadɪ | *sf.* trinity; (*cap.*) the Trinity

trinta | 'trīta | *sm. num.* thirty

tripa | 'tripa | *sf.* gut, intestine (esp. of animals); tripe

tripé | tri'pɛ | *sm.* tripod

triplo -pla | 'triplʋ | *sm. a.* triple

tripudiar | tripudi'aʀ | *vi.* to gloat, to rejoice malignantly

tripulação | tripula'sãw | *sf.* crew

tripulante | tripu'lãtɪ | *smf.* crew member

tripular | tripu'laʀ | *vt.* (naut., aeron.) to man

triste | 'triʃtɪ | *a.* sad, sorrowful; wretched. **-fazer um papel t.** to cut a sorry figure

tristeza | triʒ'teza | *sf.* sadness, sorrow, melancholy

triturar | tritu'raʀ | *vt.* to grind to powder, to pound

triunfar | triũ'faʀ | *vi.* to triumph (over), to prevail (over)

triunfo | tri'ũfʋ | *sm.* triumph, conquest, victory

trivial | trivi'al | *sm.* plain home--cooked dishes / *a.* commonplace, trite; trivial, trifling

triz | 'triʃ | *sm.* used in the expression **por um t.** by or with the skin of one's teeth

troar | trʋ'aʀ | *vi.* to roar, to thunder

troca | 'trɔka | *sf.* exchange; trade, barter. **-em t. de** in exchange for

troça | 'trɔsa | *sf.* mockery, jeering. **-fazer t. de** to make fun of

trocadilho | troka'diLʋ | *sm.* pun, play on words

trocador -dora | troka'doʀ | *smf.* fare collector (in buses)

trocados | tro'kadʋʃ | *smpl.* small

change. **-ter t.** to have change

trocar | tro'kaʀ | *vt.* to exchange; to barter; to change, to replace. **-t. idéias** to exchange views

troçar | tro'saʀ | *vt.* to mock, to gibe. **-t. de** to make fun of

trocista | tro'siʃta | *smf.* mocker; joker / *a.* mocking; joking

troco | 'trokʋ *pl.* 'trokʋʒ 'trɔkʋʒ | *sm.* change (of money); small change. **-a t.** de at the cost of

troço | 'trɔsʋ | *sm.* (colloq.) thing; (colloq.) big shot

troféu | tro'fɛw | *sm.* trophy

tromba | 'trõba | *sf.* elephant's trunk; snout; proboscis. **-t. d'água** water spout

trombada | trõ'bada | *sf.* (colloq.) collision (esp. of cars)

trombeta | trõ'beta | *sf.* trumpet, bugle

trompa | 'trõpa | *sf.* (mus.) horn

tronco | 'trõkʋ | *sm.* (anat., arch., bot.) trunk

trono | 'tronʋ | *sm.* throne

tropa | 'trɔpa | *sf.* troop, soldiers; pack animals

tropeção | trope'sãw | *sm.* stumble, tripping

tropeçar | trope'saʀ | *vi.* to stumble, to trip; to blunder

tropeço | tro'pesʋ | *sm.* stumble, false step; obstacle, impediment; blunder

trôpego -ga | 'tropegʋ | *a.* staggering, stumbling

tropeiro | tro'peyrʋ | *sm.* cattle driver

tropel | tro'pɛl | *sm.* trample, clatter of hoofs; (fig.) tumult, confusion

tropical | tropi'kal | *a.* tropicɛ'

trotar | tro'taʀ | *vi.* to trot

trote | 'trɔtɪ | *sm.* trot; (colloq.) hazing (of new students)

trouxa | 'trowxa | *sf.* bundle (esp. of clothes); *smf.* (colloq.) fool, sucker

trova | 'trɔva | *sf.* popular ballad, song or tune

trovador | trova'doR | *sm.* troubado(u)r

trovão | tro'vãw | *sm.* thunder

trovejar | trove'jaR | *vi.* to thunder

trovoada | trovu'ada | *sf.* thunderstorm

trucidar | trusi'daR | *vt.* to slaughter, to murder ruthlessly

trunfo | 'trũfʋ | *sm.* trump; (colloq.) big shot

truque | 'trukι | *sm.* trick, stratagem

truta | 'truta | *sf.* trout

tu | 'tu | *pron. 2nd person sing.* you (familiar), thou, thee

tubarão | tuba'rãw | *sm.* shark; (colloq.) commercial profiteer

tuberculose | tubeRku'lɔzι | *sf.* tuberculosis

tuberculoso -sa | tubeRku'lozʋ -'lωza | *smf.* tubercular, a tuberculous person / *a.* tubercular

tubo | 'tubʋ | *sm.* tube; pipe

tucano | tu'kanʋ | *sm.* toucan

tudo | 'tudʋ | *pron.* all, everything. **-t. quanto** all that

tufão | tu'fãw | *sm.* typhoon, hurricane

tufo | 'tufʋ | *sm.* tuft, bunch, cluster

tulipa | tu'lipa | *sf.* tulip

tumba | 'tũba | *sf.* tomb; tombstone

tumor | tu'moR | *sm.* tumo(u)r

túmulo | 'tumulʋ | *sm.* grave, tomb

tumulto | tu'multʋ | *sm.* tumult, agitation, uproar

tunda | 'tũda | *sf.* (colloq.) beating, thrashing

túnel | 'tunιl *pl.* 'tuneyʒ | *sm.* tunnel

túnica | 'tunika | *sf.* tunic

turba | 'tuRba | *sf.* mob, rabble, crowd

turbante | tuR'bãtι | *sm.* turban

turbar | tuR'baR | *vt.* to darken; to cloud. **-t. -se** to become overcast; to become clouded (wine etc.)

turbilhão | tuRbi'Lãw | *sm.* whirlwind, whirlpool

turbulência | tuRbu'lẽsia | *sf.* turbulence

turbulento -ta | tuRbu'lẽtʋ | *a.* turbulent, tumultuous, disturbed

turco -ca | 'tuRkʋ | *sm.* (ling.) Turkish; *smf.* a Turk / *a.* Turkish

turfa | 'tuRfa | *sf.* peat

turfe | 'tuRfι | *sm.* turf, horse-racing

turista | tu'riʃta | *smf.* tourist

turismo | tu'riʒmʋ | *sm.* tourism, touring

turma | 'tuRma | *sf.* gang, group; division (of a school class); (colloq.) group of friends

turno | 'tuRnʋ | *sm.* turn; shift (at work); group; school period (hour)

turquesa | tuR'keza | *sf.* turquoise

turra | 'tuRa | *sf.* quarrel, controversy. **-andar às turras com** to be on bad terms with

turvar | tuR'vaR | *vt.* to muddy, to cloud / *vt. vr.* to become turbid (also fig.)

turvo -va | 'tuRvʋ | *a.* turbid, muddy; cloudy, overcast

tutano | tu'tanʋ | *sm.* marrow. **-ter t.** (colloq.) to be tough

tutela | tu'tεla | *sf.* (law) guardianship, tutorship, custody

tutelar | tute'laR | *a.* tutelary / *vt.* to tutor

tutor -tora | tu'toR | *smf.* (law) guardian, tutor

tutu | tu'tu | *sm.* Brazilian dish of beans and manioc meal; (slang) dough, money

U

úbere, ubre | ‘uberɪ ‘ubrɪ | *sm.* udder, teat

ufanar-se | ufa‘naRsɪ | *vr.* to pride oneself on

uísque | u‘iʃkɪ | *sm.* whisky

uivar | uy‘vaR | *vi.* to howl

uivo | ‘uyvʊ | *sm.* howl

úlcera | ‘ulsera | *sf.* ulcer

ulcerar | ulse‘raR | *vt. vi. vr.* to ulcerate

ulterior | ulteri‘oR | *a.* later, future; further

ultimar | ulti‘maR | *vt.* to finish, to complete

ultimato | ulti‘matʊ | *sm.* ultimatum

último -ma | ‘ultimʊ | *smf.* last / *a.* last, latest, final. **-por ú.** finally, at last

ultrajar | ultra‘jaR | *vt.* to outrage, to insult

ultraje | ul‘trajɪ | *sm.* insult, outrage

ultramar | ultra‘maR | *sm.* overseas lands or regions

ultramarino -na | ultrama‘rinʊ | *a.* overseas

ultrapassar | ultrapa‘saR | *vt.* to go beyond; to surpass; to get ahead of, to outclass

um, uma | ‘ũ ‘uma | *sm. num.* one / *a. pron.* one / *indef. art.* a, an

umbigo | ũ‘bigʊ | *sm.* navel

umbral | ũ‘bral | *sm.* threshold

umedecer | umɪde‘seR | *vt.* to moisten, to dampen / *vi.* (also **-u. -se**) to become moist

umidade | umi‘dadɪ | *sf.* humidity, moisture, dampness

úmido -da | ‘umidʊ | *a.* humid, moist, damp

unânime | u‘nanimɪ | *a.* unanimous

unanimidade | unanimi‘dadɪ | *sf.* unanimity

unção | ũ‘sãw | *sf.* unction (also fig.)

ungir | ũ‘jiR | *vt.* to anoint; (relig.) to consecrate by unction

unha | ‘uNa | *sf.* nail claw; hoof. **-fazer as unhas** to cut or to manicure one’s nails. **-ser u. e carne com alguém** to be hand and glove with someone. **-à u.** with the bare hands

unha-de-fome | ‘uNadɪ‘fomɪ | *smf.* (colloq.) miser

unhar | u‘NaR | *vt.* to scratch (with the nails or claws)

união | uni‘ãw | *sf.* union; association, alliance. **-traço de u.** hyphen

único -ca | ‘unikʊ | *a.* only, sole; single, unique

unidade | uni‘dadɪ | *sf.* unit (also mil.); unity; one

unificar | unifi‘kaR | *vt.* to unify, to unite

uniforme | uni‘fʊRmɪ | *sm. a.* uniform

uniformizar | unifoRmi‘zaR | *vt.* to render uniform; to clothe or to supply with a uniform. **-u. -se** to put on a uniform

unir | u‘niR | *vt.* to unite; to connect; to couple, to marry. **-u. -se** to unite; to join in marriage; to associate oneself with

universal | univeR‘sal | *sm. a.* universal

universidade | univeRsi‘dadɪ | *sf.* university

universitário -ria | univeRsi‘tariʊ | *smf.* university student or professor / *a.* of or pertaining to a university

universo | uni‘veRsʊ | *sm.* universe

untar | ũ‘taR | *vt.* to grease; to smear with any fat substance

untuoso -sa | ũtu'ozʋ -'ωza | *a.* unctuous (fig.)

upa | 'upa | *interj.* up, up!, hoop-la!, oops!

urbanidade | uʀbani'dadɪ | *sf.* courtesy, urbanity

urbanismo | uʀba'niʃmʋ | *sm.* city planning

urbano -na | uʀ'banʋ | *a.* urban; (fig.) urbane, polite

urdir | uʀ'diʀ | *vt. vi.* to warp (yarn); to plot, to intrigue

urgência | uʀ'jẽsia | *sf.* urgency

urgente | uʀ'jẽtɪ | *a.* urgent, pressing

urgir | uʀ'jiʀ | *vi.* to be urgent, to be pressing. **-o tempo urge** time is pressing

urina | u'rina | *sf.* urine

urinar | uri'naʀ | *vi.* to urinate

urna | 'uʀna | *sf.* urn; ballot box

urrar | u'ʀaʀ | *vi.* to roar (as a lion); to bellow (as a bull)

urro | 'uʀʋ | *sm.* roar; bellow; howl

ursada | uʀ'sada | *sf.* (colloq.) dirty trick

urso -sa | 'uʀsʋ | *sm.* bear; *sf.* female bear

urticária | uʀti'karia | *sf.* urticaria, nettle rash

urtiga | uʀ'tiga | *sf.* nettle

urubu | uru'bu | *sm.* black vulture

uruguaio-guaia | uru'gwayʋ | *smf. a.* Uruguayan

usado -da | u'zadʋ | *a.* used; worn (out); second-hand; cus-tomary

usar | u'zaʀ | *vt.* to use; to wear; to employ; to wear out; to be in the habit of. **-u. -se** to be in fashion. **-fazer uso da palavra** to speak at a meeting

usina | u'zina | *sf.* mill, factory, works. **-u. de açúcar** sugar-mill

usineiro -ra | uzi'neyrʋ | *smf.* owner of a sugar-mill

uso | 'uzʋ | *sm.* use; usage, custom; fashion, wear

usual | uzu'al | *a.* usual, customary

usufruir | uzufru'iʀ | *vt.* to enjoy, to have the use of (advantages etc.)

usufruto | uzu'frutʋ | *sm.* usu-fruct; fruition

usura | u'zura | *sf.* usury

usurário -ria | uzu'rariʋ | *smf.* usu-rer; (colloq.) miser / *a.* usurious

usurpar | uzuʀ'paʀ | *vt.* to usurp, to appropriate unlawfully

utensílio | utẽ'siliʋ | *sm.* utensil, implement

útero | 'uterʋ | *sm.* uterus, womb

útil | 'util | *a.* useful, helpful. **-dia ú.** workday, weekday

utilidade | utili'dadɪ | *sf.* utility, use, usefulness

utilizar | utili'zaʀ | *vt.* to utilize, to use, to apply; to take advantage of

uva | 'uva | *sf.* grape

vaca | 'vaka | *sf.* cow

vacilar | vasi'laʀ | *vt.* to hesitate; to vacillate, to waver

vacina | va'sina | *sf.* vaccine; vaccination

vacinar | vasi'naʀ | *vt.* to vaccinate

vacum | va'kũ | *a.* bovine

vácuo -cua | 'vakuʋ | *sm.* vacuum, vóid / *a.* empty, void

vadiação | vadia'sãw | *sf.* idleness

vadiagem | vadi'ajẽy | *sf.* (law) va-grancy; laziness

vadiar | vadi'aʀ | *vi.* to loaf; to dawdle (said esp. of a student)

vadio -dia | va'diʋ | *smf.* vagabond, vagrant; *sf.* (slang) prostitute / *a.* loafing, idle (esp. a student)

vaga | 'vaga | *sf.* vacancy; parking space; billow, wave

vagabundagem | vagabū'dajĕy | *sf.* vagrancy

vagabundo -da | vaga'būdʋ | *smf.* vagrant, tramp; *sf.* prostitute / *a.* vagrant, loafing; (colloq.) cheap, poor in quality

vaga-lume | vaga'lumι | *sm.* firefly

vagão | va'gãw | *sm.* railway wagon

vagar | va'gaR | *sm.* spare time, leisure. **-com v.** at leisure; taking one's time / *vi.* to roam, to wander; to become vacant

vagaroso -sa | vaga'rozʋ -'rωza | *a.* slow, sluggish

vagem | 'vajĕy | *sf.* pod; green bean

vagir | va'jiR | *vi.* to cry (newborn child), to whine

vago -ga | 'vagʋ | *a.* vague, uncertain; vacant, unoccupied. **-horas vagas** spare time

vaguear | vagι'aR | *vi.* to roam, to wander; to ramble

vaia | 'vaya | *sf.* hoot, boo, jeer

vaiar | vay'aR | *vt.* to hoot, to hiss at, to boo

vaidade | vai'dadι | *sf.* vanity; conceit

vaidoso -sa | vai'dozʋ -'dωza | *a.* vain; conceited

vaivém | vay'vĕy | *sm.* to-and-fro motion; coming and going (of people)

vala | 'vala | *sf.* ditch; trench. **-v. comum** common grave, potter's field

vale | 'valι | *sm.* valley; voucher; IOU. **-v. postal** money order

valentão | valē'tãw | *sm.* bully, braggart

valente | va'lĕtι | *a.* brave, courageous

valentia | valē'tia | *sf.* valo(u)r, bravery

valer | va'leR | *vt.* to be worth; to cost. **-v. -se de** to resort to; to take advantage of. **-vale a pena** it is worth while / *vi.* to be worth; to have importance. **-assim não vale!** (colloq.) that is not fair! **-a v.** to one's fill; a great deal. **-valeu!** (colloq.) it's a deal!

valeta | va'leta | *sf.* gutter

valete | va'lĕtι | *sm.* jack (playing card)

valia | va'lia | *sf.* value, worth; merit

validade | vali'dadι | *sf.* = *validez*

validar | vali'daR | *vt.* to validate

validez | vali'deʒ | *sf.* validity

válido -da | 'validʋ | *a.* valid; able-bodied

valioso -sa | vali'ozʋ -'ωza | *a.* valious, precious

valise | va'lizι | *sf.* valise, travelling bag

valor | va'loR | *sm.* valo(u)r; merit; (*pl.*) valuables; (*pl.*) values, one's standards. **-sem v.** valueless, worthless

valorização | valoriza'sãw | *sf.* appreciation, rise in price or value; valorization

valorizar | valori'zaR | *vt.* to increase the value of; to valorize / *vi. vr.* to increase in value

valoroso -sa | valo'rozʋ -'rωza | *a.* courageous, brave

valsa | 'valsa | *sf.* waltz

válvula | 'valvυla | *sf.* valve; (electron.) tube. **-v. de segurança** safety valve

vangloriar-se | vãglori'aRsι | *vr.* to boast

vanguarda | vã'gwaRda | *sf.* vanguard, forefront

vantagem | vã'tajĕy | *sf.* advantage; superiority; profit, benefit. **-contar v.** (colloq.) to boast. **-levar v.** to get the upper hand

vão, vã | 'vãw 'vã | *sm.* space, gap / *a.* vain; delusive; vainglorious. **-em vão** in vain

vapor | va'poR | *sm.* steam; vapo(u)r; (obs.) steamship, steamer. **-a todo o v.** at full blast

vaqueiro -ra | va'keyrʋ | *sm.* cowboy, herdsman

vaquinha |va'kiɴa| *sf.* small cow; (colloq.) combination of resources or funds

vara | 'vara | *sf.* rod; wand; stick; (law) jurisdiction. **-v. de porcos** a herd of swine

varal | va'ral | *sm.* shaft (of a cart); clothesline

varanda |va'rãda| *sf.* open porch; verandah; balcony

varão | va'rãw | *sm.* man, male

varapau | vara'paw | *sm.* long pole; (colloq.) very thin and tall person

varar | va'raʀ | *vt.* to pierce through (also fig.); to ford a stream

varejar | vare'jaʀ | *vt.* to ransack, to search; to throw out or away

varejeira | vare'jeyra | *sf.* bluebottle

varejista | vare'jiʃta | *smf.* retail dealer

varejo | va'rejʋ | *sm.* retail trade

vareta | va'reta | *sf.* a slender stick; ramrod

variação | varia'sãw | *sf.* variation (also mus.); change

variar | vari'aʀ | *vt.* to vary, to change / *vi.* to vary; (colloq.) to go out of one's mind

variável | vari'avɩl | *a.* variable; changeable

variedade | varie'dadɩ | *sf.* variety

vário -ria | 'variʋ | *a. (pl.)* various, several

varíola | va'riʋla | *sf.* smallpox

varonil | varo'nil | *a.* virile, manly

varrer | va'ʀeʀ | *vt.* to sweep (off, away, out)

varrido -da | va'ʀidʋ | *a.* swept. **-doido** or **louco v.** (colloq.) raving mad

vasa | 'vaza | *sf.* slime, mire; silt

vasculhar | vaʃku'laʀ | *vt.* to pry into every nook and corner; to ransack; to sweep ceilings with a long broom

vasculho | vaʃ'kuʟʋ | *sm.* long--handled broom (to clean walls and ceiling)

vaselina | vazɩ'lina | *sf.* vaseline

vasilha | va'ziʟa | *sf.* vessel (for liquids)

vaso | 'vazʋ | *sm.* vase, pot; bowl. **-v. de guerra** warship. **-v. sangüíneo** blood vessel

vassoura | va'sowra | *sf.* broom

vasto -ta | 'vaʃtʋ | *a.* vast

vatapá | vata'pa | *sm.* highly spiced Afro-brazilian dish of shrimp, coconut milk, palm oil etc.

vaticinar | vatisi'naʀ | *vt.* to prophesy, to foresee

vau | 'vaw | *sm.* ford; shallow. **-passar a v.** to wade

vaza | 'vaza | *sf.* a trick (round of cards). **-não perder v.** to overlook no opportunity

vazamento |vaza'mẽtʋ| *sm.* leak, leakage

vazante | va'zãtɩ | *sf.* ebb tide / *a.* ebbing

vazão | va'zãw | *sf.* out flow; rate of flow. **-dar v. a** to find an outlet for

vazar |va'zaʀ| *vt.* to empty; to hollow out (something); to pierce / *vi.* to leak; to flow out, to ebb

vazio -zia | va'ziʋ | *a.* empty; vacant; futile

veado | vɩ'adʋ | *sm.* deer; (vulg.) male homosexual

vedação | veda'sãw | *sf.* stopping, sealing; prohibition

vedar | ve'daʀ | *vt.* to forbid, to prohibit; to seal; to stop up (hole, leak)

vedete | ve'detɩ | *sf.* (theat., cine.) star

veemência | vee'mẽsia | *sf.* vehemence, intensity

veemente |vee'mẽtɩ| *a.* vehement, intense

vegetação |vejeta'sãw| *sf.* vegetation

vegetal | veje'tal | *sm.* vegetable /

a. vegetal

vegetar | veje'taʀ | *vi.* to vegetate

vegetariano -na | vejetari'anʋ | *smf. a.* vegetarian

veia | 've‿ya | *sf.* vein. **-estar de v.** to be in the mood

veículo | ve'ikulʋ | *sm.* vehicle

veio | 've‿yʋ | *sm.* vein, seam; grain (of wood)

vela | 'vela | *sf.* sail; candle. **-v. de ignição** spark plug. **-fazer-se a** or **à** or **de v.** to set sail

velar | ve'laʀ | *vt.* to veil, to cloak; to watch / *vi.* to keep awake, to keep vigil

veleidade | veley'dadɪ | *sf.* velleity; whim; fancy

veleiro | ve'leyrʋ | *sm.* sailing vessel; sail-boat

velejar | vele'jaʀ | *vi.* to sail

velhaco -ca | ve'Lakʋ | *smf.* scoundrel, crook / *a.* crooked, dishonest

velharia | veLa'ria | *sf.* anything old (objects, clothes etc.); group of old people; (*pl.*) antiques

velhice | ve'Lisɪ | *sf.* old age

velho -lha | 'veLʋ | *sm.* old man; (colloq.) dad; *sf.* old woman; (colloq.) mother; (*pl.*, colloq.) parents / *a.* old

velhote -ta | ve'Lʋtɪ | *smf.* oldster

velocidade | velosi'dadɪ | *sf.* velocity, speed, swiftness

velocímetro | velo'simetrʋ | *sm.* speedometer

velório | ve'lʋriʋ | *sm.* wake, vigil, deathwatch

veloz | ve'lʋʒ | *a.* quick, fast, swift

veludo | ve'ludʋ | *sm.* velvet. **-v. piquê** corduroy

vencedor -dora | vẽse'doʀ | *smf.* winner / *a.* winning; victorious

vencer | vẽ'seʀ | *vt.* to vanquish, to conquer; to overcome. **-v. -se** to fall due, to expire / *vi.* to win, to gain

vencimento | vẽsi'mẽtʋ | *sm.* salary, wage; expiration, due date (of a note, debt etc.)

venda | 'vẽda | *sf.* sale; small grocery store; blindfold

vendar | vẽ'daʀ | *vt.* to blindfold

vendaval | vẽda'val | *sm.* gale

vendedor -dora | vẽde'doʀ | *sm.* salesman; *sf.* saleswoman, saleslady; *smf.* seller

vender | vẽ'deʀ | *vt.* to sell. **-v. à vista** to sell for cash. **-v. a prestações** to sell on instalments. **-v. fiado** to sell on credit. **-v. a varejo** to sell at retail. **-v. por atacado** to sell at wholesail

veneno | ve'nenʋ | *sm.* poison, venom

venenoso -sa | vene'nozʋ -'nwza | *a.* poisonous, venomous

veneração | venera'sãw | *sf.* veneration, reverence

venerar | vene'raʀ | *vt.* to venerate, to revere

venerável | vene'ravɪl | *a.* venerable

venéreo -rea | ve'nɛriʋ | *a.* venereal. **-doença venérea** venereal disease

veneta | ve'neta | *sf.* whim, fancy, caprice. **-dar na v.** to be struck with an idea

veneziana | venezi'ana | *sf.* Venetian blind

venezuelano -na | venezue'lanʋ | *smf. a.* Venezuelan

venta | 'vẽta | *sf.* nostril; (*pl.*) nostrils

ventania | vẽta'nia | *sf.* high wind, gale

ventar | vẽ'taʀ | *vi.* to blow, to bluster (wind)

ventarola | vẽta'rʋla | *sf.* palm-leaf fan

ventilação | vẽtila'sãw | *sf.* ventilation

ventilador | vẽtila'doʀ | *sm.* electric fan; ventilator

ventilar | vẽti'laʀ | *vt.* to ventilate; (fig.) to discuss

vento | 'vẽtʋ | *sm.* wind. **-de v. em popa** prosperously. **-pé de v.** a gust of wind

ventoinha | vẽtu'iNa | *sf.* weather-cock, weather vane

ventosa | vẽ'tωza | *sf.* (med.) cup; (zool.) sucking disk

ventoso -sa | vẽ'tozυ -'tωza | *a.* windy

ventre |'vẽtrɪ | *sm.* womb; belly. **-prisão de v.** constipation

ventura |vẽ'tura | *sf.* chance, fortune, luck

ver | 'veR | *vt.* to see. **-v. -se** to see oneself; to find oneself (in a situation). **-ficar a v. navios** (colloq.) to be left holding the bag. **-vamos a v.** let's see. **-veja lá!** watch out! **-nada ter a v. com** to have nothing to do with. **-a meu v.** in my opinion

veranear | veranɪ'aR | *vi.* to spend the summer

veranista | vera'niʃta | *smf.* vacationist (at a summer resort)

verão | ve'rãw | *sm.* summer

verba |'vɛRba | *sf.* budget; available sum or amount; allotment

verberar | veRbe'raR | *vt.* to censure, to criticize

verbete | veR'betɪ | *sm.* entry (of a dictionary or encyclopaedia)

verbo |'vɛRbυ| *sm.* verb; (*cap.*) the Word

verboso -sa | veR'bozυ -'bωza | *a.* verbose

verdade | veR'dadɪ | *sf.* truth. **-de v.** really, truly. **-na v.** or **em v.** in fact, actually

verdadeiro -ra | veRda'deyrυ | *a.* true, real, genuine

verde | 'veRdɪ | *sm.* green (colo[u]r) / *a.* green; unripe. **-carne v.** fresh meat

verdugo | veR'dugυ | *sm.* executioner, hangman

verdura | veR'dura | *sf.* verdure (also fig.), greenness, verdancy; (gen. *pl.*) vegetables

verdureiro -ra |veRdu'reyrυ |*smf.* greengrocer

vereador -dora | verɪa'doR | *sm.* councilman; *sf.* councilwoman

veredicto, vèredito | vere'diktυ

vere'ditυ | *sm.* verdict

vergalhão | veRga'Lãw | *sm.* iron bar or beam

vergão | veR'gãw | *sm.* weal (on flesh)

vergar | veR'gaR | *vt.* to bend, to curve; (fig.) to subdue. **-v. -se** to bow, to stoop

vergonha | veR'goNa | *sf.* shame; disgrace; embarrassment; shyness. **-é uma v.** it's a downright shame. **-que v.!** what a shame!

vergonhoso -sa | veRgo'Nozυ -'Nωza | *a.* shameful, disgraceful

verídico -ca | ve'ridikυ | *a.* veridical, true

verificação | vɪrifika'sãw | *sf.* verification; confirmation; checking

verificar | vɪrifi'kaR | *vt.* to verify, to check. **-v. -se** to take place

verme | 'vɛRmɪ | *sm.* worm

vermelho -lha | veR'meLυ | *sm.* red (colo[u]r); (ichth.) red snapper / *a.* red

verniz | veR'niʒ | *sm.* varnish; lacquer; gloss

verruga | ve'Ruga | *sf.* wart

verruma | ve'Ruma |*sf.* gimlet; auger; bit

versado -da | veR'sadυ | *a.* versed, experienced, skilled, proficient

versão | veR'sãw | *sf.* version, translation; particular account of some matter

versar | veR'saR | *vt.* to examine (something); to deal with (a subject) / *vi.* to deal with; to turn on, to hinge on (conversation, discussion etc.)

versátil |veR'satil | *a.* versatile

versejar | veRse'jaR | *vi.* to write verses

verso | 'vɛRsυ | *sm.* verse; reverse; side

vértebra | 'vɛRtebra | *sf.* vertebra

vertente | veR'tẽtɪ | *sf.* slope; mountainside

verter |veR'teR | *vt.* to pour out;

to shed; to spill; to translate (to a foreign language). **-v. lágrimas** to shed tears

vertical | veRti'kal | *a.* vertical, upright

vertigem | veR'tijĕy | *sf.* dizziness, giddiness

vesgo -ga | 've∫gʊ | *a.* crosseyed

vespa | 've∫pa | *sf.* wasp, hornet

véspera | 'vε∫pera | *sf.* eve, day before. **-à v.** or **em vésperas de** on the eve of

vespertino -na | ve∫peR'tinʊ | *sm.* evening newspaper / *a.* evening

veste | 'vε∫tι | *sf.* (gen. *pl.*) garment, clothes

vestiário | vι∫ti'ariʊ | *sm.* cloakroom

vestibular | vι∫tibu'laR | *sm.* college entrance examination / *a.* vestibular

vestíbulo | vι∫'tibulʊ | *sm.* vestibule, lobby, hall

vestido -da | vι∫'tidʊ | *sm.* dress, gown / *a.* dressed; covered

vestígio | vι∫'tijiʊ | *sm.* vestige, trace, sign

vestir | vι∫'tiR | *vt.* to dress, to clothe. **-v. -se** to dress oneself; to become covered

vestuário | vι∫tu'ariʊ | *sm.* clothing, wardrobe

vetar | ve'taR | *vt.* to veto; (colloq.) to prohibit, to refuse

veterano -na | vete'ranʊ | *sm.* veteran / *a.* veteran; (colloq.) old--timer; (colloq.) senior (said of a student)

veterinária | veteri'naria | *sf.* veterinary medicine

veterinário -ria | veteri'nariʊ | *smf. a.* veterinary

veto | 'vεtʊ | *sm.* veto

véu | 'vew | *sm.* veil

vexame | ve'xamι | *sm.* vexation, annoyance; shame

vexar | ve'xaR | *vt.* to vex; to trouble; to make ashamed. **-v. -se** to feel shame

vez | 've∫ | *sf.* time; turn; occasion. **-v. por outra** now and then;

once in a while. **-cada v. que** whenever. **-certa v.** once, one time. **-de uma v. por todas** once and for all. **-era uma v.** once upon a time. **-outra v.** again,. once more. **-uma v. once.** **-às** or **por vezes** sometimes

via | 'via | *sf.* way, route, road; (anat.) duct, canal; carbon copy / *prep.* by way of, via. **-(por) via aérea (marítima, terrestre)** by air mail (by sea or ship; by land, surface). **-por v. de regra** as a rule. **-chegar às vias de fato** to come to blows

viação | via'sãw | *sf.* transit system, transportation system

viaduto | via'dutʊ | *sm.* viaduct

viagem | vi'ajĕy | *sf.* trip, journey, travel

viajante | via'jãtι | *smf.* travel(l)er / *a.* travel(l)ing

viajar | via'jaR | *vi.* to travel

víbora | 'vibʊra | *sf.* viper

vibração | vibra'sãw | *sf.* vibration

vibrar | vi'braR | *vt.* to brandish; to strike (the strings of a guitar etc.); to vibrate. **-v. um golpe** to deal a blow / *vi.* to vibrate; to thrill

vicejar | vise'jaR | *vi.* to flourish; to blossom

vice-presidência | visιprιzi'dẽsia | *sf.* vice-presidency

vice-presidente | visιprιzi'dẽtι | *smf.* vice-president

vice-rei | visι'Rey | *sm.* viceroy

viciar | visi'aR | *vt.* to vitiate; to addict. **-v. -se** to become addict

vício | 'visiʊ | *sm.* vice; bad habit; addiction; corruption

vicioso -sa | visi'ozʊ -'ɔza | *a.* vicious, corrupt, depraved

viçoso -sa | vi'sozʊ -'sɔza | *a.* luxuriant, lush; vigorous; flourishing

vida | 'vida | *sf.* life. **-custo de v.** cost of living. **-estar bem de v.** to be well-off. **-meio de v.** livelihood. **-padrão de v.** standard of living. **-para toda a v.** for life

videira | vi'deyra | *sf.* grape-vine, vine

vidraça | vi'drasa | *sf.* window-pane; window glass

vidraceiro | vidra'seyrʊ | *sm.* glazier; glassworker. **-massa de v.** putty

vidrado -da | vi'dradʊ | *sm.* glaze / *a.* glazed; (slang) fascinated

vidrar | vi'draʀ | *vt.* to glaze / *vi.* (slang) to become enthusiastic, to fall (madly) in love

vidro | 'vidrʊ | *sm.* glass; small bottle

vieira | .vi'eyra | *sf.* scallop; scallop-shell

viela | vi'ɛla | *sf.* narrow alley, lane

viga | 'viga | *sf.* beam, girder. **-v. mestra** main beam

vigarice | viga'risɪ | *sf.* (colloq.) swindling game

vigário | vi'garɪʊ | *sm.* vicar; parson

vigarista | viga'riʃta | *smf.* (colloq.) swindler

vigência | vi'jẽsia | *sf.* validity, effect

vigente | vi'jẽtɪ | *a.* in force, in effect; valid

vigésimo -ma | vi'jɛzimʊ | *sm. a.* twentieth

vigia | vi'jia | *sm.* watchman, guard, sentry; *sf.* watch, vigil; lookout; (naut.) porthole

vigiar | viji'aʀ | *vt.* to watch, to guard / *vi.* to keep watch

vigilância | viji'lãsia | *sf.* vigilance, watchfulness

vigor | vi'goʀ | *sm.* vigo(u)r; validity, effect. **-em v.** in force

vigorar | vigo'raʀ | *vi.* to be valid, to be in force

vigoroso -sa | vigo'rozʊ -'rɔza | *a.* vigorous, strong

vil | 'vil | *a.* vile, base; contemptible

vila | 'vila | *sf.* village, settlement; villa

vilania | vila'nia | *sf.* vileness

vilão, -lã, -loa | vi'lãw -'lã -'loa | *smf.* villain, rascal, scoundrel / *a.* villainous

vilarejo | vila'rejʊ | *sm.* small village

vime | 'vimɪ | *sm.* wicker, withe, osier for baskets and wickerwork

vinagre | vi'nagrɪ | *sm.* vinegar

vinco | 'vĩkʊ | *sm.* crease, seam, wrinkle

vínculo | 'vĩkulʊ | *sm.* tie, link, bond of union

vinda | 'vĩda | *sf.* arrival, coming

vindicar | vĩdi'kaʀ | *vt.* to vindicate

vindima | vĩ'dima | *sf.* vintage; gathering of grapes

vindo -da | 'vĩdʊ | *a.* arrived, come, coming. **-v. de** coming or arriving from

vindouro -ra | vĩ'dowrʊ | *a.* future, coming

vingança | vĩ'gãsa | *sf.* vengeance, revenge

vingar | vĩ'gaʀ | *vt.* to revenge, to avenge **-se** to take vengeance / *vi.* to thrive, to prosper

vingativo -va | vĩga'tivʊ | *a.* vindictive, revengeful

vinha | 'viNa | *sf.* vine; vineyard

vinha-d'alhos | viNa'daʎʊʃ | *sf.* a marinade of vinegar or wine and spices

vinhateiro -ra | viNa'teyrʊ | *smf.* wine-grower / *a.* wine-producing

vinhedo | vi'Nedʊ | *sm.* large vineyard

vinho | 'viNʊ | *sm.* wine. **-v. branco** white wine. **-v. tinto** red wine. **-v. espumante** sparkling wine

vinícola | vi'nikʊla | *a.* wine-producing

vinte | 'vĩtɪ | *sm. num.* twenty

vintém | vĩ'tẽy | *sm.* former Portuguese and Brazilian copper coin; farthing. **-não ter v.** to be penniless

vintena | vĩ'tena | *sf.* set or group of twenty; twentieth

viola | vi'ɔla | *sf.* (mus.) viola;

small guitar; (ichth.) guitar fish, a kind of ray or skate

violação | viola'sãw | *sf.* violation, infringement; rape

violão | vio'lãw | *sm.* guitar

violar | vio'laʀ | *vt.* to violate; to rape. **-v. a lei** to break the law

violência | vio'lẽsıɐ | *sf.* violence

violentar | violẽ'taʀ | *vt.* to coerce, to constrain, to force. **-v. -se** to constrain oneself

violento -ta | vio'lẽtʋ | *a.* violent

violeta | vio'leta | *sf.* violet; *sm. a.* violet (colo[u]r)

violinista | vıʋli'niʃta | *smf.* violinist

violino | viʋ'linʋ | *sm.* violin

vir | 'viʀ | *vi.* to come. **-v. ao mundo** to be born. **-v. a ser** to become; to signify; to amount to. **-mandar v.** to send for; to order (at a restaurant etc.). **-ir e v.** to come and go. **-não v. ao caso** to be irrelevant. **-vamos!** come!, let's go!, let's begin!

viração | vira'sãw | *sf.* breeze, gentle wind

vira-casaca | viraka'zaka | *smf.* (colloq.) turncoat

vira-lata | vira'lata | *smf.* mongrel, street dog

virar | vi'raʀ | *vt.* to turn (down, inside out, over, upside down). **-v. -se** to turn; (colloq.) to provide for one's own needs. **-virar contra** to turn against. **-v. a cabeça de alguém** to turn a person's head. **-v. a cara** to turn away (from something); to cut dead

viravolta | vira'vɔlta | *sf.* complete turn; (fig.) sudden change

virgem | 'viʀʒẽy | *sf.* virgin; (*cap.*) Virgin Mary / *a.* virgin; chaste. **-floresta v.** virgin forest

vírgula | 'viʀgula | *sf.* comma (used also as a decimal mark). **-ponto e v.** semicolon

viril | vi'ɾil | *a.* virile, masculine

virilha | vi'ɾiʟa | *sf.* groin

virtual | viʀtu'al | *a.* virtual, poten-

tial, possible

virtude | viʀ'tudı | *sf.* virtue, uprightness, probity; power. **-em v. de** in view of, because

virtuoso -sa | viʀtu'ozʋ -'ɔza | *a.* virtuous, upright

virulento -ta | viru'lẽtʋ | *a.* virulent; acrimonious

vírus | 'viruʃ | *sm.* (*sing.* and *pl.*) virus

visão | vi'zãw | *sf.* vision, sight; apparition; dream, chimera

visar | vi'zaʀ | *vt.* to aim at (a target); to visa (a passport); to approve by countersigning. **-v. a** to look at, to intend, to have in view

visco | 'viʃkʋ | *sm.* (bot.) mistletoe

visconde | viʃ'kõdı | *sm.* viscount

viscondessa | viʃkõ'desa | *sf.* viscountess

viscoso -sa | viʃ'kozʋ -'kɔza | *a.* viscous; slimy

visgo | 'viʃgʋ | *sm.* birdlime

visibilidade | vizibili'dadı | *sf.* visibility

visionário -ria | vizio'narıʋ | *smf. a.* visionary

visita | vi'zita | *sf.* visit, call; visitor; guest. **-cartão de v.** visiting-card. **-fazer uma v.** to pay a call

visitante | vizi'tãtı | *smf.* visitor, caller / *a.* visitant, visiting

visitar | vizi'taʀ | *vt.* to visit; to go to see

visível | vi'zivıl | *a.* visible

vislumbrar | viʃlũ'braʀ | *vt.* to glimpse, to discern; to conjecture

vislumbre | viʃ'lũbrı | *sm.* glimpse; glimmer, gleam; hint

víspora | 'viʃpʋra | *sf.* lotto

vista | 'viʃta | *sf.* sight; eyesight; view, scene; (colloq.) eyes. **-até a v.** so long. **-à v.** cash (payment); exposed. **-em v. de** considering, in view of. **-fazer v. grossa** to shut one's eye to. **-ter em v.** to have in mind

visto -ta | 'viʃtʋ | *sm.* visa / *a.* seen; accepted, known. **-bem v.** well thought of. **-está v. que** of course. **-haja vista** as shown by. **-v. que** since, inasmuch as

vistoria | viʒtυ'ria | *sf.* inspection, survey

vistoso -sa | viʒ'tozυ -'tωza | *a.* showy, eye-catching

vital | vi'tal | *a.* vital

vitalício -cia | vita'lisiυ | *a.* lifelong

vitamina | vita'mina | *sf.* vitamin; (colloq.) fruit juice and pulp with milk, sugar etc.

vitelo -la | vi'tɛlυ | *smf.* calf; *sf.* veal

vítima | 'vitima | *sf.* victim

vitória | vi'tωria | *sf.* victory

vitoriano -na | vitori'anυ | *smf. a.* Victorian

vitória-régia | vi'tωria'Rεjia | *sf.* (bot.) royal watter platter

vitorioso -sa | vitori'ozυ -'ωza | *a.* victorious

vitral | vi'tral | *sm.* stained-glass window

vitrina, vitrine | vi'trina vi'trinɛ | *sf.* store window; show-window

vitrola | vi'trωla | *sf.* phonograf

viúvo -va | vi'uvυ | *sm.* widower; *sf.* widow

viuvez | viu'veʒ | *sf.* widowhood

viva | 'viva | *interj.* cheers!, hurrah!, hurray!

vivacidade | vivasi'dadɛ | *sf.* vivacity, liveliness, animation

vivaz | vi'vaʒ | *a.* vivacious, animated

viveiro | vi'veyrυ | *sm.* vivarium (warren, aviary, fish hatchery etc.); plant nursery

vivência | vi'vẽsia | *sf.* experience; (psychol.) grasp of the life experience

vivenda | vi'vẽda | *sf.* residence

viver | vi'veR | *vt.* to live / *vi.* to live, to be alive

víveres | 'vivɛrɛʒ ⌉ *smpl.* food, provisions

vívido -da | vi'vidυ | *a.* experienced (in life)

vívido -da | 'vividυ | *a.* vivid, lively, brilliant, bright

vivo -va | 'vivυ | *sm.* living creature

(esp. man); (*pl.*) the living; *smf.* (slang) shrewd. **-ao v.** to the life / *a.* alive, living, live; lively; (slang) shrewd; bright. **-à or de viva voz** orally. **-cal viva** quicklime

vizinhança | vizi'Nãsa | *sf.* vicinity; neighbo(u)rhood

vizinho -nha | vi'ziNυ | *smf.* neighbo(u)r / *a.* neighbo(u)ring; adjoining; similar, like

voador -dora | vυa'doR | *a.* flying

voar | vυ'aR | *vi.* to fly

vocabulário | vokabu'lariυ | *sm.* vocabulary

vocábulo | vo'kabulυ | *sm.* word

vocação | voka'sãw | *sf.* vocation, calling

vocal | vo'kal | *a.* vocal

você | vo'se | *pron. 2nd pers. sing.* you; (*pl.*) you

voga | 'vωga | *sm.* stroke (rower); *sf.* act of rowing; vogue, fashion

vogal | vo'gal | *sf.* vowel; *smf.* voting member

vogar | vo'gaR | *vt.* to row; to navigate / *vi.* to sail; to drift; to be in vogue

volante | vo'lãtɛ | *sm.* steering wheel; racing motorist; leaflet / *a.* flying; mobile. **-hospital v.** mobile hospital unit

volátil | vo'latil | *a.* volatile; inconstant, changeable

volatilizar | volatili'zaR | *vt. vi.* (also **v. -se**) to volatilize

volta | 'vωlta | *sf.* return; turn; revolution; bend; loop; rebound; exchange, change; restitution; short walk. **-v. e meia** frequently. **-à v. de** around. **-às voltas com** at odds with. **-de v.** back, returned. **-de v. a** back to. **-ida e v.** round trip. **-na v.** on the way back. **-por v. de** around

voltar | vol'taR | *vt.* to turn; to turn over; to turn inside out. **-v. -se** to turn. **-v. -se contra** to turn against / *vi.* to return; to go or to come back. **-v. a si** to get back to one's senses. **-v. atrás** to turn around and go back; to take back one's word

volume | vʊˈlumɪ | *sm.* volume; bulk, mass; piece of luggage; capacity, content

volumoso -sa | vʊluˈmozʊ-ˈmʊza | *a.* voluminous, bulky

voluntário -ria | vʊlũˈtariʊ | *smf.* volunteer / *a.* voluntary

voluntarioso -sa | vʊlũtariˈozʊ ˈʊza | *a.* stubborn, headstrong

voluptuoso -sa | vʊluptuˈozʊ -ˈʊza | *a.* voluptuous, sensual

volúvel | vʊˈluvɪl | *a.* inconstant, changeable, fickle

volver | volˈveʀ | *vt.* to turn (as the eyes or face); to return to. **-v. -se** to turn oneself around / *vi.* to come or to go back; to reply, to retort

vomitar | vomiˈtaʀ | *vt. vi.* to vomit; to belch forth (as a volcano) / *vi.* to vomit, to spew

vômito | ˈvomitʊ | *sm.* vomit

vontade | võˈtadɪ | *sf.* will; wish, desire; intention, purpose. **-à v.** at ease; as much as you like. **-de boa v.** gladly, willingly. **-de má v.** grudgingly

vôo | ˈvoʊ | *sm.* flight. **-levantar v.** (aeron.) to take off

voraz | voˈraʒ | *a.* voracious, rapacious, greedy

vos | ˈvʊʒ | *oblique pron. 2nd pers. pl.* (direct object) you, (indirect object) to you, to yourselves; *reflexive pron. 2nd pers. pl.* yourselves

vós | ˈvʊʒ | *pron. 2nd pers. pl.* you

(formal form of you [in official speeches etc.])

vosso -sa | ˈvʊsʊ | *poss. a.* your / *poss. pron.* yours (formal form)

votação | votaˈsãw | *sf.* voting, balloting

votar | voˈtaʀ | *vt. vi.* to vote; to vow; to consecrate. **-v. -se** to devote oneself

voto | ˈvʊtʊ | *sm.* vote; solemn promise. **-fazer votos que** to hope that

vovô | voˈvo | *sm.* (colloq.) grandpa, grandpappy

vovó | voˈvʊ | *sf.* (colloq.) grandma, granny

voz | ˈvʊʒ | *sf.* voice; right to speak; cry (of animals); tone, expression. **-a meia v.** softly. **-ao alcance da v.** within call. **-dar v. de prisão** to arrest. **-em v. alta** aloud

vozerio | vozeˈriʊ | *sm.* clamo(u)r, uproar

vulcão | vulˈkãw | *sm.* volcano

vulgar | vulˈgaʀ | *a.* vulgar, common, ordinary. **-pouco v.** rare

vulgaridade | vulgariˈdadɪ | *sf.* vulgarity; coarseness

vulgarizar | vulgariˈzaʀ | *vt.* to vulgarize

vulgo | ˈvulgʊ | *sm.* people, common people; alias. **-Fulano, v. Sicrano** Doe, alias Roe

vulnerável | vulneˈravɪl | *a.* vulnerable

vulto | ˈvultʊ | *sm.* shadowy form; volume, mass; (fig.) importance. **-de v.** considerable (in size, amount etc.). **-um grande v.** a famous figure

W, w | ˈdablɪu | *sm.* used in names and words derived from foreign names (e.g. *darwinista, wagneriano, washingtoniano* etc.)

X

xá | 'xa | sm. shah

xadrez | xa'dreʒ | sm. chess; chess-board; checked cloth, check; (colloq.) jail / a. checkered, checked

xale | 'xalι | sm. shawl

xampu | xã'pu | sm. shampoo

xará | xa'ra | sm. namesake

xaropada | xaro'pada | sf. (colloq.) boring occasion; boring speech

xarope | xa'rωpι | sm. syrup; medical syrup; (colloq.) tiresome person

xelim | xι'lĩ | sm. shilling

xeque | 'xɛkι | sm. sheik; = xeque-mate

xeque-mate | 'xɛkι'matι | sm. checkmate, mate (chess)

xereta | xe'reta | smf. (colloq.) meddler

xerez | xe'reʒ | sm. sherry wine

xerife | xe'rifι | sm. sheriff

xerocar | xero'kaʀ | vt. (colloq.) to xerox

xi | 'xi | interj. my! (expressing astonishment or inquietude)

xícara | 'xikara | sf. cup

xicrinha | xi'kriɲa | sf. (colloq.) small cup, demitasse

xilindró | xilĩ'drω | sm. (colloq.) jail

xingar | xĩ'gaʀ | vt. vi. (colloq.) to insult, to curse, to swear

xodó | xo'dω | sm. (colloq.) sweetheart

xucro -cra | 'xukrυ | a. wild, savage; unbroken (said of horses)

Y

Y, y | ipsi'lãw'ipsilõ | smi. used in words derived from foreign names (e. g. yeatsiano, byroniano etc.)

Z

zaga | 'zaga | sf. near; (Braz., soccer) fullback position

zagueiro | za'geyrυ | sm. (Braz., soccer) fullback

zanga | 'zãga | sf. anger, rage

zangado -da | zã'gadυ | a. angry

zangão | zã'gãw | sm. drône

zangar | zã'gaʀ | vi. to anger. z.-se (com) to get angry (with)

zanzar | zã'zaʀ | vi. (colloq.) to wander, to loiter

zarolho -lha | za'roʟυ | smf. a. cross-eyed, one-eyed

zarpar | zaʀ'paʀ | vt. vi. to sail, to put out to sea

zé | 'zɛ | sm. (colloq.) Joe; man in

the street

zelador -dora | zela'doR | *smf.* janitor of an apartment building; keeper

zelar | ze'laR | *vi.* to take care of, to manage with zeal

zelo | 'zelʋ | *sm.* zeal

zeloso -sa | ze'lozʋ -'lωza | *a.* zealous

zé-povinho | zεpo'vįNʋ | *sm.* lower classes

zero | 'zεrʋ | *sm.* zero, nothing; naught

ziguezague | zigι'zagι | *sm.* zigzag

ziguezaguear | zigιzagι'aR | *vi.* to zigzag

zinco | 'zĩkʋ | *sm.* zinc

zoada | zʋ'ada | *sf.* buzzing (as of bees)

zombar | zõ'baR | *vt. vi.* to mock; to scoff; to jeer at

zombaria | zõba'ria | *sf.* mock; scoff; jeer

zombeteiro -ra | zõbe'teyrʋ | *smf.* one who jeers / *a.* jeering

zona | 'zona | *sf.* zone, district; (colloq.) red light district

zonzo -za | 'zõzʋ | *a.* dizzy

zoologia | zoolo'jia | *sf.* zoology

zoológico -ca | zoo'lωjikʋ | *a.* zoological. **-jardim z.** zoo

zumbido | zũ'bidʋ | *sm.* humming, buzz

zumbir | zũ'biR | *vi.* to drone, to hum, to buzz

zunido | zu'nidʋ | *sm.* whining; whistling (of wind); whizzing (of bullet)

zunir | zu'nıR | *vi.* to buzz, to whizz

zunzum | zũ'zũ | *sm.* humming; (colloq.) gossip, rumo(u)r

zurrapa | zu'Rapa | *sf.* inferior wine

zurrar | zu'RaR | *vi.* to bray

zurro | 'zuRʋ | *sm.* bray

zurzir | zuR'ziR | *vt.* to thrash, to whip, to scourge (also fig.)

PREFÁCIO

Este livro foi planejado como pequeno dicionário prático bilíngüe das línguas portuguesa e inglesa.

Como quase todos os dicionários bilíngües, este não dá definições, mas sim "sinônimos" de uma para a outra língua em causa, isto é, palavra ou palavras ou frases usadas como correspondentes de equivalência de sentido na ordem alfabética do *Português*-Inglês e do *Inglês*-Português.

Este dicionário baseia-se nos dicionários maiores e de maior número de entradas da editora Record — o *Webster's Dicionário Inglês-Português,* de Antônio Houaiss, Ismael Cardim e outros (928 páginas) e o *Webster's Portuguese-English Dictionary,* de James L. Taylor *(revised edition,* 657 páginas). Assim, este dicionário representa uma seleção de verbetes nova e original que desejamos corresponda ao espírito dos usos modernos em inglês e português.

Os símbolos fonéticos aspiram a dar traços fonológicos principais de cada palavra na mais simples forma, mas um cuidadoso estudo desses símbolos é muito recomendado aos consulentes.

Desejamos que este dicionário seja de boa utilidade entre seus leitores e consulentes dos quais receberemos sugestões e correções e melhoras com a mais alta simpatia.

SOBRE A REPRESENTAÇÃO DA PRONÚNCIA

A representação fonológica das palavras inglesas buscou aproximar-se do inglês padrão (*Standar English*), com os seguintes sinais:

| a | é o *a* no português "*casa*", "*mesa*", "*sala*"
| ʌ | é o mesmo fonema acima, mas prolongado
| â | é o *a* fechado (mas não nasal) de "*cama*", "*câmara*"
| e | é o *e* aberto de "*certo*", "*leve*", "*pé*"
| ə | é um *e* reduzido e fechado, como no francês "*le*"
| E | é o fonema anterior, mas prolongado
| i | é um *i* muito breve, como em "*leve*"
| ɪ | é um *i* longo e como em "*aqui*", "*nítido*"
| Ī | é um *i* não tão longo como o anterior
| ĭ | é um *i* anterior a outra vogal na mesma sílaba, como quando se pronuncia "*iaiá*" em duas sílabas
| o | é um *o* aberto como em "*pote*", "*nó*"
| ó | é o *o* anterior, mas prolongado
| u | é um *u* como em "*tudo*", "*súmula*"
| U | é o anterior, mas mais longo
| ey | como em "*sei*", "*leito*"
| ow | como em "*vou*", "*estou*"
| ay | como em "*baixo*"
| aw | como em "*pauta*"
| oy | como em "*heróico*"
| b | como em português
| f | como em português
| j | como em português
| p | como em português
| v | como em português
| d | como em português
| t | como em português
| g | como em "*gato*", "*guerra*", "*guizo*", "*gosto*", "*gula*"

Sobre a representação da pronúncia

| k | como em "*qu*ilo", "*c*ara", "*c*orte", "*c*ujo"
| h | é aspirado
| m | como no português "*m*ala", "*m*esa", "*m*ito", "*m*otor", "*m*úsica", sem jamais nasalizar a vogal anterior
| n | como em português "*n*ada", "*n*ele", "*n*icho", "*n*osso", "*n*uca", sem jamais nasalizar a vogal anterior
| r | como no português "ca*r*o"; num grande número de casos, não é pronunciado, acarretando uma modificação da vogal anterior (veja-se no dicionário "*care*", *partner*, *gardener* etc.)
| s | como em português em "*s*eco", "po*ss*o", "pe*ç*a", "po*ç*o"
| z | como em português
| ζ | como um *s* ceceado (espanhol "ca*z*a" [port. caça] na pronúncia castelhana)
| δ | como na pronúncia distensa do *d* português em palavras como "da*d*o", "para*d*o"
| ś | como em português "cai*x*a", "*ch*egar"
| š | como na palavra "*tch*eco"
| j | como se fosse grafado "*dj*ovem"
A sílaba tônica é indicada pelo sinal ' logo após a mesma

ABREVIATURAS USADAS NESTE DICIONÁRIO

a.	adjetivo
abrev.	abreviatura
adv.	advérbio, adverbial
(aer.)	aeronáutica
(anat.)	anatomia
(ant.)	antiguidade, arcaico
(ant. rom.)	antiguidade romana
(arqueol.)	arqueologia
(arquit.)	arquitetura
art.	artigo
(astron.)	astronomia
(b.a.)	belas artes
(bíbl.)	bíblico
(bibliot.)	biblioteconomia
(bot.)	botânica
(cin.)	cinema
(coloq.)	coloquialismo
(com.)	comércio
(cost.)	costura
conj.	conjunção
(cul.)	culinária
def.	definido
dem.	demonstrativo
(desp.)	desporte
(dial.)	dialetal
(ecles.)	eclesiástico
(econ.)	economia
(educ.)	educação
(eletr.)	eletricidade
(eletrôn.)	eletrônica
(ent.)	entomologia
(equit.)	equitação
(Esc.)	Escócia

esp.	especialmente
(EUA)	Estados Unidos
(farmac.)	farmacologia
(ferrov.)	estrada de ferro
(fig.)	figuradamente
(fin.)	finanças
(fot.)	fotografia
(futb.)	futebol
(geog.)	geografia
(geol.)	geologia
(geom.)	geometria
ger.	geralmente
(gír.)	gíria
(gram.)	gramática
(heráld.)	heráldica
(hist.)	história
(hort.)	horticultura
(ict.)	ictiologia
(impr.)	imprensa
indef.	indefinido
(inf.)	informática
interj.	interjeição
(Irl.)	Irlanda
(jur.)	jurídico
(lat.)	latim, latinismo
(ling.)	lingüística
(liter.)	literatura
loc.	locução
(lud.)	ludismo
(maiúsc.)	maiúscula
(mat.)	matemática
(mec.)	mecânica
(med.)	medicina
(mil.)	militar
(min.)	mineralogia
(minúsc.)	minúscula
(mús.)	música
(náut.)	náutica

(ópt.)	óptica
(orn.)	ornitologia
(pej.)	pejorativo
pess.	pessoal
p. ex.	por exemplo
pl.	plural
(poét.)	poético
(polít.)	política
poss.	possessivo
pref.	prefixo
prep.	preposição, prepositivo
pron.	pronome
(quím.)	química
(rád.)	rádio
refl.	reflexivo
rel.	relativo
(relig.)	religião
s.	substantivo
sing.	singular
suf.	sufixo
tb.	também
(teat.)	teatro
(tecl.)	tecelagem
(tip.)	tipografia
(TV)	televisão
v.	verbo
v. aux.	verbo auxiliar
v. defect.	verbo defectivo
vi.	verbo intransitivo
vr.	verbo reflexivo
vt.	verbo transitivo
(veter.)	veterinária
(vulg.)	vulgarismo
(zool.)	zoologia

English-Portuguese

A

A, a | ə, ey | *s.* a; (maiúsc; mús.) lá / *art.* um, uma

aback | əbak' | *adv.* para trás. **-to be taken a.** ficar surpreso; sobressaltar-se; ficar confuso

abandon | əban'dən | *vt.* abandonar; desistir; desamparar

abandoned | əban'dənd | *a.* abandonado; arruinado, desmantelado (prédio); depravado, vicioso

abandonment | əban'dənmənt | *s.* abandono; negligência; renúncia; desistência

abasement | əbeys'mənt | *s.* humilhação; rebaixamento

abashed | əbaśt' | *a.* confuso, humilhado, envergonhado

abate | əbeyt' | *vt.* abater, reduzir, diminuir; deduzir

abatement | əbeyt'mənt | *s.* abatimento, redução, dedução

abattoir | a'batwa | *s.* matadouro, abatedouro, corte

abbey | a'bĭ | *s.* mosteiro, monastério, abadia.

abbot | a'bət | *s.* abade

abbreviate | əbrı'vieyt | *vt.* abreviar, resumir, encurtar

abbreviation | əbrıvīey'śən | *s.* abreviação, abreviatura

ABC | eybısı' | *s.* alfabeto, abecê, abecedário

abdicate | ab'dikeyt | *vt.* abdicar; renunciar

abdication | abdikey'śən | *s.* abdicação; renúncia

abdomen | ab'dəmən | *s.* abdome, ventre, barriga

abduct | abdâkt' | *vt.* seqüestrar; (coloq.) raptar; arrebatar

abduction | abdâk'śən | *s.* seqüestro; (coloq.) rapto; arrebatamento

aberration | aberey'śən | *s.* aberração; anomalia; absurdo

abet | əbet' | *vt.* instigar, incitar; (fig.) açular

abettor | əbe'tə | *s.* instigador, incitador; cúmplice

abeyance | əbey'əns | *s.* suspensão; vacância. **-in a.** temporariamente

abhor | abhó' | *vt.* abominar, detestar; odiar; repugnar

abhorrence | abho'rəns | *s.* repulsa, repugnância; aversão; horror; ódio

abhorrent | abho'rənt | *a.* repulsivo, repugnante; detestável; abominável

abide | əbayd' | *vt.* tolerar / *vi.* morar, habitar, residir; permanecer, perdurar. **-to a. by** cumprir, manter; observar; ser fiel a

abiding | əbay'ding | *a.* perdurável, permanente, constante; inabalável

ability | əbi'litĭ | *s.* habilidade, talento, capacidade, aptidão. **-to**

the best of my a. o melhor que puder

abject | ab'jekt | *a.* abjeto, vil, desprezível, miserável. **-a. poverty** extrema miséria

abjure | abʃu'ɔ | *vt.* abjurar

ablaze | əbleyz' | *a.* em chamas, ardendo; flamejante; iluminado; excitado

able | ey'bəl | *a.* capaz, competente, talentoso. **-to be a.** ser capaz de, saber (to read, to sing, to swim etc.)

able-bodied | ey'bəlbo'dĭd | *a.* robusto, fisicamente válido, capaz, apto

able seaman | əy'bəlsı'mən | *s.* marinheiro de primeira classe, marinheiro experimentado

abnegation | abnegey'ʃən | *s.* abnegação, renúncia; desprendimento, desinteresse

abnormal | abnó'məl | *a.* anormal, anômalo; disforme

abnormality | abnóma'litĭ | *s.* anormalidade, anomalia; disformidade; irregularidade

aboard | əbód' | *adv.* a bordo

abode | əbowd' | *s.* residência; estada, permanência

abolish | əbo'liʃ | *vt.* abolir, extinguir, suprimir

abolition | əbəli'ʃən | *s.* abolição, extinção, supressão

abominable | əbo'minəbəl | *a.* abominável, odioso

abominate | əbo'mineyt | *vt.* abominar; detestar, odiar

abomination | əbominey'ʃən | *s.* abominação; ódio, aversão

aboriginal | əbəri'ʃinəl | *s.a.* aborígine, indígena

abortion | əbó'ʃən | *s.* aborto

abortive | əbó'tiv | *a.* abortivo; malogrado, frustrado, inútil

abound | əbawnd' | *vi.* abundar, ser rico em

abounding | əbawn'ding | *a.* abundante, em abundância

about | əbawt' | *prep. adv.* por volta de, aproximadamente; ao redor de, em torno de; aqui e ali;

circulando, passeando em; na vizinhança; quase, a ponto de; acerca de, a respeito de; sobre. **-a. to leave a ponto de partir. -all a.** por toda a parte. **-to bring a.** ocasionar. **-to come a.** acontecer. **-what is all a.?** de que se trata? **-a. turn!** meia-volta, volver! **-wandering a.** vagueando

above | əbəv' | *adv.* em cima. **-a. all** acima de tudo, sobretudo. **-up a.** lá em cima. **-a. board** leal, franco. **-a. oneself** orgulhoso, desvanecido / *prep.* sobre; por cima de, acima de; além de, superior a. **-from a.** do alto, do céu

above-mentioned | əbəvmen'ʃənd | *a.* acima mencionado, referido

abrasion | əbrey'ʃən | *s.* abrasão, desgaste; escoriação

abrasive | əbrey'ziv | *s.a.* abrasivo

abrasive paper | əbrey'zivpey'pə | *s.* lixa

abreast | əbrest' | *adv.* lado a lado, ombro a ombro. **-to be a. of** estar a par de

abridge | əbriʃ' | *vt.* resumir, abreviar; compactar

abridgement | əbriʃ'mənt | *s.* resumo; redução, compactação

abroad | əbród' | *adv.* no exterior, no estrangeiro. **-there is a rumo(u)r a.** dizem, corre o boato. **-to spread a.** divulgar, espalhar, tornar público

abrogate | ab'rowgeyt | *vt.* abrogar, anular, revogar

abrupt | əbrâpt' | *a.* abrupto; escarpado, íngreme; inesperado, imprevisto; brusco

abruptly | əbrâpt'lĭ | *adv.* abruptamente; bruscamente

abruptness | əbrâpt'nes | *s.* brusquidão; rudeza, aspereza

abscess | ab'ses | *s.* abscesso

abscond | abskond' | *vi.* evadir-se; homiziar-se

absence | ab'səns | *s.* ausência; privação, falta. **-a. of mind** distração. **-in the a. of** na falta de

absent | ab'sənt | *a.* ausente; distraído / vr. ausentar-se

absentee | absɔntɪ' | s. pessoa ausente; absenteísta

absent-minded | ab'sɔntmayn'- did | a. distraído, desatento

absolute | ab'sɔlut | a. absoluto; completo, acabado; puro; independente

absolution | absɔlu'ʃɔn | s. absolvição; perdão; remissão

absolutism | ab'sɔlutizɔm | s. absolutismo; despotismo

absolve | abzolv' | vt. absolver; perdoar; remir

absorb | abzób' | vt. absorver, sorver; consumir; assimilar; amortecer

absorbed | abzóbd' | a. absorvido, absorto; enlevado

absorbing | abzó'bing | a. absorvente; empolgante; cativante, interessante

absorption | absóp'ʃɔn | s. absorção; assimilação; amortecimento (de golpes)

abstain | absteyn' | vi. abster-se; privar-se

abstainer | abstey'nɔ | s. abstinente, abstêmio

abstemious | abstɪ'mīɔs | a. abstinente, sóbrio; abstêmio

abstemiousness | abstɪ'mīɔsnɔs | s. abstinência; sobriedade, frugalidade

abstention | absten'ʃɔn | s. abstenção, abstinência

abstinence | ab'stinɔns | s. abstinência, sobriedade

abstinent | ab'stinɔnt | a. abstinente, sóbrio; abstêmio

abstract | ab'strakt | s. sumário, resumo. **-in the a.** em teoria / a. abstrato, difícil / vt. abstrair, separar; subtrair, retirar

abstraction | abstrak'ʃɔn | s. abstração; teoria; alheamento, recolhimento; afastamento

abstract of account | ab'straktovɔkawnt' | s. extrato de conta

abstruse | abstrus' | a. abstruso, incompreensível, obscuro, ininteligível

absurd | absɛd' | a. absurdo, disparatado; tolo

absurdity | absɛ'ditɪ | s. absurdo, disparate; tolice

abundance | ɔbân'dɔns | s. abundância, fartura; opulência

abundant | ɔbân'dɔnt | a. abundante, farto; rico, opulento

abuse | ɔbĭuz' | s. abuso; desmando, irregularidade / vt. abusar de; maltratar; insultar, ofender, injuriar

abusiveness | ɔbĭu'sivnes | s. insolência, petulância

abut | ɔbât' | vi. limitar, confinar com, tocar em

abysmal | ɔbiz'mɔl | a. abissal, abismal; insondável; total

abyss | ɔbis' | s. abismo; caos

academic | akɔde'mik | a. acadêmico; universitário; convencional, clássico

academy | ɔka'dɔmī | s. academia; sociedade (científica, literária, artística etc.)

accede | aksɪd' | vi. aceder, consentir, anuir; subir (ao trono, a um cargo etc.)

accelerate | akse'lɔreyt | vi. acelerar; apressar; abreviar

acceleration | akselɔrey'ʃɔn | s. aceleração; celeridade

accelerator | akselɔrey'tɔ | s. acelerador

accent | ak'sɔnt | s. acento; sotaque; modo de falar

accentuate | aksen'tĭueyt | vt. acentuar; salientar, frisar

accentuation | aksentĭuey'ʃɔn | s. acentuação

accept | aksept' | vt. aceitar, receber; concordar com

acceptable | aksep'tɔbɔl | a. aceitável, admissível

acceptance | aksep'tɔns | s. aceitação; aprovação, boa acolhida; (com.) aceite

access | ak'ses | s. acesso, admissão; paroxismo; (med.) ataque, acesso

accessary | akse'sarī | s. (jur.) co-autor, cúmplice

accessible | akse'sibəl | *a.* acessível; tratável, afável

accession | akse'śən | *s.* acesso; adesão; anuência; acréscimo; elevação (ao trono, a um cargo etc.); inscrição (de livro novo em biblioteca)

accessory | akse'sərī | *s.* acessório / *a.* acessório, adicional

accident | ak'sidənt | *s.* acidente; acaso, casualidade; desastre. **-by a.** por acaso

accidentally | aksiden'təlī | *adv.* acidentalmente

acclaim | əkleym' | *s.* aplauso / *vt.* aclamar, aplaudir, aprovar

acclamation | akləmey'śən | *s.* aclamação, ovação, aplauso

acclimatize | aklay'mətayz | *vt.* aclimatar, aclimar; adaptar

accolade | a'kowleyd | *s.* pranchada (toque com espada aos que são armados cavaleiros); (fig.) galardão, aprovação

accommodate | əko'mədeyt | *vt.* acomodar; alojar, hospedar; harmonizar, conciliar; fornecer, prover; atender

accommodating | əko'mədeyting | *a.* que acomoda; acomodatício; obsequioso; complacente

accommodation | əkomədey'śen | *s.* acomodação; alojamento; adaptação; reconciliação

accommodation train | əkomədey'śəntreyn | *s.* trem parador

accompaniment | əkâm'pənimənt | *s.* acompanhamento (tb. mús.)

accompanist | əkâm'pənist | *s.* (mús.) acompanhador

accompany | əkâm'pənī | *vt.* acompanhar (tb. mús.); seguir; unir, juntar a

accomplice | əkâm'plis | *s.* (jur.) co-autor, cúmplice

accomplish | əkâm'pliś | *vt.* executar, efetuar, levar a cabo, realizar, cumprir

accomplished | əkâm'pııst | *a.*

perfeito, consumado, completo; definitivo

accomplishment | əkâm'pliśmənt | *s.* realização; feito, proeza; (ger. *pl.*) méritos

accord | əkód' | *s.* acordo, pacto. **-of his own a.** espontaneamente. **-with one a.** unanimemente / *vt.* conceder, outorgar / *vi.* concordar, harmonizar-se, acordar

accordance | əkó'dəns | *s.* acordo, conformidade. **-in a. with** de acordo com

according | əkó'ding | *adv.* conformemente, conseqüentemente. **-a. to** segundo, conforme

accordingly | əkó'dinglī | *adv.* por conseguinte, portanto, conseqüentemente

accordion | əkó'diən | *s.* acordeão, sanfona

accost | əkost' | *vt.* abordar, dirigir-se a

account | əkawnt' | *s.* conta; cálculo; relatório, descrição. **-on a.** por conta. **-on a. of** por causa de. **-on no a.** de modo algum. **-of no a.** sem importância. **-to take into a.** levar em conta. **-on one's own a.** por sua conta e risco. **-to settle accounts with** ajustar contas com. **-to keep accounts** manter uma escrita. **-to turn to a.** fazer uso de. **-to pay on a.** pagar a crédito / *vt.* considerar, reputar / *vi.* **-to a. for** prestar contas de, justificar. **-to a. to** prestar contas a

accountable | əkawn'təbəl | *a.* responsável; justificável

accountancy | əkawn'tənsī | *s.* contabilidade; cargo ou função de contador

accountant | əkawn'tənt | *s.* contabilista, contador

accredited | əkre'didit | *a.* acreditado, autorizado

accretion | akrī'śən | *s.* acréscimo, adição, agregação

accrue | əkru' | *vi.* advir, originar-se, resultar; acumular-se (juros)

accumulate | əkĭu'mĭuleyt | *vt.* acumular, amontoar, ajuntar

accumulation | əkĭumĭuley'śən | *s.* acumulação, acúmulo

accuracy | a'kĭurəsī | *s.* precisão, exatidão, justeza

accurate | a'kĭureyt | *a.* preciso, exato, correto

accursed | əkɛst' | *a.* maldito, amaldiçoado; execrável, detestável; condenável. **-a. be** maldito seja

accusation | akĭuzey'śən |*s.* acusação; denúncia

accuse | əkĭuz' | *vt.* acusar; imputar; incriminar

accused | əkĭuzd' | *s.* acusado

accuser | əkĭu'zə | *s.* acusador; denunciante

accustom | əkâs'təm | *vt.* acostumar, habituar

accustomed| əkâs'təmd |*a.* acostumado, habituado; usual

ace | eys' | *s.* ás (tb. aer.). **-within an a.** por pouco, quase. **-not an a.** nem um pouco

acerbity | əsɛ'bitī | *s.* azedume; amargor; acrimônia

ache | eyk' | *s.* dor / *vi.* doer; ansiar, desejar ardentemente

achieve | əśĭv' | *vt.* realizar, concluir, completar

achievement| əśĭv'mənt |*s.* realização; empreendimento; feito, façanha, proeza

aching | ey'king | *a.* dolorido

acid | a'sid | *s.* ácido / *a.* ácido; azedo, acre

acidity | asi'ditī | *s.* acidez

acid test | a'sidtest | *s.* prova real ou decisiva

acknowledge | akno'lij | *vt.* reconhecer, admitir; agradecer. **-to a. (the) receipt** acusar o recebimento

acknowledged | akno'lijd | *a.* agradecido, reconhecido; incontestável (líder, chefe)

acknowledgement | akno'lijmənt |*s.* reconhecimento, gra-

tidão; confissão

acme| ak'mī |*s.* auge, ápice, apogeu, máximo, cúmulo

acolyte | a'kəlayt |*s.* acólito

acorn | ey'kón | *s.* bolota (de carvalho)

acoustics | əku'stiks | *s.* acústica

acquaint| əkweynt' | *vt.* comunicar, avisar, inteirar. **-to a. oneself with** inteirar-se; acostumar-se com

acquaintance | əkweyn'təns | *s.* conhecimento; relações, familiaridade. **-to make the a.** of travar conhecimento com. **-to gain a.** familiarizar-se

acquaintanceship | əkweyn'tənsśip | *s.* conhecimento

acquainted | əkweyn'tid | *a.* informado, inteirado; familiarizado. **-to be a. with** conhecer; estar familiarizado. **-to get a.** travar conhecimento, familiarizar-se

acquiesce | akwĭes' | *vi.* concordar, consentir, anuir. **-to a. in** aceitar, submeter-se a, conformar-se com

acquiescence | akwĭe'səns | *s.* consentimento, anuência

acquiescent| akwĭe'sənt |*a.* condescendente, indulgente

acquire | əkway'ə | *vt.* adquirir, comprar; conseguir; granjear; contrair (hábito)

acquisition | akwizi'śən |*s.* aquisição, obtenção; compra

acquisitive| akwi'zitiv |*a.* aquisitivo; ávido, ambicioso

acquit | əkwit' | *vt.* absolver, exculpar, inocentar

acquittal | əkwi'təl | *s.* absolvição; quitação

acre | ei'kə | *s.* acre (4.047 m^2)

acrid | a'krid | *a.* acre, picante; mordaz, virulento

acrimonious | akrimow'nĭəs | *a.* acrimonioso; áspero, rabugento, amargo; mordaz

acrimony | akrimo'nī | *s.* acrimônia, aspereza

acrobat | a'krowbat | *s.* acrobata, equilibrista

across | əkros' | *adv.* de través, transversalmente. **-to go ,a.** atravessar. **-to come a.** encontrar, topar com / *prep.* através de, de um lado para outro; por, sobre

act | akt' | *s.* ato (tb. teat.), ação; ato legislativo, lei. **-caught in the a.** apanhado em flagrante. **-to put an a.** fingir / *vt.* (teat.) representar, desempenhar. **-to a. the fool** fazer-se de tolo / *vi.* proceder, comportar-se; agir; fingir, simular. **-to a. on** atuar sobre. **-to a. as** servir de·

acting | ak'ting | *s.* (teat.) desempenho, modo de representar; simulação / *a.* ativo, em exercício; interino; (teat.) encenável

action | ak'şən | *s.* ação; ato, feito; funcionamento; atividade; (mil.) combate; mecanismo, sistema mecânico. **-to put out of a.** pôr fora de ação / *vt.* acionar, processar

actionable | ak'şənəbəl | *a.* processável, acionável

active | ak'tiv | *a.* ativo; vivo, ligeiro; enérgico, diligente; vigoroso, forte

activity | akti'vitĭ | *s.* atividade; presteza, diligência

act of sale | akt'ovseyl | *s.* instrumento de venda

actor | ak'tə | *s.* ator, protagonista

actress | ak'trəs | *s.* atriz

actual | ak'tĭuəl | *a.* real, verdadeiro; existente, presente

actual cost | ak'tĭuəlkost | *s.* custo real

actually | ak'tĭuəlĭ | *adv.* realmente, verdadeiramente, de fato, na realidade

actuary | ak'tĭuərĭ | *s.* atuário

actuate | ak'tĭueyt | *vt.* acionar, mover; impelir, impulsionar; incitar, instigar

acumen | a'kĭumen | *s.* perspicácia, agudeza, argúcia

acute | əkĭut' | *a.* agudo, aguça-

do; penetrante; fino, estridente; perspicaz, sagaz

acutely | əkĭut'lĭ | *adv.* agudamente, com perspicácia

acuteness | əkĭut'nes | *s.* agudeza, vivacidade; penetração, sagacidade

Adam | a'dəm | *s.* Adão. **-the old A.** a natureza pecaminosa do homem

adamant | a'dəmənt | *a.* inflexível, intransigente, inexorável; adamantino

Adam's ale | a'dəmzeyl' | *s.* (coloq.) água

Adam's apple | a'dəmza'pəl | *s.* pomo-de-adão

Adam's wine | a'dəmswayn | *s.* (coloq.) água

adapt | ədapt' | *vt.* adaptar, ajustar; amoldar, apropriar

adaptability | ədaptəbi'litĭ | *s.* adaptabilidade

adaptable | ədap'təbəl | *a.* adaptável; ajustável

adaptor | ədap'tə | *s.* (mec.) adaptador

add | ad' | *vt. vi.* acrescentar, adicionar, juntar, anexar; somar. **-to a. up** ou **together** somar

adder | a'də | *s.* víbora. **-deaf as an a.** (coloq.) surdo como uma porta

addict | a'dikt | *s.* viciado (esp. em drogas)

addicted | ədik'tid | *a.* dedicado, inclinado; dado a, entregue a (esp. drogas)

addiction | ədik'şən | *s.* inclinação, apego; vício

addition | ədi'şən | *s.* adição, soma; acréscimo

additional | ədi'şənəl | *a.* adicional, complementar

addle | a'dəl | *a.* oco, vazio; infecundo; confuso, desorientado

addle egg | a'dəleg | *s.* ovo gorado

address | ədres' | *s.* endereço; discurso, fala; destreza, habilidade; distinção, maneiras. **-to pay addresses to** cortejar / *vt.* endereçar; discursar; dirigir a palavra a. -to a. as tratar por

addressee | adresı' | s. destinatário

adduce | adı̆us' | vt. aduzir; alegar; citar, mencionar

adenoids | a'dənoydz | spl. (med.) vegetações adenóides

adept | a'dept | s. a. perito, entendido, conhecedor

adequacy | a'dikwəsı | s. adequação, conformidade

adequate | a'dikwit | a. adequado, apropriado

adhere | adhı'ə | vi. aderir

adherence | adhı'ərəns | s. aderência; adesão; fidelidade

adherent | adhı'ərənt | s. aderente / a. ligado, unido

adhesion | adhı'jən | s. adesão, aderência; fidelidade

adhesive | adhı'ziv | s. a. adesivo

adhesiveness | adhı'zivnes | s. adesividade

adhesive tape | adhı'zivteyp | s. (eletr.) fita isolante; espara drapo

adjacent | əˇjey'sənt | a. adjacente, contíguo, vizinho

adjective | a'jiktiv | s. adjetivo / vt. adjetivar

adjoin | əˇjoyn' | vt. vi. confinar, estar contíguo

adjoining | əˇjoy'ning | a. contíguo, adjacente, ao lado

adjourn | əˇjEn' | vt. vi. adiar; suspender (sessão)

adjournment | əˇjEn'mənt | s. adiamento; suspensão

adjudge | əˇjAˇj' | vt. (jur.) julgar, decidir; sentenciar, condenar; adjudicar

adjudicate | əˇju'dikeyt | vt. vi. = (jur.) adjudge

adjudication | əˇjudikey'ʃən | s. decisão judicial; adjudicação; declaração de estado falimentar

adjudicator | əˇjudikey'tə | s. juiz, árbitro

adjunct | a'jĭΛnkt | s. a. adjunto, anexo, acessório

adjure | əˇju'ə | vt. suplicar, implorar; insistir com

adjust | əˇjAˇst' | vt. ajustar, regular; adaptar

adjustable | əˇjAˇs'təbəl | a. ajustável, regulável; móvel

adjustment | əˇjAˇst'mənt | s. ajustamento, ajuste; adaptação, acomodação

adjutant | a'jutənt | s. ajudante (esp. mil.)

administer | ədmı'nistə | vt. administrar, dirigir; ministrar; dar, fornecer

administration | ədministrey'ʃən | s. administração; direção; governo; gestão

administrator | ədmı'nistreytə | s. administrador, gerente; curador

admirable | ad'mirəbəl | a. admirável, magnífico

admiral | ad'mirəl | s. almirante; navio capitânia

admiralty | ad'mirəltı | s. almirantado; Supremo Tribunal da Marinha

admiration | admirey'ʃən | s. admiração; reverência; alta estima e respeito

admire | ədmay'ə | vt. admirar; reverenciar; ter em alta conta

admirer | ədmay'ərə | s. admirador; pretendente, namorado

admissible | ədmi'sibəl | a. admissível, aceitável, tolerável; permissível

admission | ədmi'ʃən | s. admissão, entrada; consentimento; aprovação; confissão. -no a. entrada proibida

admission free | ədmi'ʃənfrı | s. entrada gratuita

admission ticket | ədmi'ʃəntikit | s. bilhete de ingresso

admit | ədmit' | vt. admitir, deixar entrar; permitir, consentir; reconhecer, aceitar como verdade

admittance | ədmi'təns | s. entrada, admissão. -no a. entrada proibida

admittedly | ədmi'tidlĭ | *adv.* reconhecidamente; sem dúvida

admonish | ədmo'niś | *vt.* repreender, censurar

admonition | adməni'śən | *s.* repreensão, admoestação

ado | ədʌ' | *s.* trabalho; agitação; barulho. **-much a. about nothing** tempestade em copo d'água. **-without more a.** sem mais delongas

adolescence | adowle'səns | *s.* adolescência

adolescent | adowle'sənt | *s. a.* adolescente

adopt | ədopt' | *vt.* adotar, perfilhar; admitir, aceitar; escolher, preferir

adoption | ədop'śən | *s.* adoção; aprovação, escolha

adorable | ədó'rəbəl | *a.* adorável, encantador, delicioso

adoration | adərey'śən | *s.* adoração; veneração; reverência

adore | ədó' | *vt.* adorar; idolatrar; venerar

adorn | ədón' | *vt.* adornar, ornar, enfeitar

adornment | ədón'mənt | *s.* adorno, ornato, ornamento

adrift | ədrift' | *adv.* à deriva; à garra, à matroca. **-to go a.** ir à deriva

adroit | ədroyt' | *a.* destro, hábil, jeitoso, engenhoso

adroitness | ədroyt'nes | *s.* destreza, habilidade, jeito

adulation | adiuley'śən | *s.* adulação, bajulação

adult | a'dâlt | *s. a.* adulto

adulterate | ədâl'təreyt | *a.* adulterado, falsificado; adulterino; adúltero / *vt.* adulterar, falsificar, deturpar

adulteration | ədâltərey'śən | *s.* adulteração, falsificação

adulterer | ədâl'tərə | *s.* adúltero

adulteress | ədâl'tərəs | *s.* adúltera

adultery | ədâl'tərĭ | *s.* adultério

advance | ədvʌns' | *s.* avanço; adiantamento, progresso; elevação, aumento; empréstimo, adiantamento; (*pl.*) investidas, propostas amorosas, tentativas de aproximação. **-in a.** à frente, antecipadamente / *vt.* avançar; elevar, promover; favorecer; ativar; adiantar, desenvolver; fomentar; antecipar; adiantar, fornecer antecipadamente / *vi.* avançar, progredir; melhorar

advanced | ədvʌnst' | *a.* avançado, adiantado; aperfeiçoado. **-a. in years** de idade avançada

advanced studies | ədvʌnst'-stâdiz | *spl.* estudos superiores

advancement | ədvʌns'mənt | *s.* adiantamento; progresso; promoção, elevação

advantage | ədvʌn'tiǰ | *s.* vantagem, superioridade; proveito, ganho. **-to take a. of** aproveitar-se, valer-se da oportunidade; abusar da confiança. **-to have a.** levar vantagem sobre. **-to show to a.** ficar bem, ressaltar / *vt.* favorecer, beneficiar

advantageous | advəntey'ǰəs | *a.* vantajoso, proveitoso, benéfico, favorável; útil

advent | ad'vənt | *s.* advento, chegada, vinda; instituição

adventure | ədven'ŝ̌ə | *s.* aventura / *vt.* aventurar

adventurer | ədven'ŝ̌ərə | *s.* aventureiro; especulador; impostor, embusteiro

adventuress | ədven'ŝ̌əres | *s.* aventureira; especuladora

adventurous | ədven'ŝ̌ərəs | *a.* aventuroso, arriscado

adverb | ad'vEb | *s.* advérbio

adversary | ad'vəsərĭ | *s.* adversário, antagonista; inimigo; oponente

adverse | ad'vEs | *a.* adverso, contrário, oposto

adversity | ədvE'sitĭ | *s.* adversidade, infortúnio

advert | advEt' | *vi.* atentar em, considerar; aludir a

advertise | ad'vətayz | *vt.* anunciar; apregoar, proclamar. **-to**

a. for publicar anúncio para

advertisement | ǝdvɛ'tizmǝnt | s. anúncio, publicidade

advertiser | advǝtay'zǝ | s. anunciante

advertising | advǝtay'zing | s. publicidade, propaganda

advice | ǝdvays' | s. conselho, recomendação; opinião, parecer; informação, aviso

advisability | ǝdvayzǝbi'litī | s. conveniência, prudência

advisable | ǝdvay'zǝbǝl | a. aconselhável; conveniente, prudente, oportuno

advise | ǝdvayz' | vt. aconselhar; avisar, informar

advisedly | ǝdvay'zidlī | adv. deliberadamente, intencionalmente, de caso pensado

adviser | ǝdvay'zǝ | s. conselheiro, consultor

advisory | ǝdvay'zǝrī | a. consultivo

advocacy | ad'vǝkǝsī | s. advocacia; defesa, intercessão

advocate | ad'vǝkit | s. advogado, defensor; partidário; intercessor / vt. advogar, defender; interceder

aegis | ī'jis | s. égide. -under the a. of sob o patrocínio de

aerated | eǝrey'tid | a. aerado, oxigenado

aerated drinks | eǝrey'tiddrinks | spl. bebidas gasosas

aerial | eǝ'riǝl | s. (rád.) antena / a. aéreo

aerodrome | e'ǝrǝdrowm | s. aeródromo, campo de aviação

aeronautic | eǝrǝnó'tik | a. aeronáutico

aeronautics | eǝrǝnó'tiks | s. aeronáutica

aeroplane | e'ǝrǝpleyn | s. = airplane, aircraft

aesthetics | īsϑe'tiks | s. estética

afar | ǝfa' | adv. longe, ao longe. -from a. de longe

affability | afǝbi'litī | s. afabilidade, amabilidade

affable | a'fǝbǝl | a. afável,

cortês, agradável

affair | ǝfe'ǝ | s. negócio, caso, questão; caso amoroso

affect | ǝfekt' | vt. gostar˘de, ser dado a; freqüentar, habitar; fingir, aparentar; afetar, influenciar; abalar

affectation | afektey'śǝn | s. afetação, artificialidade

affected | ǝfek'tid | a. afetado, artificial, amaneirado: inclinado, disposto; atacado (doença); impressionado. influenciado

affecting | ǝfek'ting | a. tocante, comovente; relativo a, afetando a

affection | ǝfek'śǝn | s. afeição, afeto, carinho, ternura, amor; (med.) afecção, doença, enfermidade

affectionate | ǝfek'śǝnit | a. afetuoso, terno, carinhoso; cordial, amigável

affidavit | afidey'vit | s. (jur.) declaração juramentada, depoimento; garantia

affiliate | ǝfi'līeyt | vi. filiar-se, associar-se

affiliation | ǝfilīey'śǝn | s. perfilhação, adoção; filiação; incorporação

affinity | ǝfi'nitī | s. afinidade; analogia, parentesco; atração, simpatia

affirm | ǝfɛm' | vt. afirmar, asseverar, assegurar

affirmation | ǝfɛmey'śǝn | s. afirmação; confirmação

affirmative | ǝfɛ'mǝtiv | s. afirmativa / a. afirmativo

affix | ǝfiks' | vt. afixar; colar; apor (assinatura)

afflict | ǝflikt' | vt. afligir, atormentar. -to be afflicted with sofrer de

affliction | ǝflik'śǝn | s. aflição, padecimento; doença

affluence | a'fluǝns | s. afluência; opulência, abundância, riqueza

affluent | a'fluǝnt | s. afluente / a. opulento, abundante, farto, rico

afford | əfód' | *vt.* proporcionar, conferir, oferecer; ter recursos para; permitir-se, dar-se o luxo de

afforestation | aforestey'śən | *s.* reflorestamento

affray | əfrey' | *s.* rixa; desordem; altercação, contenda

affront | əfrânt' | *s.* afronta, ultraje / *vt.* afrontar, ultrajar, injuriar, insultar

afield | əfıld' | *adv.* no campo. **-far a.** muito longe

aflame | əfleym' | *adv.* em chamas, ardendo

afloat | əflowt' | *adv.* flutuando, boiando; a bordo (de embarcação); em circulação; correndo (rumores). **-to get a boat a.** desencalhar

afoot | əfut' | *adv.* a pé, caminhando; em ação; em discussão; em marcha

aforesaid | əfó'sed | *a.* supracitado, supramencionado

aforethought | əfó'ϑót | *a.* premeditado, intencional. **-with malice a.** com intenção ou premeditação criminosa

afraid | əfreyd' | *a.* com medo, receoso; apreensivo. **-to be a.** estar com medo, temer, recear; lamentar, sentir. **-I'm a. I cannot...** lamento não poder...

afresh | əfreś' | *adv.* novamente, de novo, outra vez

African | a'frikən | *s. a.* africano

aft | Aft' | *adv.* à popa, à ré. **-fore and a.** de popa a proa

after | Af'tə | *adv.* depois; atrás / *prep.* depois de; atrás de. **-a. all** afinal de contas. **-day a. day** dia após dia. **-time a. time** repetidas vezes. **-to ask a.** perguntar por. **-to take a.** sair a, parecer-se com. **-to be a.** procurar, buscar, pretender. **-to look a.** cuidar de. **-a. the manner of** ao estilo de. **-a. the fashion of** à moda de. **-a. you!** passe primeiro; sirva-se primeiro! **-a. the example of** a exemplo de

after-dinner speech | Af'tədinəspiš' | *s.* brinde

after life | Af'təlayf | *s.* vida futura; vida depois da morte

aftermath | Af'təmaϑ | *s.* conseqüências, resultados

afternoon | Aftənʊn' | *s.* tarde / *a.* da tarde, vesperal

after-taste | Af'təteyst | *s.* ressaibo (depois de beber, comer ou fumar)

afterthought | Af'təϑót | *s.* pensamento ou reflexão posterior. **-as an a.** pensando melhor, refletindo

afterwards | Af'təwədz | *adv.* mais tarde, depois, posteriormente, em seguida

again | əgen' | *adv.* de novo, outra vez, mais uma vez. **-now and a.** de vez em quando. **-a. and a.** repetidas vezes. **-once a.** mais uma vez. **-never a.** nunca mais. **-half as much a.** mais a metade

against | əgenst' | *prep.* contra, em sentido oposto a. **-up a.** encostado a, junto de ou a. **-he is up a. it** ele está em apuros. **-a. the grain** contra a fibra (da madeira); ao revés; a contrapelo; a contragosto

agape | əgeyp' | *adv.* boquiaberto, embasbacado

age | eyj | *s.* idade; período, época. **-of middle a.** de meia-idade. **-to be under a.** ser menor. **-to come of a.** atingir a maioridade. **-what is your a.?** que idade têm? **-ages ago** há muitos e muitos anos. **-Middle Ages** Idade Média. **-Dark Ages** época de obscurantismo / *vt.* tornar velho, amadurecer / *vi.* envelhecer, ficar velho

aged | ey'jid | *a.* velho, idoso; antigo, vetusto; envelhecido; da idade de; próprio da velhice

agency | ey'jensī | *s.* agência; ação, atuação, atividade. **-by the a. of** por meio de

agenda | əjən'də | *s.* agenda; ordem do dia; coisas a fazer

agent | ey'jənt | *s.* agente; representante; delegado; comissário, corretor; (quím.) reagente

agglomeration | əglomərey'śən | *s.* aglomeração; aglomerado

aggrandizement | əgran'dizmənt | *s.* engrandecimento, enaltecimento; ampliação, desenvolvimento, aumento

aggravate | a'grəveyt | *vt.* agravar, piorar; exasperar, irritar

aggravation | agrəvey'śən | *s.* agravamento, exacerbação; circunstância agravante; irritação, provocação

aggregate | a'grəgeyt | *s. a.* agregação, conjunto / *vt.* agregar, juntar, anexar

aggression | əgre'śən | *s.* agressão, ataque; provocação

aggressive | əgre'siv | *a.* agressivo; empreendedor, dinâmico, ativo

aggressor | əgre'sə | *s.* agressor

aggrieved | əgrivd' | *a.* aflito; magoado, ferido; (jur.) lesado em seus direitos

aghast | əgʌst' | *a.* horrorizado; espantado; consternado

agile | a'jayl | *a.* ágil, vivo, ativo, ligeiro

agility | əji'litĭ | *s.* agilidade, ligeireza, vivacidade

agitate | a'jiteyt | *vt.* agitar, sacudir; perturbar, abalar; amotinar

agitation | ajitey'śən | *s.* agitação; perturbação; tumulto, comoção

agitator | a'jiteytə | *s.* agitador (esp. político)

aglow | əglow' | *a.* em brasa; afogueado; alvoroçado

ago | əgow' | *adv.* há. **-long a.** há muito tempo

agog | əgog' | *a.* impaciente, alvoroçado; ansioso

agonizing | a'gənayzing | *a.* agoniante, torturante, doloroso; agonizante

agony | a'gənĭ | *s.* agonia; angústia, tormento, dor; paroxismo; luta, esforço

agrarian | əgre'ərĭən | *a.* agrário; campestre

agree | əgrĭ' | *vi.* concordar, convir; consentir; entender-se; harmonizar-se, combinar; darse bem com, fazer bem a (comida)

agreeable | əgrĭ'əbəl | *a.* agradável, aprazível; encantador; favorável, conforme; conveniente

agreed | əgrĭd' | *a.* de acordo, concorde; convencionado. **-it was a. that** foi estabelecido que

agreement | agrĭ'mənt | *s.* acordo, ajuste, entendimento; harmonia; concordância (tb. gram.)

agricultural | agrikâl'śərəl | *a.* agrícola

agricultural engineer | agrikâl'-śərələnjĭnĭə | *s.* engenheiro agrônomo

agriculture | a'grikâlśə | *s.* agricultura

aground | əgrawnd' | *adv.* encalhado. **-to run a.** encalhar, dar à costa

ahead | əhed' | *adv.* à frente, adiante, para a frente; em frente. **-a. of** na dianteira de. **-to look a.** pensar no futuro. **-to get a. in the world** prosperar

ahoy | əhoy' | *interj.* (náut.) ó de bordo!, olá!

aid | eyd' | *s.* ajuda, auxílio; socorro, assistência; ajudante, auxiliar

aide-de-camp | eyd'dəkon | *s.* ajudante-de-campo

ail | eyl' | *vt.* doer, incomodar, molestar / *vi.* estar adoentado

ailing | ey'ling | *a.* doente

ailment | eyl'mənt | *s.* indisposição, enfermidade; achaque; inquietação

aim | eym' | *s.* pontaria; objetivo, intuito, fim. **-to take a.** fazer pontaria / *vt. vi.* apontar, fazer pontaria; visar a, aspirar a, esforçar-se por. **-to miss one's a.** errar a pontaria. **-well aimed**

certeiro. **-to a. high** ter altas aspirações

aimless | eym'les | *a.* sem direção; desorientado; vago

air | e'ə | *s.* ar; atmosfera; espaço; brisa, aragem; alento, fôlego; ar, jeito; ária, cantiga; melodia. **-in the open a.** ao ar livre. **-to put on airs** dar-se ares / *vt.* arejar, ventilar; discutir; propalar. **-to a. oneself** tomar ar

aircraft | e'əkrʌft | *s.* avião, aeronave; aviões

aircraft carrier | e'əkrʌftkariə | *s.* porta-aviões

airgun | e'əgân | *s.* espingarda ou pistola de ar comprimido

airily | e'ərilĩ | *adv.* aereamente, levemente

airiness | e'ərines | *s.* leveza, delicadeza; qualidade do que é aéreo

airing | e'əring | *s.* arejamento, ventilação

airman | e'əmən | *s.* aviador

airplane | e'əpleyn | *s.* = *aircraft*

airport | e'əpót | *s.* aeroporto, campo de aviação

air raid | e'əreyd | *s.* ataque aéreo

airsickness | e'əsiknes | *s.* enjôo (em avião etc.)

airtight | e'ətayt | *a.* hermeticamente fechado

airworthiness | e'əwεðines | *s.* aeronavegabilidade

airy | e'ərĩ | *a.* arejado, ventilado; tênue, vaporoso; vago, quimérico; delicado

aisle | ayl' | *s.* passagem (entre filas de bancos), corredor; nave (de igreja)

ajar | əjʌ' | *adv.* entreaberto

akimbo | əkim'bow | *adv.* com as mãos nos quadris

akin | əkin' | *a.* aparentado; semelhante, parecido

alacrity | əla'kritĩ | *s.* jovialidade, entusiasmo, vivacidade, presteza

alarm | əlʌm' | *s.* alarme; sobressalto, susto / *vt.* dar aviso de perigo; alarmar

alarm clock | əlʌm'klok | *s.* relógio despertador

alarming | əlʌ'ming | *a.* alarmante, assustador

alas | əlas' | *interj.* ai!, ai de mim!

albeit | ól'bĩt | *conj.* embora, conquanto, se bem que

album | al'bəm | *s.* álbum

alcohol | al'kəhol | *s.* álcool

alcoholic | alkəho'lik | *s. a.* alcoólico

alcove | al'kowv | *s.* nicho, recanto; alcova; caramanchão

alderman | ól'dəmən | *s.* vereador, edil

ale | eyl' | *s.* variedade de cerveja

ale house | eyl'haws | *s.* cervejaria, taverna

alert | əlεt' | *s.* alerta, alarme. **-to be on the a.** estar de prontidão / *a.* alerta, vigilante; vivo, ativo / *vt.* alertar

alertness | əlεt'nes | *s.* vigilância, vivacidade

algebra | al'jibrə | *s.* álgebra

alias | ey'lies | *s.* nome suposto ou falso; apelido / *adv.* aliás, de outro modo

alibi | a'libay | *s.* álibi

alien | ey'lïən | *s.* estrangeiro, forasteiro / *a.* estranho, alheio, exótico, contrário, oposto

alienate | ey'lïəneyt | *vt.* alienar, transferir a outrem; desviar, apartar; indispor, desunir, malquistar

alienation | eylïəney'śən | *s.* alienação (tb. mental)

alight | əlayt' | *a.* aceso, iluminado; em chamas / *vi.* apear, desmontar; pousar, descer suavemente

align | əlayn' | *vt.* alinhar

alike | əlayk' | *a.* parecido, semelhante, igual

aliment | a'limənt | *s.* alimento (tb. fig); comida

alimony | a'limonĩ | *s.* pensão alimentícia, alimentos

alive | əlayv' | *a.* vivo, com vida; animado, ativo. **-a. with** cheio de, a fervilhar de. **-to be a.** estar

vivo. **-a. to** ciente de, sensível a.
-man a.! homem de Deus!

all | ól' | *s.* tudo, todos, a totalida-
de, o conjunto / *adv.* todo,
completamente, inteiramente.
-once and for a. de uma vez por
todas. **-after a.** afinal. **-not at a.**
não tem de quê, de nada; de mo-
do nenhum. **-a. out** a toda velocidade. **-a. at once** de repente.
-a. the better tanto melhor. **-by
a. means** certamente!, pois
não!; de qualquer modo, por
todas as maneiras. **-a. the same**
ainda assim. **-on a. fours** de ga-
tinhas. **-he is not a.** there ele é
meio amalucado. **-a. of a sudden** repentinamente, de repente

allay | əley' | *vt.* acalmar, apazi-
guar; mitigar

allegation | alegey'śən | *s.* ale-
gação; pretexto

allege | əlej' | *vt.* alegar; asseve-
rar; pretextar

alleged | əlejd' | *a.* alegado; pre-
tenso, suposto

allegiance | əli'jəns | *s.* obe-
diência, fidelidade, lealdade;
vassalagem

allegory | a'ligərī | *s.* alegoria;
emblema, símbolo

alleviate | əli'vīeyt | *vt.* aliviar;
mitigar, minorar

alleviation | əlivīey'śən | *s.* alívio;
atenuação

alley | a'lī | *s.* aléia; passagem,
viela; bola de gude

All Hallows | ólha'lowz | *s.* dia de
Todos os Santos

alliance | əlay'əns | *s.* aliança;
união; matrimônio; pacto; pa-
rentesco, afinidade

allied | a'layd | *a.* aliado; associa-
do, unido; afim

alligator | a'ligeytə | *s.* aligátor

alligator pear | a'ligeytəpiə | *s.*
abacate

allocate | a'ləkeyt | *vt.* distribuir,
aquinhoar; destinar, designar;
pôr de parte

allocation | aləkey'śən | *s.* distri-
buição, repartição

allot | əlot' | *vt.* repartir, distri-
buir; dividir em lotes; dar em
quinhão

allotment | əlot'mənt | *s.* parti-
lha, distribuição; porção, quinhão; pensão; lote de terra; sorte,
fado

allow | əlaw' | *vt.* permitir, dei-
xar; conceder; tolerar. **-to a. for**
levar em conta. **-a. me** com
licença

allowable | əlaw'əbəl | *a.* per-
missível, admissível

allowance | əlaw'əns | *s.* per-
missão, licença; subsídio, pensão / *vt.* dar mesada ou pensão a; racionar

alloy | aloy' | *s.* liga de metais / *vt.*
ligar metais

all right | ól'rayt | *adv.* muito
bem, certamente; está bem; tu-
do bem

all-round | olrawnd' | *a.* comple-
to, total, geral

All Souls' Day | ólsowlz'dey | *s.*
dia de Finados

allude | əliud' | *vi.* aludir, fazer re-
ferência a

allure | əlïu'ə | *vt.* seduzir, aliciar;
cativar, atrair; engodar, nega-
cear; fascinar

allurement | əlïu'əmənt | *s.* en-
canto; sedução; atração

alluring | əlïu'əring | *a.* tentador,
sedutor, fascinante

allusion | əlu'jən | *s.* alusão,
referência

ally | a'lay | *s.* aliado / *vi.* aliar-se

almanac | ól'mənak | *s.* almana-
que, anuário, calendário

almighty | ólmay'tī | *a.* onipoten-
te, todo-poderoso; (gír.) tre-
mendo, formidável

almond | ʌ'mənd | *s.* amêndoa

almond eyes | ʌ'məndayz | *spl.*
olhos amendoados

almond tree | ʌ'məndtrī | *s.*
amendoeira

almost | ól'mowst | *adv.* quase; a
ponto de; perto de

alms | ʌmz' | *s.* esmola; caridade;
donativo

almshouse | Amz'haws | s. asilo de pobres

aloft | əloft' | adv. em cima; para cima; (náut.) no tope

alone | əlown' | a. adv. só, sozinho; a sós. **-to let a.** deixar em paz. **-let a.** sem mencionar. **-all a.** absolutamente só

along | əlong' | adv. para diante, adiante. **-a. with** com, em companhia de. **-all a.** ao longo de; desde o princípio. **-to get a. with** · dar-se bem com. **-to move a.** circular / prep. ao longo de, junto a

aloof | əlʊf' | a. afastado, separado; arredio / adv. à distância, ao longe

aloud | əlawd' | adv. alto; em voz alta

alphabet | al'fəbet | s. alfabeto, abecedário

alpine | al'payn | a. alpino, alpestre

Alps | alps' | s. Alpes

already | ól'redɪ | adv. já

also | ól'sow | adv. também, da mesma forma, além disso

altar | ol'tə | s. altar. **-to lead to the a.** conduzir ao altar, desposar

altar boy | ol'təboy | s. acólito

altar cloth | ol'təkloϑ | s. toalha de altar

altar piece | ol'təpis | s. painel, retábulo

altar rail | ol'təreyl | s. mesa de comunhão

altar wine | ol'təwayn | s. vinho eucarístico, vinho de missa

alter | ol'tə | vt. alterar, modificar / vi. passar por alteração

alteration | oltərey'śən | s. alteração, modificação

altercation | oltəkey'śən | s. altercação, contenda, disputa

alternate | oltə'nit | a. alternado / vt. alternar, revezar, interpolar / vi. alternar-se, revezar-se

alternating | ol'təneyting | a. alternado, alternativo

alternating current | ol'təneytingkârənt | s. corrente alter-

nada

alternation | oltəney'śən | s. alternação, revezamento

alternative | oltə'nətiv | s. alternativa / a. alternativo

although | ólðow' | conj. ainda que, posto que, embora, não obstante

altitude | al'titʃud | s. altitude, altura

altogether | óltuge'ðə | adv. totalmente, completamente, inteiramente; em conjunto; num total de, ao todo

altruism | al'truizəm | s. altruísmo, amor ao próximo

aluminium | alʲumi'nʲəm | s. alumínio

aluminum | alʲumi'nəm | s. = aluminium

always | ól'weyz | adv. sempre

a.m. l ey'em | loc. lat. (abrev. de ante meridiem) de manhã, antes do meio-dia

amalgamate | əmal'gəmeyt | vt. vi. amalgamar, misturar, fundir, combinar

amalgamation | əmalgəmey'śən | s. amálgama, amalgamação

amass | əmas' | vt. acumular, juntar, amontoar, empilhar

amateur | a'mətə | s. amador, aficionado, diletante

amateurish | amətE'riś | a. próprio de amador, tosco, imperfeito, não profissional

amaze | əmeyz' | vt. maravilhar, assombrar, pasmar

amazed | əmey'zid | a. maravilhado, assombrado, pasmado

amazement | əmeyz'mənt | s. assombro, pasmo, surpresa

amazing | əmey'zing | a. assombroso, pasmoso, surpreendente, maravilhoso

Amazon | a'məzən | s. o rio Amazonas; (minúsc.) amazona

ambassador | amba'sədə | s. embaixador; emissário

amber | am'bə | s. âmbar, âmbar amarelo

ambergris | am'bəgriz | s. âmbar,

âmbar gris

ambiguity | ambĭgĭu'itĭ | s. ambigüidade, dubiedade

ambiguous | ambi'gĭuəs | a. ambíguo, dúbio, obscuro

ambition | ambi'śən | s. ambição / vt. ambicionar

ambitious | ambi'śəs | a. ambicioso; cobiçoso

amble | am'bəl | vi. (equit.) marchar a furta-passo

ambulance | am'bĭuləns | s. ambulância

ambush | am'buś | s. emboscada, tocaia, cilada / vt. emboscar, tocaiar, armar cilada / vi. emboscar-se

ameliorate | əmĭ'lĭəreyt | vt. melhorar, aperfeiçoar

amelioration | əmĭlĭərey'śən | s. melhora, aperfeiçoamento

amenable | əmĭ'nəbəl | a. responsável; dócil, submisso. **-a. to law** responsável perante a lei. **-a. to reason** razoável, acessível

amend | əmend' | vt. emendar, modificar, corrigir

amendment | əmend'mənt | s. emenda, correção; regeneração

amends | əmendz' | s. reparação, indenização; satisfação; compensação

amenity | əmĭ'nitĭ | s. amenidade, suavidade, cortesia; (pl.) prazeres; comodidades, confortos

American | əme'rikən | s. a. norte-americano; americano

amethyst | a'məȝist | s. ametista

amiability | eymĭəbi'litĭ | s. amabilidade, afabilidade

amiable | ey'mĭəbəl | a. amável, afável, benévolo

amicable | a'mikəbəl | a. amigável, amistoso; conciliador

amid, amidst | əmid' əmidst' | prep. no meio de, entre, cercado de

amiss | əmis' | adv. erroneamente; mal; inoportuno, fora de propósito. **-to take a.** levar a mal. **-to go a.** desencaminhar-se

amity | a'mitĭ | s. amizade; harmonia, concórdia

ammunition | amĭuni'śən | s. munição; munições

amnesty | am'nistĭ | s. anistia / vt. anistiar

amok | əmok' | adv. amoque. **-to run a.** ser atacado de amoque

among, amongst | əmâng' əmângst' | prep. no meio de, entre; junto com

amorous | a'mərəs | a. amoroso, carinhoso; enamorado, apaixonado; erótico

amortize | əmətayz' | vt. (jur., fin.) amortizar

amount | əmawnt' | s. quantia, importância, soma, total / vi. **-to a.** to montar a, chegar a, equivaler a

amphibious | amfi'bĭəs | a. anfíbio

amphitheatre | am'fiȝĭətə | s. anfiteatro

ample | am'pəl | a. amplo; abundante; bastante, suficiente; folgado (peça de roupa)

amplification | amplifikey'śən | s. amplificação; ampliação

amplify | am'plifay | vt. amplificar; ampliar

amply | am'plĭ | adv. generosamente, fartamente

amputate | am'pĭuteyt | vt. amputar, cortar fora

amputation | amplutey'śən | s. amputação

amulet | a'mĭulit | s. amuleto

amuse | əmĭuz' | vt. divertir, recrear, entreter. **-to a. oneself** divertir-se

amused | amĭuzd' | a. divertido, distraído. **-we are not a.** não achamos graça

amusement | əmĭuz'mənt | s. divertimento, entretenimento, diversão, recreação

amusing | əmĭu'zing | a. engraçado, divertido

anachronism | əna'krənizəm | s. anacronismo

anaemia | ənĭ'mĭə | s. anemia

anaemic | ənĭ'mik | a. anêmico

anaesthesia | ənesϑɪ'sɪə | s. anestesia

anaesthetic | ənesϑe'tik | s. a. anestésico

analogous | əna'ləgəs | a. análogo, semelhante

analogy | əna'ləjī | s. analogia, semelhança

analyse | a'nəlayz | vt. analisar

analysis | əna'lisis | s. análise; psicanálise

analytic, -al | anəli'tik(əl) | a. analítico; psicanalítico

anarchic, -al | ənʌ'kik(əl) | a. anárquico; desordenado, caótico, desorganizado

anarchism | a'nəkizəm | s. anarquismo

anarchist | a'nəkist | s. a. anarquista

anarchy | a'nəkī | s. anarquia

anathema | əna'ϑimə | s. anátema, excomunhão; maldição; execração

anatomy | əna'təmī | s. anatomia

ancestor | an'sestə | s. antepassado; (pl.) antepassados

ancestral | anses'trəl | a. ancestral, dos antepassados

ancestry | an'sestrī | s. antepassados, ascendentes; linhagem, ascendência

anchor | ang'kə | s. âncora. -at a. ancorado. -to cast a. lançar ferro. -to weigh a. levantar ferro / vt. vi. ancorar, fundear

anchorage | an'kərij | s. ancoradouro

anchovy | an'ʃəvī | s. anchova, enchova (esp. salgada)

ancient | eyn'ʃənt | a. antigo, velho; venerável, vetusto

and | and | conj. e. -a. so on e assim por diante. -a. yet contudo, apesar disso

Andalusian | andəlʋ'jən | s. a. andaluz, da Andaluzia

anecdote | a'nikdowt | s. historieta, caso, anedota

anew | ənīu' | adv. de novo

angel | eyn'jəl | s. anjo

angelic | anje'lik | a. angélico

Angelus | an'ʃiləs | s. ângelus, ave-marias

anger | ang'gə | s. ira, raiva, cólera, sanha / vt. encolerizar, irritar

angle | ang'gəl | s. ângulo, canto, esquina; ponto de vista / vi. pescar com caniço, pescar esportivamente. -to a. for praise procurar lisonjas, pescar elogios. -to a. for procurar obter ardilosamente

angler | ang'glə | s. pescador de caniço, pescador esportivo

angry | ang'grī | a. zangado, irritado, aborrecido, irado

anguish | ang'gwiʃ | s. angústia, sofrimento, dor

angular | ang'giulə | a. angular; anguloso, pontudo; ossudo, desajeitado; intratável

animal | a'niməl | s. animal / a. animal, carnal, sensual

animate | a'nimeyt | vt. animar, encorajar

animation | animey'ʃən | s. animação; vivacidade

animosity | animo'sitī | s. animosidade, hostilidade, ressentimento

ankle | ang'kəl | s. tornozelo; artelho

annals | a'nəlz | spl. anais; crônica, história

annex | a'neks | s. anexo, dependência; acréscimo / vt. anexar; ocupar (território)

annexation | aneksey'ʃən | s. anexação, incorporação

annihilate | ənay'ileyt | vt. aniquilar, exterminar; destruir, desbaratar

annihilation | ənayiley'ʃən | s. aniquilação, extermínio

anniversary | aniveʹsərī | s. aniversário

annotate | a'nowteyt | vt. anotar / vi. tomar notas

announce | ə'nawns' | vt. anunciar; participar, proclamar; manifestar, revelar

announcement | ənawns'mənt |

s. proclamação, participação, declaração, aviso

announcer | ənawn'sə | *s.* anunciante; locutor de rádio

annoy | ənoy' | *vt.* aborrecer, irritar, incomodar, molestar

annoyance | ənoy'əns | *s.* irritação, aborrecimento

annoying | ənoy'ing | *a.* enfadonho, aborrecido, maçante

annual | a'niuəl | *s.* anuário, publicação anual / *a.* anual

annuity | aniu'itī | *s.* anuidade; renda anual

annul | ənâl' | *vt.* anular, cancelar, revogar, suprimir

annulment | ənâl'mənt | *s.* anulação, abolição, rescisão

anoint | ənoynt' | *vt.* untar; ungir, consagrar

anointing | ənoyn'ting | *s.* unção; consagração

anomalous | əno'mələs | *a.* anômalo, anormal, aberrante, irregular

anomaly | əno'məlī | *s.* anomalia, anormalidade, aberração, irregularidade

anon | ənon' | *adv.* daqui a pouco, dentro em pouco

anonymity | anəni'mitī | *s.* anonimato, anonímia

anonymous | əno'niməs | *a.* anônimo, sem nome

another | ə'nâðə | *a. pron.* outro; um outro; outra pessoa; mais um. **-to one a.** um ao outro, uns aos outros

answer | An'sə | *s.* resposta; réplica; solução de um problema; explicação / *vt.* responder; replicar; contestar, refutar. **-to a. back** replicar com insolência. **-to a. the phone** atender ao telefone. **-to a. my purpose** corresponder ao meu desejo. **-to a. the description** corresponder à descrição. **-to a. to name of** atender pelo nome de

answerable | An'sərəbəl | *a.* responsável. **-a. for something** responsável por alguma coisa

ant | ant' | *s.* formiga

antagonism | anta'gənizəm | *s.* antagonismo, oposição

antagonist | anta'gənist | *s.* antagonista, adversário

antagonistic | antagəni'stik | *a.* antagônico, antagonista, hostil; oposto, contrário

antagonize | anta'gənayz | *vt.* contrariar, resistir a, hostilizar, combater

antarctic | antAk'tik | *s.* regiões antárticas; (maiúsc.) Antártico / *a.* antártico

ant-bear | ant'beə | *s.* tamanduá; pangolim

antecedent | antisı'dənt | *s. a.* antecedente

antechamber | an'tišeymbə | *s.* antecâmara, sala de espera

antedate | an'tideyt | *vt.* antedatar; antecipar

antelope | an'tilowp | *s.* antílope; couro de antílope

anteroom | an'tirum | *s.* ante-sala, sala de espera

anthem | an'ϑəm | *s.* hino sacro; cântico

anthill | ant'hil | *s.* formigueiro; cupim

anthology | anϑo'ləjī | *s.* antologia, seleta, florilégio, crestomatia

anthracite | an'ϑrəsayt | *s.* antracito, carvão de pedra

anthropologist | anϑrəpo'ləjist | *s.* antropólogo

anthropology | anϑrəpo'ləjī | *s.* antropologia

anti-aircraft | antie'əkrAft | *a.* antiaéreo

antibiotic | antibayo'tik | *s. a.* antibiótico

anticipate | anti'sipeyt | *vt.* antecipar, fazer de antemão; antegozar; prever; prevenir; antecipar-se a

anticipation | antisipey'śən | *s.* expectativa; antecipação. **-in a.** antecipadamente, de antemão

antics | an'tiks | *spl.* extravagâncias, excentricidades, travessuras, momices. **-to be up to his a.** fazer das suas, fazer extravagâncias

antidote | an'tidowt | s. antídoto, contraveneno

antipathetic | antipəϑe'tik | a. avesso, contrário, oposto, inimigo, que tem aversão

antipathy | anti'pəϑī | s. antipatia, repugnância, aversão; objeto de aversão

antipodes | anti'pədīz | spl. antípodas

antiquarian | antikwe'ərīən | s. antiquário; arqueólogo / a. arqueológico

antiquated | antikwey'tid | a. antiquado, fora de moda ou uso, obsoleto

antique | antık' | s. (ger. pl.) antiguidades / a. antigo, vetusto

antiquity | anti'kwitī | s. antiguidade; os antigos

antiseptic | antisep'tik | s. a. anti-séptico, bactericida

antisocial | antisow'səl | a. anti-social

antithesis | anti'ϑəsis | s. antítese; oposto, contrário

antler | ant'lə | s. armação dos cervídeos, galhada

antonym | an'tənim | s. antônimo

anvil | an'vil | s. bigorna

anxiety | angzay'ətī | s. ansiedade, ânsia; desejo, afã, anseio

anxious | ank'səs | a. ansioso, apreensivo; desejoso

any | e'nī | a. pron. qualquer, quaisquer; algum, alguns, alguma(s); nenhum, nenhuma. **-a. of them** qualquer deles. **-a. more** mais. **-at a. time** a qualquer hora. **-in a. case** em todo o caso. **-not on a. account** de maneira alguma. **-at a. rate** seja de que modo for, custe o que custar

anybody | e'nibodī | pron. alguém, qualquer pessoa. **-not a.** ninguém

anyhow | e'nihaw | adv. conj. de qualquer modo, seja como for; em todo o caso; negligentemente, inconsideradamente, a esmo

anyone | e'niwon | pron. qualquer pessoa, qualquer um; alguém

anything | e'niðing | pron. qualquer coisa; alguma coisa, algo; tudo. **-a. will do** qualquer coisa serve. **-a. but** tudo menos

anyway | e'niwey | adv. conj. de qualquer modo; em todo o caso, seja como for

anywhere | e'niweə | adv. em qualquer lugar; em lugar algum; onde quer que

apace | əpeys' | adv. apressadamente, rapidamente, depressa, velozmente

apart | əpʌt' | adv. separadamente, à parte; de parte, de lado. **-to tear a.** estraçalhar. **-to fall a.** desfazer-se, cair aos pedaços. **-a. from** salvo, exceto

apartment | əpʌt'mənt | s. apartamento; (pl.) aposentos

apathetic | apəϑe'tik | a. apático, indiferente

apathy | a'pəϑī | s. apatia, indiferença, insensibilidade

ape | eyp' | s. macaco (esp. antropóide); qualquer macaco / vt. macaquear, imitar

aperient | əpi'rīənt | s. a. laxante, laxativo

aperture | a'pətīuə | s. abertura; orifício, fenda

apex | ey'peks | s. ápice, cume

aphorism | a'fərizəm | s. aforismo, máxima

apiary | ey'pīərī | s. apiário

apiece | əpīs' | adv. cada um, por peça

aplomb | əplom' | s. aprumo, segurança, confiança

apocalypse | əpo'kəlips | s. apocalipse

apogee | a'pəjī | s. apogeu

apologetic | əpoləʃe'tik | a. apologético

apologist | əpo'ləjist | s. apologista, defensor

apologize | əpo'ləᵵayz | vi. pedir desculpas, desculpar-se

apology | əpo'laᵵi | s. desculpas, escusa; apologia, defesa. **-to demand an a.** exigir satisfações

apoplexy | a'pəpleksī | s. apoplexia

apostasy | əpos'təsī |s. apostasia, abjuração

apostate | əpos'tit | s. apóstata, renegado

apostle | əpo'səl | s. apóstolo

apostolic | apəsto'lik | a. apostólico

apostrophe | əpos'trəfī | s. apóstrofe, interpelação; apóstrofo (sinal gráfico)

apothecary | əpo'ϑəkərī | s. boticário, farmacêutico

apotheosis | əpoϑīow'sis |s. apoteose, glorificação

appal | əpól' | vt. aterrorizar, aterrar, apavorar

appalling | əpó'ling | a. aterrorizante, apavorante

apparatus | apərey'təs | s. aparelhagem, maquinaria; aparelho, instrumento

apparel | əpa'rəl | s. vestuário, roupa; paramentos, vestes, atavios

apparent | əpa'rənt | a. aparente, visível, manifesto; aparente, fingido

apparently | əpa'rəntlī |adv. aparentemente, ao que parece

apparition | apəri'śən | s. aparição, espectro, fantasma

appeal | əpīl' | s. (jur.) apelo, recurso; pedido, rogo; atração, encanto / vt. fazer subir um processo a instância superior / vi. (jur.) apelar, recorrer; implorar, rogar; atrair, interessar, empolgar. **-to a. against** apelar de sentença. **-to a.** to apelar para. **-to a. to arms** recorrer às armas. **-to a. for help** rogar auxílio. **-it doesn't a. to me** não me atrai, não me interessa

appear | əpī'ə | vi. aparecer, sur-

gir; comparecer; ser publicado; manifestar-se, revelar-se. **-it a. by this** daqui se conclui

appearance | əpī'ərəns | s. aparência, aspecto; aparecimento; comparecimento, apresentação. **-to keep up appearances** manter as aparências. **-to all appearances** a julgar pelos indícios

appease | əpīz' | vt. aplacar, apaziguar, mitigar; satisfazer, saciar

appeasement | əpīz'mənt | s. apaziguamento, pacificação

append | əpend' | vt. anexar, acrescentar, apensar

appendage | əpen'diᵵ | s. acréscimo, aditamento, apêndice; dependência

appendicitis | əpendisay'tis | s. apendicite

appendix | əpen'diks | s. apêndice

appertain | a'pəteyn | vi. pertencer a; competir a

appetite | a'pitayt | s. apetite; desejo

applaud | əplód' | vt. aplaudir, bater palmas; aclamar

applause | əplóz' | s. aplauso, aclamação; aprovação

apple | a'pəl |s. maçã

apple of discord | a'pəlovdiskód | s. pomo da discórdia

apple of the eye | a'pəlovðəay |s. pupila

apple pie | a'pəlpay | s. torta de maçã

apple tree | a'pəltrī |s. macieira

appliance | əplay'əns | s. utensílio, instrumento, aparelho; aplicação, uso

applicant | a'plikənt | s. requerente, peticionário; aspirante, pretendente

application | aplikey'śən |s. aplicação, uso; requerimento, petição, pedido; aplicação, diligência; adequação, pertinência; emplastro

apply | əplay' |vt. vi. aplicar; acomodar, adaptar; usar, empregar; requerer, solicitar; referir-se a, dizer respeito a

appoint | əpoynt' | *vt.* designar, nomear; determinar, fixar / *vi.* ordenar, mandar

appointment | əpoynt'mənt | *s.* nomeação, designação; compromisso; encontro, entrevista. **-to make an a.** marcar um encontro. **-to have an a.** ter um encontro

apportion | əpó'śən | *vt.* aquinhoar, dividir, repartir equitativamente

apposite | a'pəzit | *a.* adequado, apropriado, oportuno

appraisal | əprey'zəl | *s.* avaliação, apreciação

appraise | əpreyz' | *vt.* avaliar, estimar

appreciable | əprī'śəbəl | *a.* apreciável, sensível; calculável, mensurável

appreciate | aprī'sīeyt | *vt.* apreciar, estimar; reconhecer; compreender, admirar / *vi.* subir de preço

appreciation | aprīsīey'śən | *s.* apreciação, avaliação; apreço, estima; reconhecimento, gratidão; admiração; alta de preços

appreciative | əprī'sĭətiv | *a.* apreciativo; reconhecido

apprehend | aprīhend' | *vt.* perceber, notar; (jur.) deter, prender; temer, recear / *vi.* compreender

apprehension | aprīhen'śən | *s.* prisão, captura; percepção, compreensão; apreensão, receio, temor

apprenhensive | aprīhen'siv | *a.* apreensivo, receoso; perceptivo; inteligente

apprentice | əpren'tis | *s.* aprendiz; principiante

apprenticeship | əpren'tisśip | *s.* aprendizagem

apprise | əprayz' | *vt.* informar, notificar, avisar

approach | əprowš' | *s.* aproximação; proximidade, vizinhança; acesso; maneira de abordar / *vi.* aproximar-se, dirigir-se a, falar com

approachable | əprow'śəbəl | *a.* abordável, acessível

approaching | əprow'śing | *a.* próximo, que se aproxima

approbation | aprəbey'śən | *s.* aprovação; beneplácito; consentimento; louvor

appropriate | əprow'prīt | *a.* apropriado, adequado, próprio; correspondente / *vt.* apropriar-se de, apoderar-se de; destinar, reservar

appropriateness | əprow'prīətnes | *s.* conveniência, adequação; decoro

appropriation | əprowprīey'śən | *s.* apropriação; dotação orçamentária

approval | əpru'vəl | *s.* aprovação, ratificação. **-on a.** dependendo de aprovação

approve | əpru̇v' | *vt.* aprovar, autorizar, ratificar / *vi.* estar de acordo

approximate | əpro'ksimit | *a.* aproximado; parecido / | əpro'ksimeyt | *vt.* aproximar-se de, avizinhar-se de

approximately | əpro'ksimətlī | *adv.* aproximadamente

appurtenance | əpE'tinəns | *s.* acessório, pertence

apricot | ey'prikot | *s.* damasco

apricot tree | ey'prikottrī | *s.* damasqueiro

April | ey'prəl | *s.* abril. **-A. weather** sol e chuva alternadamente

April Fool's Day | ey'prəlfʋlzdey | *s.* primeiro de abril

apron | ey'prən | *s.* avental. **-tied to the a. strings** agarrado às saias da mãe, dominado por (mãe ou mulher)

apropos | aprəpow' | *adv.* a propósito de, com respeito a

apt | apt' | *a.* adequado, oportuno; apto, competente; hábil, capaz; inclinado, predisposto, tendente, sujeito

aptitude | ap'titĭud | *s.* aptidão, capacidade, queda

aptness | apt'nes | *s.* aptidão, pertinência; talento

aqueduct | a'kwidâkt | *s.* aqueduto

aquiline | a'kwilayn | *a.* aquilino

Arab, Arabian | a'rəbərey'bĭən | *s. a.* árabe

Arabian Nights (the) | ərey'bĭən nayts | *spl.* As Mil e Uma Noites

Arabic | a'rəbik | *s. a.* árabe, a língua árabe

arable | a'rəbəl | *a.* arável, cultivável. **-a. land** terra arável

arbiter | A'bitə | *s.* árbitro

arbitrary | A'bitrərĭ | *a.* arbitrário, discricionário, despótico, tirânico

arbitrate | A'bitreyt | *vi.* arbitrar, decidir

arbitration | Abitrey'śən | *s.* arbitragem

arbitration award | Abitrey'śənawad | *s.* laudo arbitral

arbitrator | A'bitreytə | *s.* árbitro, arbitrador

arc | Ak' | *s.* arco

arcade | Akeyd' | *s.* arcada, galeria, passagem coberta

arch | Aś' | *s.* arco; abóbada; céu da boca / *vt. vi.* arquear(-se)

archaeologist | Akĭo'ləjist | *s.* arqueólogo

archaeology | Akĭo'ləjĭ | *s.* arqueologia

archaic | Akey'ik | *a.* arcaico; antiquado

archbishop | aśbi'śəp | *s.* arcebispo

archenemy | Aśe'nəmĭ | *s.* arquiinimigo

archer | A'śə | *s.* arqueiro, flecheiro

archipelago | Aśpe'ləgow | *s.* arquipélago

architect | A'kitekt | *s.* arquiteto; (fig.) criador, artífice

architectural | Akitek'śərəl | *a.* arquitetônico

architecture | Akitek'śə | *s.* arquitetura

archive | A'kayv | *s.* (ger. *pl.*) arquivo

archway | Aś'wey | *s.* arco, arcada, passagem em arco

Arctic | Ak'tik | *s.* Ártico / *a.* (minúsc.) ártico

ardent | A'dənt | *a.* ardente

ardour, ardor | A'də | *s.* ardor; fervor, entusiasmo

arduous | A'dĭuəs | *a.* árduo, difícil, laborioso, penoso

area | e'ərĭə | *s.* área, superfície; zona, região, setor

arena | ərī'nə | *s.* arena

argue | A'gĭu | *vt.* discutir, debater; provar, demonstrar / *vi.* argumentar; arrazoar

argument | A'gĭumənt | *s.* altercação, disputa acirrada, contenda; argumento, argumentação, raciocínio

arid | a'rid | *a.* árido, seco, ressequido, estéril

aridity | əri'ditĭ | *s.* aridez

aright | ərayt' | *adv.* corretamente, acertadamente

arise | ərayz' | *vi.* surgir, aparecer; provir de, resultar; erguer-se, levantar-se; elevar-se

aristocracy | aristo'krəsĭ | *s.* aristocracia; nobreza

aristocrat | a'ristəkrat | *s.* aristocrata; nobre

aristocratic | aristəkra'tik | *a.* aristocrático

arithmetic | əriϑ'mətik | *s.* aritmética

ark | Ak' | *s.* arca

arm | Am' | *s.* braço; (mil.) arma; ramo, ramal; braço de mar. **-a. in a.** de braço dado. **-with arms folded** de braços cruzados. **-infant in arms** criança de colo. **-to keep at arm's length** tratar friamente. **-to be up in arms** amotinado, sublevado / *vt.* armar

armadillo | Amədi'low | *s.* tatu

armament | A'məmənt | *s.* armamento; equipamento militar

armchair | Am'šeə | s. cadeira de braços, poltrona / a. de gabinete, teórico

armful | Am'ful | s. braçada (o que pode conter-se entre os braços)

armhole | Am'howl | s. cava (de manga)

armistice | A'mistis | s. armistício, trégua

armorial | Amó'rīəl | a. heráldico, armorial

armour, armor | A'mə | s. armadura; couraça (de navio) / vt. blindar

armour plating | A'məpleyting | s. blindagem

armoury, armory | A'mərī | s. depósito de armas, arsenal; (heráld.) armaria

armpit | Am'pit | s. axila, sovaco

army | A'mī | s. exército. -to join the a. alistar-se

aroma | ərow'mə | s. aroma, cheiro, perfume

aromatic | arowma'tik | a. aromático; perfumado, cheiroso

around | ərawnd' | prep. em volta de, em torno de, ao redor de; perto de, por volta de / adv. em redor, em volta, na vizinhança

arouse | ərawz' | vt. acordar, despertar; provocar, estimular, incitar, excitar

arraign | əreyn' | vt. (jur.) citar; acusar, denunciar

arrange | əreynj' | vt. arranjar, arrumar, dispor; organizar; (mús.) arranjar / vi. fazer preparativos, providenciar, tomar providências

arrangement | əreynj'mənt | s. arranjo, disposição; preparativo; adaptação; combinação, acordo; (mús.) arranjo

arrant | a'rənt | a. notório, rematado, refinado. -an a. scoundrel um rematado patife

array | ərey' | s. ordem, disposição; série, rol; pompa, aparato; vestes, atavio / vt. dispor em

ordem de batalha; ataviar, ornar

arrears | əri'əz | spl. atrasados, contas atrasadas, débitos, dívidas

arrest | ərest' | s. prisão, detenção; interrupção, parada / vt. prender, deter; interromper; chamar, atrair, prender (atenção)

arrival | əray'vəl | s. chegada; vinda. -a new a. um recém-chegado

arrive | ərayv' | vt. chegar; alcançar celebridade

arrogance | a'rəgəns | s. arrogância, insolência

arrogant | a'rəgənt | a. arrogante, insolente

arrogate | a'rowgeyt | vt. arrogar-se, apropriar-se de; atribuir a si mesmo

arrow | a'row | s. flecha

arrowroot | a'rowrut | s. araruta

arsenal | A'sənəl | s. arsenal

arson | A'sən | s. (jur.) incêndio criminoso

art | At' | s. arte; habilidade, perícia

artery | A'tərī | s. artéria

artful | At'fəl | a. ardiloso, astuto, manhoso; hábil, engenhoso; velhaco, finório

artfulness | At'fəlnes | s. astúcia, manha; habilidade

arthritis | Aϑray'tis | s. artrite, artritismo

article | A'tikəl | s. artigo; item, objeto; parágrafo, cláusula. -in the a. of no que concerne a

articulate | Ati'kĭuleyt | a. articulado, bem pronunciado / vt. pronunciar, articular / vi. articular-se

articulation | Atikĭuley'śən | s. articulação, junta; pronúncia clara; articulação, coordenação; sistematização

artifice | A'tifis | s. artifício, ardil, artimanha

artificial | Atifi'śəl | a. artificial; postiço; fingido; afetado, amaneirado

artificiality | Atifišia'litī | s. artificialidade, artificialismo, afetação

artillery | Ati'lərī | s. artilharia

artilleryman | Ati'lərīman | s. artilheiro; oficial ou soldado de artilharia

artisan | Atizan' | s. artífice, artesão; operário

artist | A'tist | s. artista

artistic | A'tistik | a. artístico

artless | At'les | a. simples, natural; ingênuo, franco, sincero

as | az | conj. como; pois, porque; quando, enquanto; segundo, conforme, à medida que. -a. big a. tão grande como. -a. long a. enquanto; visto que, já que. -a. soon a. logo que. -a. far a. tanto quanto, até onde. -such a. tal como. -a. to, a. for quanto a, com respeito a. -a. yet por enquanto, até agora, ainda. -a. well tão bem como outra coisa qualquer. -a. far a. I know que eu saiba. -a. best one can da melhor forma possível

asbestos | azbes'təs | s. amianto, asbesto

ascend | əsend' | vi. ascender, subir, elevar-se

ascendancy | əsen'dənsī | s. ascendência, predomínio, influência, preponderância

ascension | əsen'šən | s. ascensão, subida, escalada; (ecles.) Ascensão

ascent | əsent' | s. ascensão, elevação; subida, escalada

ascertain | əsəteyn' | vt. descobrir, averiguar, apurar

ascetic | əse'tik | s. asceta / a. ascético

ascribe | əskrayb' | vt. atribuir, imputar

asepsis | əsep'sis | s. (med.) assepsia

ash | aś' | s. cinza; freixo; cor de cinza. -A. Wednesday quarta-feira de Cinzas

ashamed | əśeymd' | a. envergo-

nhado. -to be a. ficar envergonhado

ashen | a'śən | a. cinzento, cor de cinza; pálido, baço

ashore | əśó'ə | adv. em terra. -to go a. desembarcar. -to run a. encalhar

ashpan | aś'pan | s. cinzeiro (de fogão ou lareira)

ashtray | aś'trey | s. cinzeiro

aside | əsayd' | s. aparte. -to put ou to set a. pôr de lado / adv. de parte, à parte; para longe; confidencialmente; obliquamente, de esguelha, de viés, enviesado

ask | ʌsk' | vt. perguntar; inquirir, indagar; pedir, solicitar; convidar. -to a. for ou after a person perguntar por uma pessoa. -to a. a question fazer uma pergunta. -to a. for dinner convidar para jantar

askance | əskans' | adv. de esguelha, de soslaio

askew | əskῙυ' | a. enviesado, torto / adv. obliquamente

aslant | əslʌnt' | adv. de esguelha, de soslaio

asleep | əslīp' | adv. adormecido. -to fall a. adormecer. -to be a. estar dormindo. -to be fast a. dormir profundamente. -to put a. fazer dormir

asparagus | əspa'rəgəs | s. aspargo, espargo

aspect | as'pekt | s. aspecto, aparência; ar, expressão; vista, perspectiva

asperity | aspe'ritī | s. aspereza, rudeza; rigor, severidade; inclemência

aspersion | aspE'jən | s. aspersão; calúnia, difamação

asphalt | as'falt | s. asfalto

aspirant | as'pirənt | s. aspirante, pretendente, candidato / a. que aspira

aspiration | aspirey'śən | s. aspiração; anelo, ambição

aspire | əspay'ə | vi. aspirar a, pretender, almejar

aspirin | as'pirin | s. aspirina

aspiring | əspay'əring | *a*. ambicioso; altaneiro

ass | as' | *s*. asno, jumento; (vulg.) nádegas, traseiro. **-to make an a. of oneself** fazer papel de tolo

assail | əseyl' | *vt*. assaltar

assailant | əsey'lənt | *s*. assaltante, agressor

assassin | əsa'sin | *s*. assassino; sicário

assassinate | əsa'sineyt | *vt*. assassinar

assassination | əsasiney'sən | *s*. assassinato, assassínio

assault | əsólt' | *s*. assalto, ataque, agressão. **-a. and battery** (jur.) agressão / *vt*. atacar, agredir; assaltar; investir, acometer

assay | əsey' | *vt*. ensaiar, analisar; avaliar; empreender, tentar

assemblage | əsem'blij | *s*. assembléia; reunião; congregação

assemble | əsem'bəl | *vt*. reunir, agrupar; montar, armar / *vi*. congregar-se

assembly | əsem'blī | *s*. assembléia, reunião, conclave, congregação

assembly call | əsem'blīkól | *s*. (mil.) toque de reunir

assembly line | əsem'blīlayn | *s*. linha de montagem

assent | əsent' | *s*. consentimento, anuência, aprovação / *vt*. consentir em, dar consentimento a, concordar com, anuir a

assert | əsEt' | *vt*. afirmar, asseverar, declarar; defender, sustentar. **-to a. oneself** impor-se

assertion | əsE'sən | *s*. proposição, alegação; assertiva; defesa; reivindicação

assertive | əsE'tiv | *a*. dogmático, peremptório; agressivo, arrogante

assertiveness | əsE'tivnes | *s*. maneira arrogante ou agressiva

assess | əses' | *vt*. taxar, tributar, cobrar taxa; avaliar, estimar

assessment | əses'mənt | *s*. taxação, tributação; avaliação, valorização; quota

asset | a'set | *s*. posse, propriedade; vantagem, predicado; (*pl*., com.) ativo, fundos; (jur.) massa falida. **-to be an a.** ser uma pessoa útil

asseverate ∟a'sevəreyt | *vt*. asseverar, afirmar, assegurar

assiduity | asidĭu'itī | *s*. assiduidade; zelo, aplicação; (*pl*.) atenções

assiduous | əsi'dĭuəs | *a*. assíduo; zeloso, aplicado

assign | əsayn' | *vt*. atribuir; designar (lugar, data); especificar, determinar; ceder (direitos)

assignment | əsayn'mənt | *s*. transmissão, transferência, cessão; distribuição, adjudicação; tarefa, encargo

assimilate | əsi'mileyt | *vt*. assimilar, absorver; digerir

assimilation | əsimiley'sən | *s*. assimilação, absorção

assist | əsist' | *vt*. ajudar, auxiliar, socorrer / *vi*. assistir, comparecer

assistance | əsis'təns | *s*. auxílio, assistência; colaboração, cooperação

assistant | əsis'tənt | *s*. assistente, auxiliar / *a*. auxiliar, ajudante

assistant secretary | əsis'təntsekrətrī | *s*. subsecretário

associate | əsow'sĭeyt | *s*. sócio, associado; parceiro, companheiro / *a*. associado, aliado / *vt*. associar, relacionar, unir / *vi*. associar-se, unir-se, aliar-se

association | əsowsĭey'sən | *s*. associação, sociedade; união, ligação; amizade, relação

association football | əsowsīey'sənfʊtból | *s*. futebol

assorted | əsó'tid | *a*. sortido, variado

assortment | əsót'mənt | *s*. sortimento; classificação

assuage | əsweyǰ' | *vt.* aliviar, mitigar, acalmar; saciar, satisfazer

assume | əsĭum' | *vt.* assumir, adotar; atribuir-se, arrogar-se; supor, presumir

assuming | əsĭu'ming | *a.* presunçoso, pretensioso. **-a. that** dado que, admitindo que

assumption | əsâm'śən | *s.* assunção, tomada; suposição, admissão de hipótese; (maiúsc.) Assunção de Nossa Senhora, festa da Assunção

assurance | əśu'ərəns | *s.* segurança; afirmação, garantia; certeza, convicção; firmeza, confiança; audácia; petulância; seguro de vida

assure | əśu'ə | *vt.* assegurar, asseverar. **-be a. that** fique certo de que

astern | əstɛn' | *adv.* à popa, à ré

asthma | as'mə | *s.* asma

astir | əstɛ' | *adv.* em movimento, em atividade, ativo

astonish | əsto'niś | *vt.* surpreender, espantar, causar admiração, assombrar

astonished | əsto'niśt | *a.* admirado, pasmado, espantado

astonishing | əsto'niśing | *a.* assombroso, pasmoso, estarrecedor, extraordinário

astonishment | əsto'niśmənt | *s.* assombro, espanto, surpresa, pasmo, admiração

astound | əstawnd' | *vt.* espantar, assombrar, aturdir

astray | əstrey' | *adv.* extraviado, perdido; errado, enganado. **-to lead a.** extraviar, levar para o caminho errado. **-to go a.** extraviar-se, perder-se, desviar-se

astride | əstrayd' | *adv.* cavalgando, a cavalo, montado em, escarranchado

astringent | əstrin'ǰənt | *a.* adstringente, áspero; severo, austero, rígido

astrology | əstro'ləǰi | *s.* astrologia

astronomer | əstro'nəmə | *s.* astrônomo

astronomy | əstro'nəmĭ | *s.* astronomia

astute | əstĭut' | *a.* astuto, astucioso, manhoso, sagaz

asunder | əsân'də | *adv.* apartados, separados, distantes. **-to tear a.** despedaçar. **-to force a.** separar à força. **-to burst a.** rebentar, estourar em pedaços

asylum | əsay'ləm | *s.* asilo; manicômio, hospício; abrigo, amparo, refúgio

at | at | *prep.* em; a. **-a. home** em casa, no lar. **-a. most** quando muito. **-a. least** pelo (ao) menos. **-a. once** imediatamente, já. **-a. first** a princípio. **-a. last** finalmente, enfim. **-a. the corner** à esquina. **-a. the door** à porta. **-a. a distance** à distância

atavistic | atəvis'tik | *a.* atávico

atheism | ey'ðiizəm | *s.* ateísmo

atheist | ey'ðiist | *s.* ateísta, ateu

athlete | aðlit' | *s.* atleta

athletic | aðle'tik | *a.* atlético, esportivo; vigoroso, robusto

athwart | əðwót | *prep.* de través em ou sobre

Atlantic | ətlan'tik | *s.* Atlântico / *a.* atlântico

atlas | a'tləs | *s.* atlas

atmosphere | at'məsfĭə | *s.* atmosfera; ambiente; clima (de obra de arte)

atoll | a'tol | *s.* atol

atom | a'təm | *s.* átomo

atomic | əto'mik | *a.* atômico

atomic bomb | əto'mikbâm | *s.* bomba atômica

atomize | a'təmayz | *vt.* atomizar, pulverizar

atone | ətown' | *vi.* expiar, reparar. **-to a. for a crime** expiar um crime

atonement | ətown'mənt | *s.* expiação, reparação

atrocious | ətrow'śəs | *a.* atroz, cruel, desumano; abominável, detestável

atrocity | ətro'sitī |*s.* atrocidade, crueldade

atrophy | a'trəfī |*s.* atrofia / *vt. vi.* atrofiar, definhar

attach | ətaš' | *vt.* ligar, prender, juntar; atar, amarrar; colar, fixar; unir, agregar; (jur.) arrestar, embargar. **-to a. importance to** ligar ou dar importância a

attaché | əta'šey |*s.* adido

attaché case | əta'šeykeys |*s.* pasta de documentos

attached | ətašt' |*a.* ligado, anexo; dedicado, afeiçoado, amigo; pertencente, relativo a, relacionado com

attachment | ətaš'mənt |*s.* união; ligação, fixação; acessório, pertence; afeto, amizade; devoção, apego; (jur.) arresto, embargo

attack | ətak' |*s.* ataque; agressão / *vt.* atacar

attain | ətéyn' | *vt.* atingir, alcançar; conseguir, obter, realizar; chegar a

attainable | ətey'nəbəl |*a.* atingível, alcançável; acessível; possível de ser obtido, conseguível

attainder | əteyn'də |*s.* (jur.) morte civil; infâmia, desonra, descrédito

attainment | əteyn'mənt |*s.* obtenção, realização, consecução; (*pl.*) conhecimentos, talentos, habilitações

attempt | ətempt' |*s.* tentativa, esforço; atentado, ataque / *vt.* tentar, intentar; esforçar-se

attend | ətend' | *vt.* atender a; assistir a (reunião); servir, estar a serviço de; acompanhar; (med.) tratar; aplicar-se a (trabalho, negócios etc.) / *vi.* atender, prestar atenção a; escutar; encarregar-se; estar presente

attendance | əten'dəns |*s.* assistência, cuidados; serviço; comparecimento, presença; auditório, assistência; séqüito, comitiva

attendant | əten'dənt |*s.* assistente, subordinado; acompanhante, membro de comitiva / *a.* que acompanha, concomitante

attention | əten'šən |*s.* atenção; diligência, aplicação; consideração, respeito; cortesia, fineza. **-to pay a.** prestar atenção a / *interj.* (mil.) sentido!

attentive | əten'tiv |*a.* atento, aplicado; solícito, atencioso, obsequioso

attenuate | əte'nĭueyt | *vt.* atenuar, diminuir; minorar

attest | ətest' | *vt.* atestar, certificar; autenticar; manifestar, demonstrar

attic | a'tik |*s.* sótão, mansarda, água-furtada

attire | ətay'ə |*s.* vestes, atavios, adornos / *vt.* vestir, ataviar, adornar

attitude | a'titĭud |*s.* atitude, postura; comportamento

attorney | ətE'ney |*s.* procurador, agente; advogado

attract | ətrakt' |*vt.* atrair; encantar, seduzir

attraction | ətrak'šən |*s.* atração; encanto, sedução

attractive | ətrak'tiv |*a.* atrativo, atraente, encantador, sedutor; simpático

attractiveness | ətrak'tivnes |*s.* atratividade; encanto, sedução

attributable | ətri'bĭutəbəl |*a.* atribuível, imputável

attribute | ətri'bĭut |*s.* atributo; predicado, qualidade / *vt.* atribuir, imputar; emprestar certo sentido ou intenção

attribution | ətribĭu'šən |*s.* atribuição; atributo; encargo

attrition | ətri'šən |*s.* atrito, desgaste

attune | ətĭun' | *vt.* afinar; entoar; harmonizar

atypical | əti'pikəl |*a.* atípico

auburn | ó'bən |*a.* castanho-avermelhado (cabelo)

auction | ók'šən |*s.* leilão / *vt.* leiloar

auctioneer | oksənı'ə |*s.* leiloeiro

audacious | ódey'śəs | *a.* audaz, arrojado, intrépido

audacity | óda'sitī | *s.* audácia, denodo, intrepidez

audible | ó'dibəl | *a.* audível; perceptível

audience | ó'dīəns |*s.* audiência, entrevista com autoridade; auditório, assistência, público, ouvintes

audit | ó'dit | *s.* balanço, 'verificação de contas / *vt.* fazer balanço; fiscalizar contas; examinar contas

auditor | ó'ditə |*s.* auditor; perito-contador

auditorium | óditó'rīəm |*s.* auditório; sala de conferências, concertos etc.

augment | ógment' | *vt.* aumentar, ampliar, amplificar

augmentation | ógmentey'śən | *s.* aumento, crescimento

August | ó'gəst |*s.* agosto / *a.* (minúsc.) augusto, imponente

aunt | Ant' |*s.* tia

Aunt Sally | Ant'salī |*s.* jogo de feira em que se derrubam bonecos atirando-lhes com bolas; (fig.) alvo de ataques ou insultos gratuitos

aura | ó'rə | *s.* aura; fluido, emanação

auspice | ós'pisi |*s.* patrocínio. **-under the a. of** sob o patrocínio de

auspicious | óspi'śəs | *a.* auspicioso, de bom augúrio; próspero, propício, feliz

austere | ostı'ə |*a.* austero

austerity | oste'ritī |*s.* austeridade; rigor, severidade; simplicidade

Austrian | os'trīən |*s. a.* austríaco

authentic | óðen'tik | *a.* autêntico, genuíno, verídico

authenticity | óðenti'sitī |*s.* autenticidade

author | ó'ðə |*s.* autor, escritor, homem de letras

authoritarian | óðorite'ərīən | *a.* autoritário

authoritative | óðo'ritətiv | *a.* autorizado, afiançado; autoritário, ditatorial; peremptório, definitivo

authority | óðo'ritī |*s.* autoridade; jurisdição, poder; influência, prestígio; direito, permissão. **-on good a.** de fonte limpa

authorization | óðərizey'śən | *s.* autorização

authorize | ó'ðərayz | *vt.* autorizar, permitir; justificar, ratificar

authorized | ó'ðərayzd | *a.* autorizado; permitido, facultado; licenciado

authorship | ó'ðəśip |*s.* autoria; profissão de autor

autobiography | ótowbayo'grəfī | *s.* autobiografia

autocratic | ótowkra'tik | *a.* autocrático

autograph | ó'təgrAf |*s.* autógrafo / *vt.* autografar

automatic | ótəma'tik |*s.* automática, pistola semi-automática / *a.* automático; inconsciente, maquinal

automation | ótəmey'śən |*s.* automatização, automação

automaton | óto'mətən | *s.* autômato

automobile | ó'təməbil | *s. a.* automóvel

autonomous | óto'nəməs | *a.* autônomo; independente

autonomy | óto'nəmī |*s.* autonomia; independência

autopsy | ó'təpsī |*s.* autópsia, necropsia

autumn | ó'təm |*s.* outono

auxiliary | ógzi'līərī | *a.* auxiliar; suplementar

avail | əveyl' |*s.* proveito. **-of a.** proveitoso, útil / *vt.* ajudar, valer / *vi.* ser útil, ser proveitoso

available | əvey'ləbəl | *a.* disponível; utilizável; acessível; à venda avalanche | a'vəlʌnš | *s.* avalancha, alude

avarice | a'vəris | *s.* avareza, sovinice; cobiça

avaricious | avəri'śəs |*a.* avarento, avaro; cobiçoso

avenge | əvenj' | *vt.* vingar

avenger | əven'jə | *s.* vingador

avenue | a'vəniu | *s.* avenida; alameda, aléia

aver | əvE' | *vt.* afirmar, asseverar, declarar

average | a'vərij | *s.* média. **-on the a.** em média / *a.* médio, mediano; medíocre

averse | əvES | *a.* contrário, avesso; oposto, adverso; relutante; hostil

aversion | əvE'jən | *s.* aversão, repugnância; relutância, má disposição

avert | əvEt' | *vt.* desviar, afastar; impedir, evitar

aviation | eyvīey'śən | *s.* aviação

aviator | eyvīey'tə | *s.* aviador

avid | a'vid | *a.* ávido, sôfrego; voraz

avidity | avi'ditī | *s.* avidez, sofreguidão; voracidade; cobiça

avocado | əvowka'dow | *s.* abacate; abacateiro

avoid | əvoyd' | *vt.* evitar, esquivar-se de; abster-se de; impedir; (jur.) invalidar

avoidable | əvoy'dəbəl |*a.* evitável

avow | əvaw' | *vt.* confessar, reconhecer; declarar, manifestar; manter, sustentar

avowal | əvow'əl | *s.* confissão, reconhecimento; declaração

await | əweyt' | *vt.* esperar, aguardar; estar reservado

awake | əweyk' | *a.* acordado, desperto / *vi.* acordar, despertar. **-to lie a.** passar a noite em claro. **-to a. to** inteirar-se de

awaken | əwey'kən | *vt. vi.* despertar, acordar; excitar, estimular, provocar

awakening | əwey'kəning | *s.* despertar, acordar

award | əwód' | *s.* (jur.) decisão, sentença; recompensa, prêmio; condecoração; adjudicação / *vt.* adjudicar; conceder, conferir

aware | əwe'ə | *a.* ciente, sabedor, cônscio, inteirado. **-to be a. of** estar a par de, saber

awash | əwoś | *adv.* à mercê das ondas; na superfície, à flor d'água, à tona; inundado, invadido pela água

away | əwey' | *adv.* longe; ausente, fora; à distância. **-far a.** muito longe. **-to go a.** ir-se embora. **-to run a.** fugir. **-to throw a.** atirar fora. **-straight a.** imediatamente, já. **-to send a.** mandar embora. **-to take a.** levar para longe

awe | ó' | *s.* admiração, assombro; temor reverencial

awestruck | ó'strâk | *a.* atemorizado; pasmado

awful | ó'fəl |*a.* terrível, horrível, espantoso

awfully | ó'fəlī | *adv.* terrivelmente, horrivelmente, espantosamente, medonhamente

awkward | ó'kwəd | *a.* desajeitado, desastrado; canhestro, sem graça; embaraçado; deselegante; difícil (problema, situação, questão)

awning | ó'ning | *s.* toldo

awry | əray' | *adv.* torto, de esguelha; errado, mal

axe, ax | aks' | *s.* machado

axis | ak'sis | *s.* eixo

axle | ak'səl | *s.* eixo (de roda)

ay, aye | ay' | *s.* resposta ou voto afirmativo / *adv.* (náut.) sim senhor

azure | ey'jə | *s.* azul-celeste, azul do céu

B

B, b | bı' | *s.* b; (maiúsc., mús.) si

baa | bA' | *s.* balido / *vi.* balir, balar

babble | ba'bəl | *s.* murmúrio, balbucio; tagarelice, conversa fiada; rumorejo, sussurro / *vi.* murmurar, balbuciar; tagarelar, palrar; rumorejar

baboon | bəbʊn' | *s.* babuíno

baby | bey'bī | *s.* bebê, nenê, neném / *a.* de criança; pequeno, recém-nascido

baby-sitter | bey'bīsitə | *s.* moça que cuida de criança (na ausência dos pais)

bachelor | ba'šələ | *s.* solteiro, celibatário; bacharel

Bachelor of Arts | ba'sələovʌts | *s.* (*abrev.* **B.A.**) Bacharel em Humanidades

bacillus | bəsi'ləs | *s.* bacilo

back | bak' | *s.* costas, dorso; parte traseira ou posterior; fundo; reverso; espaldar de cadeira; (desp.) zagueiro, beque / *a.* posterior, traseiro / *adv.* atrás, para trás; de volta; outra vez / *vt.* apoiar, dar apoio (causa, negócio etc.); apostar em (cavalo de corrida) / *vi.* recuar, retroceder, mover para trás. **-at the b. of** por detrás de. **-to come b.**, **to go b.** voltar. **-to get b.** voltar, chegar: recobrar. **-to give b.** devolver. **-to call someone b.** chamar alguém de volta, mandar voltar. **-to draw b.** recuar, retirar-se. **-two years b.** há dois anos. **-b. and forth** para trás e para diante. **-sometime b.** há algum tempo. **-to look b.** olhar para trás. **-to be b.** estar de volta. **-on one's b.** deitado de costas, indefeso

backbite | bak'bayt | *vi.* falar mal, falar pelas costas; caluniar

backbiter | bak'baytə | *s.* maldizente, difamador

backbiting | bak'bayting | *s.* maledicência, difamação

backbone | bak'bown | *s.* espinha dorsal, coluna vertebral. **-to the b.** até a medula dos ossos, inteiramente

backchat | bak'šat | *s.* (coloq.) insolência

back-door | bak'də | *s.* porta traseira

background | bak'grawnd | *s.* fundo, último plano; antecedentes, passado; ambiente, meio, origens; base, experiência, formação

backing | ba'king | *s.* proteção, apoio; patrocínio; forro, fundo; reserva, suplemento; reforço

backside | bak'sayd | *s.* traseiro, nádegas

backslider | bak'slaydə | *s.* apóstata; renegado; relapso, reincidente

backstairs | bakste'əz | *s.* escada de serviço / *a.* secreto, clandestino

backward | bak'wəd | *a.* para trás; às avessas; atrasado, retrógrado / *adv.* para trás; em decadência, retrospectivamente

backward motion | bak'wəd mow'šən | *s.* retrocesso, marcha à ré

backwardness | bak'wədnes | *s.* hesitação, relutância; atraso, ignorância

backwards | bak'wədz | *adv.* para trás

backwater | bak'wótə | *s.* remanso de rio

backwoods | bak'wudz | *spl.* sertão, floresta; interior, roça, região remota backyard | baki̇́Ad' | s. quintal, pátio interno

bacon | bey'kən | s. toicinho de fumeiro. -to bring home the b. tirar a sorte grande. -to save one's b. fugir, salvar a pele

bacteriology | baktərīo'ləjĭ | s. bacteriologia

bacterium | bakte'riəm | s. (pl. bacteria) bactéria

bad | bad' | a. mau, ruim; estragado, deteriorado; nocivo; malvado; vicioso. -to feel b. estar pesaroso, sentir-se indisposto

bad debt | bad'debt | s. dívida incobrável

bad form | bad'fóm | s. má educação, descortesia

badge | baj' | s. emblema, insígnia, distintivo; símbolo / vt. conferir distintivo ou insígnia a

badger | ba'jə | s. texugo / vt. importunar, atormentar

bad language | bad'langwij | s. linguagem grosseira

badly | bad'lĭ | adv. mal; insuficientemente; gravemente. -to need b. necessitar muito. -to be b. off ter pouco dinheiro. -to be b. off for ter grande necessidade de

badness | bad'nes | s. maldade, ruindade; má qualidade

bad-tempered | badtem'pərd | a. mal-humorado

bad ways | bad'weyz | spl. maus costumes

baffle | ba'fəl | vt. frustrar, fazer malograr; zombar de. -to b. description ser impossível de descrever / vi. lutar inutilmente

baffling | baf'ling | a. frustrante; desconcertante; obscuro, complicado

bag | bag' | s. saco, saca; bolsa; maleta. -to let the cat out of the b. revelar involuntariamente um segredo

baggage | ba'gij | s. bagagem

baggy | ba'gĭ | a. bambo, frouxo,

balofo, flácido

bagpipe | bag'payp | s. gaita de foles, cornamusa

bail | beyl' | s. fiança. -to go b. for ser fiador / vt. prestar fiança; pôr em liberdade sob fiança / vi. -to b. out (aer.) saltar de pára-quedas

bailiff | bey'lif | s. meirinho, oficial de diligências; intendente; bailio

bairn | be'ən | s. (Esc.) criança

bait | beyt' | s. isca, engodo; tentação / vt. iscar, engodar; tentar; perseguir, acossar; irritar, atormentar

bake | beyk' | vt. assar ou cozer (forno)

baker | bey'kə | s. padeiro

baker's dozen | bey'kəzdowzən | s. (coloq.) dúzia de frade

bakery | bey'kərĭ | s. padaria

balance | ba'ləns | s. balança; equilíbrio; saldo, balanço, diferença entre débito e crédito. -to have a b. in the bank ter saldo no banco / vt. pesar; ponderar, comparar; compensar; (com.) dar balanço em / vi. equilibrar-se; vacilar

balcony | bal'kənĭ | s. sacada; balcão de teatro

bald | bóld' | a. calvo, careca; escalvado. -as b. as a coot calvo como uma bola de bilhar

balderdash | ból'dədaś | s. disparate, lengalenga

bald lie | bóld'lay | s. mentira deslavada

baldness | bóld'nes | s. calvície; aridez, insipidez

bald spot | bóld'spot | s. calva

bale | beyl' | s. fardo, volume de mercadoria / vt. enfardar, embalar; = bail

baleful | beyl'ful | a. nocivo, daninho, pernicioso, maléfico

ball | ból' | s. bola; bala (esp. de canhão); baile; novelo de lã / a. esférico, em forma de bola

ballad | ba'ləd | s. balada; canção

popular, poesia narrativa, romance

ballast | ba'ləst | *s.* lastro

ball-bearing | bólbe'əring | *s.* rolamento de esferas

ballet | ba'ley | *s.* balé; bailado; corpo de baile

balloon | balʊn' | *s.* balão

ballot | ba'lət | *s.* cédula eleitoral; votação, sufrágio / *vi.* votar

ballot-box | ba'lətboks | *s.* urna eleitoral

balm | bʌm' | *s.* bálsamo; ungüento; alívio, lenitivo

balsam | bal'səm | *s.* bálsamo; ungüento, pomada

balustrade | ba'ləstreyd | *s.* balaustrada

bamboo | bambu' | *s.* bambu

bamboozle | bambʊ'zəl | *vt.* lograr, enganar, mistificar

ban | ban' | *s.* proibição, interdito, interdição / *vt.* proibir. proscrever

banal | bənal' | *a.* banal, trivial, corriqueiro

banana | bənʌ'nə | *s.* banana; bananeira

band | band' | *s.* banda, faixa; bando; (mús.) banda / *vt.* organizar em bando / *vi.* **-to b. together** associar-se, reunir-se; coligar-se; conspirar

bandage | ban'dij | *s.* bandagem, atadura; venda (para os olhos) / *vt.* aplicar bandagem ou atadura a

bandit | ban'dit | *s.* bandido, bandoleiro, salteador

band saw | band'só | *s.* serra de fita

band stand | band'stand | *s.* coreto

bandy | ban'dĩ | *a.* arqueado (pernas) / *vt.* jogar de um lado para outro; alternar; altercar, discutir

bane | beyn' | *s.* ruína, desgraça, perdição; veneno

baneful | beyn'ful | *a.* pernicioso, nocivo, funesto

bang | bang' | *s.* estrondo, panca-

da ruidosa, detonação; baque / *vt.* fechar ruidosamente. **-to b. on** golpear ruidosamente / *interj.* bum!

bangle | bang'gəl | *s.* bracelete

banish | ba'niš | *vt.* banir, expulsar, desterrar; excluir

banishment | ba'niśmənt | *s.* banimento, degredo; exclusão

banister | ba'nistə | *s.* corrimão de escada

bank | bank' | *s.* (com.) banco; margem (rio, lago etc.), beira, borda; ladeira, encosta; outeiro, monte / *vt.* depositar em banco. **-to b. on** confiar em

banker | ban'kə | *s.* banqueiro

bank holiday | bankho'lidey | *s.* feriado bancário

banking | bank'ing | *s.* operações bancárias; construção de barreiras / *a.* bancário

bank rate | bank'reyt | *s.* taxa de desconto

bankrupt | bank'rəpt | *a.* falido, insolvente

bankruptcy | bank'rəptsĩ | *s.* falência, bancarrota; ruína

banner | ba'nə | *s.* estandarte, bandeira

banns | banz' | *spl.* proclamas de casamento, banhos. **-to publish the b.** ler os proclamas. **-to forbid the b.** impugnar casamento

banquet | ban'kwit | *s.* banquete

banter | ban'tə | *s.* troça, gracejo, zombaria

baptism | bap'tizəm | *s.* batismo

baptize | baptayz' | *vt.* batizar

bar | bʌ' | *s.* barra; tranca; lingote; barreira, impedimento; advocacia, os advogados; barra, listra; bar; (mús.) barra / *prep.* exceto, salvo. **-b. none** sem exceção / *vt.* trancar; excluir, pôr de parte

barb | bʌb' | *s.* farpa (de flecha, anzol, arame farpado)

barbarian | bʌbe'ərĩan | *s.a.* bárbaro; ignorante

barbarism | bʌ'bərizəm | *s.* barbárie, barbarismo

barbarity | bʌba'ritĭ | s. barbaridade, brutalidade

barbarous | bʌ'bərəs | a. bárbaro, brutal

barbecue | bʌ'bikĭu | s. churrasco; grelha, fogão em que se faz churrasco / vt. fazer churrasco

barbed | bʌ'bid | a. farpado; (fig.) mordaz

barbed wire | bʌ'bidwayə | s. arame farpado

barber | bʌ'bə | s. barbeiro

barber's shop bʌ'bəʃop | s. barbearia

bard | bʌd | s. bardo, poeta

bare | be'ə | a. nu, despido; árido; deserto; desguarnecido, mal provido; destituído; simples, rudimentar; pobre, indigente, parco. -b. **hands** sem armas; sem ferramentas / vt. desnudar, descobrir

bareback | be'əbak | a. em pêlo, sem arreios / vi. montar em pêlo

barefoot, barefooted | be'əfut(id) | a. descalço

bareheaded | beəhe'did | a. adv. descoberto, sem chapéu

barely | be'əlĭ | adv. apenas, mal

bareness | be'ənes | s. nudez; aridez; pobreza

bargain | bʌ'gin | s. ajuste; transação, negócio; pechincha, boa compra. -**into the b.** de quebra, ainda por cima / vt. negociar, regatear; ajustar, estipular. -**to b. away** ter prejuízo num negócio / vi. negociar; chegar a um acordo; pechinchar

bargaining | bʌ'gining | s. regateio

bargain sale | bʌ'ginseyl | s. liquidação

barge | bʌʤ' | s. barcaça, batelão / vt. transportar em barcaça / vi. mover-se ou entrar pesadamente. -**to b. in** irromper. -**to b. into** intrometer-se (em conversa)

bark | bʌk' | s. casca de árvore; latido; (poét.) barco, pequeno veleiro / vi. latir, ladrar

barley | bʌ'lĭ | s. cevada

barm | bʌm' | s. levedura

barmy | bʌ'mĭ | a. que fermenta, espumoso; (gír.) amalucado

barn | bʌn' | s. celeiro; paiol; estábulo, cocheira

barnacle | bʌ'nəkəl | s. craca (de rochedos ou navios); pessoa importuna

barnyard | bʌn'ïʌd | s. terreiro, quintal

barometer | baro'mitə | s. barômetro

baron | ba'rən | s. barão

baronet | ba'rənet | s. baronete

barrack | ba'rək | vt. vi. vaiar, gritar (espectadores de jogos esportivos)

barracks | ba'rəks | spl. caserna, quartel

barrage | ba'rʌj | s. barragem, açude, dique; (mil.) barragem

barrel | ba'rəl | s. barril; barrica; pipa; cano (de arma de fogo)

barren | ba'rən | a. estéril; árido; improdutivo

barrenness | ba'rənnes | s. esterilidade; aridez; improdutividade

barricade | ba'rikeyd | s. barricada / vt. barricar

barrier | ba'rĭə | s. barreira; obstáculo; paliçada

barring | bʌ'ring | prep. exceto, salvo, excetuando

barrister | ba'ristə | s. advogado, causídico

barrow | ba'row | s. carrinho de mão; (arqueol.) túmulo; porco castrado

barter | bʌ'tə | s. troca, escambo, permuta / vt. trocar, permutar / vi. negociar por meio de trocas

base | beys' | s. base, alicerce / a. vil, baixo / vt. basear, fundar

baseball | beys'ból | s. beisebol

baseless | beys'les | a. sem base, sem fundamento

basement | beys'mənt | s. porão

baseness | beys'nes | s. baixeza, vileza

bash | baʃ' | s. pancada forte / vt. bater; atacar violentamente

bashful | baś'ful | *a.* tímido, acanhado, envergonhado, retraído; contrafeito

basic | bey'sik | *a.* básico

basil | bey'zil | *s.* manjericão

basin | bey'sən | *s.* bacia; tigela; lago artificial; doca seca; enseada

basis | bey'sis | *s.* base, alicerce, fundação

bask | bᴀsk' | *vi.* aquecer-se ao sol, tomar sol

basket | bᴀs'kit | *s.* cesto; cesta

basketball | bᴀs'kitból | *s.* basquetebol

basket chair | bᴀs'kitšeə | *s.* cadeira de vime

basketwork | bᴀs'kitwᴇk | *s.* obra de vime, cestaria

Basque | bask' | *s. a.* basco, vascongado

bass | bes' | *s.* perca

bass | beys' | *s.* (mús.) baixo; contrabaixo

bastard | bᴀs'təd | *s. a.* bastardo; (fig.) qualquer coisa irregular ou inferior; (fig.) pessoa ou coisa desprezível

bastion | bas'tĭən | *s.* bastião, baluarte

bat | bat' | *s.* morcego; pá (críquete); bastão (beisebol e outros jogos). -off his own b. por sua própria iniciativa. -to have bats in the belfry ter macaquinhos no sótão / *vi.* rebater (com pá, bastão etc.); espancar, surrar

batch | bas' | *s.* fornada; lote, leva, grupo, bando

bath | bᴀϑ' | *s.* banho. -to have a b. tomar banho

bathe | beyδ' | *vt.* lavar, banhar, mergulhar em banho; inundar, alagar / *vi.* banhar-se, lavar-se; tomar banho de mar, de rio etc.

bather | bey'δə | *s.* banhista

bathing | bey'δing | *s.* banho / *a.* balneário; que se banha

bathing beauty | bey'δingbĭu'tĭ | *s.* mulher bela em traje de banhista

bathing-suit | bey'δingsʋt | *s.* maiô ou calção de banho

bathrobe | baϑ'rowb | *s.* roupão de banho

bathroom | baϑ'rum | *s.* banheiro, quarto de banho

bathtub | bᴀϑ'tâb | *s.* banheira

baton | ba'tən | *s.* (mil.) bastão; (mús.) batuta

battalion | bəta'lĭən | *s.* batalhão

batten | ba'tən | *s.* tábua em grosso; ripa, sarrafo / *vt.* cevar, engordar / *vi.* prosperar; engordar, medrar

batter | ba'tə | *s.* massa mole, pasta / *vt.* bater, sovar, espancar; demolir

battering-ram | ba'təringram | *s.* aríete

battery | ba'tərĭ | *s.* (eletr., mil., mús.) bateria; trem de cozinha

battle | ba'təl | *s.* batalha. -to do ou to join b. entrar em combate / *vi.* combater

battle array | ba'təlarey | *s.* ordem de batalha

battlefield | ba'təlfĭld | *s.* campo de batalha

battlement | ba'təlmənt | *s.* (ger. pl.) ameias, muralhas, parapeito

battleship | ba'təlšip | *s.* couraçado, encouraçado

bauble | bó'bəl | *s.* quinquilharia, bugiganga; bagatela; ninharia

baulk, balk | bók' | *s.* obstáculo; contratempo / *vt.* falhar; impedir, frustrar / *vi.* refugar; rejeitar

bawd | bód' | *s.* alcoviteira, proxeneta

bawdy | bó'dĭ | *a.* obsceno, devasso, indecente

bawl | ból' | *vi.* gritar, berrar, vociferar

bay | bey' | *s.* baía; angra, enseada; louro, loureiro; baia; cavalo baio; latido, ladrido. -at b. acuado, cercado. -to keep at b. manter à distância

bayonet | bey'ənit | *s.* baioneta

bazaar, bazar | bəzA' | *s.* bazar; quermesse de caridade

be | bɪ | *vi.* ser; estar; existir; acontecer; ficar, permanecer; realizar-se. **-to b. thirsty** estar com sede. **-to b. able** poder

beach | bɪs' | *s.* praia

beacon | bɪ'kən | *s.* farol; bóia; bóia-farol; sinal

bead | bɪd' | *s.* conta; gota, baga; massa de mira

beak | bɪk' | *s.* bico

beaker | bɪ'kə | *s.* copo de boca larga; taça grande

beam | bɪm' | *s.* viga, trave; raio de luz; (rád.) feixe direcional / *vt.* irradiar, emitir / *vi.* brilhar; sorrir, estar radiante

beaming | bɪ'ming | *a.* radiante, brilhante

bean | bɪn' | *s.* feijão; favá; vagem; grão, semente

bear | be'ə | *s.* urso / *vt.* suportar; suster, sustentar; levar; agüentar, tolerar; produzir; render; parir, dar à luz. **-to b. in mind** lembrar-se, ter presente. **-to b. a grudge** guardar rancor. **-to b. arms** prestar serviço militar. **-to b. a hand** prestar auxílio, dar a mão. **-to b. down** deɪrotar; sobrepujar. **-to b. off** ganhar, conquistar prêmio. **-to b. oneself** comportar-se. **-to b. witness** prestar testemunho

bearable | be'ərəbəl | *a.* suportável, tolerável

beard | bɪ'əd | *s.* barba / *vt.* agarrar pela barba; pôr barba em; desafiar / *vi.* criar barba, barbar

bearer | be'ərə | *s.* portador

bearing | be'əring | *s.* paciência, poder de agüentar; comportamento, conduta; porte, maneira; referência, relação; (náut.) rumo, orientação; (mec.) mancal, cochinete. **-to lose one's bearings** desnortear-se, desorientar-se

beast | bɪst' | *s.* animal, besta; rês, gado

beastly | bɪst'lɪ | *a.* bestial, animalesco

beat | bɪt' | *s.* batida; pulsação, batimento; batida (caça); (mús.) compasso; toque de tambor; batida policial; furo jornalístico / *vt.* bater; surrar, espancar; superar, ultrapassar; derrotar; (mús.) marcar o compasso; bater, palpitar (coração). **-to b. about the bush** usar de rodeios, divagar, vacilar. **-to b. down** abater, abaixar; regatear. **-to b. back** rechaçar. **-to b. the devil** ser extraordinário, ser incrível. **-can you b. it?** será possível? **-it beats me** fico perplexo. **-b. it!** caia fora!, suma-se daqui!

beating | bɪ'ting | *s.* pulsação, batimento; surra, sova; derrota

beautiful | bɪu'tiful | *a.* lindo, belo, formoso

beautify | bɪu'tifay | *vt.* embelezar, ataviar

beauty | bɪu'tɪ | *s.* beleza, formosura; mulher bela

beauty parlour | bɪu'tɪpAlə | *s.* salão de beleza

beauty sleep | bɪu'tɪslɪp | *s.* sono antes da meia-noite

beauty spot | bɪu'tɪspot | *s.* pinta, sinal (na cútis); recanto pitoresco, atração turística

beaver | bɪ'və | *s.* castor

becalmed | bɪkAmd' | *a.* em calmaria, parado

because | bɪkoz' | *conj.* porque. **-b. of** por causa de

beckon | be'kən | *vt. vi.* acenar, chamar com aceno

become | bikâm' | *vt.* convir, ficar bem / *vi.* tornar-se, vir a ser, converter-se em, fazer-se

becoming | bikâ'ming | *a.* adequado, conveniente; decente, decoroso; que assenta bem; elegante, gracioso

bed | bed' | *s.* cama, leito; fundo do mar; leito de rio; camada; base. **-b. and board** cama e comida (pensão); vida conjugal.

-separation from b. and board
separação de corpos. -to go to
b. deitar-se

bedbug | bed'bʌg |s. percevejo

bedding | be'ding | s. colchão e
roupa de cama; leito, camada
que serve de base

bedeck | bidek' | vt. adornar,
enfeitar

bedevil | bide'vəl | vt. infernizar,
atormentar; baralhar, confun-
dir; corromper

bedlam | bed'ləm | s. hospício,
manicômio; balbúrdia

bedraggled | bidra'gəld | a. enla-
meado, molhado, ensopado;
desgrenhado; maltrapilho

bedridden | bed'ridən |a. acama-
do; gasto; decrépito, caduco;
entrevado, inválido

bedroom | bed'rʊm |s. quarto de
dormir

bedside | bed'sayd | s. cabeceira
(esp. de doente)

bedstead | bed'sted | s. armação
de cama

bee | bi' | s. abelha; mutirão. -to
have a b. in one's bonnet ter um
"parafuso frouxo"

beech | biš' |s. faia

beef | bif' | s. carne de boi ou de
vaca

beefeater | bifi'tə | s. carnívoro,
comedor de carne; (coloq.)
guarda da Torre de Londres

beefsteak | bif'steyk |s. bife

beef tea | bif'ti |s. caldo de carne
reduzido

beefy | bi'fi | a. carnudo, muscu-
loso; bovino, impassível, sólido

beer | bi'ə |s. cerveja

beet | bit' | s. beterraba

beetle | bɛ'təl | s. besouro, esca-
ravelho; marreta, macete

beetle-browed | bɛ'təlbrawd | a.
de sobrancelhas hirsutas; car-
rancudo, cenhudo, sombrio,
casmurro

befall | bifól' | vi. suceder, acon-
tecer, ocorrer

befit | bifit' | vt. convir, ser ade-

quado para

befitting | bifi'ting | a. adequa-
do, que cai bem

before | bifó'ə | adv. à frente.
adiante; antes / prep. diante de,
à frente de; antes de; perante,
na presença de

beforehand | bifó'hand |adv. de
antemão, com antecipação

beforelong | bifó'əlong |adv. em
breve

befriend | bifrend' | vt. ajudar,
proteger, amparar; tornar-se
amigo de

beg | beg' |vt. rogar, suplicar, im-
plorar; pedir licença para / vi.
mendigar

beget | biget' | vt. gerar, engen-
drar, procriar; produzir

beggar | be'gə | s. mendigo / vt.
empobrecer, arruinar; ultrapassar. -to b. description ser
indescritível

beggary | be'gərī | s. mendicida-
de; pobreza extrema

begin | bigin' | vt. começar, ini-
ciar, principiar / vi. começar,
iniciar-se

beginner | bigi'nə | s. iniciador;
novato, principiante

beginning| bigi'ning |s. começo,
princípio; origem

begrudge | bigrâj' | vt. invejar;
dar de má vontade

beguile | bigayl' | vt. iludir, enga-
nar; seduzir

behalf | bihʌf' | s. favor, interes-
se. -in b. of em nome de; a favor
de

behave | biheyv' | vi. comportar-
se, portar-se, conduzir-se; tra-
balhar (máquina)

behaviour, behavior | bihey'viə |
s. comportamento, conduta

behead | bihed' | vt. decapitar,
cortar a cabeça

behind | bihaynd' | adv. atrás,
detrás, nas costas. -to b. estar
atrasado / prep. atrás de, detrás
de; após

behindhand | bihaynd'hand |
adv. atrasado, com atraso

behold | bǐhowld' | vt. contemplar; ver, avistar / interj. eis aqui, eis que; veja!

behove, behoove | bǐhowv' behʋv' | vt. caber a, competir a, incumbir a

being | bɪ'ing | s. ser, ente, entidade, criatura; existência; natureza, essência

belated | bǐley'tid | a. atrasado, retardado; surpreendido pelo entardecer

belch | belš' | vt. vi. arrotar; vomitar

beleaguer | bǐlɪ'gǝ | vt. sitiar, assediar, cercar

beleaguered | bǐlɪ'gǝd | a. sitiado, assediado, cercado

belfry | bel'frī | s. campanário, torre de sinos

Belgian | bel'jǝn | s. a. belga

belie | bǐlay' | vt. desmentir, contradizer; caluniar; não corresponder a (expectativa); faltar a (promessa)

belief | bilɪf' | s. crença; fé, confiança; convicção

believe | bilɪv' | vt. vi. crer, acreditar; julgar, supor. -to make b. fazer crer. -to b. in crer em

believer | bilɪ'vǝ | s. (relig.) crente, fiel

belittle | bǐli'tǝl | vt. desdenhar; subestimar, depreciar; menosprezar

bell | bel' | s. sino; sineta; campainha; guizo. -to ring the b. acertar em cheio; acudir à lembrança

bellboy | bel'boy | s: (EUA) mensageiro (de hotel etc.)

belligerent | bǝli'jǝrǝnt | s. beligerante

bellow | be'low | vt. vi. berrar, gritar, rugir

bellows | be'lowz | s. fole

bellringer | bel'ringǝ | s. sineiro

belly | be'lī | s. barriga, ventre, pança; bojo / vt. vi. -to b. out enfunar-se; formar bojo

belong | bilong' | vi. pertencer a; ser próprio de; competir a, ser da obrigação de

belongings | bilon'gingz | spl. bens, haveres, pertences; coisas, roupas, bagagem

beloved | bilǝvd' | a. amado, querido, muito estimado

below | bilow' | adv. abaixo, debaixo, embaixo; para baixo / prep. debaixo de, por baixo de, abaixo de

belt | belt' | s. cinto, cinturão; correia; faixa, cinta; zona, região / vt. cingir

bemoan | bǐmown' | vt. lamentar / vi. lamentar-se

bench | benš' | s. banco; (jur.) o tribunal, os juízes

bend | bend' | s. curva; meandro, volta / vt. curvar, vergar, dobrar; submeter, abaixar a cabeça / vi. curvar-se, vergar-se; submeter-se; pender, dobrar

beneath | binɪϑ' | prep. sob, debaixo de, abaixo de, por baixo de; inferior a. -b. contempt abaixo da crítica

benediction | benidik'šǝn | s. bênção; ação de graças; graça divina

benefaction | benifak'šǝn | s. boa ação, ato caridoso; doação; donativo

benefactor | benifak'tǝ | s. benfeitor; doador

benefice | be'nifis | s. benefício eclesiástico; domínio feudal, feudo

beneficial | benifi'šǝl | a. benéfico, proveitoso, salutar

beneficient | benifi'šǝnt | a. beneficente; caritativo

benefit | be'nifit | s. benefício, proveito, vantagem / vt. beneficiar, favorecer / vi. ser beneficiado

benevolence | bǝne'vǝlǝns | s. benevolência, bondade

benevolent | bǝne'vǝlǝnt | a. benevolente, bondoso, benévolo, benigno, caridoso

benighted | bǐnay'tid | a. surpreendido pela noite; ignorante, inculto

benign | binayn' | *a.* benigno, benévolo

bent | bent' | *s.* pendor, queda, tendência / *a.* curvo, flexionado, envergado, torto

bequeath | bikwɪð' | *vt.* legar, transmitir por herança, deixar

bequest | bikwest' | *s.* legado, doação testamentária

berate | bĭreyt' | *vt.* admoestar, repreender, ralhar

bereaved | bĭrɪvd' | *s. a.* aflito, consternado, desolado

bereavement | bĭrɪv'mənt | *s.* aflição, desolação

bereft | bĭreft' | *a.* privado, despojado, roubado

beret | be'rey | *s.* boina

berry | be'rī | *s.* baga

berserk | bE'sEk | *a.* furioso, frenético, louco

berth | bEϑ' | *s.* beliche (em navio); leito (em carro dormitório); (náut.) ancoradouro, atracadouro

beseech | bɪsɪs' | *vt.* rogar, implorar, suplicar

beset | bĭset' | *a.* cercado, assediado / *vt.* assediar, acossar, cercar

besetting | bĭse'ting | *a.* atacante; insistente

besetting sin | bĭse'tingsin | *s.* pecado ou falta que se pratica frequentemente

beside | bĭsayd' | *prep.* ao lado de, junto de. **-b. the point** fora de propósito, irrelevante. **-b. oneself** fora de si, furioso

besides | bĭsaydz' | *adv.* além disso, fora disso, também / *prep.* além de; salvo, a não ser, senão, fora de

besiege | bĭsɪj' | *vt.* cercar, sitiar, assediar

besmirch | bĭsmEs̆ | *vt.* manchar, enodoar, macular

bespatter | bĭspa'tə | *vt.* salpicar, manchar

best | best' | *a. adv.* o melhor. **-at**

b. quando muito. **-to make one's b.** fazer o possível. **-to the b. of my knowledge** segundo creio, que eu saiba. **-to make the b. of a bad job** fazer das tripas coração. **-as b. as one can** da melhor forma possível

bestial | bes'tĭəl | *a.* bestial, brutal

bestir | bistE' | *vr.* mexer-se, mover-se; atarefar-se

best man | best'mən | *s.* padrinho de casamento

bestow | bistow' | *vt.* conceder, outorgar

best seller | best'selə | *s.* livro de grande vendagem; autor desses livros

bet | bet' | *s.* aposta / *vt.* apostar

betide | bĭtayd' | *vt.* acontecer, suceder. **-whatever b.** aconteça o que acontecer / *vi.* acontecer a, suceder a

betimes | bĭtaymz' | *adv.* cedo

betoken | bĭtow'kən | *vt.* pressagiar, anunciar; indicar, mostrar; exprimir

betray | bĭtrey' | *vt.* trair; denunciar; revelar

betrayal | bĭtrey'əl | *s.* traição; denúncia; revelação; inconfidência

betrothal | bĭtrow'ðəl | *s.* esponsais, contrato de casamento

betrothed | bitrowôd' | *a.* noivo; noiva

better | be'tə | *a. adv.* melhor, preferível. **-to get b.** melhorar. **-so much the b.** tanto melhor. **-b. off** em melhor situação. **-to know b.** estar mais bem informado. **-b. and b.** cada vez melhor. **-to get the b. of** levar a melhor / *vt.* melhorar

better half | be'təhaf | *s.* (coloq.) cara-metade, esposa

betterment | be'təmənt | *s.* melhoramento, aperfeiçoamento; melhoria; benfeitoria

between | bitwɪn' | *adv.* no meio, no intervalo. **-far b.** com longos intervalos / *prep.* entre, por entre. **-b. you and me** cá entre nós.

**-b. the devil and the deep blue
sea** entre a espada e a parede
beverage | be'vəriĵ |*s.* bebida
bevy | be'vī |*.s.* bando (de aves);
grupo (de moças)
bewail | biweyl' |*vt.* lamentar
beware | biwe'ə |*vi.* tomar cuida-
do, precaver-se / *interj.*
cuidado!
bewilder | biwil'də |*vt.* confun-
dir, desnortear
bewildering | biwil'dəring |*a.*
desnorteante; desconcertante;
estonteante
bewilderment | bīwil'dəmənt |*s.*
atordoamento; espanto, per-
plexidade
bewitch | bīwiš' |*vt.* enfeitiçar,
encantar, fascinar
beyond | bīyond' |*adv.* além,
mais longe / *prep.* além de, do
outro lado de; acima de, superior a; depois de; fora de. **-b.
doubt** fora de dúvida. **-b. dispute** indiscutível. **-b. compare**
sem comparação. **-b. belief** in-
crível
bias | bay'əs |*s.* viés; linha
oblíqua; tendência; preconcei-
to / *vt.* enviesar; predispor; in-
fluenciar
biased | bay'əst |*a.* tendencioso,
parcial
bib | bib' |*s.* babador; peitilho de
avental
Bible | bay'bəl |*s.* bíblia
Biblical | bi'blikəl |*a.* bíblico
bibliography | biblī'o'grəfī |*s.*
bibliografia
bicker | bi'kə |*vi.* altercar, discu-
tir; brigar
bickering | bi'kəring |*s.* alter-
cação, disputa
bicycle | bay'sikəl |*s.* bicicleta
bid | bid' |*s.* lanço, oferta (em
leilão) / *vt.* fazer oferta (em
leilão); dar (boas vindas,
adeus); mandar, ordenar; con-
vidar; anunciar. **-to b. farewell
to** dizer adeus. **-to b. defiance**
desafiar. **-to b. against** cobrir a
oferta (leilão)

bidding | bi'ding |*s.* lanços, ofer-
tas, licitação
bide | bayd' |*vt.* esperar, aguar-
dar. **-to b. one's time** esperar a
melhor oportunidade, aguar-
dar o momento propício
bier | bɪ'ə |*s.* esquife, ataúde; car-
reta fúnebre
big | big' |*a.* grande; volumoso,
corpulento; importante; arrogante. **-to talk b.** contar vanta-
gem. **-to think b.** ser ambicioso
bigamist | bi'gəmist |*s.* bígamo
bigamy | bi'gəmī |*s.* bigamia
big-boned | big'bownd |*a.* os-
sudo
big game | big'geym |*s.* caça
grossa
big money | bigmâ'nī |*s.* grande
soma, alto lucro
big name | big'neym |*s.* pessoa
famosa
bigot | bi'gət |*s.* fanático,
intolerante
bigotry | bi'gətrī |*s.* intolerân-
cia, fanatismo
big shot | big'šot |*s.* pessoa im-
portante, mandachuva
bike | bayk' |*s.* (coloq.) bicicleta
bile | bayl' |*s.* bile, bílis; mau hu-
mor, cólera
bilge | bilĵ' |*s.* (náut.) fundo de
embarcação; (gír.) disparate,
bobagem
bilingual | bayling'wəl |*a.*
bilíngüe
bilious | bi'lɪəs |*a.* bilioso
bilk | bilk' |*vt.* desapontar; tra-
pacear; lograr
bill | bil' |*s.* conta, fatura; cédu-
la; anúncio, cartaz; projeto de
lei; bico de ave. **-to fill the b.** satisfazer, dar conta do recado,
aprovar
billet | bi'lit |*s.* (mil.) quartel,
acantonamento; emprego; si-
necura / *vt.* aquartelar, alojar
billiards | bi'lɪədz |*spl.* bilhar
billion | bi'lɪən |*s.* trilião; (EUA)
bilião
bill of exchange | bilovekššeynj' |
s. letra de câmbio

bill of fare | bil'offe'ə | s. cardápio

billow| bi'low {s. vaga, vagalhão / vi. formar vagalhões, encapelar-se

billy | bi'lĭ | s. cassetete

billy-goat | bi'lĭgowt | s. bode

bin| bin' | s. caixa, arca; depósito

bind | baynd' | vt. atar, amarrar; juntar, ligar; vincular; encadernar; pôr atadura. -to b. over obrigar moral ou legalmente

binding | bayn'ding | s. encadernação; atadura / a. que amarra; que compromete ou empenha

binocular | bino'kĭulə bayno'-kĭulə | a. binocular

binoculars | bino'kĭuləz | spl. binóculo

biochemist | bayəke'mist | s. bioquímico

biochemistry | bayəke'mistrĭ | s. bioquímica

biographer | bayo'grəfə | s. biógrafo

biographical | bayəgrə'fikəl | a. biográfico

biography | bayo'grəfĭ | s. biografia

biologist | bayo'ləǰist | s. biólogo

biology| bayo'ləǰi | s. biologia

biopsy | bayop'sĭ | s. (med.) biopsia

biped | bay'ped | s. a. bípede

birch| bēś' | s. bétula, vidoeiro

bird| bēd' | s. pássaro, ave

bird cage | bēd'keyǰ | s. gaiola

bird dog | bēd'dog | s. cão para caça às aves

birdlime| bēd'laym | s. visgo (para apanhar pássaros); engodo, isca

bird of prey | bēd'ovprey | s. ave de rapina

birth | bēϑ' | s. nascimento, origem; princípio, começo; estirpe, linhagem. -to give b. to dar à luz

birth certificate | bēϑ'sətifikit | s. certidão de nascimento

birth control | bēϑkəntrol' | s. controle de natalidade

birthday | bēϑ'dey | s. aniversário natalício

birth pill | bēϑ'pil | s. pílula anticoncepcional

birthplace | bēϑ'pleys | s. lugar de nascimento, lugar de origem, terra natal

birth rate | bēϑ'reyt | s. coeficiente de natalidade

birthright | bēϑ'rayt | s. direito inato, direito de primogenitura

biscuit| bis'kit | s. biscoito, bolacha; biscuit (porcelana)

bishop | bi'śəp | s. bispo

bishopric | bi'śəprik | s. bispado; diocese

bit| bit' | s. pedaço; bocado; momento; freio de cavalo; pua, broca; (inf.) bit. -b. by b. pouco a pouco. -to do one's b. cumprir o dever. -not a b. nem um pouco. -wait a b.! espere um momento, espere aí! -to smash to bits quebrar em pedaços

bitch | bis' | s. cadela; (vulg.) prostituta

bite| bayt' | s. picada; mordedura; bocado, dentada / vt. morder; picar (cobra, inseto); causar dor aguda; roer; corroer (ácido)

biting | bay'ting | a. mordente; mordaz; penetrante; pungente; cáustico

bitter | bi'tə | s. amargo, bíter; amargura / a. amargo; doloroso, penoso; ofensivo, mordaz; rancoroso, implacável. -to the b. end até não poder mais, até a morte / vt. amargar

bitterness | bi'tənes | s. amargura; mordacidade; acrimônia, rancor

bitter pill | bi'təpil | s. fato desagradável, acontecimento penoso

bitumen | bi'tĭumən | s. betume

bivouac | bi'vuak | s. bivaque / vi. bivacar, acampar

blab| blab' | vi. tagarelar, revelar segredos

blabber | bla'bǝ | s. tagarela, falador; pessoa indiscreta

black | blak' | a. preto, negro; escuro; atroz; sujo; funesto. **-inb. and white** por escrito. **-b. and blue** cheio de contusões

black arts | blak'ʌts | s. magia negra

black-beetle | blak'bɛtǝl | s. barata comum

blackberry | blak'bǝrī | s. amora--preta, amora silvestre

blackbird | blak'bɛd | s. melro

blackboard | blak'bód | s. quadro-negro

blackbook | blak'buk | s. lista negra

blacken | bla'kǝn | vt. enegrecer; difamar, caluniar

blackguard | bla'gʌd | s. patife, canalha, cafajeste; pessoa desbocada / a. torpe, indecente / vt. injuriar de maneira torpe

blackhead | blak'hed | s. cravo (na pele); (orn.) negrela; (veter.) amebíase

blackleg | blak'leg | s. trapaceiro (no jogo); fura-greve

black looks | blak'luks | a. hostil, ameaçador

blackmail | blak'meyl | s. chantagem / vt. chantagear

black market | blak'mʌkit | s. mercado negro

blackness | blak'nes | s. negrume, negror; escuridão

black sheep | blak'śıp | s. ovelha ranha; ovelha negra (tb. fig.)

blacksmith | blak'smiϑ | s. ferreiro

bladder | bla'dǝ | s. bexiga

blade | bleyd' | s. lâmina (de faca etc.); instrumento cortante; folha (de grama); pá (de hélice ou remo)

blame | bleym' | s. culpa / vt. acusar, pôr a culpa em, responsabilizar. **-to be not to b.** não merecer censura. **-to put the b. on** acusar, pôr a culpa em

blameless | bleym'les | a. inocente, sem culpa

blanch | blanś' | vt. alvejar (tecido etc.); escaldar (amêndoas, legumes etc.); estanhar (metais)

blancmange | blemonj' | s. manjar branco

bland | bland' | a. brando, suave; gentil; leve, delicado; ameno

blandishments | blan'diśmǝnts | spl. agrados, lisonjas

blank | blank' | s. espaço em branco ou vazio; bilhete branco (loteria); alvo (tiro) / a. vazio, em branco; inexpressivo; perplexo

blank cartridge | blank'kʌtriǰ | s. cartucho de festim

blanket | blan'kit | s. cobertor, manta; manto (neve'etc.)

blank verse | blaɪk'vɛs | s. verso branco

blare | ble'ǝ | s. clangor, som de trombeta / vt. vi. bradar, clamar, gritar

blarney | blʌ'nī | s. adulação, lisonja, lábia

blaspheme | blasfɪm' | vt. vi. blasfemar

blasphemous | blas'fǝmǝs | a. blasfemo; irreverente

blasphemy | blas'fǝmī | s. blasfêmia

blast | blʌst' | s. rajada de vento; detonação; carga de explosivo; deslocamento de ar (de explosão); toque de corneta; clangor. **-at full b.** a todo o vapor, em pleno funcionamento / vt. fazer explodir, dinamitar; arruinar, arrasar; crestar, queimar; praguejar. **-to b. open** rebentar (com explosivos) / interj. **-b. it!, b. you!** dane-se!, raios!

blatant | bley'tǝnt | a. clamoroso, ruidoso; patente, manifesto; espalhafatoso

blaze | bleyz' | s. chama, labareda, fogo; luz brilhante; esplendor; assomo de ira. **-like blazes** furiosamente. **-go to blazes!** vá para o inferno! / vi. arder em

chamas, chamejar; resplande-
cer. -to b. away atirar continua-
mente. -to b. a trail abrir caminho. -to b. up explodir de raiva
blazer | bley'zə | s. casaco espor-
te, japona
bleach | blĭš' | vt. descorar, bran-
quear; alvejar (ao sol)
bleak | blĭk' | a. árido, deserto;
descampado;   desanimador,
sombrio; áspero, rude; gelado
blear(y)-eyed | blĭr'(ĭ)ayd | a. de
vista turva, de olhos cansados
bleat | blĭt' | s. balido / vi. balir
bleed | blĭd' | s. sangria / vt. san-
grar / vi. sangrar, deitar sangue
blemish | ble'mĭš | s. mancha, ja-
ça, falha, defeito
blend | blend' | s. mistura (de fu-
mo etc.); (min.) blenda, esfale-
rita / vt. misturar, combinar
bless | bles' | vt. abençoar, ben-
zer; consagrar; fazer feliz;
louvar
blessed | ble'sid | a. abençoado,
bendito; bem-aventurado; feliz, venturoso
blessing | ble'sing | s. bênção;
mercê, graça; ação de graças;
louvor
blight | blayt' | s. praga das plan-
tas; influência maligna; caipo-
rismo / vt. vi. mirrar, crestar
(plantas); gorar, frustrar
Blighty | blay'tī | s. (gír.)
Inglaterra
blimey | blay'mī | interj. caram-
ba!, diacho!
blind | blaynd' | s. estore; trans-
parente de janela; antolho; em-
boscada; tocaia ou espera de ca-
çador; anteparo; subterfúgio /
a. cego / vt. cegar, deslumbrar
blind alley | blaynd'alī | s. beco
sem saída (tb. fig.)
blind date | blaynd'deyt | s. en-
contro marcado entre pessoas
de sexos opostos que não se co-
nheciam previamente
blindfold | blaynd'fowld | a. de
olhos vendados, às cegas / vt.
vendar os olhos a

blinding | blayn'ding | a. ofus-
cante, deslumbrante
blind landing | blaynd'landing |
s. aterrissagem por instrumen-
tos
blindly | blaynd'lī | adv. às cegas,
cegamente
blind-man's-buff | blaynd'manz-
bâf | s. jogo de cabra-cega
blindness | blaynd'nes | s. ce-
gueira
blink | blink' | vi. pestanejar
blinkers | bling'kəz | s. antolhos
de cavalo; óculos de proteção
bliss | blis' | s. felicidade, bem-
-aventurança; prazer, êxtase;
glória
blissful | blis'ful | a. jubiloso,
bem-aventurado, ditoso. -b. ig-
norance! santa ignorância!
blister | blis'tə | s. bolha, empola
/ vt. empolar / vi. empolar,
empolar-se
blithe | blayð' | a. alegre
blizzard | bli'zəd | s. nevasca,
tempestade de neve
bloated | blow'tid | a. inchado,
intumescido
block | blok' | s. bloco; cepo;
quarteirão, quadra; (com.) lote
de ações; obstrução, bloqueio /
vt. bloquear, obstruir; impe-
dir, estorvar. -to b. up entupir
blockade | blokeyd' | s. bloqueio
/ vt. bloquear
blockhead | blok'hed | s. pessoa
estúpida; cabeça-dura
block letter | blok'letə | s. letra de
fôrma
block print | blok'print | s.
xilogravura
bloke | blowk' | s. (gír.) sujeito,
cara, camarada
blond | blond' | s. pessoa lou-
ra / a. louro
blonde | blond' | s. mulher lou-
ra / a. de cabelos louros
blood | blâd' | s. sangue. -in cold
b. a sangue-frio. -to get one's b.
up fazer subir o sangue
bloodhound | blâd'hawnd | s. sa-
bujo; (gír.) detetive

bloodless | blâd'les | a. exangue; sem sangue; sem derramamento de sangue; insensível, frio

blood-letting | blâdle'ting | s. sangria; matança

blood-poisoning | blâdpoy'zǝning | s. septicemia

blood pressure | blâdpre'śǝ | s. pressão arterial

bloodshed | blâd'śed | s. derramamamento de sangue; chacina, matança

bloodshot | blâd'śot | a. injetados (olhos)

bloodthirsty | blâd'θɛstī | a. sedento de sangue, sangüinário, cruel

blood vessel | blâdve'sǝl | s. vaso sangüíneo

bloody | blâ'dī | a. sangrento, ensangüentado; (gír.) maldito (palavra injuriosa ou simplesmente intensiva)

bloody flux | blâ'dīflâks | s. disenteria

bloom | blʊm' | s. flor; florescência; beleza, louçania; a coloração das faces. **-in b.** em flor. **-in the b. of youth** na flor da idade / vi. florescer, florir

blossom | blo'sǝm | s. flor (de árvore frutífera) / vi. florescer, desabrochar

blot | blot' | s. borrão; nódoa, mancha; rasura, emenda / vt. secar com mata-borrão; borrar, manchar. **-to b. out** riscar, rasurar

blotch | blos' | s. mancha

blotter | blo'tǝ | s. mata-borrão; (com.) borrador

blotting-paper | blo'tingpeypǝ | s. mata-borrão

blouse | blauz' | s. blusa

blow | blow' | s. golpe, pancada (com instrumento, punhos, cassetete); soco; bofetada; revés, infortúnio; sopro; rajada de vento. **-to come to blows** chegar a vias de fato / vt. (mús.) fazer soar, tocar. **-to b. down** derrubar. **-to b. out** apagar. **-to**

b. up inflar, encher; dinamitar, fazer explodir; (fot.) ampliar. **-to b. one's nose** assoar-se. **-to b. one's horn** gabar-se / vi. soprar; ventar; resfolegar

blowlamp | blow'lamp | s. maçarico

blowpipe | blow'payp | s. maçarico de boca; zarabatana

blowtorch | blow'tóś | s. maçarico; lamparina de soldador

blubber | blâ'bǝ | a. inchados (lábios) / vt. dizer por entre soluços / vi. chorar ruidosamente

bludgeon | blâ'jǝn | s. porrete, cacete

blue | blʊ' | s. azul; anil; céu; mar; (pl. com the) depressão, melancolia / a. azul; lívido (de frio); deprimido, triste. **-out of the b.** inesperadamente, caído do céu. **-once in a b. moon** uma vez na vida, outra na morte; de raro em raro. **-b. devils** estado de depressão

bluebell | blʊ'bel | s. (bot.) campainha-azul

bluebottle | blʊ'botǝl | s. mosca-varejeira

blueprint | blʊ'print | s. planta, projeto, esquema

bluestocking | blʊ'stoking | s. (pej.) mulher letrada, literata, sabichona

bluff | blâf' | s. blefe, burla; penhasco, ribanceira / a. escarpado, a pique; franco, cordial; sincero, rude / vt. blefar, enganar

blunder | blân'dǝ | s. erro crasso, asneira / vi. cometer erro crasso

blundering | blân'dǝring | a. desajeitado, estouvado

blunt | blânt' | a. rombudo, embotado; brusco, rude; indelicado

bluntly | blânt'lī | adv. sem rodeios; indelicadamente, secamente

blur | blɛ' | s. borrão, mancha; falta de clareza / vt. confundir, obscurecer; embaciar

blurb | blɛb' | s. publicidade (em quarta de capa de livro); elogio exagerado para fins publicitários

blurred | blɛd' | a. indistinto, embaçado

blurt | blɛt' | vt. falar abruptamente

blush | blâs' | s. rubor; tom rosado / vi. corar

bluster | blâs'tə | s. fanfarronada; gritaria, escarcéu; vociferação; vendaval / vi. vociferar; fanfarronar; zunir (vento)

blustery | blâs'tərī | a. tempestuoso; fanfarrão

boar | bó'ə | s. porco não castrado, varrão; javali

board | bó'əd | s. tábua; tabuleiro (de jogo); pensão, refeições; conselho, junta; quadro-negro. **-b. and lodging** casa e comida. **-on b.** a bordo. **-to go by the b.** cair ao mar; ficar arruinado. **-above b.** às claras, abertamente. **-to sweep the b.** quebrar a banca, limpar a mesa / vt. embarcar em, ir a bordo de; abordar; hospedar. **-to b. with** estar hospedado em casa de, estar hospedado com

boarder | bó'ədə | s. comensal, hóspede; pensionista; aluno interno

boarding | bó'əding | s. pensão; tabuado, madeiramento; tapume feito de tábuas

boarding-house | bó'ədinghaws | s. casa de pensão, pensão, hospedaria

boarding-school | bó'ədingskʋl | s. internato

Board of Trade | bó'ədovtreyd | s. Câmara de Comércio

boast | bowst' | s. jactância, gabolice, bazófia / vi. jactar-se, gabar-se

boaster | bows'tə | s. fanfarrão, gabola

boastful | bowst'ful | a. jactancioso; fanfarrão, gabola

boat | bowt' | s. barco. **-to push the b. out** (coloq.) celebrar. **-in the same b.** no mesmo barco, com os mesmos riscos

boat drill | bowt'dril | s. (náut.) exercício de lançamento de escaleres

boat race | bowt'reys | s. regata

boatswain | bow'sən | s. contra-mestre

bob | bob' | s. pêndulo; prumo; mecha de cabelos; (gír.) xelim; apelido de Robert / vt. balançar, bambolear / vi. balançar-se; menear-se. **-to b. up** surgir inesperadamente

bobbin | bo'bin | s. bobina; carretel; bilro

bobby | bo'bī | s. (gír.) policial, guarda

bode | bowd' | vt. pressagiar; pressentir; prometer, anunciar. **-to b. ill for** ser de mau agouro para

bodice | bo'dis | s. corpete

bodily | bo'dilī | a. corporal, corpóreo; físico, material / adv. em pessoa, em carne e osso

body | bo'dī | s. corpo; cadáver; tronco; corporação; consistência, densidade; solidez; carroceria de automóvel; unidade militar; coleção (de leis). **-the main b.** o grosso, a maioria. **-in a b.** em conjunto

bog | bog' | s. pântano, brejo, atoleiro / vt. vi. atolar(-se)

boggle | bo'gəl | vi. hesitar em; refugar (cavalo); sentir escrúpulos; equivocar-se

bogus | bow'gəs | a. falso, fictício, suposto

bohemian | bowhī'mi̇̃ən | s. a. boêmio; (maiúsc.) cigano

boil | boyl' | s. furúnculo; fervura, ebulição / vt. vi. ferver, cozinhar. **-to b. away** evaporar(-se). **-on the b.** fervendo. **-to b. over** transbordar (líquido em ebulição). **-to b. down** reduzir por ebulição

boiler | boy'lə | s. caldeira

boiling | boy'ling | s. fervura,

ebulição / *a*. fervendo, fervente

boiling point | boy'lingpoynt | *s*. ponto de fervura

boisterous | boys'tərəs | *a*. barulhento, turbulento; tempestuoso (mar, vento)

bold | bowld' | *a*. audacioso, arrojado, destemido; vigoroso; escarpado, abrupto; (tip.) negrito

bold-faced | bowld'feyst | *a*. atrevido, descarado; (tip.) negrito

boldness | bowld'nes | *s*. intrepidez, arrojo, ousadia; atrevimento, descaramento

bolster | bowls'tə | *s*. travesseiro; almofadão; suporte, reforço / *vt*. apoiar, escorar; favorecer. -**to b. up** apoiar; animar

bolt | bowlt' | *s*. flecha de besta, virote; ferrolho (de porta ou de fuzil); parafuso ou porca; pino, cavilha; raio, corisco. -**a b. from the blue** surpresa total. -**my b. is shot** fiz o possível. -**to make a b.** correr, fugir / *vt*. arremessar; aferrolhar; engolir sem mastigar / *vi*. escapar-se, fugir

bomb | bom' | *s*. bomba / *vt*. bombardear

bombard | bombʌd' | *vt*. bombardear, canhonear

bombardment | bombʌd'mənt | *s*. bombardeio, canhoneio

bombast | bom'bast | *s*. linguagem bombástica, estilo empolado ou extravagante

bombastic | bombas'tik | *a*. bombástico, empolado, pomposo, pretensioso

bomber | bo'mə | *s*. bombardeiro (avião ou aviador)

bombing | bo'ming | *s*. bombardeio, bombardeamento

bond | bond' | *s*. vínculo, obrigação, laço; (com.) título, obrigação, apólice; (*pl*.) grilhões, cadeias. -**in b.** sob fiança; sob retenção alfandegária / *vi*. unir-se, aglutinar-se

bondage | bon'dij | *s*. servidão; escravidão

bone | bown' | *s*. osso; espinha (de peixe); (*pl*.) ossada. -**to have a b. to pick with someone** ter contas a ajustar com alguém. -**to have no bones about** não hesitar em dizer

bone of contention | bown'ovkənten'śən | *s*. pomo de discórdia

boner | bow'nə | *s*. (gír.) erro estúpido, enormidade, tolice, rata

bonfire | bon'fayə | *s*. fogueira

bonnet | bo'nit | *s*. touca; gorro escocês; capota (de automóvel)

bonny | bo'nĭ | *a*. formoso, bonito; galante; robusto

bonus | bow'nəs | *s*. bônus, bonificação; dividendo

bony | bow'nĭ | *a*. ossudo

book | buk' | *s*. livro. -**by the b.** de acordo com as normas. -**to bring to b.** exigir explicação. -**the (good) b.** a Bíblia. -**closed b.** coisa incompreensível / *vt*. reservar lugar ou passagem; registrar / *vi*. registrar-se, inscrever-se

bookcase | buk'keys | *s*. estante

booking-office | bu'kingófis | *s*. bilheteria

book-keeping | buk'kıping | *s*. escrituração comercial

booklet | buk'lit | *s*. folheto, opúsculo

book of account | buk'ovəkawnt | *s*. livro de contabilidade

bookseller | buk'selə | *s*. livreiro

bookshop | buk'śop | *s*. livraria

bookworm | buk'wεm | *s*. traça; (coloq.) rato de biblioteca

boom | bʋm' | *s*. desenvolvimento, crescimento rápido, fase de prosperidade / *vi*. ribombar, retumbar

boon | bʋn' | *s*. benefício, vantagem; favor, mercê / *a*. alegre, jovial

boon companion | bʋn'kəmpanĭən | *s*. (coloq.) companheirão, amigão

boor | bʋ'ə | *s*. campônio; pessoa

rústica ou grosseira

boorish | bʋ'əriś | a. grosseiro, rústico, rude

boot | bʋt' | s. bota; porta-malas (de automóvel). -**like old boots** (gír.) muitíssimo. -**you bet your boots** (gír.) pode ter certeza. -**to get the b.** ser despedido. -**to b.** além disso, além do mais

bootblack | bʋt'blak | s. (EUA) engraxate

booth | bʋð' | s. barraca de feira; tenda; cabine (de telefone, votação etc.)

bootlace | bʋt'leys | s. cordão de sapato

bootlicker | bʋt'likə | s. adulador servil, sabujo

bootmaker | bʋt'meykə | s. sapateiro

booty | bʋ'tī | s. despojos, butim, presa, espólio

booze | bʋz' | s. bebida alcoólica; vinhaça / vi. beber muito

border | bó'də | s. fronteira, limite; borda, beira, orla / a. fronteiriço / vt. orlar, debruar; limitar com / vi. -**to b. on** confinar com; tocar as raias de

bore | bó' | s. furo, orifício; diâmetro interno, alma; calibre; pessoa importuna, cacete; maçada / vt. abrir um buraco em; furar, brocar; aborrecer, incomodar, maçar, enfadar

bored | bó'əd | a. aborrecido

boredom | bó'dəm | s. aborrecimento, tédio, enfado

boring | bó'ring | s. perfuração, escavação; sondagem / a. enfadonho, cacete

born | bón' | a. nascido, nato; inato. -**to be b.** nascer

borough | bə'rə | s. município

borrow | bo'row | vt. pedir emprestado

bosh | boś' | s. tolice, asneira, bobagem

bosom | bu'zəm | s. seio, peito / a. relativo ao seio ou ao peito. -**b. friend** amigo íntimo, amigo do peito

boss | bos' | s. bossa, protuberância; patrão, chefe / vt. mandar, dirigir

bossy | bo'sī | a. mandão

botanist | bo'tənist | s. botânico

botany | bo'tənī | s. botânica

botch | boś' | s. remendo; trabalho atamancado / vt. remendar; atamancar

both | bowϑ' | a. pron. ambos, os dois, um e outro. -**b. of** ambos, os dois. -**b. of them** eles dois

bother | bo'ðə | vt. incomodar, aborrecer, amolar. -**to b. about** preocupar-se com. -**don't b.!** não se incomode!

bothersome | bo'ðəsəm | a. aborrecido, tedioso, enfadonho

bottle | bo'təl | s. garrafa; frasco, vidro; botija; mamadeira / vt. engarrafar. -**to b. up** conter, refrear (emoções, sentimentos)

bottom | bo'təm | s. fundo; parte inferior; base; fundação; nádegas; âmago, fundamento. -**from top to b.** de alto a baixo. -**at b.** no fundo, na realidade / a. o mais baixo, último

bottomless | bo'təmles | a. sem fundo, insondável

bough | baw' | s. ramo

boulder | bowl'də | s. pedra grande, rocha (gasta pela ação da água ou do vento)

bounce | bawns' | s. pancada; pulo, salto; fanfarronada; (gír.) demissão sumária / vt. fazer saltar / vi. saltar, pular

bound | bawnd' | s. salto, pulo; (pl.) limites. -**at a b.** de um pulo. -**out of bounds** (mil.) entrada proibida. -**by leaps and bounds** rapidamente / a. ligado; compelido, obrigado; encadernado. -**b. for** com destino a. -**b. up in** concentrado em. -**where are you b. for?** para onde vai? -**b. up with** ligado com / vt. confinar, limitar / vi. saltar, pular; saltitar

boundary | bawn'dərī | s. limite, fronteira, divisa

boundless | bawnd'les | *a.* ilimitado, infinito

bountiful | bawn'tiful | *a.* generoso, dadivoso, liberal

bounty | bawn'tī | *s.* generosidade, liberalidade; subvenção; recompensa; gratificação, abono

bouquet | bukey' | *s.* buquê, ramalhete; aroma do vinho

bourgeois | bu'əjwa | *s. a.* burguês

bout | bawt' | *s.* turno, vez; acesso, ataque; assalto (luta etc.); rodada (de bebida)

bow | baw' | *s.* reverência, vênia; (náut.) proa / *vt.* curvar, vergar / *vi.* curvar-se, fazer uma reverência; submeter-se a. **-to b. and scrape** fazer reverências exageradas

bow | bow' | *s.* arco (arma, violino etc.); curva; arco-íris; laço, laçada

bowel | baw'əl | *s.* intestino, tripa; (*pl.*) tripas, entranhas

bower | baw'ə | *s.* caramanchão

bowl | bowl' | *s.* tigela; cuia; gamela; terrina de ponche; concavidade; fornilho de cachimbo; bola de madeira / *vt.* fazer rolar (bola) / *vi.* rolar (bola)

bow-legged | bowlegd' | *a.* que tem· as pernas arqueadas, cambaio

bowler-hat | bow'ləhat | *s.* chapéu-coco, chapéu-de-coco

box | boks' | *s.* caixa; arca, baú; estojo; (teat.) camarote; boléia; bofetão; (bot.) buxo. **-to be in a tight b.** estar em situação difícil / *vt.* encaixotar; esbofetear / *vi.* boxear, lutar boxe

box camera | boks'kamərɔ | *s.* (fot.) caixote

boxer | bok'sə | *s.* pugilista; bóxer (cão)

boxing | bok'sing | *s.* boxe, pugilismo

Boxing Day | bok'singdey | *s.* o dia 26 de dezembro (em que se dão presentes de Natal)

box-office | bokso'fis | *s.* (teat.) bilheteria

boy | boy' | *s.* menino, garoto; contínuo, bói; bói de hotel. **-old b.** meu velho, meu caro; ex-aluno. **-my b.** meu velho (tb. para cães)

boycott | boy'kot | *s.* boicote / *vt.* boicotar

boy-friend | boy'frend | *s.* namorado; amiguinho

boyhood | boy'hud | *s.* meninice

boyish | boy'iš | *a.* pueril, infantil; de menino

brace | breys' | *s.* braçadeira, tirante; esteio, apoio; par, dois; (*pl.*) suspensórios. **-b. and bit** berbequim e pua. **-to splice the main b.** beber, tomar um trago / *vt.* atar, apertar; retesar. **-to b. oneself** endireitar-se; concentrar-se; preparar-se para uma surpresa etc.

bracelet | breys'lit | *s.* bracelete, pulseira

bracing | brey'sing | *a.* revigorante, tônico

bracken | bra'kən | *s.* samambaia, feto

bracket | bra'kit | *s.* suporte angular, braço (metálico); (*pl.*) colchetes, parênteses, chave; categoria (incluída numa chave) / *vt.* pôr entre colchetes; incluir na mesma categoria

brackish | bra'kiš | *a.* salobro

brackish water | bra'kiśwótə | *s.* água salobra

brag | brag' | *s.* jactância, bazófia / *vi.* gabar-se, jactar-se

braggart | bra'gʌt | *s. a.* fanfarrão, gabola

braid | breyd' | *s.* trança; galão / *vi.* trançar; agaloar

brain | breyn' | *s.* cérebro; (*pl.*) inteligência, miolos. **-to rack one's brains** dar tratos à bola. **-to have on the b.** estar obcecado por / *vt.* rebentar os miolos de

brainy | brey'nī | *a.* inteligente, que tem miolos

braise | breyz' | *vt.* cozinhar lentamente (carne)

brake | breyk' | *s.* freio, trava, breque; moita, matagal / *vt.* frear, brecar, travar

bramble | bram'bəl | *s.* amoreira silvestre; espinheiro, sarça

bran | bran' | *s.* farelo (de trigo ou outro cereal)

branch | brʌnś' | *s.* ramo, galho; (com.) filial, sucursal / *vi.* -to b. off bifurcar-se. -to b. out ramificar-se; ampliar-se

brand | brand' | *s.* marca de ferro em brasa; tição; (com.) marca / *vt.* marcar (com ferro em brasa); cauterizar; estigmatizar; gravar na memória

brandish | bran'diś | *s.* floreio (de arma) / *vt.* brandir, florear (arma etc.)

brand-new | brandniu' | *a.* novo em folha, novinho

brandy | bran'dī | *s.* conhaque, aguardente

brash | braś | *a.* atrevido, impertinente; impetuoso

brass | bras' | *s.* latão; bronze; (mús.) os metais; (gír.) descaramento; (gír.) dinheiro, cobres. -to get down to b. tacks passar ao que interessa, conversar detalhes práticos

brass band | bras'band | *s.* charanga

brass farthing | bras'fʌδing | *s.* um vintém, a menor quantia possível

brassière | brasīe'ə | *s.* sutiã, corpinho

brat | brat' | *s.* (pej.) criança, pirralho

bravado | bravʌ'dow | *s.* bravata; fanfarronada

brave | breiv' | *s.* pessoa valente; guerreiro / *a.* valente, corajoso / *vt.* arrostar, desafiar

bravery | brey'varī | *s.* coragem, valentia

bravo | brʌvow' | *s.* sicário; malfeitor / *interj.* bravo!

brawl | bról' | *s.* rixa; altercação;

burburinho / *vt.* altercar, brigar

brawn | brón' | *s.* músculo; carnes rijas; força muscular; carne de porco (temperada e moldada)

brawny | bró'nī | *a.* forte, musculoso, vigoroso

bray | brey' | *s.* zurro; som de trombeta / *vi.* zurrar; trombetear, buzinar

brazen | brey'zən | *a.* descarado, insolente; feito de latão ou de bronze / *vt.* -to b. it out negar ou sustentar algo desavergonhadamente

brazier | brey'zĩə | *s.* latoeiro; braseiro

Brazilian | brəzi'lĩən | *s. a.* brasileiro

Brazil-nut | brəzil'nât | *s.* castanha-do-pará

breach | briś' | *s.* brecha; fenda, abertura; ruptura, fissura; violação, transgressão. -b. of faith ou of trust abuso de confiança. -b. of the peace atentado contra a ordem pública. -b. of promise quebra de esponsais

bread | bred' | *s.* pão; (fig.) sustento, meio de vida; (fig.) rotina diária. -b. and butter pão com manteiga. -to eat the b. of estar sujeito a (humilhação etc.). -b. and wine Eucaristia

bread-fruit | bred'frʊt | *s.* fruta-pão

breadth | bredϑ' | *s.* largura; largueza de vistas, tolerância. -by a hair's b. por um triz

bread-winner | bredwi'nə | *s.* arrimo de família

break | breyk' | *s.* quebra, ruptura; brecha; interrupção; (med.) fratura; pausa; descanso; (coloq.) oportunidade, chance. -the b. of day o raiar do dia / *vt.* quebrar, romper, partir; transgredir (lei). -to b. away separar-se de, romper com; soltar-se, fugir. -to b. down derrubar; ceder; demolir; abater-se, ficar

sucumbido; decompor, anali-
sar; estacar, parar. **-to b. in** do-
mar, amansar; amaciar, come-
çar a usar; forçar, abrir à força.
-to b. off cortar; quebrar (compromisso); suspender, interromper; separar (quebrando).
-to b. up dividir, fragmentar;
dissolver, dispersar; parar, ces-
sar (conversa); pôr fim a, suspender. **-to b. the news** dar uma
notícia / *vi.* quebrar-se, rom-
per-se; irromper, romper. **-to b.
loose** soltar-se, escapar. **-to b.
in** (com **on** ou **upon**) surgir;
irromper; interromper, per-
turbar
breakable | brey'kəbəl | *a.* que-
bradiço, frágil
breakage | brey'kiʃ' | *s.* quebra
breakdown | breyk'dawn | *s.* es-
gotamento nervoso; enguiço,
pane; falência; parada, inter-
rupção; decomposição quími-
ca; análise; divisão, classifi-
cação
breaker | brey'kə | *s.* infrator;
vagalhão, onda
breakfast | brek'fəst | *s.* desje-
jum, café da manhã / *vi.* desje-
juar, tomar café da manhã
breakup | breyk'âp | *s.* desinte-
gração; colapso; dispersão
breakwater | breyk'wótə | *s.* que-
bra-mar, talha-mar
breast | brest' | *s.* peito, seio. **-to
make a clean b.** of desabafar,
confessar
breastplate | brest'pleyt | *s.* cou-
raça; peitoral (de broca)
breastwork | brest'wɛk | *s.* para-
peito baixo
breath | breϑ' | *s.* hálito; fôlego;
respiração; brisa. **-out of b.** ofegante. **-under one's b.** a meia
voz. **-to save one's b.** poupar
palavras. **-to draw b.** tomar
fôlego. **-b. of wind** aragem
breathe | briϑ' | *vt. vi.* respirar.
-to b. in inspirar. **-to b. out** expi-
rar. **-to b. one's last** exalar o úl-
timo suspiro

breathing | brı'ϑing | *s.* respi-
ração
breathing-space | brı'ϑingspeys |
s. tempo para respirar, pausa
breathless | breϑ'les | *a.* sem vida;
ofegante; ansioso; parado, cal-
mo, sem vento
breech | brıʃ' | *s.* culatra; (*pl.*)
calções (amarrados abaixo do
joelho)
breed | brıd' | *s.* raça, casta; li-
nhagem / *vt.* produzir, procriar; criar (animais) / *vi.* repro-
duzir-se
breeder | brı'də | *s.* criador
breeding | brı'ding | *s.* educação;
criação
breeding place | brı'dingpleys | *s.*
viveiro; foco de mosquitos
breeze | brız' | *s.* brisa. **-it's a b.**
(coloq.) é fácil!, é sopa!
breezy | brı'zı | *a.* com brisa; fres-
co; animado. jovial
brethren | breϑ'rən | *spl.* irmãos;
confrades
breviary | bre'vΐərΐ | *s.* breviário
brevity | bre'vitΐ | *s.* brevidade;
concisão
brew | brv' | *s.* bebida fermenta-
da; infusão / *vt.* fazer cerveja;
fazer chá; preparar, provocar /
vi. fazer cerveja; preparar-se,
armar-se (tempestade etc.).
-there's something b. há qualquer coisa no ar
brewer | brv'ə | *s.* cervejeiro, fa-
bricante de cerveja
brewery | brv'ərΐ | *s.* fábrica de
cerveja
brewing | brv'ing | *s.* fabricação
de cerveja
bribe | brayb' | *s.* suborno / *vt.*
subornar
bribery | bray'bərΐ | *s.* suborno
brick | brik' | *s.* tijolo; bloco em
forma de tijolo; (coloq.) bom
sujeito. **-to drop a b.** cometer
uma gafe
bridal | bray'dəl | *a.* nupcial
bride | brayd' | *s.* noiva
bridegroom | brayd'grʋm | *s.*
noivo

bridesmaid | braydz'meyd | *s.* dama de honor (de noiva)

bridge | briǰ' | *s.* ponte; (náut.) ponte de comando; *bridge* (jogo); cavalete do nariz / *vt.* construir ponte, ligar com ponte

bridle | bray'dəl | *s.* cabeçada (freio, rédeas), brida / *vt.* enfrear, embridar / *vi.* empertigar-se

brief | brif' | *s.* sumário, resumo; breve pontifício; (jur.) súmula dos fatos; (náut., aer.) instruções para a tripulação / *a.* breve; conciso / *vt.* sumariar; (náut., aer.) instruir

brief-case | brif'keys | *s.* pasta para documentos

briefness | brif'nes | *s.* brevidade, concisão

brier, briar | bray'ə | *s.* roseira brava, sarça; urze-bránca; cachimbo de raiz de urze-branca

brigade | brigeyd' | *s.* brigada

brigand | bri'gənd | *s.* bandido, bandoleiro

bright | brayt' | *a.* brilhante, claro; lustroso; inteligente; promissor, favorável, auspicioso

brighten | bray'tən | *vt.* iluminar; fazer brilhar; alegrar; avivar / *vi.* animar-se, cobrar ânimo; clarear, melhorar (tempo, céu)

brightness | brayt'nes | *s.* brilho, claridade; agudeza, vivacidade, inteligência

brilliance | bri'lïəns | *s.* brilho, luminosidade; agudeza de espírito

brilliant | bri'lïənt | *s.* brilhante (gema) / *a.* brilhante, cintilante; auspicioso, favorável

brim | brim' | *s.* borda, beira; aba / *vt.* encher até a borda / *vi.* transbordar

brimful | brim'ful | *a.* cheio até a borda; repleto

brimstone | brim'stown | *s.* enxofre; virago, megera

brine | brayn' | *s.* salmoura

bring | bring' | *vt.* trazer; levar. **-to b. about** ocasionar, dar origem a. **-to b. back** devolver; recordar. **-to b. down** derrubar; abater. **-to b. forth** dar à luz. **-to b. forward** transportar (soma) para outra coluna; antecipar (data); apresentar (proposta). **-to b. in** introduzir; render, produzir. **-to b. out** apresentar; publicar; (teat.) encenar. **-to b. over** persuadir, converter. **-to b. up** criar, educar; trazer à baila

brink | brink' | *s.* beira, borda

brisk | brisk' | *a.* animado, ativo, vigoroso, vivo

bristle | bri'səl | *s.* cerda / *vi.* eriçar-se (animal); encrespar-se; arrepiar-se. **-to b. up** encolerizar-se

British | bri'tiš | *a.* britânico, inglês

Briton | bri'tən | *s.* inglês

brittle | bri'təl | *a.* quebradiço, frágil

broach | browš' | *s.* espeto; sovela / *vt.* espetar; encetar, abordar (assunto)

broad | bród' | *s.* a parte mais larga; (gír.) mulher, dona; (*pl.*) laguna, banhado / *a.* largo; extenso, vasto; geral; claro, franco; direto; tolerante; indecente (piada). **-in b. daylight** em pleno dia

broadcast | bród'kʌst | *s.* radiodifusão; programa de rádio / *a.* irradiado, transmitido / *vt.* transmitir

broadcasting | bród'kʌsting | *s.* radiodifusão; emissão, transmissão

broadcast station | bród'kʌststey'sən | *s.* emissora, radiodifusora

broaden | bró'dən | *vt. vi.* alargar(-se), ampliar(-se), desenvolver(-se)

broad hint | bród'hint | *s.* insinuação clara

broadsheet | bród'šit | *s.* folha volante

broadside| bród'sayd |s. (náut.) costado; banda de artilharia; (coloq.) torrente de injúrias

broccoli | bro'kəlī | s. (bot.) brócolis

brochure | brosĭu'ə | s. folheto, panfleto

brogue | browg' | s. borzeguim grosseiro; sotaque dialetal (esp. irlandês)

broil | broyl' | vt. grelhar

broke | browk' | a. (gír.) sem dinheiro, quebrado, duro. **-to be b.** estar quebrado

broken| brow'kən |a. quebrado, partido; interrompido; infringido; arruinado; mal falada (língua); acidentado (caminho); sucumbido; domado, domesticado

broken-hearted | brow'kənhᴧtid | a. de coração partido, quebrantado

broker | brow'kə | s. corretor, agente, comissário

bronchitis | bronkay'tis | s. bronquite

bronze | bronz' |s. bronze

brooch | browś' |s. broche

brood | brʊd' | s. ninhada / vt. chocar (galinha etc.) / vi. refletir; matutar sobre; cismar; remoer

brook| bruk' |s. arroio, regato / vt. suportar, tolerar (insultos etc.)

broom | brʊm' | s. vassoura; (bot.) giesta

broth | broϑ' |s. caldo, sopa

brothel| bro'ϑəl |s. bordel

brother | brâ'ðə |s. irmão

brotherhood | brâ'ðəhud | s. irmandade, fraternidade; confraria

brother-in-law | brâ'ðəinló | s. cunhado

brotherly | brâ'ðəlī |a. fraternal, fraterno / adv. fraternalmente

brow | braw' | s. sobrancelha; testa; cume, cimo. **-to knit one's brows** franzir a testa, franzir as sobrancelhas

browbeat | braw'bĭt | vt. intimidar, amedrontar

brown| brawn' |a. marrom, castanho; moreno / vt. tostar; bronzear(-se)

brown bread | brawn'bred | s. pão de centeio

brown paper | brawn'peypə | s. papel pardo, papel de embrulho

brown sugar | brawn'śugə | s. açúcar mascavo

brown study | brawn'stâdī | s. meditação profunda; devaneio

browse | brawz' | vi. pastar; ler aqui e ali, folhear, percorrer com os olhos (livro)

bruise | brʊz' | s. contusão, equimose, mancha roxa; ofensa / vt. contundir, machucar; pilar; ofender

brunt| brânt' |s. choque, impacto; força, violência

brush | brâś' | s. escova; pincel; escoriação, esfoladura; (mil.) escaramuça; matagal / vt. escovar. **-to b. up** fazer limpeza em; retocar. **-to b. against** roçar. **-to b. aside** afastar, repelir; pôr de lado; não fazer caso de. **-to b. over** pincelar

Brussels sprout | brâ'səlzprawt | s. couve-de-bruxelas

brutal | bru'təl | a. brutal; grosseiro; selvagem, animalesco

brutality | bruta'litī | s. brutalidade; barbaridade

brutalize| bru'təlayz |vt. embrutecer, brutalizar

brute | brʊt' | s. bruto; animal. **-by b. force** à força / a. brutal; animalesco, bestial

brutish | bru'tiś | a. brutal; animalesco, bestial

bubble | bâ'bəl | s. bolha; bolha de sabão / vi. borbulhar, espumar, fazer bolhas

buccaneer | bâ'kənǐə | s. bucaneiro, pirata

buck | bâk' | s. animal macho (esp. gamo, cervo, bode); dândi, janota; corcovo; (gír.,

EUA) dólar. **-to pass the b.** passar a responsabilidade para outro / *vi.* corcovear. **-to b. up** animar-se; criar coragem; vestir-se com elegância

bucket | bâ'kit | *s.* balde

buckle | bâ'kəl | *s.* fivela; empenamento, curvatura / *vt.* afivelar; empenar / *vi.* preparar-se, dispor-se; empenar, vergar. **-to b. with** lutar com

buckshot | bâk'şot | *s.* chumbo grosso (de caça)

bucktooth | bâk'tvϑ | *s.* dente saliente

bud | bâd' | *s.* botão, broto, rebento / *vi.* desabrochar, brotar. **-to nip the b.** cortar pela raiz

budge | bâ' | *vi.* bulir, mover-se, mexer-se

budget | bâ'jit | *s.* orçamento / *vi.* **-to b. for** incluir no orçamento

buffalo | bâ'fəlow | *s.* búfalo; bisão-americano

buffer | bâ'fə | *s.* pára-choque. **-old b.** sujeito antiquado ou incompetente

buffet | bĭu'fey | *s.* tapa, tabefe / *vt.* esbofetear

buffoonery | bâfv'nərī | *s.* bufonaria, palhaçada

bug | bâg' | *s.* percevejo; inseto, bicho

bugbear | bâg'beə | *s.* papão; fantasma; espantalho

bugle | bĭu'gəl | *s.* corneta

build | bild' | *s.* construção; compleição, constituição / *vt.* construir, edificar

builder | bil'də | *s.* construtor

building | bil'ding | *s.* edifício; construção; formação, criação / *a.* de construção

bulb | bâlb' | *s.* bulbo; lâmpada elétrica

bulge | bâlĭ' | *s.* bojo, saliência *vi.* fazer bojo

bulk | bâlk' | *s.* volume; vulto; tamanho. **-to sell in b.** vender por atacado / *vi.* sobressair, avultar

bulkhead | bâlk'hed | *s.* anteparo, tabique

bulky | bâl'kī | *a.* volumoso

bull | bul' | *s.* touro; macho de animais de grande porte; bula papal

bulldog | bul'dog | *s.* buldogue

bulldozer | bul'dowzə | *s.* buldôzer, máquina de terraplenagem

bullet | bu'lit | *s.* bala (projétil)

bullet head | bu'lithed | *s.* pessoa cabeçuda ou obstinada

bulletin | bu'lətin | *s.* boletim

bullfight | bul'fayt | *s.* tourada, corrida de touros

bullfighter | bul'faytə | *s.* toureiro

bullion | bu'lĭən | *s.* ouro ou prata em barras

bullring | bul'ring | *s.* praça de touros

bull's-eye | bulz'ay | *s.* centro do alvo, mosca

bully | bu'lī | *s.* valentão, fanfarrão; protetor de prostitutas, cáften / *vt.* perseguir, tiranizar; amedrontar

bully beef | bu'lĭbif | *s.* carne enlatada

bulwark | bul'wək | *s.* baluarte

bum | bum' | *s.* (gír.) nádegas; (gír., EUA) vagabundo, vadio / *vt.* (gír., EUA) filar (cigarros etc.) / *vi.* (gír., EUA) vagabundear, vadiar

bump | bâmp' | *s.* choque; baque; bossa; solavanco / *vt.* colidir; chocar. **-to b. into** dar um encontrão; topar com. **-to b. off** (gír.) matar, eliminar / *vi.* colidir, chocar-se

bumper | bâm'pə | *s.* copo cheio até à borda; (gír.) colosso, coisa excelente; pára-choque (de automóvel etc.); batente

bumpkin | bâmp'kin | *s.* campônio, pessoa rústica

bumptious | bâm'şəs | *a.* presunçoso, arrogante

bun | bân' | *s.* bolinho com passas; coque (cabelo)

bunch | bânś' | *s.* molho, feixe; cacho (de uvas); ramalhete; punhado; grupo / *vt. vi.* reunir(-se), agrupar(-se)

bundle | bân'dəl | *s.* trouxa; fardo; feixe, molho / *vt.* entrouxar; enfardar; enfeixar. **-to b. out, off, away** despachar rapidamente ou sem cerimônia (pessoa)

bung | bâng' | *s.* batoque, tampão / *vt.* tampar com batoque; (gír.) estropiar

bungalow | bâng'gəlow | *s.* bangalô

bungle | bâng'gəl | *vt.* atamancar, estropiar, fazer mal

bunk | bânk' | *s.* beliche; leito (carro-dormitório); tarimba. **-to do a b.** (gír.) fugir, sumir-se / *vi.* dormir em beliche, tarimba etc.

bunker | bâng'kə | *s.* (náut.) carvoeira; (mil.) casamata

bunkum | bâng'kəm | *s.* disparates, tolices

bunny | bâ'nī | *s.* coelhinho (expressão carinhosa)

bunting | bân'ting | *s.* pano para bandeiras ou decorações; bandeiras (coletivamente)

buoy | boy' | *s.* (náut.) bóia / *vt.* (náut.) balizar. **-to b. up** fazer flutuar; animar, levantar o ânimo, alentar

buoyancy | boy'ənsī | *s.* flutuabilidade; vivacidade, animação

buoyant | boy'ənt | *a.* flutuante; animado, alegre

burden | bE'dən | *s.* carga; fardo; encargo, responsabilidade; (mús.) estribilho. **-b. of proof** (jur.) ônus de prova

burdensome | bE'dənsəm | *a.* pesado, incômodo; opressivo

bureau | biu'row | *s.* escrivaninha, secretária; repartição oficial; escritório comercial; agência

bureaucracy | bĭuro'krəsī | *s.* burocracia

bureaucrat | bĭu'rowkrat | *s.* burocrata

burglar | bE'glə | *s.* ladrão, arrombador

burglary | bE'glərī | *s.* arrombamento (roubo)

burial | be'rīəl | *s.* enterro

burlap | bE'lap | *s.* aniagem

burlesque | bE'lesk | *s.* paródia; (teat.) revista / *a.* burlesco, caricato

burly | bE'lī | *a.* robusto, corpulento, musculoso

burn | bEn' | *s.* queimadura; riacho, arroio / *vt.* queimar, incendiar. **-to b. down** destruir pelo fogo / *vi.* queimar-se, incendiar-se; arder, picar. **-to b. up** consumir-se completamente

burning | bE'ning | *s.* ardor; combustão; incêndio, queima / *a.* ardente; veemente

burnish | bE'niś | *vt.* brunir, lustrar

burnt offering | bEnt'ofəring | *s.* holocausto

burrow | bə'row | *s.* toca (de animal) / *vi.* fazer toca; entocar-se; esconder-se

bursar | bE'sə | *s.* bolsista; tesoureiro

bursary | bE'sərī | *s.* tesouraria (de universidade); bolsa de estudos

burst | bEst' | *s.* explosão, estouro; ruptura, brecha; rajada (de metralhadora etc.) / *vi.* rebentar, quebrar. **-to b. out** desatar a (rir etc.). **-to b. open** rebentar. **-to b. into** irromper em. **-to b. through** passar impetuosamente

bury | be'rī | *vt.* enterrar, sepultar, inumar

bus | bâs' | *s.* ônibus

bush | buś' | *s.* arbusto; moita; matagal; sertão australiano. **-to beat around the b.** usar de rodeios ou meias palavras

bushel | bu'śəl | *s.* alqueire (medida de capacidade para cereais = c. 36 litros)

bushy | bu'śī | *a.* basto, denso, cerrado

business | biz'nis | *s.* negócio(s),

comércio; atividade, ocupação; assunto, objetivo. **-that's my b.** isso é comigo. **-this is no b.** of yours isso não é da sua conta. **-mind your own b.** trate de sua vida. **-he has no b. to come here** ele não tem nada que vir aqui. **-he means b.** ele está falando do sério. **-a strange b.** uma questão difícil, um assunto complicado

business hours | biz'nisawəz | *s.* horas de expediente

businessman | biz'nismən | *s.* homem de negócios

bust | bâst' | *s.* busto; seios, peitos

bustle | bâ'səl | *s.* animação; afobação, pressa; alvoroço / *vt.* apressar; alvoroçar / *vi.* alvoroçar-se; afobar-se

busy | bi'zĩ | *a.* ocupado, atarefado; movimentado / *vr.* ocupar-se de

busybody | bi'zĩbodĩ | *s.* intrometido, pessoa abelhuda

but | bât | *conj. prep.* mas; porém; menos, salvo, exceto; senão, a não ser. **-all b.** todos menos; quase, por um triz. **-b. for** se não fosse por. **-b. little** muito pouco. **-nothing b.** só, somente. **-cannot b.** (seguido de infinitivo) não poder deixar de / *adv.* apenas, somente

butcher | bu'šə | *s.* açougueiro; assassino, homem sangüinário. **-the b., the baker, the candlestick-maker** pessoas de todas as profissões / *vt.* matar, abater animais

butchery | bu'šərĩ | *s.* matadouro; comércio de carne; carnificina, chacina

butler | bât'lə | *s.* mordomo

butler's pantry | bâ'tləspantrĩ | *s.* copa

butt | bât' | *s.* extremidade mais grossa; toco (de árvore); (gír.) guimba, ponta de cigarro; pipa (vinho ou cerveja); coronha; alvo, talude do alvo; objeto de ridículo; (gír.) nádegas / *vt.* dar

marradas ou cabeçadas. **-to b. against** confinar com. **-to b. in** interromper, intrometer-se

butter | bâ'tə | *s.* manteiga / *vt.* amanteigar

buttercup | bâ'təkəp | *s.* (bot.) ranúnculo, botão-de-ouro

butter dish | bâ'tədiš | *s.* manteigueira

butter-fingers | bâ'təfingə | *s.* mão-furada, pessoa que deixa cair as coisas

butterfly | bâ'təflay | *s.* borboleta

butterfly-nut | bâ'təflaynât | *s.* (mec.) borboleta

butterfly stroke | bâ'təflay-strowk | *s.* nado borboleta

buttock | bâ'tək | *s.* nádega

button | bâ'tən | *s.* botão / *vt.* abotoar

buttonhole | bâ'tənhowl | *s.* casa de botão / *vt.* casear; segurar (alguém) pelo botão do paletó; deter; abordar

buttress | bâ'tres | *s.* arco botante, botaréu; escora, suporte / *vt.* apoiar, sustentar, escorar

buxom | bâk'səm | *a.* robusto, sadio; rechonchudo

buy | bay' | *s.* compra; pechincha / *vt.* comprar; subornar

buyer | bay'ə | *s.* comprador

buzz | bâz' | *s.* zumbido / *vi.* zumbir

buzzer | bâ'zə | *s.* campainha elétrica, cigarra

by | bay | *prep.* por; perto de, junto de; de. **-b. day** de dia. **-b. chance** por acaso. **-b. land** por terra. **-b. air** de avião. **-b. myself** sozinho. **-b. far!** de longe! **-b. the way** a propósito. **-b. now** a esta hora, já. **-b. heart** de cor. **-b. right** de direito. **-b. means of** mediante. **-b. and large** de modo geral. **-b. the b.** a propósito

bygone | bay'gən | *s.* passado, antigo; morto; (pl.) coisas passadas. **-to let bygones be bygones** esquecer o que passou, perdoar e esquecer

by-law | bay'ló | *s.* regulamento

bypass | bay'pʌs | *s.* passagem secundária, desvio

bypath | bay'pʌϑ |*s.* atalho

by-product | baypro'dəkt | *s.* subproduto

byre | bay'ə | *s.* estábulo (de vacas)

bystander| baystan'də |*s.* espectador, circunstante

byway | bay'wey | *s.* estrada de pouco trânsito; atalho

byword | bay'wɛd |*s.* provérbio; pessoa proverbial como tipo; objeto de escárnio

C

C, c| si' |*s.* c; (maiúsc., mús.) dó

cab | kab' | *s.* cabriolé, carro de praça; táxi

cabbage | ka'biǰ | *s.* repolho; couve

cabin| ka'bin |*s.*(náut.)camarote; (aer.) cabine de passageiros; cabana

cabin-boy | ka'binboy | *s.* criado de bordo

cabinet | ka'binit | *s.* gabinete; conselho de ministros; armário; caixa (de rádio etc.)

cabinet-maker | ka'binitmeykə | *s.* marceneiro

cable | key'bəl |*s.* cabo; cabograma, telegrama

cackle | ka'kəl | *s.* cacarejo / *vi.* cacarejar; tagarelar

cactus | kak'təs |*s.* cacto

cad | kad' | *s.* patife, grosseirão, cafajeste

caddie, caddy | ka'dī | *s.* rapaz que carrega os tacos (golfe)

cadet | kədet' |*s.* cadete

cadre | kʌ'də |*s.*(mil.)quadro de oficiais; quadro, estrutura

café | ka'fey | *s.* café, salão de chá; restaurante

cafeteria | kafitɪ'riə | *s.* restaurante em que os clientes se servem no balcão

cage | keyǰ' |*s.* gaiola; jaula / *vt.* engaiolar; enjaular

cage-bird | keyǰ'bɛd | *s.* pássaro de gaiola

cairn | ke'ən | *s.* pirâmide de pedras(marco, monumento funerário etc.)

cajole | kəǰowl' | *vt.* lisonjear, agradar, engabelar

cake | keyk' |*s.* bolo; pão (de sabão, cera etc.). **-cakes and ale** reunião alegre, festa / *vi.* coagular, aglutinar-se

calamitous | kəla'mitəs | *a.* calamitoso, desastroso

calamity| kəla'mitī |*s.* calamidade, desastre

calculate | kal'kĭuleyt | *vt.* calcular

calculation | kalkĭuley'śən | *s.* cálculo

calendar | ka'lində | *s.* calendário, almanaque

calf | kʌf' |*s.* bezerro; barriga da perna

calibre, caliber | ka'libə | *s.* calibre; qualidade, importância; competência

calico | ka'likow | *s.* tecido comum do algodão; chita

call | kól' | *s.* grito; chamado, apelo; visita breve. **-on** c. resgatável sem aviso prévio (dívida, título etc.). **-within** c. ao alcance da voz / *vt.* chamar; gritar; convocar; tocar, fazer escala (em porto). **-to c. back** mandar voltar; revogar; retratar; recordar-se de; telefonar de volta. **-to c. for** pedir; requerer, exigir; vir buscar. **-to c. forth** chamar; suscitar, provocar. **-to c. off** adiar, suspender; abandonar. **-to c. on** visitar. **-to c. up** evocar; (mil.) chamar às fileiras, convocar. **-to c. to mind** lembrar. **-to c. the roll** fazer a chamada. **-to c. to witness** chamar como testemunha, tomar por testemunha

call-box | kól'boks | *s.* cabine telefônica

caller | kó'lə | *s.* visita

calling | kó'ling | *s.* chamado; vocação; ocupação

callous | ka'ləs | *a.* calejado; endurecido, insensível, empedernido

callow | ka'low | *a.* implume; inexperiente

calm | kAm' | *s.* (náut.) calmaria; calma, tranqüilidade / *a.* calmo, sossegado, tranqüilo / *vt.* acalmar, sossegar, tranqüilizar / *vi.* acalmar-se, serenar

calm and collected | kam'andkəlek'tid | *a.* calmo, tranqüilo

calm sea | kAm'sı | *s.* mar calmo

calory | ka'lərī | *s.* caloria

calumny | ka'ləmnī | *s.* calúnia

Calvary | kal'vərī | *s.* Calvário

calve | kAv' | *vi.* parir, dar cria (vaca etc.)

camel | ka'məl | *s.* camelo

cameo | ka'mīow | *s.* camafeu

camera | ka'mərə | *s.* máquina fotográfica; câmara de TV ou cinema; gabinete de juiz. **-in c.** em particular

camouflage | ka'muflAj | *s.* camuflagem / *vt.* camuflar

camp | kamp' | *s.* acampamento. **-to break c.** levantar acampamento / *vi.* acampar

camp-bed | kamp'bed | *s.* cama de campanha

campaign | kampeyn' | *s.* campanha / *vi.* fazer ou participar de campanha

campaigner | kampey'nə | *s.* aquele que serve em campanha; veterano

camphor | kam'fə | *s.* cânfora

camping | kam'ping | *s.* campismo

campus | kam'pəs | *s.* (EUA) terrenos de uma universidade, *campus*

can | kan' | *s.* lata; caneca / *vt.* enlatar / | kan | *v. aux.* poder; saber

Canadian | kəney'dīən | *s. a.* canadense

canal | kənal' | *s.* canal

canary | kəne'ərī | *s.* canário

canary-seed | kəne'ərīsid | *s.* alpiste

cancel | kan'səl | *vt.* cancelar; anular, revogar; eliminar

cancellation | kansəley'śən | *s.* cancelamento

cancer | kan'sə | *s.* câncer; (maiúsc., astron.) Câncer

candid | kan'did | *a.* franco, sincero; cândido

candidate | kan'dideyt | *s.* candidato

candid camera | kandidka'mərə | *s.* máquina fotográfica de bolso

candle | kan'dəl | *s.* vela. **-the game is not worth the c.** não vale a pena. **-not fit to hold a c. to** não se pode comparar com

candlestick | kan'dəlstik | *s.* castiçal

candlewick | kan'dəlwik | *s.* pavio de vela

candour, candor | kan'də | *s.* sinceridade, franqueza; ingenuidade, candura

candy | kan'dī | *s.* açúcar-cande; açúcar cristalizado; (EUA) bala, confeito

cane | keyn' | *s.* cana; bambu; bengala / *vt.* vergastar

cane-brake | keyn'breyk | *s.* bambuzal, taquaral

cane chair | keyn'śeə | *s.* cadeira de vime

cane-sugar | keyn'śugə | *s.* açúcar de cana

canine | key'nayn | *a.* canino

canned | kand' | *a.* enlatado, em

conserva; (gír.) despedido, posto na rua

cannery | ka'nərī | s. fábrica de conservas

cannibal | ka'nibəl | s. canibal, antropófago

cannon | ka'nən | s. canhão; carambola (bilhar)

cannonade | kanəneyd' | s. canhoneio / vt. vi. canhonear

cannon-fodder | ka'nənfodə | s. carne de canhão

canny | ka'nī | a. cauteloso, prudente; astuto, esperto

canoe | kənu' | s. canoa

canon | ka'nən | s. cônego; cânone; regra, princípio

canonical | kəno'nikəl | a. canônico

canon law | ka'nənló | s. direito canônico

can-opener | kan'owpənə | s. abridor de latas

canopy | ka'nəpī | s. dossel; pálio (de procissão)

cant | kant' | s. bisel; canto, ângulo; jargão; gíria; cantilena; inclinação; hipocrisia

cantankerous | kantang'kərəs | a. rabugento, rixento

canteen | kantin' | s. (mil.) cantina; cantil

canter | kan'tə | s. meio galope / vi. andar a meio galope

cant phrase | kant'freyz | s. expressão corrente, frase feita

canvas | kan'vəs | s. lona; tela (pintura); pano de vela; velame. **-under c.** em barracas

canvass | kan'vəs | s. discussão, debate; solicitação de votos / vt. solicitar (votos)

canyon | ka'niən | s. garganta estreita e profunda, desfiladeiro, canhão, canyon

cap | kap' | s. boné; boina; gorro; (mil.) quépi; (mil.) cápsula de percussão; tampa, tampinha (de garrafa). **-to make the c. fit** enfiar a carapuça / vt. cobrir a cabeça (boné, boina etc.); rematar, coroar. **-to c. the climax**

ser o cúmulo, passar dos limites

capability | keypəbi'litī | s. capacidade, aptidão, habilidade, competência

capable | key'pəbəl | a. capaz; apto, competente. **-c. of** capaz de; passível; sujeito a

capacious | kəpey'śəs | a. amplo, vasto, espaçoso

capacity | kəpa'sitī | s. capacidade; aptidão, faculdade; lotação (teatro etc.). **-in the c. of** na qualidade de

cape | keyp' | s. cabo, promontório; capa, pelerine

caper | key'pə | s. cabriola, cambalhota, salto; alcaparra; extravagância / vi. cabriolar, cambalhotar

capital | ka'pitəl | s. capital (tb. fin., com.); maiúscula (letra) / a. capital, principal; essencial; excelente. **-to make c. out of** tirar proveito de

capitalism | ka'pitəlizəm | s. capitalismo

capitalist | ka'pitəlist | s. capitalista

capitalistic | ka'pitəlistik | a. capitalista

capital letter | ka'pitəlle'tə | s. letra maiúscula

capitulate | kəpi'tĭuleyt | vi. capitular, render-se

capitulation | kəpitĭuley'śən | s. capitulação, rendição

caprice | kəpris' | s. capricho

capricious | kəpri'śəs | a. caprichoso; inconstante; extravagante; volúvel

capsize | kapsayz' | vt. vi. emborcar, virar de cabeça para baixo

capstan | kap'stən | s. cabrestante

capsule | kap'sĭul | s. cápsula

captain | kap'tin | s. capitão / vt. capitanear, comandar

caption | kap'śən | s. título, legenda

captious | kap'śəs | a. capcioso; manhoso; implicante

captivate | kap'tiveyt | vt. cativar, seduzir, fascinar

captivating | kap'tiveyting | *a.* cativante, fascinante

captive | kap'tiv | *s. a.* cativo

captivity | kapti'vitī | *s.* cativeiro

capture | kap'śə | *vt.* capturar, aprisionar

car | kʌ' | *s.* carro; automóvel; vagão

carat | ka'rət | *s.* quilate

caravan | ka'rəvan | *s.* caravana; reboque de campismo; carroção coberto (de circo etc.)

carbon | kʌ'bən | *s.* carbono

carbon paper | kʌ'bənpeypə | *s.* papel carbono

carbuncle | kʌ'bângkəl | *s.* carbúnculo

carburettor, carburetor | kʌbəre'tə | *s.* carburador

carcass | kʌ'kəs | *s.* carcaça

card | kʌd' | *s.* carta (de jogar); cartão de visitas; cartão postal; convite; entrada; programa. **-to be on the cards** ser provável, possível / *vt.* cardar (lã etc.)

cardboard | kʌd'bód | *s.* papelão, cartão, cartolina

cardigan | kʌ'digən | *s.* colete ou blusão de lã (com ou sem mangas)

cardinal | kʌ'dinəl | *s.* cardeal / *a.* cardeal, principal, fundamental

cardinal number | kʌ'dinəlnâm'bə | *s.* número cardinal

cardinal points | kʌ'dinəlpoyntz | *spl.* pontos cardeais

card index | kʌd'indeks | *s.* fichário

card-sharp, card-sharper | kʌd'śʌp(ə) | *s.* trapaceiro (em jogo de cartas)

care | ke'ə | *s.* cuidado; prudência; atenção; vigilância; preocupação; ansiedade, inquietação. **-c. of** (*abrev.* c/o) aos cuidados de. **-take c.!** tome cuidado! / *vi.* cuidar de, olhar por; importar-se com; interessar-se. **-c. to, c. for** gostar de. **-I don't c.** não me importa. **-I couldn't c.** less não me importa nada, nem ligo

career | kəri'ə | *s.* carreira, profissão; corrida / *vi.* correr a toda velocidade; ir a toda brida, galopar

carefree | ke'əfrı | *a.* despreocupado, feliz, tranqüilo

careful | ke'əful | *a.* cuidadoso; prudente; meticuloso; zeloso. **-be c.!** cuidado!

careless | ke'əles | *a.* descuidado, desatento; negligente, desleixado

carelessness | ke'əlesnes | *s.* descuido, negligência

caress | kəres' | *s.* carícia / *vt.* acariciar

caretaker | ke'əteykə | *s.* zelador; vigia, porteiro

careworn | ke'əwón | *a.* ansioso, angustiado

cargo | kʌ'gow | *s.* carga

caricature | ka'rikətiuə | *s.* caricatura / *vt.* caricaturar

carnage | kʌ'nij | *s.* carnagem, carnificina

carnal | kʌ'nəl | *a.* carnal

carnal knowledge | kʌ'nəlno'ləj | *s.* relações sexuais

carnation | kʌney'śən | *s.* (bot.) cravo

carnival | kʌ'nivəl | *s.* carnaval

carnivorous | kʌ'nivərəs | *a.* carnívoro

carol | ka'rəl | *s.* cântico alegre, hino de Natal / *vt. vi.* cantar com alegria (hino de Natal)

carousal | kəraw'zəl | *s.* festança, bebedeira, farra

carp | kʌp' | *s.* carpa / *vi.* **-to c. at** criticar, censurar

carpenter | kʌ'pintə | *s.* carpinteiro

carpentry | kʌ'pintrī | *s.* carpintaria

carpet | kʌ'pit | *s.* tapete, alcatifa, alfombra. **-on the c.** sob censura; em discussão; aguardando repreensão / *vt.* atapetar, alcatifar

carping | kʌ'ping | *a.* luxento, impertinente, difícil de contentar

carriage | ka'riǰ | s. carruagem; vagão de passageiros; porte; transporte; frete. -c. **forward** frete a pagar. -c. **paid** frete pago, porte pago

carrier | karı'ə | s. carregador; portador; transportador; (med.) hospedeiro; porta-aviões

carrier pigeon | kari'əpiǰən | s. pombo-correio

carrier wave | kari'əweyv | s. (eletrôn.) onda portadora

carrion | ka'rıən | s. carniça, carne podre

carrot | ka'rət | s. cenoura

carry | ka'rı | vt. transportar, levar; trazer consigo. -to c. **on** continuar. -to c. **off** ou **away** arrebatar; empolgar, entusiasmar. -to c. **back** devolver. -to c. **forward** transportar. -to c. **through** levar a cabo. -to c. **up** to ajustar; aumentar. -to c. **weight** ter peso ou influência. -to c. **the day** ganhar, levar a palma

cart | kat' | s. carroça; carreta; aranha (de um só cavalo). -to **put the c. before the horse** pôr o carro adiante dos bois / vt. transportar em carroça

carter | ka'tə | s. carroceiro, carreteiro

cart-load | kat'lowd | s. carrada, carga de um carro

carton | ka'tən | s. caixa de papelão

cartoon | katʊn' | s. desenho humorístico, caricatura

cartridge | ka'triǰ | s. cartucho (de arma de fogo)

carve | kav' | vt. esculpir, entalhar, cinzelar; trinchar (carne). -to c. **up** dividir em vários pedaços

carving | ka'ving | s. obra de talha; gravura

carving knife | ka'vingnayf | s. trinchante, faca de trinchar

cascade | kaskeyd' | s. cascata

case | keys' | s. caso; exemplo; causa, demanda; estojo; caixa, caixote. -in any c. em todo o caso, de qualquer forma

cash | kaś' | s. dinheiro, espécie. -to pay c. pagar em dinheiro. -c. on delivery (abrev. C.O.D.) entrega contra reembolso / vt. descontar (cheque); converter em dinheiro

cashew | kəśu' | s. cajueiro; caju; castanha-de-caju

cashier | kəśı'ə | s. caixa, encarregado da caixa / vt. pôr na rua, demitir; rejeitar, pôr de lado

cash register | kaś'reǰistə | s. caixa registradora

casing | key'sing | s. invólucro, revestimento; material de embalagem; cobertura

cask | kask' | s. barrica, barril (esp. de bebidas alcoólicas)

casket | kas'kit | s. cofrezinho, caixinha ornamentada (para guardar jóias etc.)

cassock | ka'sək | s. sotaina

cast | kast' | s. arremesso, lanço; molde, fôrma; (teat.) elenco; tom de cor, matiz; inclinação; disposição; forma, aparência; deformação; ligeiro estrabismo / vt. arremessar, lançar; fundir metal; (teat.) distribuir papéis. -to c. **aside** rejeitar, pôr de parte. -to c. **away** abandonar, perder; desfazer-se de; pôr fora. -to c. **in one's teeth** lançar em rosto a. -to c. **loose** soltar-se. -to c. **lots** tirar a sorte. -to be c. **down** estar desanimado

castanets | kastənets' | spl. castanholas

castaway | kast'əwey | s. réprobo; náufrago; pária

caste | kast' | s. casta; classe social

castigate | kas'tigeyt | vt. castigar; censurar

Castilian | kəsti'łłən | s. a. castelhano

cast iron | kastay'ən | s. ferro fundido

castle | ka'səl | s. castelo; torre (no xadrez)

castor | kas'tə | s. substância obtida do castor (usada em perfumaria); rodízio (de cadeira, mesa etc.)

castor oil | kʌs'təoyl | *s*. óleo de rícino

castor sugar | kʌs'təśugə | *s*. açúcar branco refinado

castrate | kastreyt' | *vt*. castrar

casual | ca'ziuəl | *a*. fortuito, casual; eventual; despreocupado, negligente; desatento; indolente

casuality | ca'ziuǎltī | *s*. casualidade; acidente, desgraça; vítima de acidente; (mil.) soldado morto ou ferido; (mil.) baixa

casuistry | ca'ziuistrī | *s*. casuística; sofisma

cat | kat' | *s*. gato; qualquer felino; mulher maliciosa. **-to rain cats and dogs** chover a cântaros. **-to lead a c.-and-dog life** viver como cão e gato. **-to let the c. out of the bag** revelar um segredo (involuntariamente). **-a c. among the pigeons** intruso, intrometido

cataclysm | ca'təklizəm | *s*. cataclismo

catacombs | ca'təkʊmz | *spl*. catacumbas

Catalan | katəlan' | *s. a*. catalão

catalogue, catalog | ca'təlog | *s*. catálogo

catapult | ca'təpəlt | *s*. catapulta; atiradeira, estilingue / *vt*. catapultar

cataract | ca'tərakt | *s*. catarata, cachoeira; aguaceiro; (med.) catarata

catarrh | kətʌ' | *s*. catarro

catastrophe | kətas'trəfī | *s*. catástrofe, calamidade

catcall | kat'kól | *s*. apupo, vaia / *vt. vi*. apupar, vaiar

catch | kaš' | *s*. aquilo que se apanha; presa; safra de peixe; lingüeta (de fechadura); armadilha; dificuldade; manha. **-a good c. of fish** uma boa pescaria / *vt*. capturar, apanhar; perceber, ouvir. **-to c. a cold** apanhar

um resfriado / *vi*. colar; prender-se, enredar-se; pegar fogo; pegar, popularizar-se. **-to c. up with** alcançar. **-to c. out** apanhar em (erro etc.)

catching | ca'šing | *a*. contagioso; atraente

catch-phrase | kaš'freyz | *s*. frase feita

catchword | kaš'wɛd | *s*. palavra colocada no alto das páginas dos dicionários; palavra chamariz; lema político; (teat.) deixa; estribilho

catchy | ca'šī | *a*. atraente, popular (melodia etc.); fácil de lembrar; enganoso

catechism | ca'təkizəm | *s*. catecismo

categorical | katəgo'rikəl | *a*. categórico; terminante

category | ca'tigərī | *s*. categoria; classe

cater | key'tə | *vi*. fornecer (alimentos, serviços para festas etc.); prover, abastecer; satisfazer

caterer | key'tərə | *s*. fornecedor; abastecedor

caterpillar | ca'təpilə | *s*. lagarta; caterpilar, trator de lagartas

cathedral | kəʋi'drəl | *s*. catedral

catholic | ca'ʋəlik | *s. a*. católico

catholicism | ca'ʋəlisizəm | *s*. catolicismo

cattle | ca'təl | *s*. gado (vacum)

catty | ca'tī | *a*. fingido, dissimulado, maldoso

caucus | kó'kəs | *s*. comitê político; (pej.) panelinha

cauldron | kól'drən | *s*. caldeirão

cauliflower | ko'liflawə | *s*. couve-flor

caulk | kók' | *vt*. calafetar

cause | kóz' | *s*. causa, motivo, origem / *vt*. causar, originar, motivar

causeway | kóz'wey | *s*. calçada

caustic | kós'tik | *a*. cáustico

caution | kó'śən | *s*. advertência; prudência, cautela / *vt*. acautelar, prevenir

cautious | kó'śəs | *a.* cuidadoso, cauteloso, precavido; judicioso

cautiousness | kó'śəsnes | *s.* precaução, prudência

cavalcade | kavəlkeyd' | *s.* cavalgada, desfile, parada

cavalier | kavəlı'ə | *s.* cavaleiro; cavalheiro; partidário de Carlos I da Inglaterra / *a.* desdenhoso, arrogante

cavalry | ka'vəlrī | *s.* cavalaria

cave | keyv' | *s.* caverna, gruta; antro / *vi.* **-to c. in** desmoronar, ruir; sucumbir

caveat | key'vīat | *s.* advertência, aviso; (jur.) embargo de terceiro

cavern | ka'vən | *s.* caverna

cavil | ka'vil | *vi.* cavilar, sofismar, chicanar

cavity | ka'vitī | *s.* cavidade; cárie dentária

caw | kó' | *vi.* grasnar, crocitar

cease | sɪs' | *vt. vi.* cessar, parar, acabar, terminar

ceaseless | sɪs'les | *a.* contínuo, incessante

cedar | sɪ'də | *s.* cedro

cede | sɪd' | *vt.* ceder, conceder, transferir

cedilla | sədi'lə | *s.* cedilha

ceiling | sɪ'ling | *s.* teto

celebrate | se'libreyt | *vt.* celebrar; comemorar; festejar ruidosamente

celebrated | se'libreytid | *a.* célebre, notável, ilustre

celebration | selibrey'śən | *s.* celebração; comemoração

celebrity | sǝle'britī | *s.* celebridade; pessoa célebre

celery | se'lərī | *s.* aipo

celestial | səles'tīəl | *a.* celeste; celestial

celibacy | se'libəsī | *s.* celibato

cell | sel' | *s.* cela; (med., bot. etc.) célula

cellar | se'lə | *s.* adega; porão; abrigo subterrâneo

Celt | kelt' | *s.* celta

Celtic | kel'tik | *a.* céltico

cement | siment' | *s.* cimento / *vt.* cimentar

cemetery | se'mətrī | *s.* cemitério

cenotaph | se'nowtʌf | *s.* cenotáfio

censor | sen'sə | *s.* censor / *vt.* censurar, cortar

censorious | sensó'rīəs | *a.* severo, censurador, reprovador

censorship | sen'səśip | *s.* censura

censure | sen'śə | *s.* censura, reprovação, condenação / *vt.* censurar, reprovar

census | sen'səs | *s.* recenseamento, censo

cent | sent' | *s.* centavo

centenary | sentı'nərī | *s.* centenário

centigrade | sen'tigreyd | *s.* centígrado

centimetre, centimeter | sen'timıtə | *s.* centímetro

centipede | sen'tipıd | *s.* centopéia

central | sen'trəl | *a.* central; fundamental, básico

centralize | sen'trəlayz | *vt.* centralizar

centre, center | sen'tə | *s.* centro; meio; núcleo / *vt.* centrar, concentrar / *vi.* centralizar-se, concentrar-se

century | sen'ťurī | *s.* século; centúria; centena

ceramics | sira'miks | *s.* cerâmica

cereal | sı'rīəl | *s.* cereal

ceremonial | serimow'nıəl | *s.* cerimonial / *a.* cerimonial, formal

ceremonious | serimow'nīəs | *a.* cerimonioso

ceremony | se'rimənī | *s.* cerimônia, solenidade. **-to stand on c.** fazer cerimônia

certain | sᴇ'tin | *a.* certo; seguro; estabelecido. **-for c.** com certeza, certamente

certainty | sᴇ'tintī | *s.* certeza, segurança

certificate | səti'fikeyt | *s.* certificado; certidão; diploma

certified copy | SE'tifaydkopī | *s.* cópia autenticada

certify | SE'tifay | *vt.* certificar; declarar; atestar

cessation | sesey'śən | *s.* cessação; parada, suspensão

cession | se'śən | *s.* cessão

cesspool | ses'pʊl | *s.* fossa sanitária, esgoto

chafe | šeyf' | *vt.* esfregar, friccionar; esfolar, irritar / *vi.* irritar-se, agastar-se, impacientar-se

chaff | šaf' | *s.* farelo; palha cortada / *vt.* troçar de

chaffinch | ša'finś | *s.* (orn.) tentilhão

chagrin | ša'grin | *s.* desgosto, pesar, mortificação

chain | šeyn' | *s.* corrente; cadeia, série, sucessão / *vt.* acorrentar

chain smoker | šeyn' smowkə | *s.* fumante inveterado

chair | še'ə | *s.* cadeira; cátedra; (EUA) cadeira elétrica. **-to take the c.** presidir (abrir) a sessão

chairman | še'əmən | *s.* presidente (de conselho, comissão, sessão etc.)

chalet | ša'ley | *s.* chalé

chalice | ša'lis | *s.* cálice

chalk | šók' | *s.* giz; greda branca. **-not by a long c.** longe disso. **-as different as c. from cheese** inteiramente diferente, da água para o vinho

challenge | ša'lenǰ | *s.* desafio / *vt.* desafiar; (mil.) pedir senha

challenger | ša'lənǰə | *s.* desafiante; competidor

chamber | šeym'bə | *s.* câmara; (jur.) sala de audiência; aposento, quarto

chamber-maid | šeym'bəmeyd | *s.* criada de quarto

chamber music | šeym'bəmǐuzik | *s.* música de câmara

chamber-pot | šeym'bəpot | *s.* urinol

chameleon | kəmɪ'lǐən | *s.* camaleão

chamois | ša'mwa | *s.* camurça

champion | šam'pǐən | *s.* campeão; paladino / *vt.* defender

championship | šam'pǐən'śip | *s.* campeonato; defesa

chance | śAns' | *s.* oportunidade, chance; sorte, fortuna; casualidade; contingência; risco. **-by c.** por acaso. **-not a c.!** de jeito nenhum! **-even c.** igual probabilidade / *a.* acidental, fortuito / *vt.* arriscar / *vi.* acontecer, suceder. **-to c. on** ou **upon** topar com

chancellor | šAn'sələ | *s.* chanceler

Chancellor of the Exchequer | śAn'sələovðəeksše'kə | *s.* ministro da Fazenda

chandelier | śandəlɪ'ə | *s.* candelabro, lampadário

chandler | šan'dlə | *s.* (ant.) mercador, negociante (de velas, sabão etc.)

change | seynǰ' | *s.* mudança, alteração, transformação; variação; diversão, distração; muda de roupa; câmbio; troco, dinheiro trocado. **-for a c.** para variar / *vt.* mudar (de), trocar; alterar; substituir / *vi.* mudar, modificar(-se), transformar(-se)

changeable | seynǰ'ǰəbəl | *a.* variável, mutável, inconstante

changeableness | šeynǰ'ǰəbəlnes | *s.* variabilidade

changeless | šeynǰ'les | *a.* constante, imutável

channel | ša'nəl | *s.* canal; sulco, rego; estreito (de mar); lejto (de rio); meio, via. **-the C.** canal da Mancha / *vt.* canalizar, abrir valas; encaminhar

chant | śAnt' | *s.* canção, cântico; salmo; cantilena, melopéia / *vt. vi.* cantar, entoar. **-to c. the praises of** entoar louvores a

chaos | key'os | *s.* caos

chaotic | keyo'tik | *a.* caótico

chap | šap' | *s.* homem, rapaz, sujeito, camarada; rachadura, greta / *vt.* rachar, gretar

chapel | ša'pəl | *s.* capela; oratório;

coro de capela; associação de tipógrafos

chaperon | ša'pərown | *s.* acompanhante (de moça solteira), dama de companhia / *vt.* acompanhar (senhorita)

chaplain | ša'plin | *s.* capelão

chapter | šap'tə | *s.* capítulo; (ecles.) cabido; assunto, matéria; episódio

char | šA' | *s.* (*abrev.* de **charwoman**) faxineira / *vt.* carbonizar, queimar, torrar / *vi.* fazer faxina

character | ka'rəktə | *s.* caráter; personalidade; índole, temperamento; (teat.) personagem, papel; pessoa excêntrica; letra, escrita; (tip.) estilo de tipo

characteristic | karəktəris'tik | *s.* característica / *a.* característico, típico

characterize | ka'rəktərayz | *vt.* caracterizar, definir; distinguir, assinalar

charade | šərAd' šəreyd' | *s.* charada; enigma

charcoal | šA'kowl | *s.* carvão de lenha

charcoal-burner | šA'kowlbEnə | *s.* carvoeiro

charge | šAJ' | *s.* carga (arma de fogo, eletricidade etc.); encargo, ônus; responsabilidade; despesa, débito; (mil.) assalto, ataque; comando, ordem; (jur.) acusação; custódia, tutela; (ecles.) exortação, alocução; (*pl.*) despesas. **-in c. of** encarregado de / *vt.* cobrar; carregar (arma etc.) / *vi.* atacar, acometer

chariot | ša'rïət | *s.* carro (antigo, de guerra); carruagem leve

charitable | ša'ritəbəl | *a.* caridoso; tolerante

charity | ša'ritï | *s.* caridade; esmola, donativo

charlatan | šA'lətən | *s.* charlatão, embusteiro

charm | šAm' | *s.* encanto, charme; amuleto, talismã / *vt.* en-

cantar; enfeitiçar; agradar, deleitar

charming | šA'ming | *a.* encantador, fascinante

charnel-house | šA'nəlhaws | *s.* ossuário, capela mortuária

chart | šAt' | *s.* mapa; quadro, tabela, diagrama / *vt.* mapear; (náut.) traçar a rota; demonstrar graficamente; projetar, traçar

charter | šA'tə | *s.* carta (régia ou constitucional); carta patente; afretamento / *vt.* conceder privilégio, alvará etc.; fretar

charwoman | šA'wəmən | *s.* faxineira; arrumadeira

chary | še'ərï | *a.* cuidadoso, cauteloso; frugal, parcimonioso; pouco inclinado a

chase | šeys' | *s.* perseguição, caçada / *vt.* perseguir, dar caça, acossar. **-to c. away** afugentar

chasm | ka'zəm | *s.* abismo

chassis | ša'sï | *s.* chassi

chaste | šeyst' | *a.* casto; modesto, decente, singelo

chasten | šey'sən | *vt.* castigar, punir; abrandar

chastise | šastayz' | *vt.* castigar; disciplinar; açoitar

chastity | šas'titï | *s.* castidade; modéstia, continência; pureza de estilo

chat | šat' | *s.* conversa leve, bate-papo / *vt.* conversar, tagarelar

chattel | ša'təl | *s.* bem móvel

chatter | ša'tə | *s.* tagarelice; bater de dentes; vibração (de ferramenta etc.)

chatterbox | ša'təboks | *s.* tagarela, palrador, falador

chauffeur | šow'fə | *s.* chofer, motorista

cheap | šïp' | *a.* barato, econômico; ordinário. **-c. and nasty** barato e ordinário. **-to hold c.** desprezar

cheapen | šï'pən | *vt.* baixar o preço de, depreciar

cheapjack | šïp'jak | *s.* mascate, bufarinheiro

cheap labour | ší pley'bə | s. mão--de-obra barata

cheat | šıt' | s. trapaceiro, impostor, escroque; burla, logro, fraude / vt. vi. trapacear, enganar

check | šek' | s. xeque (xadrez); padrão xadrez (tecido); parada; revés; (EUA) cheque; (EUA) conta (restaurante) / vt. pôr em xeque; refrear, conter; moderar; verificar, investigar; fiscalizar; conferir (conta etc.); embargar, impedir. **-to c. off** conferir, verificar. **-to c. up on** investigar (costumes de alguém) / vi. conferir, estar conforme. **-to c. in** registrar-se (em hotel). **-to c. out** pagar a conta e sair (de hotel)

checkmate | šek'meyt | s. xeque--mate / vt. dar xeque-mate; derrotar

check-up, checkup | šek'âp | s. exame cuidadoso (esp. med.)

cheek | šík' | s. face, bochecha; atrevimento, descaramento, insolência

cheek-bone | šık'bown | s. maçã do rosto

cheeky | ší'kī | a. petulante, insolente

cheep | šíp' | vi. piar

cheer | ší'ə | s. ânimo, disposição; viva. **-what c.?** como está?, como se sente? **-to be of good c.** estar animado, animar-se / vt. alegrar, animar; dar vivas / vi. animar-se. **-c. up!** ânimo!, anime-se!

cheerful | ší'əful | a. alegre, animado, jovial

cheerfulness | ší'əfulnes | s. alegria, animação

cheering | ší'əring | s. vivas, aplausos / a. animador

cheerio | ší'rīow | interj. saudação ou palavra de encorajamento (na despedida, antes de beber etc.)

cheerless | ší'əles | a. desanimado, melancólico, sombrio

cheers | sí'əz | interj. saúde!, viva!, apoiado!

cheery | ší'ərī | a. alegre, animado, vivo

cheese | šīz' | s. queijo

chef | šef' | s. chefe de cozinha, cozinheiro

chemicals | ke'mikəlz | spl. produtos químicos

chemist | ke'mist | s. químico; farmacêutico

chemistry | ke'mistrī | s. química

cheque, check | šek' | s. cheque. **-crossed c.** cheque cruzado

cheque-book | šek'buk | s. talão de cheques

chequered, checkered | še'kərd | a. quadriculado; (fig.) acidentado (carreira, vida)

cherish | se'riš | vt. cuidar bem de, tratar com carinho; alimentar, nutrir (esperança etc.); acalentar; ter, guardar (no coração)

cheroot | sərvt' | s. espécie de charuto com as duas pontas cortadas

cherry | še'rī | s. cereja

chess | šes' | s. xadrez

chess-board | šes'bóəd | s. tabuleiro de xadrez

chest | šest' | s. arca, baú, caixa (de ferramentas, remédios etc.); cofre; peito

chestnut | šest'nət | s. castanha; (coloq.) anedota velha / a. castanho

chest of drawers | šestovdró'əz | s. cômoda

chew | šv' | s. mastigação; pedaço de fumo de mascar / vt. mastigar, mascar. **-to c. the cud** ruminar, meditar. **-to c. the rag** (gír.) discutir assunto do qual se guarda ressentimento, remoer

chewing-gum | šu'inggâm | s. goma de mascar, chiclete

chic | šík' | a. chique, elegante

chick | šík' | s. pinto, pintinho; (coloq.) criança

chicken | ší'kin | s. frango

chide | šayd' | vt. vi. ralhar, repreender

chief| sɪf' |s. chefe /a. principal, o mais importante

chieftain| šɪf'tən |s. chefe (de salteadores); chefe (de clã ou tribo)

child | sayld' | s. criança; filho. **-with c.** grávida. **-this c.** (gír.) eu. **-from a c.** desde criança

childhood | šayld'hud | s. meninice, infância

childish | šayl'diš | a. infantil, pueril, de criança

childishness | šayl'dišnes | s. infantilidade

childlike | šayld'layk |a. inocente, próprio de criança

chill | šil' | s. calefrio, arrepio; frio; resfriado. **-to catch a c.** apanhar um resfriado. **-to take the c. off** amornar / a. frio / vt. esfriar, resfriar; (fig.) desanimar

chilled | šild' | a. gelado; congelado

chilliness| ši'lɪnes |s. frio; frieza, indiferença

chilly | ši'lɪ |a. um tanto frio; friorento; insensível, indiferente

chime | šaym' |s. carrilhão; repique; sons harmoniosos / vt. repicar, bimbalhar. **-to c. in with** harmonizar-se com, concordar com

chimera | kɪmɪ'rə |s. quimera

chimney | šim'nī | s. chaminé; lareira; chaminé (de vulcão ou montanha)

chimney-corner | šim'nīkónə |s. canto da lareira

chimney-sweep, chimney-sweeper | šim'nīswɪp(ə) |s. limpador de chaminés

chimpanzee | šim'panzɪ |s. chimpanzé, chipanzé

chin | šin' | s. queixo

china | šay'nə |s. porcelana

Chinese| šay'nɪz |s. a. chinês

chink| šink' | s. fenda, greta, racha; tinido metálico

chip | šip' | s. cavaco, lasca (de madeira ou pedra), estilhaço; (pl.) batatas fritas (em lascas) / vt. lascar, quebrar / vi. lascar-se

chiropodist| kiro'pədist |s. pedicuro

chirp | šɛp' | s. trilo (de passarinho, grilo etc.) / vi. trilar, chilrear

chirpy| šɛ'pɪ |a. alegre, vivaz, jovial, animado

chirrup | ši'rəp | s. série de trilos ou chilreios / vi. trilar, chilrear

chisel | ši'zəl | s. cinzel; formão / vt. cinzelar

chit | šit' | s. criança, pirralho; mulher franzina; pequena insolente; nota, papel escrito, vale

chit-chat | šit'šat | s. conversa leve, bate-papo

chivalrous | ši'vəlrəs | a. cavalheiresco, nobre

chivalry | ši'vəlrī | s. cavalaria (medieval); cavalheirismo, nobreza, cortesia

chock-full | šokful' |a. abarrotado, à cunha

chocolate | šok'lit | s. chocolate; bombom

choice | šoys' | s. escolha, preferência; sortimento, variedade (de mercadorias etc.); alternativa / a. seleto, escolhido, superior

choir | kway'ə | s. coro, orfeão, grupo coral, coro de igreja / vt. vi. cantar em coro

choirboy | kway'əboy | s. menino de coro

choke| šowk' |vt. vi. sufocar, estrangular. **-to c. off** desencorajar (pessoa), dissuadir. **-to c. down** engolir com dificuldade

cholera| ko'lərə |s. (med.) cólera

choleric | kole'rik | a. colérico, irascível

choose| šuz' |vt. escolher, preferir. **-I cannot c. but** não tenho outra alternativa senão

chop | šop' | s. costeleta (de porco, carneiro etc.); talhada / vt. rachar (lenha); picar, cortar.

-to c. off cortar fora. **-to c. logic** discutir, argumentar. **-to c. and change** variar constantemente, ser inconstante

chop-house | sop'haws | *s.* restaurante barato

chopper | šo'pə | *s.* cortador; cutelo; máquina de picar; (coloq.) helicóptero; (gír.) metralhadora

choppy | šo'pī | *a.* agitado, picado, encapelado (mar)

choppy sea | šo'pīsɪ | *s.* mar encapelado

chord | kód' | *s.* acorde; corda (vocal etc.); (geom.) corda; (poét. ou fig.) corda de harpa. **-to touch the right c.** tocar na corda sensível

chore | šó'ə | *s.* rotina diária, tarefa tediosa

chorister | ko'ristə | *s.* menino de coro, membro de coro

chortle | šó'tɘl | *vi.* casquinar, soltar risadinhas

chorus | kó'rəs | *s.* coro, estribilho / *vt. vi.* cantar em coro, dizer em coro

chorus-girl | kó'rəsɡɛl | *s.* corista

chowder | šow'də | *s.* (EUA) sopa de peixe ou mariscos

Christ | krayst' | *s.* Cristo

christen | kri'sən | *vt. vi.* batizar; dar nome a

Christendom | kri'səndəm | *s.* cristandade

christening | kri'səning | *s.* batismo; batizado

Christian | kris'tɪən | *s. a.* cristão

Christian burial | kris'tɪənbe'-rɪɐl | *s.* enterro cristão, enterro religioso

Christianity | kristɪa'nitɪ | *s.* cristianismo

Christian name | kris'tɪənneym | *s.* nome de batismo

Christmas | kris'məs | *s.* Natal

Christmas Eve | kris'məsɪv | *s.* véspera de Natal

chronic | kro'nik | *a.* crônico; inveterado

chronicle | kro'nikəl | *s.* crônica; narrativa / *vt.* narrar, registrar, relatar

chronicler | kro'niklə | *s.* cronista

chronological | kronəlo'jikəl | *a.* cronológico

chrysanthemum | krisan'təməm | *s.* crisântemo

chubby | šâ'bɪ | *a.* bochechudo, rechonchudo, roliço

chuck | šâk' | *s.* pancadinha amigável debaixo do queixo; (mec.) mandril. **-to give someone the c.** dar o fora em alguém / *vt.* afagar; atirar, jogar (com desprezo ou descuidadamente). **-to c. out** expulsar (de bar, reunião etc.). **-c. it!** (gír.) pare com isso!, acabe com isso!

chuckle | šâ'kəl | *vi.* rir por entre os dentes; exultar discretamente

chuckle-head | šâ'kəlhed | *s.* palerma, estúpido, idiota

chum | šâm' | *s.* camarada, companheiro, amigo íntimo; engodo (para atrair peixes) / *vi.* partilhar o mesmo quarto; acamaradar-se; engodar, atirar engodo

chunk | šânk' | *s.* pedaço grande, tora

church | šɛš' | *s.* igreja

churchman | šɛš'mən | *s.* clérigo, eclesiástico; membro zeloso de uma igreja, devoto de comunidade religiosa

churchyard | šɛs'ɪAd | *s.* cemitério (anexo a uma igreja); terreno de igreja

churlish | šɛ'liš | *a.* grosseiro, descortês; avarento

churn | šɛn' | *s.* batedeira de manteiga; latão de leite / *vt.* bater leite, fazer manteiga; fazer espuma

chute | šut | *s.* calha; rampa; (coloq.) pára-quedas

cider | say'də | *s.* sidra

cigar | sigA' | *s.* charuto

cigarette, cigaret | sigəret' | *s.* cigarro

cigarette-case | sigəret'keys | *s.* cigarreira

cigarette-holder | sigəret'holdə | *s.* piteira

cigarette-lighter | sigəret'laytə | *s.* isqueiro

cigarette-paper | sigəret'peypə | *s.* papel para fazer cigarros, mortalha

cinch | sinš' | *s.* (EUA) cincha, barrigueira; (gír., EUA) coisa fácil e segura, sopa, canja

cinder | sin'də | *s.* cinza vulcânica; escória; borralho; (*pl.*) cinzas

Cinderella | sindəre'lə | *s.* Gata Borralheira; pessoa desprezada etc.

cinema | si'nəmə | *s.* cinema

cipher, cypher | say'fə | *s.* zero; pessoa ou coisa sem importância; algarismo (arábico); código secreto; chave de código; monograma

circle | SE'kəl | *s.* círculo; grupo; camada social; (teat.) balcão. **-to come full c.** dar uma volta completa / *vt.* girar em volta de, dar a volta a

circuit | SE'kit | *s.* circuito; volta; itinerário; rodada, acontecimentos esportivos; cadeia (de cinema, teatro)

circuitous | SEkĭu'itəs | *a.* circundante; indireto

circular | SE'kĭulə | *s.* circular / *a.* circular, redondo; indireto

circulate | SE'kĭuleyt | *vt.* circular; difundir / *vi.* circular, girar; difundir-se

circulation | SEkĭuley'šən | *s.* circulação; tiragem (de jornais, publicações periódicas)

circumcise | SE'kəmsayz | *vt.* circuncidar

circumference | SEkâm'fərəns | *s.* circunferência

circumflex | SE'kəmfleks | *a.* circunflexo (acento)

circumlocution | SEkəmləkĭu'šən | *s.* circunlóquio

circumnavigate | SEkəmna'vi-geyt | *vt.* circunavegar

circumscribe | SE'kəmskrayb | *vt.* circunscrever, limitar, fixar, abranger

circumspect | SE'kəmspekt | *a.* circunspecto, discreto

circumspection | SE'kəmspek'šən | *s.* circunspecção

circumstance | SE'kəmstans | *s.* circunstância

circumstantial | SEkəmstan'šəl | *a.* circunstancial; pormenorizado, circunstanciado

circumvent | SEkəmvent' | *vt.* apanhar com armadilha; evadir, evitar (dificuldade etc.)

circus | SE'kəs | *s.* circo

cistern | sis'tən | *s.* cisterna, reservatório

citadel | si'tədəl | *s.* cidadela

citation | saytey'šən | *s.* citação, intimação; referência; (mil.) menção honrosa

cite | sayt' | *vt.* citar, intimar; mencionar; (mil.) citar em menção honrosa

citizen | si'tizən | *s.* cidadão

citizenship | si'tizənšip | *s.* cidadania

citron | si'trən | *s.* cidra, cidrão; cidreira

city | si'tī | *s.* cidade (importante). **-the C.** centro comercial e financeiro de Londres

city council | si'tīkawn'sil | *s.* municipalidade; câmara de vereadores

city fathers | si'tīfaðəz | *spl.* vereadores

city hall | si'tīhól | *s.* prefeitura

civic | si'vik | *a.* cívico

civil | si'vil | *a.* civil; cortês, polido

civil disobedience | si'vildizowbI'dĭənz | *s.* desobediência (resistência) passiva

civilian | sivi'lĭən | *s.* civil / *a.* civil. **-in c. clothes** à paisana

civility | sivi'litī | *s.* civilidade

civilization | sivilayzey'šən | *s.* civilização

civilize | si'vilayz | vt. civilizar; educar; refinar

civilizing | si'vilayzing | a. civilizador

civil law | si'villó | s. direito civil

civil servant | si'vilsɛvənt | s. funcionário público

civil service | si'vilsɛvis | s. serviço público

civil war | si'vilwó | s. guerra civil

clad | klad' | a. vestido; recoberto

claim | kleym' | s. reivindicação; pretensão; reclamação / vt. reivindicar; pretender; reclamar, exigir

claimant | kley'mənt | s. reclamante, requerente; pretendente (ao trono)

clairvoyant | kleəvoy'ənt | s. vidente

clam | klam' | s. marisco, amêijoa etc. (bivalves)

clamber | klam'bə | s. escalada / vt. vi. escalar, subir com dificuldade

clammy | kla'mī | a. pegajoso; viscoso; úmido

clamour, clamor | kla'mə | s. clamor; gritaria / vi. vociferar; gritar

clamp | klamp' | s. grampo, braçadeira / vt. segurar com grampo ou braçadeira. **-to c. down on** suprimir, proibir, fazer parar

clan | klan' | s. clã; grupo

clandestine | klandes'tin | a. clandestino

clang | klang' | s. tinido; clangor / vt. fazer tinir / vi. retinir, ressoar

clank | klank' | vi. tinir

clannish | kla'niś | a. de ou relativo a clã; exclusivo

clap | klap' | s. estampido, estrondo (trovão) / vi. aplaudir, bater palmas. **-to c. eyes on** avistar. **-to c. on the back** dar pancadinhas nas costas

claptrap | klap'trap | s. bazófia, palavrório

clarify | kla'rifay | vt. esclarecer; clarificar

clarion | kla'rīən | s. clarim

clarity | kla'ritī | s. claridade

clash | klaś' | s. colisão, choque; discordância, conflito / vi. colidir, chocar-se; discordar, entrar em conflito

clasp | klʌsp' | s. fivela; fecho; aperto de mão / vt. afivelar; apertar a mão; abraçar; estreitar; segurar na mão

clasp-knife | klʌsp'nayf | s. faca de mola

class | klʌs' | s. classe; espécie, categoria; camada social; aula; turma de alunos / vt. classificar, agrupar

classic | kla'sik | s. a. clássico. **-the classics** os clássicos; letras clássicas

classification | klasifikey'śən | s. classificação

clatter | kla'tə | s. algazarra, vozerio; ruído, barulho, estrépito

clause | klóz' | s. cláusula; parágrafo; artigo; oração gramatical

claw | kló' | s. garra, unha; pinça, tenaz (lagosta etc.) / vt. arranhar, lacerar, rasgar (com garras)

clay | kley' | s. barro, argila

clay pipe | kley'payp | s. cachimbo de barro

clean | klīn' | a. limpo; puro, imaculado; perfeito; audível; visível; manifesto; honesto, inocente

cleaner | klī'nə | s. encarregado(a) da limpeza; preparado para limpar, removedor. **-to take to the cleaners** roubar todo o dinheiro de alguém; criticar asperamente.

cleanliness | klen'lines | s. limpeza, asseio; arrumação

cleanse | klenz' | vt. limpar; purificar; absolver

clean-shaven | klīn'śeyvn | a. escanhoado, bem barbeado

clear | klī'ə | a. claro; distinto; evidente, manifesto; limpo, puro, transparente / vt. clarear; limpar; dissolver; desobstruir; saltar, passar sobre (obstáculo); tirar a mesa; abrir caminho; saldar, liquidar. **-to c. up** esclarecer (problema); fazer a limpeza; aclarar (tempo) / *vi.* clarear-se, limpar-se. **-to c. off** ir-se embora. **-to c. up** melhorar, abrir (tempo)

clearance | klı'ərəns | *s.* esclarecimento; desobstrução; liberação; (mec.) folga, espaço livre; (náut.) desembaraço de navio

clearance sale | klı'ərənsseyl | *s.* (com.) liquidação total

clearing | klı'əring | *s.* esclarecimento; clareira; (com.) compensação de cheques

clearness | klı'ənes | *s.* claridade; clareza; limpidez

cleavage | klı'vij | *s.* divisão; corte; fissura, fenda

cleave | klı́v' | *vt.* rachar, fender / *vi.* fender-se, rachar-se; abrir caminho; aderir, apegar-se

cleft | klɛft' | *s.* fissura, rachadura; reentrância

clemency | kle'mənsī | *s.* clemência, indulgência

clench |klɛnś | *vt.* rebitar; cerrar (punho, dentes)

clergy | klɛ'jī | *s.* clero

clergyman | klɛ'jĭmən | *s.* pastor, ministro protestante

cleric | kle'rik | *s.* clérigo / *a.* clerical

clerk | klʌk' | *s.* escrevente, empregado (de escritório, banco); empregado leigo (de paróquia); (EUA) caixeiro, balconista. **-c. in holy orders** clérigo

clerk of the works | klʌk'ovðəwɛks | *s.* supervisor de obras

clever | kle'və | *a.* hábil, destro; inteligente, esperto, perspicaz, arguto

cleverness | kle'vənes | *s.* habilidade, destreza; inteligência, sagacidade

cliché | klı'śey | *s.* clichê; lugar comum, idéia feita

click | klik' | *s.* estalido, clique / *vt.* fazer estalar. **-to c. the heels** bater os calcanhares / *vi.* produzir um estalido

client | klay'ənt | *s.* cliente; freguês ou freguesa

clientele | klıəntel' | *s.* clientela; freguesia

cliff | klif' | *s.* penhasco, rochedo escarpado

climate | klay'mit | *s.* clima

climax | klay'maks | *s.* clímax; ápice, auge, culminância

climb | klaym' | *s.* subida / *vt. vi.* subir, escalar. **-to c. down** descer (declive íngreme); (fig.) desistir, abandonar

climber | klay'mə | *s.* alpinista, escalador

climbing | klay'ming | *a.* ascendente; que forma subida

clinch | klinś' | *s.* (boxe) *clinch,* agarrado; (coloq.) abraço / *vt.* confirmar; decidir, resolver (negócio etc.)

cling | kling' | *vi.* agarrar-se, unir-se; aderir

clinic | klı'nik | *s.* clínica

clink | klink' | *s.* tinido; (gír.) cadeia, prisão / *vi.* tinir, tilintar

clip | klip' | *s.* clipe (para papéis); fecho (de jóia etc.); pente, carregador de cartuchos / *vt.* cortar, aparar; tosquiar; podar; perfurar (bilhete, entrada)

clipper | kli'pə | *s.* tosquiador; máquina de cortar (cabelo, lã); clíper (navio ou avião); cavalo veloz; (gír.) pessoa ou coisa excelente

clipping | kli'ping | *s.* tosquia; recorte de jornal

clique | klık' | *s. clique,* igrejinha, panelinha

cloak | klowk' | *s.* capa, manto; disfarce / *vt.* encapotar; disfarçar, encobrir

cloakroom | klowk'rʊm | *s.* vestiário, guarda-roupa

clock | klok' | *s.* relógio (exceto os de pulso ou bolso). **-it is ten o'c.** são dez horas / *vt.* cronometrar / *vi.* **-to c. in** ou **out** bater o ponto (entrando ou saindo) clockwise | klok'wayz | *a.* da esquerda para a direita

clockwork | klok'wɛk | *s.* mecanismo de relógio

clod | klod' | *s.* torrão (de terra); palerma, pateta

clog | klog' | *s.* tamanco, soco / *vt.* entupir, obstruir

cloister | kloys'tə | *s.* claustro

close | klows' | *s.* encerramento, término / *a.* fechado; encerrado; abafado; reservado; íntimo (amigo); disputado (concurso, corrida etc.); cuidadoso, minucioso; bem guardado (segredo); compacto (textura); apertado, justo. -at c. quarters de perto; em contato. -to have a c. shave escapar por um triz. -c. range pequena distância / *adv.* perto, próximo. -c. on perto de / | klowz' | *vt. vi.* fechar, encerrar; acabar, terminar. -to c. in aproximar-se; fechar, encerrar. -to c. down fechar ou parar totalmente. -to c. ranks cerrar fileiras. -to c. with cair sobre, lutar com

closeness | klows'nes | *s.* proximidade, intimidade; densidade (textura); fidelidade (tradução)

closet | klo'zit | *s.* gabinete; armário embutido; guarda-roupa; privada / *a.* confidencial, privado

closet play | klo'zitpley | *s.* peça para ser lida e não representada

closure | klow'jə | *s.* encerramento, término

clot | klot' | *s.* coágulo; coalho; grumo / *vt.* coagular; coalhar / *vi.* coagular-se

cloth | kloϑ' | *s.* tecido, fazenda, pano. -the c. o clero

cloth-binding | kloϑ'baynding | *s.* encadernação em pano

clothe | klowð' | *vt.* vestir; cobrir, revestir; investir

clothes | klowðz' | *spl.* roupas, vestuário; roupa de cama

clothing | klow'ðing | *s.* roupa, vestuário

cloud | klawd' | *s.* nuvem. -in the clouds nas nuvens, sonhando. -under a c. desacreditado, sob suspeita / *vi.* turvar-se. -to c. over nublar-se, enevoar-se

cloudburst | klawd'bɛst | *s.* aguaceiro, temporal

cloudiness | klaw'dines | *s.* nebulosidade; obscuridade

cloudless | klawd'les | *a.* sem nuvens, claro, límpido

cloudy | klaw'dī | *a.* nublado, nebuloso; turvo (líquido)

clout | klawt' | *s.* (coloq.) bofetão, bofetada

clove | klowv' | *s.* cravo-da-índia; dente de alho

clover | klow'və | *s.* trevo. -inc.na abastança e no luxo

clown | klawn' | *s.* palhaço / *vi.* fazer palhaçadas

cloy | kloy' | *vt.* empanturrar; saciar, enfadar

club | klâb' | *s.* clube, sociedade, associação; bastão, cacete; clava, maça; taco de golfe; (*pl.*) paus (cartas). -in the c. (gír.) grávida / *vt.* dar cacetadas em; associar. -to c. up reunir quantia (cotização) / *vi.* associar-se, juntar-se

cluck | klâk' | *s.* cacarejo / *vi.* cacarejar

clue | klu' | *s.* indício, sinal, pista, chave / *vt.* dar uma pista. -to c. in ou up (gír.) informar

clump | klâmp' | *s.* grupo, aglomeração; grumo; sola grossa

clumsiness | klâm'zines | *s.* falta de jeito; inépcia

clumsy | klâm'zī | *a.* desajeitado, desastrado; tosco

cluster | klâs'tə | *s.* grupo; molho; cacho; enxame; cardume

clutch | klâs̄' | *s.* garra; (*pl.*) garras; (mec.) embreagem; (gír.) aperto, situação difícil / *vt.* agarrar, empunhar / *vi.* -to c. at agarrar-se a

clutter | klâ'tə | *s.* monte de coisas, desordem / *vt.* pôr em desordem, atravancar

c/o | kow' | *abrev.* de **care of** | ke'rov | aos cuidados de

coach | kowš' | *s.* vagão (de trem); coche, carruagem; ônibus (de turismo etc.); treinador; explicador / *vt.* transportar (em vagão, coche, ônibus etc.); treinar; ensinar

coach-house | kowš'haws | *s.* cocheira; abrigo para carruagem

coachman | kowš'mən | *s.* cocheiro

coagulate | kowa'gĭuleyt | *vi.* coagular, coalhar

coal | kowl' | *s.* carvão de pedra, hulha. **-to carry coals to Newcastle** levar água ao rio. **-to be hauled over the coals** ser repreendido

coalesce | kowəles' | *vi.* unir-se, fundir-se; misturar-se

coal field | kowl'fĭld | *s.* mina de carvão

coal gas | kowl'gas | *s.* gás de hulha

coal-house | kowl'haws | *s.* carvoeira

coalition | kowəli'šən | *s.* coligação, coalizão, liga

coal-scuttle | kowl'skâtəl | *s.* balde para carvão

coal-seam | kowl'sɪm | *s.* filão, veio de hulha

coarse | kó'əs | *a.* grosseiro; grosso; áspero; ordinário; descortês; obsceno

coarseness | kó'əsnes | *s.* asperidade; grosseria, rudeza

coast | kowst' | *s.* costa. **-the c. is clear** o caminho está desimpedido / *vi.* costear

coastal | kows'təl | *a.* costeiro

coastal trade | kows'təltreyd | *s.* cabotagem

coaster | kows'tə | *s.* navio de cabotagem

coast guard | kowst'gʌd | *s.* guarda costeira

coastline | kowst'layn | *s.* contorno litorâneo

coat | kowt' | *s.* paletó; sobretudo; cor do pêlo (animais); de-

mão (tinta); camada (poeira etc.) / *vt.* cobrir

coat-hanger | kowt'hangə | *s.* cabide de guarda-roupa

coati | kow'ətɪ | *s.* (zool.) quati

coating | kow'ting | *s.* camada, cobertura, capa

coat of arms | kowt'ovʌmz | *s.* brasão, armas de família

co-author | kow'óϑə | *s.* co-autor

coax | kowks' | *vt.* persuadir com doçura, induzir

coaxing | kow'ksing | *s.* súplicas, blandícias

cob | kob' | *s.* sabugo (de milho)

cobbler | kob'lə | *s.* sapateiro remendão; operário inábil; sangria (bebida)

cobweb | kob'web | *s.* teia de aranha

cocaine, cocain | kow'k̆əin | *s.* cocaína

cock | kok' | *s.* galo; válvula; torneira; cão (arma de fogo); (gír.) besteira; (vulg.) pênis / *vt.* engatilhar; levantar (sobrancelhas); arrebitər (nariz). **-to c. one's nose at** olhar com desprezo

cock-and-bull story | kok'andbulstó'rĭ | *s.* patranha, história mentirosa

cockatoo | kokətu' | *s.* cacatua

cockerel | ko'krəl | *s.* galo novo, frango

cock-eyed | kok'ayid | *a.* (gír.) vesgo; ridículo, estúpido; bêbado

cockle | ko'kəl | *s.* (bot.) joio; (zool.) amêijoa

cockles of the heart | ko'kəlzovðϑhʌt | *s.* o fundo do coração

cockney | kok'nĭ | *s.* londrino (pessoa do povo); dialeto londrino / *a.* relativo ao dialeto londrino

cock of the walk | kok'ovðəwók | *s.* mandão, mandachuva

cockpit | kok'pit | *s.* rinha; arena; carlinga, nacele

cockroach | kok'rowš | *s.* barata

cocksure | kok'šuə | *a.* convenci-

do (de alguma coisa), dogmáti-
co, infalível

cocktail | kok'teyl | *s.* coquetel,
cocktail

cocky | ko'kī | *a.* arrogante, petu-
lante, atrevido

cocoa | kow'kow | *s.* chocolate
em pó; chocolate (bebida)

cocoa bean | kow'kowbɪn |
s. chocolate em pó; chocolate
(bebida)

cocoa butter | kow'kowbətə|*s.*
manteiga de cacau

cocoa tree | kow'kowtrɪ | *s.* ca-
caueiro

coconut | kow'kownət | *s.* coco

coconut butter | kow'kownətbâ-
tə | *s.* gordura de coco

coconut palm | kow'kownət-
pᴀm | *s.* coqueiro

C.O.D. | sᴇowdɪ' | *abrev.* de **cash
on delivery** a cobrar na entrega

cod| kod' | *s.* bacalhau / *vt.* enga-
nar, lograr

coddle | ko'dəl | *vt.* afagar, mi-
mar

code| kowd' | *s.* código (leis); có-
digo secreto, cifra

cod-liver oil | kod'livəoyl' | *s.*
óleo de fígado de bacalhau

coerce | kowᴇs' | *vt.* coagir, com-
pelir, constranger

coercion | kowᴇ'śən | *s.* coerção,
coação, compulsão

coexistence | kowegzis'təns | *s.*
coexistência

coffee | ko'fī | *s.* café

coffee-bean | ko'fībɪn | *s.* grão de
café

coffee-mill | ko'fīmil | *s.* moinho
de café

coffee plant| ko'fīplᴀnt | *s.* cafe-
eiro

coffee plantation | ko'fīplᴀn-
tey'śən | *s.* cafezal

coffee-pot | ko'fīpot | *s.* cafeteira

coffin | ko'fīn | *s.* ataúde, caixão.
-to drive a nail into someone's c.
apressar a morte de alguém

cog | kog' | *s.* dente (de engrena-
gem); (fig.) membro irrelevante
de uma organização

cogency | kow'jənsī | *s.* irrefuta-
bilidade

cogent | kow'jənt | *a.* convincen-
te, irrefutável

cogitate| ko'jiteyt | *vi.* ponderar,
considerar, pensar

cognac | kow'nīᴀk | *s.* conhaque

cognate | kog'neyt | *a.* cognato,
análogo, afim, aparentado

cognizance | kog'nizəns | *s.* co-
nhecimento

cog-wheel | kog'wɪl | *s.* roda den-
tada

cohabit | kowha'bit | *vi.* coabitar

coherence | kowhɪ'ərəns | *s.* coe-
rência, congruência, nexo

cohesion | kowhɪ'jən | *s.* coesão

cohort | kowhót' | *s.* coorte

coiffure | kwaffu'ə | *s.* penteado,
toucador

coil | koyl' | *s.* bobina; enrola-
mento; serpentina; rolo / *vt.* en-
rolar / *vi.* enroscar-se (serpen-
te)

coin | koyn' | *s.* moeda. **-the other
side of the c.** o reverso da meda-
lha / *vt.* cunhar (moeda)

coinage | koy'nij | *s.* cunhagem;
moedas; sistema monetário

coincide | kowinsayd' | *vi.* coinci-
dir

coincidence | kowin'sidəns | *s.*
coincidência; concordância

coke | kowk' | *s.* coque; (gír.) co-
caína; (coloq.) coca-cola

colander | ko'ləndə | *s.* coador

cold | kowld' | *s.* frio; resfriado.
-to catch a c. apanhar um resfriado / *a.* frio; (fig.) insensível,
indiferente

cold colours | kowld'kâləz | *spl.*
cinzento ou azul

cold cuts | kowld'kâts | *spl.* frios,
carnes frias

coldness | kowld'nes | *s.* frio;
frieza, indiferença

cold shoulder | kowld'šowl'də |
s. tratamento inamistoso

collaborate | kəla'bəreyt | *vt.* co-
laborar

collaboration | kəlabərey'śən | *s.*
colaboração

collapse | kəlaps' | *s.* colapso; desmoronamento; ruína / *vi.* sofrer um colapso; desmoronar-se, ruir

collapsible | kəlap'sibəl | *a.* dobrável; desmontável

collar | ko'lə | *s.* colarinho; gola; coleira; colar (de ordem honorífica). **-hot under the c.** em situação embaraçosa / *vt.* agarrar pelo colarinho; pôr colarinho ou gola em; (coloq.) dominar

collate | kəleyt' | *vt.* cotejar, comparar, confrontar

colleague | ko'līg | *s.* colega

collect | kəlekt' | *vt.* reunir; colecionar; coletar; cobrar (dívida etc.); coligir; colher; acumular. **-to c. one's thoughts** concentrar-se / *vi.* reunir-se, juntar-se

collected | kəlek'tid | *a.* reunido; calmo, senhor de si

collected works | kəlek'tidwɛks | *spl.* obras completas

collection | kəlek'şən | *s.* coleção; conjunto; compilação; coleta; arrecadação; cobrança

collective | kəlek'tiv | *s.* (gram.) coletivo / *a.* coletivo; conjunto

collector | kəlek'tə | *s.* colecionador; cobrador, arrecadador

collector's item | kəlek'təzaytəm | *s.* peça digna de coleção

colleen | ko'lin | *s.* (Irl.) moça, menina

college | ko'lij | *s.* universidade, faculdade; colégio; corporação; agremiação

collide | kəlayd' | *vi.* colidir, chocar; conflitar

collier | ko'līə | *s.* mineiro de carvão; navio carvoeiro; marinheiro de navio carvoeiro

colliery | ko'līərī | *s.* mina de carvão

collision | kəli'jən | *s.* colisão, choque

colloquial | kəlow'kwīəl | *a.* coloquial, familiar; falado

colloquialism | kəlow'kwīəlizəm | *s.* coloquialismo

collusion | kəlu'jən | *s.* conluio; conspiração; maquinação

colon | kow'lən | *s.* dois pontos; (med.) cólon

colonel | kɛ'nəl | *s.* coronel

colonial | kəlow'nīəl | *a.* colonial

colonist | ko'lənist | *s.* colono; colonizador

colonization | kolənayzey'şən | *s.* colonização

colonize | ko'lənayz | *vt.* colonizar / *vi.* fundar colônia

colonizer | kolənay'zə | *s.* colonizador

colonizing | kolənay'zing | *a.* colonizador

colony | ko'lənī | *s.* colônia

colossal | kəlo'səl | *a.* colossal

colour, color | kâ'lə | *s.* cor; (pl.) cores, bandeira. **-to change c.** empalidecer ou enrubescer. **-to join the colours** alistar-se. **-to show one's colours** revelar suas idéias ou projetos / *vt.* colorir / *vi.* **-to c. up** corar

colour bar | kâ'ləbA | *s.* barreira de cor, discriminação racial

colour-blind | kâ'ləblaynd | *a.* daltônico

coloured, colored | kâ'ləd | *a.* colorido; de cor, negro (raça); exagerado, influenciado

colourful, colorful | kâ'ləful | *a.* brilhante, colorido; pitoresco; animado, vivo

colouring, coloring | kâ'ləring | *s.* colorido; tez; disfarce, aparência enganosa

colourless, colorless | kâ'ləles | *a.* incolor; (fig.) insípido

colt | kowlt' | *s.* potro; (maiúsc.) marca de revólver

column | ko'ləm | *s.* coluna

coma | kow'mə | *s.* (med.) coma

comb | kowm' | *s.* pente; crista (galo etc.); favo de mel; carda / *vt.* pentear; cardar (lã); (fig.) vasculhar

combat | kom'bat | *s.* combate, batalha, luta / *vt.* combater

combatant | kom'bətənt | *s.* combatente

combination | kombiney'śən | *s.* combinação; associação

combine | kombayn' | *vt.* combinar; associar

combustible | kəmbâs'tibəl | *s. a.* combustível

combustion | kəmbâs'śən | *s.* combustão

come | kâm' | *vi.* vir. -**to c. about** acontecer, suceder. -**to c. across** encontrar, topar com. -**to c. along** acompanhar, ir junto; apressar-se. -**to c. apart** ou **asunder** partir-se em pedaços. -**to c. away** sair, ir-se embora. -**to c. back** voltar. -**to c. by** passar perto de; ganhar, obter. -**to c. down** descer, baixar; decair. -**to c. for** vir buscar; vir para. -**to c. forth** aparecer, sair. -**to c. forward** apresentar-se. -**to c. from** vir de; descender de. -**to c. in** entrar, chegar. -**c. in!** entre! -**to c. off** sair, desprender-se; realizar-se. -**to c. of age** atingir a maioridade. -**to c. on** avançar; fazer progressos. -**c. on!** venha!, vamos! -**to c. out** sair; revelar-se. -**to c. out with** propor (plano); sair-se com. -**to c. short** não alcançar; ser insuficiente. -**to c. to vir a ser,** montar a (conta); tratar-se de. -**to c. to blows** chegar às vias de fato. -**to c. to hand** vir ou chegar à mão. -**to c. to grief** sair mal. -**to c. together** reunir-se. -**to c. true** realizar-se. -**to c. under** pertencer a; incluir-se em; cair sob o controle de. -**to c. up** subir; aparecer; vir visitar. -**to c. up for air** parar para tomar fôlego; fazer uma pausa. -**to c. up to** alcançar, chegar a; corresponder a, satisfazer. -**to c. upon** encontrar, achar. -**to c. up with** propor, sugerir; alcançar, apanhar. -**how c.?** como assim?

comedian | kəmı'dïən | *s.* comediante; comediógrafo

comedy | ko'mədĩ | *s.* comédia

comely | kâm'lī | *a.* bonito, atraente; gracioso; próprio

comet | ko'mit | *s.* cometa

comfort | kâm'fət | *s.* conforto; alívio, consolação. -**cold c.** triste consolação / *vt.* confortar, consolar; animar; encorajar; fortificar

comfortable | kəm'fətəbəl | *a.* confortável; contente, satisfeito; desafogado. -**make yourself c.** esteja à vontade

comfortably | kâm'fətəblī | *adv.* confortavelmente; comodamente. -**c. off** bem de vida, com meios suficientes

comforting | kâm'fəting | *a.* confortante; encorajador

comic | kó'mik | *s.* cômico; comediante; comicidade; (*pl.*) história em quadrinhos / *a.* cômico

comical | ko'mikəl | *a.* cômico, engraçado, divertido

comic strip | kó'mikstrip | *s.* história em quadrinhos

coming | kə'ming | *s.* chegada, vinda; advento / *a.* próximo, futuro, vindouro. -**c. into force** entrada em vigor. -**the c. thing** algo que entrará em moda ou será popular

coming man | kə'mingmən | *s.* pessoa de futuro

coming of age | kə'mingoveyj | *s.* maioridade

comity | ko'mitī | *s.* cortesia, urbanidade. -**c. of nations** reconhecimento de leis e costumes (entre as nações)

comma | ko'mə | *s.* vírgula. -**inverted c.** aspas

command | kəmAnd' | *s.* ordem; (mil.) comando; domínio / *vt.* comandar; dominar

commandant | koməndant' | *s.* comandante

commandeer | koməndı'ə | *vt.* requisitar, confiscar, tomar

commander | kəmAn'də | *s.* comandante

commander in chief | kəmAn'də-inśif | *s.* comandante-em-chefe

commanding | kəmAn'ding | *a.*

dominante, imponente. **-c. position** posição dominante

commandment | kəmʌnd'mənt | *s.* mandamento; preceito

commando | kəmʌn'dow | *s.* (mil.) comando

commemorate | kəme'məreyt | *vt.* comemorar, celebrar

commemoration | kəmeməreý'-śən | *s.* comemoração, celebração

commemorative | kəme'mərətiv | *a.* comemorativo

commence | kəmens' | *vt. vi.* começar; iniciar(-se)

commencement | kəmens'mənt | *s.* começo, princípio, início

commend | kəmend' | *vt.* encomendar, confiar; recomendar, louvar, elogiar

commendable | kəmend'əbəl | *a.* recomendável; louvável

commensurate | kəmen'śurit | *a.* coincidente (em extensão ou duração); correspondente, proporcional; equiparável

comment | ko'ment | *s.* observação, comentário; crítica, censura / *vt.* comentar, anotar; criticar, censurar

commentary | ko'mentrī | *s.* comentário; observação

commentator | ko'menteytə | *s.* comentarista, comentador

commerce | ko'mEs | *s.* comércio

commercial | kəmE'śəl | *a.* comercial

commiserate | kəmi'zəreyt | *vt. vi.* compadecer-se, apiedar-se, condoer-se (de)

commission | kəmi'śən | *s.* comissão; encargo; delegação; (mil.) posto, patente; cometimento, perpetração. **-in** c. em serviço ativo, comissionado. **-out of** c. fora de serviço / *vt.* encarregar; comissionar

comission-agent | kəmi'śəney'-jənt | *s.* agenciador de apostas, *bookmaker*

commissionaire | kəmiśəne'ə | *s.* porteiro uniformizado (de teatro, cinema etc.)

commissioner | kəmi'śənə | *s.* comissário; delegado; membro de uma comissão

commit | kəmit' | *vt.* cometer, praticar; entregar, confiar. **-to c. oneself** comprometer-se. **-to c. to memory** decorar. **-to c. to paper** ou **to writing** pôr por escrito. **-to c. to printing** imprimir. **-to c. to prison** encarcerar, deter, prender

commitment | kəmit'mənt | *s.* compromisso; incumbência

committee | kəmi'tī | *s.* comitê, comissão, delegação

commodious | kəmow'dīəs | *a.* espaçoso, amplo; folgado

commodity | kəmo'ditī | *s.* utilidade; mercadoria

commodore | ko'mədó | *s.* comodoro

common | ko'mən | *s.* propriedade pública; propriedade em comunhão; (jur.) servidão / *a.* comum; habitual; ordinário, grosseiro. **-in** c. em comum

common law | ko'mənló | *s.* direito consuetudinário

commonplace | ko'mənpleys | *s.* banalidade, lugar-comum / *a.* banal, corriqueiro

Commons | ko'mənz | *s.* Câmara dos Comuns

common sense | ko'mənsens | *s.* bom senso, senso comum

commonweal | ko'mənwɪl | *s.* bem público, bem-estar público

Commonwealth | ko'mənwelθ | *s.* Comunidade Britânica; (minúsc.) comunidade, nação, Estado

commotion | kəmow'śən | *s.* comoção, agitação; tumulto, distúrbio

commune | kəmiun' | *s.* comuna, comunidade / *vi.* ter conversa íntima; (relig.) comungar

communicant | kəmĭu'nikənt | *s.* (relig.) comungante / *a.* participante; comunicante

communicate | kəmĭu'nikeyt | *vt. vi.* comunicar; informar, transmitir; estar ligado

communication | kəmĭunikey'šən | *s.* comunicação; comunicado; mensagem; ofício

communion | kəmĭu'nĭən | *s.* comunhão; Santa Comunhão

communiqué | kəmĭu'nikey | *s.* comunicado oficial, boletim

communism | kó'mĭunizəm | *s.* comunismo

communist | kó'mĭunist | *s. a.* comunista

community | kəmĭu'nitĭ | *s.* comunidade

commute | kəmĭut' | *vt.* (jur.) comutar para / *vi.* compensar; substituir; (EUA) comprar e usar (passe de trem)

compact | kəmpakt' | *s.* pacto, acordo; estojo de maquilagem / *a.* compacto, sólido; sucinto, resumido

companion | kəmpa'nĭən | *s.* companheiro, colega

companionship | kəmpa'nĭən-šip | *s.* companheirismo, camaradagem

company | kâm'pənĭ | *s.* companhia; convivência; empresa, companhia. **-to bear** ou **to keep someone c.** fazer companhia a alguém. **-to keep c. (with)** associar-se a. **-to part c. (with)** separar-se

comparable | kom'pərəbəl | *a.* comparável

comparative | kəmpa'rətiv | *a.* comparativo

compare | kəmpe'ə | *vt.* comparar, confrontar; cotejar (textos)

comparison | kəmpa'risən | *s.* comparação; cotejo

compartment | kəmpʌt'mənt | *s.* compartimento

compass | kâm'pas | *s.* (náut.) bússola; âmbito; limite; perímetro; alcance; (mús.) registro (de voz ou instrumento); (*pl.*) compasso (instrumento).

-points of the c. rumos da bússola / *vt.* planear, maquinar; fazer o circuito de; circundar

compass card | kâm'paskʌd | *s.* (náut.) rosa-dos-ventos

compassion | kəmpa'šən | *s.* compaixão, piedade, dó

compassionate | kəmpa'šənit | *a.* compassivo, piedoso

compatible | kəmpa'tibəl | *a.* compatível, conciliável

compatriot | kəmpa'trĭət | *s.* compatriota, patrício

compel | kəmpel' | *vt.* compelir, constranger, obrigar

compendium | kəmpen'dĭəm | *s.* compêndio, resumo, sumário

compensate | kom'penseyt | *vt.* compensar; indenizar

compensation | kompensey'šən | *s.* compensação; indenização

compete | kəmpĭt' | *vi.* competir, concorrer, rivalizar

competence | kom'pitəns | *s.* competência, capacidade; meios suficientes, renda adequada para viver

competent | kom'pitənt | *a.* competente; adequado

competition | kompiti'šən | *s.* competição; disputa; rivalidade, concorrência

competitive | kəmpe'titiv | *a.* relativo a competição. **-c. prices** preços competitivos

competitor | kəmpe'titə | *s.* competidor; concorrente; rival

compilation | kompiley'šən | *s.* compilação

compile | kəmpayl' | *vt.* compilar, coligir

complacency | kəmpley'sənsĭ | *s.* satisfação de si mesmo; fatuidade, presunção

complacent | kəmpley'sənt | *a.* satisfeito (de si mesmo); presunçoso, enfatuado

complain | kəmpleyn' | *vi.* queixar-se de

complainant | kəmpley'nənt | *s.* (jur.) queixoso, querelante

complaint | kəmpleynt' | *s.* quei-

xa, lamúria; (jur.) queixa,
denúncia; achaque, doença,
enfermidade
complaisance | kəmpley'zəns | s.
complacência; afabilidade
complaisant | kəmpley'zənt | a.
complacente; afável
complement | kom'plimənt | s.
complemento; (mil.) efetivo;
(náut.) lotação, tripulação com-
pleta
complete | kəmplıt' | a. comple-
to; absoluto, total; integral / vt.
completar, perfazer; acabar,
terminar
completeness | kəmplıt'nes | s.
plenitude, totalidade, integra-
lidade, perfeição
completion | kəmplı'ʃən | s. con-
clusão, acabamento
complex | kom'pleks | s. comple-
xo / a. complicado, complexo
complexion | kəmplek'ʃən | s.
tez, cútis, cor (esp. do rosto);
compleição, natureza; (fig.)
caráter, aspecto
complexity | kəmplek'sitī | s.
complexidade
compliance | kəmplay'əns | s.
aquiescência, concordância;
obediência, submissão; complacência, condescendência.
-in c. with de acordo com
compliant | kəmplay'ənt | a. con-
descendente, complacente; sub-
misso
complicate | kom'plikeyt | a.
complicado / vt. complicar
complication | komplikey'ʃən |
s. complicação
complicity | kəmpli'sitī | s. cum-
plicidade
compliment | kom'plimənt | s.
elogio; cumprimento, cortesia;
(pl.) cumprimentos / vt. elogiar; felicitar
complimentary | komplimen'tə-
rī | a. lisonjeiro, cortês
complimentary ticket | kompli-
men'tərīti'kit | s. entrada de
cortesia
comply | kəmplay' | vi. cumprir,

obedecer. **-to c. with** agir de
acordo com
component | kəmpow'nənt | s.
componente; parte, ingredien-
te / a. componente
compose | kəmpowz' | vt. com-
por; ajustar, arranjar; acal-
mar, aquietar. **-to c. oneself**
acalmar-se
composite | kom'pəzit | s. a.
composto
composition | kompəzi'ʃən | s.
composição; composto, mistura; redação
composure | kəmpow'jə | s. com-
postura; serenidade
compote | kəmpowt' | s. com-
pota
compound | kom'pawnd | s. com-
posto; combinação, mistura / a.
composto, combinado / vt.
compor, combinar
comprehend | komprīhend' | vt.
compreender; incluir
comprehensible | komprīhen'si-
bəl | a. compreensível
comprehension | komprīhen'ʃən |
s. compreensão
comprehensive | komprīhen'siv |
a. compreensivo; pormenori-
zado
comprehensiveness | komprīhen'-
sivnes | s. alcance; extensão
(de matérias, assuntos etc.)
compress | kompres' | s. com-
pressa / vt. comprimir; conden-
sar; resumir
compression | kəmpre'ʃən | s.
compressão; condensação, redução, abreviação
compressor | kəmpre'sə | s. com-
pressor
comprise | kəmprayz' | vt. in-
cluir, abranger, compreender
compromise | kom'prəmayz | s.
compromisso; transigência, aco-
modamento / vi. transigir; comprometer-se, enlear-se (dificuldades)
compromising | kom'prəmay-
zing | a. transigente; compro-
metedor (situação etc.)

compulsion | kəmpâl'śən | s. compulsão; coação, coerção

compulsory | kəmpâl'sərī | a. compulsório, obrigatório

compunction | kəmpânk'śən | s. compunção; contrição

computation | kempĭutey'śən | s. computação; cômputo; cálculo

compute | kəmpĭut' | vt. vi. computar, calcular

computer | kəmpĭu'tə | s. máquina de calcular; computador

comrade | kom'rid, kom'reyd | s. camarada, companheiro

comradeship | kom'ridśip | s. camaradagem; companheirismo

conceal | kənsīl' | vt. ocultar, esconder; disfarçar

concealment | kənsīl'mənt | s. ocultação, encobrimento. -**inc**. escondido

concede | kənsīd' | vt. admitir, conceder, reconhecer

conceit | kənsīt' | s. vaidade, presunção; comparação rebuscada, afetação de estilo. -**to be out of c. with** estar descontente com

conceited | kənsī'tid | a. vaidoso, presunçoso

conceivable | kənsī'vəbəl | a. concebível; imaginável

conceive | kənsīv' | vt. conceber, imaginar, fazer idéia de / vi. engravidar, conceber

concentrate | kon'səntreyt | vt. vi. concentrar(-se) em

concentration | konsəntrey'śən | s. concentração; aplicação, atenção

concentration camp | konsəntrey'śənkamp | s. campo de concentração

concept | kon'sept | s. conceito; idéia, noção; opinião

conception | kənsep'śən | s. concepção; (relig.) conceição

concern | kənsEn' | s. preocupação, cuidado; relação, referência; interesse, consideração; (com.) firma, empresa / vt. dizer respeito a; inquietar-se

por. -**as far as I am concerned** pelo que me diz respeito. -**that's no c. of mine** nada tenho com isso

concerning | kənsE'ning | prep. concernente a, relativo a; sobre, acerca de

concert | kon'sət | s. (mús.) concerto; acordo, combinação. -**in c.** de comum acordo

concert-goer | kon'sətgowə | s. freqüentador de concertos

concert grand | kon'sətgrand | s. piano de cauda para concertos

concertina | konsətī'nə | s. concertina, sanfona

concerto | kon'sEtow | s. (mús.) concerto

concession | kənse'śən | s. concessão; privilégio

conch | konk' | s. concha, búzio; abóbada

conciliate | kənsī'līeyt | vt. conciliar; apaziguar

conciliation | kənsīlīey'śən | s. conciliação; apaziguamento

conciliatory | kənsī'līətrī | a. conciliatório, conciliador

concise | kənsayz' | a. conciso, sucinto, resumido

conciseness | kənsays'nes | s. concisão; brevidade

conclave | kon'kleyv | s. conclave; reunião

conclude | kənklʋd' | vt. vi. concluir, acabar, terminar; chegar à conclusão, deduzir; chegar a um acordo

conclusion | kənklʋ'jən | s. conclusão; resultado; decisão, acordo. -**in c.** em conclusão, para concluir. -**to jump to conclusions** inferir apressadamente

conclusive | kənklʋ'siv | a. conclusivo, decisivo; terminante, definitivo

concoct | kənkokt' | vt. preparar (misturando ingredientes); tramar, maquinar; engendrar, inventar

concoction | kənkok'śən | s. mistura; comida ou bebida; maqui-

nação, trama; história inventa-
da, elaboração de inverdades
ou fantasias

concomitant | kənko'mitənt | *s.*
coisa concomitante, acompa-
nhamento / *a.* concomitante;
simultâneo; concorrente

concord | kon'kód | *s.* concór-
dia, harmonia; (gram.) concordância

concordance | kənkó'dəns | *s.*
concordância; harmonia;
acordo

concordat | kənkó'dat | *s.*
convênio, convenção; (ecles.)
concordata

concourse | kon'kós | *s.* con-
corrência, afluência, concurso

concrete | kon'krɪt | *s.* concreto /
a. concreto; sólido; real. -in the
c. na realidade

concubine | kon'kľubayn | *s.*
concubina, amásia

concur | konkE' | *vi.* coincidir;
concordar; concorrer; coope-
rar; combinar-se

concurrence | kənkâ'rəns | *s.*
concorrência; coincidência;
cooperação; consentimento

concurrent | kənkâ'rənt | *a.* con-
corrente; simultâneo

concussion | kənkâ'ʃən | *s.* con-
cussão; abalo; choque

condemn | kəndem' | *vt.* conde-
nar; censurar; proibir o uso de;
desapropriar (prédios)

condemnation | kondəmney'-
ʃən | *s.* condenação; censura

condensation | kondənsey'ʃən |
s. condensação

condense | kəndens' | *vt.* conden-
sar; abreviar, resumir

condescend | kondisend' | *vi.*
dignar-se; condescender

condescending | kondisen'ding |
a. condescendente; superior;
que se dá ares protetores

condescension | kondisen'ʃən | *s.*
afabilidade para com inferio-
res, ares protetores

condign | kəndayn' | *a.* condigno

condiment | kon'dimənt | *s.* con-

dimento, tempero

condisciple | kondisay'pəl | *s.*
condiscípulo

condition | kəndi'ʃən | *s.* con-
dição; estipulação; estado; cir-
cunstância / *vt.* condicionar;
induzir; habituar

conditional | kəndi'ʃənəl | *a.*
condicional

conditional mode | kəndi'ʃənəl-
mowd | *s.* (gram.) modo condi-
cional, futuro do pretérito

conditioning | kəndi'ʃəning | *s.*
condicionamento

condole | kəndowl' | *vi.* com-
padecer-se; expressar pesar ou
condolência

condolence | kəndow'lens | *s.*
condolência; (*pl.*) pêsames

condone | kəndown' | *vt.* per-
doar, tolerar, desculpar

condor | kon'dó | *s.* condor

conduce | kəndľus' | *vi.* conduzir;
concorrer, contribuir para;
tender a

conduct | kon'dəkt | *s.* conduta,
procedimento; atividade, ação;
administração, direção / *vt.*
conduzir, acompanhar; dirigir;
(mús.) reger / *vr.* comportar-se

conductor | kəndâk'tə | *s.* chefe,
guia; (mús.) regente; (fís.) condutor; condutor (de ônibus,
bonde); (EUA) chefe de trem;
diretor, gerente

cone | kown' | *s.* cone; casquinha
de sorvete

confab | kon'fab | *s.* (coloq.) ba-
te-papo, conversa

confection | kənfek'ʃən | *s.* con-
fecção, preparação; confeito,
bala, doce

confectioner | kənfek'ʃənə | *s.*
confeiteiro, doceiro

confectionery | kənfek'ʃənrī | *s.*
doces; pastelaria

confederacy | kənfe'dərəsī | *s.*
confederação

confederate | kənfe'dərit | *s. a.*
confederado / *vt. vi.* confede-
rar(-se)

confer | kənfE' | *vt.* conferir, conceder, dar; condecorar / vi. conferenciar, deliberar

conference | kon'fǝrǝns | s. conferência; congresso; reunião

confess | kǝnfes' | vt. confessar; admitir, reconhecer

confession | kǝnfe'śǝn | s. confissão

confessional | kǝnfe'śǝnǝl | s. confessionário / a. confessional, confissional

confession of faith | kǝnfe'śǝnoffeyϑ' | s. profissão de fé

confetti | kǝnfe'tī | s. confete

confidant | konfidant' | s. confidente

confide | kǝnfayd' | vt. confiar / vi. confiar, ter confiança. **-to c. in** confiar em

confidence | kon'fidǝns | s. confiança, fé; confidência, segredo; atrevimento

confidence man | kon'fidǝnsmǝn | s. vigarista

confidence trick | kon'fidǝnstrik | s. vigarice, conto-do--vigário

confident | kon'fidǝnt | s. confidente / a. confiante; confiado, ousado, atrevido

confidential | konfiden'śǝl | a. confidencial, secreto, reservado; de confiança

confine | kǝnfayn' | vt. confinar; aprisionar; limitar; restringir. **-confined to bed** acamado. **-confined to barracks** detido no quartel. **-to be confined** estar em trabalho de parto

confinement | kǝnfayn'mǝnt | s. reclusão, clausura; restrição; parto

confines | kon'faynz | spl. confins, limites, fronteiras

confirm | kǝnfɛm' | vt. confirmar; ratificar; verificar; corroborar; (ecles.) crismar

confirmation | konfǝmey'śǝn | s. confirmação; comprovação; ratificação; (ecles.) crisma

confirmed | konfǝmd' | a. inveterado, incorrigível (bêbedo etc.)

confiscate | kon'fiskeyt | vt. confiscar; apreender

confiscation | konfiskey'śǝn | s. confisco, confiscação

conflagration | konflǝgrey'śǝn | s. conflagração, incêndio devastador e incontrolável

conflict | kon'flikt | s. conflito; luta; divergência / vi. estar em conflito com

conflicting | kǝnflik'ting | a. conflitante; incompatível

conform | kǝnfóm' | vi. conformar-se, submeter-se

conformist | kǝnfó'mist | s. conformista

conformity | kǝnfó'mitī | s. conformidade

confound | kǝnfawnd' | vt. frustrar, destruir; desconcertar. **-c. it!** com os diabos!

confounded | kǝnfawn'did | a. confuso; (coloq.) odioso, maldito, abominável

confront | kǝnfrɔnt' | vt. defrontar, arrostar; enfrentar; confrontar, comparar

confrontation | konfrǝntey'śǝn | s. confrontação; comparação

confuse | kǝnfɪuz' | vt. confundir; desconcertar

confusion | kǝnfɪu'jǝn | s. confusão; desordem; perplexidade, perturbação

confute | kǝnfɪut' | vt. refutar; rebater

congeal | kǝnǰil' | vi. congelar-se

congener | kon'ǰinǝ | s. congênere

congenial | kǝnǰi'niǝl | a. satisfatório; agradável; apropriado, conveniente

congenital | kǝnǰe'nitǝl | a. congênito; inerente

congested | kǝnǰes'tid | a. (med.) congestionado; abarrotado (de gente); congestionado (trânsito)

congestion | kǝnǰes'śǝn | s. (med.) congestão; congestionamento (trânsito)

conglomerate | kǝnglo'mǝreyt | s. a. conglomerado / vt. vi. conglomerar(-se)

conglomeration | kənglomərey'śən |
s. conglomeração; aglomeração; acumulação

congratulate | kəngra'tĭuleyt | *vt.*
congratular, felicitar

congratulations | kəngratʃuley'-
śənz | *spl.* parabéns

congregate | kon'grigeyt | *a.* con-
gregado / *vt. vi.* congregar(-se),
reunir(-se)

congregation | kongrigey'śən | *s.*
congregação; assembléia; (ecles.)
os fiéis

congress | kon'gres | *s.* congres-
so; assembléia

congressman | kon'grəsmən | *s.*
congressista; deputado ou se-
nador

congresswoman | kon'grəswu-
mən | *s.* congressista; deputada
ou senadora

conjecture | kənǰek'śə | *s.* con-
jetura, hipótese, suposição / *vt.
vi.* conjeturar

conjugal | kon'ǰugəl | *a.* conju-
gal, matrimonial

conjugate | kon'ǰugeyt | *s.* cog-
nato, palavra cognata / *a.* con-
jugado / *vt.* conjugar

conjugation | konǰugey'śən | *s.*
conjugação

conjunction | kənǰənk'śən | *s.*
conjunção; associação

conjunctivitis | kənǰənktivay'tis |
s. conjuntivite

conjuration | kənǰiurey'śən | *s.*
apelo solene; magia, feitiçaria

conjure | kənju'ə | *vt.* invocar;
| kân'ǰə | conjurar, esconju-
rar; afastar. **-to c. away** exorci-
zar. **-to c. up** evocar / *vi.* invocar
(espíritos ou demônios); praticar feitiçaria; escamotear

conjurer | kân'ǰərə | *s.* prestidigi-
tador, ilusionista; feiticeiro,
mago

conjuring | kân'ǰəring | *s.* ilusio-
nismo, prestidigitação; magia,
feitiçaria

connect | kənekt' | *vt.* ligar, jun-
tar, unir; associar, relacionar /

vi. fazer conexão

connection, connexion | kənek'-
śən | *s.* conexão, relação

conning-tower | ko'ningtaw'ə |
s. (náut.) cabine blindada do pi-
loto; torre de submarino

connivance | kənay'vəns | *s.* co-
nivência, cumplicidade

connive | kənayv' | *vi.* ser coni-
vente com, fazer vista grossa a,
tolerar

conniver | kənay'və | *s.* cúmplice

connoisseur | konəsE' | *s.* conhe-
cedor, apreciador; especialista,
perito

conquer | kong'kə | *vt.* conquis-
tar; dominar, vencer

conqueror | kong'kərə | *s.* con-
quistador; vencedor

conquest | kong'kwest | *s.* con-
quista; vitória

conscience | kon'śəns | *s.* cons-
ciência. **-in all c.** em sã consciência

conscience-stricken | kon'śəns-
tri'kən | *a.* atormentado pelo
remorso

conscientious | konśien'śəs | *a.*
consciencioso, escrupuloso,
cuidadoso

conscientiousness | konśien'śəs-
nes | *s.* integridade, escrupu-
losidade, retidão

conscientious objector | konśien'-
s'əsəb'ǰek'tə | *s.* (mil.) aquele
que se recusa a combater por
razões religiosas ou morais

conscious | kon'śəs | *a.* conscien-
te, cônscio; ciente; premedita-
do, intencional. **-to be c. of** ter
consciência de, perceber

consciousness | kon'śəsnes | *s.*
consciência; conhecimento;
percepção; mente

conscript | kon'skript | *s.* (mil.)
sorteado, recruta

conscription | kənskrip'śən | *s.*
(mil.) recrutamento

consecrate | kon'sikreyt | *a.* con-
sagrado / *vt.* consagrar; (ecles.)
sagrar

consecration | konsikrey'śən | *s.*

consagração; dedicação; (ecles.) sagração

consecutive | kənse'kĩutiv | *a.* consecutivo, sucessivo

consent | kənsent' | *s.* consentimento, aprovação; autorização, permissão. -by common c. de comum acordo / *vi.* consentir em, permitir

consequence | kon'sikwəns | *s.* conseqüência; significação, importância. -of no c. sèm importância. -in c. por conseqüência, conseqüentemente

consequent | kon'sikwənt | *a.* conseqüente, resultante

consequential | konsikwen'śəl | *a.* conseqüente; pretensioso

consequently | kon'sikwəntlĩ | *adv.* portanto, por conseguinte

conservation | konsərvey'śən | *s.* conservação

conservationist | kənsəvey'śənist | *s.* conservacionista

conservatism | kənsE'vətizəm | *s.* conservantismo

conservative | kənsE'vətiv | *a.* conservador; (maiúsc.) membro do partido conservador

conservatory | kənsE'vətrĩ | *s.* (mús.) conservatório; estufa (de plantas)

conserve | kənsEv' | *vt.* conservar, preservar

consider | kənsi'də | *vt.* considerar; ter consideração; julgar, apreciar / *vi.* considerar; refletir

considerable | kənsi'dərəbəl | *a.* considerável; notável

considerate | kənsi'dərit | *a.* atencioso, cortês, delicado

consideration | kənsidərey'śən | *s.* consideração; reflexão; respeito, estima; estimativa; (jur.) compensação. -in c. of em recompensa por, em atenção a. -without due c. sem a devida consideração

considering | kənsi'dəring | *prep.* considerando, tendo em vista que, atendendo a

consign | kənsayn' | *vt.* consignar (tb. com.); confiar, entregaɪ; ceder, transferir

consignment | kənsayn²mənt | *s.* consignação; mercadorias consignadas

consist | kənsist' | *vi.* consistir em; ser constituído por; constar de

consistency | kənsis'tənsĩ | *s.* consistência; densidade; firmeza, solidez; coerência

consistent | kənsis'tənt | *a.* consistente; compatível; coerente, lógico; constante, fiel a seus princípios

consolation | konsəley'śən | *s.* consolação, consolo

consolation prize | konsəley'śən-prayz | *s.* prêmio de consolação

console | kənsowl' | *vt.* consolar, confortar

consolidate | kənso'lideyt | *vt.* consolidar, fortalecer, firmar

consonant | kon'sənənt | *s.* consoante / *a.* harmonioso

consort | kon'sót | *s.* consorte, cônjuge / *vi.* associar-se

conspicuous | kənspi'kĩuəs | *a.* conspícuo, notável; visível, evidente, manifesto

conspiracy | kənspi'rəsĩ | *s.* conspiração, conjuração

conspirator | kənspi'rətə | *s.* conspirador, conjurado

conspire | kənspay'ə | *vi.* conspirar, tramar

constable | kon'stəbəl | *s.* policial, guarda; (hist.) condestável; (hist.) chefe de fortaleza ou castelo

constabulary | kənsta'bĩulərĩ | *s.* guarda, polícia / *a.* policial, da polícia

constancy | kon'stənsĩ | *s.* constância, persistência

constant | kon'stənt | *a.* constante; permanente, contínuo

constellation | konstəley'śən | *s.* constelação

consternation | konstəney'śən | *s.* consternação

constipated | kon'stipeytid | *a.* com prisão de ventre

constipation | konstipey'śən | *s.* prisão de ventre

constituency | kənsti'tīuənsī | *s.* eleitorado; círculo eleitoral

constituent | kənsti'tīuənt | *s.* componente; constituinte; eleitor / *a.* constituinte

constitute | kon'stitīut | *vt.* constituir, estabelecer

constitution | konstitīu'śən | *s.* constituição; estabelecimento

constrain | kənstreyn' | *vt.* constranger; compelir

constraint | kənstreynt' | *s.* coação, constrangimento; retraimento, reserva

constrict | kənstrikt' | *vt.* constringir, apertar

construct | kənstrâkt' | *vt.* construir, edificar; traçar

construction | kənstrâk'śən | *s.* construção (tb. gram.); explicação, interpretação (de texto, lei etc.)

constructive | kənstrâk'tiv | *a.* construtivo, positivo

construe | kənstru' | *vt.* interpretar, explicar; deduzir

consul | kon'səl | *s.* cônsul

consular | kon'sīulə | *a.* consular

consulate | kon'sīulit | *s.* consulado

consulate general | kon'sīulit-je'nərəl | *s.* consulado geral

consult | kənsâlt' | *vt.* consultar; considerar

consultant | kənsâl'tənt | *s.* consultor; consulente

consultation | konsəltey'śən | *s.* consulta; reunião, conferência; junta médica

consume | kənsīum' | *vt.* consumir; gastar; destruir; devorar; dissipar (tempo, dinheiro etc.)

consumer | kənsīu'mə | *s.* consumidor

consummate | kənsâ'mit | *a.* consumado; acabado, completo / | kon'sâmeyt | *vt.* consumar

consummation | kənsīumey'-śən | *s.* consumação, conclusão; resultado, fim desejado

consumption | kənsâm'śən | *s.* consumo, gasto; (med.) tuberculose pulmonar

consumptive | kənsâm'tiv | *s.* tuberculoso / *a.* consumidor

contact | kon'takt | *s.* contato / *vt.* pôr-se em contato com

contact lens | kon'taktlens | *s.* lente de contato

contagion | kəntey'jən | *s.* contágio, infecção

contagious | kəntey'jəs | *a.* contagioso

contain | kənteyn' | *vt.* conter, encerrar, compreender; reprimir / *vr.* conter-se, dominar-se, reprimir-se

container | kəntey'nə | *s.* recipiente (caixa, frasco etc.)

contaminate | kənta'mineyt | *vt.* contaminar, contagiar

contamination | kəntaminey'śən | *s.* contaminação

contemplate | kon'təmpleyt | *vt.* contemplar; meditar em; tencionar, projetar

contemplation | kontəmpley'śən | *s.* contemplação

contemporaneous | kəntempə-rey'nīəs | *a.* contemporâneo

contemporary | kəntem'pərərī | *s. a.* contemporâneo, coetâneo

contempt | kəntempt' | *s.* desprezo, desdém; (jur.) contumácia, desacato à autoridade

contemptible | kəntemp'tibəl | *a.* deprezível, vil, ignóbil

contempt of court | kəntempt'-ovkót | *s.* desacato a um tribunal

contemptuous | kəntemp'tīuəs | *a.* desdenhoso; insolente

contend | kəntend' | *vt.* sustentar, afirmar / *vi.* lutar; litigar; discutir

contender | kənten'də | *s.* contendor; concorrente

content | kəntent' | *s.* contentamento, satisfação; (*pl.*) conteúdo / *a.* satisfeito, contente. **-to**

one's heart c. à vontade, tanto quanto se deseja / *vt.* contentar, satisfazer; apaziguar

contented | kənten'tid | *a.* contente, satisfeito

contention | kənten'śən | *s.* disputa, altercação; afirmação, opinião

contentment | kəntent'mənt | *s.* contentamento, satisfação

contest | kon'test | *s.* debate, controvérsia; luta, disputa; competição; concurso / *vt.* disputar; (jur.) contestar

context | kon'tekst | *s.* contexto

contiguous | kənti'gŭəs | *a.* contíguo, adjacente

continent | kon'tinənt | *s.* continente. **-the C.** o continente europeu / *a.* moderado; continente, casto

continental | kontinen'təl | *a.* continental

contingency | kəntin'jənsī | *s.* contingência

contingent | kəntin'jənt | *s.* (mil.) contingente; cota, quota / *a.* contingente; incerto. **-c. on** ou **upon** dependendo de, com a condição de

continual | kənti'nĭuəl | *a.* contínuo, sucessivo

continuance | kənti'nĭuəns | *s.* continuação; seqüência; (jur.) adiamento

continuation | kəntinĭuey'śən | *s.* continuação, prosseguimento; continuidade

continue | kənti'nĭu | *vt. vi.* continuar, prosseguir; prolongar; manter; recomeçar

continuity | kontinĭu'itī | *s.* continuidade, seqüência

continuous | kənti'nĭuəs | *a.* contínuo, ininterrupto, incessante; permanente

contort | kəntót' | *vt.* contorcer; retorcer; deformar

contortion | kəntó'śən | *s.* contorção; deformação

contraband | kon'trəband | *s.* contrabando / *a.* contraban-deado, de contrabando

contrabass | kon'trəbeys | *s.* (mús.) contrabaixo

contraceptive | kontrəsep'tiv | *s. a.* anticoncepcional

contract | kon'trakt | *s.* contrato; ajuste, acordo; contrato de casamento / | kəntrakt' | *vt.* contrair (doença, costume, dívida etc.) / *vi.* contratar; encolher; contrair-se. **-contracted ideas** idéias mesquinhas

contraction | kəntrak'śən | *s.* contração; forma abreviada

contractor | kəntrak'tə | *s.* empreiteiro; contratante

contradict | kontrədikt' | *vt.* contradizer; contrariar

contradiction | kontrədik'śən | *s.* contradição; contestação; oposição, desacordo

contradictory | kontrədik'tərī | *a.* contraditório

contrary | kon'trərī | *s.* contrário, oposto. **-on the c.** pelo contrário. **-by contraries** contrário ao esperado / *a.* | kəntre'ərī | voluntarioso, caprichoso; teimoso / *adv.* contrariamente

contrast | kon'trast | *s.* contraste. **-in c. to** em contraste com / *vt.* contrastar, opor, confrontar / *vi.* contrastar, formar contraste

contravene | kontrəvin' | *vt.* transgredir, infringir, contravir; contraditar, contestar

contravention | kontrəven'śən | *s.* contravenção, infração

contribute | kəntri'bŭut | *vt.* contribuir; concorrer, cooperar; colaborar (na imprensa)

contribution | kəntribĭu'śən | *s.* contribuição; colaboração (na imprensa); donativo; imposto; cota, quota

contributor | kəntri'bĭutə | *s.* colaborador (na imprensa); contribuinte (impostos etc.)

contrite | kon'trayt | *a.* contrito,

arrependido

contrition | kəntri'ʃən | s. contrição, arrependimento

contrivance | kəntray'vəns | s. tramóia, artimanha; invenção; aparelho; engenhoca, instrumento, dispositivo

contrive | kəntrayv' | vt. inventar; planejar, maquinar; conseguir, dar um jeito

control | kəntrowl' | s. controle; governo; domínio; (mec.) regulador, freio / vt. controlar; dominar, comandar; dirigir, guiar; fiscalizar; refrear

controller | kəntrow'lə | s. controlador; tesoureiro; superintendente, fiscal

controversial | kɔntrəvE'ʃəl | a. controverso, discutível; polêmico; litigioso

controversialist | kɔntrəvE'ʃəlist | s. polemista

controversy | kɔn'trəvəsī | s. controvérsia; polêmica

controvert | kɔntrəvEt' | vt. controverter, discutir / vi. entrar em controvérsia

contumacious | kɔntĭumey'ʃəs | a. contumaz; (jur.) revel

contusion | kəntĭu'jən | s. contusão

conundrum | kənân'drəm | s. adivinhação, enigma, adivinha, quebra-cabeça

convalesce | kɔnvəles' | vi. convalescer

convalescence | kɔnvəle'səns | s. convalescença, recuperação

convalescent | kɔnvəle'sənt | s. a. convalescente

convene | kənvin' | vt. convocar; (jur.) intimar, citar / vi. reunir-se, juntar-se

convenience | kənvi'nĭəns | s. conveniência, comodidade; conforto; utensílio. -at your c. quando lhe convier. -at your earliest c. o mais cedo possível. -to make a c. of someone abusar da boa vontade de alguém

convenient | kənvi'nĭənt | a. con-

veniente, oportuno; vantajoso; cômodo; útil

convent | kon'vənt | s. convento (de freiras)

convention | kənven'ʃən | s. convenção, assembléia; membros (de assembléia); convênio, pacto; convenção social

conventional | kənven'ʃənəl | a. convencional, costumeiro; formal; sem originalidade; estipulado, contratual

conventionality | kənvenʃənə'litī | s. convencionalismo

convent school | kon'vəntskʋl | s. colégio de freiras

converge | kənvEʤ' | vt. fazer convergir / vi. convergir

conversant | kənvE'sənt | a. familiarizado com, versado em

conversation | kɔnvəsey'ʃən | s. conversação, conversa

conversation piece | kɔnvəsey'ʃənpis | s. objeto que serve como assunto para conversa (por ser raro, inusitado etc.)

converse | kon'vEs | s. conversa, conversação; oposto, inverso / vi. conversar / kənvEs' | a. oposto, contrário; invertido

conversely | kənvE'səlī | adv. inversamente, ao invés

conversion | kənvE'jən | s. conversão; transformação; (jur.) apropriação indébita

convert | kon'vEt | s. convertido; prosélito / vt. converter; transformar; (jur.) apropriar-se indevidamente / vi. converter-se

convertibility | kənvEtəbi'litī | s. convertibilidade

convex | kon'veks | a. convexo

convey | kənvey' | vt. transportar, carregar; transmitir, comunicar, exprimir; transferir, ceder (propriedade)

conveyance | kənvey'əns | s. transporte; comunicação, transmissão; meio de comunicação, veículo; escritura de transmissão (propriedade)

convict | kon'vikt | s. presidiário,

sentenciado / *vt.* sentenciar, condenar

conviction | kənvik'śən | *s.* (jur.) condenação; convicção, crença

convince | kənvins' | *vt.* convencer, persuadir

convincing | kənvin'sing | *a.* convincente, persuasivo

convivial | kənvi'vĭəl | *a.* festivo, alegre, jovial

convocation | konvəkey'śən | *s.* convocação; reunião, assembléia; sínodo (Igreja anglicana)

convoke | kənvowk' | *vt.* convocar, chamar

convolution | konvəlu'śən | *s.* circunvolução cerebral

convoy | kon'voy | *s.* comboio, escolta, comboiamento / *vt.* comboiar, escoltar

convulse | kənvâls' | *vt.* convulsionar, agitar; transtornar; sacudir (soluço, riso, raiva etc.)

convulsion | kənvâl'śən | *s.* convulsão; comoção

cony, coney | ko'nī | *s.* coelho; pele de coelho

coo | kʋ' | *vi.* arrulhar

cook | kuk' | *s.* cozinheiro, cozinheira / *vt.* cozinhar. -to c. up inventar (desculpa, história falsa)

cooker | ku'kə | *s.* fogão; panela; fruta (que se come preferencialmente cozida)

cookery | ku'kərī | *s.* arte culinária, cozinha

cookie | ku'kī | *s.* biscoito; (EUA) bolinho (doce)

cooking | ku'king | *s.* cozimento; arte culinária. -what's c.? (coloq.) que há de novo?

cool | kʋl' | *a.* fresco; indiferente, frio; moderado, ponderado; audacioso / *vt.* refrescar; arrefecer; refrigerar. -to c. down ou off esfriar; (fig.) acalmar-se

coolie, cooly | kʋ'lī | *s.* cule, trabalhador chinês

cooling | kʋ'ling | *s.* arrefecimento; refrigeração / *a.* refrigerante, refrescante

coolness | kʋl'nes | *s.* frescor, frescura; indiferença; serenidade, calma

coop | kʋp' | *s.* gaiola, capoeira / *vt.* engaiolar; prender

co-op | kow-op' | *abrev.* de **co--operative**

co-operate, coöperate | kowo'pəreyt | *vi.* cooperar

co-operation, coöperation | kowopərey'śən | *s.* cooperação

co-operative, coöperative | kowo'pərətiv | *s.* cooperativa / *a.* cooperativo

co-opt, coöpt | kowopt' | *vt.* cooptar, admitir (em sociedade de classe)

co-ordinate, coördinate | kowó'dineyt | *vt.* coordenar

coot | kʋt' | *s.* frangão-d'água; (coloq.) simplório. -bald as a c. completamente calvo

cop | kop' | *s.* (gír.) policial, guarda, tira / *vt.* (gír.) roubar, furtar; (gír.) apanhar, capturar

cope | kowp' | *s.* (ecles.) pluvial, capa de asperges; abóbada / *vt.* cobrir, recobrir / *vi.* -to c. with lutar, bater-se, enfrentar

copious | kow'pīəs | *a.* copioso, abundante, farto

copiousness | kow'pīəsnes | *s.* abundância, fartura

copper | ko'pə | *s.* cobre; moeda de cobre; caldeira de cobre; (gír.) guarda, policial, polícia

coppice | ko'pis | *s.* capão (de arbustos)

copulate | ko'pʎuleyt | *vi.* copular

copy | ko'pī | *s.* cópia; exemplar (de livro, jornal etc.); matéria para publicação

copyright | ko'pīrayt | *s.* copirraite, direitos autorais

coquettish | kowke'tiś | *s.* coquete, namoradeira

coral | ko'rəl | *s.* coral

cord | kód' | *s.* corda; cordão; fio elétrico

cordial | kó'dĭəl | *s.* licor, cordial / *a.* cordial

cordiality | kódīa'litī | *s.* cordialidade; afetuosidade

cordillera | kódile'rə | s. cordilheira (esp. os Andes)

cordon | kó'dən | s. cordão, alamar; cordão sanitário; cordão de isolamento; fita honorífica. **-c. bleu** cozinheiro exímio / vt. **-to c. off** isolar

corduroy | kó'dəroy | s. veludo piquê, belbutina

core | kó' | s. centro; cerne; âmago; miolo; medula

co-respondent, corespondent | korispon'dənt | s. (jur.) co-réu (esp. homem) em processo de divórcio litigioso

cork | kók' | s. cortiça; rolha (cortiça ou outro material) / vt. arrolhar

corkscrew | kók'skrυ | s. saca-rolhas / a. espiralado

corn | kón' | s. grão, cereal; trigo; (EUA) milho; calo (esp. nos pés) / vt. preservar com sal

corn-cob | kón'kəb | s. espiga de milho

corned beef | kónd'bɪf | s. carne em conserva

corner | kó'nə | s. canto (de um quarto, do olho etc.); (futb.) córner, escanteio; esquina; curva (de estrada); ângulo. **-to round a c.** dobrar uma esquina. **-in a tight c.** em apuros / vt. (com.) monopolizar, açambarcar; cercar, encurralar (pessoa)

cornet | kó'nit | s. cornetim

corollary | kəro'ləri | s. corolário; conseqüência

coronation | korəney'śən | s. coroação (de rei ou rainha)

coroner | kə'rənə | s. magistrado que investiga casos de morte suspeita

coronet | ko'rənit | s. pequena coroa (de titular)

corporal | kó'pərəl | s. (mil.) cabo / a. corpóreo

corporate | kâ'pərit | a. incorporado, unido

corporation | kópərey'śən | s. corporação, associação; socie-

dade anônima; (coloq.) barriga grande, pança

corps | kó' | s. corpo (militar, diplomático etc.). **-c. de ballet** corpo de baile

corpse | kóps' | s. cadáver; defunto

corpulent | kó'pʲulənt | a. corpulento, gordo, forte

Corpus-Christi | kó'pəskris'tɪ | s. Corpo de Deus

correct | kərekt' | a. correto, exato, certo / vt. corrigir, emendar

correction | kərek'śən | s. correção, emenda, retificação; punição. **-I speak under c.** posso estar errado

corrective | kərek'tiv | s. a. corretivo

correctness | kərekt'nes | s. correção, exatidão

correlate | ko'rileyt | vt. correlacionar

correspond | korispon'd | vi. corresponder a; corresponder-se, cartear-se

correspondence | korispon'dəns | s. correspondência; correlação; equivalência

correspondent | korispon'dənt | s. correspondente / a. correspondente, correlativo

corresponding | korispon'ding | a. correspondente; análogo; adequado, apropriado

corridor | ko'ridə | s. corredor; galeria

corroborate | kəro'bəɾeyt | vt. corroborar, confirmar

corrode | kərowd' | vt. corroer, desgastar, consumir

corrosion | kərow'jən | s. corrosão

corrosive | kərow'ziv | s. a. corrosivo

corrugated | koɾʲugey'tid | a. corrugado, ondulado

corrupt | kərâpt' | a. corrupto, corrompido / vt. vi. corromper(-se)

corrupting | kərâp'ting | a. corruptor

corruption | kərâp'sən | s. corrupção

corsair | kó'seə |s. corsário

corset | kó'sit |s. espartilho

cortège | kóteyj' | s. comitiva; cortejo (esp. fúnebre)

corvette | kó'vet |s. corveta

cosiness | kow'zines |s. conchego

cosmetic | kozme'tik | s. a. cósmético

cosmic | koz'mik |a. cósmico

cosmopolitan | kozmэpo'litэn | s. a. cosmopolita

cosset | ko'sit | vt. afagar, acariciar

cost | kost' | s. preço; custo; despesa; (pl., jur.) custas. -at all costs custe o que custar

costly | kos'tlĭ | a. caro, custoso; suntuoso, luxuoso

cost of living | kost'ovliving | s. custo de vida

cost price | kost'prays | s. preço de custo

costume | kos'tĭum | s. indumentária; traje (típico, de época etc.); fantasia

costume jewellery | kos'tĭumjʋ'эlrĭ |s. jóias de fantasia

cosy, cozy | kow'zĭ | a. aconchegado, confortável

cot | kot' | s. catre; (náut.) rede (para dormir); cama de criança; leito de hospital

coterie | kow'tərĭ |s. coterie, círculo seleto; panelinha

cottage | ko'tij |s. chalé, pequena casa de campo

cottage cheese | ko'tijšĭz | s. espécie de requeijão

cotton | ko'tэn |s. algodão

cotton mill | ko'tэnmil | s. cotonifício

cotton-plant | ko'tэnplʌnt |s. algodoeiro

cotton wool | ko'tэnwʋl | s. algodão em rama

couch | kawš' | s. divã, sofá / vt. deitar em divã etc.; redigir, enunciar

cough | kof' |s. tosse / vi. tossir; (gír.) confessar

coughing | ko'fing |s. tosse, tossir. -fit of c. acesso de tosse

cough mixture | kof'mikssə | s. xarope para tosse

council | kawn'sil | s. conselho, assembléia administrativa ou consultiva; conselho de Estado; (ecles.) concílio

councillor | kawn'silə |s. membro de câmara municipal; membro de concílio; conselheiro

council of war | kawn'silovwó |s. conselho de guerra

counsel | kawn'sэl | s. conselho; opinião, parecer; advogado / vt. aconselhar, recomendar

count | kawnt' | s. conta, contagem; cálculo; soma, total; conde (título estrangeiro correspondente a earl); (jur.) artigo de acusação. -to lose c. perder a conta / vt. contar; calcular; somar; considerar, julgar. -to c. on contar com. -to c. in incluir. -to c. out excluir. -to c. off separar em grupos iguais (contando)

countenance | kawn'tinэns |s. fisionomia, semblante, face. -out of c. desconcertado. -to lose c. ficar embaraçado, desapontado / vt. aprovar; apoiar, encorajar

counter | kawn'tэ | s. (com.) balcão; ficha de jogo / adv. em sentido contrário / vt. vi. opor-se (a); rebater

counteract | kawntэrakt' | vt. agir contra, contrapor-se a

counter-attack | kawn'tэrэtak | s. contra-ataque

counterbalance | kawn'tэbalэns | s. contrapeso / vt. contrabalançar, compensar

counterblast | kawn'tэblʌst | s. declaração enérgica (contra alguém ou alguma coisa)

counterfeit | kawn'tэfit | s. contrafação, falsificação / a. falsificado, falso / vt. falsificar, contrafazer, imitar

counterfoil | kawn'tэfoyl | s.

talão, canhoto (de cheque, protocolo etc.)

counterpart | kawn'təpʌt | s. complemento; contrapartida

counter-revolution | kawn'tərevəlu'śən | s. contra-revolução

countersign | kawn'təsayn | vt. rubricar; autenticar; referendar

countless | kawnt'les | a. sem conta, incontável

country | kân'trī | s. país; pátria; campo, zona rural; região; território; (jur.) júri /a. rural, campestre, do campo

country cousin | kân'trīkəzən | s. parente de maneiras rústicas

country gentleman | kântrījen'təlmən | s. senhor rural

countryman | kân'trīmən | s. habitante, homem de determinado país; compatriota; camponês

country people | kântrīpı'pəl | s. gente do campo

countryside | kân'trīsayd | s. campo, região ou zona rural

county | kawn'tī | s. condado; distrito; município

couple | kâ'pəl | s. par (pessoas ou coisas); parelha; dupla; junta (de bois); (coloq.) alguns / vt. ligar, juntar, associar / vi. acasalar-se

couplet | kâp'let | s. dístico, parelha de versos

coupling | kâp'ling | s. acoplamento, conexão; engate

coupon | ku'pən | s. cupom

courage | kâ'rij | s. coragem, bravura, valentia

courageous | kərey'jəs | a. corajoso, intrépido, valente

courier | kə'rīə | s. mensageiro especial; estafeta; guia de turistas

course | kó'əs | s. curso; (náut.) rota; trajeto; marcha (dos acontecimentos); decurso, decorrer (tempo); curso, série de aulas; campo de corridas; campo de golfe; prato (de refeição). -in due c. no devido tempo. -in the c. of no decorrer de. -of c.

claro, naturalmente. -as a matter of c. naturalmente, normalmente, como rotina

court | kó'ət | s. corte; tribunal; pátio; beco; quadra de tênis. -in open c. abertamente; publicamente. -to pay c. to cortejar / vt. namorar; procurar, buscar

courteous | kE'tīəs | a. cortês, polido, afável

courtesy | kE'tisī | s. cortesia, urbanidade, polidez

courtier | kó'tīə | s. cortesão

court martial | kó'ətmʌśəl | s. conselho de guerra

courtship | kót'śip | s. corte, namoro

courtyard | kót'ïʌd | s. pátio, quintal

cousin | kə'zən | s. primo

cove | kowv' | s. angra, enseada; vale estreito; (gír.) sujeito, camarada, cara

covenant | kâ'vənənt | s. acordo, pacto; contrato; aliança / vi. comprometer-se a

cover | kâ'və | s. coberta; abrigo; proteção; cobertura (tb. da imprensa); tampa; capa; pretexto, disfarce; capa (de livro etc.). -in paper covers brochado. -in cloth covers encadernado. -under c. em lugar seguro. -under separate c. em envelope separado. -from c. to c. do princípio ao fim (livro etc.) / vt. cobrir (tb. imprensa); tapar; abrigar; abranger, incluir; proteger (com arma de fogo). -to c. up esconder, encobrir

covering | kə'vəring | s. cobertura; capa, invólucro; revestimento

covering letter | kə'vəringletə | s. carta anexa (a documento etc.)

covert | kə'vət | s. abrigo; esconderijo (de caça) / a. velado, encoberto

covet | kâ'vit | vt. cobiçar, ambicionar; almejar

covetous | kâ'vitəs | a. cobiçoso; ávido, ganancioso

covetousness| kâ'vitəsnes |s. cobiça; ganância; avidez

cow| kaw' |s. vaca; fêmea (deelefante, baleia etc.) / vt. intimidar, atemorizar

coward | kaw'əd | s. covarde, poltrão, medroso; tímido

cowardice | kaw'ədis | s. covardia, pusilanimidade

cowardly| kaw'ədlī |a. covarde/ adv. covardemente

cowboy| kaw'boy | s. vaqueiro, boiadeiro

cower| kaw'ə |vi. agachar-se; encolher-se; humilhar-se

cowl| kawl' |s. capuz; hábito de monge (com capuz); cobertura de chaminé; capô de motor (carro, avião)

coxswain| kok'sən |s. (náut.) patrão, timoneiro

coy | koy' | a. tímido, modesto, esquivo

coyness | koy'nes | s. timidez, acanhamento

crab | krab' |s. caranguejo

crab-apple | krab'apəl |s. maçã-brava, maçã silvestre

crabbed | krabd' |a. arrevezado (estilo); carrancudo, rabugento; garranchosa, difícil de entender (letra)

crack| krak' |s. fenda, racha, fissura; estalido; estampido (tiro, trovão etc.); (coloq.) tapa, murro; (coloq.) piada; (gír.) tentativa / a. excelente, de primeira (cavalo, jogador etc.) / vt. quebrar; contar (piada); arrombar; solucionar (problema), decifrar (código) / vi. estalar, rachar, partir-se. **-to c. up** (gír.) cair, despencar (avião)

crack-brained | krak'breynd | a. maluco, doido, biruta

cracker | kra'kə | s. bomba (de são João); bolacha; quebra-nozes; (pl., gír.) maluco, doido, biruta

crackle| kra'kəl | vi. crepitar

crack-shot| krak'şot |s. atirador de elite

cradle | krey'dəl | s. berço / vt. embalar; criar

craft | krʌft' | s. ofício, arte; perícia; astúcia; (pl.) embarcação, avião, foguete espacial. **-the C.** a maçonaria. **-the gentle c.** a pesca esportiva

craftiness | krʌf'tīnes | s. habilidade, astúcia, manha

craftsman | krʌfts'mən |s. artífice, artesão; homem habilidoso (trabalhos manuais)

crafty| krʌf'tī |a. habilidoso, astuto, manhoso

crag | krag' | s. penhasco, rochedo

craggy | kra'gī | a. escarpado, alcatilado, íngreme

cram| kram' |vt. encher, abarrotar; apinhar / vi. encher-se, fartar-se

cramp| kramp' |s. cãibra; grampo de carpinteiro / vt. prender com grampo; restringir, limitar

crane | kreyn' | s. (orn.) grou; guindaste, grua / vt. vi. guindar, suspender (com guindaste); espichar o pescoço

crank| krank' |s. manivela; (coloq.) excêntrico; (coloq.) excentricidade, mania, extravagância

crash| kraś'| s. estrondo, estampido; desastre (de carro, avião etc.); falência, quebra / vt. causar desastre / vi. cair com estrondo; colidir; abrir falência, falir

crass| kras' |a. crasso, grosseiro

crate | kreyt' | s. engradado; caixote; (coloq.) lata velha (automóvel)

crater | krey'tə |s. cratera

crave | kreyv' | vt. implorar, rogar; suspirar por; almejar

craven | krey'vən | a. covarde; medroso; tímido, encolhido

craving| krey'ving |s. avidez; desejo ardente; anelo

crawl| król' |vi. rastejar, arrastar-se; engatinhar; ferver, fervilhar (de animais rastejantes, insetos etc.)

crayfish | krey'fiś | *s.* lagostim (fluvial), pitu

crayon | krey'ən | *s.* pastel; desenho a pastel / *vt.* desenhar ou colorir com pastel

craze | kreyz' | *s.* mania, paixão, novidade passageira

craziness | krey'zīnes | *s.* loucura, doidice

crazy | krey'zī | *a.* louco, maluco, doido. -c. for louco por, doido por

creak | krīk' | *s.* rangido, chiado / *vi.* ranger, chiar

cream | krīm' | *s.* creme; nata / *vt.* desnatar; adicionar creme a. -to c. off tirar a melhor parte (de alguma coisa) / *vi.* formar nata

crease | krīs' | *s.* vinco; ruga, prega / *vt.* vincar; enrugar, amarrotar

create | krīeyt' | *vt.* criar; produzir; causar, provocar; conferir (título de nobreza etc.), elevar a

creation | krīey'śən | *s.* criação; universo, natureza; invenção; instituição

creative | krīey'tiv | *a.* criativo, criador; inventivo

creator | krīey'tə | *s.* criador; (maiúsc.) Deus

creature | krī'sə | *s.* criatura; ser vivo; ser humano; animal

credence | krī'dəns | *s.* crédito, confiança, fé. -to give c. to acreditar

credentials | krədən'śəlz | *spl.* credenciais

credibility | kredibi'litī | *s.* credibilidade

credible | kre'dibəl | *a.* crível, verossímil

credibly | kre'diblī | *adv.* de modo digno de crédito

credit | kre'dit | *s.* crédito; confiança; boa reputação; mérito; certificado de aprovação em curso, disciplina ou matéria; indicação de fonte (citação etc.). -to give someone c. for atribuir mérito a alguém. -to his c. para

sua honra / *vt.* acreditar, confiar; (com.) creditar, dar crédito a. -to c. one with reconhecer o mérito de, julgar capaz de

creditable | kre'ditəbəl | *a.* honroso, meritório, estimável

creditor | kre'ditə | *s.* credor

credulity | kredīu'litī | *s.* credulidade

credulous | kre'dīuləs | *a.* crédulo; ingênuo

creed | krīd' | *s.* credo; crença

creek | krīk' | *s.* riacho, córrego; enseada estreita

creep | krīp' | *vi.* rastejar, arrastar-se. -to c. up ou in subir (entrar) em silêncio

creeper | krī'pə | *s.* (bot.) trepadeira; (orn.) trepador; (gír.) sapatos de sola de borracha

creepy | krī'pī | *a.* rastejante; arrepiado, horripilado; arrepiante, horripilante

cremate | krimeyt' | *vt.* cremar

crescent | kre'sənt | *s.a.* crescente

crest | krest' | *s.* crista (de galo, onda, montanha etc.); timbre (de brasão)

crestfallen | krestfó'lən | *a.* abatido, cabisbaixo, desanimado

crevice | kre'vis | *s.* fissura, racha, fenda

crew | krū' | *s.* tripulação; grupo, turma; quadrilha

crib | krib' | *s.* manjedoura; caminha de criança (de grades); presépio; (coloq.) plágio; pequeno furto / *vt.* encerrar, confinar; (coloq.) plagiar; furtar

cricket | kri'kit | *s.* grilo; críquete. -not c. (coloq.) desleal. -merry as a c. alegre como um passarinho

crier | kray'ə | *s.* pregoeiro público; arauto

crime | kraym' | *s.* crime / *vt.* (mil.) acusar ou punir por ofensa ao regulamento

criminal | kri'minəl | *s.a.* criminoso

criminal law | kri'minəlló | *s.* direito penal

crimson | krim'zən | *s. a.* carmesim, escarlate

cringe | krinǰ' | *vi.* humilhar-se, encolher-se

crinkly | kring'klĭ | *a.* sinuoso; enrugado; encrespado

crinoline | kri'nəlın | *s.* crinolina

cripple | kri'pəl | *s.* aleijado, coxo / *vt.* aleijar; incapacitar

crisis | kray'sis | *s.* crise

crisp | krisp' | *a.* tostado; quebradiço; agudo, preciso; vivo, animado; conciso, vigoroso, seco; crespo; ondulado, enrugado / *vt. vi.* encrespar(-se), encaracolar(-se)

criss-cross | kriskros' | *a.* cruzado / *adv.* em cruz

criterion | kraytı'rǐən | *s.* critério, padrão

critic | kri'tik | *s.* crítico

critical | kri'tikəl | *a.* crítico; hostil, severo; crucial

criticism | kri'tisizəm | *s.* crítica; censura; desaprovação

criticize, criticise | kri'tisayz | *vt.* criticar; censurar, desaprovar; comentar

croak | krowk' | *s.* coaxo; crocito; queixa / *vi.* coaxar; crocitar; agourar; queixar-se

crock | krok' | *s.* pote ou jarro de barro; caco de barro; (gír.) calhambeque (carro, navio etc.)

crockery | kro'kərĭ | *s.* louça

crocodile | kro'kədayl | *s.* crocodilo

crocus | krow'kəz | *s.* açafrão

crony | krow'nĭ | *s.* amigo íntimo, companheiro inseparável

crook | kruk' | *s.* cajado de pastor; báculo; trapaceiro, vigarista; ladrão, criminoso. **-on the c.** desonestamente

crooked | kru'kid | *a.* torto, recurvado; tortuoso (rua); desonesto, fraudulento

croon | krʊn' | *vi.* cantar, cantarolar (em surdina)

crooner | krʊ'nə | *s.* cantor (de canções populares)

crop | krop' | *s.* colheita, safra; papo de ave; rebenque; couro curtido; cabelo à escovinha / *vt.* ceifar; tosar; colher; plantar / *vi.* produzir safra. **-to c. up** surgir

crosier, crozier | krow'ziə | *s.* báculo, croça (de bispo)

cross | kros' | *s.* cruz; cruzeiro (monumento); cruzamento (de praças); encruzilhada; provação, infortúnio / *a.* cruzado; transversal; zangado, irritado; recíproco; híbrido / *vt.* atravessar (rua etc.); cruzar; contrariar, contradizer. **-to c. out** riscar, eliminar. **-to c. oneself** benzer-se. **-to c. the mind** ocorrer a, vir ao pensamento. **-to c. a horse** ou **a saddle** cavalgar

crossbow | kros'baw | *s.* besta (arma antiga)

cross-examination | kros'egzaminey'śən | *s.* (jur.) interrogatório (no júri etc.)

cross-eyed | kros'ayid | *a.* vesgo

cross-fire | kros'fayə | *s.* (mil.) fogo cruzado

cross-grained | kros'greynd | *a.* mal-humorado, intratável

crossing | kro'sing | *s.* cruzamento (de ruas, raças etc.); travessia (viagem, de rio etc.); passagem (de pedestres)

cross-reference | kros'refrəns | *s.* remissão recíproca (em dicionário etc.)

crossroad | kros'rowd | *s.* encruzilhada (tb. *pl.*)

cross-section | kros'seksǝn | *s.* corte transversal; grupo típico (amostragem, apanhado)

crossword | kros'wɛd | *s.* palavras cruzadas

crouch | krawš' | *vi.* agachar-se

croup | krʊp' | *s.* (med.) crupe, difteria; garupa (de cavalo)

crow | krow' | *s.* corvo; canto de galo; alavanca, pé-de-cabra. **-as the c. flies** em linha reta. **-a white c.** uma raridade / *vi.* cantar (galo); exultar, dar um grito de vitória, prazer etc.

crowbar | krow'bʌ | s. pé-de-
-cabra, alavanca

crowd | krawd' | s. multidão,
muita gente, povo; (coloq.)
turma, grupo / vt. comprimir;
encher, abarrotar / vi.
aglomerar-se

crowded | kraw'did | a. abarrota-
do, atulhado, apinhado

crown | krawn' | s. coroa; cume;
alto da cabeça; copa (de chapéu
ou árvore); moeda de cinco xe-
lins (até 1971) / vt. coroar; (fig.)
concluir, rematar

crown prince | krawn'prins | s.
príncipe herdeiro

crown wheel | krawn'wıl | s. en-
grenagem de coroa

crucial | kru'śəl | a. crucial; críti-
co, decisivo

crucible | kru'sibəl | s. cadinho,
crisol

crucifix | kru'sifiks | s. crucifixo

crucifixion | krusifik'śən | s. cru-
cificação, crucifixão

crucify | kru'sifay | vt. crucificar

crude | krʋd' | a. rude, tosco;
grosseiro; cru, em bruto

crudity | krʋ'ditī | s. crueza; rude-
za; realismo brutal

cruel | krʋ'əl | a. cruel, desuma-
no, atroz, impiedoso

cruelty | krʋ'əltī | s. crueldade,
barbaridade, impiedade

cruet | krʋ'it | s. galheta; galhe-
teiro

cruise | krʋz' | s. (náut.) cruzeiro
/ vi. navegar

cruiser | krʋ'zə | s. cruzador

crumb | krâm' | s. migalha

crumble | krâm'bəl | vt. esmiga-
lhar / vi. desmoronar-se

crumple | krâm'pəl | s. prega, ru-
ga / vt. amarrotar, enrugar / vi.
amassar-se, ficar amarrotado;
(coloq.) sofrer desequilíbrio
nervoso

crunch | krânš' | vt. vi. roer ou
mastigar ruidosamente; esmi-
galhar ruidosamente

crusade | kru'seyd | s. cruzada

crusader | krusey'də | s. cruzado;

paladino, campeão

crush | krâś' | s. espremedura, es-
magamento; aglomeração; be-
bida feita com suco de frutas;
(gír.) paixão. **-to have a c. on** estar apaixonado por / vt. espre-
mer, esmagar, triturar; impren-
sar; amarrotar (roupa); aniqui-
lar / vi. ser ou ficar espremido,
comprimido, esmagado etc.

crusher | krâ'śə | s. triturador;
britadeira

crushing | krâ'śing | s. trituração
/ a. esmagador, triturador;
aniquilador

crust | krâst' | s. crosta, casca,
côdea; crosta terrestre; (med.)
escara; (gír.) petulância,
audácia, insolência

crusty | krâs'tī | a. áspero; gros-
seiro; rabugento, mal-humora-
do, irritável

crutch | krâś | s. muleta; apoio;
forqueta (de remo)

crux | krâks' | s. dilema; enigma;
ponto crucial; momento crítico

cry | kray' | s. grito, brado; excla-
mação; choro; pregão. **-a far c.**
grande distância / vt. procla-
mar; apregoar / vi. gritar, bra-
dar; exclamar; chorar. **-to c.
down** diminuir, menoscabar.
-to c. for implorar. **-to c. off** desistir. **-to c. up** enaltecer, louvar, exaltar

crying | kray'ing | a. que grita,
que chora; clamoroso, notório.
-a c. need uma necessidade pre-
mente, urgente

crypt | kript' | s. cripta

cryptic | krip'tik | a. críptico,
oculto, secreto

crystal | kris'təl | s. cristal / a. de
cristal, cristalino

cub | kâb' | s. filhote (de certos
animais); repórter novato, foca

cube | kıʋb' | s. cubo / vt. dar for-
ma cúbica

cube root | kıʋb'rʋt | s. raiz
cúbica

cubicle | kıʋ'bikəl | s. cubículo

cubism | kıʋ'bizəm | s. (b.a.)

cubismo

cuckoo | ku'ku | *s.* cuco

cucumber | kiukâm'bə | *s.* pepino

cud | kâd | *s.* bolo alimentar dos ruminantes. **-to chew the c.** ruminar; (fig.) refletir

cuddle | kâ'dəl | *s.* abraço; carinho, afago / *vt.* abraçar; acariciar, afagar; aninhar / *vi.* aconchegar-se, aninhar-se

cudgel | kâ'jəl | *s.* cacete, pau; clava / *vt.* esbordoar

cue | kiu' | *s.* taco (de bilhar); (teat.) deixa; insinuação

cuff | kâf' | *s.* punho (de manga); bainha das calças; tabefe, bofetada / *vt.* esbofetear

cuff-link | kâf'link | *s.* abotoadura, botão de punho

cul-de-sac | kul'dəsak | *s.* beco sem saída

culminate | kâl'mineyt | *vi.* culminar

culmination | kâlminey'sən | *s.* culminação, auge

culpable | kâl'pəbəl | *a.* culpável, repreensível

culprit | kâl'prit | *s.* réu, acusado; culpado

cult | kâlt' | *s.* culto

cultivate | kâl'tiveyt | *vt.* cultivar; amanhar, lavrar

cultivation | kâltivey'sən | *s.* cultivo, cultivação, cultura

cultivator | kâl'tiveytə | *s.* cultivador, agricultor

cultural | kâl'sərəl | *a.* cultural

culture | kâl'sə | *s.* cultura; educação, refinamento

cumbersome | kâm'bəsəm | *a.* incômodo, pesado, molesto

cunning | kâ'ning | *s.* astúcia, manha, esperteza / *a.* astucioso, astuto, manhoso

cup | kâp' | *s.* xícara; cálice; (desp.) taça. **-one's c. of tea** (coloq., fig.) coisa que interessa a alguém

cupboard | kâp'bəd | *s.* armário, guarda-louça

Cup Final | kâp'faynəl | *s.* (desp.) jogo final

cupidity | kiupi'ditī | *s.* cupidez; cobiça; avareza

cur | kE' | *s.* cachorro vira-lata; cão vadio; (fig.) patife, homem desprezível

curable | kiu'rəbəl | *a.* curável

curate | kiu'rit | *s.* (ecles.) coadjutor, adjunto

curator | kiurey'tə | *s.* diretor, administrador; conservador (museu); (jur.) curador

curb | kEb' | *s.* meio-fio; freio, bridão / *vt.* pôr meio-fio em (calçada); refrear, reprimir

curdle | kE'dəl | *vt. vi.* coalhar, coagular. **-to c. the blood** gelar o sangue, horrorizar, aterrorizar

cure | kiu'ə | *s.* cura; tratamento; cura (de almas); cura (de queijos etc.) / *vt.* curar; tratar; curar, secar; conservar, defumar / *vi.* curar-se; curar

curfew | kE'fīu | *s.* toque de recolher; hora de recolher

curiosity | kiurīo'sitī | *s.* curiosidade; objeto raro

curious | kiu'rīəs | *a.* curioso; indiscreto; raro, estranho

curl | kEl' | *s.* cacho, anel (de cabelo) / *vt.* anelar, encaracolar; enrolar; enroscar / *vi.* formar anéis; encrespar-se. **-to c. up** enrolar-se

currant | kâ'rənt | *s.* passa de Corinto; groselha

currency | kâ'rənsī | *s.* moeda corrente, dinheiro

current | kâ'rənt | *s.* corrente; tendência, curso / *a.* corrente; comum, geral

current account | kâ'rənt-əkawnt | *s.* conta corrente

curriculum | kâri'kiuləm | *s.* currículo, curso de estudos

curry | kâ'rī | *s.* caril / *vt.* sovar (couro curtido); tratar de cavalo (passando raspadeira). **-to c. favour** lisonjear, bajular

curse | kEs' | *s.* maldição, praga; blasfêmia, imprecação; casti-

go, calamidade / *vt.* amaldi-
çoar / *vi.* praguejar; blasfemar
cursed| kɛ'st | *a.* maldito
cursory | kɛ'sərī | *a.* apressado,
breve, superficial
curt| kɛt' |*a.* seco, lacônico; cur-
to, breve; brusco
curtail| kɛteyl' | *vt.* abreviar, re-
duzir, diminuir
curtain| kɛ'tin |*s.* cortina; (teat.)
pano de boca
curve| kɛv' |*s.* curva / *a.* curvo /
vt. vi. encurvar(-se)
cushion | ku'ʃən | *s.* almofada,
coxim / *vt.* almofadar, acol-
choar; proteger
custard | kâs'təd | *s.* creme (de
ovos, leite etc.)
custodian | kâstow'dĩən |*s.* guar-
da; zelador; administrador
custody | kâs'tədī |*s.* custódia,
guarda. -**to take into c.** prender,
deter
custom | kâs'təm | *s.* costume,
hábito; (*pl.*) alfândega; (*pl.*) direitos alfandegários
customary| kâs'təmərī |*a.* costu-
meiro, usual
custom-built | kâs'təmbilt | *a.*
feito sob medida
customer | kâs'təmə | *s.* freguês,
cliente, comprador; (coloq.)
camarada, sujeito
cut | kât | *s.* corte, talho; ferida;
abertura; atalho; fatia, talha-
da / *a.* cortado / *vt.* cortar; baixar (preços). -**to c. classes** matar
aula. -**to c. down** cortar, abater;
reduzir (despesas). -**to c. out** su-
primir, cortar. -**to c. off** ou
away cortar fora. -**to c. short**
abreviar; interromper. -**to be c.
out for** estar talhado para. -**to c.
dead** fingir não ver, recusar

cumprimento **a.** -**to c. no ice**
não ter valor (opiniões alheias
etc.). -**to c. up** afligir, magoar
cute | kĩut' | *a.* astuto, esperto;
(EUA) gracioso, mimoso, atra-
ente, bonito
cut glass | kât'glɑs | *s.* cristal
cuticle | kĩu'tikəl | *s.* cutícula;
epiderme; película
cutlass | kât'ləs |*s.* cutelo; facão;
espada curta; sabre de aborda-
gem
cutlery | kât'lərī | *s.* talheres;
cutelaria
cutlet| kât'lit |*s.* costeleta
cutting | kâ'ting | *s.* corte; esca-
vação; recorte (de jornal); pedaço cortado; muda de planta;
redução (de preços) / *a.* cortan-
te (frio); mordaz (resposta etc.)
cutting edge| kâ'tingej |*s.* gume
cybernetics | sibəne'tiks | *s.*
cibernética
cycle | say'kəl |*s.* ciclo, período;
época, idade; bicicleta; motoci-
cleta / *vi.* andar de bicicleta etc.
cycling | say'kling |*s.* ciclismo
cyclist | say'klist |*s.* ciclista
cyclone | say'klown |*s.* ciclone
cylinder| si'lində |*s.* cilindro
cymbals | sim'bəls | *spl.* (mús.)
pratos
cynic | si'nik | *s.* cínico; descren-
te, céptico
cynical | si'nikəl | *a.* cínico; cépti-
co, descrente, desdenhoso
cynicism| si'nisizəm |*s.* cinismo;
cepticismo
cynosure| say'nəjuə |*s.* centro de
atenção, alvo de admiração, foco de atração
cypress | say'prəs |*s.* cipreste
cyst| sist' | *s.* quisto; (med.) cisto
Czech| ʃek' |*s. a.* tcheco

D

D, d | di' | *s.* d; (maiúsc., mús.) ré

dab | dab' | *s.* toque de leve; pancadinha; pincelada / *vt.* tocar de leve (com pincel, esponja etc.)

dabble | da'bəl | *vt.* salpicar, borrifar, umedecer / *vi.* chapinhar na água; dedicar-se a algo como diletante

dad, daddy | dad' da'dĭ | *s.* (coloq.) papai, paizinho

daffodil | da'fədil | *s.* (bot.) narciso

daft | daft' | *a.* tolo; maluco

dagger | da'gə | *s.* adaga, punhal; (tip.) cruz

daily | dey'lĭ | *a.* diário, cotidiano / *adv.* diariamente

daintiness | deyn'tines | *s.* delicadeza, refinamento, elegância, graça

dainty | deyn'tĭ | *a.* delicado, refinado, elegante; saboroso, delicioso, gostoso

dairy | de'ərĭ | *s.* leiteria; indústria de laticínios

dais | dey'is | *s.* tablado

daisy | dey'zĭ | *s.* margarida

dale | deyl' | *s.* vale

dally | da'lĭ | *vi.* brincar; flertar; perder tempo

dam | dam' | *s.* represa, barragem; dique / *vt.* represar

damage | da'mij | *s.* dano, avaria; prejuízo, estragos; (*pl.*, jur.) indenização / *vt.* danificar, avariar

dame | deym' | *s.* dama, senhora; (gír.) mulher, moça; (maiúsc.) título honorífico

damn | dam' | *vt.* amaldiçoar; praguejar; imprecar. **-d. it!** maldito seja!

damnable | dam'nəbəl | *a.* detestável, execrável

damnation | damney'śən | *s.* danação eterna; maldição

damned | damd' | *a.* danado, condenado; maldito. **-the d.** os condenados (ao inferno)

damning | da'ming | *a.* condenatório, que traz condenação

damp | damp' | *s.* umidade; neblina; abatimento, depressão / *a.* úmido; enevoado / *vt.* umedecer; deprimir, abater; amortecer

dampen | dam'pən | *vt.* umedecer; desanimar, deprimir; amortecer

damper | dam'pə | *s.* (mús.) abafador; amortecedor; regulador (de chaminé). **-to put a d. on** (coloq.) desanimar

dampness | damp'nes | *s.* umidade

damson | dam'zən | *s.* espécie de ameixa pequena

dance | dΛns' | *s.* dança; baile; bailado / *vt.* dançar. **-to d. attendance (on)** ser deixado esperando; seguir obsequiosamente; embalar (criança)

dancer | dΛn'sə | *s.* dançarino, bailarino

dancing | dΛn'sing | *s.* dança / *a.* dançante

dancing-hall | dΛn'singhól | *s.* salão de baile (público)

dandelion | dan'dilayən | *s.* (bot.) dente-de-leão

dandruff | dan'drΛf | *s.* caspa

dandy | dan'dĭ | *s.* janota, dândi

Dane | deyn' | *s.* dinamarquês

danger | deyn'jə | *s.* perigo

dangerous | deyn'jərəs | *a.* perigoso; grave (doença)

dangle | dang'gəl | *vt.* balançar; oscilar / *vi.* balançar-se; estar suspenso

Danish | dey'niś | *s. a.* dinamarquês (língua)

dank | dank' | *a.* frio e úmido (tempo, ar etc.)

dapper | da'pǝ | *a.* vestido com apuro, limpo; vivaz, ativo

dapple | da'pǝl | *s.* mancha, malha / *a.* malhado

dare | de'ǝ | *vt.* desafiar, provocar. **-I d.** say é muito provável / *vi.* atrever-se, ousar

daredevil | de'ǝdevǝl | *s.* pessoa temerária / *a.* temerário, intrépido, arrojado

daring | de'ǝring | *s.* audácia, ousadia, arrojo / *a.* audacioso, ousado, arrojado; perigoso, arriscado

dark | dʌk' | *s.* escuridão, escuro / *a.* escuro; moreno; sombrio, triste; atroz, sinistro; misterioso, oculto. **-to get** ou **grow d.** anoitecer; escurecer. **-to keep d.** ocultar, calar

darken | dʌ'kǝn | *vt. vi.* escurecer(-se); obscurecer(-se); anuviar(-se); entristecer(-se). **-to d. someone's door** visitar alguém

darkness | dʌk'nes | *s.* escuridão; (fig.) ignorância

darling | dʌ'ling | *s.* querido(a), meu bem / *a.* querido; favorito, predileto

darn | dʌn' | *vt.* cerzir; (coloq.) maldizer

darning-needle | dʌn'ingnɪdǝl | *s.* agulha de cerzir

dart | dʌt' | *s.* dardo; ferrão de inseto / *vt.* atirar, arremessar; dardejar / *vi.* correr, disparar

dash | daś' | *s.* pancada; colisão; salpico; pequena quantidade; travessão (pontuação); ímpeto; arremetida. **-to make a d. for** tentar alcançar (correndo). **-to cut a d.** fazer figura / *vt.* arremessar; despedaçar, destroçar; destruir, frustrar; diluir, temperar. **-to d. off** rabiscar / *vi.* arremessar-se; chocar-se; atirar-se. **-to d. into** entrar subitamente. **-to d. by** passar correndo. **-to d. out** ou **off** sair precipitadamente

dashing | da'śing | *a.* precipitado; arrojado; vistoso; garboso;

animado, vivo

dastardly | das'tǝdlĭ | *a.* covarde, traiçoeiro, vil / *adv.* covardemente

data | dey'tǝ | *spl.* dados, fatos, elementos, referências

date | deyt' | *s.* data; período, época; tâmara; (coloq., EUA) encontro, namoro. **-out of d.** antiquado. **-up to d.** moderno. **-to d.** até esta data. **-to bring up to d.** atualizar / *vt.* datar; (coloq., EUA) marcar um encontro / *vi.* **-to d. from** datar de. **-to be dated** estar fora de moda, ser obsoleto

datum | dey'tǝm | *s.* (*pl.* **data**) dado

daub | dób' | *s.* borrão, mancha / *vt.* borrar; besuntar

daughter | dó'tǝ | *s.* filha

daughter-in-law | dó'tǝinló | *s.* nora

daunt | dónt' | *vt.* desencorajar, desanimar; assustar, atemorizar, intimidar

dauntless | dónt'les | *a.* intrépido, audaz, destemido

dawdle | dó'dǝl | *vi.* perder tempo, vadiar, fazer cera

dawn | dón' | *s.* madrugada, aurora / *vi.* amanhecer, raiar o dia. **-to d. (up) on** começar a ser perceptível, vir ao pensamento

day | dey' | *s.* dia. **-all d.** long o dia inteiro. **-by d.** de dia. **-by the d.** por dia. **-d. by d.** dia a dia. **-d. off** dia de folga. **-from this d. on** doravante. **-in the days of old** outrora. **-the d. after tomorrow** depois de amanhã. **-the d. before** na véspera. **-every other d.** dia sim dia não. **-d. in d. out** dia após dia. **-to call it a d.** desistir de; (coloq.) parar de trabalhar

daybreak | dey'breyk | *s.* aurora, romper do dia

day-dream | dey'drɪm | *s.* devaneio, fantasia / *vi.* devanear

daylight | dey'layt | *s.* luz do dia. **-in broad d.** em pleno dia

daytime| dey'taym |s. dia. **-in the d.** de dia

daze | deyz' | s. atordoamento / vt. deslumbrar; atordoar, aturdir

dazzle | da'zəl | s. deslumbramento, fascinação / vt. deslumbrar, fascinar

dazzling | da'zəling | a. deslumbrante, ofuscante

deacon | dI'kən |s. diácono

dead | ded' | a. morto; extinto; monótono, triste (paisagem); total, completo (silêncio); antiquado; improdutivo; exausto. **-as d. as a herring** completamente morto. **-a d. shot** atirador certeiro. **-at d. of night** a horas mortas, tarde da noite

dead-and-alive | ded'andəlayv | a. inerte, entre vivo e morto; triste, monótono (lugar)

deadbeat | ded'bIt | s. (gír.) indivíduo caloteiro, parasita / a. totalmente exausto; quebrado, sem tostão, falido

deaden | de'dən | vt. amortecer, abafar, enfraquecer

dead end | ded'end | s. beco sem saída

dead heat | ded'hIt | s. empate (em corrida)

deadline | ded'layn | s. prazo de entrega, limite de tempo

deadliness | ded'lines | s. poder letal

deadlock | ded'lok |s. (fig.) beco sem saída, impasse, empate

deadly | ded'lI | a. mortal, letal, fatal / adv. mortalmente; muito, extremamente

deadness | ded'nes |s. marasmo, entorpecimento, estagnação, apatia; insipidez

deaf | def' | a. surdo. **-to turn a d. ear** ser insensível a (pedido etc.). **-as d. as a post** surdo como uma porta. **-to make d.** ensurdecer

deaf-aid | def'eyd |s. aparelho de surdez

deaf-and-dumb | def'anddâm | a. surdo-mudo

deafen | de'fən | vt. ensurdecer; aturdir; abafar (som)

deafening | de'fəning | a. ensurdecedor, atroador

deafmute | def'mľut | s. surdo-mudo

deafness | def'nes |s. surdez

deal | dIl' | s. (com.) negócio, acordo, transação; quantidade, bocado; pranchas de pinho. **-great** ou **good d.** muito, em quantidade. **-raw** ou **rough d.** tratamento injusto. **-it's a d.** (coloq.) negócio fechado / vt. **-to d. out** distribuir, repartir. **-to d. with** tratar com, negociar com / vi. dar cartas (no jogo); tratar, ter relações; negociar; lutar, medir-se; portar-se, proceder

dealer| dI'lə |s. comerciante, negociante; concessionário

dealing | dI'ling | s. procedimento, conduta; comércio; (pl.) negócios; entendimentos

dean | dIn' |s. deão; reitor

dear | dI'ə |s. querido, amor / a. caro, prezado; custoso, caro. **-d. me!** meu Deus! / adv. caro, custosamente; amorósamente, com estima

dearth | dEϑ' |s. escassez, carência; carestia; falta

death | deϑ' | s. morte; falecimento, óbito. **-to d.** ou **to the d.** até a morte; até não poder mais. **-to put to d.** executar, matar. **-as sure as d.** absolutamente certo

death-blow | deϑ'blow |s. golpe fatal

death certificate | deϑ'sEtifikit | s. atestado de óbito

death duty | deϑ'dľutI |s. imposto de transmissão (em heranças)

deathless | deϑ'les | a. imortal, imorredouro

death rate | deϑ'reyt |s. índice de mortalidade

debar | dibʌ' | vt. excluir; proibir; interditar

debase| dibeys' |vt. rebaixar, degradar, aviltar; desvalorizar ou adulterar (moeda)

debasement | dibeys'mənt | s. degradação; aviltamento; desvalorização (moeda)

debatable | dibey'təbəl | a. debatível, discutível

debate | dibeyt' | s. debate, discussão / vt. discutir

debauch | dibóš' | vt. corromper, depravar

debauchery | dibó'šərī | s. devassidão, libertinagem

debenture | diben'šə | s. debênture, obrigação

debilitate | dibi'liteyt | vt. debilitar, enfraquecer

debility | dibi'litī | s. debilidade, fraqueza

debit | de'bit | s. débito / vt. debitar

debonair | debəne'ə | a. alegre, jovial; afável

debris | de'brī | s. escombros, ruínas, entulho

debt | det' | s. dívida. **-to pay the d. of nature** morrer

debtor | de'tə | s. devedor

debunk | dibânk' | vt. (coloq.) desmascarar (pessoa, instituição, culto etc.); desprestigiar

debut | de'biu | s. estréia

decade | de'keyd | s. década, decênio

decadence | de'kədəns | s. decadência, declínio

decadent de'kədənt | a. decadente

decamp | dikamp' | vi. fugir, escapar-se, safar-se

decant | dikant' | vt. decantar

decanter | dikan'tə | s. garrafa de mesa (para vinho etc.)

decapitate | dika'piteyt | vt. decapitar, degolar

decay | dikey' | s. decadência; declínio; decomposição, deterioração; degenerescência; cárie dentária / vi. decair, declinar; deteriorar-se; degenerar; cariar (dentes)

decaying | dikey'ing | a. decadente; cariado (dente)

decease | disis' | s. óbito, falecimento

deceased | disi'sid | s. a. falecido, finado, defunto

deceit | disit' | s. engano, fraude, logro; trapaça

deceitful | disit'ful | a. enganoso; mentiroso; fraudulento; ilusório; insincero

deceitfulness | disit'fulnes | s. falsidade, perfídia

deceive | disiv' | vt. enganar, iludir, lograr; decepcionar; (gír.) tapear

December | disem'bə | s. dezembro

decency | di'sənsī | s. decência, decoro, recato, pudor

decent | di'sənt | a. decente, decoroso, respeitável; (coloq.) razoável

decentralization | disentrəlayzey'šən | s. descentralização

decentralize | disen'trəlayz | vt. descentralizar

deception | disep'šən | s. engano, burla, fraude; dissimulação; ilusão

deceptive | disep'tiv | a. ilusório; enganoso, fraudulento; falso, fingido

decide | disayd' | vt. vi. decidir(-se)

decidedly | disay'didlī | adv. decididamente, definitivamente

decimal | de'siməl | s. a. decimal

decimate | de'simeyt | vt. dizimar

decipher | disay'fə | vt. decifrar; interpretar

decision | disi'jən | s. decisão, resolução; sentença; firmeza, determinação

decisive | disay'siv | a. decisivo, categórico; resoluto

decisiveness | disay'sivnes | s. determinação, firmeza

deck | dek' | s. (náut.) convés, tombadilho; andar (de ônibus); (EUA) baralho; (gír., EUA) pacote de entorpecentes / vt. enfeitar, embelezar, adornar; vestir

declaim | dikleym' | vt. vi. declamar, recitar

declaration | diklərey'śən | s. declaração; proclamação; manifesto; notificação

declare | dikle'ə | vt. declarar; proclamar; afirmar. -to d. oneself revelar-se, declarar-se

decline | diklayn' |s. declínio, decadência; baixa (preços); enfraquecimento / vt. declinar; rejeitar; eximir-se a / vi. declinar; diminuir

decode | dikowd' | vt. descodificar, decifrar

decompose | dikəmpowz' | vt. decompor; analisar / vi. decompor-se, apodrecer

decomposition | dī'kompəzi'śən | s. decomposição

decorate | de'kəreyt |vt. decorar, ornamentar; condecorar

decoration | dekərey'śən | s. decoração, ornamentação; condecoração

decorative | de'kərətiv | a. decorativo, ornamental

decorator | de'kəreytə | s. decorador

decorous | de'kərəs | a. decoroso, decente, correto

decorum | dikó'rəm | s. decoro, decência; moderação

decoy | dikoy' | s. chamariz, engodo / vt. vi. atrair, engodar; seduzir

decrease | dīkris' | s. diminuição; redução, abatimento; baixa / vt. vi. diminuir; reduzir, baixar; abater

decree | dikri' | s. decreto; decisão ou mandato judicial / vt. decretar; ordenar, mandar; decidir

decrepit | dikre'pit | a. decrépito, caduco

decry | dikray' | vt. desacreditar; depreciar, rebaixar; censurar

dedicate | de'dikeyt | vt. dedicar; consagrar, devotar

dedication | dedikey'śən |s. dedicação; consagração; dedicatória (em livro etc.)

deduce | didĺus' | vt. deduzir, inferir, concluir

deduct | didâkt' | vt. descontar, deduzir

deduction | didâk'śan | s. dedução; desconto, redução, abatimento

deed | dīd' | s. ação, feito; proeza, façanha; (jur.) escritura, documento, contrato

deem | dīm' |vt. vi. julgar, supor, achar; estimar

deep | dīp' | a. fundo, profundo; forte (cor); intenso, vívido; íntimo, sincero. -a d. one (gír.) pessoa astuciosa ou reservada

deepen | dī'pən | vt. vi. aprofundar(-se); agravar(-se)

deepmourning | dīp'móəning |s. luto fechado

deep-rooted | dīp'rʋtid | a. arraigado, inveterado

deep sea | dīp'sı | s. mar alto

deep therapy | dīp'ϑerəpī | s. tratamento com raios X (ondas curtas)

deer | dī'ə | s. veado, cervo

deface | difeys' | vt. desfigurar, deformar; estragar; sujar, borrar; apagar

defamation | difəmey'śən | s. difamação, calúnia; injúria

defamatory | difə'mətrī | a. difamatório, calunioso

defame | difeym' | vt. difamar, caluniar

default | difolt' | s. falta; omissão; negligência; (jur.) contumácia, revelia. -by d. (jur.) à revelia. -in d. of por falta de / vt. vi. faltar, negligenciar; não pagar; (jur.) condenar à revelia; ocultar-se; ausentar-se

defaulter | difol'tə | s. infrator; (jur.) revel

defeat | difit' |s. derrota / vt. derrotar, vencer; frustrar, malograr. -to d. one's purposes ser contraproducente

defeatist | difi'tist | s. derrotista

defect | di'fekt | s. defeito

defection | difek'śən | s. deserção, defecção

defective | difek'tiv | *a.* defeituoso, imperfeito, incompleto, defectivo

defence, defense | difens' | *s.* defesa

defenceless | difens'les | *a.* indefeso, desprotegido, inerme

defend | difend' | *vt.* defender, proteger, amparar; justificar; (jur.) contestar

defendant | difen'dənt | *s.* (jur.) réu, acusado

defender | difen'də | *s.* defensor, protetor; paladino

defensive | difen'siv | *s.* defensiva / *a.* defensivo

defer | difε' | *vt.* adiar, pospor; retardar / *vi.* procrastinar. -**to d. to** condescender com; acatar

deference | de'fərəns | *s.* deferência, respeito, consideração, acatamento

deferential | defərən'śəl | *a.* deferente, respeitoso

defiance | difay'əns | *s.* desafio; provocação; rebeldia. -**ind. of** a despeito de, em conflito com. -**to bid d.** desafiar, afrontar, arrostar

defiant | difay'ənt | *a.* desafiante, desafiador; provocador; rebelde; arrogante

deficiency | difi'śənsī | *s.* deficiência, insuficiência

deficient | difi'śənt | *a.* deficiente; insuficiente

defile | dı'fayl | *s.* desfiladeiro / | difayl' | *vt.* sujar, manchar; corromper; profanar

define | difayn' | *vt.* definir; determinar; caracterizar

definite | de'finit | *a.* definido; claro, preciso; limitado

definition | defini'śən | *s.* definição; conceituação

definitive | defi'nitiv | *a.* definitivo, conclusivo, terminante, decisivo

deflate | difleyt' | *vt.* esvaziar, desinflar; (econ.) desinflacionar, deflacionar

deflation | difley'śən | *s.* esvazia-

mento; (econ.) deflação

deflect | diflekt' | *vt.* desviar

deform | difóm' | *vt.* deformar

deformity | difó'mitī | *s.* deformidade, deformação

defraud | difród' | *vt.* defraudar, espoliar, enganar

defray | difrey' | *vt.* custear, assumir as despesas de

defrost | difrost' | *vt.* degelar, descongelar

deft | deft' | *a.* destro, hábil, perito; ágil, ativo

deftness | deft'nes | *s.* destreza, agilidade, habilidade

defunct | difãnkt' | *a.* defunto, falecido, extinto

defy | difay' | *vt.* desafiar; afrontar; desacatar, desrespeitar; desdenhar

degeneracy | diže'nərəsī | *s.* degeneração, degenerescência

degenerate | diže'nəreyt | *vi.* degenerar

degradation | degrədey'śən | *s.* degradação, aviltamento

degrade | digreyd' | *vt.* degradar, aviltar; rebaixar

degrading | digrey'ding | *a.* degradante, aviltante

degree | digrı' | *s.* grau; diploma; extensão, intensidade; estágio, etapa; categoria. -**by degrees** gradualmente. -**to a d.** até certo ponto. -**to take a d.** colar grau, graduar-se

dehydrate | di'haydreyt | *vt. vi.* desidratar(-se)

deify | dı'ifay | *vt.* endeusar

deign | deyn' | *vi.* dignar-se

deity | dı'itī | *s.* divindade

dejected | diźek'tid | *a.* desanimado, desalentado

dejection | diźek'śən | *s.* desânimo, depressão

delay | diley' | *s.* demora; atraso (de trem, avião etc.); adiamento / *vt.* demorar; atrasar; adiar

delegate | de'ligit | *s.* delegado, representante / | de'ligeyt | *vt.* delegar, comissionar

delegation | deligey'śən | *s.* delegação, representação

delete| dilıt' |vt. riscar, eliminar; apagar, suprimir

deleterious| dilitı'rīəs |a. deletério, nocivo, danoso

deletion| dilı'śən |s. eliminação, supressão

deliberate| dili'bərit |a. deliberado, premeditado, intencional; cuidadoso, cauteloso; vagaroso, pausado / | dili'bəreyt | vt. vi. deliberar, considerar

deliberation | dilibərey'śən | s. deliberação, reflexão

delicacy| de'likəsī |s. delicadeza; elegância, fineza; cortesia; sutileza; iguaria, especialidade; fragilidade; debilidade (saúde)

delicate | de'likit | a. delicado, sensível, frágil; débil (saúde); suave, sutil

delicatessen | delikətə'sən |s. casa de comestíveis finos

delicious | dili'śəs | a. delicioso, saboroso

delight | dilayt' | s. delícia, deleite; encanto / vt. deliciar, deleitar / vi. deleitar-se em, deliciar-se com

delighted | dilay'tid | a. encantado, muito contente. -to be d. to ter muito prazer em (aceitar convite etc.)

delightful | dilayt'ful | a. encantador, delicioso

delimit | dili'mit | vt. delimitar, demarcar, definir

delineate | dili'nieyt | vt. deli- -near, esboçar; traçar

delineation | diliniey'śən |s. delineamento, esboço, descrição

delinquency | diling'kwensī | s. delinqüência, criminalidade

delinquent | diling'kwənt |s. delinqüente, criminoso

delirious | dili'rīəs | a. delirante; desvairado

delirium | dili'rīəm |s. delírio

deliver | dili'və | vt. livrar, libertar; entregar; distribuir; proferir, pronunciar (discurso); emitir (opinião); desfechar, desfe-

rir (golpe). -to be delivered of dar à luz. -to d. oneself of aliviar-se, tirar do peito

deliverance | dili'vərəns |s. libertação; salvação; resgate

deliverer | dili'vərə | s. libertador; salvador

delivery | dili'vərī |s. libertação; entrega (de mercadorias); distribuição (de cartas etc.); estilo, forma (de discursar, apresentar etc.); parto. -to take d. of receber (mercadoria comprada)

dell| del' |s. pequeno vale

delude | diluud' | vt. iludir, enganar, tapear

deluge | de'lïuj | s. dilúvio, inundação, aguaceiro / vt. inundar, alagar

delusion | dilïu'jən | s. ilusão; alucinação

delve | delv' | vi. pesquisar laboriosamente (documentos etc.)

demagogue | de'məgog | s. demagogo

demand | dimʌnd' | s. exigência; procura, demanda. -supply and d. oferta e procura. -to be in d. estar em demanda, ser solicitado. -on d. à vista, contra apresentação vt. exigir; demandar; requerer

demanding | dimʌn'ding | a. exigente

demarcation | dimʌkey'śən | s. demarcação, delimitação

demean | dimīn' | vt. rebaixar, degradar / vi. portar-se, conduzir-se, comportar-se

demeanour, demeanor| dimī'nə |s. conduta, comportamento

demented | dimen'tid | a. louco, doente mental

demerit | dime'rit | s. demérito; falta

demise| dimayz' |s. morte, falecimento

demitasse | de'mitas | s. xícara pequena de café

demobilization | dimowbilayzey'śən |s. desmobilização

demobilize | dimow'bilayz | vt.

desmobilizar

democracy | dimo'krəsī | *s.* democracia

democrat | de'məkrat | *s.* democrata

democratic | deməkra'tik | *a.* democrático

demolish | dimo'liś | *vt.* demolir, arrasar, destruir

demolition | deməli'śən | *s.* demolição; arrasamento

demon | dı'mən | *s.* demônio

demonstrate | de'mənstreyt | *vt.* demonstrar

demonstration | demənstrey'śən | *s.* demonstração; prova; manifestação (política etc.)

demonstrative | dimons'trətiv | *a.* demonstrativo; expansivo, efusivo, comunicativo

demonstrator | de'mənstreytə | *s.* manifestante (político); demonstrador (em laboratório, de um produto industrial etc.)

demoralize, demoralise | dimo'rəlayz | *vt.* desmoralizar; perverter; indisciplinar

demur | dimE' | *vi.* objetar, contestar; vacilar; (jur.) argüir exceção

demure | dimǐu'ə | *a.* recatado, reservado, sério; pudico

den | den' | *s.* antro, covil; recanto, refúgio (para trabalho, leitura etc.)

denationalize | dina'śənəlayz | *vt.* desnacionalizar

denial | dinay'əl | *s.* negativa, recusa; rejeição; contradição

denizen | de'nizən | *s.* habitante, estrangeiro residente; palavra, animal ou planta adaptada ou naturalizada

denomination | dinominey'śən | *s.* denominação; valor (moeda); (relig.) igreja, seita, denominação

denote | dinowt' | *vt.* denotar, indicar, significar

denouement | deynʊ'mon | *s.* desenlace

denounce | dinawns' | *vt.* denunciar, acusar; condenar; delatar;

protestar, verberar publicamente

dense | dens' | *a.* denso, espesso; cerrado, fechado

density | den'sitī | *s.* densidade

dent | dent' | *s.* mossa; entalhe em forma de dente / *vt.* amolgar

dentifrice | den'tifris | *s.* dentifrício, creme dental

dentist | den'tist | *s.* dentista

dentistry | den'tistrī | *s.* odontologia

denture | den'šə | *s.* dentadura postiça

denude | dinǐʊd' | *vt.* privar, despojar; desnudar

denunciation | dinânsĩey'śən | *s.* denúncia, acusação; condenação; delação; denunciação

deny | dinay' | *vt.* negar; repudiar; rejeitar, recusar; desconhecer; renunciar

deodorant | diow'dərənt | *s. a.* desodorante, desodorizante

depart | dipʌt' | *vi.* partir; desviar-se de, afastar-se de (verdade etc.); divergir; falecer, morrer. **-the departed** os defuntos, os mortos

department | dipʌt'mənt | *s.* departamento; repartição (do governo); ramo (do saber)

department store | dipʌt'-məntstóə | *s.* loja de departamentos

departure | dipʌ'śə | *s.* partida, saída; divergência, desvio; abandono

depend | dipend' | *vi.* depender de; confiar em; estar sujeito a. **-that depends** talvez

dependable | dipen'dəbəl | *a.* seguro, digno de confiança; fidedigno, em que se pode crer

dependance | dipen'dəns | *s.* dependência

dependants | dipen'dənts | *spl.* dependentes (filhos etc.)

dependent | dipen'dənt | *s.a.* dependente, subordinado

depict | dipikt' | *vt.* pintar; retratar; descrever

deplete | diplīt' | *vt.* esgotar; esvaziar; reduzir

deplorable | dipló'rəbəl | *a.* deplorável, lamentável

deplore | dipló'ə | *vt.* deplorar, lamentar

deploy | diploy' | *vt.* colocar (argumentos etc.) em ação / *vt. vi.* espalhar ou distribuir (soldados) para combate

depopulation | dipopĭuley'śən | *s.* despovoamento

deport | dipót' | *vt.* deportar, exilar, desterrar, degredar. **-to d. oneself** comportar-se, portar-se, conduzir-se

deportation | dipótey'śən | *s.* deportação; expatriação

deportment | dipót'mənt | *s.* comportamento, procedimento; porte, postura

depose | dipowz' | *vt.* depor, destituir; destronar / *vi.* (jur.) depor em juízo

deposit | dipo'zit | *s.* depósito; sinal, penhor; sedimento; armazém. **-on d.** depositado (no banco) / *vt.* depositar; sedimentar; dar como sinal (transação comercial)

deposition | dipəzi'śən | *s.* deposição, destituição; (jur.) depoimento, testemunho; depósito; sedimento

depot | de'pow | *s.* depósito, armazém; (mil.) almoxarifado; (mil.) quartel-general de regimento; (EUA) estação ferroviária ou de ônibus

deprave | dipreyv' | *vt.* depravar, corromper

depravity | dipra'vitī | *s.* depravação, devassidão

deprecate | de'prəkeyt | *vt.* desaprovar; censurar; protestar

depreciate | diprɪ'sieyt | *vt.* depreciar, menoscabar / *vi.* depreciar-se, baixar

depreciation | diprɪsiey'śən | *s.* depreciação

depredation | deprədey'śən | *s.* depredação, devastação

depress | dipres' | *vt.* deprimir, desanimar; abaixar; achatar; depreciar; diminuir

depressed | diprest' | *a.* deprimido, triste, desanimado

depressing | dipre'sing | *a.* deprimente, triste

depression | dipre'śən | *s.* depressão; tristeza, abatimento

deprivation | deprivey'śən | *s.* privação; despojamento; perda; (ecles.) destituição

deprive | diprayv' | *vt.* privar; despojar; (ecles.) destituir (funções clericais)

depth | depϑ' | *s.* profundidade; intensidade, gravidade; (*pl.*) profundezas, abismo. **-in d. a** fundo. **-out of one's d.** lugar onde não dá pé. **-to be beyond one's d.** estar fora do alcance de alguém

deputation | depĭutey'śən | *s.* delegação; comissão

depute | dipĭut' | *vt.* delegar

deputize | de'pĭutayz | *vt.* delegar / *vi.* substituir

deputy | de'pĭutī | *s.* representante, delegado; substituto; representante no parlamento. **-by d.** por procuração

derail | direyl' | *vt. vi.* descarrilar

derange | direynj' | *vt.* desarrumar, desordenar; perturbar; enlouquecer

deranged | direynjd' | *a.* demente, doente mental

derelict | de'rəlikt | *s.* propriedade abandonada; navio abandonado; pária / *a.* abandonado; desprezado

deride | dirayd' | *vt.* escarnecer, zombar de

derision | diri'jən | *s.* escárnio, menosprezo

derisive | diray'siv | *a.* escarnecedor, zombeteiro

derisory | diray'zərī | *a.* irrisório, ridículo

derivation | derivey'śən | *s.* derivação; origem; descendência

derive | dirayv' | *vt.* derivar; tirar

(prazer, lucro etc.) / *vi.* proceder

derogatory | diro'gɔtrĪ | *a.* pejorativo, insultante

derrick | de'rik | *s.* guindaste

descend | disend' | *vi.* descer; baixar; descender, proceder

descendant | disen'dɔnt | *s.* descendente; (*pl.*) descendência, posteridade

descendent | disen'dɔnt | *a.* descendente; decrescente; decadente

descent | disent' | *s.* descida; declive, ladeira; descendência, origem; rebaixamento; declínio; queda; (mil.) assalto, ataque

describe | diskrayb' | *vt.* descrever; narrar; delinear, traçar

description | diskrip'śɔn | *s.* descrição; narrativa, exposição; espécie, classe. **-beyond d.** indescritível

descriptive | diskrip'tiv | *a.* descritivo

descry | diskray' | *vt.* avistar

desecrate | de'sikreyt | *vt.* profanar; desconsagrar

desert | de'zɔt | *s.* deserto / *a.* deserto, ermo, desolado, árido / | dizEt' | *vt.* desertar, abandonar; desamparar / *vi.* (mil.) desertar, fugir

desert | dizEt' | *s.* mérito; valor, virtude; paga, castigo ou recompensa devidos. **-to get one's deserts** ter o que se merece

deserter | dizE'tɔ | *s.* desertor

desertion | dizE'śɔn | *s.* deserção, abandono; (jur.) abandono do lar

deserve | dizEv' | *vt.* merecer

deservedly | dizE'vidlĪ | *adv.* merecidamente, condignamente

deserving | dizE'ving | *a.* merecedor, digno (de recompensa etc.)

design | dizayn' | *s.* projeto, desígnio, plano; desenho (industrial etc.), esboço; intenção. **-by d.** propositadamente. **-to have designs on** cobiçar, ter em mira / *vt.* desenhar; delinear; planejar; intentar, objetivar; destinar

designate | de'zigneyt | *vt.* designar; nomear, indicar

designation | dezigney'śɔn | *s.* designação; nomeação

designer | dizay'nɔ | *s.* desenhista; projetista (desenho industrial etc.); planejador; figurinista; cenarista

designing | dizay'ning | *a.* engenhoso, ardiloso; intrigante

desirability | dizayrɔbi'litĪ | *s.* conveniência; necessidade

desirable | dizay'rɔbɔl | *a.* desejável; apetecível

desire | dizay'ɔ | *s.* desejo; anseio, aspiração; paixão; cobiça; pedido / *vt.* desejar; ansiar, aspirar; cobiçar; pedir

desirous | dizay'ɔrɔs | *a.* desejoso; anelante

desist | disist' | *vi.* desistir, renunciar; parar, cessar

desk | desk' | *s.* escrivaninha, secretária; (mús.) estante

desolate | de'sɔlit | *a.* desolado, desconsolado; solitário, deserto; devastado

desolation | desɔley'śɔn | *s.* desolação, abandono; tristeza, desconsolação; solidão, isolamento; ruína

despair | dispe'ɔ | *s.* desespero / *vi.* desesperar

despairing | dispe'ɔring | *a.* desesperançado; desesperado

despatch | dispaś' | *s.* = *dispatch*

desperado | despɔra'dow | *s.* criminoso, facínora, malfeitor

desperate | des'pɔrit | *a.* desesperado; irremediável; temerário; arrebatado, violento

desperation | despɔrey'śɔn | *s.* desespero, desesperação

despicable | despi'kɔbɔl | *a.* desprezível, indigno, vil

despicableness | despi'kɔbɔlnes | *s.* vileza, indignidade

despise | dispayz' | *vt.* desprezar, desdenhar, menosprezar

despite | dispayt' | *prep.* apesar de, não obstante

despoil | dispoyl' | *vt.* despojar; saquear; espoliar

despondency | dispon'dənsī | *s.* desalento, desânimo, abatimento

despondent | dispon'dənt | *a.* desanimado, desalentado

despot | des'pot | *s.* déspota

despotic | despo'tik | *a.* despótico, tirânico

despotism | des'pətizəm | *s.* despotismo, tirania

dessert | dizɛt' | *s.* sobremesa

dessert spoon | dizɛt'spʋn | *s.* colher de sobremesa

destination | destiney'śən | *s.* destino, ponto de destino; objetivo, meta

destine | des'tin | *vt.* destinar

destiny | des'tinī | *s.* destino

destitute | des'titiut | *a.* indigente, necessitado. **-d. of** desprovido de

destitution | destitĭu'śən | *s.* penúria, miséria, indigência

destroy | distroy' | *vt.* destruir, demolir; exterminar

destroyer | distroy'ə | *s.* destruidor, destrutor; (náut.) destróier, contratorpedeiro

destruction | distrâk'śən | *s.* destruição, arrasamento; extermínio; aniquilamento

destructive | distrâk'tiv | *a.* destrutivo, daninho

destructiveness | distrâk'tivnes | *s.* capacidade de destruir, destrutividade

desultory | de'səltrī | *a.* desconexo; incoerente; confuso

detach | ditaś' | *vt.* destacar (tb. mil.), separar

detachable | dita'śəbəl | *a.* destacável, separável

detached house | ditaśt'haws | *s.* casa isolada

detachment | ditaś'mənt | *s.* (mil.) destacamento; separação; imparcialidade, neutralidade; indiferença

detail | dɪ'teyl | *s.* pormenor, detalhe. **-in d.** pormenorizada-

mente / *vt.* pormenorizar, detalhar; especificar

detailed | dɪ'teyld | *a.* pormenorizado, detalhado

detain | diteyn' | *vt.* deter, retardar; sustar; prender

detect | ditekt' | *vt.* descobrir; detectar; investigar, averiguar

detection | ditek'śən | *s.* descoberta; revelação; detecção

detective | ditek'tiv | *s.* detetive

detective story | ditek'tivstorī | *s.* romance ou conto policial

detector | ditek'tə | *s.* detector

detention | diten'śən | *s.* detenção, prisão

deter | ditɛ' | *vt.* sustar; dissuadir, desanimar, desencorajar

detergent | ditɛ'jənt | *s.* detergente

deteriorate | ditɪ'rīəreyt | *vi.* deteriorar-se, estragar-se; arruinar-se, decair

deterioration | ditīrīərey'śən | *s.* deterioração; degeneração; decadência, ruína

determination | ditɛminey'śən | *s.* determinação; delimitação; resolução, decisão; firmeza

determine | ditɛ'min | *vt.* determinar, decidir; resolver

determined | ditɛ'mind | *a.* determinado, decidido, resoluto; teimoso, pertinaz

deterrent | dite'rənt | *s.* impedimento, embaraço. **-to act as a d.** servir de freio / *a.* impeditivo; dissuasivo

detest | ditest' | *vt.* detestar

detestable | dites'təbəl | *a.* detestável, execrável

detestation | ditestey'śən | *s.* aversão, execração, detestação

dethrone | diϑrown' | *vt.* destronar

detonate | de'towneyt | *vt.* detonar

detonator | de'towneytə | *s.* detonador

detour | ditu'ə | *s.* desvio, mudança de direção

detract | ditrakt' | *vi.* difamar, denegrir, denigrir, prejudicar

detractor | ditrak'tə | *s.* detrator,

caluniador

detriment | de'trimənt | s. detrimento, prejuízo

detrimental | detrimen'təl | a. nocivo, prejudicial, danoso

deuce | dīus' | s. dois, duque (cartas ou dados). -**what the d.!** que diacho!

devastate | de'vəsteyt | vt. devastar, assolar; saquear

devastation | devəstey'śən | s. devastação, destruição

develop | dive'ləp | vt. desenvolver; fomentar; expandir; ampliar; contrair (doença); (fot.) revelar / vi. progredir, avançar; crescer, desenvolver-se; evoluir

development | dive'ləpmənt | s. desenvolvimento; progresso, crescimento, aumento; (fot.) revelação

deviate | dı'vīeyt | vt. vi. desviar(-se), afastar(-se), apartar(-se)

deviation | dıvīey'śən | s. desvio, afastamento

device | divays' | s. dispositivo, aparelho; plano, projeto, esquema; expediente, estratagema; divisa, moto; emblema heráldico

devil | de'vəl | s. diabo, demônio. -**the d. to pay!** vai haver o diabo! -**between the d. and the deep blue sea** entre a espada e a parede. -**to raise the d.** armar barulho

devilish | de'viliś | a. diabólico, endiabrado

devilment | de'vilmənt | s. diabrura; travessura; bruxaria, feitiçaria

devious | dı'vīəs | a. remoto; afastado; tortuoso; inescrupuloso; insincero

devise | divayz' | vt. (jur.) legar; planejar; maquinar

devitalize | divay'təlayz | vt. desvitalizar, debilitar

devoid | divoyd' | a. destituído de, privado, carente

devolution | divəlu'śən | s. devolução; transferência, transmissão; delegação

devolve | divolv' | vt. transferir, delegar / vi. passar, caber, incumbir. -**tod. to, on ou upon** caber por sucessão

devote | divowt' | vt. devotar, dedicar, consagrar; destinar

devoted | divow'tid | a. devotado, dedicado, leal; afetuoso, extremoso; destinado

devotee | devowtı' | s. adepto, entusiasta; devoto; sectário

devotion | divow'śən | s. devoção; dedicação; (pl.) orações, preces

devotional | divow'śənəl | a. devoto, religioso, piedoso

devour | divaw'ə | vt. devorar, destruir, consumir

devout | divawt' | a. devoto, piedoso, religioso; dedicado

devoutness | divawt'nes | s. devoção, piedade

dew | dīu' | s. orvalho, sereno, rocio

dexterity | dekste'ritī | s. destreza, agilidade

dexterous | deks'trəs | a. destro, hábil, ágil

diabetes | dayəbı'tīz -tis | s. diabetes, diabete

diabetic | dayəbe'tik | s. a. diabético

diabolic, -al | dayəbo'lik(əl) | a. diabólico, demoníaco

diagnose | day'əgnowz | vt. diagnosticar

diagnosis | dayəgnow'sis | s. diagnóstico

diagram | day'əgram | s. diagrama, esquema

dial | day'əl | s. mostrador (de relógio, rádio etc.); relógio de sol; disco de telefone / vt. discar (telefone); sintonizar (rádio)

dialect | day'əlekt | s. dialeto

dialogue, dialog | day'əlog | s. diálogo

diameter | daya'mitə | s. diâmetro

diametrical | dayəme'trikəl | a. diametral

diamond | day'əmənd | *s.* diamante; (*pl.*) ouros (naipe)

diaper | day'əpə | *s.* fralda de criança

diarrhoea, diarrhea | dayəri'ə | *s.* diarréia

diary | day'ərī | *s.* diário; agenda, livro de anotações

diatribe | day'ətrayb | *s.* diatribe, ataque, invectiva

dice | days' | *spl.* dados / *vt. vi.* jogar dados

dickens | di'kinz | *s.* (coloq.) diacho, diabo. **-what the d.!** que diacho!

dictate | dik'teyt | *s.* preceito, ditame / *vt.* ditar; impor / *vi.* ditar; dar ordens

dictation | diktey'śən | *s.* ditado; prescrição; imposição

dictator | diktey'tə | *s.* ditador; déspota

dictatorial | diktətó'rīəl | *a.* ditatorial; despótico

dictatorship | diktey'təśip | *s.* ditadura

diction | dik'śən | *s.* dicção

dictionary | dik'śənərī | *s.* dicionário

dictum | dik'təm | *s.* dito, máxima, sentença, aforismo

didactic | didak'tik | *a.* didático

diddle | di'dəl | *vt.* (gír.) enganar, trapacear, iludir

die | day' | *s.* (*pl. dice*) dado. **-the d. is cast** a sorte está lançada; (mec.) molde, cunho, matriz

die | day' | *vi.* morrer, falecer. **-to d. away** desvanecer, extinguir-se. **-to d. in harness** morrer trabalhando. **-to be dying for** ansiar por

die-hard | day'hʌd | *s.* pessoa conservadora ou teimosa / *a.* obstinado, teimoso

diet | day'ət | *s.* dieta; regime alimentar. **-to be on a d.** estar de dieta

differ | di'fə | *vi.* diferir, distinguir-se; discordar

difference | dif'rens | *s.* diferença, distinção; divergência (opinião etc.)

different | dif'rənt | *a.* diferente, distinto

differential | difərən'śəl | *s. a.* diferencial

differentiate | difərən'śīeyt | *vt.* distinguir, diferençar

difficult | di'fikʌlt | *a.* difícil; exigente (pessoa)

difficulty | di'fikʌltī | *s.* dificuldade

diffidence | di'fidəns | *s.* modéstia excessiva; timidez, acanhamento; hesitação

diffident | di'fidənt | *a.* pessoa excessivamente modesta; acanhado, tímido

diffuse | diffuz' | *vt.* difundir, propagar / *a.* difuso; prolixo, verborrágico

diffusion | diffu'jən | *s.* difusão; prolixidade

dig | dig' | *s.* escavação; (coloq.) cotovelada, cutucada; (coloq.) censura, comentário sarcástico / *vt.* cavar; desenterrar; cutucar; cravar, meter. **-to d. out** ou **up** descobrir, desencavar; averiguar. **-to d. up the hatchet** preparar-se para a guerra

digest | day'jest | *s.* sumário, compilação, coleção / | di'jest' | *vt.* digerir; sintetizar, condensar

digestible | dijes'tibəl | *a.* digerível, digestível

digestion | dijes'śən | *s.* digestão

digestive | dijes'tiv | *s. a.* digestivo

digger | di'gə | *s.* cavador; escavadora; (coloq.) pessoa trabalhadora ou estudiosa

digit | di'jit | *s.* algarismo, dígito; (anat., zool.) dedo; medida linear (3/4 de polegada)

dignified | dig'nifayd | *a.* sério, grave; majestoso; nobre, augusto, excelso

dignify | dig'nifay | *vi.* dignificar, honrar, exaltar

dignitary | dig'nitərī | *s.* dignitário

dignity | dig'nitī | *s.* dignidade; nobreza; decoro, respeitabilidade

digress | daygres' | *vi.* divagar; desviar-se

digression | daygre'ʃən | *s.* digressão, divagação

dike | dayk' | *s.* dique

dilapidated | dila'pideytid | *a.* dilapidado, arruinado

dilapidation | dilapidey'ʃən | *s.* dilapidação, decadência

dilate | dayleyt' | *vt. vi.* dilatar(-se), expandir(-se)

dilation | dayley'ʃən | *s.* dilação

dilatoriness | di'lətrīnes | *s.* lentidão, demora; indolência

dilatory | di'lətrī | *a.* vagaroso, lento; negligente

dilemma | dile'mə | *s.* dilema

dilettante | 'dilitan'ti | *s.* diletante, amador

diligence | di'liʃəns | *s.* diligência, zelo, aplicação

diligent | di'liʃənt | *a.* diligente, zeloso, aplicado

dilute | dayʎut' | *vt.* diluir

dim | dim' | *a.* escuro; baço, pouco claro; indistinto, confuso; fraco (som). **-to take a d. view of** não fazer fé em, ver com pessimismo

dime | daym' | *s.* (EUA) moeda de dez centavos

dimension | dimen'ʃən | *s.* dimensão, extensão

diminish | dimi'niʃ | *vt.* diminuir, atenuar / *vi.* minguar, diminuir

diminution | diminʎu'ʃən | *s.* diminuição, redução

diminutive | dimi'niʎutiv | *s.* (gram.) diminutivo / *a.* diminuto, minúsculo

dimness | dim'nes | *s.* obscuridade; falta de clareza

dimple | dim'pəl | *s.* covinha (nas faces ou queixo)

din | din' | *s.* barulho, alarido, gritaria / *vt.* aturdir, ensurdecer / *vi.* atroar

dine | dayn' | *vi.* jantar

diner | day'nə | *s.* aquele que janta; comensal, conviva; vagão-restaurante

ding-dong | ding'dong | *s.* tilintar de sino / *a.* renhido, duro (batalha, jogo etc.) / *vt. vi.* tilintar

dinginess | din'ʃines | *s.* escuridão; sujidade, deslustre, empanamento

dingy | din'ʃi | *a.* sombrio; embaçado, encardido

dining-car | day'ningkʌ | *s.* vagão-restaurante

dining-room | day'ningrum | *s.* sala de jantar

dinner | di'nə | *s.* jantar

dinner-jacket | di'nəjakit | *s. smoking*

dint | dint' | *s.* (ant.) pancada, golpe. **-by d. of** à força de

diocese | day'əsis | *s.* diocese

dip | dip' | *s.* mergulho, imersão; depressão, buraco; inclinação, declividade / *vt.* mergulhar, molhar, banhar, ensopar; saudar com a bandeira / *vi.* mergulhar; baixar, inclinar-se; desaparecer subitamente. **-to d. into a book** folhear um livro

diphtheria | difϑi'rīə | *s.* difteria

diphthong | dif'ϑong | *s.* ditongo

diploma | diplow'mə | *s.* diploma

diplomacy | diplow'məsī | *s.* diplomacia; habilidade, tato

diplomat | di'pləmat | *s.* diplomata

diplomatic | dipləma'tik | *a.* diplomático; prudente, sagaz

dire | day'ə | *a.* medonho; terrível, horrendo; calamitoso

direct | direkt' dayrekt' | *a.* direto; direito, reto; franco; imediato; completo, absoluto; pessoal / *adv.* diretamente / *vt.* dirigir; encaminhar, guiar; ordenar / *vi.* dar ordens, mandar

direction | direk'ʃən | *s.* direção; governo; orientação

directive | direk'tiv | *s.* diretiva, diretriz

directly | direk'tlī | *adv.* diretamente; imediatamente, já / *conj.* logo que, assim que

directness | direkt'nes | *s.* franqueza; retidão, integridade

director | direk'tə dayrek'tə | *s.* diretor; superintendente

directory | direk'tərī | *s.* registro profissional, anuário comercial, lista telefônica

dirge | dEɤ̆' | *s.* missa de réquiem; endecha, canto fúnebre

dirt | dɛt' | *s.* sujeira, imundície; lama, lodo; poeira, pó; lixo, dejetos. -**d. cheap** muito barato

dirtiness | dɛ'tines | *s.* sujeira; imundície; sordidez

dirty | dɛ'tī | *a.* sujo; indecente, obsceno; tempestuoso, borrascoso / *vt.* sujar / *vi.* sujar-se

dirty joke | dɛ'tiɤ̆owk | *s.* piada obscena

dirty trick | dɛ'tītrik | *s.* trapaça

disability | disəbi'litī | *s.* incapacidade, inépcia, inaptidão, inabilidade; invalidez

disable | disey'bəl | *vt.* incapacitar, inabilitar; estropiar, aleijar; invalidar

disabled | disey'bəld | *a.* incapacitado; mutilado

disabuse | disəbi̇̆uz' | *vt.* desenganar; desiludir

disadvantage | disədvʌn'tiɤ̆ | *s.* desvantagem; inconveniente

disadvantageous | disədvəntey'ɤ̆əs | *a.* desvantajoso, desfavorável; prejudicial

disaffected | disəfek'tid | *a.* desafeto, inimigo; descontente, insatisfeito; desleal

disagree | disəgri' | *vi.* discordar, divergir. -**to d. with** não se dar bem com (comida, clima etc.)

disagreeable | disəgrī'əbəl | *a.* desagradável; antipático; mal-humorado, irritadiço

disagreement | disəgrī'mənt | *s.* desentendimento, desacordo, divergência, discordância

disallow | disəlaw' | *vt.* rejeitar; negar, recusar; proibir; reprovar

disappear | disəpī'ə | *vi.* desaparecer, sumir; cessar

disappearance | disəpī'ərəns | *s.* desaparecimento

disappoint | disəpoynt' | *vt.* desapontar; frustrar

disappointed | disəpoyn'tid | *a.* desapontado; frustrado

disappointment | disəpoynt'mənt | *s.* desapontamento

disapproval | disəprʊ'vəl | *s.* desaprovação; rejeição; reprovação, censura

disapprove | disəprʊv' | *vt. vi.* desaprovar; censurar

disarm | disʌm' | *vt. vi.* desarmar, depor as armas

disarmament | disʌ'məmənt | *s.* desarmamento

disarrange | disəreynɤ̆' | *vt.* transtornar, perturbar

disarrangement | disəreynɤ̆'mənt | *s.* desordem; contratempo

disarray | disərey' | *s.* desordem, confusão; desalinho

disaster | dizʌs'tə | *s.* desastre, catástrofe, calamidade

disastrous | dizʌs'trəs | *a.* desastroso, calamitoso

disavow | disəvnaw' | *vt.* repudiar, negar; desautorizar; desmentir; refutar

disavowal | disəvaw'əl | *s.* repúdio, rejeição; refutação, desmentido

disband | disband' | *vt.* (mil.) debandar, dispersar; dissolver / *vi.* debandar, dispensar

disbelief | disbilif' | *s.* incredulidade, descrença, ceticismo, dúvida

disbelieve | disbilīv' | *vt.* descrer, duvidar de / *vi.* não ter fé em

disburse | disbɛs' | *vt.* desembolsar, gastar, pagar

disc, disk | disk' | *s.* disco; gravação fonográfica; placa, chapa

discard | discʌd' | *vt.* descartar; desfazer-se de, livrar-se de; rejeitar, excluir / *vi.* descartar

discern | disɛn' | *vt.* discernir; ver, avistar; reconhecer, apreciar

discernible | disɛ'nibəl | *a.* discernível, perceptível

discernment | disɛn'mənt | *s.* discernimento; perspicácia, agudeza, penetração

discharge | dis'ŝAJ | s. descarga (elétrica, de arma de fogo etc.); descarregamento; desempenho, execução; demissão; exoneração (de cargo); liberação (de preso); absolvição; alta (de hospital); (mil.) baixa; evacuação, emissão; supuração / | disŝAJ' | vt. descarregar (navio, arma de fogo etc.); cumprir (dever); (mil.) dar baixa a; absolver; libertar, soltar; demitir, despedir; dar alta a (de hospital); exonerar, isentar (de incumbência); aliviar (de responsabilidade etc.)

disciple | disay'pǝl | s. discípulo; adepto, seguidor

disciplinarian | disipline'ǝrīǝn | s. disciplinador / a. disciplinar

disciplinary | di'siplinǝrī | a. disciplinar

discipline | di'siplin | s. disciplina / vt. disciplinar

disc jockey | disk'jokī | s. locutor de programa de discos

disclaim | diskleym' | vt. repudiar, rejeitar, repelir

disclose | disklowz' | vt. revelar, descobrir

disclosure | disklow'jǝ | s. revelação, divulgação; mostra, exposição, exibição

discolour, discolor | diskǝ'lǝ | vt. vi. descorar, desbotar; manchar(-se)

discolouration, discoloration | diskǝlǝrey'ŝǝn | s. descoloração, desbotamento; mancha

discomfit | diskâm'fit | vt. desbaratar, derrotar; desconcertar; frustrar

discomfort | diskâm'fǝt | s. desconforto; mal-estar; inquietação; privação

disconcert | diskǝnsEt' | vt. desconcertar, perturbar, confundir, desnortear

disconcerting | diskǝnsE'ting | a. desconcertante, embaraçoso

disconnect | diskǝnekt' | vt. desli-

gar; separar, desunir

disconsolate | diskon'sǝlit | a. desconsolado, desolado

discontent | diskǝntent' | s. descontentamento; insatisfação; desgosto, desagrado

discontented | diskǝnten'tid | a. descontente, insatisfeito

discontinue | diskǝnti'nĩu | vt. interromper, suspender, cessar

discord | diskód' | s. discórdia, desavença; desarmonia

discordant | diskó'dǝnt | a. discordante, divergente

discount | dis'kawnt | s. desconto, abatimento, redução

discourage | diskâ'rij | vt. desencorajar, desanimar; dissuadir; desaprovar

discouragement | diskâ'rijmǝnt | s. desânimo, desalento; desaprovação, reprovação

discouraging | diskâ'rijing | a. desanimador, desalentador

discourse | dis'kós | s. discurso; dissertação; (ecles.) sermão, exortação; exposição, tratado; conversação / vi. discorrer, tratar

discourteous | diskE'tĩǝs | a. descortês, indelicado, rude

discourtesy | diskE'tisĩ | s. descortesia, indelicadeza

discover | diskâ'vǝ | vt. descobrir, encontrar; revelar

discoverer | diskâ'vǝrǝ | s. descobridor

discovery | diskâ'vǝrī | s. descobrimento, achado; descoberta; revelação; invenção

discredit | diskre'dit | s. descrédito; desonra, vergonha; desconfiança; dúvida / vt. desacreditar, duvidar

discreditable | diskre'ditǝbǝl | a. desabonador; vergonhoso

discreet | diskrit' | a. discreto; prudente; moderado

discrepancy | diskre'pǝnsī | s. discrepância, disparidade

discretion | diskre'ŝǝn | s. discrição; prudência; moderação. **-at**

d. à discrição, à vontade

discriminate | diskri'mineyt | *vt.* discriminar; distinguir; diferençar; separar

discriminating | diskriminey'ting | *a.* perspicaz, arguto, que sabe discernir

discrimination | diskriminey'śən | *s.* discriminação

discursive | diskE'siv | *a.* discursivo; divagador, digressivo

discuss | diskâs' | *vt.* discutir, debater; comentar

discussion | diskâ'śən | *s.* discussão, debate

disdain | disdeyn' | *s.* desdém, desprezo / *vt.* desdenhar, desprezar

disdainful | disdeyn'ful | *a.* desdenhoso, arrogante

disease | diziz' | *s.* doença, enfermidade

diseased | dizizd' | *a.* doente; doentio; infeccionado

disembark | disembAk' | *vt. vi.* desembarcar; descarregar

disembarkation | disembAkey'śən | *s.* desembarque

disembody | disembo'dī | *vt.* desencarnar, desencorporar

disengage | disengeyj' | *vt.* soltar, desprender; desembaraçar, desimpedir; livrar, liberar / *vi. vr.* soltar-se, livrar-se; afastar-se, retirar-se

disentangle | disentang'gəl | *vt.* soltar, desenredar, desemaranhar; deslindar, destrinçar

disfavour, disfavor | disfey'və | *s.* desfavor, desagrado; desaprovação

disfigure | disfi'gə | *vt.* desfigurar, deformar

disfranchise | disfran'śayz | *vt.* privar de (direitos civis, voto, imunidades etc.)

disgorge | disgój' | *vt.* vomitar, expelir; devolver (com relutância); desaguar

disgrace | disgreys' | *s.* vergonha, desonra; desfavor, desgraça, descrédito / *vt.* desonrar, aviltar; degradar

disgraceful | disgreys'ful | *a.* infame, vergonhoso, desonroso

disgruntled | disgrân'təld | *a.* descontente, aborrecido; desapontado, frustrado

disguise | disgayz' | *s.* disfarce / *vt.* disfarçar, dissimular; encobrir, ocultar

disgust | disgâst' | *s.* repugnância, aversão; nojo, asco / *vt.* repugnar, nausear

disgusted | disgâs'tid | *a.* enojado, enfastiado; aborrecido

disgusting | disgâs'ting | *a.* repugnante, asqueroso, nojento, repulsivo; infame, vil

dish | diś' | *s.* prato; travessa; iguaria; (*pl.*) louça. **-to do the dishes** lavar a louça / *vt.* servir (comida). **-to d. up** servir, apresentar; (*gír.*) defraudar, enganar, lograr

dishabille | dis'əbil | *s.* traje caseiro; chambre, roupão, penhoar, *déshabillé*

disharmony | dishA'mənī | *s.* desarmonia, discórdia

dishearten | dishA'tən | *vt.* desencorajar, desanimar

dishevelled | diśe'vəld | *a.* desgrenhado, despenteado

dishonest | diso'nist | *a.* desonesto, fraudulento; insincero, desleal

dishonesty | diso'nistī | *s.* desonestidade, improbidade; insinceridade, deslealdade

dishonour, dishonor | diso'nə | *s.* desonra, vergonha / *vt.* desonrar; infamar; envergonhar; (*com.*) deixar de pagar (cheque, título etc.)

dishonourable, dishonorable | diso'nərəbəl | *a.* desonroso, indigno, vergonhoso, vil

disillusion | disilʋ'jən | *s.* desilusão, desengano / *vt.* desiludir, desenganar

disinclination | disinkliney'śən | *s.* aversão, relutância

disinclined | disinklaynd' | *a.*

pouco disposto, avesso, relutante

disinfect | disinfekt' | vt. desinfetar, tornar asséptico

disinfectant | disinfek'tənt | s. a. desinfetante

disinfection | disinfek'šən | s. desinfecção

disingenuous | disinje'nĭuəs | a. dissimulado, falso

disinherit | disinhe'rit | vt. deserdar

disintegrate | disin'tigreyt | vt. vi. desintegrar(-se), desagregar(-se)

disintegration | disintigrey'šən | s. desintegração

disinter | disintE' | vt. desenterrar, exumar

disinterested | disin'trəstid | a. desinteressado, imparcial

disinterestedness | disin'trəstidnes | s. desinteresse

disjointed | disjoyn'tid | a. desconjuntado; desarticulado; desconexo, incoerente

dislike | dislayk' | s. aversão, antipatia; repugnância / vt. ter aversão a

dislocate | dis'ləkeyt | vt. deslocar; desarticular, desconjuntar; transtornar

dislodge | disloĵ' | vt. desalojar; expulsar; desentocar; deslocar

disloyal | disloy'əl | a. desleal, falso, pérfido

disloyalty | disloy'əltī | s. deslealdade, falsidade, perfídia, infidelidade

dismal | diz'məl | a. triste, sombrio, desolador, lúgubre

dismantle | disman'təl | vt. desmantelar, demolir; desmontar, desarmar

dismay | dismey' | s. desalento, desânimo; consternação; assombro / vt. desalentar; consternar; assombrar

dismember | dismem'bə | vt. desmembrar, destroçar

dismiss | dismis' | vt. demitir, despedir; dissolver (reunião etc.); dispensar (turma, classe); repudiar, rejeitar; (jur.) absol-

ver; (mil.) excluir, dar baixa

dismissal | dismi'səl | s. demissão, destituição, exoneração; repúdio, rejeição; (jur.) indeferimento

dismount | dismawnt' | vt. desmontar, apear; (mec.) desarmar; desengastar (jóia) / vi. apear-se, desmontar-se

disobedience | disəbi'dĭəns | s. desobediência; insubordinação

disobedient | disəbi'dĭənt | a. desobediente; insubordinado

disobey | disəbey' | vt. desobedecer, transgredir, infringir

disorder | disó'də | s. desordem, desalinho; confusão; tumulto; indisposição, doença

disorderly | disó'dəlī | a. desordenado; confuso; tumultuado; desregrado, irregular / adv. desordenadamente

disorganization | disógənayzey'šən | s. desorganização

disorganize | disó'gənayz | vt. desorganizar, desordenar

disown | disown' | vt. repudiar, rejeitar; renunciar

disparage | dispa'riĵ | vt. desacreditar, menoscabar

disparagement | dispa'riĵmənt | s. descrédito; depreciação

disparaging | dispa'riĵing | a. depreciativo; degradante

disparity | dispa'ritī | s. disparidade, desproporção

dispassionate | dispa'šənit | a. desapaixonado, imparcial

dispatch | dĭspaš' | s. despacho; expedição; comunicado, telegrama; diligência, presteza; ato de matar / vt. expedir, enviar; matar

dispel | dispel' | vt. dissipar

dispensary | dispen'sərī | s. dispensário

dispensation | dispensey'šən | s. (teol.) dispensação; dispensa; isenção; distribuição, repartição; administração, regime; (teol.) graça, revelação

dispense | dispens' | vt. dispensar; distribuir, repartir; administrar; isentar, eximir; aviar (receita) / *vi.* conceder dispensas. **-to d. with** prescindir de, passar sem

dispenser | dispen'sǝ | *s.* farmacêutico, boticário

dispersal | dispE'sǝl | *s.* dispersão; debandada

disperse | dispES' | *vt.* dispersar; disseminar; dissipar

dispirited | dispi'ritid | *a.* desanimado, abatido, desalentado

displace | displeys' | *vt.* deslocar, desalojar; remover, transferir; substituir

display | displey' | *s.* exposição; manifestação; ostentação / *vt.* expor, exibir; manifestar; ostentar

displease | displiz' | *vt.* desagradar, desgostar; irritar; ofender

displeased | displizd' | *a.* descontente; irritado; ofendido

displeasure | disple'jǝ | *s.* desprazer, desagrado; descontentamento; enfado

disport | dispót' | *vi. vr.* brincar, divertir-se

disposal | dispow'zǝl | *s.* disposição; emprego, uso (dinheiro); arranjo, disposição; distribuição, venda; alienação; controle. **-at your d.** às suas ordens, ao seu dispor

dispose | dispowz' | *vt.* dispor, arrumar; predispor, inclinar; colocar, distribuir. **-to d. of** dispor de, desfazer-se de; descartar-se de; acabar com, consumir; alienar, vender, passar adiante

disposition | dispozi'śǝn | *s.* disposição, distribuição; índole, temperamento; tendência; gênio, humor; regulamento; alienação, venda

dispossess | dispǝzes' | *vt.* despossar; desalojar, despejar; despojar, privar de

disproportionate | disprǝpó'śǝnit | *a.* desproporcionado, desconforme, desigual

disprove | dispruv' | *vt.* refutar; invalidar

disputable | dispǐu'tǝbǝl | *a.* discutível, contestável

disputant | dis'pǐutǝnt | *s.* disputador, discutidor, contendor, argumentador

dispute | dispǐut' | *s.* disputa, contenda; controvérsia, discussão, altercação / *vt.* disputar, discutir / *vi.* disputar, altercar

disqualification | diskwolifikey'śǝn | *s.* desqualificação, inabilitação, incapacidade

disqualify | diskwo'lifay | *vt.* desqualificar, desclassificar, incapacitar, inabilitar

disquiet | diskway'ǝt | *s.* inquietação, desassossego; perturbação / *vt.* perturbar

disquieting | diskway'ǝting | *a.* inquietante, perturbador

disquisition | diskwizi'śǝn | *s.* tratado, dissertação ou estudo minucioso

disregard | disrigʌd' | *s.* desatenção, negligência, descuido; desdém / *vt.* descuidar, desatender; desprezar, desdenhar

disrepair | disripe'ǝ | *s.* dilapidação, mau estado, abandono

disreputable | disre'pǐutǝbǝl | *a.* vergonhoso, indecoroso, de má fama; desacreditado; de má aparência, maltrapilho

disrepute | disripǐut' | *s.* descrédito, desonra, má fama

disrespect | disrispekt' | *s.* desrespeito, desacato, irreverência / *vt.* desrespeitar

disrespectful | disrispekt'ful | *a.* desrespeitoso, irreverente; grosseiro, rude, incivil

disrobe | disrowb' | *vt. vi.* desvestir(-se), desnudar(-se)

disrupt | disrãpt' | *vt.* quebrar, despedaçar; interromper, descontinuar

dissatisfaction | disatisfak'śǝn | *s.* descontentamento

dissatisfied | disa'tisfayd | *a.* insatisfeito, descontente

dissect | disekt' | vt. dissecar

dissemble | disem'bəl | vt.disfarçar, dissimular, ocultar / vi. dissimular, fingir

dissembler | disem'blə | s. dissimulador, hipócrita

disseminate | dise'mineyt | vt. disseminar, propagar

dissension | disen'śən | s. dissensão, discórdia, desavença

dissent | disent' | s. dissenção, discordância / vi. dissentir, discordar, divergir

dissenter | disen'tə | s. dissidente, não-conformista

dissentient | disen'śənt | a. dissidente, discordante

dissertation | disətey'śən | s. dissertação; tese

disservice | disɛ'vis | s. desserviço, dano, prejuízo

dissimilar | disi'milə | a. diferente, dessemelhante

dissimilarity | disimila'ritī | s. diferença, dessemelhança, dissimilitude

dissimulation | disimīuley'śən | s. dissimulação

dissipate | di'sipeyt | vt. dissipar; esbanjar, desperdiçar (dinheiro)

dissipated | di'sipeytid | a. dissoluto, devasso; pródigo

dissipation | disipey'śən | s. dissipação, libertinagem; esbanjamento; dispersão

dissociate | disow'sīeyt | vt. dissociar; separar, desligar

dissolute | di'səlut | a. dissoluto, devasso, libertino, licencioso

dissoluteness | di'səlutnes | s. devassidão, depravação

dissolution | disəlu'śən | s. dissolução; extinção

dissolve | dizolv' | vt. dissolver; desintegrar

dissuade | disweyd' | vt. dissuadir, fazer desistir

distaff | dis'taf | s. roca

distaff side | dis'tafsayd | s. o ramo feminino da família

distance | dis'təns | s. distância.
-in the d. ao longe. -from a d. de certa distância. -to keep one's d. guardar distância. -in the d. distante

distant | dis'tənt | a. distante, afastado; frio, reservado (temperamento)

distaste | disteyst' | s. nojo, repugnância, aversão

distasteful | disteyst'ful | a. repugnante, nojento; aborrecido

distemper | distem'pə | s. destempero, desarranjo; pintura a têmpera / vt. desarranjar, indispor; pintar (à têmpera)

distend | distend' | vt. vi. distender(-se), dilatar(-se)

distil | distil' | vt. destilar

distillation | distiley'śən | s. destilação

distillery | disti'lərī | s. destilaria

distinct | distinkt' | a. distinto, claro; diferente

distinction | distink'śən | s. distinção; diferença

distinctive | distink'tiv | a. distintivo, característico

distinctness | distinkt'nes | s. clareza, nitidez

distinguish | disting'gwiś | a. distinguir, diferençar

distinguished | disting'gwiśt | a. distinto, eminente, notável

distort | distót' | vt. torcer; falsear, deturpar; deformar

distortion | distó'śən | s. distorção; torção; deformação

distract | distrakt' | vt. distrair, desviar a atenção de; enlouquecer, pôr fora de si

distracted | distrak'tid | a. enlouquecido, desesperado

distraction | distrak'śən | s. distração, passatempo; perturbação nervosa. -to love to d. amar loucamente

distraught | distrót' | a. transtornado, quase louco (de preocupação etc.)

distress | distres' | s. aflição, sofrimento, angústia; perigo; pobreza, miséria / *vt.* afligir, angustiar

distressing | distre'sing | *a.* aflitivo, angustiante

distress-signal | distres'signəl | *s.* sinal de socorro

distribute | distri'bĭut | *vt.* distribuir, repartir

distribution | distribĭu'śən | *s.* distribuição

distributor | distri'bĭutə | *s.* distribuidor

district | dis'trikt | *s.* distrito; região

district attorney | dis'triktə-tE'nĭ | *s.* (EUA) promotor público

distrust | distrâst' | *s.* desconfiança / *vt.* desconfiar de

distrustful | distrâst'ful | *a.* desconfiado, suspeitoso

disturb | distEb' | *vt.* perturbar, incomodar; inquietar

disturbance | distE'bəns | *s.* perturbação; distúrbio, tumulto

disunite | disĭunayt' | *vt.* desunir, separar, dividir

disuse | disĭus' | *s.* desuso

ditch | diš' | *s.* vala, rego / *vt.* abrir valas ou regos

ditto | di'tow| *s.* idem, o mesmo. -**to say d. to** concordar com, apoiar

ditty | di'tĭ | *s.* canção

divan | divan' | *s.* divã, sofá

dive | dayv' | *s.* mergulho; (coloq.) tasca, antro / *vi.* mergulhar; atirar-se

diver | day'və | *s.* mergulhador

diverge | dayvEj' | *vi.* divergir; desviar-se, afastar-se

divergence | dayvE'jəns | *s.* divergência, desacordo

divers | day'vəz | *a.* vários, diversos, diferentes

diverse | dayvEs' | *a.* diverso, diferente, variado

diversify | dayvE'sifay | *vt.* diversificar, variar

diversion | dayvE'jən | *s.* desvio, afastamento; diversão, distração

diversity | dayvE'sitĭ | *s.* diversi-

dade, variedade, diferença, dessemelhança

divert | dayvEt' | *vt.* desviar, afastar; distrair, entreter

divest | dayvest' | *vt.* despir, despojar; desapossar, privar

divide | divayd' | *vt.* dividir, repartir, partilhar

dividend | di'vidənd | *s.* dividendo; lucro

divine | divayn' | *s.* teólogo / *a.* divino / *vt.* adivinhar

divinity | divi'nitĭ | *s.* divindade; teologia

division | divi'jən | *s.* divisão, partilha; grupo, seção; limite; discórdia, cisão

divorce | divós' | *s.* divórcio / *vt.* divorciar; divorciar-se de; repudiar

divulge | dayvâlj' | *vt.* divulgar, revelar, propagar

dizziness | di'zines | *s.* tonteira, vertigem

dizzy | di'zĭ |*a.* tonto, vertiginoso / *vt.* estontear

do | dʊ' | *vt. vi.* fazer; arrumar (quarto etc.); arranjar (penteado etc.); fazer-se de, bancar; (coloq.) bastar, servir. -**to d. away with** suprimir, abolir. -**to d. one's best** fazer o possível. -**to d. over** refazer, repetir. -**to have nothing to d. with** nada ter a ver com. -**that will d.** basta assim, isso serve. -**how d. you d.?** muito prazer em conhecê-lo; como tem passado?, como vai?

docile | dow'sayl | *a.* dócil, submisso, obediente

dock | dok' | *s.* doca; dique; banco dos réus; sabugo, coto (da cauda de animal) / *vt.* cortar (cauda); reduzir, diminuir (salários etc.); despojar; levar à doca (navio)

dockyard | do'kĭad | *s.* estaleiro

doctor | dok'tə | *s.* doutor; médico. -**you're the d.** (coloq.) você é quem decide / *vt.* conferir grau de doutor; tratar; (coloq.) consertar, remendar; adulterar, falsificar

doctorate | dok'tərit | s. doutorado, grau de doutor

doctrinaire | doktrine'ə | a. doutrinário, teórico; ideológico; dogmático

doctrine | dok'trin | s. doutrina; crença, dogma

document | do'kĭumənt | s. documento / vt. documentar

doddering | do'dəring | a. trêmulo; vacilante; senil

dodge | doj' | s. esquiva; evasiva, escapatória; artimanha / vt. evadir, evitar / vi. esquivar-se, furtar-se

doe | dow' | s. corça, cerva

doer | dʊ'ə | s. agente, autor; pessoa ativa

doff | dof' | vt. tirar, retirar (chapéu, roupa)

dog | dog' | s. cão, cachorro; (coloq.) sujeito, camarada. **-not a d.'s chance** nem a menor chance. **-d. in manger** desmancha-prazeres. **-a d.'s age** (coloq.) um tempão. **-an old d. at it** perito, conhecedor / vt. seguir, perseguir

dog-collar | dog'kolə | s. coleira

dog days | dog'deys | spl. canícula

dog-ear | dog'ıə | s. canto de página dobrado

dogged | do'gid | a. teimoso, persistente, obstinado

doggerel | do'gərəl | s. versos de pé quebrado

dog Latin | dog'latin | s. latim macarrônico

dogma | dog'mə | s. dogma

dogmatic | dogma'tik | a. dogmático; autoritário

dog-tired | dog'tayəd | a. totalmente exausto

dog-watch | dog'woš | s. (náut.) meio quarto (de duas horas)

doldrums | dol'drəmz | spl. depressão, melancolia; (fig.) zona de calmaria

dole | dowl' | s. dádiva; pensão dada a desempregados / vt. **-to d. out** repartir, distribuir parcimoniosamente

doleful | dowl'ful | a. triste; desconsolado, pesaroso

doll | dol' | s. boneca / vt. vi. embonecar(-se)

dollar | do'lə | s. dólar

dolphin | dol'fin | s. golfinho; (ict.) dourado (do mar)

dolt | dowl' | s. imbecil, tolo

domain | dəmeyn' | s. domínio, território; terras

dome | dowm' | s. cúpula

domestic | dəmes'tik | s. criado / a. doméstico; nacional

domesticate | dəmes'tikeyt | vt. domesticar, domar, amansar

domicile | do'misayl | s. domicílio, residência

domiciled | do'misayld | a. domiciliado, residente

dominant | do'minənt | a. dominante, predominante

dominate | do'mineyt | vt. dominar; controlar / vi. predominar, prevalecer

domination | dominey'šən | s. domínio, dominação

domineer | dominı'ə | vt. vi. dominar, oprimir, tiranizar

domineering | dominı'əring | a. tirânico, prepotente, opressor

dominion | dəmi'nı̆ən | s. domínio; soberania; controle

domino | do'minow | s. dominó (fantasia); (pl.) dominó (jogo), pedras de dominó

don | don' | s. Don (título espanhol); professor universitário (Oxford ou Cambridge) / vt. vestir, pôr

donate | downeyt' | vt. contribuir, fazer doação, doar

donation | downey'šən | s. contribuição, doação

donkey | don'kī | s. asno, burro; estúpido, idiota

donor | dow'nə | s. doador

doom | dʊm' | s. ruína, perdição; Juízo Final / vt. pronunciar julgamento contra; condenar, sentenciar

doomed | dᴜmd' | *a*. fadado, destinado (à perdição)

doomsday | dᴜmz'dey | *s*. dia do Juízo Final

door | dɔ́'ə | *s*. porta. **-out of doors** ao ar livre. **-to lay the blame at one's d**. pôr a culpa em alguém. **-to see somebody to the d**. acompanhar alguém à porta. **-to show somebody the d**. pôr na rua, mandar embora. **-behind closed doors** a portas fechadas. **-next d**. na casa ao lado, no vizinho

doorknob | dó'ənob | *s*. maçaneta de porta

doormat | dó'əmat | *s*. capacho (tb. fig.)

doorway | dó'əwey | *s*. entrada, vão de porta

dope | dowp' | *s*. (gír.) entorpecente, droga; (gír., EUA) informações confidenciais / *vt*. drogar, intoxicar

dope-fiend | dowp'fɪnd | *s*. (gír., EUA) viciado em drogas

dormant | dó'mənt | *a*. inativo, inoperante, imóvel

dormitory | dó'mɪtrī | *s*. dormitório

dose | dows' | *s*. dose, porção / *vt*. dosar, administrar em doses ou porções; adulterar (esp. vinho, bebidas)

doss | dos' | *s*. (gír.) cama (esp. em albergue) / *vi*. (gír.) **-to d. down** dormir (esp. em albergue)

doss-house | dos'haws | *s*. albergue, estalagem

dossier | do'sɪə | *s*. dossiê, documentos relativos a um assunto ou a uma pessoa

dot | dot' | *s*. ponto. **-on the d**. em ponto, pontualmente / *vt*. pontear, pontilhar; salpicar, semear, juncar. **-to d. the i's and cross the t's** ser extremamente minucioso

dotage | dow'tɪj | *s*. senilidade; imbecilidade

dote | dowt' | *vi*. caducar. **-to d.**

on ou **upon** ser louco por, ter um fraco por

doting | dow'tɪng | *a*. caduco, senil; excessivamente afeiçoado

dotty | do'tī | *a*. pontilhado; (coloq.) doido

double | dâ'bəl | *s*. dobro, duplo; sósia. **-at the d**. em passo acelerado / *a*. duplo, dobrado / *adv*. duplamente, em dobro / *vt*. duplicar, dobrar / *vi*. dobrar(-se). **-to d. back** voltar atrás rapidamente. **-to d. up** torcer-se (de dor)

double bed | dâ'bəlbed | *s*. cama de casal

double-breasted | dâ'bəlbrestid | *a*. de tipo jaquetão, trespassado

double-cross | dâ'bəlkros | *s*. traição / *vt*. trair, atraiçoar

double-dealing | dâ'bəldɪling | *s*. traição, trapaça

double Dutch | dâ'bəldâš | *s*. algaravia

double-faced | dâ'bəlfeysid | *a*. hipócrita

double meaning | dâ'bəlmɪning | *s*. duplo sentido

double-quick | dâ'bəlkwik | *s*. marcha acelerada / *a*. acelerado / *adv*. aceleradamente, rapidamente

doubt | dawt' | *s*. dúvida / *vt*. duvidar

doubtful | dawt'ful | *a*. duvidoso, incerto; indeciso

doubtless | dawt'les | *adv*. sem dúvida, indubitavelmente

dough | dow' | *s*. massa (de pão); (gír.) dinheiro

doughnut | dow'nât | *s*. rosca frita

doughty | daw'tī | *a*. forte, valente

dour | du'ə | *a*. severo, obstinado, teimoso

dove | dâv' | *s*. pomba

dovecot, dovecote | dâv'kot | *s*. pombal

dovetail | dâv'teyl | *vt*. encaixar, adaptar; relacionar

dowager | daw'əǰə | *s*. viúva que herda títulos de nobreza e propriedades do marido

dowdy | daw'dī | *s.* mulher mal vestida ou desmazelada / *a.* desalinhado, fora de moda

down | dawn' | *s.* penugem; queda, baixa; (*pl.*) terrenos ondulados. **-ups and downs** altos e baixos, vicissitudes / *a.* descendente; em declive / *adv.* para baixo, abaixo, embaixo. **-d. below** lá embaixo. **-d. and out** nocaute; (fig.) arrasado, liquidado/ *vt.* derrubar; (coloq.) tragar, engolir / *vi.* descer; cair; abaixar-se

downcast | dawn'kast | *a.* desanimado, abatido

downfall | dawn'fól | *s.* aguaceiro; queda, ruína

down-hearted | dawn'hʌtid | *a.* deprimido, desanimado, triste

downpour | dawn'póə | *s.* aguaceiro, chuvarada

downright | dawn'rayt | *a.* perfeito, completo, acabado / *adv.* completamente

downstairs | dawnste'əz | *s.* andar de baixo / *a.* do andar de baixo / *adv.* para baixo, lá embaixo

downstream | dawn'strɪm | *adv.* rio abaixo; correnteza abaixo

down-to-earth | dawntʋEϑ' | *a.* realista, sensato, com os pés na terra

downtown | dawntawn' | *s.* cidade, centro comercial / *a.* central, comercial / *adv.* na, para ou em direção à cidade

downtrodden | dawn'trodən | *a.* oprimido, humilhado

downward | dawn'wəd | *a.* descendente / *adv.* para baixo; para diante (no tempo)

dowry | daw'rī | *s.* dote

doze | dowz' | *s.* cochilo, soneca / *vi.* cochilar

dozen | dâ'zən | *s.* dúzia

drab | drab' | *s.* mulher desmazelada; prostituta / *a.* monótono, enfadonho, depressivo; pardo, acinzentado (cor); desbotado, sujo

draft | drʌft' | *s.* desenho, plano; rascunho, esboço; saque bancário, ordem de pagamento; (mil.) destacamento; (mil., EUA) recrutamento / *vt.* rascunhar, esboçar; (mil.) destacar; (mil., EUA) recrutar

drag | drag' | *s.* freio, trava; draga / *vt.* arrastar; dragar / *vi.* arrastar-se

dragon | dra'gən | *s.* dragão

dragon-fly | dra'gənflay | *s.* libélula

dragoon | drəgʋn' | *s.* dragão (soldado) / *vt.* acossar, oprimir, coagir, constranger

drain | dreyn' | *s.* dreno, escoadouro; cano, conduto; bueiro, cano de esgoto / *vt.* drenar; secar, enxugar; exaurir, extenuar; esgotar (forças etc.)

drainage | drey'nij | *s.* drenagem; esgotos

drake | dreyk' | *s.* pato

drama | drʌ'mə | *s.* drama

dramatic | drəma'tik | *a.* dramático; teatral

dramatist | drʌ'mətist | *s.* dramaturgo, autor teatral

drape | dreyp' | *vt.* colgar, ornar com colgaduras

draper | drey'pə | *s.* negociante de fazendas

drastic | dras'tik | *a.* drástico, enérgico, violento

draught | drʌft' | *s.* corrente de ar; tiragem (de chaminé); esboço, rascunho, plano; (náut.) calado. **-to feel the d.** (gír.) sofrer adversidades (esp. financeiras)

draught beer | drʌft'bɪə | *s.* chope

draught horse | drʌft'hós | *s.* cavalo de tiro

draughtsman | drʌfts'mən | *s.* desenhista, planejador

draw | dró' | *s.* ato de puxar; extração; tração; empate (jogo, luta); rifa, sorteio; atração, atrativo / *vt.* tirar, puxar, sacar; desenhar; atrair; correr (cortinas); receber (salário) / *vi.* (desp.) empatar. **-to d. back** puxar para trás, retirar-se. **-to**

d. in atrair, seduzir. **-to d. near**
aproximar-se. **-to d. out** arrancar (informações etc.), extrair.
-to d. up redigir, minutar; parar
(carro etc.); (mil.) alinhar, dispor (tropas). **-to d. attention**
chamar a atenção. **-to d. the line**
não passar de, fixar o limite em.
-to d. lots tirar sorte, fazer sorteio. **-to d. together** aproximar,
juntar, unir

drawback | dró'bak | s. desvan-
tagem, inconveniente

drawer | dró' | s. gaveta; (pl.) ce-
roulas; | dró'ə | desenhista;
(com.) sacador

drawing | dró'ing | s. desenho;
esboço; sorteio

drawing-room | dró'ingrʊm | s.
sala de estar; sala de visitas

drawl | dról' | s. fala arrastada /
vi. arrastar a voz

drawn | drón' | a. contraído de
dor ou medo (rosto)

drawn battle | drón'batəl | s. ba-
talha indecisa

drawn butter | drón'bâtə | s.
manteiga derretida

dread | dred' | s. terror, pavor;
apreensão, medo / a. terrível,
pavoroso / vt. temer / vi. apa-
vorar-se

dreadful | dred'ful | a. terrível,
pavoroso, espantoso; (coloq.)
intragável

dreadfully | dred'fulĩ | adv. pavo-
rosamente, horrivelmente, es-
pantosamente

dream | drim' | s. sonho; fanta-
sia, devaneio / vt. sonhar, imaginar / vi. sonhar, ter um so-
nho. **-to d. of** sonhar com

dreamer | drɪ'mə | s. sonhadór;
visionário

dreamy | drɪ'mĩ | a. sonhador;
distraído; vago, indistinto

dreary | drɪ'ərĩ | a. monótono,
enfadonho; sombrio, lúgubre

dredge | drej' | vt. dragar

dredger | dre'jə | s. draga

dreg | dreg' | s. (ger. pl.) borra; re-
síduo; (fig.) escória, ralé

drench | drenś' | vt. encharcar,
embeber, ensopar

dress | dres' | s. vestido, roupa,
traje / vt. vestir; fazer curativo.
-to d. down repreender / vi. vestir-se; vestir traje a rigor. **-to d.
up** vestir-se elegantemente, vestir a rigor

dress circle | dres'sɛkəl | s. (teat.)
balcão nobre

dress coat | dres'kowt | s. casaca

dressing | dre'sing | s. curativo;
tempero (salada etc.); adubo

dressing-case | dre'singkeys | s.
estojo de toucador

dressing down | dre'singdawn |
s. reprimenda, repreensão

dressing-gown | dre'singgawn |
s. roupão, chambre, penhoar

dressing-table | dre'singteybəl |
s. penteadeira

dressmaker | dres'meykə | s. mo-
dista, costureira

dress rehearsal | dres'rihɛsəl | s.
ensaio geral

dribble | dri'bəl | vi. gotejar; ba-
bar; (desp.) driblar

drier | dray'ə | s. secador

drift | drift' | s. impulso; corrente;
curso; tendência, intenção; mu-
dança, deslocamento / vi. ir à deriva (na correnteza ou vento);
deixar-se levar; perambular;
mover-se passivamente ou sem
direção; amontoar-se (areia, detritos etc.)

driftwood | drift'wud | s. madei-
ra flutuante à deriva

drill | dril' | s. broca, furadeira;
(mil.) exercícios; dril, brim / vt.
brocar, furar; treinar, adestrar;
(mil.) ministrar instrução

drink | drink' | s. bebida; gole,
trago / vt. vi. beber

drinkable | drin'kəbəl | a. potável,
bebível

drinker | drin'kə | s. bebedor, be-
berrão, alcoólatra

drinking | drin'king | s. ato de
beber

drip | drip' | vi. pingar, gotejar

drive | drayv' | s. passeio, excursão; estrada para veículos; direção (de automóvel); ímpeto, energia; tendência; (desp.) golpe, tiro, pancada; avenida; (mil.) ataque, assalto; (mec.) acionamento, impulsão / vt. dirigir (esp. automóvel); levar, tocar (gado); cravar (prego); obrigar, compelir, impulsionar; pressionar. -to d. at dar a entender. -to d. away ou off afugentar. -to d. back repelir. -to d. in cravar; forçar a entrada. -to d. on impelir, induzir, incitar. -to d. out expulsar. -to d. mad exasperar, enlouquecer. -to d. (something) home insistir (em idéia etc.), martelar; convencer; demonstrar. -to d. over atropelar

drive-in | drayv'in | s. cinema ao ar livre (visto do próprio carro); bar ou restaurante (em que se é servido no próprio carro)

drivel | dri'vəl | s. baba; bobagem / vt. vi. babar(-se); dizer bobagens ou disparates

driver | dray'və | s. motorista, chofer; maquinista (de trem etc.); cocheiro; capataz

driving | dray'ving | a. violento, impetuoso, forte (curva etc.)

driving-force | dray'vingfós | s. força motriz

driving-licence | dray'vinglaysəns | s. carteira de habilitação, carteira de motorista

drizzle | dri'zəl | s. chuvisco / vi. chuviscar

droll | drowl' | a. brincalhão, divertido; engraçado, cômico; excêntrico

drone | drown' | vi. zumbir

droop | drup' | vt. pender, curvar, inclinar / vi. vergar; desfalecer; desanimar; murchar, enlanguescer

drooping | druv'ping | a. vergado, curvo, caído

drop | drop' | s. gota, pingo; baixa (de preços); queda (de temperatura); declive, escarpa; (pl.) balas, pastilhas / vt. deixar cair; abandonar; desistir; cessar de. -to d. a hint fazer uma insinuação. -to d. a line (coloq.) escrever um bilhete / vi. cair, deixar-se cair. -to d. back ficar para trás. -to d. off adormecer; (coloq.) sair, cair fora

dropper | dro'pə | s. conta-gotas

dropsy | drop'sĩ | s. (med.) hidropisia

dross | dros' | s. escória

drought, drouth | drawt' | s. seca, estiagem; aridez

drove | drowv' | s. manada (de bois); rebanho (de carneiros); multidão (esp. em movimento)

drover | drow'və | s. vaqueiro, tropeiro

drown | drawn' | vt. afogar; inundar; submergir; abafar (som) / vi. afogar-se

drowse | drawz' | vi. cochilar

drowsiness | draw'zinəs | s. sonolência, entorpecimento

drowsy | draw'zĩ | a. sonolento; entorpecido

drubbing | drâ'bing | s. surra, sova; derrota

drudge | drâj' | s. escravo do trabalho, burro de carga / vi. trabalhar como burro de carga (esp. em tarefa tediosa)

drudgery | drâ'jərĩ | s. lida, labuta; trabalho penoso, trabalho servil ou tedioso

drug | drâg' | s. droga; tóxico, narcótico / vt. drogar

drug addict | drâg'adikt | s. toxicômano

drug addiction | drâgədik'śən | s. toxicomania

druggist | drâ'gist | s. farmacêutico; droguista

drugstore | drâg'stoə | s. (EUA) farmácia e drogaria (tb. loja de miudezas)

drum | drâm' | s. tambor; barril; (mec.) cilindro de máquina / vt. martelar, repetir, bater na mesma tecla. -to d. into repetir. -to

d. out of (mil.) expulsar a toque de caixa

drummer | drâ'mə | s. tambor (executante); (coloq., EUA) caixeiro-viajante

drunk | drânk' | a. bêbedo, bêbado; (gír.) bebedeira. **-blind** ou **dead d.** bêbedo como um gambá

drunkard | drâng'kəd | s. beberrão, bêbedo, bêbado

drunken | drân'kən | a. bêbedo; causado pela embriaguês

drunkenness | drâng'kənnes | s. bebedeira, embriaguez

dry | dray' | a. seco, enxuto; árido, ressequido; insípido; seco distante (temperamento) / vt. secar, enxugar / vi. **-to d. up** secar-se; mirrar-se; (gír.) calar-se

dry-cleaning | draykli'ning | s. lavagem a seco

dryness | dray'nes | s. secura

dry toast | dray'towst | s. torrada sem manteiga

dubious | dŭu'biəs | a. duvidoso, incerto; ambíguo; suspeito

duchess | dâ'šes | s. duquesa

duchy | dâ'ši | s. ducado

duck | dâk' | s. pato; brim / vt. mergulhar por um momento / vi. abaixar a cabeça

duckling | dâk'ling | s. patinho

dud | dâd' | s. coisa falsificada; granada que não explodiu

dudgeon | dâ'jən | s. ressentimento, raiva. **-in high d.** ressentido, com raiva

due | dŭu | s. dívida, taxa; (pl.) direitos / a. devido. **-d.** to graças a; (coloq.) por causa de. **in d. time** no momento devido. **-when d.** no vencimento / adv. diretamente

due date | dŭu'deyt | s. vencimento

duel | dŭu'əl | s. duelo. **-to fight a d.** duelar

duet | dŭuet' | s. dueto

dug-out | dâg'awt | s. canoa (de um só tronco); abrigo em trincheiras (com teto)

duke | dŭuk' | s. duque

dull | dâl' | a. estúpido, obtuso; nublado, toldado (tempo); sombrios (olhos); baço, fosco (cor); surdo, abafado (som); enfadonho, tedioso; embotado, sem fio / vt. vi. embotar(-se); entorpecer(-se); obscurecer(-se); entediar(-se)

dullness, dulness | dâl'nes | s. embotamento; tédio, tristeza; fosco, cor fosca; nebulosidade, embaciamento.

duly | dŭu'li | adv. devidamente

dumb | dâm' | a. mudo; (coloq.) tolo, bobo, pateta

dumbfound, dumfound | dâmfawnd' | vt. assombrar, aturdir; emudecer, embatucar

dummy | dâ'mi | s. manequim (de alfaiate); morto (em jogos de baralho); testa-de-ferro; palerma; simulacro

dump | dâmp' | s. monturo; (mil.) depósito. **-to be in the dumps** estar deprimido / vt. despejar, descarregar; jogar fora

dumpling | dâmp'ling | s. bolinha de massa cozida ou assada; pessoa baixa e gorda

dumpy | dâm'pi | a. atarracado e gordo

dunce | dâns' | s. estúpido, ignorante, burro

dune | dŭun' | s. duna

dung | dâng' | s. esterco, estrume / vt. estercar

dungeon | dân'jən | s. masmorra, calabouço

dupe | dŭup' | s. simplório, papalvo, vítima, crédulo

duplicate | dŭu'plikeyt | s. duplicata / a. duplicado, duplo / vt. duplicar

duplicity | dŭu'plisiti | s. duplicidade, velhacaria, fraude

durability | dŭurəbi'liti | s. durabilidade, duração

durable | dŭu'rəbəl | a. durável

duration | dŭurey'šən | s. duração

duress | dŭures' | s. encarceramento; coação, constrangimento

during | dĭu'ring | *prep.* durante

dusk | dâsk' | *s.* anoitecer, crepúsculo, obscuridade

dusky | dâs'kĭ | *a.* escurecido, sombrio

dust | dâst' | *s.* pó, poeira. **-to bite the d.** morder o pó, ser derrotado. **-to make the d. fly** agir com energia. **-to raise a d.** arranjar briga. **-to shake the d. off one's feet** sair enojado ou com raiva / *vt.* polvilhar; empoar; tirar o pó de

dustbin | dâst'bin | *s.* lata de lixo, caixa de lixo ou cisco

dust-cover | dâst'kâvə | *s.* capa (de móveis); capa ou cobertura de papel (em livros)

duster | dâs'tə | *s.* espanador; faxineiro; guarda-pó

dustman | dâst'mən | *s.* lixeiro, empregado da limpeza urbana

dustpan | dâst'pan | *s.* pá de lixo

dusty | dâs'tĭ | *a.* empoeirado, poeirento

Dutch | dâš' | *s. a.* holandês. **-to go D.** dividir as despesas

Dutch courage | dâš'kârĭj | *s.* coragem produzida por bebida

Dutchman | dâš'mən | *s.* holandês

dutiable | dĭu'tiəbəl | *a.* sujeito a impostos, taxável

dutiful | dĭu'tiful | *a.* zeloso; obediente, respeitoso

duty | dĭu'tĭ | *s.* dever; obrigação; acatamento; taxa, direitos. **-on d.** de serviço. **-off d.** de folga. **-to do somebody's d.** substituir alguém. **-to do d. for** substituir a, servir de

duty-free | dĭu'tĭfrĭ | *a.* isento de taxas

dwarf | dwóf | *s. a.* anão / *vt.* ultrapassar, sobrepujar

dwell | dwel' | *vi.* viver, residir, habitar; ficar; demorar-se. **-to d. on** ou **upon** estender-se, falar longamente

dwelling | dwe'ling | *s.* casa, morada, residência, moradia

dwindle | dwin'dəl | *vi.* minguar, diminuir, reduzir

dye | day' | *s.* corante, tinta. **-of deepest d.** da pior espécie / *vt.* tingir

dyed | dayd' | *a.* tingido, tinto

dyer | day'ə | *s.* tintureiro

dyestuff | day'stâf | *s.* corante, matéria corante

dying | day'ing | *a.* agonizante; que está desaparecendo (luz etc.); mortal, morredouro

dynamic | dayna'mik | *a.* dinâmico

dynamite | day'nəmayt | *s.* dinamite

dynamo | day'nəmow | *s.* dínamo

dynastic | dinas'tik | *a.* dinástico

dynasty | di'nəstĭ | *s.* dinastia

dysentery | di'səntrĭ | *s.* disenteria

dyspepsia | dispep'sĭə | *s.* dispepsia

E

E, e | ĭ' | *s.* e; (maiúsc., mús.) mi

each | ĭš' | *a.* cada / *pron.* cada um, cada qual. **-e. other** um ao outro

eager | ĭ'gə | *a.* desejoso, ansioso, impaciente

eagerness | ĭ'gənes | *s.* ânsia, ardor, impaciência

eagle | ĭ'gəl | *s.* águia

ear | ĭ'ə | *s.* orelha; ouvido; alça, asa; espiga. **-within e. shot** ao alcance da voz. **-to prick up one's ears** apurar o ouvido. **-to fall on deaf ears** não ser atendido. **-to be wet behind the ears** ser imaturo, ser inexperiente

earache | ɪ'əeyk | s. dor de ouvido

ear-drum | ɪ'ədrâm | s. (anat.) tímpano

earl | El' | s. conde (título britânico)

earliness | E'lines | s. precocidade; presteza

early | E'lĭ | a. prematuro, precoce; primitivo; matinal; próximo. **-at an e. age** na infância, na mocidade. **-in the e. morning** de manhã cedo. **-at your earliest convenience** o mais cedo que puder **-the e. part** o começo. **-to keep e. hours** deitar-se e levantar-se cedo / adv. cedo; de madrugada; no começo

early riser | E'liray'zə | a. madrugador

early schooling | Elĭskʋ'ling | s. escola primária, primeiras letras

earmark | ɪ'əmʌk | s. marca na orelha (gado) / vt. marcar na orelha (gado); reservar, designar; destinar

earn | En' | vt. ganhar; merecer; conseguir, obter

earnest | E'nist | s. seriedade. **-in good e.** a sério / a. sério, austero; zeloso, cuidadoso; fervoroso, ardente

earnestness | E'nistnes | s. seriedade, gravidade; sinceridade; cuidado, zelo; solicitude; fervor, ardor

earnings | E'ningz | spl. ganhos, vencimentos, salário; lucro, féria

earphone | ɪ'əfown | s. (rád.) fone de ouvido

earring | ɪ'əring | s. brinco

earth | Eϑ' | s. terra, solo; mundo, orbe. **-down to e.** terra-a-terra. **-to run to e.** perseguir até capturar. **-what on e.?** por que cargas-d'água?

earthen | E'ϑən | a. de barro, de terra

earthenware | E'ϑənweə | s. louça de barro

earthiness | E'ϑines | s. sabor popular; grosseria

earthly | Eϑ'lĭ | a. terrestre; mundano, carnal. **-no e. reason** nenhuma razão imaginável

earthquake | Eϑ'kweyk | s. terremoto, tremor de terra

earthwork | Eϑ'wEk | s. fortificação; terraplenagem

earthworm | Eϑ'wEm | s. minhoca

earthy | E'ϑĭ | a. térreo; grosseiro

earthy juke | E'ϑĭjowk | s. piada grosseira; graça pesada

earwig | ɪ'əwig | s. (ent.) tesoura; (EUA) lacrainha

ease | ɪz' | s. facilidade; tranqüilidade, sossego; desembaraço, desenvoltura; naturalidade. **-to be at e.** estar à vontade. **-ill at e.** constrangido; inquieto / vt. aliviar (dor), consolar, suavizar; desembaraçar, facilitar. **-to e. someone of** ou **out of** (coloq.) furtar

easel | ɪ'zəl | s. cavalete

easiness | ɪ'zines | s. facilidade; espontaneidade, naturalidade; tranqüilidade

east | ɪst' | s. este, leste, levante, oriente

Easter | ɪs'tə | s. Páscoa

eastern | ɪs'tən | s. oriental / a. oriental, do Oriente

Easter Saturday | ɪs'təsatədey | s. sábado de Aleluia

easy | ɪ'zĭ | a. fácil; complacente, condescendente; descontraído; natural, simples. **-e. of belief** crédulo. **-on e. street** (coloq.) em boa maré, em boas circunstâncias. **-free and e.** afável; sem-cerimonioso. **-within e. reach** de fácil acesso. **-on e. payments** pagamento a prestações. **-take it e.!** calma!, devagar! **-stand e.!** (mil.) à vontade!, descansar!

easy chair | ɪ'zĭeə | s. poltrona, espreguiçadeira

easy-going | ɪ'zigowing | a. pacato; condescendente; calmo

eat | ɪt' | vt. comer. **-to e. away** destruir, corroer. **-to e. humble pie** humilhar-se desculpar-se. **-to e. one's heart out** sofrer em silêncio. **-to e. one's words** retratar-se

eatable | ı'təbəl | *a.* comestível, comível

eaves ıvz' | *spl.* beiral (do telhado)

eavesdrop | ıvz'drop | *vi.* escutar às escondidas

ebb | eb' | *s.* baixa-mar, vazante. **-e. of life** senilidade. **-at a low e.** em má situação

ebb-tide | eb'tayd | *s.* maré vazante, baixa-mar

ebony | e'bɔnı | *s.* ébano

ebullient | ibâ'lĩənt | *a.* efervescente; entusiasmado, exaltado, entusiástico

eccentric | eksen'trik | *a.* excêntrico, extravagante

ecclesiastical | ekklĩzĩas'tikəl | *a.* eclesiástico

echo | e'kow | *s.* eco, ressonância; reminiscência / *vt. vi.* ecoar, repercutir; ressoar

éclat | eyklʌ' | *s.* brilho

eclipse | iklips' | *s.* eclipse / *vt.* eclipsar

ecology | iko'ləjĩ | *s.* ecologia

economic | ikəno'mik | *a.* econômico; parco

economical | ikəno'mikəl | *a.* econômico; frugal

economics | ikəno'miks | *s.* economia (ciência)

economize | iko'nəmayz | *vt. vi.* economizar, poupar

economy | iko'nəmy | *s.* economia; parcimônia

ecstasy | eks'təsĩ | *s.* êxtase, enlevo; arrebatamento

ecstatic | eksta'tik | *a.* extático, enlevado; arrebatado

ecumenical | ikĩume'nikəl | *a.* ecumênico

eczema | ek'simə | *s.* eczema

eddy | e'dĩ | *s.* redemoinho / *vt.* redemoinhar

Eden | e'dən | *s.* éden, paraíso

edge | ej' | *s.* borda, orla; margem (de rio); fio, gume (de lâmina). **-on e.** nervoso, impaciente. **-to have the e. on** levar vantagem / *vt.* afiar, amolar; guarnecer; exasperar / *vi.* avançar de flan-

co, flanquear

edgeways | ej'weyz | *adv.* de lado, de esguelha, de soslaio

edgy | e'jĩ | *a.* afiado; irascível, irritável

edible | e'dibəl | *s. a.* comestível

edict | ı'dikt | *s.* edi(c)to, decreto, lei, ordem

edifice | e'difis | *s.* edifício

edify | e'difay | *vt.* edificar

edict | ı'dikt | *s.* edito, decreto, compilar; revisar

editing | e'diting | *s.* correção (de redação)

edition | idi'śən | *s.* edição, publicação

editor | e'ditə | *s.* organizador de uma edição; redator de jornal; editor (periódico)

editorial | editó'rĩəl | *s.* editorial, artigo de fundo / *a.* editorial

editorial staff | editó'rĩəlstaf' | *s.* corpo de redatores

editorship | e'ditəśip | *s.* função de editor (jornal etc.); cargo de redator ou organizador de edições

educable | e'dĩukəbəl | *a.* educável

educate | e'dĩukeyt | *vt.* educar, ensinar, instruir

education | edĩukey'śən | *s.* educação, ensino, instrução

eel | ıl' | *s.* enguia

eerie | ı'ərĩ | *a.* assustador, sinistro, lúgubre, soturno

efface | ifeys' | *vt.* apagar, eliminar; eclipsar, ofuscar

effect | ifekt' | *s.* efeito, consequência, resultado; impressão; repercussão; (*pl.*) bens, propriedades, posses. **-in e.** de fato, realmente; em vigor (lei). **-to that e.** nesse sentido. **-to carry into e.** pôr em execução. **-to give e. to** dar cumprimento a. **-for e.** para impressionar

effective | ifek'tiv | *a.* eficaz, eficiente, efetivo

effectiveness | ifek'tivnes | *s.* eficácia, eficiência

effeminate | ife'minit | *a.* efeminado, afeminado

effervescent | efəve'sənt | *a.* efervescente; (fig.) exuberante, agitado

effete | efit' | *a.* cansado, exausto; fraco, incapaz

efficacious | efikey'šəs | *a.* eficaz, eficiente

efficacy | e'fikəsī | *s.* eficácia, eficiência

efficiency | ifi'šənsī | *s.* eficiência, eficácia

efficient | ifi'šənt | *a.* eficiente, eficaz; ativo, competente

effigy | e'fijī | *s.* efigie

effort | e'fət | *s.* esforço

effrontery | efrân'tərī | *s.* atrevimento, desfaçatez

effusive | efiu'siv | *a.* efusivo, expansivo

egg | eg' | *s.* ovo. **-boiled** e. ovo cozido. **-fried** e. ovo estrelado. **-poached** e. ovo pochê, ovo escalfado. **-scrambled** e. ovo mexido / *vt.* **-to e. on** incitar, instigar, impelir

egg-beater | eg'bɪtə | *s.* batedor de ovos; (gír., EUA) helicóptero

egg-plant | eg'plant | *s.* berinjela

eggshell | eg'šel | *s.* casca de ovo

egg-white | eg'wayt | *s.* clara de ovo

egoism | e'gowizəm | *s.* egoísmo

egregious | igrı'jəs | *a.* grande, enorme; notório; (ant.) insigne, eminente

Egyptian | iJip'šən | *s. a.* egípcio

eiderdown | ay'dədawn | *s.* edredom, edredão

eider duck | ay'dədâk | *s.* (orn.) êider

eight | eyt' | *s. a.* oito

eighteen | eytin' | *s. a.* dezoito

eighth | eytϑ' | *s.* oitavo; (mús.) oitava / *a.* oitavo

either | ay'ðə | *a. pron.* cada, cada um (de dois); um ou (e) outro, ambos / *adv.* também não, tampouco / *conj.* **-e. ... or** ou ... ou, ou isto ou aquilo

ejaculation | iJakĩuley'šən | *s.* ejaculação; exclamação

eject | iJekt' | *vt.* ejetar, expelir, expulsar

eke | ık' | *vt.* acrescer, aumentar. **-to e. out** aumentar; ampliar; suplementar; sobreviver (com dificuldade), ganhar o pão

elaborate | ila'bərit | *a.* elaborado, esmerado; rebuscado / | ila'bəreyt | *vt.* elaborar; aperfeiçoar

elapse | ilaps' | *vi.* decorrer

elastic | ilas'tik | *s. a.* clástico

elated | iley'tid | *a.* exultante, radiante, jubiloso

elation | iley'šən | *s.* júbilo

elbow | el'bow | *s.* cotovelo; ângulo, esquina / *vt.* acotovelar / *vi.* abrir caminho com os cotovelos

elder | el'də | *s.* ancião; antepassado / *a.* mais velho; primogênito

elderly | el'dəlī | *a.* idoso

eldest | el'dist | *a.* o mais velho; primogênito

elect | ilekt' | *vt.* eleger

election | ilek'šən | *s.* eleição

elector | ilek'tə | *s.* eleitor

electric | ilek'trik | *a.* elétrico

electrician | elektri'šən | *s.* eletricista

electricity | elektri'sitī | *s.* eletricidade

electric sign | ilek'triksayn | *s.* anúncio (letreiro) luminoso

electrify | ilek'trifay | *vt.* eletrificar; (fig.) eletrizar

electrocute | ilek'trəkĩut | *vt.* eletrocutar

electronics | ilektro'niks | *s.* eletrônica

elegance | e'ligəns | *s.* elegância, distinção

elegant | e'ligənt | *a.* elegante

elegy | e'ləJī | *s.* elegia

element | e'limənt | *s.* elemento; (pl.) elementos, rudimentos, primeiras noções

elementary | elimen'tərī | *a.* elementar; primário

elephant | e'lifənt | *s.* elefante

elevate | e'liveyt | *vt.* elevar

elevated | e'liveytid | *a.* elevado; nobre, sublime

elevating | e'liveyting | *a.* que eleva; edificante

elevation | elivey'śən | *s.* elevação; sublimidade; exaltação; (ecles.) Elevação, Consagração

elevator | e'liveytə | *s.* (EUA) elevador, ascensor

eleven | ile'vən | *s. a.* onze

eleventh | ile'vənϑ | *s.a.* décimo primeiro. **-at the e. hour** no último momento

elf | elf' | *s.* elfo, gnomo, duende

elicit | ili'sit | *vt.* tirar, extrair; evocar; obter; deduzir; provocar (resposta)

eligible | e'liʃibəl | *a.* elegível; qualificado; idôneo

eliminate | eli'mineyt | *vt.* eliminar, suprimir, excluir

elision | ili'jən | *s.* elisão

élite | elit' | *s.* elite

elm | elm' | *s.* olmo, ulmeiro

elocution | ilakiu'śən | *s.* elocução, dicção; declamação

elongate | i'longgeyt | *a.* alongado, prolongado / *vt.* alongar, prolongar / *vi.* estender-se, alongar-se

elope | ilowp' | *vi.* fugir com namorado (mulher); fugir para se casar (casal)

eloquence | e'ləkwəns | *s.* eloquência

eloquent | e'ləkwənt | *a.* eloqüente; expressivo

else | els' | *a.* outro; mais. **-anything e.?** algo mais? **-nobody e.** ninguém mais. **-what e.?** que mais? / *adv.* de outro modo, em outro lugar. **-where e.?** em que outro lugar? / *conj.* ou, senão. **-or e.** ou então (ameaça ou advertência)

elucidate | iłłu'sideyt | *vt.* elucidar, esclarecer

elude | iłłu'd | *vt.* evitar, escapar a; iludir, lograr

elusion | iłłu'jən | *s.* evasiva, subterfúgio

elusive | ilu'siv | *a.* esquivo; impreciso, indistinto

emaciated | ima'sīeytid | *a.* macilento, emaciado

emanate | i'məneyt | *vi.* provir, originar-se, emanar

emancipate | iman'sipeyt | *vt.* emancipar, liberar, libertar

emancipation | imansipey'śən | *s.* emancipação, libertação

embalm | embʌm' | *vt.* embalsamar, conservar; preservar

embankment | embank'mənt | *s.* dique; aterro, terraplenagem

embargo | embʌ'gow | *s.* embargo, proibição; impedimento

embark | embʌk' | *vt. vi.* embarcar; meter-se em (negócio, empresa etc.)

embarkation | embʌkey'śən | *s.* embarque

embarrass | emba'rəs | *vt.* embaraçar, confundir, enlear, desconcertar; endividar

embarrassed | emba'rəst | *a.* embaraçado, confuso, enleado, desconcertado; endividado

embarrassing | emba'rəsing | *a.* embaraçoso, desagradável

embarrassment | emba'rəsmənt | *s.* embaraço; impedimento, dificuldade, empecilho

embassy | em'bəsī | *s.* embaixada

embedded | embe'did | *a.* engastado, embutido; encravado, implantado, fincado

embellish | embe'liś | *vt.* enfeitar, adornar, embelezar

ember | em'bə | *s.* brasa, tição; (*pl.*) borralho

embezzle | embe'zəl | *vt.* apropriar-se fraudulentamente de, dar desfalque

embezzlement | embe'zəlmənt | *s.* desfalque, peculato

embitter | embi'tə | *vt.* amargurar; angustiar; exasperar, exacerbar, acirrar

embittered | embi'təd | *a.* amargurado, ressentido

emblem | em'bləm | *s.* emblema

embodiment | embo'dimənt | *s.*

personificação; encarnação

embody | embo'dī | vt. personificar, corporificar; incluir, compreender

embolden | embowl'dən | vt. encorajar, animar, estimular

embrace | embreys' | s. abraço / vt. abraçar; abranger, incluir; adotar, seguir

embroider | embroy'də | vt. bordar; (fig.) adornar

embroidery | embroy'dərī | s. 'bordado; (fig.) ornamento

embroil | embroyl' | vt. enredar, confundir, envolver

embryo | em'brīow | s. embrião

embryonic | embrīo'nik | a. embrionário; incipiente

emend | imend' | vt. emendar

emendation | imendey'śən | s. emenda, correção

emerald | e'mərəld | s. esmeralda

emerge | imEĵ' | vt. emergir

emergence | imE'ĵəns | s. emergência, aparecimento

emergency | imE'ĵənsī | s. emergência, situação crítica

emery | e'mərī | s. esmeril

emigrant | e'migrənt | s. a. emigrante

emigrate | e'migreyt | vi. emigrar

emigration | emigrey'śən | s. emigração

eminence | e'minəns | s. eminência; colina, elevação. -Your E. Vossa Eminência

eminent | e'minənt | a. eminente, elevado; insigne, ilustre

emissary | e'misərī | s. emissário (esp. agente secreto)

emit | imit' | vt. emitir

emolument | imo'līumənt | s. salário, vencimentos, emolumento

emotion | imow'śən | s. emoção

emotional | imow'sənəl | a. emocional, emotivo; emocionante

emotionalism | imow'śənəlizəm | s. emocionalismo, sentimentalismo, emotividade

emotive | imow'tiv | a. emotivo, emocionante

empathy | em'pəðī | s. empatia

emphasis | em'fəsis | s. ênfase. **-to lay e. on** dar relevo a, dar importância a

emphasize | em'fəsayz | vt. enfatizar, salientar, acentuar

emphatic | emfa'tik | a. enfático; enérgico; significativo

empire | em'payə | s. império

employ | employ' | s. emprego; ocupação / vt. empregar

employee | employī' | s. empregado

employer | employ'ə | s. patrão

employment | employ'mənt | s. emprego; uso, utilização

empower | empaw'ə | vt. autorizar, dar poderes a

empress | em'pres | s. imperatriz

emptiness | emp'tines | s. vacuidade; vazio, vácuo

empty | emp'tī | a. vazio; desocupado; oco / vt. esvaziar; despejar; drenar / vi. esvaziar-se; desaguar

emulate | e'mĭuleyt | vt. emular, rivalizar com

enable | eney'bəl | vt. habilitar; permitir; capacitar

enact | enakt' | vt. decretar, ordenar; representar, atuar

enamel | ena'məl | s. esmalte / vt. esmaltar, laquear

enamoured, enamored | ena'məd | a. enamorado, apaixonado

encase | enkeys' | vt. encaixotar

enchant | enśAnt' | vt. encantar; cativar

enchanting | enśAn'ting | a. encantador; cativante

enchantment | enśAnt'mənt | s. encantamento; feitiço

encircle | ensE'kəl | vt. cercar, rodear, cingir

enclose | enklowz' | vt. cercar, rodear; mandar incluso

enclosed | enklowzd' | a. incluso (em carta); cercado (terra); circundado

enclosure | enklow'ĵə | s. cercado, cerca; inclusão (em correspondência)

encompass | enkâm'pəs | *vt.* rodear, cercar; abranger, envolver, encerrar, conter

encore | eng'kó | *s.* bis / *vt.* bisar

encounter | enkawn'tə | *s.* encontro; batalha, combate

encourage | enkâ'riĵ | *vt.* encorajar, animar, fomentar, estimular; promover

encouragement | enkâ'riĵmənt | *s.* encorajamento, incitamento, estímulo, animação

encouraging | enkâ'rijing | *a.* encorajador, animador

encroach | enkrowš' | *vi.* usurpar; transgredir; abusar

encroachment | enkrowš'mənt | *s.* usurpação; transgressão

encumber | enkâm'bə | *vt.* estorvar; onerar; entulhar

encumbrance | enkâm'brəns | *s.* obstáculo, estorvo, empecilho

encyclical | ensi'klikəl | *s.* encíclica

encyclopaedia | ensayklǝpı'dıǝ | *s.* enciclopédia

end | end' | *s.* fim, conclusão; extremidade; limite; objetivo; finalidade; morte / *vt. vi.* terminar, acabar. **-é. to e.** do princípio ao fim. **-in the e.** no fim, afinal. **-on e.** a fio, sem interrupção. **-to bring to an e.** pôr termo. **-at loose ends** desarrumado, em desordem. **-odds and ends** bugigangas, miudezas

endanger | endeyn'ĵə | *vt.* pôr em perigo; arriscar, expor

endear | ındı'ə | *vt.* fazer amar ou estimar; tornar benquisto

endearing | endı'əring | *a.* afetivo, afetuoso, carinhoso

endearment | endı'əmənt | *s.* estima; afeto, meiguice

endeavour, endeavor | endə'və | *s.* esforço, empenho / *vi.* esforçar-se, empenhar-se; tentar, procurar

ending | en'ding | *s.* fim, término, conclusão, desenlace

endless | end'les | *a.* sem fim, incessante, interminável

endorse | endós' | *vt.* (com.) endossar; (fig.) aprovar

endorsement | endós'mənt | *s.* endosso; (fig.) aprovação

endow | endaw' | *vt.* dotar

endurable | endĭu'ərəbəl | *a.* suportável, tolerável; resistente

endurance | endĭu'ərəns | *s.* resistência; persistência, paciência; durabilidade. **-beyond e.** insuportável

endure | endĭu'ə | *vt.* suportar, agüentar / *vi.* perseverar, resistir; durar

enduring | endĭu'əring | *a.* duradouro; continuado

enemy | e'nəmī | *s.* inimigo

energetic | enəĵe'tik | *a.* enérgico, ativo, operoso

energy | e'nəĵī | *s.* energia

enervating | e'nəveyting | *a.* enervante, exasperante

enfeeble | enfı'bəl | *vt.* enfraquecer, debilitar

enforce | enfós' | *vt.* impor, fazer respeitar (a lei)

enfranchise | enfran'šayz | *vt.* conceder direitos civis a; libertar, alforriar

engage | engeyĵ' | *vt.* comprometer, empenhar; contratar, engajar; convidar; travar (conversa); empenhar em combate (tropas) / *vi.* comprometer-se; (mec.) engrenar. **-to e. in** envolver-se

engaged | engeyĵd' | *a.* ocupado; comprometido; noivo; contratado; em comunicação (telefone); -(mec.) engrenado; (mil.) em combate

engagement | engeyĵ'mənt | *s.* compromisso; promessa de casamento; contrato; (mec.) engreno; (mil.) combate

engaging | engey'ĵing | *a.* atraente, cativante, insinuante

engender | enĵen'də | *vt.* engendrar, gerar, produzir

engine | en'ĵin | *s.* motor; máquina, mecanismo; locomotiva; máquina a vapor

engine-driver | en'jindrayvə | s. maquinista de locomotiva

engineer | enjini'ə | s. engenheiro; (EUA) maquinista de locomotiva / vt. construir, planejar, planear

engineering | enjini'əring | s. engenharia

English | ing'lis | s.a. inglês

engrave | engreyv' | vt. gravar

engraving | engrey'ving | s. gravura; gravação

engross | engrows' | vt. açambarcar, monopolizar

engrossed | engrowst' | a. açambarcado; absorto

engulf | engâlf' | vt. submergir; tragar, engolir

enhance | enhans' | vt. intensificar; acentuar, realçar

enigma | enig'mə | s. enigma

enigmatic | enigma'tik | a. enigmático, obscuro

enjoin | enjoyn' | vt. impor, mandar, ordenar

enjoy | enjoy' | vt. ter prazer em, gostar de; gozar (de), desfrutar; deleitar-se com

enjoyable | enjoy'əbəl | a. agradável, que se pode gozar

enjoyment | enjoy'mənt | s. prazer, gozo, deleite

enlarge | enlaJ' | vt. ampliar, aumentar, alargar; estender, desenvolver (assunto); (fot.) ampliar

enlargement | enlaJ'mənt | s. aumento, alargamento; expansão; (fot.) ampliação

enlighten | enlay'tən | vt. esclarecer, ilustrar; instruir, ensinar; informar

enlightenment | enlay'tənmənt s. esclarecimento, ilustração; explicação; (maiúsc.) Iluminismo

enlist | enlist' | vt. alistar, recrutar / vi. alistar-se

enliven | enlay'vən | vt. animar, avivar; estimular

enmeshed | enmest' | a. enredado, emaranhado

enmity | en'miti | s. inimizade

ennoble | enow'bəl | vt. nobilitar, enobrecer; exaltar

ennui | onwi' | s. tédio, enfado, aborrecimento

enormity | inó'miti | s. enormidade; atrocidade, crime

enormous | inó'məs | a. enorme, imenso; atroz, chocante

enormousness | inó'məsnes | s. enormidade; atrocidade

enough | inâf' | a. adv. bastante / interj. basta!

enquire, enquiry | enkway'ə enkway'əri | vt. vi. = inquire, inquiry

enrage | enreyj' | vt. enfurecer

enrapture | enrap'šə | vt. arrebatar, enlevar, extasiar

enrich | enris' | vt. enriquecer; embelezar; tornar mais saboroso; fertilizar (solo)

enrol, enroll | enrowl' | vt. registrar; matricular; (mil.) alistar, recrutar

enrolment, enrollment | enrowl'mənt | s. inscrição; alistamento

ensconced | enskonst' | a. escondido, oculto; abrigado

enshrine | ensrayn' | vt. guardar em relicário; entesourar

ensign | en'sayn | s. insignia, estandarte, bandeira; (mil.) porta-bandeira; (EUA) guarda-marinha

enslave | ensleyv' | vt. escravizar

ensue | ensiu' | vi. decorrer, resultar, seguir-se

ensuing | ensiu'ing | a. seguinte; resultante, decorrente

ensure | ensu'ə | vt. assegurar, garantir; proteger

entail | enteyl' | s. (jur.) vínculo / vt. (jur.) vincular (bens de raiz); acarretar, trazer

entangle | entang'gəl | vt. embaraçar, enredar; emaranhar

enter | en'tə | vt. entrar; introduzir, penetrar; inscrever, matricular; filiar-se; apresentar (petição etc.) / vi. entrar; introduzir-se em; inscrever-se, matricular-se; ser admitido; (mil.) alistar-se em. **-to e. into** entrar em, começar · (conversa, relações, acordo etc.)

enteritis| entəray'tis |s. enterite

enterprise| en'təprayz |s. empresa, empreendimento; aventura; audácia, arrojo

enterprising | en'təprayzing | a. empreendedor, ativo; arrojado, audacioso

entertain| entəteyn' |vt. divertir; receber (convidados); ser hospitaleiro; cogitar (idéias); nutrir (esperanças)

entertaining| entətey'ning |a. divertido, alegre

entertainment | entəteyn'mənt | s. diversão, divertimento; espetáculo; recepção (de convidados)

enthral, enthrall| enϑról' |vt. cativar, encantar, fascinar; enfeitiçar; subjugar

enthrone| inϑrown' |vt. entronizar; exaltar

enthusiasm | enϑuziazəm |s. entusiasmo; arrebatamento

enthusiast | enϑuziast' | s. entusiasta

enthusiastic | enϑuzias'tik | a. entusiasmado; ardoroso, arrebatado

entice | entays' | vt. atrair, seduzir; aliciar; tentar

enticing | entay'sing |a. atraente, sedutor; aliciante

entire | entay'ə |a. inteiro, total, completo; pleno, irrestrito, total, puro

entirety| entay'ətī |s. totalidade, conjunto, soma total

entitle | entay'təl | vt. intitular, denominar; dar direito a, autorizar. **-to be entitled to** ter direito a

entity| en'titī |s. entidade

entomb | entυm' | vt. sepultar, enterrar

entourage| onturʌj' |s. séquito, companhia, comitiva

entrails | en'treylz | spl. entranhas, tripas, intestinos

entrance | en'trəns | s. entrada; admissão; porta, portão. **-no e.** entrada proibida / | entrʌns' | vt. encantar, extasiar

entrance fee | en'trənsfī | s. jóia (de clube)

entrance permit| en'trənspEmit | s. visto de entrada

entreat | entrīt' | vt. rogar, suplicar, implorar

entreaty | entri'tī | s. rogo, súplica, pedido

entrust | entrâst' | vt. confiar

entry | en'trī | s. entrada, ingresso; entrada solene; (jur.) tomada de posse; verbete (dicionário etc.); (com.) lançamento

enumerate| inϑu'məreyt |vt. enumerar, relacionar

enunciate | inân'sīeyt | vt. enunciar; expor, articular

envelop | enve'ləp | vt. envolver; rodear, cercar

envelope | en'vəlowp | s. envelope; invólucro, capa

enviable | en'vīəbəl | a. invejável; cobiçável

envious| en'vīəs |a. invejoso; cobiçoso

environment | envay'rənmənt |s. meio ambiente, meio; circunstâncias, ambiência

environs | en'virənz | spl. arrabaldes, subúrbios

envisage | envi'zij | vt. considerar, analisar; imaginar

envoy| en'voy |s. enviado; emissário; mensageiro

envy| en'vī |s. inveja / vt. invejar

epaulette, epaulet | e'powlet | s. dragona

ephemeral | ife'mərəl | a. efêmero, passageiro

epic | e'pik | s. poema épico / a. épico, heróico

epicure | e'pikĭuə | s. epicurista, epicureu

epidemic | epide'mik | s. epidemia / a. epidêmico

epilepsy | e'pilepsī |s. epilepsia

epilogue | e'pilog | s. epílogo

episode | e'pisowd | s. episódio

epistle | ipi'səl | s. epístola

epitaph | e'pitʌf | s. epitáfio

epithet | e'piðet | s. epíteto

epitome | epi'təmī | s. epítome

epitomize | epi'təmayz | vt. resumir, sintetizar

epoch | ɪ'pok | s. época

equable | e'kwəbəl | a. invariável, igual; calmo, sereno

equal | ɪ'kwəl | s. igual, pessoa da mesma categoria / a. igual, equivalente. **-to be e. to** estar à altura de (tarefa etc.). **-on an e. footing** em pé de igualdade / vt. igualar, ser igual a, rivalizar com, igualar-se a

equality | ikwo'litī | s. igualdade; eqüidade

equalize, equalise | ɪ'kwəlayz | vt. igualar / vi. (desp.) empatar

equanimity | ikwəni'mitī | s. equanimidade; serenidade

equate | ikweyt' | vt. igualar; equiparar

equation | ikwey'jən | s. equação

equator | ikwey'tə | s. equador

equidistant | ikwidis'tənt | a. equidistante

equilibrium | ikwili'brīəm | s. equilíbrio

equinox | e'kwinoks | s. equinócio

equip | ikwɪp' | vt. equipar; guarnecer, aparelhar, prover

equipment | ikwip'mənt | s. equipamento; petrechos; armamento; aparelhamento

equitable | e'kwitəbəl | a. equitativo, imparcial, justo

equitation | ekwitey'jən | s. equitação

equity | e'kwitī | s. eqüidade, justiça, imparcialidade

equivalent | ikwi'vələnt | a. equivalente

equivocal | ikwi'vəkəl | a. equívoco; ambíguo, duvidoso

era | ɪ'rə | s. era; época

eradicate | ira'dikeyt | vt. erradicar; extirpar

erase | ireyz' | vt. apagar, raspar, rasurar; eliminar

eraser | irey'zə | s. apagador, esponja (de quadro-negro); borracha (de apagar)

ere | e'ə | prep. conj. (poét. ou ant.) antes de, antes que

erect | irekt' | a. ereto / vt. erigir, erguer

erection | irek'jən | s. ereção; construção, elevação

eremite | e'rimayt | s. eremita, ermitão

ermine | e'min | s. arminho

erode | irowd' | vt. corroer, carcomer, desgastar

erosion | irow'jən | s. erosão

erotic | iro'tik | a. erótico

eroticism | iro'tisizəm | s. erotismo, caráter erótico

erotism | e'rətizəm | s. erotismo, desejo sexual

err | e' | vi. errar; desviar-se; enganar-se; pecar

errand | e'rənd | s. recado; incumbência, mandado; propósito (de uma viagem)

errand-boy | e'rəndboy | s. moço de recados, mensageiro

errant | e'rənt | a. errante (em busca de aventuras); pecador, extraviado

erratic | era'tik | a. errático, irregular; errante; caprichoso, extravagante

erring | e'ring | a. transviado; pecador, culpado

erroneous | erow'nīəs | a. errôneo, errado

error | e'rə | s. erro, engano, equívoco, desacerto

erstwhile | est'wayl | adv. (ant.) antigamente, outrora

erudite | e'rʃudayt | a. erudito

erudition | erʃudi'jən | s. erudição

erupt | irʌpt' | vi. entrar em erupção; rebentar, explodir

escalator | es'kəleytə | s. escada rolante

escapade | es'kəpeyd | s. escapada, fuga; leviandade

escape| eskeyp' |s. fuga, evasão;
escapamento (de gás etc.). **-to
have a narrow e.** escapar por um
triz / vi. escapar(-se), evadir-se;
salvar-se. **-to e. notice** passar
despercebido

eschew| issʊ' | vt. evitar, abster-
se de

escort| es'kót |s. escolta; séquito
/ vt. escoltar; acompanhar (se-
nhora etc.)

Eskimo | es'kimow | s. a. esqui-
mó

especially | ispe'śəlī |adv. especi-
almente, principalmente

espionage | es'pīənʌj | s. espio-
nagem

espouse | espawz' |vt. desposar;
abraçar (causa, idéia)

esprit de corps| es'prīdəkó |s. es-
pírito de corporação (solidarie-
dade)

esquire| eskway'ə |s. (hist.) escu-
deiro; (maiúsc., *abrev.* Esq.)
Exmo. Sr. (título acrescentado
a um nome quando não precedi-
do de Mr., Dr. etc.)

essay | e'sey |s. ensaio / vt. ten-
tar, experimentar

essayist | e'seyist |s. ensaísta (es-
critor)

essence | e'səns |s. essência

essential | isen'śəl | a. essencial,
indispensável

establish | esta'bliś |vt. estabele-
cer; fundar, instituir; determi-
nar; instalar

establishment | esta'bliśmənt | s.
estabelecimento; fundação,
instituição; sistema eclesiástico
estabelecido pela lei. **-the E.**
grupo social que exerce a auto-
ridade

estate| esteyt' |s. estado; bens de
raiz; propriedade; éstado, condição

esteem | estīm' | s. estima, apre-
ço; avaliação / vt. estimar,
apreciar; avaliar

estimate | es'timeyt |s. cálculo,
estimativa / vt. calcular; avaliar; julgar

estimation | estimey'śən | s. esti-
ma, apreço; opinião

estrange | estreynj' | vt. alienar,
desavir, separar

estrangement | estreynj'mənt | s.
alienação, desavença, malque-
rença

estuary| es'tɪ̆uərī |s. estuário, de-
sembocadura, foz

etching | e'śing | s. água-forte,
gravura a água-forte

eternal | itE'nəl | a. eterno

eternity | itE'nitī |s. eternidade

ether | ɪ'ϑə |s. éter

ethereal | iϑɪ'rīəl | a. etéreo; sutil,
delicado

ethic | e'ϑik | s. ética / a. moral,
ético

ethical | e'ϑikəl | a. ético

ethics | e'ϑiks | s. (*sing.* e *pl.*) éti-
ca; tratado de ética

ethos | ɪ'ϑos | s. espírito caracte-
rístico (de obra de arte, povo,
pessoa etc.)

etiquette | e'tiket | s. etiqueta,
protocolo

etymology | etimo'ləĵī | s. etimo-
logia

Eucharist | ɪ̆u'kərist | s. Eucaris-
tia

eulogize | ɪ̆u'ləĵayz | vt. elogiar,
louvar, gabar

eulogy | ɪ̆u'ləĵī |s. elogio

eunuch | ɪ̆u'nək |s. eunuco

euphemism | ɪ̆u'fəmizəm | s. eu-
femismo

European | ɪ̆urəpɪ'ən | s.a. eu-
ropeu

euthanasia | ɪ̆uϑəney'jə | s. euta-
násia

evacuate | iva'kɪ̆ueyt | vt. vi.
evacuar; esvaziar; abandonar

evade | iveyd' |vt. evadir, evitar,
fugir a, eximir-se de

evaluate | iva'lɪ̆ueyt | vt. avaliar,
estimar (preço)

evanescent | ivəne'sənt | a. eva-
nescente; fugidio

evangelical | ivənĵe'likəl |s. evan-
gelista / a. evangélico

evaporate | iva'pəreyt | vt. vi.
evaporar(-se)

evasion | ivey'jən | *s.* evasão, fuga; evasiva, subterfúgio

evasive | ivey'ziv | *a.* evasivo, ambíguo

eve | ıv' | *s.* véspera. -**on the e. of** em vésperas de

even | ı'vən | *a.* liso, plano; constante, regular; paralelo, equilibrado; calmo, sereno; par (número). -**to be e.** estar quite(s). -**to get e. with** vingar-se de / *adv.* até, mesmo; ainda. -**e. so** ainda assim. -**e. if** ainda que. -**not e.** nem mesmo / *vt.* igualar, nivelar, alisar; equilibrar; equiparar

evening | ıv'ning | *s.* entardecer, anoitecer / *a.* vespertino

evening dress | ıv'ningdres | *s.* traje a rigor

evening gown | ıv'ninggawn | *s.* vestido de baile, vestido de gala

evensong | ı'vənsong | *s.* (ecles.) vésperas

event | ivent' | *s.* acontecimento; (desp.) prova, competição. -**in the e. of** em caso de. -**at all events, in any e.** de qualquer maneira

eventful | ivent'ful | *a.* notável, memorável, momentoso

eventual | iven'tʃuəl | *a.* eventual; conseqüente; final

eventuality | iventʃua'litī | *s.* eventualidade, acontecimento possível

ever | e'və | *adv.* sempre; já, alguma vez; nunca, jamais. -**for e.** para sempre. -**e. since** desde então. -**hardly e.** quase nunca. -**more than e.** mais do que nunca. -**did you e.?** você já viu (ouviu) coisa igual?

evergreen | e'vəgrin | *s.a.* sempre-verde, planta sempre-verde; conífera

everlasting | evəlʌs'ting | *s.* eternidade; (bot.) sempre-viva; tecido de la resistente / *a.* perpétuo, eterno

every | ev'rī | *a.* cada, todo. -**e. day** todos os dias. -**e. other day** dia sim, dia não. -**e. now and then** de vez em quando. -**e. bit** (coloq.) tudinho, cada. pedacinho

everybody | ev'rıɒodı | *pron.* todo (o) mundo, toda (a) gente

everything | ev'rīƀing | *pron.* tudo

everywhere | ev'rıwe'ə | *adv.* em (por) toda a parte

evict | ivikt' | *vt.* (jur.) expulsar, despejar

evidence | e'vidəns | *s.* evidência; (jur.) testemunho, depoimento. -**to give e.** depor em juízo

evident | e'vidənt | *a.* evidente, óbvio, claro

evil | ı'vil | *s.* mal, maldade / *a.* mau, ruim; maligno, malfazejo. -**the E. One** o diabo

evil days | ı'vildeyz | *s.* tempo de infortúnio

evil eye | ı'vilay | *s.* mau-olhado

evince | ivins' | *vt.* manifestar, evidenciar

evocation | ivowkey'ʃən | *s.* evocação

evoke | ivowk' | *vt.* evocar; invocar; despertar

evolution | ivəlu'ʃən | *s.* evolução

evolve | ivolv' | *vi.* evoluir; desenvolver-se; expandir; evolucionar; derivar-se

ewe | ıv' | *s.* ovelha

ewe lamb | īv'lam | *s.* (fig.) o "tesouro" de alguém, o seu bem mais precioso, a menina dos olhos

ewer | iu'ə | *s.* jarro (para água), cântaro

exacerbate | eksa'səbeyt | *vt.* exacerbar, agravar

exacerbation | eksasəbey'ʃən | *s.* exacerbação

exact | egzakt' | *a.* exato, correto; preciso, justo / *vt.* exigir; cobrar; extorquir

exacting | egzak'ting | *a.* exigente, severo; rigoroso

exaction | egzak'ʃən | *s.* cobrança; extorsão

exactly | egzakt'lī | *adv.* exatamente, justamente

exactness | egzakt'nes | *s.* exatidão, precisão

exaggerate | egza'jəreyt | *vt.* exagerar

exaggeration | egzajərey'śən | *s.* exageração, exagero

exalt | egzolt' | *vt.* exaltar, louvar, enaltecer

exaltation | egzoltey'śən | *s.* exaltação; elevação; excitação

examination | egzaminey'śən | *s.* exame; inspeção; inquérito, investigação; fiscalização. **-e. paper** lista de questões em prova escrita; exame escrito

examine | egza'min | *vt.* examinar, interrogar

examiner | egza'minə | *s.* examinador; inspetor

example | egzam'pəl | *s.* exemplo

exasperate | egzʌs'pəreyt | *vt.* exasperar, irritar, enfurecer; exacerbar

exasperation | egzʌspərey'śən | *s.* exasperação; exacerbação

excavate | eks'kəveyt | *vt.* escavar; desenterrar

excavation | ekskəvey'śən | *s.* escavação; cavidade

exceed | eksıd' | *vt.* exceder, ultrapassar

exceedingly | eksı'dinglı | *adv.* extremamente, muitíssimo

excel | eksel' | *vt.* sobrepujar, superar / *vi.* distinguir-se, sobressair

excellence | ek'sələns | *s.* excelência, perfeição

excellent | ek'sələnt | *a.* excelente, ótimo

except | eksept' | *prep.* exceto, salvo, a não ser / *vt.* excetuar / *vi.* objetar

excepting | eksep'ting | *prep.* exceto, salvo, menos

exception | eksep'śən | *s.* exceção. **-to take e.** fazer objeção; ofender-se

exceptional | eksep'śənəl | *a.* excepcional

excerpt | ek'sɛpt | *s.* excerto, tre-

cho, extrato

excess | ekses' | *s.* excesso, demasia; intemperança. **-in e. of** mais que. **-to e.** em demasia / *a.* em excesso

excessive | ekse'siv | *a.* excessivo, demasiado

exchange | eksšeynǰ' | *s.* troca; substituição; câmbio (moedas etc.). **-in e. for** em troca de / *vt.* trocar; cambiar (dinheiro)

exchange rate | eksšeynǰ'reyt | *s.* taxa de câmbio

exchequer | eksše'kə | *s.* erário, tesouro (público)

excise | ek'sayz | *s.* impostos internos, impostos de consumo / *vt.* aplicar e obrigar a pagar esses impostos

excitable | eksay'təbəl | *a.* excitável; irritável

excite | eksayt' | *vt.* excitar; irritar; estimular

excited | eksay'tid | *a.* excitado; irritado; estimulado; entusiasmado, alvoroçado

excitement | eksayt'mənt | *s.* excitação, entusiasmo; agitação, alvoroço, arrebatamento

exciting | eksay'ting | *a.* excitante, empolgante, estimulante, emocionante

exclaim | ekskleym' | *vi.* exclamar, bradar, gritar

exclamation | ekskləmey'śən | *s.* exclamação

exclamation mark | ekskləmey'śənmʌk | *s.* ponto de exclamação

exclude | eksklʊd' | *vt.* excluir; eliminar; expulsar

exclusion | eksklʊ'jən | *s.* exclusão; expulsão

exclusive | eksklʊ'siv | *a.* exclusivo; privativo; restrito; de alta classe

exclusiveness | eksk_lʊ'sivnes | *s.* exclusividade

excommunicate | ekskə.nĩu'nikeyt | *s. a.* excomungado / *vt.* excomungar

excrement | eks'krimənt | *s.* excremento

excruciating| ekskrʋ'sĩeyting |a. cruciante, torturante (dor, angústia etc.)

excursion | ekskE'sən | s. excursão, viagem de recreio

excuse| ekskĩus' |s. desculpa, justificativa; pretexto / | ekskĩuz' | vt. desculpar; justificar; dispensar. **-e. me!** desculpe-me!, com licença! (para passar)

execrable | ek'sikrəbəl | a. execrável

execute | eksikĩut' | vt. executar, realizar; executar (pená capital)

execution | eksikĩu'sən |s. execução; realização; execução (de pena capital)

executioner | eksikĩu'sənə | s. carrasco, verdugo, algoz

executive | egze'kĩutiv |s. poder executivo; executivo (de uma empresa) / a. executivo, realizador

executor| egze'kĩutə |s. executor testamentário

exemplary | egzem'plərī | a. exemplar, modelar; típico

exemplify | egzem'plifay | vt. exemplificar; fazer cópia autenticada de, transladar

exempt | egzempt' | vt. isentar, eximir / a. isento, livre

exemption | egzem'sən | s. isenção, dispensa

exercise | eksəsayz' | s. exercício; adestramento, ginástica; dever escolar / vt. exercer; desempenhar; adestrar; praticar, usar / vi. exercitar-se, treinar

exert | egzEt' | vt. exercer; pôr em ação / vi. esforçar-se

exertion | egzE'sən | s. esforço, diligência; emprego, aplicação

exhale | eksheyl' | vt. exalar

exhaust | egzóst' | s. escapamento, **descarga** / vt. **esgotar, exaurir**

exhausted | egzós'tid | a. exausto, esgotado

exhausting| egzós'ting |a. exaustivo, fatigante

exhaustion | egzós'šən | s. exaustão, esgotamento

exhaustive | egzós'tiv |a. exaustivo; completo

exhibit | egzi'bit |vt. exibir, apresentar

exhibition | egzibi'sən |s. exposição; demonstração

exhilarating | egzilərey'ting | a. excitante, estimulante, animador; tonificante (clima)

exhilaration | egzilərey'sən | s. jovialidade, alegria, animação, hilaridade

exhort | egzót' | vt. exortar, incitar; aconselhar

exhumation | ekshĩumey'sən | s. exumação

exigence, exigency | egzi'jəns egzi'jɔnsī | s. exigência; necessidade urgente

exiguous | egzi'gĩuəs | a. exíguo; escasso

exile | eksayl' |s. exílio, desterro; exilado (pessoa) / vt. exilar, desterrar

exist | egzist' | vi. existir

existence | egzis'təns | s. existência, vida

exit | ek'sit | s. saída

exodus| ek'sədəs |s. êxodo; emigração

exonerate | egzo'nəreyt | vt. exonerar; desobrigar

exorbitant | egzó'bitənt | a. exorbitante, excessivo

exorcise | ek'sósayz | vt. exorcizar, esconjurar

exotic | egzo'tik | a. exótico

expand | ikspand' |vt. expandir, dilatar; desenvolver, **aumentar** / vi. expandir-se

expanse | ekspans' | s. extensão; vastidão

expansion | ekspan'sən | s. expansão; progresso, desenvolvimento, aumento

expansive | ikspan'siv |a. expansivo; (fig.) efusivo; extenso, vasto

expatiate | ekspey'sĩeyt | vi. estender-se, alargar-se; divagar

expatriate | ekspa'trīeyt |s. a. expatriado / vt. expatriar

e..pect | ekspekt' | vt. esperar, aguardar; contar com

expectancy | ekspek'tənsī |s. expectativa

expectation | ekspektey'śən | s. expectativa; esperança

expedient | ekśpi'di̇̃ənt |s. expediente, recurso / a. conveniente, adequado

expedite | eks'pidayt | vt. expedir; promulgar; lavrar; executar prontamente

expedition | ekspidi'śən |s. expedição; desembaraço, rapidez; expedição, excursão

expel | ekspel' | vt. expulsar (de país etc.); expelir

expenditure | ekspen'diśə |s. despesa, gasto, consumo

expense | ekspens' |s. custo; despesas. **-at any e.** a qualquer custo

expensive | ekspen'siv | a. caro, de alto preço

experience | ekspi'rīəns |s. experiência, prática; acontecimento / vt. experimentar, sentir; sofrer; conhecer ou aprender por experiência

experienced | ekspi'rīənst |a. experimentado, experiente

experiment | ekspe'rimənt |s. experiência, ensaio / vt. fazer experiências

expert | eks'pɛt |s. perito, especialista, autoridade / a. perito; versado, hábil

expiate | eks'pīeyt | vt. expiar

expiration | ekspirey'śən |s. expiração; ar expirado; término, fim; morte

expire | ekspay'ə | vt. expirar; expelir (ar) / vi. expirar, morrer; terminar, vencer-se (prazo)

explain | ekspleyn' | vt. explicar, esclarecer. **-to e. away** explicar satisfatoriamente, justificar

explanation | eksplaney'śən | s. explicação; explanação

explanatory | ekspla'nətrī | a. explicativo, explanatório

expletive | eksplı'tiv | s. expletivo; imprecação / a. expletivo, completivo

explicit | ekspli'sit | a. explícito, claro, inequívoco

explode | eksplowd' |vt. fazer explodir / vi. explodir

exploit | eks'ployt | s. façanha, proeza / | eksployt' | vt. explorar, utilizar

exploitation | eksploytey'śən |s. exploração, utilização

exploration | eksplərey'śən | s. exploração; investigação

explore | eksplo' | vt. explorar; sondar, pesquisar

explorèr | eksplo'rə | s. explorador, descobridor

explosion | eksplow'jən | s. explosão; estampido

explosive | eksplow'ziv | s.a. explosivo

exponent | ekspow'nənt | s. exponente; expositor, expoente; intérprete, representante

export | eks'pót | s. exportação; artigo de exportação / a. de exportação / vt. exportar

expose | ekspowz' |vt. expor; exibir; descobrir, desnudar

exposition | ekspozi'śən |s. exposição, exibição; abandono (de criança)

expostulate | ekspos'tĭuleyt | vi. protestar, reclamar

exposure | ekspow'jə | s. exposição (tb. fot.); exibição; desmascaramento

exposure meter | ekspow'jəmıtə | s. fotômetro

expound | ekspawnd' | vt. expor, explicar

express | ekspres' | s. expresso (trem) / a. expresso, explícito; rápido / vt. expressar, exprimir

expression | ekspre'śən | s. expressão; palavra, locução

expressive | ekspre'siv |a. expressivo

expropriate | eksprow'prīeyt |vt. expropriar, desapropriar

expulsion | ekspâl'śən | s. expulsão

expunge | ekspânĵ' | vt. apagar, cancelar, riscar

expurgate | eks'pɛgeyt | vt. expurgar; purificar

exquisite | ekskwi'zit | a. requintado, primoroso

ex-serviceman | eksse'vismən | s. veterano de guerra

extant | ekstant' | a. existente, subsistente

extemporary | ekstem'pərərī | a. improvisado, extemporâneo

extempore | ekstem'pərī | a. improvisado, extemporâneo / adv. de improviso (falar)

extend | ekstend' | vt. estender, prolongar, aumentar

extension | eksten'śən | s. extensão, prolongamento; expansão; dependência, puxado (casa); prorrogação

extensive | eksten'siv | a. extensivo; extenso; amplo

extensively | eksten'sivlī | adv. extensamente, largamente

extent | ekstent' | s. extensão; grau, proporção. **-to a certaine.** até certo ponto. **-to a great e.** em grande parte

extenuate | ekste'nĭueyt | vt. atenuar, mitigar; desculpar

extenuating | ekste'nĭueyting | a. atenuante

exterior | ekstı'rīə | s. exterior, parte exterior / a. exterior, externo

exterminate | ekstɛ'mineyt | vt. exterminar, aniquilar

extermination | ekstɛminey'śən | s. extermínio

external | ekstɛ'nəl | a. externo, exterior

extinct | ekstinkt' | a. extinto; suprimido; morto

extinction | ekstink'śən | s. extinção, supressão, abolição

extinguish | eksting'gwiś | vt. extinguir (fogo etc.); abolir, destruir, aniquilar

extinguisher | eksting'gwiśə | s.

extintor (tb. de incêndio); **apagador de vela**

extirpate | eks'tɛpeyt | vt. extirpar, erradicar

extol, extoll | ekstowl' | vt. exaltar, louvar, elogiar

extort | ekstót' | vt. extorquir, arrancar

extortion | ekstó'śən | s. extorsão; (jur.) concussão

extortionate | ekstó'śənit | a. extorsivo, exorbitante, excessivo (preço)

extra | eks'trə | s. extra; suplemento, adicional; edição extra (jornal) / a. extra, suplementar; superior (qualidade), excepcional / adv. excepcionalmente

extract | eks'trakt | s. extrato; excerto, trecho (de livro etc.) / | ekstrakt' | vt. extrair, tirar; separar; extorquir; transcrever, copiar

extraction | ekstrak'śən | s. extração; origem (social), descendência

extradite | eks'trədayt | vt. extraditar

extraneous | ekstrey'nĭəs | a. extrínseco; estranho, alheio; irrelevante

extraordinarily | ekstró'dinərilī | adv. extraordinariamente, extremamente

extraordinary | ekstró'dinərī | a. extraordinário, excepcional

extravagance | ekstra'vəgəns | s. extravagância; exorbitância; prodigalidade

extravagant | ekstra'vəgənt | a. extravagante; excessivo

extreme | ekstrım' | s. extremo, extremidade. **-in the e.** ao extremo / a. extremo; distante; final; exagerado

extremely | ekstrım'lī | adv. extremamente, muito

extremist | ekstrı'mist | s. a. extremista

extremity | ekstre'mitī | s. extremidade

extricate| eks'trikeyt |*vt.* desembaraçar, soltar, livrar

extroversion | ekstrovɛ'śən | *s.* extroversão

extrude| ekstrʊd' |*vt.* expelir, expulsar

exuberance | egzĭu'bərəns | *s.* exuberância; efusão

exuberant| egzĭu'bərənt |*a.* exuberante; copioso, farto; efusivo, alegre

exude | eksĭʊd' | *vt. vi.* exsudar, destilar

exult| egzãlt' | *vi.* exultar, regozijar-se

eye | ay' | *s.* olho; olhar, visão; acuidade visual; fundo (de agulha). -**to keep an e. on** vigiar. -**to turn a blind e. to** fazer vista grossa a. -**to have an e. to** estar muito atento a. -**up to the eyes in** sobrecarregado de. -**to make eyes at** namorar com os olhos / *vt.* olhar, fitar; vigiar

eyeball | ay'bol ⌊*s.* globo ocular

eyebrow | ay'braw | *s.* sobrancelha

eyelash | ay'laś |*s.* pestana

eyelet | ay'lit |*s.* ilhós; ocelo; seteira / *vt.* fazer ilhós em

eyelid | ay'lid |*s.* pálpebra

eye-shade | ay'śeyd |*s.* pala

eyesight | ay'sayt |*s.* visão, vista

eyewash | ay'woś | *s.* colírio; (gir.) tolice; fanfarronice; lábia, lisonja

eyewitness | ey'witnes | *s.* testemunha ocular

F

F, f | ef'| *s.* f; (maiúsc., mús.) fá

fable | fey'bəl | *s.* fábula; lenda

fabric | fa'brik | *s.* estrutura; tecido, pano; construção

fabricate | fa'brikeyt | *vt.* inventar, engendrar, urdir

fabulous | fa'bĭuləs | *a.* fabuloso, prodigioso, espantoso.

façade | fəsʌd' | *s.* fachada

face | feys' | *s.* rosto, cara, face; semblante, fisionomia; face (da terra); mostrador (de relógio); atrevimento, descaro. -**f. to f.** face a face. -**in the f. of** diante de. -**to pull a long f.** aparentar desapontamento. -**to save f.** salvar as aparências / *vt.* encarar, enfrentar, arrostar, fazer face a; dar para, estar voltado para (casa etc.). -**to f. the idea that** acostumar-se à idéia de. -**to f. the music** enfrentar as conseqüências / *vi.* voltar-se; olhar de frente

facet | fa'sit | *s.* faceta

facetious | fəsi'śəs |*a.* zombeteiro, brincalhão

face value | feysva'lĭu |*s.* (com.) valor nominal (moeda, nota)

facile | fa'sayl | *a.* simples, fácil; fluente, abundante; (ant.) dócil, afável

facilitate | fəsi'liteyt | *vt.* facilitar, simplificar

facility | fəsi'litĭ | *s.* facilidade; (*pl.*) facilidades, meios; comodidades

fact | fakt' | *s.* fato. -**in f.** de fato. -**as a matter of f.** em verdade, aliás. -**to know for a f.** saber sem dúvida. -**the f. of the matter is** a verdade é que

faction | fak'śən | *s.* facção

factor | fak'tə | *s.* fator, elemento, coeficiente; (com.) administrador

factory | fak'tərĭ | *s.* fábrica

faculty | fa'kəltĭ | *s.* faculdade

faculty of arts | fa'kəltĭov'Ats | s. faculdade de letras

fad | fad' | s. moda; mania passageira; excentricidade

fade | feyd' | vi. desbotar, perder a cor ou o viço; murchar; extinguir-se

fag | fag' | s. trabalho árduo; maçada; (gír.) cigarro. -**what a f.!** que trabalheira!

fagged | fagd' | a. esfalfado

faggot, fagot | fa'gət | s. feixe de lenha ou gravetos

fail | feyl' | s. reprovação (em exame). -**without f.** sem falta / vt. falhar; (coloq.) ser reprovado (em exames) / vi. faltar, minguar; fracassar; (com.) falir. -**I f. to see** não compreendo. -**don't f. to come** não deixe de vir. -**words f. me** não tenho palavras

failing | fey'ling | s. falta; malogro; imperfeição; fraqueza / a. enfraquecido; reduzido / prep. em lugar de, na falta de

failure | fey'lĭə | s. malogro, fracasso, fiasco; deficiência, falta; enguiço (de motor etc.); (com.) falência. -**f. of issue** não deixar descendência

faint | feynt' | s. desmaio / a. tênue, fraco, vago, indistinto / vi. desmaiar

fair | fe'ə | s. feira / a. justo, lícito; belo, formoso; regular, mediano; moderado; sofrível (nota); louro (cabelo); claro (pele); favorável (vento). -**sense of f. play** lealdade. -**f. and square** justo e leal. -**f. to middling** sofrível. -**f. trial** julgamento imparcial. -**f. enough!** (coloq.) de acordo!

fair copy | fe'əkopĭ | s. cópia a limpo

fairly | fe'əlĭ | adv. bastante, razoavelmente, sofrivelmente

fairly good | fe'əlĭgud | a. regular, sofrível

fairness | fe'ənes | s. formosura, beleza; alvura (da pele); probidade, honestidade

fair play | fe'əpley | s. jogo limpo

fairy | fe'ərĭ | s. fada

fairy-tale | fe'ərĭteyl | s. conto de fadas

faith | feyϑ' | s. fé; confiança; crença religiosa. -**to break f. with** faltar com a palavra. -**in f.** na verdade

faithful | feyϑ'ful | a. fiel, leal; verdadeiro, exato, fidedigno. -**the f.** os fiéis

faithfully | feyϑ'fulĭ | adv. fielmente, lealmente, sinceramente; pontualmente

faithfulness | feyϑ'fulnes | s. fidelidade, lealdade

faithless | feyϑ'les | a. infiel, incrédulo; desonesto, desleal; descrente

faithlessness | feyϑ'lesnes | s. infidelidade; deslealdade; falsidade

fake | feyk' | s. contrafação; fraude / a. fraudulento, falso / vt. falsificar

fall | fól' | s. queda; baixa (preços, temperatura); (EUA) outono / vi. cair; baixar. -**to f. asleep** adormecer. -**to f. away** emagrecer; apostatar; desertar. -**to f. apart** cair aos pedaços. -**to f. back** cair para trás; retroceder. -**to f. on** ou **upon** recorrer a. -**to f. behind** ficar para trás. -**to f. in love with** apaixonar-se por. -**to f. in with** adaptar-se a, conformar-se com. -**to f. out** discutir, brigar. -**to f. short** faltar, ser insuficiente. -**to f. under** ficar sob a influência de; estar compreendido em. -**to f. through** falhar (planos). -**to f. within** estar na categoria de

fallacious | fəley'şəs | a. falaz, enganador, ilusório

fallacy | fa'ləsĭ | s. falácia, ilusão, engano, mentira

fallen | fó'lən | a. caído; decaído, arruinado; degradado; morto

fallibility | falibi'litī | s. falibilidade

falling | fó'ling | a. cadente, que cai; caduco, decadente

falling star | fó'lingstA | s. estrela cadente

fallow | fa'low | a. sem cultivo; maninho; (fig.) sem cultura; amarelo avermelhado

false | fols' | a. falso; errado; artificial; postiço

false alarm | fols'əlAm | s. rebate falso

falsehood | fols'hud | s. mentira, falsidade

falseness | fols'nes | s. falsidade, perfídia

false tooth | fols'tʋϑ | s. dentadura postiça

falsify | fol'sifay | vt. falsificar

falter | fol'tə | vt. gaguejar / vi. vacilar, hesitar; tropeçar, cambalear; recuar

fame | feym' | s. fama, renome, reputação, celebridade

famed | feymd' | a. famoso, célebre, afamado

familiar | fəmi'līə | a. familiar, doméstico, conhecido. -to make f. with someone tomar liberdades com alguém. -to become f. with familiarizar-se com

familiarity | fəmilīa'ritī | s. familiaridade; intimidade

familiarize | fəmi'līərayz | vt. familiarizar, acostumar. -to f. oneself with familiarizar-se com

family | fa'milī | s. família / a. familiar, de família. -in the f. way grávida

family allowance | fa'milīəlaw'-əns | s. abono de família

family name | fa'milīneym | s. nome de família, sobrenome

famine | fa'min | s. fome, escassez, penúria

famished | fa'mist | a. esfaimado, faminto, esfomeado

famous | fey'məs | a. famoso,

célebre, renomado, insigne

fan | fan' | s. leque; (mec.) ventoinha; ventarola; fã, entusiasta / vt. abanar / vr. abanar-se

fanatic | fəna'tik | s.a. fanático

fanatical | fəna'tikəl | a. fanático

fanaticism | fəna'tisizəm | s. fanatismo

fanciful | fan'siful | a. fantástico; extravagante

fancy | fan'sī | s. fantasia, imaginação; inclinação, gosto; capricho, extravagância. -to take a f. for agradar-se de / a. fantástico, extravagante; exorbitante (preço) / vt. imaginar, supor; gostar de, desejar; atrair, interessar; simpatizar com. -f. that! imagine só! -to f. oneself imaginar-se. -f.! imagine!, faça idéia!

fancy dress | fan'sīdres | s. fantasia (roupa)

fancy goods | fan'sīgudz | spl. objetos de fantasia, artigos de luxo

fancy woman | fan'sīwəmən | s. amante

fanfare | fan'feə | s. fanfarra, clarinada

fang | fang' | s. presa (de serpente ou animal)

fantastic | fantas'tik | a. fantástico; irreal

fantasy | fan'təsī | s. fantasia

far | fA' | a. distante, remoto. -on the f. side of do lado mais afastado. -f. and wide por toda a parte / adv. longe; muito; em alto grau; a grande distância. -as f. as I am concerned quanto a mim. -as f. as I know que eu saiba. -by f. em muito. -f. better muito melhor. -how f.? a que distância? -so f. até agora. -so f. so good até aqui tudo bem

farce | fAs' | s. farsa

farcical | fA'sikəl | a. grotesco, ridículo

fare | fe'ə | s. passagem, bilhete;

preço de passagem; frete; comida, alimentação / vi. viajar; passar, ser tratado ou tratar-se (comida)

far-end | fʌ'end | a. a outra extremidade

farewell | feəwel' | s. despedida; adeus. **-to bid f. to** despedir-se de / a. de despedida / interj. adeus!

far-famed | fʌ'feymd | a. muito conhecido, renomado

far-fetched | fʌ'feŝid | a. forçado, afetado, rebuscado

far-flung | fʌ'flâng | a. vasto, extenso

farm | fʌm' | s. fazenda, granja / vt. cultivar, lavrar. **-to f. out** arrendar

farmer | fʌ'mə | s. fazendeiro, lavrador, agricultor

farm-hand | fʌm'hand | s. trabalhador rural

farming | fʌ'ming | s. agricultura, lavoura

far-off | fʌ'of | a. longe, afastado; remoto

far-reaching | fʌ'riŝing | a. de longo alcance

far-seeing | fʌ'siing | a. previdente

fascicle | fa'sikəl | s. fascículo

fascinate | fa'sineyt | vt. fascinar, encantar, cativar

fascinating | fa'sineyting | a. fascinante, sedutor

fascination | fasiney'śən | s. fascinação, sedução, encanto

fascism | fa'śizəm | s. fascismo

fascist | fa'śist | s. fascista

fashion | fa'śən | s. moda, estilo. **-in f.** na moda. **-out of f.** fora de moda. **-to set the f.** lançar a moda / vt. amoldar, adaptar, ajustar

fashionable | fa'śənəbəl | a. na moda, elegante, em voga

fast | fʌst' | s. (relig.) jejum / a. veloz, rápido, adiantado (relógio); fixado, firme; fixa (cor); dissoluto. **-to lead a f. life** levar vida dissoluta / adv. firmemente; ve-

lozmente; dissolutamente. **-f. asleep** em sono profundo. **-f. by** perto de. **-to hold f.** segurar firmemente, não soltar

fasten | fʌ'sən | vt. fixar, prender, apertar; trancar, aferrolhar; fixar, cravar (olhos); depositar (esperanças); atribuir, imputar (culpa, crime)

fastener | fʌ'sənə | s. fecho

fastening | fʌ'səning | s. fecho; colchete

fastidious | fəsti'diəs | a. exigente; delicado; melindroso

fastness | fʌst'nes | s. firmeza, solidez; rapidez; dissipação; (mil.) forte

fat | fat' | s. gordura / a. gordo; rico, fértil; lucrativo; abundante. **-the f. of the land** o melhor pedaço. **-a f. lot** (gír.) muito pouco (ironicamente)

fatal | fey'təl | a. fatal, inevitável; mortal, funesto

fatality | fəta'litî | s. fatalidade

fate | feyt' | s. destino, sorte, fortuna, fado

fated | fey'tid | a. fadado, predestinado

fateful | feyt'ful | a. fatal, funesto, desastroso

father | fʌ'ðə | s. pai; (ecles.) padre / vt. engendrar, procriar; adotar, reconhecer (filho); assumir a paternidade; apadrinhar. **-to f. on** ou **upon** atribuir, imputar

Father Christmas | fʌ'ðəkrisməs | s. Papai Noel

fatherhood | fʌ'ðəhud | s. paternidade

father-in-law | fʌ'ðəinló | s. sogro

fatherland | fʌ'ðəland | s. pátria, terra natal

fatherless | fʌ'ðəles | a. órfão de pai; (fig.) anônimo

fatherly | fʌ'ðəlî | a. paternal, paterno

fathom | fa'ðəm | s. (náut.) braça / vt. sondar, aprofundar; esquadrinhar

fatigue | fətig' | *s.* fadiga, cansaço; (mil.) faxina / *vt.* fatigar, cansar

fatiguing | fəti'ging | *a.* fatigante, cansativo, penoso

fatten | fa'tən | *vt.* cevar, engordar

fatty | fa ıɪ | *s.* (coloq.) gorducho / *a.* gordurento; adiposo (tecido)

fatuous | fa'tɪ̆uəs | *a.* fátuo, néscio; ilusório

fatuousness | fa'tɪ̆uəsnes | *s.* fatuidade, tolice

fault | folt' | *s.* culpa; defeito imperfeição. -at f. errado; culpado. -to a f. excessivamente. -to find f. with criticar

faultfinder | folt'fayndə | *s.* crítico; reclamador

faultless | folt'les | *a.* impecável, perfeito

faulty | fol'tī | *a.* defeituoso, imperfeito

favour, favor | fey'və | *s.* favor; parcialidade; proteção; distintivo, emblema. -to be in f. with contar com o apoio de. -to be out of f. perder o apoio. -to lose f. cair em desgraça / *vt.* favorecer, auxiliar, proteger

favourable, favorable | fey'vərəbəl | *a.* favorável

favoured | fey'vəd | *a.* favorecido; protegido; propício, conveniente

favourite, favorite | fey'vərit | *s.a.* favorito, predileto; protegido

favouritism, favoritism | fey'vəritizəm | *s.* favoritismo

fawn | fón' | *s.* filhote de corça; castanho claro / *vi.* moı ɪr afeição (diz-se do cão). -to f. on adular

fear | fɪ'ə | *s.* medo, receio, temor. -for f. of, that, lest para evitar que. -without f. or favour imparcialmente. -no f. (coloq.) é pouco provável / *vt.vi.* recear, temer

fearful | fɪ'əful | *a.* medroso, receoso; medonho, terrível

fearless | fɪ'əles | *a.* destemido, intrépido

fearlessness | fɪ'əlesnes | *s.* intrepidez, audácia, arrojo

fearsome | fɪ'əsəm | *a.* temível (esp. na aparência)

feasibility | fɪzəbi'litī | *s.* praticabilidade, exeqüibilidade

feasible | fɪ'zibəl | *a.* factível, praticável

feast | fīst' | *s.* festim, banquete / *vt.* festejar, banquetear; (fig.) deleitar / *vi.* banquetear-se; deleitar-se. -to f. one's eyes deleitar a vista

feat | fīt' | *s.* façanha, feito

feather | fe'ðə | *s.* pluma, pena. -in high ou full f. de bom humor

feather-brained | fe'ðəbreynd | *a.* tolo; estouvado

featherweight | fe'ðəweyt | *s.* coisa ou pessoa muito leve; peso-pena (no boxe)

feature | fɪ'šə | *s.* feição; característica; (EUA) filme principal; (*pl.*) feições, traços

February | fe'bruərī | *s.* fevereiro

feckless | fek'les | *a.* fraco; ineficiente; fútil, sem sentido

fecundation | fikəndey'šən | *s.* fecundação

fecundity | fikân'ditī | *s.* fecundidade

fed | fed' | *a.* alimentado. -f. up (gír.) farto, irritado

federation | fedərey'šən | *s.* federação, confederação

fee | fī' | *s.* honorários; joia; taxa de exame; gratificação, propina

feeble | fɪ'bəl | *a.* fraco, débil; tênue, delicado

feeble-minded | fɪ'bəlmayn'did | *a.* fraco de espírito

feebleness | fɪ'bəlnes | *s.* fraqueza, debilidade

feed | fīd' | *s.* comida; forragem, ração; (mec.) alimentação / *vt.* alimentar. -to f. up engordar, cevar. **-to f. upon** ou **on** alimentar-se de / *vi.* pastar; nutrir-se

feedback | fid'bak | *s.* (eletr.) regeneração, realimentação / *a.* de regeneração

feeding | fi'ding | *s.* alimentação; forragem / *a.* alimentar, alimentício

feel | fil' | *s.* tato; sensação / *vt.* sentir; apalpar; examinar. **-to f. one's way** tatear o caminho / *vi.* sentir-se. **-to f. better** sentir-se melhor. **-to f. oneself again** sentir-se restabelecido. **-to f. like** estar com vontade de. **-to f. soft** ser macio ao tato. **-how do you f. about it?** que tal lhe parece?

feeler | fi'lə | *s.* antena (de insetos); tentáculo; insinuação, indireta

feeling | fi'ling | *s.* tato; impressão; sensação; pressentimento; sensibilidade. **-to hurt one's feelings** magoar alguém / *a.* sensível; sensitivo; emotivo; agudo

feign | feyn' | *vt. vi.* fingir, simular; falsificar

feint | feynt' | *s.* (mil.) ataque simulado; finta (esgrima etc.); estratagema; subterfúgio / *vi.* aplicar finta

felicity | fəli'siti | *s.* felicidade, ventura; expressão ou idéia feliz

fell | fel' | *s.* pele (animal); charneca / *a.* cruel / *vt.* derrubar, deitar por terra

fellow | fe'low | *s.* camarada, companheiro; sujeito; igual, par; membro de conselho universitário; (EUA) estudante graduado. **-good f.** bom companheiro. **-old f.** meu velho. **-poor f.!** coitado!

fellow-countryman | fe'low-kân-trimən | *s.* compatriota

fellow creature | fe'lowkri'šə | *s.* semelhante, criatura

fellow-feeling | fe'lowfiling | *s.* solidariedade

fellow-member | fe'lowmembə |

s. confrade

fellowship | fe'lowšip | *s.* companheirismo, coleguismo; solidariedade; amizade; associação; bolsa de estudos

fellow-traveller | fe'lowtravələ | *s.* companheiro de viagem

felon | fe'lən | *s.* réu, delinqüente; (med.) panarício / *a.* cruel, malvado

felony | fe'lənī | *s.* (jur.) crime envolvendo violência

felt | felt' | *s.* feltro

female | fi'meyl | *s.* mulher; fêmea (animal) / *a.* feminino, fêmeo

feminine | fe'minin | *a.* feminino, feminil

fen | fen' | *s.* pântano, brejo

fence | fens' | *s.* cerca; tapume; esgrima. **-to be on the f.** ficar neutro; vacilar / *vt.* cercar; pôr tapume / *vi.* esgrimir

fencing | fen'sing | *s.* esgrima; cercas; tapumes

fend | fend' | *vt.* repelir. **-to f. for oneself** arranjar-se

fender | fen'də | *s.* defesa, proteção; (náut.) defensa; pára-lama; limpa-trilhos

fennel | fe'nəl | *s.* funcho, erva-doce

ferment | fɛ'ment | *s.* fermento; fermentação; agitação / *vi.* fermentar

fermentation | fɛmentey'šən | *s.* fermentação

fern | fɛn' | *s.* samambaia

ferocious | fərow'šəs | *a.* feroz, cruel, selvagem

ferocity | fəro'sitī | *s.* ferocidade, violência

ferret | fe'rit | *s.* (zool.) furão / *vt.* **-to f. out** indagar

Ferris wheel | fe'riswil | *s.* roda-gigante

ferroconcrete | ferow'kənkrit | *s.* cimento armado

ferry | fe'rī | *s.* barca; estação de barcas / *vt.* transportar em barca

ferryboat | fe'rībowt | *s.* barca

(de passagem ou transporte); balsa

fertile | fE'tayl | *a.* fértil, fecundo, produtivo

fertility | fEti'liti | *s.* fertilidade, produtividade

fertilize | fE'tilayz | *vt.* fertilizar, fecundar

fertilizer | fE'tilayzə | *s.* fertilizante, adubo químico

fervent | fE'vənt | *a.* fervoroso, fervente; ardoroso

fervour, fervor | fE'və | *s.* fervor, devoção; zelo

festival | fes'tivəl | *s.* festa; (mús.) festival / *a.* festivo

festive | fes'tiv | *a.* festivo

festivity | festi'viti | *s.* festividade; festejos, festa

festoon | festun' | *s.* festão, grinalda / *vt.* engrinaldar

fetch | fes' | *vt.* ir buscar; trazer; extrair, arrancar (lágrimas etc.); alcançar (preço); dar, soltar (suspiro etc.). **-to f. up** vomitar / *vi.* ir buscar e trazer; (náut.) rumar. **-to f. and carry** servir de criado; ser bisbilhoteiro

fête, fete | feyt' | *s.* festa ao ar livre / *vt.* festejar

fetish | fI'tiś | *s.* fetiche, amuleto, talismã

fetter | fe'tə | *s.* trava, grilhão; prisão; (*pl.*) grilhões / *vt.* agrilhoar

fettle | fe'təl | *s.* condição, estado. **-in good f.** em boas condições, em bom estado

feud | fiud | *s.* feudo; contenda, hostilidade (entre famílias)

feudal | fIu'dəl | *a.* feudal

feudalism | fIu'dəlizəm | *s.* feudalismo

fever | fI'və | *s.* febre

feverish | fI'vəriś | *a.* febril; (fig.) exaltado

few | fIu' | *s.* pouco. **-the f.** a minoria / *a.* poucos, alguns. **-a f.** poucos. **-not a f.** não poucos. **-quite a f.** muitos, um grande número

fewness | fIu'nes | *s.* raridade, pequeno número

fiancé | fion'sey | *s.* noivo

fiancée | fion'sey | *s.* noiva

fiasco | fias'kow | *s.* fiasco

fib | fib' | *s.* mentira leve

fibre, fiber | fay'bə | *s.* fibra; (fig.) caráter

fickle | fi'kəl | *a.* volúvel, caprichoso

fickleness | fi'kəlnes | *s.* volubilidade, inconstância

fiction | fik'śən | *s.* ficção

fictitious | fikti'śəs | *a.* fictício; imaginário

fiddle | fi'dəl | *s.* rabeca, violino; (gír.) trapaça. **-fit as a f.** em boa condição física. **-to play second f.** estar em segundo plano / *vt.* tocar rabeca; desperdiçar (tempo); (gír.); falsificar, trapacear, lograr

fiddlestick | fi'dəlstik | *s.* arco de rabeca / *interj.* (*pl.*) tolice!, bobagem!

fidelity | fide'liti | *s.* fidelidade, lealdade

fidget | fi'jit | *s.* desassossego; pessoa irrequieta / *vt.* desassossegar, inquietar / *vi.* remexer-se

fidgety | fi'jiti | *a.* irrequieto, inquieto

field | fIld' | *s.* campo; (fig.) domínio, setor; (mil.) campo de batalha. **-to take the f.** (mil.) entrar em campanha

field-glasses | fIld'glAsiz | *spl.* binóculo

fiend | fInd' | *s.* demônio, diabo, espírito mau; fanático. **-to be a f. for** ter mania por alguma coisa

fiendish | fIn'diś | *a.* demoníaco, diabólico

fierce | fI'əs | *a.* feroz, violento; impetuoso

fierceness | fI'əsnes | *s.* ferocidade; impetuosidade

fiery | fay'ərI | *a.* fogoso, impetuoso; inquieto; belicoso

fife | fayf' | *s.* pífano

fifteen | fif'tin | *s. a.* quinze

fifth | fifϑ' | *s.* quinto; (mús.) quinta / *a.* quinto

fifty | fif'tĭ | *s. a.* cinqüenta

fig | fig' | *s.* figo

fight | fayt' | *s.* luta, combate; briga, rixa; disputa / *vt.* lutar, combater. **-to f. off** repelir / *vi.* travar combate; sustentar causa. **-to f. against odds** enfrentar obstáculos. **-to f. shy of** esquivar-se a

fighter | fay'tə | *s.* lutador; pugilista; combatente; paladino; avião de caça

fighting | fay'ting | *s.* luta, combate / *a.* combatente; aguerrido; de combate

fighting cock | fay'tingkok | *s.* galo-de-briga

figment | fig'mənt | *s.* invenção, ficção

figure | fi'gə | *s.* figura, forma; número, algarismo; preço, valor. **-to cut a f.** fazer figura. **-good at figures** forte em contas / *vt.* calcular; imaginar / *vi.* figurar em. **-to f. on** contar com

figure-head | fi'gəhed | *s.* figura de proa; testa-de-ferro, chefe nominal

filbert | fil'bət | *s.* avelã; aveleira

filch | filš' | *vt. vi.* furtar, surripiar, abafar

file | fayl' | *s.* (mec.) lima; arquivo; (mil.) fila. **-on f.** arquivado. **-the rank and f.** os soldados rasos / *vt.* limar; arquivar (papéis) / *vi.* desfilar, marchar em fila

filigree | fi'ligrĭ | *s.* filigrana

fill | fil' | *s.* o suficiente, o bastante; cavidade ou imperfeição remendada com massa (em madeira etc.); o bastante para encher alguma coisa (cachimbo etc.); enchimento. **-to eat one's f.** comer até não poder mais / *vt.* encher; preencher (formulário etc.); ocupar; obturar (dente). **-to f. in** inserir; preencher; completar. **-to f. the bill** (coloq.) encher as medidas. **-to**

have one's f. of fartar-se de / *vi.* encher-se, enfunar-se

filling | fi'ling | *s.* enchimento; aterro; recheio; obturação (de dente)

filling station | fi'lingstey'šən | *s.* posto de gasolina

fillip | fi'lip | *s.* estímulo, incentivo

film | film' | *s.* filme; membrana; película; camada fina (de poeira) / *vt.* filmar; envoar, toldar

film-goer | film'gowə | *s.* freqüentador de cinema

filter | fil'tə | *s.* filtro / *vt.* filtrar / *vi.* filtrar-se, penetrar, infiltrar-se

filth | filϑ' | *s.* imundície, sujidade

filthy | fil'ϑĭ | *a.* imundo; indecente, obsceno

fin | fin' | *s.* barbatana

final | fay'nəl | *a.* final

finale | finA'lĭ | *s.* final

finally | fay'nəlĭ | *adv.* finalmente, por fim

finance | finans' faynans' | *s.* finanças / *vt.* financear / *vi.* realizar operações financeiras

financial | finan'šəl | *a.* financeiro

financier | finan'sĭə | *s.* financista; capitalista

find | faynd' | *s.* achado / *vt.* achar, encontrar, descobrir; averiguar; perceber. **-to f. out** descobrir. **-to f. favour with** cair nas boas graças de. **-to f. fault with** censurar, criticar, desaprovar

finding | fayn'ding | *s.* descobrimento; (jur.) veredicto; (*pl.*) ferramentas

fine | fayn' | *s.* multa / *vt.* multar / *a.* fino; requintado; belo, vistoso; seleto; agradáve!; afiado; saboroso / *interj.* excelente!, muito bem!, ótimo!

fine arts | fayn'Ats | *spl.* belas artes

finery | fay'nərĭ | *s.* refinamento (de maneiras); ornamentos, atavios

finesse | fines' | *s.* tato, sutileza, delicadeza; astúcia

finger | fing'gə | *s.* dedo. **-to lay a f. on** tocar (ainda que de leve). **-to shake one's f.** at reprovar asperamente / *vt.* tocar com os dedos; (mús.) dedilhar; (gír.) apontar (criminoso à polícia etc.)

fingerling | fing'gəling | *s.* filhote de salmão; peixinho

fingerprint | fing'gəprint | *s.* impressão digital

fingertip | fing'gətip | *s.* ponta do dedo. **-to the fingertips** completamente

finicky | fi'nikī | *a.* melindroso, exigente; precioso

finish | fi'niś | *s.* fim; remate, acabamento / *vt.* acabar, terminar, dar acabamento; liquidar, matar. **-to f. off** completar, rematar; matar / *vi.* acabar, cessar. **-to f. with** acabar com; liquidar; cortar relações com

finished | fi'niśt | *a.* acabado, completo; esgotado, exausto; (coloq.) liquidado

finishing | fi'niśing | *s.* acabamento. **-f. touch** último retoque

finishing blow | fi'niśingblow | *s.* golpe de misericórdia

finite | fay'nayt | *a.* finito, limitado, terminável

fir | fE' | *s.* abeto

fire | fay'ə | *s.* fogo; incêndio; fogueira; (fig.) paixão, veemência, vivacidade. **-to go through f. and water** passar por grandes dificuldades. **-to miss f.** falhar o tiro; fracassar. **-to set the Thames on f.** fazer algo notável. **-on f.** em chamas. **-to catch f.** incendiar-se; (fig.) exaltar-se / *vt.* incendiar; disparar (arma de fogo); (coloq.) despedir (empregado) / *vi.* fazer fogo, atirar

fire-alarm | fay'əəlAm | *s.* alarma contra incêndio

firearm | fay'əAm | *s.* arma de fogo

fire brigade | fay'əbrigeyd' | *s.* corpo de bombeiros

fire-eater | fay'əitə | *s.* homem que engole fogo (em circos etc.); valentão

fire-engine | fay'əenǰin | *s.* bomba contra incêndio; carro equipado com bomba

fire-escape | fay'əeskeyp' | *s.* saída de emergência; escada de incêndio

firefly | fay'əflay | *s.* vagalume

fireman | fay'əmən | *s.* (ferrov.) foguista; bombeiro

fireplace | fay'əpleys | *s.* lareira

firewood | fay'əwud | *s.* lenha

firework | fay'əwEk | *s.* fogo de artifício

firing | fay'əring | *s.* queima; tiroteio, fuzilaria, tiros; cauterização

firing-party, firing-squad | fay'əringpAtī fay'əringskwad | *s.* guarda fúnebre, pelotão de fuzilamento

firm | fEm' | *s.* (com.) firma, empresa / *a.* firme, sólido, inflexível

firmament | fE'məmənt | *s.* firmamento, céu

firmness | fEm'nes | *s.* firmeza, resolução

first | fEst' | *a.* primeiro. **-at f.** a princípio. **-f. of all** antes de mais nada. **-at f. hand** em primeira mão, diretamente

first floor | fEst'fló'ə | *s.* primeiro andar

first-rate | fEst'reyt | *a.* excelente, da melhor categoria

firth | fEϑ' | *s.* estuário; braço de mar

fish | fiś' | *s.* peixe. **-to have other f. to fry** ter coisa mais importante a fazer / *vt. vi.* pescar

fisherman | fi'śəmən | *s.* pescador

fishing | fi'śing | *s.* pesca

fishing story | fi'śingstorī | *s.* relato exagerado, história mentirosa

fishmonger | fiʃ'məngə | s. peixeiro, vendedor de peixe

fishy | fi'ʃĭ | a. piscoso; de peixe; (coloq.) suspeito, improvável

fission | fi'ʃən | s. fissão (nuclear)

fissure | fi'ʃə | s. fissura, fenda, rachadura

fist | fist' | s. punho; letra. **-to write a good f.** ter boa letra. **-a blow with the f.** murro / vt. socar, esmurrar; agarrar

fit | fit' | s. (med.) ataque, acesso, convulsão; capricho; ajuste, encaixe. **-to have a f.** dar um ataque. **-by fits and starts** aos trancos, espasmodicamente. **-to give someone a f.** surpreender ou escandalizar alguém. **-it is a good f.** está bem ajustado (roupa, ajuste mecânico). **-if the f. takes me** (coloq.) se me der na telha / a. apto, habilitado; adequado, conveniente; vigoroso, bem de saúde, em forma; pronto, em condições. **-f. for a king** digno de um rei. **-to see** ou to think f. decidir fazer algo (embora extravagante). **-as f. as a fiddle** (coloq.) em grande forma / vt. ajustar, adaptar; fixar; encaixar; convir a, ficar bem a (roupas). **-to f. out** (mil., náut.) armar, prover. **-to f. together** combinar. **-to f. up** montar (negócio, máquina etc.) / vi. assentar, ajustar-se; corresponder exatamente

fitful | fit'ful | a. caprichoso, intermitente

fitment | fit'mənt | s. (ger. pl.) peça de mobiliário (fixa)

fitness | fit'nes | s. aptidão; idoneidade; conveniência, oportunidade

fitter | fi'tə | s. ajustador mecânico (operário)

fitting | fi'ting | s. instalação, montagem; (pl.) acessórios / a. oportuno, conveniente, adequado, próprio

five | fayv' | s. a. cinco

fiver | fay'və | s. (gír.) nota de cinco (libras ou dólares)

fix | fiks' | s. apuro, dificuldade. **-to be in a f.** estar em apuros / vt. fixar; prender; consertar, reparar; (coloq.) subornar; (coloq.) castigar, ajustar contas. **-to f. up** (coloq.) compor, arrumar

fixed | fikst' | a. fixo; estável; estabelecido; determinado, permanente

fixity | fik'sitĭ | s. fixidez; rigidez; firmeza

fixture | fiks'ʃə | s. fixidez, rigidez; fixação; artefato, acessório; (desp.) jogo, encontro, desafio

fizzy | fi'zĭ | a. efervescente, espumante, gasoso

flabbergasted | fla'bəgᴀstid | a. pasmado, estupefato

flabby | fla'bĭ | a. frouxo, flácido, débil

flag | flag' | s. bandeira, estandarte, pavilhão; bandeirola. **-to keep the f. flying** continuar a luta. **-to put the f. out** celebrar uma vitória / vt. embandeirar; sinalizar com bandeira / vi. pender; enfraquecer; desanimar; vacilar

flagrant | fley'grənt | a. flagrante, manifesto, notório

flagstone | flag'stown | s. laje de pavimentação

flail | fleyl' | s. mangual

flair | fle'ə | s. faro, instinto especial, perspicácia

flake | fleyk' | s. floco (de neve); lasca (de madeira ou metal); escama; fagulha / vt. cobrir de flocos / vi. formar flocos; esfarelar-se

flamboyant | flamboy'ənt | a. ostentoso, extravagante, vistoso, empolado

flame | fleym' | s. chama, labareda; fulgor, brilho / vt. inflamar, incendiar / vi. flamejar, chamejar

flaming | fley'ming | *a*. flamejante, chamejante; ardente

flammable | fley'məbəl | *a*. inflamável

flank | flank' | *s*. flanco, costado; ilharga / *vt*. flanquear, ladear

flannel | fla'nəl | *s*. flanela; (*pl*.) roupa de flanela

flap | flap' | *s*. aba; borda; palmada; (aer.) flape / *vt*. agitar; bater (asas) / *vi*. agitar-se (bandeira)

flapper | fla'pə | *s*. mata-moscas; cauda de crustáceo; (gír., ant.) mocinha, garota

flare | fle'ə | *s*. fulgor, brilho, clarão; chama; (mil.) sinal luminoso (foguete) / *vt*. ostentar / *vi*. brilhar, refulgir; enfurecer-se

flash | flaś | *s*. clarão; lampejo; relâmpago; brilho intenso e passageiro. **-in a f**. num instante. **-a f. in the pan** fracasso, fogo de palha / *vt*. lampejar, cintilar; despachar (telegrama, mensagem etc.) / *vi*. faiscar, cintilar; relampejar; arrojar-se

flashback | flaś'bak | *s*. (cin., liter. etc.) interrupção de cena ou narrativa com volta ao passado

flashlight | flaś'layt | *s*. projetor de sinais luminosos; (EUA) lanterna elétrica

flashy | fla'śī | *a*. vistoso, ostentoso, espalhafatoso

flask | flʌsk' | *s*. frasco

flat | flat' | *s*. apartamento; superfície plana / *a*. chato, plano, nivelado; tedioso, aborrecido; deprimido, desanimado; (mús.) menor; categórico, formal (recusa); invariável, uniforme; vazio (pneu). **-to fall f**. ser um fracasso, não dar certo

flat-iron | flat'ayən | *s*. ferro de passar roupa

flatten | fla'tən | *vt*. achatar, aplanar, nivelar

flatter | fla'tə | *vt*. lisonjear, adular; satisfazer, agradar a. **-to f. oneself** alimentar a esperança (ilusão) de

flatterer | fla'tərə | *s*. adulador, lisonjeador

flattering | fla'təring | *a*. lisonjeiro; promissor

flattery | fla'tərī | *s*. lisonja, adulação

flaunt | flónt' | *vt*. exibir, ostentar, pavonear, alardear

flavour, flavor | fley'və | *s*. sabor, gosto; aroma, tempero

flavouring, flavoring | fley'vəring | *s*. condimento

flaw | fló' | *s*. defeito, imperfeição; rachadura, fenda

flax | flaks' | *s*. linho

flay | fley' | *vt*. esfolar, pelar; (fig.) fustigar, descompor; esbulhar, espoliar

flea | flī' | *s*. pulga

flee | flī' | *vi*. fugir, escapar-se

fleece | flīs' | *s*. velocino, tosão / *vt*. tosquiar; (fig.) espoliar, roubar

fleet | flīt' | *s*. frota, esquadra / *a*. (poét.) veloz

fleeting | flī'ting | *a*. fugaz, rápido, passageiro

Flemish | fle'miś | *a*. flamengo (língua)

flesh | fleś' | *s*. carne; polpa (de frutas). **-in the f**. em pessoa, em carne e osso. **-to lose f**. emagrecer. **-to put on f**. engordar

flesh-fly | fleś'flay | *s*. mosca-varejeira

fleshly | fles'lī | *a*. carnal, sensual

flex | fleks' | *s*. fio elétrico / *vt. vi*. dobrar(-se), curvar(-se)

flexibility | fleksibi'litī | *s*. flexibilidade

flexible | flek'sibəl | *a*. flexível; maleável; complacente

flick | flik' | *s*. piparote; movimento repentino / *vt*. dar um piparote em; sacudir, agitar

flicker | fli'kə | *s*. luz bruxuleante; oscilação, meneio / *vt*. fazer bruxulear ou tremular / *vi.* adejar; palpitar, tremular

flickering | fli'kəring | *a.* vacilante, bruxuleante

flier | flay'ə | *s.* aviador

flight | flayt' | *s.* vôo; fuga; lance de escada. **-to put to f.** afugentar. **-in the first f.** na vanguarda

flighty | flay'tī | *a.* leviano

flimsy | flim'zī | *s.* coisa ou material fino, frágil; papel de cópia, papel fino, documento escrito nesse papel / *a.* frágil, inconsistente; trivial; frívolo, superficial

flinch | flinš' | *vi.* recuar; hesitar, titubear, vacilar

fling | fling' | *vt.* arremessar, lançar; atirar ao chão. **-to f. open** abrir com violência. **-to f. away** jogar fora. **-to f. off** abandonar, renegar. **-to f. in one's teeth** lançar em rosto

flint | flint' | *s.* pederneira, sílex; pedra de isqueiro

flip | flip' | *s.* piparote; toque leve; sacudidela / *vt.* pôr em movimento com um piparote (moeda etc.) / *vi.* dar um piparote

flippancy | fli'pənsī | *s.* leviandade; petulância, insolência, irreverência

flippant | fli'pənt | *a.* impertinente, irreverente

flirt | flɛrt' | *s.* namorador, namoradeira / *vi.* flertar, coquetear; brincar com, namorar (idéia)

flirtation | flɛtey'śən | *s.* flerte, namorico

flit | flit' | *s.* mudança de domicílio (esp. para evitar credores) / *vi.* esvoaçar

float | flowt' | *s.* jangada; bóia (de pesca); flutuador / *vt.* fazer flutuar; desencalhar; lançar à água (navio); (com.) lançar no mercado; fundar (empresa) / *vi.* flutuar; pairar

floater | flow'tə | *s.* o que flutua; certificado oficial de compra de ações; eleitor que vota ilegal-

mente; pessoa que troca de emprego com freqüência

floating | flow'ting | *a.* flutuante

flock | flok' | *s.* rebanho; bando (de pássaros) / *vi.* congregarse, reunir-se; afluir, concorrer

floe | flow' | *s.* massa de gelo flutuante; banquisa

flog | flog' | *vt.* chicotear

flogging | flo'ging | *s.* fustigação, varadas

flood | flâd' | *s.* enchente, inundação. **-the F.** o Dilúvio / *vt.* inundar

floor | fló'ə | *s.* soalho, chão; andar, pavimento. **-to ask for the f.** pedir a palavra / *vt.* assoalhar; (coloq.) confundir, derrotar

flooring | fló'ring | *s.* pavimento, soalho; material para pavimentação

flop | flop' | *s.* baque; (gír.) fracasso, fiasco / *vi.* sacudir-se; bater as asas; baquear; mudar subitamente de atitude; (gír.) fracassar totalmente

florid | flo'rid | *a.* corado, rosado; ostentoso; floreado, ornado (estilo)

florin | flo'rin | *s.* florim; moeda de dois xelins (até 1971)

florist | flo'rist | *s.* florista

flotilla | fləti'lə | *s.* flotilha

flotsam | flot'səm | *s.* destroços flutuantes de naufrágio. **-f. and jetsam** (fig.) pessoas desocupadas e errantes, destroços humanos

flounce | flawns' | *s.* folho (de saia), babados / *vi.* **-to f. out** sair dando rabanadas, sair indignada

flounder | flawn'də | *s.* linguado / *vi.* debater-se

flour | flaw'ə | *s.* farinha

flourish | flâ'riś | *s.* floreado, floreio; arabesco / *vt.* florir; brandir, florear (espada etc.) / *vi.* florescer, vicejar; prosperar

flourishing | flâ'riśing | *a.* próspero, florescente

flout | flawt' | *vt.* escarnecer, zombar de

flow | flow' | *s.* fluxo, escoamento; curso d'água, torrente; maré enchente / *vt.* inundar, alagar / *vi.* fluir, correr; encher (maré); escorrer; deslizar. **-to f. into** desaguar em. **-to f. together** confluir. **-to f. with** abundar

flower | flaw'ə | *s.* flor. **-in f.** em flor / *vi.* florescer, florir, desabrochar; (fig.) prosperar

flower-bed | flaw'əbed | *s.* canteiro de flores

flowerpot | flaw'əpot | *s.* vaso de flores

flowery | flaw'ərī | *a.* florido

flowing | flow'ing | *a.* fluente, corrente; gracioso, harmonioso; contínuo, ininterrupto (linha, curva etc.)

flu | flv' | *s.* (coloq.) gripe

fluctuate | flâk'tǐueyt | *vi.* flutuar; oscilar

fluctuation | flâktǐuey'śən | *s.* flutuação; oscilação

flue | flv' | *s.* cano de chaminé; conduto de ar quente, tubo de caldeira

fluency | flv'ənsī | *s.* fluência, facilidade

fluent | flv'ənt | *a.* fluente, copioso; espontâneo

fluently | flv'əntlī | *adv.* fluentemente, correntemente

fluff | flâf' | *s.* cotão, lanugem; (gír.) fala que o ator não diz ou diz errado / *vt.* (gír.) estropiar (fala em teatro, TV etc.)

fluffy | flâ'fī | *a.* penugento, peludo, felpudo; fofo

fluid | flv'id | *s. a.* fluido

fluke | flvk' | *s.* linguado; farpa (de flecha ou arpão); (coloq.) sorte no jogo

flummox | flâ'məks | *vt.* (gír.) atrapalhar, desconcertar

flunkey, flunky | flân'kī | *s.* lacaio; adulador, bajulador

fluorescent | fluəre'sənt | *a.* fluorescente

flurry | flâ'rī | *s.* lufada, rajada (de vento); agitação

flush | flâś' | *s.* jorro, jato, descarga (de água); rubor, ruborização; entusiasmo, excitação / *a.* rente a, nivelado; transbordante / *vt.* lavar, dar descarga / *vi.* jorrar; corar, ruborizar

fluster | flâs'tə | *s.* confusão, agitação, atrapalhação / *vt.* confundir, perturbar, atrapalhar

flute | flvt' | *s.* flauta

flutter | flâ'tə | *s.* agitação; alvoroço / *vt.* alvoroçar, agitar, alarmar / *vi.* esvoaçar, adejar; tremular, ondear (bandeira)

flux | flâks' | *s.* fluxo; corrente, curso. **-in a state of f.** em contínua alteração, mudando freqüentemente / *vt.* fundir / *vi.* fluir

fly | flay' | *s.* mosca / *vt.* pilotar (avião); soltar (papagaio, pipa); hastear, desfraldar (bandeira) / *vi.* voar, fugir. **-to f. at** lançar-se sobre. **-to f. away** escapar-se. **-to f. off the handle** (coloq.) perder as estribeiras. **-to f. open** abrir-se subitamente

flyer, flier | flay'ə | *s.* voador, que voa; aviador

flying | flay'ing | *s.* o voar; vôo; aviação / *a.* voador, volante

flying bomb | flay'ingbom | *s.* bomba voadora

flying colours | flay'ingkâ'ləz | *spl.* bandeiras desfraldadas; (fig.) vitória. **-with f. c.** brilhantemente

flying fish | flay'ingfiś | *s.* peixe--voador

flying saucer | flay'ingsósə | *s.* disco voador

flywheel | flay'wil | *s.* (mec.) volante

fly-whisk | flay'wisk | *s.* enxota--moscas

foal | fowl' | *s.* potro

foam | fowm' | *s.* espuma / *vi.* espumar, fazer espuma

fob | fob' | *vt.* enganar, lograr.

-to f. off iludir, pregar uma peça

focalize, focalise | fowkəlayz' | vt. focalizar, enfocar

focus | fow'kəs | s. foco / vt. focalizar, concentrar / vi. ser focalizado

focussing, focusing | fow'kəsing | s. focalização

fodder | fo'də | s. forragem

foe | fow' | s. inimigo

foetus | fi'təs | s. feto

fog | fog' | s. nevoeiro denso

foggy | fo'gī | a. nevoento

fogy, fogey | fow'gī | s. pessoa antiquada, caturra

foible | foy'bəl | s. ponto fraco, fraqueza, defeito

foil | foyl' | s. folha delgada de metal; florete embolado; esgrima com florete

foist | foyst' | vt. impingir

fold | fowld' | s. dobra; curral, aprisco (de ovelhas) / vt. dobrar; cruzar (braços); juntar (mãos). -to f. away ou up tornar mais compacto, dobrando

-fold | fowld | suf. forma adjetivos e advérbios multiplicativos (twofold duas vezes mais; manyfold múltiplo, multiforme)

folder | fowl'də | s. pasta (para papéis); folheto

folding | fowl'ding | a. dobrável, dobradiço

foliage | fow'līij | s. folhagem, folhas

folk | fowk' | s. povo; gente, pessoas; (pl., coloq.) família, parentes

folk-dance | fowk'dʌns | s. dança popular tradicional

folklore | fowk'ló | s. folclore

folk-song | fowk'song | s. canção popular tradicional

folkways | fowk'weyz | s. comportamento tradicional de um povo

follow | fo'low | vt. seguir; acompanhar; suceder; compreender / vi. seguir-se, vir depois;

suceder; continuar; resultar; concluir-se. -it follows that segue-se que, portanto, logo

follower | fo'lowə | s. seguidor, partidário

following | fo'lowing | a. seguinte; próximò

folly | fo'lī | s. loucura; extravagância; tolice

foment | fowment' | vt. fomentar, estimular

fomentation | fowmentey'śən | s. fomento, fomentação

fomenter | fowmen'tə | s. fomentador; instigador

fond | fond' | a. extremoso; afetuoso. -to be f. of gostar de, ser amigo de

fondle | fon'dəl | vt. acariciar, afagar

fondness | fond'nes | s. carinho, afeição, afeto

font | font' | s. pia batismal

food | fʊd' | s. alimento, comida, comestíveis; víveres, mantimentos; sustento

fool | fʊl' | s. tolo, louco; bobo da corte. -to play the f. bufonear, bobear, brincar. -to make a f. of oneself fazer papel de tolo / vt. enganar, iludir / vi. bobear; brincar, gracejar

foolhardy | fʊlhʌ'dī | a. temerário, arriscado

foolish | fʊ'liś | a. louco, tolo, insensato; ridículo; absurdo

foolishness | fʊ'liśnes | s. loucura, insensatez, tolice, imprudência

foolscap | fʊlz'kap | s. gorro de bufão; carapuça de papel (castigo para alunos relapsos); papel almaço

foot | fut' | s. (pl. feet | fit' |) pé (tb. medida); pata; sopé de montanha. -on f. a pé. -to set on f. lançar, iniciar (empresa etc.). -to put one's f. down fazer finca-pé. -to carry someone off his feet empolgar, entusiasmar uma pessoa. -to keep one's feet manter-se em pé, não cair. **-to put one's f. in it** meter os pés pelas mãos

football | fut'ból | *s.* futebol; rúgbi, futebol americano; bola de futebol ou rúgbi

footballer | fut'bólə | *s.* jogador de futebol

foot-bridge | fut'briǰ | *s.* ponte para pedestres

foothold | fut'howld | *s.* apoio para os pés; posição segura

footing | fu'ting | *s.* passada; lugar onde apoiar o pé; (fig.) fundamento, base. **-on a war f.** em pé de guerra. **-on an equal f.** em pé de igualdade. **-to get a f.** tomar pé. **-to lose one's f.** perder pé; escorregar

foot-passenger | fut'pasinǰə | *s.* pedestre, transeunte

footprint | fut'print | *s.* pegada, pisada

foot-soldier | fut'sowlǰə | *s.* soldado de infantaria

footstep | fut'step | *s.* passo

footwear | fut'weə | *s.* sapatos, meias etc.

fop | fop' | *s.* janota, almofadinha, peralvilho

for | fó | *prep.* para; por. **-f. all that** apesar disso. **-f. good** para sempre. **-f. life** para toda a vida. **-as f.** enquanto a. **-f. the moment** por enquanto. **-I f. one** quanto a mim. **-but f. this** se não fosse isto. **-f. how long?** por quanto tempo? **-now f. it!** mãos à obra! **-f. all the world** exatamente, tal qual / *conj.* pois, porque, visto que

forage | fo'riǰ | *s.* forragem; pilhagem; / *vt. vi.* dar forragem a; saquear, pilhar

foray | fo'rey | *s.* pilhagem; incursão, correria

forbear | fóbe'ə | *vt. vi.* abster-se de, deixar de

forbearance | fóbe'ərəns | *s.* tolerância, indulgência

forbid | fəbid' | *vt.* proibir. **-God f.!** Deus nos livre!

forbidding | fəbi'ding | *a.* severo, ameaçador; proibitivo

force | fós' | *s.* força, vigor; violência; vigência (de lei); (mil.) força, tropa. **-by f. of** por meio de. **-the f.** a polícia / *vt.* forçar, obrigar, coagir; violar. **-to f. open** abrir à força. **-to f. out** fazer sair, expulsar, arrancar

forceful | fós'ful | *a.* vigoroso, poderoso; eficaz

forcibly | fó'siblī | *adv.* à força; energicamente, violentamente; eficazmente

ford | fód' | *s.* vau, passo / *vt.* vadear, passar a vau

fore | fó'ə | *s.* frente, parte dianteira; (náut.) proa. **-to the f.** à frente; conspícuo / *a.* dianteiro; (náut.) de proa / *adv.* à proa. **-f. and aft** (náut.) de popa à proa

forearm | fó'ʌm | *s.* antebraço

foreboding | fóbow'ding | *s.* pressentimento

forecast | fó'kʌst | *s.* previsão do tempo; prognóstico, opinião / *vt.* prever

forefathers | fó'fʌðəz | *spl.* antepassados

forefinger | fó'fing'gə | *s.* dedo indicador

forefront | fó'frânt | *s.* vanguarda, dianteira

forego | fógow' | *vt. vi.* preceder, adiantar-se a

foregoing | fógow'ing | *a.* precedente, anterior

foregone | fógon' | *a.* precedente, antecedente

foregone conclusion | fógon'-kənklʊ'jən | *s.* conclusão precipitada; resultado previsto

foreground | fó'grawnd | *s.* primeiro plano

forehead | fo'rid fó'hed | *s.* testa, fronte

foreign | fo'rin | *a.* estrangeiro; estranho, alheio

foreign body | fo'rinbodī | *s.* corpo estranho

foreigner | fo'rinə | *s.* estrangeiro

Foreign Office | forino'fis | *s.*

ministério das Relações Exteriores

foreign policy | fo'rinpo'lisĩ | s. política externa

foreman | fó'mən | s. capataz; chefe de seção

forementioned | fómen'śənd | a. acima mencionado

foremost | fó'mowst | a. primeiro / adv. em primeiro lugar. -first and f. primeiramente, antes de tudo

forenoon | fó'nʊn | s. manhã

forerunner | fó'rânə | s. precursor

foresee | fósı' | vt. prever, antever, prognosticar

foreshadow | fósá'dow | vt. prenunciar, prefigurar

foresight | fó'sayt | s. previsão; previdência; perspicácia

forest | fo'rist | s. floresta, mata; selva tropical

forestall | fóstól' | vt. prevenir, antecipar; frustrar

forester | fo'ristə | s. guarda--florestal; silvícola; animal da floresta

forestry | fo'ristrĩ | s. silvicultura

foretaste | fó'teyst | s. antegozo; prelibação

foretell | fótel' | vt. predizer

forethought | fó'ϑót | s. previsão, prudência

forewarn | fówón' | vt. prevenir, avisar, advertir

forewoman | fó'wəmən | s. contramestra; primeira jurada

foreword | fó'wεd | s. prefácio; preâmbulo

forfeit | fó'fit | s. multa; prenda (jogo); (pl.) jogo de prendas / a. confiscado / vt. prender, ser privado de

forfeiture | fó'fisə | s. confisco; penalidade

forge | fój' | s. forja / vt. forjar; falsificar, contrafazer / vi. trabalhar em forja. -to f. ahead avançar gradualmente, tomar a dianteira lentamente

forger | fó'jə | s. forjador, ferreiro; falsário

forgery | fó'jərĩ | s. falsificação; contrafação

forget | fəget' | vt. esquecer. -f. it! (coloq.) não pense mais nisto!

forgetful | fəget'ful | a. esquecido, descuidado

forgetfulness | fəget'fulnes | s. esquecimento; negligência, descuido

forget-me-not | fəget'minot | s. (bot.) miosótis

forgive | fəgiv' | vt. perdoar; desculpar; relevar

forgiveness | fəgiv'nes | s. esquecimento, descuido

forgiving | fəgi'ving | a. indulgente, complacente

fork | fók' | s. garfo; forcado; forquilha; bifurcação / vi. bifurcar-se

forlorn | fəlón' | a. desamparado, abandonado, solitário; desolado, triste, deprimido

forlorn hope | fəlón'howp | s. esperança vã; empresa arriscada

form | fóm' | s. forma, figura; modo, maneira; formalidade, cerimônia; formulário. -in due f. na devida forma, em regra. -in f. em forma, em boa forma; satisfatoriamente / vt. formar, constituir; modelar; organizar

formal | fó'məl | a. formal; cerimonioso; convencional

formality | fóma'litĩ | s. formalidade

formation | fómey'śən | s. formação

former | fó'mə | a. anterior, precedente; antigo, ex-. -in f. times outrora. -the f. o primeiro, aquele (em oposição a **the latter**)

formerly | fó'məlĩ | adv. antigamente, em outros tempos

formidable | fó'midəbəl | a. temível, tremendo, formidável

formula | fó'mĭulə | s. fórmula; receita; preceito

formulate | fó'm̃uleyt | vt. formular; manifestar; expor sistematicamente

forsake | fəseyk' | vt. abandonar, deixar

forswear | fóswe'ə | vt. abjurar, renunciar

fort | fót' | s. (mil.) fortaleza, forte

forte | fót' | s. ponto forte, forte

forth | fóθ' | adv. para diante, em diante. -and so f. e assim por diante

forthcoming | fóθkâ'ming | a. próximo, a chegar, por vir; à mão, acessível. -not very f. (coloq.) reservado, pouco comunicativo, frio

forthright | fóθ'rayt | a. franco, enérgico, decidido

forthwith | fóθwiθ' | adv. imediatamente, sem demora

fortification | fótifikey'śən | s. fortificação

fortify | fó'tifay | vt. fortificar, fortalecer

fortitude | fó'titĭud | s. fortaleza, força moral

fortnight | fót'nayt | s. quinzena, quinze dias

fortnightly | fót'naytlī | a. quinzenal / adv. quinzenalmente

fortress | fót'res | s. (mil.) fortaleza, forte

fortuitous | fótĭu'itəs | a. fortuito, casual, acidental

fortunate | fó'śənit | a. feliz, afortunado

fortune | fó'śən | s. fortuna; sorte, destino. -to tell someone's f. ler a sorte a alguém. -to try one's f. tentar a sorte

fortune-teller | fó'śənte'lə | s. adivinho, cartomante, quiromante

forty | fó'tī | s. a. quarenta

forum | fo'rəm | s. foro, fórum; (fig.) tribunal, foro

forward | fó'wəd | s. (desp.) dianteiro, atacante / a. dianteiro; disposto, ansioso; impertinente, atrevido; precoce; zeloso, ativo; exagerado, radical / adv. para a frente, para diante. -to bring f. trazer à baila. -to look f. to aguardar, antegozar / vt. enviar, remeter, mandar, expedir

forwarding | fó'wəding | s. remessa, expedição

forwards | fó'wədz | adv. para diante, para a frente

fossil | fo'sil | s. fóssil

foster | fos'tə | a. adotivo, de criação / vt. alimentar, nutrir; criar; acalentar; fomentar, favorecer

foster-brother | fos'təbrâðə | s. irmão de criação, irmão de leite

foster-child | fos'təśayld | s. filho adotivo

foster-parents | fos'təpeərents | spl. pais adotivos

foster-sister | fos'təsistə | s. irmã de criação, irmã de leite

foul | fawl' | s. falta, infração / a. sujo, imundo; fétido; viciado (ar); mau (tempo); (fig.) infame, abominável, obsceno / vt. sujar, emporcalhar; (náut.) abalroar

foul language | fawl'langwiĵ | s. linguagem obscena

foul play | fawl'pley | s. jogo sujo; trapaça; crime

found | fawnd' | vt. fundar

foundation | fawndey'śən | s. fundação; alicerce, fundamento; fundação (beneficência)

foundation stone | fawndey'śənstown | s. pedra fundamental

founder | fawn'də | s. fundador, instituidor; fundidor / vi. ir a pique, afundar-se

foundling | fawnd'ling | s. enjeitado, criança exposta

foundry | fawn'drī | s. fundição

fount | fawnt' | 's. fonte; (fig.) origem

fountain | fawn'tin | s. fonte; repuxo; bebedouro

fountain-pen | fawn'tinpen | s. caneta-tinteiro

four | fó'ə | *s. a.* quatro. **-on all fours** de gatinhas

foursome | fó'səm | *s.* grupo de quatro pessoas

four-square | fó'skweə | *a.* quadrado, quadrangular; firme, de base sólida; resoluto, firme, franco, honesto

fourteen | fó'tɪn | *s. a.* catorze, quatorze

fourth | fóϑ' | *s.* quarto; (mús.) quarta / *a.* quarto

fowl | fawl' | *s.* ave doméstica; galinha / *vt.* caçar aves

fox | foks' | *s.* raposa / *vt.* enganar, lograr

foxy | fok'sɪ | *a.* manhoso

foyer | fo;'ey | *s. foyer*, vestíbulo (de teatro etc.)

fracas | fra'kʌ | *s.* tumulto, balbúrdia, desordem; rixa

fraction | frak'sən | *s.* fração; fragmento, parte

fracture | frak'sə | *s.* fratura, fenda / *vt.* fraturar

fragile | fra'jayl | *a.* frágil

fragment | frag'mənt | *s.* fragmento

fragrance | frey'grəns | *s.* perfume, aroma, fragrância

fragrant | frey'grənt | *a.* fragrante, perfumado, aromático

frail | freyl' | *a.* frágil, delicado, quebradiço

frailty | freyl'tɪ | *s.* fragilidade; fraqueza

frame | freym' | *s.* moldura (de quadro); armação (de óculos); caixilho (de janela); arcabouço (de barco); constituição (do corpo humano ou de animal) / *vt.* emoldurar; colocar armação etc. **-to f. up** (gír.) maquinar, tramar, forjar acusação

frame of mind | freym'ov-maynd | *s.* disposição de ânimo

framework | freym'wɛk | *s.* armação, esqueleto, arcabouço, travejamento

franchise | fran'sayz | *s.* fran-

quia; imunidade, isenção; direito de voto

frank | frank' | *a.* franco, sincero / *vt.* franquear (carta)

frankly | frank'lɪ | *adv.* francamente, sinceramente

frankness | frank'nes | *s.* franqueza, sinceridade

frantic | fran'tik | *a.* frenético, furioso, desvairado

fraternize | fra'tənayz | *vi.* fraternizar(-se)

fraud | fród' | *s.* fraude, trapaça; (coloq.) impostor

fraudulent | fro'dÏulənt | *a.* fraudulento

fraught | frót' | *a.* carregado, cheio. **-f. with** cheio de

fray | frey' | *s.* rixa, conflito; combate; puimento / *vi.* puir (roupa)

frayed | freyd' | *a.* puído, desgastado; (fig.) irritado

freak | frɪk' | *s.* capricho, extravagância; aleijão, monstruosidade, aberração

freckle | fre'kəl | *s.* sarda

freckled | fre'kəld | *a.* sardento

free | frɪ' | *a.* livre; gratuito; voluntário; isento; público; liberal; espontâneo. **-to make f. with** tomar liberdades. **-to set f.** libertar / *adv.* livremente, gratuitamente / *vt.* libertar; desembaraçar; isentar; desimpedir, desobstruir

freedom | frɪ'dəm | *s.* liberdade; familiaridade; atrevimento; autonomia

freedom of speech | frɪ'dəmov-spɪš' | *s.* liberdade de expressão

freedom of the city | frɪ'dəmov-ðəsi'tɪ | *s.* direito de cidadania

freehold | frɪ'howld | *s.* (jur.) propriedade livre e alodial

free of charge | frɪ'ovšʌǰ | *a.* grátis

free will | frɪ'wil | *s.* livre-arbítrio

freeze | frɪz' | *vt.* gelar, congelar

freezer | frɪ'zə | *s.* congelador (de geladeira); frigorífico

freezing | frı'zing | s. congelamento / a. glacial

freezing point | frı'zingpoynt | s. ponto de congelamento

freight | freyt' | s. frete; fretamento; carga / vt. fretar; transportar; despachar (como mercadoria)

French | frenś' | s. a. francês. **-to take F. leave** sair sem se despedir, sair à francesa

French dressing | frenś'dresing | s. molho de azeite e vinagre

Frenchman | frenś'mən | s. francês (pessoa)

French vermouth | frenś-vE'mʋt | s. vermute seco

frenzied | fren'zĩd | a. frenético, enfurecido

frenzy | fren'zĩ | s. frenesi

frequency | frı'kwənsĩ | s. frequência

frequent | frı'kwənt | a. freqüente / vi. freqüentar

frequenter | frikwen'tə | s. freqüentador

fresh | freś' | a. fresco; novo, recente; (coloq.) atrevido, confiado

freshen | fre'śən | vt. refrescar / vi. refrescar-se

fresher | fre'śə | s. (gír.) = *freshman*

freshman | freś'mən | s. calouro, novato

freshness | freś'nes | s. frescura, frescor

freshwater | freś'wótə | a. de água doce

fret | fret' | s. aflição / vt. desgastar; atormentar / vi. afligir-se; gastar-se

fretful | fret'ful | a. aflito; impaciente, irritável, rabugento; agitado

fretsaw | fret'só | s. serra tico-tiço

friar | fray'ə | s. frade; frei (antes de prenome)

friction | frik'śən | s. fricção; atrito; desinteligência

Friday | fray'dey | s. sexta-feira

fried | frayd' | a. frito

friend | frend' | s. amigo. **-to make friends with** fazer amizade com; fazer as pazes com. **-to have a f. at court** ter amigo influente, ter pistolão

friendliness | frend'lines | s. amizade; benevolência

friendly | frend'lĩ | a. amigável, afável, cordial / adv. amigavelmente

friendship | frend'śip | s. amizade

frieze | frĩz' | s. (arquit.) friso

frigate | fri'git | s. fragata

fright | frayt' | s. medo; susto; terror; pavor; pessoa de aparência grotesca ou ridícula. **-to take f.** assustar-se. **-to give a f.** pregar um susto a, assustar / vt. (poét.) aterrorizar, apavorar, horrorizar

frighten | fray'tən | vt. assustar, amedrontar, meter medo a. **-to f. off** ou **away** afugentar / vi. assustar-se

frightened | fray'tend | a. assustado. **-to be f. at** assustar-se com

frightening | frayt'ning | a. horripilante, horrível, apavorante

frightful | frayt'ful | a. medonho, horroroso, terrível

frightfulness | frayt'fulnes | s. horror, pavor

frigid | fri'jid | a. frígido, frio; insensível, indiferente

frigidity | friji'ditĩ | s. frialdade, frigidez; indiferença, insensibilidade

frill | fril' | s. babado, folho; (coloq.) enfeite supérfluo. **-to put on frills** dar-se ares

fringe | frinj' | s. franja, orla, margem

fringe benefits | frinj'benifits | spl. suplemento de salário

frisk | frisk' | s. salto, cambalhota / vi. saltar, saltitar, cabriolar

frisky | fris'kĩ | a. alegre, vivo, brincalhão

fritter | fri'tə | *s.* filhó, massa recheada e frita / *vt.* fragmentar. **-to f. away** desperdiçar, gastar à toa

frivolity | frivo'litĩ | *s.* frivolidade, leviandade

frivolous | fri'vələs | *a.* frívolo, fútil

frizzy | fri'zĩ | *a.* frisado, encrespado, encaracolado

frock | frok' | *s.* vestido; batina (de padre), hábito (de monge)

frog | frog' | *s.* rã; (pej.) francês. **-to have a f. in one's throat** estar rouco

frogman | frog'mən | *s.* (mil.) homem-rã

frolic | fro'lik | *s.* brincadeira, travessura; divertimento / *vi.* brincar

from | from' | *prep.* de, da parte de (origem); desde (tempo); por (causa)

front | frânt' | *s.* frente; fachada; testa; aparência; ousadia. **-in f. of** em frente de / *vi.* fazer frente a

front door | frânt' dóə | *s.* porta principal

frontier | frânt'Iə | *s.* fronteira

frontispiece | frân'tispIs | *s.* frontispício, fachada

frost | frost' | *s.* geada

frost-bite | frost'bayt | *s.* inflamação ou gangrena causada pelo frio

frosted | fros'tid | *a.* congelado

frosted glass | fros'tidglAs | *s.* vidro fosco

frosty | fros'tĩ | *a.* gelado; coberto de geada; glacial

froth | froϑ' | *s.* espuma

frown | frawn' | *s.* carranca, cenho / *vi.* franzir o cenho

frugal | fru'gəl | *a.* frugal

frugality | frʊga'litĩ | *s.* frugalidade, sobriedade

fruit | frʊt' | *s.* fruta, fruto / *vi.* frutificar

fruit cup | frʊt'kâp | *s.* salada de frutas

fruitful | frʊt'ful | *a.* fértil, frutífero; (fig.) útil

fruitless | frʊt'les | *a.* estéril, infrutífero

fruit salts | frʊt'solts | *spl.* sais efervescentes

fruit-tree | frʊt'trī | *s.* árvore frutífera

fruity | frʊ'tī | *a.* que tem sabor ou aroma de fruta

frustrate | frâstreyt' | *vt.* frustrar, baldar, decepcionar

frustration | frâstrey'sən | *s.* frustração, decepção

fry | fray' | *s.* prole, filhotes / *vt.* fritar

frying-pan | fray'ingpan | *s.* frigideira. **-out of the f.-p. into the fire** de mal a pior

fuchsia | fʃu'śə | *s.* fúcsia, brinco-de-princesa

fuddled | fâ'dəld | *a.* bêbedo; intoxicado; aturdido

fuel | fʃu'əl | *s.* combustível

fugitive | fʃu'jitiv | *s.* fugitivo / *a.* fugidio, fugaz, efêmero, fugitivo

fulfil, fulfill | fulfil' | *vt.* preencher (condições etc.)

fulfilment | fulfil'mənt | *s.* cumprimento; preenchimento

full | ful' | *a.* cheio; completo; minucioso; farto, saciado. **-in f.** por extenso, integralmente. **-at f. blast** em pleno andamento. **-to the f.** completamente

full age | ful'eyỹ | *s.* maioridade

full dress | ful'dres | *s.* traje a rigor

full-length | ful'lengϑ | *a.* de tamanho natural

fullness, fulness | ful'nes | *s.* plenitude; amplitude

full stop | ful'stop | *s.* ponto, ponto final; cessação completa

full-time | ful'taym | *a.* de horário integral

fully | fu'lī | *adv.* completamente, totalmente

fulminate | ful'mineyt | *s.* fulminato / *vt. vi.* fulminar; trovejar; detonar

fulsome | ful'səm | *a.* enjoativo,

nojento, repugnante

fumble | fâm'bɔl | *vi.* remexer em, manejar desajeitadamente. -to f. for ou after procurar desordenadamente

fumigate | fĭu'migeyt | *vt.* fumigar, desinfetar

fun | fân' | *s.* graça; brincadeira; prazer, diversão. -for f. por brincadeira. -to make f. of zombar de. -to play for f. jogar de brincadeira. -like f. vigorosamente, rapidamente, abundantemente, muito

function | fânk'sən | *s.* função; exercício, uso; obrigação, ofício; festa, reunião / *vi.* funcionar

functioning | fânk'səning | *s.* funcionamento

fund | fând' | *s.* fundo

fundamental | fândəmen'təl | *a.* fundamental, essencial

funeral | fĭu'nərəl | *s.* funeral, enterro / *a.* fúnebre

funereal | fĭuni'rīəl | *a.* fúnebre, sombrio, funéreo

fungus | fun'gəs | *s.* fungo

funicular | fĭuni'kīulə | *a.* funículaɪ

funk | fânk' | *s.* medo, pânico. -in a blue f. apavorado / *vt.* (coloq.) esquivar-se a; ter medo de

funnel | fâ'nəl | *s.* funil; chaminé (de navio ou locomotiva); tubo de exaustor

funnily | fâ'nilī | *adv.* estranhamente. -f. enough bem estranhamente

funny | fâ'nī | *a.* engraçado, divertido; (coloq.) curioso, esquisito, estranho

funny business | fânĭbiz'nes | *s.* (coloq.) fraude, trapaça

fur | fɛ' | *s.* pele (de animal); pêlo; casaco de peles. -to make the f. fly (coloq.) puxar briga, provocar confusão

furious | fĭu'rĭəs | *a.* furioso, enfurecido

furl | fɛl' | *vt.* enrolar, dobrar;

(náut.) ferrar (vela)

furlong | fɛ'long | *s.* 1/8 de milha (201,164 m)

furlough | fɛ'low | *s.* licença (esp. mil.)

furnace | fɛ'nis | *s.* forno, fornalha (de máquina etc.)

furnish | fɛ'niš | *vt.* mobiliar; suprir, fornecer, dar, prover

furnished room | fɛ'nĭštrʋm | *s.* quarto mobiliado

furnishings | fɛ'nišings | *spl.* mobília, móveis

furniture | fɛ'nišə | *s.* mobília, móveis; equipamentos; acessórios

furore, furor | fĭuró'rī fĭu'rə | *s.* furor, sensação, entusiasmo popular

furrow | fâ'row | *s.* sulco, rego; esteira (de navio); ruga (na face)

further | fâ'ðə | *a.* mais longe, mais distante; ulterior, adicional. -until f. orders até nova ordem. -f. particulars mais pormenores. -f. to em aditamento a / *adv.* mais longe; ademais, além disso / *vt.* promover, incrementar

furtherance | fɛ'ðərəns | *s.* fomento, promoção, incremento, favorecimento

furthermore | fɛ'ðəmó | *adv.* além disso, ademais

furthermost | fɛ'ðəmowst | *a.* o' mais afastado, o mais distante ou remoto

furtive | fɛ'tiv | *a.* furtivo

fury | fĭu'rī | *s.* fúria; violência. -in a f. num acesso de raiva

furze | fɛz' | *s.* (bot.) tojo

fuse | fĭuz' | *s.* estopim; detonador; espoleta; (eletr.) fusível / *vt.* fundir, amalgamar / *vi.* derreter-se; amalgamar-se, fundir-se

fuselage | fĭu'zilʌj | *s.* fuselagem

fusillade | fĭuzileyd' | *s.* fuzilaria

fusion | fĭu'jən | *s.* fusão

fuss | fâs' | *s.* espalhafato, alvoroço; azáfama. -to make a f.

of ou **over** demonstrar excessiva afeição (ao encontrar alguém). **-to make a f.** fazer espalhafato

fussy | fâ'sī | *a.* meticuloso, exagerado; espalhafatoso; complicado, difícil

fustian | fâs'tīən | *s.* fustão; (fig.) linguagem empolada / *a.* de fustão; (fig.) bombástico, empolado

futile | fīu'tayl | *a.* fútil, inútil, frívolo, vão; infrutífero, improfícuo

futility | fīuti'litī | *s.* futilidade, frivolidade

future | fīu'sə | *s.* futuro / *a.* futuro, vindouro

fuzzy | fâ'zī | *a.* felpudo, penugento; puído, esfiapado; encrespado, frisado; indistinto, vago; aturdido, confuso

G

G, g | ǰi' | *s.* g; (maiúsc., mús.) sol

gab | gab' | *s.* (coloq.) tagarelice. **-the gift of the g.** o dom da palavra, loquacidade. **-stop your g.!** cale a boca!

gabardine | ga'bədın | *s.* gabardina (tecido)

gabble | ga'bəl | *s.* tagarelice, lenga-lenga; mexerico / *vi.* tagarelar, palrar; mexericar

gable | gey'bəl | *s.* (arquit.) empena

gabled roof | gey'bəldrʋf | *s.* (arquit.) teto de duas águas

gad | gad' | *vi.* vaguear, errar

gadfly | gad'flay | *s.* mutuca

gadget | ga'ǰit | *s.* dispositivo, aparelho, engenhoca

gaff | gaf' | *s.* bicheiro (vara ou bastão com anzol ou gancho na ponta)

gag | gag' | *s.* mordaça; piada, brincadeira; (teat.) enxerto, caco / *vt.* amordaçar

gaiety | gey'ətī | *s.* alegria, vivacidade, jovialidade

gain | geyn' | *s.* ganho, lucro, proveito; vantagem; progresso / *vt.* ganhar, obter, conseguir; lucrar / *vi.* ganhar; progredir; adiantar-se (relógio). **-to g. on** ou **upon** ganhar caminho, avançar, aproximar-se de

gainful | geyn'ful | *a.* vantajoso, proveitoso

gainsay | geyn'sey | *vt.* contradizer, contestar

gait | geyt' | *s.* modo de andar

gaiter | gey'tə | *s.* polaina

gala | gʌ'lə | *s.* gala, festa

galaxy | ga'ləksī | *s.* galáxia; plêiade (de pessoas talentosas, ilustres etc.)

gale | geyl' | *s.* vendaval

Galician | gəli'sən | *s.a.* galego (na Espanha); galiciano (na Polônia)

gall | gól' | *s.* bílis; (fig.) fel; amargura / *vt.* atormentar, irritar, afligir

gallant | ga'lənt | *a.* intrépido, bravo; cortês

gallantry | ga'ləntrī | *s.* bravura, coragem, valentia; cortesia

gallery | ga'lərī | *s.* galeria (tb. de arte); passagem, corredor. **-to play to the g.** cortejar pessoas de gosto pouco refinado

galley | ga'lī | *s.* galé; cozinha (de navio)

galley proof | ga'līprʋf | *s.* (impr.) prova de paquê, prova de granel

galley-slave | ga'līsleyv | s. galeriano, sentenciado

galling | gó'ling | a. irritante, exasperante

gallivant | galivant' | vi. vadiar, vagabundear

gallon | ga'lən | s. galão (medida de capacidade para líquidos)

galloon | gəlʊn' | s. galão (tira de tecido bordado)

gallop | ga'ləp | vi. galopar. **-at full g.** a toda a brida

gallows | ga'lowz | s. forca

galore | gəló' | adv. em abundância, em quantidade

galosh | gəloš' | s. galocha

galvanize | gal'vənayz | vt. galvanizar

gambit | gam'bit | s. gambito (lance de xadrez); (fig.) artimanha, ardil

gamble | gam'bəl | vi. jogar; arriscar. **-to g. away** perder no jogo (dinheiro)

gambler | gam'blə | s. jogador

gambling | gam'bling | s. jogo

gambol | gam'bəl | vi. cabriolar, saltar; brincar

game | geym' | s. jogo; brinquedo, passatempo; plano, estratagema; caça (animais). **-big g.** caça grossa. **-to give the g. away** revelar um segredo. **-to make g. of** ridicularizar / a. corajoso, valente; (coloq.) aleijado; (coloq.) pronto para qualquer eventualidade

game of chance | geym'ovšans | s. jogo de azar

gamut | ga'mət | s. (mús.) gama escala (tb. fig.)

gander | gan'də | s. ganso

gang | gang' | s. quadrilha, bando; turma (de trabalhadores); corja, súcia, malta

gangrene | gang'grīn | s. gangrena

gangster | gang'stə | s. gângster, bandido, pistoleiro

gangsterism | gang'stərizəm | s. gangsterismo, banditismo

gangway | gang'wey | s. passagem, coxia; (náut.) passadiço; prancha de desembarque; galeria (de mina)

gaol | jeyl' | s. prisão / vt. condenar à prisão

gap | gap' | s. abertura, fenda; intervalo; lacuna; desfiladeiro, ravina, passo

gape | geyp' | s. bocejo; boca aberta (estupefação, pasmo) / vi. ficar boquiaberto

gaping | gey'ping | a. aberto, escancarado; boquiaberto

garage | ga'rAj | s. garagem

garb | gAb' | s. vestimenta; roupagem / vi. vestir(-se) (com traje característico)

garbage | gA'biǰ | s. lixo

garble | gA'bəl | vt. adulterar, deturpar, mutilar

garden | gA'dən | s. jardim / vi. jardinar

garden bed | gAdən' bed | s. canteiro

gardener | gAd'nə | s. jardineiro; hortelão

gardening | gAd'ning | s. jardinagem; horticultura

garden party | gA'dənpAtī | s. recepção em parque ou jardim, garden party

gargle | gA'gəl | s. gargarejo / vi. gargarejar

gargoyle | gA'goyl | s. (arquit.) gárgula

garish | ge'əriš | a. brilhante, vistoso; berrante (cor); ostentoso

garland | gA'lənd | s. grinalda, coroa. **-to win the g.** levar a palma / vt. engrinaldar, coroar, enfeitar

garlic | gA'lik | s. alho

garment | gA'mənt | s. peça de roupa; (pl.) roupas

garnish | gA'niš | vt. guarnecer; adornar, enfeitar

garret | ga'rit | s. sótão

garrison | ga'risən | s. (mil.) guarnição / vt. (mil.) guarnecer

garrulous | ga'rĭuləs | a. tagarela, loquaz, palrador

garrulousness | ga'rĭuləsnes | s.

garrulice, loquacidade

garter | gᴀ'tə |s. liga (que segura a meia). -the G. insígnia da Ordem da Jarreteira

gas | gas' | s. gás; (coloq., EUA) gasolina

gash | gaś' |s. corte, talho; cutilada / vt. cortar

gasket | gas'kit | s. gaxeta, junta de vedação

gas mask | gas'mᴀsk |s. máscara contra gases

gas meter | gas'mitə | s. medidor de gás

gasoline | ga'sowlin |s. gasolina

gasp | gᴀsp' | s. suspiro; arfada; grito sufocado

gasping | gᴀs'ping | a. arquejante, ofegante

gas station | gas'steysən | s. (EUA) posto de gasolina

gastritis | gastray'tis | s. gastrite

gasworks | gas'wᴇks | s. fábrica de gás, gasômetro

gate | geyt' | s. portão; porta (de cidade, fortaleza etc.); (ferrov.) cancela, barreira; total de espectadores, público (em jogo esportivo)

gatecrasher | geyt'kraśə |s. intruso, penetra

gatekeeper | geyt'kipə |s. porteiro; guarda-cancela

gateway | geyt'wey | s. porta de entrada; portal

gather | ga'ðə | vt. reunir; colher; juntar; acumular; coligir; colecionar; deduzir, concluir. -to g. in armazenar. -to g. up apanhar; arregaçar (mangas etc.). -to g. strength tomar forças, recuperar-se

gathering | ga'ðəring |s. colheita; vindima; reunião, assembléia; aglomeração (de pessoas); abscesso; (cost.) franzido, prega

gauche | gowś' | a. desajeitado, canhestro; tímido

gaudy | gó'dī | a. berrante, vistoso, espalhafatoso

gauge | geyj' | s. padrão, medida; calibre; bitola; medidor, indi-

cador / vt. medir, aferir; calibrar; estimar, avaliar, calcular

gaunt | gónt' | a. macilento, descarnado; lúgubre

gauntlet | gónt'lit | s. manopla; luva comprida (de punho largo). -to take up the g. aceitar desafio. -to run the g. sofrer castigo; expor-se (a críticas etc.)

gauze | góz' | s. gaze

gawky | gó'kī |a. tímido, acanhado, desajeitado

gay | gey' | a. alegre, festivo; jovial, folgazão; vistoso, brilhante; dissoluto, imoral; (gír.) homossexual

gaze | geyz' |s. olhar / vi. olhar fixamente, contemplar

gazette | gəzet' |s. gazeta, diário, jornal

gazetteer | gaziti'ə |s. dicionário geográfico

gear | gi'ə |s. engrenagem; mecanismo; equipamento, acessórios, apetrechos; marcha, velocidade. -in g. engrenado. -out of g. desengrenado. -first (second, third) g. primeira (segunda, terceira) marcha / vt. engrenar; equipar; preparar

gearbox | gi'əboks | s. caixa de mudança; caixa de engrenagens

gearwheel | gi'əwil | s. (mec.) roda de transmissão

gelding | gel'ding | s. animal castrado (esp. cavalo)

gelignite | je'lignayt | s. gelignite (explosivo)

gem | jem' | s. gema, jóia

gender | jen'də | s. (gram.) gênero; (coloq.) sexo

genealogy | jinia'ləjī |s. genealogia, linhagem

general | je'nərəl | s. general; geral (dos jesuítas etc.). -in g. em geral / a. geral, comum, corrente. -to become g. generalizar-se

generalization | jenərəlayzey'śən | s. generalização

generally | je'nərəlī | adv. geralmente, em geral

general practitioner | ˇĕnərəl·
prakti'śənə | s. clínico geral

generalship | ˇĕ'nərəlśip | s. gene-
ralato; habilidade militar (como general)

generate | ˇĕ'nəreyt | vt. gerar,
produzir; originar

generation | ˇĕnərey'śən | s. ge-
ração; procriação; produção,
criação

generosity | ˇĕnəro'sitī | s.
generosidade, liberalidade

generous | ˇĕ'nərəs | a. generoso,
liberal; abundante

genesis | ˇĕ'nisis | s. gênese (tb.
maiúsc.)

genial | ˇjI'nĭəl | a. cordial, jovial,
afável, simpático; ameno, agradável (clima)

genius | ˇjI'nĭəs | s. gênio

Genoese | ˇĕnowIz' | s.a. genovês

genre | jonr' | s. gênero, estilo

genteel | ˇĕntil' | a. gentil, cortês,
polido, requintado

gentile | ˇĕn'tayl | s.a. não judeu
(pessoa), cristão (tb. maiúsc.);
gentio

gentility | ˇĕnti'litī | s. nobreza, fi-
dalguia; polidez, cortesia

gentle | ˇĕn'təl | a. suave, dócil,
meigo; nobre, aristocrático;
tranqüilo; propício (tempo); le-
ve (pancada, golpe, vento etc.)

gentleman | ˇĕn'təlmən | s. cava-
lheiro, senhor

gentlemanly | ˇĕn'təlmənlī | a. ca-
valheiresco; generoso; honra-
do, cortês; nobre

gentleness | ˇĕn'təlnes | s. bran-
dura, mansidão, delicadeza;
cortesia; bondade

gently | ˇĕnt'lī | adv. delicada-
mente, suavemente; bondosa-
mente, meigamente

gentry | ˇĕn'trī | s. gente de boa fa-
mília, gente de qualidade; no-
breza menor

genuflect | ˇĕ'nĭuflekt | vi. dobrar
o joelho, ajoelhar(-se)

genuine | ˇĕ'nĭuin | a. genuíno,
autêntico, legítimo; típico; sincero (pessoa)

genuineness | ˇĕ'nĭuinnes | s. au-
tenticidade; sinceridade

geography | ˇjo'grəfī | s. geografia

geology | ˇjo'ləˇjī | s. geologia

geometry | ˇjo'mətrī | s. geo-
metria

geranium | ˇjərey'nĭəm | s. gerâ-
nio

germ | ˇĕm' | s. germe, micróbio,
bacilo; embrião

German | ˇĕ'mən | s.a. alemão

germane | ˇĕmeyn' | a. adequa-
do, apropriado, pertinente

German measles | ˇĕ'mən-
mIz'əlz | s. (med.) rubéola

germicide | ˇĕmisayd' | s. germi-
cida

germinate | ˇĕ'mineyt | vi. germi-
nar, brotar

gerrymander | ˇĕ'rimandə | vt.
manipular (eleições)

gesticulate | ˇĕsti'kĭuleyt | vi. ges-
ticular

gesticulation | ˇĕstikĭuley'śən | s.
gesticulação

gesture | ˇĕs'śə | s. gesto, aceno,
sinal, trejeito

get | get' | vt. conseguir, obter;
apanhar, pegar; ir buscar; chegar; ganhar, receber; comprar;
preparar, fazer. **-to g. across**
atravessar; (coloq.) explicar.
-to g. back recuperar, reaver.
-to get it (coloq.) entender. **-to
g. in touch with** entrar em con-
tato com. **-to have got to** ter de /
vi. chegar; ir; vir; ficar; tornar-
se, fazer-se. **-to g. about** circular. **-to g. along** andar; ser bem-
-sucedido; passar, ir, viver. **-to
g. along (well, badly) with** dar-
se (bem, mal) com. **-to g. angry
(old, sick)** ficar zangado (velho,
doente). **-to g. back** voltar. **-to
g. off** descer, saltar. **-to g. ready**
preparar-se. **-to g. rid of** livrar-se de

getaway | ge'təwey | s. fuga

get-together | gettəge'ðə | s. (co-
loq.) reunião informal

geyser | gı'zə | s. gêiser

ghastly | gʌst'lī | a. horrível, assustador; (coloq.) lívido, cadavérico; (coloq.) forçado (sorriso)

gherkin | gə'kin | s. pepininho (usado em picles)

ghost | gowst' | s. fantasma. **-not a g. of a doubt** sem sombra de dúvida. **-to give up the g.** morrer; (fig.) perder a esperança

ghoul | gawl' gul' | s. espírito maléfico, vampiro

giant | jay'ənt | s. gigante

gibberish | gi'bəriś | s. algaravia, palavreado sem sentido

gibbet | ji'bit | s. forca

gibe | jayb' | s. zombaria, chacota, escárnio / vi. zombar de, mofar de

giblets | jib'lits | s. miúdos de ave

giddiness | gi'dines | s. vertigem, tonteira

giddy | gi'dī | a. tonto, atordoado. **-to feel g.** ter vertigens. **-to play the g. goat** fazer papel de tolo

gift | gift' | s. presente, dádiva; dom, talento; ato de dar, doação. **-I would not have it at a g.** não quero nem de graça

gift of the gab | gift'ovðəgab | s. dom da palavra; lábia

gift-wrap | gift'rap | s. embrulho de presente / vt. embrulhar para presente

gig | gig' | s. cabriolé; escaler, baleeira (esp. de regata); anzóis montados em conjunto (para pescar garateando); espantalho, monstrengo, coisa estranha ou grotesca

gigantic | jaygan'tik | a. gigantesco, enorme, imenso

giggle | gi'gəl | s. risadinha, riso espremido, riso alvar / vi. rir(-se)

gild | gild' | vt. dourar

gill | gil' | s. guelra, brânquia (ger. pl.); (pl.) barbela das aves / vt. estripar, limpar (peixe); levantar segurando pelas guelras

gilt | gilt' | s. douradura / a. dourado

gilt-edged | gilt'eĵid | a. de corte dourado (livro); (fig.) excelente

gilt securities | giltsikĭu'ritiz | spl. títulos ou ações de inteira confiança

gilt stocks | gilt'stokz | spl. = gilt securities

gin | jin | s. gim, genebra

ginger | jin'jə | s. gengibre; amarelo arruivado pálido (cor)

gingerly | jin'jəli | adv. cuidadosamente, cautelosamente, pouco a pouco

gipsy | jip'si | s. cigano

giraffe | jiraf' | s. girafa

gird | gɛd' | vt. cingir, pôr a cintura. **-to g. oneself (up) one's loins** preparar-se para a ação

girder | gɛ'də | s. viga, trave, barrote

girdle | gɛ'dəl | s. cinto, cinturão; cinta; faixa / vt. cintar; cingir; rodear

girl | gɛl' | s. menina, moça; filha; namorada; empregada (em loja etc.)

girl-friend | gɛl'frend | s. namorada

girth | gɛθ' | s. cilha; perímetro, circunferência

gist | jist' | s. essência, substância, ponto principal, ponto essencial

give | giv' | s. elasticidade, flexibilidade / vt. dar; conceder; entregar; dedicar; oferecer; legar. **-to g. away** dar; desfazer-se de; revelar. **-to g. back** devolver. **-to g. ground** retirar-se; recuar. **-to g. off** emitir, desprender (vapores). **-to g. oneself away** trair-se. **-to g. oneself up** entregar-se. **-to g. rise to** ocasionar. **-to g. up** desistir. **-to g. up the ghost** morrer, expirar; (fig.) perder a esperança. **-to g. the lie to** desmentir. **-to g. way** recuar; ceder; transigir

given | gi'vən | a. dado, presenteado; inclinado; (mat.) conhecido; (mat.) suposto. **-g. that**

supondo que. **-g. to** dado a, propenso a

given name | gi'vənneym | *s.* (EUA) nome de batismo

gizzard | gi'zəd | *s.* moela (de ave). **-to stick in one's g.** ficar atravessado na garganta, ser desagradável

glacier | gla'sīə | *s.* glaciar, geleira

glad | glad' | *a.* alegre, contente, satisfeito. **-to be g.** to ter prazer em

gladden | gla'dən | *vt.* alegrar

glade | gleyd' | *s.* clareira

gladness | glad'nes | *s.* alegria, satisfação

glamour, glamor | gla'mə | *s.* magia, encanto, feitiço

glamour girl | gla'məgɛl | *s.* jovem encantadora

glance | glᴀns' | *s.* olhadela, relance. **-at a g.** num relance. **-at first g.** à primeira vista / *vt.* **-to g. at** olhar de relance, dar uma olhadela, passar os olhos / *vi.* roçar, resvalar, desviar-se. **-to g. off** resvalar

glancing | glᴀn'sing | *a.* de relance; de raspão

gland | gland' | *s.* glândula

glare | gle'ə | *s.* clarão deslumbrante, brilho ofuscante / *vi.* lançar olhares penetrantes ou furiosos, olhar com raiva

glaring | gle'əring | *a.* ofuscante, fulgurante; (fig.) manifesto, óbvio

glass | glᴀs' | *s.* vidro; copo; (*pl.*) óculos, óculo de alcance, binóculo

glass case | glᴀs'keys | *s.* redoma de vidro, vitrine

glass-cutter | glᴀs'kâtə | *s.* diamante de vidraceiro; cortador de vidro, lapidador (operário)

glasshouse | glᴀs'haws | *s.* vidraria; estufa (de plantas); (gír.) prisão militar

glassware | glᴀs'weə | *s.* artigos de vidro

glaze | gleyz' | *vt.* vidrar; esmaltar; lustrar

glazier | gley'zīə | *s.* vidraceiro

gleam | glīm' | *s.* raio de luz; clarão; brilho / *vt.* brilhar, fulgurar

glean | glīn' | *vt.* rebuscar, catar; (fig.) compilar

glee | glī' | *s.* (mús.) composição para três vozes masculinas; alegria, júbilo

glen | glen' | *s.* vale estreito

glib | glib' | *a.* loquaz, corrente, fluente; volúvel

glibness | glib'nes | *s.* fluência, facilidade

glide | glayd' | *vi.* planar, deslizar; escorregar

glider | glay'də | *s.* (aer.) planador, avião sem motor

glimmer | gli'mə | *s.* vislumbre; luz frouxa e trêmula / *vi.* bruxulear

glimpse | glimps' | *s.* vislumbre / *vt.* vislumbrar, entrever / *vi.* bruxulear

glint | glint' | *s.* clarão, brilho / *vi.* cintilar, reluzir, faiscar

glisten | gli'sən | *vi.* cintilar, brilhar, faiscar

glitter | gli'tə | *s.* brilho, fulgor / *vi.* brilhar, cintilar, resplandecer

glittering | gli'təring | *a.* brilhante, resplandecente

gloat | glowt' | *vi.* contemplar com maldade, volúpia ou cobiça; exultar com o mal alheio

globe | glowb' | *s.* globo; mundo, globo terrestre

gloom | glᴜm' | *s.* escuridão; melancolia, tristeza

gloomy | glᴜ'mī | *a.* sombrio, lúgubre; triste, melancólico; desalentador

glorification | glórifikey'sən | *s.* glorificação

glorious | gló'rīəs | *a.* glorioso; magnífico, soberbo

glory | gló'rī | *s.* glória; brilho, esplendor, magnificência. **-to go to g.** (gír.) morrer / *vi.* gloriar-se em, jactar-se de

gloss| glos' |*s.* verniz, brilho; comentário, glosa

glossary| glo'sərī |*s.* glossário

glossy| glo'sī |*a.* lustroso

glove | glâv' | *s.* luva. **-to treat with kid gloves** tratar com luvas de pelica

glove compartment | glâvkəmpʌt'mənt |*s.* porta-luvas

glove money | glâv'mânī |*s.* gorjeta

glow| glow' |*s.* fulgor, brilho; ardor, entusiasmo / *vi.* incandescer-se; reluzir, brilhar; animar-se

glower | glow'ə | *vi.* olhar de modo ameaçador

glowing| glow'ing |*a.* resplandecente, brilhante; afogueado; apaixonado

glow-worm| glow'wεm |*s.* vaga-lume, pirilampo

glue | glu' | *s.* cola / *vt.* colar, grudar

glum | glâm' |*a.* taciturno, deprimido; mal-humorado

glut | glât' | *s.* superabundância, excesso, superprodução / *vt.* saciar, saturar

glutinous | glu'tinəs | *a.* glutinoso, pegajoso

glutton| glâ'tən |*s.* glutão, comilão; (zool.) glutão, carcaju

gluttonous | glâ'tənəs |*a.* glutão, guloso, devorádor

gluttony | glâ'tənī |*s.* gula

glycerine | gli'sərin |*s.* glicerina

gnarl | nʌl' |*s.* nó (de madeira ou tronco de árvore) / *vt.* torcer, retorcer / *vi.* formar nós (madeira); rosnar

gnarled, gnarly | nʌld' nʌ'lī | *a.* nodoso; retorcido

gnash| naś' |*vt.* ranger, rilhar (os dentes)

gnat | nat' |*s.* mosquito

gnaw | nó' |*vt.* roer

gnawing| nó'ing |*a.* roedor, que rói; (fig.) torturante

gnome | nowm' |*s.* gnomo

go | gow⁻ |*s.* ida; sucesso, êxito; vitalidade, energia, animação.

-all the g. (coloq.) na moda. **-it's a g.!** (coloq.) combinado!, feito! **-it's no g.** (coloq.) é impossível. **-always on the g.** sempre ativo. **-to have a g.** experimentar a sorte, tentar fazer / *vi.* ir; avançar; funcionar, andar; fazer-se, tornar-se. **-to g. across** atravessar, cruzar. **-to g. after** seguir. **-to g. against** ser contrária a. **-to g. ahead** continuar, ir adiante. **-to g. away** ir-se embora. **-to g. back** voltar. **-to g. backward** retroceder, ir para trás. **-to g. by** passar (por); passar por perto de; passar despercebido; ser conhecido pelo nome de. **-to g. down** descer, baixar; pôr-se (sol). **-to g. for** ir buscar. **-to g. in** entrar. **-to g. in for** (coloq.) interessar-se por, tomar parte em. **-to g. off** sair; ir-se embora; disparar, explodir. **-to g. on** continuar, seguir; acontecer. **-to g. out** sair; apagar-se. **-to g. over** passar pôr cima de; revisar; refazer; atravessar; passar (a outro lado, partido etc.). **-to g. up** subir. **-to g. up with** acompanhar; harmonizar-se com. **-to g. without** passar sem. **-to let g.** largar; soltar; desistir; abandonar

goad | gowd' | *s.* aguilhão; aguilhada; (fig.) sofrimento; (fig.) estímulo

go-ahead | gow'əhed | *a.* enérgico, empreendedor

goal| gowl' |*s.* objetivo, fim, meta; (desp.) gol, tento; gol, arco (futb. etc.)

goat| gowt' |*s.* cabra; (gír.) bode expiatório. **-to get someone's g.** irritar alguém, enfurecer alguém

goatee| gowtī' |*s.* cavanhaque

gobble | go'bəl | *vt.* engolir; devorar, tragar / *vi.* grugulejar (voz do peru)

go-between | gow'bitwin | *s.* alcoviteiro; intermediário

goblin| gob'lin |*s.* duende

god| god' |s. deus, divindade (tb. maiúsc.). -G. forbid Deus me (te, nos etc.) livre. -the gods (teat.) público das galerias

godchild | god'šayld | s. afilhado, afilhada

god-daughter | god'dótə | s. afilhada

goddess | go'des | s. deusa

godfather | god'fʌðə | s. padrinho (de batismo)

god-fearing | god'fɪəring | a. temente a Deus

god-forsaken | god'fəseykən | a. abandonado, solitário; triste; deserto; miserável

godless | god'les | a. ateu; ímpio; perverso, desalmado

godliness| god'lines |s. devoção, piedade

godly | god'lī | a. devoto, piedoso, religioso

godmother | god'mâðə | s. madrinha

godparents | god'peərənts | spl. padrinhos

God's acre | godz'eykə | s. cemitério

godsend | god'send | s. mercê divina, dádiva de Deus; acaso ou acontecimento feliz

godson | god'sân | s. afilhado

Godspeed | godspíd' | s. voto de feliz viagem. -G. you! feliz viagem!

goggle | go'gəl | s. revirar de olhos; (pl.) óculos de proteção (de operário, aviador, nadador etc.) / vi. arregalar os olhos

going | gow'ing | s. ida, partida; modo de andar (dirigir etc.); condições da estrada (pista etc.). -while the g. is good enquanto as condições são favoráveis / a. que vai etc.; existente, disponível; em atividade. -a g. concern um negócio (empresa) florescente

goitre, goiter | goy'tə | s. bócio, papeira

gold| gowld' |s. ouro / a. de ouro

gold-bearing | gowld'beəring | a. aurífero

golden | gowld'ən | a. dourado, de ouro; precioso; favorável, propício

gold-field| gowld'fɪld |s. terreno aurífero

goldfish | gowld'fiś | s. peixe dourado (de aquário)

gold-mine | gowld'mayn | s. mina de ouro (tb. fig.)

gold-smith | gowld'smið | s. ourives

golf| golf' |s. golfe

golfer | gol'fə | s. golfista

golf-links | golf'links | s. campo de golfe

golliwog | go'liwog |s. boneco de trapos (imitando um negrinho)

gong| gong' |s. gongo

good | gud' | s. bem; proveito, vantagem; (pl.) mercadorias; (pl.) bens, haveres; (pl.) fazendas, tecidos. -for g. para sempre. -to be up to no g. estar com más intenções. -to come to no g. acabar mal / a. bom. -that's a g. one! boa piada!, essa é boa! -a g. way uma boa distância. -in g. time em tempo, oportunamente. -g. and late bem tarde, muito tarde. -to be g. for servir para; ter crédito até. -it is no g. não vale a pena, não adianta. -as g. as done quase pronto. -to have a g. mind to estar disposto a. -to be g. at ser bom em. -to hold g. ser verdadeiro, vigorar. -to make g. ser bem-sucedido; confirmar; indenizar, compensar / adv. bem

good afternoon| gudaf'tənvn |s. boa-tarde

good breeding | gudbrɪ'ding | s. boas maneiras

good-bye | gudbay' | s. interj. adeus. -to say g. despedir-se, dizer adeus

good evening | gudiv'ning | s. boa-noite (na chegada)

good form| gud'fóm |s. = good breeding

good-for-nothing | gudfónâ'-ðing |*s.* vadio, vagabundo / *a.* que não presta para nada, imprestável (pessoa)

Good Friday | gudfray'dey | *s.* sexta-feira da Paixão

good-looking | gud'luking | *a.* bonito, bem-parecido

goodness | gud'nes | *s.* bondade; benevolência; virtude, mérito; excelência. -to have the g. ter a gentileza de / *interj.* valha-me Deus! -for g. sake! pelo amor de Deus! -I wish to g. Deus queira!, Oxalá!

good night | gudnayt' | *s.* boa-noite (na despedida, na hora de dormir)

goods and chattels | gudz'andšAtəlz | *spl.* bens e haveres

good-tempered | gudtem'pəd | *a.* bem-disposto

goose | gʊs' | *s.* ganso

gooseberry | gʊz'bərī | *s.* groselha (fruto)

goose-flesh | gʊs'fleš | *s.* pele arrepiada (pelo frio, medo etc.)

gore | gó'ə | *s.* sangue coagulado / *vt.* escornar, ferir com os chifres

gorge | gój' | *s.* desfiladeiro, garganta / *vt.* engolir, tragar; empanturrar / *vi.* comer vorazmente; empanturrar-se, fartar-se

gorgeous | gó'jəs | *a.* magnífico, esplêndido, suntuoso

gorilla | gəri'lə | *s.* gorila

gorse | gós' | *s.* (bot.) tojo

gospel | gos'pəl | *s.* evangelho (tb. maiúsc.)

gossamer | go'səmə | *s.* teia de aranha flutuante; fio de teia de aranha; tecido diáfano / *a.* diáfano, transparente

gossip | go'sip | *s.* mexerico, tagarelice, bisbilhotice / *a.* mexeriqueiro, tagarela, bisbilhoteiro / *vi.* mexericar, tagarelar, bisbilhotar

gossip column | go'sipkəlum | *s.* crônica social (em jornal)

Gothic | go'ðik | *a.* gótico

gouge | gawj' | *s.* goiva; (coloq.)

trapaça / *vt.* goivar; arrancar (olho); (coloq.) trapacear

gourd | gu'əd | *s.* cabaça

gourmet | gu'əmey | *s.* gastrônomo

gout | gawt' | *s.* (med.) gota

govern | gâ'vən | *vt.* governar

governess | gâ'vənes | *s.* governanta, preceptora

governing | gâ'vəning | *a.* governante (classe)

governing body | gâ'vəningbodī | *s.* direção (de hospital etc.)

government | gâ'vənmənt | *s.* governo; direção

governor | gâ'vənə | *s.* governador; diretor (de empresa etc.); (mil.) comandante (de forte etc.); (gír.) empregador; pai

governorship | gâ'vənəšip | *s.* governo (cargo e mandato)

gown | gawn' | *s.* vestido; roupão; camisola; toga; batina; beca (de professor etc.)

grab | grab' | *vt.* agarrar; apoderar-se de; arrebatar

grace | greys' | *s.* graça, distinção, elegância; clemência; (relig.) graça. -with a good g. de boa vontade. -with a bad g. relutando. -to say graces dar graças (antes das refeições). -days of g. período de tolerância (concedido a devedor) / *vt.* ornar; honrar; dignificar

graceful | greys'ful | *a.* elegante, gracioso

graceless | greys'les | *a.* desajeitado, desgracioso

gracious | grey'šəs | *a.* atraente, gracioso; cortês, afável; misericordioso. -good g.! santo Deus!, meu Deus!, valha-me Deus!

graciousness | grey'šəsnes | *s.* gentileza, cortesia, afabilidade; benevolência, benignidade

grade | greyd' | *s.* grau; classe, categoria, tipo / *vt.* graduar; classificar. -to be on the up g. subir, melhorar. -to be on the down g. descer, decair

gradient | grey'dĭənt | s. declive, rampa, inclinação

gradual | gra'dĭuəl | a. gradual, gradativo

gradually | gra'dĭuəlĭ | adv. gradualmente, pouco a pouco; paulatinamente

graduate | gra'dĭuit | s. diplomado / | gra'dĭueyt | vt. vi. diplomar(-se)

graft | grʌft' | s. enxerto; (coloq., EUA) suborno, fraude; (gír.) trabalho duro / vt. enxertar

grain | greyn' | s. grão; grânulo; grão (64,8 mg); veio (madeira); cereais. -against the g. a contrapelo

grammar | gra'mə | s. gramática

grammar school | gra'məskʋl | s. curso secundário

grammatical | grəma'tikəl | a. gramático

granadilla | grənədi'lə | s. maracujá

granary | gra'nərĭ | s. celeiro

grand | grand' | a. magnífico; grandioso; esplêndido

grandchild | grand'šayld | s. neto, neta

grand-dad | gran'dad | s. vovô

granddaughter | gran'dótə | s. neta

grandee | gran'dɪ | s. grande de Espanha; magnata

grandeur | gran'dĭə | s. grandeza; magnificência; majestade; esplendor; imponência

grandfather | grand'fʌðə | s. avô; antepassado

grandiloquent | grandi'ləkwənt | a. grandiloqüente

grandiose | grand'dĭowz | a. grandioso, imponente; pomposo, ostentoso

grandma | grand'mə | s. vovó

grandmother | grand'mâðə | s. avó; antepassada

grandpa | grand'pə | s. vovô

grandparent | grand'peərənt | s. avô ou avó

grand piano | grand'pĭanow | s. piano de cauda

grandson | grand'sân | s. neto

grange | greynǰ' | s. granja

granite | gra'nit | s. granito

granny | gra'nĭ | s. vovó

grant | grʌnt' | s. concessão; doação; subvenção, subsídio / vt. conceder, admitir. -to take for granted admitir, supor; contar com

grape | greyp' | s. uva; videira, parreira. -the juice of the g. vinho

grapefruit | greyp'frʋt | s. grapefruit, toranja, toranja

grape juice | greyp'ǰʋs | s. suco de uva

grape-shot | greyp'šot | s. metralha (de canhão)

graph | grʌf' | s. gráfico, diagrama; (ling.) grafe

graphic | gra'fik | a. gráfico; vívido, animado, pitoresco, bem delineado

graphology | grafo'ləǰĭ | s. grafologia

graph paper | grafpey'pə | s. papel quadriculado

grapple | gra'pəl | vt. agarrar / vi. agarrar-se; lutar (com problema etc.)

grappling-iron | gra'plingay'ən | s. arpéu, gancho de abordagem, croque, fateixa

grasp | grʌsp' | s. ato de agarrar; domínio. -to have a good g. ter bom domínio de. -within the g. of ao alcance de / vt. agarrar(-se) a; apertar; compreender

grasping | grʌs'ping | a. ganancioso, cobiçoso; ávido

grass | grʌs' | s. relva, capim, erva; grama

grasshopper | grʌs'hopə | s. gafanhoto

grate | greyt' | s. grade; grelha; lareira / vt. ralar / vi. irritar; ranger

grateful | greyt'ful | a. grato, agradecido, reconhecido

grater | grey'tə | s. ralador

gratification | gratifikey'šən | s.

satisfação, prazer

gratify | gra'tifay | *vt.* satisfazer, deleitar

gratifying | gra'tifaying | *a.* agradável, deleitoso, grato

grating | grey'ting | *s.* grade, gradil / *a.* áspero, dissonante, irritante

gratis | gra'tis | *a. adv.* grátis

gratitude | gra'titiud | *s.* gratidão, reconhecimento

gratuitous | grətĭu'itəs | *a.* gratuito; injustificado

gratuity | grətĭu'itĭ | *s.* gratificação, gorgeta

gravamen | grəvey'mən | *s.* gravame; (jur.) ponto essencial de uma acusação

grave | greyv' | *s.* sepultura, cova / *a.* grave, sério

grave-digger | greyv'digə | *s.* coveiro, sepultureiro

gravel | gra'vəl | *s.* cascalho, pedregulho / *vt.* pavimentar com cascalho ou pedregulho

gravestone | greyv'stown | *s.* lápide, pedra tumular

graveyard | grey'vĭAd | *s.* cemitério

gravity | gra'vitĭ | *s.* gravidade; seriedade, compostura

gravure | grəvĭu'ə | *s.* (*abrev.* de) fotogravura

gravy | grey'vĭ | *s.* molho

gravy-boat | grey'vĭbowt | *s.* molheira

graze | greyz' | *s.* arranhadura, escoriação / *vt.* apascentar; roçar; esfolar / *vt. vi.* pastar

grease | gris' | *s.* graxa, lubrificante; gordura / *vt.* lubrificar; untar

greasy | gri'sĭ | *a.* gorduroso; escorregadio

great | greyt' | *a.* grande; imenso; célebre, notável; excelente, ótimo; esplêndido, magnificente

great age | greyt'eyj | *s.* idade avançada

great-grandfather | greyt'grandfAðə | *s.* bisavô

great-grandmother | greyt' grand-

mâðə | *s.* bisavó

great-grandparent | greyt'grandpeərənt | *s.* bisavô, bisavó

greatness | greyt'nes | *s.* grandeza; extensão; magnitude

greatly | greyt'lĭ | *adv.* extremamente, enormemente

greed | grid' | *s.* cobiça, ganância; avareza; voracidade

greedy | gri'dĭ | *a.* cobiçoso; avaro; voraz, ávido

Greek | grık' | *s.a.* grego

green | grin' | *a.* verde; (coloq.) inexperiente, novato, simplório

greenback | grin'bak | *s.* (coloq., EUA) nota, cédula (dólar)

greenery | gri'nərĭ | *s.* folhagem, vegetação

greengage | grin'geyj | *s.* ameixa rainha-cláudia

greengrocer | grin'growsə | *s.* verdureiro

greenhouse | grin'haws | *s.* estufa para o cultivo de plantas delicadas

greet | grit' | *vt.* saudar, cumprimentar; dar as boas-vindas a, acolher. -to g. the eye deparar(-se)

greeting | gri'ting | *s.* saudação; cumprimento; (*pl.*) cumprimentos / *interj.* greetings! salve!, bons olhos o vejam!

gregarious | grige'ərĭəs | *a.* gregário; sociável

grenade | grəneyd' | *s.* (mil.) granada

grenadilla | grənədi'lə | *s.* = *granadilla*

grey, gray | grey' | *a.* cinzento, cinza (cor); pardacento; grisalho (cabelo)

greyhound | grey'hawnd | *s.* galgo

grid | grid' | *s.* grade; rede; grelha; (eletr.) placa de acumulador, rede (válvula)

grief | grif' | *s.* pesar, mágoa, desgosto. -to come to g. fracassar, falhar

grievance | gri'vəns | *s.* motivo de

queixa, ressentimento; injustiça, ofensa

grieve | grīv' | *vt.* afligir; causar sofrimento / *vi.* afligir-se; entristecer-se

grievous | grī'vəs | *a.* doloroso, penoso, angustiante, angustioso

grill | gril' | *s.* grelha / *vt.* grelhar

grille | gril' | *s.* grade

grill-room | gril'rum | *s.* restaurante (esp. de hotel, cassino etc.)

grim | grim' | *a.* severo, carrancudo; cruel; implacável; horrível, horrendo, sinistro

grimace | grimeys' | *s.* careta; esgar / *vi.* fazer careta

grime | graym' | *s.* fuligem, sujidade

grimness | grim'nes | *s.* severidade; crueldade; terror, horror

grimy | gray'mī | *a.* fuliginoso, sujo, encardido

grin | grin' | *s.* sorriso, arreganhar de dentes / *vi.* sorrir, arreganhar os dentes (num sorriso)

grind | graynd' | *s.* moagem; (coloq.) trabalho penoso / *vt.* moer, triturar; amolar, afiar; ranger (dentes); polir (lentes). **-to g. down** reduzir a pó; atormentar, oprimir

grinder | grayn'də | *s.* moedor; afiador; moinho (de pimenta-do-reino, café etc.)

grindstone | graynd'stown | *s.* rebolo, pedra de amolar. **-to keep one's nose to the g.** trabalhar arduamente

grip | grip' | *s.* ato de segurar; aperto de mão; punho, cabo; (fig.) compreensão. **-to be in the g. of** estar nas garras de. **-to come to grips (with)** lutar com / *vt.* pegar, agarrar, apertar; prender a atenção de

grippe | grip' | *s.* (med.) gripe

grisly | griz'lī | *a.* horrível

gristle | gri'səl | *s.* cartilagem

grit | grit' | *s.* areia; granulação (pedra de amolar); (fig.) firme-

za de caráter

grizzly | griz'lī | *s.* urso pardo norte-americano / *a.* cinzento, acinzentado; grisalho

grizzly bear | griz'lībeə | *s.* urso pardo norte-americano

groan | grown' | *s.* gemido / *vi.* gemer

grocer | grow'sə | *s.* comerciante de secos e molhados

groceries | grow'səriz | *spl.* secos e molhados

grocer's shop | grow'səzśop | *s.* mercearia

grocery | grow'sərī | *s.* (EUA) armazém, mercearia

groggy | gro'gī | *a.* vacilante, inseguro, cambaleante; fraco das pernas (cavalo)

groin | groyn' | *s.* virilha

groom | grʋm' | *s.* cavalariço; noivo; oficial da Casa Real / *vt.* tratar de cavalos. **-well groomed** bem arrumado, bem penteado, bem vestido

groove | grʋv' | *s.* ranhura, encaixe; rego, sulco

grope | growp' | *vi.* andar às apalpadelas. **-to g. for** procurar às apalpadelas

gross | grows' | *s.* grosa. **-by the g.** em grandes quantidades / *a.* grosso, corpulento; crasso, gritante

gross weight | grows'weyt | *s.* peso bruto

grotesque | growtesk' | *a.* grotesco, absurdo

grotto | gro'tow | *s.* gruta

ground | graynd' | *s.* terra, solo; terreno; base, motivo, fundamento; (*pl.*) terras; (*pl.*) razões, motivos. **-above g.** (fig.) vivo. **-to stand one's g.** manter-se firme. **-to gain g.** ganhar terreno. **-on (the) ground(s) of** com o motivo (pretexto) de / *vt.* pôr no chão; basear, estabelecer; apoiar; (náut.) encalhar

ground floor | graynd'floə | *s.* andar térreo. **-to get in on the g. f.** ser admitido em empresa,

projeto etc. como um dos fun-
dadores

groundless | grawnd'les | *a.* in-
fundado, sem fundamento

group | grʊp' | *s.* grupo / *vt.*
agrupar

grouse | graws' | *s.* galo silvestre;
(gír.) queixa, murmúrio (de
descontentamento) / *vi.* (gír.)
queixar-se

grove | growv' | *s.* pequeno bos-
que; arvoredo; alameda

grovel | gro'vəl | *vi.* rastejar;
humilhar-se; aviltar-se

grow | grow' | *vt.* cultivar, produ-
zir / *vi.* crescer, desenvolver-se;
ficar, tornar-se, fazer-se

grower | grow'ə | *s.* plantador,
produtor, agricultor

growing | grow'ing | *s.* cultivo,
cultura, produção

growl | grawl' | *vi.* rosnar

grown | grown' | *a.* crescido;
adulto, maduro

grown-up | grown'âp | *s. a.*
adulto

growth | growϑ' | *s.* crescimento,
desenvolvimento; incremento;
vegetação; (med.) tumor

grub | grâb' | *s.* larva de inseto, la-
garta; (gír.) comida, bóia / *vi.*
cavar, revolver, cavoucar

grudge | grâǰ' | *s.* rancor, ressenti-
mento, má vontade / *vi.* queixar-se de; dar de má vontade;
invejar

grudgingly | grâ'ǰinglī | *adv.* de
má vontade; com relutância

gruel | grʊ'əl | *s.* mingau, papa

gruelling, grueling | grʊ'əling | *a.*
árduo, estafante, extenuante

gruesome | grʊ'səm | *a.* horripi-
lante, medonho

gruff | grâf' | *a.* áspero, rude

grumble | grâm'bəl | *vi.* resmun-
gar, queixar-se

grumbler | grâmb'lə | *s.* resmun-
gão

grumpy | grâm'pī | *a.* rabugento,
mal-humorado, irritadiço

grunt | grânt' | *s.* grunhido / *vi.*
grunhir

guarantee | garəntī' | *s.* garantia /
vt. garantir

guaranty | ga'rəntī | *s.* garantia;
fiança; penhor, caução

guard | gʌd' | *s.* guarda, prote-
ção; sentinela, guarda; vigia;
guarda-freios, guarda-cance-
la. **-off g.** desprevenido. **-on g.**
prevenido; em guarda; de sentinela, de vigia / *vt.* guardar, vigiar; proteger

guarded | gʌ'did | *a.* protegido;
cauteloso, prudente

guardian | gʌ'dĩən | *s.* protetor;
(jur.) tutor, curador

guardian angel | gʌ'dĩəneynǰəl |
s. anjo da guarda

guardianship | gʌ'dĩənśip | *s.*
proteção; guarda; (jur.) tutela,
curadoria

guava | gwa'və | *s.* goiaba

guerrilla, guerilla | gəri'lə | *s.*
guerrilheiro

guerrilla war | gəri'ləwó | *s.* guer-
rilha

guerrilla warfare | gəri'ləwófeə |
s. = guerrilla war

guess | ges' | *s.* suposição; estima-
tiva / *vt. vi.* adivinhar; pensar,
imaginar. **-to g. at** fazer conje-
turas

guesswork | ges'wɛk | *s.* conje-
tura; adivinhação

guest | gest' | *s.* hóspede; convi-
dado; pensionista

guffaw | gâfó' | *s.* gargalhada

guidance | gay'dəns | *s.* direção,
governo; liderança

guide | gayd' | *s.* guia; roteiro,
manual / *vt.* guiar, dirigir,
orientar

guild | gild' | *s.* associação, socie-
dade, corporação

guile | gayl' | *s.* engano; astúcia,
manha, malícia

guileless | gayl'les | *s.* ingênuo,
sincero, sem malícia

guillotine | gi'lətın | *s.* guilhotina

guilt | gilt' | *s.* culpa

guiltless | gilt'les | *a.* inocente, li-
vre de culpa

guilty | gil'tī | *a.* culpado; culpável. **-not g.** inocente

guinea | gi'nı | *s.* guinéu; moeda inglesa de cálculo (£1.05) usada para honorários, propriedades etc.

guinea-fowl | gi'nıfawl | *s.* galinha-d'angola

guinea-hen | gi'nıhen | *s.* = *guinea-fowl*

guinea-pig | gi'nıpig | *s.* cobaia, porquinho-da-índia

guise | gayz' | *s.* disfarce, máscara, falsa aparência. **-under** ou **in the g. of** sob a capa de, com o pretexto de

guitar | gitA' | *s.* violão

gulf | gâlf' | *s.* golfo, baía; abismo, redemoinho. **-the G.** golfo do México

gull | gâl' | *s.* gaivota; simplório, crédulo

gullet | gâ'lit | *s.* garganta, goela; ravina

gullible | gâ'libəl | *a.* crédulo, simplório, ingênuo

gully | gâ'lī | *s.* barranco

gulp | gâlp' | *s.* gole, trago / *vt.* tragar, engolir

gum | gâm' | *s.* gengiva; goma; secreção (dos olhos) / *vt.* engomar; colar, grudar

gumption | gum'şən | *s.* (coloq.) iniciativa, bom senso, senso prático

gun | gân' | *s.* canhão; arma de fogo (de caça, guerra etc.). **-big g.** (gír.) figurão

gun-metal | gân'metəl | *s.* cinza-escuro, cinza-metálico escuro (cor)

gunner | gâ'nə | *s.* artilheiro

gunnery | gâ'nərī | *s.* artilharia; técnica do tiro de artilharia; fabricação de canhões

gunny | gâ'nī | *s.* aniagem; saco de aniagem

gunpowder | gân'pawdə | *s.* pólvora

gurgle | gE'gəl | *vi.* gorgolejar, borbotar, rumorejar

gush | gâş' | *s.* jorro, golfada; arroubo, arrebatamento / *vi.* jorrar, golfar; brotar; (coloq.) falar com arrebatamento

gushing | gâ'şing | *a.* (fig.) efusivo, arrebatado

gust | gâst' | *s.* rajada de vento; pancada de chuva

gusto | gâs'tow | *s.* animação, satisfação, prazer

gut | gât' | *s.* tripa; (*pl.*) tripas, intestinos; (fig.) coragem / *vt.* estripar; pilhar, esvaziar (casa)

gutter | gâ'tə | *s.* sarjeta; calha; valeta; canaleta

guy | gay' | *s.* (gír.) sujeito, ''cara''; espantalho / *vt.* (coloq.) zombar, ridicularizar

guzzle | gâ'zəl | *vt. vi.* empanturrar-se, comer ou beber em demasia

gymnasium | ǰimney'z¹am | *s.* ginásio, sala de ginástica; liceu (Europa continental)

gymnastics | ǰimnas'tiks | *s.* ginástica

gynaecology | gayniko'ləǰī | *s.* ginecologia

gypsy | ǰip'sī | *s.* = *gipsy*

gyrate | jay'reyt | *vi.* girar

H

haberdasher | ha'bədaşə | *s.* comerciante de miudezas e armarinho; (EUA) camiseiro

habit | ha'bit | *s.* hábito, costume, praxe

habitable | ha'bitəbəl | *a.* habitável

habitation | habitey'śən | s. moradia, habitação, casa

habitual | həbi'tĭuəl | a. costumeiro, habitual, comum

habituate | həbi'tĭueyt | vt. habituar(-se), acostumar

hack | hak' | s. picareta; talho, corte; cavalo velho e cansado; cavalo de aluguel; trabalhador mercenário; escritor assalariado / a. alugado, mercenário; rotineiro

hackney | hak'nī | s. cavalo pequeno (de montaria) / a. de aluguel

hackney carriage | hak'nīkariǰ | s. carruagem de aluguel

hackneyed | hak'nid | a. gasto, velho; trivial

hack-saw | hak'só | s. serra para metais

haemorrhage | he'məriǰ | s. hemorragia

haemorrhoids | he'məroydz | spl. hemorróidas

haft | haft' | s. cabo (de faca, adaga etc.)

hag | hag' | s. velha feia; bruxa, feiticeira

haggard | ha'gəd | a. pálido, macilento, desfigurado

haggle | ha'gəl | vi. regatear

hail | heyl' | s. granizo, saraiva; saudação; aclamação. -within h. ao alcance da voz / vt. saudar; aclamar; chamar / vi. chover pedras. -to h. from proceder de, vir de

Hail Mary | heylme'ərī | s. ave-maria

hair | heyl' | s. cabelo; pêlo. -to a h. exatamente. -to split hairs discutir minúcias. -without turning a h. sem pestanejar. -by a h.'s breadth por um triz

haircut | he'əkât | s. corte de cabelo

hairdresser | he'ədresə | s. cabeleireiro

hairless | he'əles | a. calvo

hairpin | he'əpin | s. grampo de cabelo

hair-raising | he'əreyzing | a. horripilante

hairy | he'ərī | a. peludo, cabeludo, hirsuto

hake | heyk' | s. (ict.) abrótea (peixe semelhante ao bacalhau)

hale | heyl' | a. robusto, vigoroso, saudável

half | haf' | s. (pl. halves) metade, meio; (desp.) primeiro ou segundo tempo. -in h. ao meio / a. meio; quase; semi-. -h. an hour meia hora. -h. a share meio quinhão

half-and-half | haf'andhaf | s. meio a meio

half-baked | haf'beykid | a. mal assado; (fig.) simplório, tolo, estúpido

half-breed | haf'brīd | s. mestiço

half-hearted | haf'hatid | a. indiferente; desanimado

half-opened | haf'owpend | a. entreaberto

halfpenny | heyp'nī | s. meio pêni / a. trivial

half-time | haf'taym | s. intervalo

half-way | haf'wey | adv. a meio caminho

half-wit | haf'wit | s. idiota, imbecil

half-yearly | haf'iəlī | a. semestral

hall | hól' | s. vestíbulo, entrada, saguão; sala, salão; mansão, solar; prédio de universidade

hallmark | hól'mak | s. marca de autenticidade (em prata, ouro etc.)

hallow | ha'low | vt. santificar, consagrar

Hallowe'en | ha'lowin | s. véspera do Dia de Todos os Santos

hallucination | həlusiney'śən | s. alucinação; ilusão

halo | hey'low | s. halo; auréola; (fig.) prestígio

halt | hólt' | s. parada; pausa / vt. fazer parar, deter / vi. parar, deter-se / interj. alto!

halve | hav' | vt. reduzir à metade; partir ao meio

ham | ham' | *s.* presunto
hamlet | ham'lit | *s.* povoado
hammer | ha'mə | *s.* martelo; malho; cão (de arma de fogo) / *vt.* martelar; malhar; forjar; (fig.) produzir com esforço
hammock | ha'mək | *s.* rede (de dormir)
hamper | ham'pə | *s.* cesto grande (com tampa) / *vt.* estorvar, embaraçar
hamstring | ham'string | *vt.* estropiar, incapacitar
hand | hand' | *s.* mão; ponteiro (de relógio); letra, caligrafia; trabalhador; marujo; ajuda, auxílio; mão, cartas de um jogador. **-a good h.** pessoa habilidosa. **-on the other h.** por outro lado. **-out of h.** ingovernável, indisciplinado. **-to live from h. to mouth** viver precariamente. **-to have a h. in** ter parte em. **-to have the upper h.** levar vantagem (sobre). **-to lend a h.** ajudar. **-to turn one's h.** to começar uma nova tarefa / *vt.* dar, entregar; passar; transmitir. **-to h. down** passar, transmitir, legar. **-to h. round** passar de mão em mão
handbag | hand'bag | *s.* bolsa de senhora; maleta de mão
hand-baggage | hand'bagiǰ | *s.* bagagem de mão
handbook | hand'buk | *s.* manual; compêndio
handcuff | han'kəf | *s.* (ger. *pl.*) algemas / *vt.* algemar
handful | hand'ful | *s.* punhado
hand-gun | hand'gån | *s.* pistola ou revólver
handicap | han'dikap | *s. handicap*, desvantagem; (fig.) empecilho
handicapped | han'dikapt | *s.* deficiente (físico ou mental), aleijado
handicraft | han'dikrʌft | *s.* artesania; trabalhos manuais; habilidade manual
handiwork | han'diwɛk | *s.* obra, trabalho manual

handkerchief | han'kəšif | *s.* lenço
handle | han'dəl | *s.* cabo; punho (de espada etc.); asa (de bule, de cesta etc.); puxador (de gaveta, de porta etc.); maçaneta; manivela / *vt.* manusear; manejar
handmade | hand'meyd | *a.* feito à mão
handshake | hand'šeyk | *s.* aperto de mão
handsome | han'səm | *a.* belo, garboso, vistoso, elegante; (fig.) generoso, magnânimo
handwriting | hand'rayting | *s.* talhe de letra, letra, caligrafia
handy | han'dī | *a.* acessível, à mão; jeitoso; conveniente; hábil. **-to come in h.** vir a calhar
hang | hang' | *vt.* pendurar, suspender; pôr; enforcar; revestir, forrar (parede) / *vi.* pender, estar pendurado; cair (vestido, cortina etc.). **-to h. around** ou **about** rondar, fazer ponto. **-to h. back** hesitar. **-to h. on to** agarrar-se a; pendurar-se em. **-to h. up** desligar o telefone
hanger | han'gə | *s.* cabide; carrasco, algoz, verdugo
hanger-on | han'gəron | *s.* dependente; parasita; freqüentador habitual
hanging | hang'ing | *s.* enforcamento / *a.* pendente
hangman | hang'mən | *s.* carrasco, verdugo
hangover | hang'owvə | *s.* (gír.) ressaca (mal-estar causado pelo álcool)
hanker | han'kə | *vi.* ansiar, almejar. **-to h. after** ou **for** ansiar por
haphazard | hapha'zəd | *a.* acidental, fortuito. **-by h.** casualmente
hapless | hap'les | *a.* infeliz, desgraçado
happen | ha'pən | *vi.* acontecer, ocorrer, suceder. **-as it happens** acontece que... **-to h. in** entrar ou chegar por acaso. **-to h. on** ou **upon** encontrar por acaso,

topar com. **-no matter what happens** aconteça o que acontecer

happening | ha'pƏning | *s.* acontecimento

happiness | ha'pines | *s.* felicidade; contentamento

happy | ha'pī | *a.* feliz; satisfeito, contente. **-to be h. to** ter muito prazer em

happy-go-lucky | ha'pīgowlâ'kī | *a.* despreocupado, negligente, descuidado

harangue | hƏrang' | *s.* arenga / *vt.* arengar; discursar veementemente

harass | ha'rƏs | *vt.* importunar, estorvar, molestar; (mil.) hostilizar, inquietar

harassing fire | ha'rƏsingfay'Ə | *s.* (mil.) fogo contínuo (para inquietar o inimigo)

harbinger | hʌ'binǰƏ | *s.* precursor, anunciador

harbour, harbor | hʌ'bƏ | *s.* ancoradouro, porto; abrigo, refúgio / *vt.* abrigar, acolher; nutrir (esperanças)

hard | hʌd' | *a.* duro; rígido, firme; sólido; difícil, trabalhoso; enérgico, severo; inflexível; perseverante; áspero, desagradável. **-h. and fast** estrito, inflexível. **-to be h. on** tratar com severidade. **-to be h. up for** (coloq.) precisar urgentemente / *adv.* duramente; diligentemente; com dificuldade. **-h. by** próximo. **-to drink h.** beber muito. **-to be h. put to it** enfrentar dificuldades. **-to try h.** tentar com empenho

hard-boiled | hʌd'boyld | *a.* cozido, duro (ovo); (fig.) calejado, insensível; brutal, rude; astuto; teimoso; "da pesada"

hard cash | hʌd'kaś | *s.* moedas (por oposição a papel-moeda); dinheiro em espécie

harden | hʌ'dƏn | *vt.* endurecer; temperar (metais) / *vi.* endure-

cer-se; aumentar, subir (preços)

hardening | hʌ'dƏning | *s.* endurecimento; solidificação; têmpera (metais)

hard-fisted | hʌd'fistid | *a.* avarento, avaro

hard-fought | hʌd'fót | *a.* encarniçado, renhido

hard-handed | hʌd'handid | *a.* de mãos calejadas; (fig.) despótico

hard-headed | hʌd'hedid | *a.* teimoso, cabeçudo, obstinado

hardiness | hʌ'dines | *s.* audácia, intrepidez; vigor, robustez; firmeza

hardly | hʌd'lī | *adv.* dificilmente, apenas, quase; mal; duramente. **-h. ever** quase nunca. **-it is h. credible** mal se pode crer

hardness | hʌd'nes | *s.* dureza; rigidez; severidade

hardship | hʌd'šip | *s.* sofrimento, miséria; privação; trabalho; dificuldade; injustiça, opressão

hardware | hʌd'weƏ | *s.* ferragens; armas, máquinas

hard-wearing | hʌd'weƏring | *a.* resistente, durável

hard-working | hʌd'wƏking | *a.* trabalhador, diligente

hardy | hʌ'dī | *a.* valente, audacioso; robusto, resistente, vigoroso

hare | he'Ə | *s.* lebre. **-to start a h.** levantar a lebre, suscitar um assunto

hare-brained | he'Əbreynd | *a.* leviano; insensato; doido

harelip | he'Əlip | *s.* lábio leporino

harem | he'ƏrƏm | *s.* harém, serralho

haricot | ha'rikow | *s.* guisado (de cordeiro ou carneiro)

haricot bean | ha'rikowbin | *s.* feijão branco

hark | hʌk' | *vi.* ouvir, escutar. **-to h. back** voltar atrás; retornar (a assunto já discutido)

harlot | hʌ'lƏt | *s.* prostituta

harm | hʌm' | *s.* mal; dano; prejuízo; ofensa. **-to mean no h.** não querer ofender / vt. fazer mal, prejudicar

harmful | hʌm'ful | a. nocivo, pernicioso, perigoso

harmless | hʌm'les | a. inofensivo, inocente

harmonious | hʌmow'nĭəs | a. harmonioso

harmonize | hʌ'mənayz | vt. harmonizar; conciliar

harmony | hʌ'mənĭ | s. harmonia, concordância

harness | hʌ'nes | s. arreios / vt. arrear; atrelar; (fig.) subordinar; aproveitar, utilizar

harp | hʌp' | s. harpa / vi. harpejar. **-to h. on the same string** repisar, bater na mesma tecla

harpoon | hʌpʋn' | s. arpão / vt. arpoar

harpsichord | hʌp'sikód | s. (mús.) cravo

harpy | hʌ'pĭ | s. harpia

harpy-eagle | hʌ'pĭïgəl | s. gavião-real

harridan | ha'ridən | s. megera, bruxa velha

harrow | ha'row | s. grade (de arado). **-under the h.** em situação angustiosa

harrowing | ha'rowing | a. angustiante, lancinante

harry | ha'rĭ | vt. assolar; pilhar; atormentar

harsh | hʌś' | a. áspero; cruel; duro; severo

harshness | hʌś'nes | s. aspereza; severidade

harum-scarum | he'ərəmske'ərəm | a. leviano, temerário, insensato, estouvado

harvest | hʌ'vist | s. colheita; ceifa; (fig.) fruto, resultado / vt. colher, fazer a colheita; ceifar

harvester | hʌ'vistə | s. ceifeiro, segador; (mec.) segadeira, ceifeira

hash | haś' | s. qualquer coisa picada; picadinho (de carne). **-to make a h. of** estropiar, estragar

haste | heyst' | s. pressa, rapidez,

celeridade. **-in h.** às pressas. **-to make h.** apressar-se

hasten | hey'sən | vt. apressar / vi. apressar-se

hastily | heys'tilĭ | adv. apressadamente; precipitadamente, irrefletidamente

hasty | heys'tĭ | a. apressado; impaciente; rápido; impetuoso, violento

hat | hat' | s. chapéu. **-at the drop of a h.** prontamente. **-under one's h.** em segredo

hatch | haś' | s. postigo, portinhola; escotilha; ninhada, cria. **-under hatches** no porão / vt. chocar; (fig.) tramar

hatchet | ha'śit | s. machadinha

hatchway | haś'wey | s. escotilha; alçapão

hate | heyt' | s. ódio, raiva, aversão / vt. odiar

hateful | heyt'ful | a. odioso, detestável

hatred | heyt'rid | s. ódio, rancor; aversão; inimizade

haughtiness | hó'tines | s. arrogância, insolência, soberba; altivez

haughty | hó'tĭ | a. arrogante, insolente, soberbo

haul | hól' | s. puxão, arrasto; lanço de rede (pesca); aquisição; roubo, pilhagem / vt. puxar, arrastar. **-to h. down** arriar

haulage | hó'lĭj | s. transporte, carreto, frete

haunch | hónś' | s. anca, quadril, cadeiras

haunt | hónt' | s. lugar freqüentado assiduamente; comedouro de animais; antro, covil (de criminosos) / vt. freqüentar, visitar; assombrar, perseguir

haunted house | hón'tidhaws' | s. casa mal-assombrada

have | hav' | vt. ter, possuir; receber, obter; comer; beber, tomar. **-to h. lunch** almoçar. **-to h. to go** ter de ir. **-you don't h. to** você não é obrigado a. **-to h. a good time** divertir-se. **-to h. a try**

tentar. **-to h. a mind to** querer, desejar; ter em vista. **-to h. it out with** chegar a um acordo (discutindo)

haven | hey'vən | s. porto, enseada; (fig.) abrigo

haversack | ha'vəsak | s. mochila

havoc | ha'vək | s. dano, estrago, devastação

hawk | hók' | s. falcão / vt. apregoar mercadorias

hawker | hó'kə | s. vendedor ambulante, mascate

hawthorn | hó'ϑón | s. (bot.) pilriteiro, espinheiro-alvar

hay | hey' | s. feno. **-it's not h.** não é pouco dinheiro, é uma boa soma

hay fever | hey'fivə | s. febre do feno

hay-fork | hey'fók | s. forcado

hayloft | hey'loft | s. palheiro

haymaker | hey'meykə | s. ceifeiro; (gír.) soco violento

haystack | hey'stak | s. monte de feno, meda

hazard | ha'zəd | s. acaso, casualidade; risco, perigo / vt. arriscar

hazardous | ha'zədəs | a. arriscado, perigoso

haze | heyz' | s. névoa, bruma

hazel | hey'zəl | s. aveleira / a. castanho-claro

hazel-nut | hey'zəlnât | s. avelã

hazy | hey'zĭ | a. enevoado; confuso, indistinto

he | hĭ | pron. ele

head | hed' | s. cabeça; cabeceira; cabeleira; diretor, chefe; nascente (rio). **-from h. to foot** dos pés à cabeça. **-to come to a h.** tornar-se crítico (situação, momento etc.). **-to keep one's h.** conservar a serenidade. **-to go to one's h.** subir à cabeça / vt. chefiar, dirigir, estar à frente de; vir à cabeça de; cabecear (futebol etc.). **-to h. for** dirigir-se para. **-to h. back** voltar

headache | he'deyk | s. dor de cabeça

head-dress | hed'dres | s. toucado; penteado

heading | he'ding | s. título; cabeceio (futb. etc.)

headland | hed'lənd | s. promontório, cabo

headlight | hed'layt | s. farol dianteiro

headline | hed'layn | s. título, cabeçalho, manchete / vt. dar relevo a

headlong | hed'long | adv. de cabeça, precipitadamente

headmaster | hedmʌs'tə | s. diretor de escola

headmistress | hedmis'trəs | s. diretora de escola

headphone | hed'fown | s. fone de ouvido (rádio)

headquarters | hedkwó'təz | spl. quartel-general

head shawl | hed'śól | s. lenço de cabeça

headstrong | hed'strong | a. cabeçudo, obstinado, teimoso

headway | hed'wey | s. progresso, adiantamento

heady | he'dĭ | a. impetuoso, temerário; capitoso, inebriante, embriagador

heal | hĭl' | vt. curar, sanar, remediar

healing | hĭ'ling | a. curativo, medicinal; benéfico

health | helϑ' | s. saúde; brinde, saudação. **-your h.!** à sua saúde!

healthful | helϑ'ful | a. saudável

healthiness | hel'ϑines | s. saúde, salubridade

healthy | hel'ϑĭ | a. saudável, são, sadio, salutar

heap | hĭp' | s. pilha, monte. **-top (bottom) of the h.** ganhador (perdedor)

hear | hĭ'ə | vt. ouvir; atender; ouvir dizer. **-to h. out** ouvir até o fim / vi. ouvir, escutar. **-h., h.!** apoiado!, muito bem! **-to h. from (someone)** ter notícias de (alguém)

hearing | hɪ'ɔring | s. audição; audiência; interrogatório

hearing-aid | hɪ'ɔringeyd | s. aparelho de surdez

hearsay | hɪ'ɔsey | s. boato. -by h. por ouvir dizer

hearse | hɛs' | s. carro fúnebre

heart | hɑt' | s. coração; centro, âmago; copas (baralho). -at h. no fundo. -by h. decor. -to learn by h. decorar. -change of h. mudança de idéia ou de sentimento. -have a h.! tenha dó! -to lay to h. refletir seriamente, levar a sério. -to h. íntimo, sincero. -to take to h. levar a sério, preocupar-se. -to one's heart's content a mais não poder. -to take the h. out of desanimar, desencorajar

heartache | hɑt'eyk | s. aflição de espírito

heart attack | hɑt'ɔtak | s. ataque cardíaco

heart-broken | hɑt'browkɔn | a. abatido, desanimado

heartburn | hɑt'bɛn | s. azia

hearten | hɑt'ɔn | vt. animar, encorajar

heartening | hɑt'ning | a. encorajador

heartfelt | hɑt'felt | a. profundamente sentido

hearth | hɑϑ' | s. lareira

heartily | hɑ'tilī | adv. cordialmente; entusiasticamente; vorazmente

heartless | hɑt'les | a. desumano; insensível

heart-rending | hɑt'rending | a. de partir o coração

heart-searching | hɑt'šɛsing | a. penetrante (exame de consciência)

hearty | hɑ'tī | a. cordial, sincero; entusiástico; vigoroso; abundante (refeição)

heat | hīt' | s. calor, (fig.) paixão, ardor, veemência; cio; (desp.) competição eliminatória. -at a h. de uma assentada. -in h. no cio / vt. aquecer

heater | hɪ'tɔ | s. aquecedor; aparelho de aquecimento, calorífero

heath | hɪϑ' | s. charneca

heathen | hɪ'ðɔn | s. a. pagão, gentio

heather | hɪ'ðɔ | s. (bot.) urze

heating | hɪ'ting | s. aquecimento, calefação

heat-stroke | hɪt'strowk | s. insolação

heave | hɪv' | s. esforço / vt. levantar, suspender; suspirar, arfar. -to h. a sigh suspirar / vi. crescer; inchar; engrossar (o mar); sentir náuseas

heaven | he'vɔn | s. céu; paraíso. -for h.'s sake! pelo amor de Deus! -good heavens! santo Deus! -h. forbid! Deus me (nos) livre!

heavenly | he'vɔnlī | a. celeste, celestial; encantador, maravilhoso

heavily | he'vilī | adv. pesadamente; opressivamente; densamente; lentamente

heaviness | he'vines | s. peso; densidade; opressão

heavy | he'vī | a. pesado; difícil; opressivo; excessivo; sobrecarregado; importante; violento

heavy-duty | he'vīďutī | a. de serviço pesado

heavy sea | he'vīsī | s. mar grosso

heavyweight | he'vīweyt | s. peso-pesado (no boxe etc.)

Hebrew | hɪ'brʊ | s. hebreu / a. hebraico

heckle | he'kɔl | vt. contrariar; interromper; apartear, importunar (orador)

hectic | hek'tik | a. febril

hedge | hej' | s. sebe / vt. cercar com sebes; resguardar; confinar; garantir / vi. esconder-se; esquivar-se; usar de evasivas

hedgehog | hej'hog | s. ouriço-cacheiro

heed | hɪd' | s. atenção. -to take h. prestar atenção / vt. prestar atenção a; considerar atentamente

heedful | hɪd'ful | *a*. atento

heedless | hɪd'les | *a*. desatento, descuidado

heel | hɪl' | *s*. calcanhar; salto de sapato. **-at one's heels** no encalço de. **-down at the h**. pobre, maltrapilho. **-to take to one's heels** fugir. **-h. of bread** bico de pão / *vt*. colocar salto / *vi*. adernar (embarcação)

hefty | hef'tɪ | *a*. vigoroso, robusto; pesado, corpulento

hegemony | hije'mənɪ | *s*. hegemonia, supremacia

heifer | he'fə | *s*. novilha

height | hayt' | *s*. altura; estatura (de pessoa); outeiro, monte; auge, ponto culminante; ápice

heighten | hay'tən | *vt*. aumentar, intensificar, realçar; exaltar, elevar

heinous | hey'nəs | *a*. hediondo; atroz

heir | e'ə | *s*. herdeiro; sucessor

heir apparent | e'əəparənt | *s*. herdeiro (de pessoa viva), herdeiro presuntivo

heir-at-law | e'əətló | *s*. herdeiro legítimo

heirloom | e'əlʊm | *s*. bens móveis herdados, herança

helicopter | he'likoptə | *s*. helicóptero

hell | hel' | *s*. inferno

hellish | he'liś | *a*. infernal

hello | helow' | *s*. alô / *interj*. alô! (ao telefone etc.)

helm | helm' | *s*. leme, timão

helmet | hel'mit | *s*. capacete

helmsman | helmz'mən | *s*. timoneiro

help | help' | *s*. ajuda, auxílio; empregado, ajudante / *vt*. ajudar, aliviar. **-I cannot h**. it não posso evitar. **-I cannot h. but** não posso deixar de. **-it can't be helped** não há remédio. **-so h. me God!** e tomo a Deus por testemunha! (em juramentos) / *interj*. socorro!

helpful | help'ful | *a*. útil, proveitoso; prestativo, prestimoso (pessoa)

helpless | help'les | *a*. desamparado, indefeso; abandonado; sem remédio

helter-skelter | hel'təskel'tə | *adv*. precipitadamente; confusamente

hem | hem' | *s*. orla, bainha

hemisphere | he'misfɪə | *s*. hemisfério

hemp | hemp' | *s*. cânhamo

hen | hen' | *s*. galinha

hence | hens' | *adv*. daqui, deste lugar; portanto, por conseqüência. **-to go h**. ir embora daqui

henceforth | hensfóϑ' | *adv*. = *henceforward*

henceforward | hensfó'wəd | *adv*. daqui por diante

henchman | hens'mən | *s*. partidário, adepto, sequaz

henpecked | hen'pekt | *a*. dominado pela mulher (marido)

her | hə | *pron*. a, a ela; lhe, a ela; dela

herald | he'rəld | *s*. arauto; precursor / *vt*. anunciar, proclamar; introduzir

heraldry | he'rəldrɪ | *s*. heráldica

herb | hɛb' | *s*. erva; planta medicinal ou aromática

herbalist | hɛ'bəlist | *s*. ervanário, herbanário

herd | hɛd' | *s*. manada, rebanho, bando. **-the common h.** a plebe, o vulgo / *vt*. arrebanhar, pastorear, guardar

herd instinct | hɛd'instinkt | *s*. instinto gregário

here | hɪ'ə | *adv*. aqui, cá. **-h. and there** aqui e ali; às vezes. **-h.'s to you** à sua saúde. **-that is neither h. nor there** isto não vem ao caso / *interj*. presente!

hereabouts | hɪ'ərəbawts | *adv*. por aqui, aqui por perto

hereafter | hɪərʌf'tə | *s*. futuro; vida futura / *adv*. daqui em diante, doravante

hereby | hɪ'əbay | *adv*. pelo presente, por este meio

hereditary | here'ditrī | a. hereditário

heresy | he'rəsī | s. heresia

heretic | he'rətik | s. herege / a. herético, herege

heretical | here'tikəl | a. herético

herewith | hı'əwiᵭ | adv. incluso, junto

heritage | he'ritiᵭ | s. herança

hermit | hɛ'mit | s. eremita, ermitão, solitário

hermitage | hɛ'mitiᵭ | s. ermida, eremitério

hero | hı'ərow | s. herói

heroic | herow'ik | a. heróico

heroin | he'rowin | s. (farmac.) heroína

heroine | he'rowin | s. heroína

heroism | he'rowizəm | s. heroísmo

heron | he'rən | s. garça

herring | he'ring | s. arenque

hers | hɛz | pron. o(s) seu(s) (dela); a(s) sua(s) (dela)

herself | həself' | pron. se; si (ela) própria; si (ela) mesma. -by h.ʼ sozinha. -to h. consigo mesma

hesitate | he'ziteyt | vi. hesitar

hesitation | hezitey'śən | s. hesitação, indecisão

hew | hĭ'v' | vt. cortar, talhar, fender. -to h. down abater, derrubar

hey | hey' | interj. olá!

heyday | hey'dey | s. auge, apogeu; flor da idade; alegria, animação, vigor

hiatus | hayey'təs | s. hiato, interrupção, intervalo

hibernate | hay'bəneyt | vi. hibernar

hiccup, hiccough | hi'kâp | s. soluço / vi. soluçar

hickory | hi'kərī | s. (bot.) hicória, nogueira americana

hidden | hi'dən | a. escondido, oculto; secreto

hide | hayd' | s. pele, couro / vt. esconder, ocultar / vi. esconder-se, ocultar-se

hide-and-seek | hayd'andsık | s. esconde-esconde

hidebound | hayd'bawnd | a. (fig.) obstinadamente tacanho e rotineiro

hideous | hi'dīəs | a. hediondo, repugnante, abominável

hide-out | hayd'awt | s. (coloq.) esconderijo

hiding | hay'ding | s. (coloq.) surra, sova; ato de esconder-se

hiding-place | hay'dingpleys | s. esconderijo

hierarchy | hay'ərʌkī | s. hierarquia

higgledy-piggledy | hi'gəldīpigəldī | adv. em desordem, desordenadamente

high | hay' | a. alto, elevado; forte, rijo (vento); principal (rua); grande (velocidade); (mús.) agudo; no auge. -in h. spirits alegre, animado. -h. and mighty (coloq.) arrogante. -h. and dry em seco; abandonado, sem recursos

high altar | hay'oltə | s. altar-mor

highbrow | hay'braw | s. a. intelectual

highlander | hay'ləndə | s. montanhês (esp. da Escócia)

Highlands | hay'ləndz | s. (Esc.) região montanhosa

highlight | hay'layt | s. ponto culminante, momento de maior interesse / vt. realçar, ressaltar

highly | hay'lī | adv. altamente, em alto grau

highness | hay'nes | s. elevação, altura. -His (Her) Royal H. Sua Alteza Real. -Your H. Vossa Alteza

high noon | hay'nʋn | s. meio-dia em ponto

high road | hay'rowd | s. estrada principal; (fig.) caminho direto

high school | hay'skʋl | s. escola secundária

high sea | hay'sı | s. alto-mar

high-spirited | hayspi'ritid | a. alegre, vivaz; valente

high spirits | hay'spirits | spl. bom humor. -to be in h. s. estar bem-humorado

high time | hay'taym | s. (gír.) grande divertimento, farra / adv. mais do que na hora

highway | hay'wey | s. estrada de·

rodagem, rodovia

highwayman | hay'weymən | *s.* salteador de estrada

hike | hayk' | *s.* caminhada; excursão / *vi.* caminhar, andar a pé

hilarious | hile'əriəs | *a.* muito divertido ou alegre

hill | hil' | *s.* morro, colina, outeiro. **-old as the hills** muito antigo

hillock | hi'lək | *s.* morro, colina, outeiro

hillside | hil'sayd | *s.* encosta

hilly | hi'li | *a.* montanhoso; escarpado

hilt | hilt' | *s.* punho (de espada, adaga etc.)

him | him | *pron.* o, lhe, com ele

himself | himself' | *pron.* se; si (ele) próprio; si (ele) mesmo. **-by h.** sozinho. **-to h.** consigo mesmo

hind | hind' | *a.* traseiro, posterior

hinder | hin'də | *a.* situado atrás, traseiro / *vt.* impedir, atrapalhar, estorvar

hindmost | haynd'mowst | *a.* o que está mais atrás, último

hindrance | hin'drəns | *s.* obstáculo, impedimento

hinge | hinj' | *s.* dobradiça, gonzo, charneira

hint | hint' | *s.* sugestão, insinuação, palpite. **-to drop a h.** dar a entender. **-to take the h.** compreender ou aceitar uma indireta / *vi.* dar a entender

hinterland | hin'tələnd | *s.* interior, sertão

hip | hip' | *s.* quadril

hire | hay'ə | *s.* aluguel / *vt.* alugar; empregar; contratar; assalariar

hireling | hay'əling | *s. a.* mercenário

hire-purchase | hay'əpɛšis | *s.* crediário / *vt.* comprar a prestações

his | hiz | *pron.* o(s) seu(s); a(s) sua(s); o(s), a(s) dele / *a. poss.* seu(s); sua(s); dele

Hispanic | hispa'nik | *a.* nispânico

hiss | his' | *s.* silvo, sibilação; vaia / *vt. vi.* silvar. sibilar; vaiar

historian | histó'riən | *s.* historiador

historic, -al | histo'rik(əl) | *a.* histórico

history | his'təri | *s.* história

hit | hit' | *s.* golpe, pancada; tiro certeiro; impacto; sucesso (teatral etc.) / *vt.* bater, golpear; atingir, acertar (alvo); esbarrar com, chocar-se contra. **-to h. it off** (coloq.) fazer camaradagem com. **-to h. the road** (coloq.) por-se a caminho. **-to h. the spot** (coloq.) satisfazer plenamente

hitch | hiš' | *s.* puxão, repelão; obstáculo, impedimento; (náut.) volta (de cabo) / *vt.* puxar; prender, atar, ligar

hither | hi'ðə | *a.* de cá, próximo, mais perto / *adv.* cá, para cá, aqui, até este ponto. **-h. and thither** aqui e acolá

hitherto | hi'ðətu | *adv.* até agora, até este ponto

hive | hayv' | *s.* colmeia, colméia

hoard | hód' | *s.* provisão, reserva; tesouro / *vt.* armazenar; acumular; entesourar; esconder; açambarcar

hoarding | hó'ding | *s.* açambarcamento; entesouramento, acumulação; tapume

hoarse | hó'əs | *a.* rouco

hoarseness | hó'əsnes | *s.* rouquidão

hoary | hó'əri | *a.* encanecido, grisalho; esbranquiçado; antigo, venerável

hoax | howks' | *s.* engano, burla, embuste / *vt.* enganar

hobble | ho'bəl | *s.* manqueira, coxeadura / *vi.* mancar, coxear

hobby | ho'bi | *s.* passatempo favorito; mania, paixão

hobby-horse | ho'bihós | *s.* cavalinho de pau; cavalinho de carrossel; mania, paixão

hob-nob | hob'nob | *vi.* ter intimidade com alguém

hobo | how'bow | *s.* vadio, vagabundo, desocupado

hockey | ho'kĭ |*s.* hóquei

hodgepodge | hoj'poÿ | *s.* = *hotchpotch*

hoe | how' | *s.* enxada, sacho

hog | hog' | *s.* porco; (fig.) grosseiro, glutão. **-to go the whole h.** (gír.) ir até ao fim

hoist | hoyst' | *s.* monta-cargas / *vt.* içar, guindar, levantar

hold | howld' | *s.* (náut.) porão; domínio, influência, controle; pegada, golpe (luta livre). **-to get h. of** agarrar-se, apoderar-se de / *vt.* segurar; agüentar, sustentar; conter, encerrar; possuir; celebrar, realizar (reunião etc.); ocupar (cargo); manter (opinião); crer (idéia). **-to h. back** refrear; deter; ocultar. **-to h. down** dominar, sujeitar. **-to h. good** ser válido. **-to h. over** adiar. **-to h. out** estender; agüentar, resistir. **-to h. on to** agarrar-se. **-to h. up** suspender; sustentar; assaltar. **-to h. with** aprovar, consentir em

holder | howl'də | *s.* possuidor; arrendatário; portador; cabo, pegador, alça

hold-up | howld'âp | *s.* assalto à mão armada; congestionamento do trânsito; impedimento, empecilho

hole | howl' |*s.* buraco, furo, orifício; toca / *vt.* esburacar, furar, cavar

holiday | ho'lidey |*s.* feriado; dia santo; (*pl.*) férias. **-on h.** de férias

holiday-maker | ho'lideymeykə | *s.* veranista

holiness | how'lines |*s.* santidade

hollow | ho'low |*s.* cavidade; depressão, vale /*a.* oco; falso, frívolo; surdo (som) / *vt.* escavar, tornar oco

hollow cheeks | ho'lowsĭks | *spl.* faces encovadas

hollow-eyed | ho'lowayid | *a.* de olhos encovados

hollowness | ho'lownes | *s.* (fig.) futilidade

holly | ho'lĭ | *s.* azevinho (planta usada como decoração na época do Natal)

holocaust | ho'ləkóst | *s.* holocausto, sacrifício

holster | howl'stə |*s.* coldre

holy | how'lĭ | *a.* santo, sagrado

Holy Ghost | how'lĭgowst |*s.* Espírito Santo

holy-water | howlĭwó'tə |*s.* água benta

homage | ho'miÿ | *s.* homenagem. **-to pay h.** homenagear

home | howm' | *s.* lar, casa, residência; terra, região; abrigo, asilo (de pessoas idosas etc.) /*a.* caseiro, doméstico; nacional; interno, interior. **-at h.** em casa. **-to feel at h.** estar à vontade

home-bred | howm'bred |*a.* criado em casa

home county | howm'kawntĭ |*s.* distrito (nas cercanias de Londres)

homeland | howm'land | *s.* terra natal (esp. a Inglaterra)

homeless | howm'les | *a.* sem casa, sem lar; desabrigado

homelike | howm'layk | *a.* confortável, familiar

homeliness | howm'lines |*s.* simplicidade; afabilidade

homely | howm'lĭ | *a.* simples; sem graça; rude; caseiro

home-made | howm'meyd | *a.* feito em casa

Home Office | howmo'fis |*s.* ministério do Interior

home rule | howm'rʋl |*s.* autonomia, governo próprio

homesick | howm'sik | *a.* nostálgico, saudoso (de casa, da pátria etc.). **-to be h.** estar saudoso (da casa, da pátria etc.)

homesickness | howmsik'nes | *s.* nostalgia, saudade (da casa, da pátria etc.)

homestead | howm'sted | *s.* propriedade rural

homeward | howm'wəd | *adv.* para casa

homeward-bound | howm'wəd-bawnd | *a.* de regresso à casa; rumo à pátria (navio etc.)

homey, homy | how'mī | *a.* (coloq., EUA) acolhedor

homicide | ho'misayd | *s.* homicídio

homily | ho'milī | *s.* homilia

hone | hown' | *s.* pedra de amolar (esp. para navalhas) / *vt.* amolar, afiar

honest | o'nist | *a.* honesto, honrado, íntegro, probo; verdadeiro, genuíno

honestly | o'nistlī | *adv.* honestamente; francamente, sinceramente

honesty | o'nistī | *s.* honestidade, probidade, retidão; franqueza, sinceridade

honey | hâ'nī | *s.* mel

honeycomb | hânīkowm | *s.* favo de mel / *vt.* esburacar; minar, solapar

honeymoon | hâ'nīmᴜn | *s.* lua-de-mel

honorary | o'nərərī | *a.* honorário

honour, honor | o'nə | *s.* honra, honradez; retidão; dignidade, cargo, posição; pureza, castidade; glória, fama; (*pl.*) distinção (universitária). **-to do h. to** honrar, fazer honra a / *vt.* honrar, respeitar, venerar; pagar (dívida etc.)

honourable, honorable | o'nərəbəl | *a.* honrado, digno, probo, respeitável; excelentíssimo (título)

hood | hud' | *s.* capuz; touca (de mulher, criança, religiosa etc.); carapuça; capô (de automóvel); capelo (acadêmico ou monástico)

hoodwink | hud'wink | *vt.* enganar, lograr, ludibriar

hoof | huf' | *s.* casco

hook | huk' | *s.* gancho; anzol. **-by h. or by crook** de qualquer

maneira, por bem ou por mal / *vt.* prender com gancho; prender no anzol, ferrar

hook and eye | huk'anday | *s.* colchete (de roupa)

hooligan | hᴜ'ligən | *s.* desordeiro, arruaceiro

hoop | hᴜp' | *s.* aro, arco (de pipa, brinquedo infantil)

hoot | hᴜt' | *vt.* apupar, vaiar / *vi.* piar (coruja); apitar (navio). **-to not give ou care a h.** não se importar, não ligar

hop | hop' | *s.* salto, pulo; (bot.) lúpulo / *vi.* pular num pé só ou de pés juntos

hope | howp' | *s.* esperança / *vt.* esperar, desejar muito

hopeful | howp'ful | *a.* esperançoso; promissor

hopeless | howp'les | *a.* desesperado; desesperançado; irremediável; inútil

hopelessness | howp'lesnes | *s.* desesperança; inutilidade

horde | hód' | *s.* horda

horizon | həray'zən | *s.* horizonte

horizontal | horizon'təl | *a.* horizontal

horn | hón' | *s.* chifre; trompa, corneta; buzina

hornet | hó'nit | *s.* vespão, marimbondo

horny | hó'nī | *a.* córneo, feito de chifre; caloso

horoscope | ho'rəskowp | *s.* horóscopo

horrible | ho'ribəl | *a.* horrível, espantoso; horrendo

horrid | ho'rid | *a.* horrível

horrify | ho'rifay | *vt.* horrorizar; escandalizar

horror | ho'rə | *s.* horror

horse | hós' | *s.* cavalo. **-like a h.** com extremo vigor. **-that's a h. of another colour** isso é outra história, são outros quinhentos

horseback | hós'bak | *adv.* a cavalo

horse-fly | hós'flay | *s.* mutuca, moscardo

horsehair | hós'heə | *s.* crina de

cavalo / *a.* feito de crina

horseman| hós'mən |*s.* cavaleiro

horsemanship | hós'mənsip | *s.* equitação; habilidade em lidar com cavalos

horsepower| hós'pawə |*s.* (mec.) cavalo-vapor

horse-race | hós'reys | *s.* corrida de cavalos

horse-radish| hós'radiś |*s.* (bot.) raiz-forte

horseshoe | hós'śυ |*s.* ferradura

horsewoman | hós'wəmən | *s.* amazona

horticulture| hó'tikálŚə |*s.* horticultura

hose | howz' | *s.* (tb. **hose-pipe**) mangueira (de borracha); (*pl.*) meias

hospitable | hos'pitəbəl hospi'təbəl | *a.* hospitaleiro

hospital | hos'pitəl |*s.* hospital

hospitality | hospita'litī | *s.* hospitalidade

host | howst' | *s.* anfitrião; hoteleiro; hospedeiro; multidão; bando; (mil.) hoste, exército; (relig.) hóstia

hostage | hos'tiĵ |*s.* refém

hostel | hos'təl |*s.* albergue, hospedaria; residência de estudantes

hostess | hows'tes | *s.* dona-de--casa; hospedeira; aeromoça

hostile | hos'tayl | *a.* hostil; agressivo; inimigo

hostility | hosti'litī | *s.* hostilidade

hot| hot' |*a.* quente; ardente, impetuoso; picante; apimentado / *adv.* ardentemente; veementemente

hot-blooded | hot'blâdid | *a.* de sangue quente; fogoso, impetuoso

hotchpotch | hoŚ'poŚ |*s.* mixórdia, confusão

hot dog | hot'dog | *s.* cachorro--quente

hotel | howtel' |*s.* hotel

hothead | hot'hed | *s.* pessoa exaltada, pessoa impetuosa

hot-house | hot'haws |*s.* estufa

hot-pot| hot'pot |*s.* (cul.) cozido (de cordeiro, batatas etc.)

hound | hawnd' | *s.* cão de caça / *vt.* caçar com cães; acossar, perseguir

hour | aw'ə |*s.* hora. **-after hours** depois do expediente. **-by the h.** por hora. **-in the small hours** altas horas da noite. **-to keep late hours** deitar-se tarde da noite

hourly | aw'əlī | *adv.* de hora em hora; a toda a hora; continuamente

house | haws' | *s.* casa. **-the H.** (coloq.) a Bolsa; (polít.) Câmara dos Comuns ou dos Lordes. **-like a h. on fire** vigorosamente, rapidamente. **-to bring the h. down** provocar aplausos (ou risadas) estrondosos. **-on the h.** por conta da casa / *vt.* alojar; acolher

house-fly | haws'flay | *s.* mosca comum ou doméstica

household| haws'howld |*s.* casa, família / *a.* doméstico

household arts | haws'howld-Ats |*spl.* trabalhos domésticos

householder | haws'howldə | *s.* dono de casa; chefe de família

household word | haws'howld-wEd |*s.* nome ou dito familiar

housekeeper | haws'kıpə | *s.* governanta

housekeeping | haws'kıping | *s.* economia doméstica

housemaid | haws'meyd | *s.* empregada doméstica

house of cards| haws'ovkAdz |*s.* castelo de cartas

housewife | haws'wayf ·|*s.* dona--de-casa

housewifery | haws'wayfərī | *s.* afazeres domésticos

housework | haws'wEk |*s.* trabalho doméstico

housing| haw'zing |*s.* alojamento, habitação, moradia

hovel | ho'vəl | *s.* cabana, choupana; alpendre, galpão

hover| ho'və | *vi.* pairar

how | haw | *adv.* como; de que modo. **-h. far?** a que distância?, até onde? **-h. long?** quanto tempo?; qual é o comprimento de? **-h. much?** quanto? **-h. many?** quantos? **-h. often?** quantas vezes? **-h. are you?** como está?, como vai? **-h. do you do?** muito prazer (em conhecê-lo). **-h. about it?** então?, que tal? **-h. about this?** que acha disso (disto)? **-h. so?** como assim?

however | hawe'vɔ | *adv. conj.* como quer que; por mais que; entretanto, contudo, não obstante

howl | hawl' | *s.* uivo / *vi.* uivar; rugir, bramir (vento); ulular

hub | hâb' | *s.* cubo (de roda); centro, ponto central

hubbub | hâ'bâb | *s.* tumulto, alarido, gritaria

huddle | hâ'dəl | *vt.* amontoar; fazer (algo) apressadamente / *vi.* amontoar-se; aconchegar-se

hue | hĭu' | *s.* cor, matiz. **-h. and cry** clamor público

huff | hâf' | *s.* ressentimento, amuo. **-in a h.** ofendido

hug | hâg' | *s.* abraço / *vt.* abraçar, apertar nos braços

huge | hĭuj' | *a.* enorme, vasto

hulk | hâlk' | *s.* casco (de navio desmantelado); (fig.) pessoa pesada, desajeitada

hull | hâl' | *s.* (náut.) casco; casca (de fruta, semente etc.) / *vt.* descascar, debulhar

hullaballoo | halǝbǝlu' | *s.* tumulto, clamor, algazarra

hum | hâm' | *s.* zumbido / *vt.* cantarolar (de boca fechada). **-h. and haw** hesitar, vacilar / *vi.* zumbir

human | hĭu'mǝn | *a.* humano

humane | hĭumeyn' | *a.* humanitário, humano, compassivo

humanitarian | hĭumanite'ǝrĭǝn | *a.* humanitário

humanity | hĭuma'nitĭ | *s.* humanidade

humble | hâm'bǝl | *a.* humilde, modesto / *vt.* humilhar

humbug | hâm'bâg | *s.* charlatanice, mistificação; logro; impostor, charlatão

humdrum | hâm'drâm | *a.* enfadonho, monótono, rotineiro

humid | hĭv'mid | *a.* úmido

humiliate | hĭumi'lĭeyt | *vt.* humilhar, rebaixar, vexar

humiliation | hĭumilĭey'śǝn | *s.* humilhação

humility | hĭumi'litĭ | *s.* humildade

humming-bird | hâ'mingbᴇd | *s.* beija-flor

humorist | hĭv'mǝrist | *s.* humorista

humorous | hĭv'mǝrǝs | *a.* humorístico, jocoso, engraçado

humour, humor | hĭv'mǝ | *s.* humor; temperamento, índole. **-out of h.** descontente, aborrecido / *vt.* comprazer, fazer a vontade de, satisfazer

hump | hâmp' | *s.* corcunda, corcova, giba; outeiro, elevação; protuberância

hunch | hânś | *s.* pedaço, naco; calombo; corcova; palpite, pressentimento

hunchback | hânś'bak | *s.* corcunda; pessoa corcunda

hundred | hân'drǝd | *s. a.* cem; cento, centena

Hungarian | hânge'ǝrĭǝn | *s. a.* húngaro

hunger | hân'gǝ | *s.* fome; (fig.) desejo ardente / *vi.* sentir fome; (fig.) desejar ardentemente

hungry | hân'grĭ | *a.* com fome, faminto; (fig.) ansioso

hunk | hânk' | *s.* pedaço grande, naco

hunt | hânt' | *s.* caça, caçada / *vt.* caçar; perseguir

hunter | hân'tǝ | *s.* caçador; cão ou cavalo de caça

hunting | hân'ting | *s.* caça, caçada; perseguição

huntsman | hânts'mǝn | *s.* caçador

hurdle | hᴇ'dǝl | *s.* barreira

hurdy-gurdy | hᴇ'dĭgᴇdĭ | *s.* realejo

hurl | hɛl’ | *vt.* arremessar, atirar, lançar, arrojar

hurrah | hərʌ’ | *s. interj.* hurra!, viva!

hurray | hərey’ | *s. interj.* = *hurrah*

hurricane | hâ’rikən | *s.* furacão, tufão, tempestade

hurry | hâ’rī | *s.* pressa; precipitação, urgência. -**to be in a h.** estar com pressa / *vt.* apressar / *vi.* apressar-se. -**h. up!** depressa!, vamos!, ande logo!

hurt | hɛt’ | *s.* ferida; dano, prejuízo; dor (moral ou física) / *a.* ferido; magoado, ofendido / *vt.* ferir, machucar; ofender, afligir, melindrar / *vi.* doer

hurtle | hɛ’təl | *vi.* chocar-se, colidir; zunir, assobiar; arremessar-se

husband | hâz’bənd | *s.* marido, esposo / *vt.* desposar; economizar; administrar cuidadosamente, conservar

hush | hâš’ | *s.* silêncio / *vt.* silenciar, acalmar / *vi.* calar-se / *interj.* silêncio!

husk | hâsk’ | *s.* casca; vagem; palha de milho / *vt.* debulhar

husky | hâs’k̩ī | *s.* cão esquimó / *a.* palhento; rouco

hustle | hâ’səl | *vt.* empurrar, atropelar / *vi.* abrir caminho aos empurrões; azafamar-se, apressar-se

hut | hât’ | *s.* cabana, choça, choupana

hyacinth | hay’əsinϑ | *s.* jacinto

(pedra e flor)

hybrid | hay’brid | *s. a.* híbrido

hydrant | hay’drənt | *s.* hidrante

hydraulic | haydro’lik | *a.* hidráulico

hydro | hay’drow | *s.* (coloq.) estabelecimento hidroterápico

hydrogen | hay’drəɹ̣ən | *s.* hidrogênio

hyena | hayɪ’nə | *s.* hiena

hygiene | hay’ɹ̣in | *s.* higiene

hygienic | hayɹ̣ɪ’nik | *a.* higiênico

hymn | him’ | *s.* hino

hyperbole | haypɛ’bəlī | *s.* hipérbole

hyphen | hay’fən | *s.* hífen, traço de união

hypnosis | hipnow’sis | *s.* hipnose

hypnotic | hipno’tik | *a.* hipnótico

hypnotism | hip’nətizəm | *s.* hipnotismo

hypnotize | hip’nətayz | *vt.* hipnotizar

hypochondria | haypowkon’drīə | *s.* hipocondria

hypocrisy | hipo’krəsī | *s.* hipocrisia

hypocrite | hi’pəkrit | *s.* hipócrita

hypocritical | hipəkri’tikəl | *a.* hipócrita, falso

hypothesis | haypo’ϑəsis | *s.* hipótese

hypothetical | haypəϑe’tikəl | *a.* hipotético

hysteria | histɪ’rīə | *s.* histeria, histerismo

hysterical | histe’rikəl | *a.* histérico

I

I, i | ay’ | *s.* i / *pron.* (maiúsc.) eu

Iberian | aybɪ’rīən | *s.a.* ibérico

ice | ays’ | *s.* gelo. -**to cut no i.** não dar resultado

iceberg | ays’bɛg | *s. iceberg*

ice cream | ays’krɪm | *s.* sorvete

iced | ayst’ | *a.* gelado; coberto com glace (bolo)

Icelandic | ayslan’dik | *s.a.* islandês

icicle | ay'sikəl | s. sincelo, pingente de gelo

icy | ay'sī | a. gelado, glacial, gélido

idea | aydı'ə | s. idéia, noção; projeto, propósito, intenção; impressão indefinida

ideal | aydı'əl | s. ideal / a. ideal; perfeito, modelar

idealist | aydı'əlist | s. idealista

identical | ayden'tikəl | a. idêntico

identification | aydentifikey'śən | s. identificaçao

identification papers | aydentifikey'śənpey'pəz | spl. documentos de identidade

identify | ayden'tifay | vt. identificar

identity | ayden'titɪ | s. identidade

ideology | aydio'ləɟī | s. ideologia

idiocy | i'dīəsī | s. idiotia; idiotice, imbecilidade

idiom | i'dīəm | s. expressão idiomática; idioma, língua

idiosyncrasy | idīəsin'krəsī | s. idiossincrasia

idiot | i'dīət | s. idiota

idiotic | idīo'tik | a. idiota, tolo, néscio, estúpido

idle | ay'dəl | a. preguiçoso, indolente; ocioso, inativo; desempregado; fútil, vão; inútil / vi. mandriar; estar inativo, desocupado ou desempregado. **-to i. away** dissipar, gastar ociosamente, desperdiçar

idleness | ay'dəlnes | s. ociosidade; indolência; frivolidade; inatividade

idler | ayd'lə | s. ocioso, preguiçoso, mandrião

idol | ay'dəl | s. ídolo

idolatrous | aydo'lətrəs | a. idólatra

idolatry | aydo'lətrī | s. idolatria

idolize | ay'dəlayz | vt. idolatrar, adorar

idyll, idyl | ay'dil i'dil | s. idílio

idyllic | idi'lik | a. idílico

if | if | conj. se; embora. **-i. not** se-

não, do contrário. **-i. so** sendo assim

ignite | ignayt' | vt. inflamar, acender, pôr fogo a / vi. inflamar-se, pegar fogo

ignition | igni'śən | s. ignição

ignoble | ignow'bəl | a. ignóbil, vil, desprezível

ignominious | ignəmi'nīəs | a. ignominioso, vergonhoso

ignominy | ig'nəminī | s. ignomínia, opróbrio, desonra

ignoramus | ignərey'məs | s. ignorante

ignorance | ig'nərəns | s. ignorância

ignorant | ig'nərənt | a. ignorante; inculto; inexperiente; grosseiro

ignore | ignó' | vt. não fazer caso de; desprezar, desconsiderar; ignorar

ill | il' | s. mal / a. doente; mau, malvado / adv. mal. **-to be taken i.** adoecer. **-with an i grace** de má vontade. **-i. at ease** embaraçado, acanhado. **-we can i. afford** mal podemos, não podemos

ill-bred | il'bred | a. mal-educado, grosseiro

ill-disposed | il'dispowzd | a. mal-intencionado

illegal | ill'gəl | a. ilegal

illegible | ile'ɟibəl | a. ilegível

illegitimacy | iləɟi'timəsī | s. ilegitimidade

illegitimate | iləɟi'timit | a. ilegítimo

ill-fated | il'feytid | a. mal-aventurado, malfadado

ill-favoured, ill-favored | il'feyvəd | a. feio

ill feeling | il'fɪling | s. hostilidade, má vontade

ill-gotten | il'gotən | a. obtido por meios ilícitos

illicit | ili'sit | a. ilícito

illiteracy | ili'tərəsī | s. analfabetismo; ignorância

illiterate | ili'tərit | a. analfabeto; ignorante

ill-mannered | il'manəd | *a.* grosseiro, descortês

ill-natured | il'neyšəd | *a.* de má índole; rabugento, mal-humorado

illness | il'nes | *s.* doença, enfermidade

illogical | ilo'ǰikəl | *a.* ilógico; absurdo

ill-starred | il'steəd | *a.* = ill--fated

illuminate | iliu'mineyt | *vt.* iluminar

illumination | iliuminey'šən | *s.* iluminação; inspiração; iluminura; (*pl.*) luminárias

illumine | iliu'min | *vt.* iluminar

ill-use | il'iuz | *vt.* maltratar; insultar

illusion | iluʹjən | *s.* ilusão

illusory | iluʹzərī | *a.* ilusório

illustrate | i'ləstreyt | *vt.* ilustrar; esclarecer

illustration | iləstrey'šən | *s.* ilustração, gravura

illustrious | ilâs'trīəs | *a.* ilustre, notável, eminente

ill will | il'wil | *s.* má vontade; rancor

image | i'miǰ | *s.* imagem; representação; efígie; símbolo

imagery | i'miǰərī | *s.* imagens

imaginable | ima'ǰinəbəl | *a.* imaginável, concebível

imaginary | ima'ǰinərī | *a.* imaginário, fictício; quimérico, ilusório

imagination | imaǰiney'šən | *s.* imaginação; fantasia

imaginative | ima'ǰinətiv | *a.* imaginativo; inventivo

imagine | ima'ǰin | *vt. vi.* imaginar; conceber, supor

imbecile | im'bəsil | *s.a.* imbecil; estúpido; idiota

imbibe | imbayb' | *vt.* beber; inalar; absorver; assimilar (idéias)

imbue | imbiu' | *vt.* impregnar; saturar; embeber; imbuir, compenetrar

imitate | i'miteyt | *vt.* imitar, copiar; arremedar; contrafazer

imitation | imitey'šən | *s.* imitação; cópia; arremedo; contrafação

imitator | i'miteytə | *s.* imitador

immaculate | ima'kĭulit | *a.* imaculado; irrepreensível; inocente, sem pecado

immaterial | iməti'rīəl | *a.* imaterial; irrelevante

immature | imətiu'ə | *a.* imaturo; inexperiente

immeasurable | ime'ǰərəbəl | *a.* imenso, incomensurável

immediate | imi'dīət | *a.* imediato, urgente; adjacente

immediately | imi'dīətlī | *adv.* imediatamente, sem demora, em seguida, já

immemorial | imimó'rīəl | *a.* imemorial

immense | imens' | *a.* imenso

immerse | imɛs' | *vt.* mergulhar, imergir, submergir

immersion | imɛ'šən | *s.* imersão

immigrant | i'migrənt | *s.a.* imigrante

immigration | imigrey'šən | *s.* imigração

imminent | i'minənt | *a.* iminente

immobile | imow'bayl | *a.* imóvel, parado, fixo

immobilize | imow'bilayz | *vt.* imobilizar, paralisar

immoderate | imo'dərit | *a.* imoderado; exagerado

immodest | imo'dist | *a.* imodesto; impudico, indecente

immoral | imo'rəl | *a.* imoral, desonesto; licencioso

immorality | imərə'litī | *s.* imoralidade

immortal | imó'təl | *a.* imortal, imorredouro

immortality | imóta'litī | *s.* imortalidade

immortalize | imó'təlayz | *vt.* imortalizar

immovable | imv'vəbəl | *s.* imóvel / *a.* imóvel, sólido, fixo; impassível

immune | imiʋn' | *a.* imune, isento, livre, imunizado

immunity | imĭu'nitī | *s.* imuni-
dade, isenção

immunize | i'mĭunayz | *vt.* imu-
nizar

immutable | imĭu'təbəl | *a.* imu-
tável, inalterável

imp | imp' | *s.* diabete, diabi-
nho; criança levada

impact | im'pakt | *s.* impacto;
choque, colisão, embate

impair | impe'ə | *vt.* prejudicar;
danificar, avariar

impalpable | impal'pəbəl | *a.*
impalpável

impart | impʌt' | *vt.* dar, empres-
tar, conferir; aquinhoar; co-
municar, participar

impartial | impʌ'śəl | *a.* impar-
cial; equitativo

impartiality | impʌśīa'litī | *s.* im-
parcialidade

impassable | impʌ'səbəl | *a.* in-
transitável; intransponível

impasse | am'pas im'pas | *s.* im-
passe, beco sem saída

impassioned | impa'śənd | *a.*
apaixonado, veemente

impassive | impa'siv | *a.* impassí-
vel, indiferente

impatience | impey'śəns | *s.* im-
paciência

impatient | impey'śənt | *a.* impa-
ciente. -i. of intolerante com

impeccable | impe'kəbəl | *a.* im-
pecável, perfeito

impecunious | impikĭu'nĭəs | *a.*
sem dinheiro, pobre

impede | impĭd' | *vt.* impedir,
dificultar

impediment | impe'dimənt | *s.*
impedimento, obstáculo; defeito da fala

impel | impel' | *vt.* obrigar, cons-
tranger, compelir; impelir,
propelir; incitar

impending | impen'ding | *a.* imi-
nente (perigo etc.)

impenetrable | impe'nitrəbəl | *a.*
impenetrável

impenitent | impe'nitənt | *a.*
impenitente

imperative | impe'rətiv | *s.* impe-
rativo / *a.* imperativo, impres-
cindível

imperceptible | impɛsep'tibəl | *a.*
imperceptível

imperfect | impɛ'fikt | *s.* (gram.)
imperfeito / *a.* defeituoso, imperfeito

imperial | impɪ'rĭəl | *a.* imperial

imperialism | impɪ'rĭəlizəm | *s.*
imperialismo

imperialist | impɪ'rĭəlist | *s.a.* im-
perialista

imperil | impe'ril | *vt.* arriscar,
pôr em perigo

imperious | impɪ'rĭəs | *a.* impe-
rioso, arrogante; urgente

imperishable | impe'riśəbəl | *a.*
imperecível, imorredouro

impermeable | impə'mĭəbəl | *a.*
impermeável

impersonal | impɛ's nəl | *s.* ver-
bo impessoal / *a.* impessoal;
indefinido

impersonate | impɛ'səneyt | *vt.*
representar, fazer o papel de;
fazer-se passar por

impersonation | impɛsəney'śən |
s. representação, imitação

impertinence | impɛ'tinəns | *s.*
impertinência; insolência; atrevimento

impertinent | impɛ'tinənt | *a.* im-
pertinente; insolente; atrevido;
arrogante

imperturbable | impɛtɛ'bəbəl |
a. imperturbável, sereno

impervious | impɛ'vĭəs | *a.* indi-
ferente; impenetrável; impermeável; inacessível

impetigo | impitay'gow | *s.* impe-
tigo

impetuosity | impetŭuo'sitī | *s.*
impetuosidade; arrebatamen-
to; violência, fúria

impetuous | impe'tŭuəs | *a.* impe-
tuoso, arrebatado; precipita-
do, irrefletido

impetus | im'pitəs | *s.* ímpeto

impinge | impinj' | *vi.* chocar-se,
colidir; infringir, violar; in-
vadir

impish | im'piś | *a.* travesso, traquinas, levado

implacable | impla'kəbəl | *a.* implacável, inexorável

implant | implʌnt' | *vt.* estabelecer, implantar

implement | im'plimənt | *s.* implemento, utensílio / *vt.* aparelhar, apetrechar; cumprir, executar

implicate | im'plikeyt | *vt.* implicar, comprometer

implication | implikey'śən | *s.* implicação, comprometimento; sugestão, dedução; ilação

implicit | impli'sit | *a.* implícito, subentendido, tácito; inquestionável, absoluto

implore | imploʹ | *vt.* implorar, suplicar

imply | implay' | *vt.* implicar; envolver; sugerir, significar

impolite | impəlayt' | *a.* descortês, indelicado, incivil

imponderable | impon'dərəbəl | *a.* imponderável

import | impótʹ | *s.* importação; artigo importado; importância, significação / *vt.* importar (tb. com.); significar, implicar; dizer respeito a

importance | impó'təns | *s.* importância; influência

important | impó'tənt | *a.* importante

importation | impótey'śən | *s.* importação

importer | impóʹtə | *s.* importador

importunate | impóʹtĭunit | *a.* importuno, insistente, impertinente; premente

impose | impowz' | *vt.* impor. -to i. on incomodar, abusar

imposing | impow'zing | *a.* imponente, grandioso

imposition | impəzi'śən | *s.* imposição; intrusão

impossibility | imposibi'litĭ | *s.* impossibilidade

impossible | impo'sibəl | *a.* impossível; irrealizável; (coloq.)
insuportavel

impostor | impos'tə | *s.* impostor, embusteiro

imposture | impos'šə | *s.* impostura, embuste

impotence | im'pətəns | *s.* impotência

impotent | im'pətənt | *a.* impotente; incapaz

impoverish | impo'vəriś | *vt.* empobrecer; exaurir

impracticable | imprak'tikəbəl | *a.* impraticável, inexeqüível

imprecation | imprəkey'śən | *s.* imprecação, maldição, praga

impregnable | impreg'nəbəl | *a.* inexpugnável; inconquistável

impregnate | im'pregneyt | *a.* prenhe (tb. fig.); fertilizado, fecundado; impregnado / *vt.* emprenhar; fertilizar; impregnar, saturar; imbuir

impress | impres' | *s.* impressão, marca / *vt.* imprimir; impressionar; inculcar, infundir; recrutar; requisitar

impression | impre'śən | *s.* impressão

impressive | impre'siv | *a.* impressionante, imponente

imprint | im'print | *s.* sinal, traço, vestígio, marca; (tip.) colofão, cólofon / | imprint' | *vt.* imprimir; gravar na mente

imprison | impri'zən | *vt.* prender, encarcerar

imprisonment | impri'zənmənt | *s.* prisão, encarceramento

improbable | impro'bəbəl | *a.* improvável, duvidoso

impromptu | impromp'tĭu | *s.* improvisação, improviso; (mús.) *impromptu* / *a.* de improviso / *adv.* improvisadamente

improper | impro'pə | *a.* impróprio, inconveniente; impreciso; indecoroso

impropriety | imprəpray'ətĭ | *s.* impropriedade, inexatidão; inconveniência, indecência

improve | imprʊv' | *vt.* aperfeiçoar, melhorar / *vi.* melho-

rar(-se); aperfeiçoar-se; pro-
gredir

improvement | impruv'mənt ǀ *s.*
aperfeiçoamento

improvident | impro'vidənt | *a.*
improvidente; imprevidente

improvise | im'prəvayz | *vt.*
improvisar

imprudent | impru'dənt | *a.*
imprudente

impudence | im'pĭudəns |*s.* inso-
lência, atrevimento

impudent | im'pĭudənt | *a.* inso-
lente, atrevido, petulante

impugn | impĭυn' | *vt.* impugnar;
contestar, discutir

impulse | im'pâls | *s.* impulso

impulsive| impâl'siv |*a.* impulsi-
vo, impetuoso

impunity | impĭu'nitĭ |*s.* impuni-
dade. **-with i.** impunemente

impure| impĭυ'ə | *a.* impuro

impurity | impĭu'ritĭ | *s.* im-
pureza

impute| impĭut' | *vt.* imputar (tb.
jur., teol.); atribuir

in | in |*prep.* em; dentro de. **-i. the
morning** de (pela) manhã / *adv.*
dentro; em casa; na sua estação
ou época (fruta, peixe, caça
etc.)

inability| inəbi'litĭ |*s.* inaptidão,
incapacidade

inaccessible | inakse'sibəl | *a.*
inacessível; inatingível

inaccuracy | ina'kĭurəsĭ | *s.* ine-
xatidão, imprecisão

inaccurate | ina'kĭurit | *a.* inexa-
to, impreciso

inactive | inak'tiv | *a.* inativo;
ocioso; inerte

inadequacy | ina'dikwəsĭ |*s.* ina-
dequabilidade; impropriedade;
inadaptação; inadequação

inadequate | ina'dikwit | *a.* ina-
dequado; insuficiente

inadmissible | inədmi'sibəl | *a.*
inadmissível, inaceitável

inadvertently | inədvε'təntlĭ | *adv.*
inadvertidamente

inalienable | iney'lĭənəbəl | *a.*
inalienável

inane | ineyn' | *a.* inane, vazio,
fútil; tolo, pateta

inanimate | ina'nimit | *a.* inani-
mado, sem vida

inapplicable | inəpli'kəbəl | *a.*
inaplicável

inappropriate| inəprow'prĭit |*a.*
impróprio, inadequado

inarticulate | inᴧti'kĭulit |*a.* inar-
ticulado; indistinto; inarticula-
do (fala); mudo

inasmuch | inəzmâš' | *adv.* (com
as) visto que, porquanto

inattentive | inəten'tiv | *a.* desa-
tento, distraído

inaudible | inó'dibəl | *a.* inau-
dível

inaugural| inó'gĭurəl |*a.* inaugu-
ral, inaugurativo

inaugurate | inó'gĭureyt | *vt.*
inaugurar

inauguration | inógĭurey'śən | *s.*
inauguração; início, estabelecimento, fundação

inauspicious | inóspi'śəs | *a.* in-
fausto, desfavorável

inboard | inbód' | *s.* (náut.) mo-
tor de centro / *a.* (náut.) inter-
no, interior / *adv.* (náut.) dentro da amurada

inborn | inbón' | *a.* inato, ingêni-
to; instintivo

inbred | inbred' | *a.* inato, congê-
nito; endógamo

inbreeding | inbrĭ'ding | *s.* pro-
criação consangüínea

incalculable | inkal'kĭuləbəl | *a.*
incalculável

incapable | inkey'pəbəl | *a.* inca-
paz; incompetente, inabilita-
do, desqualificado

incapacitate | inkəpa'siteyt | *vt.*
incapacitar

incapacity | inkəpa'sitĭ | *s.* inca-
pacidade

incarnation| inkᴧney'śən |*s.* en-
carnação

incendiarism| insen'dĭərizəm |*s.*
incêndio doloso, incêndio cri-
minoso

incendiary| insen'dĭərĭ |*a.* incen-
diário

incense | in'sɔns | s. incenso; lisonja / vt. incensar; lisonjear; enraivecer, encolerizar, enfurecer

incentive | insen'tiv | s. incentivo; estímulo

inception | insɛp'ʃɔn | s. inauguração, começo

incessant | inse'sɔnt | a. ininterrupto, contínuo

incest | in'sest | s. incesto

inch | inʃ' | s. polegada. -i. by i. pouco a pouco. -every i. sob todos os aspectos / vt. vi. mover(-se) pouco a pouco. -to i. forward avançar gradualmente

incident | in'sidɔnt | s. incidente, acontecimento, casualidade / a. possível, provável, eventual

incidental | insiden'tɔl | a. incidental, acidental, eventual, casual

incidentally | insiden'tɔlĭ | adv. incidentalmente; a propósito, por falar nisso

incinerator | insi'nɔreytɔ | s. incinerador

incipient | insi'pĭɔnt | a. incipiente, em início

incision | insi'jɔn | s. incisão, corte; entalhe

incisive | insay'siv | a. incisivo, penetrante; mordaz

incite | insayt' | vt. incitar, instigar, estimular

incivility | insivi'litĭ | s. incivilidade, indelicadeza

inclemency | inkle'mɔnsĭ | s. inclemência (do tempo), intempérie

inclination | inkliney'ʃɔn | s. inclinação, tendência, propensão, disposição

incline | in'klayn | s. inclinação; declive, aclive / | inklayn' | vt. inclinar, predispor / vi. inclinar-se, estar propenso a

include | inklʊd' | vt. incluir; abranger, conter

inclusion | inklʊ'jɔn | s. inclusão

inclusive | inklʊ'siv | a. inclusivo. -i. of incluindo

incoherence | inkowhɪ'rɔns | s. incoerência

incoherent | inkowhɪ'rɔnt | a. incoerente, desconexo

income | in'kɔm | s. rendimento

income tax | in'kɔmtaks | s. imposto de renda

incoming | in'kâming | s. chegada, entrada; (pl.) renda / a. que entra, entrante

incomparable | inkom'pɔrɔbɔl | a. incomparável

incompatible | inkɔmpa'tibɔl | a. incompatível

incompetence | inkom'pitɔns | s. incompetência

incompetent | inkom'pitɔnt | a. incompetente

incomplete | inkɔmplĭt' | a. incompleto, inacabado

incomprehensible | inkomprihen'sibɔl | a. incompreensível

inconceivable | inkɔnsɪ'vɔbɔl | a. inconcebível, incrível

inconclusive | inkɔnklʊ'siv | a. não decisivo, inconvincente (argumento, prova ou ação)

incongruous | inkon'gruɔs | a. incongruente; absurdo

inconsiderable | inkɔnsi'dɔrɔbɔl | a. insignificante

inconsiderate | inkɔnsi'dɔrit | a. inconsiderado

inconsistency | inkɔnsis'tɔnsĭ | s. incoerência, contradição; inconseqüência; inconstância

inconsistent | inkɔnsis'tɔnt | a. incoerente, contraditório; inconstante, volúvel

inconsolable | inkɔnsow'lɔbɔl | a. inconsolável

inconspicuous | inkɔnspi'kŭɔs | a. insignificante; obscuro, modesto, humilde

inconstancy | inkon'stɔnsĭ | s. inconstância; instabilidade

inconstant | inkon'stɔnt | a. inconstante; instável

incontestable | inkɔntes'tɔbɔl | a. incontestável

inconvenience | inkɔnvɪ'nĭɔns | s. inconveniência, transtorno /

vt. incomodar, transtornar, estorvar

inconvenient | inkənvı'nĭənt | *a.* inconveniente, inoportuno

incorporate | inkó'pəreyt | *vt.* incorporar, incluir

incorrect | inkərekt' | *a.* incorreto, errado

incorrigible | inko'rĭjibəl | *a.* incorrigível

incorruptible | inkərâp'tibəl | *a.* incorruptível

increase | in'krĭs | *s.* aumento; crescimento / | inkrĭs' | *vt. vi.* aumentar; crescer

increasing | inkrĭ'sing | *a.* crescente, progressivo

incredible | inkre'dibəl | *a.* incrível, inacreditável

incredulous | inkre'dĭuləs | *a.* incrédulo

increment | in'krimənt | *s.* incremento; aumento, acréscimo; desenvolvimento

incriminate | inkri'mineyt | *vt.* incriminar

incubate | in'kĭubeyt | *vt.* incubar, chocar

inculcate | in'kâlkeyt | *vt.* inculcar, incutir

inculcation | inkâlkey'śən | *s.* ato de incutir (idéia etc.)

incumbent | inkâm'bənt | *s.* (ecles.) beneficiado. **-to be i. upon** incumbir a, ser obrigação de, caber a

incur | inkE' | *vt.* incorrer em; contrair (dívida)

incurable | inkĭv'rəbəl | *a.* incurável; incorrigível

incursion | inkE'śən | *s.* incursão, invasão

indebted | inde'tid | *a.* endividado; grato, reconhecido

indebtedness | inde'tidnes | *s.* dívida; gratidão

indecency | indı'sənsĭ | *s.* indecência; obscenidade

indecent | indı'sənt | *a.* indecente; desonesto; obsceno

indecipherable | indisay'fərəbəl | *a.* indecifrável; ilegível

indecision | indisi'śən | *s.* indecisão, irresolução

indecisive | indisay'siv | *a.* indeciso; hesitante

indecorous | inde'kərəs | *a.* indecoroso, vergonhoso

indeed | indıd' | *adv.* na verdade, realmente, decerto, com certeza, de fato / *interj.* é possível?, é mesmo?

indefatigable | indifa'tigəbəl | *a.* infatigável, incansável

indefensible | indifen'sibəl | *a.* indefensável

indefinite | inde'finit | *a.* indefinido, indeterminado

indefinitely | inde'finitlĭ | *adv.* indefinidamente

indelible | inde'libəl | *a.* indelével, permanente

indelible pencil | inde'libəlpen'səl | *s.* lápis-tinta

indelicate | inde'likit | *a.* indelicado, rude; inconveniente, indecoroso

indemnify | indem'nifay | *vt.* indenizar, ressarcir

indemnity | indem'nitĭ | *s.* indenização, ressarcimento

indent | indent' | *s.* endentação; contrato; encomenda (mercadorias) / *vt.* dentear; recortar; picotar; endentar; penetrar em profundidade; dividir (contrato em duas partes iguais) / *vi.* recortar (reentrância); contratar; encomendar; requisitar

independence | indipen'dəns | *s.* independência

independent | indipen'dənt | *a.* independente; separado

indescribable | indiskray'bəbəl | *a.* indescritível, indizível

indestructible | indistrâk'tibəl | *a.* indestrutível

indeterminate | inditE'minit | *a.* indeterminado, indefinido

index | in'deks | *s.* índice; (ecles.) índice expurgatório / *vt.* classificar, catalogar; indexar, fazer índice

index card | in'dekskʌd' | *s.* ficha

de arquivo

index finger | in'deksfing'gə | *s.* dedo indicador

Indian | in'dǐən | *s.a.* indiano (da Índia); índio (da América)

Indian summer | in'dǐənsâ'mə | *s.* veranico; (EUA) dias anormalmente quentes (no fim do outono ou princípio do inverno); (fig.) dias tranqüilos (do último período da vida)

indicate | in'dikeyt | *vt.* indicar; apontar, mostrar; significar; mencionar

indication | indikey'śən | *s.* indicação; menção; indício

indicative | indi'kətiv | *s.a.* indicativo

indicator | in'dikeytə | *s.* indicador

indict | indayt' | *vt.* processar, acusar

indictment| indayt'mənt |*s.* acusação; (jur.) pronúncia

indifference | indi'frəns | *s.* indiferença

indifferent| indif'rənt |*a.* indiferente; medíocre

indigenous | indi'jinəs | *a.* indígena

indigent| in'dijənt |*a.* indigente, pobre

indigestible | indiǰes'tibəl | *a.* indigerível, indigesto

indigestion | indiǰes'śən | *s.* indigestão, dispepsia

indignant | indig'nənt | *a.* indignado; furioso

indignation | indigney'śən | *s.* indignação

indignity | indig'nitǐ | *s.* indignidade, afronta

indigo | in'digow | *s.* índigo, anil / *a.* cor de anil

indirect | indirekt' | *a.* indireto; secundário; remoto

indiscipline | indi'siplin | *s.* indisciplina

indiscreet | indiskrit' | *a.* indiscreto, incauto

indiscretion | indiskre'śən |*s.* indiscrição, irreflexão

indiscriminate | indiskri'minit | *a.* indiscriminado

indispensable | indispen'səbəl | *a.* indispensável

indisposed | indispowzd' | *a.* indisposto; relutante

indisposition | indispəzi'śən | *s.* indisposição; relutância

indisputable | indispǐu'təbəl | *a.* incontestável

indissoluble| indiso'lǐubəl |*a.* indissolúvel, firme, permanente, indestrutível

indistinct | indistinkt' | *a.* indistinto, indefinido, vago

indistinguishable | indistin'gwiśəbəl | *a.* indistinguível

individual | indivi'dǐuəl | *s.* indivíduo / *a.* individual

individuality | individǐua'litǐ | *s.* individualidade, personalidade; particularidade

indivisible | indivi'zibəl | *a.* indivisível

indolence | in'dələns |*s.* indolência, preguiça

indolent | in'dələnt | *a.* indolente, preguiçoso

indomitable | indo'mitəbəl | *a.* indomável, indômito

indoor| in'dó |*a.* doméstico, caseiro, que se faz dentro de casa, de salão

indoors | indóz' | *adv.* dentro de casa, portas adentro

induce | indǐus' | *vt.* induzir; persuadir; produzir, causar

inducement | indǐus'mənt |*s.* indução, persuasão; incentivo, estímulo; chamariz

indulge | indâlj' | *vt.* satisfazer, saciar (desejos); comprazer / *vi.* entregar-se a; deliciar-se com

indulgence | indâl'jəns |*s.* indulgência, condescendência; apego (a alguma coisa), prazer, deleite; (com.) moratória, prorrogação

indulgent | indâl'jənt | *a.* indulgente, condescendente

industrial | indâs'trīəl | *a*. industrial

industrialism | indâs'trīəlizəm | *s*. industrialismo

industrialist | indâs'trīəlist | *s*. industrial

industrious | indâs'trīəs | *a*. diligente, trabalhador, esforçado, industrioso

industry | in'dâstrī | *s*. indústria; atividade, diligência

inebriated | inī'brīeytid | *a*. embriagado, ébrio, bêbedo

inedible | ine'dibəl | *a*. que não é comestível, incomível

ineffable | ine'fəbəl | *a*. inefável, indizível

ineffective | inifek'tiv | *a*. ineficaz, ineficiente

ineffectiveness | inifek'tivnes | *s*. ineficácia

inefficiency | inifi'śənsī | *s*. ineficiência, ineficácia

inefficient | inifi'śənt | *a*. ineficiente, ineficaz

ineligible | ine'lijibəl | *a*. inelegível

inept | inept' | *a*. inepto; desajeitado; ineficiente

inequality | inikwo'lītī | *s*. desigualdade; desproporção

inequitable | ine'kwitəbəl | *a*. injusto, iníquo

ineradicable | inira'dikəbəl | *a*. inerradicável, inextirpável

inert | inēt' | *a*. inerte; neutro; inanimado

inertia | inē'śə | *s*. inércia; inação, indolência

inescapable | iniskey'pəbəl | *a*. inevitável, inelutável

inexcusable | inekskïu'zəbəl | *a*. imperdoável, indesculpável

inexhaustible | inegzós'tibəl | *a*. inesgotável, inexaurível

inexorable | inek'sərəbəl | *a*. inexorável, implacável

inexpedient | inekspɪ'dïənt | *a*. inoportuno, desaconselhável

inexpensive | inekspen'siv | *a*. barato, econômico

inexperience | inekspɪ'rīəns | *s*. inexperiência

inexperienced | inekspɪ'rīənst | *a*. inexperiente

inexplicable | inekspli'kəbəl | *a*. inexplicável

inexpressible | inekspre'sibəl | *a*. inexprimível, indescritível, indizível, inefável

inextricable | inekstri'kəbəl | *a*. inextricável; insolúvel

infallibility | infalibi'litī | *s*. infalibilidade

infallible | infa'libəl | *a*. infalível; indubitável

infamous | in'fəməs | *a*. infame; abominável, vil

infamy | in'fəmī | *s*. infâmia

infancy | in'fənsī | *s*. infância

infant | in'fənt | *s*. bebê, criança / *a*. infantil

infantry | in'fəntrī | *s*. infantaria

infatuated | infa'tïueytid | *a*. apaixonado, enamorado; arrebatado, entusiasmado

infatuation | infatïuey'śən | *s*. paixão; fascinação, arrebatamento; obsessão

infect | infekt' | *vt*. infectar, infeccionar; contaminar, contagiar

infection | infek'śən | *s*. infecção; contaminação

infectious | infek'śəs | *a*. infeccioso, contagioso

infer | infE' | *vt*. inferir, deduzir, concluir / *vi*. tirar inferências

inference | in'fərənś | *s*. inferência, conclusão, dedução

inferior | infɪ'rīə | *s.a*. inferior

inferiority | infirïo'ritī | *s*. inferioridade

infernal | infE'nəl | *a*. infernal

infest | infest' | *vt*. infestar

infidel | in'fidəl | *s*. infiel

infidelity | infide'litī | *s*. infidelidade; deslealdade

infiltrate | in'filtreyt | *vt*. infiltrar, introduzir / *vi*. infiltrar-se, introduzir-se

infinite | in'finit | *s.a*. infinito

infinitely | in'finitlī | *adv*. infinitamente; imensamente

infinitive| infi'nitiv |*s*. infinitivo
infinity | infi'nitĭ | *s*. infinidade, infinito
infirm | infɛm' | *a*. inválido; enfermo; fraco; (fig.) irresoluto, vacilante
infirmary | infɛ'mərĭ | *s*. hospital; enfermaria
infirmity| infɛ'mitĭ |*s*. fraqueza, debilidade; enfermidade, doença; invalidade
inflame | infleym' | *vt*. inflamar, excitar / *vi*. inflamar-se, pegar fogo
inflammable| infla'məbəl |*a*. inflamável; excitável
inflammation | infləmey'śən | *s*. inflamação
inflammatory | infla'mətərĭ | *a*. inflamatório, inflamativo; excitante, apaixonante
inflate | infleyt' | *vt*. inflar; (econ.) inflacionar / *vi*. inflar; causar inflação
inflated | infley'tid | *a*. inflado; inflacionado; empolado, bombástico (estilo)
inflation | infley'śən |*s*. inflação (esp. fin.)
inflection | inflek'śən | *s*. inflexão; modulação (de voz); (gram.) flexão
inflexible | inflek'sibəl | *a*. inflexível; intransigente
inflict | inflikt' | *vt*. infligir; impor
influence | in'fluəns | *s*. influência; ascendência, prestígio / *vt*. influenciar, influir em; alterar
influential | influen'śəl | *a*. influente; poderoso, importante, prestigioso
influenza | influen'zə | *s*. gripe, influenza
influx| in'flâks |*s*. afluência
inform | infóm' | *vt*. informar, notificar / *vi*. **-to i. against** ou **on** denunciar
informal | infó'məl | *a*. à vontade, sem-cerimonioso, sem formalidade, não oficial
informality | infóma'litĭ | *s*. in-

formalidade, sem-cerimônia
informant | infó'mənt | *s*. informante; denunciante
information | infəmey'śən |*s*. informação; informações (dados, fatos etc.), esclarecimentos
informer | infó'mə | *s*. denunciante, delator; informante
infrequent| infri'kwənt |*a*. raro, pouco freqüente
infringe | infrinj' | *vt*. infringir, transgredir, violar
infringement | infrinj'mənt | *s*. infração, transgressão
infuriate| infʊ'rīeyt |*vt*. enfurecer, enraivecer
infuse | infʊz' | *vt*. infundir
ingenious| injî'nɩəs |*a*. engenhoso; artificioso
ingenuity | injinĭu'itĭ | *s*. engenhosidade, habilidade; inventividade
ingenuous | inje'nĭuəs | *a*. ingênuo, simples, inocente
inglorious | ingló'rīəs | *a*. inglório, vergonhoso
ingrained | ingreynd' | *a*. inveterado; arraigado
ingratiate | ingrey'śieyt | *vt*. insinuar-se nas boas graças de alguém, ganhar a simpatia de alguém
ingratitude | ingra'titĭud | *s*. ingratidão
ingredient | ingrɩ'diənt | *s*. ingrediente; componente
inhabit | inha'bit | *vt*. habitar
inhabitant| inha'bitənt |*s*. habitante; morador, residente permanente
inhale | inheyl' | *vt*. inalar, aspirar; tragar (fumaça de cigarro, charuto etc.)
inherent| inhi'ərənt |*a*. inerente, inato, intrínseco
inherit | inhe'rit | *vt*. herdar
inheritance | inhe'ritəns | *s*. herança; sucessão; patrimônio
inheritor | inhe'ritə |*s*. herdeiro
inhibit| inhi'bit |*vt*. inibir, reprimir, impedir

inhibition| inibi'śən |*s.* inibição, impedimento

inhospitable | inhospi'təbəl | *a.* inóspito (lugar); inospitaleiro (pessoa)

inhuman | inhĭu'mən | *a.* desumano, inumano, atroz, brutal

inhumanity | inhĭuma'nitĭ |*s.* desumanidade, atrocidade

inimical | ini'mikəl | *a.* inimigo, hostil; prejudicial

inimitable| ini'mitəbəl |*a.* inimitável

iniquitous| ini'kwitəs |*a.* iníquo, injusto; mau, ruim

iniquity | ini'kwitĭ |*s.* iniqüidade

initial| ini'śəl |*s.a.* inicial / *vt.* assinar, rubricar, marcar com iniciais

initiate| ini'śĭeyt |*s.* iniciado, iniciando /*a.* iniciado / *vt.* iniciar, começar; inaugurar

initiative | ini'śĭətiv | *s.* iniciativa / *a.* iniciativo, inicial, preliminar

inject | inȷekt' | *vt.* injetar

injection | inȷek'śən |*s.* injeção

injudicious| inȷudi'śəs |*a.* indiscreto, imprudente, insensato, leviano

injunction| inȷânk'śən |*s.* injunção, imposição; mandado; (jur.) interdito

injure | in'ȷə | *vt.* prejudicar, lesar; ferir, machucar; danificar, avariar

injured | in'ȷəd |*a.* prejudicado; ferido; magoado

injurious | inȷυ'rĭəs | *a.* prejudicial, danoso, nocivo

injury | in'ȷərĭ |*s.* ferimento; dano, prejuízo; mal

injustice | inȷâs'tis | *s.* injustiça; iniqüidade

ink | ink' | *s.* tinta (de escrever ou de impressão)

ink-blot | ink'blot | *s.* borrão de tinta

inkling | ink'ling | *s.* insinuação, alusão vaga; noção

ink-pad | ink'pad | *s.* almofada para carimbos

inkstand | ink'stand | *s.* tinteiro (com porta-canetas)

ink-well | ink'wel |*s.* tinteiro

inlaid | in'leyd | *a.* embutido, marchetado, incrustado

inland | in'lənd | *s.* interior (de um país) / *a.* interior; do interior / *adv.* para ou no interior

in-law| inló' |*s.* (coloq.) parente por afinidade

inlet | in'let | *s.* enseada, angra; estreito; entrada

inmate | in'meyt | *s.* interno, recluso (em prisão, hospital etc.); residente

inmost | in'mowst |*a.* íntimo, recôndito, mais profundo

inn | in' | *s.* estalagem, taberna, hospedaria

innate | ineyt' | *a.* inato

inner | i'nə | *a.* interior

inner tube | i'nətĭub | *s.* câmara de ar (de pneu)

innings| i'ningz |*s.* vez de jogar, turno; (*pl.*) gestão, governo, administração

innkeeper | in'kɪpə | *s.* estalajadeiro, hospedeiro

innocence | i'nəsəns | *s.* inocência; pureza, simplicidade

innocent | i'nəsənt | *a.* inocente; ingênuo, puro

innocuous | ino'kĭuəs | *a.* inócuo, inofensivo

innovation | inəvey'śən | *s.* inovação, novidade

Inns of Court | inz'ofkóət | *spl.* nome de quatro sociedades de advogados londrinos

innuendo| inĭuen'dow |*s.* indireta, alusão, insinuação

innumerable | inĭu'mərəbəl | *a.* inumerável, incontável

inoculate | ino'kĭuleyt | *vt.* inocular

inoculation | inokĭuley'śən | *s.* inoculação

inoffensive | inəfen'siv | *a.* inofensivo, inócuo, anódino

inopportune | ino'pətĭun |*a.* inoportuno, intempestivo

inordinate | inó'dinit | *a.* desordenado; imoderado

inorganic| inóga'nik |*a.* inorgânico

in patient, in-patient | in-pey'sənt |*s.* doente internado

inquest | in'kwɛst |*s.* inquérito judicial; investigação

inquire, enquire | inkway'ə |*vt.* perguntar, indagar / *vi.* inquirir. **-to i. after** pedir notícias de

inquiry, enquiry | ɪnkway'ərɪ |*s.* investigação oficial, inquérito. **-to make inquiries** colher informações

inquisition| inkwizi'ʃən |*s.* (jur.) inquérito judicial; (maiúsc., ecles.) Inquisição

inquisitive| inkwi'zitiv |*a.* curioso, perguntador, indagador; intrometido

inquisitor| inkwi'zitə |*s.* inquisidor; inquiridor

inroad | in'rowd | *s.* incursão; invasão

insane | inseyn' | *a.* louco, demente, alienado mental

insanitary| insa'nitərɪ |*a.* insalubre; anti-higiênico

insanity | insa'nitɪ | *s.* loucura, demência

insatiable | insey'ʃəbəl | *a.* insaciável; ávido, voraz

inscribe | inskrayb' | *vt.* inscrever, gravar; dedicar, fazer dedicatória (livro)

inscription | inskrip'ʃən | *s.* inscrição; dedicatória

inscrutability inskrutəbi'litɪ *s.* impenetrabilidade, inescrutabilidade

inscrutable | inskru'təbəl | *a.* impenetrável, inescrutável

insect | in'sekt |*s.* inseto

insecticide | insek'tisayd | *s.* inseticida

insecure | insikɪu'ə | *a.* inseguro; perigoso

insecurity| insikɪu'ritɪ |*s.* insegurança, inseguridade

insensibility | insensibi'litɪ | *s.* insensibilidade

inseparable | inse'pərəbəl | *a.* inseparável

insert | insɛt' | *s.* suplemento (de jornal, livro etc.) / *vt.* inserir, introduzir; pôr, publicar (anúncio em jornal)

inside| insayd' |*s.* interior / *a.* interior, interno; confidencial / *adv.* dentro, por dentro. **-i. out** às avessas / *prep.* em, dentro de; no interior

insidious | insi'dīəs | *a.* ınsidioso; traiçoeiro

insight | in'sayt | *s.* penetração, perspicácia, percepção, discernimento

insignia | insig'nīə | *spl.* insígnias; emblemas

insignificance | ınsigni'fikəns |*s.* insignificância

ınsignificant | insigni'fikənt | *a.* insignificante

insincere| insinsı'ə |*a.* insincero, falso, dissimulado

insincerity | insinse'ritɪ | *s.* insinceridade, falsidade

insinuate | insi'nʎueyt | *vt.* insinuar, dar a entender / *vr.* insinuar-se

insinuation | insinʎuey'ʃən | *s.* insinuação, sugestão, **indireta**, alusão

insipid | insi'pid | *a.* insípido, sem sabor

insist | in'sist | *vi.* insistir, persistir. **-to i. on** ou **upon** insistir em

insistence, insistency | insıs'təns insis'tənsɪ | *s.* insistência, persistência

insistent | insis'tənt | *a.* insistente, persistente

insobriety | insowbray'ətɪ | *s.* intemperança, embriaguez

insolence | in'sələns | *s.* insolência, atrevimento

insolent | in'sələnt | *a.* insolente, atrevido

insoluble | inso'lʎubəl | *a.* insolúvel

insolvent | insol'vənt | *a.* insolvente

insomnia | insom'nɪə | *s.* insônia

insomuch| insowmʌs |*adv.* (com

as ou **that)** a tal ponto que, de tal modo que

inspect | inspekt' | *vt.* inspecionar, fiscalizar, examinar; (mil.) passar revista (a)

inspection | inspek'ʃən | *s.* inspeção, fiscalização; (mil.) revista, inspeção

inspector | inspek'tə | *s.* inspetor, fiscal; comissário de polícia

inspiration | inspirey'ʃən | *s.* inspiração; inalação

inspire | inspay'ə | *vt.* inspirar; animar, incitar / *vi.* inspirar; influenciar

inspiring | inspay'əring | *a.* inspirador, animador

inst. *abrev.* de **instant. -the 6th. inst.** 6 do corrente; *abrev.* de **institute, institution**

instability | instəbi'litĭ | *s.* instabilidade

install | instól' | *vt.* instalar, montar; estabelecer

installation | instəley'ʃən | *s.* instalação, montagem

instalment, installment | instól'mənt | *s.* prestação; episódio (história seriada)

instalment plan | instól'mənt-plan | *s.* (EUA) crediário

instance | in'stəns | *s.* exemplo; caso, situação. **-for i.** por exemplo

instant | in'stənt | *s.* instante, momento / *a.* imediato, urgente; corrente, atual

instantaneous | instəntey'nĭəs | *a.* instantâneo; imediato

instantly | in'stəntlĭ | *adv.* imediatamente, logo

instead | insted' | *adv.* em vez de. **-i. of** em lugar de

instep | in'step | *s.* peito do pé. **-to be high in the i.** ser arrogante

instigate | in'stigeyt | *vt.* instigar, provocar

instigation | instigey'ʃən | *s.* instigação, incitação

instigator | in'stigeytə | *s.* instigador, incitador

instil, instill | instil' | *vt.* instilar; infundir, incutir

instinct | in'stinkt | *s.* instinto

instinctive | instink'tiv | *a.* instintivo

institute | in'stitĭut | *s.* instituto / *vt.* instituir

institution | institĭu'ʃən | *s.* instituição; instituto

instruct | instrâkt' | *vt.* instruir, ensinar; adestrar

instruction | instrâk'ʃən | *s.* instrução, ensino; (*pl.*) instruções, ordens

instructor | instrâk'tə | *s.* instrutor; professor

instrument | in'strumənt | *s.* instrumento (musical etc.) / *vt.* (mús.) instrumentar

instrumental | instrumen'təl | *a.* instrumental. **-to be i. in** ajudar a, concorrer para

insubordinate | insəbó'dinit | *a.* insubordinado, rebelde

insubordination | insəbódiney'ʃən | *s.* insubordinação

insufferable | insâ'fərəbəl | *a.* intolerável, insuportável

insufficient | insəfi'ʃənt | *a.* insuficiente, deficiente

insular | in'sĭulə | *a.* insular, ilhéu; estreito, limitado; insulado, separado; (fig.) retraído, isolado

insulate | in'sĭuleyt | *vt.* isolar

insulation | insĭuley'ʃən | *s.* isolamento

insult | in'sâlt | *s.* insulto, ofensa, injúria / | insâlt' | *vt.* insultar, ofender, injuriar

insulting | insâl'ting | *a.* insultante, ultrajante

insuperable | insu'pərəbəl | *a.* insuperável, invencível

insupportable | insəpó'təbəl | *a.* insuportável, intolerável

insurance | inśu'ərəns | *s.* seguro; prêmio de seguro

insurance broker | inśu'ərəns-brow'kə | *s.* corretor de seguros

insurance policy | inśu'ərəns po'lisĭ | *s.* apólice de seguro

insure | inśu'ə | *vt.* segurar, fazer

seguro

insurgent | insɛ'jənt | *s.a.* insurgente, insurrecto, rebelde, revoltoso

insurmountable | insəmawn'təbəl | *a.* insuperável, intransponível

insurrection | insərek'śən | *s.* insurreição, sublevação

intact | intakt' | *a.* intacto

intangible | intan'jibəl | *a.* intangível; impalpável

integral | in'tigrəl | *a.* integral, completo, total

integrate | in'tigreyt | *vt.* integrar, unir, unificar

integration | intigrey'śən | *s.* integração; assimilação racial; harmonização

integrity | inte'gritī | *s.* integridade, probidade

intellect | in'tilekt | *s.* intelecto, inteligência

intellectual | intilek'tǐuəl | *s.a.* intelectual

intelligence | inte'lijəns | *s.* inteligência; sagacidade; discernimento; serviço secreto, serviço de informações

intelligence officer | inte'lijənso'fisə | *s.* agente do serviço secreto

intelligent | inte'lijənt | *a.* inteligente

intelligentsia | intelijent'sīa | *s.* classe dos intelectuais, intelectualidade, *intelligentsia*

intelligible | inte'lijəbəl | *a.* inteligível; compreensível

intemperate | intem'pəriṭ | *a.* imoderado; excessivo

intend | intend' | *vt.* tencionar, projetar; intentar

intense | intens' | *a.* intenso, veemente, apaixonado

intensification | intensifikey'śən | *s.* intensificação

intensify | inten'sifay | *vt.* intensificar

intensity | inten'sitī | *s.* intensidade, energia

intensive | inten'siv | *a.* intensivo, intenso, concentrado

intent | intent' | *s.* intento, intenção. **-to all intents and purposes** para todos os efeitos / *a.* atento; concentrado

intention | inten'śən | *s.* intenção, propósito

intentionally | inten'śənəlī | *adv.* intencionalmente, deliberadamente, de propósito

inter | intɛ' | *vt.* enterrar

interaction | intərak'śən | *s.* interação, ação recíproca

intercede | intəsīd' | *vi.* interceder, intervir

intercept | intəsept' | *vt.* interceptar; impedir; deter

intercession | intəse'śən | *s.* intercessão, mediação

interchange | intəśeynj' | *s.* intercâmbio / *vt.* intercambiar / *vi.* alternar-se

interchangeable | intəśeyn'jəbəl | *a.* intercambiável

intercommunication | intəkəmǐunikey'śən | *s.* intercomunicação

intercourse | in'təkós | *s.* intercâmbio; comunicação; relações sexuais

interdependence | intədipən'dəns | *s.* interdependência

interdict | intədikt' | *s.* interdito / *vt.* proibir

interest | in'trəst | *s.* interesse; (com.) participação; influência; (pl.) juros. **-to make i. with someone** interceder junto a alguém / *vt.* interessar; (com.) dar participação a

interested | in'trəstid | *a.* interessado

interesting | in'trəsting | *a.* interessante

interfere | intəfī'ə | *vi.* interferir, interpor; intrometer-se; estorvar

interference | intəfī'ərəns | *s.* interferência, intervenção

interfering | intəfī'əring | *a.* intrometido, metediço

interim | in'tərim | *s.* ínterim. **-in the i.** entrementes, no ínterim /

a. interino, provisório

interior | intɪ'rɪə |*s.a.* interior

interjection | intəjek'śən | *s.* interjeição; exclamação

interlace | intəleys' | *vt.* entrelaçar; misturar

interleave | intəliv' | *vt.* entrefolhar, intercalar (uma folha)

interloper | in'təlowpə | *s.* intruso, intrometido

interlude | in'təlud |*s.* interlúdio; entreato

intermarriage | intəma'rij |*s.* casamento entre diferentes castas, tribos etc.; (coloq.) casamento entre parentes próximos

intermarry | intəma'rɪ | *vi.* unir-se por casamento (famílias, castas etc.)

intermediary | intəmɪ'dɪərɪ | *s.a.* intermediário

intermediate | intəmɪ'dɪət | *s.a.* intermédio, intermediário / | intəmɪ'dɪeyt | *vi.* intermediar

interminable | intE'minəbəl | *a.* interminável

intermission | intəmi'śən | *s.* intervalo; interrupção

intermittent | intəmi'tənt | *a.* intermitente; periódico

intern | intEn' |*s.* interno / *vt.* internar, confinar

internal | intE'nəl |*a.* interno

international | intənaś'nəl | *a.* internacional

internecine | intənɪ'sayn |*a.* mutuamente destrutivo

internee | intEnɪ' | *vt.* confinar (esp. inimigo ou prisioneiro de guerra)

internment | intEn'mənt | *s.* internamento

internment camp | intEn'məntkamp | *s.* campo de internamento (de prisioneiros)

interplanetary | intəpla'nitrɪ | *a.* interplanetário

interplay | in'təpley | *s.* ação ou efeito recíproco

interpolate | intE'powleyt |*vt.* interpolar; inserir

interpret | intE'prit | *vt.* interpre-

tar; representar; explicar, esclarecer

interpretation | intEpritey'śən |*s.* interpretação

interpreter | intE'pritə | *s.* intérprete (tb. mús., teat., cin.)

interracial | intərey'śəl | *a.* inter--racial

interrogate | inte'rəgeyt | *vt. vi.* interrogar

interrogation | interəgey'śən | *s.* interrogação; interrogatório; pergunta

interrogation mark | interəgey'śənmAk | *s.* = *interrogation point*

interrogation point | interəgey'śən poynt | *s.* ponto de interrogação

interrogative | intəro'gətiv | *a.* interrogativo

interrogator | inte'rəgeytə | *s.* interrogador

interrupt | intərâpt' | *vt.* interromper, suspender

interruption | intərâp'śən | *s.* interrupção; intervalo

intersect | intəsekt' | *vt. vi.* cruzar(-se), entrecortar(-se)

intersperse | intəspEs' | *vt.* entremear; espalhar

interval | in'təvəl | *s.* intervalo; pausa. **-at intervals** de tempo em tempo

intervene | intəvin' | *vi.* interferir, intervir; ocorrer; sobrevir; interceder

intervention | intəven'śən | *s.* intervenção, mediação

interview | in'təvɪʊ |*s.* entrevista / *vt.* entrevistar

intestate | intes'tit | *a.* intestado

intimacy | in'timəsɪ |*s.* intimidade; relações sexuais

intimate | in'timit | *a.* íntimo / | intimeyt' | *vt.* anunciar, comunicar; insinuar, sugerir, dar a entender

intimation | intimey'śən |*s.* notificação, comunicação; insinuação, sugestão

intimidate | inti'mideyt | *vt.* intimidar, atemorizar

intimidation | intimidey'śən | *s.* intimidação

into | in'tu | *prep.* em, para dentro de. **-i. the bargain** de quebra. **-two i. four** quatro dividido por dois

intolerable | into'lərəbəl | *a.* intolerável, insuportável

intolerance | into'lərəns | *s.* intolerância

intolerant | into'lərənt | *a.* intolerante

intonation | intəney'śən | *s.* entonação; modulação, inflexão da voz

intoxicant | into'ksikənt | *s.* bebida alcoólica / *a.* inebriante

intoxicate | into'ksikeyt | *vt.* inebriar, embriagar

intoxicating | into'ksikeyting | *a.* intoxicante, inebriante

intoxication | intoksikey'śən | *s.* intoxicação; embriaguês; (fig.) excitação

intractable | intrak'təbəl | *a.* intratável, refratário, selvagem, indomável

intransigent | intran'ziǰənt | *a.* intransigente

intransitive | intran'zitiv | *a.* intransitivo

intrepid | intre'pid | *a.* intrépido, destemido

intricacy | in'trikəsī | *s.* complicação

intricate | in'trikit | *a.* intrincado, complicado

intrigue | intrig' | *s.* intriga, trama / *vt.* intrigar, tramar, conspirar

intriguer | intri'gə | *s.* intrigante; conspirador; mexeriqueiro

intrinsic | intrin'zik | *a.* intrínseco, inerente

introduce | intrədſus' | *vt.* introduzir; apresentar (pessoas)

introduction | intrədak'śən | *s.* introdução, prefácio; apresentação (de pessoas)

introductory | intrədâk'tərī | *a.* in-

trodutório; preliminar

introspection | intrəspek'śən | *s.* introspecção

introversion | introwvE'jən | *s.* introversão

introvert I in'trovEt | *s. a.* introvertido

intrude | intrud' | *vi.* intrometer-se, interromper

intruder | intru'də | *s.* intruso, intrometido

intrusion | intru'jən | *s.* intrusão, intromissão

intuition | intſui'śən | *s.* intuição

intuitive | intſiu'itiv | *a.* intuitivo

inundate | i'nândeyt | *vt.* inundar, alagar

inure | inſu'ə | *vt.* acostumar, habituar, disciplinar

invade | inveyd' | *vt.* invadir

invader | invey'də | *s.* invasor

invalid | invə'lid | *s.* inválido, doente, enfermo / | inva'lid | *a.* inválido, doente; sem efeito, sem validade / | in'vəlid | *vt.* invalidar; tornar inválido (pessoa) por doença; (mil.) reformar por invalidez / *vi.* tornar-se inválido

invalidate | inva'lideyt | *vt.* invalidar, anular

invaluable | inva'lſubəl | *a.* inestimável, inapreciável

invariable | inve'əríəbəl | *a.* invariável, constante

invasion | invey'jən | *s.* invasão; intrusão

invective | invek'tiv | *s.* invectiva; denúncia

inveigle | invı'gəl | *vt.* induzir, persuadir

invent | invent' | *vt.* inventar; imaginar

invention | inven'śən | *s.* invenção; invento (coisa)

inventive | inven'tiv | *a.* inventivo, engenhoso

inventiveness | inven'tivnes | *s.* inventiva, espírito inventivo

inventor | inven'tə | *s.* inventor

inventory | in'vəntrī | *s.* inventário

invert | invɛt' | *vt*. inverter

invertebrate | invɛ'tibrit | *a*. invertebrado

invest | invest' | *vt*. investir; (mil.) sitiar; inverter capital / *vi*. fazer investimentos; aplicar capital

investigate | inves'tigeyt | *vt*. investigar, indagar, pesquisar, examinar / *vi*. fazer investigações

investigation | investigey'ʃən | *s*. investigação, inquérito

investigator | inves'tigeytə | *s*. investigador

investiture | inves'tiʃə | *s*. investidura

investment | invest'mənt | *s*. investimento

investor | inves'tə | *s*. investidor, acionista

inveterate | inve'tərit | *a*. inveterado, crônico

invidious | invi'ɗĩəs | *a*. odioso, hostil, antipático

invigilate | invi'ʃileyt | *vt*. vigiar; fiscalizar exame

invigilation | invijiley'ʃən | *s*. vigilância

invigorate | invi'gəreyt | *vt*. robustecer, fortalecer

invigorating | invi'gəreyting | *a*. tonificante (ar); animador, fortalecedor

invincible | invin'sibəl | *a*. invencível, insuperável

inviolable | invay'ələbəl | *a*. inviolável

invisible | invi'zibəl | *a*. invisível

invitation | invitey'ʃən | *s*. convite

invite | invayt' | *vt*. convidar; pedir, solicitar; (fig.) provocar, atrair

inviting | invay'ting | *a*. convidativo; atraente, sedutor

invocation | invowkey'ʃən | *s*. invocação, prece; evocação, fórmula mágica

invoice | in'voys | *s*. fatura / *vt*. faturar

invoke | invowk' | *vt*. invocar, rogar, suplicar

involuntary | invo'ləntrī | *a*. involuntário

involve | involv' | *vt*. envolver; enrolar; implicar; incluir, compreender; acarretar, trazer consigo

invulnerable | invâl'nərəbəl | *a*. invulnerável

inward | in'wəd | *a*. interior, interno; intrínseco / *adv*. para o interior, para o centro, para dentro

inwardly | in'wədlī | *adv*. interiormente, no interior

iodine | ay'ədin | *s*. iodo

I.Q. | ay'kĩu' | *s*. (abrev. de **intelligence quotient**) Q.I. (quociente de inteligência)

irascible | ira'sibəl | *a*. irascível, irritável

irate | ayreyt' | *a*. zangado, irritado, colérico, irado

Irish | ay'əriś | *s.a*. irlandês

Irishman | ay'əriśmən | *s*. irlandês

irk | ɛk' | *vt*. incomodar, aborrecer; enfadar, cansar

irksome | ɛk'səm | *a*. maçante, fatigante; aborrecido

iron | ay'ən | *s*. ferro; (pl.) grilhões. **-in irons** a ferros, algemado / *a*. férreo; forte; cruel / *vt*. passar a ferro. **-to i. out** remover (dificuldades etc.)

ironic, -al | ayro'nik(al) | *a*. irônico

ironing board | ay'əningbód' | *s*. tábua de passar roupa

ironmonger | ay'ənmângə | *s*. negociante de ferragens

ironmongery | ay'ənmângərī | *s*. ferragens

iron ration | ay'ənra'ʃən | *s*. ração enlatada (de emergência)

irony | ay'rənī | *s*. ironia

irradiate | irey'ɗīeyt | *vt*. irradiar

irrational | ira'ʃənəl | *a*. irracional

irreconcilable | irekənsay'ləbəl | *a*. irreconciliável

irreducible | iriɗĩu'sibəl | *a*. irredutível

irrefutable | iriʃʃu'təbəl | *a.* irrefutável, incontestável

irregular | ire'gʲulə | *a.* irregular

irrelevant | ire'livənt | *a.* irrelevante, descabido, fora de propósito

irreligious | irili'ʤəs | *a.* irreligioso, descrente, ímpio

irremediable | irimɪ'dĩəbəl | *a.* irremediável

irreplaceable | iripley'səbəl | *a.* insubstituível

irrepressible | iripre'sibəl | *a.* irreprimível, irrefreável

irresistible | irizis'təbəl | *a.* irresistível

irrespective | irispek'tiv | *a.* independente de, sem levar em consideração

irresponsible | irispon'sibəl | *a.* irresponsável

irretrievable | iritrɪ'vəbəl | *a.* irrecuperável, irreparável

irreverent | ire'vərənt | *a.* irreverente, desrespeitoso

irreversible | irivE'sibəl | *a.* irreversível, irrevogável

irrevocable | ire'vəkəbəl | *a.* irrevogável; definitivo

irrigate | i'rigeyt | *vt.* irrigar, regar; (med.) lavar

irrigation | irigey'ʃən | *s.* irrigação; (med.) lavagem

irritability | iritəbi'litī | *s.* irritabilidade

irritable | i'ritəbəl | *a.* irritável, irascível

irritate | i'riteyt | *vt.* irritar, enervar; excitar

irritation | iritey'ʃən | *s.* irritação; excitação

Islam | iz'lAm | *s.* Islã; islamismo

Islamic | izla'mik | *a.* islâmico, muçulmano

island | ay'lənd | *s.* ilha / *vt.* ilhar, insular

islander | ay'ləndə | *s.* ilhéu

islet | ay'lit | *s.* ilhota

isolate | ay'səleyt | *vt.* isolar

isolation | aysɔley'ʃən | *s.* isolamento; solidão

Israeli | izrey'lĪ | *s. a.* israelense

issue | i'sĩu | *s.* saída; desembocadura; resultado; prole; emissão (de dinheiro, ações, selos etc.); questão, disputa; conclusão; resultado / *vt.* distribuir; publicar; emitir; promulgar; lançar / *vi.* sair, brotar, manar; resultar; ser publicado, divulgado ou emitido

isthmus | is'məs | *s.* istmo

Italian | ita'lĩən | *s. a.* italiano

italics | ita'liks | *spl.* itálico, grifo

itch | iʃ' | *s.* sarna; coceira, comichão; (fig.) grande desejo / *vi.* sentir comichão. **-to be itching to** sentir grande desejo de

itchy | i'ʃĩ | *a.* sarnento; que comicha

item | ay'təm | *s.* item, artigo; notícia, informação

itinerant | iti'nərənt | *a.* itinerante, ambulante

itinerary | iti'nərərĨ | *s.* itinerário

ivory | ay'vərĪ | *s.* marfim / *a.* ebúrneo, de marfim

ivy | ay'vĪ | *s.* hera

J

jab | ʤab' | *s.* espetadela; pontada; soco, murro / *vt.* cutucar; espetar; socar

jabber | ʤa'bə | *s.* algaravia. tazãrelice / *vi.* tagarelar, palrar, falar confusamente

jack | ǰak' | *s.* (mec.) macaco. -**j. of all trades** pau para toda obra, homem dos sete instrumentos

jackal | ǰa'kol | *s.* chacal

jackass | ǰa'kas | *s.* burro, asno; (fig.) tolo, idiota

jackdaw | ǰak'dó | *s.* gralha

jacket | ǰa'kit | *s.* paletó; casaco; blusão; capa, sobrecapa (de livro)

jack-knife | ǰak'nayf | *s.* canivete grande (de bolso)

jackpot | ǰak'pot | *s.* apostas acumuladas (pôquer); acumulada (turfe); o prêmio mais alto. -**to hit the j.** tirar o prêmio mais alto (loteria etc.)

jacks | ǰaks' | *s.* três-marias (jogo); (*pl.*) pedrinhas usadas nesse jogo

jade | ǰeyd' | *s.* jade; mulher de pouca virtude; cavalo cansado, matungo

jaded | ǰey'did | *a.* exausto

jagged | ǰa'gid | *a.* dentado, denteado; recortado; irregular; pontudo, pontiagudo

jaguar | ǰa'giuə | *s.* jaguar, onça-pintada

jail, gaol | ǰeyl' | *s.* cadeia, prisão, cárcere

jailbird, gaolbird | ǰeyl'bɛd | *s.* (coloq.) prisioneiro, criminoso inveterado

jailer, gaoler | ǰey'lə | *s.* carcereiro

jam | ǰam' | *s.* geléia; aglomeração, congestionamento; (coloq.) enrascada / *vt.* apertar, espremer; apinhar, entupir; emperrar; fazer interferência (rádio) / *vi.* ser comprimido; ficar emperrado

Jamaican | ǰəmey'kən | *s. a.* jamaicano

jammed | ǰamd' | *a.* emperrado, enguiçado; preso, entalado (dedo etc.); cheio, apinhado, entupido, bloqueado

jam session | ǰam'sesən | *s.* reunião de executantes de *jazz*; estilo de *jazz* improvisado

janitor | ǰa'nitə | *s.* zelador, porteiro

January | ǰa'nïuərï| *s.* janeiro

Japanese | ǰapəniz' | *s. a.* japonês

jar | ǰA' | *s.* jarro, vaso, pote; rangido, som áspero / *vt.* sacudir, tremer; abalar; fazer vibrar / *vi.* irritar; chocar; vibrar

jargon | ǰA'gən | *s.* jargão; gíria; algaravia

jarring | ǰA'ring | *a.* dissonante, discordante, desafinado; estridente

jasmine | ǰaz'min | *s.* jasmim

jaundice | ǰón'dis | *s.* icterícia; (fig.) inveja ou ciúme

jaundiced | ǰón'dist | *a.* ictérico; (fig.) invejoso, despeitado ou ciumento

jaunt | ǰónt' | *s.* caminhada, passeio, excursão

jaunty | ǰón'tï | *a.* elegante; lépido, vivaz, desenvolto

javelin | ǰa'vəlin | *s.* dardo

jaw | ǰó' | *s.* maxila, maxilar, queixada; mandíbula

jay | ǰey' | *s.* (orn.) gaio; (gír.) pessoa tola ou tagarela

jazz | ǰaz' | *s. jazz*

jealous | ǰe'ləs | *a.* ciumento; invejoso

jealousy | ǰe'ləsï | *s.* ciúme; inveja

jeans | ǰinz' | *spl.* calças de tecido grosso de algodão, *jeans, blue jeans*

jeep | ǰip' | *s.* jipe

jeer | ǰï'ə | *s.* zombaria, mofa, troça, escárnio / *vt. vi.* escarnecer, zombar (de)

Jehovah | ǰihow'və | *s.* Jeová

jelly | ǰe'lï | *s.* geléia

jellyfish | ǰe'lïfiš | *s.* (zool.) água-viva

jeopardize | ǰe'pədayz | *vt.* comprometer, expor a risco

jeopardy | ǰe'pədï | *s.* perigo, risco, prejuízo

jerk | ǰɛk' | *s.* solavanco, empurrão, tranco, arranco; guinada; charque; (gír.) tolo / *vt.* sacudir; empurrar, dar um tranco em / *vi.* mover-se aos trancos

jerked beef | ǰɛ'kidbɪf | *s.* carne-
-seca, charque

jerky | ǰɛ'kī | *a.* convulsivo, es-
pasmódico; que anda aos ar-
rancos ou trancos; titubeante,
hesitante

jerry-builder | ǰe'rībildə | *s.* cons-
trutor negligente (de casas etc.)

jerry-built | ǰe'rībilt | *a.* mal cons-
truído, malfeito, atamancado,
ordinário

jest | ǰest' | *s.* gracejo, graça, pi-
lhéria / *vi.* gracejar, pilheriar

jester | ǰes'tə | *s.* pilheriador; bu-
fão, bobo da corte

Jesuit | ǰe'ziuit | *s.* jesuíta

jet | ǰet' | *s.* (mín.) azeviche; jato
(de ar, vapor ou líquido); avião
a jato

jet-black | ǰet'blak | *a.* negro co-
mo azeviche

jetsam | ǰet'səm | *s.* carga atirada
ao mar

jettison | ǰe'tisən | *vt.* atirar ao
mar; jogar fora

jetty | ǰe'tī | *s.* quebra-mar, mo-
lhe, cais, píer

Jew | ǰu' | *s.* judeu

jewel | ǰu'əl | *s.* jóia

jeweller, jeweler | ǰu'ələ | *s.*
joalheiro

jewellery, jewelry ǰu'əlrī | *s.* joa-
lheria; jóias

Jewess | ǰu'əs | *s.* judia

jew-fish | ǰu'fiš | *s.* (ict.) mero

Jewish | ǰu'iš | *a.* judaico

jew's harp | ǰus'hap | *s.* berimbau
(de boca)

jib | ǰib' | *s.* (náut.) bujarrona;
(mec.) braço (móvel) de guin-
daste; (gír.) jeitão, cara, pinta;
empacamento / *vi.* empacar, la-
dear (cavalo); (náut.) cambar

jibe | ǰayb' | *s.* zombaria, mofa /
vi. zombar de

jiffy | ǰi'fī | *s.* instante

jig | ǰig' | *s.* jiga (música e dança);
(mec.) guia; (gír.) brincadeira,
truque

jigsaw | ǰig'só | *s.* serra de recor-
tar, serra tico-tico

jigsaw puzzle | ǰig'sópâzəl | *s.*
quebra-cabeça (de montagem)

jilt | ǰilt' | *s.* mulher que se nega
depois de encorajar / *vt.* romper, acabar (namoro)

jingle | ǰin'gəl | *s.* tinido; rima,
aliteração; (rád., TV) *jingle*
/ *vi.* tinir

jingo | ǰin'gow | *s.* patrioteiro,
chauvinista, jingoísta

job | ǰob' | *s.* emprego, ocupa-
ção; trabalho, serviço; obra, ta-
refa; dever, ofício. **-on the j.**
(coloq.) a postos. **-to lie on the j.**
(coloq.) atamancar o serviço.
-that's your j. (coloq.) isso é
com você

jobber | ǰo'bə | *s.* atacadista (co-
merciante); empreiteiro; tare-
feiro; traficante

jobbery | ǰo'bərī | *s.* negociata,
traficância, concussão

jobless | ǰob'les ǰob'les | *a.*
desempregado

jockey | ǰo'kī | *s.* jóquei

jocular | ǰo'kĭulə | *a.* alegre, joco-
so, jovial, galhofeiro

jog | ǰog' | *s.* sacudidela, solavan-
co; meio trote / *vt.* sacudir; em-
purrar; espertar (memória) / *vi.*
mover-se ou andar aos trancos;
correr a passo curto (exercício
físico). **-I'm jogging along** vou
indo, vou levando, vou andando

jogtrot | ǰog'trot | *s.* meio trote,
trote lento; (fig.) marcha roti-
neira ou lenta

John Bull | ǰon'bul | *s.* personifi-
cação da Inglaterra; o inglês
típico

John Doe | ǰon'dow | *s.* Fulano de
Tal

join | ǰoyn' | *vt.* juntar, ligar,
unir; combinar; ingressar em;
associar-se a; alistar-se; fazer-
se sócio de. **-to j. battle** travar
batalha. **-to j. up** alistar-se (no
exército etc.)

joiner | ǰoy'nə | *s.* marceneiro ou
carpinteiro

joinery | ǰoy'nərī | *s.* marcenaria,
carpintaria

joint | ǰoynt' | s. junta, junção, articulação; peso de carne (com osso); (gír.) taberna, tasca. **-out of j.** desconjuntado, fora de lugar / a. unido, combinado, associado, solidário / vt. unir por articulação, juntar; desmembrar

jointed | ǰoyn'tid | a. articulado, que tem juntas

joint heir | ǰoynt'eə | s. co-herdeiro

jointly | ǰoynt'lī | adv. juntamente, conjuntamente

joint owner | ǰoynt'ownə | s. co--proprietário

joint stock | ǰoynt'stok | s. (com.) capital social

joint-stock company | ǰoynt'stokkâm'pənī | s. sociedade anônima

joist | ǰoyst' | s. trave, barrote, viga

joke | ǰowk' | s. gracejo, pilhéria, piada. **-to play a j. on** pregar uma peça em / vi. dizer piadas; falar de brincadeira. **-no joking** fora de brincadeira

joker | ǰow'kə | s. piadista, pessoa que gosta de pregar peças; artifício contratual; curinga

jolly | ǰo'lī | a. divertido, alegre, agradável. **-j. good** muito bom. **-the j. god** Baco

jolt | ǰowlt' | s. solavanco, sacudidela / vt. sacudir / vi. dar solavancos

jostle | ǰo'səl | s. encontrão / vt. vi. empurrar, acotovelar

jot | ǰot' | s. mínimo, tiquinho (em frases negativas). **-not a j.** nada / vt. **-to j. down** tomar nota, anotar

jottings | ǰo'tingz | spl. notas

journal | ǰE'nəl | s. jornal, periódico, revista; diário (contábil); diário de bordo

journalism | ǰEnəli'zəm | s. jornalismo

journalist | ǰE'nəlist | s. jornalista

journey | ǰE'nī | s. viagem / vt. viajar

Jove | ǰowv | s. Júpiter. **-by J.!** caramba!, puxa! (exclamação de surpresa ou aprovação)

jovial | ǰow'viəl | a. jovial, prazenteiro, alegre

jowl | ǰawl' | s. queixada; papada; bochecha. **-cheek by j.** lado a lado

joy | ǰoy' | s. alegria; deleite, felicidade, júbilo

joyful | ǰoy'ful | a. alegre, contente, satisfeito

jubilant | ǰu'bilənt | a. jubiloso, exultante

jubilation | ǰubiley'śən | s. júbilo, exultação; festividade

jubilee | ǰu'bilī | s. jubileu; aniversário

Judaism | ǰu'deyizəm | s. judaísmo

judge | ǰâ' | s. juiz; árbitro; conhecedor, perito; entendido, apreciador / vt. julgar; avaliar, calcular / vi. julgar; entender, opinar

judgement, judgment | ǰâ'mənt | s. (jur.) julgamento, sentença; juízo, critério, opinião. **-the Last J.** o Juízo Final

judicial | ǰudi'śəl | a. judicial

judiciary | ǰudi'śərī | s. magistratura, poder judiciário

judicious | ǰudi'śəs | a. judicioso, sensato, ponderado

judo | ǰu'dow | s. judô

jug | ǰâg' | s. jarro; cântaro

juggle | ǰâ'gəl | s. prestidigitação; malabarismo; trapaça / vi. fazer prestidigitação ou malabarismo. **-to j. with** lograr, iludir (pessoas); baralhar, falsear (idéias)

juggler | ǰâg'lə | s. prestidigitador; malabarista; trapaceiro

juice | ǰus' | s. suco; secreção, humor orgânico; (gír.) gasolina, eletricidade, óleo diesel etc.

juicy | ǰu'sī | a. suculento

juke-box | ǰuk'boks | s. toca-discos automático que funciona por meio de fichas (em bares, restaurantes etc.)

July | ǰulay' | s. julho

jumble | ǰâm'bəl | s. mistura; confusão; desordem; artigos baratos / *vt.* misturar, confundir, atrapalhar

jumble sale | ǰâm'bəlseyl | *s.* bazar de caridade

jumbo I jâm'bow I *a.* enorme, gigantesco

jump | ǰâmp' | *s.* salto, pulo / *vt.* saltar, pular; galgar / *vi.* saltar, pular; dar solavancos

jumper | ǰâm'pə |*s.* saltador; blusão (de vestir pela cabeça); macacão (de criança)

junction | ǰânk'šən | *s.* junção; entroncamento ferroviário; cruzamento (de estradas); confluência (de rios)

juncture | ǰânk'šə |*s.* junção; conexão; conjuntura, momento crítico, concorrência de acontecimentos

June | ǰʊn' | *s.* junho

jungle | ǰân'gəl | *s.* selva

junior | ǰʊ'niə | *s.* jovem, rapaz; calouro; estudante no penúltimo ano do primeiro grau (antigo ginásio) / *a.* júnior, mais jovem; subordinado

junk | ǰânk' | *s.* refugo, rebotalho; sucata, ferro velho; (náut.) junco; (gír.) narcótico (esp. heroína)

junket| ǰân'kit |*s.* espécie de coalhada (com frutas etc.); (EUA) pândega, farra

junkman | ǰânk'mən | *s.* negociante de ferro velho

junta | ǰân'tə |*s.* junta, conselho; facção política

jurisdiction | ǰurisdik'šən | *s.* jurisdição, competência; autoridade, poder

jurist | ǰu'rist | *s.* jurista

juror | ǰʊə'rə | *s.* jurado

jury | ǰʊə'rī | *s.* júri

just | ǰâst' | *a.* justo; imparcial; merecido, justificado; apropriado; certo, exato; honrado / *adv.* justamente, exatamente; por pouco, há pouco; somente. **-j. a little** só um pouco. **-j. once** só uma vez. **-j. now** agora mesmo

justice | ǰâs'tis | *s.* justiça; juiz, magistrado. **-to do j.** to fazer justiça a

justice of the peace | ǰâs'tisovðepis' | *s.* juiz de paz

justifiable I jâstifay'əbəl I *a.* justificável, defensável

justification | ǰâstifikey'šən | *s.* justificação; justificativa, desculpa, razão

justify | ǰâs'tifay | *vt.* justificar, desculpar, explicar / *vi.* (jur., tip.) justificar

justness | ǰâst'nes |*s.* justiça; imparcialidade; exatidão; precisão

jut | ǰât' | *s.* protuberância, ponta / *vi.* sobressair. **-to j. out** projetar-se

jute | ǰʊt' | *s.* juta

juvenile | ǰʊ'vənayl | *s.* jovem, rapaz, moço / *a.* juvenil

juxtaposition | ǰâkstəpəzi'šən | *s.* justaposição

K

Kaffir | ka'fə | *s.* cafre

kale | keyl' | *s.* couve

kaleidoscope | kəley'deskowp | *s.* caleidoscópio, calidoscópio

kangaroo | kangərʊ' | *s.* canguru

keel | kil' | *s.* quilha / *vi.* **-to k. over** virar, emborcar

keen | kin' | *a.* agudo, afiado; penetrante; perspicaz, alerta; mordaz; interessado, entusiasmado; aplicado. **-to be k. on** gostar muito de

keenness | kin'nes | *s.* agudeza; perspicácia, penetração; intensidade, profundeza; diligência, entusiasmo

keep | kıp’ | s. manutenção; meios de sustento; fortaleza, torre de menagem. **-for keeps** (EUA) para sempre, definitivamente / vt. guardar, conservar; ter, possuir; ficar com, reter; sustentar; deter; observar, cumprir, obedecer; comemorar, celebrar, respeitar. **-to k. away** manter afastado. **-to k. back** deter, reter; ocultar (segredos). **-to k. from** impedir, proteger. **-to k. in** manter, guardar. **-to k. off** afastar, manter à distância. **-to k. on** conservar, manter nas mesmas condições. **-to k. out** excluir, ficar fora. **-to k. up** manter, continuar / vi. ficar, continuar; conservar-se. **-to k. at** persistir. **-to k. away** afastar-se; abster-se. **-to k. off** afastar-se. **-to k. on** continuar, persistir. **-to k. out** não se intrometer. **-to k. quiet** calar-se. **-to k. up with** andar a par de; acompanhar, não ficar atrás

keeper | kı’pə | s. guarda, zelador; encarregado; protetor; carcereiro

keeping | kı’ping | s. custódia, guarda; conservação. **-in k. with** de acordo com. **-out of k.** em desacordo com. **-in safe k.** a salvo

keepsake | kıp’seyk | s. lembrança, recordação, presente

keg | keg’ | s. barrilete, barril pequeno

ken | ken’ | s. alcance da vista ou da percepção. **-beyond one’s k.** fora do alcance de / vt. (Esc.) conhecer, saber

kennel | ke’nəl | s. canil

keno | kı’now | s. loto, víspora

kerb | kεb’ | s. meio-fio (da calçada)

kerchief | kə’s̄íf | s. lenço de cabeça

kernel | kE’nəl | s. semente, caroço; parte comestível de uma noz; miolo; (fig.) cerne, âmago, parte central

kerosene | ke’rosin | s. querosene

kettle | ke’təl | s. chaleira

kettledrum | ke’təldrâm | s. (mús.) tímpano, timbale

key | kı’ | s. chave; tecla; (mús.) clave, tonalidade; interruptor, comutador; solução, explicação / vt. fechar à chave. **-to k. up** incitar, estimular.

keyboard | kı’bóəd | s. teclado

keyhole | kı’howl | s. buraco da fechadura

keynote | kı’nowt | s. (mús.) tônica; (fig.) idéia básica, princípio fundamental

khaki | kA’ki | s. a. cáqui

kick | kik’ | s. pontapé; chute; coice (de animal ou arma de fogo). **-to get a k. out of** (gír.) ter prazer em, divertir-se com / vt. dar pontapé; chutar; escoicear; dar coice, recuar (arma de fogo). **-to k. down** derrubar a pontapés / vi. dar pontapés; escoicear; espernear. **-to k. at** ou **against** reclamar, protestar. **-to k. the bucket** (gír.) morrer

kid | kid’ | s. cabrito; criança; garoto; garota; pelica / vt. vi. lograr, enganar; zombar, escarnecer; brincar

kidnap | kid’nap | vt. seqüestrar, raptar

kidnapper | kid’napə | s. seqüestrador, raptor

kidney | kid’nĭ | s. rim; (fig.) disposição, temperamento; espécie, tipo

kidney bean | kid’nĭbın | s. feijão comum

kill | kil’ | s. matança; ato de matar; golpe final / vt. matar; abater (gado); destruir, aniquilar; fazer parar (motor); cortar (eletricidade). **-to k. time** matar o tempo

killer | ki’lə | s. matador, assassino

kiln | kiln’ | s. forno (para tijolos etc.)

kilogram, kilogramme | ki’lowgram | s. quilograma, quilo

kilometre, kilometer | ki'lowmitə kilo'mitə | *s.* quilômetro

kilt | kilt' | *s.* saiote escocês

kin | kin' | *s.* parente; parentesco. **-next of k.** o parente mais próximo / *a.* aparentado; consangüíneo

kind | kaynd' | *s.* espécie; gênero; tipo; qualidade. **-in k.** em espécie, na mesma moeda. **-to repay in k.** pagar na mesma moeda. **-nothing of the k.** nada disso / *a.* amável, bondoso, gentil, cordial. **-to be k. enough to** ter a gentileza de

kindergarten | kin'dəgʌtən | *s.* jardim de infância

kindle | kin'dəl | *vt.* atear fogo, acender

kindliness | kaynd'lines | *s.* bondade, amabilidade; generosidade; compaixão

kindling | kind'ling | *s.* gravetos, aparas de lenha (para começar fogueira)

kindly | kaynd'lĩ | *a.* bondoso; amável, afável, gentil. **-to take k. to** afeiçoar-se a. **-k. accept** digne-se aceitar. **-I would take k** ... ficar-lhe-ia muito grato...

kindness | kaynd'nes | *s.* bondade, amabilidade; generosidade; favor, gentileza

king | king' | *s.* rei

kingdom | king'dəm | *s.* reino

kingfisher | king'fíʃə | *s.* martim-pescador

kingship | king'ʃip | *s.* monarquia; realeza; majestade

king-size | king'sayz | *a.* de tamanho gigante

kink | kink' | *s.* torcedura, volta, coxa (em cabo, linha de pesca etc.) / *vi.* enroscar, torcer, dar coxa

kinship | kin'ʃip | *s.* parentesco; afinidade

kinsman | kinz'mən | *s.* parente

kiosk | ki'osk | *s.* quiosque

kipper | ki'pə | *s.* arenque defumado

kirk | kɛk' | *s.* (Esc.) igreja

kiss | kis' | *s.* beijo / *vt.* beijar. **-to k. one's hand to** atirar beijo a

kit | kit' | *s.* conjunto de utensílios ou petrechos; gatinho

kitbag | kit'bag | *s.* mochila (de soldado ou viajante)

kitchen | ki'ʃin | *s.* cozinha

kitchenware | ki'ʃinwɛə | *s.* utensílios de cozinha

kite | kayt' | *s.* milhafre; papagaio, pipa (brinquedo)

kitten | ki'tən | *s.* gatinho

kitty | ki'tĩ | *s.* gatinho; barato (em jogo de cartas)

knack | nak' | *s.* jeito, queda, aptidão, destreza

knapsack | nap'sak | *s.* mochila

knave | neyv' | *s.* patife, tratante; valete (de baralho)

knavery | ney'vərĩ | *s.* patifaria, desonestidade

knead | nid' | *vt.* amassar (massa de pão etc.)

knee | nĩ' | *s.* joelho. **-on one's knees** de joelhos

kneecap | nĩ'kap | *s.* rótula

kneel | nĩl' | *vi.* ajoelhar-se, ficar de joelhos

knell | nel' | *s.* dobre de sino (a finados) / *vt.* anunciar com dobre de sinos

knick-knack | nik'nak | *s.* bugiganga, quinquilharia

knife | nayf' | *s.* faca / *vt.* esfaquear, cortar com faca

knight | nayt' | *s.* cavaleiro; cavalo (jogo de xadrez) / *vt.* armar cavaleiro

knight errant | nayt'erənt | *s.* cavaleiro andante

knit | nit' | *vt.* tricotar; fazer malha. **-to k. one's brows** franzir a testa. **-to k. together** unir, ligar / *vi.* fazer tricô ou malha; enrugar-se, franzir-se

knitting | ni'ting | *s.* tricô, malha

knitting-needle | ni'tingnidəl | *s.* agulha de tricô

knob | nob' | *s.* maçaneta; puxador (de gaveta etc.)

knock | nok' | *s.* pancada, batida

-a k. at the door uma batida na porta / vt. bater. -to k. down derrubar; desmontar; rematar em leilão. -to k. off abater (preço); largar, interromper (trabalho). -to k. out pôr fora de combate, pôr (a) nocaute / vi. bater; colidir com. -to k. about perambular

knockabout | nokəbawt' | a. violento, turbulento; forte, resistente; apropriado para viagens; que vagueia, errante

knockdown | nokdawn' | s. derrubamento, queda (no boxe) / a. que derruba, arrasador

knocker | no'kə | s. aldrava; o que bate (à porta etc.)

knock-kneed | nok'nıd | a. cambaio, que tem os joelhos para dentro

knock-out | nok'awt | s. nocaute (no boxe)

knoll | nol' | s. outeiro

knot | not' | s. nó; laço; grupo, agrupamento / vt. amarrar, dar nós em

knotty | no'tī | a. espinhoso, difícil (problema)

know | now' | s. conhecimento. -to be in the k. estar informado, estar por dentro / vt. saber, conhecer. -to k. of saber de. -to k. one's mind saber o que se quer. -to k. by name (by sight) conhecer de nome (de vista). -to k. by heart saber de cor. -as far as I k. que eu saiba

know-how | now'haw | s. conhecimento prático, perícia técnica, destreza

knowing | now'ing | a. astuto, sagaz; conhecedor. -there is no k. não há meio de saber

knowledge | no'lij | s. saber; sabedoria; erudição. -not to my k. não que eu saiba. -I have no k. of não tenho conhecimento de. -to the best of my k. tanto quanto posso saber

knuckle | nâ'kəl | s. nó dos dedos / vi. dedicar-se com afinco. -to k. down ou under submeter-se, ceder, sujeitar-se

K.O. | key'ow' | s. (abrev. de knock-out) nocaute

Koran | korʌn' | s. Alcorão

kotow, kowtow | kətaw' kawtaw' | vi. prostrar-se (tocando o chão com a testa)

kudos | kĭu'dos | s. (coloq.) glória, renome, fama

L

label | ley'bəl | s. rótulo, etiqueta / vt. rotular, etiquetar; (fig.) classificar

laboratory | ləbo'rətrı | s. laboratório

laborious | ləbo'rīəs | a. laborioso, penoso, árduo

labour, labor | ley'bə | s. trabalho; esforço, fadiga; labuta; mão-de-obra; operariado, classe operária; trabalho de parto / vi. trabalhar; labutar, esforçar-se

labourer, laborer | ley'bərə | s. operário, trabalhador

labour force | ley'bəfós | s. força de trabalho, mão-de-obra (de um país etc.)

Labour Party | ley'bəpʌtı | s. Partido Trabalhista

labour union | ley'bəĭʊnĭən | s. sindicato operário

labyrinth | la'birinð | s. labirinto

lace | leys' | *s.* cordão de sapato; renda / *vt.* amarrar com cordão; enfeitar com renda

lacerate | la'sɔreyt | *vt.* lacerar, dilacerar; afligir

lack | lak' | *s.* falta, carência / *vt.* faltar a; carecer de / *vi.* carecer de

lackadaisical | lakɔdey'zikɔl | *a.* indiferente, apático; negligente; lânguido

lackey | la'kī | *s.* lacaio

lacking | la'king | *a.* desprovido de; com falta de

laconic | lɔko'nik | *a.* lacônico

lacquer | la'kɔ | *s.* laca / *vt.* laquear

lad | lad' | *s.* rapaz, moço

ladder | la'dɔ | *s.* escada de mão; fio corrido (em meia) / *vi.* correr o fio (em meia)

laden | ley'dɔn | *a.* carregado; oprimido; acabrunhado

ladle | ley'dɔl | *s.* colherão, concha de sopa

lady | ley'dī | *s.* senhora, dama; dona-de-casa; amada, namorada. -Our L. Nossa Senhora. -she is no l. ela não tem educação. -ladies and gentlemen minhas senhoras e meus senhores

ladybird | ley'dībɛd | *s.* (ent.) joaninha

lady-killer | ley'dīkilɔ | *s.* conquistador, homem sedutor

ladylike | ley'dīlayk | *a.* próprio de senhora; elegante, distinto; adamado (homem)

lag | lag' | *s.* retardamento, atraso; (gír.) recluso penal; revestimento (de cilindros etc.) / *vt.* revestir (cilindros etc.); (gír.) encarcerar / *vi.* -to l. behind atrasar-se, ficar para trás

lager | la'gɔ | *s.* cerveja clara (do tipo usado na Europa continental)

lagoon | lɔgʊn' | *s.* laguna, lagoa

laid | leyd' | *a.* -to be l. up estar de cama; estar incapacitado. -l. off desempregado; sem trabalho (temporariamente)

lair | le'ɔ | *s.* covil / *vi.* entocar-se

laird | le'ɔd | *s.* (Esc.) proprietário de terras (o mesmo que *lord*)

laity | ley'itī | *s.* os leigos, a classe leiga

lake | leyk' | *s.* lago; laca

lake-dwelling | leyk'dweling | *s.* palafita, habitação lacustre

lamb | lam' | *s.* cordeiro

lambaste, lambast | lam'beyst | *vt.* (coloq.) criticar severamente; surrar, sovar

lambskin | lam'skin | *s.* pele de cordeiro (com a lã); espécie de pelica

lame | leym' | *a.* coxo, manco / *vt.* aleijar, estropiar

lament | lɔment' | *s.* lamento, queixume, pranto; elegia / *vt. vi.* lamentar, queixar

lamentable | la'mɔntɔbɔl | *a.* lamentável, deplorável

lamentation | lamentey'śɔn | *s.* lamentação

lamented | lɔmen'tid | *a.* saudoso, pranteado (morto)

lamp | lamp' | *s.* lâmpada, candeeiro, lampião, lamparina

lamp-chimney | lamp'śimnī | *s.* manga de candeeiro

lampoon | lampʊn' | *s.* pasquim, panfleto, sátira / *vt.* satirizar

lampshade | lamp'śeyd | *s.* abajur, quebra-luz

lance | lʌns' | *s.* lança. -to break a l. for quebrar lanças por / *vt.* lancear; lancetar

lancet | lan'sit | *s.* bisturi

land | land' | *s.* terra; país, nação; terreno; propriedades, terras / *vt. vi.* desembarcar, pôr em terra; descarregar / *vi.* aterrar

landing | lan'ding | *s.* desembarque; aterrissagem, aterragem; desembarcadouro; patamar de escada

landing-stage | lan'dingsteyǰ | *s.* plataforma flutuante (de desembarque)

landlady | land'leydī | *s.* senhoria, proprietária

landlord | land'lód | *s.* senhorio, proprietário

landmark | land'mʌk | *s.* marco divisório; marco, ponto de referência

landowner | land'ownə | *s.* proprietário de terras

landscape | land'skeyp | *s.* paisagem, panorama

landslide | land'slayd | *s.* deslizamento de terras; vitória eleitoral esmagadora

lane | leyn' | *s.* senda, vereda; viela, beco. **-ocean l.** curso regular de navios

language | lan'gwiǰ | *s.* língua; linguagem; idioma. **-bad l.** linguagem grosseira, obscenidades

languid | lan'gwid | *a.* lânguido; apático, indolente

languish | lan'gwiś | *vi.* enlanguescer; enfraquecer, debilitar-se

lank | lank' | *a.* esguio, delgado; liso (cabelo)

lantern | lan'tən | *s.* lanterna; clarabóia

lanyard | la'nĭəd | *s.* tira de couro; cordão usado ao pescoço (de onde pende apito, cronômetro etc.); cordão de disparo (em canhões)

lap | lap' | *s.* colo, regaço; (desp.) volta completa (da pista). **-in the l. of luxury** afundado em luxo / *vt.* envolver, sobrepor; lamber, beber (como cão etc.); (fig.) banhar, tocar levemente

lap-dog | lap'dog | *s.* cãozinho fraldeiro

lapel | ləpel' | *s.* lapela

lapse | laps' | *s.* lapso; erro leve; intervalo (tempo) / *vi.* extinguir-se, acabar-se, anular-se; passar (tempo); (jur.) caducar. **-to allow to l.** deixar prescrever

larceny | lʌ'sənĭ | *s.* furto

lard | lʌd' | *s.* toucinho, banha de porco / *vt.* lardear, entremear; engordurar

larder | lʌ'də | *s.* despensa

large | lʌǰ' | *a.* grande, amplo, extenso; espaçoso; numeroso, considerável, abundante. **-at l.** em liberdade; em geral. **-by and l.** de modo geral

largely | lʌ'lĭ | *adv.* grandemente; em grande parte

lark | lʌk' | *s.* (orn.) cotovia; travessura, brincadeira, divertimento, pândega. **-to rise with the l.** levantar-se cedo, madrugar

laryngitis | larinǰay'tis | *s.* laringite

larynx | la'rinks | *s.* laringe

lascivious | ləsi'vĭəs | *a.* lascivo, licencioso, sensual

lasciviousness | ləsi'vĭəsnes | *s.* lascívia, sensualidade

lash | laś' | *s.* chicote, látego, açoite; chicotada; pestana / *vt.* chicotear, açoitar; criticar, censurar; estimular; amarrar, atar / *vi.* dar chicotadas; lançar-se. **-to l. out** escoicear; desembestar

lass | las' | *s.* moça, jovem; namorada

lassitude | la'sitĭud | *s.* lassitude, lassidão, cansaço

lasso | la'sow | *s.* laço (para laçar animais)

last | lʌst' | *s.* último; final; fôrma de sapato / *a.* último; anterior, passado. **-l. but one** penúltimo. **-l. night** ontem à noite. **-l. but not least** último mas não menos importante. **-at l.** por fim, finalmente. **-to the l.** até ao fim. **-l. post** (mil.) toque de silêncio / *adv.* em último lugar; por fim, para terminar / *vi.* durar; continuar; conservar-se, resistir

lasting | lʌst'ing | *a.* permanente, duradouro

last name | last'neym | *s.* nome de família

last rites | last'rayts | *spl.* últimos sacramentos

latch | laś' | *s.* trinco

late | leyt' | *a.* tarde, tardio, atrasado; último; recente, avançado; falecido. **-to keep l. hours** deitar-se tarde. **-of l.** ultimamente, recentemente / *adv.* tarde. -l. in the year no fim do ano. -to be l. estar atrasado. -to grow l. ficar tarde. -too l. tarde demais

lately | leyt'lī | *adv.* recentemente, ultimamente

lateness | leyt'nes | *s.* hora adiantada; idade avançada; data ou caráter recente (de acontecimento); demora

latent | ley'tənt | *a.* latente, adormecido; oculto

latest | ley'tíst | *a.* último, mais recente. -at the l. o mais tarde

lath | laϑ' | *s.* ripa

lathe | leyδ' | *s.* torno mecânico

lather | la'δə | *s.* espuma (de sabão); suor espumoso (esp. de cavalo). -in a l. agitado, suando / *vt.* ensaboar

Latin | la'tin | *s.* latim; latino / *a.* latino

Latin-American | la'tinəme'rikən | *s.a.* latino-americano

latitude | la'titĭud | *s.* latitude; largueza, extensão; liberdade (de palavra ou de ação)

latrine | lətrin' | *s.* latrina, privada (esp. de quartel, acampamento etc.)

latter | la'tə | *a.* mais recente; final; último, este

lattice | la'tis | *s.* treliça; gelosia, rótula

laud | lód' | *vt.* louvar

laudable | ló'dəbəl | *a.* louvável; (med.) saudável

laudatory | ló'dətrĭ | *a.* laudatório

laugh | lᴧf' | *s.* riso; gargalhada, risada / *vi.* rir. -to l. at rir-se de. -to l. one's head off rir a bandeiras despregadas. -to l. up one's sleeve rir à socapa. -to l. on the wrong side of one's mouth rir amarelo

laughable | lᴧ'fəbəl | *a.* risível, engraçado

laughing | lᴧ'fing | *a.* risonho; que provoca riso. -to be no l. matter ser assunto sério

laughing-stock | lᴧ'fingstok | *s.* pessoa ou coisa ridícula

laughter | lᴧf'tə | *s.* risada, gargalhada

launch | lónś' | *s.* escaler de navio; lancha / *vt.* lançar à água; iniciar, lançar. -to l. out lançar (navio ao mar); empreender ou iniciar algo

launching | lón'śing | *s.* lançamento; inauguração

launder | lón'də | *vt.* lavar e passar (roupa)

laundress | lón'dres | *s.* lavadeira

laundry | lón'drī | *s.* lavanderia; roupa para lavar (ou lavada)

laureate | ló'rīeyt ló'rīit | *s. a.* laureado

laurels | ló'rəlz | *spl.* louros, glórias, honrarias

lava | lᴧ'və | *s.* lava

lavatory | la'vətrī | *s.* banheiro, toalete, WC

lavender | la'vində | *s.* alfazema, lavanda / *a.* da cor da alfazema

lavish | la'viś | *a.* pródigo; generoso, liberal; copioso, abundante / *vt.* prodigalizar

lavishness | la'viśnes | *s.* prodigalidade; abundância

law | ló' | *s.* lei; direito; jurisprudência; justiça, tribunais. -to go to l. recorrer aos tribunais. -to lay down the l. pontificar. -to take the l. into one's hands fazer justiça pelas próprias mãos. -to study l. estudar direito

law-abiding | ló'əbay'ding | *a.* cumpridor das leis

lawful | ló'ful | *a.* legítimo, legal, lícito

lawgiver | ló'givə | *s.* legislador

lawless | ló'les | *a.* ilegal, sem lei; arbitrário

lawn | lón' | *s.* gramado, relvado; cambraia, batista

lawn-mower | lón'mowə | *s.* máquina de cortar grama

lawn tennis | lón'tenis | *s.* tênis, jogo de tênis

law office | ló'ofis | *s.* (EUA) escritório de advocacia

lawyer | ló'īə | *s.* advogado

lax | laks' | *a.* frouxo, mole; negligente, descuidado

laxative | laks'ətiv | *s. a.* laxativo, laxante

lay | ley' | *s.* disposição, configuração; canção, trova / *a.* leigo / *vt.* pôr, colocar; armar (armadilha, cilada); pôr (ovos, mesa); apostar. -to l. **aside** ou by pôr de lado. -to l. **bare** expor, revelar. -to l. **before** submeter, apresentar, expor. -to l. **down** estabelecer, estipular, declarar; depor (armas). -to l. **hold of** segurar, pegar em. -to l. **in** acumular, armazenar. -to l. **on** pôr, colocar; dispor. -to l. **out** dispor, ordenar; preparar. -to l. **up** armazenar, guardar; prostrar; obrigar, forçar (alguém) a ficar acamado

layer | ley'ə | *s.* camada; mão, demão

layman | ley'mən | *s.* leigo

layout | ley'awt | *s.* plano, esquema; planta, esboço; (tip.) leiaute, boneca

laziness | ley'zines | *s.* preguiça

lazy | ley'zĭ | *a.* preguiçoso, indolente

lead | led' | *s.* chumbo

lead | lid' | *s.* liderança; direção; vanguarda; (eletr.) fio condutor; mão (de cartas). -to take the l. tomar a iniciativa; assumir o comando ou a dianteira (corrida) / *vt.* conduzir, levar; comandar, chefiar; ir à frente de / *vi.* levar a dianteira, ir à frente; levar a, conduzir a (estrada). -to l. **astray** desencaminhar. -to l. **a life of** levar vida de. -to l. **the way** ir à frente. -to l. **up to** preparar o caminho; conduzir a conversa (para determinado assunto)

leaden | le'dən | *a.* de chumbo, plúmbeo

leader | lĭ'də | *s.* chefe; guia; (mil.) comandante; editorial, artigo de fundo; linha pontilhada (em índice); (EUA) chefe de orquestra

leadership | lĭ'dəsip | *s.* chefia, comando, direção

leading | lĭ'ding | *s.* guia; direção (tb. de orquestra) / *a.* principal; dominante

leading article | lĭ'dingA'tikəl | *s.* artigo de fundo, editorial

leading lady | lĭ'dingley'dĭ | *s.* (teat.) primeira dama, estrela

leading man | lĭ'dingmən | *s.* primeiro ator, astro

leaf | lĭf' | *s.* folha; aba (de mesa). -to turn over a new l. emendar-se, mudar de vida. -to l. **through** folhear (livro, revista)

leaflet | lĭf'let | *s.* folha pequena; folheto; panfleto

leafy | lĭ'fĭ | *a.* frondoso; folhudo; de folhas grandes

league | lĭg' | *s.* liga; associação, sociedade, aliança; confederação; légua. -in l. with em associação com / *vt. vi.* aliar(-se); coligar(-se); mancomunar(-se)

leak | lĭk' | *s.* vazamento; escapamento; goteira / *vi.* vazar; fazer água (navio); (fig.) transpirar, divulgar-se

leakage | lĭ'kĭj | *s.* escapamento, vazamento; perda

leaky | lĭ'kĭ | *a.* esburacado, com goteiras; (coloq.) indiscreto

lean | lĭn' | *s.* inclinação, pendor; carne magra / *a.* magro, enxuto de carnes; sem gordura / *vt. vi.* inclinar(-se); apoiar(-se). -to l. **against** encostar-se; apoiar-se. -to l. **back** recostar-se; inclinar-se para trás. -to l. **out of** debruçar-se. -to l. **toward** tender, pender; inclinar-se para

leaning | lĭ'ning | *s.* propensão, inclinação / *a.* encostado a, apoiado a

leanness | lĭn'nes | *s.* magreza

lean-to | lĭn'tu | *s.* telhado de meia-água, alpendre

leap | lĭp' | *s.* salto, pulo / *vi.* saltar, pular. -a l. in the dark um pulo no escuro. -by leaps and bounds aos trancos e barrancos; a passos largos

leap year | lip'ɪə | s. ano bissexto

learn | lɛn' | vt. vi. aprender. **-to l. by heart** aprender de cor. **-to l. of** tomar conhecimento de. **-to l. that** saber que

learned | lɛ'nid | a. erudito

learner | lɛ'nə | s. estudante; principiante; aprendiz

learning | lɛ'ning | s. aprendizado; erudição, saber

lease | lis' | s. arrendamento / vt. alugar, arrendar

leash | liš' | s. correia, trela. **-to hold in l.** dominar

least | list' | s. o mínimo; o menor, o menos. **-at l.** pelo (ao) menos. **-not in the l.** de maneira alguma. **-when you l. expect it** quando menos se espera. **-last but not l.** por último mas não de menor importância. **-to say the l. of it** para dizer pouco / a. menor, mínimo / adv. o menos

leather | le'ðə | s. couro / a. de couro

leave | liv' | s. licença, permissão; despedida. **-on l.** de licença. **-to give l.** permitir. **-to take l.** despedir-se / vt. deixar; abandonar; legar, deixar em testamento. **-to l. behind** deixar para trás, abandonar. **-to l. undone** deixar por fazer. **-to l. word** deixar recado / vi. ir-se embora; partir; enfolhar

leaven | le'vən | s. levedura

leave-taking | liv'teyking | s. despedida, partida

leaving | li'ving | s. partida; (pl.) restos, sobras

lecherous | le'šərəs | a. libidinoso, lúbrico, lascivo

lechery | le'šərī | s. luxúria

lectern | lek'tɛn | s. atril; (EUA) suporte, estante

lecture | lek'šə | s. conferência; preleção; repreensão / vt. repreender, censurar / vi. dar uma conferência; fazer uma preleção

lecturer | lek'šərə | s. conferencista; lente, leitor

lectureship | lek'šəšip | s. cargo

ou função de leitor ou lente; leitorado

ledge | leǰ' | s. saliência; borda; aba; sacada; recife submarino

ledger | le'ǰə | s. livro-razão (de escrituração)

lee | li' | s. (náut.) sotavento; abrigo (contra o vento)

leech | liš' | s. sanguessuga

leek | lik' | s. alho-poró

leer | li'ə | s. olhar malicioso, olhar de esguelha

leeway | li'wey | s. (náut.) abatimento; (aer.) deriva; (coloq.) oportunidade

left | left' | s. esquerda / a. esquerdo. **-on the l.** à esquerda. **-to the l.** para a esquerda / adv. à esquerda

left-handed | left'handid | a. canhoto; insincero

leftover | left'owvə | s. a. restante, sobra

left-winger | left'wingə | s. esquerdista

leg | leg' | s. perna; pé (de mesa ou cadeira). **-to give a l. up** ajudar a montar ou subir. **-not a l. to stand on** não ter desculpa, não ter defesa. **-to be on one's last legs** estar nas últimas. **-to pull somebody's l.** brincar com alguém, fazer de bobo. **-to stretch one's legs** estirar as pernas

legacy | le'gəsī | s. legado, herança

legal | li'gəl | a. legal

legal channels | li'gəlšanəlz | spl. trâmites legais

legality | liga'litī | s. legalidade

legalization | ligəlayzey'śən | s. legalização

legalize | li'gəlayz | vt. legalizar

legal tender | li'gəltendə | s. moeda corrente

legate | le'geyt | s. legado

legation | legey'śən | s. legação (missão diplomática)

legend | le'ǰond | s. lenda; legenda, inscrição

legendary | le'ǰondərī | a. lendário, legendário

legibility | leˇjibi'litī |s. legibilidade

legible | le'ˇjibəl | a. legível

legion | lı'jən |s. legião

legislate | le'ˇjisleyt | vt. vi. legislar, fazer leis

legislation | leˇjisley'śən |s. legislação

legislature | le'ˇjisləˇśə |s. legislatura

legist | li'ˇjist | s. pessoa versada em leis, jurisconsulto

legitimacy | leˇji'timəsī |s. legitimidade

legitimate | leˇji'timit | a. legítimo; autêntico / vt. legitimar

leisure | le'jə | s. vagar; lazer; ociosidade. **-at l.** devagar, sem pressa. **-at your l.** à sua conveniência

leisurely | le'jəlī | a. vagaroso, lento / adv. lentamente, vagarosamente

lemon | le'mən |s. limão

lemonade | leməneyd' | s. limonada

lemon tree | le'məntrı |s. limoeiro

lend | lend' | vt. emprestar. **-to l. a hand** ajudar. **-to l. itself to** prestar-se a / vi. fazer empréstimo

length | lengɤ' |s. comprimento; duração; extensão; alcance. **-at full l.** estirado, esticado. **-at l.** finalmente; detalhadamente; extensivamente; largamente. **-to go to any l.** fazer todo o possível. **-to go to great lengths to** fazer todos os esforços para

lengthen | leng'ɤən | vt. vi. alongar(-se), estender(-se)

lengthways | lengɤ'weyz | adv. em comprimento, ao comprido

lengthy | leng'ɤī | a. comprido, longo; (fig.) prolixo, cansativo, maçante

leniency, lenience | lı'nˇiənsī lı'nˇiəns | s. indulgência, clemência

lenient | lı'nˇiənt | a. clemente

Leninism | le'ninizəm | s. leninismo

lens | lenz' | s. lente

Lent | lent' | s. quaresma

lentil | len'til | s. lentilha

leopard | le'pəd | s. leopardo

leper | le'pə | s.a. leproso

leprosy | le'prəsī | s. lepra

lesion | lı'jən | s. lesão

less | les' | s. a. adv. prep. menos. **-none the l.** apesar disso, não obstante

lessen | le'sən | vt. diminuir, reduzir / vi. diminuir, tornar-se menor; amainar (vento)

lesser | le'sə | a. menor

lesson | le'sən | s. lição / vt. lecionar, ensinar; repreender

lest | lest' | conj. para que não, a fim de que não; com medo de que

let | let' | vt. deixar, permitir; alugar, arrendar. **-to l. alone** deixar em paz, não interferir. **-to l. down** deixar cair; desapontar, desiludir. **-to l. fly** (coloq.) soltar, disparar. **-to l. go** ou **loose** largar, soltar. **-to l. know** avisar, inteirar. **-to l. off** descarregar, disparar (arma); perdoar, absolver. **-to l. on** (coloq.) dar a entender. **-to l. through** deixar passar. **-l.'s go** vamos (embora). **-l. me (us) see** vejamos

lethal | lı'ɤəl | a. letal, mortífero

lethargic | leɤʌ'jik | a. letárgico; apático, inerte

lethargy | le'ɤəˇjī |s. letargia; apatia, torpor

letter | le'tə |s. carta; letra (do alfabeto). **-to the l.** ao pé da letra, precisamente / vt. marcar com letras, inscrever; desenhar letras

letter-box | le'təboks | s. caixa postal, caixa do correio ⋅

letter-head | le'təhed |s. timbre, cabeçalho

letter of credit | le'təovkre'dit |s. carta de crédito

letter-scale | le'təskeyl | s. pesa-cartas

lettuce | le'tis |s. alface

level | le'vəl | s. nível. **-on the l.** (gír.) honestamente!, palavra!; leal, sincero. **-above sea l.** acima do nível do mar / *vt.* nivelar, aplanar; arrasar, destruir; apontar (arma); igualar

level-headed | le'vɔlhedid | *a.* prudente, sensato, judicioso, equilibrado

levelling | le'vɔling | *s.* nivelamento

lever | lɪ'vɔ | *s.* alavanca

levity | le'vɪtī | *s.* leviandade, frivolidade

levy | le'vī | *s.* arrecadação, coleta; (mil.) recrutamento / *vt.* impor (tributos, taxas etc.); arrecadar, cobrar; (mil.) recrutar, alistar

lewd | lʋd' | *a.* lascivo, impudico; obsceno

lexicon | leks'ikən | *s.* léxico

liability | layəbi'litī | *s.* responsabilidade; obrigação; (*pl.*) dívida, passivo; compromissos financeiros; risco, perigo, probabilidade. **-l. to diseases** etc. tendência a doenças etc.

liable | lay'əbəl | *a.* responsável; sujeito, exposto; propenso a. **-something l. to happen** algo que pode acontecer

liaison | liey'zən | *s.* ligação, relação amorosa; contato

liaison officer | liey'zəno'fisə | *s.* (mil.) oficial de ligação

liar | lay'ə | *s.* mentiroso

libation | libey'śən | *s.* libação

libel | lay'bəl | *s.* calúnia, difamação; (jur.) libelo / *vt.* difamar, caluniar

libellous | lay'bələs | *a.* difamatório

liberal | li'brəl | *s.* liberal / *a.* liberal, generoso, dadivoso

Liberalism | li'brəlizəm | *s.* liberalismo

liberality | libərə'litī | *s.* liberalidade

liberate | li'bəreyt | *vt.* libertar

libertine | li'bətɪn | *s. a.* libertino, devasso, licencioso

liberty | li'bətī | *s.* liberdade; permissão, licença; independência. **-to take liberties with** tomar liberdades com; abusar

de. **-at l.** em liberdade

librarian | laybre'ərĩən | *s.* bibliotecário

library | lay'brərī | *s.* biblioteca

licence, license | lay'səns | *s.* licença, permissão; certificado universitário; libertinagem / *vt.* licenciar

licentious | laysen'śəs | *a.* licencioso, depravado

licentiousness | laysen'śəsnes | *s.* libertinagem, depravação

lick | lik' | *s.* lambida, lambidela / *vt.* lamber

licking | li'king | *s.* (coloq.) sova, surra; derrota

lid | lid' | *s.* tampa; tampo; pálpebra; (gír.) chapéu

lie | lay' | *s.* mentira; posição, situação, estado. **-the l. of the land** (fig.) estado de coisas / *vi.* mentir; estar situado; residir, consistir. **-to l. down** deitar-se. **-to l. in wait** estar de emboscada. **-to l. on** estar (deitado ou colocado) em; pesar sobre (direitos, taxas etc.). **-here lies** aqui jaz

lieutenant | lefte'nənt (EUA) lute'nənt | *s.* (mil.) tenente; capitão-tenente (na marinha)

lieutenant-colonel | lefte'nəntkɛ'nəl | *s.* tenente-coronel

life | layf' | *s.* vida; biografia; vivacidade. **-as big as l.** de tamanho natural. **-for l.** por toda a vida. **-not on your l.** de maneira alguma. **-to see l.** ser vivido. **-true to l.** fiel à realidade

lifebelt | layf'belt | *s.* cinto salva-vidas

lifeboat | layf'bowt | *s.* barco salva-vidas

life buoy | layf'boy | *s.* bóia de salvação

lifelong | layf'long | *a.* para toda a vida; de longa data

life-saver | layf'seyvə | *s.* pessoa ou coisa que salva da morte ou de sérias dificuldades

life-size | layf'sayz | *a.* de tamanho natural

lifetime | layf'taym | *s.* a vida, a existência. **-during the l. of** em vida de

lift | lift' | *s.* elevador, ascensor; levantamento; auxílio; (coloq.) carona / *vt.* levantar, erguer

light | layt' | *s.* luz; fogo, lume; sinal (de trânsito); farol (de carro). **-in the l. of** à luz de. **-to strike a l.** riscar um fósforo / *a.* claro; leve (peso); suave; louro (cabelo); ligeiro, ágil; leviano. **-to make l. of** dar pouca importância, não levar a sério. **-to travel l.** viajar com pouca bagagem / *vt.* iluminar; acender. **-to l. up** acender (cigarro etc.) / *vi.* iluminar-se; acender-se; brilhar; pousar. **-to l. into** (gír.) atacar, cair em cima de. **-to l. on** ou **upon** encontrar por acaso

light blue | layt'blʊ | *s.* azul-claro

lighten | lay'tən | *vt.* aliviar (peso); iluminar / *vi.* relampejar; tornar-se mais leve

lighter | lay'tə | *s.* isqueiro; batelão, barcaça / *vt. vi.* transportar em barcaça

lighthouse | layt'haws | *s.* farol (para guiar navegantes)

lighthouse keeper | layt'hawskı'pə | *s.* faroleiro

lighting | layt'ing | *s.* iluminação; ignição

lightly | layt'lī | *adv.* levemente; ligeiramente; agilmente; alegremente; levianamente

lightness | layt'nes | *s.* ligeireza

lightning | layt'ning | *s.* relâmpago

lightning-conductor | layt'ningkəndâk'tə | *s.* pára-raios

lightship | layt'ship | *s.* barco-farol

like | layk' | *s.* igual; semelhante; (*pl.*) gostos, preferências. **-and the l.** etc., e outros mais / *a. prep.* como, à semelhança de; parecido com. **-to be l.** parecer-se com. **-to feel l.** estar disposto a; gostar de. **-it looks l.** parece que, está com jeito de (chuva etc.). **-what is he l.?** como é ele? **-l. father, l. son** tal pai, tal filho /

vt. gostar de; agradar-se de; preferir. **-as you l.** como quiser

likeable, likable | lay'kəbəl | *a.* simpático, agradável

likelihood | layk'lihud | *s.* probabilidade

likely | layk'lī | *a.* provável; promissor. **-to be l.** to ser provável / *adv.* provavelmente

like-minded | laykmayn'did | *a.* da mesma opinião, que pensa do mesmo modo

liken | lay'kən | *vt.* comparar

likeness | layk'nes | *s.* semelhança; forma, aspecto. **-it is a good l.** está muito parecido. **-family l.** ar de família. **-to take someone's l.** fazer o retrato de alguém

likewise | layk'wayz | *adv.* igualmente

liking | lay'king | *s.* gosto, predileção. **-to take a l. to** tomar gosto por; simpatizar(-se) com, interessar-se por (pessoas)

lilac | lay'lək | *s.* (bot.) lilás (tb. a cor lilás) / *a.* de cor lilás, lilá

lilt | 'lilt' | *s.* ritmo, cadência

lily |.li'lī | *s.* lírio / *a.* como lírio, lirial, puro

limb | lim' | *s.* membro (do corpo); ramo (de árvore); braço (de mar); traquinas, moleque; borda, orla, extremidade

lime | laym' | *s.* cal; lima (fruta); visgo; tília

limelight | laym'layt | *s.* luzes da ribalta. **-in the l.** em evidência

limestone | laym'stown | *s. a.* calcário

limit | li'mit | *s.* limite, restrição, fim, termo. **-that's the l.!** é o cúmulo! / *vt.* limitar, restringir

limitation | limitey'śən | *s.* limitação, restrição

limited | li'mitid | *a.* limitado, restrito; pouco, escasso

limp | limp' | *s.* manqueira, claudicação / *a.* mole, flácido; fraco / *vi.* mancar, claudicar

limy | lay'mī | *a.* visguento; calcário; que contém cal

line | layn' | s. linha; fila; fileira; traço, risco; negócio, ramo de atividade; (pl.) versos. **-on a l.** na mesma linha, nivelado. **-to get a l. on** (coloq.) colher informações sobre. **-to drop someone a l.** (coloq.) escrever a alguém. **-to take a l.** adotar uma posição, tomar uma atitude. **-to stand in l.** fazer fila. **-hard lines** má sorte / vt. enfileirar; forrar, revestir. **-to l. up** alinhar / vi. alinhar-se, enfileirar-se. **-to l. up** pôr-se em fila

lineage | li'nĭĭj | s. linhagem, estirpe

linen | li'nən | s. linho; roupa branca (de cama e mesa) / a. de linho

liner | lay'nə | s. navio ou avião de carreira

linesman | laynz'mən | s. (desp.) juiz de linha

linger | lin'gə | vi. demorar-se

lingering | lin'gəring | a. prolongado, demorado

lingo | lin'gow | s. algaravia, gíria, jargão

linguist | lin'gwist | s. lingüista

linguistic | lingwis'tik | a. lingüístico

linguistics | lingwis'tiks | s. lingüística

liniment | li'nimənt | s. linimento

lining | lay'ning | s. forro

link | link' | s. elo / vt. ligar / vi. ligar-se

linoleum | linow'liəm | s. linóleo

linseed | lin'sıd | s. linhaça

lint | lint' | s. gaze (para curativos)

lion | lay'ən | s. leão

lioness | lay'ənes | s. leoa

lip | lip' | s. lábio; beira, borda; (gír.) linguagem insolente

lipstick | lip'stik | s. batom

liqueur | likĭu'ə | s. licor

liquid | li'kwid | s. líquido / a. líquido; claro, transparente; suave, puro (som); instáveis (opiniões, princípios)

liquidate | li'kwideyt | vt. liquidar

liquor | li'kə | s. bebida alcoólica

liquorice | li'kəris | s. alcaçuz

lisp | lisp' | s. ceceio / vt. vi. cecear

list | list' | s. lista; ourela; (náut.) adernagem; (pl.) liça, arena / vt. fazer uma lista de, catalogar, classificar, inventariar / vi. (náut.) adernar

listen | li'sən | vi. escutar, dar ouvidos a; prestar atenção; atender, obedecer. **-to l. to** escutar (a)

listener | li'sənə | s. ouvinte; radiouvinte

listless | list'les | a. apático, cansado, abatido

litany | li'tənĭ | s. ladainha

literacy | li'tərəsĭ | s. alfabetização, instrução primária

literal | li'tərəl | a. literal

literary | li'tərərĭ | a. literário

literature | lit'ərisə | s. literatura

lithe | layð' | a. flexível; ágil; esbelto

litigant | li'tigənt | s. a. litigante

litigation | litigey'sən | s. litígio, pleito, demanda

litigious | liti'jəs | a. litigioso; dado a demandas (pessoa)

litre, liter | lı'tə | s. litro

litter | li'tə | s. liteira; padiola; palha (para ninho de animais); lixo / vi. espalhar lixo; dar cria

little | li'təl | s. pouco. **-in l.** em pequena escala / a. pequeno, pouco / adv. pouco. **-l. by l.** pouco a pouco

little finger | li'təlfing'gə | s. dedo mínimo

littleness | li'təlnes | s. pequenez; mesquinharia

liturgy | li'təjĭ | s. liturgia

live | layv' | a. vivo, ativo; (eletr.) carregado; não riscado (fósforo); não detonada (bomba) / | liv' | vt. viver (experiência, aventura etc.) / vi. viver; morar, habitar, residir. **-to l. on** viver de (alimento); viver à custa de. **-to l. up to** corresponder a; cumprir o prometido. **-to l. from hand to mouth** viver ao deus-dará. **-long l.!** viva!

livelihood | layv'lihud | s. vida, subsistência

liveliness | layv'lines | s. vivacidade, viveza, rigor

lively | layv'lĭ | a. vivo, vivaz; animado, ativo; alegre, jovial

liver | li'və | s. fígado

livery | li'vərī | s. libré

livery stable | li'vərīstey'bəl | s. estabelecimento onde se alugam cavalos ou carruagens

livestock | layv'stok | s. gado

livid | li'vid | a. lívido; (coloq.) furioso

living | li'ving | s. vida, modo de vida, subsistência; benefício eclesiástico. -to make a l. ganhar a vida / a. vivo; ativo; aceso; exato

living-room | li'vingrʊm | s. sala de estar, *living*

lizard | li'zəd | s. lagarto

load | lowd' | s. carga; peso, fardo / vt. carregar; sobrecarregar; cumular; adulterar, chumbar (dados)

loaded | low'did | a. carregado (arma, navio etc.); chumbado (dados, bengala etc.); (gír.) cheio de (dinheiro, bebida etc.)

loading | low'ding | s. carga / a. de carga

loaf | lowf' | s. pão. -half a l. is better than no bread antes pouco do que nada; (gír.) inteligência / vi. vadiar

loafer | low'fə | s. vadio, mandrião, vagabundo

loan | lown' | s. empréstimo / vt. emprestar. -may I have the l. of? posso tomar emprestado?

loath | lowθ' | a. relutante. -nothing l. desejoso de, disposto

loathe | lowδ' | vt. detestar

loathing | low'δing | s. aversão, abominação, repugnância

loathsome | lowδ'səm | a. repugnante, abominável, asqueroso; odioso

lobby | lo'bĭ | s. vestíbulo, saguão; (polít.) grupo que procura influenciar legisladores

lobe | lowb' | s. lobo; lóbulo

lobster | lob'stə | s. lagosta

local | low'kəl | a. local, regional

locality | lowka'litĭ | s. localidade

locate | low'keyt | vt. localizar, situar, instalar

location | lowkey'sən | s. localização, posição. -on l. (cin.) local exterior de filmagem fora dos estúdios

loch | loš' | s. (Esc.) lago; braço de mar

lock | lok' | s. fechadura; comporta, eclusa; madeixa, cacho (cabelo). -under l. and key debaixo de chave / vt. fechar à chave. -to l. up fechar, trancar; meter na cadeia / vi. trancar-se

locker | lo'kə | s. armário, compartimento com chave

locket | lo'kit | s. medalhão

lockjaw | lok'jó | s. tétano

locksmith | lok'smiθ | s. serralheiro, fabricante de fechaduras

locomotive | lowkəmow'tiv | s. locomotiva

locust | low'kəst | s. gafanhoto

lodge | loj' | s. casa de zelador (esp. em parque etc.); cabana; loja maçônica / vt. alojar; fixar; apresentar protesto / vi. alojar-se

lodger | lo'jə | s. inquilino; hóspede

lodging | lo'jing | s. alojamento. -board and l. cama e mesa

lodging-house | lo'jinghaws | s. hospedaria; pensão

loft | loft' | s. sótão

lofty | lof'tĭ | a. alto, elevado, sublime; orgulhoso, arrogante, altivo

log | log' | s. cepo; tronco, toro; diário ou livro de bordo; (aer.) caderneta de vôo. -to sleep like a l. dormir como uma pedra

loggerhead | lo'gəhed | s. palerma, idiota. -to be at loggerheads estar em total desacordo

logic | lo'jĭk | s. lógica

logical | lo'jikəl | a. lógico

loin | loyn' | s. lombo

loincloth | loyn'kloθ | s. tanga

loiter | loy'tə | vt. matar o tempo / vi. vaguear; perder tempo;

demorar-se

loll | lol' | *vt.* deixar pender (a língua) / *vi.* reclinar-se, recostar-se

Londoner| lân'dənə |*s.* londrino

loneliness | lown'līnes | *s.* solidão; isolamento

lonely | lown'lī | *a.* solitário, isolado; deserto

long | long' | *a.* longo, comprido (esp. objeto); prolongado, de longo alcance. -**in the l. run** no fim de contas. -**the l. and the short of** para encurtar a história / *adv.* longamente, muito tempo. -**as l. as** enquanto. -**l. ago** há muito tempo. -**before l.** breve , daqui a pouco. -**all day l.** durante todo o dia. -**to be l.** demorar-se. -**not by a l. way** nem por sombras / *vi.* desejar ardentemente; ter saudades de; ansiar por, ambicionar

long-distance | long'distəns | *a.* interurbano; de longa distância

longing | long'ing | *s.* desejo ardente, anelo; ânsia; saudade / *a.* desejoso; ansioso; saudoso

longitude | lon'jitiud |*s.* longitude

longways | long'weyz | *adv.* em comprimento, ao comprido

look | luk' | *s.* olhar; olhada, olhadela; aspecto, aparência, ar. -**let me have a l.** deixe-me ver. -**good looks** beleza / *vt.* olhar; mostrar; parecer. -**to l. over** examinar; folhear. -**to l. up** procurar, pesquisar / *vi.* olhar, ver; procurar; encarar. -**to l. after** cuidar de. -**to l. alike** parecer-se. -**to l. at** olhar para. -**to l. back** relembrar. -**to l. down on** desprezar. -**to l. for** procurar; esperar. -**to l. forward to** aguardar ansiosamente. -**to l. like** parecer-se com; parecer que. -**to l. ill** parecer doente. -**to l. well** ter bom aspecto; ficar bem a (roupas etc.). -**to l. upon** considerar, estimar. -**l. here!** um momento!, ouça! -**l. out!** cuidado!

looker-on | lu'kəron |*s.* especta-

dor, observador

looking-glass | lu'kingglʌs | *s.* espelho

look-out | luk'awt |*s.* vigia (pessoa); posto de observação. -**to be on the l. -o.** ficar de vigia, ficar de olho. -**to be on the l. -o. for** procurar; estar à espreita de

loom | lum |*s.* tear / *vi.* assomar, surgir, aparecer

loop | lup' |*s.* laço, laçada; curva fechada; alça, presilha / *vt.* fazer alça; dar laçada (em corda etc.); dar voltas em / *vi.* (aer.) fazer *loop*

loophole | lup'howl | *s.* seteira; brecha; (fig.) saída, evasiva, escapatória

loose | lus' | *a.* solto, livre; frouxo, folgado; livre (conduta, costumes). -**to break l.** libertar-se, soltar-se; fugir. -**to let** ou **set l.** soltar; pôr em liberdade

loosen | lu'sən |*vt. vi.* soltar(-se), desatar(-se); alargar(-se)

looseness | lus'nes |*s.* frouxidão

loot | lut' |*s.* pilhagem, saque / *vt. vi.* saquear, pilhar

looter | lu'tə |*s.* saqueador

lop | lop' |*vt.* podar; cortar fora, decepar

lop-sided | lop'saydid | *a.* torto, desequilibrado

loquacious | ləkwey'śəs | *a.* loquaz, verboso, falador

lord | lód' | *s.* senhor; amo; (maiúsc.) Deus; lorde / *vi.* dominar, ser senhor de. -**to l. it over** ser senhor absoluto

lordly | lód'lī |*a.* altivo, soberbo / *adv.* altivaménte

lordship | lód'śip | *s.* senhorio. -**your l.** Vossa Excelência (tratamento de lordes e juízes)

lore | ló'ə | *s.* conjunto de tradições (sobre determinado assunto); anedotário

lorry | ló'rī |*s.* caminhão

lose | luz' | *vt.* perder. -**to l. ground** perder terreno. -**to l. sight of** perder de vista. -**to l. one's way** perder o caminho.

-to l. one's temper perder a calma. -to l. face perder o prestígio ou a dignidade / vi. perder, ser derrotado; atrasar (relógio)

loss | los' | s. perda; prejuízo. -to be at a l. ficar perplexo. -to sell at a l. vender com prejuízo

lost | lost' | a. perdido; desperdiçado; perplexo. -to be l. perder o caminho. -to be l. in ficar absorto. -to get l. perder-se, extraviar-se. -to be l. to ser insensível a

lot | lot' | s. sorteio; lote; quinhão; grupo. -to be a bad l. não prestar. -to draw lots tirar a sorte. -a l. of muito, grande quantidade

lotion | low'śǝn | s. loção

lottery | lo'tǝrī | s. loteria

lotus | low'tǝs | s. (bot.) lótus, loto

loud | lawd' | a. alto, forte (som); berrante (cor) / adv. ruidosamente

loudspeaker | lawdspı'kǝ | s. alto-falante

lounge | lawnj' | s. sala de estar; espreguiçadeira; lugar de descanso; ociosidade / vi. mover-se preguiçosamente, perambular; vadiar

louse | laws' | s. piolho

lousy | law'zī | a. piolhento; (gír.) nojento, ordinário

lout | lawt' | s. labrego; rústico, boçal, homem sem maneiras

lovable | lâ'vǝbǝl | a. amorável, que merece ser amado

love | lâv' | s. amor. -to fall in l. with enamorar-se. -for l. por amor, de graça. -not for l. or money por nada deste mundo. -give my l. to lembranças, recomendações / vt. amar; gostar muito de / vi. amar

loveliness | lâv'lines | s. encanto, beleza

lovely | lâv'lī | a. formoso, lindo; adorável

lover | lâ'vǝ | s. amante, namorado; (pl.) par de amantes; amigo, amante (da verdade

etc.); apaixonado de (livros, teatro etc.)

low | low' | s. primeira (marcha de automóvel) / a. baixo; vil, grosseiro. -in l. spirits deprimido, desalentado / vi. mugir / adv. baixo, em voz baixa. -to bow l. curvar-se, fazer reverência profunda; prostrar-se

lower | low'ǝ | a. inferior, mais baixo / vt. baixar; arriar (bandeira); (náut.) amainar, reduzir (velas) / vi. abaixar-se; diminuir

lower case | low'ǝkeys | s. (tip.) caixa baixa

lowly | low'lī | a. humilde / adv. humildemente

low-necked | lowne'kid | a. decotado

low-spirited | lowspi'ritid | a. desanimado, triste

loyal | loy'ǝl | a. leal, fiel

loyalty | loy'ǝltī | s. lealdade

lubricant | lu'brikǝnt | s. lubrificante

lubricate | lu'brikeyt | vt. lubrificar

lucid | lʊ'sid | a. lúcido

luck | lâk' | s. sorte. -to be in l. estar com sorte. -to be down in one's l. estar sem sorte; estar em dificuldades. -to try one's l. tentar a sorte. -worse l.! tanto pior!

luckily | lâ'kilī | adv. felizmente, por sorte

luckless | lâk'les | a. sem sorte, desafortunado

lucky | lâ'kī | a. com sorte, afortunado. -l. dog! (coloq.) felizardo!

lucrative | lu'krǝtiv | a. lucrativo, vantajoso

ludicrous | lu'dikrǝs | a. risível, cômico, absurdo

luggage | lâ'gij | s. bagagem

luggage-van | lâ'gijvan | s. vagão de bagagens

lukewarm | lʊk'wóm | a. morno, tépido; (fig.) indiferente

lull | lâl' | s. intervalo de calma, estiada, calmaria / vt. acalentar; acalmar / vi. acalmar-se

lullaby | lâ'ləƀay | *s.* cantiga de ninar, acalanto

lumber | lâm'bə | *s.* móveis velhos, trastes; (EUA) madeira, pranchas / *vt.* entulhar (sala, quarto etc.); empilhar / *vi.* mover-se pesadamente

lumbering | lâm'bəring |*s.* exploração e comércio de madeiras, serraria

lumberjack | lâm'bəjak | *s.* lenhador; madeireiro ou negociante de madeiras

luminous| lu'minəs |*s.* luminoso

lump | lâmp' |*s* pedaço; torrão, tablete; inchaço; nó (na garganta) / *a.* em torrões / *vt.* amontoar; encaroçar / *vi.* encaroçar-se; mover-se pesadamente

lump sum| lâmp'sâm |*s.* quantia total, soma total

lunacy| lu'nəsī |*s.* insensatez, tolice; loucura, demência

lunatic| lu'nətik |*s. a.* louco, demente, lunático

lunch| lânś' |*s.* almoço; merenda / *vi.* almoçar

lung| lâng' |*s.* pulmão

lunge | lânj' | *s.* estocada; salto, mergulho; investida / *vi.* investir, atacar

lurch | lɛš' |*s.* guinada. **-to leave in the l.** abandonar / *vi.* dar guinadas, desviar subitamente; dar solavancos (carro)

lure | lïu'ə |*s.* engodo, chamariz; isca artificial; atração, encanto

/ *vt.* atrair, seduzir, fascinar, tentar

lurid | lïu'rid | *a.* lívido, pálido; sombrio; sinistro

lurk | lɛk' | *vi.* estar emboscado ou escondido; mover-se furtivamente, rondar

luscious | lâ'śəs |*a.* suculento, saboroso; excessivamente doce; demasiadamente rico (linguagem ou estilo)

lush | lâś' |*a.* luxuriante

lust | lâst' | *s.* luxúria, lascívia; ambição, cobiça, desejo ardente / *vi.* desejar ardentemente, ansiar por

lustful | lâst'ful |*a.* lascivo, sensual

lustre, luster | lâs'tə | *s.* lustre, brilho, esplendor

lusty | lâs'tī |*a.* robusto, forte, vigoroso, saudável

lute | lut' |*s.* alaúde

luxuriance | lâgju'rīəns | *s.* exuberância, abundância

luxuriant | lâgju'rīənt | *a.* luxuriante, viçoso

luxurious | lâgju'rīəs | *a.* luxuoso, de luxo, suntuoso

luxury | lâk'śərī |*s.* luxo

lying | lay'ing |*s.* mentira; ato de deitar-se / *a.* mentiroso; estendido; situado, colocado

lynch | linś' | *vt.* linchar

lynx | links' |*s.* lince

lyre | lay'ə |*s.* (mús.) lira

lyric | li'rik |*s.* poema lírico; (*pl.*, mús.) letra / *a.* lírico

M

macaroni | makərow'nī | *s.* macarrão

macaw | məkó' |*s.* arara

mace | meys' |*s.* maça, clava; macis (arilo da noz-moscada)

macerate | ma'səreyt | *vt.* macerar

machete | maśe'ti ma'śet | *s.* facão de mato

machination | makiney'śən | *s.* maquinação, intriga, trama

machine| məśin' |*s.* máquina

machine-gun | məśin'gân | *s.* metralhadora

machine-made | məsɪn'meyd | *a.* feito à máquina

machinery | məsí'nərī | *s.* maquinaria, máquinas

mackerel | mak'rəl | *s.* (ict.) cavala

mackintosh | ma'kintoś | *s.* capa impermeável

mad | mad' | *a.* louco, doido; imprudente; furioso. **-like m.** furiosamente, como louco. **-to go m.** enlouquecer

madam | ma'dəm | *s.* minha senhora (forma de tratamento)

madden | ma'dən | *vt.* enlouquecer; enfurecer

made | meyd' | *a.* feito, fabricado

made-to-order | meydtuó'də | *a.* feito sob medida, de encomenda

made-up | meyd'âp | *a.* fictício, inventado; artificial; maquilado

madhouse | mad'haws | *s.* manicômio, hospício

madman | mad'mən | *s.* doido, louco, maluco, maníaco

madness | mad'nes | *s.* loucura, demência; raiva (animais)

madwoman | mad'wəmən | *s.* louca

magazine | magəzin' | *s.* revista; paiol (de pólvora); carregador, pente (de arma de fogo)

maggot | ma'gət | *s.* larva de mosca; bicho de queijo; fantasia, capricho

magic | ma'ʝik | *s.* magia, encanto; fascinação / *a.* mágico; maravilhoso

magician | məji'śən | *s.* mágico

magistrate | ma'ʝistreyt | *s.* magistrado, juiz

magnanimous | məgna'niməs | *a.* magnânimo, generoso

magnate | mag'neyt | *s.* magnata

magnet | mag'nit | *s.* ímã

magnetic | magne'tik | *a.* magnético (tb. fig.)

magnificence | məgni'fisəns | *s.* magnificência, esplendor

magnificent | məgni'fisənt | *a.* magnificente; suntuoso

magnifier | mag'nifayə | *s.* (eletr.) amplificador; lente de aumento

magnify | mag'nifay | *vt.* aumentar, ampliar; exagerar

magnifying glass | mag'nifayingglAs | *s.* lente de aumento

magnitude | mag'nitʃud | *s.* magnitude; importância

magpie | mag'pay | *s.* (orn.) pega; (fig.) tagarela

mahogany | məho'gənī | *s.* mogno

Mahometan | meho'midən | *s.a.* = *Muhammadan*

maid | meyd' | *s.* donzela; criada, empregada

maiden | mey'dən | *s.* donzela, moça solteira / *a.* solteira; virginal

maiden name | mey'dənneym | *s.* nome de solteira

mail | meyl' | *s.* correio; cartas, correspondência

mail-bag | meyl'bag | *s.* mala postal, saco do correio

mailman | meyl'mən | *s.* carteiro

mail order | meyl'ódə | *s.* encomenda postal, pedido por correio

maim | meym' | *vt.* mutilar, aleijar

main | meyn' | *s.* parte principal; cano principal; mastro grande. **-in the m.** principalmente. **-with might and m.** com toda a força / *a.* principal, precípuo

mainland | meyn'lənd | *s.* continente, terra firme

mainly | meyn'lī | *adv.* principalmente, geralmente; mormente

mainmast | meyn'mast | *s.* (náut.) mastro grande

mainspring | meyn'spring | *s.* mola principal; (fig.) motivo principal

mainstay | meyn'stey | *s.* amparo, suporte, sustentáculo

maintain | meynteyn' | *vt.* manter, sustentar; defender; afirmar, asseverar

maintenance | meyn'tinəns | *s.* manutenção, conservação; sustento; subsistência

majestic | məʝes'tik | *a.* majestoso, imponente, grandioso

majesty | ma'jistī | s. majestade, grandeza, imponência; monarca, soberano. -**His(Her)M.** Sua Majestade. -**Your M.** Vossa Majestade

major | mey'jɔ | s. major; superior; (educ., EUA) matéria de maior interesse ou principal nos estudos / a. maior; principal; importante

majority | mɔjo'ritī | s. maioria, maior parte; maioridade

make | meyk' | s. feitura, fabricação; marca, modelo. -**to be on the m.** ser arrivista / vt. fazer; produzir; concluir, inferir; obrigar; tornar. -**to m. as if** fingir. -**to m. for** dirigir-se para, ir para. -**to m. fun of** zombar de, troçar de. -**to m. good** compensar, indenizar; ressarcir; comprovar; cumprir. -**to m. headway** avançar, fazer progressos. -**to m. known** tornar conhecido. -**to m. of** deduzir, tirar; fazer de. -**to m. off** fugir. -**to m. out** compreender, deduzir; decifrar; avistar, ver. -**to m. the most of** tirar o maior proveito de. -**to m. over** transformar (roupa); transmitir, ceder. -**to m. room for** fazer ou dar lugar para. -**to m. short work of** fazer ou livrar-se de rapidamente. -**to m. up** fazer; inventar; completar; aviar (receita); recobrar (tempo); maquilar-se; conciliar. -**to m. it up** fazer as pazes. -**to m. up one's mind** resolver-se. -**to m. way** abrir caminho

make-believe | meyk'bilɪv | s. simulação, fingimento; simulacro / a. fingido, falso

maker | mey'kɔ | s. fabricante; criador

makeshift | meyk'śift | s. substituto; paliativo; recurso / a. provisório, temporário

make-up | meyk'ȃp | s. composição; constituição (física ou mental); modo de ser; maquilagem, pintura

making | mey'king | s. fabricação, manufatura, preparo; · (pl.) qualidades essenciais. -**in the m.** em formação, em desenvolvimento

maladjusted | malɔjȃs'tid | a. desajustado, inadaptado

maladministration | malɔdministrey'śɔn | s. má administração

malady | ma'lɔdī | s. doença

malaise | maleyz' | s. mal-estar, indisposição; inquietação

malaria | mɔle'ɔrīɔ | s. malária

malarial | mɔle'ɔrīɔl | a. malárico

malcontent | mal'kɔntɔnt | s.a. descontente

male | meyl' | s. varão, homem, macho / a. macho, másculo, viril

malediction | malidik'śɔn | s. maldição, praga; maledicência

malefactor | ma'lifaktɔ | s. malfeitor

malevolence | mɔle'vɔlɔns | s. malevolência, má vontade

malevolent | male'vɔlɔnt | a. malevolente, malévolo, maligno

malice | ma'lis | s. malícia, malignidade, malevolência; (jur.) dolo, intenção criminosa. -**to bear m. to** guardar rancor a

malicious | mɔli'śɔs | a. malicioso; malévolo

malign | mɔlayn' | a. maligno, malévolo; maléfico / vt. difamar, caluniar

malignant | malig'nɔnt | a. maligno; maléfico

malinger | melin'gɔ | s. detrator, aquele que calunia / vi. fingir-se doente

mallard | ma'lɔd | s. pato selvagem

mallet | ma'lit | s. marreta (esp. de madeira)

malpractice | malprak'tis | s. mau procedimento; (jur.) imperícia (esp. de médico)

malt | malt' | s. malte

maltreat | maltrɪt' | vt. seviciar, maltratar

maltreatment | maltrɪt'mənt | *s.* maus tratos, mau tratamento

mammal | ma'məl | *s.* mamífero

mammoth | ma'məϑ | *s.* mamute / *a.* gigantesco, enorme

man | man' | *s.* homem. -**m. and wife** marido e mulher. -**to a m.** todos, sem exceção. -**m. and boy** desde menino, toda a vida. -**to be one's own m.** ser livre, ter pleno domínio de si. -**m. alive!** homem de Deus! / *vt.* (náut.) tripular; guarnecer; fortalecer; manejar

manacle | ma'nəkəl | *s.* (ger. *pl.*) grilheta, algema / *vt.* algemar, agrilhoar

manage | ma'niĵ | *vt.* manejar, manipular; administrar, dirigir, ser gerente ou diretor de; conseguir, lograr. -**to m.** to conseguir, arranjar meio de ser capaz de. -**could you m. to come?** daria um jeito de vir? -**how did she m.** ? como se arranjou ela?, como conseguiu sobreviver? / *vi.* administrar (empresa, negócio); sair-se bem (em tarefa)

manageable | ma'nijəbəl | *a.* manejável; tratável

management | ma'niĵmənt | *s.* administração, gerência; manejo, controle; capacidade administrativa

manager | ma'nijə | *s.* gerente; administrador; (teat.) empresário

manageress | manijəres' | *s.* administradora, gerente

managerial | maniĵi'rīəl | *a.* administrativo, gerencial

mandate | man'deyt | *s.* mandato

mandatory | man'dətərī | *a.* imperativo, obrigatório

mandible | man'dibəl | *s.* mandíbula

mandolin | man'dəlin | *s.* bandolim

mane | meyn' | *s.* crina; juba (de leão)

manfully | man'fulī | *adv.* varonilmente, corajosamente

mange | manĵ' | *s.* sarna (de cães), ronha (de cavalos, ovelhas)

manger | meyn'ĵə | *s.* manjedoura

mangle | man'gəl | *s.* (mec.) calandra / *vt.* calandrar; lacerar; estropiar, mutilar

mango | man'gow | *s.* (bot.) manga

mango-tree | man'gowtrɪ | *s.* (bot.) mangueira

manhole | man'howl | *s.* poço de inspeção (em rede de esgotos etc.)

manhood | man'hud | *s.* virilidade; maioridade; população masculina

mania | mey'nīə | *s.* mania

maniac | mey'nīək | *s.a.* maníaco

manicure | ma'nikīuə | *s.* manicure

manifest | ma'nifest | *s.* manifesto (de carga) / *a.* manifesto, patente, evidente / *vt.* manifestar, mostrar, expressar

manifestation | manifestey'śən | *s.* manifestação

manifesto | manifes'tow | *s.* manifesto

manifold | ma'nifowld | *a.* múltiplo; multiforme, complexo

manipulate | məni'pĭuleyt | *vt.* manipular, manejar

mankind | mankaynd' | *s.* gênero humano, humanidade, os homens

manliness | man'lines | *s.* virilidade, coragem

manly | man'lī | *a.* varonil, másculo, viril

mannequin | ma'nikin | *s.* manequim, modelo; manequim (de vitrine)

manner | ma'nə | *s.* modo, maneira; civilidade; conduta; prática, hábito, costume; espécie; estilo; (*pl.*) maneiras. -**after the m. of** à maneira de. -**in a m.** de certo modo. -**in a m. of speaking** por assim dizer. -**lack of manners** falta de maneiras, falta de cortesia

mannerism | ma'nərizəm | *s.* maneirismo

mannish | ma'niś | *a.* masculino, masculinizado

manoeuvre, maneuver | mənʋ'-və | *s.* manobra / *vt.* manobrar

man-of-war | man'ovwʌ | *s.* navió de guerra

manor | ma'nə | *s.* domínio feudal, herdade nobre

manor house | ma'nəhaws | *s.* solar, casa senhorial

manse | mans' | *s.* residência de pároco (esp. na Esc.)

mansion | man'śən | *s.* mansão

manslaughter | man'slótə | *s.* homicídio; (jur.) homicídio involuntário

mantelpiece | man'təlpıs | *s.* parapeito de lareira

mantilla | manti'lə | *s.* mantilha

mantis | man'tis | *s.* louva-a-deus

mantle | man'təl | *s.* manto; camisa de lampião / *vt.* cobrir, encobrir; envolver

manual | ma'ñiuəl | *s.a.* manual

manufacture | manĭufak'śə | *s.* manufatura, fabricação / *vt.* manufaturar, fabricar

manufacturer | manĭufak'śərə | *s.* fabricante, industrial

manufacturing | manĭufak'śəring | *s.* fabricação / *a.* manufatureiro

manure | manĭu'ə | *s.* estrume, esterco, adubo / *vt.* estrumar, estercar, adubar

manuscript | ma'ñiuskript | *s.* manuscrito

Manx | manks' | *s.* habitante da ilha de Man; língua da ilha de Man / *a.* da ilha de Man

many | me'ñi | *a.* muitos. **-a great m.** muitos. **-as m. as** tantos quanto. **-how m.?** quantos? **-one too m.** um de mais, um de sobra. **-very m.** muitíssimos

map | map' | *s.* mapa. **-to put on the m.** (coloq.) colocar em evidência / *vt.* fazer mapa; planejar

maple | mey'pəl | *s.* (bot.) bordo

mar | mʌ' | *vt.* estragar, danificar, desfigurar

marathon | ma'rəϑən | *s.* maratona (tb. fig.)

marauder | məró'də | *s.* saqueador, pirata

marble | mʌ'bəl | *s.* mármore; bola de gude; (*pl.*) jogo de gude / *a.* de mármore

march | mʌś' | *s.* marcha. **-on the m.** em marcha; (maiúsc.) março / *vt.* pôr em marcha, fazer marchar / *vi.* marchar. **-to m. in.** entrar

marchioness | mʌ'śənes | *s.* marquesa

mare | me'ə | *s.* égua

margarine | mʌgərin' | *s.* margarina

margin | mʌ'ĭin | *s.* margem; limite; reserva, provisão

marijuana | marĭua'nə | *s.* maconha

marine | mərin' | *s.* (EUA) fuzileiro naval / *a.* marinho, marítimo, naval

mariner | ma'rinə | *s.* marinheiro, marujo

marionette | marĭənet' | *s.* marionete, fantoche

maritime | ma'ritaym | *a.* marítimo

mark | mʌk' | *s.* marca; sinal; nota, grau; cicatriz, mancha; prova, testemunho; alvo, meta, mira; carimbo, sinete; marco (moeda). **-to be beside the m.** não vir ao caso. **-not up to the m.** não satisfatório; doente. **-to hit the m.** acertar no alvo. **-of m.** notável, importante / *vt.* marcar; distinguir; indicar; notar; dar nota ou grau. **-to m. down** reduzir o preço. **-to m. out** traçar, delimitar. **-to m. time** marcar passo

marked | mʌkt' | *a.* marcado; acentuado; distinto, notável

market | mʌ'kit | *s.* mercado. **-on the m.** à venda. **-to make a m. of** barganhar. **-to buy (to sell) at the m.** comprar (vender) ao preço da praça / *vt.* colocar na praça; vender / *vi.* negociar no mercado

marking | mʌ'kɪŋ | *s.* marcação

marksman | mʌks'mən | *s.* atirador de elite

marksmanship | mʌks'mənʃip | *s.* boa pontaria

marmalade | mʌ'məleyd | *s.* geléia de laranja (ou outra fruta cítrica)

maroon | mərʊn' | *s.* negro fugido; pessoa abandonada em praia deserta; cor castanha / *vt.* abandonar (em costa deserta); isolar

marquee | mʌkɪ' | *s.* grande barraca; toldo colocado à entrada de edifício

marquis, marquess | mʌ'kwis | *s.* marquês

marriage | ma'riĵ | *s.* casamento, matrimônio, núpcias

marriageable | ma'rijəbəl | *a.* casadouro

marriage portion | ma'riĵpóśən | *s.* dote

married | ma'rid | *a.* casado; matrimonial, conjugal. **-to get m.** casar-se

married couple | ma'ridkâ'pəl | *s.* casal

marrow | ma'row | *s.* tutano, medula; (fig.) o cerne, o essencial

marry | ma'rī | *vt.* casar; dar em casamento; (fig.) unir / *vi.* casar-se

Mars | mʌz' | *s.* Marte

marsh | mʌś' | *s.* pântano

marshal | mʌ'śəl | *s.* marechal / *vt.* dispor, colocar em ordem de batalha; conduzir, dirigir

marshy | mʌ'śī | *a.* pantanoso

martial | mʌ'śəl | *a.* marcial, bélico, militar

martyr | mʌ'tə | *s.* mártir

martyrdom | mʌ'tədəm | *s.* martírio

martyred | mʌ'təd | *a.* martirizado

marvel | mʌ'vəl | *s.* maravilha, prodígio / *vt.* maravilhar / *vi.* maravilhar-se

marvellous, marvelous | mʌ'vələs | *a.* maravilhoso

Marxism | mʌk'sizəm | *s.* marxismo

Marxist | mʌk'sist | *s.a.* marxista

marzipan | mʌzipan' | *s.* marzipã

mascot | mas'kət | *s.* mascote

masculine | mas'kĭulin | *s.a.* masculino

mash | maś' | *vt.* triturar, esmagar, amassar

mashed potatoes | maśdpətey'təz | *spl.* purê de batatas

mask | mʌsk' | *s.* máscara / *vt.* mascarar; disfarçar

mason | mey'sən | *s.* pedreiro; (maiúsc.) maçom

masonry | mey'sənrī | *s.* alvenaria; (maiúsc.) maçonaria

masquerade | maskəreyd' | *s.* baile de máscaras

mass | mas' | *s.* massa (esp. povo); montão, conjunto; missa / *a.* maciço; popular (fenômeno de massa) / *vi.* aglomerar-se; juntar-se em massa

massacre | ma'səkə | *s.* massacre, carnificina / *vt.* massacrar, chacinar

massage | ma'sʌỹ | *s.* massagem / *vt.* massagear

masseus | masE' | *s.* massagista (homem)

masseuse | masEz' | *s.* massagista (mulher)

massive | ma'siv | *a.* maciço; sólido; compacto; grande, importante

mast | mʌst' | *s.* mastro. **-to serve before the m.** servir como marinheiro / *vt.* mastrear

master | mʌs'tə | *s.* mestre; senhor, patrão; dono da casa; proprietário; (náut.) capitão; (náut.) mestre, arrais, patrão; título de tratamento para um menino / *a.* mestre, principal / *vt.* subjugar, dominar, vencer; tornar-se perito (em algum assunto)

masterly | mʌs'təlī | *a.* magistral / *adv.* magistralmente

masterpiece | mAs'təpis | s. obra-
-prima

master-stroke | mAs'təstrowk | s.
golpe de mestre

mastery | mAs'təri | s. domínio

mastiff | mas'tif | s. mastim

mastoid | mas'toyd | s. (anat.) apó-
fise mastóide / a. (anat.) mastóide

mat | mat' | s. capacho; esteira /
a. mate, fosco / vt. atapetar; es-
teirar; emaranhar

match | maš' | s. fósforo; igual,
semelhante; (desp.) partida;
casamento, aliança / vt. igualar; rivalizar; emparelhar; ca-
sar, combinar / vi. igualar;
casar-se, combinar; corres-
ponder

matchless | maš'les | a. incompa-
rável, inigualável

matchlock | maš'lok | s. fecho de
mecha; arcabuz, mosquete ou
pistola de mecha

matchwood | maš'wud | s. ma-
deira para fazer fósforos; las-
cas, estilhas

mate | meyt' | s. companheiro,
camarada; parceiro; (náut.)
imediato; macho ou fêmea
(animais) / vt. acasalar / vi.
acasalar-se

material | mətı'rīəl | s. material;
(pl.) utensílios, implementos /
a. material; substancial; importante

materialism | mətı'rīəlizəm | s.
materialismo

materialize | matı'rīəlayz | vi.
concretizar-se, materializar-se

maternal | mətE'nəl | a. mater-
nal, materno

maternity | mətE'nitī | s. materni-
dade

maternity hospital | mətE'nitī-
hos'pitəl | s. maternidade

mathematician | maϑiməti'śən |
s. matemático

mathematics | maϑima'tiks | s.
matemática

matinée, matinee | ma'tiney |
matinê; vesperal

matins | ma'tinz | spl. (ecles.)

matinas

matriculation | mətrikľuley'śən |
s. matrícula; exame de admissão

matrimonial | matrimow'nľəl | a.
matrimonial

matrimony | ma'trimənī | s.
matrimônio

matron | mey'trən | s. matrona;
supervisora (de escola etc.); en-
fermeira-chefe

matter | ma'tə | s. matéria; subs-
tância; coisa; negócio, questão;
caso; (med.) pus. **-as a m. of fact**
aliás, na verdade. **-for that m.**
quanto a isso. **-no m.** não obstan-
te. **-what is the m.?** que é que há?
-it is a m. of trata-se de / vi. signi-
ficar; importar; (med.) supurar.
-it doesn't m. não importa, não
faz mal

mattress | ma'trəs | s. colchão

mature | mətľu'ə | a. maduro;
(com.) vencido (nota, conta
etc.) / vt. amadurecer / vi.
(com.) vencer

maturity | mətľu'ritī | s. maturi-
dade; (com.) vencimento

maudlin | mód'lin | a. sentimen-
tal, piegas, choroso

maul | mól' | s. malho / vt. ma-
lhar; (fig.) criticar severamente

mauve | móv' | s. cor de malva / a.
de cor malva

mawkish | mó'kiš | a. sentimen-
tal, piegas

maxim | mak'sim | s. máxima

maximum | mak'siməm | s.a.
máximo

may | mey | v. aux. poder

May | mey' | s. maio

maybe | mey'bī | adv. talvez

mayonnaise | meyəneyz' | s. maio-
nese

mayor | me'ə | s. prefeito

maze | meyz' | s. labirinto. **-in a**
m. perplexo, confuso

me | mī | pron. me; mim

meadow | me'dow | s. prado,
campina

meagre, meager | mī'gə | a. escas-
so, mesquinho, exíguo, parco,
insuficiente, minguado

meagreness | mı'gənes | s. exigüidade, pobreza, insuficiência

meal | mıl' | s. refeição; farinha (de qualquer grão); (EUA) farinha de milho

mean | mın' | s. média, meio-termo; meio, modo, método; instrumento; (pl.) meios, recursos, rendimentos. **-by all means** sem dúvida, certamente. **-by any means** de qualquer maneira. **-by means of** por meio de. **-by no means** de modo nenhum. **-to live beyond one's means** viver além de seus recursos / a. médio; intermediário; medíocre; vil, baixo; indigno, desprezível; mesquinho; miserável; (coloq., EUA) ruim, mau, maldoso / vt. querer dizer, significar; tencionar, pensar; representar, denotar; exprimir; destinar. **-what do you m. by it?** que quer dizer com isso? **-I didn't m. it** não fiz por querer; não falei a sério. **-he means well** ele está com boas intenções

meander | mıan'də | s. meandro, sinuosidade; (pl.) meandro (de rio) / vi. serpentear

meaning | mı'ning | s. significado, significação; intenção, propósito. **-double m.** duplo sentido / a. intencional, significativo

meaningful | mı'ningful | a. significativo, expressivo

meaningless | mı'ningles | a. sem sentido, sem significado

meanness | mın'nes | s. mesquinhez, vileza; maldade

meantime | mın'taym | s. ínterim. **-in the m.** neste (nesse) meio-tempo / adv. entrementes; enquanto isso

meanwhile | mın'wayl | s.adv. = meantime

measles | mı'zəlz | s. (sing. ou pl.) sarampo

measurable | me'jərəbəl | a. mensurável

measure | me'jə | s. medida; dimensão; quantidade, grau;

compasso; providência; ato legislativo, projeto de lei. **-beyond m.** sem limite. **-in a m.** até certo ponto. **-in some m.** em parte. **-made to m.** feito sob medida. **-to take measures** tomar providências / vt. medir, tomar a medida de; estimar

measurement | me'jəmənt | s. medição; medida; sistema de medidas

meat | mıt' | s. carne (como alimento); (EUA) polpa, parte comestível (de fruta etc.). **-to be m. and drink to** (coloq.) ser tudo para

meat ball | mıt'ból | s. almôndega

meat-safe | mıt'seyf | s. guarda-comida

meaty | mı'tı | a. carnudo

mechanic | mika'nik | s. mecânico

mechanical | mika'nikəl | a. mecânico

mechanism | mə'kənizəm | s. mecanismo

medal | me'dəl | s. medalha

medallion | məda'lïən | s. medalhão

meddle | me'dəl | vi. intrometer-se; interferir

meddlesome | me'dəlsəm | a. intrometido, metediço

meddling | med'ling | s. intromissão, ingerência

mediate | mı'dïeyt | a. mediato, indireto / vt. mediar; tratar como intermediário; ser mediador de; reconciliar / vi. mediar, servir como intermediário

mediation | mıdıey'śən | s. mediação, intercessão

mediator | mı'dıeytə | s. mediador; árbitro

medical | me'dikəl | a. médico

medicine | me'disin | s. medicina; remédio, medicamento

medicine-man | me'disinmən | s. feiticeiro, curandeiro

medieval, mediaeval | medıi'vəl | a. medieval

mediocre | mɪ'diowkə | a. medíocre

mediocrity| mɪdĩo'kritĩ |s. mediocridade

meditate | me'diteyt | vi. meditar; refletir

meditation | meditey'śən | s. meditação

Mediterranean | meditərey'nĩən | s. Mediterrâneo (mar) / a. (minúsc.) mediterrâneo

medium | mɪ'dĩəm | s. meio; instrumento; médium (espírita). -through the m. of por intermédio de / a. médio; mediano

medley | med'lĩ | s. mistura, miscelânea; confusão, mixórdia / a. misturado, confuso

meek | mɪk' | a. manso, dócil

meekness| mɪk'nes |s. mansidão

meet | mɪt' | vt. encontrar; ser apresentado a, travar relações; fazer junção com, cruzar; aparecer; satisfazer (desejos, dívidas); pagar (contas); refutar (argumentos). -to m. a charge responder a uma acusação. -to m. one's match encontrar seu igual. -to m. with an accident sofrer um acidente / vi. encontrar-se (com); conhecer-se; reunir-se (grupo). -to arrange to m. combinar um encontro

meeting | mɪ'ting | s. encontro; reunião, assembléia; entrevista; duelo

meeting-house | mɪ'tinghaws |s. casa de culto (dos quacres)

meeting-place | mɪ'tingpleys | s. ponto de reunião (assembléia); confluência (de rios)

megaphone | me'gəfown] s. megafone

melancholy | me'lənkəlĩ | s. melancolia / a. melancólico

mêlée, melee | me'ley |s. refrega, contenda, combate; tumulto, confusão

mellow| me'low |a. maduro; capitoso(vinho); (mús.)melodioso, suave; rico (solo); jovial,

bem-humorado, afável; alegre (levemente embriagado) / vt. amadurecer, abrandar / vi. amadurecer-se

melodious | məlow'dĩəs | a. melodioso, harmonioso

melodramatic | məlowdrəma'-tik | a. melodramático

melody | me'lədĩ | s. melodia

melon | me'lən | s. melão

melt | melt' | vt. derreter; fundir; dissolver; liquefazer / vi. derreter-se; fundir-se; desfazer-se

melting | mel'ting | s. fusão; fundição; derretimento / a. enternecedor, lânguido (olhar); comovente

melting-point | mel'tingpoynt | s. ponto de fusão

melting-pot | mel'tingpot | s. cadinho; (fig.) mistura de raças, mistura de etnias

member | mem'bə | s. membro, sócio; (anat.) membro; parte, elemento

membership | mem'bəśip | s. qualidade ou estado de membro ou sócio; número de sócios, quadro de membros

memento | məmen'tow | s. memento, lembrança, recordação

memoir | me'mwʌ | s. memória, dissertação; biografia; (pl.) autobiografia

memorable| me'mərəbəl |a. memorável, célebre

memorandum | meməran'dəm | s. memorando, lembrete, nota

memorial | məmó'rĩəl | s. monumento comemorativo; feriado comemorativo / a. comemorativo

memorize | me'mərayz |vt. decorar, memorizar

memory | me'mərĩ | s. memória; lembrança, recordação. - from m. de memória. -to commit to m. decorar

menace | me'nis | s. ameaça / vt. ameaçar

mend | mend' | s. remendo / vt. consertar, reparar. -to m. one's

ways emendar-se. **-to be on the
m.** estar melhorando

mendacious | mendey'ŝəs | *a.*
mentiroso, falso, mendaz

mendacity | menda'sitĭ | *s.* mendacidade; embuste, mentira

mending | men'ding | *s.* conserto, reparo; remendo

menial | mɪ'nɪˈəl | *a.* humilde, servil; desprezível, vil

meningitis | menĭnjay'tis | *s.* meningite

menstruation | menstruey'ŝən | *s.* menstruação

mensuration | mensˇuərey'ŝən | *s.* mensuração, medição

mental | men'təl | *a.* mental; intelectual

mention | men'ŝən | *s.* menção, alusão, referência / *vt.* citar, mencionar, falar de. **-don't m.
it** de nada, não há de quê

menu | me'nĭu | *s. menu,* cardápio

mercantile | mE'kəntayl | *a.* mercantil, comercial

mercenary | mE'sinərĭ | *s. a.* mercenário

merchandise | mE'ŝəndayz | *s.* mercadoria / *vt. vi.* negociar, comerciar

merchant | mE'ŝənt | *s.* comerciante / *a.* mercantil

merchantman | mE'ŝəntmən | *s.* navio mercante

merchant navy | mE'ŝəntneyvĭ | *s.* marinha mercante

marchant ship | mE'ŝəntŝip | *s.* navio mercante

merciful | mE'siful | *a.* misericordioso, compassivo

merciless | mE'siles | *a.* implacável, inexorável, cruel

mercury | mE'kĭurĭ | *s.* mercúrio; (maiúsc.) Mercúrio (planeta, deus)

mercy | mE'sĭ | *s.* misericórdia, clemência; piedade, compaixão. **-at the m. of** à mercê de. **-to
cry for m.** pedir misericórdia /
interj. misericórdia!

mere | mɪ'ə | *s.* (poét.) lagoa, lago / *a.* mero, simples

merely | mɪ'əlĭ | *adv.* meramente, simplesmente

merge | mEȷ' | *vt.* amalgamar, unir / *vi.* fundir-se, unir-se, incorporar-se

merit | me'rit | *s.* mérito / *vt. vi.* merecer

meritorious | meritó'rɪəs | *a.* meritório

mermaid | mE'meyd | *s.* sereia; (fig.) ótima nadadora

merriment | me'rimənt | *s.* alegria, divertimento

merry | me'rĭ | *a.* alegre, jovial, festivo. **-to make m.** divertir-se

Merry Christmas | me'rĭkris'məs | *interj.* Feliz Natal!

merry-go-round | me'rĭgowrawnd | *s.* carrossel; (fig.) turbilhão, tumulto

merry-making | me'rĭmeyking | *s.* divertimento, brincadeira, festividade, folguedo

mesh | meŝ' | *s.* malha (de rede); engrenagem. **-in m.** engrenado

mesmerize | mes'mərayz | *vt.* hipnotizar, magnetizar

mess | mes' | *s.* desordem, confusão; embrulhada, trapalhada; enrascada, apuros; ração, prato; rancho de soldados. **-to be in
a m.** estar em maus lençóis. **-to
make a m. of** fazer uma mixórdia de. **-to m. about** mexer em; intrometer-se em; desperdiçar o tempo

message | me'siȷ | *s.* mensagem; recado. **-to run messages** levar e trazer recados

messenger | me'sinȷə | *s.* mensageiro; moço de recados

Messiah | məsay'ə | *s.* Messias

messmate | mes'meyt | *s.* companheiro de rancho (esp. marinheiro ou embarcadiço)

messy | me'sĭ | *a.* desalinhado, enxovalhado, sujo

metal | me'təl | *s.* metal; (pl., ferrov.) trilhos / *a.* metálico

metalic | məta'lik | *a.* metálico

metamorphosis | metəmó'fəsis | s. metamorfose

metaphor | me'təfə | s. metáfora

metaphysics | metəfi'ziks | s. metafísica; (coloq.) linguagem abstrusa

meteor | mɪ'tīə | s. meteoro

meter | mɪ'tə | s. medidor (de gás, água etc.); = metre

method | me'θəd | s. método

methodical | məθo'dikəl | a. metódico; ordenado, sistemático

Methodist | me'θədist | s. metodista

meticulous | məti'kĭuləs | a. meticuloso, escrupuloso

metre, meter | mɪ'tə | s. metro; (poét.) metro; (mús.) compasso

metric | me'trik | a. métrico

metropolis | mətro'pəlis | s. metrópole, capital

mettle | me'təl | s. índole, feitio; vivacidade; brio, valor. -to be on ou upon one's m. meter-se em brios

mew | mĭʋ' | s. gaivota; miado, miau; (pl.) cavalariças / vi. miar

mewing | mĭʋ'ing | s. miado

microbe | may'krowb | s. micróbio

microfilm | may'krowfilm | s. microfilme

microphone | may'krəfown | s. microfone

microscope | may'krəskowp | s. microscópio

mid | mid' | a. meio, relativo ao meio; meado / prep. (poét.) entre, em meio a

midday | mid'dey | s. meio-dia

midden | mi'dən | s. estrumeira, monturo; monte de lixo

middle | mi'dəl | s. meio, centro; meados (mês); cintura / a. médio, mediano; intermediário. -of m. height de estatura mediana

middle-aged | mi'dəleyǰid | a. de meia-idade

Middle Ages | mi'dəleyǰis | spl. Idade Média

middle class | mi'dəlklas | s. clas-

se média

Middle East | mi'dəlıst | s. Oriente Médio

midge | mij' | s. mosquito-pólvora; nanico, pigmeu

midget | mi'jit | s. anão / a. minúsculo, diminuto, miniatura

midnight | mid'nayt | s. meia-noite

midriff | mid'rif | s. diafragma; boca do estômago

midshipman | mid'śipmən | s. aspirante de marinha

midst | midst' | s. meio

midsummer | midsâ'mə | s. meio do verão, pleno verão

Midsummer's Day | midsâ'məzdey | s. o 24 de junho (no hemisfério norte, é meio do verão)

midway | mid'wey | s. o meio do caminho / a. no meio do caminho / adv. a meio caminho

midwife | mid'wayf | s. parteira

midwinter | midwin'tə | s. meio do inverno

mien | mɪn' | s. semblante, fisionomia

might | mayt' | s. força, poder; vigor, pujança

mighty | may'tī | a. poderoso, potente; enorme, vasto, imenso

migraine | mɪ'greyn | s. enxaqueca

migrant | may'grənt | s. migrador / a. migrador, migrante; migratório

migrate | maygreyt' | vi. migrar

migration | maygrey'śən | s. migração

migratory | maygrey'tərī | a. migratório

mild | mayld' | a. suave, brando; meigo; manso; benigno; ameno; moderado

mildew | mil'dĭu | s. mofo, bolor / vi. mofar, embolorar

mildness | mayld'nes | s. suavidade, brandura; indulgência

mile | mayl' | s. milha (equivalente a 1.609,35m)

mileage | may'lij | s. milhagem; preço por milha

milestone | mayl'stown | *s.* marco miliário

militant | mi'litənt |*s.* pessoa que milita em algo, ativista / *a.* militante, combatente

military | mi'litərī |*s.* tropa, exército / *a.* militar; bélico, guerreiro

militate | mi'liteyt |*vi.* militar; influir, pesar (contra, raramente a favor)

militia | mili'ʃə |*s.* milícia

milk | milk' | *s.* leite / *vt.* ordenhar; (fig.) extrair, tirar, arrancar (dinheiro etc.)

milk and water | milk'andwótə | *a.* insípido, desenxabido, chocho

milkman | milk'mən |*s.* leiteiro

milksop | milk'sop | *s.* homem sem energia, molenga

milky | mil'kī | *a.* leitoso; efeminado, fraco

Milky Way | mil'kīwey | *s.* Via Láctea

mill | mil' | *s.* moinho; fábrica; engenho; serrilhador; laminador / *vt.* moer, triturar; serrilhar (moedas) / *vi.* rodopiar, remoinhar

mill-dam | mil'dam |*s.* açude, represa de moinho

millennium | mile'nĭəm | *s.* milênio

miller | mi'lə |*s.* moleiro

milliner | mi'linə | *s.* chapeleiro(a) de senhora

milling | mi'ling |*s.* moagem; fresagem; laminação

million | mi'lĭən |*s.a.* milhão

millionaire | milĭəne'ə | *s.* milionário

mill-pond | mil'pond |*s.* reservatório, pequeno açude. **-like a m.-p.** como um lago (diz-se do mar quando calmo)

millstone | mil'stown |*s.* mó

milt | milt' |*s.* leita, láctea (esperma dos peixes); (anat.) baço / *vt.* fecundar (ovos de peixe)

mime | maym' | *s.* pantomima / *vt.* imitar

mimic | mi'mik | *s.* mímico / *vt.* imitar; arremedar

mimicry | mi'mikrī | *s.* imitação; paródia; (zool.) mimetismo

mince | mins' | *s.* picadinho (de carne) / *vt.* picar (carne); dizer com afetação ou rodeios. **-to not m. matters** não ter papas na língua / *vi.* andar com passos miúdos ou de elegância afetada

mincemeat | mins'mīt |*s.* recheio de passas, maçãs, especiarias etc. (para tortas)

mincing | min'sing | *a.* afetado, amaneirado. **-m. steps** passos miudinhos ou de elegância afetada

mind | maynd' |*s.* mente, mentalidade; entendimento; inteligência, compreensão; intenção, propósito. **-absence of m.** distração. **-presence of m.** presença de espírito. **-to bear in m.** ter em mente. **-to be of one m.** estar de comum acordo. **-to be out of one's m.** não estar no seu juízo perfeito. **-to make up one's m.** decidir-se. **-to my m.** a meu ver. **-to set one's m. on** empenhar-se em. **-to be in two minds** hesitar, vacilar / *vt.* atender, dar ou prestar atenção; cuidar de; vigiar; importar-se com; fazer objeção a, opor-se a. **-I don't m.** não me importo, não me incomodo, não faço caso (de). **-do you m.?** não se importa que?, incomoda-o? **-never m.** não importa; não faz mal; não dê importância. **-m. the step!** cuidado com o degrau! **-m. you** lembre-se; repare. **-m. your own business** meta-se com a sua vida

minded | mayn'did | *a.* disposto, inclinado

mindful | maynd'ful | *a.* cônscio; cuidadoso, atento

mine | mayn' | *s.* mina / *vt.* extrair minério; minar; solapar / *pron.* meu, minha

minefield | mayn'fīld | *s.* (mil.) campo minado

miner | may'nə | s. mineiro

mineral | mi'nərəl | a. mineral

mineral water | mi'nərəlwótə | s. água mineral

minesweeper | mayn'swɪpə | s. (náut.) caça-minas

mingle | min'gəl | vi. misturar-se, mesclar-se, combinar-se; confundir-se com (multidão etc.); participar de; associar-se com

miniature | mi'niǩə | s. miniatura

minimize | mi'nimayz | vt. minimizar; subestimar, dar pouca importância a

minimum | mi'niməm | s.a. mínimo

minimum wage | mi'niməmweyǰ | s. salário mínimo

mining | may'ning | s. mineração; (mil.) ato de minar / a. mineiro

minion | mi'nǐən | s. favorito, predileto, valido

minister | mi'nistə | s. ministro; (ecles.) ministro, pastor / vi. prestar auxílio; servir, prover a; (ecles.) oficiar

ministry | mi'nistrĩ | s. ministério

mink | mink' | s. (zool.) visão, vison

minor | may'nə | s. menor; (educ., EUA) matéria de menor interesse ou secundária nos estudos / a. menor, de menor idade; secundário, de pouca importância, inferior

minor key | may'nəkɪ | s. (mús.) tom menor

minority | mino'ritĩ | s. menoridade; minoria

minster | mins'tə | s. catedral, basílica; igreja de mosteiro

minstrel | mins'trəl | s. menestrel, trovador; (pl.) cantores cômicos caracterizados de negros

mint | mint' | s. casa da moeda; (bot.) hortelã, menta / a. novo, não usado / vt. cunhar

minus | may'nəs | prep. menos, sem

minute | mi'nit | s. minuto; momento, instante; (pl.) minuta,

ata de reunião / vt. cronometrar; minutar; lavrar ata / | may'nĭut | a. miúdo, diminuto, minucioso

minuteness | maynĭut'nes | s. extrema pequenez; minudência; minuciosidade

minx | minks' | s. mulher petulante, sirigaita

miracle | mi'rəkəl | s. milagre

miraculous | mira'kʼuləs | a. milagroso, miraculoso

mirage | mi'rʌj | s. miragem, ilusão

mire | may'ə | s. lodaçal; lodo, lama. -in the m. em apuros

mirror | mi'rə | s. espelho / vt. refletir

mirth | mɛϑ | s. alegria

misadventure | misədven'šə | s. revés, desventura, infortúnio

misapplication | misaplikey'šən | s. má aplicação, mau uso; malversação

misapplied | misəplayd' | a. mal-empregado; desperdiçado

misapprehension | misaprihen'šən | s. mal-entendido, equívoco

misappropriation | misəprowprĩey'šən | s. desvio, desfalque, apropriação indébita

misbehave | misbĩheyv' | vi. portar-se mal, comportar-se mal

misbehaviour, misbehavior | misbĩhey'vǐə | s. mau comportamento, má conduta

miscalculation | miskalkʼuley'šən | s. erro de cálculo, cálculo errado

miscarriage | miska'riǰ | s. aborto; (fig.) malogro

miscarry | miska'rĩ | vi. abortar; (fig.) malograr

miscellaneous | misəley'nǐəs | a. variado, misto, misturado

miscellany | mise'lənĩ | s. miscelânea

mischance | misčʌns' | s. infortúnio; azar, má sorte

mischief | mis'šif | s. discórdia; dano, prejuízo; travessura. -The M. (coloq.) o demônio

mischief-maker | mis'šifmeykə |
s. mexeriqueiro; traquinas

mischievous | mis'šivəs | a. travesso; malicioso, nocivo

misconduct | miskon'dəkt | s.
mau procedimento; prevaricação; adultério

misconstrue | miskənstrv' | vt.
compreender ou interpretar
mal

miscreant | mis'krīənt |s.a. patife, vilão, tratante, depravado

misdeed | misdīd' | s. delito, má
ação; crime

misdemeanour, misdemeanor
| misdimī'nə |s. delito, ofensa

misdirect | misdirekt' | vt. orientar ou dirigir mal; informar ou
endereçar mal

miser | may'zə | s. avaro, avarento, sovina

miserable | mi'zərəbəl |a. miserável, infeliz; pobre; tristonho;
mesquinho, ruim

miserliness | may'zəlines | s. avareza, mesquinhez

miserly | may'zəlī | a. avarento,
mesquinho

misery | mi'zərī | s. miséria, pobreza; desolação, aflição; tormento, angústia

misfire | misfay'ə | s. falha (de arma ou motor) / vi. negar fogo
(arma); falhar, malograr (plano)

misfit | mis'fit | s. desajuste, desajustamento; pessoa desajustada ou deslocada

misfortune | misfó'šən | s. desventura, infortúnio

misgiving | misgi'ving |s. dúvida;
receio; desconfiança

misgovern | misgâ'vən | vt. governar mal

misgovernment | misgâ'vənmənt |
s. mau governo

misguided | misgay'did | a. mal
orientado; desencaminhado

mishap | mis'hap | s. contratempo, acidente, infortúnio

misinform | misinfóm' |vt.informar mal; dar informações
erradas

misinterpret | misintE'prit | vt.
interpretar mal

misjudge | misjâj' | vt.vi. julgar
incorretamente, fazer juízo errado de

mislay | misley' | vt. perder, pôr
em lugar errado. **-to be mislaid**
extraviar-se

mislead | mislīd' | vt. desencaminhar, enganar, iludir; extraviar

mismanage | misma'nij | vt. administrar mal

misnomer | misnow'mə |s. nome
inadequado; denominação errônea, termo impróprio

misplaced | mispleyst' | a. mal-empregado, imerecido

misprint | mis'print | s. erro de
impressão, erro tipográfico

mispronounce | misprənowns' |
vt. pronunciar mal

misread | misrīd' | vt. ler mal, interpretar mal

misrepresent | misreprəzent' | vt.
representar erroneamente; desfigurar, deturpar

misrepresentation | misreprəzentey'šən | s. descrição enganosa; deturpação, falsificação

miss | mis' | s. menina, moça; senhorita; malogro; omissão; engano / vt. perder (trem, oportunidade); errar (alvo); sentir a
falta de; dar pela falta de; não
entender (sentido); não encontrar (pessoa); faltar a, não aparecer em / vi. falhar; não surtir
efeito

missal | mi'səl |s. missal

misshapen | misšey'pən | a. disforme, malformado

missile | mi'sayl |s. projétil, míssil

missing | mi'sing | a. que falta,
ausente, desaparecido. **-to be
m.** faltar, fazer falta; estar ausente ou desaparecido

mission | mi'šən |s. missão; (pl.,
ecles.) missões

missionary | mi'šənrī | s. missionário

missive | mi'siv |s. missiva, carta

misspell| misspel' |vt.soletrar ou

escrever erradamente

misspent | misspent' | *a.* desperdiçado, mal gasto, esbanjado

misstatement | missteyt'mənt | *s.* afirmação errada, inexatidão

mist | mist' | *s.* neblina, névoa

mistake | misteyk' | *s.* erro, engano, equívoco. **-to make a m.** enganar-se. **-by m.** por engano. **-and no m.** (coloq.) com toda certeza

mistaken | mistey'kən | *a.* errado, errôneo. **-to be m.** estar enganado. **-if I'm not m.** se não estou enganado. **-to be m. for** ser tomado por

mister | mis'tə | *s.* senhor

mistletoe | mi'səltow | *s.* (bot.) visco

mistranslation | mistranzley'-şən | *s.* tradução incorreta

mistreat | mistrıt' | *vt.* maltratar

mistress | mis'tris | *s.* senhora; patroa, ama; amante (mulher); soberana, dona

mistrust | mistrâst' | *s.* desconfiança / *vt. vi.* desconfiar

misty | mis'tī | *a.* enevoado

misunderstand | misândəstand' | *vt.* entender ou interpretar mal

misunderstanding | misândəstan'ding | *s.* mal-entendido; desentendimento

misuse | mis 'ı̆ uz | *s.* uso incorreto / ı misı̆ uz | *vt.* abusar; empregar mal; maltratar

mite | mayt' | *s.* pequena quantia, óbolo; bichinho; migalha; criancinha. **-not a m.** nem um bocadinho

mitigate | mi'tigeyt | *vt.* mitigar, aliviar

mitigation | mitigey'şən | *s.* mitigação, alívio

mitre, miter | may'tə | *s.* mitra

mix | miks' | *s.* mistura / *vt.* misturar. **-to m. up** misturar bem; confundir, embaralhar / *vi.* misturar-se; mesclar-se; associar-se

mixed | mikst' | *a.* misturado; misto; sortido, variado; (co-

loq.) confuso. **-m. up** atrapalhado, confuso. **-m. up in (with)** envolvido em, implicado em

mixture | miks'şə | *s.* mistura (tabaco etc.); mescla (tecido etc.); preparação farmacêutica

mix-up | miks'âp | *s.* confusão, trapalhada

moan | mown' | *s.* gemido, lamento / *vt.* lamentar / *vi.* lamentar-se, lastimar-se

moat | mowt' | *s.* fosso, vala

mob | mob' | *s.* populaça; turba, horda; súcia, malta; (gír.) quadrilha (de criminosos) / *vt.* aglomerar-se em torno de / *vi.* reunir-se em turba

mobile | mow'bayl | *s.* móbile / *a.* móvel; movediço; versátil, expressivo

mobility | mowbi'litī | *s.* mobilidade

mobilization | mowbilayzey'şən | *s.* mobilização

mobilize | mow'bilayz | *vt.* mobilizar / *vi.* mobilizar-se

mock | mok' | *a.* falso, fingido; de imitação; simulado / *vt.* zombar, escarnecer de, ridicularizar / *vi.* **-to m. at** fazer zombaria

mockery | mo'kərī | *s.* zombaria, troça, escárnio

mocking | mo'king | *a.* zombeteiro, escarnecedor

mode | mowd' | *s.* modo; (mús.) modo, tom; maneira, método; moda, estilo, costume

model | mo'dəl | *s.* modelo; maquete / *a.* modelar, exemplar / *vt.* modelar

moderate | mo'dərit | *s.* pessoa moderada / *a.* moderado; módico (preço); comedido / | mo'dəreyt | *vt.* moderar, suavizar; presidir / *vi.* moderar-se; presidir como moderador

moderation | modərey'şən | *s.* moderação, comedimento

modern | mo'dən | *a.* moderno, recente

modernize | mo'dənayz | *vt.* modernizar / *vi.* modernizar-se

modest | mo'dist | *a.* modesto; recatado, simples, decoroso

modesty | mo'disti | *s.* modéstia, recato, decoro

modicum | mo'dikəm | *s.* pequena quantidade ou porção

modification | modifikey'ʃən | *s.* modificação

modify | mo'difay | *vt.* modificar, alterar

Mohammedan | mowha'midən | *s. a.* = *Muhammadan*

moist | moyst' | *a.* úmido, molhado

moisten | moy'sən | *vt. vi.* umedecer(-se), molhar(-se)

moisture | moys'ʃə | *s.* umidade

molasses | mowla'siz | *s.* melado, melaço

mole | mowl' | *s.* toupeira; quebra-mar; sinal (da pele), lunar

molecule | mo'likʲul | *s.* molécula

molest | məlest' | *vt.* importunar, molestar

mollify | mo'lifay | *vt.* apaziguar, pacificar, abrandar

·molly-coddle | mo'likodəl | *s.* homem efeminado / *vt.* mimar, mimosear

molten | mowl'tən | *a.* fundido

moment | mow'mənt | *s.* momento. **-of great m.** de grande importância. **-for the m.** por enquanto

momentary | mow'məntri | *a.* momentâneo

momentous | mowmen'təs | *a.* momentoso, importante, sério

monarch | mo'nək | *s.* monarca (tb. fig.)

monarchist | mo'nəkist | *s. a.* monarquista

monarchy | mo'nəki | *s.* monarquia

monastery | mo'nəstri | *s.* mosteiro, convento

monastic | mənas'tik | *a.* monástico

monasticism | mənas'tisizəm | *s.* monasticismo; monaquismo

Monday | mân'dey | *s.* segunda-feira

monetary | mo'nitəri | *a.* monetário

money | mâ'ni | *s.* dinheiro

money-box | mâ'niboks | *s.* mealheiro

money-changer | mâ'niʃeyn'ʲə | *s.* cambista

moneyed | mâ'nid | *a.* endinheirado, rico

money-lender | mâ'nilen'də | *s.* agiota

money order | mâ'nió'də | *s.* ordem de pagamento; vale postal

mongoose | mon'gʊs | *s.* (zool.) mangusto

mongrel | mân'grəl | *s.* vira-lata (cão); mestiço / *a.* mestiço, cruzado; híbrido

monk | mânk' | *s.* monge, frade

monkey | mân'ki | *s.* macaco; criança travessa. **-to make a m. of** ridicularizar / *vt.* macaquear, imitar / *vi.* (coloq.) traquinar

monkey-wrench | mân'kirenš | *s.* chave inglesa, chave de mandíbula ajustável

monocle | mo'nəkəl | *s.* monóculo

monologue | mo'nəlog | *s.* monólogo

monopolist | məno'pəlist | *s.* monopolista

monopolistic | mənopəlis'tik | *a.* monopólico, monopolizador, monopolístico

monopolize | məno'pəlayz | *vt.* monopolizar, açambarcar

monopoly | məno'pəli | *s.* monopólio

monotonous | məno'tənəs | *a.* monótono

monotony | məno'təni | *s.* monotonia

monsoon | monsʊn' | *s.* monção; estação chuvosa

monster | mon'stə | *s.* monstro / *a.* monstruoso; enorme

monstrosity | monstro'siti | *s.* monstruosidade

monstrous | mon'strəs | a. mons-
truoso

month | mânϑ' | s. mês

monthly | mânϑ'lī | a. mensal /
adv. mensalmente

monthly allowance | mân'ϑliǝla-
wǝns | s. mesada

monument | mo'nĭumǝnt | s.
monumento

mooch | mυś' | vt. (gír.) furtar;
(EUA) pechinchar / vi. (gír.)
vaguear, vadiar

mood | mυd' | s. humor; disposi-
ção; capricho; modo (de ver-
bo). -in the m. for disposto para. -in a bad m. de mau humor,
de má disposição

moody | mυ'dī | a. de mau hu-
mor; (fig.) melancólico, taci-
turno

moon | mυn' | s. lua

moonlight | mυn'layt | s. luar

moonlit | mυn'lit | a. enluarado

moonshine | mυn'śayn | s. luar;
devaneio; (coloq.) bebida fa-
bricada ilegalmente

moor | mυ'ǝ | s. charneca; terre-
no de caça; (maiúsc.) mouro /
vi. amarrar, atracar

mooring | mu'ǝring | s. amarra-
ção, atracação

Moorish | mu'ǝriś | a. mouro,
mourisco

mop | mop' | s. esfregão (de as-
soalho) / vt. esfregar ou limpar
o assoalho; limpar (lágrimas,
suor). -to m. up limpar; absor-
ver (lucros etc.); (mil.) fazer
operação de limpeza

mope | mowp' | s. pessoa apática
/ vi. sentir-se deprimido

moral | mo'rǝl | s. moral; (pl.)
princípios de conduta / a. mo-
ral, ético; virtuoso

morale | morAl' | s. moral, estado
de espírito

morality | mǝra'litī | s. moralida-
de, honestidade

moralize | mo'rǝlayz | vi. mora-
lizar

morass | mǝras' | s. pântano, bre-
jo; lamaçal, atoleiro

moratorium | morǝto'rĭǝm | s.
(com.) moratória

morbid | mó'bid | a. mórbido,
doentio

mordant | mó'dǝnt | a. mordaz,
mordente, sarcástico; corrosi-
vo, cáustico

more | mó' | a. adv. mais. -m. and
m. cada vez mais. -m. or less
mais ou menos. -once m. mais
uma vez, outra vez. -the m. he
has, the m. he wants quanto
mais ele tem, mais quer

moreover | mórow'vǝ | adv. além
disso, ademais

morgue | móg' | s. necrotério

moribund | mó'ribând | a. mori-
bundo, agonizante

morn | món' | s. (poét.) manhã

morning | mó'ning | s. manhã / a.
matinal, matutino, da manhã

Moroccan | mǝro'kǝn | s. a.
marroquino

morocco | mǝro'kow | s. marro-
quim

moron | mo'rǝn | s. débil mental,
retardado mental

morose | mǝrowz' | a. taciturno,
sorumbático, triste; mal-humorado

morrow | mo'row | s. (ant.) dia
seguinte. -on the m. no dia
seguinte

morsel | mó'sǝl | s. bocado; naco,
pedaço, fragmento

mortal | mó'tǝl | s. a. mortal

mortality | móta'litī | s. mortali-
dade; mortandade

mortar | mó'tǝ | s. argamassa; al-
mofariz; (mil.) morteiro / vt.
cimentar

mortgage | mó'giǰ | s. hipoteca.
-on m. hipotecado / vt.
hipotecar

mortification | mótifikey'śǝn | s.
mortificação; penitência; hu-
milhação, vexame

mortified | mó'tifayd | a. aborre-
cido, desgostoso; humilhado,
vexado

mortify | mó'tifay | vt. mortifi-
car; humilhar

mortuary | mó'tĭuərĭ | *s.* casa ou sala mortuária / *a.* mortuário, funerário

mosaic | mowzey'ik | *s. a.* mosaico

Moslem | moz'ləm | *s.* = *Muslim*

mosque | mosk' | *s.* mesquita

mosquito | moskı'tow | *s.* mosquito

mosquito-net | moskı'townet | *s.* mosquiteiro

moss | mos' | *s.* musgo

most | mowst' | *s.* a maior parte de, a maioria de. **-at m.** quando muito. **-to make the m.** of tirar o máximo proveito de, aproveitar-se de / *a.* o mais; na maior parte, na maioria dos casos. **-for the m. part** em geral / *adv.* muito, extremamente; principalmente, acima de tudo

mostly | mowst'lĭ | *adv.* na maior parte; principalmente

moth | moϑ' | *s.* mariposa; traça

moth-ball | moϑ'ból | *s.* naftalina, bola de naftalina

mother | mâ'ðə | *s.* mãe / *a.* materno, maternal / *vt.* ser mãe de; dar origem a; cuidar ou proteger como mãe

Mother Church | mâ'ðəšɛš | *s.* igreja matriz

motherhood | mâ'ðəhud | *s.* maternidade

mother-in-law | mâ'ðəinló | *s.* sogra; madrasta

motherland | mâ'ðəland | *s.* pátria, terra natal

motherly | mâ'ðəlĭ | *a.* maternal / *adv.* maternalmente

Mother Superior | mâ'ðəsupı'rĭə | *s.* madre superiora

mother tongue | mâ'ðətâng | *s.* língua materna

motif | mowtĭf' | *s.* motivo, tema principal

motion | mow'šən | *s.* movimento; gesto, sinal; ação; moção, proposta / *vi.* acenar

motionless | mow'šənles | *a.* imóvel, parado

motion picture | mow'šənpik'šə | *s.* filme de cinema, fita, película

(espetáculo)

motivate | mow'tiveyt | *vt.* motivar, causar, provocar

motive | mow'tiv | *s.* motivo, razão / *a.* motriz

motley | mot'lĭ | *a.* variegado; mosqueado, sarapintado

motor | mow'tə | *s.* motor / *a.* motriz, motor / *vi.* viajar ou ir de automóvel

motor boat | mow'təbowt | *s.* barco a motor, lancha

motor car | mow'təkA | *s.* automóvel

motor coach | mow'təkowš | *s.* ônibus de turismo

motor cycle | mow'təsaykəl | *s.* motocicleta

motoring | mow'təring | *s.* automobilismo

motorist | mow'tərist | *s.* motorista, chofer

mottled | mo'təld | *a.* mosqueado, pintadinho

motto | mo'tow | *s.* divisa, lema

mould, mold | mowld' | *s.* molde, fôrma; bolor, mofo; humo, terra vegetal / *vt.* moldar, amoldar; (fig.) formar, adaptar / *vi.* mofar, embolorar

mouldy, moldy | mowl'dĭ | *a.* bolorento, mofado

mound | mawnd' | *s.* monte, montão, montículo; outeiro

mount | mawnt' | *s.* monte, montanha; cavalo, cavalgadura, montaria; encaixe, montagem / *vt.* escalar; cavalgar; armar, montar / *vi.* subir; montar (cavalo); crescer, aumentar

mountain | mawn'tin | *s.* montanha

mountain dweller | mawn'tindwelə | *s.* montanhês

mountaineer | mawntinı'ə | *s.* montanhista, alpinista; montanhês

mountaineering | mawntinı'əring | *s.* montanhismo, alpinismo

mountain lion | mawn'tinlayən |

s. puma, onça-parda, suçua-rana

mountainous | mawn'tinəs | *a.* montanhoso

mountain range | mawn'tinreynǰ | *s.* cordilheira, cadeia de montanhas

mountebank | mawn'tibank | *s.* charlatão de feira

mourn | món' | *vt. vi.* lamentar, carpir, chorar

mourner | mó'nə | *s.* carpideira; pranteador, lamentador; acompanhante de enterro

mournful | món'ful | *a.* pesaroso; lamentoso; lúgubre; deplorável; lutuoso

mourning | mó'əning | *s.* luto. **-in m.** de luto

mouse | maws' | *s.* camundongo, rato

mousetrap | maws'trap | *s.* ratoeira

moustache, mustache | məstaś' | *s.* bigode

mouth | mawϑ' | *s.* boca; foz, desembocadura. **-by word of m.** de viva voz. **-down in the m.** desapontado; deprimido, abatido. **-to have a big m.** falar demais. **-to laugh on the wrong side of one's m.** rir amarelo / *vt.* levar à boca; falar afetadamente

mouthful | mawϑ'ful | *s.* bocado; gole, trago, sorvo

mouthpiece | mawϑ'pɪs | *s.* (mús.) embocadura, bocal; piteira (de cachimbo); porta-voz (pessoa)

movable, moveable | mu'vəbəl | *s.* móvel; (*pl.*, jur.) bens móveis / *a.* móvel; transportável

movable feast | mu'vəbəlfɪst | *s.* festa móvel

movable property | mu'vəbəlpro'pəṭī | *s.* bens móveis

move | muv' | *s.* movimento; jogada, lance; medida, providência; golpe, rasgo; mudança (de residência). **-on the m.** em movimento, em marcha, viajan-do. **-to get a m. on** apressar-se / *vt.* mover; pôr em movimento; fazer funcionar; comover; deslocar, transferir; fazer moção, propor. **-to m. away** afastar. **-to m. in with** ir morar com. **-to m. to anger** provocar raiva / *vi.* mover-se; partir; mudar-se. **-to m. back** recuar. **-to m. out** sair. **-to m. forward** avançar, progredir. **-to m. in** instalar-se, mudar-se (para nova casa). **-to m. off** afastar-se, ir andando, ir embora

movement | muv'mənt | *s.* movimento, transferência

movie | mu'vī | *s.* (gír.) filme de cinema, fita (espetáculo). **-the movies** o cinema

moving | mu'ving | *a.* comovente; móvel, movediço; (mec.) giratório, rolante; motriz

mow | mow' | *vt.* ceifar; segar; cortar (grama)

mower | mow'ə | *s.* ceifadeira; máquina de cortar grama; segador

much | mâś' | *a. adv.* muito, grande quantidade; grande parte. **-too m.** demasiado, demais. **-how m?** quanto? **-as m. as** tanto como. **-so m. the better** tanto melhor. **-very m.** muito

muck | mâk' | *s.* estrume, esterco; imundície, sujeira

mucous | mīu'kəs | *a.* mucoso

mucus | mīu'kəs | *s.* muco

mud | mâd' | *s.* lama

muddle | mâ'dəl | *s.* confusão, desordem / *vt.* confundir, baralhar, atrapalhar / *vi.* confundir-se, atrapalhar-se

muddler | mâ'dlə | *s.* trapalhão, desastrado

muddy | mâ'dī | *a.* lamacento

mudguard | mâd'gʌd | *s.* pára-lama

mud-slinging | mâdslin'ging | *s.* (coloq.) maledicência, difamação

muffle | mâ'fəl | *vt.* embuçar; abafar, amortecer (som)

mufti| mâf'tī |s. trajecivil. -**in m.**
à paisana

mug| mâg' |s. caneca; (gír.)cara,
face; (gír.)simplório / vt. -**to m.
up** (coloq.) decorar, aprender
decorando

muggy | mâ'gī |a. abafado

Muhammadan, Mohammedan
| məha'mədən mowha'midən |
s.a. muçulmano, islamita

mulatto | mǐula'tow |s. mulato

mulberry | mâl'berī |s. amora

mule | mǐʋl' |s. mula

muleteer | mǐulətī'ə |s. arrieiro,
condutor de bestas de carga,
almocreve

mullet | mâ'lit |s. (ict.) tainha;
(ict.) parati

multifarious | mâltife'ərīəs | a.
variado, multíplice, multiforme, multifário

multiple | mâl'tipəl | a. multíplice; (mat.)múltiplo

multiplication | mâltiplikey'śən |
s. multiplicação

multiply | mâl'tiplay | vt. multiplicar (tb. mat.) / vi. multiplicar-se

multitude | mâl'titǐud |s. multidão

mum | mâm' | interj. silêncio!,
psiu!

mumble | mâm'bəl | s. murmúrio, resmungo / vt. vi. resmungar; murmurar

mummy | mâ'mī |s. múmia; (coloq.) mãezinha, mamãezinha

mumps | mâmps' |s. caxumba

munch | mânś' | vt. mastigar

mundane | mân'deyn | a. mundano

municipal | mǐuni'sipəl |a. municipal

municipality | mǐunisipa'litī | s.
municipalidade

munificent | mǐuni'fisənt | a. generoso, munificente

munition | mǐuni'śən | s. munição; (pl.) munições / vt. municionar; abastecer

murder | me'də | s. homicídio,
assassinato / vt. assassinar,
matar

murderer | me'dərə |s. assassino,
homicida

murderous | me'dərəs | a. homicida; mortal; mortífero

murky | me'kǐ | a. escuro, sombrio, lôbrego

murmur | me'mə | s. murmúrio,
sussurro / vt. murmurar, segredar / vi. murmurar, sussurrar;
resmungar, rezingar

muscle | mâ'səl | s. músculo;
musculatura / vi. empregar a
força

muscular | mâs'kǐulə | a. muscular; musculoso

muse| mǐʋz' |s. musa / vi. meditar, pensar

museum | mǐuzī'əm |s. museu

mushroom | mâś'rum | s. cogumelo

music | mǐʋ'zik | s. música. -**to
face the m.** enfrentar as conseqüências. -**to set to m.** musicar, pôr música em

musical | mǐu'zikəl | s. comédia
musical / a. musical

musical comedy | mǐu'zikəlko'mədī | s. comédia musical

music-hall | mǐʋ'zikhól |s. teatro
de variedades

musician | mǐuzi'śən | s. musicista, músico

music-stand | mǐʋ'zikstand | s.
estante para música

musk | mâsk' | s. almíscar

musket | mâs'kit |s. mosquete

musketry | mâs'kitrī | s. (mil.)
instrução de tiro

Muslim | mâs'lim | s. muçulmano

muslin | mâz'lin |s. musselina

mussel | mâ'səl |s. mexilhão

must | mâst' |s. mosto; mofo, bolor; (coloq.)imperativo, necessidade / v. defect. dever, ter de,
ser necessário, ser preciso

mustard | mâs'təd |s. mostarda;
cor de mostarda

muster | mâs'tə | vt. reunir,
juntar

mustiness | mâs'tines | s. mofo,

bolor; bafio

musty | mâs'tĭ | *a.* mofado, bolorento; (fig.) antiquado

mutability | mĭutəbi'litĭ | *s.* mutabilidade, instabilidade

mutation | mĭutey'śən | *s.* mutação

mute | mĭut' | *s.* mudo; (mús.) surdina / *a.* mudo. **-to stand m. of malice** (jur.) recusar-se deliberadamente a falar

muted | mĭu'tid | *a.* amortecido, suave

mutilate | mĭu'tileyt | *vt.* mutilar

mutilation | mĭutiley'śən | *s.* mutilação

mutineer | mĭutinı'ə | *s.* amotinado, revoltoso

mutinous | mĭu'tinəs | *a.* amotinado, rebelde

mutiny | mĭu'tinĭ | *s.* motim, rebelião, insurreição / *vi.* amotinar-se

mutter | mâ'tə | *vi.* resmungar, rezingar

mutton | mâ'tən | *s.* carne de carneiro

mutton chop | mâ'tənšop | *s.* costeleta de carneiro; (*pl.*) suíças

mutual | mĭu'tĭuəl | *a.* mútuo, recíproco

muzzle | mâ'zəl | *s.* focinho; boca (de arma de fogo); açaimo, mordaça, focinheira / *vt.* amordaçar

muzzle-loader | mâ'zəllowdə | *s.* arma de carregar pela boca

my | may | *a. poss.* meu(s), minha(s)

myopia | mayow'pĭə | *s.* miopia

myriad | mi'rĭəd | *s.* miríade; grande quantidade

myrrh | mε' | *s.* mirra

myrtle | mε'təl | *s.* (bot.) mirto, murta

myself | mayself' | *pron.* me; eu mesmo; eu próprio. **-by m.** sozinho, por mim mesmo

mysterious | mistı'rĭəs | *a.* misterioso

mistery | mis'tərĭ | *s.* mistério

mystic | mis'tik | *s.a.* místico

mysticism | mis'tisizəm | *s.* misticismo

mystify | mis'tifay | *vt.* mistificar

myth | miϑ' | *s.* mito

mythical | mi'ϑikəl | *a.* mítico, fabuloso

mythologic, -al | miϑəlo'ǰik(əl) | *a.* mitológico

mythology | miϑo'ləǰĭ | *s.* mitologia

N

nag | nag' | *s.* (coloq.) cavalo, matungo / *vt.* criticar; repreender; importunar

nagging | na'ging | *a.* importuno, enfadonho, aborrecido; incômodo (dor)

nail | neyl' | *s.* prego; unha; garra. **-to hit the n. on the head** acertar em cheio. **-as hard as nails** duro como o aço. **-tooth and nails** com unhas e dentes / *vt.* pregar; cravar. **-to n. up (down)** pregar, segurar com pregos; condenar (porta, janela etc.)

nail-brush | neyl'brâś | *s.* escova de unhas

nail-file | neyl'fayl | *s.* lima de unhas

nail varnish | neyl'vʌniś | *s.* verniz de unhas

naïve, naive | naıv' | *a.* ingênuo, simples; crédulo

naked | ney'kid | *a.* nu, despido. **-to strip n.** despir-se. **-with the n. eye** a olho nu

nakedness | ney'kidnes | *s.* nudez

name | neym' | *s.* nome. **-by n.** de nome. **-in the n. of** em nome de;

da parte de. **-to call somebody names** descompor, xingar / *vt.* chamar; nomear; dar ou pôr nome a; designar; indicar

nameless | neym'les | *a.* sem nome; anônimo; ilegítimo; indefinível

namely | neym'lĩ | *adv.* a saber, isto é

namesake | neym'seyk | *s.* homônimo, xará

nap | nap' | *s.* soneca, sesta; pêlo, lanugem. **-against the n.** a contrapelo. **-to be caught napping** ser apanhado desprevenido

napkin | nap'kin | *s.* guardanapo; (Ing.) fralda, cueiro

nappy | na'pĩ | *s.* (coloq.) fralda, cueiro

narcotic | nʌko'tik | *s. a.* narcótico

narrate | nəreyt' | *vt.* narrar

narration | nərey'śən | *s.* narração, narrativa

narrative | na'rətiv | *s.* narrativa / *a.* narrativo

narrator | nərey'tə | *s.* narrador

narrow | na'row | *a.* estreito; limitado, restrito. **-to have a n. escape** escapar por um triz. **-to n. down** reduzir, limitar. **-in n. circumstances** em dificuldades financeiras / *vt.* estreitar; reduzir, limitar / *vi.* estreitar-se, tornar-se estreito

narrow-minded | na'rowmayndid | *a.* tacanho, intolerante, de mentalidade estreita

narrowness | na'rownes | *s.* estreiteza

nasal | ney'zəl | *a.* nasal

nasalize | ney'zəlayz | *vt. vi.* nasalizar

nasty | nʌs'tĩ | *a.* desagradável, detestável; repulsivo; horrível; obsceno; desprezível; vil, grosseiro; úmido, desagradável (tempo); tempestuoso (mar); perigoso, malévolo; grave (ferimento). **-to turn n.** zangar-se

nation | ney'śən | *s.* nação, país

national | naś'nəl | *a.* nacional; patriótico

national anthem | naś'nəlan-ϑəm | *s.* hino nacional

national debt | naś'nəldebt | *s.* dívida pública

nationalism | naś'nəlizəm | *s.* nacionalismo

nationalist | naś'nəlist | *s. a.* nacionalista

nationality | naśəna'litĩ | *s.* nacionalidade

native | ney'tiv | *s.* nativo; indígena. **-a n. of London** natural de Londres (pessoa) / *a.* nativo, natural; natal (terra); indígena; inato; materno (idioma)

native sod | ney'tivsod | *s.* torrão natal

nativity | nəti'vitĩ | *s.* natividade, nascimento; horóscopo; (maiúsc.) Natividade, Natal

natty | na'tĩ | *a.* elegante, garboso, alinhado

natural | na'śərəl | *a.* natural, espontâneo, simples

naturalize | na'śərəlayz | *vt.* naturalizar

naturally | na'śərəlĩ | *adv.* naturalmente, claro

naturalness | na'śərəlnes | *s.* naturalidade, simplicidade

nature | ney'śə | *s.* natureza. **-by n.** por natureza. **-in the course of n.** na ordem natural das coisas. **-debt of n.** morte

naught | nót' | *s.* nada. **-to come to n.** reduzir-se a nada; frustrar-se

naughty | nó'tĩ | *a.* travesso, levado; malcomportado; malicioso, picante

nausea | nó'zĩə | *s.* náusea

nauseating | nó'zĩeyting | *a.* nauseante; asqueroso, repugnante, nojento

nautical | nó'tikəl | *a.* náutico, marítimo

nautical mile | nó'tikəlmayl | *s.* milha marítima

naval | ney'vəl | *a.* naval, marítimo

nave | neyv' | *s.* nave (de igreja)

navel | ney'vəl | *s.* umbigo

navigability | navigəbi'litĩ | *s.*

navegabilidade

navigable | na'vigəbəl | *a.* navegável

navigate | na'vigeyt | *vt. vi.* navegar; pilotar

navigation | navigey'sən | *s.* navegação

navigator | na'vigeytə | *s.* navegador

navvy | na'vï | *s.* (Ing.) trabalhador em escavações, dragagens etc.

navy | ney'vï | *s.* marinha

navy blue | ney'vïblʋ | *s.* azul-marinho

nay | ney' | *s.* não; negativa / *adv.* mais ainda, não somente isso

near | nı'ə | *a.* perto, próximo; vizinho; por um triz; próximo; íntimo / *adv.* perto; quase; intimamente; aproximadamente. **-n. by** perto / *prep.* perto de; próximo de (a); junto de (a) / *vi.* aproximar-se de. **-to draw n.** aproximar-se

Near East | nı'əıst | *s.* Oriente Próximo

nearly | nı'əlï | *adv.* quase, aproximadamente. **-I n. fell** quase caí. **-I n. went** estava a ponto de ir. **-not n. as** muito menos que, bem menos que

nearness | nı'ənes | *s.* proximidade

neat | nıt' | *a.* limpo, arrumado; elegante, de bom gosto; puro, sem mistura; líquido (quantia, lucro)

neatness | nıt'nes | *s.* limpeza, elegância; esmero, capricho

nebula | ne'bïulə | *s.* nebulosa

nebulous | ne'bïuləs | *a.* nebuloso, vago, impreciso

necessary | ne'səsərï | *a.* necessário, essencial

necessitate | nəse'siteyt | *vt.* tornar necessário ou inevitável; exigir, obrigar a

necessity | nəse'sitï | *s.* necessidade

neck | nek' | *s.* pescoço; colo; gola; colarinho; gargalo; língua (de terra). **-low n.** decote. **-n. and n.** emparelhados. **-n. or nothing** a todo custo

necklace | nek'ləs | *s.* colar

necktie | nek'tay | *s.* gravata

née, nee | ney' | *a. née*, em solteira, nascida

need | nıd' | *s.* necessidade; indigência, penúria. **-to be in n. of** necessitar, precisar de. **-if n. be** se for preciso. **-in case of n.** em caso de necessidade. **-there is no n.** não é necessário / *vt.* necessitar, precisar de

needle | nı'dəl | *s.* agulha

needless | nıd'les | *a.* desnecessário, inútil

needlewoman | nı'dəlwəmən | *s.* costureira

needlework | nı'dəlwɛk | *s.* trabalho de agulha, costura

needy | nı'dï | *a.* necessitado, indigente, pobre

nefarious | nəfe'ərïəs | *a.* nefando, execrável, nefário

negation | negey'sən | *s.* negação; negativa; anulação

negative | ne'gətiv | *s.* negativa; (fot.) negativo / *a.* negativo

neglect | niglekt' | *s.* negligência; descuido, desleixo; esquecimento, abandono / *vt.* negligenciar; abandonar; esquecer-se de; desprezar

neglectful | niglekt'ful | *a.* negligente, descuidado

negligence | ne'gliǰəns | *s.* negligência, descuido, desleixo

negligent | ne'gliǰənt | *a.* negligente, descuidado

negligible | ne'gliǰəbəl | *a.* insignificante, sem importância, desprezível

negotiate | nigow'sïeyt | *vt.* negociar; (coloq.) vencer, transpor / *vi.* negociar

negotiation | nigowsïey'sən | *s.* negociação

negotiator | nigow'sïeytə | *s.* negociador

Negro | nı'grow | *s. a.* negro

neigh | ney' | *s.* relincho / *vi.* relinchar

neighbour, neighbor | ney'bə | *s.* vizinho / *a.* vizinho, adjacente

neighbourhood, neighborhood | ney'bəhud |s. vizinhança, arredores. **-in the n. of** perto de; mais ou menos, quase

neighbouring, neighboring | ney'bəring | a. vizinho, próximo, adjacente

neighbourly, neighborly | ney'bəlĭ | a. amistoso; amável, prestativo

neither | nay'ðə (EUA) nĭ'ðə | a. pron. nenhum; nem um nem outro / conj. nem; também não; tampouco. **-n.... nor...** nem ... nem ...

nephew | ne'fĭu |s. sobrinho

nerve | nɛv' |s. nervo; (fig.) coragem, sangue-frio; (gír.) atrevimento, descaro

nerve-racking | nɛv'raking | a. aflitivo, torturante, insuportável

nervous | nɛ'vəs | a. nervoso; apreensivo

nervous breakdown | nɛ'vəsbrey'dawn | s. esgotamento nervoso

nervousness | nɛ'vəsnes | s. nervosismo; agitação

nest | nest' |s. ninho / vt. encaixar em, aninhar / vi. aninhar-se

nestle | ne'səl | vi. aninhar-se, aconchegar-se

net | net' | s. rede / vt. apanhar com rede; cobrir ou proteger com rede

net, nett | net' |a. líquido (preço, peso etc.)

netting | ne'ting | s. rede; pesca com rede; ato de pegar na rede ou de cobrir com rede; feitura de filé ou rede

nettle | ne'təl | s. urtiga / vt. irritar; exasperar

nettle-rash | ne'təlraś | s. urticária

network | net'wɛk | s. rede; tela, filó; (rád.) cadeia de emissoras

neuralgia | nĭural'jə |s. nevralgia

neuritis | nĭuray'tis | s. neurĭte

neurotic | nĭuro'tik | s. a. neurótico

neuter | nĭu'tə |s. a. neutro

neutral | nĭu'trəl |s. (mec.) ponto morto / a. neutro

neutrality | nĭutra'litĭ | s. neutralidade

never | ne'və |adv. nunca, jamais

nevertheless | nevəðəles' | adv. conj. apesar disso, ainda assim, contudo

new | nĭu' | a. novo; recente

new-born | nĭu'bón | a. recém-nascido; renascido

newcomer | nĭu'kâmə | s. recém-chegado

new departure | nĭudipA'šə | s. nova perspectiva (pensamento), nova orientação (ação)

newly | nĭu'lĭ |adv. recentemente

newness | nĭu'nes | s. novidade

news | nĭuz' | s. notícia(s); novidade(s)

news-boy | nĭuz'boy |s. jornaleiro (menino)

news bulletin | nĭuz'bulətin | s. (rád. etc.) noticiário

newspaper | nĭuz'peypə |s. jornal

newspaper clipping | nĭuz'peypəkliping | s. recorte de jornal

newspaperman | nĭuz'peypəmən | s. jornalista

news-reel | nĭuz'rĭl | s. cine-jornal, atualidades

news-stand | nĭuz'stand |s. banca de jornais

next | nekst' |s. seguinte / a. próximo; seguinte; vizinho; ao lado. **-n. door** a casa ao lado, o vizinho. **-n. time** da próxima vez / adv. a seguir; logo depois; da próxima vez / prep. junto de, ao lado de, perto de

nib | nib' | s. pena (de escrever); bico

nibble | ni'bəl | s. mordidinha; naco, bocado / vt. mordiscar. **-to n. at** beliscar (comida)

nice | nays' | a. simpático, amável; bonito, belo, elegante; agradável; atraente; correto; bom, excelente; de bom gosto

nicety | nay'sitĭ | s. sutileza

niche | niš' |s. nicho

nickel | ni'kəl |s. níquel

nickname | nik'neym | *s.* alcunha, apelido / *vt.* alcunhar, apelidar

niece | nīs | *s.* sobrinha

niggardly | ni'gǝdlī | *a.* avarento, sovina, miserável / *adv.* sovinamente

nigger | ni'gǝ | *s.* (pej.) negro, preto

nigh | nay' | *a.adv.prep.* (ant., dial., liter.) = *near*

night | nayt' | *s.* noite. **-at** ou **by n.** à noite, de noite. **-at dead of n.** na calada da noite / *a.* noturno

nightcap | nayt'kap | *s.* barrete ou touça de dormir; trago (de bebida) tomado antes de dormir

night-club | nayt'klâb | *s.* clube noturno, cabaré

nightfall | nayt'fól | *s.* o anoitecer

nightingale | nay'tingeyl | *s.* rouxinol

nightly | nayt'lī | *a.* noturno / *adv.* todas as noites

nightmare | nayt'meǝ | *s.* pesadelo

night-shift | nayt'šift | *s.* serão

night-shirt | nayt'šɛt | *s.* camisa (camisola) de dormir

night-watchman | naytwoš'mǝn | *s.* guarda-noturno

nil | nil' | *a.* zero, nada

nimble | nim'bǝl | *a.* ágil, rápido, ligeiro, veloz

nincompoop | nin'kǝmpup | *s.* tolo, pateta, idiota

nine | nayn' | *s.a.* nove

nineteen | nayn'tīn | *s.a.* dezenove

ninety | nayn'tī | *s.a.* noventa

ninth | naynϑ' | *s.* nono; (mús.) nona/*a.* nono

nip | nip' | *s.* beliscão; mordida, naco; trago (de bebida) / *vt.* beliscar; mordiscar. **-to n. in the bud** cortar pela raiz, frustrar

nipple | ni'pǝl | *s.* mamilo

nit | nit' | *s.* lêndea

nitwit | nit'wit | *s.* estúpido, tolo, pateta

no | now | *a.* nenhum. **-n. matter** não importa. **-n. smoking** proibido fumar / *adv.* não. **-n**

longer já não. **-n. sooner** nem bem

Noah's arc | nowaz'ʌk | *s.* arca de Noé

nobility | nowbi'litī | *s.* nobreza, aristocracia

noble | now'bǝl | *a.* nobre

nobleman | now'bǝlmǝn | *s.* nobre, fidalgo, aristocrata

nobody | now'bǝdī | *s.* joãoninguém / *pron.* ninguém

nocturnal | noktɛ'nǝl | *a.* noturno

nod | nod' | *s.* inclinação de cabeça; cabeceio, cochilo / *vt.* inclinar (cabeça); aprovar, concordar (inclinando a cabeça) / *vi.* cabecear, dormitar; acenar com a cabeça, nutar; aprovar (inclinando a cabeça)

noise | noyz' | *s.* barulho, ruído; tumulto, algazarra

noisy | noy'zī | *a.* barulhento

nomad | now'mad | *s. a.* nômade

nominal | no'minǝl | *a.* nominal, módico, insignificante (preço, custo)

nominate | no'mineyt | *vt.* nomear, designar

nomination | nominey'šǝn | *s.* nomeação; indicação (de candidato)

nonchalant | non'šólǝnt | *a.* indiferente, negligente

nonconformist | nonkǝnfó'mist | *s. a.* não-conformista

nondescript | non'diskript | *a.* indefinível; indescritível

none | nân' | *pron.* nenhum; ninguém; nada / *adv.* de nenhum modo, nada; não

nonentity | nonen'titī | *s.* coisa não existente; nulidade

nonplussed | nonplâst' | *a.* confuso, perplexo

nonprofit | nonpro'fit | *a.* que não tem o lucro como principal objetivo (empresa), sem fins lucrativos

nonsense | non'sǝns | *s.* tolice, asneira, ninharia / *interj.* tolice!

non-stop | nonstop' | *a.* direto /

adv. diretamente

noodle | nu'dəl |*s.* talharim; simplório, pateta, idiota

nook | nuk' | *s.* canto; recanto, esconderijo

noon | nun' |*s.* meio-dia

no one | now'wân |*pron.* ninguém

noose | nus' |*s.* laço, nó corredio

nor | nó | *conj.* nem. **-neither ... n. ...** nem ... nem ...

norm | nóm' |*s.* norma

normal | nó'məl |*a.* normal

normally | nó'məlĭ |*adv.* normalmente; geralmente

Norman | nó'mən |*s. a.* normando

Norse | nós' | *s. a.* norueguês; escandinavo

north | noð' |*s.* norte

north-east | nóð'ıst |*s.* nordeste / *a.* nordeste, nordestino

northern | nó'ðən |*a.* do norte, setentrional

North Pole | nóð'powl |*s.* pólo norte

North Star | nóð'stA | *s.* estrela polar

north-west | nóð'wəst | *s. a.* noroeste

Norwegian | nówı'jən | *s. a.* norueguês

nose | nowz' | *s.* nariz; focinho (animais). **-by a n.** por focinho, por pequena margem. **-on the n.** (coloq.) exatamente / *vt.* farejar, descobrir. **-to n. out** farejar. **-to pay through the n.** pagar caro, custar caro. **-to turn up one's n. at** desdenhar

nostalgia | nostal'jə | *s.* nostalgia, saudade

nostril | nos'tril |*s.* narina

nostrum | nos'trəm |*s.* panacéia, remédio de charlatão

nosy, nosey | now'zĭ |*a.* (coloq.) abelhudo, intrometido

not | not |*adv.* não. **-n. even** nem mesmo. **-n. at all** de modo algum. **-to think n.** achar que não

notable | now'təbəl |*a.* notável; memorável

notch | noš' |*s.* entalhe, corte, chanfradura

note | nowt' | *s.* nota; apontamento. **-of n.** notável. **-to compare notes** trocar idéias / *vt.* notar, observar; anotar; registrar

notebook | nowt'buk |*s.* agenda, caderno de notas

noted | now'tid |*a.* notável

notepaper | nowt'peypə |*s.* papel de carta

noteworthy | nowt'wɛðĭ |*a.* notável, digno de nota

nothing | nâ'ðing |*s.* nada. **-forn.** grátis, de graça; em vão, inutilmente. **-n. but** só, somente, apenas. **-n. else** nada mais. **-to have n. to do with** não ter nada que ver com. **-to come to n.** não dar resultado, fracassar. **-to think n. of** não fazer caso de

notice | now'tis | *s.* aviso; notícia; comunicação; notificação; participação; atenção, observação. **-on short n.** em cima da hora, de repente. **-without previous n.** sem aviso prévio. **-to give (somebody) n.** despedir. **-to give n. of** informar, avisar, fazer saber. **-to take n. of** observar, reparar, notar / *vt.* notar, observar, reparar em; tratar com cortesia; notificar, intimar

noticeable | now'tisəbəl |*a.* visível, claro, perceptível; notável, digno de nota

notification | nowtifikey'śən | *s.* aviso, notificação

notify | now'tifay | *vt.* avisar, informar, notificar

notion | now'śən |*s.* noção

notoriety | nowtəray'ətĭ |*s.* notoriedade; má reputação

notorious | nowto'ri̇̆əs |*a.* notório; de má reputação

notwithstanding | notwiðstan'ding |*prep.* apesar de, não obstante / *adv.* entretanto, ainda assim, não obstante / *conj.* apesar de

nought | nót' | *s.* zero. **-noughts and crosses** jogo-da-velha

noun | nawn' |*s.* substantivo

nourish | nâ'riś | *vt.* nutrir

nourishing | nâ'riśing | *a.* nutritivo

nourishment | nâ'riśmənt | *s.* alimento; nutrição

novel | no'vəl | *s.* romance / *a.* novo, inesperado, inusitado

novelist | no'vəlist | *s.* romancista

novelty | no'vəltī | *s.* novidade

November | nowvem'bə | *s.* novembro

novice | no'vis | *s.* (ecles.) noviço; aprendiz, principiante

now | naw' | *adv.* agora. **-n. and then** de vez em quando. **-just n.** agora mesmo, há pouco. **-by n.** a esta hora. **-from n. on** daqui por diante. **-right n.** já / *conj.* agora; já que; agora que. **-n. then** ora, pois bem / *interj.* ora!, vamos!

nowadays | naw'ədeyz | *adv.* hoje em dia

nowhere | now'weə | *adv.* em parte alguma, em lugar nenhum. **-n. near** longe de

noxious | nok'śəs | *a.* nocivo, prejudicial, daninho; doentio

nozzle | no'zəl | *s.* bico, esguincho; (gír.) nariz, focinho

nuance | nĭu'óns | *s.* matiz

nuclear | nĭu'klĭə | *a.* nuclear

nucleus | nĭu'klĭəs | *s.* núcleo

nude | nĭvd' | *s.* nu / *a.* nu, despido

nudge | nâj' | *s.* cotovelada / *vt.* acotovelar

nudity | nĭu'ditī | *s.* nudez

nugget | nâ'git | *s.* pepita (de ouro); (fig.) coisa de valor

nuisance | nĭu'səns | *s.* maçada, incômodo, amolação; pessoa cacete, coisa que incomoda. **-what a n.!** que maçada!

null | nâl' | *a.* nulo. **-n. and void** nulo, sem efeito, írrito e nulo

nullify | nâ'lifay | *vt.* anular

numb | nâm' | *a.* entorpecido, paralisado / *vt.* entorpecer, paralisar

number | nâm'bə | *s.* número / *vt.* contar; enumerar; montar a

numberless | nâm'bəles | *a.* inumerável, sem número

numbness | nâm'nes | *s.* entorpecimento

numeral | nĭu'mərəl | *s.* numeral, algarismo

numerous | nĭu'mərəs | *a.* numeroso

nun | nân' | *s.* freira

nunnery | nâ'nərī | *s.* convento (de freiras)

nuptial | nâp'śəl | *spl.* núpcias / *a.* nupcial

nurse | nɛs' | *s.* enfermeira; ama-seca; ama-de-leite / *vt.* amamentar; criar; cuidar (de doente); alimentar, acalentar (idéia, sentimento etc.) / *vi.* mamar, ser amamentado; dar de mamar

nursery | nɛ'sərī | *s.* quarto de criança; sementeira, viveiro de plantas

nursery rhymes | nɛ'sərīraymz | *spl.* versos para crianças

nursery school | nɛ'sərīskʋl | *s.* escola maternal

nursing | nɛ'sing | *s.* enfermagem

nursing home | nɛ'singhowm | *s.* sanatório, clínica de repouso

nurture | nɛ'śə | *s.* alimentação; criação; educação / *vt.* alimentar; educar

nut | nât' | *s.* noz; (mec.) porca; (gír.) maluco, louco. **-a hard n. to crack** um osso duro de roer

nutcracker | nât'krakə | *s.* quebra-nozes

nutmeg | nât'meg | *s.* noz-moscada

nutrition | nĭutri'śən | *s.* nutrição, alimentação

nutritious | nĭutri'śəs | *a.* nutritivo

nutshell | nât'śel | *s.* casca de noz. **-in a n.** em poucas palavras

nylon | nay'lən | *s.* náilon

nymph | nimf' | *s.* ninfa

O

o | ow' | *s.* zero (nos números de telefone) / *interj.* oh!

oaf | owf' | *s.* idiota, imbecil; pessoa estúpida ou desastrada

oak | owk' | *s.* carvalho

oar | ó'ə | *s.* remo

oasis | owey'sis | *s.* oásis

oat | owt' | *s.* (ger. *pl.*) aveia

oath | owθ' | *s.* juramento; imprecação, praga. -to take an o. jurar. -to take the o. prestar juramento

oatmeal | owt'mıl | *s.* farinha de aveia

obdurate | ob'dĭurit | *a.* obstinado, teimoso

obedience | owbı'dĭəns | *s:* obediência

obedient | owbı'dĭənt | *a.* obediente, submisso

obese | owbıs' | *a.* obeso

obey | owbey' | *vt.* obedecer / *vi.* ser obediente

obituary | əbi'tĭuərı | *s.* obituário, nota necrológica

object | ob'jekt | *s.* objeto, coisa; objetivo, finalidade, propósito, fim; (gram.) complemento / *vi.* fazer objeção a, opor-se a; discordar. -to o. to fazer objeção a; não gostar de

objection | əbjek'šən | *s.* objeção; oposição. -to have no o. não fazer objeção a

objectionable | əbjek'šənəbəl | *a.* objetável; desagradável, censurável

objective | əbjek'tiv | *s.* objetivo, propósito; (ópt.) objetiva / *a.* objetivo; real; impessoal; imparcial

objector | əbjek'tə | *s.* objetante, opositor, oponente

obligation | obligey'šən | *s.* obrigação; dever; responsabilidade

obligatory | əbli'gətrı | *a.* obrigatório

oblige | əblayĭ' | *vt.* obrigar, forçar; fazer favor a, obsequiar. -much obliged muito grato. -to be obliged to someone ficar agradecido a alguém. -to o. oneself comprometer-se

obliging | əblay'jing | *a.* obsequiador

obliterate | əbli'təreyt | *vt.* obliterar; apagar, riscar

oblivion | əbli'vĭən | *s.* esquecimento, olvido

oblivious | əbli'vĭəs | *a.* esquecido, desatento, distraído

oblong | ob'long | *s.* figura oblonga / *a.* oblongo, alongado

obloquy | ob'ləkwı | *s.* censura, reprovação; difamação, calúnia; ignomínia, vergonha

obnoxious | əbnok'šəs | *a.* antipático, detestável; irritante, odioso

obscene | obsın' | *a.* obsceno, imoral, indecente

obscenity | obse'nitĭ | *s.* obscenidade, indecência

obscure | əbskĭu'ə | *a.* obscuro; confuso, ininteligível; vago, indistinto; humilde (nascimento) / *vt.* obscurecer, encobrir, ofuscar, eclipsar

obscurity | əbskĭu'ritĭ | *s.* obscuridade

obsequious | obsı'kwĭəs | *a.* bajulador, subserviente

obsequiousness | obsı'kwĭəsnes | *s.* subserviência

observance | əbzE'vəns | *s.* observância; uso, prática, costume; formalidade, rito

observant | əbzE'vənt | *a.* observador, perspicaz; observante, cumpridor, obediente

observation | obzəvey'šən | *s.* observação

observatory | əbzE'vətrı | *s.* observatório

observe | əbzɛv' | *vt. vi.* observar, notar, ver; cumprir, respeitar

observer | əbzɛ'və | *s.* observador

obsess | obses' | *vt.* perseguir, atormentar; preocupar, obsedar

obsession | obse'ʃən | *s.* obsessão

obsolete | ob'səlit | *a.* obsoleto

obstacle | ob'stəkəl | *s.* obstáculo, impedimento

obstinacy | ob'stinəsĩ | *s.* obstinação, teimosia

obstinate | ob'stinit | *a.* obstinado, teimoso

obstreperous | obstre'pərəs | *a.* barulhento; turbulento

obstruct | əbstrâkt' | *vt.* obstruir; dificultar, retardar

obstruction | əbstrâk'ʃən | *s.* obstrução, impedimento

obtain | əbteyn' | *vt.* obter; conseguir, alcançar

obtainable | əbtey'nəbəl | *a.* obtenível; conseguível; à venda

obtuse | obtĩus' | *a.* obtuso (tb. fig.); estúpido, bronco

obviate | ob'vĩeyt | *vt.* obviar, esclarecer; evitar, prevenir

obvious | ob'vĩəs | *a.* óbvio, evidente, claro

obviously | ob'vĩəslĩ | *adv.* obviamente

occasion | əkey'jən | *s.* ocasião, oportunidade; acontecimento; motivo. **-on o.** de vez em quando. **-on the o. of** por ocasião de. **-to rise to the o.** enfrentar uma emergência / *vt.* ocasionar, causar

occasional | əkey'jənəl | *a.* ocasional, pouco freqüente

occasionally | əkey'jənəlĩ | *adv.* ocasionalmente, de vez em quando

occident | ok'sidənt | *s.* ocidente (tb. maiúsc.)

occult | okâlt' | *a.* oculto

occupant | o'kĩupənt | *s.* ocupante; morador, inquilino

occupation | okĩupey'ʃən | *s.* ocupação; profissão, trabalho

occupier | o'kĩupayə | *s.* inquilino, morador

occupy | o'kĩupay | *vt.* ocupar

occur | əkɛ' | *vi.* ocorrer; acontecer, suceder; encontrar-se; vir à mente

occurrence | əkɛ'rəns | *s.* ocorrência; acontecimento

ocean | ow'ʃən | *s.* oceano

o'clock | əklok' | *s.* hora(s) (forma abreviada de **of the clock**: *five o'clock* cinco horas, *ten o'clock* dez horas)

October | oktow'bə | *s.* outubro

octopus | ok'təpəs | *s.* polvo

oculist | o'kĩulist | *s.* oculista

odd | od' | *a.* estranho, singular; bizarro, curioso; excêntrico, original (pessoa); avulso; ímpar (número); desirmanado (objeto); tanto(s) (*one hundred and odd books* cento e tantos livros); pouco(s) (*fifty odd years ago* há cinqüenta e poucos anos). **-at o. times** de vez em quando. **-in o. places** aqui e ali

oddity | o'ditĩ | *s.* singularidade, estranheza; excentricidade

odd job | od'job | *s.* biscate

oddment | od'mənt | *s.* (tb. *pl.*) sobra, retalho, pedaço

odds | odz' | *spl.* desigualdade; vantagem; diferença. **-by all o.** com ampla margem. **-to be at o. with** estar em desacordo com. **-o. and ends** miudezas; peças avulsas; retalhos; bugigangas; restos

ode | owd' | *s.* ode

odious | ow'dĩəs | *a.* odioso

odium | ow'dĩəm | *s.* ódio geral, reprovação geral, repulsa

odour, odor | ow'də | *s.* odor, cheiro; perfume; (fig.) traço, vestígio

odourless, odorless | ow'dəles | *a.* inodoro, sem cheiro

of | ov | *prep.* de. **-o. course** certamente, sem dúvida, claro que sim. **-o. oneself** por si mesmo

off | of | *adv.* à distância, para longe / *prep.* de; a certa distância de; fora de / *a.* desligado (aparelho etc.); transversal, que sai de

off chance | of'ʃans | *s.* possibilidade remota

off-day | of'dey | *s.* dia de folga

offence, offense | əfens' | *s.* ofensa; infração, delito

offend | əfend' | *vt.* ofender; ferir; transgredir

offended | əfen'did | *a.* ofendido, indignado

offender | əfen'də | *s.* infrator, transgressor

offensive | əfen'siv | *s.* (mil.) ofensiva / *a.* ofensivo, insultante; agressivo; desagradável (cheiro etc.); repugnante

offer | o'fə | *s.* oferta; proposta / *vt.* oferecer

offering | o'fəring | *s.* oferta; oferenda

offhand | of'hand | *a.* de improviso / *adv.* imediatamente, logo; bruscamente; precipitadamente

office | o'fis | *s.* escritório; repartição pública; emprego; cargo; ofício. **-to take o.** tomar posse (cargo público); (*pl.*) ofícios (*good offices* bons ofícios)

officer | o'fisə | *s.* (mil.) oficial; guarda, policial; funcionário, dignitário

official | əfi'śəl | *s.* funcionário público / *a.* oficial

officialdom | əfi'śəldəm | *s.* funcionalismo, burocracia

official gazette | əfi'śəlgəzet' | *s.* diário oficial

officiate | əfi'śieyt | *vi.* oficiar, celebrar; exercer funções oficiais

officious | əfi'śəs | *a.* intrometido; oficioso, não oficial

offing | o'fing | *s.* mar alto. **-in the o.** (náut.) ao largo; (fig.) em futuro próximo

offprint | of'print | *s.* separata

off-season | of'sizən | *s.* estação morta

offset | of'set | *s.* compensação; (impr.) ofsete / *vt.* compensar, contrabalançar; imprimir em ofsete

offshoot | of'śut | *s.* ramo; rebento; ramificação, ramal

offshore | ofśó'ə | *adv.* ao largo (no mar)

offside | ofsayd' | *s.* (desp.) jogada em impedimento / *a.* (desp.) impedido

offspring | of'spring | *s.* prole, filhos

often | o'fən | *adv.* muitas vezes

ogle | ow'gəl | *s.* olhar cobiçoso / *vt. vi.* comer com os olhos

ogre | ow'gə | *s.* ogre, papão

oil | oyl' | *s.* óleo; azeite; petróleo / *vt.* lubrificar

oilcloth | oyl'kloϑ | *s.* linóleo

oil-colour, oil-color | oyl'kolə | *s.* = *oil-painting*

oil-painting | oyl'paynting | *s.* pintura a óleo; quadro a óleo

oilskin | oyl'skin | *s.* oleado

oil well | oyl'wel | *s.* poço de petróleo

oily | oy'lĩ | *a.* oleoso; oleaginoso; gorduroso

ointment | oynt'mənt | *s.* ungüento

O.K., okay | owkey' | *s.* (coloq.) aprovação, consentimento / *a. adv.* (coloq.) certo, correto, bom / *interj.* (coloq.) está bem!, está certo!

okra | ow'krə | *s.* quiabo

old | owld' | *s.* tempo antigo. **-of o.** de outrora / *a.* velho; cansado; gasto. **-how o. are you?** quantos anos tem você?

old age | owld'eyĵ | *s.* velhice

old bachelor | oldba'śələ | *s.* solteirão

old country | oldkân'trĩ | *s.* país natal de imigrante

old-fashioned | owld'faśənd | *a.* fora de moda, antiquado

old fogy, old fogey | oldfo'gĩ | *s.* pessoa antiquada, caturra

old folks | oldfolks' | *spl.* (coloq.) velhos (os pais)

old maid | old'meyd | *s.* solteirona

old man | old'mən | *s.* (gír.) velho, o pai; (gír.) chefe, patrão, comandante etc.; (gír.) velho, meu velho (tratamento)

old-timer | oldtay'mə | *s.* (coloq.) veterano

old wives' tale | oldwayvzteyl' |s. crendice, superstição

oligarchy | o'ligaki |s. oligarquia

olive | o'liv | s. azeitona / a. oliváceo

olive grove | o'livgrowv |s. olival

olive oil | o'livoyl' | s. azeite de oliva

omelette, omelet | om'lit |s. omelete

omen | ow'men | s. agouro, presságio / vt. pressagiar

ominous | o'minəs | a. sinistro, funesto

omission | owmi'śən |s. omissão

omit | owmit' | vt. omitir

omnibus | om'nibəs |s. ônibus

omnipotent | omni'pətənt | a. onipotente

on | on | adv. por diante. -and so o. e assim por diante. -o. and o. sem parar / prep. em, sobre, em cima de. -o. horseback a cavalo. -o. purpose de propósito. -o. the left à esquerda

once | wâns' | adv. uma vez. -o. in a while às vezes. -o. upon a time… era uma vez… -at o. imediatamente. -all at o. de repente; ao mesmo tempo, todos juntos. -just this o. só por esta vez. -o. and for all de uma vez por todas. -o. or twice uma vez ou duas, algumas vezes

oncoming | on'kâming | s. aproximação / a. próximo, que se aproxima, que avança

one | wân |s. um, uma. -o. and all todos. -o. by o. um por um. -to be at o. estar de acordo / a. um, uma; único, só; um tal, um certo. -for o. thing em primeiro lugar / pron. um, uma; o(s), a(s). -o. another um ao outro. -o. of these days um dia desses. -this o. este, esta. -that o. aquele, aquela

onerous | ow'nərəs | a. oneroso; pesado, molesto

oneself | wânself' | pron. se, si, a si mesmo, a si próprio. -by o. sozinho

one-sided | wânsay'did | a. desigual, injusto, unilateral

one-time | wântaym' | a. de uma só direção, de mão única; descartável

onion | ə'nĭon |s. cebola

onlooker | on'lukə | s. espectador, circunstante

only | own'lĭ | a. único / adv. só, somente, unicamente. -if o. se ao menos / conj. (coloq.) mas, porém

onset | on'set |s. assalto, ataque; início, começo

onslaught | on'slôt | s. ataque, assalto, arremetida

onto | ontu | prep. em; para; sobre

onus | ow'nəs | s. ônus, encargo; responsabilidade

onward | on'wəd | a. adv. para frente

ooze | vz' | vi. exsudar, ressumar, destilar

opaque | owpeyk' | a. opaco

open | ow'pən | s. abertura / a. aberto; descoberto, desprotegido; franco, sincero. -to be o. to estar disposto a (aceitar, discutir assunto etc.). -to throw o. abrir de par em par / vt. abrir; revelar. -to o. up franquear, abrir caminho / vi. abrir(-se); revelar-se; estrear (peça). -to o. into abrir para; desembocar em

opener | ow'pənə | s. abridor (de latas etc.)

open-handed | owpənhan'did | a. generoso

open house | owpənhaws' | s. casa aberta aos amigos (sem convite); dia de visita pública (em edifício público etc.)

opening | owp'ning | s. abertura; entrada; inauguração; estréia; oportunidade (emprego) / a. primeiro; inaugural

openly | ow'pənlĭ | adv. abertamente, publicamente

opera | o'pərə | s. ópera

opera-glasses | o'pərəglasiz | s. binóculo de teatro

opera-house| o'pərəhaws |s. teatro lírico

operate| o'pəreyt |vt. operar; fazer funcionar; acionar; gerir, administrar / vi. operar; trabalhar; funcionar. **-to o. on** produzir ou causar efeito em; (med.) operar

operation| opərey'śən |s. (med., mil.) operação; funcionamento; ação; influência; administração

operative| o'pərətiv |s. operário / a. operativo, operante

operator| o'pəreytə / s. operador; maquinista; telefonista; especulador

opinion | əpi'nïən | s. opinião; parecer

opinionated | əpi'nïəneytid | a. dogmático; opiniático

opium | ow'pïəm |s. ópio

opossum | əpo'səm | s. gambá

opponent | əpow'nənt | s. oponente, adversário

opportune | o'pətïun |a. oportuno, conveniente

opportunity | opətïu'nitī |s. oportunidade, ocasião

oppose | əpowz' | vt. opor, resistir / vi. opor-se

opposed | əpowzd' |a. contrário; hostil

opposite | o'pəzit | s.a. oposto, contrário / prep. em frente a, defronte a; (teat., cin., TV) ao lado de, junto com

opposition | opəzi'śən |s. oposição; resistência

oppress | əpres' | vt. oprimir

oppression| əpre'śən |s. opressão; tirania

oppressive | əpre'siv | a. opressivo; despótico; carregado, pesado (tempo)

oppressiveness | əpre'sivnes | s. opressão

oppressor | əpre'sə | s. opressor, tirano

opprobrium | əprow'brïəm | s. opróbrio, infâmia

opt | opt' | vi. optar por

optical illusion | op'tikəlilʋ'jən | s. ilusão de ótica

optician | opti'śən | s. fabricante ou vendedor de instrumentos ópticos (esp. óculos)

optics | op'tiks | s. óptica (ciência)

optimism | op'timizəm | s. otimismo

optimist | op'timist | s. otimista

optimistic | optimis'tik | a. otimista, otimístico

option | op'śən | s. opção, alternativa, escolha

optional | op'śənəl | a. optativo, facultativo

opulence | o'pïuləns | s. opulência, riqueza

opulent | o'pïulənt | a. opulento, abundante, rico

or | ó | conj. ou; nem (em frases negativas). **-either...o....ou... ou ... . -whether ... o. not** quer ... quer não

oracle | o'rəkəl | s. oráculo

oral | o'rəl | a. oral

orange | o'rinj | s. laranja (tb. cor)

orangeade | órinjeyd' | s. laranjada

orange-blossom | o'rinjblosəm | s. flor de laranjeira

orange-grove | o'rinjgrowv | s. laranjal

orange-tree | o'rinjtrī | s. laranjeira

oration | orey'śən | s. discurso

orator | o'rətə | s. orador

oratorical | orəto'rikəl | a. oratório

orb | ób' | s. orbe, globo

orbit | ó'bit | s. órbita

orchard | ó'śəd | s. pomar

orchestra | ó'kistrə | s. orquestra; (teat., cin.) platéia

orchid | ó'kid | s. orquídea

ordain | ódeyn' | vt. ordenar. **-to be ordained** (ecles.) ser ordenado

ordeal | ó'dīl | s. ordálio; provação, transe

order | ó'də | s. ordem; (com.) pedido, encomenda; pedido (em restaurante). **-in o.** em ordem;

por ordem; em boa condição.
-in o. to a fim de, para. -in o.
that a fim de que. -in short o. em
pouco tempo. -on o. encomen-
dado. -out of o. enguiçado. -to
o. de encomenda, sob medida.
-to put in o. arrumar, arranjar;
consertar / vt. ordenar, mandar; encomendar; pedir (no restaurante)

orderly | ó'dəlĭ | s. ordenança;
servente de hospital, enfermei-
ro / a. ordeiro; obediente; paca-
to; metódico / adv. ordenada-
mente; metodicamente

ordinance | ó'dinəns | s. decreto,
regulamento; costume, práti-
ca; postura municipal

ordinary | ó'dinərĭ | a. habitual,
ordinário, costumeiro; medío-
cre, ordinário

ordination | ódiney'śən | s. (ecles.)
ordenação

ordnance | ód'nəns | s. (mil.)
artilharia; (mil.) material bé-
lico

ore | ó'ə | s. minério

organ | ó'gən | s. órgão

organist | ó'gənist | s. organista

organization | ógənayzey'śən | s.
organização

organize | ó'gənayz | vt. organi-
zar / vi. organizar-se

organizer | ó'gənayzə | s. organi-
zador

orgy | ó'jĭ | s. orgia

orient | o'rīənt | s. oriente (tb.
maiúsc.)

orientate | o'rīənteyt | vt. orien-
tar / vi. orientar-se

origin | o'rijin | s. origem

original | əri'jinəl | s. original / a.
original; originário

originality | ərijina'litĭ | s. origina-
lidade

originally | əri'jinəlĭ | adv. origi-
nalmente; originariamente

originate | əri'jineyt | vt. origi-
nar, criar / vi. originar-se, começar, surgir

oriole | o'riowl | s. (orn.) pa-
pa-figo

ornament | ó'nəmənt | s. orna-
mento; (pl., ecles.) paramentos
/ vt. ornamentar, adornar

ornamentation | ónəmentey'
śən | s. ornamentação

ornate | óneyt' | a. adornado; pom-
poso, floreado

orphan | ó'fən | s. órfão

orphanage | ó'fənij | s. orfanato

orthodox | ó'θədoks | a. orto-
doxo

orthodoxy | ó'θədoksĭ | s. orto-
doxia

oscillate | o'sileyt | vi. oscilar;
vacilar

ostensible | osten'sibəl | a. ostensi-
vo; aparente

ostensibly | osten'siblĭ | adv. os-
tensivamente; aparentemente

ostentation | ostentey'śən | s.
ostentação

ostentatious | ostentey'śəs | a.
ostentoso

ostracize | os'trəsayz | vt. banir,
condenar ao ostracismo, expa-
triar; rejeitar

ostrich | os'trij | s. avestruz

other | â'ðə | a. outro(s), outra(s).
-each o. um ao outro. -every o.
um sim um não. -the o. day outro dia, recentemente / adv.
diferentemente

otherwise | â'ðəwayz | adv. de
outra maneira, de outro modo,
diferentemente; senão, do contrário

otter | ó'tə | s. lontra

ought | ót' | s. zero; algo / v. de-
fect. dever

ounce | awns' | s. onça (peso)

our | aw'ə | a. (o) nosso, (a) nossa

oust | awst' | vt. expulsar; desalo-
jar; despejar (inquilino)

out | awt | s. saída. -at the outs em
desacordo / adv. fora (de).
-nine o. of ten nove entre dez.
-o. of doors ao ar livre. -o. of
print esgotado (edição, livro).
-o. of the way remoto, distante.
-o. and o. completo, consumado; pertinaz. -to be o. não estar
em casa; estar apagado (fogo).

-to be o. of não ter mais, estar sem. **-to be made o. of** ser feito de. **-get o.!** fora!, saia daqui! **-way o.** saída / *prep.* por

outboard | awt'bóəd | *a. adv.* do lado externo; de popa (motor)

outboard motor | awt'bóədmowtə | *s.* motor de popa

outbreak | awt'breyk | *s.* erupção; explosão; eclosão (epidemia); deflagração (de guerra)

outbuilding | awt'bilding | *s.* anexo, dependência

outburst | awt'bɛst | *s.* explosão

outcast | awt'kʌst | *s.* pária, proscrito, exilado; vagabundo

outclass | awtklʌs' | *vt.* exceder, ultrapassar

outcome | awt'kâm | *s.* resultado, conseqüência

outcrop | awt'krop | *s.* (geol.) afloramento / *vi.* aflorar

outcry | awt'kray | *s.* clamor, protesto, grita

outdated | awtdey'tid | *a.* antiquado

outdo | awtdʋ' | *vt.* exceder

outdoors | awtdóz' | *s.* ar livre, espaço ao ar livre / *adv.* ao ar livre

outer | aw'tə | *a.* exterior, externo, da parte de fora

outfit | awt'fit | *s.* roupa, traje; equipamento, petrechos

outfitter | awt'fitə | *s.* fabricante (fornecedor) de roupas ou equipamentos

outflank | awtflank' | *vt.* flanquear, cercar

outflow | awt'flow | *s.* escoamento, saída

outgoing | awt'gowing | *a.* que está de partida; demissionário; sociável, expansivo

outgrow | awtgrow' | *vt.* exceder em crescimento; ficar pequena (roupa); superar

outhouse | awt'haws | *s.* dependência, anexo

outing | aw'ting | *s.* excursão, passeio; saída

outlandish | awtlan'diś | *a.* estranho; exótico, bizarro; remoto, longínquo

outlast | awtlʌst' | *vt.* durar mais que; sobreviver

outlaw | awt'ló | *s.* proscrito, foragido, criminoso

outlay | awt'ley | *s.* dispêndio, desembolso, despesa, gasto

outlet | awt'let | *s.* saída, escape; escoadouro; (eletr.) tomada; (com.) distribuidor

outline | awt'layn | *s.* contorno, perfil; esboço; resumo, esquema, sumário / *vt.* delinear, esboçar; resumir

outlive | awtliv' | *vt.* sobreviver a

outlook | awt'luk | *s.* perspectiva, probabilidade; ponto de vista; posto de observação; panorama

outlying | awt'laying | *a.* distante, remoto

outnumber | awtnâm'bə | *vt.* superar em número

out-patient | awt'peysənt | *s.* paciente de ambulatório

outpost | awt'powst | *s.* (mil.) posto avançado

outpouring | awt'póring | *s.* efusão; derramamento

output | awt'put | *s.* produção; rendimento; (eletr.) saída

outrage | awt'reyʤ | *s.* ultraje, afronta; violência, atrocidade; violação (da lei etc.) / *vt.* ultrajar; abusar; infringir (lei etc.)

outrageous | awtrey'ʤəs | *a.* ultrajante, ofensivo, insultuoso, afrontoso; horrendo

outright | awt'rayt | *a.* completo, total; sincero, sem rodeios / *adv.* completamente; francamente; sem rodeios; logo, imediatamente

outset | awt'set | *s.* princípio, começo, início

outshine | awtśayn' | *vt.* superar em brilho, eclipsar

outside | awtsayd' | *s.* exterior, parte externa. **-at the o.** no máximo / *a.* externo, exterior, de fora / *adv.* fora, externamente, para fora / *prep.* fora de; além dos limites de; (coloq.) exceto

outsider | awtsay'də | *s.* estranho; intruso; forasteiro

outskirts | awt'skEts | *spl.* arredores, cercanias, subúrbios

outspoken | awtspow'kən | *a.* franco, sincero; atrevido, ousado; arrebatado; que fala sem rebuços

outstanding | awtstan'ding | *a.* notável, importante, proeminente; pendente, a resolver

outstrip | awtstrip' | *vt.* exceder, ultrapassar

outvote | awtvowt' | *vt.* superar em número de votos

outward | awt'wəd | *s.* exterior, mundo exterior / *a.* externo, exterior; de fora; visível, aparente / *adv.* para fora. **-to o. seeming** aparentemente

outwardly | awt'wədlĩ | *adv.* exteriormente

outweigh | awtwey' | *vt.* exceder em peso; (fig.) ter mais valor ou importância que

outwit | awtwit' | *vt.* exceder em astúcia, levar a melhor; enganar

outworn | awt'wón | *a.* usado, gasto; velho, antiquado

oval | ow'vəl | *a.* oval

ovation | owvey'śən | *s.* ovação, aclamação, aplausos

oven | â'vən | *s.* forno

over | ow'və | *a.* excessivo, demasiado / *adv.* para (do) o outro lado; para baixo, para o chão; e mais; de sobra; excessivamente; acabado, terminado; de novo, novamente; do princípio ao fim; todo; lá; cá. **-all o.** completo, terminado. **-o. again** novamente. **-o. and o.** repetidamente. **-o. here** aqui. **-to be o.** terminar. **-to turn o.** virar / *prep.* sobre, por cima de; mais de, além; através. **-o. one's head** acima da compreensão de

overall | ow'vəról | *a.* total, global

overalls | ow'vərólz | *spl.* macacão

overawe | owvəró' | *vt.* intimidar; apavorar

overbalance | owvəba'ləns | *vt.* pesar mais que, sobrepujar; desequilibrar, fazer perder o equilíbrio / *vi.* desequilibrar-se, perder o equilíbrio

overbearing | owvəbe'əring | *a.* arrogante, insolente

overboard | ow'vəbód | *adv.* (náut.) pela borda fora

overburden | owvəbE'dən | *vt.* sobrecarregar

overcast | owvəkAst' | *a.* encoberto, nublado

overcharge | owvəšAĵ' | *vt.* sobrecarregar; cobrar demais; exagerar

overcoat | ow'vəkowt | *s.* sobretudo

overcome | owvəkâm' | *vt.* vencer, subjugar, sobrepujar

overdone | owvədân' | *a.* passado demais, cozido demais

overdraft | ow'vədrAft | *s.* (com.) saque a descoberto

overdue | owvədĩu' | *a.* (com.) já vencido; atrasado

overestimate | owvæs'timeyt | *vt.* superestimar

overflow | owvəflow' | *vi.* transbordar

overgrown | owvəgrown' | *a.* crescido em demasia

overhang | owvəhang' | *s.* (arquit.) balanço; (arquit.) saliência, projeção / *vt.* pender sobre; (fig.) ameaçar / *vi.* projetar-se sobre alguma coisa

overhaul | ow'vəhól | *s.* exame, revisão, vistoria / *vt.* vistoriar, examinar

overhead | owvəhed' | *s.* (ger. *pl.*) despesas gerais / *a.* aéreo; superior, elevado / *adv.* por cima; acima da cabeça

overhear | owvəhI'ə | *vt.* ouvir por acaso ou secretamente

overjoyed | owvəjoyd' | *a.* cheio de alegria

overland| owvəland' |*a. adv.* por terra, por via terrestre

overlap | owvəlap' | *vt. vi.* sobrepor(-se)

overlay | owvəley' | *vt.* revestir, cobrir

overleaf| owvəlif' |*adv.* no outro lado da página, no verso

overload | owvəlowd' | *s.* sobrecarga / *vt.* sobrecarregar

overlook | owvəluk' | *s.* mirante, belvedere / *vt.* dar vista para, estar sobranceiro a; ver, contemplar (do alto); fazer vista grossa a, perdoar, não reparar em

overlord | owvəlód | *s.* senhor feudal, suserano

overnight | owvənayt' | *adv.* de um dia para outro; de pernoite; da noite anterior. **-to stay o.** passar a noite

overpower| owvəpaw'ə |*vt.* subjugar; sobrepujar

overproduction | owvəprədak'-sən |*s.* superprodução

overrate| owvəreyt' |*vt.* superestimar; avaliar acima do preço; exagerar o valor

overreach | owvəriš' | *vt.* ultrapassar; exceder / *vr.* fazer esforço excessivo, exceder-se

override| owvərayd' |*vt.* atropelar; ultrapassar, valer mais; estafar (cavalo)

overriding | owvəray'ding |*a.* supremo, dominante

overripe | owvərayp' |*a.* maduro demais

overrule | owvərʊl' | *vt.* rejeitar; anular; revogar

overrun | owvərân' | *vt.* invadir, devastar; cobrir, inundar; infestar; alastrar; exceder, ultrapassar / *vi.* transbordar

overseas | owvəsiz' |*a.* ultramarino / *adv.* no ultramar, no (do, para o) estrangeiro

overseer | ow'vəsiə | *s.* capataz, feitor; superintendente, inspetor

oversight | ow'vəsayt | *s.* inadvertência, descuido; supervisão, superintendência

overstep | owvəstep' | *vt.* ultrapassar, exceder; transgredir, infringir

overstrain | owvəstreyn' | *s.* excesso de tensão ou esforço / *vt.* esticar, estirar; sobrecarregar; submeter a esforço excessivo

overt | ow'vɛt | *a.* claro, manifesto, público

overtake | owvəteyk' | *vt.* alcançar, ultrapassar

overthrow | ow'vəðrow |*s.* deposição, destronamento; derrota / *vt.* derrubar, destronar, depor; derrotar

overtime | ow'vətaym | *s.* horas extraordinárias (de trabalho)

overture | ow'vətĺuə | *s.* (mús.) abertura; oferta, proposta inicial

overturn| owvətɛn' |*vt.* virar; derrubar, depor / *vi.* emborcar, virar de borco

overweening| owvəwi'ning |*a.* arrogante, presunçoso

overweight | owvəweyt' | *s.* excesso de peso

overwhelm | owvəwelm' | *vt.* esmagar; soterrar; dominar; cobrir (de favores etc.), cumular

overwhelming | owvəwel'ming |*a.* esmagador; irresistível

overwork| owvəwɛk' |*s.* trabalho excessivo

overwrought | owvə'rót | *a.* superexcitado; fatigado por excesso de trabalho

owe | ow' | *vt. vi.* dever

owing | ow'ing | *a.* devedor; devido. **-o. to** devido a; por causa de

owl | awl' | *s.* coruja

own | own' | *a.* próprio. **-on his o.** sozinho, independente. **-on his o. account** por conta própria. **-to get one's o. back** tirar a desforra / *vt.* possuir, ter, ser dono de; admitir, reconhecer / *vi.* reconhecer

owner | own'ə | *s.* dono, proprietário

ownership| ow'nəsip |*s.* propriedade, posse, domínio

ox | oks' | *s.* boi
ox-blood | oks'blâd | *s.* verme-
lho-escuro

ox-cart | oks'kʌt | *s.* carro de boi
oxygen | ok'sijən | *s.* oxigênio
oyster | oys'tə | *s.* ostra

P

pace | peys' | *s.* passo; modo de an-
dar; marcha, velocidade. -**at a
slow p.** a passo lento. -**to keep p.
with** ir na mesma velocidade;
acompanhar os passos de. -**to set
the p.** regular a marcha; dar o
exemplo. -**to take a p. forward** dar
um passo em frente / *vt.* percorrer
passo a passo / *vi.* andar pausada-
mente; medir a passos (distância),
regular a marcha etc.
pacific | pəsi'fik | *s.* (maiúsc.)
oceano Pacífico / *a.* pacífico,
tranqüilo
pacification | pasifikey'sən | *s.*
pacificação
pacifist | pa'sifist | *s.* pacifista
pacify | pa'sifay | *vt.* pacificar,
apaziguar
pack | pak' | *s.* fardo; pacote, em-
brulho; maço; mochila; bara-
lho; malta (malfeitores); mati-
lha (cães); alcatéia (lobos);
monte (de mentiras) / *vt.* empa-
cotar, embrulhar; embalar;
acondicionar; fazer (malas).
-**to p. down** apertar, comprimir. -**to p. in** atulhar, amontoar
(gente). -**to p. up** embrulhar; fazer (mala). -**to p. off** despachar
packet | pa'kit | *s.* embrulho, pa-
cote; fardo; maço (de cigarros)
packet-boat | pa'kitbowt | *s.*
(náut.) paquete
packing | pa'king | *s.* empacota-
mento, embalagem
pack-mule | pak'miʋl | *s.* besta de
carga
pack-saddle | pak'sadəl | *s.* albar-
da, sela para animais de carga
pact | pakt' | *s.* pacto, acordo;
tratado
pad | pad' | *s.* almofada; enchi-
mento / *vt.* almofadar / *vi.* ir a
pé; caminhar pesadamente; andar a passos cadenciados
padding | pa'ding | *s.* estofamen-
to; acolchoamento; enchimen-
to; (fig.) palavreado desnecessá-
rio
paddle | pa'dəl | *s.* remo (de cabo
curto), pagaia / *vt.* remar (com
pagaia)
paddle-boat | pa'dəlbowt | *s.* va-
por movido a rodas
paddock | pa'dək | *s.* recinto de
pesagem etc. (em hipódromo),
padoque
padlock | pad'lok | *s.* cadeado
paean, pean | pɪ'ən | *s.* peã; hino
de louvor ou triunfo
pagan | pey'gən | *s. a.* pagão
paganism | pey'gənizəm | *s.*
paganismo
page | peyǰ' | *s.* página; pajem, es-
cudeiro; mensageiro (de hotel
etc.) / *vt.* pajear
pageant | pa'ǰənt | *s.* cortejo cívi-
co, préstito; espetáculo
pageantry | pa'ǰəntrī | *s.* fausto,
pompa; cerimonial
pail | peyl' | *s.* balde
pain | peyn' | *s.* dor; pena, pesar;
amargura, mágoa; (*pl.*) traba-
lhos, esforços, cuidados. -**to
take pains** esforçar-se / *vt.* causar dor a; dar desgosto a / *vi.*
causar dor; doer. -**it pains me** la-
mento muito
painful | peyn'ful | *a.* doloroso;
difícil, árduo

painstaking | peynz'teyking | *a.* cuidadoso, esmerado

paint | peynt' | *s.* tinta (de pintar) / *vt.* pintar

painter | peyn'tə | *s.* pintor

painting | peyn'ting | *s.* pintura; quadro, tela

pair | pe'ə | *s.* par; casal; parelha (de cavalos); junta (de bois). -**in pairs** aos pares / *vt.* emparelhar; acasalar; dispor aos pares / *vi.* emparelhar-se; acasalar-se. -**to p. off** formar pares

pajamas | pəjʌ'məz | *spl.* = *pyjamas*

pal | pal' | *s.* companheiro, amigo, camarada

palace | pa'lis | *s.* palácio

palatable | pa'lətəbəl | *a.* saboroso, gostoso, apetitoso; (fig.) agradável

palate | pa'lit | *s.* (anat.) palato; paladar; gosto

palatial | pəley'śəl | *a.* magnífico, suntuoso

palaver | pəlʌ'və | *s.* negociação (esp. com nativos africanos etc.); (fig.) palavreado

pale | peyl' | *s.* estaca; limite. -**beyond the p.** além dos limites, inadmissível, inaceitável / *a.* pálido; claro; descorado / *vt.* cercar com paliçada / *vi.* empalidecer

paleness | peyl'nes | *s.* palidez

palisade | paliseyd' | *s.* paliçada, estacada

pall | pól' | *s.* pano mortuário; (fig.) manto, nuvem; (ecles.) pátena; (ecles.) toalha de altar / *vi.* tornar-se insípido, perder o sabor; saciar-se

pallbearer | pólbe'ərə | *s.* pessoa que carrega o caixão (num funeral)

palliasse | pa'lïas | *s.* colchão de palha

palliate | pa'lïeyt | *vt.* mitigar, aliviar, atenuar

pallid | pa'lid | *a.* pálido

pallor | pa'lə | *s.* palidez

palm | pʌm' | *s.* palmeira; palma (tb. da mão) / *vt.* empalmar, escamotear. -**to p. off** impingir (alguma coisa a alguém)

palmist | pʌ'mist | *s.* quiromante

palmistry | pʌ'mistrī | *s.* quiromancia

palmy | pʌ'mī | *a.* florescente, próspero

palpable | pal'pəbəl | *a.* palpável, evidente

palpitate | pal'piteyt | *vi.* palpitar, latejar, pulsar

paltry | pól'trī | *a.* insignificante, miserável

pamper | pam'pə | *vt.* mimar

pamphlet | pam'flit | *s.* folheto; panfleto (esp. político)

pan | pan' | *s.* panela, frigideira, assadeira

pancake | pan'keyk | *s.* panqueca

pandemonium | pandimow'nïəm | *s.* balbúrdia, pandemônio

pander | pan'də | *s.* alcoviteiro / *vt.* alcovitar / *vi.* mostrar-se indulgente

pane | peyn' | *s.* vidraça; painel; almofada (de porta etc.)

panegyric | panəji'rik | *s.* panegírico, elogio

panel | pa'nəl | *s.* almofada (de porta); painel; lista de jurados; júri; painel (mesa-redonda, jurados etc.)

pang | pang' | *s.* pontada, dor cruciante; agonia, tormento, sofrimento, pena

panic | pa'nik | *s.* pânico, terror pânico / *a.* pânico / *vt.* infundir terror pânico a, aterrar / *vi.* ser tomado de pânico

pannier | pa'nïə | *s.* cesto, canastra

panorama | panərʌ'mə | *s.* panorama, vista

pansy | pan'zī | *s.* (bot.) amor--perfeito

pant | pant' | *s.* arquejo, palpitação / *vi.* ofegar, arfar. -**to p. for** ou **after** suspirar por

panther | pan'ϑə | *s.* pantera

pantomime | pan'təmaym | *s.* pantomima; peça produzida no Natal (com cantos, danças etc.)

pantry | pan'trī | *s.* despensa; copa

pants | pants' | *spl.* (coloq.) calças; (coloq.) ceroulas

papacy | pey'pəsī | *s.* papado

papal | pey'pɔl | *a.* papal, pontifical

papaw, pawpaw | pəpó' | *s.* = *papaya*

papaya | pəpay'ə | *s.* mamão; mamoeiro

paper | pey'pə | *s.* papel; jornal; dissertação; documento; relatório; prova escrita / *a.* de, feito de ou semelhante a papel; hipotético / *vt.* empapelar (parede)

paperback | pey'pəbak | *s.* brochura, livro brochado

paper money | pey'pəmânī | *s.* papel-moeda

par | pA' | *s.* (com.) par. **-to be on a p. with** ser igual a / *a.* médio ou normal; (fin.) nominal; (fin.) ao par

parable | pa'rəbəl | *s.* parábola

parachute | pa'rəʃut | *s.* pára-quedas / *vt.* lançar de pára-quedas / *vi.* saltar de pára-quedas

parachutist | pa'rəʃutist | *s.* pára-quedista

parade | pəreyd' | *s.* parada, desfile; ostentação, exibição / *vt.* fazer desfilar; ostentar, alardear / *vi.* desfilar, marchar; exibir-se

parade-ground | pəreyd'grawnd | *s.* praça de armas, local de revistas militares

paradise | pa'rədays | *s.* paraíso

paradox | pa'rədoks | *s.* paradoxo

paradoxical | parədok'sikəl | *a.* paradoxal

paraffin | pa'rəfin | *s.* parafina / *vt.* parafinar

paraffin oil | pa'rəfinoyl | *s.* querosene

paragon | pa'rəgən | *s.* modelo

paragraph | pa'rəgrʌf | *s.* parágrafo

parakeet, parrakeet | pa'rəkit | *s.* periquito

parallel | pa'rəlel | *s.* paralelo / *a.* paralelo, semelhante, análogo.

-to draw a p. estabelecer um paralelo. **-to run p. with** correr paralelo com / *vt.* competir com, rivalizar

paralyse | pa'rəlayz | *vt.* paralisar

paralysed | pa'rəlayzd | *s. a.* paralítico

paralysis | pərə'lisis | *s.* paralisia

paramount | pa'rəmawnt | *a.* superior, supremo, predominante

parapet | pa'rəpit | *s.* parapeito

paraphernalia | parəfəney'lı̃ə | *s.* parafernália; pertences; acessórios; aprestos

paraphrase | pa'rəfreyz | *s.* paráfrase / *vt.* parafrasear

parasite | pa'rəsayt | *s.* parasito

paratroops | pa'rətrups | *spl.* pára-quedistas; paratropa

parcel | pA'səl | *s.* volume, embrulho; lote; encomenda postal / *vt.* empacotar. **-to p. out** repartir, dividir

parch | pAʃ' | *vt.* crestar, queimar; ressecar

parched | pAʃt' | *a.* ressequido

parchment | pAʃ'mənt | *s.* pergaminho

pardon | pA'dən | *s.* perdão; (jur.) indulto. **-I beg your p.** desculpe-me; como?, como disse? / *vt.* perdoar

pardonable | pA'dənəbəl | *a.* perdoável, desculpável

pare | pe'ə | *vt.* aparar; podar; reduzir (despesas)

parentage | pe'ərəntiỹ | *s.* pais; ascendência, origem

parental | pəren'təl | *a.* relativo aos pais

parenthesis | pəren'ϑəsĩs | *s.* parêntese

parents | pe'ərənts | *spl.* pais

pariah | pa'rĩə | *s.* pária

parish | pa'riʃ | *s.* paróquia / *a.* paroquial

parishioner | pəri'ʃənə | *s.* paroquiano

parity | pa'ritī | *s.* paridade

park | pAk' | *s.* parque / *vt.* estacionar (veículo)

parking | pA'king | *s.* estacionamento (de veículos)

parley | pA'lī |s. conferência / vi. parlamentar, conferenciar

parliament | pA'ləmənt | s. parlamento

parlour, parlor | pA'lə |s. sala de visitas; locutório (de convento); salão (de beleza)

parochial | pərow'kĩəl |a. paroquial

parody | pa'rədī |s. paródia

parole | pərowl' | s. palavra de honra; (jur.) livramento condicional; (mil.) senha

parrot | pa'rət |s. papagaio

parry | pa'rī | vt. aparar (golpe); desviar / vi. defender-se

parse | pAz' | vt. (gram.) analisar

parsimonious | pAsimow'niəs | a. parcimonioso, econômico; sovina, avarento

parsley | pAs'lī |s. salsa

parsnip | pAs'nip | s. pastinaga, cenoura-branca

parson | pA'sən | s. pároco, pastor, sacerdote

part | pAt' |s. parte; (teat.) papel; elemento, componente; peça (de máquina etc.). -for my p. quanto a mim. -for the most p. geralmente. -p. and parcel parte integrante. -a man of parts homem de talento. -to take in good p. não levar a mal. -to take the p. of tomar o partido de, defender; desempenhar o papel de. -to do one's p. fazer a sua obrigação / a. parcial / adv. parcialmente / vt. dividir, partir. -to p. company separar-se de. -to p. the hair repartir o cabelo / vi. dividir-se; separar-se; partir; morrer. -to p. with desfazer-se de

partake | pAteyk' | vi. participar de, compartilhar de. -to p. of participar de; comer; beber

partial | pA'šəl | a. parcial. -to be p. to ter predileção por

partiality | pAšĩa'litī |s. parcialidade; predileção

participant | pAti'sipənt | s. participante

participate | pAti'sipeyt | vi. participar, tomar parte

particular | pəti'kĩulə |s. particularidade, pormenor; (pl.) informação. -in p. em particular / a. particular, especial; curioso, estranho; exigente, escrupuloso, cuidadoso; preciso, exato

parting | pA'ting | s. partida; despedida; separação; divisão. -p. of the ways encruzilhada; (fig.) ponto em que se deve tomar uma decisão

parting words | pA'tingwEdz spl. palavras de despedida

partisan, partizan | pAtizan' |s. partidário, adepto; (mil.) guerrilheiro / a. partidário; de guerrilha

partition | pAti'šən | s. divisão; tabique / vt. dividir

partly | pAt'lī | adv. em parte; até certo ponto

partner | pAt'nə |s. sócio; par (de dança); parceiro; cônjuge; companheiro

partnership | pAt'nəšip | s. sociedade

partridge | pA'riĵ |s. perdiz

part-time | pAt'taym | a. de meio expediente; horista

party | pA'tī |s. partido; festa, recepção; (jur.) parte; (mil.) destacamento; (coloq.) sujeito, pessoa

pass | pAs' | s. desfiladeiro; passo, passagem; passe, salvo-conduto; conjuntura, transe, situação difícil; (desp.) passe / vt. vi. passar (por); proferir (sentença). -to p. away falecer; passar. -to p. by passar por cima, não levar em conta; perdoar. -to p. off fazer passar por, impingir. -to p. on transmitir; passar adiante, ir para mais longe. -to p. out (coloq.) desmaiar. -to p. over atravessar, transpor; perdoar, passar em cima; preterir (promoção). -to p. muster ser aprovado ou aceito. -to p. water urinar. -to come to p. acontecer. -to p. the time of day trocar saudações

passable | pʌ'səbəl | *a.* sofrível, tolerável; passável, transitável (estrada)

passage | pa'siɏ | *s.* passagem; trânsito; galeria, corredor; trecho (musical etc.)

passenger | pa'sinjə | *s.* passageiro

passer-by | pasəbay' | *s.* transeunte, passante

passing | pʌ'sing | *s.* o ato de passar, passagem; passamento, falecimento. **-in p.** de passagem

passion | pa'śən | *s.* paixão (tb. maiúsc., ecles.)

passionate | pa'śɒnit | *a.* apaixonado; entusiasmado, arrebatado; violento

passion-fruit | pa'śɒnfrʊt | *s.* maracujá

passive | pa'siv | *s.* (gram.) voz passiva / *a.* passivo

passivity | pəsi'vitɪ | *s.* passividade

Passover | pʌ'sowvə | *s.* páscoa (dos judeus)

passport | pʌs'pót | *s.* passaporte

password | pʌs'wɛd | *s.* senha; santo-e-senha; contra-senha

past | pʌst' | *s.* passado (tb. gram.) / *a.* passado, acontecido; pretérito, passado; ex-; terminado / *prep.* diante de, perante; além de; depois de; sem, fora de. **-a quarter p.** five cinco e um quarto (hora). **-she is p. forty** ela tem mais de quarenta anos

paste | peyst' | *s.* massa; pasta; grude, cola / *vt.* colar, grudar; afixar (cartaz etc.)

pastime | pʌs'taym | *s.* passatempo

pastoral | pʌs'tərəl | *s.* pastoral / *a.* pastoral; pastoril, bucólico

pastry |ˌpeys'trɪ | *s.* pastelaria (massas, tortas etc.)

pasture | pas'śə | *s.* paśto, pastagem / *vt.* apascentar / *vi.* pastar

pat | pat' | *s.* tapa, tapinha; carícia, afago / *a.* oportuno, adequado / *adv.* oportunamente; exatamente / *vt.* tocar levemente, afagar; dar palmadinhas em

patch | paš' | *s.* remendo; mancha; malha (de animal); sinal (na face etc.); pedaço de terreno; retalho. **-it is not a p. on** (coloq.) não se pode comparar com / *vt.* remendar

patent | pey'tɒnt | *s.* patente / *a.* patente, evidente / *vt.* patentear

patent leather | pey'tɒntleðə | *s.* verniz (couro)

paternal | pətɛ'nəl | *a.* paterno

paternity | pətɛ'nitɪ | *s.* paternidade

path | pʌϑ' | *s.* trilha, senda, vereda, picada; (fig.) linha de conduta, procedimento

pathetic, -al | pəϑe'tik(əl) | *a.* comovente, tocante, patético

pathos | pey'ϑos | *s.* patos, patético

patience | pey'śəns | *s.* paciência (tb. lud.)

patient | pey'śənt | *s.* (med.) paciente, doente; (med.) cliente / *a.* paciente, resignado

patrimony | pa'trimənɪ | *s.* patrimônio

patriot | pey'trɪət pa'trɪət | *s.* patriota

patriotic | peytrɪo'tik patrɪo'tik | *a.* patriótico

patriotism | pey'trɪətizəm pa'trɪ̄ətizəm | *s.* patriotismo

patrol | pətrowl' | *s.* patrulha / *vt.* patrulhar

patron | pey'trən | *s.* patrono; protetor, defensor; patrocinador; cliente, freguês

patronage | pey'trənɪj pa'trənɪɏ | *s.* patrocínio; suporte, apoio; clientela; (ecles.) padroado

patronize | pa'trənayz | *vt.* patrocinar; proteger; freqüentar, ser freguês de

patronizing | pa'trənayzing | *a.* com ares protetores

patron saint | pey'trənseynt | *s.* padroeiro (santo)

pattern | pa'tən | *s.* modelo, padrão; molde (de vestido); padrão, desenho decorativo / *vt.* modelar, moldar

paucity | pó'sitɪ | *s.* pequena quantidade; escassez

paunch| pónś' |s. pança, barriga

pauper | pó'pə | s. indigente, mendigo

pause| póz' |s. pausa, intervalo; hesitação / vi. fazer uma pausa; hesitar; calar(-se)

pave| peyv' |vt. calçar, pavimentar; lajear. -to p. the way preparar o terreno para

pavement | peyv'mənt | s. pavimento, calçamento

pavilion | pəvi'lĩən | s. pavilhão; pavilhão auricular

paw| pó' |s. pata; garra / vt. vi. escarvar (cavalo)

pawn| pón' |s. peão (xadrez); penhor, garantia / vt. empenhar. -in p. empenhado

pawnbroker | pón'browkə | s. penhorista, agiota, prestamista

pawnshop | pón'śop | s. casa de penhor

pawn-ticket| pón'tikit |s. cautela de penhor

pay| pey' |s. salário; remuneração; (mil.) soldo. -in the p. of a soldo de / vt. vi. pagar. -to p. attention to prestar atenção a. -to p. back pagar; devolver. -to p. a call ou a visit fazer uma visita. -to p. off saldar (dívida etc.); pagar e despedir (empregado); ajustar contas. -to p. the fiddler ou the piper (coloq.) pagar o pato

payable | pey'əbəl | a. pagável; a pagar

payment | pey'mənt | s. pagamento; recompensa; castigo

pay office | pey'ofis | s. pagadoria, tesouraria

pea| pi' |s. ervilha

peace | pis' | s. paz; calma, tranqüilidade. -to hold ou keep one's p. calar-se

peaceful| pis'ful | a. sossegado, tranqüilo, quieto

peacefulness| pis'fulnes |s. paz, tranqüilidade, quietude

peacemaker| pis'meykə |s. pacificador, mediador

peach| pis' |s. pêssego

peach-tree | piś'tri | s. pessegueiro

peacock| pi'kok |s. pavão

peak| pik' |s. pico, cume; auge, apogeu; pala (de boné)

peak hour | pik'awə | s. hora de trânsito mais intenso, hora do pique (tráfego, trânsito, circulação, atendimento)

peak-load | pik'lowd | s. (eletr.) carga máxima

peal | pil' | s. repique (de sinos); ribombo (trovão); rajada, salva. -p. of laughter gargalhada / vt. vi. repicar; ribombar, soar

peanut| pi'nât | s. amendoim

pear| pe'ə |s. pêra

pearl| pEl' |s. pérola

pear-tree| pe'ətri |s. pereira

peasant | pe'zənt | s. camponês, pequeno agricultor

peat| pit' |s. turfa

pebble| pe'bəl |s. seixo

peck | pek' | s. bicada; (coloq.) beijinho / vt. bicar; beliscar (alimento)

peculiar | pikĩu'lĩə | a. estranho; esquisito; privativo; próprio, característico de

peculiarity| pikĩulĩa'rit̃ |s. peculiaridade; singularidade

pedal| pe'dəl |s. pedal

pedantic | pidan'tik | a. pedante, pedantesco

pedantry| pe'dəntri |s. pedantismo; pedantice

pedestal| pe'distəl |s. pedestal

pedestrian| pides'trĩən |s. pedestre / a. pedestre; (fig.) prosaico, corriqueiro

pedigree| pe'digri |s. linhagem, estirpe

pedigreed | pe'digrid | a. de boa linhagem, de raça pura

pedlar| ped'lə |s. vendedor ambulante

peel | pil' | s. casca (de fruta); pá de forno / vt. descascar, pelar

peep | pip' | vi. pipilar; espreitar

peer | pi'ə |s. par, nobre; igual / vi. examinar, espreitar

peerage| pi'ərij |s. pariato; nobreza; nobiliário

peerless| pɪ'əles |*a.* sem-par, sem igual, incomparável

peevish| pɪ'viš | *a.* rabugento, mal-humorado

peg| peg' |*s.* cavilha; cabide; pequena estaca; (fig.) pretexto, ocasião

pelican| pe'likən |*s.* pelicano

pellet | pe'lit |*s.* pílula; bolinha; bago de chumbo

pell-mell | pelmel' |*s.* confusão, desordem / *a.* confuso, tumultuado / *adv.* confusamente, em desordem; atropeladamente, de roldão

pelt | pelt' |*s.* pele, peliça / *vt.* atirar (pedras etc.) a; (fig.) cobrir, crivar / *vi.* bater, martelar; cair torrencialmente

pen | pen' |*s.* pena (de escrever); cercado (para animais) / *vt.* escrever, redigir; cercar, encurralar

penal | pɪ'nəl | *a.* penal

penalize | pɪ'nəlayz | *vt.* tornar punível; impor penalidade

penal servitude | pɪ'nəlsɛ'vitȟud | *s.* prisão com trabalhos forçados

penalty | pe'nəltī |*s.* penalidade, punição; multa; (desp.) pênalti, penalidade

penance | pe'nəns |*s.* penitência

pencil | pen'səl |*s.* lápis. -in p. a lápis

pencil-case | pen'səlkeys |*s.* portalápis, lapiseira

pencil-sharpener | pen'səlšʌ'pənə |*s.* apontador de lápis

pending| pen'ding |*a.* pendente; iminente / *prep.* durante, enquanto; à espera de, até

pendulum| pen'dȟuləm |*s.* pêndulo

penetrate | pe'nitreyt | *vt. vi.* penetrar, entrar em

penetrating| pe'nitreyting |*a.* penetrante, forte (cheiro); (fig.) agudo, perspicaz

penetration | penitrey'šən | *s.* penetração

penguin | pen'gwin |*s.* pingüim

peninsula| penin'sȟulə |*s.* península

penitence| pe'nitəns |*s.* penitência, arrependimento

penitent | pe'nitənt | *a.* penitente

penitentiary | peniten'šərī | *s.* penitenciária

penknife| pen'nayf |*s.* canivete

pen-name| pen'neym |*s.* pseudônimo literário

pennant | pe'nənt | *s.* flâmula, bandeirola

penny | pe'nī |*s.* pêni; (EUA) centavo

pension | pen'šən | *s.* pensão, aposentadoria, subsídio / *vt.* pensionar. -to p. off aposentar

pensioner| pen'šənə |*s.* pensionista

pensive | pen'siv | *a.* pensativo; preocupado

penthouse| pent'haws |*s.* telheiro, alpendre; cobertura (apartamento); toldo, marquise

pent-up | pent'âp | *a.* contido, reprimido

penultimate | penâl'timit | *a.* penúltimo

penury| pe'nȟurī |*s.* penúria, indigência, miséria

people | pɪ'pəl |*s.* povo; gente / *vt.* povoar

pepper | pe'pə |*s.* pimenta

peppermint | pe'pəmint |*s.* hortelã-pimenta (tb. pastilha)

per| pə |*prep.* por, mediante; por cada. -as p. conforme

perambulator | pəram'bȟuleytə | *s.* carrinho de bebê

perceive | pɛsiv' | *vt.* perceber, compreender; ver

percentage| pɛsen'tiȟ |*s.* percentagem, porcentagem

perceptible | pɛsep'tibəl | *a.* perceptível; visível

perception | pɛsep'šən | *s.* percepção

perch| pɛš' |*s.* (ict.) perca; poleiro / *vi.* empoleirar-se; pousar (aves)

percolate | pɛ'kəleyt | *vt.* coar; filtrar / *vi.* coar-se; filtrar-se

percussion | pɛkâ'šən |*s.* percussão

perdition | pɛdi'šən |*s.* perdição

peremptory | pəremp'tərī | *a.* peremptório; dogmático; ditatorial, autoritário

perennial | pəre'nĭəl | *a.* perene, permanente

perfect | pE'fikt | *a.* perfeito / | pEfekt' | *vt.* aperfeiçoar

perfection | pEfek'śən | *s.* perfeição

perfectly | pE'fiktlĭ | *adv.* perfeitamente; completamente

perfidious | pEfi'dĭəs | *a.* pérfido, desleal, falso

perfidy | pE'fidĭ | *s.* perfídia

perforate | pE'fəreyt | *vt.* perfurar / *vi.* penetrar

perform | pəfóm' | *vt.* (teat.) representar; executar; desempenhar; realizar / *vi.* executar; atuar; funcionar (máquina)

performance | pəfó'məns | *s.* (teat.) representação; (mús.) execução; recital, récita; exibição (filme); realização; desempenho; proeza, feito

performer | pəfó'mə | *s.* ator, atriz; executante, músico

perfume | pE'fĭum | *s.* perfume / *vt.* perfumar

perfunctory | pəfânk'tərĭ | *a.* perfunctório, superficial; negligente, indiferente

perhaps | pəhaps' | *adv.* talvez

peril | pe'ril | *s.* perigo

perilous | pe'riləs | *a.* perigoso, arriscado

period | pɪ'rĭəd | *s.* período; ponto (no fim de uma frase); ciclo, época; era

periodical | pirĭo'dikəl | *s.* periódico, publicação periódica / *a.* periódico

periphery | pəri'fərĭ | *s.* periferia

periscope | pe'riskowp | *s.* periscópio

perish | pe'riś | *vi.* perecer, morrer; deteriorar

perishable | pe'riśəbəl | *s.* (ger. *pl.*) gêneros deterioráveis / *a.* perecível

perjury | pE'ĵərĭ | *s.* perjúrio; falso testemunho

perky | pE'kĭ | *a.* vivo, ativo

permanence | pE'mənəns | *s.* permanência

permanent | pE'mənənt | *a.* permanente

permeate | pE'mĭeyt | *vt.* permear; penetrar; impregnar

permissible | pəmi'sibəl | *a.* permissível, admissível

permission | pəmi'śən | *s.* permissão, autorização

permit | pE'mit | *s.* licença, permissão / *vt.* permitir, consentir, autorizar; tolerar

permutation | pEmĭutey'śən | *s.* permutação

pernicious | pEni'səs | *a.* pernicioso

pernickety | pEni'kətĭ | *a.* (coloq.) exigente demais; impertinente; espinhoso

peroration | perərey'śən | *s.* peroração

perpendicular | pEpəndi'kĭulə | *a.* perpendicular

perpetrate | pE'pitreyt | *vt.* perpetrar, praticar (ato condenável)

perpetrator | pE'pitreytə | *s.* autor (de ato condenável)

perpetual | pEpe'tĭuəl | *a.* perpétuo

perpetuate | pEpe'tĭueyt | *vt.* perpetuar, eternizar

perplex | pEpleks' | *vt.* deixar perplexo, confundir

perplexed | pEplekst' | *a.* perplexo; desconcertado

perplexing | pEplek'sing | *a.* embaraçoso, desconcertante

perplexity | pEplek'sitĭ | *s.* perplexidade

perquisite | pE'kwizit | *s.* emolumento, lucro eventual; gratificação habitual; rendimento; remuneração

persecute | pE'sikĭut | *vt.* perseguir, oprimir; atormentar

persecution | pEsikĭu'śən | *s.* perseguição; opressão

perseverance | pEsivĭ'ərəns | *s.* perseverança, persistência

persevere | pEsivĭ'ə | *vi.* perseverar, persistir

persevering | pɛsivı'ɔring | *a.* perseverante, persistente

Persian | pɛ'śɔn | *s. a.* persa

persimmon | pɔsi'mɔn | *s.* caqui; caquizeiro

persist | pɛsist' | *vi.* persistir

persistence | pɔsis'tɔns | *s.* persistência

persistent | pɔsis'tɔnt | *a.* persistente; insistente; permanente, contínuo

person | pɛ'sɔn | *s.* pessoa, indivíduo

personage | pɛ'sɔnij | *s.* personagem

personal | pɛ'sɔnɔl | *a.* pessoal

personal effects | pɛ'sɔnɔlifekts' | *s.* objetos de uso pessoal

personality | pɛsɔna'litĩ | *s.* personalidade

personify | pɛso'nifay | *vt.* personificar

personnel | pɛsɔnel' | *s.* pessoal, corpo de empregados

perspective | pɛspek'tiv | *s.* perspectiva

perspicacious | pɛspikey'śɔs | *a.* perspicaz, sagaz, astuto

perspicacity | pɛspika'sitĩ | *s.* perspicácia, argúcia

perspiration | pɛspirey'śɔn | *s.* suor, transpiração

perspire | pɛspay'ɔ | *vi.* suar, transpirar

persuade | pɛsweyd' | *vt.* persuadir, convencer

persuasion | pɛswey'jɔn | *s.* persuasão; convicção, crença, credo

persuasive | pɛswey'ziv | *a.* persuasivo, convincente

pert | pɛt' | *a.* petulante, atrevido, descarado; (coloq.) animado, esperto

pertain | pɛteyn' | *vi.* pertencer; concernir, dizer respeito, referir-se

pertinacious | pɛtiney'śɔs | *a.* pertinaz

pertinacity | pɛtina'sitĩ | *s.* pertinácia

pertinent | pɛ'tinent | *a.* perti-

nente; concernente

pertness | pɛt'nes | *s.* petulância, atrevimento

perturb | pɛtɛb' | *vt.* perturbar, transtornar

perturbation | pɛtɛbey'śɔn | *s.* perturbação, transtorno; desordem; confusão; agitação

perusal | pɔrʊ'zɔl | *s.* leitura atenta, exame

peruse | pɔrʊz' | *vt.* ler atentamente, examinar, estudar com vagar

pervade | pɛveyd' | *vt.* difundir-se em, impregnar, saturar, penetrar

pervasive | pɛvey'siv | *a.* penetrante; difuso

perverse | pɔvɛs' | *a.* perverso; persistente no erro; malvado; contra as provas (veredicto)

perversion | pɔvɛ'jɔn | *s.* perversão; corrupção; deturpação

perversity | pɔvɛ'sitĩ | *s.* obstinação; impertinência; maldade, perversidade

pervert | pɔvɛt' | *s.* pervertido (esp. sexual) / *vt.* perverter, depravar, corromper

pessimism | pe'simizɔm | *s.* pessimismo

pessimist | pe'simist | *s.* pessimista

pessimistic | pesimis'tik | *a.* pessimista

pest | pest' | *s.* peste, praga; pessoa importuna; coisa nociva; inseto ou animal nocivo

pester | pes'tɔ | *vt.* importunar, incomodar

pestilence | pes'tilɔns | *s.* peste (esp. bubônica)

pestilential | pestilen'śɔl | *a.* pestilencial; pernicioso

pestle | pe'sɔl | *s.* mão de almofariz, pilão

pet | pet' | *s.* animal de estimação; mau humor, amuo / *a.* favorito; especial / *vt.* afagar, acariciar

petal | pe'tɔl | *s.* pétala

pet dog | pet'dog | *s.* cãozinho de estimação

peter | pɪ'tə | vi. (gír.) enfraque-cer-se, esgotar-se. **-to p. out** (co-loq.) desaparecer aos pouços

petition | pəti'ʃən | s. petição, re-querimento; súplica / vt. dirigir requerimento ou petição a; ro-gar / vi. peticionar

petitioner | pəti'ʃənə | s. peticio-nário; requerente

pet name | pe'neym | s. apelido carinhoso, hipocorístico

petrify | pe'trifay | vt. petrificar

petrol | pe'trəl | s. gasolina

petroleum | pətrow'liəm | s. petróleo

petrol-pump | pe'trəlpâmp | s. bomba de gasolina

petticoat | pe'tikowt | s. anágua / a. feminino

pettifogging | pe'tifoging | a. chi-canista, velhaco

pettiness | pe'tines | s. insignifi-cância, mesquinhez, banalida-de; intolerância

petty | pe'ʧi | a. insignificante, mesquinho, trivial

petty larceny | pe'ʧilAsənɪ | s. (jur.) furto de pouca monta

petty officer | pe'ʧio'fisə | s. (náut.) suboficial

petulant | pe'ʧiulənt | a. mal-hu-morado, rabugento

pew | pɪu' | s. banco (de igreja). **-take a p.** (coloq.) sente-se

pewter | pɪu'tə | s. peltre, liga de estanho; (gír.) taça que se ganha como prêmio

phalanx | fa'lənks | s. falange

phantom | fan'təm | s. fantas-ma / a. fantasmal

pharmaceutical | fAməʃiu'tikəl | a. farmacêutico

phase | feyz' | s. fase; período. **-out of p.** (eletr.) em defasa-gem; em desarmonia

pheasant | fe'zənt | s. faisão

phenomenal | fino'minəl | a. fenomenal

phenomenon | fino'minən | s. fenômeno

philander | filan'də | vi. namo-rar, flertar (diz-se de homem)

philanthropic | filənϑro'pik | a. filantrópico, humanitário

philanthropist | filan'ϑrəpist | s. filantropo

philanthropy | filan'ϑrəpɪ | s. fi-lantropia

philately | fila'təlɪ | s. filatelia

philologist | filo'ləʝist | s. filólogo

philology | filo'ləʝɪ | s. filologia

philosopher | filo'səfə | s. filósofo

philosophic | filəso'fik | a. filosó-fico

philosophy | filo'səfɪ | s. filosofia

phlegm | flem' | s. catarro, expec-toração; fleuma, calma

phlegmatic | flegma'tik | a. fleu-mático, calmo; apático

phoenix | fɪ'niks | s. fênix

phone | fown' | s. telefone; (gram.) fonema / vt. vi. telefonar

phonetic | fowne'tik | a. fonético

phonetician | fowniti'ʃən | s. foneticista

phonetics | fowne'tiks | s. fonética

phoney, phony | fow'nɪ | s. (gír.) coisa ou pessoa falsa / a. (gír.) falso, falsificado

phosphorescence | fosfəre'səns | s. fosforescência

photograph | fow'təgrAf | s. fo-tografia / vt. fotografar

photographer | fəto'grəfə | s. fotógrafo

photography | fəto'grəfɪ | s. foto-grafia

phrase | freyz' | s. frase / vt. vi. frasear, exprimir com frases

physical | fi'zikəl | a. físico

physician | fizi'ʃən | s. médico

physicist | fi'zisist | s. físico

physics | fi'ziks | s. física

physiognomy | fizio'nəmɪ | s. fisio-nomia; semblante; aparência

physiological | fiziəlo'ʝikəl | a. fisiológico

physiology | fizio'ləʝɪ | s. fisiologia

physique | fizik' | s. físico, com-pleição, corpo

pianist | pɪ'ənist | s. pianista

piano | pɪa'now | s. piano

piano-stool | pɪa'nowstʋl | s. banço de piano

pick | pik' | *s.* picareta; colheita; (fig.) nata, escol / *vt.* apanhar, colher; escolher; palitar (dentes); esgaravatar, escarafunchar. **-to p. off** tirar, apanhar. **-to p. on** (coloq.) atormentar. **-to p. out** escolher; reconhecer, distinguir; indicar, apontar; avistar, enxergar. **-to p. up** apanhar; recolher; captar, pegar; melhorar (saúde). **-to p. a quarrel with** puxar briga com, procurar questões com

pickaxe, pickax | pik'aks | *s.* picareta / *vt. vi.* trabalhar com picareta

picket | pi'kit | *s.* estaca; (mil.) piquete; grevista / *vt.* (mil.) guardar com piquete; rondar; impedir a entrada (grevista), fazer piquete

pickle | pi'kəl | *s.* escabeche; (*pl.*) picles. **-to be in a p.** estar em maus lençóis; estar em desordem (coisas) / *vt.* pôr de escabeche; conservar em vinagre

pick-me-up | pik'miāp | *s.* (coloq.) estimulante, trago de bebida alcoólica

pickpocket | pik'pokit | *s.* batedor de carteiras

picnic | pik'nik | *s.* piquenique / *vi.* fazer um piquenique

pictorial | pikto'riəl | *s.* revista ou jornal ilustrado / *a.* pictórico; pitoresco

picture | pik'šə | *s.* quadro, imagem; estampa; ilustração, figura; fotografia, filme; visão, idéia / *vt.* pintar; fotografar; descrever; imaginar

picturesque | pikšəresk' | *a.* pitoresco

pie | pay' | *s.* torta; empadão, pastelão. **-as p.** (coloq.) muito fácil, sopa

piece | pis' | *s.* pedaço; peça (de fazenda, de artilharia, de xadrez, musical, teatral). **-a p. of advice** um conselho. **-a p. of news** uma notícia. **-a p. of work** uma obra, um trabalho. **-of a p.**

da mesma qualidade. **-to take to pieces** desmontar / *vt.* acrescentar partes ou peças; remendar; juntar. **-to p. together** consertar, reconstituir

piecemeal | pis'mil | *adv.* peça por peça, pouco a pouco

piece of cloth | pis'ovkloϑ | *s.* corte de fazenda

piece-work | pis'wεk | *s.* trabalho por tarefa

pier | pi'ə | *s.* cais, embarcadouro; píer; cais flutuante; pilar de ponte

pierce | pi'əs | *vt.* perfurar; penetrar; (fig.) afligir, trespassar

piercing | pi'əsing | *a.* penetrante, cortante (vento); estridente, agudo (grito); pungente (sofrimento, pena)

pierrot | pi'ərow | *s.* pierrô; menestrel itinerante; comediante

piety | pay'əti | *s.* piedade, religiosidade; ato piedoso

piffle | pi'fəl | *s.* (gír.) disparate / *vi.* dizer disparates ou tolices

pig | pig' | *s.* porco

pigeon | pi'jən | *s.* pombo

pigheaded | pig'hedid | *a.* obstinado; teimoso, cabeçudo

pigment | pig'mənt | *s.* pigmento

pigmy | pig'mī | *s.* pigmeu

pigtail | pig'teyl | *s.* fumo em corda; rabicho (de chinês); rabo--de-cavalo (cabelo)

pike | payk' | *s.* pique, chuço; (ict.) lúcio; pedágio, estrada de pedágio

pile | payl' | *s.* pilha, montão; pilha, bateria; estaca; (*pl.*) hemorróidas / *vt.* empilhar, amontoar; estacar / *vi.* amontoar-se

pilfer | pil'fə | *vt.* surripiar, surrupiar, furtar

pilfering | pil'fəring | *s.* furto

pilgrim | pil'grim | *s.* peregrino

pilgrimage | pil'grimij | *s.* peregrinação, romaria

pill | pil' | *s.* pílula, comprimido

pillage | pi'lij | *s.* pilhagem / *vt.* pilhar, saquear

pillar | pi'lə | *s.* pilar, coluna.

-from p. to post de Herodes para Pilatos

pillar-box | pi'ləboks | *s.* marco postal, caixa de correio

pillar-box red | pi'ləboks red | *s. a.* vermelho vivo

pillory | pi'lərī | *s.* pelourinho

pillow | pi'low | *s.* travesseiro

pillowcase | pi'lowkeys | *s.* fronha

pillowsleep | pi'lowslıp | *s.* fronha

pilot | pay'lət | *s.* piloto / *vt.* pilotar

pimp | pimp' | *s.* alcoviteiro, proxeneta / *vi.* alcovitar

pimple | pim'pəl | *s.* espinha (da pele), acne

pin | pin' | *s.* alfinete; pino; grampo de cabelo; broche; (fig.) ninharia. **-to be on pins and needles** estar ansioso para, estar louco para / *vt.* prender com alfinete; alfinetar. **-to p. someone down** (coloq.) obrigar alguém a cumprir uma promessa, pegar na palavra

pinafore | pi'nəfó | *s.* espécie de avental (vestuário infantil ou feminino)

pincers | pin'səz | *spl.* tenaz, torquês

pinch | pinš' | *s.* beliscão; pitada. **-in a p.** (coloq.) num aperto / *vt.* beliscar; atormentar, extorquir; (gír.) surripiar, furtar

pincushion | pin'kušən | *s.* almofada de alfinetes

pine | payn' | *s.* pinheiro / *vi.* definhar, enfraquecer; diminuir; ansiar. **-to p. for** suspirar por

pineapple | pay'napəl | *s.* abacaxi, ananás; (gír.) granada de mão

pine-cone | payn'kown | *s.* pinha

pinion | pi'niən | *s.* segmento terminal de asa; (poét.) asa / *vt.* amarrar, prender

pink | pink' | *s.* (bot.) cravo / *a.* cor-de-rosa, rosado

pin-money | pin'mânī | *s.* dinheiro miúdo, caixa-pequena

pinnacle | pi'nəkəl | *s.* pináculo,

píncaro, cume; (fig.) auge, culminância

pinpoint | pin'poynt | *s.* ponta de alfinete / *vt.* apontar com precisão; definir exatamente

pioneer | payənı'ə | *s.* pioneiro; (mil.) sapador / *vt.* ser pioneiro em ou de

pious | pay'əs | *a.* pio, piedoso, devoto

pip | pip' | *s.* caroço, semente, pevide; sinal sonoro / *vi.* piar

pipe | payp' | *s.* tubo, cano, canudo; cachimbo; flauta / *vi.* tocar instrumento de sopro. **-to p. down** calar a boca. **-to p. up** começar a tocar, cantar ou falar. **-to p. one's eyes** chorar

piper | pay'pə | *s.* flautista; tocador de gaita de foles

piquant | pı'kənt | *a.* picante; estimulante

pique | pık' | *s.* ressentimento, amuo; melindre

piqued | pıkt' | *a.* amuado

piquet | pi'kit | *s.* piquê (jogo de cartas)

piracy | pay'rəsī | *s.* pirataria

pirate | pay'rit | *s.* pirata

piratical | payra'tikəl | *a.* de pirata, de corsário

pistol | pis'təl | *s.* pistola

piston | pis'tən | *s.* êmbolo, pistão (de motor etc.)

pit | pit' | *s.* cova, buraco; armadilha; poço de mina; (teat.) platéia (esp. últimas filas); fosso da orquestra; (EUA) caroço (de fruta). **-p. of the stomach** boca do estômago / *vt.* pôr, lançar, guardar em buraco ou fosso; (EUA) descaroçar

pitch | pıš' | *s.* piche; breu; (desp.) lance, arremesso; altura do som, tom de voz; (mús.) diapasão / *vt.* armar (barraca); (desp.) atirar, lançar / *vi.* acampar; arfar (o navio). **-to p. into** atacar com vigor. **-to p. forward** cair de cabeça

pitcher | pi'šə | *s.* jarro, cântaro

pitchfork | piš'fók | *s.* forcado

pitfall | pit'fól | s. armadilha, cilada, laço

pitiful | pi'tiful | a. piedoso; lamentável

pitiless | pi'tiles | a. desapiedado, impiedoso

pittance | pi'təns | s. mesada ou remuneração miserável; bagatela, insignificância

pitted | pi'tid | a. descaroçado (ameixa, tâmara etc.)

pity | pi'tī | s. compaixão, piedade. **-what a p.!** que pena! / vt. compadecer-se de, ter pena de

pivot | pi'vət | s. pino, eixo / vi. girar em torno de um eixo

placard | pla'kʌd | s. cartaz

placate | pləkeyt' | vt. aplacar, apaziguar

place | pleys' | s. lugar; local, ponto; localidade, cidade; residência, casa; emprego, colocação; lugar, colocação (corridas etc.). **-p. of birth** naturalidade. **-all over the p.** por toda a parte. **-to take p.** acontecer, ter lugar. **-in p.** apropriado; oportuno. **-out of p.** deslocado; inoportuno. **-to put someone in his p.** pôr alguém em seu lugar, corrigir a arrogância de alguém / vt. colocar, pôr, meter; fazer (uma encomenda) / vi. (desp.) colocar-se entre os vencedores; aplicar (dinheiro)

placid | pla'sid | a. plácido, sossegado, sereno, tranqüilo

plagiarize | pley'jərayz | vt. plagiar

plague | pleyg' | s. peste; praga (de insetos) / vt. atormentar; importunar

plaice | pleys' | s. (ict.) linguado

plain | pleyn' | s. planície / a. claro, evidente; simples; modesto; comum; franco; desgracioso, feio. **-in p. clothes** à paisana. **-in p. English** em bom inglês

plaintiff | pleyn'tif | s. (jur.) autor, queixoso, querelante

plaintive | pleyn'tiv | a. lamentoso; triste, melancólico

plait | pleyt' | s. trança / vt. trançar

plan | plan' | s. plano; esboço; projeto, planta / vt. planejar / vi. fazer planos

plane | pleyn' | s. plano; nível; plaina; avião / a. plano, liso / vt. aplainar / vi. trabalhar com plaina; planar (avião)

planet | pla'nit | s. planéta

planetary | pla'nitrī | a. planetário

plank | plank' | s. prancha

planner | pla'nə | s. planejador, projetista

planning | pla'ning | s. planificação

plant | plʌnt | s. (bot.) planta; fábrica; aparelhagem, instalação / vt. plantar; estabelecer, colocar; fundar

plantation | plantey'şən | s. plantação; fazenda

planter | plʌn'tə | s. plantador, fazendeiro

plaque | plak' | s. placa; lápide; distintivo

plaster | plʌs'tə | s. estuque, reboco; (med.) emplastro / vt. estucar, rebocar

plasterer | plʌs'tərə | s. estucador

plaster of Paris | plʌs'təovpa'ris | s. gesso

plastic | plas'tik | s. a. plástico

plate | pleyt' | s. placa; chapa; cliché, ilustração; prato; baixela; (ecles.) coleta; chapa, dentadura postiça / vt. chapear (de ouro, prata etc.); blindar

plateau | pla'tow | s. platô, planalto

platform | plat'fóm | s. plataforma; tablado, estrado

platitude | pla'tit̆ud | s. lugar-comum, chavão

platitudinous | platitĭu'dinəs | a. banal, trivial

platoon | plətʊn' | s. pelotão

plaudits | pló'dits | spl. aplauso, aclamação

plausible | pló'zibəl | a. plausível; insinuante e falso (pessoa)

play | pley' | s. jogo; divertimento; atuação, funcionamento; (mec.) folga; liberdade de ação;

(teat.) peça, drama. **-a p. on
words**trocadilho. **-to bring into
p.** pôr em jogo; pôr em movi-
mento. **-to give free p.** to dar lar-
gas a / *vt.* jogar; (mús.) tocar;
(teat.) representar. **-to p. the
part of** fazer o papel de. **-to p. a
trick on** pregar uma peça a. **-to
p. the game** comportar-se leal-
mente / *vi.* jogar; brincar. **-to p.
at** tomar parte em; fingir ser ou
fazer algo. **-to p. for time** ganhar tempo. **-to p. up to** (coloq.) adular. **-played out** gasto;
exausto; antiquado; liquidado

player | pley'ə | *s.* jogador; músi-
co, tocador; ator

playful | pley'ful | *a.* brincalhão,
alegre

playgoer | pley'gowə | *s.* freqüen-
tador de teatros

playground | pley'grawnd | *s.* pá-
tio de recreio (esp. de escola);
lugar de recreação

playhouse | pley'haws | *s.* teatro;
casa de brinquedo

playing-field | pley'ingfɪld | *s.*
campo de esportes

playmate | pley'meyt | *s.* compa-
nheiro de jogos

plaything | pley'ɵing | *s.* brin-
quedo

playwright | pley'rayt | *s.* drama-
turgo, comediógrafo

plea | plı' | *s.* apelo, súplica; des-
culpa, justificativa; (jur.) ale-
gação

plead | plɪd' | *vt.* pleitear; alegar;
(jur.) declarar-se (inocente
etc.); interceder, suplicar

pleasant | ple'zənt | *a.* agradável;
prazenteiro, alegre

pleasantry | ple'zəntrī | *s.* grace-
jo, brincadeira

please | plız' | *vt.* agradar, con-
tentar, dar prazer a. **-p. God** se
Deus quiser. **-to p. oneself** fazer
o que se deseja. **-I should be
pleased** to teria muito prazer
em. **-to be pleased with** estar
contente com / *vi.* ser agradável.
-if you p. faça o favor, tenha a

bondade, com a sua permissão

pleasing | plı'zing | *a.* agradável

pleasurable | ple'jərəbəl | *a.* pra-
zeroso, agradável

pleasure | ple'jə | *s.* prazer, delei-
te, gozo; vontade, desejo; re-
creio, passatempo

pleasure-boat | ple'jəbowt | *s.*
barco de recreio

plebeian | plibı'ən | *s. a.* plebeu

plebiscite | ple'bisit | *s.* plebiscito

pledge | plej' | *s.* promessa; voto;
garantia, penhor / *vt.* empe-
nhar, penhorar

plentiful | plen'tiful | *a.* abun-
dante, copioso, farto

plenty | plen'tī | *s.* abundância,
fartura. **-p. of** muito, grande
quantidade. **-that is p.** basta

pleurisy | plu'risī | *s.* pleurisia

pliable | play'əbəl | *a.* flexível;
dobradiço

pliers | play'əz | *spl.* alicate

plight | playt' | *s.* situação difícil,
transe / *vt.* comprometer-se a

plod | plod' | *vi.* mover-se pesa-
damente; labutar

plot | plot' | *s.* porção, pedaço,
lote (de terreno); enredo (de romance etc.); conspiração, con-
juração / *vt.* traçar mapa; fazer
gráfico de; tramar; planejar
(enredo) / *vi.* conspirar

plotter | plo'tə | *s.* conspirador

plough | plaw' | *s.* arado, char-
rua; (astron.) Ursa Maior / *vt.*
arar, lavrar; sulcar. **-to p. the
seas** sulcar os mares. **-to p. back**
(fig.) reinvestir (lucros)

ploughing | plaw'ing | *s.* lavoura

ploughman | plaw'mən | *s.* lavrador

plow | plaw' | *s.* = *plough*

pluck | plâk' | *s.* arranco, puxão;
coragem; ânimo, valor / *vt.* co-
lher, apanhar; depenar; (mús.)
dedilhar. **-to p. up courage** criar
coragem, cobrar ânimo

plug | plâg' | *s.* tampão; batoque;
(eletr.) plugue, tomada / *vt.*
tampar, tapar; inserir (tomada). **-to p. in** fazer ligação
elétrica

plum | plâm' | s. ameixa; ameixeira

plumage | plʊ'miȝ | s. plumagem

plumb | plâm' | s. prumo / vt. sondar

plumber | plâ'mə | s. bombeiro, encanador; funileiro

plumb-line | plâm'layn | s. fio de prumo

plum-cake | plâm'keyk | s. bolo inglês (com ameixas, passas etc.)

plump | plâmp' | a. rechonchudo, roliço; direto, franco

plum pudding | plâm'puding | s. pudim de passas (tradicionalmente servido no Natal)

plunder | plân'də | s. saque, pilhagem / vt. saquear, pilhar

plunge | plânj' | s. mergulho. -to take the p. arriscar-se / vt. mergulhar; lançar, precipitar / vi. mergulhar ou afundar-se em

plural | plu'ərəl | s. plural

plus | plâs' | s. sinal de somar / a. adicional; (coloq.) extra / prep. mais

ply | play' | s. camada; espessura; fio; tendência / vt. dobrar, torcer; exercer; encher de, cumular de; transitar (navio, ônibus etc.) / vi. ocupar-se com

pneumatic | nĩuma'tik | a. pneumático

pneumonia | nĩumow'nĩə | s. pneumonia

poach | powš' | vt. furtar (caça ou peixe); caçar ou pescar ilicitamente; escaldar, escalfar (ovos) / vi. invadir (terras alheias)

poacher | pow'šə | s. caçador ou pescador furtivo

pock | pok' | s. pústula (esp. de varíola)

pocket | po'kit | s. bolso; cavidade; foco (de resistência, doença etc.). -in one's p. totalmente sob a influência de alguém. -out of p. gasto, perdido / vt. embolsar; reprimir (afronta)

pocket-book | po'kitbuk | s. caderno de notas; carteira (de dinheiro)

pocket-knife | po'kitnayf | s. canivete

pock-market | pok'mʌkit | a. bexigoso, marcado de varíola

pod | pod' | s. vagem; casulo de bicho-da-seda

podgy | po'jĩ | a. atarracado, socado, rechonchudo

poem | pow'im | s. poema, poesia

poet | pow'it | s. poeta

poetic | powe'tik | a. poético

poetry | pow'itrĩ | s. poesia

poignancy | poy'nənsĩ | s. pungência; sabor picante; mordacidade

poignant | poy'nənt | a. pungente; comovente, tocante

point | poynt' | s. ponto; ponta, extremidade; assunto, caso, questão; (pl.) agulha de chave. -p. of view ponto de vista. -to be on the p. of estar a ponto de. -to come to the p. vir ao caso. -to be beside the p. ser irrelevante. -to make a p. of fazer questão de. -there is no p. in não há razão para. -that is not to the p. isso não vem ao caso. -to stretch ou to strain a p. fazer uma concessão / vt. pontuar; apontar; aguçar / vi. apontar para; indicar; insinuar

pointed | poyn'tid | a. aguçado, pontiagudo; picante, penetrante (observação)

pointless | poynt'les | a. despropositado, sem sentido

poise | poyz' | s. equilíbrio, estabilidade; porte; pausa; indecisão / vi. estar equilibrado; pairar

poison | poy'zən | s. veneno / a. venenoso / vt. envenenar, intoxicar

poison gas | poy'zəngas | s. gás asfixiante

poisonous | poy'zənəs | a. venenoso, tóxico

poke | powk' | s. empurrão; aguilhoada / vt. meter, empurrar; atiçar (fogo). -to p. fun at zombar de. -to p. one's nose into

meter o nariz em / *vi.* cutucar;
intrometer-se

poker | pow'kə | *s.* atiçador; pôquer
(jogo de cartas)

poky | pow'kī | *a.* pequeno, acanhado (aposento)

pole | powl' | *s.* (geog.) pólo; vara;
haste; poste; mastro; (maiúsc.)
polonês. **-poles apart** em pólos
opostos, em extremos diametralmente opostos

polemics | pole'miks | *spl.* polêmica, controvérsia

police | pəlīs' | *s.* polícia / *a.* policial / *vt.* policiar

policeman | pəlīs'mən | *s.* policial, guarda

police station | pəlīs'steysən | *s.*
delegacia de polícia

policewoman | pəlīs'wəmən | *s.*
policial (feminina)

policy | po'lisī | *s.* política; sistema, plano de ação; diplomacia;
apólice (de seguro)

polish | po'liś | *s.* brilho, polimento; pasta para polimento;
(fig.) polidez, urbanidade / *vt.*
polir; dar brilho a (sapatos
etc.). **-to p. off** engolir, devorar; acabar; dar o toque final; livrar-se de (competidor etc.);
dar cabo de (inimigo). **-to p. up**
(coloq.) aperfeiçoar, aprimorar

Polish | pow'liś | *s. a.* polonês

polished | po'liśt | *a.* polido; elegante, refinado

polite | pəlayt' | *a.* polido, cortês

politeness | pəlayt'nes | *s.* polidez, cortesia

politic | po'litik | *a.* político; diplomático; oportunista

political | pəli'tikəl | *a.* político

politician | politi'śən | *s.* político

politics | po'litiks | *spl.* política

poll | powl' | *s.* votação (eleição);
apuração, contagem de votos;
(*pl.*, EUA) local de votação /
vt. votar; receber votos; recolher votos / *vi.* votar em eleição

polling | pow'ling | *s.* votação

poll-tax | powl'taks | *s.* taxa *per*

capita; (EUA) taxa cobrada a
votantes

pollute | pəllut' | *vt.* poluir; contaminar; corromper

pollution | pəllū'śən | *s.* poluição;
contaminação

pomegranate | po'migranit | *s.*
romã; romãzeira, romeira

pomp | pomp' | *s.* pompa, fausto

pompous | pom'pəs | *a.* pomposo; afetado, pretensioso; empolado, bombástico

pond | pond' | *s.* pequeno açude,
reservatório, tanque

ponder | pon'də | *vt.* ponderar,
considerar. **-to p. on** meditar
sobre, pensar em

ponderous | pon'dərəs | *a.* pesado, maciço; trabalhoso, enfadonho; tedioso (estilo)

pontiff | pon'tif | *s.* pontífice

pontoon | pontʊn' | *s.* barca (de
fundo chato); ponte de barcas
ou de cilindros metálicos

pony | pow'nī | *s.* pônei

poodle | pʊ'dəl | *s. poodle*, *caniche*, cão-d'água

pool | pʊl' | *s.* poça d'água; píscina; poço (em rio); tanque, lago
(artificial); poça (de sangue);
bolo, fundo comum; bilhar;
(EUA) sinuca / *vt.* reunir, agrupar; contribuir para um fundo
comum

poop | pʊp' | *s.* popa

poor | pu'ə | *a.* pobre; inferior, de
má qualidade; fraco, insatisfatório. **-to take a p. view of** olhar
com pessimismo ou desagrado.
-p. thing! coitado!, coitadinho!

poorly | pu'əlī | *a.* indisposto,
adoentado / *adv.* insuficientemente, imperfeitamente

poor-spirited | puəspi'ritid | *a.* tímido, pusilânime

pop | pop' | *s.* estouro; bebida gasosa / *vi.* estourar. **-to p. up** ou
out aparecer, surgir; rebentar.
-to p. at atirar em (com arma de
fogo)

popcorn | pop'kón | *s.* pipoca

pope | powp' | *s.* (relig.) papa;

(fig.) pessoa que se crê infalível; pope

popery | pow'pərĭ | s. papismo; (pej.) a religião católica romana

poplar | pop'lə | s. choupo

poplin | pop'lin | s. popeline

poppy | po'pĭ | s. papoula

poppycock | po'pĭkok | s. (gír.) tolices, conversa fiada

populace | po'pĭulis | s. populaça, ralé

popular | po'pĭulə | a. popular

popularity | popĭula'ritĭ | s. popularidade

popularization | popĭulərayzey'sən | s. divulgação, difusão (de livros etc.)

popularize | po'pĭulərayz | vt. popularizar, vulgarizar

populate | po'pĭuleyt | vt. povoar

population | popĭuley'sən | s. população

populous | po'pĭuləs | a. populoso

porcelain | pó'selin | s. porcelana

porch | pós' | s. portal, pórtico; (EUA) varanda

porcupine | pó'kĭupayn | s. porco-espinho

pore | pó' | s. poro / vi. -to p. over examinar ou ler com atenção

pork | pók' | s. carne de porco

pork chop | pók'śop | s. costeleta de porco

porous | pó'rəs | a. poroso

porpoise | pó'pəs | s. toninha, marsuíno, boto

porridge | po'riĵ | s. mingau de aveia

port | pót' | s. porto; vinho-do-porto

portable | pó'təbəl | a. portátil

portend | pótend' | vt. prenunciar, pressagiar

portent | pó'tənt | s. presságio; prodígio, maravilha

portentous | póten'təs | a. agourento; portentoso, prodigioso, maravilhoso

porter | pó'tə | s. porteiro; carregador; (EUA) cabineiro de trem; tipo de cerveja preta

portfolio | pótfow'lĭow | s. pasta

para documentos; pasta ministerial

porthole | pót'howl | s. (náut.) vigia; (mil.) portinhola

portion | pó'śən | s. porção; pedaço / vt. -to p. out repartir, dividir

portly | pót'lĭ | a. corpulento

portmanteau | pótman'tow | s. maleta, valise

portmanteau word | pótman'tow wɛd | s. palavra formada pela combinação de outras duas (p. ex. *motel* [*motor car* + *hotel*])

portrait | pó'trit | s. retrato

portray | pótrey' | vt. retratar, pintar, descrever

portrayal | pótrey'əl | s. descrição, representação

Portuguese | pótĭugiz' | s. a. português

pose | powz' | s. pose; postura; (fig.) pose, atitude / vt. embaraçar (com pergunta); declarar, afirmar; propor (problema) / vi. posar; dar-se ares de, fazer-se passar por

position | pazi'śən | s. posição, situação; colocação, emprego, lugar / vt. colocar, pôr em posição; localizar

positive | po'zitiv | a. positivo; seguro, certo

posse | po'sĭ | s. pelotão, corpo; bando armado; força civil

possess | pəzes' | vt. possuir

possessed | pəzest' | a. possuidor, dotado; possuído, possesso; louco; endemoninhado

possession | pəze'śən | s. poder, posse; possessão (território). -to take p. of tomar posse de, apoderar-se de; (pl.) posses, haveres, bens; (pl.) possessões, colônias

possessor | pəze'sə | s. possuidor

possibility | posibi'litĭ | s. possibilidade

possible | po'sibəl | a. possível

possibly | po'siblĭ | adv. possivelmente

post | powst' | s. correio, caixa de

correio; poste, pilar; posto (de trabalho, militar etc.); guarnição, forte; cargo. **-by p.** pelo correio. **-by return of p.** na volta do correio / *vt.* postar, expedir (pelo correio); afixar (cartaz, aviso etc.); (mil.) postar (sentinela); publicar, anunciar. **-to keep (somebody) posted** avisar, pôr ao corrente, inteirar

post- | powst |*pref.* post-, pós-

postage | pows'tij | *s.* franquia postal, porte

post-box | powst'boks | *s.* caixa de correio

postcard | powst'kʌd | *s.* cartão postal

post-date | powstdeyt' | *vt.* pós-datar

poster | pows'tə | *s.* cartaz

poste restante | powstres'tónt |*s.* posta-restante

posterity | poste'ritī |*s.* posteridade

post-free | powst'frɪ | *a.* com franquia postal gratuita

posthumous | pos'tĩuməs | *a.* póstumo

postman | powst'mən |*s.* carteiro

postmark | powst'mʌk |*s.* carimbo do correio

postmaster | powst'mʌstə | *s.* agente dos correios

Postmaster General | powst'mʌstəje'nərəl | *s.* ministro das Comunicações; diretor geral dos correios

post-mortem | powstmó'təm | *s.* autópsia, necrópsia

post office | powst'ofis | *s.* agência dos correios

postpone | powspown' | *vt.* adiar, protelar

postponement | powspown'mənt| *s.* adiamento, protelação

postscript | powskript' | *s.* pós-escrito

postulate | pos'tĩuleyt | *s.* postulado; condição, requisito / *vt.* exigir; postular, pressupor / *vi.* **-to p. for** pedir, solicitar, insistir em

posture | pos'šə | *s.* postura, ati-

tude; estado (de espírito) / *vi.* fazer pose; posar

pot | pot' | *s.* pote, vaso; panela; (coloq.) urinol; cadinho; (gír.) maconha. **-to go to p.** arruinar-se, acabar-se. **-to keep the p. boiling** manter (algo) em atividade; ganhar a vida / *vt.* fazer conserva; plantar em vaso; matar caça (para comer) / *vi.* atirar (de perto)

potash | po'taś |*s.* potassa

potato | pətey'tow |*s.* batata

potency | pow'tənsī |*s.* potência

potent | pow'tənt | *a.* potente, forte

potential | powten'śəl | *s. a.* potencial, possível

potentiality | powtensĩa'litī | *s.* potencialidade; *(pl.)* possibilidades

pot luck | pot'lâk | *s.* trivial, comida caseira. **-to take p.l.** aceitar convite para comer o que houver

potter | po'tə | *s.* oleiro / *vt.* desperdiçar tempo / *vi.* fazer biscates

pottery | po'tərī | *s.* cerâmica; olaria; louça de barro

pouch | pawś' | *s.* bolsa; cartucheira; mala postal / *vt.* embolsar

poulterer | powl'tərə | *s.* comerciante de aves domésticas

poultice | powl'tis | *s.* cataplasma / *vt.* aplicar cataplasma

poultry | powl'trī |*s.* aves domésticas

pounce | pawns' | *vt.* agarrar, apoderar-se de; alisar com pedra-pomes / *vi.* saltar sobre, atacar

pound | pawnd' | *s.* libra / *vt.* triturar, esmagar, pilar, bater / *vi.* pulsar com força (coração)

pounder | pawn'də | *s.* pilão, almofariz

pound sterling | pawndstɛ'ling | *s.* libra esterlina *(abrev.* £)

pour | pó' | *s.* chuvarada, aguaceiro / *vt.* derramar; extravasar. **-to p. out** servir (chá, café etc.) / *vi.* fluir, correr; chover

torrencialmente; sair em bor-
botões. **-to p. with rain** chover a
potes. **-to p. out of** jorrar

pout | pawt’ | *vi.* amuar, fazer
beiço

poverty | po’vətī |*s.* pobreza

powder| paw’də |*s.* pó; pólvora /
vt. empoar, pulverizar / *vi.* em-
poar-se, pulverizar-se

power | paw’ə |*s.* poder; potência;
força, energia; eficácia. **-the
powers that be** as autoridades
constituídas. **-more p. to you ou
to your elbow!** expressão de en-
corajamento ou aprovação

powerful | paw’əful | *a.* podero-
so, potente

powerless | paw’əles | *a.* sem po-
der, sem forças, impotente

power of attorney | paw’əovə-
tE’nī | *s.* (jur.) procuração

practicable | prak’tikəbəl | *a.*
praticável, factível

practical | prak’tikəl | *a.* prático;
útil

practical joke | prak’tikəļjowk |
s. peça, brincadeira, logro

practically | prak’tiklī | *adv.* pra-
ticamente, quase

practice| prak’tis |*s.* prática; costu-
me; procedimento; exercício de
uma profissão; clientela (de advo-
gado); clínica. **-to make a p.** of ter
o costume de. **-out of p.** fora de
forma, sem prática

practise, practice | prak’tis | *vt. vi.*
praticar, exercitar(-se) em; exer-
cer (profissão)

practised | prak’tist | *a.* experi-
mentado, experiente, hábil

practitioner | prakti’śəna |*s.* pro-
fissional (esp. médico)

prairie | pre’ərī |*s.* (EUA) prada-
ria, planície, campina

praise | preyz’ |*s.* louvor, elogio /
vt. louvar, elogiar; glorificar.
-in p. of em louvor de

praiseworthy | preyz’wEδī | *a.*
louvável, digno de louvor

pram | pram’ | *s.* carrinho de be-
bê; carrinho de leiteiro

prance | prAns’ | *vt.* empinar, ca-

briolar / *vt. vi.* empertigar(-se)

prank | prAnk’ | *s.* peça, trote,
brincadeira; travessura

prattle | pra’təl | *s.* tagarelice;
balbucio / *vi.* palrar

prawn | prón’ | *s.* camarão gran-
de (marinho)

pray | prey’ | *vt.* pedir a, rogar a;
solicitar, implorar; por favor,
diga-me / *vi.* rezar

prayer | pre’ə | *s.* oração, prece;
súplica. **-the Lord’s p.** o pai-
-nosso

praying mantis | pre’ingmantis |
s. louva-a-deus

preach | priś’ | *vt.* pregar (ser-
mão) / *vi.* pregar, exortar, dar
conselhos

preacher| prı’śə |*s.* pregador

preamble| prı̃am’bəl |*s.* preâmbulo

precarious | prike’ərīəs |*a.* precário

precariousness | prike’ərīəsnes |
s. precariedade

precaution | prikó’śən | *s.*
precaução

precautionary | prikó’śənərī | *a.*
preventivo, acautelador; pre-
cavido, cauteloso

precede | prisıd’ | *vt.* preceder

precedence | pre’sidəns | *s.* prece-
dência

precedent | pre’sidənt | *s.* prece-
dente, exemplo / *a.* precedente

preceding| prisı’ding |*a.* anterior

precept| prı’sept | *s.* preceito

precinct | prı’sinkt | *s.* recinto;
área limitada; zona eleitoral;
distrito policial

precious | pre’śəs | *a.* precioso,
valioso; afetado, empolado

precipice | pre’sipis |*s.* precipício

precipitate| prəsi’pitit | *s.* (quím.)
precipitado / *a.* precipitado /
| prəsi’piteyt | *vt.* precipitar

precipitation | prəsipitey’śən | *s.*
precipitação

precipitous| prəsi’pitəs |*a.* íngre-
me, escarpado

précis | prey’sī | *s.* sumário, resu-
mo / *vt.* resumir

precise| prisays’ |*a.* preciso, exa-
to; minucioso

precision | prisi'jən | *s.* precisão

preclude | priklʊd' | *vt.* excluir; impedir

precocious | prikow'ʃəs | *a.* precoce

precociousness | prikow'ʃəsnes | *s.* precocidade

preconceived | prikənsıvd' | *a.* preconcebido

precursor | prikE'sə | *s.* precursor

predatory | pre'dətərī | *a.* predatório

predecessor | prɪ'disesə | *s.* predecessor, antecessor

predestine | prides'tin | *vt.* predestinar

predetermine | prɪditE'min | *vt.* predeterminar

predicament | pridi'kəmənt | *s.* situação difícil ou embaraçosa, transe

predict | pridikt' | *vt.* predizer, prognosticar

prediction | pridik'ʃən | *s.* predição, prognóstico

predilection | predilek'ʃən | *s.* predileção

predispose | prɪdispowz' | *vt.* predispor

predominance | prido'minəns | *s.* predomínio

predominant | prido'minənt | *a.* predominante

pre-eminence | prie'minəns | *s.* preeminência, superioridade

prefabricate | prifa'brikeyt | *vt.* pré-fabricar

preface | pré'fis | *s.* prefácio / *vt.* prefaciar

prefect | prɪ'fekt | *s.* (ant. rom.) magistrado; aluno (encarregado da disciplina)

prefer | prifE' | *vt.* preferir

preferable | pre'fərəbəl | *a.* preferível

preference | pre'fərəns | *s.* preferência

preferential | prefəren'ʃəl | *a.* preferencial

preferment | prifE'mənt | *s.* promoção; cargo honorífico ou lucrativo

prefix | prɪ'fiks | *s.* prefixo

pregnancy | preg'nənsī | *s.* gravidez

pregnant | preg'nənt | *a.* grávido; significativo; fértil

prehistoric | prɪhisto'rik | *a.* pré-histórico

prejudge | prijãȷ̆' | *vt.* prejulgar, julgar antecipadamente

prejudice | pre'ȷ̆udis | *s.* preconceito; parcialidade; prejuízo, dano. **-to the p. of** em detrimento de. **-without p.** sem abrir mão dos seus direitos / *vt.* prejudicar, causar dano; induzir a preconceito. **-to be prejudiced** ter preconceitos

prejudicial | preȷ̆udi'ʃəl | *a.* prejudicial, nocivo, danoso

prelate | pre'lit | *s.* prelado

preliminary | prili'minərī | *s.* (ger. *pl.*) preliminar / *a.* preliminar, introdutório

prelude | pre'lĭud | *s.* prelúdio / *vt. vi.* preludiar

premature | pre'mətĭuə | *a.* prematuro; precipitado

premeditated | prime'diteytid | *a.* premeditado

premier | prɪ'mĭə | *s.* primeiro-ministro / *a.* principal

premise | pre'mis | *s.* premissa; (*pl.*) instalações, local, estabelecimento, prédio, recinto

premium | prɪ'mĭəm | *s.* prêmio. **-at a p.** raro, difícil de obter. **-to put a p. on** estimular, incentivar

premonition | prɪməni'ʃən | *s.* pressentimento

preoccupation | prɪokĭupey'ʃən | *s.* preocupação

preoccupied | prɪo'kĭupayd | *a.* absorto, distraído, preocupado; ocupado previamente

preoccupy | prɪo'kĭupay | *vt.* preocupar; ocupar previamente

preparation | prepərey'ʃən | *s.* preparação, preparativo

preparatory | pripa'rətərī | *a.* preparatório

prepare | pripe'ə | *vt.* preparar / *vi.* preparar-se

prepared | pripe'əd | *a.* preparado; pronto, disposto

preparedness| pripe'ədnes |s. estado de preparação (esp. para a guerra)

preponderance | pripon'dərəns | s. preponderância

preponderant | pripon'dərənt | a. preponderante

preposition | pripəzi'śən | s. preposição

prepossessing | pripəze'sing | a. atraente, simpático

preposterous | pripos'tərəs | a. absurdo, despropositado; grotesco, ridículo

prerogative | priro'gətiv | s. prerrogativa

presage | pre'siǰ | s. presságio, pressentimento / vt. pressagiar, predizer

prescribe | priskrayb' | vt. prescrever; (med.) receitar

prescription | priskrip'śən | s. (med.) receita

presence | pre'zəns | s. presença; aparência, porte, apresentação. -in the p. of em presença de

presence of mind | pre'zənsovmaynd' |s. presença de espírito

present | pre'zənt | s. presente, dádiva; tempo presente. -at p. atualmente. -for the p. por enquanto / a. presente, atual; em apreço/ | prizent' |vt. apresentar; presentear; expor, explicar. -to p. oneself apresentar-se

presentable | prizen'təbəl | a. apresentável

presentation | prezəntey'śən | s. apresentação; representação; espetáculo; símbolo, imagem. -on p. (com.) à vista

presentiment | prizen'timənt | s. pressentimento

presently| pre'zəntlī |adv. daqui a pouco, em breve

preservation | prezəvey'śən | s. preservação, conservação

preservative | prizE'vətiv | s. a. preservativo

preserve | prizEv' | s. compota, geléia; conserva; reserva (de caça) / vt. conservar, preservar,

proteger

preside | prizayd' | vi. presidir (a)

presidency | pre'zidənsī | s. presidência

president | pre'zidənt |s. presidente

presidential | preziden'śəl | a. presidencial

press| pres' |s. prensa; prelo; impressão; imprensa. -to have a good p. ter boa crítica (nos jornais) / vt. prensar; pressionar; imprimir; espremer (uvas etc.); passar a ferro; compelir; fazer pressão. -to p. down apertar, segurar; apertar, carregar em (botão, pedal etc.) / vi. -to p. on (forward) avançar, abrir caminho, continuar

pressing | pre'sing | a. urgente, premente, insistente

pressure | pre'śə | s. pressão; opressão; premência. -p. of circumstances força das circunstâncias

pressure-cooker | pre'śəkukə |s. panela de pressão

pressure gauge | pre'śəgeyǰ | s. manômetro

prestige | prestiǰ' | s. prestígio, influência

presumably | prəźu'məblī | adv. presumivelmente

presume | priźu'm' | vt. presumir, supor; imaginar, julgar; pressupor; atrever-se a, ousar / vi. mostrar presunção; tomar liberdades. -to p. on abusar de

presumption | priźâm'śən |s. suposição, conjetura; presunção; atrevimento, arrogância, insolência

presumptive | priźâm'tiv | a. presuntivo

presumptuous | priźâm'tŭəs | a. presunçoso, presumido; arrogante; audacioso

presuppose | prisəpowz' | vt. pressupor

pretence, pretense | pritens' | s. pretexto

pretend | pritend' | vt. vi. fingir(-se); pretender, aspirar a

pretender | priten'də | s. pretendente

pretension | priten'śən | s. pretensão

pretentious | priten'śəs | a. pretensioso

preterite | pre'tərit | s. a. (gram.) pretérito

pretext | pri'tekst | s. pretexto / vt. pretextar

pretty | pri'tĭ | a. bonito, gracioso; galante / adv. bastante; muito; um tanto; regularmente

prevail | priveyl' | vi. prevalecer, predominar; triunfar. -to p. on ou upon persuadir a

prevailing | privey'ling | a. dominante; corrente, em voga; superior; eficaz

prevalence | pre'vələns | s. prevalência

prevalent | pre'vələnt | a. predominante

prevaricate | priva'rikeyt | vi. usar de evasivas, tergiversar, mentir

prevarication | privarikey'śən | s. evasivas, tergiversação

prevent | privent' | vt. impedir, prevenir, evitar

prevention | priven'śən | s. prevenção, impedimento

preventive | priven'tiv | a. preventivo

previous | pri'vĭəs | a. prévio, anterior

prey | prey' | s. presa; vítima. -to be a p. to ser vítima de / vi. -to p. on ou upon pilhar, saquear; oprimir, afligir, atormentar

price | prays' | s. preço. -at any p. custe o que custar

priceless | prays'les | a. inestimável, precioso; (coloq.) engraçadíssimo, impagável

prick | prik' | s. picada, pontada; alfinetada / vt. picar, alfinetar. -to p. up one's ears empinar as orelhas (cavalo); apurar o ouvido

prickle | pri'kəl | s. espinho; sensação de picada / vi. sentir alfinetadas; formigar

prickly | prik'lĭ | a. espinhoso; irritadiço (pessoa)

prickly heat | prik'lĭhit | s. brotoeja

pride | prayd' | s. orgulho; soberba; arrogância, altivez. -to take p. in ter orgulho de (em). -p. of the morning nevoeiro matinal (indicando a vinda de bom tempo)

priest | prist' | s. sacerdote, padre

priestess | pris'tes | s. sacerdotisa

priesthood | prist'hud | s. sacerdócio

priestly | prist'lĭ | a. sacerdotal; sagrado

prig | prig' | a. pedante, afetado; presumido

prim | prim' | a. afetado, empertigado; moralista (esp. mulher)

primacy | pray'məsĭ | s. supremacia; primazia, prioridade

primary | pray'mərĭ | a. primário; original, primordial; fundamental; elementar

prime | praym' | s. apogeu. -in the p. of life na flor da idade, na plenitude da vida / a. primeiro; principal / vt. aprontar, preparar; escorvar (bomba hidráulica); instruir; prevenir

primer | pray'mə | s. espoleta, escorva; cartilha; manual; livro elementar

primeval | praymĭ'vəl | a. primevo

primitive | pri'mitiv | s. pessoa ou coisa primitiva; (b.a.) primitivo / a. primitivo; tosco, rudimentar

primrose | prim'rowz | s. primavera (flor) / a. amarelo-claro; florido, alegre

prince | prins' | s. príncipe

princely | prins'lĭ | a. principesco, magnífico

princess | prinses' | s. princesa

principal | prin'sipəl | s. reitor, diretor; capital, principal / a. principal

principality | prinsipa'litĭ | s. principado

principle | prin'sipəl | s. princípio, teoria; (pl.) princípios. -in p. em princípio, teoricamente. **-on p.** por princípio

print | print' | s. impressão; estampa; publicação, impresso; marca, vestígio. **-small p.** tipo miúdo. **-out of p.** esgotado (livro) / vt. imprimir; estampar; gravar (na memória etc.). **-printed matter** impressos

printer | prin'tə | s. impressor, tipógrafo

printer's devil | prin'tǝzdevǝl | s. aprendiz de tipógrafo, menino de recados (em oficina tipográfica)

printing-press | prin'tingpres | s. prelo

prior | pray'ǝ | s. prior / a. prévio, anterior / adv. previamente. **-p. to** antes de

priority | prayo'ritī | s. prioridade, precedência

prise | prayz' | vt. = *prize*

prison | pri'zǝn | s. prisão, cárcere, cadeia

prisoner | pri'zǝnǝ | s. preso, prisioneiro. **-to take p.** fazer prisioneiro

prisoner of conscience | pri'zǝnǝovkon'śǝns | s. pessoa presa por protesto social

prisoner of state | pri'zǝnǝovsteyt | s. prisioneiro político

prisoner of war | pri'zǝnǝovwó | s. prisioneiro de guerra

prison van | pri'zǝnvan | s. carro para o transporte de presos

privacy | pri'vǝsī | s. intimidade, isolamento, recato; reserva, segredo

private | pray'vit | s. (mil.) soldado raso / a. particular, privado; confidencial, secreto. **-in p.** em particular, em segredo, confidencialmente

privateer | prayvǝtī'ǝ | s. corsário (navio ou capitão)

privation | prayvey'śǝn | s. privação; penúria, miséria

privet | pri'vit | s. (bot.) alfena

privilege | pri'vilij | s. privilégio

privileged | pri'vilijd | a. privile-

giado

privy | pri'vī | s. privada, latrina / a. secreto, clandestino; privado, particular. **-to be p. to** ter conhecimento de, saber de

prize | prayz' | s. prêmio, recompensa; presa, propriedade capturada do inimigo; força ou emprego ou ação de alavanca / a. premiado / vt. prezar, apreciar; apresar, capturar; mover ou arrombar com alavanca

pro | prow' | s. argumento, voto ou pessoa favorável. **-the pros and cons** os prós e os contras / a. favorável / adv. pró, a favor

pro- | prow | pref. pró-

probability | probǝbi'litī | s. probabilidade

probable | pro'bǝbǝl | a. provável

probation | prǝbey'śǝn | s. prova, experiência; aprendizado, noviciado; (jur.) liberdade condicional

probationer | prǝbey'śǝnǝ | s. praticante, principiante, aprendiz; (jur.) delinquente em liberdade condicional

probe | prowb' | s. sonda / vt. sondar, explorar

problem | pro'blǝm | s. problema

procedure | prowsī'dīǝ | s. procedimento, processo; ação, ato; norma, uso; prosseguimento, continuação

proceed | prowsīd' | vi. prosseguir, continuar; proceder, provir de; proceder, comportar-se. **-to p. against** mover ação contra. **-to p. from** derivar de, provir de

proceeding | prowsī'ding | s. prosseguimento, continuação; processo, maneira de operar; (pl.) ata (de assembléia etc.). **-legal proceedings** medidas legais

proceeds | prowsīdz' | spl. produto, lucro (de venda, transação comercial etc.)

process | prow'ses | s. processo, sistema. **-in p. of time** com o decorrer do tempo. -**in the p. of** no decurso de

procession | prəse'śən |s. procissão; cortejo; passeata

proclaim | prowkleym' | vt. proclamar, declarar

proclamation | prokləmey'śən | s. proclamação

proclivity | prəkli'vitī |s. propensão, inclinação

procrastinate | prowkras'tineyt | vi. procrastinar

procrastination | prowkrastiney'śən |s. procrastinação, adiamento

procreation | prowkriey'śən | s. procriação

procure | prəkĭu'ə | vt. obter, arranjar / vi. praticar o lenocínio, alcovitar

procurer | prəkĭu'rə |s. proxeneta (homem ou mulher)

procuress | prəkĭu'əris |s. alcoviteira, caftina

prod | prod' | s. aguilhoada; cutucão; cotovelada / vt. aguilhoar; incitar, estimular

prodigal| pro'digəl |s.a. pródigo

prodigious | prədi'jəs | a. prodigioso

prodigy | pro'dijī |s. prodígio

produce | pro'dĭus | s. produto, produção / | prədĭus' | vt. produzir; fabricar; apresentar, exibir; escrever, compor (livro etc.); apresentar ao público (peça, ator)

producer | prədĭu'sə | s. produtor (tb. cin., TV); (teat.) financiador (de peça)

product | pro'dəkt | s. produto

production | prədâk'śən |s. produção (tb. teat., cin., TV)

productive | prədâk'tiv | a. produtivo

productivity | prədâkti'vitī | s. produtividade

profane | prəfeyn' | a. profano; sacrílego; irreverente / vt. profanar

profanity | prəfa'nitī | s. impiedade; irreverência; blasfêmia,

praga

profess | prəfes' | vt. professar; declarar; afirmar, confessar; pretender, aparentar, afetar

professed | prəfest' | a. professo; declarado, ostensivo

profession | prəfe'śən |s. profissão

professional | prəfe'śənəl | s. a. profissional

professor | prəfe'sə |s. professor universitário (esp. catedrático)

professorship | prəfe'səśip | s. professorado, cadeira de professor universitário

proffer | pro'fə |s. oferecimento / vt. oferecer

proficiency | prəfi'śənsī |s. proficiência, competência

proficient | prəfi'śənt | a. proficiente, competente

profile | prow'fayl | s. perfil. -**in p. de perfil**

profit | pro'fit | s. lucro, ganho; provento, proveito. -**to derive p. from** tirar proveito de. -**to make a p. from** obter lucro de / vt. servir a, aproveitar a, ser vantajoso a. -**to p. by** ou **from** aproveitar-se de; lucrar com / vi. lucrar; beneficiar-se

profitable | pro'fitəbəl | a. proveitoso; lucrativo

profiteer | profitī'ə | s. especulador, aproveitador

profligacy | pro'fligəsī | s. devassidão, libertinagem; dissipação, desperdício

profligate | pro'fligit | a. devasso, libertino; pródigo

profound | prəfawnd' | a. profundo; intenso

profundity | prəfân'ditī | s. profundidade

profuse | prəfĭus' | a. abundante, copioso; extravagante, dissipador

profusion | prəfĭv'jən | s. profusão, abundância

progeny | pro'jinī | s. prole, progênie, descendência

prognosis | prognow'sis | s. prognóstico

prognosticate | prəgnos'tikeyt | vt. prognosticar

programme, program | prow'-grəm | s. programa (tb. de computador)

progress | prow'gres | s. progresso / | prəgres' | vi. progredir

progressive | prəgre'siv | s. progressista / a. progressivo; progressista

prohibit | prəhi'bit | vt. proibir, interdizer, obstar

prohibition | prowibi'śən | s. proibição

project | pro'jekt | s. projeto, plano / vt. projetar, lançar, atirar; projetar, planejar / vi. sobressair, ressaltar, prolongar-se

projectile | prəjek'tayl | s. projetil, projétil

projection | prəjek'śən | s. projeção

projector | prəjek'tə | s. projetor

proletarian | prowlite'əriən | s. a. proletário

proletariat | prowlite'əriət | s. proletariado

proliferate | prəli'fəreyt | vi. proliferar, multiplicar-se

prolific | prəli'fik | a. prolífico, fecundo

prologue | prow'log | s. prólogo, prefácio / vt. prefaciar

prolong | prəlong' | vt. prolongar

promenade | promənAd' | s. passeio; passeio público / vi. passear

prominence | pro'minəns | s. proeminência; notoriedade, importância

prominent | pro'minənt | a. proeminente; elevado; notável; saliente

promiscuous | prəmis'k∫uəs | a. promíscuo; libertino

promise | pro'mis | s. promessa; compromisso; esperança. -of high p. muito prometedor / vt. prometer; comprometer-se a; dar esperanças de. -to p. well prometer muito, dar boas esperanças / vi. prometer, fazer promessa

promised land | pro'mistland | s. terra da promissão

promising | pro'mising | a. prometedor

promontory | pro'məntrī | s. promontório

promote | prəmowt' | vt. promover; estimular

promotion | prəmow'śən | s. promoção; estímulo

prompt | prompt' | a. pronto, imediato; preparado, disposto; rápido / vt. incitar, estimular; induzir; mover; fazer lembrar; (teat.) servir de ponto a; "soprar" a (estudante)

prompter | promp'tə | s. (teat.) ponto

prompting | promp'ting | s. instigação, sugestão

promptly | prompt'lī | adv. prontamente, imediatamente

promptness | prompt'nes | s. prontidão

promulgate | pro'məlgeyt | vt. promulgar; propagar, disseminar

prone | prown' | a. inclinado, propenso; prostrado, de bruços; deitado. -p. to dado a, propenso a

prong | prong' | s. dente de garfo; ponta aguçada

pronoun | prow'nawn | s. pronome

pronounce | prənawns' | vt. pronunciar; declarar, anunciar / vi. pronunciar-se, declarar-se, manifestar-se

pronounced | prənawnst' | a. acentuado, pronunciado, forte

pronunciation | prənânsīey'śən | s. pronúncia

proof | prʊf' | s. prova; evidência; ensaio, experiência / a. de prova, usado em ensaios; resistente; refratário

-proof | prʊf | suf. à prova de

prop | prop' | s. escora, estaca, suporte / vt. -to p. up sustentar, escorar

propaganda | propəgan'də | s. propaganda

propagate | pro'pəgeyt | *vt.* propagar

propel | prəpel' | *vt.* propelir, impulsionar, mover

propeller | prəpe'lə | *s.* hélice

propensity | prəpen'sitĩ | *s.* propensão, tendência

proper | pro'pə | *a.* correto, exato; oportuno, próprio, apropriado; conveniente, decente; natural, próprio; propriamente dito; (coloq.) rematado, completo

properly | pro'pəlĩ | *adv.* propriamente, exatamente; devidamente, corretamente

property | pro'patĩ | *s.* propriedade, bens; senhorio, domínio; qualidade, propriedade

prophecy | pro'fisĩ | *s.* profecia

prophesy | pro'fisay | *vt.* profetizar

prophet | pro'fit | *s.* profeta

prophetic | prəfe'tik | *a.* profético

propitiate | prəpi'śĩeyt | *vt.* propiciar, favorecer; conciliar

propitious | prəpi'śəs | *a.* propício, favorável

proportion | prəpó'śən | *s.* proporção; relação; simetria. -**in p. as** à proporção que. -**out of p.** desproporcionado

proposal | prəpow'zəl | *s.* proposta (tb. de casamento)

propose | prəpowz' | *vt.* propor, sugerir; tencionar, pretender; apresentar, indicar / *vi.* propor-se, dispor-se a; propor casamento

proposer | prəpow'zə | *s.* proponente

proposition | propəzi'śən | *s.* proposta, proposição

propound | prəpawnd' | *vt.* propor, sugerir; apresentar

proprietor | prəpray'ətə | *s.* proprietário

propriety | prəpray'ətĩ | *s.* propriedade, adequação, conveniência; (*pl.*) conveniências, convenções sociais

propulsion | prəpâl'śən | *s.* propulsão

prosaic | prowzey'ik | *a.* prosaico; vulgar, trivial

proscribe | prowskrayb' | *vt.* proscrever

prose | prowz' | *s.* prosa

prosecute | pro'sikĩut | *vt.* (jur.) processar; prosseguir, continuar, levar avante

prosecution | prosikĩu'śən | *s.* (jur.) acusação, denúncia, instauração de processo; prosseguimento; realização, execução

proselyte | pro'silayt | *s.* prosélito

prospect | pros'pekt | *s.* perspectiva; probabilidade, esperança. -**in p.** em perspectiva / | prospekt' | *vt.* explorar (terreno, jazida) / *vi.* -**to p. for** explorar (jazida etc.)

prospective | prəspek'tiv | *a.* provável, presumível; em perspectiva

prospectus | prəspek'təs | *s.* prospecto, programa

prosper | pros'pə | *vi.* prosperar, crescer

prosperity | prospe'ritĩ | *s.* prosperidade

prosperous | pros'pərəs | *a.* próspero, florescente

prostitute | pros'titĩut | *s.* prostituta / *vt.* prostituir; degradar

prostitution | prostitĩu'śən | *s.* prostituição

prostrate | pros'treyt | *a.* prostrado; abatido / *vt.* prostrar

prostration | prostrey'śən | *s.* prostração

protagonist | prowta'gənist | *s.* protagonista

protect | prətekt' | *vt.* proteger, resguardar

protecting | prətek'ting | *a.* protetor

protection | prətek'śən | *s.* proteção, defesa, salvaguarda; imunidade garantida por malfeitores (sob pagamento extorquido)

protective | prətek'tiv | *a.* protetor, de proteção, defensivo

protector | prətek'tə | *s.* protetor

protégé | pro'tejey | s. protegido

protein | prow'tɪn | s. proteína

protest | prow'test | s. protesto / | prɔtest' | vt. vi. protestar

protestant | pro'tistənt | s. a. protestante (maiúsc. tb. relig.)

protester | prɔtes'tə | s. reclamante; manifestante

protocol | prow'təkol | s. protocolo

prototype | prow'tətayp | s. protótipo

protract | prətrakt' | vt. prolongar, demorar

protrude | prətrʊd' | vi. sair, ressaltar, projetar-se

protruding | prətrʊ'ding | a. saliente

proud | prawd' | a. orgulhoso, altivo; arrogante, vaidoso, presunçoso. -to do oneself p. ufanar-se

prove | prʊv' | vt. provar, comprovar; demonstrar / vi. revelar-se; mostrar ser. -to p. true confirmar-se

proverb | pro'vEb | s. provérbio, ditado, adágio

proverbial | prəvE'bləl | a. proverbial; conhecido, notório

provide | prəvayd' | vt. prover, proporcionar; fornecer, abastecer, munir; (jur.) estatuir, estipular, determinar / vi. -to p. for prover as necessidades de; preparar-se para

provided | prəvay'did | a. provido, munido / conj. -p. that contanto que, desde que

providence | pro'vidəns | s. providência

provident | pro'vidənt | a. providente; previdente; prudente; econômico

providential | providen'śəl | a. providencial

provider | prəvay'də | s. fornecedor, abastecedor

providing | prəvay'ding | conj. -p. that desde que, contanto que

province | pro'vins | s. província; território, região; competência, esfera de ação

provincial | prəvin'śəl | s. (ecles.) provincial; provinciano

provision | prəvi'jən | s. provisão; fornecimento, abastecimento; cláusula, disposição; (pl.) provisões (comestíveis e bebidas) / vt. fornecer provisões

provisional | prəvi'jənəl | a. provisório

provocation | provəkey'śən | s. provocação

provocative | prəvo'kətiv | a. provocador, estimulante; provocante

provoke | prəvowk' | vt. provocar, excitar; irritar; causar, ocasionar

provost | pro'vəst | s. reitor (Oxford, Cambridge etc.); (EUA) alto funcionário administrativo (em universidade); (Esc.) prefeito; preboste

provost marshal | pro'vəstMAśəl | s. chefe da polícia militar

prow | praw' | s. proa

prowess | praw'es | s. bravura; proeza, façanha; perícia, habilidade

prowl | prawl' | vi. rondar, espreitar; vaguear, errar

proximity | proksi'mitī | s. proximidade; arredores; (pl.) cercanias

proxy | prok'sī | s. procuração; procurador. -by p. por procuração

prude | prʊd' | s. pessoa puritana (esp. afetadamente), santarrão

prudence | prʊ'dəns | s. prudência

prudent | prʊ'dənt | a. prudente, cauteloso

prudery | prʊ'dərī | s. pudicícia, afetação de virtude

prudish | prʊ'diś | a. puritano, santarrão

prune | prʊn' | s. ameixa seca / vt. podar, aparar

pruning | prʊ'ning | s. poda

pruning-hook | prʊ'ninghʊk | s. podão, podadeira

pry | pray' | vt. erguer, abrir etc. com alavanca. **-to p. up** levantar com alavanca / vi. **-to p. into** espreitar; intrometer-se, meter o nariz em

psalm | sam' | s. salmo

pseudonym | sĭu'dənim | s. pseudônimo

psychiatrist | saykay'ətrist | s. psiquiatra

psychoanalysis | saykowəna'lisis | s. psicanálise

psychologist | sayko'ləjist | s. psicólogo

psychology | sayko'ləji | s. psicologia

pub | pâb' | s. (coloq.) taberna, cervejaria, bar

puberty | pĭu'bəti | s. puberdade

public | pâb'lik | s. público, povo. **-in p.** em público / a. público; comum; notório, conhecido. **-to make p.** tornar público

publican | pâb'likən | s. taberneiro; publicano

publication | pâblikey'śən | s. publicação

public convenience | pâb'likkənvĭ'nĭəns | s. lavatório público

public house | pâb'likhaws | s. = pub

publicity | pâbli'sitī | s. publicidade

publicize | pâb'lisayz | vt. dar publicidade a

publish | pâb'liś | vt. publicar, editar; divulgar

publisher | pâb'liśə | s. editor; casa editora

pucker | pâ'kə | vt. vi. franzir(-se), enrugar(-se)

pudding | pu'ding | s. pudim

puddle | pâ'dəl | s. poça; argila amassada

puerile | pĭu'ərayl | a. pueril, infantil

puff | pâf' | s. sopro, baforada; jato de vapor; lufada, rajada (de vento) / vt. inflar; enfunar; fumar, tirar fumaça / vi. so-

prar; ofegar, arfar. **-to p. out** apagar com um sopro. **-to p. up** inchar

puffed | pâft' | a. ofegante, esbaforido. **-p. out** inchado

puffy | pâ'fī | a. inchado

pugilist | pĭu'jilist | s. pugilista

pugnacious | pâgney'śəs | a. pugnaz, brigão

pugnacity | pâgna'sitī | s. combatividade

puke | pĭuk' | s. vômito / vt. vi. vomitar

pull | pul' | s. puxão; (gír.) influência; (gír.) empenho, recomendação / vt. puxar. **-to p. away** ou **out** tirar, arrancar. **-to p. away from** afastar-se de. **-to p. down** abaixar; humilhar; demolir. **-to p. off** tirar, arrancar. **-to p. up** arrancar; parar, fazer alto; deter; avizinhar. **-to p. ones's leg** caçoar com alguém, implicar com alguém

pulley | pu'lī | s. roldana, polia; cadernal

pullover | pu'lowvə | s. pulôver

pulp | pâlp' | s. polpa / vt. reduzir a polpa

pulpit | pul'pit | s. púlpito

pulsate | pâl'seyt | vi. pulsar, palpitar

pulse | pâls' | s. pulso. **-to feel the p.** tomar o pulso / vi. pulsar, palpitar

pulverize | pâl'vərayz | vt. pulverizar, triturar

pumice-stone | pâ'misstown | s. pedra-pome(s)

pump | pâmp' | s. bomba (de bombear água, ar etc.); sapatilhas (de dança etc.) / vt. bombear / vi. dar à bomba

pumpkin | pâmp'kin | s. abóbora

pun | pân' | s. trocadilho

punch | pânś | s. soco, murro; (mec.) punção; ponche; (fig.) energia, vitalidade; (maiúsc.) Polichinelo / vt. socar, esmurrar; furar, abrir furos em

Punch and Judy show | pân'sand- Ju'dĭsow | s. teatro de mario- netes

punctilious | pânkti'lĭəs | a. es- crupuloso, meticuloso; for- mal; suscetível

punctual | pânk'tĭuəl | a. pontual

punctuality | pânktĭua'litĭ | s. pontualidade

punctuate | pânk'tĭueyt | vt. pon- tuar; destacar; interromper, entrecortar

punctuation | pânktĭuey'sən | s. pontuação

puncture | pânk'sə | s. furo, picada, perfuração / vt. perfu- rar; (med.) puncionar

pungency | pân'jənsĭ | s. sabor (odor) forte ou picante; mordacidade

pungent | pân'jənt | a. acre, forte (odor, sabor); (fig.) mordaz, cáustico

punish | pâ'nĭs | vt. punir, castigar

punishable | pâ'nĭsəbəl | a. punível

punishment | pâ'nĭsmənt | s. cas- tigo, punição; (coloq.) trata- mento severo, maus tratos

punitive | pĭu'nitiv | a. punitivo

punk | pânk' | s. isca (para acen- der fogo); (coloq.) coisa ou pes- soa sem valor; (coloq.) jovem brutal e turbulento / a. de pou- co valor ou qualidade

punt | pânt' | s. embarcação de fundo chato impelida com varejão

puny | pĭu'nĭ | a. fraco, pequeno, miúdo; insignificante

pup | pâp' | s. cachorrinho novo

pupil | pĭu'pil | s. aluno; (anat.) pupila

puppet | pâ'pit | s. marionete, fantoche, boneco

puppet-show | pâ'pitsow | s. tea- tro de marionetes

purchase | pE'sĭs | s. compra; aparelho de içar, talha / vt. comprar

pure | pĭu'ə | a. puro

purely | pĭu'əlĭ | adv. puramente, exclusivamente

purgatory | pE'gətrĭ | s. purga- tório

purge | pEj' | s. purgante; depu- ração (esp. polít.) / vt. purgar; depurar / vi. purgar-se, purifi- car-se

purification | pĭurifikey'sən | s. purificação

purify | pĭu'rifay | vt. purificar; depurar; clarificar; isentar (de culpa ou pecado)

puritan | pĭu'ritən | s. a. puritano

purity | pĭu'ritĭ | s. pureza

purple | pE'pəl | s. púrpura / a. purpúreo, de púrpura

purport | pE'pət | s. significado, tεor, sentido, conteúdo / vt. pretender; significar, querer dizer

purpose | pE'pəs | s. propósito, intenção, intento, fim; utilida- de; resolução. -on p. de propósi- to. -for what p.? para que fim?, com que intenção? -to no p. em vão, debalde / vt. tencionar

purposeful | pE'pəsful |a. propo- sitado, intencional; decidido, resoluto

purposely | pE'pəslĭ | adv. de propósito

purr | pE' | s. som de ronronar ou semelhante / vi. ronronar

purse | pEs' | s. bolsa / vt. franzir, enrugar (lábios)

purser | pE'sə | s. (náut.) comissá- rio de bordo

purse-strings | pEs'stringz | spl. cordões da bolsa. -to hold the p.-s. controlar as despesas

pursuance | pəsĭu'əns | s. prosse- guimento; execução, cumpri- mento. -in p. of de conformida- de com

pursue | pEsĭu' | vt. perseguir, acossar, dar caça a; dedicar-se a; importunar; seguir (curso, carreira etc.)

pursuer | pəsĭu'ə | s. perseguidor

pursuit | pəsĭut' | s. perseguição; busca, procura; atividade, pro- fissão; investigação. -in p. of à procura de, no encalço de

purvey | pɛvey' | *vt.* fornecer (provisões) / *vi.* ser fornecedor. **-to p. for** abastecer

purveyor | pɛvey'ə | *s.* fornecedor

push | puś' | *s.* empurrão; repelão; esforço; arremetida; (coloq.) iniciativa, dinamismo / *vt.* empurrar, impelir. **-to p. away** afastar

pussy | pu'sī | *s.* bichano, gatinho

put | put' | *vt.* pôr, colocar, botar; meter; expressar, exprimir. **-to p. aside** pôr de lado; pôr de parte; guardar; abandonar. **-to p. back** repor, recolocar; atrasar (relógio). **-to p. by** guardar, pôr de lado. **-to p. down** abaixar, arriar; tomar nota, assentar, escrever; debelar (revolta); inscrever, registrar; rebaixar (preço); degradar. **-to p. forward** apresentar, submeter; adiantar (relógio). **-to p. in** meter, introduzir; inserir; apresentar (queixa, documento etc.). **-to p. in at** fazer escala, arribar a (porto). **-to p. in mind** lembrar. **-to p. in writing** pôr por escrito. **-to p. in for** concorrer a (um lugar ou posto). **-to p. in an appearance** fazer ato de presença, comparecer. **-to p. into** pôr em, redigir em. **-to p. into one's head** meter na cabeça de. **-to p. off** protelar, adiar; desconcertar, confundir; livrar-se de; desfazer-se de; despir, tirar. **-to p. on** pôr; adiantar (relógio); aparentar, simular; representar, encenar. **-to p. on airs** dar-se ares de grande personagem. **-to p. out** apagar (luz); estender (mão); desconcertar; intimidar; transtornar, incomodar.

-to p. out of pôr fora de. **-to p. right** consertar, ajustar. **-to p. through** passar; ligar (telefone). **-to p. to sea** zarpar, largar, fazer-se ao mar. **-to p. to death** executar (pena capital). **-to p. to flight** afugentar. **-to p. up** levantar, erguer; guardar; apresentar (candidato); alojar (hóspede); (coloq.) instigar; (coloq.) tramar. **-to p. up with** tolerar, suportar. **-to p. a stop to** pôr termo a. **-to p. to shame** envergonhar

putrefaction | pĭutrifak'śən | *s.* putrefação

putt | pât' | *vt. vi.* (golfe) dar uma tacada leve

putty | pâ'tī | *s.* massa de vidraceiro / *vt.* emassar

puzzle | pâ'zəl | *s.* quebra-cabeça; enigma, problema; perplexidade / *vt.* confundir, embaraçar, intrigar / *vi.* estar perplexo; ponderar sobre problema. **-to be puzzled** estar confuso

puzzled | pâ'zəld | *a.* perplexo, desorientado

puzzling | pâz'ling | *a.* enigmático, embaraçoso

pygmy | pig'mī | *s.* pigmeu, pigméia

pyjamas, pajamas | pəjʌ'məz | *spl.* pijama

pylon | pay'lən | *s.* (arquit.) pilone, entrada monumental; (aer.) mastro, torre; estrutura ou suporte (para cabos elétricos)

pyramid | pi'rəmid | *s.* pirâmide

pyrotechnics | payrowtek'niks | *s.* pirotecnia, espetáculo pirotécnico

python | pay'ϑən | *s.* jibóia

Q

quack | kwak' | *s.* curandeiro, charlatão; grasnido (de pato etc.) / *a.* charlatanesco, de curandeiro / *vi.* grasnar

quadrangle | kwo'drangǝl | *s.* quadrângulo; pátio quadrangular

quaff | kwof' | *s.* gole grande, sorvo / *vt.* tragar, beber aos goles grandes

quagmire| kwag'mayǝ |*s.* atoleiro, lamaçal

quail | kweyl' | *s.* codorniz, codorna / *vi.* desanimar, recuar; intimidar-se

quaint| kweynt' | *a.* curioso, singular, extraordinário; mimoso, gracioso

quaintness | kweynt'nes | *s.* singularidade, encanto estranho e peculiar

quake| kweyk' |*s.* tremor, terremoto / *vi.* tremer, estremecer; trepidar; tiritar

qualification | kwolifikey'śǝn |*s.* habilitação, aptidão, qualificação; requisito

qualified | kwo'lifayd | *a.* habilitado, qualificado; idôneo, competente

qualify | kwo'lifay | *vt.* qualificar; habilitar / *vi.* qualificar-se; habilitar-se

qualifying examination | kwo'lifayingegzaminey'śǝn | *s.* exame de habilitação ou de admissão

qualifying round | kwo'lifayingrawnd' |*s.* = *qualifying examination*

quality | kwo'litī |*s.* qualidade

qualm | kw'om kwʌm' |*s.* escrúpulo; receio

quandary| kwon'dǝrī |*s.* dilema, perplexidade, dúvida

quantity | kwon'titī | *s.* quantidade

quarantine | kwo'rǝntin |*s.* quarentena

quarrel | kwo'rǝl |*s.* altercação, disputa, contenda. **-to pick a q. with** puxar briga com / *vi.* disputar, altercar; zangar-se; ficar de mal com

quarrelsome | kwo'rǝlsǝm | *a.* rixento, turbulento, briguento, brigão

quarry | kwo'rī | *s.* pedreira; (fig.) fonte de informações; caça; (fig.) presa / *vt.* extrair (de pedreira)

quarryman | kwo'řĩmǝn | *s.* trabalhador em pedreira

quart| kwót' |*s.* medida de capacidade (esp. para líquidos). **-to put q. into pint pot** fazer o impossível

quarter | kwó'tǝ | *s.* quarto, quarta parte; bairro; quarto (de animal); trimestre; quarto (da lua); quartel, graça, perdão; (EUA) moeda de 25 centavos; (*pl.*) alojamento. **-from all quarters** de todos os lados. **-at close quarters** de perto. **-to take up one's quarters** alojar-se (com, em etc.). **-to give no q. to** não dar quartel, atacar sem piedade / *a.* igual à quarta parte / *vt.* esquartejar; aquartelar, alojar / *vi.* alojar-se

quarterly | kwó'tǝlī | *s.* revista trimestral / *a.* trimestral / *adv.* por trimestre

quartermaster | kwó'tǝmʌstǝ |*s.* (náut.) contramestre; (mil.) oficial de intendência

quartet | kwótet' | *s.* (mús.) quarteto

quash | kwoś' | *vt.* dominar; reprimir, sufocar; (jur.) anular

quaver | kwey'və | s. trêmulo (da voz); (mús.) colcheia / vi. tremular; (mús.) trinar

quay | kı' | s. cais

queen | kwın' | s. rainha; dama (baralho)

queen bee | kwın'bı | s. abelha-mestra

queen mother | kwın'mâðə | s. rainha-mãe

queer | kwı'ə | s. (gír.) dinheiro falso; (gír.) homossexual / a. estranho, esquisito; suspeito (pessoa); extraordinário, curioso; (gír.) falsificado. **-to feel q.** sentir-se mal ou estranho. **-in Q. Street** (gír.) em dificuldades / vt. (gír.) atrapalhar, prejudicar, impedir

quell | kwel' | vt. sufocar, reprimir, esmagar; mitigar

quench | kwenś' | vt. apagar, extinguir; reprimir; matar (sede)

querulous | kwe'r̃ıuləs | a. queixoso, lamuriento

query | kwı'ərī | s. pergunta, pedido de informação; objeção, dúvida / vt. perguntar; duvidar (de)

quest | kwest' | s. busca, procura. **-in q. of** em demanda de, em busca de

question | kwes'šən | s. pergunta; questão; assunto, tema; contenda, litígio. **-beside the q.** que não vem ao caso. **-beyond all q.** indubitavelmente. **-out of q.** fora de cogitação. **-to call in q.** fazer objeção; duvidar; debater / vt. questionar; perguntar; contestar; debater; duvidar / vi. fazer perguntas, indagar

questionable | kwes'šənəbəl | a. duvidoso, controverso; suspeito

question mark | kwes'šənmAk | s. ponto de interrogação

questionnaire | kwestĭŏne'ə | s. questionário

queue | kĭu' | s. rabicho, trança de cabelo; fila (de pessoas, carros etc.) / vi. **-to q. up** fazer fila

quibble | kwi'bəl | s. sofisma, rodeio, evasiva; cavilação, chicana; trocadilho / vi. apelar para subterfúgios, fazer chicana

quick | kwik' | s. sabugo (sob a unha); sensibilidade, parte vital. **-the q. and the dead** os vivos e os mortos. **-to the q.** (coloq.) verdadeiro, genuíno. **-to cut to the q.** ferir profundamente / a. veloz, rápido; inteligente, vivo / adv. rapidamente; prontamente

quicken | kwi'kən | vt. apressar; estimular; excitar / vi. animar-se; agitar-se; apressar-se

quickly | kwik'lī | adv. depressa, rapidamente

quick march | kwik'mAš | s. (mil.) passo acelerado

quickness | kwik'nes | s. rapidez; vivacidade

quicksand | kwik'sand | s. areia movediça

quicksilver | kwik'silvə | s. azougue (tb. fig.), mercúrio, argento-vivo

quick-tempered | kwik'tempərd | a. irascível, genioso

quick-witted | kwik'witid | a. sagaz, perspicaz, esperto

quid | kwid' | s. pedaço de fumo de mascar; (gír.) libra esterlina

quiescent | kwaye'sənt | a. quiescente, imóvel, inerte

quiet | kway'ət | s. quietude; calma; repouso; paz. **-on the q.** secretamente, na surdina / a. sossegado; calmo; silencioso; calado; discreto; suave (cor); sutil (humor); oculto, secreto (ressentimento) / vt. acalmar / vi. acalmar-se

quieten | kway'ətən | vt. tranqüilizar, sossegar

quietness | kway'ətnes | s. paz, tranqüilidade, sossego

quill | kwil' | s. pena (da asa ou da cauda); espinho (de porco-espinho)

quilt | kwilt' | s. edredom

quince | kwins' | s. marmelo;

marmeleiro

quince jelly | kwins'jelī | *s.* marmelada

quinine | kwinɪn' | *s.* quinino

quinsy | kwin'zī | *s.* amigdalite, ⁀angina

quintessence | kwinte'səns | *s.* quinta-essência

quip | kwip' | *s.* observação sarcástica; dito espirituoso; trocadilho

quirk | kwɛk' | *s.* trocadilho, dito espirituoso; singularidade (de comportamento); arabesco

quit | kwit' | *a.* quite, desobrigado / *vt.* deixar, abandonar / *vi.* desistir, largar, ir embora

quite | kwayt' | *adv.* totalmente, inteiramente; verdadeiramente; (coloq.) muito. -q. other muito diferente. -q. something algo de notável. -q. a few bastante, um número considerável. -q. right! perfeitamente! -q. so

quiver | kwi'və | *s.* aljava; tremor, estremecimento / *vi.* tremer, estremecer

quixotic | kwikso'tik | *a.* quixotesco

quiz | kwiz' | *s.* teste, questionário; (rád., TV) teste de conhecimentos / *vt.* submeter a questionário.

quizzical | kwi'zikəl | *a.* excêntrico, curioso; zombeteiro, irônico, trocista

quoits | kwoyts' | *s.* jogo semelhante à malha

quota | kwow'tə | *s.* cota, quota, quota-parte; quinhão; máxima quantidade (imigrantes etc.)

quotation | kwowtey'śən | *s.* citação; (com.) cotação

quotation-marks | kwowtey'śənmʌks | *spl.* aspas

quote | kwowt' | *vt.* citar; (com.) cotar

R

rabbi | ra'bay | *s.* rabino

rabbit | ra'bit | *s.* coelho

rabble | ra'bəl | *s.* turba, multidão; ralé, populacho

rabid | rey'bid | *a.* furioso, raivoso

rabies | rey'bɪz | *s.* (med.) raiva, hidrofobia

race | reys' | *s.* corrida, páreo; raça (humana ou animal); corrente, torrente / *vt.* fazer correr / *vi.* correr

racehorse | reys'hós | *s.* cavalo de corridas

race-track | reys'trak | *s.* pista de corridas (de cavalos, automóveis etc.)

racial | rey'śəl | *a.* racial

raciness | rey'sines | *s.* vigor, vivacidade, energia

racing | rey'sing | *s.* corrida (de cavalos etc.)

racism | rey'sizəm | *s.* racismo

racist | rey'sist | *s.a.* racista

rack | rak' | *s.* prateleira, estante; cabide; manjedoura; cremalheira. -to go to r. and ruin arruinar-se totalmente / *vt.* torturar, atormentar; oprimir. -to r. one's brains dar tratos à bola

racket | ra'kit | *s.* raquete (de tênis etc.); algazarra, barulho; (gír.) trapaça, tramóia, negociata; (gír.) extorsão

racketeer | rakitɪ'ə | *s.* (gír.) traficante, bandido; (gír.) extorsionário / *vi.* (gír.) extorquir

racy | rey'sī | *a.* animado, vigoroso, vivo

radar | rey'dʌ |s. radar

radiance | rey'dĭəns |s. brilho, fulgor, radiância

radiant | rey'dĭənt | a. radiante, brilhante

radiate | rey'dĭeyt |vt. irradiar, emitir

radiation | reydĭey'śən |s. radiação

radiator | reydĭey'tə |s. radiador

radical | ra'dikəl |s.a. radical

radio | rey'dĭow |s. rádio / vt. vi. transmitir ou comunicar-se por rádio

radioactive | reydĭowak'tiv | a. radioativo

radiogram | rey'dĭowgram | s. radiograma

radish | ra'diś |s. rabanete

radium | rey'dĭəm | s. (quím.) rádio

radius | rey'dĭəs |s. raio; circunferência; (anat.) rádio

raffle | ra'fəl |s. rifa / vt. rifar

raft | rʌft' |s. balsa, jangada

rafter | rʌf'tə |s. caibro, viga, trave

rag | rag' |s. trapo, farrapo; (pl.) andrajos. -**in rags** em farrapos, andrajoso / vt. atormentar, zombar de; (gír.) passar um carão, admoestar

ragamuffin | ragəmâ'fin | a. maltrapilho

rag-and-bone man | rag'and-bownmən |s. negociante (ambulante) de roupas velhas

rage | reyj' |s. fúria, raiva, cólera; voga, moda; paixão, mania. -**to be in a r.** estar furioso. -**to be all the r.** fazer furor / vt. enfurecer-se; alastrar-se (epidemia)

ragged | ra'gid | a. esfarrapado, roto; surrado; imperfeito, inacabado

raging | rey'jing | s. fúria / a. furioso

raid | reyd' |s. ataque de surpresa; reide; batida policial / vt. invadir, assaltar, atacar

raider | rey'də |s. invasor, assaltante, atacante

rail | reyl' |s. barra de grade; cerca; corrimão; parapeito; amurada (de navio); trilho. -**by r.** por via férrea. -**to run off the rails** descarrilar / vt. prover de barra ou viga; cercar; pôr trilhos em. -**tor. in** cercar. -**tor. off** separar com cerca ou barreira / vi. -**to r. against** injuriar; ralhar com; zombar de

railing | rey'ling |s. balaustrada; grade

rail road | reyl'rowd |s. (EUA) estrada de ferro

railway | reyl'wey |s. estrada de ferro

railway man | reyl'weymən |s. ferroviário

raiment | rey'mənt |s. vestuário, roupa, traje

rain | reyn' |s. chuva. -**come r. or come shine** chova ou faça sol / a. de chuva / vi. chover. -**to r. cats and dogs** chover a cântaros

rainbow | reyn'bow |s. arco-íris

rain coat | reyn'kowt |s. capa de chuva, impermeável

raindrop | reyn'drop |s. pingo de chuva

rainfall | reyn'fól |s. chuva, precipitação atmosférica

rain storm | reyn'stóm |s. tempestade de chuva

rainy | rey'nĭ |a. chuvoso, de chuva

raise | reyz' |s. aumento; elevação / vt. levantar; criar (gado etc.); educar (crianças); aumentar (salário); cultivar, produzir; tirar (chapéu); provocar (risos); ressuscitar

raisin | rey'zən |s. passa (uva)

rake | reyk' |s. ancinho; rodo; libertino, devasso; inclinação, caimento / vt. limpar com ancinho; raspar; esquadrinhar; explorar; (mil.) varrer (a tiros ou rajadas). -**to r. together** juntar com o ancinho (tb. fig.). -**to r. out** tirar, raspar. -**to r. up** recolher (dinheiro de aposta); esquadrinhar, revolver

rake-off | reyk'of | s. (coloq., pej.) comissão ilícita (ou lucro)

rakish | rey'kiś | *a.* libertino, licencioso, dissoluto. **-at a r. angle** inclinado, de lado

rally | ra'lī | *s.* reunião, concentração, reagrupamento; recuperação (de energias); rali (competição automobilística etc.); (EUA) comício monstro; (desp.) contra-ataque / *vt.* reunir; reanimar / *vi.* cobrar ânimo, reagir. **-to r. round** reunir-se ao redor de, tomar o partido de

ram | ram' | *s.* carneiro / *vt.* abalroar; bater; calcar, comprimir, socar; fincar, cravar. **-to r. in** meter à força

ramble | ram'bəl | *s.* passeio, caminhada / *vi.* passear a pé, caminhar; divagar; devanear

rambler | ram'blə | *s.* excursionista, caminhante

rambling | ram'bling | *a.* incoerente, desconexo; perambulante; divagador; torta, irregular (rua, casa)

ramification | ramifikey'śən | *s.* ramificação

ramp | ramp' | *s.* rampa; ladeira; (gír.) trapaça

rampage | rampeyĵ' | *s.* agitação, comportamento violento. **-to be on a r.** estar furioso / *vt.* agitar-se; esbravejar; grassar (vício, doença)

rampant | ram'pənt | *a.* exaltado, agressivo (animal); exuberante; extravagante; desenfreado; luxuriante (vegetação); (heráld.) rampante

rampart | ram'pʌt | *s.* baluarte, muralha

ramshackle | ram'śakəl | *a.* desmoronado, em ruínas

ranch | ranś' | *s.* (EUA) fazenda de gado

rancid | ran'sid | *a.* rançoso

rancour, rancor | ran'kə | *s.* rancor, ressentimento

random | ran'dəm | *s.* acaso. **-at r.** ao acaso

range | reynĵ' | *s.* alcance; raio de ação; fileira; série; classe; com-

petência, jurisdição; limites (de variações); pastagens; fogão de cozinha. **-at close r.** a curta distância; à queima-roupa. **-within r.** ao alcance de / *vt.* enfileirar, alinhar; classificar; percorrer / *vi.* estender-se, prolongar-se; colocar-se; enfileirar-se; vaguear; variar; ter o alcance de

range-finder | reynĵ'fayndə | *s.* telêmetro

ranger | reyn'ĵə | *s.* guarda-florestal, guarda-parque

rank | rank' | *s.* fileira; linha; classe social; (mil.) posto. **-r. and file** soldados rasos; a plebe, as massas / *a.* luxuriante, viçoso; fértil; grosseiro, indecoroso; repelente; fétido; rançoso; imperdoável; rematado, consumado / *vt.* enfileirar; (mil.) formar; ser superior a / *vi.* enfileirar-se; ser considerado, ser contado; ser superior a; ter grau ou posto superior a. **-to r. with** equiparar-se com. **-to r. first** ocupar o primeiro lugar. **-to r. high** ser muito cotado ou estimado. **-to r. past** ou **off** marchar, desfilar

rankle | ran'kəl | *vi.* irritar

ransack | ran'sak | *vt.* saquear; esquadrinhar

ransom | ran'səm | *s.* resgate / *vt.* resgatar

rant | rant' | *s.* arenga; linguagem empolada / *vt.* arengar; dizer em linguagem empolada; declamar, perorar

rap | rap' | *s.* golpe seco, pancada rápida / *vi.* bater rapidamente

rapacious | rəpey'śəs | *a.* ávido; voraz; rapinante

rapacity | rəpa'sitī | *s.* avidez; voracidade; rapacidade

rape | reyp' | *s.* violação; estupro / *vt.* violar; estuprar

rapid | ra'pid | *s.* (ger. *pl.*) rápidos, parte encachoeirada (de rio) / *a.* rápido, veloz; escarpado

rapidity | rəpi'ditī | *s.* rapidez, velocidade

rapprochement | raproś'mon | *s.* estreitamento de relações (esp. entre países)

rapt | rapt' | *a.* enlevado, arrebatado, extasiado

rapture | rap'śə | *s.* arrebatamento, êxtase. -**to be** ou **to go into raptures** ficar encantado

rapturous | rap'šərəs | *a.* enlevado, extático

rare | re'ə | *a.* raro; invulgar; de alta qualidade; (cul.) malpassado

rareness | re'ənes | *s.* raridade

rarity | re'əritī | *s.* raridade; coisa incomum; (*pl.*) curiosidades

rascal | ras'kəl | *s.* velhaco, patife; malandro

rase, raze | reyz' | *vt.* arrasar

rash | raś' | *s.* erupção (na pele) / *a.* precipitado, irrefletido

rasher | ra'śə | *s.* fatia fina (de presunto ou *bacon*)

rashness | raś'nes | *s.* precipitação, imprudência

rasp | rʌsp' | *s.* grosa (ferramenta)

raspberry | rʌz'bərī | *s.* framboesa

rasping | rʌs'ping | *a.* áspero, dissonante

rat | rat' | *s.* ratazana; (gír.) traidor. -**to smell a r.** ter suspeitas, desconfiar / *interj.* -**rats!** droga! / *vi.* desertar, virar a casaca

rate | reyt' | *s.* taxa; tarifa; preço, custo; classe, ordem; ritmo; índice; velocidade, marcha. -**at any r.** de qualquer maneira. -**at the r. of** à razão de. -**at that r.** (coloq.) a julgar por isso. -**first r.** de primeira ordem. -**second r.** de qualidade inferior. -**r. of exchange** câmbio. -**r. of progress** cadência, ritmo / *vt.* avaliar, classificar / *vi.* estar avaliado (classificado) em

rather | rʌ'ðə | *adv.* antes, preferivelmente, mais precisamente; pelo contrário; bastante, muito. -**had r.** preferiria. -**r. than**

em vez de. -**the r.** mormente. -**the r. that** tanto mais que

ratify | ra'tifay | *vt.* ratificar

rating | rey'ting | *s.* (náut.) posto, posição; classificação

ratio | rey'śow | *s.* proporção

ration | ra'śən | *s.* ração / *vt.* racionar

rational | ra'śənəl | *a.* racional

rationalism | ra'śənəlizəm | *s.* racionalismo

rationalize | ra'śənəlayz | *vt.* racionalizar; justificar, explicar

ration card | ra'śənkʌd | *s.* cartão de racionamento

rattle | ra'təl | *s.* barulhada; algazarra; animação; matraca; chocalho; rufo (de tambor); guizo (de cascavel); tagarelice / *vt.* chocalhar; sacudir, agitar; (coloq.) confundir, desconcertar / *vi.* chocalhar; mover-se ruidosamente; bater (porta, janela); tagarelar. -**to r. down** avançar ruidosamente (carroça, carro etc.). -**to get rattled** (coloq.) agitar-se; inquietar-se; zangar-se

rattle-brain | ra'təlbreyn | *a.* desmiolado, frívolo

rattlesnake | ra'təlsneyk | *s.* cascavel

rattling | rat'ling | *s.* ruído / *a.* chocalhante; animado; ruidoso / *adv.* extremamente

raucous | ró'kəs | *a.* rouco

ravage | ra'viĵ | *s.* estrago, devastação / *vt. vi.* arruinar, devastar; pilhar

rave | reyv' | *s.* delírio / *vi.* delirar

ravel | ra'vəl | *vt.* emaranhar

raven | rey'vən | *s.* corvo

ravening | ra'vəning | *a.* voraz

ravenous | ra'vənəs | *a.* ávido, voraz, sôfrego, faminto

ravine | rəvin' | *s.* ravina

raving | rey'ving | *a.* delirante; furioso; frenético

ravish | ra'viś | *vt.* raptar; estuprar, violentar; arrebatar, extasiar

ravishing | ra'viśing | *a.* encantador, arrebatador

raw | ró' | *s.* esfoladura, ferida; ponto sensível. **-to touch on the r.** tocar na ferida / *a.* cru; bruto, em estado natural; em rama (algodão); inexperiente; dolorido; (coloq.) obsceno; (coloq.) injusto

raw-boned | ró'bownd | *a.* ossudo

raw cotton | ró'kotən | *s.* algodão em rama

rawhide | ró'hayd | *s.* couro cru; corda ou chicote de couro cru

raw material | ró'mətı'rīəl | *s.* matéria-prima

ray | rey' | *s.* raio; arraia

rayon | rey'ən | *s.* raiom, seda artificial

razor | rey'zə | *s.* navalha de barbear; aparelho de barbear

reach | riš' | *s.* alcance. **-out of r.** fora de alcance. **-within r. of** ao alcance de / *vt.* alcançar; passar; estender. **-to r. out** estender a mão / *vi.* estender-se

react | rīakt' | *vi.* reagir

reaction | rīak'šən | *s.* reação

reactionary | rīak'šənrī | *s.a.* reacionário

read | rid' | *vt.* ler; interpretar; adivinhar; dizer, rezar (inscrição, documento etc.); estudar. **-to r. out** ou **aloud** ler em voz alta. **-to r. between the lines** ler nas entrelinhas. **-to be well r.** ter muita leitura, ter muitos conhecimentos

readable | rı'dəbəl | *a.* legível; agradável de ler

reader | rı'də | *s.* leitor; professor; revisor; manual de leitura

readily | re'dilĭ | *adv.* prontamente; de boa vontade

readiness | re'dines | *s.* presteza; boa vontade; facilidade. **-to be in r.** estar alerta, estar pronto

reading | rı'ding | *s.* leitura; interpretação

ready | re'dĭ | *a.* pronto; disposto; alerta; vivo, esperto, vivaz; fácil, espontâneo (sorriso). **-to**

get r. preparar(-se), aprontar(-se)

ready-made | re'dĭmeyd | *a.* feito, já pronto (*ready-made suit* roupa feita); comum, pouco original

ready money | re'dĭmânĭ | *s.* dinheiro à vista

real | rı'əl | *a.* verdadeiro, genuíno, autêntico; real

real estate | rı'əlesteyt' | *s.* bens imóveis

realism | rı'əlizəm | *s.* realismo

realist | rı'əlist | *s.* realista

realistic | rıəlis'tik | *a.* realístico

reality | rıa'litĭ | *s.* realidade

realization | rıəlayzey'śən | *s.* realização, concretização; percepção; conversão em dinheiro

realize | rı'əlayz | *vt.* dar-se conta de, fazer idéia de; imaginar; compreender; realizar (capital), lucrar / *vi.* converter em dinheiro

really | rı'əlĭ | *adv.* realmente, na verdade

realm | relm' | *s.* reino, domínio

ream | rim' | *s.* resma

reap | rip' | *vt. vi.* ceifar, colher

reaper | rı'pə | *s.* ceifeiro, segador

reaping-machine | rı'pingmə-śín' | *s.* segadeira mecânica

reappear | rıəpı'ə | *vi.* reaparecer

reapply | rıəplay' | *vi.* requerer ou solicitar novamente

reappoint | rıəpoynt' | *vt.* nomear novamente (cargo)

rear | rı'ə | *s.* retaguarda, traseira. **-to bring up the r.** ser o último, chegar ou vir na retaguarda / *a.* posterior, último / *vt.* erguer; criar, educar (criança) / *vi.* empinar; levantar-se

rear-admiral | rı'əad'mirəl | *s.* contra-almirante

rearguard | rı'əgʌd | *s.* retaguarda

rear-view mirror | rı'əvĭumi'rə | *s.* espelho retrovisor

reason | rı'zən | *s.* razão; causa, motivo; argumento, fundamento; premissa. **-by r. of** por causa de. **-within** r. dentro do razoável. **-out of** r. absurdo. **-to bring to** r. convencer, persuadir (alguém) / vi. pensar, raciocinar. **-to** r. **with (somebody)** chamar (alguém) à razão

reasonable| rɪ'zənəbəl |a. razoável

reasonably | rɪ'zənəblī | adv. razoavelmente

reasoning | rɪ'zəning | s. raciocínio; argumentação

reassert | rɪəsEt' | vt. reafirmar

reassurance | rɪəsu'rəns | s. reafirmação, afirmação reiterada; confiança renovada

reassure | rɪəsu'ə | vt. reassegurar, assegurar novamente; tranqüilizar

rebate | rɪ'beyt | s. abatimento, desconto

rebel | re'bəl |s.a. rebelde, revoltado / | ribel' | vi. revoltar-se, sublevar-se

rebellion | ribe'lĭən | s. rebelião, revolta

rebellious | ribe'lĭəs | a. rebelde, insurrecto, insurgente; desobediente

rebound | ribawnd' |s. ricochete / vi. ricochetear

rebuff | ribâf' | s. repulsa, recusa /vt. repelir, rejeitar

rebuke | ribĭuk' | s. repreensão, censura / vt. repreender, censurar

rebut | ribât' | vt. refutar

recalcitrant | rikal'sitrənt | s.a. recalcitrante, obstinado

recall | rikól' | s. revogação / vt. chamar de volta; lembrar, recordar; revogar, cancelar; demitir. **-beyond** r. totalmente esquecido

recant | rikant' | vt. vi. retratar(-se), desdizer(-se)

recapitulate | rikəpi'tĭuleyt | vt. recapitular

recede | risid' | vi. retroceder, recuar; retirar-se; baixar (maré)

receipt | risit' | s. recibo; receita, fórmula; recebimento; (pl.) re-

ceitas, rendimentos. **-on** r. **of** após recepção de. **-to acknowledge** r. **of** acusar o recebimento de. **-to be in** r. **of** estar de posse de. **-to pay on** r. pagar ao receber, pagar contra entrega (encomenda etc.) / vt. passar recibo

receive | risiv' | vt. receber

receiver | risi'və | s. receptor (rádio, telégrafo etc.); fone; recebedor; (jur.) receptador; (jur.) síndico de massa falida; (jur.) depositário de bens em litígio

receiving | risi'ving | a. recebedor; receptor

receiving set | risi'vingset | s. receptor (de rádio etc.)

recent | rɪ'sənt | a. recente

recently | rɪ'səntlī | adv. recentemente

receptacle | risep'təkəl | s. receptáculo

reception | risep'şən | s. recepção; acolhimento

recess | rises' | s. reentrância, vão; nicho (na parede); escaninho; recreio (escolar); férias (parlamentares); suspensão, interrupção (de atividades)

recession | rise'şən |s. retrocesso, recuo; (econ.) recessão

recipe | re'sipī | s. receita

reciprocal | rəsi'prəkəl | a. recíproco

reciprocate | rəsi'prəkeyt | vt. retribuir

recital | risay'təl | s. (mús.) recital; narrativa, narração

recitation | resitey'şən | s. recitação; declamação

recite | risayt' | vt. recitar; declamar

reckless | rek'les | a. precipitado, irrefletido, imprudente; negligente

recklessness| rek'lesnes |s. temeridade, ousadia, atrevimento; negligência

reckon| re'kən | vt. calcular, avaliar, computar; considerar, julgar, supor / vi. contar, calcular.

-to r. on ou upon contar com.
-to r. up avaliar, calcular. -to r.
with ajustar contas com; levar
em conta

reckoning| re'kǝning |s. cálculo;
avaliação, estimativa; ajuste de
contas. -to be out in one's r. en-
ganar-se no cálculo. -day of r.
dia do Juízo Final

reclaim | rikleym' | vt. regenerar,
reformar (pessoa); recuperar,
aproveitar (terras); recuperar
(borracha, papel etc.); reivindicar

recline | riklayn' | vt. vi. recli-
nar(-se), recostar(-se), apoiar(-se)

recluse | riklʋs' | s. a. recluso,
solitário

recognition | rekǝgni'sǝn | s. re-
conhecimento

recognize | re'kǝgnayz | vt. reco-
nhecer, admitir

recoil| rikoyl' |s. recuo; coice (de
arma de fogo) / vi. recuar

recollect | re'kǝlekt | vt. vi. lem-
brar(-se), recordar(-se)

recollection | rekǝlek'śǝn |s. lem-
brança, recordação, reminis-
cência

recommend | re'kǝmend | vt. re-
comendar; aconselhar

recommendation | rekǝmendey'-
śǝn |s. recomendação

recompense | re'kǝmpens | s. re-
cómpensa / vt. recompensar;
indenizar, ressarcir

reconcile | re'kǝnsayl | vt. reconci-
liar. -to r. oneself to conformar-
se com

reconciliation | rekǝnsilĩey'śǝn |
s. reconciliação

reconnaissance | riko'nisǝns | s.
(mil., náut.) reconhecimento

reconnoitre, reconnoiter | rekǝ-
noy'tǝ | vt. (mil., náut.) fazer
um reconhecimento de

record | re'kód | s. registro; ins-
crição; disco fonográfico; re-
corde; (pl.) arquivos, anais /
| rikód' | vt. registrar; anotar

recorder | rikó'dǝ | s. registra-
dor; amanuense, escrivão; gra-
vador, aparelho de gravação

(som); (mús.) espécie de flauta
antiga

recount | rikawnt' | vt. narrar ou
contar minuciosamente

recoup | rikʋp' | vt. recuperar;
reembolsar

recourse | rikós' | s. recurso. -to
have r. to recorrer a, apelar
para

recover | rikâ'vǝ | vt. recobrar,
recuperar; (jur.) retomar / vi.
restabelecer-se

recovery | rikâ'vǝrī | s. recupera-
ção; restabelecimento (saúde).
-past r. sem remédio, incurável

recreation | rekrīey'śǝn |s. diverti-
mento, passatempo, recreação

recrimination | rikriminey'śǝn |
s. recriminação

recruit| rikrut' |s. recruta; nova-
to / vt. recrutar

rectangle | rek'tangǝl | s. retân-
gulo

rectify | rek'tifay | vt. retificar,
corrigir

rectitude | rek'titĩud | s. retidão,
integridade

rector | rek'tǝ | s. reitor, pároco,
prior

recumbent | rikâm'bǝnt | a. dei-
tado, reclinado; em repouso

recuperate | rikĩu'pǝreyt | vi. res-
tabelecer-se

recur| rikE' | vi. repetir-se; voltar
a um assunto; acudir à memó-
ria; (med.) recair

recurrence | rikâ'rǝns | s. repeti-
ção; retorno; recordação

recurrent | rikâ'rǝnt | a. periódi-
co; que reaparece

red | red' | s. a cor vermelha; (co-
loq.) comunista, extremista.
-to grow r. corar. -in the r. endi-
vidado. -to see r. (coloq.) enfu-
recer-se / a. vermelho; corado
(rosto); tinto (vinho); (coloq.)
comunista, extremista

redden | re'dǝn | vt. vi. averme-
lhar(-se), tornar(-se) vermelho,
corar

redeem | ridım' | vt. remir, redi-
mir; resgatar; cumprir (pro-

messa); contrabalançar

redeemer | rɪdɪ'mə | s. redentor (tb. maiúsc.)

redeem feature | ridɪm'fɪ'sə | s. aspecto compensador, lado favorável

redelivery | rɪdili'vərī | s. nova entrega

redemption | ridem'śən | s. redenção; amortização (de dívida). **-beyond r.** sem esperança, sem remédio; incorrigível

red-haired | red'heərd | a. ruivo

red-handed | red'handid | a. em flagrante

red herring | red'hering | s. arenque defumado; (fig.) pista falsa

redirect | rɪdirekt' | vt. reexpedir (cartas)

redistribution | rɪdistribɪu'śən | s. redistribuição

red-letter | red'letə | a. feliz, memorável (data)

redness | red'nes | s. vermelhidão, rubor

redolent | re'dowlənt | a. fragrante. **-r. of** que cheira a, que está impregnado de

redouble | rɪdâ'bəl | vt. redobrar, intensificar

redoubtable | ridaw'təbəl | a. temível, terrível

redound | ridawnd' | vi. redundar em

red pepper | redpe'pə | s. pimenta malagueta; pimentão (maduro)

redress | rɪdres' | s. compensação, reparação / vt. reparar, compensar; desagravar; retificar, corrigir

redskin | red'skin | s. pele-vermelha (índio norte-americano)

reduce | ridɪus' | vt. reduzir; abater (preço); diminuir; forçar a; ser forçado a; obrigar, constranger. **-to r. to the ranks** (mil.) rebaixar a soldado. **-in reduced circumstances** na miséria / vi. ser reduzido; emagrecer

reduction | ridâk'śən | s. redução; abatimento (de preço); emagre-

cimento; (mil.) rebaixamento de posto

redundancy | ridân'dənsī | s. redundância

redundant | ridân'dənt | a. redundante; supérfluo

redwood | red'wud | s. (bot.) espécie de sequóia da Califórnia

re-echo | rie'kow | vt. vi. repercutir, ressoar; repetir

reed | rɪd' | s. junco, cana; (mús.) palheta (de instrumento de sopro)

reef | rif' | s. recife; (min.) veio

reef-knot | rif'not | s. (náut.) nó direito

reek | rik' | s. mau cheiro (de alho, tabaco etc.), fartum / vi. cheirar mal

reel | ril' | s. carretel, bobina; carretilha ou molinete de pesca; escocesa (dança) / vt. enrolar / vi. rodopiar, cambalear

refectory | rifek'tərī | s. refeitório

refer | rifɛ' | vt. referir; classificar; atribuir; submeter; recomendar / vi. referir-se; consultar

referee | refərī' | s. árbitro / vt. vi. arbitrar

reference | ref'rəns | s. referência; recomendação. **-with r. to** com referência a; em resposta a / a. de referência, de consulta

reference book | ref'rənsbuk | s. livro, obra de consulta

refill | rɪ'fil | s. carga (de caneta, isqueiro etc.) / vt. encher novamente, reabastecer

refine | rifayn' | vt. refinar, purificar; aperfeiçoar, requintar

refined | rifaynd' | a. refinado; polido; requintado

refinement | rifayn'mənt | s. refinamento; requinte

refinery | rifay'nərī | s. refinaria

refining | rifay'ning | s. refinação

reflect | riflekt' | vt. refletir; mostrar, revelar / vi. refletir; meditar, pensar; refletir-se em (favorável ou desfavoravelmente)

reflection, reflexion | riflek'ʃən | *s.* reflexão; meditação; censura, acusação. **-to cast reflections on** criticar, censurar. **-on r.** pensando bem, reconsiderando

reflex | rɪ'fleks | *s.* reflexo / *a.* reflexo, refletido

reflex action | rɪ'fleksak'ʃən | *s.* ato reflexo

reform | rifóm' | *s.* reforma / *vt.* reformar / *vi.* reformar-se, corrigir-se

re-form | rɪ'fóm | *vt. vi.* formar(-se) de novo; refazer, remodelar

reformation | refəmey'ʃən | *s.* reforma (tb. maiúsc., hist.)

reformatory | rifó'mətrī | *s.* reformatório

refractory | rifrak'tərī | *a.* refratário; obstinado, teimoso

refrain | rifreyn' | *s.* estribilho, refrão / *vi.* abster-se. **-to r. from** abster-se de

refresh | rifreʃ' | *vt.* refrescar; reabastecer; refazer-se / *vi.* restaurar as forças

refreshing | rifre'ʃiŋ | *a.* refrescante

refreshment | rifreʃ'mənt | *s.* refresco; revigoramento; refeição leve

refreshment room | rifreʃ'məntrum | *s.* bufê (esp. em estações ferroviárias)

refrigeration | rifrijərey'ʃən | *s.* refrigeração

refrigerator | rifrijərey'tə | *s.* geladeira, refrigerador

refuel | riffu'əl | *vt. vi.* reabastecer(-se) de combustível

refuge | re'ffuj | *s.* refúgio, abrigo. **-to take r.** refugiar-se

refugee | reffuji' | *s.* refugiado

refund | rɪ'fând | *s.* reembolso / *vt.* reembolsar, restituir, devolver

refusal | riffu'zəl | *s.* recusa

refuse | re'ffʊz | *s.* refugo, rebotalho / | riffʊz' | *vt.* recusar, rejeitar; negar-se a / *vi.* recusar-se

refute | riffut' | *vt.* refutar, rebater

regal | rɪ'gəl | *a.* real, régio; suntuoso

regale | ri'geyl | *vt. vi.* regalar(-se), deleitar(-se)

regalia | rigey'liə | *spl.* insígnias reais

regard | rigâd' | *s.* consideração, estima, respeito; (*pl.*) saudações, lembranças. **-with r. to** com respeito a. **-having r. for** ou **out of r. for** em atenção a. **-with due r.** com o devido respeito / *vt.* olhar, observar, considerar. **-as regards** quanto a / *vi.* olhar, prestar atenção

regarding | rigâ'ding | *prep.* com respeito a, a respeito de

regardless | rigâd'les | *a.* indiferente, desatento. **-r. of** independentemente de, sem levar em conta / *adv.* sem ligar às conseqüências

regatta | riga'tə | *s.* regata

regency | rɪ'jənsī | *s.* regência

regenerate | rije'nəreyt | *a.* regenerado / *vt. vi.* regenerar(-se)

regicide | rijisayd' | *s.* regicídio; regicida

regime | rejim' | *s.* regime

regiment | re'jimənt | *s.* regimento / *vt.* arregimentar, organizar

region | rɪ'jən | *s.* região. **-in the r. of** aproximadamente

regional | rɪ'jənəl | *a.* regional

register | re'jistə | *s.* registro; inscrição; lista / *vt. vi.* registrar(-se); inscrever(-se)

registrar | rejistrâ' | *s.* escrivão; oficial do registro civil

registration | rejistrey'ʃən | *s.* registro; matrícula

registry | re'jistrī | *s.* registro, arquivo, cartório

regret | rigret' | *s.* pesar, mágoa; arrependimento. **-to express regrets** pedir desculpas; lamentar. **-to send one's regrets** escrever lamentando não poder aceitar / *vt.* lamentar; arrepender-se de

regrettable | rigre'təbəl | a. lamentável

regular | re'g̃ulə |a. regular; metódico; habitual; (coloq.) perfeito, rematado

regular army | re'g̃uləʌ'mī | s. exército efetivo

regularity | reg̃iula'ritī | s. regularidade

regulate | re'g̃uleyt | vt. regular; acertar (relógio)

regulation | reg̃iuley'śən | s. regulamento / a. regulamentar, usual

regulator | re'g̃uleytə |s. regulador

rehearsal | rɪhE'səl | s. (teat.) ensaio

rehearse | rihEs' |vt. ensaiar; recitar; repetir do princípio ao fim

reign | reyn' | s. reinado / vi. reinar; prevalecer

reigning | rey'ning | a. reinante; predominante

reimburse | rɪimbEs' | vt. reembolsar, indenizar

rein | reyn' | s. rédea (tb. pl.). -to give free reins to dar rédeas a / vt. controlar, refrear

reindeer | reyn'dɪə |s. rena

reinforce | rɪinfós' | vt. reforçar, fortalecer

reinforcement | rɪinfós'mənt | s. reforço; (pl., mil.) reforços

reinstate | rɪinsteyt' | vt. restabelecer, reintegrar

reiterate | rɪi'təreyt | vt. reiterar, repetir

reject | riȷ̌ekt' | s. refugo / vt. rejeitar; repelir; vomitar

rejection | riȷ̌ek'śən | s. rejeição, recusa; rebotalho, refugo

rejoice | riȷ̌oys' | vt. vi. alegrar(-se)

rejoicing | riȷ̌oy'sing |s. regozijo, júbilo; comemoração, festa/ a. festivo, jubiloso

rejoin | riȷ̌oyn' | vt. ingressar novamente em ; reincorporar-se, alistar-se de novo / vi. reunir-se; (jur.) treplicar

rejoinder | riȷ̌oyn'də |s. resposta; réplica; (jur.) tréplica

rejuvenate | riȷ̌fu'vəneyt | vt. rejuvenescer; remoçar

rekindle | rɪkin'dəl | vt. reacender

relapse | rilaps' | s. (med.) recaída, recidiva / vi. recair, reincidir

relate | rileyt' | vt. relatar, narrar; relacionar / vi. relacionar-se com; referir-se a

related | riley'tid | a. relacionado, ligado; aparentado; narrado, contado. -it is r. (that) diz-se (que)

relation | riley'śən |s. relação, conexão; parente; parentesco; (pl.) relações. -in r. to com respeito a

relationship | riley'śənśip | s. relação, conexão; parentesco

relative | re'lətiv | s. parente / a. relativo, conexo

relax | rilaks' |vt. descansar, relaxar; mitigar, suavizar / vi. descansar, repousar, estar à vontade; afrouxar, abrandar

relaxation | rilaksey'śən | s. descanso; passatempo, divertimento; abrandamento, afrouxamento

relay | ri'ley | s. revezamento, turno, substituição; muda (de cavalos); retransmissão (de rádio etc.); (eletr.) relé / vt. revezar; retransmitir (por rádio etc.)

relay race | ri'leyreys | s. corrida de revezamento

release | rilis' |s. libertação; liberação; dispensa; recibo, quitação; exoneração; permissão para exibir ou divulgar / vt. libertar; livrar; exonerar; permitir a exibição ou divulgação (de livro, filme etc.)

relegate | re'ligeyt | vt. relegar, pôr de parte; desterrar; rebaixar; submeter, confiar (a outrem)

relent | rilent' | vi. enternecer-se, abrandar-se; ceder, afrouxar

relentless | rilent'les | a. inexorável, implacável

relevance | re'livəns | *s.* relevância; pertinência

relevant | re'livənt | *a.* relevante; pertinente

reliability | rilayəbi'litī | *s.* confiança, segurança; integridade; fidedignidade

reliable | rilay'əbəl | *a.* seguro, digno de confiança; resistente; fidedigno

reliance | relay'əns | *s.* confiança

relic | re'lik | *s.* relíquia; (*pl.*) ruínas, restos mortais

relief | rilif' | *s.* alívio; auxílio, socorro; substituto; reforço; (mil.) levantamento (de cerco); revezamento (de sentinela); relevo; (jur.) reparação, compensação

relieve | riliv' | *vt.* aliviar, mitigar; socorrer; render, revezar (sentinela); (mil.) levantar (cerco); exonerar, desobrigar. **-to r. nature** fazer uma necessidade fisiológica

religion | rili'jən | *s.* religião

religious | rili'jəs | *a.* religioso

relinquish | rilin'kwiś | *vt.* abandonar, renunciar, abrir mão de

relish | re'liś | *s.* sabor, gosto; atrativo; condimento; aperitivo (de comer) / *vt.* saborear; condimentar; gostar de / *vi.* ter gosto de; agradar

reluctance | rilâk'təns | *s.* relutância

reluctant | rilâk'tənt | *a.* relutante, hesitante. **-to be r. to** hesitar em

reluctantly | rilâk'təntlī | *adv.* com relutância

rely | rilay' | *vi.* confiar em, contar com

remain | rimeyn' | *vi.* ficar, permanecer; sobrar, restar; perdurar; persistir. **-it remains to be seen** resta saber-se

remainder | rimeyn'də | *s.* resto; restante; sobejo; saldo / *a.* restante

remains | rimeynz' | *spl.* restos; vestígios; obras póstumas

remand | rimʌnd' | *vt.* reenviar; (jur.) mandar voltar à prisão

remark | rimʌk' | *s.* observação / *vt.* observar, notar, reparar em / *vi.* fazer comentários. **-tor. on** ou **upon** fazer comentários ou observações sobre

remarkable | rimʌ'kəbəl | *a.* notável, excepcional, singular

remarry | rima'ri | *vi.* casar em segundas núpcias

remedial | rimi'diəl | *a.* terapêutico, que cura; corretivo, reparador

remedy | re'mədī | *s.* remédio / *vt.* remediar

remember | rimem'bə | *vt.* lembrar, recordar. **-r. me to** dê lembranças minhas a / *vi.* lembrar-se, recordar-se

remembrance | rimem'brəns | *s.* lembrança, recordação; reminiscência; (*pl.*) lembranças

remind | rimaynd' | *vt. vi.* lembrar, fazer lembrar

reminder | rimayn'də | *s.* lembrete; advertência; lembrança; momento, monumento

reminisce | reminis' | *vi.* recordar, relembrar

reminiscence | remini'səns | *s.* reminiscência; recordação; (*pl.*) memórias

reminiscent | remini'sənt | *a.* rememorativo; que tem reminiscências. **-to be r.** of lembrar

remiss | rimis' | *a.* negligente, descuidado; apático, indolente

remission | rimi'śən | *s.* remissão

remit | rimit' | *vt.* remeter, enviar; remitir, perdoar (dívidas, pecados)

remittance | rimi'təns | *s.* pagamento, remessa

remnant | rem'nənt | *s.* remanescente, resto; retalho (de fazenda)

remonstrate | re'mənstreyt | *vi.* advertir, censurar

remorse | rimós' | *s.* remorso. **-without r.** sem piedade

remorseless| rimós'les |*a.* implacável, inexorável

remote| rimowt' |*a.* remoto, distante; isolado, solitário; vaga (idéia)

remoteness | rimowt'nes | *s.* isolamento, afastamento

removable | rimʋ'vəbəl |*a.* removível; transferível (funcionário, magistrado etc.)

removal | rimʋ'vəl | *s.* remoção, transferência; demissão; afastamento; mudança

remove| rimʋv' |*s.* remoção / *vt.* remover; transferir; mudar; exonerar; afastar; extirpar, extrair / *vi.* mudar-se (de residência)

remuneration | rimʏunərey'śən | *s.* remuneração; salário, ordenado

remunerative | rimʏu'nərətiv | *a.* lucrativo, rendoso

renaissance | rəney'səns | *s.* renascença, renascimento (tb. maiúsc.)

rend| rend' |*vt.* arrancar, dilacerar. **-to r. one's hairs** arrancar os cabelos (de desespero)

render| ren'də |*vt.* tornar, fazer; dar; ceder; traduzir; prestar (homenagem, auxílio)

rendering | ren'dəring | *s.* tradução, versão; interpretação; pintura; camada de tinta, reboco

rendezvous | ron'divu | *s.* encontro, entrevista; lugar de encontro

renegade | re'nigeyd | *s.* renegado, apóstata

renew | rinʏv' | *vt.* renovar; recomeçar; restabelecer; repetir, reiterar

renewable | rinʏv'əbəl |*a.* renovável, prorrogável

renewal | rinʏv'əl | *s.* renovação (tb. de contrato etc.); reatamento (de amizade etc.); prorrogação; restauração

renounce | rinawns' | *vt.* renunciar a, desistir de, abandonar; repudiar

renovate| re'nəveyt |*vt.* renovar, restaurar

renovation | renəvey'śən | *s.* renovação, restauração

renown | rinawn' | *s.* renome, fama

renowned | rinawnd' |*a.* célebre, famoso, renomado

rent| rent' |*s.* renda; aluguel / *vt.* alugar

renunciation | rinânsiey'śən | *s.* renúncia

reopening | rıow'pəning | *s.* reabertura

repair | ripe'ə | *s.* conserto; reparação, restauração. **-in good r.** em bom estado. **-out of r.** em mau estado. **-under r.** em obras / *vt.* consertar; reparar (erro); remediar; recompensar

reparation | ripərey'śən | *s.* reparação; restauração; indenização; (*pl.*) reparações de guerra

repartee | repatı' | *s.* resposta pronta, réplica viva

repast | ripast' | *s.* repasto, refeição

repay | rıpey' | *vt.* pagar; reembolsar; recompensar; retribuir

repayment | rıpey'mənt | *s.* reembolso

repeal | ripıl' |*s.* revogação, anulação / *vt.* revogar, anular, cancelar

repeat | ripıt' | *vt.* repetir; reproduzir; recitar

repeatedly | ripı'tidlī | *adv.* repetidamente

repel| ripel' |*vt.* repelir, rebater, rechaçar; não se misturar com

repellent | ripe'lənt | *s.* repelente (esp. contra insetos) / *a.* repulsivo, repugnante, repelente

repent | ripent' | *vt.* *vi.* arrepender-se (de)

repentance | ripen'təns | *s.* arrependimento

repentant | ripen'tənt | *a.* arrependido

repercussion | ripєkâ'śən | *s.* repercussão

repertoire | re'pɔtwʌ | s. repertório

repertory | re'pɔtrī | s. repositório, compilação, coleção; repertório

repetition | repiti'śən | s. repetição

repetitive | ripe'titiv | a. repetido, repetitivo

replace | rɪpleys' | vt. repor, substituir

replacement | ripleys'mənt | s. reposição, substituição; reforço; restituição

replenish | riple'niś | vt. reabastecer, encher de novo; repovoar

replete | riplīt' | a. repleto, cheio; empanturrado

replica | re'plikə | s. cópia, réplica

reply | riplay' | s. resposta / vi. responder, replicar; (jur.) contestar

report | ripót' | s. relatório; comunicação; parecer; rumor, boato; reportagem; detonação / vt. informar, relatar, expor; noticiar; fazer um relatório de; denunciar, acusar / vi. apresentar-se, comparecer; apresentar relatório; trabalhar como repórter. **-to r. for duty** apresentar-se para receber ordens ou para trabalhar

reporter | ripó'tə | s. repórter

repose | ripowz' | s. repouso, descanso; tranqüilidade / vi. repousar, descansar; basear-se

reprehend | reprihend' | vt. repreender, ralhar

reprehensible | reprihen'sibəl | a. repreensível

represent | reprizent' | vt. representar; descrever; imaginar; retratar; corresponder a; mostrar, fazer ver

representation | reprizentey'śən | s. representação

representative | reprizen'tətiv | s. representante / a. representativo

repress | ripres' | vt. reprimir, subjugar

repression | ripre'śən | s. repressão

repressive | ripre'siv | a. repressivo

reprieve | riprɪv' | s. adiamento de execução de pena capital / vt. suspender a execução

reprimand | re'primʌnd | s. reprimenda, repreensão / vt. repreender

reprint | rɪ'print | s. reimpressão / vt. reimprimir

reprisal | ripray'zəl | s. represália

reproach | riprowś' | s. reprovação. **-above** ou **beyond r.** perfeito / vt. reprovar, censurar, exprobar

reprobate | re'prəbeyt | s.a. depravado; réprobo; patife

reproduce | riprədīus' | vt. reproduzir

reproduction | riprədâk'śən | s. reprodução

reproof | riprʊf' | s. reprovação; censura; reprimenda, repreensão

reprove | riprʊv' | vt. reprovar, condenar

reptile | rep'tayl | s. réptil

republic | ripâb'lik | s. república

republican | ripâb'likən | s. a. republicano

repudiate | ripɪʊ'dīeyt | vt. repudiar, rejeitar, repelir

repudiation | ripɪʊdīey'śən | s. repúdio; rejeição; negação (de dívida)

repugnance | ripâg'nəns | s. repugnância; aversão, repulsa

repugnant | rɪpâg'nənt | a. repugnante; repulsivo

repulse | ripâls' | s. repulsa / vt. repelir

repulsion | ripâl'śən | s. repugnância; nojo, repulsa

repulsive | ripâl'siv | a. repulsivo; repelente, nojento

reputable | re'pɪʊtəbəl | a. respeitável, honrado

reputation | repɪʊtey'śən | s. reputação; renome

repute | ripɪʊt' | s. reputação; boa fama. **-of ill r.** de má fama / vt. considerar, reconhecer

reputed | ripǐu'tid | *a.* suposto, putativo. **-to be r.** to be ter fama de

reputedly | ripǐu'tidlī | *adv.* de acordo com o conceito geral

request | rikwest' | *s.* pedido; solicitação. **-at the r. of** ou **by r.** a pedido de. **-to be in great r.** estar em voga / *vt.* solicitar, pedir; rogar

requiem | re'kwīem | *s.* réquiem

requiem mass | re'kwīemmas | *s.* missa de réquiem

require | rikway'ə | *vt.* requerer, pedir, solicitar; exigir, mandar; precisar, necessitar

requirement | rikway'əmənt | *s.* exigência; necessidade

requisite | re'kwizit | *s.* requisito, condição / *a.* necessário, essencial

requisition | rekwizi'śən | *s.* requisição / *vt.* requisitar

requite | rikwayt' | *vt.* retribuir; recompensar; revidar. **-to r. like for like** pagar na mesma moeda

rescind | risind' | *vt.* rescindir, revogar

rescue | res'kǐu | *s.* salvação / *vt.* livrar, salvar, libertar; resgatar

rescuer | res'kǐuə | *s.* salvador, libertador

rescuing | res'kǐuing | *s.* salvamento

research | risɛs' | *s.* pesquisa, investigação

resemblance | rizem'bləns | *s.* semelhança, parecença

resemble | rizem'bəl | *vt.* parecer-se com

resent | rizent' | *vt.* levar a mal

resentful | rizent'ful | *a.* ressentido, ofendido

resentment | rizent'mənt | *s.* ressentimento, rancor

reservation | rezəvey'śən | *s.* reserva (de hotel etc.); restrição; (EUA) reserva (de tribo indígena)

reserve | rizɛv' | *s.* reserva; restrição / *vt.* reservar, guardar

reserved | rizɛvd' | *a.* reservado

reservoir | re'zəvwʌ | *s.* reservatório, barragem

reset | rı'set | *vt.* (tip.) recompor; recolocar, tornar a engastar

reside | rizayd' | *vt.* residir, habitar, morar. **-to r. in** consistir em

residence | re'zidəns | *s.* residência, moradia, morada

resident | re'zidənt | *s.* residente, habitante, morador / *a.* residente; sedentário

residential | rezidən'śəl | *a.* residencial

residue | re'zidǐu | *s.* resíduo; resto; remanescente

resign | rizayn' | *vt.* renunciar, abandonar / *vi.* demitir-se, pedir demissão

resignation | rezigney'śən | *s.* resignação; demissão; pedido de demissão

resigned | rizaynd' | *a.* resignado, conformado

resilience | rəzi'līəns | *s.* elasticidade, energia; capacidade de recuperação

resilient | rəzi'līənt | *a.* elástico; capaz de recuperação

resin | re'zin | *s.* resina

resist | rizist' | *vt.* resistir a, impedir; repelir

resistance | rizis'təns | *s.* resistência

resolute | re'zəlut | *a.* resoluto, corajoso, decidido

resoluteness | re'zəlutnes | *s.* determinação, coragem

resolution | rezəlu'śən | *s.* resolução; deliberação, decisão. **-to pass a r.** aprovar uma proposta. **-good resolutions** bons propósitos, decisão de adotar boa conduta

resolve | rizolv' | *s.* resolução; determinação; deliberação / *vt.* resolver; decompor; analisar; transformar; solucionar; decidir / *vi.* resolver-se; decidir-se

resolved | rizolvd' | *a.* decidido, determinado

resonant | re'zənənt | *a.* ressoante, ressonante

resort | rizót' | s. lugar de veraneio, férias etc.; ponto de reunião; antro, covil (de ladrões etc.). **-as a last r.** em último recurso / vi. dirigir-se a, ir freqüentar. **-to r. to** recorrer a, lançar mão de

resound | rizawnd' | vi. ressoar, retumbar; ecoar

resounding | rizawn'ding | a. ressoante, retumbante

resource | risós' | s. recurso

resourceful | risós'ful | a. engenhoso, fértil em recursos, atilado, despachado

respect | rispekt' | s. respeito; consideração; estima, acatamento; (pl.) saudações. **-in r. of** com respeito a, a respeito de. **-with r. to** com respeito a. **-out of r. for** em atenção a. **-in some respects** sob certos aspectos. **-in all respects** em tudo / vt. respeitar

respectability | rispektəbi'litī | s. respeitabilidade

respectable | rispek'təbəl | a. respeitável; honesto; digno; considerável

respected | rispek'tid | a. respeitado, considerado

respectful | rispekt'ful | a. respeitoso

respecting | rispek'ting | prep. a respeito de

respective | rispek'tiv | a. respectivo, correspondente

respiration | respirey'śən | s. respiração

respiratory | rispay'rətrī | a. respiratório

respite | res'payt | s. adiamento; interrupção, intervalo, pausa

resplendent | risplen'dənt | a. resplandecente

respond | rispond' | vi. responder, replicar; reagir, obedecer; mostrar-se sensível

response | rispons' | s. resposta; reação; (ecles.) responso

responsibility | risponsibi'litī | s. responsabilidade; dever

responsible | rispon'sibəl | a. responsável; digno de confiança, respeitável

responsive | rispon'siv | a. sensível, impressionável; receptivo, compreensível

rest | rest' | s. descanso, repouso; folga; intervalo, interrupção, pausa; suporte, apoio, descanso; (mús.) pausa; resto, restante; morte, repouso final. **-at r.** em repouso; em paz; morto. **-to take a r.** repousar. **-to set at r.** resolver (questão). **-all the r. of it** e tudo mais. **-for the r.** quanto ao mais / vt. descansar; apoiar, colocar; fixar (os olhos) / vi. descansar. **-to r. assured (that)** poder ficar descansado (de que). **-to r. on** ou **upon** confiar. **-it rests with you** depende de você, está em suas mãos

restaurant | res'tərən | s. restaurante

restful | rest'ful | a. sossegado, tranqüilo

restitution | restitĩu'śən | s. restituição

restive | res'tiv | a. agitado, inquieto, impaciente; indócil (cavalo)

restiveness | res'tivnes | s. inquietação, agitação

restless | rest'les | a. inquieto, agitado; turbulento; insone

restlessness | rest'lesnes | s. inquietação; impaciência; descontentamento

restoration | restərey'śən | s. restauração

restore | ristó' | vt. restaurar, restabelecer; devolver; reintegrar

restrain | ristreyn' | vt. restringir; reprimir, refrear; limitar; impedir

restraining | ristrey'ning | a. restritivo, moderador; tranqüilizador

restraint | ristreynt' | s. restrição, controle; contenção, comedimento

restrict | ristrikt' | vt. restringir, limitar; sujeitar

restricted | ristrik'tid | a. restrito, limitado

restriction | ristrik'śən | s. restrição, limitação

restrictive | ristrik'tiv | a. restritivo

result | rizâlt' | s. resultado; conseqüência. -as a r. por conseguinte. -as a r. of em conseqüência de / vi. resultar, proceder, provir de

resume | riziúm' | vt. reassumir; retomar; prosseguir / vi. recomeçar, prosseguir

résumé | re'ziúmey | s. resumo, sumário

resumption | rizâm'śən | s. recomeço; retomada

resurrect | rezərekt' | vt. ressuscitar; reanimar; desenterrar, exumar / vi. ressuscitar; ressurgir

resurrection | rezərek'śən | s. ressurreição; restabelecimento, restauração; exumação

resuscitate | risâ'siteyt | vt. vi. ressuscitar

retail | ri'teyl | s. venda a varejo. -at r. a varejo / a. varejista / vt. vender a varejo; contar minuciosamente; repetir a outros / vi. vender a varejo; ser vendido a varejo

retailer | ri'teylə | s. varejista

retain | riteyn' | vt. reter, guardar; contratar (advogado etc.)

retaining | ritey'ning | a. retentor; de retenção

retaining fee | ritey'ningfi | s. honorários pagos como sinal

retaining wall | ritey'ningwól | s. muro ou parede de sustentação

retaliate | rita'lieyt | vi. retaliar, revidar

retaliation | ritaliey'śən | s. retaliação, represália

retard | ritAd' | vt. retardar; impedir

retention | riten'śən | s. retenção; conservação; memória

retentive | riten'tiv | a. retentivo;

tenaz (memória)

reticence | re'tisəns | s. reticência, reserva; retraimento, modéstia

reticent | re'tisənt | a. reticente, reservado; retraído, calado

retinue | re'tiniú | s. séquito; escolta; acompanhamento

retire | ritay'ə | vt. retirar, remover; aposentar, reformar / vi. retirar-se; aposentar-se, reformar-se; recuar, retroceder

retired | ritay'əd | a. retirado, isolado (lugar); aposentado; retirado (dos negócios); (mil.) reformado

retirement | ritay'əmənt | s. aposentadoria; reforma; afastamento; isolamento, solidão; refúgio, retiro

retirement pension | ritay'əməntpen'śən | s. aposentadoria, pensão de aposentado ou reformado

retiring | ritay'əring | a. retraído; tímido; reservado, modesto

retort | ritót' | s. réplica, retorta / vt. replicar, retrucar; destilar em retorta / vi. replicar, redarguir

retrace | ritreys' | vt. voltar atrás, retroceder; rememorar, relembrar; reconstituir (história etc.)

retract | ritrakt' | vt. retrair, encolher; abjurar, revogar; retirar, desdizer / vi. desdizer-se, retratar-se

retraction | ritrak'śən | s. retratação (de declaração); retração, encolhimento

retreat | ritrit' | s. retirada; reclusão, retiro; (mil.) toque de retirada; toque de recolher. -to beat a r. bater em retirada / vi. retirar-se, retroceder

retrenchment | ritrenś'mənt | s. redução; economia, poupança; (mil.) entrincheiramento

retribution | retribiú'śən | s. castigo, punição; revide, retaliação

retrieve | ritriv' | vt. reaver, recuperar; salvar, resgatar; trazer a caça (o cão)

retriever | ritrī'və | s. cão de busca (cão que traz a caça abatida)

retrograde | re'trowgreyd | a. retrógrado / vi. degenerar; deteriorar; piorar

retrospect | re'trowspekt | s. retrospecto. **-in r.** retrospectivamente

return | ritEn' | s. volta, retorno; devolução; recompensa; lucro; declaração; relatório; reaparição; repetição (de data, comemoração etc.); recaída (de doença); (pl). ganhos, rendimentos. **-in r. (for)** em troca de. **-r. ticket** bilhete de ida e volta. **-many happy returns!** que esta data se repita por muitos anos! / vt. devolver; retribuir; reeleger; desviar; corresponder a; repor, recolocar / vi. voltar, regressar; responder, replicar

return address | ritEn'ədres' | s. endereço do remetente

reunion | rīĭu'nĭən | s. reunião

reunite | rī'ĭunayt | vt. reunir; reconciliar; congregar, juntar / vi. reunir-se

reveal | rivīl' | vt. revelar; divulgar; exibir, mostrar

reveille | riva'lī | s. (mil.) toque de alvorada

revel | re'vəl | s. (sing. ou pl.) festança, farra, pândega, folia / vi. divertir-se, folgar, farrear

revelation | revəley'śən | s. revelação; (maiúsc., bíbl.) Apocalipse

reveller | re'vəle | s. farrista, folião

revelry | re'vəlrī | s. orgia, folia; festança

revenge | rivenǰ' | s. vingança, desforra, retaliação / vt. vingar-se de

revengeful | rivenǰ'ful | a. vingativo

revenue | ri'vənĭu | s. rendimento, renda; rendimèntos públicos; (pl.) rendas

reverberate | rivE'bəreyt | vi. reverberar; repercutir; ecoar

reverberation | rivEbərey'śən | s. reverberação; repercussão; eco

revere | rivī'ə | vt. reverenciar, venerar

reverence | re'vərəns | s. veneração, reverência / vt. reverenciar, venerar

reverend | re'vərənd | a. reverendo (esp. como título de sacerdotes); venerável

reverent | re'vərənt | a. reverente, respeitoso

reverie | re'vərī | s. devaneio, sonho, fantasia

reversal | rivE'səl | s. reversão, inversão

reverse | rivEs' | s. reverso; avesso; revés; contratempo. **-to go into r.** fazer marcha à ré / a. inverso; oposto, contrário / vt. inverter; mudar (decisão etc.); anular; revogar; inverter a marcha, fazer marcha à ré

reversible | rivE'sibəl | a. de duas faces (capa etc.); reversível

revert | rivEt' | vt. reverter, voltar

review | rivĭu' | s. revista; revisão; crítica, apreciação (literária etc.); (jur.) revisão / vt. rever, examinar; (mil.) passar em revista; (jur.) rever; fazer crítica (literária etc.)

reviewer | rivĭu'ə | s. crítico (de jornal ou revista)

revile | rivayl' | vt. ultrajar, injuriar, insultar

revise | rivayz' | vt. revisar, atualizar, melhorar; repassar, reestudar; mudar (de opinião etc.)

revision | rivi'ǰən | s. revisão, correção

revival | rivay'vəl | s. ressurgimento, renascimento; (teat.) reapresentação; movimento religioso

revive | rivayv' | vt. ressuscitar, reanimar, renovar / vi. voltar a si; reanimar-se

revoke | rivowk' | vt. revogar

revolt | rivowlt' | s. revolta, rebelião, insurreição / vt. revoltar;

indignar; repugnar / *vi.* revoltar-se; indignar-se

revolting | rivowl'ting | *a.* revoltante, repugnante

revolution | revəlu'śən | *s.* revolução

revolutionary | revəlu'śənrī | *s. a.* revolucionário

revolutionize| revəlu'śənayz |*vt.* revolucionar

revolve| rivolv' |*vt.* revolver, fazer girar; ponderar, revolver (mentalmente) / *vi.* girar, dar voltas; andar em círculos; acontecer periodicamente

revolver | rivol'və | *s.* revólver

revolving | rivol'ving | *a.* giratório

revulsion | rivâl'śən |*s.* (med.) revulsão; reviravolta, mudança súbita

reward | riwód' |*s.* recompensa / *vt.* recompensar, premiar

rhapsody | rap'sədī |*s.* rapsódia

rhetoric | re'tərik |*s.* retórica

rheumatism | rʋ'mətizəm | *s.* reumatismo

rhinoceros | rayno'sərəs | *s.* rinoceronte

Rhodesian | rowdɪ'jən | *s. a.* rodesiano

rhubarb | rʋ'bʌb | *s.* (bot.) ruibarbo; cor marrom-amarelada; (gír., EUA) disputa acalorada

rhyme, rime | raym' | *s.* rima. **-without r. or reason** sem quê nem para quê / *vt. vi.* rimar

rhythm | ri'ðəm |*s.* ritmo

rib | rib' | *s.* costela; viga, trave; vareta de guarda-chuva

ribald | ri'bəld |*a.* irreverente, licencioso, impudico, obsceno

ribaldry | ri'bəldrī |*s.* linguagem impudica e irreverente

ribbing | ri'bing | *s.* costelas; (náut.) cavername; (gír.) zombaria

ribbon | ri'bən |*s.* fita, faixa, tira / *vt.* enfeitar com fitas

rice | rays' |*s.* arroz

rich | riś' |*s.* **-the rich** os ricos /*a.*

rico; precioso; opulento; suntuoso; generoso (vinho); abundante; fértil (solo); brilhante (cor); suculento; gordo, que engorda. **-r. in** rico em

riches | ri'śiz |*spl.* riquezas

richly | riś'lī |*adv.* ricamente, esplendidamente, abundantemente

richness | riś'nes | *s.* riqueza; fertilidade

rickets| ri'kits |*s.* raquitismo

rickety | ri'kitī | *a.* raquítico, franzino; vacilante

ricochet | ri'kəśey | *s.* ricochete / *vi.* ricochetear

rid | rid' | *vt.* livrar, desembaraçar. **-to get r. of** livrar-se de

riddance | ri'dəns | *s.* livramento (de mal ou estorvo etc.). **-to make a clean r. of** desembaraçar-se de. **-good r.!** bons ventos o levem!

riddle | ri'dəl |*s.* adivinha, charada; peneira, crivo / *vt.* crivar (de balas etc.)

ride | rayd' | *s.* passeio (a cavalo, de carro etc.). **-to go for a r.** dar uma volta (de carro etc.) / *vt.* cavalgar, montar; andar de; sulcar (as ondas). **-to r. down** esfalfar (cavalo); atropelar. **-to r. out** resistir a / *vi.* viajar, andar de (cavalo, carro etc.)

rider | ray'də | *s.* cavaleiro; amazona; jóquei; ciclista; passageiro (de ônibus etc.); aditamento, cláusula suplementar

ridge | rij' | *s.* cume, crista; cadeia de montanhas; espinhaço; aresta; sulco; lomba (em campo arado); cumeeira (telhado)

ridicule | ri'dikʋl | *s.* escárnio, zombaria / *vt.* zombar de, escarnecer

ridiculous| ridi'kʋləs |*a.* ridículo

riding | ray'ding |*s.* equitação /*a.* de andar a cavalo

riding-breeches | ray'dingbriśiz | *spl.* culote, calça de montaria

riding-habit | ray'dinghabit | *s.* roupa de amazona

riding-school | ray'dingskʊl | *s.* escolá de equitação

rife | rayf' | *a.* comum, corrente, freqüente

riff-raff | rif'raf |*s.* ralé, gentalha

rifle | ray'fəl |*s.* carabina, fuzil / *vt.* pilhar, saquear

rift | rift' | *s.* racha, fenda; desavença (entre amigos)

rig | rig' | *vt.* aparelhar, equipar (navio). -**to r. out** ou **up** montar, armar; guarnecer, adornar. -**to r. up** armar às pressas, improvisar

rigging | ri'ging |*s.* (náut.) corda-me, massame

right | rayt' |*s.* direito, justiça; direita, lado direito; (polít.) direita; bem, razão. -**to be in the r.** ter razão. -**by r.** ou **rights** de direito. -**to turn to the r.** dobrar à direita / *a.* exato, correto, certo; justo, equitativo; adequado; conveniente (ocasião); normal, perfeito; direito (lado oposto ao avesso); reto; certo (relógio). -**to be all r.** ir bem. -**to be r.** ter razão / *adv.* certo; corretamente, exatamente, justamente. -**r. away** imediatamente, já. -**r. here** aqui mesmo. -**r. opposite** exatamente em frente. -**it serves (you) r!** é bem feito! -**if I remember r.** se não me falha a memória / *interj.* bom!, certo! -**all r.!** está certo! -**quite r.!** muito bem!, perfeito! / *vt.* endireitar; corrigir; fazer justiça a / *vi.* endireitar-se, aprumar-se

righteous | ray'šəs | *a.* justo, virtuoso, honesto

righteousness | ray'šəsnes | *s.* justiça

rightful | rayt'ful | *a.* legitimo; justo; direito

rightly | ray·'lī | *adv.* justamente, com justiça; adequadamente

rightness | rayt'nes |*s.* justiça, retidão, correção

rigid | ri'jid |*a.* rígido; inflexível

rigidity | riji'ditī | *s.* rigidez; severidade

rigmarole | rig'mərowl | *s.* palavrório, fala incoerente

rigorous | ri'gərəs | *a.* rigoroso

rigour, rigor | ri'gə | *s.* rigor; exatidão; severidade; calafrio

rig-out | rig'awt | *s.* (coloq.) roupas, roupagens, equipamentos, atavios

rile | rayl' | *vt.* (coloq.) irritar; (EUA) toldar a água

rim | rim' | *s.* bordo, rebordo, margem; aba; aro

rime | raym' | *s.* geada

rind | raynd' | *s.* casca (de árvore, queijo); pele (de fruta); couro (de toicinho)

ring | ring' | *s.* anel; argola; círculo, roda; grupo, panelinha; arena; ringue (boxe); olheiras; toque, tinido; repique, badalada; (coloq.) telefonema / *vt.* cercar, rodear; tocar, soar (sino, campa). -**to r. off** desligar (telefone). -**to r. up** telefonar / *vi.* tocar; repicar, soar. -**to r. for** chamar ou mandar pedir. -**to r. true (false)** soar bem (mal)

ringed | ringd' | *a.* anelado; que tem anel

ring-finger | ring'fingə | *s.* dedo anular

ringing | ring'ing | *s.* toque (de campainha, sino etc.); zumbido (nos ouvidos) / *a.* sonoro, ressoante

ringleader | ring'lıdə | *s.* chefe de motim

ringworm | ring'wɛm | *s.* tinha; impingem

rink | rink' | *s.* rinque (de patinação etc.)

rinse | rins' | *vt.* enxaguar

riot | ray'ət | *s.* tumulto, motim; rixa. -**to run r.** desenfrear-se; crescer desordenadamente / *vi.* participar de tumulto ou rixa

rioter | ray'ətə |*s.* arruaceiro, desordeiro; amotinado

riotous | ray'ətəs |*a.* devasso, dissipado; turbulento; amotinado

rip | rip' |*s.* rasgão / *vt.* rasgar. -**to r. off** ou **out** arrancar rasgando

/ *vi.* rasgar-se

riparian| ripa'rĩən |*s.* proprietário ribeirinho / *a.* ribeirinho

ripe | rayp' | *ą.* maduro, amadurecido

ripen | ray'pən | *vt. vi.* amadurecer

ripeness | rayp'nes | *s.* amadurecimento

ripper | ri'pə |*s.* estripador; (gír.) pessoa ou coisa notável

ripple | ri'pəl | *s.* ondulação, encrespamento (das águas); murmúrio, sussurro / *vt.* encrespar / *vi.* encrespar-se

rise | rayz' | *s.* aumento; subida (de temperatura, maré, preços); encosta, elevação. **-to get a r.** ter um aumento salarial. **-to giver. to** dar origem a, motivar / *vt.* levantar (caça); fazer subir à tona (peixe) / *vi.* levantar-se; rebelar-se; subir; nascer (do sol, de rio); surgir; aumentar. **-to r. up** levantar-se. **-to r. to one's feet** pôr-se de pé. **-to r. above** ser superior a. **-to r. to the occasion** estar à altura da situação. **-to r. in the world** atingir posição social elevada

rising | ray'zing |*s.* nascer (do sol, da lua); revolta, insurreição / *a.* nascente, crescente; nova (geração)

risk | risk' | *s.* risco, perigo. **-at all risks** a todo custo / *vt.* arriscar

risky | ris'kĩ | *a.* perigoso, arriscado

rissole | ri'sowl |*s.* almôndega de carne ou peixe; rissole

rite | rayt' | *s.* rito, ritual, cerimônia

ritual | ri'tĩuəl |*s. a.* ritual

rival | ray'vəl |*s. a.* rival, concorrente / *vt.* rivalizar com

rivalry | ray'vəlrĩ | *s.* rivalidade, competição

river | ri'və | *s.* rio. **-to sell down the r.** (coloq.) fraudar, trair, atraiçoar

riverside | ri'vəsayd | *s.* margem de rio

rivet| ri'vit |*s.* rebite / *vt.* rebitar, cravar, fixar

rivulet | ri'vĩulit | *s.* riacho, arroio, regato

roach | rowš' | *s.* (ent.) barata; peixe da família da carpa

road| rowd' |*s.* estrada; (*pl.*) ancoradouro. **-on the r.** na estrada, em viagem. **-to observe the rule of the r.** observar a mão de direção. **-to take the r.** ir viajar

road-hog | rowd'hog | *s.* motorista que dirige agressivamente

road-house | rowd'haws |*s.* hospedaria à beira da estrada

road-metal | rowd'metəl |*s.* cascalho, pedra britada

roam| rowm' | *vi.* vaguear, errar, vagar, perambular

roar| ró' |*s.* rugido, urro, bramido (do mar, vento); ribombar (de trovão, caminhões) / *vt. vi.* rugir, urrar; bramir; troar (canhões); roncar (motores). **-to r. with laughter** rir às gargalhadas

roast | rowst' | *s.* assado, carne assada; torrefação / *a.* assado / *vt.* assar; torrar (café etc.); zombar de, criticar; (EUA) repreender / *vi.* assar; torrar; calcinar-se

rob | rob' | *vt.* roubar; privar de; saquear, pilhar

robber | ro'bə |*s.* ladrão

robbery | ro'bərĩ |*s.* roubo

robe | rowb' | *s.* manto; túnica; toga (de juiz); roupão / *vt. vi.* vestir manto, toga etc.

robin | ro'bin | *s.* (orn.) papo-roxo; espécie de tordo norte-americano

robot | row'bot | *s.* robô, autômato

robust | rowbâst' | *a.* robusto

rock | rok' | *s.* rocha, rochedo, penhasco; (EUA) pedra; bala (esp. de hortelã) cilíndrica. **-on the rocks** bebida alcoólica servida sobre pedras de gelo. **-to be on the rocks** estar sem dinheiro ou em apuros. **-the R.** Gibraltar

/ *vt*. balançar, oscilar; embalar, acalentar; abalar

rock candy | rok'kandī | *s*. açúcar--cande

rocket | ro'kit | *s*. foguete; (gír.) reprimenda / *vi*. subir como um foguete

rocking | ro'king | *a*. que balança, balouçante

rocking-chair | ro'kingše'ǝ | *s*. cadeira de balanço

rocky | ro'kī | *a*. rochoso, pedregoso

rod | rod' | *s*. vara; haste; vara de pescar; vareta; varinha; medida de comprimento (5 1/2 jardas)

rodent | row'dǝnt | *s*. *a*. (zool.) roedor

roe | row' | *s*. ova de peixe; corço, cabrito montês

roebuck | row'bâk | *s*. (zool.) corço (cervídeo macho)

rogue | rowg' | *s*. patife, velhaco, tratante

roguery | row'gǝrī | *s*. velhacaria

roguish | row'giš | *a*. maroto, brincalhão, travesso, brejeiro, gaiato

roister | roys'tǝ | *vi*. divertir-se ruidosamente, fazer algazarra

role | rowl' | *s*. (teat.) papel. **-to play a r**. desempenhar um papel

roll | rowl' | *s*. rolo (de papel etc.); rol, lista; pãozinho; rufo (de tambor); rebôo (de trovão); balanço (de navio). **r. of honour** lista dos mortos pela pátria. **-to call the r**. fazer a chamada. **-to strike off the rolls** expulsar por desonestidade / *vt*. rolar; laminar (metal); rufar (tambor); revirar (olhos); rolar, fazer vibrar os *rr*; enrolar (cigarro, cobertor etc.). **-to. r. up** enrolar / *vi*. rolar; rodar; correr (tempo); retumbar (trovão); balançar, jogar (navio). **-to r. away** sumir, dissipar-se. **-to r. by** passar (de carro etc.). **-to r. in ease** viver confortavelmente. **-to r. up** enrolar-se, enroscar-se

roller | row'lǝ | *s*. rolo; cilindro, tambor; rolo compressor; vagalhão, onda

roller-coaster | row'lǝkows'tǝ | *s*. montanha-russa

roller-skate | row'lǝskeyt | *s*. patim de rodas

rollicking | ro'liking | *a*. alegre, divertido, brincalhão

rolling | row'ling | *s*. rodar; balanço, jogo (de navio); laminação (de metais) / *a*. rolante; ondulado (terreno); bamboleante; encapelado (mar)

rolling-mill | row'lingmil | *s*. laminação de metais (oficina)

rolling-pin | row'lingpin | *s*. rolo de pasteleiro

rolling-stock | row'lingstok | *s*. material (ferroviário) rodante

Roman | row'mǝn | *s*. *a*. romano

romance | rowmans' | *s*. romance, línguas românicas / *a*. românico, neolatino / *vi*. romancear, distorcer a verdade

Romance languages | rowmans'-langwiǰiz | *spl*. línguas românicas

Romanesque | rowmǝnesk' | *a*. (arquit.) românico

Roman law | row'mǝnló | *s*. direito romano

romantic | rowman'tik | *s*. *a*. romântico / *a*. fabuloso, romanesco, sentimental

romanticism | rowman'tisizǝm | *s*. romantismo

Romany | row'mǝnī | *s*. cigano; (ling.) romani / *a*. cigano, relativo ao cigano ou ao romani

romp | romp' | *s*. travessura / *vi*. brincar ruidosamente, fazer travessuras. **-to r. home** ganhar facilmente

roof | ruf' | *s*. telhado. **-r. of the mouth** céu da boca. **-to raise the r**. enfurecer-se / *vt*. telhar, cobrir com telhas

rook | ruk' | *s*. gralha; torre (no jogo de xadrez) / *vt*. trapacear

rookie | ru'kī | *s*. (gír.) recruta; novato

room | rʊm’ | s. quarto, aposento; sala; espaço ou lugar. **-to make r.** dar lugar. **-to make r. for** deixar passar; conseguir lugar para. **-there is r. for improvement** as condições não são muito boas. **-there is no r. for doubt** não cabe dúvida / vt. hospedar, alojar

room-mate | rʊm’meyt | s. companheiro de quarto

roomy | rʊ’mī | a. espaçoso

roost | rʊst’ | s. poleiro. **-to rule the r.** mandar / vi. empoleirar-se

rooster | rʊs’tə | s. galo

root | rʊt’ | s. raiz; origem. **-to take** ou **strike r.** enraizar; criar raízes. **-to r. out** arrancar

rooted | rʊ’tid | a. arraigado, radicado

rope | rowp’ | s. corda, cabo. **-on the ropes** (coloq.) em péssima situação. **-to know the ropes** ser entendido no assunto / vt. amarrar, atar. **-to r. in** (gír.) enganar, persuadir a participar. **-to r. off** cercar, isolar

rope-maker | rowp’meykə | s. cordoeiro

rosary | row’zərī | s. rosário

rose | rowz’ | s. rosa. **-under the r.** confidencialmente / a. rosado

rose-bud | rowz’bâd | s. botão de rosa; (fig.) moça bonita

rose-bush | rowz’bâś | s. roseira

rosemary | rowz’mərī | s. alecrim, rosmaninho

rosewood | rowz’wʊd | s. jacarandá

roster | ros’tə | s. rol, lista

rostrum | ros’trəm | s. tribuna; (zool., bot.) rostro

rosy | row’zī | a. rosado; (fig.) cor-de-rosa, propício

rot | rot’ | s. podridão; caruncho; (gír.) disparate, loucura. **-the r.** distomíase (doença das ovelhas) / vt. vi. apodrecer / interj. bolas!, droga!

rotary | row’tərī | a. rotativo, giratório

rotate | row’teyt | vt. fazer girar; alternar, variar / vi. girar, rodar; alternar-se

rotation | rowtey’śən | s. rotação. **-in** ou **by r.** por turnos, alternadamente

rote | rowt’ | s. rotina. **-by r.** por simples hábito, maquinalmente

rotten | ro’tən | a. podre; (fig.) estragado; (gír.) péssimo, horrível

rotter | ro’tə | s. (gír.) canalha, patife

rouble, ruble | rʊ’bəl | s. rublo

rouge | rʊj’ | s. ruge ou batom (cosméticos); ruge de joalheiro (polidor) / vi. usar ruge ou batom

rough | râf’ | s. aspereza. **-in the r.** em bruto; impolido / a. acidentado, áspero (terreno); tempestuoso (tempo); encapelado (mar); rude, grosseiro (aparência, conduta); duro, brutal (tratamento); áspero (superfície); rude (vida); tosco (trabalho, acabamento). **-a so u at a r. guess** aproximadamente. **-a r. time** maus momentos / vt. tornar áspero. **-to r. out** esboçar

rough-and-ready | râf’andre’dī | a. tosco e eficaz, feio e forte

rough-and-tumble | râf’andtâm’bəl | s. luta violenta / a. desordenado, irregular

rough coat | râf’kowt | s. primeira camada de argamassa

rough copy | râf’kopī | s. rascunho

roughly | râf’lī | adv. asperamente; grosseiramente; aproximadamente; de modo geral

roughness | râf’nes | s. aspereza; grosseria; rudeza; severidade; indelicadeza

roulette | rulet’ | s. roleta (jogo de azar)

Romanian, Rumanian | rʊmey’nĩən | s. a. romeno

round | rawnd’ | s. círculo; anel; cartucho, tiro; salva (de palmas); assalto, round (boxe); ciclo; série; sucessão. **-to fire a r.**

dar uma descarga (tiros). **-ar. of beer** uma rodada de cerveja. **-the daily r.** a rotina diária. **-to go the r.** ou **rounds** andar de boca em boca: rondar / *a.* redondo; circular; esférico; redondo (soma); arredondado. **-r. trip** viagem de ida e volta. **-all r.** completo / *adv.* à (em) roda; ao (em) redor. **-r. about** em direção oposta; em volta. **-to bring r.** persuadir. **-to come r.** recuperar os sentidos; (coloq.) ceder; (coloq.) visitar / *prep.* à volta de; ao ou em redor de. **-r. the corner** ali na esquina, pertinho. **-to go r.** rodear, contornar / *vt.* arredondar, tornear; completar, perfazer; rematar; contornar, dar a volta a; circundar. **-to r. up** arrebanhar; reunir. **-to r. off** completar; terminar; dar acabamento

roundabout | rawnd'əbawt | *s.* rodeio, tergiversação; carrossel / *a.* indireto; circundante; que cerca

rounded | rawnd'id | *a.* redondo; arredondado

roundness | rawnd'nes | *s.* redondeza; franqueza; severidade

rouse | rawz' | *vt.* despertar; excitar; levantar (caça). **-to r. oneself** dominar a indolência

rousing | raw'zing | *a.* vibrante (discurso etc.); caloroso, animador

rout | rawt' | *s.* turba, ralé; debandada, retirada desordenada / *vt.* derrotar; desbaratar, pôr em fuga

route | rʊt' | *s.* rota, caminho; itinerário; (náut.) rumo, rota / *vt.* traçar a rota de; enviar; encaminhar (documento etc.)

route-map | rʊt'map | *s.* roteiro, itinerário

route march | rʊt'maš | *s.* (mil.) marcha de treinamento

routine | rʊtɪn' | *s.* rotina / *a.* rotineiro

rove | rowv' | *vi.* vaguear, perambular, errar

rover | row'və | *s.* vagabundo, nômade; aventureiro; bucaneiro, pirata

roving | row'ving | *s.* vida errante / *a.* errante, vadio, aventureiro, nômade

row | row' | *s.* fila, fileira; remada; passeio em bote de remos. **-in a r.** seguidos, em fila / *vt.* enfileirar; remar

row | raw' | *s.* (coloq.) rixa; (coloq.) clamor, estrépito, algazarra / *vi.* brigar, disputar com algazarra

row-boat | row'bowt | *s.* bote, barco de remos

rowdiness | raw'dines | *s.* algazarra, gritaria

rowdy | raw'dī | *s.* desordeiro / *a.* turbulento, barulhento

rowdyism | rawdī'zəm | *s.* desordem, violência, turbulência

rower | row'ə | *s.* remador

rowing | row'ing | *s.* (desp.) remo; remada

royal | roy'əl | *a.* real, régio

royalist | roy'əlist | *s. a.* monarquista

royalty | roy'əltī | *s.* realeza; (*pl.*) direitos

rub | râb' | *s.* fricção; (fig.) dificuldade / *vt.* esfregar; friccionar. **-to r. against** roçar. **-to r. in** aplicar (esfregando). **-to r. out** apagar (com borracha); (gír.) matar. **-to r. the wrong way** exasperar, irritar / *vi.* friccionar; esfregar-se; roçar

rubber | râ'bə | *s.* borracha

rubber band | râ'bəband | *s.* elástico, fita elástica

rubber cement | râ'bəsiment' | *s.* cola de borracha, cola de contato

rubber plant | râ'bəplant | *s.* seringueira

rubber plantation | râbəplantey'sən | *s.* seringal

rubber stamp | râ'bəstamp | *s.* carimbo de borracha

rubber tree | râ'bətrɪ | s. seringueira

rubbing | râ'bing | s. fricção

rubbish | râ'biś | s. lixo, refugo; sucata; asneira, tolice, bobagem; porcaria, droga

rubble | râ'bəl | s. pedregulho; cascalho; entulho

ruby | rʊ'bī | s. rubi

rucksack | râk'sak | s. mochila

ruction | râk'śən | s. (coloq.) tumulto

rudder | râ'də | s. leme

ruddy | râ'dī | a. corado

rude | rʊd' | a. descortês, grosseiro; brusco; rude, bruto; tosco, simples; inclemente (tempo)

rudely | rʊd'lī | adv. grosseiramente; toscamente; bruscamente

rudeness | rʊd'nes | s. grosseria, descortesia

rudiment | rʊ'dimənt | s. (ger. pl.) rudimento

rudimentary | rʊdimen'tərī | a. rudimentar

rue | rʊ' | vt. lamentar, arrepender-se de

ruffian | râ'fīən | s. desordeiro, valentão

ruffianly | râ'fīənlī | a. violento, desordeiro

ruffle | râ'fəl | vi. encrespar-se, encapelar (mar, águas); desfraldar-se; exaltar-se; rufar (tambor)

rug | râg' | s. tapete

rugby | râg'bī | s. (desp.) rúgbi

rugged | râ'gid | a. acidentado, escarpado; robusto, vigoroso, duro; tempestuoso, turbulento; rude, grosseiro; austero, severo

ruin | rʊ'in | s. ruína; destruição, perda / vt. arruinar, destruir

ruinous | rʊ'inəs | a. ruinoso, desastroso

rule | rʊl' | s. regra, regulamento; lei, código; costume; domínio, autoridade; régua. -as a r. via de regra / vt. governar, dominar; traçar linhas. -to r. out não admitir, excluir; rejeitar / vi.

governar; prevalecer; decretar

ruled | rʊld' | a. governado; pautado (papel)

rule of thumb | rʊl'ovϑâm | s. maneira prática de proceder

ruler | rʊ'lə | s. rei, rainha, soberano ou governador; régua

ruling | rʊ'ling | s. lineamento (com régua); decisão / a. reinante, dominante; dirigente (classe)

rum | râm' | s. rum / a. (gír.) estranho, esquisito; perigoso

rumble | râm'bəl | s. ruído; ribombo, troar, estrondo / vt. ribombar, retumbar

ruminate | rʊ'mineyt | vi. ruminar; (fig.) meditar

rummage | râ'miĵ | vi. remexer, revolver; explorar

rumour, rumor | rʊ'mə | s. boato, rumor / vt. boatar. -it is rumoured that corre o boato que, dizem que

rump | râmp' | s. rabada; garupa, anca; alcatra; (fig.) rebotalho

rumple | râm'pəl | s. dobra, vinco / vt. vi. amarrotar(-se); despentear(-se), desgrenhar(-se)

rump steak | râmp'steyk | s. bife de alcatra

run | rân' | s. corrida; percurso; passeio, viagem curta; duração, período; grande procura ou aceitação (de artigos à venda); corrida (ao banco); migração (de cardume de peixes etc.); permanência em cartaz (esp. peça teatral). -in the long r. afinal de contas, com o passar do tempo. -on the r. correndo, em fuga. -the ordinary r. a maioria, o povo. -to have the r. of ter livre acesso a. -a r. of good luck período de boa sorte / vt. vi. correr; circular (trem, ônibus); fazer regularmente o percurso (navio, avião); funcionar (motor, máquina etc.); dirigir, administrar (negócio, hotel etc.); disputar (eleição); organizar. -to r. about correr para cá e para lá. -to r. **across** encontrar por acaso, topar com; atravessar correndo. -to r. **against** ou **up** chocar-se com; deparar. -to r. **aground** encalhar. -to r. **ahead** adiantar-se, correr na frente. -to r. **away** ou **off** fugir. -to r. **amuck** ficar desvairado. -to r. **down** parar; reduzir; atropelar; falar mal de. -to feel r. **down** sentir-se exausto. -to r. **dry** secar; esgotar-se. -to r. **for** candidatar-se a. -to r. **from** fugir de. -to r. **into** chocar-se com; topar com (pessoa etc.). -to r. **into debt** endividar-se. -to r. **into money** receber uma boa soma. -to r. **low** escassear. -to r. **out** sair correndo; acabar-se. esgotar-se. -to r. **over** atropelar; inundar; dar um pulo até; examinar, passar os olhos sobre; repetir; ensaiar. -to r. **short** não dispor de. -to r. **through** examinar, folhear; ensaiar rapidamente; gastar, esgotar; desperdiçar (dinheiro); trespassar. -to r. **to** importar em, montar a (soma, dinheiro). -to r. **to waste** dissipar-se, perder-se. -to r. **up** hastear (bandeira); acumular (dívidas). -to r. **its course** seguir o seu curso. -to r. **the risk** correr o risco. -to r. **wild** tornar-se selvagem; levar vida desregrada

runaway | râ'nəwey | s. fugitivo, desertor; vitória fácil / a. fugitivo

runner | râ'nə | s. corredor (esportista)

runner-up | râ'nəâp | s. segundo colocado (em corrida etc.)

running | râ'ning | s. correr, corrida, carreira. -**in the** r. em competição, com possibilidade de ganhar / a. corredor, veloz; corrente (água); (med.) supurado, purulento. -**for ten days** r. por dez dias seguidos

running commentary | râ'ning-ko'məntrī | s. comentário ao vivo, comentário oral

running conditions | râ'ningkəndi'śənz | spl. condições vigentes, condições de funcionamento

running headline | râ'ninghed'-layn | s. título de página

running knot | râ'ningnot | s. nó corrediço

run of the mill | rân'ovðəmil | a. ordinário, comum

rupture | râp'śə | s. rompimento, quebra; (med.) hérnia, quebradura / vt. vi. romper(-se), quebrar(-se)

rural | ru'rəl | a. rural

ruse | ruz' | s. ardil, estratagema

rush | râś' | s. rush; investida, assalto; afluxo, afluência; corrida (em busca de ouro etc.); precipitação, pressa; grande procura (de artigo, entradas de teatro etc.); (bot.) junco. -**with a** r. de repente, precipitadamente / vt. apressar, precipitar; ativar, acelerar; assaltar, investir / vi. apressar-se, precipitar-se; lançar-se. -to r. **about** correr de um lado para outro. -to r. **forward** lançar-se. -to r. **in** entrar correndo. -to r. **off** sair correndo. -**don't** r.! devagar!, não corra!

rushing | râ'śing | a. precipitado

rusk | râsk' | s. fatia de pão torrada no forno; farinha de rosca

russet | râ'sit | s. cor castanho-avermelhada; espécie de maçã de casca arruivada e grossa / a. castanho-avermelhado

Russian | râ'śən | s. a. russo

rust | râst' | s. ferrugem / vt. vi. criar ferrugem

rustic | râs'tik | s. rústico, camponês; pessoa incivil / a. rústico, rural, campestre

rustle | râ'səl | s. sussurro; ruge-ruge / vt. vi. sussurrar; roçar: roçagar, farfalhar; rumorejar; crepitar, estalar (folhas secas)

rusty | râs'tī | a. ferrugento, enferrujado

rut | rât' | s. cio, brama; sulco de

carros; costume arraigado, rotina. **-inar** ser escravo da rotina / vt. sulcar (com rodas) / vi. estar no cio
ruthless | ruϑ'les | a. inexorável,

desapiedado, implacável, cruel
ruthlessness | ruϑ'lesnes | s. desumanidade, crueldade
rye | ray' | s. centeio; uísque de centeio

S

Sabbath | sa'baϑ | s. domingo (cristão); sábado (judaico)
sabotage | sa'bɔtAj | s. sabotagem
saccharine | sa'kɔrin | s. sacarina
sack | sak' | s. saco, saca; (mil.) saque / vt. ensacar; saquear; (gír., EUA) despedir (de emprego), pôr na rua
sacrament | sa'krɔmɔnt | s. sacramento. **-the Blessed S.** o Santíssimo Sacramento
sacred | sey'krid | a. sacro, sagrado. **-s. to** consagrado a
sacredness | sey'kridnes | s. santidade, inviolabilidade
sacrifice | sa'krifays | s. sacrifício / vt. vi. sacrificar(-se)
sacrilege | sa'krilij | s. sacrilégio
sacrilegious | sakrili'jɔs | a. sacrílego
sad | sad' | a. triste, aziago, sombrio
sadden | sa'dɔn | vt. entristecer, afligir
saddle | sa'dɔl | s. sela, selim / vt. selar. **-to s. with** carregar de
saddle-bag | sa'dɔlbag | s. alforje, alforge
sadness | sad'nes | s. tristeza, pesar
safe | seyf' | s. cofre / a. seguro, (a) salvo, intacto. **-s. and sound** são e salvo
safe-conduct | seyf'kondɔkt | s. salvo-conduto
safeguard | seyf'gAd | s. salvaguarda, proteção, defesa / vt. salvaguardar, proteger

safely | seyf'li | adv. seguramente, a salvo, sem perigo
safety | seyf'ti | s. segurança. **-to play for s.** evitar riscos
safety-pin | seyf'tipin | s. alfinete de fralda, alfinete de segurança
sag | sag' | vi. vergar, abater-se, cair (queixo)
sagacity | sɔga'siti | s. esperteza, sagacidade
sage | seyj' | s. sábio; (bot.) sálvia; (bot.) artemísia / a. sábio; judicioso, prudente
sago | sey'gow | s. sagu
sail | seyl' | s. (náut.) vela. **-to set s.** velejar / vt. governar, pilotar, levar (o barco) / vi. navegar, viajar; voar, deslizar
sailing | sey'ling | s. navegação, vela (esporte)
sailing-boat | sey'lingbowt | s. barco a vela
sailing-ship | sey'lingsıp | s. navio (barco) a vela
sailing-vessel | sey'lingvesɔl | s. veleiro
sailor | sey'lɔ | s. marinheiro
saint | seynt' | s. santo, santa, são / a. santo, sagrado
saintliness | seynt'lines | s. santidade
saintly | seynt'li | a. de santo, santificado
Saint Vitus's dance | seynt'vitɔzdans | s. (med.) coréia, dança de São Guido ou de São Vito
sake | seyk' | s. causa, motivo; bem, amor. **-for the s. of** por amor de, em atenção a, por cau-

sa de. **-for my s.** por mim. **-for my own s.** no meu próprio interesse. **-for God's (heaven's, goodness')** s. por amor de Deus. **-for pity's s.** por piedade

salacious | səley'śəs | *a.* lascivo, lúbrico

salad | sa'ləd | *s.* salada

salad days | sa'ləddeys | *spl.* os verdes anos, os tempos da juventude

salad dressing | sa'ləddresing | *s.* molho de salada

salary | sa'lərī | *s.* salário, ordenado, vencimentos

sale | seyl' | *s.* venda; saldos, liquidação. **-for s.** à venda

salesman | seylz'mən | *s.* caixeiro, vendedor

saleswoman | seylz'wəmən | *s.* caixeira, vendedora

salient | sey'lǐənt | *s.* (mil.) saliente / *a.* relevante, principal; saliente

saliva | səlay'və | *s.* saliva

sallow | sa'low | *s.* (bot.) salgueiro / *a.* pálido, amarelo / *vt.* empalidecer, amarelar

sally | sa'lī | *s.* surtida, saída; arranco, ímpeto; chiste, dito espirituoso / *vi.* investir; arrancar. **-to s. forth** sair (com ímpeto)

salmon | sa'mən | *s.* salmão

saloon | səlʊn' | *s.* bar; salão

salt | solt' | *s.* sal / *a.* salgado / *vt.* salgar. **-to s. away** ou **down** pôr de lado, poupar. **-old s.** velho marinheiro

salt-cellar | solt'selə | *s.* saleiro

salt-pan | solt'pan | *s.* salina

salty | solt'ī | *a.* salgado

salutary | sa'ĺutərī | *a.* salutar, benéfico, saudável

salutation | salĺutey'śən | *s.* saudação

salute | səlut' | *s.* saudação; cumprimento; (mil.) continência; (mil.) salva. **-to fire a s.** dar uma salva. **-to take the s.** passar em revista / *vi.* saudar; (mil.) fazer continência; (mil.) dar salva

salvage | sal'vij | *s.* salvamento;

salvados / *vt.* salvar (de incêndio, naufrágio etc.)

salvation | salvey'śən | *s.* salvação

Salvation Army | salvey'śənAmī | *s.* Exército da Salvação

salver | sal'və | *s.* salva, bandeja

salvo | sal'vow | *s.* (mil.) salva

same | seym' | *a.* mesmo; igual; idêntico / *pron.* (o[s], a[s]) mesmo(s), mesma(s). **-the very s.** precisamente o mesmo. **-much the s.** quase o mesmo. **-all the s.** mesmo assim, apesar disso, ainda assim. **-at the s. time** mas, contudo, todavia

sameness | seym'nes | *s.* semelhança, identidade; mesmice, monotonia

sample | sʌm'pəl | *s.* amostra; prova / *vt.* provar, experimentar

sanatorium | sanətó'rǐəm | *s.* sanatório

sanctify | sank'tifay | *vt.* santificar

sanctimonious | sanktimow'nǐəs | *a.* que aparenta santidade, santimonial

sanctimoniousness | sanktimow'nǐəsnes | *s.* santimônia

sanction | sank'śən | *s.* sanção, autorização, aprovação / *vt.* sancionar, autorizar, aprovar

sanctity | sank'titī | *s.* santidade

sanctuary | sank'tǐuərī | *s.* santuário; abrigo; homizio

sand | sand' | *s.* areia; (*pl.*) praia; (*pl.*) areal

sandal | san'dəl | *s.* sandália, sapatilha, alpercata

sandalwood | san'dəlwʊd | *s.* (bot.) sândalo

sandbag | sand'bag | *s.* saco de areia

sandbank | sand'bank | *s.* banco de areia

sand-hill | sand'hil | *s.* duna de areia

sandpaper | sand'peypə | *s.* lixa / *vt.* lixar

sand-pit | sand'pit | *s.* caixa de areia, areeiro, bueiro de areia

sandstone | sand'stown | s. (min.) arenito, grés

sandwich | san'wij | s. sanduíche / vt. intercalar, pôr apertado entre duas coisas

sandy | san'dī | a. arenoso; ruivo (cabelo)

sane | seyn' | a. são, saudável (do juízo); sensato, racional

sanguinary | san'gwinərī | a. sangüinário; feroz

sanguine | san'gwin | a. confiante, otimista

sanitary | sa'nitrī | a. sanitário, higiênico

sanitation | sanitey'şən | s. higiene, saúde pública; (pl.) condições sanitárias

sanity | sa'nitī | s. sanidade mental, bom juízo, bom senso

Santa Claus | san'təklóz | s. Papai Noel

sap | sap' | s. seiva; (gír.) boboca, tolo

sapling | sap'ling | s. árvore nova

sapper | sa'pə | s. sapador

sapphire | sa'fayə | s. safira

sarcasm | sʌ'kazəm | s. sarcasmo

sarcastic | sʌkas'tik | a. sarcástico

sardine | sʌdin' | s. sardinha

sardonic | sʌdo'nik | a. sardônico

sash | saś' | s. banda, cinta, faixa; caixilho (esp. de janela de guilhotina)

sash-window | saś'window | s. janela de guilhotina, janela de correr

Sassenach | sa'sənak | s. (Esc.) inglês

Satan | sey'tən | s. Satanás, Satã

satchel | sat'şəl | s. bolsa ou pasta de colegial (usada a tiracolo)

satellite | sa'təlayt | s. satélite

satiate | sey'śīeyt | a. saciado, farto / vt. saciar

satiety | sətay'itī sey'śətī | s. saciedade

satin | sa'tin | s. cetim / a. acetinado / vt. acetinar

satire | sa'tayə | s. sátira

satirical | səti'rikəl | a. satírico

satirist | sa'tirist | s. satírico, satirista (escritor)

satirize | sa'tirayz | vt. satirizar

satisfaction | satisfak'şən | s. satisfação

satisfactory | satisfak'tərī | a. satisfatório

satisfied | sa'tisfayd | a. satisfeito

satisfy | sa'tisfay | vt. satisfazer, contentar; cumprir (lei)

saturate | sa'tĭureyt | vt. saturar

Saturday | sa'tədey | s. sábado

saturnine | sa'tənayn | a. mal-humorado, sombrio; saturnino

satyr | sa'tə | s. sátiro

sauce | sós' | s. molho, tempero; (coloq.) atrevimento, petulância / vt. temperar

saucepan | sós'pan | s. caçarola

saucer | só'sə | s. pires

sauciness | só'sines | s. petulância, atrevimento, insolência

saucy | só'sī | a. respondão, insolente, atrevido; esperto, irrequieto

saunter | són'tə | s. passeio, volta a pé; passo vagaroso / vi. andar devagar

sausage | só'sij | s. salsicha

savage | sa'vij | s. selvagem / a. brutal, selvagem / vt. atacar

savagery | sa'vijrī | s. selvageria, brutalidade, ferocidade

save | seyv' | vt. salvar; guardar, poupar, economizar. -to s. up economizar, fazer pé-de-meia. -God s. the King (the Queen) Deus proteja o rei (a rainha). -to s. one's face salvar as aparências / prep. menos, exceto, salvo

saving | sey'ving | s. salvação, salvamento; (pl.) economias, poupanças / a. salvador; econômico / prep. salvo, exceto / conj. senão

savings bank | sey'vingzbank | s. caixa econômica

saviour, savior | sey'vĭə | s. salvador

savour, savor | sey'və | s. sabor /

vt. saborear / *vi.* cheirar a

savoury, savory | sey'vərī |*s.* (bot.) segurelha; pitéu, delícia (comida) / *a.* delicioso, saboroso

saw | só' |*s.* serra / *vt.* serrar

sawdust | só'dâst | *s.* serragem (pó)

sawmill | só'mil |*s.* serraria

Saxon | sak'sən |*s.a.* saxão

saxophone | sak'səfown | *s.* saxofone

say | sey' | *vt.* dizer. -**to s. nothing of** para não falar de. -**that is to s.** isto é, noutros termos. -**it goes without saying** obviamente. -**no sooner said than done** dito e feito

saying | sey'ing |*s.* provérbio, dito, rifão. -**as the s. goes** como diz o refrão

scab | skab' |*s.* crosta, casca (de ferida)

scabbard | ska'bəd |*s.* bainha (de espada)

scabies | skey'bız |*s.* sarna

scaffold | ska'fowld |*s.* patíbulo, forca; cadafalso

scaffolding | ska'fəlding |*s.* andaime

scald | skóld' |*s.* queimadura, escaldadura / *vt. vi.* escaldar(-se)

scale | skeyl' |*s.* escala (cartografia); tarifa; (*pl.*) balança; escama / *vt.* escalar, subir. -**to s. down** diminuir. -**to s. up** elevar

scallop | ska'ləp |*s.* (zool.) vieira, concha de romeiro

scalp | skalp' |*s.* couro cabeludo, escalpo / *vt.* escalpelar, arrancar o couro cabeludo

scalpel | skal'pəl | *s.* escalpelo, lanceta, bisturi

scaly | skey'lī |*a.* escamoso

scamp | skamp' | *s.* malandro, maroto / *vt.* atabalhoar, atamancar

scamper | skam'pə |*s.* fuga precipitada; correria / *vi.* fugir precipitadamente; sair em disparada

scan | skan' |*vt.* esmiuçar, esquadrinhar; explorar (algo com

aparelhagem própria); discriminar

scandal | skan'dəl |*s.* escândalo, vexame; (*pl.*) mexericos

scandalize | skan'dəlayz |*vt.* ofender; escandalizar

scandal monger | skan'dəlmângə | *s.* mexeriqueiro

scandalous | skan'dələs | *a.* vergonhoso, escandaloso

Scandinavian | skandiney'vĭən | *s.a.* escandinavo

scant | skant' | *a.* pouco, insuficiente, escasso, parco / *vt.* restringir; limitar

scantiness | skan'tines |*s.* insuficiência, escassez

scanty | skan'tī | *a.* apoucado, exíguo; sumário (roupa)

scapegoat | skeyp'gowt |*s.* bode expiatório

scar | skA' | *s.* escara, cicatriz / *vt.* cicatrizar, marcar / *vi.* deixar cicatrizes

scarce | ske'əs | *a.* escasso, pouco, raro

scarcely | ske'əslī | *adv.* quase, mal . -**s. ever** quase nunca

scarcity | ske'əsitī | *s.* escassez, falta

scare | ske'ə |*s.* susto; medo; pânico. -**to get a s.** levar um susto / *vt.* assustar, pregar um susto. -**to s. off** afugentar. -**to s. up** arranjar, obter / *vi.* assustar-se; amedrontar-se

scarecrow | ske'əkrow | *s.* espantalho

scarf | skAf' |*s.* cachecol

scarlet | skA'lit |*s.a.* escarlate

scarlet fever | skA'litfıvə | *s.* escarlatina

scathing | skey'ðing | *a.* severo, mordaz

scatter | ska'tə | *vt.* espalhar; dispersar (pessoas)

scatter-brained | ska'təbreynd | *a.* irresponsável, atirado, disparatado; avoado

scattered | ska'təd |*a.* espalhado, disperso; raro

scattering | ska'təring | *s.* espalhamento, dispersão

scavenge | ska'vinʒ | *vi.* remexer, rebuscar, vasculhar; comer carniça

scavenger | ska'vinʒə | *s.* varredor de rua, gari; animal necrófago (esp. besouro)

scene | sin' | *s.* cena; panorama; espetáculo. **-behind the s.** nos (atrás dos) bastidores. **-to make a s.** fazer cenas

scenery | sı'nərī | *s.* (teat.) cenário; paisagem, panorama

scent | sent' | *s.* aroma, cheiro, perfume. **-on the right s.** na boa pista. **-on the wrong s.** na pista errada. **-to throw off the s.** despistar / *vt.* farejar; perfumar

scented | sen'tid | *a.* fragrante, aromático, perfumado

sceptic | skep'tik | *a.* céptico

sceptical | skep'tikəl | *a.* céptico. **-to be s. of** duvidar de, ter dúvidas sobre

scepticism | skep'tisizəm | *s.* cepticismo

sceptre, scepter | sep'tə | *s.* cetro

schedule | ʃe'dĭul ske'dıul | *s.* lista, rol, catálogo; horário; cronograma; programa / *vt.* arrolar, catalogar; marcar a hora de, fixar horário

scheme | skım' | *s.* esquema, plano, projeto / *vt.* planejar / *vi.* intrigar, tramar

schemer | skı'mə | *s.* planejador; intrigante

scheming | skı'ming | *a.* interesseiro, calculista; intrigante

schism | si'zəm | *s.* cisma (tb. relig.)

scholar | sko'lə | *s.* erudito, sábio; aluno, estudante; bolsista (de estudo)

scholarly | sko'ləlī | *a.* erudito, douto, estudioso

scholarship | sko'ləsip | *s.* erudição, cultura; bolsa de estudo

scholastic | skəlas'tik | *s.* escolástico / *a.* escolar, acadêmico, universitário; escolástico

scholasticism | skəlas'tisizəm | *s.* escolástica

school | skʋl' | *s.* escola; cardume / *vt.* ensinar, adestrar, disciplinar / *vi.* nadar em cardume

school-book | skʋl'buk | *s.* livro didático, livro escolar

schoolboy | skʋl'boy | *s.* aluno, estudante

schoolfellow | skʋl'felow | *s.* colega, condiscípulo

schoolgirl | skʋl'gEl | *s.* aluna, estudante

schooling | skʋ'ling | *s.* ensino, disciplina, matéria (escolar)

schoolroom | skʋl'rʋm | *s.* sala de aula

schooner | skʋ'nə | *s.* escuna

sciatica | saya'tikə | *s.* ciática

science | say'əns | *s.* ciência

scientific | sayənti'fik | *a.* científico

scientist | say'əntist | *s.* cientista

scintillate | sin'tileyt | *vi.* cintilar

scintillating | sin'tileyting | *a.* cintilante

scion | say'ən | *s.* broto, rebento, vergôntea; filho, descendente, herdeiro

scissors | si'zəz | *spl.* tesoura

scoff | skof' | *s.* escárnio, zombaria / *vi.* escarnecer, zombar

scold | skowld' | *s.* mulher ranzinza / *vt.* censurar, ralhar

scoop | skʋp' | *s.* concha; pá côncava; caçamba / *vt.* apanhar; tirar (com concha). **-to. s. out** escavar

scoot | skʋt' | *s.* correria, disparada / *vi.* correr, sair como uma bala

scooter | skʋ'tə | *s.* patinete

scope | skowp' | *s.* alcance; mira telescópica; campo de ação

scorch | skóʃ' | *vt. vi.* chamuscar(-se)

scorching | skó'ʃing | *a.* calorento, abrasador

score | skó'ə | *s.* (desp.) escore; marcação, pontos; resultado; (mús.) partitura. **-on that s.** a tal respeito. **-on what s.?** por que motivo? / *vt.* marcar (pontos); conquistar (vitória);

(mús.) orquestrar; rasgar, gastar, cortar. **-to s. out** riscar / vi. ganhar (pontos); alcançar sucesso, ter êxito; fazer riscos ou marcas

scoring | skó'ring | s. (mús.) instrumentação. **-to open the s.** abrir o escore, fazer o primeiro tento (gol etc.)

scorn| skón' |s. desprezo, desdém / vt. desprezar, desdenhar

scornful| skón'ful |a. desdenhoso

scorpion | skó'p˅ən |s. escorpião

Scot | skot' |s. escocês

Scotch | skoš' |s. forma de inglês (esp. usada no sul da Esc.); uísque escocês (tb. minúsc.); os escoceses; (minúsc.) calço, cunha (de roda) / a. escocês

scot-free | skot'frı | a. ileso; impune

Scottish | sko'tiš |a. escocês

scoundrel | skawn'drəl |s. velhaco, vigarista, patife

scour | skaw'ə |s. esfregão, limpeza / vt. esfregar (alfaias); polir; percorrer; perlindar, vagar (campos)

scourge | skɛj' | s. açoite, chicote; castigo, flagelo. **-s. of God** flagelo de Deus / vt. flagelar, açoitar

scout | skawt' |s. observador; escuta; explorador; escoteiro / vt. explorar; vigiar; refugar, rejeitar; desdenhar / vi. explorar; espionar. **-to s. round** investigar. **-to s. at** zombar de

scouting | skaw'ting | s. escoteirismo, escotismo

scowl | skawl' | s. carranca / a. carrancudo / vi. fazer carranca

scraggy | skra'gı̃ | a. magro, esquálido

scramble | skram'bəl | vi. esbarrar-se; andar aos trancos; lutar. **-to s. up** subir com dificuldade. **-to s. over** arrastar-se

scrambled eggs | skram'bəldegz | spl. ovos mexidos

scrap | skrap' | s. pedaço, lasca; (gir.) briga; (pl.) restos (de comida) / vt. desfazer-se de, abandonar / vi. (gir.) brigar

scrap-book | skrap'buk | s. álbum (pasta) de recortes

scrape| skreyp' | s. (coloq.) aperto, embaraço / vt. raspar. **-to s. through** (gír.) passar pela tangente

scrappy | skra'pı̃ | a. remexido, embaralhado; desconexo

scratch | skraš' |s. arranhão; unhada; coçadura; risca. **-not up to s.** abaixo da expectativa. **-from s.** sem aviso prévio, de improviso / vt. arranhar; coçar, riscar

skrawl | skról' | s. rabisco, garatuja / vi. rabiscar, garatujar

scream | skrım' |s. grito. **-to be a s.** ser divertida (pessoa) / vi. gritar

screech | skrıš' |s. grito, guincho / vi. gritar, guinchar; piar

screen | skrın' | s. tela, écran; cinema; anteparo; biombo / vt. abrigar, anteparar, proteger; esconder; (cin.) exibir, passar (filme); investigar, vasculhar, examinar

screw| skrʊ' |s. parafuso. **-to put the s. on** exercer pressão sobre. **-to have a s. loose** (coloq.) ter um parafuso de menos / vt. aparafusar, parafusar, fixar, apertar

screwdriver | skrʊ'drayvə | s. chave de fenda, chave de parafuso

scribble | skri'bəl | s. rabisco / vt. vi. rabiscar

script | skript' | s. letra, caráter; escrita; (cin.) texto, roteiro

scripture | skrip'šə | s. escritura. **-Holy S.** (tb. pl.) Sagrada Escritura

scroll | skrol' | s. rolo (de papel, pergaminho etc.); (arquit.) voluta

scrounge | skrawnj' | vt. cravar; mendigar, pedinchar

scrub | skrâb' | s. matagal, mata, mato / a. inferior; pequeno / vt. esfregar

scrubbing-brush | skrâ'bingbrâŝ |
s. escova (de esfregar)

scruff | skrâf' | s. nuca, cachaço

scruffy | skrâ'fī | a. sujo, mal-
-ajambrado, desmazelado

scruple | skru'pəl | s. escrúpulo /
vi. ter escrúpulos, titubear

scrupulous | skru'pʾuləs | a. es-
crupuloso

scrupulousness | skru'pʾuləsnes |
s. escrúpulo, escrupulosidade

scrutinize | skru'tinayz | vt. in-
vestigar, examinar; estudar

scrutiny | skru'tinī | s. investiga-
ção, exame, pesquisa

scuffle | skâ'fəl | s. rixa, briga; al-
gazarra, escaramuça / vi. lutar
renhidamente

scullery | skâ'lərī | s. copa (sepa-
rada da cozinha)

sculptor | skâlp'tə | s. escultor

sculpture | skâlp'ŝə | s. escultura
/ vt. esculpir

scum | skâm' | s. escuma; ralé,
gentalha

scurf | skEf' | s. caspa

scurrility | skâri'litī | s. baixeza;
insolência

scurrilous | skâ'riləs | a. agressi-
vo, injurioso, grosseiro

scurry | skâ'rī | s. disparada, cor-
reria / vt. pôr em fuga / vi. sair
correndo; apressar-se

scurvy | skE'vī | s. escorbuto / a.
vil, reles

scuttle | skâ'təl | s. (náut.) escoti-
lha; fuga precipitada / vt. pôr a
pique (navio) por meio de rom-
bo / vi. -to s. off fugir

scythe | sayð' | s. foice, gadanha /
vt. ceifar, gadanhar

sea | sī' | s. mar. -at s. no mar. -to
go to s. engajar-se marinheiro.
-to put to s. ir-se (fazer-se) ao
mar

seafarer | sīfe'ərə | s. navegante,
marinheiro

seafaring | sīfe'əring | s. navega-
ção, viagens marítimas / a. na-
vegante, marítimo

seafood | sī'fʊd | s. frutos do mar
(ostras, mariscos etc.)

seal | sīl' | s. selo; (zool.) foca / vt.
selar; lacrar; (fig.) decidir (sorte, destino)

sealing-wax | sī'lingwaks | s. lacre

seam | sīm' | s. costura; camada;
veio

seaman | sī'mən | s. marinheiro

seamstress | sem'stris | s. cos-
tureira

seamy | sī'mī | a. ruim. -s. side lado
avesso; o lado pior (da vida etc.)

séance | sey'óns | s. sessão (no
espiritismo)

seaplane | sī'pleyn | s. hidroavião

seaport | sī'pót | s. porto (de mar)

sear | sī'ə | s. trava de cão de arma
de fogo; chamusco, marca de
queimadura / vt. queimar; (fig.)
cicatrizar

search | sEŝ' | s. busca; pesquisa, in-
vestigação / vt. procurar; examinar, investigar

searching | sE'sing | a. indaga-
dor, inquisitivo

searchlight | sEŝ'layt | s. holofo-
te, lanterna

sea-shore | sī'ŝóə | s. praia, beira-
-mar

seasick | sī'sik | a. mareado, en-
joado

seasickness | sī'siknes | s. enjôo
(de mar)

seaside | sī'sayd | s. praia, litoral

season | sī'zən | s. estação; época,
tempo; período. -to be in s. of
ser tempo de / vt. sazonar; tem-
perar, condimentar

seasonable | sī'zənəbəl | a. sazo-
nal; oportuno

seasonal | sī'zənəl | a. periódico,
sazonal

seasoned | sī'zənd | a. tempera-
do, condimentado; amadure-
cido, seco (lenho); experimen-
tado

seasoning | sī'zəning | s. tempe-
ro, condimento

seat | sīt' | s. cadeira, assento; sí-
tio, local. -to keep a s. guardar
um lugar. -to take a s. sentar-
se / vt. pôr, colocar; sentar(-se)

seat-belt | sīt'belt | s. cinto de segurança (usado esp. em aviões)

sea-urchin | sɪ'ɛšin | *s.* ouriço-
-do-mar

seawards | sɪ'wɔdz | *adv.* em direção ao mar, para o lado do mar

seaweed | sɪ'wɪd | *s.* alga marinha

seaworthiness | sɪ'wɛðines | *s.* navegabilidade

seaworthy | sɪ'wɛðɪ | *a.* seguro, navegável, em boas condições de navegar

secede | sisɪd' | *vi.* separar-se

secession | sise'šən | *s.* secessão

secluded | siklʊ'did | *a.* separado, remoto, isolado

seclusion | siklʊ'jən | *s.* separação, isolamento, solidão

second | se'kənd | *s.* segundo; instante, momento; padrinho (em duelo). **-s. to none** sem-par, insuperável. **-on s. thoughts** pensando melhor / *adv.* em segundo lugar / *vt.* apoiar (moção)

secondary | se'kəndrɪ | *a.* secundário, acessório

second-hand | se'kəndhand | *a.* de segunda mão

second-in-command | se'kəndin-kəmand' | *s.* (mil.) imediato, subcomandante, comandante auxiliar

secondly | se'kəndlɪ | *adv.* em segundo lugar

second-rate | se'kəndreyt | *a.* de segunda ordem

secrecy | sɪ'krəsɪ | *s.* segredo, sigilo, mistério

secret | sɪ'krit | *s.* segredo / *a.* secreto

secretariat | sekrite'ərɪət | *s.* secretariado

secretary | se'krətrɪ | *s.* secretário; secretário de Estado, ministro; secretária, escrivaninha

secretaryship | se'krətrɪšip | *s.* secretariado

secrete | sikrɪt' | *vt.* esconder, apartar; secretar, segregar

secretive | sɪ'kritiv | *a.* furtivo, clandestino

sect | sekt' | *s.* seita

sectarian | sekte'ərɪən | *s.a.* sec-

tário

section | sek'šən | *s.* seção; secção; divisão; artigo, parágrafo

sectional | sek'šənəl | *a.* particular, seccional, divisional

sector | sek'tə | *s.* setor

secular | se'kľulə | *a.* secular, temporal, leigo, mundano

secure | sikiʊ'ə | *a.* seguro, a salvo; firme / *vt.* conseguir, ter, obter; fixar, fechar seguro / *vi.* assegurar-se

security | sikiʊ'ritɪ | *s.* segurança; seguridade, seguro; (jur.) garantia; (jur.) fiança, aval; (*pl.*) títulos (ações, valores etc.)

sedate | sideyt' | *a.* comedido, recatado; grave, sóbrio

sedative | se'dətiv | *s.a.* sedativo, calmante

sedentary | se'dəntərɪ | *a.* sedentário

sediment | se'dimənt | *s.* sedimento

sedition | sidi'šən | *s.* sedição

seditious | sidi'šəs | *a.* sedicioso

seduce | sidľus' | *vt.* seduzir; desonrar, enganar, desencaminhar

seducer | sidľu'sə | *s.* sedutor

seduction | sidâk'šən | *s.* sedução

seductive | sidâk'tiv | *a.* sedutor

sedulous | se'dľuləs | *a.* pertinaz; diligente; constante, assíduo

see | sɪ' | *s.* sé, bispado / *vt. vi.* ver; notar, perceber. **-to s. about** tratar de. **-to s. off** despedir-se de. **-to s. that** fazer (com) que. **-as far as I can s.** ou **as I s. it** a meu ver

seed | sɪd' | *s.* semente, pevide. **-to run to s.** semear; (fig.) desmazelar-se; perder forças. **-to sow s.** semear

seed-bed | sɪd'bed | *s.* viveiro (de plantas)

seedling | sɪd'ling | *s.* broto, rebento, muda, plantinha nova

seed-time | sɪd'taym | *s.* sementeira, época de semear

seedy | sɪ'dɪ | *a.* (coloq.) maltrapilho, mendigo

seek | sɪk' | *vt.* buscar, procurar: tentar, pretender

seem | sɪm' | *vi.* parecer, dar a impressão de

seemingly | sɪ'mɪnglī | *adv.* aparentemente

seemly | sɪm'lī | *a.* decente, decoroso

seep | sɪp' | *s.* nascente / *vi.* verter; infiltrar-se, penetrar

seer | sɪ'ə | *s.* vidente

see-saw | sɪ'só | *s.* balanço, gangorra; vaivém (movimento) / *vi.* gangorrear, oscilar

seethe | sɪð' | *vi.* ferver

segment | seg'mənt | *s.* segmento

segregate | se'grigeyt | *vt.* segregar, separar

segregation | segrigey'śən | *s.* segregação

seize | sɪz' | *vt.* segurar, pegar; agarrar; aproveitar; confiscar; assaltar; agarrar-se a; apoderar-se de

seizure | sɪ'jə | *s.* roubo; confisco; seqüestro; (med.) congestão, apoplexia

seldom | sel'dəm | *adv.* raramente, poucas vezes

select | silekt' | *a.* seleto, fino, exclusivo / *vt.* escolher, selecionar

selection | silek'śən | *s.* seleção

self | self' | *s.* ego, o eu, a individualidade / *pron.* mim; (coloq.) o próprio; (coloq.) o mesmo

self-centred | selfsen'təd | *s.a.* egocêntrico, egoísta

self-confidence | selfkon'fidəns | *s.* confiança em si mesmo, autoconfiança

self-conscious | selfkon'śəs | *a.* introvertido, acanhado

self-control | selfkəntrowl' | *s.* autodomínio

self-defence | selfdifens' | *s.* (jur.) legítima defesa, autodefesa

self-denial | selfdinay'əl | *s.* abnegação

self-determination | selfditEminey'śən | *s.* autonomia, auto-determinação

self-devotion | selfdivow'śən | *s.* dedicação

self-educated | selfidľukey'tid | *s.a.* autodidata

self-employed | selfemployd' | *s.* trabalhador autônomo

self-esteem | selfestim' | *s.* amor-próprio

self-examination | selfegzaminey'śən | *s.* exame de consciência

self-government | selfgà'vənmənt | *s.* autonomia, autogoverno

self-important | selfimpó'tənt | *a.* vaidoso, arrogante

self-indulgent | selfindâl'jənt | *a.* comodista, preguiçoso

selfish | sel'fíś | *a.* egoísta, interesseiro, avarento

selfishness | sel'fíśnes | *s.* egoísmo, egotismo

selfless | self'les | *a.* altruísta, abnegado

self-operating | selfo'pəreyting | *a.* automático

self-possessed | selfpəzest' | *a.* confiante, calmo, sereno

self-reliant | selfrilay'ənt | *a.* confiante, confiado

self-respect | selfrispekt' | *s.* amor-próprio, pundonor

self-service | selfsE'vis | *s.* auto-serviço

self-sufficiency | selfsəfi'śənsī | *s.* auto-suficiência (tb. econ.); (econ.) autarcia

sell | sel' | *s.* fraude, logró; habilidade em vender / *vt.* vender

seller | se'lə | *s.* vendedor

semaphore | se'məfó | *s.* semáforo

semblance | sem'bləns· | *s.* aparência, semblância

semester | simes'tə | *s.* semestre

semicolon | semikow'lən | *s.* ponto e vírgula

semi-detached | semiditaś' | *a.* geminada (casa)

semifinal | semifay'nəl | *s.a.* (desp.) semifinal

seminary | se'minərī | *s.* seminário

Semitic | səmi'tik | *s.a.* semítico, semita

senate | se'nit | *s.* senado

senator | se'nətə | *s.* senador

send | send' | *vt.* mandar, remeter. **-to s. away** despedir, mandar embora. **-to s. back** devolver, restituir. **-to s. for** mandar buscar. **-to s. word** mandar dizer

sender | sen'də | *s.* remetente

sending | sen'ding | *s.* envio, remessa

send-off | sen'dof | *s.* despedida

senile | sı'nayl | *a.* senil

senile decay | sı'nayldikey | *s.* senilidade

senior | sı'nĭə | *s.* chefe, o mais velho (em grupo, profissão) / *a.* mais velho; superior; principal

seniority | sınĭo'rıtĭ | *s.* antiguidade (em serviço, grupo organizado)

sensation | sensey'śən | *s.* sensação

sensational | sensey'śənəl | *a.* sensacional

sensationalism | sensey'śənəlizəm | *s.* sensacionalismo

sense | sens' | *s.* senso, sentido, juízo; sentimento; sensação. **-to talk s.** falar a sério. **-to have no s.** não ter juízo. **-to make s.** fazer sentido. **-to bring one to one's. s.** fazer alguém chegar à razão / *vt.* sentir; adivinhar, perceber

senseless | sens'les | *a.* sem sentido; insensato

sense of duty | sens'ovďutĭ | *s.* sentimento do dever

sensibility | sensibi'litĭ | *s.* sensibilidade

sensible | sen'sibəl | *a.* sensato

sensitive | sen'sitiv | *a.* sensitivo; sensível; impressionável; delicado; suscetível

sensitiveness | sen'sitivnes | *s.* sensibilidade; suscetibilidade

sensual | sen'sĭuəl | *a.* sensual, carnal; sensorial

sensuous | sen'sĭuəs | *a.* sensual

sentence | sen'təns | *s.* frase;

(jur.) sentença / *vt.* (jur.) condenar, sentenciar

sententious | senten'śəs | *a.* pomposo; sentencioso; acaciano

sentient | sen'śənt | *a.* sensível

sentiment | sen'timənt | *s.* sentimento, sentimentalidade; opinião pessoal; significado (de frase etc.)

sentimental | sentimen'təl | *a.* sentimental

sentimentality | sentimenta'litĭ | *s.* sentimentalidade

sentinel | sen'tinəl | *s.* sentinela

sentry | sen'trĭ | *s.* sentinela

sentry-box | sen'trĭboks | *s.* guarita

separable | se'pərəbəl | *a.* separável

separate | se'pərit | *a.* separado / | se'pəreyt | *vt.* separar; dividir

separation | sepərey'śən | *s.* separação

September | septem'bə | *s.* setembro

septic | sep'tik | *a.* infectado, séptico

septicaemia | septisı'mĭə | *s.* (med.) septicemia

sepulchre | se'pəlkə | *s.* sepulcro

sequel | sı'kwəl | *s.* seqüela; resultado, conseqüência

sequence | sı'kwəns | *s.* seqüência, série

sequestered | sikwes'təd | *a.* retirado, isolado, apartado

sequestrate | sı'kwestreyt | *vt.* seqüestrar, confiscar

serenade | serəneyd' | *s.* serenata / *vi.* fazer serenata

serene | sərin' | *a.* sereno

serenity | sərə'nitĭ | *s.* serenidade

serf | sef' | *s.* servo

serfdom | sef'dəm | *s.* servidão

sergeant | sa'ĵənt | *s.* sargento

serial | sı'riəl | *s.* filme ou romance em episódio; folhetim / *a.* serial, periódico, em série

series | sı'rĭz | *s.* série, seqüência

serious | sı'rĭəs | *a.* sério; grave, crítico (estado de saúde)

seriously | sı'rĭəslĭ | *adv.* seriamente; gravemente

seriousness | sɪ'rīəsnes | *s.* serie-
dade; gravidade

sermon | SE'mən | *s.* sermão

serpent | SE'pənt | *s.* serpente

serried | se'rid | *a.* apertado

serum | sɪ'rəm | *s.* soro

servant | SE'vənt | *s.* empregado,
criado, serviçal

serve | SEV' | *s.* (desp.) saque /
vt. vi. servir, cumprir (uma pena). **-to s. as** servir de

service | SE'vis | *s.* serviço; ceri-
mônia religiosa. **-to be at one s.**
estar ao dispor de

serviceable | SE'visəbəl | *a.* útil,
usável; prático

service station | SE'visstey'śən | *s.*
posto de gasolina, posto de
abastecimento

serviette | SEviet' | *s.* guardanapo

servile | SE'vayl | *a.* servil; sub-
serviente

servility | SEvi'litī | *s.* servilidade;
subserviência

servitude | SE'vitſud | *s.* servidão

session | se'śən | *s.* sessão; (*pl.*)
tribunal

set | set' | *s.* coleção, série; con-
junto, jogo; grupo, classe, cír-
culo (de pessoas); (cin., teat.)
cenário; aparelho (de rádio, de
louça etc.). **-s. of tea** aparelho
de chá. **-s. of teeth** dentadura
postiça / *a.* estabelecido, marcado; fixado, fixo / *vt.* colocar,
pôr; fixar; estabelecer; dar;
acertar (relógio); (tip., mús.)
compor; congelar; pôr-se (sol).
-to s. about dedicar-se a, começar a. **-to s. aside** pôr de lado. **-to
s. back** (fazer) retroceder. **-to s.
before** indicar. **-to s. down** escrever; registrar; depor, depo-
sitar. **-to s. forth** expor. **-to s.
free** soltar, libertar. **-to s. in**
chegar, começar. **-to s. off** sair,
partir; correr; realçar. **-to s. out**
sair. **-to s. up** levantar, erigir.
-to s. upon investir, atacar

set-back | set'bak | *s.* revés, con-
tratempo

settee | setɪ' | *s.* sofá, canapé

setting | se'ting | *s.* situação, lo-
cal; paisagem; pôr-do-sol; mú-
sica; (cin., teat., TV) montagem, cenário. **-s. of jewels** en-
gaste

settle | se'təl | *s.* canapé / *vt.* ajus-
tar; resolver, decidir; compor;
liquidar, pagar; fixar / *vi.* fixar
residência, estabelecer-se; acos-
tumar-se; começar a

settled | se'təld | *a.* firme, sereno,
calmo (tempo); estável; deci-
dido

settlement | se'təlmənt | *s.* estabe-
lecimento; ajuste, liquidação
(de contas); povoamento, po-
voação, povoado

settler | set'lə | *s.* colono, povoa-
dor, colonizador

set-to | set'tυ | *s.* rixa, briga; luta,
combate; ajuste físico de contas

set-up | se'tâp | *s.* estado de coi-
sas, situação; organização

seven | se'vən | *s.a.* sete

seventeen | se'vəntɪn | *s.a.* dezes-
sete

seventh | se'vənϑ | *s.a.* sétimo

seventy | se'vəntī | *s. a.* setenta

sever | se'və | *vt.* cortar, romper, cin-
dir / *vi.* separar-se; desligar-se

several | se'vərəl | *a.* vários, al-
guns, diversos, certos

severally | se'vərəlī | *adv.* separa-
damente

severe | səvi'ə | *a.* severo, austero,
rigoroso

severity | səve'ritī | *s.* severidade,
rigor; dureza; austeridade

sew | sow' | *vt.* costurar, coser.
-to s. on pregar (botão)

sewage | sυ'ij | *s.* sujidade, deje-
tos; (*pl.*) despejos, detritos, es-
gotos

sewer | sυ'ə | *s.* (cano de) esgoto

sewing | sow'ing | *s.* costura

sewing-machine | sow'ingməśin | *s.*
máquina de costura

sex | seks' | *s.* sexo. **-the fair s.** o
belo sexo

sexton | seks'tən | *s.* sacristão; co-
veiro

sexual | sek'sîuǝl | *a.* sexual

shabby | śa'bī | *a.* mal-ajambrado; gasto, esfarrapado; reles

shackle | śa'kǝl | *s.* grilhão, algema (tb. *pl.*) / *vt.* agrilhoar, algemar

shade | śeyd' | *s.* sombra; cor, tom, matiz / *vt.*. dar sombra, proteger (do sol); sombrear (desenho)

shading | śey'ding | *s.* sombreado

shadow | śa'dow | *s.* sombra; escuro, escuridão; (*pl.*) trevas / *vt.* proteger (contra a luz); sombrear; obscurecer; seguir (a alguém como sua sombra), perseguir (como policial às escondidas)

shadowy | śa'dowī | *a.* difuso, indefinido, obscuro

shady | śey'dī | *a.* sombreado, ensombrado; suspeito; ambíguo, indefinido

shaft | śAft' | *s.* seta, flecha; poço (de mina, de elevador); varal; haste; fuste; raio (de luz); veio

shaggy | śa'gī | *a.* peludo

shake | śeyk' | *s.* sacudida, safanão, sacudidela; aceno ou nuto (da cabeça) / *vt.* sacudir, agitar; acenar (com a cabeça); apertar (as mãos); vibrar; estremecer

shaking | śey'king | *s.* tremor, vibração / *a.* trêmulo, vibrátil

shaky | śey'kī | *a.* trêmulo; hesitante; dúbio; inseguro

shale | śeyl' | *s.* xisto; piçarra

shallow | śa'low | *s.* banco de areia; (*pl.*) baixios / *a.* raso, pouco profundo; superficial, leviano

sham | śam' | *s.* imitação; impostura; simulacro / *a.* imitado; falso / *vt.* simular, fingir. **-to s. dead** fazer-se de morto

shamble | śam'bǝl | *s.* andar desajeitado; (*pl.*) açougue; (*pl.*, coloq.) trapalhada; ruínas

shambling | śamb'ling | *a.* arrastado, pesadão; canhestro, desajeitado

shame | śeym' | *s.* vergonha.
-what a s.! que vergonha!; que pena! **-for s.!** que vergonha! / *vt.* envergonhar

shamefaced | śeym'feyst | *a.* envergonhado

shameful | śeym'ful | *a.* vergonhoso

shamefulness | śeym'fulnes | *s.* indignidade, baixeza, ignomínia, vergonha, infâmia

shameless | śeym'les | *a.* sem--vergonha, descarado, desaforado

shampoo | śampv' | *s.* xampu

shamrock | śam'rok | *s.* trevo

shank | śank' | *s.* canela (da perna); perna, tarso (de ave)

shanty | śan'tī | *s.* choupana, choça, casebre

shape | śeyp' | *s.* forma, feitio. **-in bad s.** em mau estado. **-in good s.** em boa forma / *vt.* dar forma, formar, modelar; produzir

shaped | śeypt' | *a.* feito. **-well s.** bem proporcionado

shapeless | śeyp'les | *a.* informe, disforme; mal cortado (traje)

shapely | śeyp'lī | *a.* bem proporcionado, bem feito; escultural

share | śe'ǝ | *s.* parte, cota-parte; porção, quinhão / *vt.* partilhar, repartir. **-to s. out** dividir

shareholder | śe'ǝhowldǝ | *s.* acionista

sharing | śe'ǝring | *s.* participação; divisão, partilha, distribuição

shark | śAk' | *s.* tubarão; (fig.) achacador, vigarista, chantagista

sharp | śAp' | *s.* (mús.) sustenido; (coloq.) perito; (coloq.) trapaceiro / *a.* agudo, pontiagudo; afiado; apertado, justo; vivaz, inteligente; picante, amargo; fechada (curva); brusco / *adv.* abruptamente; agudamente; em ponto (*at five o'clock sharp* às cinco horas em ponto)

sharpen | śA'pǝn | *vt.* afiar, amolar; aparar; aguçar

sharpener | śA'pǝnǝ | *s.* afiador,

amolador; apontador (de lápis)

sharpness | śAp'nes | s. agudeza; aspereza; (fig.) esperteza; vivacidade mental, inteligência

shatter | śa'tə | vt. quebrar, romper, espatifar; destruir

shave | śeyv' | vt. vi. fazer a barba, barbear. -to s. off cortar, rapar

shaving-brush | śey'vingbrȧš | s. pincel de barba

shavings | śey'vingz | spl. aparas, lascas, raspas

shaving-soap | śey'vingsowp | s. sabão de barba

shawl | śól' | s. xale, xaile

she | śı | pron. ela

sheaf | śıf' | s. feixe, molho, maço

shear | śı'ɔ | s. (ger. pl.) tesoura / vt. tosquiar

sheath | śıϑ' | s. bainha

sheathe | śıð' | vt. embainhar

shed | śed' | s. refúgio, abrigo; telheiro; barracão, cabana / vt. espalhar; derramar, verter; perder (folhas). -to s. light on esclarecer

sheen | śın' | s. brilho, lustro, resplendor

sheep | śıp' | s. carneiro, ovelha. -flock of s. rebanho

sheep-fold | śıp'fowld | s. redil, aprisco

sheepish | śı'piś | a. arisco, tímido, envergonhado

sheer | śı'ɔ | s. desvio / a. absoluto, puro; fino, seleto; escarpado, abrupto

sheet | śıt' | s. lençol; folha (de papel, de metal etc.); chapa; cortina (de chuva)

shelf | śelf' | s. prateleira; estante; escarpa saliente

shell | śel' | s. casca; concha; carcaça, carapaça / vt. descascar; (mil.) bombardear

shellac | śe'lək | s. goma-laca / vt. envernizar com goma-laca

shellfish | śel'fiś | s. marisco, mexilhão, amêijoa

shelling | śe'ling | s. (mil.) bombardeamento

shell-shock | śel'śok | s. neurose de guerra

shelter | śel'tə | s. refúgio, abrigo, asilo. -to take s. abrigar-se / vt. proteger, abrigar; homiziar; asilar

shelve | śelv' | vt. adiar; separar; evitar; esquecer

shepherd | śe'pəd | s. pastor

shepherdess | śe'pədes | s. pastora

sheriff | śe'rif | s. (EUA) xerife, comissário de polícia

sherry | śe'rı | s. xerez (vinho)

shield | śıld' | s. escudo; amparo, anteparo, proteção / vt. resguardar, proteger

shift | śıft' | s. mudança, deslocamento; turno, meio expediente; deslizamento. -to make s. to esforçar-se; mudar, transferir / vi. mudar. -to s. for oneself viver por conta própria

shifting | śif'ting | s. mudança, transporte, transferência / a. alternativo; dobradiço, movediço

shifty | śif'tı | a. escorregadio; fugidio; vacilante; manhoso

shilling | śı'ling | s. xelim

shimmer | śi'mə | s. vislumbre; luz trêmula / vi. cintilar, tremeluzir

shin | śin' | s. canela (da perna)

shindy | śin'dı | s. tumulto, arruaça; vozerio

shine | śayn' | s. brilho, lustre / vi. brilhar, reluzir; distinguir-se

shingle | śin'gəl | s. seixo miúdo, cascalho; pedrinhas; (med., ger. pl.) herpes

shining | śay'ning | a. luzente, reluzente; brilhante; notável

shiny | śay'nı | a. lustroso, reluzente

ship | śıp' | s. barco, navio, nau / vt. navegar; embarcar; remeter, enviar

shipment | śıp'mənt | s. carga, embarque

shipping | śı'ping | s. navegação, marinha mercante, navios; embarque, transporte / *a.* marítimo

shipshape | ʃip'ʃeyp | *a. adv.* asseado, em boa ordem

shipwreck | ʃip'rek | *s.* naufrágio

shipwright | ʃip'rayt | *s.* construtor naval

shipyard | ʃip'ɪᴀd | *s.* estaleiro

shirk | ʃᴇk' | *vi.* esquivar-se, fugir de; negligenciar

shirker | ʃᴇ'kə | *s.* malandro; fujão, desertor

shirt | ʃᴇt' | *s.* camisa

shiver | ʃi'və | *s.* calefrio, calafrio, tremor / *vt.* despedaçar, espatifar / *vi.* tremer, tiritar de frio

shoal | ʃowl' | *s.* cardume; (geog.) baixio

shock | ʃok' | *s.* choque (tb. med.); susto, espanto; tufo (de cabelo) / *vt.* chocar; ofender; escandalizar

shock absorber | ʃok'absóbə | *s.* (mec.) amortecedor

shocking | ʃo'king | *a.* chocante; escandaloso; ofensivo; lamentável; horrível

shock-proof | ʃok'pruf | *a.* à prova de choque, antichoque

shock-troops | ʃok'trʊps | *spl.* (mil.) tropas de choque, tropas de assalto

shoddy | ʃo'dɪ | *a.* ruim, baixo, inferior, ordinário

shoe | ʃuʹ | *s.* sapato; ferradura / *vt.* calçar; ferrar (cavalo)

shoe brush | ʃuʹbrâʃ | *s.* escova de sapato

shoe-lace | ʃuʹleys | *s.* cordão de sapato

shoemaker | ʃuʹmeykə | *s.* sapateiro

shoe-polish | ʃuʹpowliʃ | *s.* graxa de sapato

shoe-shop | ʃuʹʃop | *s.* sapataria

shoo | ʃuʹ | *interj.* xô! / *vt.* espantar, afugentar

shoot | ʃut' | *s.* caça; tiro ao alvo; (bot.) rebento, broto / *vt.* fuzilar; ferir (com bala); disparar (flecha etc.); caçar; filmar; fotografar; correr (ferrolho). **-to s. down** matar, abater / *vi.* disparar; (futb.) rematar, arrematar. **-to s. ahead** passar adiante. **-to s. past** passar como relâmpago

shooting | ʃuʹting | *s.* tiro, tiroteio; caça de tiro; pontaria

shooting party | ʃuʹtingpᴀtɪ | *s.* grupo de caçadores

shooting star | ʃuʹtingstᴀ | *s.* estrela cadente, meteoro

shop | ʃop' | *s.* loja; armazém / *vi.* fazer compras

shop assistant | ʃop'əsistənt | *s.* comerciário, caixeiro

shopkeeper | ʃop'kɪpə | *s.* lojista, comerciante

shop-lifting | ʃop'lifting | *s.* pequeno furto (geralmente em lojas de vendas)

shop-steward | ʃop'stɪ̌vəd | *s.* representante sindical (no local de trabalho)

shop-window | ʃop'window | *s.* vitrine

shore | ʃóʹə | *s.* praia, costa, litoral / *vt.* (ger. com **up**) suster, escorar, acochar

shorn | ʃón' | *a.* tosquiado; privado de

short | ʃót' | *a.* pequeno; curto; breve; baixo; pouco, insuficiente, escasso; limitado, restrito. **-in a s. time** daqui a pouco, em breve. **-a s. while ago** faz pouco, há pouco. **-to be s. of** ter falta de. **-to fall s. of** não corresponder a, ficar abaixo de. **-to run s.** faltar. **-nothing s. of** nada menos que

shortage | ʃó'tij | *s.* escassez, carência, falta; carestia, indigência

shortcoming | ʃót'kâming | *s.* defeito; deficiência, falta

short cut | ʃót'kât | *s.* atalho

shorten | ʃó'tən | *vt.* diminuir, reduzir, abreviar

shorthand | ʃót'hand | *s.* taquigrafia, estenografia

shortly | ʃót'lɪ | *adv.* brevemente,

em breve; em resumo

shortness | śót'nes | *s*. brevidade; pequenez, curteza

shorts | śóts' | *spl*. calção, *short*

short-sighted | śót'saytid | *a*. míope, curto de vista

shot | śot' | *s*. tiro; chumbo; atirador; remate; tentativa. **-to be off like a s.** partir como um raio / *a*. fuzilado; furtacor; entretecido

shoulder | śowl'də | *s*. ombro / *vt*. encarregar-se de, tomar a si. **-s. arms!** (mil.) ombro armas!

shoulder-blade | śowl'dəbleyd | *s*. espádua, omoplata

shout | śawt' | *s*. grito / *vi*. gritar, exclamar

shove | śâv' | *s*. empurrão / *vt*. empurrar; introduzir

shovel | śâ'vəl | *s*. pá, pazinha / *vt*. trabalhar (areia, terreno, massa etc.) com pá

shovelful | śâ'vəlful | *s*. pazada

show | śow' | *s*. exposição, mostra, exibição; espetáculo; pompa, ostentação; indício, sinal. **-for s.** não para valer, para inglês ver. **-in s.** em exibição, em exposição. **-to run the s.** dirigir um grupo ou uma empresa / *vt*. mostrar, demonstrar. **-tos. in** mandar entrar, conduzir para dentro. **-to s. out** conduzir para fora. **-to s. off** pavonear-se, exibir-se. **-to s. up** fazer subir; desmistificar, desmascarar

shower | śaw'ə | *s*. chuvarada, aguaceiro; chuveiro / *vt*. regar; derramar, entornar / *vi*. chover

shower-bath | śaw'əbaϑ | *s*. banho de chuveiro

showery | śaw'əri | *a*. pluvioso, de aguaceiros, de chuvaradas

showy | śow'ī | *a*. espetaculoso, ostentoso, aparatoso, pomposo

shred | śred' | *s*. tira, farrapo; fragmento / *vt*. esfrangalhar; fazer em tiras ou em pedaços; esmigalhar

shrew | śrʊ' | *s*. megera; (zool.) musaranho

shrewd | śrʊd' | *a*. astuto, esperto, sagaz; prudente

shrewdness | śrʊd'nes | *s*. astúcia, perspicácia, sagacidade

shrew-mouse | śrʊ'maws | *s*. (zool.) musaranho

shriek | śrīk' | *s*. grito, guincho / *vi*. gritar, guinchar

shrift | śrift' | *s*. (ecles.) confissão; confissão e absolvição. **-to make short s.** of demitir sumariamente; despachar; rejeitar

shrill | śril' | *a*. agudo; estridente; perfurante, penetrante

shrimp | śrimp' | *s*. camarão

shrine | śrayn' | *s*. santuário; relicário

shrink | śrink' | *vi*. encolher (pano). **-to s. back** encolher-se de medo. **-to s. from** fugir de; abster-se de; recuar

shrinkage | śrink'iǰ | *s*. encolhimento, contração; redução

shrivel | śri'vəl | *vt*. secar; enrugar, mirrar

shroud | śrawd' | *s*. mortalha; enxárcias / *vt*. envolver, cobrir, encobrir

Shrove Tuesday | śrowv'tⁱʊzdey | *s*. terça-feira gorda; dia do entrudo

shrub | śrâb' | *s*. arbusto

shrug | śrâg' | *vt*. *vi*. encolher os ombros, dar de ombros

shudder | śâ'də | *s*. estremecimento, tremor / *vi*. estremecer, tremer

shuffle | śâ'fəl | *vt*. baralhar (cartas); misturar; arrastar os pés, andar tropegamente

shun | śân' | *vt*. evitar, furtar-se a; distanciar-se de

shunt | śânt' | *vt*. desviar

shut | śât' | *vt*. fechar. **-to s. in** encerrar. **-to s. off** isolar, fechar cerrado. **-to s. from** excluir, impedir a entrada. **-s. up!** cale-se!

shutter | śâ'tə | *s*. (fot.) obturador; veneziana; postigo; taipa, biombo

shuttle | šâ'təl |s. (tecl.)lançadeira, laçadeira

shuttlecock | šâ'təlkok |s. peteca (de cortiça); (desp.) volante

shy | šay' | a. acanhado, tímido, arredio, retraído/ vt. atirar/ vi. espantar-se (animal)

shyness | šay'nes |s. acanhamento, timidez

sick | sik' | a. doente; enjoado, mareado(mar, ar, viagem etc.). **-to be s.** enjoar, vomitar. **-to fall s.** adoecer, acamar-se. **-to feel s.** sentir-se enjoado, ter náuseas. **-to report s.** dar parte de doente

sick-bay | sik'bey |s. enfermaria

sicken | si'kən | vt. aborrecer, desgostar / vi. adoecer

sickening | si'kəning | a. enjoativo, repugnante, nauseante

sickle | si'kəl | s. foice, foicinha, roçadeira

sickly | si'klī | a. doentio, pálido; repugnante

sickness | sik'nes |s. doença; enjôo, náusea

side | sayd' |s. lado; (desp.)time, equipe. **-this s. up** este lado para cima **-s. by s.** lado a lado / a. lateral, de lado; secundário, complementar / vi. **-to s. with** tomar o partido de

sideboard | sayd'bód | s. console, aparador

sideburns | sayd'bEns | spl. suíças, costeletas

side-door | sayd'dóə | s. porta lateral

sidelong | sayd'long |a. transversal, oblíquo

side-step | sayd'step | vt. evitar, esquivar-se, desguiar-se de

side-street | sayd'strit | s. rua lateral; travessa

side-track | sayd'trak | s. (ferrov.) desvio / vt. vi. evitar; adiar; pospor

sidewalk | sayd'wók | s. (EUA) calçada, passeio (de rua)

sideways | sayd'weyz |a. oblíquo / adv. lateralmente

siding | say'ding |s. tapume; (ferrov.) desvio

sidle | say'dəl | vi. achegar-se furtivamente

siege | sīj' |s. cerco, sítio, assédio

siesta | sIes'tə |s. sesta

sieve | siv' |s. crivo, joeira, peneira / vt. peneirar, joeirar

sift | sift' | vt. peneirar, joeirar; esmiuçar, perscrutar, sondar, investigar

sigh | say' | s. suspiro, sussurro / vi. suspirar, sussurrar

sight | sayt' |s. vista; cena; aspecto; espetáculo. **-at first s.** à primeira vista. **-by s.** de vista / vt. avistar; apontar, mirar

sightseer | sayt'sIə | s. turista, excursionista

sign | sayn' |s. sinal; aviso, tabuleta, letreiro; signo / vi. assinar, assinalar. **-to s. away** conceder, ceder

signal | sig'nəl |s. sinal / a. notável / vi. fazer sinais, acenar

signalize | sing'nəlayz | vt. assinalar

signalling | sig'nəling | s. sinalização

signalman | sig'nəlmən | s. sinaleiro

signatory | sig'nətərī | s. signatário

signature | sig'nəšə |s. assinatura

signboard | sayn'bód | s. tabuleta, placar, quadro de avisos

significance | signi'fikəns |s. significação, significado; importância

significant | signi'fikənt |s. significante / a. significativo, relevante; importante

signify | sig'nifay | vt. significar

signpost | sayn'post | s. poste indicador, marco

silence | say'ləns |s. silêncio / vt. silenciar, impor silêncio

silent | say'lənt |a. silencioso, calado, silente, mudo

silently | say'ləntlī | adv. silenciosamente, silentemente

silhouette | silvet' | s. silhueta

silk | silk' |s. seda

silkworm | silk'wεm | s. bicho-
-da-seda

silliness | si'lines | s. bobice, toli-
ce; estupidez

silly | si'lī | a. bobo, tolo; estú-
pido

silt | silt' | s. lama; vasa; resíduo;
sedimento

silver | sil'vǝ | s. prata; dinheiro;
(fot.) sal de prata / a. de prata;
prateado / vt. pratear

silver paper | sil'vǝpeypǝ | s. pa-
pel estanhado

silver plate | sil'vǝpleyt | s. baixe-
la de prata

silver plated | sil'vǝpleytid | a.
prateado

silversmith | sil'vǝsmiθ | s. pra-
teiro (ourives de prata)

silverware | sil'vǝweǝ | s. objetos
de prata, baixela de prata

silver wedding | sil'vǝweding | s.
bodas de prata

silvery | sil'vǝrī | a. prateado

similar | si'milǝ | a. similar, seme-
lhante, parecido

similarity | simila'ritī | s. similari-
dade, semelhança

similarly | si'milǝlī | adv. do mes-
mo modo, igualmente, se-
melhantemente

simile | si'milī | s. símile

simmer | si'mǝ | vi. ferver (a fogo
lento)

simper | sim'pǝ | s. sorriso força-
do / vt. sorrir afetadamente

simple | sim'pǝl | a. simples; ingê-
nuo, inocente; tolo, simplório

simpleton | sim'pǝltǝn | s. tolo,
bobo, simplório

simplicity | simpli'sitī | s. simpli-
cidade; ingenuidade

simplify | sim'plifay | vt. sim-
plificar

simply | sim'plī | adv. simplesmente

simulate | si'm˘uleyt | vt. simular

simultaneous | saymǝltey'nīǝs |
a. simultâneo

sin | sin' | s. pecado. -besetting s.
pecador inveterado. -deadly s.
pecado mortal / vi. pecar

since | sins | prep. desde; após;
depois de / conj. desde (que);
visto que / adv. desde então.
-not long s. faz pouco, há pouco tempo

sincere | sinsɪ'ǝ | a. sincero

sincerity | sinse'ritī | s. sin-
ceridade

sinecure | si'nik˘uǝ say'nik˘uǝ |
s. sinecura

sinew | si'n˘u | s. tendão, músculo

sinewy | si'n˘uī | a. tendinoso,
musculoso

sinful | sin'ful | a. pecaminoso

sing | sing' | vt. vi. cantar

singe | sinj' | vt. chamuscar

singer | sin'gǝ | s. cantor

singing | sin'ging | s. canto; (fig.)
zumbido

single | sin'gǝl | a. só, único; sol-
teiro / vt. -to s. out escolher;
apontar, indicar

single combat | sin'gǝlkom'bat |
s. duelo

single ticket | sin'gǝltikit | s. pas-
sagem de ida

singly | sing'lī | adv. individual-
mente; um a um, um por um, de
um em um

singular | sin'g˘ulǝ | s. singular /
a. singular, diferente, curioso

singularity | sing˘ula'ritī | s.
singularidade

singularly | sin'g˘ulǝlī | adv. ex-
traordinariamente, singular-
mente

sinister | si'nistǝ | a. sinistro

sink | sink' | s. pia (de cozinha) /
vt. afundar; empregar, colocar
(dinheiro); abrir (poço); pregar, cravar / vi. afundar(-se),
mergulhar; pôr-se (sol); sumir;
declinar, enfraquecer

sinking | sin'king | s. afundamen-
to, naufrágio

sinking feeling | sin'kingfɪling |
s. receio, temor; desânimo, de-
salento

sinking fund | sin'kingfând | s.
fundo de amortização, fundo
de garantia

sinner | si'nǝ | s. pecador

sinuous | si'n˘uǝs | a. sinuoso

sinusitis| saynəsay'tis |s. sinusite

sip| sip' |s. sorvo, traguinho / vt. sorver

siphon | say'fən |s. sifão

sir | se' | s. senhor (seguido de prenome)

siren | say'rən |s. sereia

sirloin | se'loyn |s. filé (de carne de vaca); (EUA) alcatra

sister| sis'tə |s. irmã

sister-in-law | sis'təinló |s. cunhada

sit | sit' | vt. sentar, assentar; colocar / vi. sentar-se, estar sentado; reunir-se. -to s. down sentar-se. -to s. up velar (à noite). -to s. for an exam fazer exame

site | sayt' |s. local, sítio, lugar; situação / vt. localizar, situar

sitting| si'ting |s. reunião; audiência, sessão; turno / a. sentado

sitting-room | si'tingrʋm |s. sala de visitas

situated | si'tʃueytid | a. situado, sito

situation| sitʃuey'şən |s. situação, posição; emprego

six | siks' |s.a. seis

sixteen | siks'tın |s.a. dezesseis

sixty | siks'tı |s.a. sessenta

size | sayz' | s. medida; tamanho; estatura / vt. -to s. up medir; estimar, avaliar

sizeable | sayz'əbəl | a. grande, bastante, considerável

sizzle | si'zəl | s. chiado / vi. chiar (de fritura)

skate | skeyt' | s. (ict.) espécie de raia ou arraia (tb. pl.); patim / vi. patinar

skater | skey'tə |s. patinador

skating | skey'ting |s. patinação

skating-rink | skey'tingrink | s. rinque de patinação

skeleton | ske'litən |s. esqueleto

skeleton key | ske'litənkı |s. chave-mestra

skeptical | skep'tikəl | a. (EUA) = sceptical

sketch | skeč | s. rascunho, esboço; croqui; bosquejo; desenho; (teat.) esquete / vt. rascunhar,

esboçar, debuxar; desenhar

sketchy | ske'şi | a. esboçado; vago, incompleto

ski | ski' |s. esqui / vi. esquiar

skid | skid' | s. derrapagem / vi. derrapar

skilful | skil'ful |a. habilidoso, hábil, destro; competente

skill | skil' | s. habilidade, perícia, destreza; competência

skilled | skild' | a. adestrado, especializado, treinado (operário etc.)

skim | skim' | vt. roçar. -to s. off desnatar. -to s. through folhear (livro)

skim milk | skim'milk | s. leite desnatado

skimp | skimp' | vt. inibir, restringir, cercear / vi. poupar, economizar

skin | skin' | s. pele; casca; cutícula; nata (de leite) / vt. depelar, esfolar

skinflint | skin'flint | s.a. avaro, avarento, sovina

skinny | ski'nı | a. avarento, miserável; magro

skip | skip' | s. salto, pulo / vi. saltar; omitir

skipper | ski'pə | s. (náut.) patrão, capitão, mestre

skirmish | ske'miş | s. escaramuça / vi. fazer escaramuça

skirt | sket' |s. saia; aba / vt. orlar, rodear; passar perto de; roçar; tangenciar

skirting-board | ske'tingbód | s. rodapé

skit | skit' | s. sátira, verrina, pasquim; (teat.) esquete

skittish | ski'tiş | a. caprichoso, dengoso; brincalhão

skittle| ski'təl |s. pau; (pl.) boliche

skulk | skålk' | vi. esconder-se

skull | skål' | s. crânio

skull-cap | skål'kap |s. solidéu

skunk | skånk' | s. espécie de gambá; doninha-fedorenta

sky | skay' | s. céu

skylark | skay'lʌk |s. cotovia / vi. brincar, fazer travessuras

skylight | skay'layt | *s.* clarabóia

skyscraper | skay'skreypə | *s.* arranha-céu

slab | slab' | *s.* pedregulho, matacão; fatia grande (de bolo)

slack | slak' | *a.* frouxo; desequilibrado, bambo; descuidado, relaxado; inativo, imobilizado; folgado (traje); (*pl.*) calças, *slack* / *vi.* malandrear, gazetear, fazer cera

slacken | sla'kən | *vt. vi.* afrouxar, diminuir, folgar

slackening | sla'kəning | *s.* afrouxamento, frouxidão, folga

slacker | sla'kə | *s.a.* malandro, folgado, boa-vida, vigarista

slackness | slak'nes | *s.* frouxidão; indolência; negligência

slag | slag' | *s.* escória

slain | sleyn' | *vt.* apagar; mitigar, saciar

slam | slam' | *s.* pancada ruidosa; baque / *vt.* bater com força (porta etc.) / *vi.* fechar barulhentamente

slander | slʌn'də | *s.* difamação, injúria, calúnia / *vt.* difamar, injuriar, caluniar

slanderous | slʌn'dərəs | *a.* difamante, infamante, calunioso

slang | slang' | *s.* gíria, calão

slant | slʌnt' | *s.* ângulo, inclinação / *vi.* inclinar-se, estar de esguelha, de soslaio

slanting | slʌn'ting | *a.* inclinado, de banda, de soslaio

slap | slap' | *s.* palmada; bofetada / *vt.* dar palmada; dar bofetada, esbofetear

slapdash | slap'daś | *a.* afogueado, impetuoso, violento; descuidado

slash | slaś' | *s.* facada, cutilada / *vt.* cortar, ferir, acutilar; chicotear, açoitar

slat | slat' | *s.* tabuinha, ripa

slate | sleyt' | *s.* lousa, ardósia; quadro-negro / *vt.* (gir.) dar uma surra, dar uma esfrega

slatternly | sla'tənlī | *a.* desmazelado

slaughter | sló'tə | *s.* chacina, massacre, mortandade, matança / *vt.* chacinar, massacrar, matar; abater (gado)

slaughterer | sló'tərə | *s.* açougueiro, magarefe, carniceiro

slaughter-house | sló'təhaws | *s.* matadouro, abatedouro

Slav | slav' | *s.a.* eslavo˙

slave | sleyv' | *s.* escravo / *vt.* trabalhar de sol a sol, mourejar

slavery | sley'vərī | *s.* escravidão

slave-ship | sleyv'śip | *s.* navio negreiro

slave-trade | sleyv'treyd | *s.* tráfico negreiro

slavish | sley'viś | *a.* servil

slay | sley' | *vt.* matar, assassinar

sledge | slej' | *s.* trenó

sleek | slık' | *a.* liso, suave, macio; insinuante, persuasivo

sleep | slıp' | *s.* sono. -to go to s. adormecer / *vi.* dormir. -to s. on it consultar o travesseiro. -I didn't s. a wink não preguei olho

sleeper | slı'pə | *s.* adormecido; (ferrov.) dormente; (ferrov.) carro-dormitório

sleepily | slı'pilī | *adv.* sonolentamente, com sono

sleepiness | slı'pines | *s.* sonolência

sleeping | slı'ping | *a.* adormecido

sleeping-car | slı'pingkʌ | *s.* (ferrov.) carro-dormitório

sleeping sickness | slı'pingsiknes | *s.* doença do sono

sleepless | slıp'les | *a.* sem dormir, em vigília, desvelado

sleepless night | slıp'lesnayt | *s.* noite em claro

sleep-walker | slıp'wókə | *s.* sonâmbulo

sleepy | slı'pī | *a.* sonolento. -to feel s. ter (estar com) sono

sleepyhead | slı'pīhed | *a.* dorminhoco

sleet | slıt' | *s.* chuva com neve; granizada

sleeve | slıv' | *s.* manga (de roupa); (mec.) manga, camisa, bucha

sleigh | sley' | *s.* trenó

sleight | slayt' | s. destreza. **-s. of hand** prestidigitação, presteza de mãos, escamoteação

slender | slen'də | a. esbelto, esguio, magro; fraco

sleuth | slυϑ' | s. investigador, detetive

slice | slays' | s. fatia, pedaço / vt. cortar em fatias

slick | slik' | s. mancha de óleo (na superfície da água) / a. (coloq.) jeitoso, esperto, rápido

slide | slayd' | s. lugar escorregadio; (ópt.) lâmina de microscópio; (ópt.) diapositivo, *slide* / vt. fazer deslizar / vi. deslizar; escorregar

sliding | slay'ding | a. escorregadio, corrediço

slight | slayt' | s. desrespeito, descortesia, desconsideração / a. pequeno; leve; fraco, frágil; fino, esguio, delicado / vt. desprezar, menosprezar, desconsiderar, fazer pouco caso de

slighting | slay'ting | a. pejorativo, desconsiderado, menosprezado

slightly | slayt'lī | adv. levemente, ligeiramente, um pouco. **-to know s.** conhecer vagamente

slim | slim' | a. esbelto, esguio, delgado, elegante; ligeiro, fraco / vi. emagrecer, adelgaçar

slime | slaym' | s. lodo, limo, visgo, vasa

slimness | slim'nes | s. esbeltez, delgadez; fragilidade

slimy | slay'mĭ | a. viscoso, pegajoso; sebento; sujo

sling | sling' | s. funda, atiradeira; tipóia, ligadura / vt. lançar, atirar; elevar, suspender

slink | slink' | vi. esgueirar-se. **-to s. off** sair de esguelha, sair a furtivas; escapulir

slip | slip' | s. escorregão; erro, deslize, falta; lapso; combinação (roupa); pedaço, tira. **-s. of the pen** lapso de escrita / vt. introduzir, meter, pôr dentro; escorregar, resvalar; equivocar-se, errar. **-to s. off** tirar; sair, ir-se embora. **-to s. out** sair, escapar-se, retirar-se

slip-knot | slip'not | s. nó corredio

slipper | sli'pə | s. chinelo

slippery | sli'pərĭ | a. escorregadio

slipshod | slip'śod | a. malfeito, descuidado; desmazelado

slipway | slip'wey | s. plano inclinado, declive de dique seco, canteiro inclinado de obra

slit | slit' | s. fenda estreita, abertura; corte, incisão; rasgão / vt. cortar (esp. em tiras), rasgar

slobber | slo'bə | s. saliva, baba / vi. babar(-se)

slog | slog' | vt. bater / vi. esforçarse, mourejar

slogan | slow'gən | s. divisa, lema, palavra de ordem, *slogan*

slope | slowp' | s. ladeira; aclive; declive; encosta, vertente; rampa; inclinação / vi. inclinar-se. **-to s. up** subir. **-to s. down** descer

sloping | slow'ping | a. enviesado, oblíquo, inclinado

sloppy | slo'pī | a. lamacento; manchado, sujo; desmazelado; piegas, sentimental

slops | slops' | spl. despejos, águas usadas, lavaduras

slot | slot' | s. fenda, ranhura

sloth | slowϑ' | s. preguiça (tb. zool.); indolência

slouch | slawš' | vi. girŕgar, andar sem aprumo

slovenliness | slâ'vənlines | s. desmazelo, desalinho

slovenly | slâ'vənlī | a. desmazelado, desalinhado; desleixado, sujo

slow | slow' | a. lento, moroso; tardio; atrasado (relógio) / vt. vi. retardar. **-to s. down** diminuir (velocidade, marcha)

slowcoach | slow'kowš | s.a. bronco, molenga, malandro

slowly | slow'lī | adv. lentamente, pouco a pouco, devagar

slow motion | slowmow'śən | s. (cin., TV) movimento retardado

slowness | slow'nes | *s.* lentidão, morosidade, vagareza

slug | slâg' | *s.* lesma / *vt.* esmurrar, socar

sluggard | slâ'gəd | *s.a.* preguiçoso, indolente, malandro, vadio

sluggish | slâ'giś | *a.* moroso, lento, vagaroso; preguiçoso

sluice | slʊs' | *s.* comporta / *vt.* abrir comporta. **-to s. down** lavar (com jorro de água) / *vi.* jorrar

slum | slâm' | *s.* favela; cortiço

slumber | slâm'bə | *s.* sono / *vi.* dormir

slump | slâmp' | *s.* (econ.) depressão / *vi.* cair (preços) rapidamente; deixar-se cair

slur | slɛ' | *s.* mancha, nódoa; pronúncia ininteligível; insulto, labéu / *vt.* gaguejar. **-to s. over** referir-se ligeiramente a

slush | slâś' | *s.* lama; neve semiderretida

slut | slât' | *s.* mulher porcalhona ou desmazelada

sly | slay' | *a.* esperto, astuto, manhoso, finório, matreiro. **-on the s.** às escondidas, furtivamente

slyness | slay'nes | *s.* malícia, esperteza, astúcia

smack | smak' | *s.* palmada, bofetada; gosto, sabor (esp. leve) / *vt.* dar palmadas em, esbofetear; lamber os lábios. **-to s. of** cheirar a

small | smól' | *s.* cintura (pelas costas); (*pl.*) roupa miúda, roupa branca / *a.* péqueno, reduzido, exíguo. **-to make (somebody) feel s.** humilhar, espezinhar

small beer | smól'bɪə | *s.* bagatela, coisa sem importância

small change | smól'śeynj | *s.* dinheiro miúdo, troco

small hours | smól'awəz | *spl.* altas horas (da noite)

smallness | smól'nes | *s.* pequenez

smallpox | smól'poks | *s.* varíola

small talk | smól'tók | *s.* mexerico, lero-lero

smart | smʌt' | *s.* dor aguda, pontada / *a.* agudo; elegante, de bom-tom; desembaraçado; esperto, inteligente / *vi.* doer agudamente

smartness | smʌt'nes | *s.* elegância; destreza; esperteza; garbo

smash | smaś' | *s.* choque, colisão, trombada, desastre / *vt.* quebrar, esmagar, espatifar. **-to s. down** derrubar, arrombar. **-to s. to pieces** fazer em pedaços / *vi.* despedaçar-se. **-to s. into** ou **against** ir de encontro a, bater em, arrebentar-se em

smashing | sma'śing | *a.* esmagador; (coloq.) ótimo, formidável, estupendo

smattering | sma'təring | *s.* conhecimento superficial, tinturas de, noções vagas de

smear | smɪ'ə | *s.* mancha (de gordura) / *vt.* untar; manchar

smell | smel' | *s.* cheiro; olfato / *vt. vi.* cheirar. **-to s. of** cheirar a

smelly | sme'lī | *a.* fedorento

smelt | smelt' | *vt.* fundir

smile | smayl' | *s.* sorriso / *vi.* sorrir

smiling | smay'ling | *a.* risonho, sorridente

smirk | smɛk' | *s.* sorriso afetado

smite | smayt' | *vt.* bater, ferir

smith | smiϑ' | *s.* ferreiro; ferrador (de cavalos)

smithereens | smiðərɪnz' | *spl.* fragmentos, pedacinhos, ciscos, poeira de

smitten | smi'tən | *a.* golpeado, ferido; (coloq.) enamorado

smog | smog' | *s.* névoa seca, mistura de fumaça e nevoeiro, *smog*

smoke | smowk' | *s.* fumo, fumaça, fumarada, fumaceira / *vt.* enfumaçar; defumar; fumar / *vi.* expelir fumaça

smoker | smow'kə | *s.* fumante; vagão (carro, local) para fumantes

smoke-screen | smowk'skrɪn | s. cortina de fumaça

smoking | smow'king | s. o ato de fumar. **-nos.** é proibido fumar / a. fumegante

smoky | smow'kī | a. enfumarado; fumegante

smooth | 'smʊð | a. liso, macio, suave; fácil; calmo, sereno (mar); insinuante, persuasivo / vt. aplainar, alisar; serenar

smoothness | smʊð'nes | s. lisura, maciez; suavidade

smooth sea | smʊð'sɪ | s. mar sereno

smother | smâ'ðə | vt. suprimir, sufocar, debelar, liquidar

smoulder | smowl'də | vi. queimar (sem chama); ficar (estar) latente

smudge | smǎǰ' | s. mancha, nódoa, borrão / vt. borrar, manchar

smug | smǎg' | a. contente (consigo mesmo), eufórico

smuggle | smâ'gəl | vt. vi. contrabandear

smuggler | smâ'glə | s. contrabandista

smuggling | smâ'gling | s. contrabando

smut | smât' | s. mancha, tisna, ferrugem (nas plantas); desaire, indecência

snack | snak' | s. refeição ligeira; (pl.) petiscos, iguarias, acepipes

snag | snag' | s. toco; dificuldade, obstáculo

snail | sneyl' | s. caracol; lesma. **-at s.'s pace** a passo de cágado

snake | sneyk' | s. cobra, serpente / vi. colear, serpentear

snap | snap' | s. estalido, estalo; fotografia / vt. dar estalos (dedos); mordiscar, tentar morder (cão); tirar foto ou instantâneo, fotografar / vi. quebrar-se, partir-se

snapshot | snap'ŝot | s. (fot.) instantâneo

snare | sne'ə | s. armadilha, laço

snarl | snɑl' | s. rosnado / vi. rosnar

snatch | snaŝ' | vt. pegar, apanhar, agarrar, lançar mão de. **-to s. away** arrancar, arrebatar

sneak | snɪk' | s. patife, velhaco / vt. roubar, furtar; ir (vir) furtivamente / vi. mover-se sorrateiramente. **-to s. in** imiscuir-se, intrometer-se, infiltrar-se. **-to s. off** livrar-se, safar-se. **-to s. on** delatar, trair, denunciar

sneaking | snɪ'king | a. oculto, inconfesso (sentimento)

sneak-thief | snɪk'ϑɪf | s. gatuno, larápio, ladrão, descuidista

sneer | snɪ'ə | s. sorriso de mofa, desdém / vi. sorrir desdenhosamente

sneering | snɪ'əring | a. desdenhoso, zombeteiro

sneeze | snɪz' | s. espirro / vi. espirrar

sniff | snif' | vt. fungar; cheirar, inalar

snip | snip' | s. pique, corte pequeno / vt. cortar

sniper | snay'pə | s. atirador

snippet | sni'pit | s. pedaço, retalho

snivel | sni'vəl | vi. choramingar

snob | snob' | s. pretensioso, esnobe

snobbery | sno'bərī | s. pretensão, vaidade, esnobismo

snobbish | sno'biŝ | a. pretensioso, vaidoso, esnobe

snobbishness | sno'biŝnes | s. pretensão, vaidade, esnobismo

snooze | snʊz' | s. soneca / vi. dormitar, cochilar, tirar uma pestana

snore | snó'ə | s. ronco / vi. roncar, ressonar

snort | snót' | s. resfolgo, resfôlego / vi. bufar, resfolegar

snotty | sno'tī | a. moncoso, ranhoso; desprezível

snout | snawt' | s. focinho

snow | snow' | s. neve / vi. nevar

snowball | snow'bol | s. bola de neve

snowdrop | snow'drop | s. (bot.)

furane, campânula-branca, galanto

snowfall | snow'fol | *s.* nevada, nevasca

snub | snâb' | *s.* repulsa / *vt.* humilhar, desprezar, repelir

snuff | snâf' | *s.* rapé; inalação, fungada / *vt.* inalar profundamente; fungar

snug | snâg' | *a.* agasalhado, aconchegado; confortável

snuggle | snâ'gəl | *vi.* aconchegar-se, acomodar-se, aninhar-se

so | sow | *adv.* assim, desse (deste) modo; tão / *conj.* portanto, por isso. **-s. many** tantos. **-s. that** de modo que. **-quite s.** isso mesmo. **-and s. on** e assim por diante. **-s. and s.** fulano, beltrano / *interj.* **-s. long!** até logo!

soak | sowk' | *vt.* ensopar, molhar. **-to s. up** embeber, absorver

soap | sowp' | *s.* sabão / *vt.* ensaboar

soar | só'ə | *vi.* planar alto, voar muito alto; ascender; elevar-se

sob | sob' | *vi.* soluço / *vi.* soluçar

sober | sow'bə | *a.* sóbrio; sensato; comedido

sobriety | səbray'ətī | *s.* sobriedade; abstinência, temperança; moderação

so-called | sowkóld' | *a.* pretenso, suposto

soccer | so'kə | *s.* futebol

sociable | sow'śəbəl | *a.* sociável; afável

social | sow'śəl | *s.* reunião social, sarau / *a.* social

social climber | sow'śəlklay'mə | *s.* arrivista

socialism | sow'śəlizəm | *s.* socialismo

socialist | sow'śəlist | *s. a.* socialista

social science | sow'śəlsayəns | *s.* ciências sociais, sociologia

social service | sow'śəlsEvis | *s.* assistência social, serviço social

society | səsay'ətī | *s.* sociedade

sock | sok' | *s.* meia soquete; murro, soco

socket | so'kit | *s.* encaixe; (eletr.) tomada; alvéolo (dentário); órbita (ocular)

sod | sod' | *s.* torrão, terra natal

soda | sow'də | *s.* soda (tb. quím.)

sodden | so'dən | *a.* ensopado, molhado, alagado

sofa | sow'fə | *s.* sofá

soft | soft' | *a.* mole, macio; suave, manso; tolerante; fraco, brando; doce; tolo; sem álcool. **-to have a s. spot for** ter um fraco por

soft drink | soft'drink | *s.* refrigerante (não alcoólico)

soften | so'fən | *vt.* abrandar, suavizar, amolecer; enternecer. **-to s. up** desmoralizar; enfraquecer; desanimar

softening | so'fəning | *a.* amolecedor; enternecedor

soft job | soft'job | *s.* sinecura

softly | soft'lī | *adv.* suavemente, mansamente; devagar; baixinho (voz)

softness | soft'nes | *s.* maciez, moleza, brandura; tolerância

soil | soyl' | *s.* solo, gleba, terreno, terra / *vt.* sujar

sojourn | sə'jən | *s.* estada; estadia / *vi.* morar, residir, ficar

solace | so'lis | *s.* consolo, alívio / *vt.* consolar, aliviar

sold | sowld' | *a.* vendável, vendível, à venda. **-s. out** vendido, esgotado, em falta

solder | sowl'də | *vt.* soldar

soldier | sowl'jə | *s.* (mil.) soldado / *vt.* servir (como soldado)

soldierly | sowl'jəlī | *a.* marcial, militar, soldadesco

soldier of fortune | sowl'jəovfó-tĭun | *s.* aventureiro

soldiery | sowl'jərī | *s.* soldadesca

sole | sowl' | *s.* sola (de sapato, pé); (ict.) linguado, solha / *a.* só, único / *vt.* pôr sola em

solely | sowl'lī | *adv.* unicamente, exclusivamente, somente

solemn | so'ləm | *a.* solene, sério, imponente, grave

solemnity | sɔlem'nitī | *s.* solenidade

solemnize | so'ləmnayz | *vt.* celebrar, solenizar

sol-fa | solfʌ' | *s.* solfa, solfejo

solicit | səli'sit | *vt.* requerer, pedir, solicitar, rogar

solicitor | səli'sitə | *s.* procurador, advogado

solicitous | səli'sitəs | *a.* solícito

solid | so'lid | *s. a.* sólido

solidarity | solida'ritī | *s.* solidariedade, unidade

solidify | səli'difay | *vt. vi.* solidificar(-se)

solidity | səli'ditī | *s.* solidez, resistência, dureza

soliloquy | səli'ləkwī | *s.* solilóquio, monólogo

solitariness | so'litərīnes` | *s.* solidão

solitary | so'litərī | *a.* solitário, isolado, só, único

solitary confinement | so'litərīkənfayn'mənt | *s.* prisão celular, prisão na cela solitária ,

solitude | so'litʃud | *s.* solidão

solo | sow'low | *s.* (mús.) solo / *a.* solitário, só, sozinho

soloist | sow'lowist | *s.* solista

soluble | so'lʃubəl | *a.* solúvel

solution | səlu'śən | *s.* solução

solve | solv' | *vt.* solver, resolver

solvency | sol'vənsī | *s.* solvência

solvent | sol'vənt | *s. a.* solvente

sombre | som'bə | *a.* sombrio, ensombrado

sombreness | som'bənes | *s.* escuridão; gravidade, seriedade, taciturnidade

some | sâm | *a.* algum(a), alguns; uns, umas / *pron.* alguns, uns

somebody | sâm'bədī | *pron.* alguém. **-s. else** outra pessoa, outro

somehow | sâm'haw | *adv.* de qualquer modo; de certo modo

some more | sâm'móə | *adv.* mais

someone | sâm'wân | *pron.* alguém

somersault | sâ'məsolt | *s.* salto mortal

something | sâm'ðing | *pron.* alguma coisa. **-s. else** outra coisa

sometimes | sâm'taymz | *adv.* às vezes, por vezes, algumas vezes

somewhat | sâm'wot | *adv.* algo, um tanto

somewhere | sâm'weə | *adv.* em algum lugar

somnolent | som'nələnt | *a.* sonolento

son | sân' | *s.* filho

song | song' | *s.* canto, canção; gorjeio

son-in-law | sân'inló | *s.* genro

sonnet | so'nit | *s.* soneto

sonneteer | sonitꞮ'ə | *s.* sonetista; (pej.) poetastro

sonnet writer | so'nitraytə | *s.* sonetista

sonorous | so'nərəs | *a.* sonoro

soon | sʊn' | *adv.* brevemente, breve; logo; cedo, em breve. **-too** *s.* muito cedo, antes da hora. **-s. after** logo em seguida, pouco depois

sooner | sʊ'nə | *adv.* antes, mais cedo. **-s. or later** mais cedo ou mais tarde. **-the s. the better** quanto mais cedo, melhor

soot | sut' | *s.* fuligem

soothe | sʊð' | *vt.* abrandar; acalmar; aliviar

soothing | sʊ'ðing | *a.* calmante

soothsayer | sʊð'seyə | *s.* adivinho

sop | sop' | *s.* bocado ou migalha de pão (embebido de leite etc.); gorjeta, propina / *vt.* empapar, ensopar

sophisticated | səfis'tikeytid | *a.* afetado, rebuscado; artificial; fino, elegante; complexo; culto; elaborado, sofisticado

sophistry | so'fistrī | *s.* sofisma

soporific | sopəri'fik | *a.* soporífico

sorcerer | só'sərə | *s.* bruxo, feiticeiro

sorcery | só'sərī | *s.* bruxaria; encantamento, sortilégio

sordid | só'did | *a.* sórdido, sujo, nauseante

sore | só' | *s.* ferida, chaga, úlcera / *a.* dorido; inflamado, inchado; desagradável, difícil, grave. **-s. point** caso (ponto) delicado

sorely | só'lī | *adv.* dificilmente; gravemente; excessivamente

soreness | só'nes | *s.* dor; desespero; irritação

sorrow | so'row | *s.* dor, pesar, desgosto, tristeza / *vi.* entristecer-se; maldizer-se; lamentar-se

sorrowful | so'rowful | *a.* triste, magoado, macambúzio, infeliz

sorry | so'rī | *a.* triste; lamentável; infeliz. **-s.!** desculpe-me! **-I am s. for** lamento que

sort | sót' | *s.* espécie, qualidade, gênero, tipo / *vt.* classificar, selecionar, grupar por classes, escolher; atribuir

sortie | só'tī | *s.* (mil.) surtida

soul | sowl' | *s.* alma; essência, espírito; pessoa. **-not a s.** ninguém

soulful | sowl'ful | *a.* sentimental; nostálgico, saudoso; lastimoso

sound | sawnd' | *s.* som, ruído; braço de mar, estreito / *a.* são; válido, seguro, confiável / *vt.* pronunciar; tocar (instrumento de cordas); auscultar; sondar / *vi.* soar; parecer

sound-film | sawnd'film | *s.* filme sonoro

sounding | sawnd'ing | *s.* sondagem. **-to take soundings** sondar

sounding-apparatus | sawnd'ingaparey'təs | *s.* sonda

sounding-rod | sawnd'ingrod | *s.* sonda

soundness | sawnd'nes | *s.* firmeza, solidez; pureza; saúde, sanidade

sound-track | sawnd'trak | *s.* (cin., TV) trilha sonora

sound-wave | sawnd'weyv | *s.* onda sonora

soup | svp' | *s.* sopa. **-in the s.** em maus lençóis

sour | saw'ə | *a.* azedo; acre; ácido; rabugento; mal-humorado, amargo / *vt.* azedar / *vi.* azedar; irritar-se

source | sós' | *s.* fonte, nascente, origem

south | sawϑ' | *s.* sul / *a.* meridional, do sul

south-east | sawϑ'ıst | *s.* sudeste

southerly | sâ'ðəlī | *a.* meridional / *adv.* para o sul, do sul

southern | sâ'ðən | *a.* meridional, do sul. **-the S. Cross** Cruzeiro do Sul

southwards | sawϑ'wədz | *adv.* para o sul

south-west | sawϑ'west | *s.* sudoeste

souvenir | svvənı'ə | *s.* lembrança

sovereign | sov'rin | *s.* soberano; libra (moeda) / *a.* supremo, soberano

sovereignty | sov'rintī | *s.* soberania

soviet | sow'vïet | *s.* soviete

sow | saw' | *s.* porca / | sow' | *vt.* semear; propagar

sowing | sow'ing | *s.* semeadura; disseminação, difusão

sowing-time | sow'ingtaym | *s.* (época de) sementeira

soy | soy' | *s.* molho de soja

soy bean | soy'bın | *s.* soja, feijão-soja

spa | spʌ' | *s.* estância termal

space | speys' | *s.* espaço; lugar / *vt.* espaçar, espacejar

spaceship | speys'ʃip | *s.* astronave, cosmonave, nave espacial

spacious | spey'ʃəs | *a.* espaçoso, amplo, vasto

spaciousness | spey'ʃəsnes | *s.* vastidão, amplidão

spade | speyd' | *s.* pá; espada (em baralho); (coloq.) negro, preto. **-s. work** trabalhos (operações, obras) iniciais (preparatórias)

span | span' | *s.* extensão; abertura (medida da); comprimento; vão (de ponte); espaço (de tempo) / vt. atravessar, cobrir, estender

Spaniard | spa'nîəd | s. espanhol

spaniel | spa'nîəl | s. *spaniel* (cão)

Spanish | spa'niš | s.a. espanhol

spank | spank' | vt. bater, espancar, dar palmadas

spanking | spank'ing | s. palmada, pancada / a. rápido

spanner | spa'nə | s. chave inglesa; chave de porcas; travessão de ponte

spar | spʌ' | s. verga (de velame) / vi. boxear; negacear, fazer negaças (no boxe)

spare | spe'ə | a. moderado, sóbrio, frugal; magro; a mais, em excesso, de sobra / vt. poupar, economizar; dispensar, dar, desfazer-se de; dispor de

spare parts | spe'əpʌts | spl. peças sobressalentes, acessórios

spare room | spe'ərum | s. quarto vago, quarto disponível

spare time | spe'ətaym | s. vagar, lazer, horas vagas

spare tyre | spe'ətay'ə | s. pneu sobressalente; (coloq.) gordura acumulada na cintura

sparing | spe'əring | a. moderado, sóbrio; frugal; poupado, econômico

spark | spʌk' | s. centelha, chispa, fagulha, faísca / vi. faiscar, lançar fagulhas

sparking-plug | spʌ'kingplâg | s. vela (de ignição)

sparkle | spʌ'kəl | s. brilho; cintilação; revérbero / vi. brilhar; reluzir, cintilar; reverberar

sparkling | spʌk'ling | a. brilhante; reluzente, cintilante; espumante; efervescente

sparkling wine | spʌk'lingwayn | s. vinho espumante

sparrow | spa'row | s. pardal

sparse | spʌs' | a. raro, escasso; esparso, disperso

spasm | spa'zəm | s. espasmo

spasmodic | spazmo'dik | a. espasmódico, convulsivo

spastic | spas'tik | s. paralítico cerebral / a. paralítico cerebral; espástico, espasmódico

spate | speyt' | s. enchente, cheia, enxurrada

spatter | spa'tə | s. salpico, respingo / vt. salpicar, respingar

spawn | spón' | s. ovas; prole; progênie; descendência; rebentos

spawning | spó'ning | s. desova (de peixes, moluscos, batráquios, crustáceos)

speak | spık' | vt. vi. falar. -to s. out falar sem rodeios. -to s. up falar (mais) alto. -to s. one's mind confessar, falar com franqueza. -so to s. por assim dizer. -Paul speaking (ao telefone) quem fala é o Paulo

speaker | spı'kə | s. orador, falante; conferencista; locutor; presidente (na Câmara dos Comuns etc.)

spear | spı'ə | s. lança; fisga; arpão / vt. arpoar; fisgar

spearmint | spı'əmint | s. hortelã

special | spe'šəl | a. especial; especializado; extraordinário

specialist | spe'šəlist | s. especialista

speciality | spešîa'litĩ | s. especialidade

specialize | spe'šəlayz | vi. especializar-se

species | spı'šız | s. espécie

specific | spəsi'fik | a. específico; explícito

specification | spesifikey'šən | s. especificação

specific gravity | spəsi'fikgra'vitĩ | s. peso específico

specify | spe'sifay | vt. especificar; particularizar, pormenorizar

specimen | spe'simən | s. espécime, amostra, exemplar

specious | spı'šəs | a. especioso

speck | spek' | s. partícula, grão (de poeira); manchinha, argueiro (no olho)

speckled | spe'kəld | a. salpicado; variegado; manchado

spectacle | spek'təkəl | s. espetáculo

spectacles | spek'takəkzlz | spl. óculos

spectacular | spekta'kɪ̆ulə | a. magnífico, grandioso, espetacular

spectator | spektey'tə | s. espectador, observador; (pl.) assistência

spectre, specter | spek'tə | s. espectro

speculate | spe'kɪ̆uleyt | vi. especular; refletir, meditar; considerar

speculation | spekɪ̆uley'śən | s. especulação

speculator | spe'kɪ̆uleytə | s. especulador

speech | spɪx̌' | s. linguagem; fala; discurso

speechless | spɪš'les | a. sem fala, mudo, estupefato

speed | spɪd' | s. velocidade; pressa; rapidez. **-at full s.** a toda velocidade. **-Godspeed!** boa viagem!

speed limit | spɪd'limit | s. limite de velocidade

speedometer | spɪdo'mitə | s. velocímetro

speedy | spɪ'dĭ | a. veloz, rápido; imediato

spell | spel' | s. feitiço, bruxaria, encantamento, magia, sortilégio; fascínio, encanto, fascinação; período, temporada; turno, intervalo. **-to cast a s.** enfeitiçar / vt. escrever, soletrar / vi. soletrar

spellbound | spel'bawnd | a. encantado, enfeitiçado; fascinado

spelling | spe'ling | s. ortografia; soletração

spelling-book | spe'lingbuk | s. cartilha

spend | spend' | vt. gastar, pagar; passar (tempo) / vi. gastar

spendthrift | spend'ϑrift | s. perdulário, esbanjador, mão-aberta

spew | spĭu' | vt. vi. vomitar

sphere | sfɪ'ə | s. esfera; globo

spherical | sfe'rikəl | a. esférico

sphinx | sfinks' | s. esfinge

spice | spays' | s. especiaria; condimento, tempero / vt. temperar

spick-and-span | spikənspan' | a. asseado; alinhado, elegante

spider | spay'də | s. aranha

spike | spayk' | s. espigão; bico, ponta; espeque

spill | spil' | s. (coloq.) queda; derramamento; desaguadouro / vt. derrâmar, entornar, transbordar; deixar cair

spin | spin' | s. rodopio, volteio; giro; rotação; (aer.) parafuso / vt. fiar; girar; contar; tecer / vi. girar, rodopiar. **-to go for a s.** dar uma volta, passear

spinach | spi'nij | s. espinafre

spinal cord | spay'nəlkód | s. medula espinhal

spindle | spin'dəl | s. fuso

spine | spayn' | s. espinha dorsal, coluna vertebral; lombada (de livro)

spineless | spayn'les | a. invertebrado; (fig.) pusilânime, desfibrado, fraco

spinner | spi'nə | s. fiandeiro, dono de fiação; colher giratória para pesca; (ent.) efêmera

spinning | spi'ning | s. fiação; pesca com molinete de tambor fixo / a. que fia

spinning-wheel | spi'ningwil | s. roca (de fiar)

spinster | spin'stə | s. solteirona

spiny | spay'nĭ | a. espinhoso

spiny lobster | spay'nĭlobstə | s. lagosta sem pinças (*Palinurus*)

spiral | spay'rəl | s. espiral; alta ou baixa (de preços) / a. espiralado

spire | spay'ə | s. agulha (de campanário), flecha

spirit | spi'rit | s. alma, espírito; fantasma, espectro; ânimo, energia, coragem; caráter, disposição; (pl.) espírito de álcool, bebidas alcoólicas brancas / vt. **-to s. away** arrebatar, entusiasmar

spirited | spi'ritid | *a.* enérgico, vigoroso; ardente, fogoso

spiritual | spi'ritʃuəl | *s.* **-negro s.** (EUA) *spiritual*, canção sacra negra / *a.* espiritual

spiritualism | spi'ritʃulizəm | *s.* espiritualismo, espiritismo

spiritualist | spi'ritʃulist | *s. a.* espírita, espiritista; espiritualista

spit | spit' | *s.* cuspe; escarro; espeto (de assar) / *vt. vi.* cuspir

spite | spayt' | *s.* má vontade, malevolência, despeito. **-out of s.** por despeito. **-in s. of** a despeito de, apesar de / *vt.* irritar, acabrunhar, vexar

spiteful | spayt'ful | *a.* malévolo; desrespeitoso; rancoroso

spittle | spi'təl | *s.* cuspe, saliva; catarro

spittoon | spitvn' | *s.* escarradeira

splash | splaʃ' | *s.* salpico, gotejamento. **-to make a big s.** fazer estrépito, fazer estardalhaço / *vt.* borrifar; espadanar; salpicar / *vi.* chapinhar

spleen | splin' | *s.* baço; (fig.) mau humor, *spleen*, melancolia

splendid | splen'did | *a.* magnífico, esplêndido; excelente / *interj.* ótimo!, esplêndido!

splendidly | splen'didli | *adv.* esplendidamente; otimamente; admiravelmente

splendour, splendor | splen'də | *s.* esplendor, brilho; magnificência; glória; gala, pompa

splint | splint' | *s.* farpa, lasca, estilhaço; (med.) tala, tipóia

splinter | splin'tə | *s.* estilhaço, lasca / *vt. vi.* espatifar(-se), despedaçar(-se)

split | split' | *s.* racha, fenda, greta; cisão, cisma / *a.* dividido; rachado / *vt.* rachar, fender, gretar; dividir; desintegrar. **-to s. on** (coloq.) denunciar, delatar / *vi.* estalar, partir-se, quebrar-se

splutter | splâ'tə | *s.* som ou fala sibilante ou explosiva / *vt.* ga-

guejar; respingar / *vi.* cuspir, cuspinhar; crepitar (fogo); balbuciar

spoil | spoyl' | *s.* espólio; despojo / *vt.* estragar, inutilizar, frustrar; mimar, amimar. **-to be spoiling for a fight** ameaçar com sete pedras / *vi.* estragar-se

spoiled | spoyld' spoylt' | *a.* estragado; mimado (criança)

spoke | spowk' | *s.* raio

spokesman | spowks'mən | *s.* porta-voz

sponge | spânʒ' | *s.* esponja. **-to throw up the s.** entregar os pontos, dar-se por vencido / *vt.* lavar com esponja. **-to s. on** viver à custa de (alguém)

sponsor | spon'sə | *s.* patrocinador / *vt.* patrocinar

spontaneous | spontey'nїəs | *a.* espontâneo

spook | spvk' | *s.* fantasma

spool | spvl' | *s.* bobina, carretel

spoon | spvn' | *s.* colher (tb. artefato de pesca) / *vt.* tirar com colher

spoonful | spvn'ful | *s.* colherada

spoor | spv'ə | *s.* rasto, rastro

sporadic | spərə'dik | *a.* esporádico

sport | spót' | *s.* esporte, desporte; diversão. **-field sports** caça; pesca. **-to make s. of** zombar de / *a.* esportivo, desportivo / *vt.* ostentar, luzir

sporting | spó'ting | *a.* esportivo, desportivo

sportsman | spóts'mən | *s.* esportista, desportista

spot | spot' | *s.* mancha, mácula, nódoa; sítio, lugar, localidade; pinta, sinal. **-sore s.** ponto sensível, ponto nevrálgico. **-on the s.** imediatamente, ato contínuo, em seguida / *vt.* manchar; sarapintar, salpicar; (coloq.) ver

spout | spawt' | *s.* bica, biqueira (d'água); bico (de chaleira etc.); jato, jorro / *vi.* esguichar, borbotar, jorrar / *vt. vi.* (coloq.) dizer, falar

sprain | spreyn' | *s.* torcedura / *vt.* torcer

sprawl | spról' | *vi.* estirar-se, alongar-se, estender-se

spray | sprey' | *s.* espuma; borrifo; raminho; aspersão; vaporizador, pulverizador, borrifador / *vt.* borrifar, pulverizar, vaporizar, espalhar

spread | spred' | *s.* extensão, dilatação, expansão; difusão, divulgação; envergadura (de asa, vela); banquete, festim; disseminação / *vt.* divulgar, difundir, noticiar; cobrir de (manteiga etc.) / *vi.* estender-se, difundir-se, alargar-se

spree | sprɪ' | *s.* farra, pândega. **-to be out on the s.** andar na farra

sprig | sprig' | *s.* vergôntea, ramo novo, haste

sprightly | sprayt'lī | *a.* vigoroso, ativo; alegre, animado / *adv.* vigorosamente, animadamente

spring | spring' | *s.* primavera; salto, pulo; fonte, nascente, mina, manancial; corda (de relógio); motivo, motivação, móvel / *a.* primaveril; elástico; de molas; de fonte / *vt.* fazer saltar / *vi.* saltar; nascer, resultar, provir de. **-to s. up** surgir; levantar-se. **-to s. out** saltar de

springboard | spring'bód | *s.* trampolim

sprinkle | sprin'kəl | *s.* borrifo; pitada; salpico; chuvisco / *vt.* aspergir, espalhar por sobre; borrifar / *vi.* chuviscar

sprint | sprint' | *vt.* correr

sprout | sprawt' | *s.* broto (de planta) / *vt.* fazer brotar; fazer crescer / *vi.* brotar; crescer rápido

spruce | sprʊs' | *a.* limpo, correto, escorreito / *vt.* **-to s. up** adornar, enfeitar

spud | spâd' | *s.* (gír.) batata

spur | spE' | *s.* espora; esporão; espigão (de montanha); estímulo, incentivo, empurrão.

-on the s. of the moment de repente, repentinamente / *vt.* **-to s. on** esporear; estimular

spurious | spɪ'riəs | *a.* falso, espúrio

spurn | spEn' | *vt.* rejeitar, desdenhar, recusar

spurt | spEt' | *s.* jorro, jato. **-to put on a s.** fazer um esforço, acelerar (a marcha) / *vt.* lançar / *vt. vi.* jorrar ou esguichar

spy | spay' | *s.* espião / *vt.* **-tos. on** investigar, perscrutar. **-tos. out** investigar, espionar

spyglass | spay'glas | *s.* óculo-de--alcance; telescópio pequeno

squabble | skwo'bəl | *s.* disputa, altercação / *vi.* disputar, altercar

squad | skwod' | *s.* pelotão, grupo de combate

squadron | skwo'drən | *s.* esquadra (mar); esquadrão (cavalaria); esquadrilha (ar)

squalid | skwo'lid | *a.* imundo, sujo; esquálido; mesquinho

squall | skwól' | *s.* pé-de-vento, borrasca / *vi.* gritar, berrar

squalor | skwo'lə | *s.* imundície, miséria; mesquinhez

squander | skwon'də | *vt.* esbanjar, desperdiçar, dissipar

square | skwe'ə | *s.* quadrado; praça; casa (xadrez); esquadro / *a.* quadrado (tb. fig.); honesto; direto / *vt.* quadrar, saldar, liquidar; chegar a acordo, subornar / *vi.* harmonizar-se, concordar

square dance | skwe'ədAns | *s.* quadrilha (dança)

square deal | skwe'ədıl | *s.* bom tratamento

squash | skwoś' | *s.* abobrinha; suco, refresco (de fruta espremida) / *vt.* espremer, esmagar; apertar; achatar

squat | skwot' | *a.* atarracado; acocorado / *vi.* agachar-se, ficar de cócoras

squatter | skwo'tə | *s.* intruso, invasor; colono (povoamento)

squawk | skwók' | s. grasnado; crocitar; chio / vt. grasnar; crocitar / vi. grasnar; (gír.) reclamar, estrilar

squeak | skwɪk' | s. chio, chiado. **-to have a narrow s.** escapar por um triz. **-not a s.** nem um pio / vi. chiar

squeal | skwɪl' | s. guincho / vi. guinchar; (gír.) delatar

squeamish | skwɪ'miś | a. melindroso; sensível, delicado; escrupuloso

squeeze | skwɪz' | s. aperto; compressão / vt. apertar; espremer (limão etc.) / vi. **-to s. through** abrir caminho, intrometer-se. **-to. s. up** apertar-se, comprimir-se

squid | skwid' | s. lula

squint | skwint' | s. estrabismo / vi. ser vesgo, ter estrabismo

squint-eyed | skwint'ay | a. zarolho, vesgo, estrábico

squire | skway'ə | s. morgado; escudeiro (medieval); título conferido por amabilidade

squirm | skwɛm' | s. contorção, torção / vi. retorcer-se, agitar-se

squirrel | skwi'rəl | s. esquilo

squirt | skwɛt' | s. esguicho / vt. vi. esguichar

stab | stab' | s. punhalada / vt. apunhalar

stability | stabi'litī | s. estabilidade, solidez

stabilize | sta'bilayz | vt. estabilizar

stable | stey'bəl | s. cavalariça; baia; estábulo / a. estável, sólido, compacto

stack | stak' | s. pilha; montão / vt. empilhar, amontoar; ensarilhar (armas)

stadium | stey'diəm | s. estádio

staff | staf' | s. cajado, bordão, báculo; suporte, apoio; conjunto de empregados de uma empresa; conjunto de professores; conjunto de funcionários; (mil.) estado-maior; redação (de jornal etc.); conjun-

to de empregados (de uma casa)

stag | stag' | s. cervo, macho de animais; homem só

stage | steyǰ' | s. palco, teatro; estrado; fase, período; parada / vt. encenar, representar

stage-coach | steyǰ'kowš | s. diligência, carruagem (coletivo)

stage-manager | steyǰma'niǰə | s. diretor (de cena, peça etc.)

stagger | sta'gə | vt. deixar estupefato; alternar (função, horas de trabalho etc.) / vi. tropeçar; cambalear

staggering | sta'gəring | a. cambaleante; esmagador; enorme

staging | stey'ǰing | s. representação, encenação (teatral etc.); andaime

stagnant | stag'nənt | a. parado, estagnado; inerte, sem ação

stagnation | stagney'śən | s. estagnação

staid | steyd' | a. grave, comedido, sóbrio; imperturbável

stain | steyn' | s. nódoa, mancha; corante / vt. manchar; tingir, pintar / vi. manchar-se

stainless | steyn'les | a. inoxidável; imaculado (esp. reputação)

stainless steel | steyn'lesstɪl | s. aço inoxidável

stair | ste'ə | s. degrau; (pl.) escada

staircase | ste'əkeys | s. escada

stake | steyk' | s. estaca; poste; baliza; aposta, parada; fogueira; interesse, participação (em negócios). **-at s.** em jogo, em perigo / vt. apostar; arriscar; reclamar. **-to s. out** delimitar com balizas; marcar

stale | steyl' | a. não fresco; choco (cerveja); dormido (pão); rançoso (manteiga); viciado (ar); gasto, velho / vt. vi. tornar(-se) velho, choco, viciado etc.

stalemate | steyl'meyt | s. impasse; empate (em xadrez) / vt. colocar em empate; paralisar

stalk | stók' | s. caule; haste; talo; pé (de copo) / vt. espreitar a caça; aproximar-se furtivamente de / *vi.* aproximar-se (de caça ou presa) furtivamente

stall | stól' | *s.* baia; estábulo; barraca (de feira); banco de coro (de igreja); (*pl.*, teat.) platéia / *vi.* envelhecer, estragar-se; urinar (cavalo ou gado)

stallion | sta'lŀən | *s.* garanhão

stalwart | stol'wət | *s.* pessoa robusta; partidário leal / *a.* destemido, valente; forte, robusto; resoluto, firme

stamina | sta'minə | *s.* resistência física, vigor, robustez; perseverança

stammer | sta'mə | *s.* gagueira / *vi.* gaguejar

stammerer | sta'mərə | *s.* gago

stamp | stamp' | *s.* selo; carimbo; sinal, marca; estampa; impressão; cunho; (fig.) marca característica (de personalidade) / *vt.* selar, pôr selo em; carimbar; imprimir, marcar; calcar com o pé; pisar; gravar, fixar (na memória); caracterizar, qualificar. **-to s. on** pisar. **-to s. out** apagar com os pés (fogo); reprimir / *vi.* bater o pé no chão

stampede | stampid' | *s.* estouro de boiada; debandada / *vt.* causar estouro ou debandada / *vi.* estourar (com respeito a boiada); debandar

stance | stans' | *s.* postura, atitude; posição

stanch | stónś' | *a.* firme, forte; leal / *vt.* estancar

stand | stand' | *s.* suporte, pedestal; estante; banca, posto de venda; tribuna; posição, opinião; pausa; resistência, oposição. **-to take a s.** oferecer resistência, opor-se. **-to take one's s.** fundar-se (em argumentos). **-to make a s.** declarar-se contra ou a favor (de princípio, idéia etc.) / *vt.* colocar, pôr; fazer ficar de pé; agüentar, suportar; resistir; ser submetido a; (coloq.) pagar. **-to s. a chance** ter uma pro-

babilidade. **-to s. one's ground** manter-se firme / *vi.* estar de pé, ficar; encontrar-se, estar situado; permanecer, manter-se, durar; apresentar-se (como candidato); estar em vigor, vigorar; agüentar, resistir; ter determinada altura. **-to s. alone** estar só, ser o único **-s.by!** a postos! **-to s. by** dar apoio a. **-to s. aside** sair do caminho, manter-se alheio a. **-to s. for** tolerar, aturar. **-to s. on ceremony** fazer cerimônia. **-to s. to attention** perfilar-se. **-to s. out** sobressair; manter-se firme; opor-se. **-to s. up** levantar-se, pôr-se de pé. **-to s. up for** defender. **-to s. up to** resistir, fazer face a. **-to s. upon** insistir em. **-to s. still** ficar imóvel

standard | stan'dəd | *s.* padrão; *standard*; norma, critério; bandeira, estandarte; símbolo / *a.* que serve de padrão; oficial; normal, regular, corrente, clássico

standard-bearer | standəbe'ərə | *s.* porta-estandarte; chefe

Standard English | stan'dədingliś | *s.* o inglês padrão

standardization | standədayzey'śən | *s.* estandardização, padronização, uniformização

standardize | stan'dədayz | *vt.* estandardizar, uniformizar

standard of living | stan'dəovliving | *s.* padrão de vida

standing | stan'ding | *s.* posição; reputação, prestígio; parada, estacionamento; tempo de serviço; antiguidade; duração. **-of long s.** de longa data / *a.* em pé, vertical; permanente; estacionário; estagnado (água)

standing room | stan'dingrʊm | *s.* lugar para ficar em pé; lugar em pé

standpoint | stand'poynt | *s.* ponto de vista

standstill | stand'stil | *s.* paralisação, interrupção; imobilização. **-to come to a s.** parar, deter-se

stanza | stan'zə | s. estância, estrofe

staple | stey'pəl | s. grampo (de grampeador e tb. mec.); produto básico (de uma região etc.); matéria-prima; (pl.) gêneros de primeira necessidade / a. básico, principal; de primeira necessidade; de maior produção ou consumo; estabelecido, reconhecido / vt. grampear

stapler | stey'plə | s. máquina de grampear, grampeador

star | stA' | s. estrela; astro ou estrela (de cinema etc.) / a. talentoso, brilhante; principal, destacado

starboard | stA'bód | s. estibordo

starch | stAš' | s. goma (tb. de roupa); amido; (fig.) formalidade / vt. engomar

starchy | stA'ši | a. amiláceo (alimento); (fig.) empertigada

stare | ste'ə | s. olhar fixo / vi. olhar fixamente, fitar. **-to s. down** desconcertar, fazer baixar os olhos

starfish | stA'fiś | s. estrela-do-mar

stark | stAk' | a. completo, acabado, rematado; rígido, hirto; nu; árido / adv. completamente

starlet | stA'lit | s. jovem e promissora estrela de cinema

starling | stA'ling | s. (orn.) estorninho

starry | stA'rī | a. estrelado; estelar; brilhante; cintilante

start | stAt' | s. começo, princípio; partida, saída; largada; sobressalto, susto; dianteira, vantagem (em corrida etc.). **-by fits and starts** aos trancos e barrancos. **-for a s.** para começar. **-to make a new s.** começar de novo / vt. começar, iniciar, principiar; inaugurar; pôr em marcha ou em movimento (motor); provocar (questão); lançar (boato); levantar (caça) / vi. partir, pôr

se a caminho; sobressaltar-se; mover-se subitamente; surgir, aparecer

starting-point | stA'tingpoynt | s. ponto de partida

starting price | stA'tingprays | s. preço inicial

startle | stA'təl | s. susto, sobressalto / vt. assustar / vi. assustar-se

startling | stAt'ling | a. surpreendente, assustador; chocante, alarmante

starvation | stAvey'šən | s. inanição; fome

starve | stAv' | vt. matar de fome / vi. morrer de fome

starving | stA'ving | a. faminto

state | steyt' | s. estado (tb. maiúsc.); condição, situação; fausto, pompa, gala. **-to lie in s.** estar exposto em câmara ardente / a. de estado; estatal; estadual; público / vt. declarar, afirmar; manifestar, apresentar; formular; fixar

stated | stey'tid | a. fixo, determinado, estabelecido

stateless | steyt'les | a. sem estado, sem governo

stately | steyt'lī | a. imponente, majestoso / adv. imponentemente, majestosamente

statement | steyt'mənt | s. declaração, afirmação; relatório; (com.) extrato de conta, balanço

statement of account | steyt'məntəvəkawnt' | s. extrato de conta

statement of witness | steyt'məntofwit'nes | s. (jur.) depoimento da testemunha

state of siege | steyt'əvsij | s. estado de sítio

statesman | steyts'mən | s. estadista

statesmanship | steyts'mənšip | s. habilidade de estadista, habilidade política

station | stey'šən | s. estação; posto, lugar; posição social, situação / vt. colocar, postar; designar para um posto

stationary| stey'śənrī |*a.* estacionário, imóvel

stationer | stey'śənə |*s.* dono ou empregado de papelaria

stationery | stey'śənrī |*s.* artigos de papelaria ou de escritório; papel de carta

station-master | stey'śənmastə |*s.* (ferrov.) chefe de estação

station-wagon | stey'śənwa'gən |*s.* caminhonete

statistician | statisti'śən |*s.* estatístico

statistics | stətis'tiks |*s.* estatística; dados estatísticos

statue| sta'tĭu |*s.* estátua

stature | sta'śə |*s.* estatura

status | stey'təs |*s.* posição, categoria, *status*; estado civil

statute | sta'tĭut |*s.* estatuto

statutory | sta'tĭutərī |*a.* estatutário; estabelecido por lei; regulamentar

staunch, stanch | stónś' |*a.* leal, fiel (amigo); estanque, impermeável (navio, conexão, junta etc.) /*vt.* estancar (esp. sangue)

stave| steyv' |*s.* aduela (de barrica etc.) /*vt.* fazer rombo em (barrica, barco etc.) pôr aduelas em. **-to s. in** arrombar. **-to s. off** protelar; afugentar, repelir

stay | stey' |*s.* (náut.) estai; esteio; permanência, estada, estadia; pausa; adiamento; suspensão /*vt.* estaiar; escorar /*vi.* ficar, permanecer; estar hospedado. **-to s. away** ficar de fora; ausentar-se. **-to s. up** não se deitar

stead | sted' |*s.* lugar. **-in someone's s.** em lugar de alguém. **-to stand in good s.** ser útil, vantajoso

steadfast | sted'fast |*a.* fixo, firme; resoluto, inabalável; imutável

steadiness | ste'dines |*s.* estabilidade; perseverança, constância; sobriedade

steady| ste'dī |*s.* (gír.) namorado firme, par constante /*a.* fixo,

firme; estável, equilibrado; resoluto, decidido; ininterrupto /*vt. vi.* fixar(-se); estabilizar(-se), firmar(-se); acalmar(-se) /*interj.* devagar!, firme!, cuidado!

steak | steyk' |*s.* bife; posta

steal | stīl' |*vt. vi.* furtar, roubar. **-to s. away** afastar-se silenciosamente, esquivar-se, furtar-se. **-to s. into** insinuar-se, penetrar em. **-to s. a march on** passar à frente de alguém, ganhar vantagem sobre (por meios sub-reptícios)

stealing| stī'ling |*s.* furto, roubo

stealth | stelθ' |*s.* procedimento secreto ou sub-reptício. **-by s.** sub-repticiamente, às escondidas

stealthy| stel'θī |*a.* clandestino, secreto; furtivo

steam | stīm' |*s.* vapor; névoa; exalação /*a.* de ou relativo a vapor /*vt.* tratar com vapor; cozinhar no vapor /*vi.* lançar vapor; fumegar; navegar a vapor

steamer| stī'mə |*s.* vapor (navio)

steamship | stīm'śip |*s.* (navio a) vapor

steed | stīd' |*s.* corcel (esp. de guerra)

steel | stīl' |*s.* aço /*a.* de ou relativo ao aço /*vt.* fortalecer, endurecer; insensibilizar

steel-plated | stīl'pleytid |*a.* blindado

steel wool| stīl'wul |*s.* palha de aço; esponja de limpeza (de aço)

steelworks | stīl'weks |*s.* fundição de aço, aciaria

steely | stī'lī |*a.* acerado; duro; inflexível

steep | stīp' |*s.* ladeira íngreme /*a.* íngreme; escarpado; exorbitante (preço) /*vt.* embeber; encharcar; pôr de molho

steeple | stī'pəl |*s.* campanário, torre de igreja

steeplechase | stī'pəlśeys |*s.* corrida (hípica) de obstáculos

steeplejack | stī'pəljak |*s.* operário que conserta chaminés, torres etc.

steeply | stɪ'plī | *adv.* abruptamente; escarpadamente, a pique

steer | stɪ'ə | *s.* novilho (esp. castrado) / *vt.* dirigir; governar, pilotar (embarcação). **-to s. clear of** passar ao largo de, evitar

steerage | stɪ'ərɪj | *s.* terceira classe (em navio); pilotagem; (náut.) governo

steering | stɪ'əring | *s.* pilotagem de embarcação; direção (de automóvel ou avião)

steering-column | stɪ'əringko'ləm | *s.* coluna da direção

steering-wheel | stɪ'əringwɪl | *s.* volante de automóvel; roda do leme, timão

stellar | ste'lə | *a.* estelar, sideral

stem | stem' | *s.* haste, talo, caule; tronco, ramo; linhagem; tubo (de cachimbo). **-from s. to stern** de popa à proa / *vt.* tirar os talos; represar; refrear, deter; resistir a, opor-se a / *vi.* provir de, derivar

stench | stenś' | *s.* fedor

stenographer | steno'grəfə | *s.* estenógrafo, taquígrafo

step | step' | *s.* passo; degrau; fase, etapa; providência, medida; (*pl.*) escada. **-in s.** em cadência, com passo certo. **-out of s.** fora da cadência. **-s. by s.** gradualmente. **-to take steps** providenciar, tomar medidas. **-to watch one's s.** tomar cuidado / *vt.* **-to s. up** aumentar / *vi.* dar um passo; andar; pisar; andar rapidamente. **-to s. aside** desviar-se. **-to s. back** dar um passo atrás, retroceder. **-to s. down** descer; demitir-se. **-to s. forward** avançar, dar um passo à frente. **-to s. in** entrar. **-to s. out** sair

stepbrother | step'brâðə | *s.* meio-irmão

stepchild | step'śayld | *s.* enteado; enteada

stepfather | step'fʌðə | *s.* pa-
drasto

stepmother | step'mâðə | *s.* madrasta

steppe | step' | *s.* estepe

stepping-stone | ste'pingstown | *s.* (ger. *pl.*) alpondras; (fig.) meios para atingir um objetivo

stepsister | step'sistə | *s.* meia-irmã

stepson | step'sân | *s.* enteado

stereotyped | stɪ'rɪətaypt | *a.* estereotipado; convencional

sterile | ste'rayl | *a.* estéril

sterility | steri'liti | *s.* esterilidade; aridez

sterilization | sterilayzey'śən | *s.* esterilização

sterilize | ste'rilayz | *vt.* esterilizar

sterling | stE'ling | *s.* moeda legal inglesa / *a.* esterlino; de prata de ɪeɪ; genuíno, legítimo, verdadeiro

sterling silver | stE'lingsilvə | *s.* prata de lei

stern | stEn' | *s.* (náut.) popa / *a.* severo; austero

sternness | stEn'nes | *s.* severidade; austeridade; rigor

stethoscope | ste'ϑəskowp | *s.* estetoscópio

stevedore | stɪ'vidó | *s.* estivador

stew | stŭ' | *s.* cozido, ensopado / *vt. vi.* cozinhar a fogo lento, ensopar

steward | stŭ'əd | *s.* administrador, intendente; ecônomo; (aer.) comissário de bordo; (náut.) criado de bordo, camareiro

stewardess | stŭ'ədes | *s.* aeromoça; camareira (esp. de bordo)

stick | stik' | *s.* graveto; vara; vareta; bastão; pauzinho; lenha (miúda) / *vt.* meter, cravar; fixar, inserir; colar; afixar (cartazes); aturar, suportar / *vi.* estar fincado ou cravado; agarrar-se, colar-se; perseverar; encalhar; atolar; emperrar. **-to s. by** ficar ao lado de. **-to s. out** estar visível, assomar a cabeça. **-to s.**

together manter-se unidos. **-to s. at nothing** não ter escrúpulos

stick-in-the-mud | stik'inðɔmâd | s. pessoa de idéias retrógradas

stickler | stik'lɔ | s. defensor obstinado, partidário fanático. **-a s. for** um defensor obstinado de

sticky | sti'kĭ | a. pegajoso; sebento; (coloq.) úmido (tempo); (coloq.) obstinado, teimoso, exigente. **-to come to a s. end** (gír.) ter um fim penoso

stiff | stif' |s. (gír.) cadáver / a. rígido; teso, duro; emperrado; dolorido (músculo); tenso; forte (vento); inflexível, obstinado; severo (castigo); engomado (colarinho); alto (preço)

stiffen | sti'fən | vt. vi. enrijecer; endurecer, fortalecer; formalizar-se; empertigar-se

stiffening | sti'fəning | s. endurecimento; reforço

stiff neck | stif'nek | s. torcicolo

stiff-necked | stifnekt' | a. de pescoço duro; obstinado, duro, teimoso

stiffness | stif'nes | s. rigidez; dificuldade

stifle | sti'fəl | vt. sufocar

stifling | sti'fling | a. sufocante

stigma | stig'mɔ | s. estigma

stigmatize | stig'mɔtayz | vt. estigmatizar

still | stil' | s. (litɛ..) quietude, paz, silêncio; alambique / a. imóvel; quieto; silencioso; calmo / adv. ainda / conj. mas, contudo, apesar disso / vt. acalmar, fazer calar / vi. acalmar-se; serenar

stillborn | stil'bón | a. nascido morto

still life | stil'layf | s. (b.a.) natureza-morta

stillness | stil'nes | s. quietude, silêncio, paz

stilt | stilt' | s. pernas de pau; estacas (de construção); (pl.) palafita, estacaria

stilted | stil'tid | a. posto sobre estacas; pomposo, empolado, afetado

stimulant | sti'm'ulɔnt | s. a. estimulante

stimulate | sti'm'uleyt | vt. estimular; excitar

stimulation | stim'uley'sɔn |s. estímulo; excitamento

stimulus | sti'm'ulɔs |s. estímulo; excitação; (bot.) pêlo urticante

sting | sting' | s. ferroada; ferrão; aguilhão; ardência, ardor; (bot.) pêlo urticante; incitamento / vt. picar; ferroar; aguilhoar; afligir, atormentar; (gír.) explorar (no preço) / vi. picar; arder; doer

stingy | stin'jĭ | a. sovina, miserável, avarento

stink | stink' | s. fedor, mau cheiro / vi. feder, cheirar mal; (gír.) ser uma droga, não prestar

stinking | stin'king | a. fedorento

stint | stint' | s. limitação, restrição; tarefa; quota / vt. limitar, restringir / vi. poupar

stipend | stay'pend | s. estipêndio, salário

stipulate | sti'p'uleyt | vt. estipular, estabelecer

stipulation | stip'uley'sɔn |s. estipulação, condição, convenção

stir | stɛ' | s. agitação, perturbação; comoção; tumulto; empurrão. **-to make a great s.** ser muito discutido, causar sensação / vt. excitar, estimular; comover; mexer (líquido). **-to s. up** agitar, excitar; despertar / vi. mexer-se; agitar-se; estar fervendo (acontecimentos)

stirring | stɛ'ring | a. emocionante; movimentado, agitado

stirrup | sti'rɔp | s. estribo

stitch | stiš' | s. (cost.) ponto; pontada, dor aguda / vt. coser

stoat | stowt' | s. (zool.) arminho (esp. com pelagem de verão)

stock | stok' | s. estoque, sortimento; provisão; (com.) capital; ações (de empresas etc.); caldo (de carne, galinha etc.); linhagem, estirpe; coronha;

matéria-prima; quantidade, cabedal; (hort.) enxerto; gado; (*pl.*) tronco, pelourinho. **-in s.** em estoque. **-on the stocks** em construção, no estaleiro; em preparação / *a.* conservado em estoque; corriqueiro / *vt.* estocar; abastecer, sortir; armazenar; pôr coronha em

stockade | sto'keyd | *s.* paliçada, estacada

stockbroker | stok'browkə | *s.* corretor de fundos públicos, corretor da Bolsa

stock company | stokkâm'pənī | *s.* sociedade anônima, sociedade por ações; teatro de repertório

stock exchange | stok'eksšeynǰ | *s.* Bolsa de Valores

stockfish | stok'fiś | *s.* peixe seco (sem sal)

stockholder | stok'howldə | *s.* (com.) acionista

stocking | sto'king | *s.* meia

stock-in-trade | stok'intreyd | *s.* estoque, mercadorias à venda

stock-market | stok'mʌkit | *s.* Bolsa de Valores. **-to play the s.-m.** jogar na Bolsa

stock phrase | stok'freyz | *s.* frase feita

stockpile | stok'payl | *s.* reserva, estocagem

stock raising | stok'reyzing | *s.* criação de gado

stock-room | stok'rʊm | *s.* depósito, armazém; almoxarifado

stock-still | stok'stil | *a.* imóvel, parado

stock-taking | stok'teyking | *s.* (com.) ato de fazer o inventário de

stocky | sto'kī | *a.* atarracado, entroncado

stodgy | sto'ǰī | *a.* indigesto

stoic | stow'ik | *s. a.* estóico

stoical | stow'ikəl | *a.* estóico

stoicism | stow'isizəm | *s.* estoicismo

stoke | stowk' | *vt.* alimentar (fornalha); atiçar (fogo)

stole | stowl' | *s.* estola

stolid | sto'lid | *a.* impassível, imperturbável; obstinado

stomach | stâ'mək | *s.* estômago; apetite, desejo, disposição / *vt.* suportar, sofrer, tolerar

stone | stown' | *s.* pedra; caroço (de fruta); medida de peso (esp. para pessoas) equivalente a 6,35kg. **-within a s.'s throw** a um tiro de pedra, muito perto / *a.* de pedra / *vt.* apedrejar; tirar o caroço a (fruta)

stone-deaf | stown'def | *a.* completamente surdo

stonemason | stown'meysən | *s.* pedreiro, canteiro

stone slab | stown'slab | *s.* laje

stonework | stown'wɛk | *s.* cantaria, trabalho em pedra

stony | stow'nī | *a.* pedregoso; (fig.) empedernido. **-to be s. broke** estar sem tostão

stool | stʊl' | *s.* banquinho, tamborete; privada; evacuação; fezes

stoop | stʊp' | *s.* inclinação ou posição curvada (do corpo); degraus à entrada (de casa) / *vt.* inclinar, curvar / *vi.* curvar-se, inclinar-se; andar curvado; rebaixar-se, humilhar-se. **-to s. to** (fig.) rebaixar-se a; condescender, dignar-se a

stop | stop' | *s.* parada; pausa; interrupção; fim; termo; ponto (sinal de pontuação); (fot.) diafragma. **-to put a s. to** pôr fim a / *interj.* alto!, pare!, basta! / *vt.* fazer parar, deter; interromper, suspender; proibir; impedir; obstruir, bloquear; obturar (dente); estancar (sangue). **-to s. short** interromper; refrear-se, conter-se. **-to s. up** tapar, obstruir. **-s. thief!** pega ladrão! / *vi.* parar, cessar; fazer alto; parar de; interromper-se; permanecer, hospedar-se; ficar obstruído. **-to s. at** hospedar-se em; deter-se em. **-to s. dead** ou **short** parar de repente. **-to s. off**

fazer uma parada em. **-to s.** over fazer escala, fazer parada (em viagem)

stoppage | sto'piɏ | s. parada; cessação; interrupção; obstrução (de tráfego); suspensão de pagamentos, falência

stopper | sto'pə | s. tampão, batoque, rolha

stop-watch | stop'woš | s. cronômetro

storage | sto'riɏ | s. armazenagem; estocagem; depósito (guarda-móveis); (eletr.) acumulação. **-in s.** armazenado. **-in cold s.** frigorificado

store | sto'ə | s. loja; armazém, depósito; estoque, reserva; abundância, provisão; (pl.) provisões, víveres, materiais. **-what is in s. for us** o que nos espera, o que teremos que enfrentar / vt. guardar, acumular; armazenar, depositar. **-to s. up** acumular; fazer provisão de

storehouse | sto'əhaws | s. armazém, depósito; (fig.) fonte (de informações); (fig.) repertório

storekeeper | sto'əkipə | s. fiel de armazém; (EUA) lojista, dono de loja

store-room | sto'ərʊm | s. depósito; almoxarifado; (náut.) paiol

storey | sto'ri | s. andar (de casa etc.)

stork | stók' | s. cegonha

storm | stóm' | s. tempestade; (fig.) tumulto, perturbação. **-to take by s.** (mil.) tomar de assalto / vt. assaltar, tomar de assalto / vi. **-to s. at** fulminar, invectivar; esbravejar

storm-bound | stóm'bawnd | a. detido pela tempestade (em porto etc.)

stormy | stó'mī | a. tempestuoso; (fig.) violento, agitado

story | stó'ri | s. história, narrativa, conto; anedota; enredo, argumento (de romance etc.); boato. **-the s. goes that** dizem que. **-to cut a long s. short** em

poucas palavras, resumindo

stout | stawt' | s. tipo de cerveja preta / a. corpulento, vigoroso; bravo, destemido, valente; sólido, resistente, forte

stove | stowv' | s. estufa, aparelho de calefação; fogão; fogareiro

stow | stow' | vt. pôr, meter; acondicionar; arrumar. **-to s. away** pôr de lado, guardar

stowaway | stow'əwey | s. passageiro clandestino

straddle | stra'dəl | s. posição escarranchada / vt. cavalgar, pôr a cavalo em; abrir muito as pernas; enquadrar (com fogo de artilharia) / vi. escarranchar-se

straggler | strag'lə | s. pessoa ou coisa desgarrada, errante, apartada dos outros

straight | streyt | a. reto; liso (cabelo); direto, contínuo; franco, honesto; simples, fácil; puro, sem mistura; lógico, metódico; ereto; em ordem, arrumado / adv. em linha reta; diretamente; sem rodeios. **-s. ahead** sempre em frente, bem em frente. **-s. on** sempre em linha reta. **-s. away** ou **off** logo, imediatamente. **-to go s.** emendar-se, corrigir-se. **-to put things s.** desfazer mal-entendidos

straighten | strey'tən | vt. endireitar, tornar reto; esticar; arrumar, pôr em ordem / vi. endireitar-se

straightforward | streyt'fówəd | a. franco; direto; simples / adv. francamente; diretamente

strain | streyn' | s. esforço, tensão; peso, pressão; distensão; deformação; linhagem, estirpe; (mús.) melodia, som; tipo, variedade, raça; traço (de caráter); estilo, modo (de falar, escrever etc.). **-to stand the s.** suportar o esforço / vt. estender; retesar; exercer pressão sobre; forçar (os nervos, a vista etc.); torcer, distender (músculo);

retorcer, deformar; coar, filtrar; abraçar, estreitar, apertar / *vi.* esforçar-se; deformar-se, retorcer-se; criar dificuldades; dar puxões; filtrar-se

strained | streynd' | *a.* tenso, preocupado; constrangido (sorriso); coado, peneirado

strainer | strey'nə | *s.* coador

strait | streyt' | *s.* (ger. *pl.*) (geog.) estreito, passo, canal; situação difícil, aperto

strait-jacket | streyt'jakit | *s.* camisa-de-força

strait-laced | streyt'leysd | *a.* austero, severo

strand | strand' | *s.* filamento, fio (que forma um cabo ou corda); (poét.) praia (de mar, lago ou rio); fio de pérolas; (fig.) elemento / *vt. vi.* encalhar (navio); ficar em dificuldades

stranded | stran'did | *a.* em dificuldades, abandonado; encalhado (navio)

strange | streynj' | *a.* estranho; singular, extraordinário; novo, desconhecido; curioso, esquisito. **-to feel s.** estar indisposto, tonto etc.; não se sentir à vontade, não estar familiarizado com

strangeness | streynj'nes | *s.* estranheza; singularidade; raridade

stranger | streyn'jə | *s.* desconhecido, estranho; forasteiro, visitante; intruso; novato, principiante. **-to make a s. of** tratar como a um estranho. **-to be a s. to the town** não conhecer a cidade. **-the little s.** criança recém-nascida

strangle | stran'gəl | *vt.* estrangular; sufocar; reprimir

strap | strap' | *s.* correia; cinta, fita; tirante; presilha; assentador (de navalha) / *vt.* prender com correia

strapping | stra'ping | *a.* forte, robusto; alto e forte. **-a s. fellow** um homenzarrão. **-a s. woman** uma mulheraça

stratagem | stra'tijəm | *s.* estratagema

strategic | strəti'jik | *a.* estratégico

strategy | stra'tiji | *s.* estratégia

stratum | strey'təm | *s.* camada

straw | stró' | *s.* palha; canudinho (de refresco). **-to be the last s.** ser a última gota, o cúmulo / *a.* de palha; cor de palha, amarelado

strawberry | stró'bərĩ | *s.* morango

strawberry-mark | stró'bərĩmAk | *s.* sinal de nascença avermelhado

stray | strey' | *a.* abandonado (animal); desgarrada (ovelha); extraviado, errante; isolada, fortuita (observação) / *vi.* extraviar-se; desviar-se; desgarrar-se; divagar

stray bullet | strey'bulit | *s.* bala perdida

streak | strik' | *s.* risca, raia; veio; traço (tb. de caráter) / *vt.* riscar, fazer traços ou raias; passar como um raio

streak of lightning | strik'əvlayt'ning | *s.* raio, relâmpago

stream | strim' | *s.* riacho, arroio, ribeirão; corrente; desfile, sucessão; jorro (de sangue); torrente (tb. de lágrimas). **-to swim against the s.** nadar contra a corrente / *vi.* correr, fluir; jorrar; flutuar, ondear (bandeira). **-to s. in** entrar em tropel. **-to s. out** sair em tropel

streamer | stri'mə | *s.* flâmula, bandeirola; cabeçalho de jornal (sobre toda a extensão da página), manchete

streamlined | strim'laynd | *a.* aerodinâmico

street | strit' | *s.* rua. **-one way s.** rua de mão única. **-man in the s.** homem comum

street arab | strit'arəb | *s.* garoto de rua

streetcar | strit'kA | *s.* (EUA) bonde

street-walker | strit'wókə | *s.* prostituta

strength | strengϑ' | *s.* força, vigor; energia, intensidade; (mil.) número de soldados, efetivo; resistência (de materiais). **-on the s. of** baseando-se em; em atenção a; valendo-se de. **-in great s.** em grande número. **-in full s.** sem faltar ninguém

strengthen | streng'ϑən | *vt. vi.* fortalecer(-se), reforçar(-se), fortificar(-se); intensificar(-se)

strenuous | stre'nĭuəs | *a.* árduo, difícil; enérgico, vigoroso; pertinaz, porfiado

stress | stres' | *s.* tensão; ênfase, importância; acento tônico, intensidade; (med.) estresse. **-to lay s. on** dar ênfase a, acentuar, insistir em, sublinhar / *vt.* submeter a tensão ou pressão

stretch | stre͜ʃ' | *s.* extensão (de terreno, estrada etc.); período (de tempo); esforço (de imaginação); esticamento; espreguiçamento. **-at a s.** de uma só vez, sem interrupção. **-by a s. of language** por força de expressão / *vt.* estender, estirar; prolongar; forçar, exagerar, torcer (significado etc.) / *vi.* estender-se, estirar-se; espreguiçar-se

stretcher | stre'ʃə | *s.* esticador; padiola; (gír.) exagero

stretcher-bearer | stre'ʃəbeərə | *s.* padioleiro

stricken | stri'kən | *a.* atacado, acometido

strict | strikt' | *a.* estrito; rigoroso, severo; austero; meticuloso, escrupuloso

strictly | strikt'lĬ | *adv.* estritamente, rigorosamente. **-s. speaking** no sentido estrito das palavras

strictness | strikt'nes | *s.* rigor; exatidão; severidade

stride | strayd' | *s.* passo largo. **-to take in one's s.** superar (obstáculo) sem mudar o passo; (fig.) enfrentar com facilidade e sem hesitar (situação); (pl.) progresso / *vt.* galgar / *vi.* andar a

passos largos, caminhar empertigado

strident | stray'dənt | *a.* estridente, penetrante

strife | strayf' | *s.* conflito, luta, disputa, contenda; rivalidade, competição

strike | strayk' | *s.* golpe, ataque; greve; (EUA) descoberta (de ouro, petróleo etc.) / *vt.* bater em; dar pancadas; ferir, atingir; chocar com; riscar, acender (fósforo); arriar (bandeira); desarmar (barraca); fisgar com anzol, ferrar; assumir (atitude); levantar (acampamento); cunhar (moedas); descobrir (ouro, petróleo etc.); ocorrer (idéia); impressionar; (mil.) atacar, investir. **-to s. a blow** dar um golpe. **-to s. a bargain** fechar um negócio. **-to s. root** criar raízes. **-to s. back** revidar. **-to s. down** derrubar. **-to s. off** riscar, eliminar. **-to s. up** (mús.) atacar, começar a tocar (ou cantar). **-how does it s. you?** que pensa disso? / *vi.* fazer greve; dar (horas); dar bote (animal ou peixe, atacando outro menor ou isca)

striker | stray'kə | *s.* grevista

striking | stray'king | *a.* notável, impressionante, extraordinário, surpreendente, admirável

string | string' | *s.* barbante; fio (de pérolas); fieira (de peixes); enfiada, chorrilho (de mentiras); (mús.) corda; (pl., mús.) instrumentos de cordas; (coloq.) condição, restrição. **-to pull strings** exercer influência, mexer (os) pauzinhos / *vt.* enfiar (em cordão) / *vi.* enfiar, formar fio. **-to s. along with** (coloq.) ser leal a; seguir; confiar. **-to s. up** (gír.) enforcar

stringency | strin'jənsī | *s.* rigor, severidade; escassez (de dinheiro); força (de argumentação, de raciocínio)

stringent | strin'jənt | *a.* rigoroso,

estrito, rígido; escasso (dinheiro)

stringy | strin'gī | *a.* fibroso

strip | strip' | *s.* tira, fita (de couro, papel etc.); história em quadrinhos; faixa (de terra) / *vt.* despir; despojar; pelar; desfolhar; (mec.) desmontar / *vi.* despir-se, desnudar-se

stripe | strayp' | *s.* lista, listra; (mil.) divisa, galão; vergastada, vergão

strive | strayv' | *vi.* empenhar-se em; esforçar-se por; lutar com

striving | stray'ving | *s.* esforço; luta

stroke | strowk' | *s.* golpe; pancada; batida; (med.) ataque (esp. apoplético); tacada; braçada; remada; pincelada; pulsação; chicotada. **-at one s.** de um só golpe. **-on the s. of** ao dar (horas) / *vt.* afagar, acariciar; alisar, passar a mão por

stroll | strowl' | *s.* volta, passeio. **-to take a s.** dar uma volta, um passeio / *vt.* passear por ou através de / *vi.* passear; andar lentamente; vaguear, deambular

strong | strong' | *a.* forte; vigoroso, robusto; enérgico; intenso, profundo; acentuado, pronunciado. **-to use s. language** dizer grosserias, usar expressões ofensivas ou vulgares. **-a thousand s.** de mil homens (regimento etc.) / *adv.* fortemente; vigorosamente

stronghold | strong'howld | *s.* praça forte, fortaleza, baluarte

strongly | strong'lĭ | *adv.* fortemente; vigorosamente; solidamente; energicamente; intensamente; poderosamente

strontium | stron'tĭəm | *s.* estrôncio

structure | străk'šə | *s.* estrutura; construção

struggle | stră'gəl | *s.* luta / *vi.* lutar

strum | străm' | *vt.* dedilhar (instrumento de corda)

strumpet | strâm'pit | *s.* (ant.) prostituta

strut | strât' | *s.* andar pomposo; escora, esteio / *vi.* pavonear-se

stub | stăb' | *s.* ponta (de cigarro ou charuto), guimba; talão, canhoto (de cheque etc.) / *vt.* destocar, tirar tocos (de um campo etc.). **-to s. one's toe** dar uma topada

stubble | stă'bəl | *s.* restolho, raiz das gramíneas (que fica no solo depois da ceifa)

stubborn | stă'bən | *a.* teimoso; tenaz, persistente; intratável; inflexível

stubbornness | stă'bənnes | *s.* teimosia; persistência, tenacidade

stubby | stă'bĭ | *a.* atarracado; curto e grosso

stucco | stă'kow | *s.* estuque

stuck | stăk' | *a.* imobilizado, emperrado, enguiçado; (gír., EUA) apaixonado, embeiçado

stuck-up | stăk'ăp | *a.* (coloq.) convencido, presumido; presunçoso

stud | stăd' | *s.* coudelaria; botão de colarinho; tacha, cravo; (mec.) pino; garanhão, reprodutor / *a.* reprodutor, destinado à reprodução

student | stĭu'dənt | *s.* estudante

stud-horse | stăd'hós | *s.* garanhão

studied | stă'did | *a.* estudado; premeditado, calculado

studio | stĭu'dĭow | *s.* estúdio

studious | stĭu'dĭəs | *a.* estudioso, aplicado; cuidadoso, zeloso

studiousness | stĭu'dĭəsnes | *s.* aplicação aos estudos, diligência

study | stă'dĭ | *s.* estudo; sala de leitura, gabinete; empenho, zelo, desejo. **-to be in a brown s.** estar em devaneio, estar absorto / *vt. vi.* estudar

stuff | stăf' | *s.* material, matéria-prima; coisa; substância; pano, tecido; coisa sem valor, droga;

bagagem; tolice, disparate. -that's the s. to give' em ou to give the troops! (coloq.) isto é o que se quer!, assim é que se faz! / vt. rechear; encher / vi. empanturrar-se

stuffing | stâ'fing | s. estofamento, enchimento; recheio

stuffy | stâ'fĭ | a. sufocante, abafado, mal ventilado; entupido (nariz); (coloq.) conservador, antiquado; (coloq.) puritano; amuado

stultify | stâl'tifay | vt. ridicularizar; frustrar, baldar

stumble | stâm'bəl | s. tropeção; passo em falso / vi. tropeçar; dar uma topada

stumbling-block | stâm'blingblok | s. obstáculo, empecilho

stump | stâmp' | s. cepo; coto (de braço ou perna); talo; toco (tb. de charuto ou lápis). -to be up a s. (gír., EUA) estar em dificuldades / vt. reduzir a toco; destocar (terreno); dar uma topada; confundir, desnortear, atrapalhar. -to s. the country percorrer em campanha eleitoral. -to s. up (gír.) pagar, desembolsar / vi. andar com passos pesados

stun | stân' | s. assombro; atordoamento / vt. atordoar, aturdir, estontear

stunt | stânt' | s. proeza, habilidade / vt. atrofiar, limitar; enfezar / vi. realizar proezas

stupefied | stĭu'pifayd | a. estupefato, pasmado; entorpecido (com bebida etc.)

stupendous | stĭupen'dəs | a. estupendo; assombroso; prodigioso, maravilhoso

stupid | stĭu'pid | s. pessoa estúpida, imbecil / a. estúpido, idiota, pateta; maçante, enfadonho

stupidity | stĭupi'ditī | s. tolice, estupidez

stupor | stĭu'pə | s. torpor, entorpecimento

sturdiness | stE'dines | s. robustez, vigor; solidez, resistência; inflexibilidade

sturdy | stE'dĭ | a. robusto, vigoroso; sólido; resoluto; inflexível

sturgeon | stE'jən | s. (ict.) esturjão

stutter | stâ'tə | s. gagueira / vt. vi. gaguejar

stutterer | stâ'tərə | s. gago

sty | stay' | s. chiqueiro; terçol / vt. pôr em chiqueiro / vi. viver em chiqueiro

stye | stay' | s. terçol

style | stayl' | s. estilo; maneira, moda; estilete; buril; tratamento, título honorífico. -in s. na moda. -to live in s. viver à grande / vt. intitular, denominar, chamar. -to s. oneself entitular-se

stylish | stay'liś | a. elegante, na moda

suave | swAv' | a. suave, ameno; urbano, delicado, cortês

subconscious | sâbkon'śəs | s.a. subconsciente

subdue | səbdĭu' | vt. subjugar, dominar, sujeitar; reprimir, conter; moderar, baixar (tom)

subject | sâb'jikt | s. súdito; sujeito (tb. gram.); assunto, tema; matéria (tb. de estudos). -on the s. of com respeito a. -to change the s. mudar de assunto / a. sujeito (a); exposto (a), com tendência para / | səbjekt' | vt. subjugar; subordinar, submeter

subjection | səbjek'śən | s. sujeição, submissão, dependência

subjugate | sâb'jugeyt | vt. subjugar, dominar, submeter

subjunctive | səbjânk'tiv | s.a. (gram.) subjuntivo

sublet | sâblet' | vt. sublocar; subarrendar

sublime | sâblaym' | a. sublime; supremo, magnífico

submarine | sâbmərin' | s. a. submarino

submerge | səbmEʤ' | vt. vi. submergir, mergulhar

submission | səbmi'ʃən | s. submissão; resignação; proposta, proposição

submissive | səbmi'siv | a. submisso; humilde; obediente

submit | səbmit' | vt. submeter, apresentar; sugerir, propor / vi. submeter-se; entregar-se; resignar-se

subordinate | səbó'dinit | s.a. subordinado / | səbó'dineyt | vt. subordinar; controlar; sujeitar

subscribe | səbskrayb' | vt. subscrever, assinar; contribuir com / vi. subscrever-se, assinar um documento; subscrever, endossar; aceitar

subscriber | səbskray'bə | s. assinante (de jornal etc.); contribuinte; subscritor

subscription | səbskrip'ʃən | s. subscrição, contribuição; assinatura (de jornal)

subsequent | sâb'sikwənt | a. subseqüente, posterior; seguinte. -s. to depois de

subsequently | sâb'sikwəntli | adv. mais tarde, subseqüentemente

subservient | səbsE'viənt | a. subserviente, servil

subside | səbsayd' | vi. acalmar-se; abater-se, diminuir; depositar-se (sedimento)

subsidence | səbsay'dəns | s. abrandamento, diminuição; sedimentação; abaixamento (de nível etc.); baixa (de maré)

subsidiary | səbsi'diəri | s. complemento / a. subsidiário; subsidiado; suplementar; tributário (rio)

subsidize | sâb'sidayz | vt. subsidiar, subvencionar

subsidy | sâb'sidi | s. subsídio, subvenção

subsist | səbsist' | vi. subsistir, manter-se

subsistence | səbsis'təns | s. subsistência

subsistence allowance | səbsis'tənsəlaw'əns | s. ajuda de custo

substance | sâbs'təns | s. substância. -a man of s. um homem de posses. -to waste one's s. ser perdulário

substantial | səbstan'ʃəl | a. substancial; sólido; rico

substantiate | səbstan'ʃieyt | vt. confirmar; comprovar, provar; fundamentar

substantive | sâbs'təntiv | s. substantivo / | səbstan'tiv | a. substantivo (tb. gram.); importante, essencial; real; explícito

substitute | sâbs'titfut | s.a. substituto / vt. substituir

substitution | sâbstitfu'ʃən | s. substituição

substratum | sâbstrey'təm | s. substrato

subtenant | sâbte'nənt | s. sublocatário; subarrendatário

subterfuge | sâb'təffuʤ | s. subterfúgio, evasiva

subterranean | sâbtərey'niən | a. subterrâneo

subtitle | sâb'taytəl | s. subtítulo; legenda (de filme)

subtle | sâ'təl | a. sutil; fino, delicado; perspicaz; insidioso

subtlety | sâ'təlti | s. sutileza

subtract | səbtrakt' | vt. subtrair, diminuir, tirar

subtraction | səbtrak'ʃən | s. subtração

suburb | sâ'bEb | s. subúrbio; (pl., fig.) arredores

subversion | sâbvE'jən | s. subversão

subversive | sâbvE'siv | s.a. subversivo

subvert | sâbvEt' | vt. subverter

subway | sâb'wey | s. passagem subterrânea para pedestres; (EUA) metrô

succeed | səksid' | vt. suceder; seguir; suceder a; suceder-se a / vi. ser bem-sucedido, sair-se bem; suceder (no trono etc.)

succeeding | səksi'ding | a. sucessivo; subseqüente, seguinte; vindouro, futuro

success | səkses' | *s.* sucesso, êxito, triunfo

successful | səkses'ful | *a.* bem-sucedido; afortunado; vitorioso, triunfante

succession | səkse'śən | *s.* sucessão; seqüência, série

successor | səkse'sə | *s.* sucessor

succinct | səksinkt' | *a.* sucinto, breve, conciso

succour, succor | sâ'kə | *s.* socorro, auxílio / *vt.* socorrer, auxiliar

succulent | sâ'kĭulənt | *a.* suculento; sumarento

succumb | səkâm' | *vi.* sucumbir; ceder, render-se; falecer, expirar

such | sâś' | *a.* tal, semelhante, assim; tanto, tamanho. **-s. as** tal como / *adv.* tão, em tal grau / *pron.* tal

suck | sâk' | *s.* sorvo; chupada / *vt.* chupar; sorver; mamar; aspirar. **-to s. up** ou **in** absorver (umidade); aspirar (pó); inalar

sucker | sâ'kə | *s.* criança de peito; leitão; (coloq.) trouxa, otário; (zool.) ventosa; tubo de sucção

suckle | sâ'kəl | *vt.* amamentar

suction | sâk'śən | *s.* sucção, aspiração

sudden | sâ'dən | *a.* súbito, repentino, inesperado. **-all of a s.** de repente

suddenly | sâ'dənlī | *adv.* subitamente, de repente

suddenness | sâ'dənnes | *s.* rapidez, precipitação, pressa

suds | sâdz' | *spl.* espuma de sabão

sue | sʊ' | *vt.* (jur.) processar; solicitar, pedir

suede | sweyd' | *s.* camurça

suet | sʊ'it | *s.* sebo

suffer | sâ'fə | *vt. vi.* sofrer, padecer; ser submetido a

sufferer | sâ'fərə | *s.* sofredor, padecedor, vítima. **-to be a s.**

from sofrer de

suffering | sâ'fəring | *s.* sofrimento, padecimento; aflição / *a.* paciente, tolerante

suffice | səfays' | *vt.* bastar para, ser suficiente a / *vi.* bastar

sufficient | səfi'śənt | *s.* suficiente, bastante

suffix | sâ'fiks | *s.* sufixo

suffocate | sâ'fəkeyt | *vt. vi.* sufocar, asfixiar

suffocation | sâfəkey'śən | *s.* sufocação, asfixia

suffrage | sâ'frij | *s.* sufrágio, voto

suffuse | səfĭʊz' | *vt.* espalhar-se por, banhar, tingir, cobrir

sugar | śu'gə | *s.* açúcar / *vt.* adoçar / *vi.* açucarar-se

sugar-beet | śu'gəbit | *s.* beterraba

sugar-bowl | śu'gəbowl | *s.* açucareiro

sugar-cane | śu'gəkeyn | *s.* cana-de-açúcar

sugar plum | śu'gəplâm | *s.* (ant.) bala, rebuçado

suggest | səjest' | *vt.* sugerir; indicar; fazer lembrar

suggestion | səjes'śən | *s.* sugestão; recomendação

suicidal | suisay'dəl | *a.* suicida

suicide | suisayd' | *s.* suicídio. **-to commit s.** suicidar-se

suit | sʊt' | *s.* petição, pedido; ação judicial; terno, traje completo; costume (de senhora); naipe (de cartas). **-to follow s.** seguir o exemplo / *vt.* convir a; ficar bem a (roupas); corresponder a, satisfazer; ir bem com / *vi.* convir, servir

suitable | sʊ'təbəl | *a.* oportuno; conveniente, adequado, adaptado

suitcase | sʊt'keys | *s.* mala

suite | swit' | *s.* comitiva, séquito; conjunto, jogo; (mús.) suíte; apartamento (em hotel etc.)

suite of furniture | swit'əffɛnišə | *s.* mobília

suitor | sʊ'tə | *s.* litigante; peticionário; pretendente (a casamento)

sulk | sâlk' | s. amuo / vi. amuar, zangar-se

sulky | sâl'kī | a. amuado, zangado, mal-humorado

sullen | sâ'lən | a. soturno, sombrio, mal-humorado; pouco sociável; melancólico

sully | sâ'lī | vt. conspurcar, macular, sujar

sulphur | sâl'fə | s. enxofre

sultan | sâl'tən | s. sultão

sultana | səlta'nə | s. sultana (mulher e tb. a passa)

sultry | sâl'trī | a. abafado, sufocante (atmosfera, tempo, ambiente)

sum | sâm' | s. soma, adição; importância, quantia / vt. **-to s. up** resumir, recapitular

summarily | sâ'mərilī | adv. sumariamente

summarize | sâ'mərayz | vt. resumir

summary | sâ'mərī | s. sumário, síntese / a. sumário (julgamento etc.)

summary conviction | sâ'mərīkənvik'śən | s. condenação por magistrado (sem júri)

summer | sâ'mə | s. verão

summer-time, summertime | sâ'mətaym | s. verão, temporada de verão

summer time | sâ'mətaym' | s. hora ou horário de verão

summery | sâ'mərī | a. estival

summing-up | sâ'mingâp | s. recapitulação

summit | sâ'mit | s. cume

summon | sâ'mən | vt. (jur.) citar; chamar, convocar; concentrar (energias etc.). **-to s. up courage** tomar coragem

summons | sâ'mənz | s. (jur.) citação; convocação, chamada; notificação, aviso

sumptuous | sâmp'tǐuəs | a. suntuoso

sun | sân' | s. sol / vi. expor-se ao sol, tomar sol

sunbathe | sân'beyð | vi. tomar banho de sol

sunbeam | sân'bim | s. raio de sol

sunburn | sân'bEn | s. queimadura de sol / vt. vi. queimar-se ao sol

sunburnt | sân'bEnt | a. bronzeado, queimado de sol

sundae | sân'dey | s. sorvete com calda, nozes etc.

Sunday | sân'dey | s. domingo

sundial | sân'dayəl | s. relógio de sol

sundown | sân'dawn | s. pôr-do-sol

sundry | sân'drī | a. vários, diversos. **-all and s.** todo (o) mundo

sunflower | sân'flawə | s. girassol

sun-glasses | sân'glasis | spl. óculos escuros

sunken | sân'kən | a. afundado, submerso; fundo; encovado (face, olhos)

sunlight | sân'layt | s. luz do sol, luz solar

sunlit | sân'lit | a. iluminado pelo sol

sunny | sâ'nī | a. banhado de sol, ensolarado; (fig.) jovial, radiante

sunrise | sân'rayz | s. nascer do sol, alvorecer

sunset | sân'set | s. pôr-do-sol, ocaso

sunshade | sân'śeyd | s. guarda-sol; toldo

sunshine | sân'śayn | s. luz do sol, sol

sunstroke | sân'strowk | s. insolação

sun-tanned | sân'tand | a. bronzeado (de sol)

superannuation | supəranǔey'śən | s. pensão de aposentadoria ou reforma (por limite de idade)

superb | supEb' | a. esplêndido, soberbo

supercilious | supəsi'lǐəs | a. arrogante, desdenhoso

superficial | supəfi'śəl | *a.* superficial

superfluous | supE'fluəs | *a.* supérfluo, excessivo

superhuman | supəhĭu'mən | *a.* sobre-humano

superimpose | supərimpowz' | *vt.* sobrepor

superintend | supərintend' | *vt.* superintender

superintendent | supərinten'dənt | *s.* superintendente; policial (de grau superior ao de inspetor)

superior | supĭ'rĭə | *s.a.* superior

superiority | supĭrĭo'ritĭ | *s.* superioridade

superlative | supE'lətiv | *s.a.* superlativo

superman | sʋ'pəmən | *s.* super-homem

supermarket | supəmA'kit | *s.* supermercado

supernatural | supənə'śərəl | *s.a.* sobrenatural

supersede | supəsɪd' | *vt.* substituir

superstition | supəsti'śən | *s.* superstição

superstitious | supəsti'śəs | *a.* supersticioso

superstructure | sʋ'pəstrâkśə | *s.* superestrutura

supervene | supəvɪn' | *vi.* sobrevir

supervise | sʋ'pəvayz | *vt.* supervisionar; superintender

supervision | supəvi'jən | *s.* supervisão, superintendência

supine | sʋ'payn | *s.* supino / *a.* supino; inativo, indolente; inerte

supper | sâ'pə | *s.* ceia, jantar

supplant | səplAnt' | *vt.* suplantar; substituir

supple | sâ'pəl | *a.* flexível, macio; ágil, elástico

supplement | sâ'plimənt | *s.* suplemento / *vt.* suprir, completar, complementar

supplementary | sâplimen'tərĭ | *a.* suplementar

suppleness | sâ'pəlnes | *s.* maciez, flexibilidade; agilidade

suppliant | sâ'plĭənt | *s.a.* suplicante

supplication | sâplikey'śən | *s.* súplica, petição

supplier | səplay'ə | *s.* fornecedor

supply | səplay' | *s.* suprimento, fornecimento; provisão; (*pl.*) suprimentos; verbas / *vt.* fornecer, suprir; prover; remeter; substituir temporariamente. **-to s. a want** suprir uma falta

supply and demand | səplay'ənddimAnd' | *s.* oferta e procura

support | səpót' | *s.* suporte, apoio; sustento, manutenção / *vt.* sustentar, apoiar; suportar, agüentar; proteger; favorecer; patrocinar

supporter | səpó'tə | *s.* partidário, adepto; defensor; patrocinador

suppose | səpowz' | *vt.* supor, presumir, crer / *vi.* supor

supposed | səpowzd' | *a.* suposto, pretenso

supposing | səpow'zing | *conj.* supondo que, no caso de

supposition | səpəzi'śən | *s.* suposição, hipótese

suppress | səpres' | *vt.* suprimir, eliminar; sufocar, reprimir (revolta, emoção etc.)

suppression | səpre'śən | *s.* supressão, eliminação; repressão

suppurate | sâ'pĭureyt | *vi.* supurar

supremacy | supre'məsĭ | *s.* supremacia

supreme | suprĭm' | *a.* supremo

surcharge | sE'śAj | *s.* sobrecarga; sobretaxa

sure | śu'ə | *a.* certo; seguro; confiante. **-to be s.** estar certo. **-to be s. to** não deixar de. **-to make s.** verificar, certificar-se de / *adv.* (coloq.) certamente / *interj.* claro!, sem dúvida!

surely | śu'əlĭ | adv. certamente, seguramente

sureness | śu'ənes | s. certeza, confiança; segurança; exatidão

surety | śu'ətĭ | s. certeza, segurança; fiador

surf | sEf' | s. rebentação (das ondas); (desp.) surfe

surface | sE'fis | s. superfície / a. superficial; exterior / vt. trazer à tona / vi. vir à superfície, vir à tona

surf-board | sEf'bóəd | s. prancha de surfe

surfeit | sE'fit | s. excesso, intemperança / vt. saciar, fartar / vi. fartar-se

surfer | sE'fə | s. surfista

surf-riding | sEf'rayding | s. (desp.) surfe

surge | sEj' | s. onda, vagalhão / vi. ondear; engrossar, encapelar-se (mar); avolumar-se, subir

surgeon | sE'jən | s. cirurgião; (mil., náut.) médico

surgery | sE'jərĭ | s. cirurgia; sala de operações

surgical | sE'jikəl | a. cirúrgico

surly | sE'lĭ | a. grosseiro, rude; carrancudo; intratável

surmise | sE'mayz | s. conjetura, suspeita / | sEmayz' | vt.vi. conjeturar, suspeitar

surmount | sEmawnt' | vt. superar, vencer; galgar; coroar

surname | sE'neym | s. nome de família, sobrenome; (ant.) cognome, alcunha / vt. dar sobrenome; (ant.) cognominar, alcunhar

surpass | sEpas' | vt. exceder, ultrapassar

surplice | sE'pləs | s. sobrepeliz

surplus | sE'pləs | s. excesso; (com.) superávit, saldo / a. excedente, de sobra

surplus value | sE'pləsvalĭu | s. mais-valia

surprise | sE'prayz' | s. surpresa/ vt. surpreender; tomar de surpresa; causar surpresa;

maravilhar

surprised | sEprayzd' | a. surpreendido

surprising | sEpray'zing | a. surpreendente

surrender | sərən'də |s. rendição, capitulação; renúncia, desistência; resgate (de apólice de seguro); cessão (de propriedade) / vi. render-se, entregar-se, dar-se por vencido

surreptitious | sârepti'śəs | a. sub-reptício, secreto, furtivo

surround | sərawnd' | vt. rodear, circundar

surrounding | sərawn'ding | a. circunvizinho, circundante; adjacente, vizinho

surrounding area | sərawn'dingeərĭə |s. arredores

surroundings | sərawn'dingz | spl. arredores; meio, ambiente

surtax | sE'taks | s. imposto adicional, sobretaxa / vt. sobretaxar

surveillance | sEvey'ləns | s. vigilância

survey | sE'vey | s. exame, inspeção; relatório; vistoria; quadro, estudo, panorama; (geog.) levantamento / | sEvey' | vt. examinar; estudar; fazer vistoria, fazer inventário de; fazer levantamento topográfico ou medição / vi. fazer levantamento topográfico

surveying | səvey'ing | s. agrimensura; hidrografia; levantamento topográfico; medição; inspeção

surveyor | səvey'ə | s. agrimensor; hidrógrafo; superintendente; observador, estudioso

survival | səvay'vəl | s. sobrevivência; sobrevivente; remanescente; herança, legado (do passado)

survive | səvayv' | vt. sobreviver a / vi. sobreviver

survivor | səvay'və |s. sobrevivente

susceptibility | səseptibi'litĭ | s. suscetibilidade

susceptible | səsep'təbəl | *a.* suscetível (de)

suspect | sâs'pəkt | *s.* suspeito, pessoa suspeita | səspekt' | *vt. vi.* suspeitar (de), duvidar (de); presumir, supor

suspend | səspend' | *vt.* suspender

suspense | səspens' | *s.* incerteza, expectativa; *suspense*

suspension | səspen'śən | *s.* suspensão

suspension bridge | səspen'śənbrij | *s.* ponte pênsil

suspicion | səspi'śən | *s.* suspeita, desconfiança; traço, indício; noção vaga

suspicious | səspi'śəs | *a.* desconfiado, suspeitoso; duvidoso, suspeito

sustain | səsteyn' | *vt.* sustentar; manter. **-to s. a loss** sofrer uma perda

sustenance | sâs'tinəns | *s.* sustento, meio de subsistência

swab | swob' | *s.* esfregão; mecha de algodão; (gír.) pessoa desprezível / *vt.* limpar com esfregão

swag | swag' | *s.* ornamento de flores; oscilação; (gír.) produto de roubo, lucro ilícito / *vi.* oscilar, cambalear

swagger | swa'gə | *s.* arrogância, insolência, fanfarronada / *vt.* intimidar com blefe / *vi.* pavonear-se; fanfarronear

swain | sweyn' | *s.* jovem camponês; namorado (rústico)

swallow | swo'low | *s.* andorinha; trago (de bebida) / *vt. vi.* engolir, tragar; beber. **-to s. one's words** desdizer-se, retirar

swallow-tailed coat | swo'lowteyldkowt | *s.* fraque

swamp | swomp' | *s.* pântano, lodaçal / *a.* relativo a pântano; palustre / *vt.* inundar, alagar; atolar / *vi.* atolar-se

swampy | swom'pī | *a.* pantanoso

swan | swon' | *s.* cisne

swank | swank' | *s.* (coloq.) ostentação, presunção / *a.* jano-

ta, almofadinha / *vi.* exibir-se com elegância aparatosa

swan-song | swon'song | *s.* canto do cisne

swap | swop' | *s.* (coloq.) troca, barganha / *vt.* trocar

swarm | swóm' | *s.* exame / *vi.* enxamear (abelhas); afluir em grande número (pessoas). **-to s. with** fervilhar de. **-to s. up** trepar, subir (em mastro, corda, árvore)

swarthy | swó'ðī | *a.* moreno, trigueiro

swashbuckling | swoś'bâkling | *s.* fanfarronada / *a.* fanfarrão

swastika | swos'tikə | *s.* suástica

swat | swot' | *vt.* esmagar de um golpe (mosca etc.)

sway | swey' | *s.* balanço, oscilação; ascendência; domínio / *vi.* oscilar, balançar-se; mexer (com os quadris)

swear | swe'ə | *vt. vi.* jurar; praguejar; rogar pragas. **-tos. at** injuriar. **-to s. by** ter confiança ilimitada em. **-to s. off** renunciar sòlenemente a

swearing | swe'əring | *s.* blasfêmia, praga

sweat | swet' | *s.* suor / *vi.* suar

sweater | swe'tə | *s.* suéter

Swede | swid' | *s. a.* sueco

Swedish | swi'diś | *s.* (ling.) sueco / *a.* sueco

sweep | swip' | *s.* varredura; vassourada (tb. fig.); movimento impetuoso; curva, trajetória; extensão, vastidão; gesto largo; rasgo (de eloquência). **-at one s.** de um só golpe. **-to make a clean s. of** fazer a limpeza geral de / *vt.* varrer, limpar; arrebatar, empolgar; arrastar; devastar; abranger, abarcar; (coloq.) vencer espetacularmente. **-to s. away** arrebatar. **-to s. the board** ganhar todos os prêmios; limpar a mesa / *vi.* **-to s. past** passar ou mover-se rapidamente. **-to s. through (down, out etc.)** precipitar-se, passar (sair, andar etc.) impetuosamente

sweepings | swɪ'pingz |*spl.* varreduras, cisco, lixo

sweet | swɪt' | *s.* doce; doçura / *a.* doce; perfumado; melodioso; suave; agradável; meigo, gentil; encantador (pessoa) / *adv.* docemente; suavemente

sweeten | swɪ'tən | *vt.* adoçar; suavizar

sweetheart | swɪt'hʌt | *s.* querido; namorado

sweetish | swɪt'tɪʃ | *a.* adocicado

sweetness | swɪt'nes | *s.* doçura; suavidade

sweet pea | swɪtpɪ' | *s.* ervilha-de--cheiro

swell | swel' | *s.* inchação; ondulação do mar; (coloq.) pessoa elegante / *a.* (coloq.) elegante; (gír.) ótimo / *vt.* inchar, aumentar / *vi.* inchar-se

swelling | swe'ling | *s.* inchação, inchaço, tumor

swelter | swel'tə | *s.* calor sufocante / *vi.* arder de calor, sufocar, abafar

sweltering | swel'təring | *a.* sufocante, abrasador

swerve | swɛv' | *s.* desvio; guinada / *vi.* desviar-se

swift | swift' | *s.* andorinhão; dobadoura, carretel / *a.* rápido, veloz; repentino

swiftness | swift'nes | *s.* rapidez, ligeireza

swig | swig' | *s.* (coloq.) gole, trago / *vt.* beber sofregamente, emborcar

swill | swil' | *s.* restos de cozinha; lavagem, comida para porcos

swim | swim' | *s.* natação; nado / *vi.* nadar; deslizar; ter vertigens, estar tonto. **-to take a s.** ir nadar, cair n'água. **-to be in the s.** (coloq.) estar informado, saber dos acontecimentos

swimmer | swi'mə | *s.* nadador

swimming | swi'ming | *s.* natação; nado

swimming-pool | swi'mingpʊl |

s. piscina

swim-suit | swim'sʊt | *s.* roupa de banho

swindle | swin'dəl | *s.* trapaça, logro, tratantada / *vt.* trapacear, lograr

swindler | swin'dlə | *s.* trapaceiro, ladrão, vigarista

swine | swayn' | *s.* porco

swing | swing' | *s.* balanço; oscilação; impulso; ímpeto; ritmo; golpe lateral (boxe); (mús.) *swing.* **-in full s.** em plena atividade / *vt.* balançar; lançar; arremessar; brandir; menear, agitar. **-to s. round** fazer girar / *vi.* balançar, oscilar; lançar-se. **-to s. open** abrir-se subitamente; escancarar-se. **-to s. round** girar, rodar

swinging | swing'ing | *a.* oscilante, giratório

swinging-door | swing'ingdóə |*s.* porta de vaivém

swipe | swayp' | *s.* golpe violento; braço (de alavanca etc.) / *vt.* (coloq.) dar golpe violento; (gír.) roubar, surripiar

swirl | swɛl' | *vi.* remoinhar, rodopiar, girar

Swiss | swis' | *s. a.* suíço

switch | swis' | *s.* (eletr., ferrov.) chave; interruptor, comutador; mudança, troca; chibata, chibatada; trança postiça / *vt.* fustigar, açoitar; abanar; brandir; mudar, trocar; transferir, desviar. **-to s. off** desligar, apagar (luz). **-to s. on** ligar, acender (luz) / *vi.* desviar(-se); mudar, trocar

switchback | swiś'bak | *s.* montanha-russa; estrada íngreme em ziguezague

switchboard | swiś'bóəd | *s.* (eletr.) painel de controle; mesa telefônica

swivel | swi'vəl | *s.* tornel; destorcedor, girador / *vt.* fazer girar / *vi.* girar sobre um eixo

swivel chair | swi'vəlśeə |*s.* cadeira giratória

swollen | swow'lən | *a.* inchado; inflado; dilatado, intumescido

swoon | swʊn' | *s.* desmaio / *vi.* desmaiar

swoop | swʊp' | *s.* arremetida, investida; descida rápida; batida policial / *vt.* tomar de um golpe, arrebatar / *vi.* cair sobre (presa, inimigo)

swop | swop' | *s.* = *swap*

sword | só'əd | *s.* espada. **-to put to the s.** passar a fio de espada

sword fish | sód'fiś | *s.* (ict.) espadarte

swords-man | sódz'mən | *s.* esgrimista; espadachim

sworn | swón' | *a.* inveterado; jurado (inimigo etc.)

swot | swot' | *s.* (gír.) aplicação ao estudo; estudante esforçado / *vt. vi.* (gír.) estudar com aplicação, queimar as pestanas

sycamore | si'kəmó | *s.* sicômoro

sycophant | si'kəfant | *s.* bajulador, adulador servil

syllable | si'ləbəl | *s.* sílaba

syllabus | si'ləbəs | *s.* sumário, resumo; roteiro (de estudos); sílabo

symbol | sim'bəl | *s.* símbolo / *vt.* simbolizar

symbolical | simbo'likəl | *a.* simbólico

symbolize | sim'bəlayz | *vt.* simbolizar

symmetrical | sime'trikəl | *a.* simétrico

sympathetic | simpəϑe'tik | *a.* simpático; compassivo; humano; solidário. **-to be s. towards** simpatizar com

sympathize | sim'pəϑayz | *vi.* compadecer-se, condoer-se; dar os pêsames; solidarizar-se; simpatizar com

sympathy | sim'pəϑī | *s.* (ger. *pl.*) pêsames; mágoa, pesar; compaixão; solidariedade; afinidade; concordância. **-to be out of s. with** não simpatizar com, não estar de acordo com

symphony | sim'fənī | *s.* sinfonia

symposium | simpow'ziəm | *s.* simpósio; debate, palestra; coletânea de artigos oú opiniões

symptom | sim'təm | *s.* sintoma

symptomatic | simtəma'tik | *a.* sintomático

synagogue | si'nəgog | *s.* sinagoga

synchronize | sin'krənayz | *vt.* sincronizar

syncopation | sinkəpey'śən | *s.* (gram.) síncope; música sincopada

syndicalism | sin'dikəlizəm | *s.* sindicalismo

syndicate | sin'dikit | *s.* associação

synonym | si'nənim | *s.* sinônimo

synonymous | sino'niməs | *a.* sinônimo

synopsis | sinop'sis | *s.* sinopse, resumo, sumário

syntax | sin'taks | *s.* sintaxe

synthesis | sin'ϑəsis | *s.* síntese

synthetic | sinϑe'tik | *a.* sintético

syphilis | si'filis | *s.* sífilis

syringe | sirinj' | *s.* seringa / *vt.* seringar

syrup | si'rəp | *s.* calda de açúcar; (med.) xarope

system | sis'təm | *s.* sistema; corpo, organismo; rede (rodoviária, ferroviária, de rádio e TV etc.); (anat.) sistema, aparelho (digestivo, respiratório etc.)

systematic | sistəma'tik | *a.* sistemático

systematize | sis'təmətayz | *vt.* sistematizar

T

tab | tab' | *s.* alça, presilha. **-to keep t.** ou **tabs on** (EUA) controlar, vigiar

tabernacle | ta'bənakəl | *s.* tabernáculo, templo

table | tey'bəl | *s.* mesa; tábua (logaritmos etc.); tabela, lista. **-on the t.** adiado. **-to lay the t.** pôr a mesa. **-to clear the t.** tirar a mesa. **-to turn the tables** virar o feitiço contra o feiticeiro / *vt.* pôr na mesa; adiar (projeto de lei etc.) indefinidamente

tableau | ta'blow | *s.* quadro vivo

table-cover | tey'bəlkâvə | *s.* pano de mesa

tableland | tey'bəlland | *s.* planalto

table-linen | tey'bəlli'nən | *s.* roupa de mesa

table of contents | tey'bəlvkon'tents | *s.* conteúdo (de livro etc.), sumário, tábua da matéria

tables of the law | tey'bəlzovðəló | *spl.* (ecles.) tábuas da lei

tablespoon | tey'bəlspʊn | *s.* colher de sopa

tablet | ta'blit | *s.* comprimido; tablete (de sabão etc.); placa comemorativa; bloco de papel

taboo, tabu | təbv' | *s.a.* tabu / *vt.* declarar tabu

tabulate | ta'bĩuleyt | *vt.* catalogar

tacit | ta'sit | *a.* tácito

taciturn | ta'sitɛn | *a.* taciturno

tack | tak' | *s.* tacha, preguinho; (*pl.*) alinhavos; (náut.) amura; (fig.) norma de ação. **-to get down to brass tacks** tratar do que é importante, enfrentar a realidade / *vt.* pregar com tacha; alinhavar / *vi.* (náut.) bordejar; (fig.) mudar subitamente de política

tackle | ta'kəl | *s.* apetrechos, equipamento (esportivo etc.); (náut.) cordame, massame / *vt.* agarrar, lutar com; desafiar; empreender; atacar (problema)

tacky | ta'ki | *a.* pegajoso

tact | takt' | *s.* tato, prudência, diplomacia

tactful | takt'ful | *a.* discreto, que tem tato, diplomático

tactics | tak'tiks | *s.* tática

tactless | takt'les | *a.* indiscreto, que não tem tato

tadpole | tad'powl | *s.* (zool.) girino

Taffy | ta'fī | *s.* (coloq.) galês (alcunha)

tag | tag' | *s.* rótulo, etiqueta; farrapo; presilha; ponta; remate / *vt.* pôr etiqueta, rotular; arrematar (narrativa etc.) / *vi.* (coloq.) seguir de perto

tail | teyl' | *s.* rabo, cauda; (*pl.*) reverso da moeda; (*pl.*, coloq.) casaca. **-with t. up** com boa disposição. **-heads or tails** cara ou coroa

tailcoat | teyl'kowt | *s.* fraque

tailor | tey'lə | *s.* alfaiate

tailor-made | tey'ləmeyd | *a.* feito sob medida

tailpiece | teyl'pīs | *s.* parte terminal; decoração em fim de capítulo ou página

taint | teynt' | *vt.* manchar; contaminar, corromper

take | teyk' | *s.* tomada; coleta; (cin.) filmagem corrida / *vt.* tomar; tirar; levar; apanhar; contrair (doença etc.); pegar (planta); necessitar, exigir; supor; agüentar, tolerar; tirar (fotografia); dar (passeio). **-tot. hold of** pegar em. **-to t. home** levar para casa; acompanhar à casa. **-to t. leave** despedir-se. **-to t.**

effect ter efeito; (jur.) entrar em vigor. **-to t. time** levar tempo. **-to t. one's time** não ter pressa. **-to t. for** tomar por, considerar. **-to t. for granted** considerar necessàriamente verdadeiro. **-to t. to heart** tomar a peito. **-to t. offence** levar a mal, ofender-se. **-to t. place** realizar-se, ter lugar. **-to t. a walk** dar um passeio a pé. **-to t. after** parecer-se com. **-to t. away** tirar. **-to t. back** retirar; receber de volta ou em devolução. **-to t. care** ter cuidado. **-to t. care of** cuidar de. **-to t. a course** seguir um curso (estudos). **-to t. down** tirar; puxar para baixo; desmontar; anotar; (coloq.) humilhar (alguém); demolir (prédio etc.). **-to t. from** tirar, privar. **-to t. in** admitir, aceitar; compreender; diminuir, apertar; iludir; lograr. **-to t. off** tirar, remover; decolar (avião); (coloq.) arremedar. **-to t. out** tirar, levar para fora. **-to t. over** tomar conta (de), assumir o comando. **-to t. on** aceitar, admitir; contratar; afrontar, arrostar; encarregar-se. **-to t. to** simpatizar com; entregar-se a (lazer, esporte etc.); refugiar-se em. **-to t. up** erguer, levantar; ocupar (tempo); seguir (profissão); estudar (assunto); pegar em (armas); instalar-se (residência). **-to t. upon** ou **on oneself** aceitar a responsabilidade de

take-off | teyk'of | s. imitação, caricatura; decolagem

talcum | tal'kəm | s. (min.) talco

talcum powder | tal'kəmpaw'də | s. talco (de toalete)

tale | teyl' | s. conto; história; fábula; intriga, mexerico. **-to tell its own t.** falar por si, dispensar comentários. **-to tell tales** mexericar

talent | ta'lənt | s. talento; engenho; aptidão

talented | ta'ləntid | a. talentoso, inteligente

talisman | ta'lizmən | s. talismã

talk | tók' | s. conversa; fala; palestra; boato, mexerico. **-the t. of the town** assunto muito comentado. **-t. is cheap** falar é fácil / vt. vi. falar; conversar. **-to t. big** contar vantagem. **-to t. back** retrucar, responder com atrevimento. **-to t. through one's hat** (gír.) dizer tolices. **-to t. over** discutir. **-to t. (somebody) into** persuadir, convencer. **-to t. (somebody's) head off** falar pelos cotovelos. **-to t. turkey** (coloq., EUA) falar francamente, falar sem rodeios

talkative | tó'kətiv | a. loquaz, tagarela

talking | tó'king | s. fala, conversa / a. tagarela; sonoro (filme)

talking-to | tó'kingtʋ | s. descompostura, repreensão

tall | tól' | a. alto, de estatura elevada; exagerado, incrível

tallow | ta'low | s. sebo

tall tale | tól'teyl | s. história inverossímil

tall talk | tól'tók | s. jactância

tally | ta'lī | s. conta, cômputo; incisão usada para contar; etiqueta, rótulo / vt. etiquetar ou rotular / vi. fazer marcação; condizer com; conferir

talon | ta'lən | s. garra

tambourine | tambərin' | s. pandeiro

tame | teym' | a. domesticado, manso; insípido, enfadonho / vt. amansar, domar

tamer | tey'mə | s. domador

tamper | tam'pə | s. calcador, soquete / vi. mexer em; alterar, falsificar (documentos); violar, forçar

tan | tan' | s. cor bronzeada (do sol); cor castanho-amarelada; tanino (para curtir) / a. bronzeado; curtido / vt. curtir; bronzear / vi. ficar bronzeado

tang | tang' | s. sabor picante; cheiro penetrante

tangerine | tanǰərɪn' | *s.* tangerina

tangible | tan'jibəl | *a.* tangível, palpável, material

tangle | tang'əl | *s.* emaranhamento; confusão, complicação / *vt.* emaranhar

tank | tank' | *s.* tanque (para líquidos ou gases); cisterna; (mil.) tanque

tankard | tan'kəd | *s.* caneca

tanker | tan'kə | *s.* petroleiro

tanner | ta'nə | *s.* curtidor

tannery | ta'nərī | *s.* curtume

tantalize | tan'təlayz | *vt.* atormentar, torturar

tantalizing | tan'təlayzing | *a.* torturante, tentador

tantamount | tan'təmawnt | *a.* equivalente

tantrum | tan'trəm | *s.* acesso de fúria

tap | tap' | *s.* torneira; pancadinha; toque leve / *vt.* dar pancadinhas em; bater de leve com; abrir, perfurar; sangrar (árvore); drenar; abrir rosca; interceptar (telefonema) / *vi.* bater de leve

tape | teyp' | *s.* fita; cadarço; trena; fita de gravador / *vt.* prender com fita; medir com trena; (coloq.) gravar em fita

tape-measure | teyp'mejə | *s.* trena, fita métrica

taper | tey'pə | *s.* círio (vela); luz fraca; adelgaçamento / *vt. vi.* adelgaçar(-se), diminuir gradualmente. **-to t. off** diminuir, afilar-se

tape-recorder | teyp'rikó'də | *s.* gravador (de fita)

tapered | tey'pəd | *a.* afilado; em diminuição

tapering | tey'pəring | *a.* cônico, em diminuição gradual de espessura

tapestry | ta'pistrī | *s.* tapeçaria

tapeworm | teyp'wɛm | *s.* tênia

tapioca | tapiow'kə | *s.* tapioca

tapir | tey'pə | *s.* anta, tapir

tap water | tap'wótə | *s.* água da torneira

tar | tA' | *s.* alcatrão; (coloq.) marinheiro / *a.* alcatroado / *vt.* alcatroar

target | tA'git | *s.* alvo (de tiro); (fig.) objetivo

target practice | tA'gitprak'tis | *s.* tiro ao alvo

tariff | ta'rif | *s.* tarifa, taxa (de importação)

tarmac | tA'mak | *s.* estrada, pista ou área macadamizada

tarn | tAn' | *s.* pequeno lago das montanhas

tarnish | tA'niš | *vt.* embaciar, deslustrar; manchar

tarpaulin | tApó'lin | *s.* encerado, oleado; (náut.) chapéu de pano alcatroado

tarpon | tA'pən | *s.* (ict.) camarupim, tarpão

tarragon | ta'rəgən | *s.* (bot.) estragão

tarry | ta'rī | *a.* alcatroado / *vi.* demorar-se, atrasar-se

tart | tAt' | *s.* torta; (gír.) moça, mulher (esp. de maus costumes) / *a.* ácido; mordaz (resposta)

tartan | tA'tən | *s.* tecido axadrezado (próprio da Escócia)

task | tAsk' | *s.* tarefa; trabalho escolar. **-to take to t.** chamar à ordem, censurar / *vt.* importar a, exigir demais de

taskmaster | tAsk'mAstə | *s.* capataz: feitor

tassel | ta'səl | *s.* borla

taste | teyst' | *s.* gosto, sabor; prova, bocadinho; gota, pingo; predileção; elegância, distinção. **-to have a t. of** provar. **-there is no account for tastes** gostos não se discutem / *vt.* provar, experimentar; degustar / *vi.* ter determinado gosto. **-to t. of** ter gosto de

tasteful | teyst'ful | *a.* de bom-gosto, elegante

tasteless | teyst'les | *a.* insípido, insosso, sem graça; deselegante, de mau gosto

tasty | teys'tī | *a.* saboroso

tat | tat' | *s.* usado na expressão **-tit**

for t. pagar na mesma moeda

ta-ta | tatá' | *interj.* até logo!, adeusinho!

tatter | ta'tə | *s.* farrapo, andrajo. **-in tatters** andrajoso, maltrapilho

tattered | ta'təd | *a.* andrajoso, maltrapilho

tattoo | tətʊ' | *s.* tatuagem; (mil.) toque de recolher (tambor ou corneta). **-to beat the devil's t.** tamborilar / *vt.* tatuar

tattooing | tətʊ'ing | *s.* tatuagem

taunt | tónt' | *s.* zombaria, escárnio / *vt.* zombar, escarnecer

taut | tót' | *a.* esticado, retesado; tenso (nervo); severo, exigente; em ordem, em boas condições (navio)

tavern | ta'vən | *s.* taverna; hospedaria

tawdry | tó'drī | *a.* de mau gosto, espalhafatoso; berrante

tawny | tó'nī | *a.* castanho-amarelado ou avermelhado

tax | taks' | *s.* imposto, taxa; obrigação; gravame; encargo / *vt.* tributar, taxar; sobrecarregar; acusar. **-to t. with** tachar, acusar (de)

taxable | tak'səbəl | *a.* tributável, sujeito a impostos

taxation | taksey'śən | *s.* taxação; impostos

tax-collector | taks'kəlek'tə | *s.* coletor de impostos

tax-free | taks'frī | *a.* isento de impostos ou taxas

taxi | tak'sī | *s.* táxi / *vt.* (aer.) taxiar

taxi-driver | tak'sīdrayvə | *s.* chofer de táxi

taxpayer | taks'peyə | *s.* contribuinte (que paga impostos)

tea | tī' | *s.* chá

teach | tīš' | *vt.* ensinar, lecionar; explicar, mostrar / *vi.* ensinar, ser professor

teacher | tī'śə | *s.* professor; instrutor, preceptor

teaching | tī'šing | *s.* ensino; magistério; ensinamento, dou-

trina

teacup | tī'kâp | *s.* xícara de chá

team | tīm' | *s.* time; equipe; junta (de animais)

tea-party | tī'pʌtī | *s.* chá (reunião social)

teapot | tī'pot | *s.* bule de chá

tear | tī'ə | *s.* lágrima; (*pl.*) pranto, choro / *vi.* chorar, derramar lágrimas

tear | te'ə | *s.* rasgão / *vt.* rasgar; romper. **-to t. away** arrancar; retirar-se contra a sua vontade. **-to t. down** demolir (tb. fig.). **-to t. one's hair** arrancar os cabelos (de desespero etc.). **-to t. up** rasgar; arrancar / *vi.* rasgar-se; romper-se

tearful | tī'əful | *a.* choroso, lacrimoso

tease | tīz' | *vt.* implicar com, zombar de, atormentar, amofinar

tea-set | tī'set | *s.* serviço de chá

teat | tīt' | *s.* teta, mama

tea-time | tī'taym | *s.* hora do chá

technical | tek'nikəl | *a.* técnico

technically | tek'niklī | *adv.* tecnicamente

technician | tekni'śən | *s.* técnico

technique | teknīk' | *s.* técnica

technology | tekno'ləǰī | *s.* tecnologia

tedious | tī'dīəs | *a.* enfadonho, tedioso, aborrecido

tediousness | tī'dīəsnes | *s.* tédio, aborrecimento

teem | tīm' | *vi.* fervilhar, pulular; vazar, despejar (líquido). **-to t. with rain** chover a cântaros

teenager | tīn'eyǰə | *s.* rapaz ou moça (entre os 13 e os 19 anos)

teens | tīnz' | *spl.* adolescência (entre os 13 e os 19 anos)

teethe | tīð' | *vi.* criar dentes

teething | tī'ðing | *s.* dentição

teetotaller, teetotaler | tītow'tələ | *s.* abstêmio, que não toma álcool

telegram | te'ligram | *s.* telegrama

telegraph | te'ligrʌf | *s.* telégrafo / *vt.* telegrafar

telepathy | tile'pǝϑĩ | s. telepatia
telephone | te'lifown | s. telefone / vt. vi. telefonar
telephone-box | te'lifownboks | s. cabine telefônica
telephone call | te'lifownkól | s. chamada telefônica
telephonist | tile'fǝnist | s. telefonista
teleprinter | te'liprintǝ | s. teletipo
telescope | te'liskowp | s. telescópio
televise | te'livayz | vt. televisar
television | te'livijǝn | s. televisão
television set | te'livijǝnset' | s. aparelho de televisão
tell | tel' | vt. vi. dizer; contar (história); mandar; distinguir; notar, observar; saber; manifestar; revelar; assegurar. **-to t. someone off** distinguir, separar; (coloq.) censurar, repreender. **-to t. on** (coloq.) denunciar
telling | te'ling | s. narração. **-there is no t. when** é impossível dizer quando / a. eficaz, vigoroso
tell-tale | tel'teyl | s. mexeriqueiro, tagarela / a. denunciador, revelador
temerity | time'ritĩ | s. temeridade
temper | tem'pǝ | s. temperamento, índole, gênio; disposição; humor; calma, sangue-frio; têmpera (aço etc.). **-to lose one's t.** perder a paciência / vt. temperar, moderar
temperament | tem'pǝrǝmǝnt | s. temperamento
temperance | tem'pǝrǝns | s. sobriedade, temperança
temperance society | tem'pǝrǝnssǝsay'ǝtĩ | s. liga antialcoólica
temperate | tem'pǝrit | a. moderado, comedido; temperado (clima)
temperature | tem'prǝšǝ | s. temperatura
tempest | tem'pist | s. tempestade, temporal; (fig.) tumulto, agitação

tempestuous | tempes'tĩuǝs | a. tempestuoso; (fig.) violento (temperamento)
temple | tem'pǝl | s. templo
tempo | tem'pow | s. (mús.) tempo; cadência
temporary | tem'pǝrǝrĩ | a. temporário
temporize | tem'pǝrayz | vi. contemporizar; ganhar tempo
tempt | tempt' | vt. tentar, seduzir; instigar
temptation | tem(p)tey'šǝn | s. tentação
tempting | tem(p)'ting | a. tentador, sedutor
ten | ten' | s. a. dez
tenable | te'nǝbǝl | a. sustentável, defensável
tenacious | tǝney'šǝs | a. tenaz; pertinaz, persistente
tenacity | tǝna'sitĩ | s. tenacidade, persistência
tenancy | te'nǝnsĩ | s. posse de bens imóveis; locação, arrendamento
tenant | te'nǝnt | s. inquilino; rendeiro (lavrador)
tend | tend' | vt. cuidar de, zelar por, vigiar, guardar; cultivar / vi. **-to t. to** tender a. **-to t. on** ou **upon someone** servir, atender
tendency | ten'dǝnsĩ | s. tendência, inclinação
tender | ten'dǝ | s. encarregado, zelador; tênder (de locomotiva); navio-tênder; proposta, orçamento / a. tenro, macio; frágil, delicado; afetuoso, terno; sensível, impressionável; sensitivo; melindroso, delicado. **-t. of age** jovem, imaturo / vt. oferecer, apresentar
tenderfoot | ten'dǝfʋt | s. novato
tender-hearted | ten'dǝhʌtid | a. terno, sensível, compassivo
tenderness | ten'dǝnes | s. ternura, carinho, afeto; compaixão; delicadeza
tendril | ten'dril | s. (bot.) gavinha; anel (de cabelo)
tenement | te'nimǝnt | s. habita-

ção, moradia; prédio de apartamentos

tenement-house | te'nimənthaws | *s.* (EUA) casa de apartamentos; casa de cômodos, cortiço

tenet | te'nit | *s.* princípio, doutrina; opinião

tennis | te'nis | *s.* (desp.) tênis

tenor | te'nə | *s.* (mús.) tenor; teor, conteúdo

tense | tens' | *s.* tempo de verbo / *a.* tenso, ansioso

tension | ten'śən | *s.* tensão; ansiedade, nervosismo

tent | tent' | *s.* barraca, tenda

tentacle | ten'təkəl | *s.* tentáculo

tentative | ten'tətiv | *a.* experimental; hipotético

tentatively | ten'tətivlī | *adv.* a título de experiência

tenth | tenϑ' | *s.* décima parte / *a.* décimo

tenuous | te'nỉuəs | *a.* tênue, débil; vago, sutil

tenure | te'nỉə | *s.* posse

tepid | te'pid | *a.* morno, tépido

term | tEm' | *s.* termo, palavra; prazo; período letivo; (*pl.*) cláusulas, condições. **-to be on good (bad) terms with** estar em boas (más) relações com. **-to bring to terms** obrigar a concordar. **-to come to terms** chegar a um acordo. **-on easy terms** com facilidades de pagamento / *vt.* chamar, denominar

terminate | tE'mineyt | *vt. vi.* terminar, concluir

termination | tEminey'śən | *s.* terminação, desinência; término, fim

terminology | tEmino'ləĵi | *s.* terminologia

terminus | tE'minəs | *s.* estação terminal (de trem etc.)

termite | tE'mayt | *s.* cupim, térmite

terms of reference | tEmz'ovre'fərəns | *spl.* atribuições; normas de procedimento; definição de competência

terrace | te'ris | *s.* terraço; renque de casas contíguas e iguais; renque de casas em ladeira

terrain | te'reyn | *s.* terreno; (geol.) formação

terrestrial | təres'trīəl | *a.* terrestre

terrible | te'ribəl | *a.* terrível

terrific | teri'fik | *a.* terrífico, terrível; (coloq.) formidável, tremendo

terrified | te'rifayd | *a.* aterrorizado

terrify | te'rifay | *vt.* aterrorizar, apavorar

terrifying | te'rifaying | *a.* aterrorizante, apavorante

territorial | teritó'rīəl | *a.* territorial

territorial waters | teritó'rīəlwó-təs | *spl.* águas territoriais

territory | te'ritrī | *s.* território; região, distrito

terror | te'rə | *s.* terror

terrorism | te'rərizəm | *s.* terrorismo

terrorist | te'rərist | *s.a.* terrorista

terrorize | te'rərayz | *vt.* aterrorizar

terse | tEs' | *a.* conciso, sóbrio, sucinto

test | test' | *s.* prova; exame; teste (psicológico); critério, padrão; pedra de toque. **-to put to the t.** pôr à prova. **-to stand the t.** resistir à prova / *vt.* testar, examinar

testament | tes'təmənt | *s.* testamento

testify | tes'tifay | *vt. vi.* testemunhar, depor

testimonial | testimow'nỉəl | *s.* atestado, certificado; presente ou soma em dinheiro (em sinal de reconhecimento público)

testimony | tes'timənī | *s.* testemunho

testy | tes'tī | *a.* irascível, rabugento, ranzinza

tether | te'ðə | *s.* corda, corrente (de atar animais). **-to be at the end of one's t.** ter atingido os limites de seus recursos (paciência etc.) / *vt.* prender, atar (animal)

Teutonic | tĭuto'nik | *a.* teutônico, germânico

text | tekst' | *s.* texto

textbook | tekst'buk | *s.* compêndio, livro escolar

textile | teks'tayl | *s.* tecido, pano / *a.* têxtil

texture | teks'šə | *s.* textura, contextura; tecido

than | ðan | *conj.* que, do que

thank | ϑank' | *s.* (ger.*pl.*) agradecimentos. -**thanks!** obrigado! -**thanks to** graças a, por causa de / *vt.* agradecer (a)

thankful | ϑank'ful | *a.* agradecido, reconhecido, grato

thankless | ϑank'les | *a.* ingrato, mal-agradecido

thanksgiving | ϑanksgi'ving | *s.* ação de graças

that | ðat | *a. pron.* esse, essa; aquele, aquela / *conj.* que / *pron.* que, o que; isso; o. -**like t.** dessa maneira. -**t. is to say** isto é, quer dizer. -**t.'s t.!** (coloq.) pronto!, acabou-se! -**t. will do** basta, chega

thatch | ϑaš' | *s.* telhado de colmo, sapé etc. / *vt.* cobrir com colmo etc.

thaw | ϑó' | *s.* degelo / *vt. vi.* degelar, descongelar(-se)

the | ðəðiði (enfático) | *a. art.* o(s); a(s)

theatre, theater | ϑi'ətə | *s.* teatro

theatrical | ϑia'trikəl | *s.* (ger. *pl.*) representações teatrais (particulares ou de amadores) / *a.* teatral; afetado

theft | ϑeft' | *s.* furto

their | ðe'ə | *a. poss.* deles, delas; seu(s), sua(s)

them | ðem | *pron.* os; as; lhes; eles, elas

theme | ϑim' | *s.* tema; assunto; prefixo musical

then | ðen | *adv.* depois, em seguida, logo; então, nessa ocasião, naquele tempo; a essa hora, nessa altura; além disso, também; nesse caso, pois então. -**but t.** mas por outro lado, mas ao mesmo tempo. -**from t. on** desde então, daí por diante. -**now and t.** de vez em quando. -**now t.** pois bem. -**there and t.** em seguida. -**well t.** pois então; pois bem

thence | ðens' | *adv.* dali, daí; desde então; por isso

theologian | ϑiəlow'ϳən | *s.* teólogo

theology | ϑio'ləϳi | *s.* teologia

theorem | ϑi'ərəm | *s.* teorema

theoretical | ϑiəre'tikəl | *a.* teórico

theory | ϑi'ərī | *s.* teoria

therapeutic | ϑerəpĭu'tik | *a.* terapêutico

there | ðe'ə | *adv.* aí, ali, lá, acolá. -**over t.** lá, por lá; por aí. -**then and t.** aí mesmo; aí, nesse momento. -**t. is** ou **t. are** há. -**he is not all t.** (coloq.) ele não regula bem / *interj.* eis!, toma!

thereabouts | ðe'rəbawts | *adv.* por aí, mais ou menos, aproximadamente

thereafter | ðerʌf'tə | *adv.* depois disso, daí em diante

therefore | ðe'əfó | *adv. conj.* portanto, por conseguinte

therein | ðe'rin | *adv.* nisto; nisso; naquilo; nesse lugar, aí

thereupon | ðerəpon' | *adv.* depois disso; em conseqüência disso; a esse respeito

thermometer | ϑəmo'mitə | *s.* termômetro

thermos | ϑE'məs | *s.* garrafa térmica

these | ðiz | *a. pron.* estes, estas; esses, essas

thesis | ϑi'sis | *s.* tese

they | ðey | *pron.* eles, elas

thick | ϑik' | *s.* o grosso; a parte mais grossa; auge. -**in the t. of** no meio de. -**through t. and thin** em quaisquer circunstâncias. -**that's a bit t.!** (gír.) isso é demais!, essa não! / *a.* grosso; espesso (líquido, floresta); denso (nevoeiro); bronco, obtuso

thicken | ϑi'kən | vt. vi. engrossar, espessar(-se); anuviar(-se)

thicket | ϑi'kit | s. moita; mata espessa, matagal

thickness | ϑik'nes | s. espessura, grossura; densidade

thief | ϑif' | s. ladrão, gatuno

thieve | ϑiv | vt. vi. furtar, roubar

thigh | ϑay' | s. coxa

thimble | ϑim'bəl | s. dedal

thin | ϑin' | a. delgado, magro, fino; leve, transparente (tecido); rala (sopa); tênue (nuvem); reduzido, escasso (público); fraca, inconsistente (desculpa). -to grow t. emagrecer; escassear (cabelo) / vt. vi. -to t. down ou out adelgaçar(-se), diminuir; diluir(-se); rarefazer(-se)

thing | ϑing' | s. coisa. -for one t. em primeiro lugar. -the latest t. a última novidade. -not a living t. nem vivalma. -to make a good t. of (coloq.) tirar proveito. -poor t.! coitado!

thingamy, thingumajig | ϑin'gəmī ϑin'gəmajig | s. (coloq.) engenhoca, negócio, troço

think | ϑink' | vt. pensar; julgar, achar, crer. -tot. out cogitar, resolver. -to t. over pensar, refletir sobre; reconsiderar. -to t. up inventar, imaginar / vi. pensar; raciocinar; refletir. -to t. better of mudar de opinião sobre. -to t. nothing of não ligar nenhuma importância a. -to t. of pensar em. -to t. so achar. -don't you t. so? não acha?

thinker | ϑin'kə | s. pensador, filósofo

thinly | ϑin'lī | adv. escassamente; pobremente; fracamente; tenuemente

third | ϑEd' | s. terço, terça parte / a. terceiro

thirst | ϑEst' | s. sede. -to quench one's t. matar a sede / vi. estar com sede

thirsty | ϑEs'tī | a. sedento. -to be t. estar com sede

thirteen | ϑE'tin | s. a. treze

thirty | ϑE'tī | s. a. trinta

this | ðis | a. este, esta / pron. isto; este, esta

thistle | ϑi'səl | s. (bot.) cardo

thither | ϑi'ðə | a. de lá / adv. (ant.) para lá

thorn | ϑón' | s. espinho

thorny | ϑó'nī | a. espinhoso

thorough | ϑâ'rə | a. completo, perfeito; rematado, acabado; escrupuloso, minucioso

thoroughbred | ϑâ'rəbred | s. puro-sangue; animal de raça / a. de raça, puro-sangue

thoroughgoing | ϑâ'rəgowing | a. completo, perfeito; rematado, radical, extremo

those | ðowz | a. pron. esses, essas; aqueles, aquelas

though | ðow | conj. embora, ainda que, apesar de

thought | ϑót' | s. pensamento, idéia; reflexão; consideração, cuidado. -on second thoughts pensando bem. -the t. struck me ocorreu-me a idéia

thoughtful | ϑót'ful | a. atencioso, solícito; pensativo; refletido

thoughtfulness | ϑót'fulnes | s. solicitude, atenção

thoughtless | ϑót'les | a. irrefletido, inconsiderado, impensado; desatencioso, negligente; leviano

thoughtlessness | ϑót'lesnes | s. desconsideração; descuido, leviandade, imprudência

thousand | ϑaw'zənd | s. mil; milheiro. -by the thousands aos milhares / a. mil

thrall | ϑról' | s. escravo, servo; escravidão, servidão / vt. escravizar

thrash | ϑraś' | s. debulha / vt. debulhar; bater, surrar, açoitar, fustigar / vi. sacudir-se, agitar-se

thread | ϑred' | s. fio, linha; rosca

(de parafuso); fio (de narrativa) / vt. enfiar (agulha etc.); passar ou ziguezaguear por. **-to t. one's way through** penetrar, introduzir-se por entre / vi. ziguezaguear

threadbare | θred'beə | a. gasto, puído; (fig.) batido, vulgar, muito conhecido

threat | θret' | s. ameaça

threaten | θre'tən | vt. ameaçar

threatening | θre'təning | a. ameaçador

three | θri' | s. a. três

thresh | θreś' | vt. debulhar, malhar (cereais)

threshing-machine | θre'śingmə-śin' | s. debulhadora

threshold | θre'śowld | s. limiar, soleira; (fig.) começo

thrice | θrays' | adv. três vezes

thrift | θrift' | s. economia, frugalidade

thriftless | θrift'les | a. pródigo, gastador

thrifty | θrif'tī | a. econômico, frugal

thrill | θril' | s. emoção, estremecimento; frêmito, sensação / vt. impressionar, excitar, emocionar / vi. estremecer, vibrar

thriller | θri'lə | s. (cin.) romance policial

thrilling | θri'ling | a. empolgante, sensacional, vibrante, emocionante

thrive | θrayv' | vi. prosperar, florescer

thriving | θray'ving | a. próspero, florescente

throat | θrowt' | s. garganta. **-to clear one's t.** pigarrear. **-lump in one's t.** nó na garganta

throaty | θrow'tī | a. rouco

throb | θrob' | s. palpitação, pulsação / vi. palpitar, pulsar, latejar

thrombosis | θrombow'sis | s. trombose

throne | θrown' | s. trono

throng | θrong' | s. multidão; aglomeração / vt. vi. encher, apinhar-se, aglomerar-se; afluir em multidão

thronged | θrongd' | a. apinhado (de gente)

throttle | θro'təl | s. garganta; acelerador de mão, afogador / vt. estrangular, sufocar

through | θru | prep. por; através de; entre; por intermédio de; durante; por causa de. **-t. and t.** totalmente. **-to be t.** acabar, terminar; encerrar. **-to be t. with** acabar, terminar; cortar relações com. **-to go t.** efetuar; sofrer; atravessar; chegar ao fim de; ligar (telefone)

throughout | θruawt' | adv. por toda a parte, a cada passo, do começo ao fim; completamente / prep. através de; durante todo; por todo

throw | θrow' | s. lançamento, arremesso / vt. lançar, arremessar. **-to t. away** jogar fora; desperdiçar (dinheiro); perder (oportunidade). **-to t. down** derrubar. **-to t. out** jogar fora; rejeitar; expelir; desligar. **-to t. open** abrir (de par em par). **-to t. over** ou **up** (fig.) abandonar, renunciar / vi. lançar ou arremessar algo. **-to t. up** vomitar

throwing | θrow'ing | s. lançamento

thrush | θrâś' | s. (orn.) tordo; (med.) afta

thrust | θrâst' | s. estocada, golpe de ponta (de espada, punhal, faca etc.); empurrão; investida, arremetida; (mec.) empuxo, impulso / vt. cravar, meter, enfiar; empurrar. **-to t. aside** empurrar (para o lado). **-to t. upon** impor, jogar em cima de (responsabilidade etc.). **-to t. out** expulsar. **-to t. one's way** abrir caminho à força

thud | θâd' | s. baque, pancada surda

thug | θâg' | s. bandido, assassino, facínora

thumb | θâm' | s. polegar. **-under**

the t. of sob o domínio de. -all
thumbs desajeitado / vt. manu-
sear. -to t. through folhear. -to
t. a ride (coloq.) pedir carona.
-to t. one's nose fazer fiau

thump | ϑâmp' | s. pancada, cho-
que, baque / vt. dar pancadas
em; esmurrar; martelar (piano)
/ vi. bater; caminhar pesadamente (fazendo ruído)

thunder | ϑân'də | s. trovão; es-
trondo (canhoneio); ribombo
(trovão) / vi. trovejar

thunderbolt | ϑân'dəbowlt | s.
raio

thunderous | ϑân'dərəs | a. trove-
jante; atroador; terrificante

thunderstorm | ϑân'dəstóm | s.
tempestade com raios e trovões

thunderstruck | ϑân'dəstrâk | a.
estupefato, aterrado

thundery | ϑân'dərī | a. tempes-
tuoso, de trovoada

Thursday | ϑEz'dey | s. quinta-
-feira

thus | ðâs | adv. assim, deste mo-
do; portanto, por conseguinte.
-t. far até aqui, até este ponto

thwart | ϑwót' | vt. frustrar; im-
pedir

thyme | taym' | s. tomilho

tick | tik' | s. tique-taque; carra-
pato; tique (sinal de conferên-
cia, revisão, contagem etc.);
(coloq.) momento, instante.
-on t. fiado. -to ou on the t. pon-
tualmente / vt. marcar, ticar,
pôr sinal de conferido. -to t. off
(gír.) repreender / vi. tiqueta-
quear

ticket | ti'kit | s. bilhete, passa-
gem; ingresso, entrada; eti-
queta

ticket-collector | ti'kitkəlék'tə | s.
condutor (em trens etc.)

ticket-office | ti'kitofis | s. bilhe-
teria (de teatro etc.)

tickle | ti'kəl | s. cócegas / vt. fazer
cócegas; (fig.) agradar, deli-
ciar; estimular (apetite) / vi.
sentir cócegas

ticklish | tik'liś | a. cocēguento;

delicado (problema); inconstante

tidal | tay'dəl | a. de maré

tidal wave | tay'dəlweyv | s. vaga-
lhão provocado por maremo-
to; moda, onda

tide | tayd' | s. maré. -to go against
the t. remar contra a corrente /
vt. carregar; arrastar. -to t. over
sustentar temporariamente, tirar de apuros

tidiness | tay'dines | s. cuidado, or-
dem, apuro (na vestimenta etc.)

tidings | tay'dingz | spl. notícias,
novidades

tidy | tay'dī | a. arrumado, ordei-
ro (diz-se de roupas, ambiente
etc.); (coloq.) grande, conside-
rável / vt. vi. arrumar, pôr em
ordem

tie | tay' | s. laço, cordão (para
amarrar); gravata; vínculo, lia-
me; empate; (ferrov., EUA)
dormente / vt. atar, ligar; unir,
vincular. -to t. down limitar,
restringir; impossibilitar o mo-
vimento. -to t. up (náut.) atracar; embrulhar e amarrar; atar

tier | ti.'ə | s. fila, fileira, renque;
arquibancada; camada / vt. vi.
dispor em filas sobrepostas ou
em camadas

tiger | tay'gə | s. tigre

tight | tayt' | a. apertado; estica-
do; hermético, estanque; rígido, severo; (coloq.) bêbedo;
(coloq.) sovina. -to be in a t.
spot (gír.) estar em má situação,
estar num aperto / adv. firmemente, hermeticamente. -to sit
t. manter-se firme (opinião
etc.)

tighten | tay'tən | vt. vi.
apertar(-se); retesar(-se); inten-
sificar

tights | taytz' | spl. malha, roupa
de malha (de dançarino, acro-
bata etc.); meia-calça (feminina)

tile | tayl' | s. telha; ladrilho; azu-
lejo / vt. ladrilhar

till | til' | s. gaveta em que se guarda dinheiro / *vt.* lavrar, cultivar o solo / | til | *conj.* até que / *prep.* até

tiller | ti'lə | *s.* lavrador; (náut.) cana do leme

tilt | tilt' | *s.* inclinação. **-at full t.** a toda velocidade / *vi.* inclinar-se, pender. **-to t. at** investir contra

timber | tim'bə | *s.* madeira de construção; floresta

timber-wolf | tim'bəwulf | *s.* lobo cinzento norte-americano

time | taym' | *s.* tempo; hora; vez; prazo; período; (mús.) compasso. **-ahead of t.** antes do tempo, antes da hora marcada. **-at no t.** nunca. **-any t.** a qualquer hora, quando quiser; em qualquer época. **-at times** às vezes. **-at that t.** nessa altura. **-for the t. being** por enquanto. **-from t. to t.** de vez em quando. **-in due t.** oportunamente. **-in no t.** num instante. **-t. and again** repetidamente, continuamente. **-to have a good t.** divertir-se. **-to keep good t.** regular bem (relógio). **-take your t.!** não se apresse! **-this t. next week** daqui a oito dias. **-in the course of t.** com o correr do tempo. **-many times** muitas vezes. **-some other t.** em outra ocasião (no futuro). **-what t. is it?** que horas são? / *a.* temporal; temporário; a prazo / *vt.* marcar o tempo; escolher a ocasião de; cronometrar (corrida etc.)

time-honoured | taymon'ərd | *a.* tradicional

timekeeper | taym'kıpə | *s.* apontador, encarregado da contagem das horas de trabalho; cronometrista

time-limit | taym'limit | *s.* prazo

timely | taym'lī | *a.* oportuno

timepiece | taym'pıs | *s.* relógio (esp. de mesa)

timetable | taym'teybəl | *s.* horário (escolar, de transportes etc.)

timid | ti'mid | *a.* tímido

timidity | timi'ditī | *s.* timidez

timing | tay'ming | *s.* sincronização; escolha do momento oportuno

timorous | ti'mərəs | *a.* temeroso, tímido

tin | tin' | *s.* estanho; lata, folha-de-flandres; lata (de conserva etc.) / *a.* de estanho; de folha-de-flandres

tincture | tink'šə | *s.* tintura

tinder | tin'də | *s.* isca (com que outrora se fazia fogo)

tin foil | tin'foyl | *s.* papel prateado, papel de estanho

tinge | tinj' | *s.* quê, toque; tom, matiz / *vt.* tingir, matizar

tingle | tin'gəl | *s.* tinido; picada; comichão / *vi.* zunir (ouvidos); formigar

tinker | tin'kə | *s.* funileiro, latoeiro / *vt.* remendar, atamancar / *vi.* **-to t. at** tentar consertar. **-to t. with** mexer ou brincar com

tinkle | tin'kəl | *s.* tinido / *vi.* tinir

tinned | tind' | *a.* em conserva, em lata

tinned goods | tind'gʊdz | *spl.* enlatados, conservas

tinny | ti'nī | *a.* de estanho; metálico (diz-se de som ou sabor)

tin plate | tin'pleyt | *s.* folha-de-flandres

tinsel | tin'səl | *s.* ouropel; (fig.) brilho superficial

tint | tint' | *s.* cor, tom, matiz / *vt.* tingir; matizar

tiny | tay'nī | *a.* muito pequeno, minúsculo

tip | tip' | *s.* ponta, extremidade; gorjeta; informação confidencial (corridas, cotações da bolsa etc.); indicação; inclinação, caimento; depósito de lixo. **-on the t. of the tongue** na ponta da língua (pronto para dizer) / *adv.* **-on tiptoe** nas pontas dos pés / *vt.* rematar, guarnecer a extremidade; dar gorjeta a; inclinar; tocar levemente. **-to t. off** avisar. **-to t. over** tombar, derrubar. **-to t. up** levantar / *vi.*

inclinar-se; dar gorjeta

tipsy | tip'sĭ | *a.* ligeiramente alcoolizado, "alegre"

tiptop | tip'top | *s.* topo, cimo; a parte mais alta / *a.* (coloq.) o melhor, excelente

tirade | tireyd' | *s.* invectiva; rasgo, tirada; trecho longo (declamação etc.)

tire | tay'ə | *s.* pneumático / *vt.* cansar. -to t. out esgotar, estafar / *vi.* cansar-se, fatigar-se

tired | tay'əd | *a.* cansado. -to be t. of estar farto de

tiredness | tay'ədnes | *s.* cansaço, fadiga

tireless | tay'əles | *a.* incansável

tiresome | tay'əsəm | *a.* enfadonho, aborrecido

tiro, tyro | tay'row | *s.* principiante, noviço

tissue | ti'sʸu | *s.* tecido

tissue-paper | ti'sʸupeypə | *s.* papel de seda

tit | tit' | *s.* (vulg.) bico do peito; (*pl.*) seios. -to give t. for tat pagar na mesma moeda

titbit, tidbit | tit'bit tid'bit | *s.* petisco, guloseima

tithe | tayð' | *s.* dízimo (imposto); décima parte

title | tay'təl | *s.* título (tb. jur.) / *vt.* entitular

titled | tay'təld | *a.* que tem título de nobreza

titter | ti'tə | *vi.* rir-se às escondidas

tittle-tattle | ti'təltatəl | *s.* tagarelice; mexerico / *vi.* tagarelar; mexericar

to | tʊ | *prep.* a, para, até. -t. and fro de um lado para o outro, para cima e para baixo

toad | towd' | *s.* sapo

toady | tow'dĭ | *s.* bajulador, sabujo / *vi.* bajular, rebaixar-se

toast | towst' | *s.* torrada; brinde, saúde / *vt.* torrar; brindar, beber à saúde

toaster | tows'tə | *s.* torradeira

tobacco | təba'kow | *s.* fumo, tabaco

tobacconist | təba'kənist | *s.* dono de tabacaria; fabricante ou negociante de tabaco

tobacco-pouch | təba'kowpawš | *s.* bolsa para tabaco

toboggan | təbo'gən | *s.* tobogã

today, to-day | tədey' tudey' | *s. adv.* hoje. -a week t. de hoje(daqui) a oito dias

toddler | tod'lə | *s.* criança na idade de aprender a andar

to-do | tədu' | *s.* agitação, alvoroço

toe | tow' | *s.* dedo do pé; ponta da meia; bico do sapato. -from top to t. da cabeça aos pés. -to tread on somebody's toes pisar nos calos de alguém. -to t. the line seguir a orientação (de partido etc.)

toffee | to'fĭ | *s.* caramelo

together | təge'ðə | *adv.* juntos, juntamente; um com o outro. -t. with junto com. -to get t. reunir(-se)

toil | toyl' | *s.* labuta, lida, trabalho penoso / *vi.* labutar

toiler | toy'lə | *s.* trabalhador

toilet | toy'lit | *s.* toalete; banheiro / *a.* de toucador

toilet-paper | toy'litpeypə | *s.* papel higiênico

toilet powder | toy'litpawdə | *s.* talco

toilet soap | toy'litsowp | *s.* sabonete

toilet water | toy'litwótə | *s.* água-de-colônia

token | tow'kən | *s.* sinal; prova, testemunho; símbolo

tolerable | to'lərəbəl | *a.* tolerável, sofrível

tolerance | to'lərəns | *s.* tolerância

tolerant | to'lərənt | *a.* tolerante

tolerate | to'ləreyt | *vt.* tolerar

toleration | tolərey'šən | *s.* tolerância

toll | towl' | *s.* pedágio; dobre (de sinos); taxa, tarifa, imposto. -to take a heavy t. of causar grandes perdas em / *vt. vi.* dobrar (sinos)

tomahawk | to'məhók |s. macha-
dinha de guerra dos índios nor-
te-americanos

tomato | təmΛ'tow təmey'tow |
s. tomate

tomb | tυm' |s. túmulo, sepultura

tombstone | tum'stown |s. pedra
tumular, lápide

tome | towm' | s. livro, volume
(esp. grande e pesado)

tomorrow, to-morrow | tu-
mo'row | s. adv. amanhã. -t.
morning amanhã de manhã.
-the day after t. depois de amanhã

ton | tân' |s. tonelada

tone | town' |s. tom / vt. dar o tom
a; afinar. -to t. **down** suavizar o
tom de; moderar (som)

tongs | tongz' | spl. tenaz (par)

tongue | tâng' | s. língua; idioma;
linguagem. -to put out one's t.
pôr a língua (careta). -to hold
one's t. calar a boca. -slip of the
t. lapso da língua

tongue-lashing | tâng'lasing | s.
repreensão severa

tongue-tied | tâng'tayd | a. que
tem a língua presa; calado

tonic | to'nik | s. tônico; (mús.)
tônica / a. tonificante, tônico

tonight, to-night | tunayt' | s.
adv. esta noite, hoje à noite

tonnage | tâ'nij |s. tonelagem

tonsil | ton'sil | s. amígdala

tonsillitis | tonsilay'tis | s. amíg-
dalite, angina

tonsure | ton'sə | s. tonsura

too | tυ' | adv. demais, demasia-
do, muito; igualmente, tam-
bém. -t. **many** demais. -t. **much**
demais. -one t. **many** um de
mais. -t. **bad!** que pena!

tool | tυl' |s. ferramenta

toot | tυt' |s. toque breve (de buzi-
na, corneta etc.)

tooth | tυϑ' |s. dente. -t. **and nail**
com unhas e dentes. -in the t. of
em oposição a, a despeito de,
desafiando. -by the skin of one
t. por um triz

toothache | tυϑ'eyk | s. dor de
dentes

tooth-brush | tυϑ'brâs | s. escova
de dentes

toothless | tυϑ'les | a. desdentado

toothpaste | tυϑ'peyst |s. pasta de
dentes, creme dental

toothpick | tυϑ'pik | s. palito

top | top' |s. cume, alto, topo; ca-
beceira (de cama); copa (de chapéu, de árvore); capota (de carro); pião, piorra; apogeu, auge.
-on t. por cima, em cima. -on t.
of all that ainda por cima. -from
t. to bottom de alto a baixo.
-from t. to toe da cabeça aos
pés. -to come to the t. distin-
guir-se, ficar famoso / a. o mais
alto; superior; principal; máximo. -at t. speed a toda velocidade / vt. encimar, rematar; cobrir, coroar; encher; superar,
ultrapassar

top brass | top'bras |s. (gír., mil.)
oficiais superiores

topcoat | top'kowt |s. sobretudo

top floor | top'flóə |s. último an-
dar

top gear | top'giə | s. terceira (ou
quarta) velocidade, prise

top hat | top'hat |s. cartola

topic | to'pik | s. tópico, assunto

topical | to'pikəl |a. tópico; local;
alusivo a assunto do momento

topmost | top'mowst | a. o mais
alto

top-notch | top'nos | a. (coloq.)
de primeira classe

topple | to'pəl | vt. derrubar / vi.
tombar

top secret | top'sıkrit |a. extrema-
mente sigiloso

topsy-turvy | top'sıtevı | adv. às
avessas, de pernas para o ar

torch | tós' |s. tocha, archote, fa-
cho; maçarico; lanterna elétrica

torment | tó'mənt | s. tormento,
suplício, aflição / | tóment' | vt.
atormentar

tornado | tóney'dow |s. tornado,
ciclone, tufão

torpedo | tópı'dow |s. torpedo

torpedo-boat | tópɪ'dowbowt | *s.* torpedeiro

torpid | tó'pɪd | *a.* entorpecido, dormente; apático

torpor | tó'pə | *s.* entorpecimento, letargia, apatia

torrent | to'rənt | *s.* torrente

torrential | tərən'śəl |*a.* torrencial

torso | tó'sow | *s.* torso, tronco

tortoise | tó'təs | *s.* cágado, tartaruga terrestre

tortoise-shell | tó'təsśel | *s.* concha de tartaruga (marinha) de que se fazem pentes etc.

tortuous | tó'tĭuəs | *a.* tortuoso; (fig.) ardiloso

torture | tó'śə | *s.* tortura / *vt.* torturar

torturer | tó'śərə | *s.* torturador; algoz, carrasco

Tory | tó'rī | *s.* (polít.) conservador

toss | tos' | *s.* lançamento; sacudidela; distância a que alguma coisa pode ser lançada; meneio (de cabeça). **-to win the t.** ganhar (em cara ou coroa) / *vt.* atirar, lançar; sacudir; agitar. **-to t. over** ou **up** virar. **-to t. off** despachar rapidamente, fazer depressa / *vi.* balançar-se (navio etc.), ser sacudido ou agitado; revolver-se (na cama etc.). **-to t. up** tirar a sorte, lançar uma moeda

tot | tot' | *s.* criancinha; (coloq.) gole de bebida / *vt.* **-to t. up** somar

total | tow'təl |*s. a.* total / *vt.* totalizar, atingir o total de

totter | to'tə | *vi.* cambalear, vacilar (esp. criança começando a andar); estar trôpego; ameaçar cair (torre ou [fig.] governo etc.)

touch | tâś' | *s.* toque; tato; contato; pancada leve; pouquinho, pontinha. **-in t. with** em contato com. **-t. and go** situação precária / *vt.* tocar; roçar levemente; provar (comer, beber); atingir, chegar a; igualar, comparar-se com; comover; tocar, fazer escala (navio etc.). **-to t. off** descarregar; dar origem a, motivar, causar. **-to t. on** mencionar. **-to t. up** retocar, embelezar / *vi.* tocar-se, estar em contato

touch-and-go | tâś'andgow | *a.* apressado; atamancado; arriscado, precário

touching | tâ'śing |*a.* comovente, enternecedor / *prep.* com respeito a

touchstone | tâś'stown | *s.* pedra de toque

touchy | tâ'śĭ |*a.* melindroso, suscetível, delicado

tough | tâf" | *s.* valentão, arruaceiro / *a,* duro, rijo; robusto, resistente; vigoroso; difícil, árduo

toughen | tâ'fən | *vt.* endurecer; temperar (aço); fortificar, tornar robusto

toughness | tâf'nes | *s.* dureza; resistência, tenacidade; agressividade

tour | tʊ'ə | *s.* excursão, viagem; turno de serviço / *vt.* excursionar em / *vi.* fazer viagem de recreio

touring | tʊ'əring | *s.* turismo

tourist | tʊ'ərist | *s.* turista / *a.* de ou para turistas

tourist class | tʊ'əristklas |*s.* classe turista (em navio, avião etc.)

tournament | tó'nəmənt | *s.* torneio

tout | tawt' | *s.* vendedor importuno; angariador de clientes, corretor (de hotel etc.); indicador de palpites (de corridas etc.) / *vt.* importunar; solicitar / *vi.* angariar clientela

tow | tow' | *s.* reboque. **-to take in t.** levar de reboque; ser responsável por alguém / *vt.* rebocar

towards, toward | təwódz' təwód' |*prep.* para, em direção a, na direção de; para com (atitude); perto de, pouco antes de. **-t. noon** pouco antes de meio-dia

towel | taw'əl |*s.* toalha / *vt.* enxugar com toalha

tower| taw'ə |s. torre / vi. **-tot. up** erguer-se, elevar-se. **-to t. over** ou **above** dominar, elevar-se sobre

town| tawn' |s. cidade; vila; Londres (ou a cidade mais importante da região)

town council | tawn'kawnsil | s. câmara municipal

town hall | tawn'hól | s. câmara municipal

toxic | tok'sik | a. tóxico

toy | toy' | s. brinquedo / a. de brinquedo, em miniatura / vi. brincar; divertir-se com. **-to t. with** brincar com (sentimentos alheios); entreter (idéia); manusear distraidamente

trace | treys' | s. traço, vestígio, indício / vt. traçar, delinear; rastrear; descobrir

tracer | trey'sə | s. investigador; (mil.) bala traçadora

track | trak' | s. pista; caminho; via férrea; trajetória, curso / vt. **-to t. down** seguir a pista de, descobrir

trackless | trak'les | a. deserto, sem caminhos; que não deixa vestígios

tract| trakt' |s. extensão de terreno, região; (anat.) trato; brochura, folheto (esp. de propaganda religiosa)

tractable | trak'təbəl | a. tratável; dócil

traction | trak'sən | s. tração

tractor | trak'tə | s. trator

trade | treyd' | s. negócio; ofício (esp. manual: carpinteiro etc.), ocupação. **-foreign t.** exportação e importação / vt. trocar, permutar / vi. negociar. **-to t. in** negociar em. **-to t. on** ou **upon** explorar, aproveitar-se de

trademark| treyd'mʌk |s. marca registrada

trader | trey'də | s. comerciante, negociante; navio mercante

tradesman | treydz'mən | s. comerciante; lojista; artífice

tradesman's entrance | treydz' mənzentrəns |s. entrada de serviço

trade union | treyd'ỹunỹən | s. sindicato / a. sindical

trade-unionist | treydỸʋ'nỸənist | s. sindicalista

trading | treyd'ing | s. comércio / a. comercial

tradition | trədi'sən | s. tradição

traditional | trədi'sənəl | a. tradicional

traduce | trədĭus' | vt. caluniar, difamar, denegrir, denigrir

traffic | tra'fik |s. trânsito, tráfego; tráfico, comércio / vi. traficar

traffic jam | tra'fik jam |s. engarrafamento de trânsito

tragedy | tra'jidỸ |s. tragédia

tragic | tra'jik | a. trágico

trail | treyl' |s. trilha, picada, vereda; rasto, pista; cauda (de vestido); tropa; fileira / vt. arrastar; pisar; seguir a pista de / vi. arrastar(-se); rastejar; seguir (rasto)

train | treyn' | s. trem; cortejo; cauda (de vestido); fila; série; seqüência, endeamento; fileira, renque; jogo (de engrenagens) / vt. treinar; instruir; apontar (canhão) / vi. treinar, preparar-se; pôr-se em forma; estudar

trainee | treynı' | s. estagiário, pessoa em treinamento

trainer | trei'nə | s. treinador (de atletas ou animais)

training | treyn'ing | s. treinamento / a. de treinamento

training-college | treyn'ingkolỸ | s. escola de treinamento especializado; escola normal

training-ship | treyn'ingsip | s. navio-escola

trait | trey' | s. característica

traitor | trey'tə | s. traidor

traitorous | trey'tərəs | a. traiçoeiro

traitress | trey'tres | s. traidora

tram | tram' | s. bonde; vagonete (de mineração)

trammels | tra'məlz | spl. empecilhos

tramp | tramp' | s. vagabundo; som de passadas (ou cascos de animais); marcha; (gír.) mulher de má vida. **-on the t.** vagueando / vt. pisar ou andar pesadamente / vi. marchar, andar; palmilhar; errar, vaguear

trample | tram'pəl | s. tropel / vt. pisar; esmagar, destruir / vi. pisar ou andar pesadamente

trance | trʌns' | s. arrebatamento; estupor; catalepsia; transe (estado mediúnico)

tranquil | tran'kwil | a. tranqüilo, sossegado

tranquillity | trankwi'litī | s. tranqüilidade

tranquillizer | trankwilay'zə | s. tranqüilizante (medicamento) / vt. tranqüilizar

transact | tranzakt' | vt. transacionar, negociar

transaction | tranzak'śən | s. transação, negócio

transatlantic | tranzətlan'tik | a. transatlântico (vôo, navio etc.); (EUA) europeu

transcend | transend' | vt. transcender; sobrepujar, ultrapassar

transcribe | transkrayb' | vt. transcrever, copiar

transfer | trans'fə | s. transferência; (EUA) passagem (de ônibus etc.) com baldeação; ponto de baldeação; (jur.) transferência / | transfē' | vt. transferir / vi. transferir-se, ser transferido

transferable | trans'fərəbəl | a. transmissível

transfigure | transfi'gə | vt. transfigurar, transformar

transfix | transfiks' | vt. trespassar

transform | transfóm' | vt. transformar

transformation | transfəmey'śən | s. transformação

transfusion | transf̃ŭ'jən | s. transfusão

transgress | tranz'gres | vt. transgredir

transgression | tranzgre'śən | s. transgressão; pecado

transient | tran'ziənt | a. transitório, passageiro

transistor | tranzis'tə | s. transistor

transit | tran'zit | s. trânsito

transition | tranzi'śən | s. transição

transitive | tran'zitiv | s. verbo transitivo / a. transitivo

translate | tranzleyt' | vt. traduzir, verter; trasladar; transformar; transferir

translation | tranzley'śən | s. tradução

translator | tranzley'tə | s. tradutor

transliteration | tranzlitərey'śən | s. transliteração

transmission | tranzmi'śən | s. transmissão

transmit | tranzmit' | vt. transmitir

transmitter | tranzmi'tə | s. transmissor

transom | tran'səm | s. travessão; dintel; bandeira (de porta); (náut.) gio

transparent | transpa'rənt | a. transparente

transpire | transpay'ə | vt. transpirar; exalar / vi. transpirar; tornar-se conhecido

transplant | transplʌnt' | s. transplante / vt. transplantar

transport | trans'pót | s. transporte(s); arrebatamento, arroubo / vt. transportar; (fig.) arrebatar

transportation | transpótey'śən | s. transporte; (EUA) meio de condução; (hist.) remoção para colônia penal; desterro

transpose | trans'powz | vt. transpor

trap | trap' | s. armadilha; cilada / vt. apanhar em armadilha

trapeze | trapız' | *s.* trapézio

trapper | tra'pə | *s.* caçador de peles (com armadilhas)

trappings | tra'pingz | *spl.* arreios; (fig.) adornos

trash | traś' | *s.* lixo; escória, refugo, rebotalho

trashy | tra'śĭ | *a.* desprezível, sem valor, insignificante

travel | tra'vəl | *s.* viagem / *vi.* viajar; mover-se, andar; percorrer; propagar-se

traveller, traveler | tra'vələ | *s.* viajante; caixeiro-viajante

travel-sickness | tra'vəlsiknes | *s.* enjôo (de locomoção, viagem etc.)

traverse | trovɛs' | *vt.* atravessar, percorrer; examinar; contrariar

travesty | tra'vistĭ | *s.* paródia; imitação grotesca

trawler | tró'lə | *s.* traineira

tray | trey' | *s.* bandeja; tabuleiro; (fot.) banheira

treacherous | tre'śərəs | *a.* traiçoeiro, desleal

treachery | tre'śərĭ | *s.* perfídia, deslealdade, traição

treacle | tri'kəl | *s.* melado; melaço

tread | tred' | *s.* passo; pisada, passadas / *vt.* pisar, esmagar. **-to t. down** esmagar; (fig.) espezinhar / *vi.* andar, caminhar; pisar

treadle | tre'dəl | *s.* pedal (de bicicleta, máquina etc.)

treason | trı'zən | *s.* traição

treasure | tre'jə | *s.* tesouro

treasure-house | tre'jəhaws | *s.* tesouro (sala ou edificação onde se guardam riquezas)

treasurer | tre'jərə | *s.* tesoureiro

treasure trove | tre'jətrowvey | *s.* tesouro descoberto (de propriedade desconhecida)

treasury | tre'jərĭ | *s.* ministério da Fazenda; tesouro nacional; tesouraria

treat | trıt' | *s.* festa; regalo, deleite / *vt.* tratar; considerar. **-to t.** to oferecer, regalar-se com / *vi.* negociar; tratar de

treatise | trı'tiz | *s.* tratado

treatment | trıt'mənt | *s.* tratamento; modo de tratar

treaty | trı'tĭ | *s.* tratado

treble | tre'bəl | *s.* triplo; soprano / *a.* triplo; três vezes maior; de soprano / *vt.* triplicar

tree | trı' | *s.* árvore

trek | trek' | *s.* jornada (esp. em carro de bois); migração / *vi.* viajar; migrar; avançar lentamente

trellis | tre'lis | *s.* treliça; latada; caramanchão

tremble | trem'bəl | *vi.* tremer, estremecer

trembling | trem'bling | *s.* estremecimento / *a.* trêmulo

tremendous | trəmen'dəs | *a.* tremendo, espantoso, terrível

tremor | tre'mə | *s.* tremor

trench | trenś' | *s.* fosso, vala; (mil.) trincheira / *vi.* cortar; abrir caminho, avançar sulcando (rio, torrente); entrincheirar-se

trenchant | tren'śənt | *a.* cortante; vigoroso; mordaz

trend | trend' | *s.* tendência; rumo, direção / *vi.* tender

trepidation | trepidey'śən | *s.* trepidação; agitação; perturbação; apreensão

trespass | tres'pəs | *s.* transgressão; violação / *vi.* entrar ilegalmente. **-to t. on** ou **upon** invadir, violar (propriedade); abusar de

trespasser | tres'pəsə | *s.* intruso; transgressor; pecador

tresses | tre'siz | *spl.* tranças

trestle | tre'səl | *s.* cavalete

trews | truz' | *spl.* calças justas (de padrão escocês)

trial | tray'əl | *s.* ensaio, teste; (jur.) julgamento; provação, sofrimento / *a.* experimental; de ensaio

trial balloon | tray'əlbəlʋn *s.* balão de ensaio (tb. fig.)

triangle | tray'angəl | *s.* triângulo

tribal | tray'bəl | *a*. tribal

tribe | trayb' | *s*. tribo

tribulation | tribiuley'śən | *s*. tribulação, aflição, sofrimento

tribunal | traybiʋ'nəl | *s*. tribunal

tributary | tri'b̃ut̃ərī | *s*. tributário, afluente / *a*. tributário, que paga tributo

tribute | tri'biut | *s*. tributo. -**to pay t.** to prestar homenagem a

trick | trik' | *s*. ardil; artifício; truque; trapaça; peça, partida; habilidade, jeito; vaza (jogo de cartas); trejeito; cacoete. -**to play a t. on** pregar uma peça a. -**to be up to his old tricks** fazer das suas / *vt*. enganar, iludir. -**to t. into** conseguir por meios astuciosos

trickery | tri'kərī | *s*. engano, logro, fraude

trickle | tri'kəl | *s*. fio de água; pingo, gota / *vi*. gotejar, escorrer

trickster ʃ triks'tə | *s*. trapaceiro, velhaco

tricky | tri'kī | *a*. astucioso; difícil, complicado (situação, problema etc.)

tricycle | tray'sikəl | *s*. triciclo

tried | trayd' | *a*. provado, experimentado; de confiança

trifle | tray'fəl | *s*. ninharia, bagatela. -**just a t.** um pouquinho / *vi*. -**to t. with** meter-se com, brincar com (sentimentos etc.)

trifling | tray'fling | *a*. superficial, fútil

trigger | tri'gə | *s*. gatilho

trilby | tril'bī | *s*. (coloq.) chapéu mole (de feltro)

trill | tril' | *s*. trilo / *vi*. trilar

trim | trim⁴ | *s*. adorno, guarnição; condição; forma, preparo físico / *a*. arrumado; em boa ordem, bem cuidado; asseado; bem aparado; elegante; esmerado / *vt*. enfeitar, guarnecer; apurar; (náut.) orientar, marear (velas); espivitar (pavio); (fig.) modificar, adaptar

trimming | tri'ming | *s*. enfeite, adorno, guarnição; (*pl*., cul.) acompanhamento, guarnição

trinity | tri'nitī | *s*. trindade

trinket | trin'kit | *s*. berloque, adorno, enfeite; bugiganga, quinquilharia

trip | trip' | *s*. excursão, viagem, passeio / *vt*. fazer tropeçar; passar uma rasteira em / *vi*. tropeçar; errar, cometer uma falta; andar, correr ou dançar agilmente

tripe | trayp' | *s*. (cul.) tripas; (*pl*., vulg.) entranhas, barriga; (gír.) droga, coisa sem valor

triple | tri'pəl | *s*. triplo / *a*. tríplice / *vt*. triplicar / *vi*. triplicar-se

triplet | tri'plit | *s*. terno, trinca; terceto (versos); (*pl*.) trigêmeo (indivíduo nascido de parto tríplice)

triplicate | tri'plikit | *s*. triplicata / *a*. triplo, tríplice

tripod | tray'pod | *s*. tripé

tripper | tri'pə | *s*. excursionista

trite | trayt' | *a*. banal

triumph | tray'əmf | *s*. triunfo / *vi*. triunfar

triumphant | trayəm'fənt | *a*. triunfante

trivia | tri'vĩə | *spl*. insignificâncias, ninharias

trivial | tri'vĩəl | *a*. insignificante, sem importância

trolley | tro'lī | *s*. vagonete; carrinho (de transporte aéreo); (EUA) bonde; carrinho (de bagagem ou de servir à mesa)

trolleybus | tro'lībəs | *s*. ônibus elétrico

trollop | tro'ləp | *s*. mulher desmazelada; prostituta

troop | trʋp' | *s*. tropa, bando; rebanho, manada; (*pl*., mil.) tropa, soldados / *vi*. reunir-se, aglomerar-se; mover-se em conjunto (entrar, sair etc.)

troop-ship | trʋp'śip | *s*. navio-transporte (de tropas)

trophy | trow'fī | *s*. troféu

tropical | tro'pikəl | *a*. tropical

tropics | tró'piks | *spl*. trópicos

trot | trot' | s. trote / vi. trotar

trotter | tro'tə | s. cavalo trotador; (pl.) pés de porco, chispe

troubadour | trʊ'bədó | s. trovador (poeta provençal)

trouble | trâ'bəl | s. perturbação; desgosto, infortúnio; inquietação; contratempo; perturbação da ordem; agitação, transtorno, distúrbio; (mec.) avaria. -to give t. to incomodar; dar desgostos a. -to be in t. estar em situação difícil. -it is not worth the t. não vale a pena. -to spare no t. não poupar trabalho. -to be looking for t. (coloq.) procurar encrenca. -to take the t. to dar-se ao trabalho de. -not t. at all! não é incômodo nenhum! -may I t. you for poderia fazer o favor de. -what's the t.? que aconteceu?, qual é o problema? / vt. perturbar, amolar

trouble-maker | trâ'bəlmeykə | s. desordeiro, arruaceiro; pessoa que cria problemas

troublesome | trâ'bəlsəm | a. enfadonho, incômodo, importuno

trough | trof' | s. cocho; gamela; alguidar; cavado (entre duas ondas); calha; masseira; bateia

trounce | trawns' | vt. espancar, surrar; derrotar

troupe | trʊp' | s. companhia (de atores etc.)

trousers | traw'zəz | spl. calças

trousseau | trʊ'sow | s. enxoval

trout | trawt' | s. truta

trowel | traw'əl | s. colher de pedreiro

truant | trʊ'ənt | s. gazeteiro, vadio (aluno). -to play t. fazer gazeta

truce | trʊs' | s. trégua

truck | trâk' | s. caminhão; carreta; carrinho (de carregador); troca, permuta. -to have no t. with não querer conversa com

truculent | trâ'kʼ ʊlənt | a. truculento, feroz, selvagem

trudge | trâj' | vi. arrastar-se, caminhar penosamente

true | trʊ' | a. verdadeiro, legítimo, autêntico; leal; fidedigno. -to come t. realizar-se

truism | trʊ'izəm | s. truísmo; lugar-comum, banalidade

trump | trâmp | s. trunfo

trumpery | trâm'pərī | s. bugiganga, quinquilharia; baboseira, tolice / a. vistoso mas falso; ilusório

trumpet | trâm'pit | s. trombeta, corneta; clarim; trompete, pistom / vt. proclamar, apregoar, trombetear

trumpeter | trâm'pitə | s. trombeteiro; (mil.) clarim; trompetista, pistonista

truncated | trânkey'tid | a. truncado

truncheon | trân'śən | s. cassetete; bastão de comando

trunk | trânk' | s. tronco (de árvore, do corpo); baú; tromba; (pl.) calção (de nadador, de pugilista), cuecas. -to put someone to his trunks reduzir alguém ao último recurso

trunk-call | trânk'kól | s. chamada interurbana

trunk-road | trânk'rowd | s. estrada principal

truss | trâs' | s. (med.) funda / vt. amarrar, enfeixar

trust | trâst' | s. confiança; custódia; guarda; crédito; truste; consórcio; (jur.) fideicomisso. -to take on t. aceitar de boa fé. -to sell on t. vender fiado, a crédito / vt. ter confiança em; confiar aos cuidados de; contar com; crer em / vi. confiar, fiar-se

trustee | trâstı' | s. depositário, fiduciário; síndico; curador; membro de conselho diretor

trusteeship | trâstı'śip | s. tutela; curatela; cargo de depositário ou fiduciário

trusting | trâs'ting | a. confiante

trustworthy | trâst'wεδī | a. fidedigno, leal

truth | trʊϑ' | *s.* verdade; veracidade; fidelidade, exatidão

truthful | trʊϑ'ful *a.* sincero, verídico, verdadeiro

try | tray' | *s.* tentativa / *vt.* experimentar; tentar; (jur.) levar a juízo, julgar; pôr à prova; refinar, purificar (óleos, metais) / *vi.* esforçar-se por, tentar

trying | tray'ing | *a.* fatigante, penoso, irritante

T-shirt | tɪ'śɛt | *s.* camiseta de mangas curtas

tub | tâb' | *s.* tina

tube | tɪʊb' | *s.* tubo; câmara de ar (de pneu). **-the t.** (coloq.) metrô (de Londres); (coloq., EUA) televisão

tubercular | tɪubɛ'kɪulə | *s.* tuberculoso

tuberculosis | tɪubɛkɪulow'sis | *s.* tuberculose

tuck | tâk' | *s.* prega, dobra / *vt.* preguear, dobrar. **-to t. away** esconder. **-to t. in** meter. **-to t. up** arregaçar

Tuesday | tɪʊz'dey | *s.* terça-feira

tuft | tâft' | *s.* tufo (de pêlos etc.) / *vi.* crescer em tufos

tug | tâg' | *s.* puxão, arranco; (náut.) rebocador / *vt.* puxar

tug of war | tâg'ovwó | *s.* cabo de guerra (jogo); luta decisiva

tuition | tɪui'śən | *s.* ensino; taxa escolar; honorários de professor

tulip | tɪʊ'lip | *s.* (bot.) tulipa

tumble | tâm'bəl | *s.* tombo, queda / *vi.* dar cambalhotas; cair aos trambolhões. **-to t. down** desmoronar-se

tumbledown | tâm'bəldawn | *a.* em ruínas, desmantelado

tumbler | tâm'blə | *s.* acrobata, saltador; copo para bebida alcoólica (sem pé)

tumour, tumor | tɪʊ'mə | *s.* tumor

tumult | tɪʊ'mâlt | *s.* tumulto; motim; desordem, algazarra

tumultuous | tɪumâl'tɪuəs | *a.* tumultuoso

tune | tɪʊn' | *s.* melodia. **-in t.** afi-

nado. **-out of t.** desafinado. **-to change one's t.** mudar de tom / *vt.* afinar. **-to t. in** sintonizar. **-to t. up** afinar (orquestra); ajustar, regular (motor etc.)

tuneful | tɪʊn'ful | *a.* melodioso, harmonioso, musical

tunic | tɪʊ'nik | *s.* túnica (tb. anat., bot., zool.)

tunnel | tâ'nəl | *s.* túnel

tunny | tâ'nī | *s.* atum

turban | tɛ'bən | *s.* turbante

turbine | tɛ'bayn | *s.* turbina

turbot | tɛ'bət | *s.* rodovalho (espécie de linguado)

turbulent | tɛ'bɪulənt | *a.* turbulento

tureen | tɪurin' | *s.* terrina

turf | tɛf' | *s.* torrão, gleba; relvado; turfa; turfe, hipismo

turgid | tɛ'jid | *a.* túrgido, inchado; bombástico, empolado

Turk | tɛk' | *s.* turco

turkey | tɛ'kī | *s.* peru; (maiúsc.) Turquia

Turkish | tɛ'kiś | *s.a.* turco

turmoil | tɛ'moyl | *s.* tumulto, agitação, desordem, confusão

turn | tɛn' | *s.* volta; vez; mudança, transformação; susto, choque. **-at every t.** a cada momento. **-by turns** alternadamente; um após outro. **-on the t.** (coloq.) no ponto de. **-t. of speech** forma de dizer. **-to take a t. for the better** estar melhorando. **-to do (someone) a bad t.** prejudicar, fazer mal (a alguém) / *vt.* fazer girar; dar voltas; enrolar; tornear; dobrar; mudar, transformar; virar (página etc.); alcançar, chegar a (idade); causar enjôo; mudar de cor. **-to t. adrift** abandonar. **-to t. away** mandar embora, despedir. **-to t. down** rejeitar; diminuir (rádio etc.). **-to t. off** desligar; fechar. **-to t. on** abrir; ligar. **-to t. out** expulsar; virar pelo avesso; dobrar para fora. **-to t. over** virar; entregar; transferir; movimentar (capital). **-to t. tail** correr, fugir. -to t. upside down virar de cabeça para baixo / *vi.* dar voltas; enrolar; virar(-se); voltar(-se); desviar; mudar, transformar-se. -to t. away afastar-se, ir embora. -to t. back voltar, retroceder. -to t. from desviar-se de, abandonar. -to t. in estar virado para dentro; (coloq.) ir deitar-se. -to t. into transformar-se em. -to t. off desviar-se. -to t. out sair; apresentar-se; revelar-se; tornar-se. -to t. over virar ao contrário; capotar. -to t. round voltar-se, virar-se; girar. -to t. to voltar-se para. -to. t. turtle capotar. -to t. up virar-se para cima; acontecer; aparecer

turncoat | tɛn'kowt | *s.* vira-casaca

turning | tɛ'ning | *s.* volta, curva, esquina; arte de tornear / *a.* giratório

turning-point | tɛ'ningpoynt | *s.* momento decisivo, crise, ponto crítico

turnip | tɛ'nip | *s.* nabo

turnout | tɛ'nawt | *s.* assembléia, concorrência, afluência; greve; cortejo, espetáculo; exibição, ostentação; traje, roupa; resultado (de eleição); via lateral; (ferrov.) desvio

turnover | tɛ'nowvə | *s.* capotagem; movimento de negócios ou dinheiro

turnstile | tɛn'stayl | *s.* torniquete

turpentine | tɛ'pəntayn | *s.* terebintina

turpitude | tɛ'piťud | *s.* torpeza, baixeza

turquoise | tɛ'kwoyz | *s.* turquesa

turret | tâ'rit | *s.* torrinha, torreão; (náut.) torre de tiro

turtle | tɛ'təl | *s.* tartaruga. -to turn t. capotar

turtle-dove | tɛ'təldowv | *s.* (orn.) rola

tusk | tâsk' | *s.* presa, colmilho (de elefante, javali etc.)

tussle | tâ'səl | *s.* luta, contenda /

vi. lutar, brigar

tutor | ťu'tə | *s.* professor particular; preceptor; diretor de estudos (de universitários), mentor / *vt.* orientar estudos

tutorial | ťutó'rīəl | *s.* período letivo individual (ministrado por um professor universitário) / *a.* relativo a tutor, tutelar

twaddle | two'dəl | *s.* tagarelice; disparate, tolice / *vt. vi.* tagarelar; dizer disparates

twang | twang' | *s.* som estridente; entonação fanhosa / *vi.* produzir som estridente; falar com voz fanhosa

tweak | twik' | *s.* beliscão / *vt.* beliscar

tweed | twid' | *s. tweed* (tecido); (*pl.*) roupa de *tweed*

tweezers | twi'zəz | *spl.* pinça

twelve | twelv' | *s.a.* doze

twenty | twen'tī | *s.a.* vinte

twice | tways' | *adv.* duas vezes; em dobro

twig | twig' | *s.* rebento, raminho, galhinho

twilight | tway'layt | *s.* crepúsculo / *a.* crepuscular

twin | twin' | *s.a.* gêmeo

twine | twayn' | *s.* fio / *vt.* torcer; trançar; enroscar / *vi.* torcer-se; trançar-se; entrelaçar-se

twin-engined | twin'enjind | *a.* bimotor

twinge | twinj' | *s.* pontada

twinkle | twin'kəl | *s.* piscadela; brilho (no olhar); cintilação; lampejo, vislumbre / *vi.* cintilar; piscar

twinkling | twink'ling | *s.* cintilação. -in the t. of an eye num abrir e fechar de olhos

twirl | twɛl' | *s.* giro / *vt.* fazer girar; torcer, enrolar / *vi.* girar

twist | twist' | *s.* torcedura, torção; trança; fumo em corda; cordão, fio forte / *vt.* torcer; (gír.) lograr / *vi.* torcer-se

twister | twis'tə | *s.* (gír.) vigarista

twitch | twis' | *s.* tique nervoso,

trejeito; puxão, safanão; crispação / vi. contrair-se

twitter | twi'tə | s. gorjeio; alvoroço; risada sufocada / vi. gorjear, pipilar; tagarelar; alvoroçar-se; rir à socapa

two | tυ' | s.a. dois. -**in twos** dois a dois. -**to put t. and t. together** tirar conclusões. -**in a day or t.** dentro de poucos dias

two-faced | tυ'feyst | a. de duas caras; insincero

twofold | tυ'fold | a. duplo, duas vezes maior / adv. duplamente

two-seater | tυ'sıtə | a. de dois lugares

tycoon | taykυn' | s. (coloq.) magnata, figurão (no mundo dos negócios)

type | tayp' | s. tipo (tb. tip.); modelo; classe / vt. vi. escrever à máquina, datilografar

typewriter | tayp'raytə | s. máquina de escrever

typhoid | tay'foyd | s. tifo / a. tifóide

typhoon | tayfυn' | s. tufão

typical | ti'pikəl | a. típico

typing | tay'ping | s. datilografia

typist | tay'pist | s. datilógrafo (esp. profissional)

tyrannical | tira'nikəl | a. tirânico

tyrant | tay'rənt | s. tirano

tyre, tire | tay'ə | s. pneu, pneumático

tyro | tay'row | s. = tiro

U

ubiquitous | ŭubi'kwitəs | a. ubíquo, onipresente

U-boat | ŭu'bowt | s. submarino (alemão)

udder | â'də | s. úbere

ugliness | â'glines | s. fealdade, feiúra

ugly | â'glĭ | a. feio; ameaçador, perigoso; grave (ferimento)

ukelele | ŭukəley'lĭ | s. ukelele, guitarra havaiana

ulcer | âl'sə | s. úlcera

ulterior | âltı'rīə | a. ulterior; oculto, dissimulado

ultimate | âl'timit | a. definitivo, final; principal, básico

ultimatum | âltimey'təm | s. ultimato

umbrage | âm'brijʸ | s. ressentimento. -**to take u.** levar a mal, ofender-se com

umbrella | âmbre'lə | s. guarda-chuva; guarda-sol

umpire | âm'payə | s. árbitro, juiz / vt. vi. arbitrar

umpteen | âmp'tın | a. (gír.) muitos, uma porção

unabashed | ânəbaśt' | a. impassível, inabalável; despudorado, descarado

unabated | ânəbey'tid | a. constante; inquebrantável

unable | âney'bəl | a. incapaz, impossibilitado

unabridged | ânəbrijd' | a. completo, integral

unacceptable | ânəkep'təbəl | a. inaceitável, inadmissível

unaccompanied | ânəkâm'pənid | a. desacompanhado, sozinho

unaccountable | ânəkawn'təbəl | a. inexplicável, extraordinário; irresponsável

unaccustomed | ânəkâs'təmd | a. desacostumado, pouco habitual, desusado, insólito

unacknowledged | ânəkno'lijd | a. não reconhecido; sem resposta (carta)

unacquainted | ânəkweyn'tid | a. que não conhece. -**to be u. with** não estar familiarizado com (assunto etc.); não conhecer (pessoa) unadaptable | ânədap'təbəl | a. inadaptável

unadorned | ânədónd' | a. simples, desataviado

unadulterated | ânədâl'tǝreytid | a. não adulterado, autêntico

unaffected | ânəfek'tid | a. natural; não afetado; sincero

unafraid | ânəfreyd' | a. destemido, sem medo

unalloyed | ânəloyd' | a. sem liga; puro, sem mistura

unalterable | ânol'tǝrəbəl | a. inalterável; invariável

unanimity | ĭunəni'mitī | s. unanimidade

unanimous | ĭuna'niməs | a. unânime

unanswerable | ânʌn'sərəbəl | a. irrefutável, incontestável

unapproachable | ânəprow'sǝbəl | a. inacessível; sem rival

unarmed | ânʌmd' | a. desarmado; indefeso

unassailable | ânəsey'ləbəl | a. inexpugnável; irrefutável (argumento,etc.)

unassuming | ânəsĭu'ming | a. modesto, simples

unattainable | ânətey'nəbəl | a. inatingível

unattractive | ânətrak'tiv | a. pouco atraente

unauthorized | âno'ϑərayzd | a. não autorizado, ilícito

unavailing | ânəvey'ling | a. ineficaz, inútil

unavoidable | ânəvoy'dəbəl | a. inevitável

unaware | ânəwe'ə | a. inconsciente, não consciente de.-to be u. of ignorar

unawares | ânəwe'əz | adv. inesperadamente, de surpresa

unbalanced | ânba'lənst | a. desequilibrado

unbar | ânbʌ' | vt. destrancar, tirar a tranca

unbearable | ânbe'ərəbəl | a. insuportável, intolerável

unbeaten | ânbɪ'tən | a. insuperado; não vencido; não trilhado

(caminho)

unbecoming | ânbikâ'ming | a. impróprio; indecoroso

unbelief | ânbilíf' | s. incredulidade, descrença

unbelievable | ânbili'vəbəl | a. inacreditável

unbeliever | ânbili'və | a. descrente; (relig.) infiel

unbend | ânbend' | vt. distender, afrouxar; desenvergar, endireitar; desfranzir (testa) / vi. endireitar-se; perder o constrangimento

unbending | ânbend'ing | a. inflexível, inabalável; rígido

unbiassed | ânbay'əst | a. imparcial, desapaixonado

unblemished | ânble'miśt | a. imaculado, impoluto, ilibado

unborn | ânbón' | a. por nascer; futuro, vindouro

unbounded | ânbawn'did | a. ilimitado

unbreakable | ânbrey'kəbəl | a. inquebrável

unbridled | ânbray'dəld | a. desenfreado, infrene

unbusinesslike | ânbiz'nislayk | a. ineficaz, mal organizado

unbutton | ânbâ'tən | vt. desabotoar

uncalled | ânkóld' | a. não chamado, não convidado

uncalled-for | ânkóld'fó | a. desnecessário; inoportuno

uncanny | ânka'nī | a. misterioso, sobrenatural

uncared-for | ânke'ədfó | a. desamparado, desprezado

unceasing | ânsɪ'sing | a. incessante, contínuo

uncertain | ânsE'tən | a. duvidoso, incerto; variável

uncertainty | ânsE'təntī | s. dúvida, incerteza; ambiguidade

unchallengeable | ânsa'lənjəbəl | a. indisputável

unchangeable | ânśeyn'jəbəl | a. imutável

unchanged | ânśeynjd' | a. inalterado

uncharitable| ânša'ritəbəl |*a*. severo (no julgamento); pouco caritativo; inclemente

uncharted| ânšA'tid |*a*. não assinalado em mapa; inexplorado, desconhecido

unchecked| ânšekt' |*a*. irreprimido; incontrolado, inverificado

uncivilized| ânsi'vilayzd |*a*. não civilizado, selvagem

unclad| ânklad' |*a*. despido, nu

unclaimed| ânkleymd' |*a*. não reclamado, não procurado

uncle| ân'kəl |*s*. tio

unclothed| ânklowôd' |*a*. despido, sem roupa

uncoil| ânkoyl' |*vt*. desenrolar, desenroscar

uncombed| ânkowmd' |*a*. não cardado, não penteado (lã); desgrenhado, despenteado

uncomfortable| ânkâm'fətəbəl |*a*. incômodo, pouco confortável; desagradável (sensação); indisposto, adoentado; constrangido.

uncommited| ânkəmi'tid |*a*. não comprometido, neutro

uncommon| ânko'mən |*a*. incomum, raro; notável

uncomplaining| ânkəmpley'ning |*a*. que não se queixa, paciente

uncomplimentary| ânkompliment'tərĭ |*a*. pouco lisonjeiro, descortês, desfavorável

uncompromising| ânkom'prəmayzing |*a*. inflexível, intransigente

unconcealed| ânkənsıld' |*a*. indisfarçado, manifesto

unconcern| ânkənsEn' |*s*. desinteresse, indiferença

unconcerned| ânkənsEnd' |*a*. indiferente; despreocupado

unconditional| ânkəndi'šənəl |*a*. incondicional

uncogenital| ânkənjĭ'nĭəl |*a*. antipático; incompatível

unconnected| ânkənek'tid |*a*. não relacionado, não ligado; desconexo

unconquerable| ânkon'kərəbəl |*a*. inconquistável, invencível

unconscious| ânkon'šəs |*s*. o inconsciente / *a*. inconsciente; desacordado

unconsciousness| ânkon'šəsnes |*s*. inconsciência

unconsidered| ânkənsi'dəd |*a*. irrefletido, impensado

unconstitutional| ânkonstitu'šənəl |*a*. inconstitucional

uncontrollable| ânkəntrow'ləbəl |*a*. incontrolável; ingovernável

unconventional| ânkənven'šənəl |*a*. invulgar, singular, fora do comum

uncouple| ânkâ'pəl |*vt*. desacoplar, desengatar; soltar

uncouth| ânkvϑ' |*a*. estranho, insólito; desajeitado, canhestro; inculto, tosco

uncover| ânkâ'və |*vt*. descobrir; desvendar, revelar

unction| ânk'šən |*s*. unção

unctuous| ânk'tǐuəs |*a*. untuoso; (fig.) melífluo

uncultivated| ânkâltivey'tid |*a*. inculto

undamaged| ânda'mĭjd |*a*. sem avarias

undaunted| ândón'tid |*a*. destemido, indômito

undecided| ândisay'did |*a*. hesitante, indeciso, incerto

undemonstrative| ândimons'trətıv |*a*. reservado, pouco expansivo

undeniable| ândinay'əbəl |*a*. inegável

under| ân'də |*prep*. sob, debaixo de; no tempo de, sob o domínio de; com menos de (idade, altura); às ordens de, sob a direção de; sujeito a, submetido a. **-u. cover of** ao abrigo de; sob o pretexto de. **-to be u. age** ser menor de idade. **-to go u.** fracassar, malograr

undercarriage| ân'dəkarĭ ̆ ĭ |*s*. chassi (de automóvel); trem de pouso

underclothes| ân'dəklowôz |spl. roupa de baixo

undercurrent | ân'dəkârənt | s. corrente submarina; (fig.) corrente oculta (opinião)

underdeveloped| ândədive'ləpt | a. subdesenvolvido (país); pouco desenvolvido; (fot.) incompletamente revelado

underdog | ân'dədog | s. aquele que sai vencido; oprimido, pobre-diabo

underdone | ândədân' | a. malpassada (carne)

underestimate | ândəres'timeyt | vt. subestimar

undergarment| ândəgA'mənt |s. roupa de baixo

undergo | ândəgow' | vt. suportar, sofrer; submeter-se a (operação)

undergraduate | ândəgra'd'ueyt | s. estudante universitário; (fig.) noviço, pessoa bisonha

underground | ân'dəgrawnd | s. metrô / a. subterrâneo; (fig.) clandestino / adv. embaixo da terra; clandestinamente, em segredo

undergrowth | ân'dəgrowϑ | s. vegetação rasteira (de floresta); matagal

underhand | ân'dəhand | a. secreto, clandestino; desleal, ilícito

underlie | ândəlay' | vt. estar debaixo de; estar sujeito a; (fig.) motivar, inspirar

underline | ândəlayn' | vt. sublinhar

underling | ân'dəling | s. subordinado, subalterno

undermanned | ândəmand' | a. com tripulação reduzida (navio, avião etc.)

undermentioned | ândəmen'sɔnd | a. abaixo mencionado

undermine | ândəmayn' | vt. solapar, minar

underneath | ândənɪϑ' | adv. debaixo, por baixo / prep. debaixo de, por baixo de

undernourished| ândənA'riśt |a. subnutrido

underrate | ândəreyt' | vt. subestimar

undersell | ândəsel' | vt. vender mais barato que

undersigned | ândəsaynd' | a. subscrito, assinado, firmado

understand | ândəstand' | vt. entender, compreender; pensar, achar que, supor; entender de. -to give to u. dar a entender. -am I to u. that...? quer dizer que...?

understandable | ândəstan'dəbəl | a. compreensível, inteligível

understanding | ândəstan'ding | s. entendimento, compreensão, razão; interpretação; acordo. -on the u. that com a condição de que / a. compreensivo; inteligente, entendedor

understatement | ândəsteyt'mənt s. declaração ou narrativa incompleta ou sem ênfase. -it would be an u. to say seria dizer pouco

understood | ândəstud' | a. implícito, subentendido; sabido. -to make oneself u. fazer-se compreender

undertake | ândəteyk' | vt. empreender, tomar a seu cargo. -to u. to comprometer-se a

undertaker| ândətey'kə |s. agente funerário; empreiteiro

undertaking | ândətey'king | s. empresa, empreendimento

undertone | ândətown' | s. voz baixa. -in an u. a meia voz

undertow | ân'dətow | s. ressaca

undervalue | ândəva'lĩu | vt. subestimar, depreciar

underwear | ân'dəweə | s. roupa de baixo

underworld | ân'dəwɛld | s. infernos; antípodas; mundo do crime, submundo

undeserved | ândizɛvd' | a. imerecido, injusto

undesirable | ândizay'rəbəl | a. indesejável

undeterred | ândit̲Ed' | *a.* não amedrontado, não assustado, inalterável

undeveloped | ândive'ləpt | *a.* não desenvolvido; primitivo; não cultivado, não plantado

undeviating | ândı'vıeyting | *a.* constante, inalterável; firme, perseverante

undignified | ândig'nifayd | *a.* sem dignidade, indecoroso

undiluted | ândaylu'tid | *a.* puro

undisclosed | ândisklowzd' | *a.* não revelado, secreto

undismayed | ândismeyd' | *a.* impávido, intrépido; impassível

undisputed | ândispĭu'tid | *a.* incontestável, inconteste

undisturbed | ândistEbd' | *a.* calmo, tranqüilo, impassível

undivided | ândivay'did | *a.* todo, inteiro; ininterrupto

undo | ândv' | *vt.* desatar, desfazer; desafivelar; decifrar; anular; frustrar

undoing | ândv'ing | *s.* ruína, desgraça, perda; anulação

undonè | ândân' | *a.* desatado; desafivelado; decifrado; anulado; frustrado. **-to leave nothing u.** não deixar nada por fazer

undoubted | ândaw'tid | *a.* indubitável, inconteste

undress | ândres' | *vt.* despir / *vi.* despir-se

undue | ân'dĭu | *a.* excessivo, desmedido; não vencido (conta); indevido, impróprio; ilegítimo

undulating | ân'dĭuleyting | *a.* ondulante; levemente acidentado (terreno)

unduly | ân'dĭulī | *adv.* indevidamente

undying | ânday'ing | *a.* imortal, eterno

unearned | ânEnd' | *a.* imerecido

unearned income | ânEnd'inkəm | *s.* rendimentos (de juros etc.)

unearned increment | ânEnd'inkrimənt | *s.* valorização imobiliária

unearth | ânEϑ' | *vt.* desenterrar

unearthly | ânEϑ'lī | *a.* sobrenatural, extraterreno. **-at an u. hour** a desoras, a horas absurdas

uneasy | ânı'zī | *a.* ansioso, inquieto, apreensivo; pouco confortável; constrangido

uneatable | ânı'təbəl | *a.* intragável, incomível

unedifying | âne'difaying | *a.* pouco edificante, indecoroso

uneducated | âne'd̲ĭukeytid | *a.* sem instrução, iletrado, ignorante

unembarrassed | ânemba'rəst *a.* despreocupado, à vontade

unemotional | ânimow'śənəl | *s.* imparcial, desapaixonado; impassível, indiferente

unemployed | ânimemployd' | *s.a.* desempregado

unemployment | ânimploy'mənt | *s.* desemprego

unending | ânen'ding | *a.* interminável, sem fim

unendurable | ânendĭu'rəbəl | *a.* intolerável

unenterprising | ânen'təprayzing | *a.* sem iniciativa

unenviable | ânen'vīəbəl | *a.* que não desperta inveja

unequal | ânı'kwəl | *a.* desigual

unequivocal | ânikwi'vəkəl | *a.* inequívoco, claro, franco

unerring | ânE'ring | *a.* infalível; certeiro

uneven | ânı'vən | *a.* irregular, desnivelado; inconstante, variável

uneventful | ânivent'ful | *a.* monótono, sossegado

unexampled | ânegzAm'pəld | *a.* sem precedentes, nunca visto; incomparável

unexpected | ânekspek'tid | *a.* inesperado, imprevisto

unexpired | ânekspay'əd | *a.* vigente, não expirado

unexplored | âneksplód' | *a.* inexplorado, desconhecido

unfading | ânfey'ding | *a.* inapagável, imperecível, inalterável; que não desbota

unfailing | ânfey'ling | *a.* inabalável, inquebrantável; inesgotável; infalível; leal

unfair | ânfe'ə | *a.* injusto, desleal

unfaithful | ânfeyð'ful | *a.* infiel, desleal

unfaltering | ânfol'təring | *a.* que não vacila (esp. a voz); inabalável, resoluto

unfamiliar | ânfəmi'ľə | *a.* estranho, desconhecido

unfashionable | ânfa'šənəbəl | *a.* antiquado, fora de moda

unfasten | ânfa'sən | *vt.* desprender, desatar, afrouxar

unfathomable | ânfa'ðəməbəl | *a.* insondável; incomensurável

unfavourable | ânfey'vərəbəl | *a.* desfavorável, adverso

unfeigned | ânfeynd' | *a.* sincero, genuíno, verdadeiro

unfinished | ânfi'ništ | *a.* inacabado, incompleto

unfit | ânfit' | *a.* inadequado, impróprio; incapaz (saúde)

unflagging | ânfla'ging | *a.* persistente, inquebrantável

unflinching | ânflin'šing | *a.* inflexível, inabalável

unfold | ânfowld' | *vt.* desdobrar; revelar, expor (idéias)

unforeseen | ânfósin' | *a.* imprevisto

unforgettable | ânfəge'təbəl | *a.* inesquecível

unforgivable | ânfəgi'vəbəl | *a.* imperdoável

unfortunate | ânfó'šənit | *a.* infeliz, desventurado; lamentável; desastroso

unfortunately | ânfó'šənitlī | *adv.* adv. iimente

unfrequented | ânfrikwen'tid | *a.* pouco freqüentado

unfriendly | ânfren'dlī | *a.* pouco amigável, hostil

unfrock | ânfrok' | *vt.* (relig.) destituir, tirar a batina

unfurl | ânfɛl' | *vt.* desfraldar (bandeira); (náut.) desenrolar, desferrar (velas)

unfurnished | ânfɛ'ništ | *a.* desmobiliado

ungainly | ângeyn'lī | *a.* desajeitado, desgracioso

ungentlemanly | ânjen'təlmənlī | *a.* não cavalheiresco, descortês, impróprio de cavalheiro

ungodly | ângod'lī | *a.* ímpio; (coloq.) medonho, atroz

ungovernable | ângâ'vənəbəl | *a.* ingovernável; desenfreado

ungrateful | ângreyt'ful | *a.* ingrato, mal-agradecido

ungrudging | ângrâ'jing | *a.* de boa vontade

ungrudgingly | ângrâ'jinglī | *adv.* de boa vontade, de bom grado

unguarded | ângʌ'did | *a.* desprotegido, vulnerável

unhampered | ânham'pəd | *a.* livre, isento

unhappiness | ânha'pines | *s.* infelicidade

unhappy | ânha'pī | *a.* infeliz; funesto (acontecimento)

unharmed | ânhʌmd' | *a.* ileso, são e salvo

unhealthy | ânhel'ðī | *a.* insalubre, malsão; enfermiço

unheard | ânhɛd' | *a.* não ouvido, despercebido

unheard-of | ânhɛd'ov | *a.* inaudito, extraordinário, sem precedente

unheated | ânhɪ'tid | *a.* sem aquecimento

unheeded | ânhɪ'did | *a.* despercebido; desdenhado

unhesitating | ânhe'ziteyting | *a.* resoluto, decidido, imediato, instantâneo

unhindered | ânhin'dəd | *a.* livre, desimpedido

unhook | ânhuk' | *vt.* tirar do anzol, desenganchar

unhoped-for | ânhowpt'fó | *a.* inesperado

unhurt | ânhɛt' | *a.* ileso

unicorn | ľu'nikón | *s.* unicórnio

uniform| ĭu'nifóm |s. uniforme, farda / a. uniforme, idêntico, homogêneo

uniformity | ĭunifó'mitĭ | s. uniformidade

unify| ĭu'nifay | vt. unificar

unimaginable| ânima'jinǝbǝl |a. inimaginável, inconcebível

unimaginative | ânima'jinǝtiv | a. sem imaginação, prosaico

unimpaired | ânimpe'ǝd |a. inalterado, intacto

unimpeachable | ânimpı'šǝbǝl | a. irrepreensível, incontestável

unimportant | ânimpó'tǝnt | a. sem importância, insignificante; despretensioso

uninhabitable | âninha'bitǝbǝl | a. inabitável

uninhabited | âninha'bitid | a. desabitado; despovoado

uninjured | ânin'jǝd | a. ileso, sem ferimentos

unintelligent | âninte'lijǝnt | a. pouco inteligente

unintelligible | âninte'lijǝbǝl | a. ininteligível

unintentional | âninten'šǝnǝl |a. involuntário, não propositado

uninteresting | ânin'trǝsting | a. desinteressante

uninterrupted | ânintǝrâp'tid |a. ininterrupto

uninvited | âninvay'tid | a. sem ser convidado; não solicitado

uninviting | âninvay'ting | a. pouco convidativo, pouco atraente; desagradável

union ı ĭu'nĭǝn ı s. união; sindicato

unique | ĭunık' | a. único; excepcional, sem-par, inimitável, inigualável

unison | ĭu'nisǝn | s. harmonia, concórdia; (mús.) uníssono

unit| ĭu'nit |s. unidade

unite| ĭunayt' | vt. unir, unificar / vi. unir-se

unity | ĭu'nitĭ | s. unidade; união, concórdia

universal | ĭunive'sǝl | a. universal

universe| ĭu'nivɛs |s. universo

university | ĭunivɛ'sitĭ | s. universidade

unjust | ânjâst' | a. injusto

unjustifiable | ânjâstifay'ǝbǝl | a. injustificável

unkempt | ânkempt' | a. desgrenhado, despenteado

unkind| ânkaynd' |a. sem piedade, cruel; grosseiro, rude

unkindness| ânkaynd'nes |s. falta de bondade, dureza, crueldade; grosseria

unknown| ânnown' |s. desconhecido; incógnita / a. desconhecido, ignorado, estranho

unladylike | ânley'dīlayk | a. impróprio de uma senhora

unlawful | ânló'ful | a. ilegal

unleash | ânlıš' | vt. desatrelar (cão); desencadear

unleavened | ânle'vǝnd | a. não fermentado, ázimo

unless | ânles' | conj. a não ser que, a menos que

unlettered | ânle'tǝd | a. iletrado, analfabeto; sem letreiros, sem letras

unlike| ânlayk' |a. diferente, não parecido, distinto / prep. de maneira diferente, ao contrário de

unlikely| ânlayk'lĭ |a. pouco provável

unlimited | ânlı'mitid |a. ilimitado; indefinido

unload| ânlowd' | vt. descarregar

unloading | ânlow'ding | s. descarga

unlock | ânlok' | vt. abrir a fechadura de, destrancar; (fig.) revelar, descobrir

unlooked-for | ânlukt'fó | a. imprevisto, inesperado

unloose | ânlʊs' | vt. desatar, soltar

unluckily | ânlâ'kilĭ | adv. infelizmente

unlucky | ânlâ'kĭ | a. sem sorte, infeliz; desastroso; aziago, infausto

unmade| ânmeyd' | a. por fazer

unmanageable| ânma'niǰəbəl |*a.* ingovernável, incontrolável, difícil de manejar; intratável (pessoa)

unmannerly| ânma'nəlī |*a.* grosseiro, malcriado / *adv.* descortesmente

unmarried| ânma'rid |*a.* solteiro

unmask| ânmʌsk' | *vt.* desmascarar

unmerciful| ânmE'siful |*a.* desapiedado, cruel, desumano

unmerited| ânme'ritid |*a.* imerecido

unmindful| ânmaynd'ful |*a.* desatento, negligente. **-to be u. of** não prestar atenção a

unmistakable | ânmistey'kəbəl | *a.* inconfundível; claro, evidente, inequívoco

unmitigated | ânmitigey'tid | *a.* não moderado; irrestrito, implacável; rematado (patife etc.)

unmixed| ânmikst' |*a.* puro, sem mistura, não misturado

unmoved | ânmʋvd' | *a.* imóvel; indiferente, impassível

unnamed | ânneymd' | *a.* anônimo; não denominado

unnatural | ânna'šərəl |*a.* anormal; artificial, afetado

unnecessary | ânne'sisərī |*a.* desnecessário; inútil, supérfluo

unnerve | ânnEv' | *vt.* intimidar; abater, desencorajar

unnoticed | ânnow'tist | *a.* despercebido

unobjectionable | ânəbǰek'šənəbəl |*a.* irrepreensível

unobservant | ânəbzE'vənt | *a.* pouco observador

unobserved | ânəbzEvd' |*a.* despercebido, inobservado

unobstructed| ânəbstrʌk'tid |*a.* desobstruído, desimpedido, livre

unobstrusive | ânəbstru'siv | *a.* modesto, discreto, moderado

unobtainable | ânəbtey'nəbəl |*a.* que não se pode obter, que não se encontra à venda

unoccupied| âno'kĭupayd |*a.* desocupado; livre (lugar)

unofficial | ânəfi'šəl | *a.* não oficial, não confirmado

unopposed | ânəpowzd' | *a.* sem oposição

unorthodox | ânó'ϑədoks | *a.* pouco ortodoxo

unpack| ânpak' | *vt.* desfazer, desarrumar (malas); desembrulhar

unpaid | ânpeyd' | *a.* por pagar; não pago

unpalatable | ânpa'lətəbəl |*a.* intragável, de mau sabor

unparalleled | ânpa'rəleld |*a.* sem paralelo, incomparável

unpardonable| ânpʌ'dənəbəl |*a.* imperdoável

unperturbed | ânpətEbd' | *a.* tranqüilo, sereno, calmo

unpleasant | ânple'zənt | *a.* desagradável

unpleasantness | ânple'zəntnes | *s.* desagrado, repugnância, dissabor; desentendimento

unpolished | ânpo'liśt |*a.* não polido; fosco, mate; grosseiro; bruto (diamante)

unpopular| ânpo'pĭulə |*a.* impopular

unprecedented | ânpre'sidəntid | *a.* sem precedente, inaudito

unprejudiced | ânpre'judist | *a.* imparcial, sem preconceitos

unpremeditated | ânprime'diteytid | *a.* sem premeditação, espontâneo

unprepared | ânpripe'əd | *a.* despreparado; desprevenido

unprepossessing | ânpripəze'sing | *a.* pouco atraente '

unpretentious | ânpriten'śəs | *a.* despretensioso

unprincipled | ânprin'sipəld | *a.* sem princípios, inescrupuloso

unproductive | ânprədʌk'tiv | *a.* improdutivo

unprofessional | ânprəfe'śənəl | *a.* pouco profissional; impróprio ou indigno de uma profissão

unprofitable | ânpro'fitəbəl | *a.* não lucrativo; inútil

unpromising | ânpro'mising | *a.* que não promete, pouco auspicioso

unprotected | ânprətek'tid | *a.* desprotegido; desamparado

unpublished | ânpâ'blĭst | *a.* inédito

unpunctuality | ânpânktĭua'litĭ | *s.* impontualidade

unpunished | ânpâ'nĭst | *a.* impune, sem castigo

unqualified | ânkwo'lifayd | *a.* sem habilitações, inepto; irrestrito, incondicional

unquenchable | ânkwen'śəbəl | *a.* insaciável

unquestionable | ânkwes'śənəbəl | *a.* indiscutível

unravel | ânra'vəl | *vt.* desembaraçar

unreal | ânrĭ'əl | *a.* irreal, ilusório; fantástico

unreasonable | ânrĭ'zənəbəl | *a.* excessivo, desmedido; pouco racional

unrecognizable | ânrekəgnay'zəbəl | *a.* irreconhecível

unrecorded | ânrikó'did | *a.* não registrado

unrefined | ânrifaynd' | *a.* não refinado

unrelated | ânriley'tid | *a.* não relacionado; sem relação, sem parentesco

unrelenting | ânrilen'ting | *a.* inflexível, inexorável

unreliable | ânrilay'əbəl | *a.* que não merece confiança; precário, duvidoso; caprichoso, incerto, inconstante

unrelieved | ânrilĭvd' | *a.* não aliviado; não rendido, não substituído (sentinela etc.); não socorrido, desamparado

unremitting | ânrimi'ting | *a.* incessante; infatigável

unrepentant | ânripen'tənt | *a.* impenitente

unrequited | ânrikway'tid | *a.* não correspondido

unreserved | ânrizɛvd' | *a.* franco; irrestrito, ilimitado; não reservado (lugar, cadeira etc.)

unrest | ânrest' | *s.* inquietação, desassossego, agitação

unrestrained | ânristreynd' | *a.* desenfreado; não reprimido

unrestricted | ânristrik'tid | *a.* sem restrição

unrewarded | ânriwó'did | *a.* sem recompensa

unrighteous | ânray'śəs | *a.* injusto, iníquo

unripe | ânrayp' | *a.* não maduro, verde

unrivalled | ânray'vəld | *a.* sem rival, incomparável

unroll | ânrowl' | *vt.* desenrolar

unruffled | ânrâ'fəld | *a.* tranqüilo, sereno, calmo

unruly | ânrŭ'lĭ | *a.* ingovernável; intratável, rebelde

unsafe | ânseyf' | *a.* inseguro, perigoso

unsatisfactory | ânsatisfak'tərĭ | *a.* insatisfatório; insuficiente

unsavoury | ânsey'vərĭ | *a.* desagradável; repugnante; sem sabor, insípido

unsay | ânsey' | *vt.* desdizer, negar

unscathed | ânskeyðd' | *a.* ileso, são e salvo, incólume

unscrew | ânskrʊ' | *vt.* desaparafusar, desatarraxar

unscrupulous | ânskru'pĭuləs | *a.* inescrupuloso

unsealed | ânsĭld' | *a.* aberto, deslacrado

unseaworthy | ânsĭ'wɛðĭ | *a.* em mau estado (diz-se de embarcação); inavegável

unseemly | ânsĭm'lĭ | *a.* impróprio, inconveniente

unseen | ânsĭn' | *a.* despercebido, não visto

unselfish | ânsel'fĭś | *a.* generoso, abnegado, desinteressado

unserviceable | ânsɛ'visəbəl | *a.* imprestável, inútil

unsettle | ânse'təl | *vt.* perturbar, transtornar

unsettled | ânse'təld | *a.* desordenado; variável, inconstante; irresoluto; não saldado (dívida); despovoado

unshakable | ânŝey'kəbəl | *a.* inabalável, inflexível

unsheathe | ânŝíð' | *vt.* desembainhar

unsightly | ânsayt'lī | *a.* feio, horrível, de má aparência

unskilled | ânskild' | *a.* não especializado, não experimentado

unsociable | ânsow'ŝəbəl | *a.* insociável

unsophisticated | ânsəfis'tikeytid | *a.* não sofisticado, simples

unsound | ânsawnd' | *a.* doentio; falso, infundado; em mau estado, defeituoso; inquieto (sono); inseguro. **-u. of mind** alienado mental

unsparing | ânspe'əring | *a.* liberal, generoso, incansável

unspeakable | ânspɪ'kəbəl | *a.* indizível, inexprimível; inqualificável, péssimo

unstable | ânstey'bəl | *a.* instável, inseguro

unsteady | ânste'dī | *a.* instável, pouco firme, vacilante; libertino, desregrado

unstinted | ânstin'tid | *a:* generoso, amplo; ilimitado

unstressed | ânstrest' | *a.* não acentuado, átono

unsuccessful | ânsəkses'ful | *a.* malsucedido; infrutífero; malogrado, fracassado

unsuccessfully | ânsəkses'fulī | *adv.* inutilmente, em vão

unsuitability | ânsʋtəbi'litī | *s.* inconveniência; inadequação; inoportunidade

unsuitable | ânsʋ't əbəl | *a.* inconveniente; inadequado; inoportuno

unsullied | ânsâ'lid | *a.* limpo, imaculado

unsurpassable | ânsəpʌ'səbəl | *a.* inexcedível, insuperável

unsurpassed | ânsəpʌst' | *a.* não superado

unsuspecting | ânsəspek'ting | *a.* confiante, insuspeitoso

unswayed | ânsweyd' | *a.* não influenciado, não dirigido, indiferente

unsympathetic | ânsimpəðe'tik | *a.* antipático, pouco indulgente, indiferente

untamable | ântey'məbəl | *a.* indomável, indômito

untarnished | ântʌ'niŝt | *a.* imaculado, não empanado

untenable | ânte'nəbəl | *a.* insustentável

unthinkable | ânðin'kəbəl | *a.* inconcebível, impensável

unthinking | ânðin'king | *a.* irrefletido, inconsiderado

untidiness | ântay'dines | *s.* desalinho, desmazelo, falta de limpeza

untidy | ântay'dī | *a.* negligente, descuidado, desasseado

untie | ântay' | *vt.* desatar, desamarrar, afrouxar / *vi.* desatar-se, afrouxar-se

until | ântil' | *prep.* até / *conj.* até que

untilled | ântild' | *a.* não cultivado, não lavrado

untimely | ântaym'lī | *a.* prematuro, inoportuno, extemporâneo, intempestivo

untiring | ântay'əring | *a.* incansável, infatigável

unto | ân'tu | *prep*ₐ a; até a

untold | ântowld' | *a.* não revelado; incontável, incalculável

untouchable | ântâ'ŝəbəl | *s.* intocável, pária / *a.* intangível, intocável

untouched | ântâŝt' | *a.* não tocado; inalterado; são e salvo; não mencionado; (fig.) não comovido, indiferente

untoward | ântuwód' | *a.* relapso, rebelde; desagradável; desfavorável

untrained | ântreynd' | *a.* inexperiente; não treinado; não adestrado; indisciplinado

untrammelled | ântra'məld | a. livre, isento, desimpedido

untranslatable | ântranzley'təbəl | a. intraduzível

untried | ântrayd' | a. não testado; não provado; (jur.) não julgado

untrodden | ântro'dən | a. não trilhado, inexplorado

untroubled | ântrâ'bəld | a. sereno, tranqüilo

untrue | ântrv' | a. falso; inexato; desleal, infiel

untrustworthy | ântrâst'wεδĩ | a. indigno de confiança

untruth | ântrvθ' | s. inverdade, falsidade

untutored | ântĩv'təd | a. sem instrução, ignorante

untwist | ântwist' | vt. desenrolar, destorcer

unused | ânĩvzd' | a. não usado, novo; | ânivst' | não acostumado

unusual | ânĩv'juəl | a. invulgar; incomum; insólito, raro; notável, extraordinário

unutterable | ânâ'tərəbəl | a. indizível, inexprimível

unvarying | ânve'əring | a. invariável, constante

unveil | ânveyl' | vt. tirar o véu a, descobrir, revelar; inaugurar (estátua)

unversed | ânvεst' | a. não versado em, inexperiente

unwarranted | ânwo'rəntid | a. não garantido; injustificado

unwary | ânwe'əri | a. desprevenido, incauto

unwavering | ânwey'vəring | a. resoluto, determinado, firme

unwearied | ânwi'ərid | a. incansável

unwelcome | ânwel'kəm | a. mal recebido; importuno, inoportuno

unwell | ânwel' | a. indisposto

unwholesome | ânhowl'səm | a. pernicioso, nocivo, insalubre

unwieldy | ânwil'dĩ | a. de difícil manejo, pesado, desajeitado

unwilling | ânwi'ling | a. relutante, de má vontade

unwillingly | ânwi'linglĩ | adv. de má vontade, com relutância

unwillingness | ânwi'lingnes | s. relutância

unwind | ânwaynd' | vt. desenrolar

unwise | ânwayz' | a. imprudente

unwitting | ânwi'ting | a. inconsciente, involuntário

unwittingly | ânwi'tinglĩ | adv. inadvertidamente, inconscientemente

unwonted | ânwown'tid | a. desusado, inabitual

unworkable | ânwε'kəbəl | a. impraticável

unworldly | ânwεld'lĩ | a. não mundano; desinteressado; ingênuo

unworthiness | ânwε'δines | s. indignidade, baixeza; falta de merecimento

unworthy | ânwε'δĩ | a. indigno, desprezível; torpe, vil, sem valor

unwrap | ânrap' | vt. desembrulhar

unwritten | ânri'tən | a. não escrito; oral, tradicional

unwritten law | ânri'tənló | s. direito consuetudinário

unyielding | ânĩil'ding | a. tenaz, persistente; inflexível, obstinado

unyoke | ânĩowk' | vt. tirar da canga; (fig.) libertar (de opressão)

up | âp | s. subida; prosperidade. -the ups and downs os altos e baixos, as vicissitudes / adv. prep. para cima, acima, em cima; de pé, em pé; acabado, terminado; todo, completamente. -u. to até a. -u. there lá em cima. -to be u. against (coloq.) enfrentar; ser confrontado com. -to be u. to estar até; estar à altura de. -to get u. levantar-se. -to keep u. manter; conservar-se. -what's u.? o que há? -it is u. to you depende de você

up-and-coming| âpandkə'ming |*a.* (coloq.) empreendedor, ativo, alerta

upbraid| âpbreyd' |*vt.* censurar, repreender

upheaval | âphɪ'vəl | *s.* sublevação; (fig.)transformação social

uphold | âphowld' | *vt.* manter, sustentar; defender, preservar

upholsterer| âphowl'stərə |*s.* estofador

upholstery | âphowl'stərī | *s.* estofo, tapeçaria

upkeep| âpkɪp' |*s.* sustento; manutenção, conservação (de prédio etc.)

uplands | âp'ləndz | *spl.* regiões montanhosas

uplift | âplift' | *s.* elevação, soerguimento; ascensão social / *vt.* levantar; enaltecer

upon | âpon' |*prep.* sobre

upper | â'pə | *a.* superior, mais alto

upper case | â'pəkeyz | *s.* (tip.) caixa alta

Upper House | â'pəhaws | *s.* Câmara Alta, *House of Lords*

upright| âp'rayt |*s.* verticalidade / *a.* vertical; honrado, justo / *adv.* verticalmente

upright piano | âp'raytpīa'now | *s.* piano de armário

uprising | âp'raysing |*s.* insurreição, revolta

uproar | âp'ró | *s.* tumulto, ruído; alvoroço

uproarious | âp'rórīəs | *a.* ruidoso; tumultuoso

uproot| âprʊt' |*vt.* erradicar, extirpar; (fig.) extinguir

upset| âpset' |*s.* transtorno, perturbação/ *a.* aflito, transtornado / *vt.* transtornar, perturbar; depor; indispor; desgostar a; fazer mal a (enfermidade)

upshot | âp'śot | *s.* desfecho, resultado final, fim

upside | âpsayd' | *s.* parte superior. -**u. down** de cabeça para baixo; em confusão

upstairs| âpste'əz |*s.* andar superior / *adv.* para cima, em cima,

no andar superior

upstart | âp'stʌt | *s.* novo-rico, arrivista

upstream | âp'strim |*adv.* rio acima, contra a corrente

uptake | âp'teyk |*s.* levantamento; compreensão, entendimento

up-to-date | âp'tudeyt | *a.* moderno, recente, atualizado

upwards | âp'wɛdz | *adv.* para cima

uranium| ɪʊrey'nīəm |*s.* urânio

urban | ɛ'bən | *a.* urbano, citadino

urbane | ɛbeyn' |*a.* polido, cortês

urchin | ɛ'śin | *s.* garoto, pirralho, moleque

urge| ɛĵ' |*s.* impeto, impulso, ânsia / *vt.* incitar; insistir em

urgency | ɛ'jənsī |*s.* urgência

urgent | ɛ'jənt |*a.* urgente

urinal | ɪʊray'nəl | *s.* urinol; mictório

urinate | ɪʊ'rineyt | *vi.* urinar

urn | ɛn' |*s.* urna (esp. funerária)

us | âs | *pron.* nos. **-for u.** para nós. **-with u.** conosco

usage| ɪʊ'ziĵ |*s.* uso

use | ɪʊs' | *s.* uso; emprego. **-it is no u.** não adianta, é inútil, não dá certo. **-to make u. of** fazer uso de; tirar proveito de / *vt.* usar; empregar; utilizar, servir-se de. **-to u. up** consumir, gastar, esgotar / *vi.* costumar

used | ɪʊzd' | *a.* usado; de segunda mão. **-to be u. to** estar acostumado a. **-to get u. to** acostumar-se a

useful | ɪʊs'ful | *a.* útil

usefulness | ɪʊs'fulnes |*s.* utilidade; proveito

useless| ɪʊs'les |*a.* inútil; imprestável

uselessness | ɪʊs'lesnes |*s.* inutilidade

user | ɪʊ'zə |*s.* usuário

usher | â'śə | *s.* (teat.) indicador de lugar; porteiro, introdutor / *vt.* conduzir; indicar o lugar; introduzir, anunciar

usual | ĭu'juəl | *a.* usual, habitual. **-as u.** como de costume

usually | ĭu'juəlĭ | *adv.* geralmente, normalmente

usurer | ĭu'jərə | *s.* usurário, agiota

usurp | ĭuzεp' | *vt.* usurpar

usurper | ĭuzε'pə | *s.* usurpador

usury | ĭu'jərĭ | *s.* usura, agiotagem

utensil | ĭuten'sĭl | *s.* utensílio

utility | ĭuti'litĭ | *s.* utilidade

utilization | ĭutilayzey'śən | *s.* utilização, emprego

utilize | ĭu'tilayz | *vt.* utilizar, empregar

utmost | ât'mowst | *s.* o máximo possível. **-to the u.** ao máximo, ao extremo / *a.* maior; extremo; máximo

Utopian | ĭutow'pĭən | *a.* utópico, quimérico

utter | â'tə | *a.* total, completo; absoluto / *vt.* proferir, pronunciar; pôr em circulação (moeda falsa)

utterance | â'tərəns | *s.* expressão, declaração; elocução, dom da palavra

utterly | â'təlĭ | *adv.* completamente, totalmente

uttermost | ât'əmowst | *a.* = *utmost*

V

vacancy | vey'kənsĭ | *s.* vaga; vacância; vacuidade mental; apatia; ociosidade

vacant | vey'kənt | *a.* livre (lugar, cadeira); vago (quarto etc.); desocupado, ocioso; idiotizado

vacate | vəkeyt' | *vt.* abandonar, deixar

vacation | vəkey'śən | *s.* férias

vaccination | vaksiney'śən | *s.* vacinação

vacillate | va'sileyt | *vi.* vacilar, hesitar

vacuum | va'kĭuəm | *s.* vácuo / *a.* vácuo, relativo a vácuo

vacuum cleaner | va'kĭuəmklĭnə | *s.* aspirador de pó

vagabond | va'gəbond | *s. a.* vadio, vagabundo

vagary | vey'gərĭ | *s.* capricho, excentricidade

vagrancy | vey'grənsĭ | *s.* vadiagem, vagabundagem; digressão

vague | veyg' | *a.* vago, indefinido

vagueness | veyg'nes | *s.* incerteza, imprecisão

vain | veyn' | *a.* fútil, vão; vaidoso, presunçoso. **-in v.** em vão

vainglorious | veyngló'rĭəs | *a.* jactancioso, vaidoso

vale | veyl' | *s.* vale (entre montes)

valedictory | validik'tərĭ | *s.* discurso de despedida / *a.* de despedida

valet | va'ley va'lit | *s.* criado, criado particular

valiant | va'liənt | *a.* valente

valid | va'lid | *a.* válido (argumento etc.)

validity | vəli'ditĭ | *s.* validez; eficácia

valise | vəlĭz' | *s.* valise, maleta

valley | va'lĭ | *s.* vale

valorous | va'lərəs | *a.* valoroso, intrépido

valour, valor | va'lə | *s.* valentia, coragem

valuable | va'lĭubəl | *s.* (ger. *pl.*) objetos de valor / *a.* valioso, precioso

valuation | valĭuey'śən | *s.* avaliação

value | va'lĭu | *s.* valor; significação / *vt*. avaliar, estimar; ter em apreço

valued | va'lĬud |*a*. avaliado, estimado; apreciado

valve | valv' | *s*. válvula

vampire | vam'páyǝ | *s*. vampiro

van | van' | *s*. pequeno caminhão coberto; (ferrov.) vagão bagageiro; vanguarda, frente

vandal | van'dǝl | *s*. vândalo

vane | veyn' | *s*. cata-vento, ventoinha; pá de hélice; vela de moinho

vanguard | van'gAd | *s*. vanguarda

vanilla | vǝni'lǝ | *s*. baunilha

vanish | va'niś | *vi*. desaparecer; dissipar-se

vanity | va'nitĭ | *s*. vaidade

vanity case | va'nitĭkeys |*s*. estojo de cosméticos, *nécessaire*

vanquish | van'kwiś | *vt*. vencer, conquistar, subjugar

vantage | van'tij | *s*. vantagem, superioridade

vantage-ground | van'tiỹgrawnd |*s*. posição vantajosa

vapid | va'pid | *a*. insípido

vapour, vapor | vey'pǝ |*s*. vapor, exalação, emanação

variability | veǝrĭǝbi'litĭ |*s*. variabilidade

variable | ve'ǝrĭǝbǝl | *a*. variável, incerto

variance | ve'ǝrĭǝns | *s*. variação; divergência; desacordo. **-to be at v.** discordar, divergir

variant | ve'ǝrĭǝnt | *s*. *a*. varianťe

variation | veǝrĭey'śǝn | *s*. variação, mudança, diferença

varicose | va'rikowz | *a*. varicoso

varicose veins | va'rikowzveynz | *spl*. varizes

varied | ve'ǝrid | *a*. variado; variegado; diversificado; modificado, mudado

variety | vǝray'ǝtĭ | *s*. variedade; sortimento (mercadorias); variação; (teat.) variedades

various | ve'ǝrĭǝs | *a*. variado; (*pl*.) vários

varnish | vA'niś |*s*. verniz / *vt*. en-

vernizar

vary | ve'ǝrĭ | *vt*. variar; alterar, modificar / *vi*. variar

varying | ve'ǝrĭing | *a*. diferente, vário, inconstante

vase | vAz' | *s*. vaso

vaseline | va'sǝlin | *s*. vaselina

vassal | va'sǝl | *s*. vassalo

vast | vAst' | *a*. vasto

vastness | vAst'nes | *s*. vastidão

vat | vat' | *s*. cuba, dorna; tonel

Vatican | va'ţikǝn | *s*. Vaticano

vault | vólt' | *s*. abóbada; casa-forte, cofre; salto (esp. com vara) / *vi*. saltar (esp. com vara)

vaulting-horse | vólt'inghós | *s*. cavalo-de-pau (de ginástica)

vaunt | vónt' | *s*. jactância, gabolice / *vt*. jactar-se

vaunted | vónt'id | *a*. gabado, apregoado

veal | vil' | *s*. vitela (carne)

veer | vĭ'ǝ |*s*. (náut.) guinada / *vi*. guinar, virar

vegetable | ve'ǰitǝbǝl | *s*. legume; verdura / *a*. vegetal

vegetable garden | ve'ǰitǝbǝl-gA'dǝn | *s*. horta

vegetable marrow | ve'ǰitǝbǝl-ma'row | *s*. abóbora-pêra

vegetarian | veǰite'ǝrĭǝn | *s*. *a*. vegetariano

vegetate | ve'ǰiţeyt | *vi*. vegetar

vegetation | veǰiţey'śǝn | *s*. vegetação

vehemence | vĭ'imǝns | *s*. veemência

vehement | vĭ'imǝnt | *a*. veemente

vehicle | vĭ'ikǝl |*s*. veículo

veil | veyl' | *s*. véu / *vt*. velar, cobrir com véu; disfarçar, ocultar

veiled | veyld' | *a*. velado, disfarçado (ameaça etc.)

vein | veyn' | *s*. veia; veio, filão

vellum | ve'lǝm | *s*. pergaminho (papel); velino

velocity | vǝlo'sitĭ | *s*. velocidade

velvet | vel'vit | *s*. veludo

vendetta | vende'tǝ | *s*. vendeta

vendor | ven'dǝ | *s*. vendedor (ger. ambulante)

veneer | vənı'ə | s. madeira chapeada; (fig.) camada superficial, aparência

venerable | ve'nərəbəl | a. venerável

venerate | ve'nəreyt | vt. venerar

veneration | venərey'śən | s. veneração

venereal | vənı'rīəl | a. venéreo

Venetian | vənı'śən | a. veneziano

venetian blind | vənı'śənblaynd | s. veneziana, persiana

Venezuelan | venizve'lən | a. venezuelano

vengeance | ven'ǰəns | s. vingança. -to take v. on vingar-se de. -with a v. furiosamente, violentamente; com exagero

vengeful | venǰ'ful | a. vingativo

venial | vı'nĭəl | a. venial

venison | ve'nisən | s. carne de veado, cervo, gamo etc.

venom | ve'nəm | s. peçonha; (fig.) rancor, maldade

venomous | ve'nəməs | a. peçonhento; (fig.) maldoso

vent | vent' | s. abertura, respiradouro; suspiro (de barril etc.). -to give v. to dar largas a / vt. dar saída a; exprimir, manifestar; desabafar

ventilate | ven'tileyt | vt. ventilar, arejar

ventilation | ventiley'śən | s. ventilação

ventilator | ven'tileytə | s. ventilador

ventriloquist | ventri'ləkwist | s. ventríloquo

venture | ven'śə | s. empreendimento / vt. aventurar, arriscar / vi. atrever-se

venturesome | ven'śəsəm | a. arrojado, atrevido

venue | ve'nĭu | s. (jur.) jurisdição, foro; local, ponto de reunião (esp. para jogos esportivos)

veracity | vərə'sitī | s. veracidade

veranda, verandah | vəran'də | s. varanda, terraço, balcão

verb | vēb' | s. verbo

verbal | vē'bəl | a. verbal, oral, de viva voz; literal (tradução)

verbatim | vēbey'tim' | adv. textualmente, palavra por palavra

verbiage | vē'biǰ | s. palavrório, verbiagem

verbose | vēbows' | a. verboso, palavroso, prolixo

verdant | vē'dənt | a. verdejante, viçoso; inexperiente, ingênuo, crédulo

verdict | vē'dikt | s. veredicto; decisão, sentença

verge | vēǰ' | s. beira, borda, margem. -on the v. of à beira de, prestes a / vi. orlar, bordar; tender; aproximar-se de

verger | vē'ǰə | s. sacristão

verify | ve'rifay | vt. verificar, comprovar; (jur.) afirmar sob juramento, provar

veritable | ve'ritəbəl | a. verdadeiro, autêntico

vermin | vē'min | spl. insetos, praga, animais nocivos

verminous | vē'minəs | a. nocivo, repugnante, infestado de parasitos

vermouth | vē'məϑ | s. vermute

vernacular | vənə'kĭulə | s. a. vernáculo

versatile | vē'sətayl | a. que tem muitos talentos, de talento versátil; jeitoso

versatility | vēsəti'litī | s. diversidade de talentos; versatilidade

verse | vēs' | s. verso; poesia; estrofe, estância; (bíbl.) versículo

versed | vēst' | a. versado, entendido, perito

versify | vē'sifay | vt. vi. versejar, versificar

version | vē'jən | s. versão

versus | vē'səs | prep. contra, versus

vertical | vē'tikəl | a. vertical

vertigo | vē'tigow | s. vertigem

verve | vēv' | s. verve, vivacidade, estro

very | ve'rī | a. verdadeiro; mesmo, próprio; exato / adv. muito; muitíssimo; extremamente;

realmente. **-v. much** muitíssi-
mo. **-v. often** freqüentemente,
muitas vezes

vespers | ves'pəz | *spl.* vésperas

vessel | ve'səl | *s.* vaso, recipiente,
vasilha; navio, barco; aerona-
ve; vaso sangüíneo

vest | vest' | *s.* colete; camiseta de
malha (lã etc.) / *vt.* investir,
outorgar

vested | ves'tid | *a.* **-v. interests,
rights etc.** bens ou direitos
adquiridos

vestibule | ves'tibʾul | *s.* vestíbu-
lo; saguão

vestige | ves'tij | *s.* vestígio

vestment | vest'mənt | *s.* vesti-
menta; (*pl.*) paramentos

vest-pocket | vest'pokit | *a.* de
bolso de colete, em miniatura

vestry | ves'trĩ | *s.* sacristia

vet | vet' | *s.* (coloq.) veterinário

veteran | ve'tərən | *s. a.* veterano

veterinarian | vet'rinəri̯ən | *s.* ve-
terinário

veterinary | vet'rinrĩ | *a.* veteriná-
ria (ciência)

veto | vī'tow | *s.* veto / *vt.* vetar

vex | veks' | *vt.* irritar, exasperar;
agastar, vexar

vexation | veksey'śən | *s.* irrita-
ção, aborrecimento

vexed | vekst' | *a.* perturbado,
aflito; aborrecido, irritado;
muito debatido (assunto)

via | vay'ə | *prep.* via, por

viable | vay'əbəl | *a.* praticável,
viável; capaz de viver

viaduct | vay'ədâkt | *s.* viaduto

vibrate | vaybreyt' | *vi.* vibrar

vibration | vaybrey'śən | *s.* vibra-
ção

vicar | vi'kə | *s.* vigário, pároco;
pastor (de paróquia anglicana)

vicarage | vi'kərij | *s.* vicariato
(residência ou benefício)

vice | vays' | *s.* vício; ̌vice- (prefi-
xo)

vice, vise | vays' | *s.* (mec.) torno,
morsa de bancada

vice-chancellor | vayss̆ʌn'sələ | *s.*

vice-chanceler, reitor de uni-
versidade

viceroy | vaysroy' | *s.* vice-rei

vicinity | visi'nitĩ | *s.* proximida-
des, arredores

vicious | vi'śəs | *a.* vicioso, depra-
vado; selvagem, brutal; trai-
çoeiro, perverso

viciousness | vi'śəsnes | *s.* depra-
vação, corrupção; ferocidade,
selvageria

vicissitude | visi'sitı̌ud | *s.* vicissi-
tude

victim | vik'tim | *s.* vítima

victimization | viktimayzey'śən |
s. ato de vitimar, enganar, de-
fraudar; ato de punir etc.

victor | vik'tə | *s.* vencedor

Victorian | viktó'rĩən | *a.* vito-
riano

victorious | viktó'rĩəs | *a.* vitorio-
so, triunfante

victory | vik'tərĩ | *s.* vitória

victual | vik'təl | *s.* (ger. *pl.*) víve-
res, provisões / *vt.* aprovisio-
nar, abastecer

vie | vay' | *vi.* rivalizar com

view | vĩu | *s.* vista, visão; pano-
rama; aspecto; opinião. **-at first
v.** à primeira vista. **-in v. of** por
causa de, devido a, em virtude
de, em consideração a. **-on v.**
em exposição. **-to have in v.** ter
em vista. **-with a v. to** com o fim
de. **-to come into v.** surgir,
tornar-se visível / *vt.* contem-
plar, observar, ver, examinar;
considerar

viewer | vĩu'ə | *s.* observador; ex-
pectador; telespectador

viewfinder | vĩu'fayndə | *s.* visor
(de câmara fotográfica etc.)

viewpoint | vĩu'poynt | *s.* ponto
de vista

vigil | vi'ǰil | *s.* vigília

vigilance | vi'ǰiləns | *s.* vigilância,
cuidado

vigilant | vi'ǰilənt | *a.* vigilante

vigorous | vi'gərəs | *a.* vigoroso,
enérgico

vigour, vigor | vi'gə | *s.* vigor,
energia

vile | vayl' | *a.* vil, infame, abominável

vileness | veyl'nes | *s.* vileza, baixeza

vilification | vilifikey'śən | *s.* difamação, calúnia

vilify | vi'lifay | *vt.* difamar, caluniar

villa | vi'lə | *s.* casa elegante, casa de campo

village | vi'liǰ | *s.* povoado, aldeia

villager | vi'liǰə | *s.* aldeão

villain | vi'lən | *s.* velhaco, patife; infame

villainous | vi'lənəs | *a.* criminoso; infame, vil

villainy | vi'lənī | *s.* vilania, vileza, baixeza

vim | vim' | *s.* (coloq.) vigor, energia

vindicate | vin'dikeyt | *vt.* justificar

vindication | vindikey'śən | *s.* justificação, defesa

vindictive | vindik'tiv | *a.* vingativo

vindictiveness | vindik'tivnes | *s.* caráter vingativo, espírito de vingança

vine | vayn' | *s.* vinha, vide, videira

vine grower | vayn'growə | *s.* viticultor, vinicultor

vinegar | vi'nigə | *s.* vinagre

vineyard | vi'nĭəd | *s.* vinha, parreiral

vintage | vin'tiǰ | *s.* vindima; vinho de alta qualidade; (fig.) coisa feita em certo ano etc. / *a.* de alta qualidade

violate | vay'əleyt | *vt.* violar, transgredir; invadir

violation | vayəley'śən | *s.* violação, transgressão; invasão

violence | vay'ələns | *s.* violência

violent | vay'ələnt | *a.* violento

violet | vay'əlit | *s.* violeta

violin | vay'əlin | *s.* violino

violinist | vayəli'nist | *s.* violinista

viper | vay'pə | *s.* víbora

virago | virA'gow | *s.* virago, megera, mulher turbulenta

virgin | vE'ǰiŋ | *s.* virgem

virginity | vEǰi'nitī | *s.* virgindade

virile | vi'rayl | *a.* viril

virility | viri'litī | *s.* virilidade

virtual | vE'tĭuəl | *a.* virtual, potencial

virtually | vE'tĭuəlī | *adv.* virtualmente

virtue | vE'tĭu | *s.* virtude. -by v. of em virtude de, em razão de

virtuous | vE'tĭuəs | *a.* virtuoso

virulence | vi'rĭuləns | *s.* virulência

virulent | vi'rĭulənt | *a.* virulento

virus | vay'rəs | *s.* vírus

visa | vī'zə | *s.* visto (em passaporte etc.)

visage | vi'ziǰ | *s.* rosto, cara, fisionomia

viscount | vay'kawnt | *s.* visconde

vise | vays' | *s.* (EUA) = *vice, vise*

visibility | vizibi'litī | *s.* visibilidade

visible | vi'zibəl | *a.* visível; evidente; aparente

vision | vi'ǰən | *s.* visão, vista; aparição, visão

visionary | vi'ǰənərī | *s. a.* visionário

visit | vi'zit | *s.* visita. -to pay a v. fazer uma visita. -to return a v. pagar uma visita / *vt.* visitar, viajar por

visitor | vi'zitə | *s.* visita, visitante; inspetor

vista | vis'tə | *s.* vista, perspectiva, panorama

visual | vi'zĭuəl | *a.* visual

visualize | vi'zĭuəlayz | *vt.* visualizar, imaginar

vital | vay'təl | *a.* vital, enérgico; básico, fundamental

vitality | vayta'litī | *s.* vitalidade, vigor

vitals | vay'talz | *spl.* órgãos vitais (coração, pulmões etc.)

vitamin | vi'təmin | *s.* vitamina

vitiate | vi'śīeyt | *vt.* viciar, corromper, arruinar

vituperation | vitĭupərey'śən | *s.* vitupério, insulto, injúria

vivacious| vivey'śǝs |*a*. vivo, animado, vivaz, ativo

vivacity| viva'sitī |*s*. vivacidade, animação

vivid | vi'vid |*a*. vivo, vívido; intenso, brilhante

vividness| vi'vidnes |*s*. vivacidade, intensidade

vivify | vi'vifay |*vt*. vivificar, estimular, animar

vivisection | vivisek'śǝn |*s*. vivissecção

vixen| vik'sǝn |*s*. fêmea da raposa; mulher briguenta

vocabulary| vǝka'bĭulǝrī |*s*. vocabulário

vocal | vow'kǝl |*a*. vocal; oral, verbal; sonoro; eloqüente, veemente

vocation | vowkey'śǝn |*s*. vocação, pendor; profissão

vocational| vowkey'śǝnǝl |*a*. vocacional; profissional

vociferate | vǝsi'fǝreyt |*vi*. vociferar, bradar, clamar

vociferous | vǝsi'fǝrǝs |*a*. vociferante, clamoroso, barulhento

vogue | vowg' |*s*. voga, moda

voice | voys' |*s*. voz / *vt*. exprimir, enunciar

voiced | voyst' |*a*. sonoro, dotado de voz; enunciado verbalmente

voiceless| voys'les |*a*. destituído de voz; surdo (consoante)

void | voyd' |*s*. vazio, vácuo /*a*. vazio, oco; desabitado, vago. -v. of desprovido de. -to make v. anular

volatile | vo'lǝtayl |*a*. volátil; volúvel, caprichoso; passageiro, transitório

volcanic | volka'nik |*a*. vulcânico

volcano | volkey'now |*s*. vulcão

volition | voli'śǝn |*s*. volição; vontade; decisão

volley | vo'lī |*s*. (mil.) descarga, salva, rajada; saraivada (de insultos etc.)

volley-ball| vo'lībol |*s*. voleibol

volt | vowlt' |*s*. volt

voltage| vowlt'iǰ |*s*. voltagem

voluble | vo'ɲubǝl |*a*. loquaz, palrador

volume | vo'lɲʋm |*s*. volume (tb. bibliot.); tomo; intensidade, volume (som)

voluminous | vǝlĭʋ'minǝs |*a*. volumoso

voluntary | vo'lǝntǝrī |*a*. voluntário

volunteer | volǝntī'ǝ |*s*. voluntário / *vt*. oferecer ou apresentar espontaneamente /*vi*. oferecer-se como voluntário

voluptuous | vǝlâp'tĭuǝs |*a*. voluptuoso, sensual

vomit | vo'mit |*s*. vômito / *vt. vi*. vomitar

voracious | vǝrey'śǝs |*a*. voraz; ávido, insaciável

vortex | vó'teks |*s*. vórtice, turbilhão, voragem

vote | vowt' |*s*. voto, sufrágio / *vt*. votar, aprovar / *vi*. votar, optar

voter | vow'tǝ |*s*. eleitor, votante

vouch| vawś' |*vt*. atestar, certificar; afirmar, garantir /*vi*.-to v. for responder por

voucher | vaw'śǝ |*s*. fiador, testemunha; comprovante, recibo, vale; talão

vouchsafe| vawśseyf' |*vt*. conceder, outorgar, conferir

vow | vaw' |*s*. promessa solene, voto / *vi*. fazer voto ou juramento

vowel | vaw'ǝl |*s*. vogal

voyage | voy'iǰ |*s*. viagem (marítima ou aérea, esp. longa); narrativa de viagem /*vt*. viajar por, percorrer / *vi*. viajar

voyager | voy'iǰǝ |*s*. viajante, navegante

vulgar| vâl'gǝ |*a*. vulgar, grosseiro, mal-educado; obsceno. -the v. era a era cristã. -the v. tongue o vernáculo

vulgarity | vâlga'ritī |*s*. vulgaridade; grosseria

Vulgate | vâl'git |*s*. (bíbl.) Vulgata

vulnerability | vâlnərəbi'litĭ | *s.* vulnerabilidade
vulnerable | vâl'nərəbəl | *a.*

vulnerável
vulture | vâl'šə | *s.* abutre; urubu

W

wad | wod' | *s.* chumaço, enchimento; bucha (de arma de fogo, de cartucho)

wadding | wo'ding | *s.* chumaço; algodão em rama; material para fazer buchas

waddle | wo'dəl | *vi.* bambolear, gingar

wade | weyd' | *vi.* passar a vau, vadear; avançar com dificuldade (na água, neve etc.)

wafer | wey'fə | *s.* obreia; hóstia (tb. ecles.); folhado, filhó

waft | woft' | *vt.* impelir ou levar suavemente (pelo ar ou pela água) / *vi.* flutuar; soprar (brisa)

wag | wag' | *s.* abano, meneio; gracejador, galhofeiro; gazeteiro. **-to play the w.** fazer gazeta

wage | weyj' | *s.* salário, ordenado; (fig.) recompensa / *vt.* empreender, manter (guerra)

wager | wey'jə | *s.* aposta / *vt.* apostar

waggle | wa'gəl | *vt.* menear, sacudir / *vi.* sacudir-se, agitar-se

wagon, waggon | wa'gən | *s.* carroça, carroção; (ferrov.) vagão de mercadorias

waif | weyf' | *s.* coisa abandonada; animal extraviado; criança abandonada; pária

wail | weyl' | *s.* lamento; gemido; queixa / *vi.* lamentar-se, gemer; queixar-se

waist | weyst' | *s.* cintura

waistband | weyst'band | *s.* cós

waistcoat | weyst'kowt | *s.* colete

waistline | weyst'layn | *s.* contorno da cintura (esp. como índice de gordura ou obesidade)

wait | weyt' | *s.* demora. **-to lie in w.** esperar de emboscada / *vt.* esperar, aguardar; servir (como garçom) / *vi.* esperar; estar à espera; servir (à mesa). **-to w. up** esperar acordado (a volta de alguém)

waiter | wey'tə | *s.* garçom

waiting | wey'ting | *s.* espera; ato de servir à mesa. **-in w.** à espera; de serviço (na corte) / *a.* que espera

waiting-room | wey'tingrʊm | *s.* sala de espera

waitress | wey'trəs | *s.* garçonete

waive | weyv' | *vt.* renunciar, desistir de; pôr de lado

wake | weyk' | *s.* esteira (de navio ou avião); vigília, velório. **-to bring in its w.** trazer como conseqüência. **-in the w. of** na esteira (dos acontecimentos) / *vt.* acordar, despertar; velar (defunto)

wakeful | weyk'ful | *a.* desperto, acordado; vigilante

waken | wey'kən | *vt.* acordar, despertar

walk | wók' | *s.* passeio; modo de andar; distância (a ser percorrida); esfera de atividade; posição social. **-to take a w.** dar um passeio. **-w. of life** posição social; profissão / *vi.*

andar a pé; caminhar; perambular. -to w. in entrar. -to w. into topar com. -to w. up subir. -to w. up to dirigir-se para. -to w. off ir-se embora. -to w. off with levar consigo; ganhar

walker | wó'kə | s. andarilho, caminhante; armação dotada de rodas (usada por criança começando a andar)

wall | wól' | s. parede; muro; muralha. -to drive to the w. encostar à parede. -to go to the w. ser derrotado; falir / vt. emparedar; murar

wallet | wo'lit | s. carteira (de dinheiro)

wallflower | wól'flawə | s. (bot.) goivo amarelo

wallop | wó'ləp | s. (gír.) pancada forte / vt. dar pancada forte; surrar

wallow | wo'low | vi. chafurdar; espojar-se; rolar; jogar (navio). -to w. in nadar em (dinheiro etc.)

walnut | wól'nət | s. noz; nogueira

walrus | wól'rəs | s. (zool.) morsa

waltz | wols' | s. valsa / vi. valsar

wan | won' | a. pálido; doentio

wand | wond' | s. varinha (tb. de condão); batuta; bastão (esp. como símbolo de autoridade)

wander | won'də | vi. errar, vagar, vaguear; perder-se; divagar; devanear; delirar

wanderer | won'dərə | s. peregrino, viandante, nômade

wandering | won'dəring | s. viagem, peregrinação; vaguear / a. errante

wandering Jew won'dəringĵu | s. judeu errante

wane | weyn' | vi. declinar, minguar (lua). -to be on the w. estar no quarto minguante

want | wont' | s. necessidade;

escassez; penúria, miséria. -for w. of por falta de / vt. necessitar; precisar; desejar; procurar (alguém); exigir, requerer / vi. passar necessidade

wanted | won'tid | a. precisa-se (coisa ou emprego); procurado (pela polícia)

wanting | won'ting | a. deficiente; desprovido de. -to be w. faltar

wanton | won'tən | s. mulher devassa / a. licencioso, devasso; caprichoso, frívolo; brincalhão; extravagante; injustificado, arbitrário

war | wó' | s. guerra / vi. guerrear, fazer guerra. -to w. on combater, lutar

warble | wó'bəl | s. gorjeio, trinado, chilreio / vi. gorjear, trinar, chilrear; cantar; murmurar (riacho)

ward | wód' | s. enfermaria; tutela; tutelado; distrito; bairro / vt. -to w. off proteger contra; desviar, aparar (golpe)

warden | wó'dən | s. diretor, administrador (de escola, hospital etc.); guarda; guardião; curador; (EUA) diretor de prisão

warder | wó'də | s. carcereiro; (ant.) sentinela, vigia

wardrobe | wód'rowb | s. guarda-roupa

wardroom | wód'rum | s. (náut.) sala dos oficiais (em navio de guerra)

ware | we'ə | s. utensílios de uso diário; (pl.) mercaḑorias, produtos

warehouse | we'əhaws | s. armazém, depósito

warfare | wó'feə | s. guerra; operações militares

wariness | we'ərines | s. cuidado, prudência

warlike | wó'layk | a. militar; bélico, belicoso

warm | wóm' | a. morno, tépido; quente; (fig.) afetuoso, caloroso, generoso. **-to be w.** sentir calor; fazer calor / *vt.* aquecer, esquentar; excitar

warmonger | wó'mângə | *s.* fomentador de guerras

warmth | wómϑ' | *s.* calor, tepidez; (fig.) ardor, fervor; cordialidade

warn | wón' | *vt.* prevenir, advertir, avisar

warning | wó'ning | *s.* advertência, aviso. **-to take w.** acautelar-se. **-without w.** inesperadamente, sem avisar

War Office | wóo'fis | *s.* ministério do Exército

warp | wóp' | *s.* (tecl.) urdidura; empenamento, empeno; aberração mental / *vt.* empenar, arquear-se (madeira)

warrant | wo'rənt | *s.* autorização, permissão; garantia; ordem de pagamento; ordem de prisão / *vt.* garantir, assegurar; justificar; comprovar

warranty | wo'rəntī | *s.* garantia

warren | wo'rən | *s.* parque de caça; terreno onde se criam coelhos; (fig.) região densamente populada

warrior | wo'riə | *s.* guerreiro

warship | wó'ṣip | *s.* navio de guerra

wart | wót' | *s.* verruga

wary | we'ərī | *a.* precavido, vigilante, cuidadoso, cauteloso

wash | woṣ' | *s.* lavagem; roupa lavada; água servida; marulho; esteira (de navio ou avião); camada de tinta; loção ou cosmético / *vt.* lavar; banhar. **-to w. away** ou **off** remover lavando (manchas etc.) / *vi*; lavar-se

washable | wo'ṣəbəl | *a.* lavável

wash-basin | woṣ'beysən | *s.* bacia de lavar as mãos; pia

washboard | woṣ'bóəd | *s.* tábua de lavar roupa

washer | wo'ṣə | *s.* (mec.) arruela

washerwoman | wo'ṣəwəmən | *s.* lavadeira

washing | wo'ṣing | *s.* lavagem; (*pl.*) água servida

washing-day | wo'ṣingdey | *s.* dia de lavar roupa

washing-machine | wo'ṣingməṣín' | *s.* máquina de lavar roupa

washing-powder | wo'ṣingpawdə | *s.* sabão em pó

wash-out | woṣ'awt | *s.* (gír.) fracasso, fiasco

wasp | wosp' | *s.* vespa

wastage | weys'tij | *s.* desperdício; perda; desgaste

waste | weyst' | *s.* desperdício, perda; estrago; desgaste; refugo, resíduo; ermo, despovoado; terra abandonada ou devastada. **-to go** ou **to run to w.** perder-se / *a.* inculto, baldio (terreno); despovoado; devastado; residual; excedente, supérfluo; de despejo, de refugo / *vt.* devastar; desgastar; desperdiçar / *vi.* enfraquecer; desgastar-se. **-to w. away** consumir-se, acabar-se

wasteful | weyst'ful | *a.* gastador, perdulário, desperdiçador

wastefulness | weyst'fulnes | *s.* prodigalidade, esbanjamento

waste land | weyst'land | *s.* terra não cultivada

waste paper | weyst'peypə | *s.* papéis sem valor

waste-paper basket | weyst'peypəbas'kit | *s.* cesta de papéis

waste-pipe | weyst'payp | *s.* cano de descarga, cano de esgoto

wastrel | weys'trəl | *s.* pródigo, esbanjador, gastador; pessoa imprestável, vagabundo

watch | woṣ' | *s.* relógio (de pulso ou bolso); vigia, vigilância; (náut.) quarto. **-on the w.** de vigia; (náut.) de quarto. **-on the w. for** à espreita de. **-to keep w.** ficar de guarda, vigiar. **-to keep w. over** zelar por

/ *vt.* vigiar; guardar; observar; ficar alerta; ver, assistir a (jogos etc.) / *vi.* velar; guardar, vigiar; olhar, observar. -to w. out ter cuidado. -to w. out for estar à espreita; precaver-se contra. -to w. over velar por; zelar por

watchful | woš'ful | *a.* vigilante, alerta; atento

watch maker | woš'meykə | *s.* relojoeiro

watchman | woš'mən | *s.* guarda, vigia

watch-tower | woš'tawə | *s.* torre de vigia

watchword | woš'wɛd | *s.* lema, divisa

water | wó'tə | *s.* água; (*pl.*) águas minerais. -by w. por mar, de navio / *a.* aquático; de água; fluvial; marítimo / *vt.* dar de beber a; regar / *vi.* encher-se d'água (olhos, boca); tomar água, aguar. -to make one's mouth w. dar água na boca

water-blister | wó'təblistə | *s.* bolha d'água

water-bottle | wó'təbotəl | *s.* garrafa de água (à mesa); cantil

water-closet | wó'təklozit | *s.* latrina, W.C.

water-colour | wó'təkâlə | *s.* aquarela

watercress | wó'təkres | *s.* agrião

water-drinker | wó'tədrinkə | *s.* abstêmio total

waterfall | wó'təfól | *s.* queda-d'água, catarata, cachoeira

waterfront | wó'təfrənt | *s.* zona portuária

water-hog | wó'təhog | *s.* capivara

water-ice | wó'təays | *s.* sorvete (feito com água e não com leite)

watering | wó'təring | *s.* rega, ato de regar

watering-can | wó'təringkan | *s.* regador

watering-place | wó'təringpleys | *s.* bebedouro, aguada (de animais); balneário (estação de águas ou praia)

waterlogged | wó'təlogd | *a.* encharcada (madeira); inundado (navio); pantanoso, inundado (terreno)

water-melon | wó'təmələn | *s.* melancia

waterproof | wó'təpruf | *s.* impermeável / *a.* à prova d'água / *vt.* impermeabilizar

watershed | wó'təšed | *s.* divisor de águas; bacia hidrográfica (de rio ou lago)

waterspout | wó'təspawt | *s.* bica; calha (de telhado); tromba-d'água

water-tank | wó'tətank | *s.* cisterna

water-way | wó'təwey | *s.* via navegável, curso d'água, canal

waterworks | wó'təwɛks | *s.* estação elevatória; usina hidráulica

watery | wó'tərī | *a.* aquático, das águas; encharcado; úmido; aguado, insípido; diluído

watt | wot' | *s.* (eletr.) watt, vátio

wattle | wo'təl | *s.* trançado de varas; latada / *vt.* cercar ou cobrir com trançado de varas

wave | weyv' | *s.* onda; ondulação; aceno / *vt.* agitar; fazer tremular; acenar, fazer sinal. -to w. aside não aceitar, não admitir / *vi.* ondear, ondular; acenar; tremular (bandeira)

waver | wey'və | *s.* hesitação, vacilação / *vi.* hesitar, vacilar

wavy | wey'vī | *a.* ondulante; ondulado (cabelo)

wax | waks | *s.* cera (de abelha, de carnaúba etc.); cerume / *a.* de cera / *vt.* encerar / *vi.* crescer, ficar cheia (lua); tornar-se, ficar. -to w. old envelhecer

way | wey' | *s.* caminho; direção; distância; modo, maneira; hábito, costume; meio, modo, saída; método; modo de proceder. **-w. in** entrada. **-w. out** saída. **-w. through** passagem. **-which w.?** por onde?; de que modo? **-across the w.** do outro lado. **-by the w.** a propósito. **-by w. of** por, por via de; para servir de. **-in a w.** de certo modo. **-in no w.** de modo algum. **-to be in the w.** incomodar, estorvar. **-on the w. (to)** a caminho (de). **-out of the w.** fora do caminho, isolado; extraordinário. **-to give w.** dar de si, ceder; abrir caminho; dar lugar; retroceder, retirar-se. **-to have a w. with** saber manejar (alguém), ter um jeito especial. **-to have one's w.** impor a sua vontade. **-to make w.** abrir caminho. **-to lead the w.** ir na frente. **-to loose one's w.** errar o caminho, perder-se. **-to meet half w.** fazer concessões. **-to mend one's ways** emendar-se, corrigir-se

wayfarer | wey'feərə | *s.* caminhante, transeunte, viandante

waylay | wey'ley | *vt.* assaltar, atacar (de emboscada); armar emboscada ou cilada a, atocaiar

wayside | wey'sayd | *s.* margem de estrada

wayward | wey'wəd | *a.* caprichoso, obstinado, desobediente

we | wi wi (enfático) | *pron.* nós

weak | wik' | *a.* fraco, débil; delicado, frágil

weaken | wi'kən | *vt.* enfraquecer, debilitar / *vi.* enfraquecer; diminuir, debilitar-se; afrouxar

weakening | wi'kəning | *s.* enfraquecimento; diminuição; afrouxamento

wealth | welϑ' | *s.* riqueza, fortuna; abundância

wealthy | wel'ϑĩ | *a.* rico, opulento; abundante

wean | win' | *vt.* desmamar; afastar. **-to w. someone from** curar alguém de (mau hábito)

weapon | we'pən | *s.* arma

wear | we'ə | *s.* uso; artigos de vestuário; desgaste. **-to get a lot of w. out of** durar muito. **-to be the worse for w.** estar gasto pelo uso. **-w. and tear** desgaste / *vt.* usar, vestir, trajar. **-to w. down** desgastar; vencer (resistência). **-to w. off** desaparecer; diminuir gradualmente. **-to w. out** gastar, consumir; desgastar; cansar / *vi.* gastar-se; desgastar-se. **-to w. on** passar gradualmente (tempo). **-to w. well** durar muito

weariness | wi'ərines | *s.* cansaço, fadiga; aborrecimento

wearing | we'əring | *a.* esgotante, fatigante, cansativo; sujeito a atrito

wearing apparel | we'əringəpa'rəl | *s.* roupas, vestuário

wearisome | wi'ərisəm | *a.* enfadonho, tedioso, maçante

weary | wi'ərī | *a.* cansado, fatigado; enfastiado, farto / *vt.* cansar, aborrecer

weasel | wi'zəl | *s.* doninha, fuinha

weather | we'ðə | *s.* tempo, condições meteorológicas / *vt.* expor às intempéries; a'güentar (tempestade); suportar (provação) / *vi.* suportar a ação do tempo

weathercock | we'ðəkok | *s.* cata-vento, ventoinha

weakling | wik'ling | *s.* pessoa ou animal débil, doentio

weak-minded | wikmayn'did | *a.* vacilante, irresoluto

weakness | wik'nes | *s.* fraqueza, debilidade. **-to have a w. for** ter um fraco por

weather-glass | we'ðəglas | *s.* barômetro

weave | wiv' | *vt.* tecer, trançar / *vi.* serpentear; avançar dando voltas

weaver | wɪ'və | *s.* tecelão

weaving | wɪ'ving | *s.* tecelagem

web | web' | *s.* teia; tecido; trama

web-footed | web'futid | *a.* palmípede

wed | wed' | *vt.* casar, unir em casamento / *vi.* casar-se. -wedded to apegado, aferrado

wedding | we'ding | *s.* casamento, núpcias; aniversário de casamento / *a.* de casamento, nupcial

wedge | weǰ' | *s.* cunha / *vt.* pôr cunha em; calçar com cunha / *vi.* introduzir-se à força

wedlock | wed'lok | *s.* casamento, vida conjugal

Wednesday | wenz'dey | *s.* quarta-feira

wee | wɪ' | *a.* pequenino. -a w. bit um pouquinho

weed | wid' | *s.* erva daninha; (*pl.*) traje de luto; fumo (faixa negra). -the soothing w. tabaco, fumo. -the w. (gír.) maconha / *vt.* arrancar (erva daninha)

weedy | wɪ'dī | *a.* cheio de ervas daninhas; (coloq.) franzino, mirrado

week | wɪk' | *s.* semana. -in a w.'s time dentro de uma semana, daqui a uma semana

weekday | wɪk'dey | *s.* dia útil

week-end | wɪk'end | *s.* fim-de-semana

weekly | wɪk'lī | *s.* semanário, hebdomadário (jornal) / *a.* semanal

weep | wɪp' | *vi.* chorar

weeping | wɪ'ping | *s.* choro, pranto / *a.* choroso; gotejante; de ramos pendentes (árvore)

weigh | wey' | *vt.* pesar; considerar, examinar; medir (pala-

vras); levantar (âncora). -to w. up considerar. -to w. down sobrecarregar, oprimir, acabrunhar / *vi.* pesar; ter importância ou influência; (náut.) levantar ferro

weighing-machine | wey'ingməśɪn' | *s.* balança para grandes pesos

weight | weyt' | *s.* peso; importância. -by w. por peso. -to carry w. ser influente, ser importante. -to put on w. engordar / *vi.* pôr peso em; sobrecarregar, oprimir

weighty | wey'tī | *a.* pesado; grave; importante, influente

weir | wɪ'ə | *s.* represa, açude, barragem

weird | wɪ'əd | *a.* misterioso, sobrenatural; sinistro; fatídico; (coloq.) esquisito

welcome | wel'kəm | *s.* recepção, boa acolhida / *a.* bem-vindo / *vt.* dar as boas-vindas a; acolher. -to be w. to ter plena liberdade para; estar à disposição. -you are w. (EUA) de nada, não há de quê

weld | weld' | *s.* solda / *vt.* soldar; (fig.) unir, consolidar

welfare | wel'feə | *s.* bem-estar, prosperidade, felicidade; saúde

welfare work | wel'feəwɛk' | *s.* obra de beneficência

well | wel' | *s.* poço; manancial / *a.* bom; conveniente, apropriado / *adv.* bem; muito; muito bem. -as w. também, igualmente. -as w. as tão bem como; tanto como, tanto quanto. -w. up in muito versado em. -it's all very w. to say é bom de dizer / *interj.* ora!, então!, bem!

well-done | wel'dân | *a.* (cul.) bem passado (bife, carne)

well-off | wel'of | *a.* em boa situação, próspero

well-to-do | wel'tʊdʊ | *a.* próspero, abastado

Welsh | welś' | s.a. galês
Welshman | welś'mən | s. galês
welter | wel'tə | s. confusão, conflito, tumulto
wench | wenś' | s. moça; (ant.) prostituta
wend | wend' | vt.vi. -to w. one's way seguir o seu caminho
werewolf | wɪ'əwulf | s. lobisomem
west | west' | s. oeste, ocidente
western | wes'tən | a. ocidental
wet | wet' | a. úmido, molhado. -to be w. behind the ears ser imaturo ou inexperiente / vt. umedecer, molhar
whack | wak' | s. pancada pesada e sonora / vt. bater
whale | weyl' | s. baleia
whale-boat | weyl'bowt | s. baleeira (pequena embarcação de duas proas)
whaler | wey'lə | s. navio baleeiro; pescador de baleias
whaling | wey'ling | s. pesca de baleia
wharf | wóf' | s. cais
what | wot' | pron. o que; que. -w. for? para quê? / pron. interrog. que?, o que?, qual? / interj. como?!, o quê?!
whatever | wote'və | pron. qualquer que; por mais... que
whatnot | wot'not | s. prateleira para pequenos objetos. -and w. e não sei mais quê, e outras coisas mais
wheal | wɪl' | s. vergão, marca empolada na pele
wheat | wɪt' | s. trigo
wheedle | wɪ'dəl | vt. persuadir (com lisonjas), engabelar, engambelar
wheel | wɪl' | s. roda; volante, direção de automóvel / vt. fazer rodar / vi. voltar-se, virar-se
wheelwright | wɪl'rayt | s. carpinteiro de carros, carpinteiro de rodas
wheeze | wɪz' | s. respiração ruidosa; chiado / vi. respirar com dificuldade
when | wen | s. momento, ocasião, data / adv. pron. quando
whence | wens | adv. de onde, donde
whenever | wene'və | adv. sempre que, todas as vezes que
where | we'ə | adv. onde
whereabouts | we'ərəbawts | s. paradeiro / adv. onde; por onde; mais ou menos em que lugar
whereas | weəraz' | conj. enquanto, enquanto que, ao passo que; visto que
whereby | weəbay' | adv. pelo que, por meio de que
wherefore | we'əfó | conj. por conseguinte, por isso
wherein | we'əin | adv. em que; onde; no que; no qual / conj. donde, e por isso, e daí
whereupon | we'ərəpon | conj. em consequência do que, depois do que, e então
wherever | weəre'və | adv. onde quer que
whet | wet' | vt. afiar, amolar; estimular; abrir (apetite)
whether | we'ðə | conj. se
which | wiš' | pron. que, qual
whiff | wif' | s. aragem, sopro (de fumaça ou cheiro); baforada / vt. soprar; tirar baforadas
while | wayl' | s. espaço de tempo. -all the w. todo o tempo. -a w. ago ainda agora, há pouco. -once in a w. de vez em quando. -to be worth one's w. valer a pena / conj. enquanto; ao passo que, embora / vt. -to w. away passar o tempo agradavelmente
whim | wim' | s. capricho, veneta, extravagância
whimper | wim'pə | s. lamúria / vi. choramingar, lamuriar
whimpering | wim'pəring | a. lamuriento
whimsical | wim'zikəl | a. capri-

choso, extravagante, excêntrico

whine | wayn' | s. queixume, lamento; ganido (de cão) / vt.vi. queixar-se, choramingar; ganir (o cão)

whining | way'ning | a. lamentoso, queixoso, lamuriento

whinny | wi'nĩ | vi. relinchar, rinchar

whip | wip' | s. chicote; chicotada / vt. chicotear, açoitar; bater (creme). **-to w. out** ou **off** arrancar, puxar, tirar, sacar. **-to w. up** estimular, excitar; (coloq.) fazer às pressas

whir | WE' | s. zunido / vi. zunir

whirl | wEl' | s. rodopio; turbilhão, remoinho; tumulto. **-to be in a w.** andar numa roda-viva; estar confuso / vi. rodopiar, girar

whirlpool | wEl'pʊl | s. remoinho, voragem, sorvedouro

whirlwind | wEl'wind | s. turbilhão, remoinho de vento

whisk | wisk' | vt. escovar, espanar (poeira); bater (ovos). **-to w. away** ou **off** tirar com movimento rápido (pó etc.); enxotar (moscas)

whisker | wis'kə | s. fio de barba; bigode (de gato, rato etc.); (pl.) suíças, costeletas

whisky, whiskey | whis'kĩ | s. uísque

whisper | wis'pə | s. murmúrio, sussurro / vt. vi. murmurar, sussurrar

whist | wist' | s. uíste (jogo)

whistle | wi'səl | s. assobio; apito; silvo. **-to pay for one's w.** pagar caro por um capricho / vt. vi. assobiar; apitar (com instrumento)

white | wayt' | s. branco; brancura; clara de ovo; branco do olho / a. branco; pálido; incolor. **-to bleed someone w.** tirar até o último tostão de alguém

whiten | way'tən | vt. branquear

whiteness | wayt'nes | s. brancura, alvura

whitewash | wayt'woś | s. cal / vt. caiar

whither | wi'ðə | adv. para onde, aonde

Whitsunday | witsân'dey | s. domingo de Pentecostes

Whitsuntide | wit'sântayd | s. Pentecostes

whittle | wi'təl | vt. aparar, desbastar, tirar lascas de (madeira); entalhar. **-to w. away** diminuir, reduzir gradualmente

whiz, whizz | wiz' | vi. zunir, zumbir

who | hʊ' | pron. quem; que, o qual

whoever | hʊe'və | pron. quem; quem quer que

whole | howl' | s. todo, totalidade; conjunto. **-on the w.** geralmente, em geral, em conjunto; em termos gerais. **-as a w.** em conjunto / a. todo, inteiro; intacto, são. **-made out of w. cloth** (EUA) fictício, imaginário, inventado

whole-hearted | howlhA'tid | a. sincero, devotado; sério; com todo o fervor

wholesale | howl'seyl | s. venda por atacado; (fig.) em massa / a. por atacado, atacadista; (fig.) indiscriminado, em grande escala

wholesome | howl'səm | a. saudável, salubre, salutar, sadio

wholly | how'li | adv. completamente, inteiramente

whom | hʊm' | pron. interrog. quem? / pron. rel. quem, que

whooping cough | hʊ'pingkof | s. coqueluche

whore | hó' | s. prostituta

whose | hʊz' | pron. cujo, de quem, do qual

why | way | s. porquê / adv. por que, por que razão / interj. ora!, ora essa!, bem!, pois bem!

wick | wik' | s. mecha, torcida; pavio (de vela)

wicked | wi'kid | *a.* mau, perverso, malvado

wickedness | wi'kidnes | *s.* maldade, perversidade

wicker | wi'kə | *s.* vime, trabalho de vime / *a.* de vime

wide | wayd' | *a.* largo, de largura; extenso, espaçoso, amplo; escancarado; variado. **-to be a metre w.** ter um metro de largura. **-w. open** aberto de par em par. **-far and w.** por toda a parte. **-w. of the mark** muito afastado do alvo

widen | way'dən | *vt.* alargar; aumentar, ampliar (conhecimentos etc.)

widespread | wayd'spred | *a.* extenso, generalizado, difundido; corrente, comum

widow | wi'dow | *s.* viúva

widower | wi'dowə | *s.* viúvo

widowhood | wi'dowhud | *s.* viuvez

widow's weeds | wi'dowzwɪdz | *spl.* traje de luto (de viúva)

width | widϑ' | *s.* largura

wield | wɪld' | *vt.* brandir, empunhar; exercer (autoridade)

wife | wayf' | *s.* esposa, mulher. **-old wives' tale** conto da carochinha, superstição

wig | wig' | *s.* cabeleira postiça, peruca

wiggle | wi'gəl | *s.* meneio / *vt.* menear, colear; sacudir / *vi.* sacudir-se

wild | wayld' | *a.* selvagem; bravo, bravio; silvestre; agreste, inculto; agressivo, turbulento (jovem); extravagante, insensato (idéia, plano); precipitado (decisão); perturbado, meio louco (aparência); desenfreado (paixão); tempestuoso, rigoroso (clima, tempo); feroz, furioso (grito). **-to be w. about** ser louco por. **-to get w.** enfurecer-se. **-to run w.** tornar-se selvagem, bravio. **-w. and wooly** selvagem, bárbaro

wilderness | wil'dənes | *s.* deserto, sertão, região inculta; imensidão

wildness | wayld'nes | *s.* estado selvagem; incultura; selvageria, ferocidade; arrebatamento, impetuosidade, ardor

wild shot | wayld'śot | *s.* tiro a esmo, tiro ao acaso

wile | wayl' | *s.* (ger. *pl.*) ardis, manhas, artimanhas, astúcias, estratagemas

wilful | wil'ful | *a.* intencional, premeditado, deliberado; obstinado, teimoso, cabeçudo

wiliness | way'lines | *s.* astúcia

will | wil' | *s.* vontade; arbítrio; (jur.) testamento. **-at his own sweet w.** a seu bel-prazer. **-at w.** à vontade; à discrição. **-with a w.** com entusiasmo, resolutamente. **-against one's w.** a contragosto / *vt.* querer; legar, deixar / *v. aux. do futuro*

willing | wi'ling | *a.* disposto, pronto, inclinado; de bom grado, com boa vontade

willingly | wi'linglĩ | *adv.* de boa vontade

willingness | wi'lingnes | *s.* boa vontade, disposição

will-o'-the-wisp | wi'ləδəwisp | *s.* fogo-fátuo

willow | wi'low | *s.* salgueiro

willowy | wi'lowĩ | *a.* esguio, esbelto; cheio de salgueiros

willy-nilly | wi'lini'lĩ | *adv.* quer queira quer não

wilt | wilt' | *vi.* murchar, definhar; enfraquecer, decair

wily | way'lĩ | *a.* manhoso, matreiro, astuto, ardiloso

win | win' | *s.* (desp.) vitória / *vt.* ganhar, vencer, conquistar / *vi.* ganhar, vencer, triunfar; prevalecer; cativar; alcançar, atingir

wince | wins' | *vi.* estremecer; recuar, encolher-se

winch | winś' | *s.* guincho / *vt.* suspender, içar com guincho

wind | wind' | s. vento; fôlego; (pl.) instrumentos de sopro. **-against the w.** contra o vento. **-down the w.** com o vento. **-in the teeth of the w.** contra o vento. **-to get w. of** vir a saber de. **-there is something in the w.** há qualquer coisa no ar. **-to have the w. up** alarmar-se, assustar-se / vt. arejar, ventilar

wind | waynd' | vt. enrolar; encher (carretel); dar corda a (relógio etc.). **-to w. up** enrolar; dar corda a (relógio etc.); (coloq.) concluir, finalizar. **-to w. off** desenrolar / vi. serpentear; dar voltas; (fig.) insinuar-se

windfall | wind'fól | s. sorte inesperada; coisa caída do céu; fruta ou árvore derrubada pelo vento

winding | wayn'ding | s. volta, curva, meandro / a. tortuoso, serpeante; cheio de meandros (rio)

winding sheet | wayn'dingsít | s. mortalha

winding staircase | wayn'dingsteakeys | s. escada de caracol

windmill | wind'mil | s. moinho de vento. **-to fight** ou **to tilt at w.** combater contra moinhos de vento

window | win'dow | s. janela; vitrine; guichê

window-ledge | win'dowlej | s. peitoril de janela

window-shopping | win'dowsóping | s. ato de olhar vitrines (sem comprar)

window-slit | win'dowslit | s. fresta

windpipe | wind'payp | s. traquéia

windscreen | wind'skrın | s. pára-brisa

windward | wind'wəd | s. barlavento

windy | win'dĩ | a. ventoso; verboso, loquaz; empolado

wine | wayn' | s. vinho

wineskin | wayn'skin | s. odre

wing | wing' | s. asa; (mil.) flanco, ala; brigada aérea, esquadrilha; (teat.) bastidores, coxias; (polít.) ala (esquerda, direita). **-on the w.** voando, em pleno vôo. **-to take w.** levantar vôo. **-under one's w.** sob a proteção de alguém / vi. voar

wing commander | wing'kəmАndə | s. comandante de esquadrilha

wing-spread | wing'spred | s. envergadura

wink | wink' | s. piscar de olhos; abrir e fechar de olhos. **-to give a w.** piscar o olho. **-to take forty winks** (coloq.) tirar uma pestana. **-to not sleep a w.** não pregar olho / vi. piscar o olho (para). **-to w. at** fazer vista grossa a, fingir ignorar

winner | wi'nə | s. vencedor

winning | wi'ning | s. vitória / a. vencedor, vitorioso; cativante, encantador

winnow | wi'now | vt. joeirar; peneirar (trigo). **-to w. out** ou **away** separar, escolher

winter | win'tə | s. inverno / a. de inverno / vt. passar o inverno, invernar

wintry | win'trĩ | a. invernal, frio e ventoso; gelado (cumprimento, sorriso)

wipe | wayp' | vt. limpar; esfregar; enxugar, secar. **-to w. off** limpar ou remover esfregando. **-to w. out** eliminar, extirpar. **-to w. the floor with someone** (gír.) infligir derrota humilhante a alguém

wire | way' | s. arame; fio elétrico; telegrama. **-to pull the wires** exercer influência secretamente / vt. ligar com arame; instalar fios elétricos; telegrafar a

wireless | way'əles | s. radiotelegrafia, radiotelefonia; rádio; receptor de rádio / vt. vi. radiografar, transmitir pelo rádio

wireless set | way'əlesset | s. receptor de rádio, rádio

wirepuller | way'əpulə | s. político que exerce influência secretamente

wiry | way'ərī | a. de arame; duro, rijo (como arame)

wisdom | wiz'dəm | s. sabedoria; bom-senso, sensatez

wise | wayz' | s. modo, maneira, forma. **-in no w.** de maneira alguma. **-in some w.** de algum modo / a. sábio; sensato, prudente; esperto, astuto. **-as w. as before** (coloq.) sem ter aprendido nada. **-to be** ou **to get w. to** (gír.) ser ou tornar-se sabedor de

wisecrack | wayz'krak | s. piada / vi. fazer piada ou observação espirituosa

wise guy | wayz'gay | s. (coloq.) sabichão

wise man | wayz'mən | s. mago, feiticeiro (esp. um dos Reis Magos)

wish | wiś' | s. desejo, vontade; anelo, anseio, aspiração; pedido, ordem; (pl.) votos de felicidades. **-the w. is father to the thought** acreditamos em alguma coisa porque desejamos que ela aconteça / vt. vi. querer, desejar. **-I don't w. him ill** não lhe desejo mal. **-I w. I could** quem me dera...

wishful | wiś'ful | a. desejoso, ansioso

wishful thinking | wiś'fulϑinking | s. desejo ilusório de que algo se torne realidade

wishy-washy | wi'śiwo'śi | a. fraco (chá, sopa etc.); frouxo, sem caráter

wisp | wisp' | s. fio (de cabelo, palha etc.); fio, filete; pouquinho, punhadinho; pedaço, lasca; anel ou madeixą de cabelo; bando de narcejas

wistful | wist'ful | a. pensativo,

melancólico; ansioso, anelante

wit | wit' | s. agudeza, espírito, finura; inteligência; bom-senso, prudência; pessoa espirituosa. **-to be at one's wits end** não saber o que fazer ou dizer. **-to be out of one's wits** estar fora de si. **-to live by one's wits** viver de expedientes / vt. vi. (ant.) saber, ter conhecimento. **-to w.** a saber, isto é

witch | wiś' | s. bruxa

witchcraft | wiś'krʌft | s. bruxaria, feitiçaria

with | wiδ | prep. com; de

withdraw | wiδdró' | vt. retirar / vi. retirar-se

withdrawal | wiδdró'əl | s. retirada; retração, retraimento

wither | wi'δə | vi. murchar, secar, definhar

withered | wi'δəd | a. murcho, decaído, seco

withering | wi'δəring | a. fulminante, mortífero, devastador (olhar etc.)

withhold | wiδhowld' | vt. reter, conter; negar, recusar

within | wiδin' | adv. por dentro, na parte interna / prep. dentro de. **-w. call** ao alcance da voz. **-w. reach** ao alcance. **-w. sight** à vista, ao alcance dos olhos. **-w. an ace of** a dois dedos de, por um triz

without | wiδawt' | adv. fora, por fora / prep. sem. **-to do w.** passar sem

withstand | wiδstand' | vt. resistir, suportar, opor-se a

witness | wit'nes | s. testemunho; testemunha; όbservador, espectador / vt. ver, presenciar; atestar, testemunhar / vi. depor, prestar testemunho

witticism | wi'tisizəm | s. dito espirituoso, gracejo

wittingly | wi'tinglī | adv. intencionalmente, propositadamente, de caso pensado

witty | wi'tī | a. espirituoso (pessoa); de espírito, gracioso, humorístico

wizard | wi'zəd | s. feiticeiro, bruxo, mago

wizardry | wi'zədrī | s. feitiçaria, bruxaria, magia

wizened | wi'zənd | a. murcho, mirrado, encarquilhado

wobble, wabble | wo'bəl | vi. oscilar, vibrar; cambalear

woe | wow' | s. mágoa, pesar, aflição; atribulação, calamidade. -w. be un(to) maldito seja. -w. is me! ai de mim!

woebegone | wow'bigon | a. abatido, sucumbido, desolado

woeful | wow'ful | a. pesaroso, aflito; calamitoso; mesquinho

wolf | wulf' | s. lobo

wolfram | wul'frəm | s. volfrâmio, tungstênio

woman | wə'mən | s. mulher

womanhood | wə'mənhud | s. feminilidade; estado ou condição de mulher; as mulheres

womanly | wə'mənlī | a. feminino, feminil / adv. femininamente

womb | wʊm' | s. útero, ventre

women | wi'min | spl. mulheres

wonder | wân'də | s. maravilha, prodígio; admiração, assombro. -no w. não admira, não é de surpreender. -for a w. por milagre / vi. -to w. at maravilhar-se de, espantar-se. -I w. at you não esperava isso de você. -I shouldn't w. if não me admiraria se

wonderful | wân'dəful | a. maravilhoso

wondrous | wân'drəs | a. maravilhoso, assombroso

wont | wownt' | s. costume, hábito. -use and w. costume tradicional. -to be w. costumar

woo | wu' | vt. cortejar, namorar, galantear

wood | wud' | s. madeira; (tb. pl.) floresta, mata. -out of the w. fora de perigo

woodcut | wud'kât | s. gravura

em madeira, xilografia

woodcutter | wud'kâtə | s. lenhador; gravador em madeira

wooded | wu'did | a. coberto de árvores, arborizado

wooden | wu'dən | a. de madeira; duro, rígido; canhestro; inexpressivo; (coloq.) pessoa sem graça

woodland | wud'lənd | s. mata, floresta, selva

woodpecker | wud'pekə | s. pica-pau

woodwork | wud'wᴇk | s. madeiramento (de casa etc.); obra ou trabalho em madeira; carpintaria; obra de talha

wool | wul' | s. lã. -dyed in the w. tingido no fio; (fig.) até a raiz dos cabelos. -against the w. a contrapelo. -to pull the w. over one's eyes jogar areia nos olhos de alguém, enganar alguém. -much cry and little w. muito esforço e pouco resultado

woollen | wu'lən | a. de lã

woolly | wu'lī | a. lanzudo; (fig.) obscuro, confuso

word | wᴇd' | s. palavra, vocábulo, termo; (ger. pl.) letra (de canção etc.); sinal, senha; notícia, aviso. -a w. to the wise a bom entendedor meia palavra basta. -in so many words exatamente; sucintamente. -the W. a Escritura. -a man of his w. um homem de palavra. -to bring w. dar notícia ou recado. -to put in a good w. for recomendar (alguém). -to take one at his w. levar alguém a sério. -upon my w. palavra de honra / vt. exprimir em palavras

wording | wᴇ'ding | s. fraseado, fraseologia; enunciação; redação

word of command | wᴇd'ovkəmʌnd' | s. voz de comando

word of honour | wᴇd'ovonə | s. palavra de honra

word-play |wɛd'pley | *s.* jogo de palavras, trocadilho

wordy | wɛ'dī | *a.* prolixo, palavroso

work | wɛk' | *s.* trabalho; obra; emprego, colocação; função, mister; ação, efeito (de remédio etc.); (*pl.*) engrenagem, mecanismo; (*pl.*) fábrica. **-out of w.** desempregado. **-to get the works** ser vítima de violências (esp. ser morto) / *vt.* fazer trabalhar, fazer funcionar; explorar (mina); lavrar (terra, minérios); produzir. **-to w. down** chegar até, atingir a. **-to w. in** introduzir, inserir; encaixar (aparte). **-to w. out** elaborar, fazer (projeto); calcular, resolver. **-to w. up** excitar, estimular; misturar, amassar; desenvolver, ampliar. **-to w. oneself up** agitar-se; irritar-se. **-to w. one's way** conseguir pelos próprios esforços. **-to w. one's w. through** trabalhar para custear (estudos etc.) / *vi.* trabalhar; funcionar, andar (mecanismo etc.); ser eficaz, dar resultado. **-to w. against** lutar contra; opor-se a. **-to w. at** trabalhar em; estudar. **-to w. free** afrouxar-se, soltar-se. **-to w. on** ou **upon** tentar persuadir

worker | wɛ'kə | *s.* operário; trabalhador rural

work-horse | wɛk'hós | *s.* cavalo de tiro ou de carga; (fig.) burro de carga; (fig.) máquina que faz trabalho pesado

workhouse | wɛk'haws | *s.* asilo de pobres; (EUA) casa de correção

working | wɛ'king | *s.* trabalho; funcionamento, operação; exploração (de mina); avanço gradual; atividade (do cérebro etc.) / *a.* que trabalha

working class | wɛ'kingklɅs | *s.* operariado, proletariado

working majority | wɛ'kingmə-ǰo'ritī | *s.* maioria suficiente, *quorum*

workman | wɛk'mən | *s.* operário

workmanlike | wɛk'mənlayk | *a.* bem acabado, bem executado / *adv.* primorosamente

workmanship | wɛk'mənṣip | *s.* habilidade (de artesão, operário etc.); acabamento

workshop | wɛk'ṣop | *s.* oficina

world | wɛld' | *s.* mundo. **-not for the w.** por nada deste mundo. **-for all the w.** sob todos os aspectos, exatamente. **-dead to the w.** profundamente adormecido ou embriagado. **-to think the w. of** ter em alta conta. **-w. without end** para todo o sempre, eternamente / *a.* mundial

worldliness | wɛld'lines | *s.* mundanidade; conhecimento da vida

worldling | wɛld'ling | *s.* pessoa mundana

worldly | wɛld'lī | *a.* mundano

world-wide | wɛld'wayd | *a.* mundial

worm | wɛm' | *s.* verme, minhoca / *vt.* **-to w. out** descobrir, arrancar / *vi.* rastejar, serpear; insinuar-se, introduzir-se

worn | wón' | *a.* usado, gasto, roto. **-well w.** trilhado (caminho)

worn out | wón'awt | *a.* cansado, exausto (pessoa)

worried | wâ'rid | *a.* preocupado; inquieto

worry | wâ'rī | *s.* preocupação, inquietação; aflição / *vt.* preocupar, inquietar; afligir; irritar; atormentar; atacar a dentadas, morder e sacudir (cão) / *vi.* preocupar-se, inquietar-se; afligir-se. **-don't w.!** fique tranqüilo! **-to w. along** ir vivendo

worrying | wâ'rīing | *a.* inquietante, que preocupa

worse | wɛs' | s. pior. **-the w. remains to tell** ainda não contei o pior / a. adv. pior. **-so much the w.** tanto pior. **-from bad to w.** de mal a pior. **-to be w. off** estar em pior situação. **-w. then ever** pior do que nunca

worsen | wɛ'sən | vt. tornar pior / vi. piorar

worship | wɛ'ʃip | s. adoração. **-Your, His W.** Vossa Excelência (tratamento de certos magistrados) / vt. adorar

worshipper | wɛ'ʃipə | s. adorador

worst | wɛst' | s.a. adv. o pior. **-at w.** na pior das hipóteses. **-to get the w. of it** sair perdendo. **-if the w. comes to the w.** se acontecer o pior / vt. derrotar, vencer

worsted | wus'tid | s. estambre, fio de lã penteada, tecido feito com essa lã

worth | wɛϑ' | s. valor; importância / a. que vale ou custa; digno ou merecedor de. **-to be w. one's salt** valer o pão que se come. **-to not be w.** não valer a pena

worthiness | wɛ'ðines | s. valor; merecimento, mérito

worthless | wɛϑ'les | a. sem valor, imprestável

worthy | wɛ'ði | s. pessoa ilustre / a. valioso; meritório; digno

would-be | wud'bi | a. que pretende ser, que quer ser, pretenso

wound | wʊnd' | s. ferimento / vt. vi. ferir

wounded | wʊn'did | a. ferido

wraith | reyϑ' | s. espectro, fantasma

wrangle | ran'gəl | s. disputa, altercação / vi. altercar

wrangler | ran'glə | s. altercador, discutidor; polemista; (EUA) cowboy, vaqueiro

wrap | rap' | s. (ger. pl.) xale, casacão; manta / vt. embru-

lhar, envolver. **-to w. up** embrulhar

wrapped | rapt' | a. embrulhado; envolto. **-to be w. up in** (fig.) estar absorvido em

wrapper | ra'pə | s. envoltório; capa de livro; capa de charuto; cinta (de jornal); roupão de senhora

wrapping | ra'ping | s. envoltório; empacotamento

wrapping paper | ra'pingpeypə | s. papel de embrulho

wrath | roϑ' | s. ira, cólera

wreak | rik' | vt. descarregar (ira); tirar (vingança); (ant.) vingar

wreath | riϑ' | s. grinalda; coroa (tb. de flores); espiral (de fumaça)

wreathe | rið' | vt. enfeitar, engrinaldar; contrair (a face com sorriso)

wreck | rek' | s. naufrágio; ruína; navio naufragado; destroços. **-to be a w.** estar uma ruína / vt. pôr a pique; destruir, arruinar / vi. naufragar

wreckage | re'kij | s. naufrágio; destroços, escombros

wren | ren' | s. cambaxirra

wrench | renʃ' | s. puxão, arranco; chave de boca, chave inglesa / vt. torcer ou puxar; arrancar, arrebatar; torcer, deslocar (o pé etc.)

wrest | rest' | vt. arrebatar, arrancar; torcer, retorcer; desvirtuar (sentido das palavras)

wrestle | re'səl | ví. lutar corpo a corpo

wrestler | res'lə | s. lutador

wrestling | res'ling | s. luta corpo a corpo

wretch | reʃ' | s. infeliz, desgraçado; patife, canalha

wretched | re'ʃid | a. desgraçado, miserável; péssimo, desprezível, odioso

wretchedness | re'ʃidnes | s. infelicidade; miséria, baixeza, vileza

wriggle | ri'gəl | *vi.* contorcer-se; serpear, colear. **-to w. out** escapar-se, esquivar-se de

wring | ring' | *s.* torção; aperto / *vt.* torcer; apertar; extorquir, arrancar; oprimir

wringer | rin'gə | *s.* rolos de espremer roupa

wrinkle | rin'kəl | *s.* ruga / *vt. vi.* enrugar(-se)

wrinkled | rin'kəld | *a.* enrugado

wrist | rist' | *s.* pulso

wristlet | rist'lit | *s.* pulseira; bracelete; algema

wrist-watch | rist'wóš | *s.* relógio de pulso

writ | rit' | *s.* (jur.) mandado, ordem. **-Holy** ou **Sacred W.** Sagrada Escritura

write | rayt' | *vt. vi.* escrever. **-to w. back** responder (carta etc.). **-to w. down** tomar nota de. **-to w. off** anular, cancelar, riscar. **-to w. out** escrever por extenso; copiar. **-to w. up** escrever a história de, narrar por extenso

writer | ray'tə | *s.* escritor

write up | rayt'âp | *s.* elogio por escrito

writhe | rayδ' | *vi.* torcer-se, contorcer-se

writing | ray'ting | *s.* escrita; letra; profissão de escritor; produção literária. **-in w.** por escrito. **-at this w.** no momento em que escrevemos. **-in one's own w.** de próprio punho

writing-paper | ray'tingpeypə | *s.* papel de escrever

written | ri'tən | *a.* escrito

wrong | rong' | *s.* injustiça; ofensa, agravo; dano, prejuízo; pecado, erro. **-to be in the w.** não ter razão; estar errado; estar enganado. **-to put someone in the w.** provar que alguém está errado. **-to take (something) the w. way** levar a mal, interpretar mal. **-what's w.?** o que aconteceu?, qual é o problema? / *adv.* erradamente; mal; impropriamente; injustamente / *vt.* prejudicar; tratar mal, ofender; enganar, seduzir (mulher)

wrongdoer | rong'dʋə | *s.* transgressor; malfeitor

wrongdoing | rong'dʋing | *s.* transgressão; má ação

wrongful | rong'ful | *a.* injusto; errado; ilegal

wrong-headed | rong'hedid | *a.* teimoso, incorrigível, obstinado no erro

wrongly | rong'lĩ | *adv.* erradamente; injustamente; impropriamente; falsamente. **-rightly or w.** com ou sem razão; em todo o caso

wrought | rót' | *a.* lavrado, forjado, trabalhado; elaborado; ornamentado, decorado

wrought iron | rótay'ən | *s.* ferro batido

wry | ray' | *a.* torto; retorcido; deturpado (sentido)

wryly | ray'lĩ | *adv.* contorcidamente; deturpadamente

wry smile | ray'smayl | *s.* sorriso amarelo

X

xenophobia | zinowfo'bĭa | *s.* xenofobia

Xerox | zi'roks | *s.* xerox / *vt.* tirar cópia *xerox*

Xmas | kris'məs | *s. abrev.* de *Christmas*

X-ray | eks'rey | *s.* (ger. *pl.*) raios X, radiografia. **-to have an X-r.** tirar uma radiografia

xylophone | zay'ləfown | *s.* xilofone

Y

yacht | ĭot' | *s.* iate / *vi.* participar de corrida ou navegar em iate

yacht-club | ĭot'clâb | *s.* iate clube, clube de iatismo

yam | ĭam' | *s.* inhame

yank | ĭank' | *s.* (coloq.) puxão / *vt.* arrancar

Yankee | ĭan'kĭ | *s. a.* ianque

yard | ĭad' | *s.* jarda (0,914m); pátio, quintal. **-by the y.** aos metros, em grande quantidade. **-the Y.** (coloq.) Scotland Yard

yarn | ĭan' | *s.* fio (de lã, algodão, seda etc.); história comprida; invencionice

yawn | ĭón' | *s.* bocejo / *vi.* bocejar

yawning | ĭó'ning | *s.* bocejo / *a.* bocejante; (fig.) aberto, enorme (abismo etc.)

year | i'ə | *s.* ano. **-last y.** o ano passado. **-next y.** o ano que vem. **-leap y.** ano bissexto. **-a man in years** um homem idoso

yearbook | i'əbuk | *s.* anuário

yearly | i'əlĭ | *a.* anual / *adv.* anualmente

yearn | ĭEn' | *vi.* desejar, ansiar, anelar; ter saudades de; enternecer-se, apiedar-se

yearning | ĭE'ning | *s.* anseio, anelo, desejo; saudade; enternecimento, piedade

yeast | ĭıst' | *s.* fermento; levedura; (fig.) agitação

yell | ĭel' | *s.* grito / *vi.* gritar, berrar

yellow | ĭe'low | *s.* amarelo (cor) / *a.* amarelo; (fig.) covarde; (fig.) invejoso. **-the y. press** imprensa marrom (sensacionalista e inescrupulosa)

yellowish | ĭe'lowiś | *a.* amarelado

yelp | ĭelp' | *s.* ganido / *vi.* ganir; gritar

yeoman | ĭow'mən | *s.* pequeno proprietário rural; oficial da casa real, camarista. **-y.'s service** ajuda eficiente em caso de necessidade

yeomanry | ĭow'mənrĭ | *s.* pequena burguesia rural; milícia montada (voluntária)

yes | ĭes' | *s.* sim. **-to say y.** consentir / *adv.* sim; certamente

yesterday | ĭes'tədey | *s. adv.* ontem. **-the day before y.** anteontem

yester-year | ĭes'təĭıə | *s.* ano passado

yesteryear | ĭes'təĭıə | *adv.* outrora

yet | ĭet' | *adv.* ainda, já / *conj.* mas, porém, todavia, contudo.

-not y. ainda não. **-as** y. até agora. **-nor** y. tampouco

yew | ĭu' | s. (bot.) teixo

yield | ĭĭld' | s. rendimento; renda, produto; lucro / vt. render, produzir; conceder; entregar. **-to** y. **up the ghost** entregar a alma, expirar; (fig.) perder as esperanças, desistir

yoke | ĭowk' | s. jugo, canga. **-y. of oxen** junta de bois / vt. jungir, pôr à canga; unir, juntar, ligar, emparelhar

yokel | ĭow'kəl | s. rústico, labrego, campônio, caipira

yolk | ĭowlk' | s. gema de ovo

yonder | ĭon'də | a. aquele / adv. lá longe, além, acolá, ao longe, do outro lado

yore | ĭó' | adv. **-in days of y.** outrora

you | ĭu' | pron. o senhor; você; tu

young | ĭăng' | s. crias, filhotes, prole (de animal) / a. jovem, moço; imaturo, inexperiente

young blood | ĭăng'blâd | s. sangue-novo, gente moça

youngster | ĭăng'stə | s. jovem, rapaz; criança, menino; (pl.) rapazes, moças, rapaziada

your | ĭó'ə | a. poss. teu, tua; seu, sua; do senhor, da senhora etc.

yours | ĭó'əz | pron. o teu, a tua; o seu, a sua; o do senhor, o da senhora etc.

yourself | ĭó'self | pron. o senhor mesmo; tu mesmo; você mesmo / pron. refl. se; te

youth | ĭuϑ' | s. mocidade, juventude; um jovem. uma jovem

youthful | ĭuϑ'ful | a. jovem, juvenil; vigoroso

youthfulness | ĭuϑ'fulnes | s. juvenilidade

yule | ĭul' | s. Natal

yule-tide | ĭul'tayd | s. (ant.) época de Natal

Z

zeal | zil' | s. zelo, fervor, entusiasmo, dedicação

zealot | ze'lət | s. fanático, entusiasta, apaixonado

zealous | ze'ləs | a. zeloso

zebra | ze'brə | s. zebra

zebra crossing | ze'brəkro'sing | s. passagem de pedestres (pintada com listras em diagonal)

zenith | ze'niϑ | s. zênite; apogeu, auge

zero | zi'row | s. zero. **-above z.** acima de zero. **-below z.** abaixo de zero

zero hour | zi'rowaw'ə | s. (mil.) hora zero, hora H; momento crítico

zest | zest' | s. gosto picante, sabor; entusiasmo

zestful | zest'ful | a. saboroso, picante; entusiasta

zigzag | zig'zag | s. ziguezague / a. em ziguezague / vi. ziguezaguear

zinc | zink' | s. zinco / vt. zincar

zinc ointment | zink'oyntmənt | s. pomada de óxido de zinco

zipper | zi'pə | s. zíper, fecho ecler

zodiac | zow'dĭak | s. zodíaco

zone | zown' | s. zona / vt. dividir em zonas

zoo | zu' | s. jardim zoológico

zoologist | zvo'ləjist | s. zoólogo

zoology | zvo'ləji | s. zoologia

Zulu | zu'lu | s. a. zulu

GLOSSARY OF MENU TERMS

Visitors to Portugal and Brazil are pleasantly surprised by the wide variety of available cuisine. The typical Portuguese cooking has been influenced by centuries of development and infusion of tastes from the world-over. The Portuguese, of course, were the first Europeans to colonize Africa, Asia and the Far East. Their vast empire spread to the new world with its special food items. So today, both Portugal and Brazil have benefitted from the reciprocal exchange of food and taste sensations.

Portuguese cuisine relies heavily upon the classic combination of garlic and olive oil. The food of Portugal in seldom overpowered by the pungent aroma of garlic (there is one soup dish that remains the obvious exception) but it is nearly always a constituent of typical Portuguese cooking. Other widely used herbs include parsley, oregano, rosemary and coriander. Seasoning includes the basic salt and pepper and sometimes the very powerful African pepper known as "piri-piri"

The cuisine of Brazil, on the other hand, focuses more on New World products. Black beans, cassava rather than potatoes, local herbs and spices, smoked pork, tropical and fresh water varieties of fish, and peppers form the basis of Brazilian cooking. Whereas in Portugal, olive oil is common, in Brazil the brusque palm oil or "dendé" can dominate the dish.

The visitor can find wide range of variation in the preparation of the Brazilian staples of beef, chicken and fish. The everyday black beans and rice, likewise take on regional flare from place to place in this huge country. For example, from the Bahia state comes the famous "xim xim". This is a stew of chicken enhanced by a variety of local herbs and served, of course, with rice. Spicey fish stew known as "moquecas" utilizes palm oil as a flavor enhancer. The visitor should try the deep-fried "acarajé" as a snack. This is a tasty doughy ball of brown beans, onions, salt and plenty of pepper. Some dishes such as "caruru" have deep African origins. It has become a Brazilian favorite over the centuries. It consists of okra, onions, salt, pepper, local herbs stewed with a heavy-fleshed saltwater or river fish.

Both cuisines are hearty, delicious and relatively simple. Rarely is a dish embellished with cream or egg sauce. They are not subject to trends but seem to be based upon recipes developed over hundreds of years using ingredients available in each country and suited to simple tastes.

"Lunch" is the main meal of the day in both Portugal and Brazil. It is taken seriously. The visitor should not expect to "do" museums, shop or conduct official business during the two-hour lunch break. Yes, two hours!! The lunch break is an important part of the traditional way-of-life. It is a time to eat, relax, refresh, gossip, joke, do some serious negotiating, but most of all to enjoy the food.

The visitor is often startled at the enormous size of the meal's portions. First-time visitors are sometimes overwhelmed by the amount of food served at lunch. An American often leaves much food uneaten. In Portugal, in particular, the huge meals are accompanied by good, inexpensive and plentiful wine. There is no reason to rush the lunch tradition. No one seems in a hurry. The visitor will quickly learn to relax and enjoy a touch of Iberian mid-day diversion.

In Portugal the meal will generally be more elaborate, more formal and a little more expensive. A true Portuguese meal begins with an appetizer of cheese, slices of sausage, ham, morsels of shrimp or other seafood, and always olives. Bread and butter accompanies this and all courses of the meal. The visitor should be aware that most items, including bread and butter, are priced "a la carte". The visitor will also be surprised by the price. In Europe, Portugal is the least expensive dining country. In Latin America, Brazil offers value despite inflation problems.

The meal continues with perhaps a glass of Port wine. In Brazil, a cold beer would be more appropriate. The soup course follows. Next comes the egg course, usually in the form of an omelette. The main course will be seafood, poultry or meat, while dessert is usually fresh fruit followed by small pastries and coffee. A bit of brandy is a fitting finale.

Coffee is the national drink of Brazil, as one would expect. Brazilian coffee is a world standard and stands on its own for richness, aroma, flavor and clout. Interestingly, the coffee of preference in Portugal is that imported from Africa. East Africa is the home of the coffee plant (later taken to Brazil by the Portuguese) and, according to the Portuguese coffee drinkers, the best in the world.

In both places, arguably, coffee is better than in most other countries. Also, in both countries, coffee consumption is taken seriously. Both countries consider their brew to be a national treasure. Each cup requires that the dark roasted beans be ground "by the cup" and then brewed by the "espresso" method. Each cup is small but potent. Both populations enjoy their coffee with a good measure of sugar (açucar). Each cup, then provides a hefty jolt of both caffeine and energy to the consumer. Coffee is a beverage for every occasion, every time of day. In Brazil, the small cups are referred to as "Cafézinho" and in Portugal the correct term is "Bica".

One will note that the effects of a full two-hour lunch last well into the afternoon. Serious business rarely takes place again until late afternoon. Offices, shops and other establishments correspondingly remain open longer than is the custom in the U.S.

The work day is long. The day typically begins with a light breakfast of coffee, hard rolls and butter. A mid-morning snack consists of coffee and a small pastry. The mid-day meal takes place between 12 and 2 pm and 1 and 3 pm. A late afternoon snack known as "lanche" is taken between 5 or 6 pm. Dinner, thankfully lighter than lunch, is served late by American standards, usually after 8:30 pm.

Table service is usually included in the price of the meal. However, a small gratuity, in addition, is left for the waiter. Service, waiting tables, is a profession and life work for most of the restaurant waiters one encounters. And, in the European tradition, service is never rushed. The check is never, ever presented without first being called for.

In both Portugal and Brazil, because of the passion for food, the tradition of the long, leisurely meal as well as the social aspects of dining out, there are a great many eating establishments per capita. They are variously termed according to the food served, the preparation style or tradition. In Portugal, restaurants are "rated". That is, each restaurant is licenced. When the licence is secured the owner or management specifies the rating level (1 to 4, with 4 being the best). In other words, the establishment states the level of service, price and food quality it intends to provide. The visitor, using the system as a guide, can choose a restaurant according to price and quality just as one chooses a hotel by its rating.

The various terms for restaurants include:

Pasteleria, pastry shop, cafe, quick meal, limited menu;

Confeitaria, limited to pastries and coffee;

Cervajaria, drinking and eating places;

Adega, drinking place, wine and sausages served;

Taberna, more respectable than an Adega;

Marisqueira, specializing in shell-fish;

Café, older pasteleria;

Churrasqueira, specializing in grilled items, chicken, etc.;

Restaurante, restaurant, generic term for all of the above.

The following list indicates very typical menu items. The "menu" itself is referred to as one of the following words: Ementa or Cardápio. Menu items include:

Sopas (soups)

-Caldo Verde, a rich, thick cabbage, kale and potato soup

-Sopa de Legumes, vegetable puree soup

-Sopa de Alentejana, garlic soup, poached egg, served over stale bread

-Açordo, garlic and bread porridge

-Sopa de Peixe, fish soup

Pão (bread)

Manteiga (butter)
Gelados (ice cream)
Queijos (cheeses)
-Queijo Flamenga, mild "edam"—like ewe's milk cheese
-Queijo Ilha, very hard cheese
-Queijo de Serra, pungent ewe's milk cheese
-Queijo de Alentejo, creamy cheese
-Queijo de Azeitão, brie-like cheese
-Queijo a Cabriero Picante, sharp goat's milk cheese
-Requeijão, unpasteurized fresh goat and ewe's milk cheese
Ovos (eggs)
-Ovos estrelado, fried eggs
-Ovos mexidos, scrambled eggs
-Ovos cozidas, boiled eggs
-Ovos escaliados, poached eggs
Carne de Vaca (beef)
-Bife, beef steak
-Bife a Portuguesa, grilled steak and egg
-Prego, hot steak sandwich
-Hamburguesa, hamburger
Vitela (veal)
-Vitela Assada, roast veal
Carne de Porco (pork)
-Costeleta de porco, pork chop
-Porco de Alentejana, pork and clam dish
-Feijoada, black beans and pork
Chourico (spicey, smoked sausage)
Vatapa (paste of dough, nuts and shrimp)
Linguiça (smoked pork tongue sausage)
Presunto (smoked ham)
Friambre (ham, less expensive)
Friambre y queijo (ham and cheese)
Frango (chicken)
-Frango na pucara, stewed chicken
-Frango Churrasco, grilled chicken
-Frango Frita, fried chicken
-Frango ao Molho Pardo, chicken with blood sauce
-Xim Xim, herb chicken stew
Peru (turkey)
Coelho (rabbit)
Carne de Veado (venison)
Carne de Carneiro (mutton)
Carne de Cordeiro (lamb)
Carne de Cabra (goat)
Carne de Cabrito (kid goat)
Carne de Sol (salt cured meat)
Frutos do Mar (seafood)
-Bacalhau, salt cod (said to be no less than 365 recipes)
-Caldeirada, fish stew
-Sardinhas Assada, grilled sardines
-Enguia, eels
-Lula, squid
-Polvo, octopus
-Lagosta, crayfish
-Lagostinos, rock lobster
-Camarões, shrimp
-Mexilhões, small mussels
-Ameijoas, small clams
-Percebes, barnacles
-Linguado, sole
-Pescada, hake
-Espadarte, swordfish
-Atum, tuna
-Salmonettes, red mullet
-Caracois, snails
-Moquecos, fish stew
-Tacacá, dried shrimp
-Siri, stuffed crab
-Caruru, fish stew
Legumes (vegetables)
-Couve, kale, cabbage

-Repolho, cabbage
-Lombarda, cabbage
-Alface, lettuce
-Salada, salad
-Tomate, tomato
-Arroz, rice
-Batatas Fritas, fried potatoes
-Farinha, manioc flour
-Farofa, deep fried farinha dough
-Pirão, flour and rice
Frutas (fruit)
-Maça, apple
-Banana, banana
-Abacaxi, pineapple
-Ananas, pineapple
-Laranja, orange
-Pera, pear
Doces (sweets)
-Flan, egg custard
-Arroz doce, rice pudding
-Bola, sweet roll
-Massa, pastry
-Ovos moles, custard
-Pateis de Nata, tart
-Marmelada, quince jelly
Bebidas (beverages)
-Vinho, wine
-Vinho do Porto, Port wine
-Vinho de Madeira, wine of Madeira Islands
-Carcavellos, sherry-like wine
-Vinho Verde, "green" or very young, light, inexpensive wine
-Branco Seco, extra dry white wine
Licors (liqueurs)
-Licor de Amendoa, almond liqueur
-Ginginha, cherry liqueur
-Brandymel, honeyed brandy
-Aguardente de Medronha, powerful liqueur
-Cachaça, sugarcane brandy
Cervejas (beers)
-Sagres, local Portuguese beer
-Sagres Europa, beer
-Cristal, beer
Agua (water)
-Agua com gas, carbonated water
-Agua sem gas, non-carbonated water
Café (coffee)
-Bica, coffee espresso style
-Cafézinho, coffee espresso style
-Galão, coffee with heated milk